RPG/400 PROGRAMMING
ON THE AS/400™

RPG/400 PROGRAMMING ON THE AS/400™

Stanley E. Myers

Professor Emeritus
Norwalk Community/Technical College

Candice E. Myers

PRENTICE HALL
Englewood Cliffs, New Jersey 07632

Library of Congress Cataloging-in-Publication Data

MYERS, STANLEY E.,
    RPG/400 programming on the AS/400 / Stanley E. Myers, Candice E.
Myers.
        p.   cm.
    Includes index.
    ISBN 0-13-096736-X
    1. IBM AS/400 (Computer)--Programming.   2. RPG/400 (Computer
program language)   I. Myers, Candice E.,   II. Title.
QA76.8.I25919M93   1995
005.245--dc20   94-25819
                                                              CIP

Acquisitions editor: Bill Zobrist
Cover designer: Bruce Kenselaar
Production manager: Judy Winthrop
Manufacturing buyer: Lori Bulwin
Editorial assistant: Phyllis Morgan

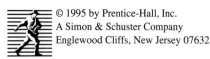 © 1995 by Prentice-Hall, Inc.
A Simon & Schuster Company
Englewood Cliffs, New Jersey 07632

The following terms, operations, commands, and select screens are used throughout this text with permission of the International Business Machines Corporation related to the AS/400™ (Version 2 Release 2) : RPG/400, DDS (Data Description Specifications), DFU (Data File Utility), SEU (Source Entry Utility), CL (Control Language), PDM (Programmer Development Method), and SDA (Screen Design Aid). The following illustrations from IBM Manual #SC09–1349.00 pages 41–42, 12, 423–424 and IBM's AS/400 New User's Guide page 1–6 are included in this text.

The author and publisher of this book have used their best efforts in preparing the program listings included in this text. These efforts include the development, research, and testing of the programs to determine their effectiveness. The author and publisher make no warranty of any kind, expressed or implied, with regard to these programs. The author and publisher shall not be liable in any event for incidental or consequential damages in connection with, or arising out of, the furnishing, performance, or use of these programs.

Printed in the United States of America
10 9 8 7 6 5 4 3 2 1

ISBN 0-13-096736-X

Prentice-Hall International (UK) Limited, *London*
Prentice-Hall of Australia Pty. Limited, *Sydney*
Prentice-Hall Canada Inc., *Toronto*
Prentice-Hall Hispanoamericana, S.A., *Mexico*
Prentice-Hall of India Private Limited, *New Delhi*
Prentice-Hall of Japan, Inc., *Tokyo*
Simon & Schuster Asia Pte. Ltd., *Singapore*
Editora Prentice-Hall do Brasil, Ltda., *Rio de Janeiro*

To our cubs

Contents

Appendices

Preface

This book is a complete text dedicated to the RPG/400 programming language and the AS/400 environment. In addition to the general syntax of the RPG/400 language, the following subjects are presented:

1. Structured RPG/400 programming is emphasized throughout the book in order to stress the importance of writing programs that may be easily maintained and debugged. RPG/400 structured operations, where applicable, are used in all program examples.
2. The creation, syntax, and processing of *Physical Files, Display Files, Logical Files, Subfiles,* and *Printer Files* are detailed in separate chapters.
3. The procedures to use the *Source Entry Utility* (**SEU**), *Data File Utility* (**DFU**), *Programmer Development Manager* (**PDM**), and *Screen Design Aid* (**SDA**), unique to the AS/400 system, are explained in separate appendices.
4. *Control Language Programming* (**CLP**) syntax and structure is discussed in a stand alone chapter.
5. A separate chapter is dedicated to the *Sort* and *Open Query File* utilities.
6. Batch and interactive methods of debugging **RPG/400** programs are detailed in a chapter.

Specifically, this textbook offers the following advantages:

1. RPG/400 procedures to externally process the AS/400 database and traditional RPG coding methods are discussed.
2. Students will be able to enter the source code, compile, debug, and load physical files after Chapter 2.
3. After Chapter 3 is completed, students will have the information to write, enter, compile, and debug RPG/400 programs that produce simple reports.

4. Over <u>seventy</u> complete RPG/400 *compiled* programs are included to support the learning of the computer language. Most of the program listings are supplemented with line-by-line explanations of the coding.

5. Over <u>eight</u> <u>hundred</u> figures are included in the text to illustrate the syntax and logic of RPG/400 programs and ***Physical, Display, Logical, Printer*** files, and **Subfiles**.

6. Chapter Summaries, Questions, and Programming Assignments are included at the end of every chapter. Summaries highlight the new subjects introduced in the chapter. Questions are designed to aid in the immediate recall of chapter materials. At least three practical Programming Assignments (some chapters have 6) that range in difficulty from the simple to the complex, enhance the learning of the RPG/400 programming language.

7. Comprehensive coverage of physical file maintenance in the batch and interactive modes is detailed in separate chapters.

8. Emphasis is placed on the importance of data and its effect on program execution and final results.

This textbook introduces the sequence of subject matter outlined in the following chapters.

In order to familiarize students with the AS/400 environment, Chapter 1 introduces basic control language commands which enable the programmer to create his or her processing environment, submit jobs and display output.

Chapter 2 explains the syntax, creation, and types of physical files. The reader is introduced to **SEU** (***Source Entry Utility***) which is needed for the entering of any source code for any file type. Specific commands are detailed which provide for the change and display of the attributes of a physical file.

Chapter 3 introduces specifics about the RPG/400 programming language. The sequence of steps followed for the completion of an RPG/400 program, which includes analysis of the application, design of input and output requirements, coding, compilation, debugging, and program execution are explained. The syntax for the processing of *externally defined* and *program defined* physical files is shown.

Chapter 4 further develops the reader's knowledge of RPG/400 syntax and coding procedures with an introduction to report headings, editing of numeric fields, the RPG/400 *Logic Cycle,* and select indicators.

RPG/400 operations that support the arithmetic functions for addition, subtraction, multiplication, division, and square root are introduced in Chapter 5. The syntax and function of other special purpose operations, including **MVR** (***Move Remainder***), **Z-ADD, Z-SUB, MOVE, MOVEL, SETON, SETOF,** and **DEFN** are presented. In addition, the use of *Resulting, Field,* and *Last Record* (**LR**) indicators are detailed in this chapter.

The syntax and use of the RPG/400 structured operations **IF/ELSE, DO, DOW** (***Do While***), **DOU** (***Do Until***), **SELEC** (***Begin a Select Group***), **WH** (***When True Then Select***), **OTHER** (***Otherwise Select***), and **END** (also **ENDIF, ENDDO, ENDSL**) are discussed in Chapter 6. Use of the **LEAVE** and **ITER** operations within a **DO, DOU,** or **DOW** group is also covered.

Chapter 7 introduces the syntax and processing logic for the **EXCPT** (***Except***) operation. RPG/400 operations unique to the processing of *internal subroutines* (i.e. **EXSR, BEGSR, ENDSR, CAS** and **ENDCS**) are discussed. Also included are the operations, syntax, and processing logic required for the *calling* of other RPG/400 programs from the current program. The **CAT** (***Concatenate Two Character Strings***) operations and *Named Constants* are also detailed in this chapter.

The RPG/400 indicators (**L1-L9**), syntax, and processing logic of generating reports that require single or multiple subtotals is discussed in Chapter 8. First, program examples are presented that use the ***RPG/400 Logic Cycle*** and second, the same programs are modified to support programmer-controlled subtotal processing.

Chapter 9 introduces ***Data Structures*** and ***Data Areas.*** The use of ***Data Structures*** to divide a field into subfields, change the format of a field, group noncontiguous data in a contiguous format, and define an area of storage in more than one format. Special purpose data structures for ***Data Areas, File Information,*** and ***Program Status*** are also explained. The commands to create, change, and display data areas are presented. *Implicit* and *explicit* processing of ***Data Areas*** by RPG/400 programs is detailed in this chapter.

The syntax and processing of *tables* is introduced in Chapter 10. Emphasis is placed on the methods of loading table data in the program cycle, alternative ways of organizing table data, and methods of processing.

Chapter 11 details the logic, syntax, and processing of *arrays*. Methods of loading arrays in the program cycle, organization of array data, and the editing of arrays on output are discussed. Also explained is array look up with and without an index. Multi-dimensional processing of arrays is simulated by syntax related to ***Multiple Occurrence Data Structures*** and the **OCUR** operation. The syntax and application of the **SORTA, SCAN,** and **SUBST** operations are also detailed in this chapter.

Data validation procedures common to the batch processing environment are introduced in Chapter 12. Individual RPG/400 programs support the learning of the syntax to control many of the commonly used validation functions.

Chapter 13 includes comprehensive coverage of *physical file maintenance* in the batch environment. The RPG/400 operations, **CHAIN, READ, READE, READP, REDPE, SETLL, SETGT, UPDAT, DELET,** and **WRITE** are included in program examples detailed in this chapter.

The syntax and procedures related to the creation and use of Display Files, used in the interactive environment, are introduced in Chapter 14.

The development of RPG/400 *maintenance programs* in the *interactive environment* is presented in Chapter 15. Many of the file processing operations discussed in Chapter 13 are required for this mode of processing.

The use, syntax, and creation of ***Logical Files*** is detailed in Chapter 16. Keywords and the processing logic of ***Non-join*** and ***Join Logical Files*** is separately discussed and supported by numerous examples.

Chapter 17 explains the purpose and syntax of ***Subfiles,*** their unique keywords, and creation. Separate RPG/400 programs are included to illustrate how *subfiles* are used in the maintenance of physical files. The syntax for ***windowing*** within a subfile is also included in this chapter.

The syntax and logic for the development of ***Printer Files*** is presented in Chapter 18. The RPG/400 syntax and logic for the processing of ***Printer Files*** is explained with a program example.

Chapter 19 introduces some of the commands and syntax used in ***Control Language Programs*** (**CLP**). The basic structure of **CLPs** is discussed and example programs are reviewed in detail to explain parameter passing, variable manipulation, display, and data file processing.

The syntax related to the often overlooked ***Sort Utility*** is discussed in Chapter 20. *Regular, summary,* and *record address sort* types are mentioned. The specification entries and procedures for the creation of a *record address sort* is detailed. In addition, the RPG/400 syntax necessary to process a *record address sort* is supported by a complete program example. The procedures required to use the ***Open Query File*** (**OPNQRYF**) command is also explained.

Chapter 21 explains RPG/400 program *debugging* techniques including *program dump interpretation,* the **DEBUG** operation, and interactive debugging commands often needed for successful program execution.

Appendix **A** instructs the reader on how to use the Source Entry Utility (**SEU**); **B,** the Programmer Development Manager (**PDM**); **C,** the Data File Utility (**DFU**); and **D,** the Screen Design Aid (**SDA**).

Teaching Tips

This book is only suitable for RPG/400 language courses taught on the AS/400. For RPG courses that use other IBM computer systems or those of other manufacturers, refer to *RPG II, RPG III, and RPG/400 With Business Applications* by Stanley E. Myers.

At the option of the instructor, the sequence of chapter, or those discussed may depend on the background of the students. The suggested sequence for students in a two semester course with no AS/400 experience is to begin with Chapter 1 and continue through Chapter 18. Chapter 21, which discusses program debugging, should be referred to when a student experiences execution time errors that cannot be identified. Within time limitations, Chapters 19 and 20 should also be covered.

For a one semester RPG/400 course with students that have no previous RPG education or experience, Chapters 2 through 8, 11, 14, 15, 16, and 17 should be assigned.

For the professional programmer who has little or no experience in the RPG/400 environment, this book provides an excellent reference source. Not only is the syntax discussed, but detailed program examples are included that put all of the elements of batch and interactive processing on the AS/400 together.

The following learning tools are available to users of this textbook:

1. An Instructor's Manual, which includes the answers to all questions and programming assignments.
2. A text bank (with answers) is included in the manual and on diskette.
3. Transparency masters of many of the example programs.
4. A compiled listings of the first program example from each chapter is available on diskette.
5. Coordinated with this text is an IBM PC compatible RPG/400 compiler that may be purchased for a nominal amount. Site license agreements are also available with attractive educational discounts.

Acknowledgments

We extend thanks to our children, Caroline, Megan, and Sean for giving us the time to write this text and supplemental Instructor's Manual.

Furthermore, we want to extend our personal thanks to Pat Pitchenik and John Cribbins for their continued support and encouragement throughout the development of this text. Good friends who have a sincere interest in what your doing is deeply appreciated.

After the manuscript is complete, the production of a text can often be a frustrating experience. Because of the skills of the production editor, Judy Winthrop, the production phase of this text was simplified. She always had an interest in the placement of figures to the related text, the print quality, and overall accuracy. Working with a manuscript that has over eight hundred figures is not an easy task. I sincerely hope that we can work on another text together.

In addition, I want to thank Bill Zobrist for his efforts in determining that a text devoted to RPG/400 and the AS/400 environment was needed. Working with him was a pleasure.

The thorough review of the original and revised manuscripts by Stephen

Cunningham of the BIC Corporation, Paul Levesque of the Lord Fairfax Community College, and Charlie Miri from the Delaware Technical College has resulted in a text that will address the needs of RPG/400 students and professional programmers. Their suggestion revisions, additions, and deletions were usually carefully followed.

Special recognition goes to the students at the Norwalk Community/Technical College who classroom tested the manuscript during the past year. Their comments and identification of topics that were not clearly presented led to modifications that have resulted in an excellent RPG/400 book.

We also want to sincerely thank IBM for the development of the AS/400 computer system and their continued improvements to the RPG compiler.

Our thanks to each and every one of you for your interest and support in the development of this textbook!

Stan and **Candy**

chapter 1

The AS/400 Environment

IBM's Application System/400 (AS/400) is a powerful family of computers intended to meet a wide range of business needs. Several types of hardware units are available: the 9402, 9404, 9406, and Advanced Series 200, 300, 310, and 320. As can be seen in Figure 1-1, the 9402, 9404, and Advanced Series 200 are compact units which, although small enough to fit under a desk, are each capable of supporting a small business. The various models of the 9406 unit (model B, model D, model E, and model F) are mounted in multiple racks, each roughly the size of a five-drawer filing cabinet, and are capable of supporting hundreds of users. The Advanced Series 300, 310, and 320, while smaller than the rack mounted units, are capable of supporting the same number of users as the 9406. To meet the needs of very large corporations, all models of the AS/400 computer may be networked together, sharing files and other resources within the same building or around the world. Indeed, it is the versatility of the AS/400 which has made it so popular.

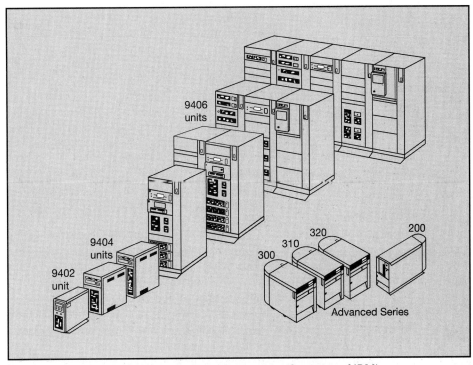

Figure 1-1   The Application System/400 models *(Courtesy of IBM).*

OS/400, the AS/400 operating system, provides the user with several tools to run the system. These tools are generally grouped together based on their functionality. *Control Language (CL)* is a set of commands which allow the user to communicate with the AS/400. *Data Management* provides the user with ways to define and access data within the AS/400's relational database. *Work Management* controls the processing of jobs in the AS/400's multiuser environment. *Programmer Services* provides development tools and utilities to assist the programmer in creating and maintaining programs and files. *System Operator Services* provides the system operator with a menu of frequently used functions. *Communication Support* provides a wide range of communication functions which allow the AS/400 to communicate with various types of systems (including, but not restricted to, other AS/400s). *Security* protects all of the data and software on the system. Together, all of these features make OS/400 a very powerful operating system.

OS/400 keeps track of millions of *objects*. An *object* can be anything; programs, files, output queues, job queues, job descriptions, and libraries are all *objects*. All *objects* are accessible via a special language called *Control Language*, or *CL*. There are a number of CL commands which a programmer uses when programming on the AS/400. We will try to explain the most common ones as we encounter them.

Let's begin by examining the programmer's environment. When an AS/400 terminal is turned on, a sign-on screen appears. The user is prompted to enter a User ID and password. The User ID allows the system to associate a job session with information stored in a *user profile*. The *user profile,* which is created by the security officer, defines the executing environment to the system. If the user is a programmer, several specific aspects of this environment are of interest.

Figure 1-2 uses the **DSPUSRPRF** command to display a typical user profile for a programmer. First there is the **profile name,** which may be up to 10 characters in length; in this case JANE. Note that JANE's password is not displayed. The AS/400 will never display a password. Passwords are encrypted and stored for use by the system. No one, not even the security officer, can display a password. If Jane forgets her password, the security officer can assign her a new one but cannot display her current password.

Many of the parameters contain the entry ***SYSVAL.** This refers to a value stored in an associated *system value*. *System values* contain information which controls the way in which an individual AS/400 system is run. For example, using a *system value* for the number of days before a user's password expires in the *Password expiration interval* parameter ensures that everyone has the same password expiration interval.

JANE has been assigned a **user class** of ***PGMR,** or programmer. This grants her two *special authorities*: ***SAVSYS** and ***JOBCTL. *SAVSYS** allows Jane to save, restore, and free storage for all objects on the system. ***JOBCTL** grants Jane the authority to hold, release, cancel, clear, or change any job on the system. She can also load the system (IPL), start writers, and stop active subsystems.

As a programmer, Jane has been associated with the QPGMR *group profile*. This "automatically" gives Jane authority to use a variety of system commands and access system objects which are reserved for programmers. Note that the security officer has also specified ***GRPPRF** for the *owner*. This means that any object which Jane creates will be owned by the QPGMR group, and the other programmers in that group will have the same rights to that object as Jane does. For example, if Jane is on vacation and a file needs to be cleared, any of the programmers who work with Jane can clear the file.

Jane's development library, JANELIB, has been specified as her *current library*. A current library is the default library for storing any objects (programs, files, and so forth) created by the user. The system has a default library, QGPL (General Purpose Library), which may also serve as a current library. But since Jane is a programmer and is expected to create a number of new objects, it is easier to put these objects in her development library and avoid storing them with the system objects that are stored in QGPL.

The profile specifies an *initial program* for Jane. The program INLPGM in JANELIB will execute every time Jane signs onto the AS/400. Jane's initial program calls the Programmer Menu for her to work from.

The *priority limit* parameter represents the highest job scheduling and output sched-

```
                    Display User Profile - *BASIC
5738SS1 V2R1M1  920306                              1/18/93  15:05:59
User Profile . . . . . . . . . . . . . . . :   JANE
Previous sign-on . . . . . . . . . . . . . :   12/31/92  08:16:59
Sign-on attempts not valid . . . . . . . . :
Status . . . . . . . . . . . . . . . . . . :   *ENABLED
Date password last changed . . . . . . . . :   12/22/92
Password expiration interval . . . . . . . :   *SYSVAL
Date password expires . . . . . . . . . :   02/20/93
Set password to expired . . . . . . . . . :   *NO
User class . . . . . . . . . . . . . . . . :   *PGMR
Special authority . . . . . . . . . . . . :   *JOBCTL
                                               *SAVSYS
Group profile . . . . . . . . . . . . . . :   QPGMR
Owner . . . . . . . . . . . . . . . . . . . :   *GRPPRF
Group authority . . . . . . . . . . . . . :   *NONE
Assistance level . . . . . . . . . . . . . :   *SYSVAL
Current library . . . . . . . . . . . . . :   JANELIB
Initial menu . . . . . . . . . . . . . . . :   MAIN
   Library . . . . . . . . . . . . . . . . :      *LIBL
Initial program . . . . . . . . . . . . . :   INLPGM
   Library . . . . . . . . . . . . . . . . :      JANELIB
Limit capabilities . . . . . . . . . . . . :   *NO
Text . . . . . . . . . . . . . . . . . . . :   Jane Smith - Programmer
Display sign-on information . . . . . . . :   *SYSVAL
Limit device sessions . . . . . . . . . . :   *SYSVAL
Keyboard buffering . . . . . . . . . . . . :   *SYSVAL
Maximum storage allowed . . . . . . . . . :   *NOMAX
   Storage used . . . . . . . . . . . . . . :      819
Highest scheduling priority . . . . . . . :   3
Job description . . . . . . . . . . . . . :   JANE
   Library . . . . . . . . . . . . . . . . :      JANELIB
Accounting code . . . . . . . . . . . . . :   DP
Message queue . . . . . . . . . . . . . . :   JANE
   Library . . . . . . . . . . . . . . . . :      QUSRSYS
Message queue delivery . . . . . . . . . . :   *NOTIFY
Message queue severity . . . . . . . . . . :   00
Output queue . . . . . . . . . . . . . . . :   JANE
Library . . . . . . . . . . . . . . . . . :   QGPL
Printer device . . . . . . . . . . . . . . :   *WRKSTN
Special environment . . . . . . . . . . . :   *NONE
Attention program . . . . . . . . . . . . :   *NONE
   Library . . . . . . . . . . . . . . . . :
Language identifier . . . . . . . . . . . :   *SYSVAL
Country identifier . . . . . . . . . . . . :   *SYSVAL
Coded character set identifier . . . . . . :   *SYSVAL
```

Figure 1-2 DSPUSRPRF display.

uling priorities which can be assigned to a user's jobs. Zero (0) is the highest priority, and 9 is the lowest. Jane has been assigned a priority limit of 3. This means that any jobs with a priority of 4 through 9 will run after Jane's jobs. However, any jobs with a priority of 0 through 2 will execute before Jane's jobs.

Jane's job description JANE in JANELIB was specified in the *job description* para-meter. The job description contains information that describes the execution environment for jobs and is used by the programmer when submitting jobs to run in the batch environ-ment.

Jane has been assigned a default *output queue* (JANE in library QGPL) for her printed output, and a *message queue* (JANE in QUSRSYS) for her messages. Because the *message queue delivery* parameter specifies ***NOTIFY,** Jane will hear a beep whenever a message arrives on her message queue. Later, when it is convenient, Jane can use the **DSPMSG** *(Display Messages)* command to display her messages.

Finally, the *special environment* parameter of JANE's user profile contains the en-try ***NONE.** Many companies have chosen to migrate software from an IBM System/36. The AS/400 has a special environment for running this software (*S36). But Jane will be developing programs that are "native" to the AS/400 and will not require a special environment for execution.

When Jane logs onto the system, the information stored in her user profile is used to establish her *job* in the interactive *subsystem,* QINTER. A subsystem is a means of grouping and controlling jobs (including the amount of memory allocated for them to run). The AS/400 has several subsystems, but programmers are generally concerned with only two of them: QINTER and QBATCH. Most interactive jobs run in the interactive subsystem, QINTER, while most batch processing is done in QBATCH.

When her initial program is executed, the *Programmer Menu* is displayed on Jane's terminal (see Figure 1-3). The Programmer Menu is a system tool intended to help programmers develop and maintain software. Programmers generally use either the Programmer Menu or **PDM,** another system tool, for programming. Information on the use of **PDM** (the *Programmer Development Manager*) may be found in Appendix B.

```
                          Programmer Menu
                                               System:   AS400
         Select one of the following:
             1. Start AS/400 Data File Utility
             2. Work with AS/400 Query
             3. Create an object from a source file   object name, type, pgm for CMD
             4. Call a program                        program name
             5. Run a command                         command
             6. Submit a job                          (job name), , ,(command)
             7. Go to a menu                           menu name
             8. Edit a source file member             (srcmbr), (type)
             9. Design display format using SDA       (srcmbr), ,(mode)
            90. Sign off                               (*nolist, *list)

         Selection . . . . . ___          Parm . . . . _____
         Type . . . . . . . _____  Parm 2 . . . _____
         Command . . . . . . _____
         Source file . . . . _____  Source library . . . . . .   *LIBL
         Object library . . _____   Job description . . . . . .  *USRPRF
         F3=Exit      F4=Prompt       F6=Display messages   F10=Command entry
         F12=Cancel   F14=Work with submitted jobs          F18=Work with output
```

Figure 1-3   The Programmer Menu.

CL commands may be entered from the Programmer Menu by selecting option 5 and typing the command on the line marked **Command.** Command prompting is available by pressing function key 4 (F4). If no command has been specified and F4 is pressed, a series of easy-to-use menus will allow the individual to find the exact command he or she needs for almost any task.

Most programmers find the command naming conventions meaningful and easy to use. The verb portion of the command is generally three consonants, such as **DSP** for *display* or **WRK** for *work with.* The remaining portion of the command describes the object type to be processed, such as **JOBD** for *job description* or **OUTQ** for *output queue.* So, to *work with* the spooled output in an *output queue,* the command to use would be **WRKOUTQ.**

If Jane wanted to display her *library list,* she would enter a **5** on the **Option** line and the command **DSPLIBL** on the **Command** line. A library list similar to the one shown in Figure 1-4 would appear. All jobs have an associated *library list,* which is a list of libraries that can be searched to find any object requested. The library list of any job is composed of four basic parts. First there is the *System Library List.* This list contains libraries associated with the AS/400 operating system. Then comes the *Product Library.* This library is associated with the specific command in use and is necessary for its execution. When the command is initiated, the *production library* is added to the *library list.* When the command finishes processing, the library is removed from the *li-

```
  5738SS1 V2R1M1  920306     Library List              1/26/93 15:47:42

     Library    Type       Text

       QSYS       SYS       System Library
       QSYS2      SYS       System Library for CPI's
       QUSRSYS    SYS
       QHLPSYS    SYS
       QPDA       PRD
       JANELIB    CUR       Jane's Development Library
       FILELIB    USR       Production File Library
       PGMLIB     USR       Production Software Library
       QTEMP      USR
       QGPL       USR       General Purpose Library
```

Figure 1-4   DSPLIBL display.

brary list. Next is the *Current Library* for the job. This library is used as the default library for storing any new objects created by the job and is generally the programmer's development library. Finally, there is the *User Library List.* This is a list of libraries selected by the programmer based on his or her requirements.

When a request for an object is made and a library is not specified in the request, each library in the library list is searched, in the order in which they appear in the list, until an object with the same name and type requested is found.

Many of a programmer's jobs are submitted to the batch subsystem for execution. The Programmer Menu allows the programmer to specify a *job description* (or **JOBD**) to be used when submitting these jobs. The job description allows the programmer to define an environment in which jobs may be executed. Although the job description may be used to define these attributes for any job, programmers are most familiar with using the job description to control jobs which they submit for batch processing. The CL command **DSPJOBD** can be used to display a job description. Refer to Figure 1-5 while we discuss the parameters of most interest to programmers.

```
                        Job Description Information

  Job description:  JANE          Library:    JANELIB
  User profile . . . . . . . . . . . . . . . . . . . :  *RQD
  CL syntax check  . . . . . . . . . . . . . . . . . :  *NOCHK
  Hold on job queue  . . . . . . . . . . . . . . . . :  *NO
  End severity . . . . . . . . . . . . . . . . . . . :  30
  Job date . . . . . . . . . . . . . . . . . . . . . :  *SYSVAL
  Job switches . . . . . . . . . . . . . . . . . . . :  00000000
  Inquiry message reply  . . . . . . . . . . . . . . :  *RQD
  Job priority (on job queue)  . . . . . . . . . . . :  5
  Job queue  . . . . . . . . . . . . . . . . . . . . :  QBATCH
     Library . . . . . . . . . . . . . . . . . . . . :    QGPL
  Output priority (on output queue)  . . . . . . . . :  5
  Printer device . . . . . . . . . . . . . . . . . . :  *USRPRF
  Output queue . . . . . . . . . . . . . . . . . . . :  JANE
     Library . . . . . . . . . . . . . . . . . . . . :    QGPL
  Message logging:
     Level . . . . . . . . . . . . . . . . . . . . . :  4
     Severity  . . . . . . . . . . . . . . . . . . . :  0
     Text . . . . . . . . . . . . . . . . . . . . . .:  *SECLVL
  Log CL program commands  . . . . . . . . . . . . . :  *NO
  Accounting code  . . . . . . . . . . . . . . . . . :  DP
  Print text . . . . . . . . . . . . . . . . . . . . :  *SYSVAL
  Routing data . . . . . . . . . . . . . . . . . . . :  QCMDB
  Request data . . . . . . . . . . . . . . . . . . . :  *NONE
  Device recovery action . . . . . . . . . . . . . . :  *SYSVAL
  Time slice end pool  . . . . . . . . . . . . . . . :  *SYSVAL
  Text . . . . . . . . . . . . . . . . . . . . . . . :  Jane Smith
  Initial library list:
     *SYSVAL
```

Figure 1-5   DSPJOBD display.

The **Job queue** parameter allows the programmer to specify the job queue to be used when the job is submitted. In most cases this will be QBATCH.

The **Job scheduling priority** and **Job output priority** parameters have a default entry of **5.** Priorities range from 0 to 9, with 0 being the highest priority and 9 being the lowest. These entries cannot be higher in priority than the value specified in the programmer's User Profile **Highest scheduling priority** parameter. An **Accounting code** may be specified for job accounting purposes. In Figure 1-5 we see that an **accounting code** of DP has been specified.

Routing data corresponds to special routing entries in the subsystem description. In this case, the entry QCMDB tells the QBATCH subsystem that jobs submitted with this job description should be processed in batch mode.

An **Initial library list** may be specified for use with jobs using the job description. This library list, just like the library list for the programmer's interactive job, can be searched for objects required for the job using this job description.

Message logging can be very helpful when debugging a batch job. The entry of **4** for **message level**, **0** for **message severity**, and ***NOLIST** for a **message text level** means that all messages with a severity of 0 or greater will be logged during the execution of the job and, should the job end abnormally, a listing of the messages (called a *joblog*) will be produced.

The option to **Log CL statements** may also be used for debugging purposes. This parameter is usually ***NO,** but if a programmer needed to log CL statements in a CL program (CLP) as they executed, he or she could change this parameter to specify ***YES.** Then the programmer could view the executed statements in the joblog.

A default **Output queue** may be specified. Programmers frequently use this parameter to place spooled output in an output queue (OUTQ) not associated with a printer. In this way they can review their output via the terminal and print only selected output.

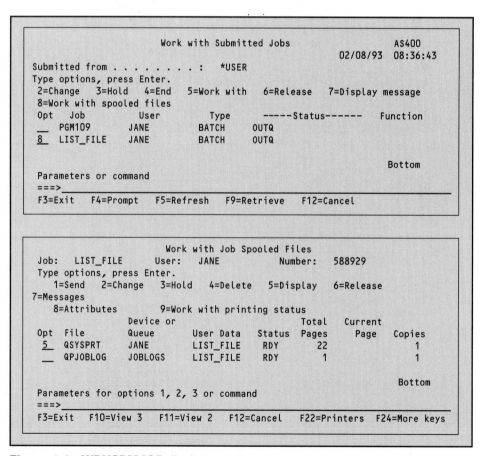

Figure 1-6 WRKSBMJOB displays.

External switches may be set ON or OFF using the **switch** parameter of the job description. A value of **0** means "OFF." A value of **1** means "ON." The values of switches are available to both RPG/400 programs and control language programs to condition operations.

To view a job which has been submitted, the programmer may use the **WRKSBMJOB** *(Work with Submitted Jobs)* command. This command will display a list of submitted jobs, with their current processing status, on the programmer's terminal (see Figure 1-6). From this display the programmer may view detailed information concerning any of the jobs listed. For example, to view a report created by the LIST_FILE job, the programmer would enter an 8 in the space next to the LIST_FILE job. Then the Work with Job Spooled Files display would show a list of all the spooled files associated with that job. To view the report from this display, the programmer would then enter a **5** *(view)* in the space next to the report.

Another way to view the same report would be to look at it in the output queue. To do this the programmer would use the **WRKOUTQ** *(Work with Output Queue)* command. An output queue may be specified when executing the command. However, if a queue is not specified, the command will display a list of output queues from which to select. Once an output queue has been selected, a list of spooled files will be displayed for review (see Figure 1-7). To view the report, the programmer would enter a **5** in the space next to the report created by the LIST_FILE job.

```
                        Work with Output Queue
Queue:    JANE              Library:    QGPL          Status:    RLS/WTR
Type options, press Enter.
   1=Send  2=Change   3=Hold   4=Delete  5=Display   6=Release  7=Messages
   8=Attributes        9=Work with printing status
Opt  File       User      User Data   Sts    Pages   Copies  Form Type   Pty
__   QSYSPRT    QSYSOPR   PGM027      RDY       1       1     *STD         5
__   QSYSPRT    JANE      PGM109      RDY      20       1     *STD         5
__   QSYSPRT    QSYSOPR               RDY       1       1     *STD         5
__   QPRINT     QSYSOPR               RDY       1       1     *STD         5
5    QSYSPRT    JANE      LIST_FILE   RDY      10       1     *STD         5


                                                                  Bottom
Parameters for options 1, 2, 3 or command
===>_____
F3=Exit   F11=View 2   F12=Cancel   F22=Printers   F24=More keys
```

Figure 1-7   WRKOUTQ display.

A third way to view the report would be to list all of the spooled files associated with the programmer. The command **WRKSPLF** *(Work with Spooled Files)* will present the programmer with a list containing all of the spooled files on the system which he or she may have created (see Figure 1-8). Again, to view the report, the programmer would enter a **5** in the space next to the report created by the LIST_FILE job.

```
                    Work with All Spooled Files
Type options, press Enter.
   1=Send  2=Change   3=Hold   4=Delete  5=Display   6=Release  7=Messages
   8=Attributes        9=Work with printing status
                                       Device or              Total    Cur
Opt  File      User      Queue       User Data   Sts  Pages  Page Copy
__   QPJOBLOG  JANE      JOBLOGS     LIST_FILE   RDY    1          1
__   QSYSPRT   JANE      JANE        PGM109      RDY   20          1
5    QSYSPRT   JANE      JANE        LIST_FILE   RDY   10          1
                                                                  Bottom
Parameters for options 1, 2, 3 or command
===>_____
F3=Exit   F10=View 3   F11=View 2   F12=Cancel   F22=Printers   F24=More keys
```

Figure 1-8   WRKSPLF display.

Output queues are usually associated with a printer. A special program called a *writer* manages the queue for the printer. Spooled files placed in such an output queue are automatically printed. However, in our example, Jane's output queue is not associated with a printer. Therefore, her spooled files will not print automatically. The technique of using an output queue not associated with a printer allows the programmer to review spooled output online to determine if a printed copy is necessary. Should the programmer decide to print the spooled file, he or she may place a **2** (*change*) in the space next to the file on any of the spooled file displays (**WRKSPLF, WRKOUTQ,** or the **WRKSB-MJOB** spooled file display) and press the ENTER key. A screen similar to the one shown in Figure 1-9 will appear. The programmer may then specify the name of a printer in the *Printer* field and press the ENTER key. The spooled file will print on the specified printer. Other attributes, such as the number of copies or the type of form on which to print the report, may be changed in the same manner.

```
                    Change Spooled File Attributes (CHGSPLFA)
 Type choices, press Enter.
 Spooled file . . . . . . . . . > QSYSPRT        Name, *SELECT
 Job name . . . . . . . . . . . > LIST_FILE      Name, *
   User . . . . . . . . . . . . > JANE           Name
   Number . . . . . . . . . . . > 588929         000000-999999
 Spooled file number . . . . . > 1               1-9999, *ONLY, *LAST
 Printer . . . . . . . . . . .   PRT01           Name, *SAME, *OUTQ
 Print sequence . . . . . . . .  *SAME           *SAME, *NEXT
 Form type . . . . . . . . . .   *STD            Form type, *SAME, *STD
 Copies . . . . . . . . . . . .  1               1-255, *SAME
 Restart printing . . . . . . .  *STRPAGE        Number, *SAME, *STRPAGE...
                    Additional Parameters
 Output queue . . . . . . . . .  JANE            Name, *SAME, *DEV
   Library . . . . . . . . . .   QGPL            Name, *LIBL, *CURLIB
                                                                    Bottom
 F3=Exit    F4=Prompt    F5=Refresh    F10=Additional parameters    F12=Cancel
 F13=How to use this display      F24=More keys
```

Figure 1-9   Change Spooled File Attributes display.

SUMMARY

IBM's AS/400 is a versatile computer which is well suited to today's business environment. Its powerful OS/400 operating system provides the programmer with an inventory of software tools with which to manage and maintain the system.

The programmer's environment is established based on parameters specified in the programmer's *user profile*. Some of the parameters rely on values maintained at the system level in *system values*. Others are maintained on the individual profile level. Parameters such as the programmer's *current library, initial program, priority limit, default message and output queues,* and *default job description* are used by the system to define the programmer's environment when the programmer signs onto the system and establishes an online session.

Job descriptions are used to define the processing environment for any job which the programmer submits to the batch subsystem for processing. They allow the programmer to specify parameters such as *run priority, job queue, output queue, message logging level* and *severity,* and a *library list* for the submitted job.

A *library list* is a list of the libraries which are searched when an *object* is referenced. Each library, in turn, is searched until an object of the same name and type referenced is found.

A high-level computer language, known as *Control Language* (or *CL*), is used to communicate with the system. The AS/400 command naming conventions are meaningful and easy to use. The first part of a command represents the action to be taken and is generally three consonants, such as **DSP** for *display* or **WRK** for *work with.* These are followed by the *object type* to be processed, such as **OUTQ** for an *output queue* or **JOBD** for a *job description*. A few useful commands were introduced in this chapter, including **WRKOUTQ, DSPLIBL, DSPJOBD, WRKSBMJOB,** and **WRKSPLF.** These are only a few of the more than 2,000 AS/400 commands.

QUESTIONS

1-1. Name the six groups of tools which OS/400 provides for the user to run the system.

1-2. What is an object?

1-3. What command would you use to display a user profile?

1-4. How are passwords protected on the AS/400?

1-5. What is a system value?

1-6. List five User Profile parameters which specified *SYSVAL in Figure 1-2.

1-7. There are two special authorities associated with the user class *PGMR. What are they and what do they allow the programmer to do?

1-8. What is a current library?

1-9. What is a priority limit?

1-10. What command may be used to display messages?

1-11. What is a library list and how is it used?

1-12. The job scheduling priority and job output priority specified in a job description (JOBD) are related to what entry on the User Profile? How are they related?

1-13. What is a joblog?

1-14. The job description (JOBD) option to log CL statements is usually set to *NO. When might a programmer change this option to *YES?

1-15. Which job description entry tells the QBATCH subsystem to process a job in batch mode?

1-16. What command would a programmer use to review output from a job which was submitted for batch processing?

1-17. What command would a programmer use to display all of his or her spooled files?

1-18. What command would a programmer use to display an output queue (OUTQ)?

PROGRAMMING ASSIGNMENTS

Programming Assignment 1-1: EXPLORE PROGRAMMER'S ENVIRONMENT

Sign-on to the AS/400 using the user ID and password provided by your instructor. If the *Programmer Menu* is not displayed, type the command **STRPGMMNU** on the command line and press the ENTER key. Complete the following steps:

1. Type a 5 (Execute a command) in the space marked **Selection.** On the **Command** line type **DSPUSRPRF** and press command function key 4 (F4). Type your user ID in the **User profile** parameter and press the ENTER key.

2. Review the display of your user profile. Note the name of your default job description (JOBD). Press command function key 3 (F3) to exit the display.

3. Type a 6 (Submit a job) in the **Selection** field, and type **DSPJOBD** on the **Command** line. Press F4. Enter the name of the job description found in step 2 in the space labeled **JOBD.** Type *PRINT in the **Output** parameter and press the ENTER key.

4. Type a 5 in the **Selection** field and WRKSBMJOB on the **Command** line.

Press the ENTER key. What output queue (OUTQ) is the spooled file created in step 3 in? Press F3 to exit each of the displays.

5. Enter a 5 in the **Selection** field and type **WRKOUTQ** followed by the name of the output queue where you found your spooled file on the **Command** line. Press F4. What parameter was filled in? Type *PRINT in the **Output** parameter and press the ENTER key.

6. Enter a 5 in the **Selection** field, type **WRKSPLF** on the **Command** line, and press ENTER. How many spooled files are there?

7. To print your spooled files, type a 2 next to each of the spooled files and press the ENTER key. Type the name of a printer in the **Printer Name** parameter and press the ENTER key. Repeat this process for each of the spooled files.

chapter 2

Physical Files

TYPES OF AS/400 DATABASE FILES

An *externally described file* is one in which the record and field descriptions are defined outside of a program. The two types supported on the AS/400 are *physical* and *logical* files. *Physical files* are explained in this chapter and *logical files* in Chapter 16.

Similar to disk files on a non–data-based computer system, physical files contain the actual data records. The attributes of the records may be databased-defined or program-defined. If they are *database-defined,* the field definitions are specified outside of a program. For *program-defined* files, the field attributes must be included in the program in the traditional RPG II way.

Physical files may be organized as *non-keyed* or *keyed sequence* files. The type of organization determines the access path followed when the file is processed.

A *non-keyed* file is similar to the standard sequential organization file in which keys are not specified. Records, which are processed in the order that they were loaded, may be read, written, and updated using sequential or relative record processing methods. Direct file organization is not supported on the AS/400. The processing methods unique to that file type, however, may be simulated for arrival of key-sequenced files.

A *keyed sequence* file is similar to the traditional indexed sequential file organization in which one or more fields may be specified as a key. Processing features unique to key sequence files are the following:

1. Records may be accessed sequentially in key value order or randomly by the value of a key.
2. Records may be accessed in arrival sequence order (ignores key value order).
3. *Composite keys* may be defined by specifying more than one field within the body of a record. These fields need not be contiguous.
4. Any field in the body of the record may be specified as a key field after the file is created. However, a logical file must be used to process the physical file by the new key(s).
5. In addition to standard sequential and random processing, files may be read backward or accessed by a relative record number.
6. The next record that is lower or higher than the specified key value may be accessed.

BUILDING A PHYSICAL FILE

The steps for building a physical file are the following:

1. Design a record format based on some application criteria.
2. Write the code on a *Data Description Specifications* (DDS) form.
3. Enter the DDS statements via the Source Entry Utility (**SEU**) and save.
4. Compile, debug, and store the error-free physical file object format.

Record Format Design

Unlike the file organization types common to the traditional computer systems, the AS/400 physical file structure will support only <u>one</u> record format. Consequently, this restriction must be considered when a user-system is designed. Note, however, that multiple record processing may be simulated by *nonjoin* and *join* logical files which are related to two or more physical files. This topic will be introduced in Chapter 16.

The record format shown in Figure 2-1 will be used as the documentation to define a *non-keyed* as well as a *keyed sequence* physical file.

```
                  PHYSICAL FILE DESCRIPTION

   SYSTEM: AS/400                        DATE: 6/10/95
   FILE NAME: GLACTS                     REV NO: 0
   RECORD NAME: GLACTSR                  KEY LENGTH: None
   SEQUENCE: Non-keyed                   RECORD SIZE: 58

                     FIELD DEFINITIONS

   FIELD    FIELD NAME   SIZE  TYPE    POSITION    COMMENTS
    NO                                 FROM   TO


     1       ACTNO         3    C        1     3
     2       NAME         27    C        4    30
     3       TYPE         20    C       31    50
     4       BALNCE        8    S       51    58   2 decimals
```

Figure 2-1 Example physical file record format.

THE DATA DESCRIPTION SPECIFICATIONS (DDS) FORM

Physical File–Non-Keyed Organization

All physical file formats (*non-keyed* and *keyed sequence*) are usually written on *Data Description Specifications* forms before the code is entered via **SEU.**

A form completed for the example *keyed sequence* physical file is illustrated and explained in Figure 2-2.

Physical File-Keyed Sequence Organization

Except for key definition requirements, the DDS coding for a *keyed sequence* physical file is similar to an non-keyed. The DDS coding for the *non-keyed* file previously

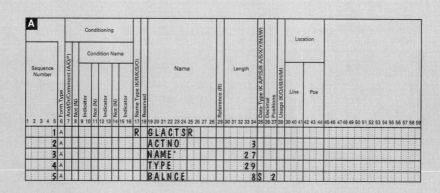

Only the fields related to the example <u>non-keyed</u> physical file are explained below:

Column 6   The letter A must be included in every statement. Entry of the DDS code via **SEU** will automatically supply this value.

<u>Record level (Line 00001):</u>
<u>Name Type</u>
Column 17   The letter R must be included to indicate the entry defines the physical file's record name. Only one record format may be defined for a physical file.

Columns 19–28   Programmer-supplied record name is entered left-justified in this field. Record names must be 10 characters or less in length and begin with an alphabetic character or one of the special characters @, $, and #. All of the other characters in the record name may be A–Z, 0–9, @, $, #, and underscore _. Embedded blanks are not permitted.

<u>Field level (Lines 00002 to 00005):</u>
<u>Name</u>
Columns 19–28   Programmer-supplied field names (ACTNO, NAME, TYPE, and BALNCE) must be left-justified in this field. For physical files that are processed by RPG/400 programs, field sizes are limited to six characters and the underscore character is not supported. Otherwise, the same syntax restrictions imposed on record names apply to field names. Note that the field names specified become a permanent part of the database and must be referenced exactly as formatted in any high-level languages that process the file.

<u>Length</u>
Columns 30–34   Unless the field is being referenced from a Field Reference file, every field must be defined with a length. For packed fields, the unpacked size is specified. The field length entry must be right-justified in the Length field.

<u>Data Type</u>
Column 35   The data types specified for this field are

Numeric Types	Alphanumeric Type
P - Packed Decimal	**A** - Any character supported
S - Zoned Decimal	by the system
B - Binary	
F - Floating Point	

If the entry is omitted, and columns 36–37 (*Decimal Positions*) are blank, the default is **A**. If columns 36–37 are not blank (they include the number from 0 to 9), the default is **P** (*Packed Decimal* field).

Column 36–37   0 through 9, indicating the number of decimal positions, must be entered for a numeric field. The entry must not be greater than the field length.

Fields ACTNO through TYPE are defined as character type and BALNCE as zoned decimal by the letter **S** in column 35.

Columns 38–44, which include fields for Usage and Location, are related to display files. The *Functions* field (columns 45–80) supports 27 keywords that are valid for physical files. None are specified for this example, however, when other DDS supported file types are discussed, some of the keywords will be introduced.

Figure 2-2   Completed Data Description Specifications non-keyed for the example physical file.

shown in Figure 2-2 is modified in Figure 2-3 to define it as a *keyed sequence* physical file.

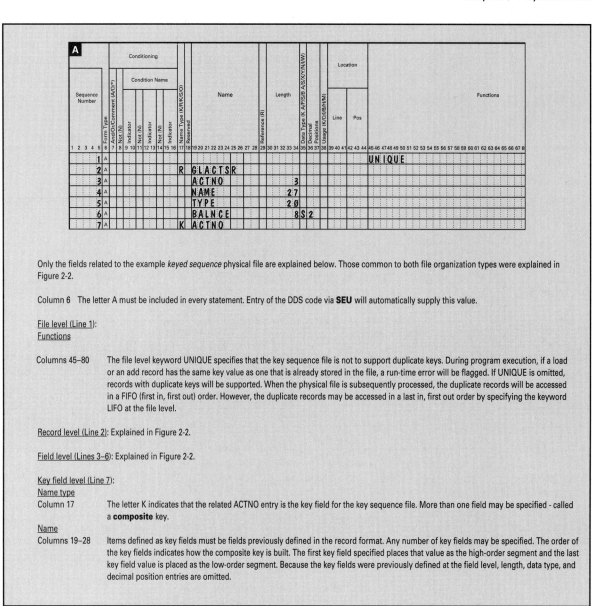

Only the fields related to the example *keyed sequence* physical file are explained below. Those common to both file organization types were explained in Figure 2-2.

Column 6   The letter A must be included in every statement. Entry of the DDS code via **SEU** will automatically supply this value.

<u>File level (Line 1):</u>
<u>Functions</u>

Columns 45–80   The file level keyword UNIQUE specifies that the key sequence file is not to support duplicate keys. During program execution, if a load or an add record has the same key value as one that is already stored in the file, a run-time error will be flagged. If UNIQUE is omitted, records with duplicate keys will be supported. When the physical file is subsequently processed, the duplicate records will be accessed in a FIFO (first in, first out) order. However, the duplicate records may be accessed in a last in, first out order by specifying the keyword LIFO at the file level.

<u>Record level (Line 2):</u> Explained in Figure 2-2.

<u>Field level (Lines 3–6):</u> Explained in Figure 2-2.

<u>Key field level (Line 7):</u>
<u>Name type</u>
Column 17   The letter K indicates that the related ACTNO entry is the key field for the key sequence file. More than one field may be specified - called a **composite** key.

<u>Name</u>
Columns 19–28   Items defined as key fields must be fields previously defined in the record format. Any number of key fields may be specified. The order of the key fields indicates how the composite key is built. The first key field specified places that value as the high-order segment and the last key field value is placed as the low-order segment. Because the key fields were previously defined at the field level, length, data type, and decimal position entries are omitted.

Figure 2-3   Completed Data Description Specifications for the example keyed sequence physical file.

DDS Function Field Keywords

Only one function field entry, the keyword **UNIQUE,** has been discussed for physical files. A total of 28 keywords are available in the definition of a physical file. They are the following:

```
      ABSVAL           *** DIGIT                RANGE
      ALIAS                EDTCDE            *  REF
   *  ALTSEQ              EDTWRD               REFFLD
      CHECK            *  FCFO                 REFSHIFT
      CMP              *  FIFO             *** SIGNED
      COLHDG              FLTPCN               TEXT (also record level)
      COMP             ** FORMAT           *  UNIQUE
  *** DESCEND          *  LIFO             *** UNSIGNED
      DFT              *** NOALTSEQ            VALUES
                                           *** ZONE

        blank - Field Level              *  - File Level
           ** - Record Level            *** - Key Field Level
```

When specified for a physical file, any of these keywords must be entered in the *Functions* field (columns 45–80). Some may be used only at the *file, record,* or *field level.* Examples showing how a few of the keywords are used are illustrated in Figure 2-4.

Line 00001   LIFO

File level keyword that specifies that the keyed file which supports records with duplicate keys is to be processed in a last in, first out mode. In other words, the last duplicate record loaded will be the first processed. If this keyword is omitted, the file will process the duplicate records in the default FIFO (first in, first-out) order.

Line 00002   TEXT('CUSTOMER MASTER')

A record or field level keyword that provides additional documentation for a record or field. The text, which must be enclosed in parenthesis and single quotes, will be included with the related field name on any source listing that includes the physical file. A maximum of 50 characters may be specified.

Line 00003   COLHDG('CUSTOMER ' 'NUMBER')

A field level keyword (column heading) that may be used as a field label or prompt in a screen design aid (SDA) utility, data file utility (DFU), and query utility. If COLHDG is not specified and the field is referenced in one of the named utilities, the default will be the field name.

The example shown will center NUMBER under CUSTOMER. Each heading line for a field must be enclosed in single quotes. A maximum of three lines of 20 characters each is supported.

If TEXT is not specified and COLHDG is, COLHDG will control the functions of both keywords.

Line 00004   COLHDG('CUSTOMER NAME')

Because the entire constant is enclosed in only one set of single quotes, it will appear as one heading.

Under most circumstances, COLHDG functions would be included for all of the fields in the body of the physical file record.

Line 00009   EDTCDE(J)

This keyword provides the same edit code control as RPG. The letter **J**, enclosed in parentheses, will edit the numeric field with zero suppression, insertion of a decimal, comma(s), and a negative sign after the low-order digit if the value is negative.

Note that the editing function will not be performed for physical file loading or maintenance functions. It is only operational for Display and Printer files and does not modify the physical file data.

Any EDTCDE entry may be overridden in a Display or Printer file by specifying the keyword **DLTEDT**.

Line 00010   DESCEND

This keyword must be specified at the key field level. When used, it will process the physical file in a descending key value sequence instead of the ascending sequence default. If the keyword is not specified, the records will be accessed in ascending key value order.

Figure 2-4 Examples of physical file keyword usage.

ENTERING DDS PHYSICAL FILE CODE

The Programmer Menu

The Programmer Menu shown in Figure 2-5 provides for a convenient method by which to access the utilities that control source code entry, compilation, program execution, de-

```
                          Programmer Menu
                                                    System:   AS400
        Select one of the following:
           1. Start AS/400 Data File Utility
           2. Work with AS/400 Query
           3. Create an object from a source file    object name, type, pgm for CMD
           4. Call a program                         program name
           5. Run a command                          command
           6. Submit a job                           (job name), , ,(command)
           7. Go to a menu                           menu name
           8. Edit a source file member             (srcmbr), (type)
           9. Design display format using SDA        (srcmbr), ,(mode)
          90. Sign off                               (*nolist, *list)

        Selection . . . . .    8       Parm . . . .    GLACTS
        Type  . . . . . . .    PF      Parm 2 . . .    _____
        Command . . . . . .            _____

        Source file . . . .   _____  Source library . . . . . . .    *LIBL
        Object library . .    _____  Job description . . . . . .     *USRPRF

        F3=Exit        F4=Prompt            F6=Display messages    F10=Command entry
        F12=Cancel     F14=Work with submitted jobs                F18=Work with output
```

The prompts to call SEU (Source Entry Utility) for DDS source code entry for a physical file are explained below:

Option: 8 must be entered to call the SEU utility.

Parm: PF must be entered for physical file source entry. The entry calls the related **SEU** screen format

Type: Programmer-supplied physical file name (limited to 8 characters for RPG) must be entered for this prompt. GLACTS is entered for this example (may be lower- or uppercase characters).

Parm 2: Used for Option 1 (**DFU** app) and Option 2 (Query app). Not used to create a physical file.

Command: Control language command may be entered for this prompt. Execution is controlled by option 5 (Run a command). For example, in lieu of using option 3 and the Parm and Type options, the physical file could be compiled by entering the command CRTPF for this prompt and pressing F4. A sequence of response screens will display to define the attributes of the file. All of the fault attributes may be taken, or specific attributes may be changed for example, (file size).

The defaults for the Source file, Source library, Object library, and Job description entries are shown in the example. Any of these values may be changed as needed.

Command keys are included at the bottom of the screen to control processing options.

The ENTER key must be pressed to display an **SEU** format for DDS PF entry. Sign-off from this menu is controlled by option 90. Prompts Parm, Type, Parm 2, and the command line must be blank for Sign off to execute.

The Programmer Menu may be accessed from any AS/400 display that has a command line by typing STRPGMMNU and pressing ENTER.

Figure 2-5   Programmer Menu filled in to call **SEU** for physical file code entry.

bugging, and so forth. The numbers at the left side relate to selection criteria that perform the related function. For example, to enter DDS source code for physical files (PF), logical files (LF), display files (DSPF), printer files (PRTF), RPG programs (RPG), or Control Language Programs (CLP) by **SEU**, Option **8** must be selected and supplemented with the related prompt responses.

Entering the DDS Code for a Physical File with SEU

After the prompts are completed to create a physical file format and the ENTER key is pressed, the **SEU** screen shown in Figure 2-6 will display.

```
Columns . . . :    1  71              Edit                 SMYERS/QDDSSRC
SEU==>                                                               GLACTS
FMT PF .....A..........T.Name++++++RLen++TDpB......Functions+++++++++++++++++
*************** Beginning of data ***********************************
''''''''

****************** End of data ****************************************
```

Figure 2-6   SEU EDIT screen (format A) for DDS physical file code.

Notice that the second line begins with the identifying format (FMT PF). The remainder of the line duplicates the fields on the DDS form. For example, the five dots after FMT PF represent the sequence number (columns 1–5) on the form; A in column 6 gives the form type, and so forth. Statements are entered horizontally by aligning the field entry with the column header. Pressing the ENTER key stores the instructions and moves the "******* END OF DATA *******" logo down one line. Figure 2-7 illustrates the EDIT screen after all of the example physical file statements have been entered.

```
Columns . . . :    1  71              Edit                 SMYERS/QDDSSRC
SEU==>                                                               GLACTS
FMT PF .....A..........T.Name++++++RLen++TDpB......Functions+++++++++++++++++
*************** Beginning of data ***********************************
0001.00    A                                          UNIQUE
0002.00    A           R GLACTSR
0003.00    A             ACTNO         3
0004.00    A             NAME         27
0005.00    A             TYPE         20
0006.00    A             BALNCE        8S 2
0007.00    A           K ACTNO
****************** End of data ****************************************
```

Figure 2-7   Filled-in **SEU EDIT** screen with example PF code.

Another method that some programmers find more convenient is to use prompt-line control. Prompt-line entry is initiated by entering P on a statement line and pressing the ENTER key.

A prompt line (for the format type) with field headers will display at the bottom of the screen as shown in Figure 2-8. Right-justification of number field entries is automatically supported when the FIELD EXIT key is pressed. After all the values for the statement are entered, the ENTER key is pressed, the statement is moved to its related location in the top section of the screen, and the prompt line is blanked out. This sequential entry of the source code will continue at the option of the programmer. With either method (line format or prompt), syntax errors will be displayed when the ENTER key is pressed. All corrections must be made before the statement is moved or stored.

The *insertion* of a line between existing lines is performed by placing the cursor above the line where the inserted line is to be entered, typing **IP** at the beginning of the statement, and pressing the ENTER key. After the prompt line is completed and the ENTER key is pressed, the new statement is inserted in the specified location. Line insertion using the line format method is executed by specifying the letter **I** at the beginning of the previous statement and pressing the ENTER key. A blank line will be displayed to enter the statement.

An instruction may be *moved* by entering **M** in the number area. The target position is identified by entering the letter **A** on the statement that will precede the moved instruction or the letter **B** on an instruction that will follow the moved statement. A group of instructions may be moved by entering **MM** in the number area of the first statement to be

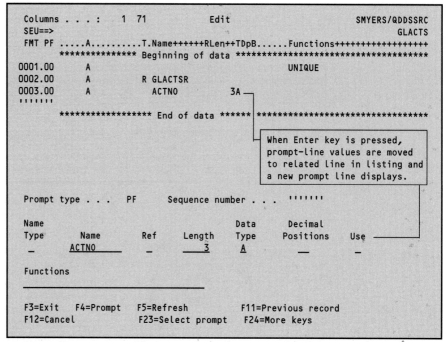

```
Columns . . . :    1  71              Edit                    SMYERS/QDDSSRC
SEU==>                                                                 GLACTS
FMT PF .....A..........T.Name++++++RLen++TDpB......Functions++++++++++++++++++
       *************** Beginning of data ************************************
0001.00     A                                        UNIQUE
0002.00     A           R GLACTSR
0003.00     A             ACTNO         3A┐
''''''
       ***************** End of data ***** │ ********************************
                                           │ ┌──────────────────────────────┐
                                           │ │ When Enter key is pressed,    │
                                           │ │ prompt-line values are moved  │
                                           │ │ to related line in listing and│
                                           │ │ a new prompt line displays.   │
                                           │ └──────────────────────────────┘
       Prompt type . . .   PF     Sequence number . . .  ''''''''
       Name                                   Data    Decimal
       Type      Name        Ref    Length    Type    Positions    Use ─────┘
        _       ACTNO_        _        3        A        __          _

       Functions
       _____

       F3=Exit   F4=Prompt   F5=Refresh       F11=Previous record
       F12=Cancel            F23=Select prompt   F24=More keys
```

Figure 2-8   Filled-in **SEU** prompt-line format for DDS physical file code entry.

moved and **MM** on the last statement to be moved. Identical to a single instruction move, the target position is specified by an **A** or **B** entry in the number area.

Copying instructions to some other location in the source program is executed similarly to moving instructions, except that **C** or **CC** is used instead of **M** or **MM.**

A line may be *deleted* by typing the letter **D** at the beginning of a statement. Consecutive lines may be deleted from the listing by typing **DD** at the beginning of the first line and **DD** at the beginning of the last line of the group to be deleted.

After all the source code for the physical file is entered, F3 is pressed to exit from the **SEU EDIT** screen into an **SEU EXIT** menu. The screen shown in Figure 2-9, which gives the programmer *exit options,* will be displayed.

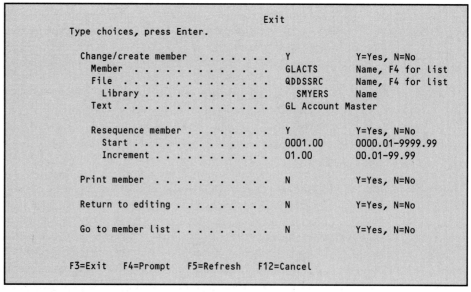

```
                                   Exit
       Type choices, press Enter.

           Change/create member . . . . . . .   Y          Y=Yes, N=No
             Member . . . . . . . . . . . .   GLACTS       Name, F4 for list
             File . . . . . . . . . . . . .   QDDSSRC      Name, F4 for list
             Library . . . . . . . . . . .    SMYERS       Name
             Text . . . . . . . . . . . . .   GL Account Master

           Resequence member . . . . . . . .   Y          Y=Yes, N=No
             Start . . . . . . . . . . . .    0001.00      0000.01-9999.99
             Increment . . . . . . . . . .    01.00        00.01-99.99

           Print member . . . . . . . . . .    N           Y=Yes, N=No

           Return to editing . . . . . . . .   N           Y=Yes, N=No

           Go to member list . . . . . . . .   N           Y=Yes, N=No


           F3=Exit   F4=Prompt   F5=Refresh   F12=Cancel
```

Figure 2-9   SEU EXIT screen.

1. The EXIT screen is displayed if **F3** is pressed when in **SEU.**

2. The variables shown in the EXIT menu are the defaults. Member, File, and Library names are accessed by the entries on the Programmer Menu or through PDM (Programmer Development Method). A Text entry provides documentation.

3. The source member currently entered (PF, LF, RPG, DSPF, PRTF, or CLP) is saved by the Y default for Change/create member. If an existing member is accessed by **SEU** and not changed, the default here will be an N (No).

4. The statements in the source file will automatically be sequenced unless the default Y is overridden with an N at the **Resequence member** prompt. Sequencing and statement incrementation may be modified by changing the Start and Increment prompts.

5. The N (No) default for Print member suppresses the printing of a source listing (before compilation). If a source listing is required, Y (Yes) must be entered for this prompt.

6. The N (No) default for Return to editing prevents return to **SEU** and the source file currently entered. Y (Yes) must be entered to return **SEU** back to the source listing.

7. The N (No) default for Go to member list will not display the names of any members in the current library. Y (Yes) must be entered to display a member list.

Figure 2-9   SEU EXIT screen. (Continued)

See Appendix A for a comprehensive discussion of the features and controls of **SEU.**

When the ENTER key is pressed, the member is saved and control is returned to the Programmer Menu. At this step of database development, the physical file source member is usually compiled. Again, this is a different procedure from that of the traditional computer system in which record formats are not compiled but are either hard-coded in the source program or included as a source code COPY member. With either method, the object will include the record format.

In the AS/400 environment, the physical file format is stored separately as a source member and the object is mutually exclusive from any high-level language program. The physical file's record format is called in during program compilation and becomes an integral part of the object.

Physical File Format Compilation

When control returns to the Programmer Menu, all the original prompt entries are retained, unless changed on the **SEU EXIT** menu. The physical file is compiled by entering a **3** in response to the Option prompt (Create object) and pressing the ENTER key.

The two listings shown in Figure 2-10 are generated when the physical file is compiled. The first includes the header information related to the physical file and lists the

```
5738SS1 V2R1M1  920306           Data Description          SMYERS/GLACTS     11/29/95 12:47:37    Page    1
File name . . . . . . . . . . . . . . . . . . . . . :   GLACTS
   Library name . . . . . . . . . . . . . . . . . :   SMYERS
File attribute . . . . . . . . . . . . . . . . . :   Physical
Source file containing DDS . . . . . . . . . . . :   QDDSSRC
   Library name . . . . . . . . . . . . . . . . . :   SMYERS
Source member containing DDS . . . . . . . . . . :   GLACTS
Source member last changed . . . . . . . . . . . :   11/29/95  12:47:23
Source listing options . . . . . . . . . . . . . :   *SOURCE    *LIST     *NOSECLVL
DDS generation severity level . . . . . . . . . :   20
DDS flagging severity level . . . . . . . . . . :   00
File type . . . . . . . . . . . . . . . . . . . :   *DATA
Authority . . . . . . . . . . . . . . . . . . . :   *LIBCRTAUT
Replace file . . . . . . . . . . . . . . . . . . :   *NO
Text . . . . . . . . . . . . . . . . . . . . . . :   GL Account Master
Compiler . . . . . . . . . . . . . . . . . . . . :   IBM AS/400 Data Description Processor
```

Figure 2-10   Listings generated from compilation of the physical file's (GLACTS) DDS source.

```
                         Data Description Source
SEQNBR *...+....1....+....2....+....3....+....4....+....5....+....6....+....7....+....8 Date
  100    A        R GLACTSR                                                           11/29/95
  200    A          ACTNO       3            COLHDG('ACCOUNT NUMBER')                  11/29/95
  300    A          NAME       27            COLHDG('ACCOUNT NAME')                    11/29/95
  400    A          TYPE       20            COLHDG('ACCOUNT TYPE')                    11/29/95
  500    A          BALNCE      8S 2         COLHDG('ACCOUNT BALANCE')                 11/29/95
                    * * * * *  E N D  O F  S O U R C E  * * * * *
5738SS1 V2R1M1 920306              Data Description         SMYERS/GLACTS        11/29/95 12:47:37    Page  2
                                   Expanded Source
                                                                        Field     Buffer position
SEQNBR *...+....1....+....2....+....3....+....4....+....5....+....6....+....7....+....8 Length   Out    In
  100    A        R GLACTSR
  200    A          ACTNO       3A B         COLHDG('ACCOUNT NUMBER')        3         1      1
                                             TEXT('ACCOUNT NUMBER')
  300    A          NAME       27A B         COLHDG('ACCOUNT NAME')         27         4      4
                                             TEXT('ACCOUNT NAME')
  400    A          TYPE       20A B         COLHDG('ACCOUNT TYPE')         20        31     31
                                             TEXT('ACCOUNT TYPE')
  500    A          BALNCE      8S 2B        COLHDG('ACCOUNT BALANCE')       8        51     51
                                             TEXT('ACCOUNT BALANCE')
                 * * * * *  E N D  O F  E X P A N D E D  S O U R C E  * * * * *
5738SS1 V2R1M1 920306              Data Description         SMYERS/GLACTS        11/29/95 12:47:37    Page  3
                                   Message Summary
    Total        Informational     Warning     Error     Severe
                     (0-9)         (10-19)    (20-29)    (30-99)
      0              0               0          0          0
* CPC7301   00             Message . . . . :  File GLACTS created in Library SMYERS.
                    * * * * *  E N D  O F  C O M P I L A T I O N  * * * * *
```

Figure 2-10 Listings generated from compliation of the physical file's (GLACTS) DDS Source. (Continued)

source member format exactly as created. A second listing, which is printed immediately after the first, is called an **EXPANDED SOURCE.** It supplements the original source with the **COLHDG** keywords for each field and identifies field lengths and the beginning position of each field in the output buffer. During program execution, *input* and *output buffers* are automatically built for all physical files processed. It is important to note that after the physical file is loaded, subsequent compilation will delete all the data in the file.

Building a Physical File without Record or Field Definitions

A physical file may be defined without record and field descriptions by the **CRTPF** (create physical file) command. This control language statement may be entered from the Programmer Menu by specifying **5** as the Option and **CRTPF** on the command line. After F4 is pressed, the prompt screens shown in Figure 2-11 will display. Most of the prompts shown in the three screens in Figure 2-11 have default values specified. However, the programmer may change any entry as needed. For a complete explanation of each prompt line, the related *IBM AS/400* Control Language manual should be referenced.

When a physical file is built without a DDS code, two parameters the user must respond to are the physical file name **(File)** entry on line 1 of the first screen and the Record length entry on line 6 of the same screen. Defaults may be taken for the remaining prompts in the other displays.

Note that the **CRTPF** command functions are automatically executed when the previously discussed method of building a DDS file and then creating an object member for it by selecting Option **3** on the Programmer Menu is followed. Unless some of the defaults on the parameter screens have to be changed, the create physical file (**CRTPF**) functions are transparent to the programmer.

Displaying the Attributes of a Physical File

The attributes of a physical file may be displayed by the **DSPFD** (*Display File Description*) command. Screens related to this command are accessed by entering a **5** in the Option field, typing **DSPFD** and the **file name** on the command line of the Programmer Menu or from the command line of any AS/400 display, and pressing F4. If the file name is omitted, a prompt screen will display in which the file name and library must be entered. Under most circumstances the default is assumed for the library name.

```
                        Create Physical File (CRTPF)

Type choices, press Enter.
File . . . . . . . . . . . . .    _____     Name
  Library . . . . . . . . . .    *CURLIB___     Name, *CURLIB
Source file . . . . . . . .      QDDSSRC___     Name
  Library . . . . . . . . .       *LIBL_____    Name, *LIBL, *CURLIB
Source member . . . . . . .      *FILE_____     Name, *FILE
Record length, if no DDS . . . .   _____        Number
Generation severity level . . .  20____          0-30
Flagging severity level . . . .  0_____          0-30
File type . . . . . . . . .      *DATA          *DATA, *SRC
Member, if desired . . . . . .   *FILE_____    Name, *FILE, *NONE
Text 'description' . . . . . .   *SRCMBRTXT_____

  _____

                                                            Bottom
F3=Exit   F4=Prompt   F5=Refresh   F10=Additional parameters   F12=Cancel
          F13=How to use this display        F24=More keys
```

Press F10
to access next
display

```
--------------------------------------------------------------------------
                        Create Physical File (CRTPF)

Type choices, press Enter.
                        Additional Parameters
Source listing options . . . .    _____     *SRC, *NOSRC, *SOURCE...
              + for more values   _____
System . . . . . . . . . . . .   *LCL_____      *LCL, *RMT, *FILETYPE
Expiration date for member . . . *NONE___       Date, *NONE
Maximum members . . . . . . .    1_____          Number, *NOMAX
Access path maintenance . . . .  *IMMED         *IMMED, *DLY, *REBLD
Access path recovery . . . . . .  _____         *NO, *AFTIPL, *IPL
Force keyed access path . . . .  *NO_           *NO, *YES
Member size:
  Initial number of records . .  10000_____    1-2147483646, *NOMAX
  Increment number of records .  1000__          Number
  Maximum increments . . . . . . 3_____          Number
Allocate storage . . . . . . .   *NO_           *NO, *YES
                                                            More...
F3=Exit   F4=Prompt   F5=Refresh   F12=Cancel   F13=How to use this display
F24=More keys
```

Roll to access
next display

```
--------------------------------------------------------------------------
                        Create Physical File (CRTPF)

Type choices, press Enter.
Contiguous storage . . . . . .   *NO_           *NO, *YES
Preferred storage unit . . . .   *ANY__         1-255, *ANY
Records to force a write . . . . *NONE_         Number, *NONE
Maximum file wait time . . . . . *IMMED         Seconds, *IMMED, *CLS
Maximum record wait time . . .   60____          Seconds, *NOMAX, *IMMED
Share open data path . . . . .   *NO_           *NO, *YES
Max % deleted records allowed .  *NONE_         1-100, *NONE
Reuse deleted records . . . . .  *NO_           *YES, *NO
Coded character set ID . . . .   *JOB_____     *JOB, *HEX...
Allow update operation . . . . . *YES           *YES, *NO
Allow delete operation . . . . . *YES           *YES, *NO
Record format level check . . .  *YES           *YES, *NO
Authority . . . . . . . . . .    *LIBCRTAUT     Name, *LIBCRTAUT, *ALL...

                                                            Bottom
F3=Exit   F4=Prompt   F5=Refresh   F12=Cancel   F13=How to use this display
F24=More keys
```

Figure 2-11 CRTPF command-generated screens to create a physical file.

The user must press ENTER if the prompt screen is displayed first to access the first of
the five displays shown in Figure 2-12. After the first screen (Page 1) is displayed, rolling

```
5738SS1 V2R1M1  920306                Display File Description                        11/18/95  15:03:20      Page   1
    File . . . . . . . . . . . :  CH1PF1
    Library . . . . . . . . . :  SMYERS
    Type of information . . . . :  *ALL
    File attributes . . . . . . :  *ALL
    System . . . . . . . . . :  *LCL
    Processor . . . . . . . . . :  IBM AS/400 Display File Description Processor

    File . :  CH1PF1       Library . :  SMYERS        Type of file . :  Physical *DATA       Auxiliary Storage Pool ID . :  01

                                          Data Base File Attributes

        Externally described file . . . . . . . . . :          Yes
        File level identifier . . . . . . . . . . . :          0921222105358
        Creation date . . . . . . . . . . . . . . :          12/22/94
        Text 'description' . . . . . . . . . . :  TEXT
        Maximum members . . . . . . . . . . . :  MAXMBRS        1
        Number of members . . . . . . . . . . . :                 1
        Member size                               SIZE
           Initial number of records . . . . . . . :          10000
           Increment number of records . . . . . . :          1000
           Maximum number of increments . . . . . :          3
        Record capacity . . . . . . . . . . . :                13000
        Allocate storage . . . . . . . . . . . :  ALLOCATE      *NO
        Contiguous storage . . . . . . . . . . :  CONTIG        *NO
        Preferred storage unit . . . . . . . . . :  UNIT        *ANY
        Records to force a write . . . . . . . . :  FRCRATIO     *NONE
        Maximum file wait time . . . . . . . . . :  WAITFILE     *IMMED
        Maximum record wait time . . . . . . . . :  WAITRCD       60
        Max % deleted records allowed . . . . . . :  DLTPCT      *NONE
        Reuse deleted records . . . . . . . . . :  REUSEDLT     *NO
        Coded character set identifier . . . . . . :  CCSID      65535
        Allow read operation . . . . . . . . . :                Yes
        Allow write operation . . . . . . . . . :                Yes
        Allow update operation . . . . . . . . . :  ALWUPD      *YES
        Allow delete operation . . . . . . . . . :  ALWDLT      *YES
        Record format level check . . . . . . . . :  LVLCHK     *YES
        Access path . . . . . . . . . . . . . :                Arrival
        Maximum record length . . . . . . . . . :               84
        File is currently journaled . . . . . . . :            No
- - - - - - - - - - - - - - - - - - - - - - - - - - - - - - - - - - - - - - - - - - - - - - - - - - - - - - - - - - -
5738SS1 V2R1M1  920306                Display File Description                        11/18/95  15:03:20      Page   2
    File . :  CH1PF1       Library . :  SMYERS        Type of file . :  Physical *DATA       Auxiliary Storage Pool ID . :  01
                                          Access Path Description
        Access path . . . . . . . . . . . . . :               Arrival
- - - - - - - - - - - - - - - - - - - - - - - - - - - - - - - - - - - - - - - - - - - - - - - - - - - - - - - - - - -
5738SS1 V2R1M1  920306                Display File Description                        1/18/93  15:03:20      Page   3
    File . :  CH1PF1       Library . :  SMYERS        Type of file . :  Physical *DATA       Auxiliary Storage Pool ID . :  01
                                          Member Description
        Member . . . . . . . . . . . . . . . :  MBR          CH1PF1
        Member level identifier . . . . . . . . . :          0921222105443
        Member creation date . . . . . . . . . . :          12/22/94
        Text 'description' . . . . . . . . . . :  TEXT
        Expiration date for member . . . . . . . :  EXPDATE     *NONE
        Member size                               SIZE
           Initial number of records . . . . . . . :          10000
           Increment number of records . . . . . . :          1000
           Maximum number of increments . . . . . :          3
        Current number of increments . . . . . . :                0
        Record capacity . . . . . . . . . . . :                13000
        Current number of records . . . . . . . :                 6
        Number of deleted records . . . . . . . :                 0
        Allocate storage . . . . . . . . . . . :  ALLOCATE      *NO
        Contiguous storage . . . . . . . . . . :  CONTIG        *NO
        Preferred storage unit . . . . . . . . . :  UNIT         *ANY
        Records to force a write . . . . . . . . :  FRCRATIO     *NONE
        Share open data path . . . . . . . . . . :  SHARE        *NO
        Max % deleted records allowed . . . . . . :  DLTPCT      *NONE
        Data space size in bytes . . . . . . . . :              4096
        Implicit access path sharing . . . . . . :            No
        Last change date/time . . . . . . . . . :            12/22/94  11:10:10
        Last save date/time . . . . . . . . . . :            11/17/95  11:25:59
        Last restore date/time . . . . . . . . . :
        Date last used . . . . . . . . . . . . :            11/18/95
        Days used count . . . . . . . . . . . :                 1
        Date use count reset . . . . . . . . :
- - - - - - - - - - - - - - - - - - - - - - - - - - - - - - - - - - - - - - - - - - - - - - - - - - - - - - - - - - -




5738SS1 V2R1M1  920306                Display File Description                        11/18/95  15:03:20      Page   4
    File . :  CH1PF1       Library . :  SMYERS        Type of file . :  Physical *DATA       Auxiliary Storage Pool ID . :  01
                                          Record Format List
                          Record  Format Level
    Format     Fields Length  Identifier
    CH1PF1R      5      84    4F7CA0E2A97A8
        Text . . . :
        Total number of formats . . . . . . . . . :          1
        Total number of fields . . . . . . . . . :          5
        Total record length . . . . . . . . . . :          84
- - - - - - - - - - - - - - - - - - - - - - - - - - - - - - - - - - - - - - - - - - - - - - - - - - - - - - - - - - -
5738SS1 V2R1M1  920306                Display File Description                        11/18/95  15:03:20      Page   5
    File . :  CH1PF1       Library . :  SMYERS        Type of file . :  Physical *DATA       Auxiliary Storage Pool ID . :  01
                                          Member List
                     Source  Creation  Last Change               Deleted
    Member      Size Type    Date      Date     Time    Records  Records   Text
    CH1PF1      4096         12/22/94  11/17/95 11:10:10    6        0
        Total number of members . . . . . . . . . :          1
        Total records . . . . . . . . . . . . . :          6
        Total deleted records . . . . . . . . . . :          0
        Total of member sizes . . . . . . . . . :
                                                    4096
```

Figure 2-12   DSPFD *(Display File Description)* displays.

up will display the other four pages sequentially. Note that each page provides different information about the physical file:

Page 1: *Data Base File Attributes* - Identifies the current attributes of the physical file. This listing is similar to the displays generated by the **CRTPF** command used to change any default attributes when the file was created.

Page 2: *Access Path Description* - Specifies how the data in the physical file will be processed. "Arrival" indicates that the data will be processed in the order it is stored in the file. "Keyed" indicates that the data will be processed in a key value order.

Page 3: *Member Description* - Provides information about the physical file **members. Members** are discussed in detail later in this chapter.

Page 4: *Record Format List* - Identifies the total number of record formats in the file (physical files may only have one), the total number of fields in the record format, and the total record length in bytes.

Page 5: *Member List* - Specifies the total number of members that the physical file supports, the total number of records stored in the file, the total number of logically deleted records, and the total number of member sizes.

A detailed explanation of each function may be found in the related *IBM AS/400 Control Language Reference* manual.

Displaying the Field Attributes of a Physical File

The record and field attributes of a physical file may be displayed by using the **DSPFFD** (*Display File Field Description*) command. The command may be executed by entering a **5** in the Option field, typing **DSPFFD** and the **file name** on the command line of the Programmer Menu or from the command line on any AS/400 display, and pressing F4. If the file name is omitted, a prompt screen will display where the library and file names must be entered. Usually the default is assumed for the library name. If the prompt screen is displayed first, press the ENTER key to access the **DSPFFD** display shown in Figure 2-13. Note that general information for Input parameters, File Information, and Record Format Information, with detailed *Field Level* information related to the fields in the physical file, is included.

```
5738SS1 V2R1M1  920306      Display File Field Description

   Input parameters
      File . . . . . . . . . . . . . . . . . . . . . :   CH1PF1
         Library . . . . . . . . . . . . . . . . . :   SMYERS

   File Information
      File . . . . . . . . . . . . . . . . . . . . . :   CH1PF1
         Library . . . . . . . . . . . . . . . . . :   SMYERS
      File location . . . . . . . . . . . . . . . :   *LCL
      Externally described . . . . . . . . . . :   Yes
      Number of record formats . . . . . . . . :       1
      Type of file . . . . . . . . . . . . . . . :   Physical
      File creation date . . . . . . . . . . . . :   12/22/92

   Record Format Information
      Record format . . . . . . . . . . . . . . . :   CH1PF1R
      Format level identifier . . . . . . . . . :   4F7CA0E2A97A8
      Number of fields . . . . . . . . . . . . . :       5
      Record length . . . . . . . . . . . . . . . :      84
```

Figure 2-13 DSPFFD (*Display File Field* Description) screen.

```
Field Level Information

                Data         Field  Buffer  Buffer      Field     Column
        Field   Type         Length Length  Position    Usage     Heading

        NAME    CHAR            25     25        1        Both     CUSTOMER NAME
          Field text . . . . . . . . . . . . . . :  CUSTOMER NAME
        . Coded Character Set Identifier . . . . . :  65535
        STREET  CHAR            29     29       26        Both      CUSTOMER AD-
DRESS
          Field text . . . . . . . . . . . . . . :  CUSTOMER ADDRESS
          Coded Character Set Identifier . . . . . :  65535
        CITY    CHAR            25     25       55        Both     CUSTOMER CITY
          Field text . . . . . . . . . . . . . . :  CUSTOMER CITY
          Coded Character Set Identifier . . . . . :  65535
        STATE   CHAR             2      2       80        Both     CUSTOMER STATE
          Field text . . . . . . . . . . . . . . :  CUSTOMER STATE
          Coded Character Set Identifier . . . . . :  65535
        ZIP     PACKED         5  0     3       82        Both     ZIP CODE
          Field text . . . . . . . . . . . . . . :  ZIP CODE
```

Figure 2-13 **DSPFFD** (*Display File Field* Description) screen. (Continued)

PHYSICAL FILE MAINTENANCE COMMANDS

Some of the common Control Language commands used to maintain physical files are detailed in the following list.

CHGPF   *(Change Physical File)* - Supports changes in the attributes of a physical file without requiring its recreation with the **CRTPF** command. The data in the physical file is <u>not</u> lost when **CHGPF** is executed.

CLRPFM   *(Clear Physical File)* - Clears a physical file member of all data records without deleting the file's structure.

CPYF   *(Copy File)* - Copies the data stored in a physical file to an output device or another physical file. Either all of the records or only selected records may be copied. A variety of selection criteria may be specified, such as a key or a relative record number range. When output is to a printer, either character or hexadecimal format may be specified. For readability, however, hexadecimal format is necessary if **packed numeric** values are stored in one or more fields of the record format.

DLTF   *(Delete File)* - Deletes the physical file's object and any data stored in the file. A physical file cannot be deleted if a logical file has been created over it or if the file is in use.

DSPPFM   *(Display Physical File Member)* - Displays the field values in the records stored in a physical file. Records are displayed in arrival sequence even if the file was created as keyed. A character or hexadecimal display of the record values may be specified. Other than printing the current display with the Print key, printer output is not supported.

RMVM   *(Remove Member)* - Removes the specified member from the physical file and deletes all of the data stored in the member.

Any of these CL commands may be executed by entering the command on the command line of an AS/400 display and pressing F4. One or more prompt screens will display, enabling the programmers to enter command specific data.

PHYSICAL FILE MEMBERS

Unless changed by the Maximum number of members option in the **CRTPF** command, a physical file will automatically be created with <u>one</u> member in which data may be stored.

The physical file's name will be assigned to this member unless specified otherwise in the **CRTPF** command. A file may be initially created with no members and still include a record definition (fields and their attributes). However, if members are to be supported later, the **CHGPF** command must be executed and the **MAXMBRS** parameter changed to the required number of members. Members may be added to a physical file without destroying the data in the existing members.

When a physical file includes more than the default member, additional members are subsets of the data in the file. Each member, which must have a unique name, is automatically assigned a structure identical to the related physical file's DDS format.

Figure 2-14 illustrates the member concept. In the example shown, a separate member is created for each of the five days of a work week. When the physical file was created with the **CRTPF** command, the *Maximum number of members* (**MAXMBRS**) parameter must be assigned 5, and DAY1 must be assigned for the member name *(MBR)* parameter. When the file is processed, DAY1 will always be considered the default member. To process the five members in any combination, a Control Language program must be written. If the physical file name were specified in an RPG/400 program without a supporting CL program, only the data in the first member, DAY1, would be accessed.

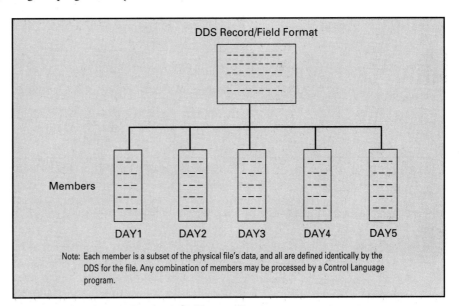

Figure 2-14 Example physical file member structure.

Maintenance Commands for Physical File Members

The following functions may be performed for physical file members:

1. Members may be added to an existing physical file.
2. Any existing member may be renamed.
3. Any member may be removed from the physical file.
4. Some of the attributes of an existing member may be changed.

The commands to perform these maintenance functions are explained in the following paragraphs.

ADDPFM *(Add Physical File Member)* - Controls the addition of a member to the physical file after it is created.

RNMM *(Rename Member)* - Changes the name of an existing member. Name of the physical file is not changed.

RMVM *(Remove Member)* - Removes the named member and its data. Any removed member cannot be referenced by the system.

CHGPFM *(Change Physical File Member)* - Supports limited changes to a member, which include only the **EXPDATE** (the member's expiration date), **SHARE** (whether the member can be shared), and **TEXT** (text description) parameters. If extensive changes are needed, such as an increase in the maximum file size, the **CHGPF** command, however, will change the selected attribute(s) for every member supported by the physical file.

Data File Terminology

The terms associated with the elements of a data file are *file, record, field, byte,* and *bit.* Figure 2-15 identifies the hierarchy and relationship of these items to each other. When a physical file is read, one record at a time is transferred from the storage device into an input buffer area in memory. Then, the field values in the record are available for processing.

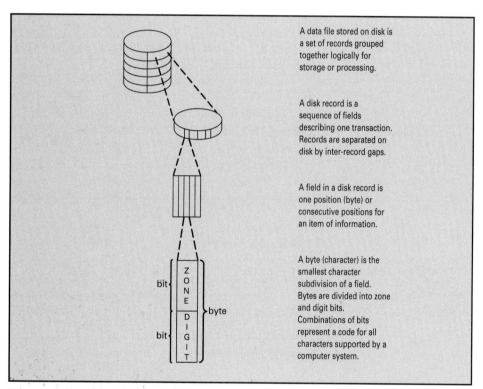

Figure 2-15   Data file terminology.

Loading Data to a Physical File

After a physical file has been created and successfully compiled, a shell exists with no data records stored. Data may be written (added) to the physical file by any of the following methods:

1. **DFU** *(Data File Utility)* - Procedures to use this utility are explained in Appendix C.
2. Output from batch or interactive **RPG/400** programs.
3. Output of a **Sort** controlled by a **CL** program.
4. Output from a tape-stored file.
5. Output from the execution of the **CPYF** *(Copy File)* utility.
6. Output from a **Query** program.

The maximum number of records that may be stored in a physical file is approximately 17 million; the maximum number of fields in the one-record format, 8,000; and the maximum number of bytes in the record, 32,766.

Until display files are introduced in Chapter 14, any physical files created by the reader of this text will have to be loaded with data using the *Data File Utility* (**DFU**).

Data Entry Considerations

In the AS/400 environment, data is initially entered through a workstation under the control of a utility (for example, **DFU**) or an interactive RPG/400 program. Regardless of the entry method, several important concepts must be understood. First, *alphabetic* and *alphanumeric* data is usually stored left-justified in its related field. Consequently, the first character of the data value is entered in the first position of the assigned field area.

Numeric data must be *right-justified* in the assigned field. Hence, the data must be entered so that the *low-order* digit of the value is stored in the low-order position of the field. When the value is stored, any unused *high-order* bytes are automatically padded with leading zeros.

Figure 2-16 illustrates the rules related to entering *alphanumeric, alphabetic,* and *numeric* data values. RPG/400 does not distinguish between *alphanumeric* and *alphabetic* values. Any field not defined as *numeric* is processed as *alphanumeric* (**character**).

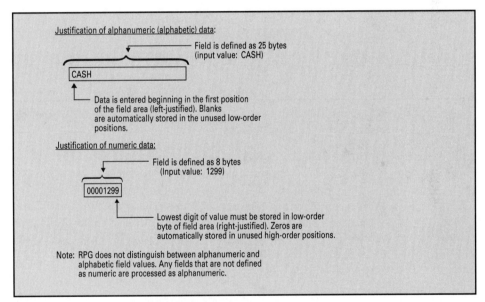

Figure 2-16 Justification rules for entering alphanumeric, alphabetic, and numeric data.

Printing a Listing of a Physical File's Data

As was previously mentioned, the **DSPPFM** or **CPYF** utility may be used to review the data stored in a physical file. The **DSPFFM** utility does not support printing (except with the Print key), whereas the **CPYF** utility does. To access the **CPYF** utility, the command **CPYF** must be entered on a command line of a display, and F4 must be pressed. The display shown in Figure 2-17 will appear.

Options are included in the **CPYF** utility to access one or more records by their key value(s) or relative position in the file. Usually, not all the records in the physical file will be accessed by this utility.

When output is directed to a printer (*PRINT selected), a partial listing in *HEX (hexidecimal) format and one in *CHAR (character) format are generated by the **CPYF**

```
                          Copy File (CPYF)

Type choices, press Enter.

From file  . . . . . . . . . .   GLACTS      Name
  Library  . . . . . . . . . .   SMYERS      Name, *LIBL, *CURLIB
To file  . . . . . . . . . .     *PRINT      Name, *PRINT
  Library  . . . . . . . . . .   *LIBL       Name, *LIBL, *CURLIB
From member  . . . . . . . . .   *FIRST         Name, generic*, *FIRST,
*ALL
To member or label . . . . . .   *FIRST      Name, *FIRST, *FROMMBR
Replace or add records . . . .   *NONE       *NONE, *ADD, *REPLACE
Create file  . . . . . . . . .   *NO         *NO, *YES
Print format . . . . . . . . .   *HEX        *CHAR, *HEX

                                                              Bottom
F3=Exit   F4=Prompt   F5=Refresh   F10=Additional parameters   F12=Cancel
F13=How to use this display        F24=More keys
```

From file

Name of the physical file accessed must be entered for this prompt. The name of a logical, diskette, tape, inline, or DDM file may also be entered for this prompt.

Library

The library name in which the physical file is stored must be entered. If the default ***LIBL** is assumed, the user's library list will be searched for the physical file. The ***CURLIB** prompt will access the currently active library.

To file

Output may be directed to another physical file, printer, diskette, tape, or **DDM** file by specifying the name of the file or to the printer by selecting the ***PRINT** option.

Library

When a disk file is specified for the To file prompt, the library name in which it is stored may be entered or the default ***LIBL** may be assumed.

From member

The default ***FIRST** specifies that the first member of the related physical file will be accessed. If the data in a specific member is to be accessed, the name of that member must be entered. If the data from all of the members supported by the physical file are to be accessed, ***ALL** must be entered for this prompt. This prompt is ignored when output is directed to a printer **(*PRINT).**

To member or label

The default ***FIRST** specifies that output is to be directed to the first member of the physical file entered for the **To file** prompt. A specific member may be specified by entering its name for this prompt. This prompt is ignored when output is direct to a printer **(*PRINT).**

Replace or add records

The default ***NONE** indicates that no records are stored in the **To file** item. The ***ADD** prompt supports the addition of records to the **To file** item. ***REPLACE** will replace records stored in the **To file** with those from the **From file.**

Create file

The default ***NO** indicates that a **To file** will not be created. A file may be created by entering ***YES** for this prompt.

Print format

In order to interpret packed numeric field values, ***HEX** is required for printed output. If packed fields are not stored in the physical file's records, ***CHAR** may be specified.

Figure 2-17 Copy file **(CPYF)** display.

command, as shown in Figure 2-18. Note that if the BALNCE field value was stored in *packed decimal* instead of *signed,* the ***CHAR** format would print unreadable characters for that field.

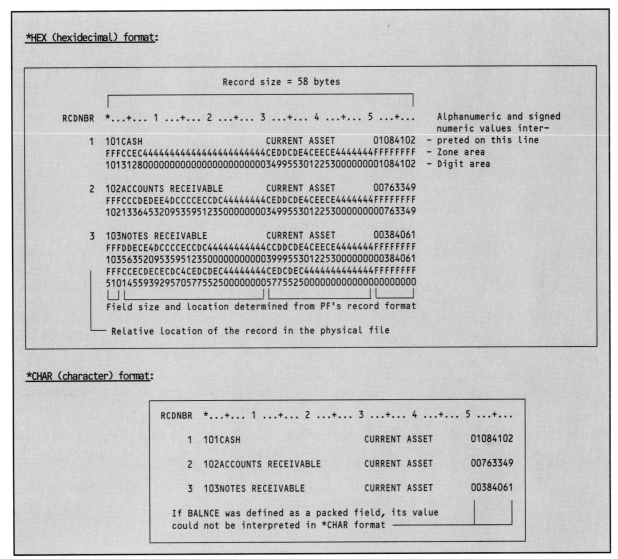

Figure 2-18   Partial ***HEX** and ***CHAR** listings generated by the **CPYF** command.

Programmer Development Manager

In lieu of using the Programmer Menu to access the environments to perform source entry and compilation, execute CL commands, access libraries, and so forth, the programmer may prefer to use the *Programmer Development Manager* (**PDM**). The procedures to use this utility are detailed in Appendix B.

SUMMARY

The AS/400 software requires that the database system define all files. Files which contain data are referred to as *physical files* and are built with or without a *data description.* Data files built with a data description are processed as **externally defined** files in an RPG/400 program. Those that do not have a data description must be *program-defined.* This topic is discussed in Chapter 3.

The **data description** for a physical file is created by entering the source code by **SEU** *(Source Entry Utility)* according to the syntax of the *Data Description Specifications.* After the source code is entered and saved, it must be compiled. The **CRTPF** *(Create Physical File)* command compiles the source code. Numerous default attributes are included with the **CRTPF** command and may be changed as needed.

Data may be loaded to the physical file by **DFU** *(Data File Utility),* interactively, or in a batch mode by an RPG/400 program.

Physical files may be created as *keyed* or *nonkeyed.* A *keyed* file will be processed in a batch mode in a default ascending key order. *Nonkeyed* files are processed in *arrival sequence.* With random processing, the records in a *keyed file* are accessed by their *key value,* whereas the records in a *non-keyed* file are accessed by their *relative position in the file.*

Twenty-eight keywords are available to control a related number of processing functions. Their use will depend on the requirements of the application.

Members, which use the same data structure, may be added to an existing physical file. Hence, a physical file may support more than one database file, all with the same record format.

Utilities are available to access the file and field attributes of a physical file. The *Display File Description* **(DSPFD)** command displays all of the default and user-supplied attributes of a physical file, and the **DSPFFD** *(Display File Field Description)* command displays the field attributes.

After the physical file is loaded with data, field values may be examined by the **CPYF** *(Copy File)* or **DSPPFM** *(Display Physical File Member)* command. The **CPYF** command generates a hard copy of the file in character or hexadecimal format, whereas the **DSPPFM** command displays the field values only, in either format. Software is also available from vendors that provides for many of the functions necessary for the maintenance of physical files.

QUESTIONS

2-1. What is an externally defined file? What two types are supported on the AS/400?

2-2. Explain the differences between a *database* and a *program-defined* file. How are the field attributes included in an RPG program for each method?

2-3. What organization types are supported for physical files?

2-4. Refer to Question 2-3, and explain the processing features of each organization type.

2-5. Explain the term *composite key.*

2-6. Explain how a physical file may be processed by any field included in the file in an ascending or descending order. "Sorting" is not an acceptable answer.

2-7. Name the steps followed for building a physical file.

2-8. What form is used to code a physical file? For a *non-keyed* file, what are the logical levels of coding? What are they for a *keyed sequence file?*

2-9. How many record formats may be included in a physical file?

2-10. What is the function of *nonjoined* and *joined* logical files?

2-11. What type of physical file is shown in the following figure? Explain the meaning of each entry.

2-12. Refer to Question 2-11, and notice that some of the fields do not include an entry in column 35. What is the default type for these fields?

2-13. Refer to Question 2-11, and explain the function of the letter P in column 35 for the QTY field. What does the length entry for this field type refer to?

2-14. Rewrite the coding in Question 2-11 to define a *keyed* sequence file. Assume that duplicate keys are not to be supported and that DEPT# and PART# are to be specified as a composite key.

2-15. What is the function of the following physical file keywords?

COLHDG	EDTWRD	REFFLD
DESCEND	LIFO	TEXT
EDTCDE	REF	UNIQUE

2-16. What entries are needed on the Programmer Menu to call the utility to enter the DDS code for a physical file?

2-17. Name the utility used to enter the DDS code for a physical file. What is a prompt line in this utility?

2-18. After the source code for a physical file is entered, explain the procedures that must be followed to exit from the utility and prepare the physical file for execution.

2-19. How many listings are generated when option **3** is selected from the Programmer Menu for the compilation of a physical file? Briefly explain how the listings differ.

2-20. What Control Language command is executed when option **3** is selected from the Programmer Menu?

2-21. Under what circumstances does the **CRTPF** command have to be explicitly specified?

2-22. What CL command is used to display the attributes of a physical file? Name the CL command needed to display the field attributes of a physical file.

2-23. Explain the function of the following physical file maintenance commands:

CHGPF	CLRPFM	CPYF
DSPPFM	RMVM	DLTF

2-24. Explain the structure of a physical file that supports four members. Where are the *file, record,* and *field* attributes defined?

2-25. How many default members are assigned when a physical file is created without changing any parameters? How is a file created to support more than one member?

2-26. What is the function of each of the following maintenance commands for members?

ADDPFM	RNMM	RMVM	CHGPFM

2-27. If a combination of the members in a physical file are to be selectively processed, what is required to provide this control? Which member(s) is/are processed if only the file name is referenced?

2-28. By what methods may data be loaded to a physical file?

PROGRAMMING ASSIGNMENTS

For all files (physical, logical, display, printer, RPG/400 programs, and CL programs) created by students, the following naming convention is recommended:

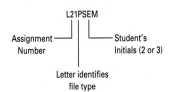

Note: File types should be identified as follows:
      P = Physical files, L = Logical files, D = Display files,
      P = Printer files, R = RPG programs, C = CL programs, S = Sort

For the following programming assignments:

1. Complete the physical file coding on a DDS form.
2. Enter the code with **SEU.** Save, compile, debug, and retain the listings.
3. Load the related data using **DFU.**
4. Generate a ***HEX** listing with the **CPYF** command.
5. Use the **DSPFD** command to display the physical file's parameters.
6. Use the **DSPFFD** command to display the field attributes in the physical file.

Programming Assignment 2-1: ACTIVE EMPLOYEE FILE

Physical File Record Format:

```
                    PHYSICAL FILE DESCRIPTION

        SYSTEM: AS/400                        DATE: Yours
        FILE NAME: Yours                      REV NO: 0
        RECORD NAME: Yours                    KEY LENGTH: 4
        SEQUENCE: Unique                      RECORD SIZE: 27

                       FIELD DEFINITIONS

        FIELD    FIELD NAME   SIZE  TYPE    POSITION      COMMENTS
         NO                                FROM    TO

          1      EMP#           4    C        1      4   Key field
          2      LNAME         16    C        5     20
          3      FINIT          1    C       21     21
          4      SINIT          1    C       22     22
          5      SSNO           9    P       23     27
```

Physical File Data:

Employee Number	Last Name	Initials 1st	2nd	Social Security Number
0001	WASHINGTON	G	G	017321799
0016	LINCOLN	A	T	018091864
0018	GRANT	U	S	018221885
0032	ROOSEVELT	F	D	018821945
0033	TRUMAN	H	S	018841973
0034	EISENHOWER	D	D	018901971
0039	CARTER	J		019771981
0040	REAGAN	R		020111989

Notes:

Specify the **COLHDG** keyword for all fields (key fields do <u>not</u> support **COLHDG**) and include a name that is more explicit than the limited six-character (or less) field name.

Observe from the description that SSNO (social security number) is defined as nine bytes in length; however, it is stored in only five positions (23–27) in the file. When the system *packs* numeric field values, it automatically uses the following formula to determine the size of the unpacked field value when it is stored in packed format:

$$\textbf{Packed size} = \frac{\textbf{Unpacked field size} + 1}{2}$$

Substituting for this example:

$$\textbf{Packed size} = \frac{9 + 1}{2} \textbf{ or 5}$$

When a *packed* numeric value is printed or displayed, it will automatically be unpacked and shown in a *signed* numeric format.

Programming Assignment 2-2: EASTERN STATE FILE

Physical File Record Format:

```
                    PHYSICAL FILE DESCRIPTION

SYSTEM: AS/400                              DATE: Yours
FILE NAME: Yours                            REV NO: 0
RECORD NAME: Yours                          KEY LENGTH: None
SEQUENCE: Non-keyed                         RECORD SIZE: 72

                     FIELD DEFINITIONS

  FIELD     FIELD NAME    SIZE   TYPE     POSITION      COMMENTS
   NO                                    FROM    TO


    1        STATE         20     C        1      20
    2        CAPITL        25     C       21      45
    3        SCODE          2     C       46      47
    4        CITY          25     C       48      72
```

Physical File Data:

State Name	State Capital	Letters	Largest City
MAINE	AUGUSTA	ME	PORTLAND
NEW HAMPSHIRE	CONCORD	NH	MANCHESTER
VERMONT	MONTPELIER	VT	BURLINGTON
MASSACHUSETTS	BOSTON	MA	BOSTON
CONNECTICUT	HARTFORD	CT	BRIDGEPORT
RHODE ISLAND	PROVIDENCE	RI	PROVIDENCE
NEW YORK	ALBANY	NY	NEW YORK
PENNSYLVANIA	HARRISBURG	PA	PHILADELPHIA
NEW JERSEY	TRENTON	NJ	NEWARK
DELAWARE	DOVER	DE	WILMINGTON
MARYLAND	ANNAPOLIS	MD	BALTIMORE
VIRGINIA	RICHMOND	VA	NORFOLK
WEST VIRGINIA	CHARLESTON	WV	HUNTINGTON
NORTH CAROLINA	RALEIGH	NC	CHARLOTTE
SOUTH CAROLINA	COLUMBIA	SC	COLUMBIA
GEORGIA	ATLANTA	GA	ATLANTA
FLORIDA	TALLAHASSEE	FL	JACKSONVILLE

Note: Use the **TEXT** keyword for all fields.

Programming Assignment 2-3: CUSTOMER MAILING FILE

Physical File Record Format:

```
                    PHYSICAL FILE DESCRIPTION

SYSTEM: AS/400                              DATE: Yours
FILE NAME: Yours                            REV NO: 0
RECORD NAME: Yours                          KEY LENGTH: None
SEQUENCE: Non-keyed                         RECORD SIZE: 44

                     FIELD DEFINITIONS

  FIELD     FIELD NAME    SIZE   TYPE     POSITION      COMMENTS
   NO                                    FROM    TO


    1        NAME          15     C        1      15
    2        STREET        14     C       16      29
    3        CITY          10     C       30      39
    4        STATE          2     C       40      41
    5        ZIP            5     P       42      44
```

```
Physical File Data:

   Name            Street        City      State    Zip

ANDREW GUMP     1 SUN AVENUE    MIAMI       FL      08881
DICK TRACY      CELL 8          ALCATRAZ    CA      07770
BEETLE BAILEY   "A" COMPANY     FORT DIX    NJ      06666
CHARLIE BROWN   8 DOGHOUSE ST.  ANYWHERE    US      00000
MOON MULLINS    16 TIDE ROAD    LAKEVILLE   CT      06497
LI`L ABNER      80 PATCH LANE   DOG PATCH   SC      99999
YOUR NAME       YOUR ADDRESS    ........    ..      .....
```

Note: Use the **COLHDG** keyword for all fields, and provide your own field text.

chapter 3

Introduction to RPG/400 Programming

DEVELOPMENT OF THE RPG PROGRAMMING LANGUAGE

In the early 1960s **RPG** *(Report Program Generator)* was developed by IBM as a computer language that would replace the manually wired boards of the IBM 1400 business machine. Because the jumper boards were column-oriented, this design was and still is included in **RPG.** During the next three decades IBM continued to make major enhancements to **RPG.** In 1969, **RPG II** was introduced. It supported major changes including disk file processing, workstation access, and array processing. When IBM introduced the System/38 in 1978, **RPG III** was also announced. **RPG III** supported new features including a built-in relational database management system and structured programming operations (including **IF/ELSE, DO, DOU,** and **DOW**). With the announcement of the AS/400 in 1988, **RPG/400** was released. New features, such as **AND/OR** support for **IF** and **DO** operations, thirty-digit numeric fields, and **SQL** *(Structured Query Language)* access, were some of the significant improvements incorporated in **RPG/400.**

Since 1978 and the introduction of **RPG III,** the language has become less *problem-oriented* and more *procedure-oriented* like COBOL. The programmer has the option of writing **RPG** programs that follow the built-in logic cycle which automatically controls **OPEN, READ, WRITE,** and **CLOSE** operations or explicitly defining these operations in the program. For performance considerations, writing programs that use the logic cycle should be avoided. The structured syntax of **RPG/400** should be used for most applications.

Most of the features included in **RPG II** and **RPG III** are fully supported by the AS/400 compiler. However, for programs which process workstation files that were written for a different computer system (IBM or other manufacturer), major modifications are usually required.

RPG CODING FORMS

As was mentioned previously, writing **RPG/400** programs requires a knowledge of the coding forms. The programmer's experience will determine whether the forms are actually used or if he or she enters the instructions directly using **SEU.** In any case, no attempt should be made to memorize the fields in every coding form. Some of the fields are special purpose and seldom used. In addition, some of the forms (for example, *Extension, Line Counter, and Input Specifications*) are required only when the related processing function is needed.

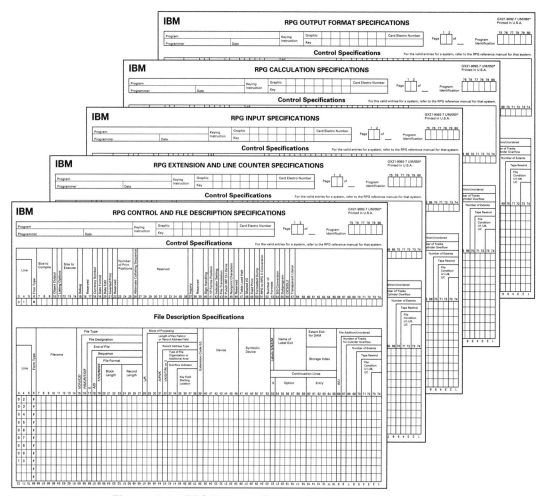

Figure 3-1 RPG/400 specification forms.

The seven commonly used RPG/400 coding forms are shown in Figure 3-1. The function of each specification form is explained in the following paragraphs.

- **Control Specifications (H in column 6)** - Only one Control instruction may be included in a program. Unless some of the functions included in this specification type are needed (such as change of date format or ignore nonprint characters), an H statement does not have to be entered. **SEU** will automatically include it as the first instruction in the compiled program.

- **File Description Specifications (F in column 6)** - Instructions for this specification define the attributes of the files (physical, logical, display, printer, and tape) processed by the RPG/400 program. Most RPG/400 programs include one or more *File Description* instructions.

- **Extension Specifications (E in column 6)** - Table, arrays, and select disk file processing functions are defined by instructions coded on this specification type.

- **Line Counter Specifications (L in column 6)** - (Lower section of the Extension Specifications). Defines and controls nonstandard page lengths directly in an RPG/400 program.

- **Input Specifications (I in column 6)** - Because physical files are usually created using DDS and are thereby externally defined, instructions for this specification type are not needed to define the record and field attributes. However, if a physical file was built without DDS, it would have to be **program-defined** and would require input statements to identify field sizes and their location in the body of the record.

- **Calculations Specifications (C in column 6)** - Arithmetic operations, table lookup, array processing, physical file maintenance functions, display file control, and internal subroutines are only a few of the controls supported by the instructions in this specification type.

- **Output Specifications (O in column 6)** - If output is directed to the system print file **(QSYSPRT),** RPG/400 output instructions are required for the report format. However, when the syntax for the report is specified in a programmer-supplied *printer file,* RPG/400 output coding is not needed. Also, for physical file maintenance (addition, update, deletion, and inquiry), output instructions do not have to be included in the program. Furthermore, the processing of display files is controlled in calculation instructions and does not require *Output Specifications.*

The preceding explanation of the specification forms indicated that those most commonly used in RPG/400 programs are the *File Description, Calculations,* and, to some extent, *Output Specifications.*

DEVELOPMENT OF AN RPG/400 PROGRAM

The steps followed in the development and processing of an RPG/400 program include

1. Program generation
2. Program execution

Figure 3-2 details the sequence of operations to create, save, compile, and execute an RPG/400 program.

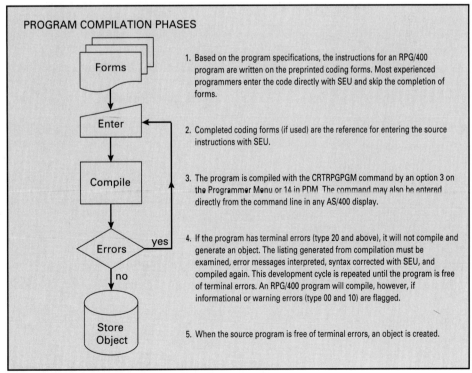

Figure 3-2 RPG/400 program development phases.

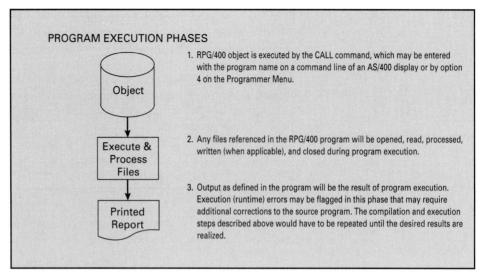

Figure 3-2   RPG/400 program development phases. (Continued)

WHAT DOES AN RPG/400 PROGRAM LOOK LIKE?

The completed specifications for an example program that reads a physical file, processes the records, and prints the field values are shown in Figure 3-3.

File Description Specifications

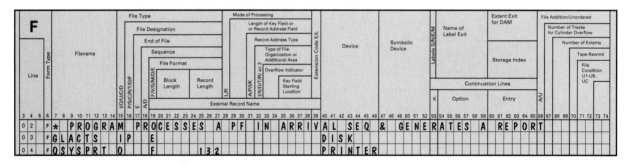

Output Specifications

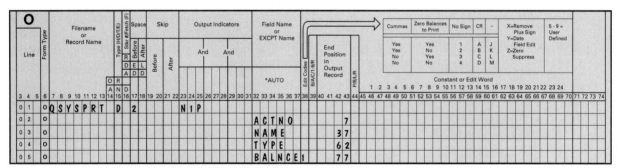

Figure 3-3   Completed RPG specifications for a program that processes a physical file and prints a report.

Examine Figure 3-3 and note the following:

1. A different form is used to define each logical section of the RPG/400 program. The *File Description Specifications* form defines the files (physical and

printer) processed by the program. *Output Specifications* reference the field values in the physical file's record format for output to a printer file.

2. Instructions to define the input record and field attributes of the physical file are not specified. Because the physical file is **externally defined** (fields defined by the database), the program does not have to explicitly reference the record and field attributes. When the RPG/400 program is compiled, the record and field definitions are included in the object generated.

3. Instructions for this example program must be arranged in an F, O *compilation order.* When all of the other form types are introduced (**H, E, L, I,** and **C**), an RPG program requires some or all of them, the instructions must be arranged in an **H, F, E, L, I, C, O** *compilation order.*

4. *Every instruction must include the related specification letter in column 6.* **SEU** will automatically supply the letter when the specific specification type is requested.

5. Each specification type includes special-function fields that are not required for every RPG/400 program. Some of the fields are not supported by RPG/400, and others are used only when the related processing feature is needed.

RPG/400 SYNTAX TO PROCESS AN EXTERNALLY DEFINED PHYSICAL FILE

File Description Specification Entries

The entries included on the *File Description* form for the example program are detailed in Figure 3-4.

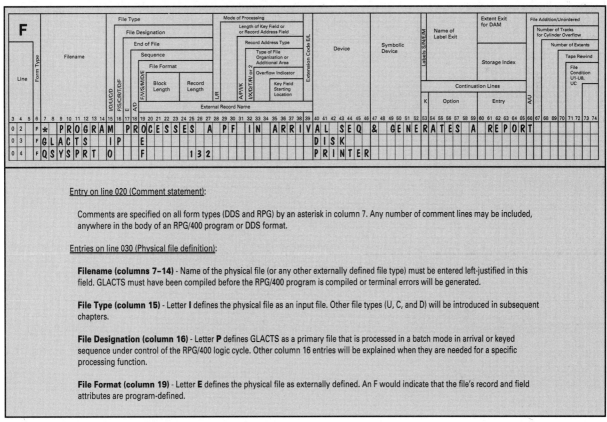

Figure 3-4   File Description form for a program that processes a physical file and prints a report.

Record Address Type (column 31) - No entry in this field indicates that the file will be processed in arrival sequence (order in which the records are stored in the file). **K** (indicating a keyed file) entered in this field would cause the file to be processed in a key value order. To process the physical file directly (without a logical file) in a key order, the file <u>must</u> have been created as a keyed file. On the other hand, a keyed file may be processed in an arrival sequence by omitting the letter K in this field.

Device (columns 40–46) - **DISK** is the required device name for all physical (and logical) files. The entry indicates the device type on which the file is stored.

<u>Entries on line 040 (Printer file definition):</u>

Filename (columns 7–14) - **QSYSPRT** is the system-supplied printer file name that is use as the default. In lieu of using **QSYSPRT,** the programmer may create his or her own printer file and include any select attributes.

File Type (column 15) - The letter **O** defines the file as output. Printer files may only be defined as output files.

File Format (column 19) - **F** in this field indicates that the record and field attributes are defined in the RPG/400 program with Output Specifications instructions.

Record Length (columns 24–27) - Because the file is program-defined (**F** in column 19), a record length value must be entered <u>right-justified</u> in this field. The entry 132 (standard width of most line printers), indicates that 132 characters will be printed on a line. A smaller value may be specified; however, the printer will still allocate 132 positions in the buffer created in memory for the printer.

Device (columns 40–46) - **PRINTER** must be used as the device name for all printer files.

Figure 3-4   File Description form for a program that processes a physical file and prints a report. (Continued)

The entries on the *Output Specifications* for the example program are explained in Figure 3-5.

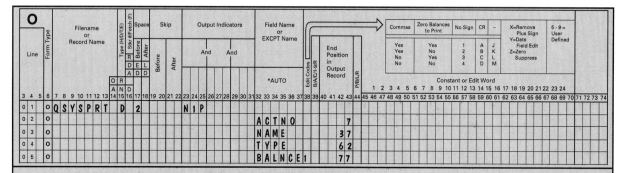

Filename or Record Name (columns 7–14) - Name of the printer or any other output file defined in the *File Description Specifications* must be entered <u>left-justified</u> in this field. The file name is entered only for the first output record and is not repeated in every instruction.

Type (column 15) - Letter D indicates that output will be executed at *Detail Time* under control of the RPG logic cycle. H (*Heading Time*), E (*Exception Time*), and T (*Total Time*) may also be specified. Each of these other line type entries will be discussed as the related subject is introduced.

Space (columns 17–18) - Line spacing in the body of a report is controlled by a Before and/or After entries. *Before* specifies that the spacing will occur <u>before</u> a line is printed and *After,* <u>after</u> the current line is printed. Value 0 through 3 may be specified for either of these fields. 0 (zero) indicates that no spacing will occur, 1 for single spacing, 2 for double spacing, and 3 for triple spacing. A maximum of five spaces may be included between lines by entering a 3 in the *Before* field and 3 in the *After* field.

Output Indicators (columns 23–31) - RPG/400 supports indicators that control processing functions in the program. Some of the indicator groups are *First Page* (**1P**), *Record Identifying* (**01–99**), *Control Level* (**L0–L9**), *Last Record* (**LR**), *Halt* (**H1–H9**), *External* (**U1–U8**), and *Matching Record* (**MR**). For this program, the **1P** (*First Page*) indicator is specified in a Not condition (instruction conditioned with the **N1P** is executed when the **1P** indicator is off). Functions performed by the On and Off status of the **1P** indicator are detailed below.

1. When an RPG/400 program is executed, the RPG/400 logic cycle automatically turns on the 1P (*First Page*) indicator.
2. All files are opened and program control branches over any E, L, I, or C instructions and executes the first output instruction conditioned by 1P (or no indicator).

Figure 3-5   *Output Specifications* form for a program that processes a physical file and prints a report.

3. Any output records conditioned by the **1P** indicator will be executed. This control is usually included in programs that have report headings.

4. After the last output instruction is tested, the **1P** indicator is automatically turned off and the first record is read from the primary file (P in column 16 of the File Description definition of the file) and processed.

5. The *Not* condition **(N1P)** of the **1P** indicator prevents any output for the first cycle **(1P)** processing. Output for the example program will occur only after the first record is read from the physical file.

6. For the example program, if **1P** was specified instead of **N1P**, no printed output would occur, other than two blank lines.

For output instructions specified with as type H, D, or T, coding cannot extend beyond column 31. Type E lines may include an EXCPT **Name** in columns 32–37.

Field Name or EXCPT Name (columns 32–37) - Names of fields from the physical file (GLACTS) are entered left-justified in this field. Entries for this section of the output form must begin in column 32 on a new line after the related record description instruction (columns 7–31). Other fields, defined in the *Input or Calculation Specifications*, may be specified as output fields.

Edit Codes (column 38) - Edit Code 1 entered in this field will suppress any leading zeros in the value stored in BALNCE, insert a comma between the thousand and hundred digits, and according to the decimal positions included in the definition of the field, insert a decimal. An edit code table is included in the upper right section of the output form. The features of each edit code will be discussed in Chapter 4.

End Position in Output Record (columns 40–43) - Numeric entries in this field must be right-justified. The entry indicates the location of the last byte in the field on the printed report. The last byte of ACTNO (defined as three bytes in the physical file) will be printed in print position 7, the second byte in 6, and the first byte in 5. The relationship of the report design to the Output Specifications instructions is detailed in Figure 3-6.

Figure 3-5 *Output Specifications* form for a program that processes a physical file and prints a report. (Continued)

Relationship of the Report Design to the Output Coding

Report designs are usually formatted on a *Printer Spacing Chart* before the *Output Specifications* are completed. This tool enables the programmer to determine heading and field locations and line spacing in the body of a report. Figure 3-6 shows the layout characteristics of a *Printer Spacing Chart.* Note that a group of **Xs** represents the maximum size of an output field which may have been defined in a physical file, in an input statement, or as the result field in a calculation instruction. Any edit characters (commas, decimals, and so forth) must be included in the output format of a numeric field. Note that the **0** (zero) in the format of the edited BALNCE field indicates where the suppression of

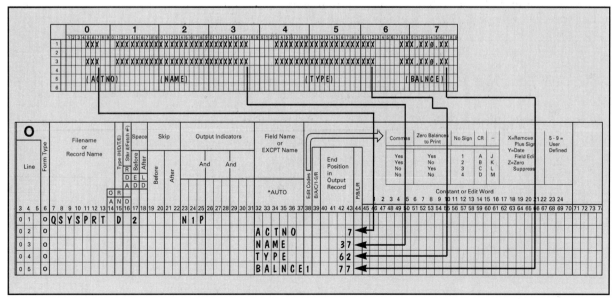

Figure 3-6 Relationship of a formatted Printer Spacing Chart to the Output Specifications coding.

leading zeros will stop. When the field value is zero, an edit code or edit word should be specified that prints .00 on output.

Line spacing is indicated by two identical rows of the **Xs** or by a supplementary note at the bottom of the *Printer Spacing Chart*. The words enclosed in parentheses— (ACTNO), (NAME), (TYPE), and (BALNCE)—identify the names of the physical file's fields and are not to be construed as headings or constants. Fields defined in the *Input* or *Calculation Specifications* may be referenced in the same manner.

Figure 3-6 also shows the relationship of the formatted *Printer Spacing Chart* to the *Output Specifications* for the example program.

The relationship of the *Output Specifications* coding to the report generated by execution of the RPG/400 program is detailed in Figure 3-7. Because of the values stored in the physical file's character fields and the editing of the BALNCE field, the printed output may not represent the actual field size.

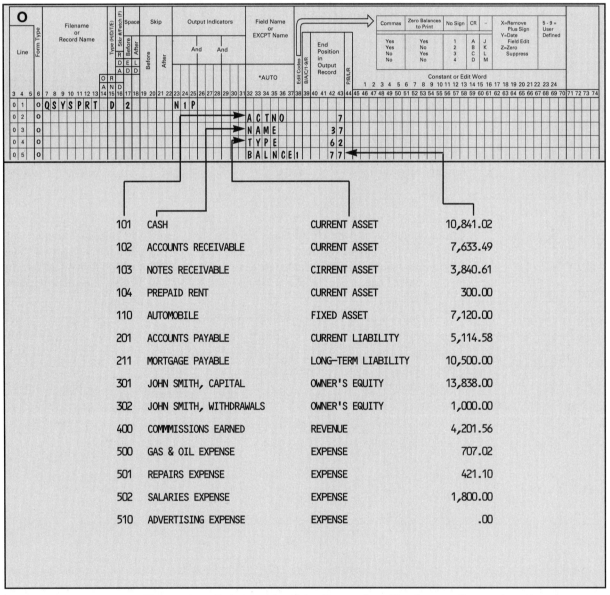

Figure 3-7 Relationship of the Output Specifications coding to the printed report.

SEU ENTRY OF RPG/400 SOURCE PROGRAM INSTRUCTIONS

Format Line Method

RPG/400 source program code is entered with **SEU** by the *Format Line* or *Prompt* method. A format line displays a horizontal definition of the fields in the related RPG/400 specification. Format lines are inserted by entering **IF** and a specification letter (for example, **IFF** displays the *File Description Specifications* layout). Figure 3-8 shows the result when **IFF** is specified and the first **F** instruction is entered for the example program.

```
Comment format line (* must be entered under column 7 format *)

FMT H   .....H........1..CDYI....S..............1.F.........................
        ************** Beginning of data **************************************
FMT *   ..... *. 1 ...+... 2 ...+... 3 ...+... 4 ...+... 5 ...+... 6 ...+... 7
''''  ┌──────────* PROGRAM PROCESSES A PF IN ARRIVAL SEQ & GENERATES A REPORT
      └──── **************** End of data ***************************************
      Programmer entered statement


File Description format line F

FMT *   ..... *. 1 ...+... 2 ...+... 3 ...+... 4 ...+... 5 ...+... 6 ...+... 7
        ************** Beginning of data **************************************
0001.00      * PROGRAM PROCESSES A PF IN ARRIVAL SEQ & GENERATES A REPORT
FMT F   .....FFilenameIPEAF....RlenLK1AIOvKlocEDevice+......KExit++Entry+A....U
''''  ┌────── FGLACTS   IP E                          DISK
      └──── **************** End of data **************************************
      Programmer entered statement
```

Figure 3-8 SEU IF* (Comment) and IFF (File Description Specification) format lines.

Comment lines are included anywhere in the program by an **IF*** entry and aligning an * (asterisk) under the displayed line format. To display the *Output Specifications* format, **IFO** must be entered to access columns 7 through 37 and **IFP** for columns 23 through 70. An example of these line formats is shown in Figure 3-9. Other SEU line formats for RPG will be introduced when the related coding form is discussed.

```
Output Specification format line O (columns 6-37)

        ************** Beginning of data **************************************
FMT O   .....OName++++DFBASbSaNO1NO2NO3Excnam................................
0001.00  ┌── OQSYSPRT D 2     N1P
         └─ **************** End of data ***************************************
         Programmer entered statement


Output Specification format line P (columns 23-70)

FMT O   .....OName++++DFBA3b3aNO1NO2NO3Excnam................................
        ************** Beginning of data **************************************
0001.00      OQSYSPRT D 2     N1P
FMT P   .....O...............NO1NO2NO3Field+YBEnd+PConstant/editword+++++++++.
''''''' ┌── O                         ACTNO     7
        └─ **************** End of data ***************************************
        Programmer entered statement
```

Figure 3-9 SEU IFO and IFP Output Specifications format lines.

Any format line may be accessed <u>without</u> inserting a statement by entering **F** and the specification letter. If the cursor is at an instruction, **F** will display the related format line above it.

Prompt Method

This method was also explained in Chapter 2 for entering DDS code for a physical file. To insert a prompt, **IP** and the related RPG/400 specification letter are entered in the statement number area. The result of an **IPF** entry is detailed in Figure 3-10. Note that the fields in the specification are displayed on four rows at the bottom of the source code. After the syntax is entered and the ENTER key is pressed, the instruction is moved to its position in the source listing. A prompt display for an existing instruction is executed by entering a **P** in the statement number area and pressing ENTER.

```
   FMT H   .....H........1..CDYI....S..............1.F.................. ..........
           ************** Beginning of data ************************* **********
   '''''''
           ***************** End of data ***************************** **********
   Prompt type . . .   F      Sequence number . . . '''''''

                  File         File          End of                     File
     Filename     Type      Designation       File       Sequence      Format
   GLACTS         I            P               _            _           E
   Record         Mode of      Length of      Record
   Length         Processing   Key Field      Address Type
     _            _            _
       File          Overflow      Key Field    Extn
     Organization    Indicator     Start Loc    Code       Device
     _               _             _            _           DISK
                                                File         File
     Continuation   Exit    Entry   Addition    Condition
     _              ___     ___      _           _

     F3=Exit   F4=Prompt   F5=Refresh        F11=Previous record
     F12=Cancel            F23=Select prompt  F24=More keys

   Programmer entered values_____
```

Figure 3-10 Prompt for File Description Specifications.

The prompt for the fields in columns 7 through 31 of the *Output Specifications* are accessed by entering **IPO** in the statement number area and **IPP** for the area from columns 32 through 74. For a complete discussion of **SEU,** refer to Appendix A.

Source Program Listing

After the instructions for the program have been entered, the source listing in Figure 3-11 may be generated by the *Print member* option in the **SEU** EXIT screen. Because compilation of the program will generate a listing, it is not always necessary to print a copy of the source. It is presented here to show the reader how a source listing differs from that generated from compilation of an RPG/400 program. However, in order to include the record formats and related fields in the files processed by an RPG/400 program, compile listings of the programs will be used throughout this text.

```
   FMT F   .....FFilenameIPEAF....RlenLK1AIOvKlocEDevice+......KExit++Entry+A....U
           ************** Beginning of data ***********************************
   0001.00     FGLACTS  IP E                    DISK
   0002.00     FQSYSPRT O  F     132             PRINTER
   0003.00     OQSYSPRT D 2      N1P
   0004.00     O                        ACTNO      7
   0005.00     O                        NAME      37
   0006.00     O                        TYPE      62
   0007.00     O                        BALNCE1   77
           ***************** End of data **************************************
```

Figure 3-11 RPG/400 program source listing.

RPG/400 PROGRAM COMPILATION

An RPG/400 source program must be *compiled* to generate the object that is executed for the processing of files. Program *compilation* is initiated by selecting option 3 on the Programmer Menu or by entering **CRTRPGPGM** and the program name on the command line of an AS/400 display and pressing ENTER. If any default parameters have to be changed, F4 must be pressed to access the displays for the **CRTRPGPGM** command. Figure 3-12 presents the listings generated from compilation of the example program.

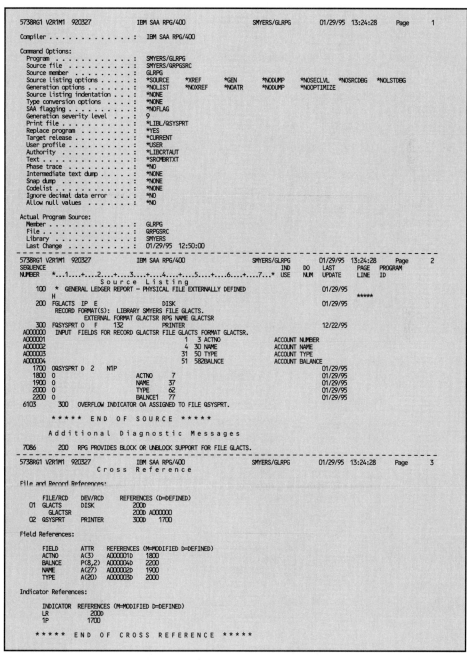

Figure 3-12 Listing generated from compilation of the example RPG/400 program (GLRPG).

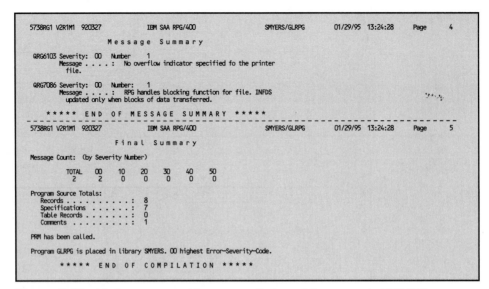

```
5738RG1 V2R1M1 920327            IBM SAA RPG/400            SMYERS/GLRPG      01/29/95  13:24:28    Page      4
                         M e s s a g e   S u m m a r y
  QRG6103 Severity:  00   Number     1
          Message . . . . :   No overflow indicator specified fo the printer
             file.

  QRG7086 Severity:  00   Number:    1
          Message . . . . :   RPG handles blocking function for file. INFDS
             updated only when blocks of data transferred.
     * * * *   E N D   O F   M E S S A G E   S U M M A R Y   * * * * *
- - - - - - - - - - - - - - - - - - - - - - - - - - - - - - - - - - - - - - - - - - - - - - - - - - - - -
5738RG1 V2R1M1 920327            IBM SAA RPG/400            SMYERS/GLRPG      01/29/95  13:24:28    Page      5
                         F i n a l   S u m m a r y
Message Count:  (by Severity Number)

             TOTAL    00   10   20   30   40   50
               2       2    0    0    0    0    0
Program Source Totals:
     Records . . . . . . . . . . :    8
     Specifications  . . . . . . :    7
     Table Records . . . . . . . :    0
     Comments  . . . . . . . . . :    1

PRM has been called.

Program GLRPG is placed in library SMYERS.  00 highest Error-Severity-Code.

        * * * * *   E N D   O F   C O M P I L A T I O N   * * * * *
```

Figure 3-12   Listing generated from compilation of the example RPG/400 program (GLRPG). (Continued)

Examine the listings and note that the source code is supplemented with the following information:

Page 1:   General information and parameter values are detailed here. Default parameters were taken for this program; however, some could be changed by entering **CRTRPGPGM** on a Command line and pressing F4.

Page 2:   *(Source Listing)* - The *externally defined* physical file and record names are included after the related *File Description* source statement (line 200).

Field names and attribute statements (A000000–A000004) from the *externally defined* physical file are inserted between the last *File Description* statement (300) and first *Output* instruction (1700).

Source instructions for the *program-defined* PRINTER file are listed on lines 1700 through 2200. An error message, **6103 OVERFLOW INDICATOR OA ASSIGNED TO FILE QSYSPRT,** for source line 300 is included at the bottom of the source. Another, **7086 RPG PROVIDES BLOCK OR UNBLOCK SUPPORT FOR, FILE GLACTS,** is specified for line 200 under the *Additional Diagnostic Messages header.* Both errors are **INFORMATIONAL** (00), not **WARNING** or **TERMINAL,** and <u>do not</u> prevent the program from compiling. Other error types may also be specified here and in the body of the *Source Listing* area.

Page 3:   *(Cross Reference)* - The statement numbers in which the *externally defined* physical file and record are described are included in the *File and Record References* section.

(Field References) - Field names, their attributes, and related statement numbers are specified here. Input fields from the physical file are referenced as being defined on lines A000001D through A000004D and the PRINTER file fields, 1800 through 2200.

(Indicator References) - Indicators *explicitly* or *implicitly* defined in the program are referenced in this area. The **LR** *(Last Record)* indicator is implicitly

assigned to the input file (GLACTS) and is turned on automatically when the end-of-file record is tested for the file. The **1P** *(First Page)* indicator is explicitly defined on line 1700 in a **Not** condition and is referenced accordingly.

Page 4:   *(Message Summary)* - This section summarizes some of the error messages generated from the compilation.

Page 5:   *(Final Summary)* - The *Message Count* area identifies the number of errors for a *Severity Number.* **00** are *Informational errors;* **10,** *Warning;* and **20** through **50,** *Terminal.* This program has two *Informational* errors related to the blocking factor and overflow indicator.

The *Program Source Totals* section lists the number of records in the source program (8), number of Specification instructions (7), number of Table records (0 in this program), and number of comment statements (1).

The last statement, **Program GLRPG is placed in library SMYERS. 00 highest-Error-Severity-Code,** indicates that the source program was successfully compiled and the object was stored in the designated library.

RPG/400 PROGRAM EXECUTION

After the RPG/400 source program has been successfully compiled and an object created, it is executed by selecting option 4 on the Programmer Menu, entering the program name in the Parm field if it isn't already entered, and pressing ENTER. The example program may also be executed by entering **CALL GLRPG** (RPG program name) on a command line and pressing ENTER.

It is unlikely that the programmer's job description will support the immediate printing of a report (or compilation). Usually the **WRKOUTQ** or **WRKSPLF** (both explained in Chapter 1) command is executed to view or print the *spooled output file.*

The printed report generated by execution of the program is shown in Figure 3-13. Note that the report does not include heading lines, page numbering, date, or additional pages. All of these commonly used report items will be discussed in Chapter 4.

101	CASH	CURRENT ASSET	10,841.02
102	ACCOUNTS RECEIVABLE	CURRENT ASSET	7,633.49
103	NOTES RECEIVABLE	CIRRENT ASSET	3,840.61
104	PREPAID RENT	CURRENT ASSET	300.00
110	AUTOMOBILE	FIXED ASSET	7,120.00
201	ACCOUNTS PAYABLE	CURRENT LIABILITY	5,114.58
211	MORTGAGE PAYABLE	LONG-TERM LIABILITY	10,500.00
301	JOHN SMITH, CAPITAL	OWNER'S EQUITY	13,838.00
302	JOHN SMITH, WITHDRAWALS	OWNER'S EQUITY	1,000.00
400	COMMMISSIONS EARNED	REVENUE	4,201.56
500	GAS & OIL EXPENSE	EXPENSE	707.02
501	REPAIRS EXPENSE	EXPENSE	421.10
502	SALARIES EXPENSE	EXPENSE	1,800.00
510	ADVERTISING EXPENSE	EXPENSE	.00

Figure 3-13   Report generated from execution of the RPG/400 program GLRPG.

RPG/400 SYNTAX TO PROCESS A PROGRAM-DEFINED PHYSICAL FILE

For some processing scenarios, a physical file shell (no *Data Description Specifications* defining a record format and fields) may be created to:

1. store the output from the sorting of one or more files
2. store the output from a magnetic tape
3. store the output from a computer system that supports multirecord (more than one record format) files
4. store the output from the electronic transfer of data
5. store the output of the **CPYF** (copy file utility).

The physical file "shell" must be created with the **CRTPF** command and the required record length entered in the *Record length (RCDLEN)* parameter (see Figure 2-11).

File Description Specification Syntax

A "shell" physical file (GLACTSF), which was created without DDS record or field definitions, is used in the following example program. Figure 3-14 details the changes needed on *File Description Specifications* to support the processing of the program-defined physical file.

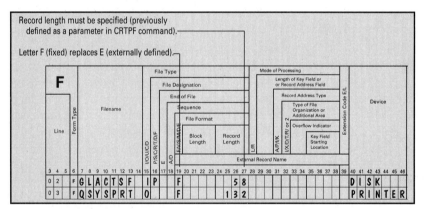

Figure 3-14   File Description Specifications syntax to support the processing of a program-defined physical file.

Input Specifications Syntax

Recall that an externally defined physical file does not require that record and field attributes be specified in the RPG/400 program. Consequently, no *Input Specifications* were included in the previous program example. Now that the file is program-defined, *Input Specifications* instructions are needed to define the fields. Figure 3-15 shows the relationship of the data in the physical file "shell" to the input coding. Identical to the traditional environment, the beginning and end positions of each field in the record must be determined and documented on a form of some suitable design. The RPG/400 syntax of each entry included in Figure 3-15 is detailed in the following paragraphs.

Record Identification Section (columns 7–42)

File or Record Name (columns 7–14).   Name of the input file defined on the *File Description Specifications* must be entered left-justified in this field.

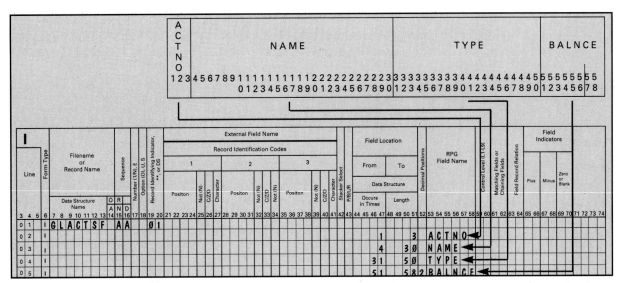

Figure 3-15 Relationship of physical file "shell" data to the Input Specifications entries.

Sequence (columns 15–16). Any two letters must be entered here. If the entry is omitted, a default value of **AA** will be assigned and a *warning error* generated.

Record Identifying Indicator (columns 19–20). The program-defined record format must be assigned a unique two-digit indicator from **01** through **99.** When a record is read from the physical file, the indicator assigned will turn on for the complete program cycle. After the last output instruction is executed, the *Record Identifying Indicator* will automatically be turned off. Program control will read another record, turn the indicator on, and continue the processing sequence until the end of file is tested.

Thirteen records are stored in the physical file processed by the example program. Consequently, the **01** indicator will be turned on and off automatically 13 times by the RPG/400 logic cycle. Any of the 99 indicators may be used for this function, not only **01.**

Record Identifying Indicators are used in a program to *condition* calculations and output instructions. The status (ON or OFF) of the indicator determines whether the *conditioned* instruction(s) will be executed.

External Field Names/Record Identification Codes (columns 21–41). *External Field Names* will be discussed in a subsequent chapter. *Record Identification Codes* are usually not used with physical files in the AS/400 environment and will be discussed later. The *Stacker/Select* (column 42) is used with punch card readers and is not functional for disk, diskette, tape, and workstation devices.

Field Description Section (columns 43–74)

Entries for this section must begin on a new line (separate from the *Record Description* instruction(s)).

Field Location (columns 44–51). This area is divided into two separate fields: the *FROM* field (columns 44–47) and the *TO* field (columns 48–51). The *FROM* field identifies the beginning (high-order) position and the *TO* field the last (low-order) position of the related field.

The rules for developing field sizes are

1. *FROM* and *TO* numeric entries must be right-justified.
2. Alphanumeric fields have a maximum size of 256 bytes.
3. Numeric fields have a maximum size of 30 bytes.

Decimal Positions (column 52).   If a data item is alphanumeric, no entry is required in this field. Fields are defined as numeric by an entry of **0** to **9.** The number of decimal positions specified cannot be larger than the field length. Figure 3-16 illustrates how a decimal entry affects stored numeric values.

Decimal Position Entry	Value in disk field	Value CPU storage	Comments
0	12345	12345 ▲	Integer value
2	12345	12345 ▲	Decimal value with 2 implied decimals
5	12345	12345 ▲	Decimal value with 5 implied decimals
blank	12345	12345	Alphanumeric value

Notes: In the last example, because the decimal position field is blank, the numeric value will be processed as alphanumeric. Calculation or editing may not be performed with that field.

Symbol ▲ indicates an implied decimal (not actual). With the exception of output edited numeric fields, actual decimals are not assigned to field storage in the CPU.

Figure 3-16   Storage result of decimal position assignment on a data value.

Numeric data stored on disk, diskette, and tape does not include an *explicit* or *implicit* decimal. For program-defined physical files, the decimal position for an input field is *specified* in the program (column 52) and *implied* in the related storage area during program execution. The *Data Description Specifications* for an externally defined physical file specify the decimal positions in columns 36–37 of the field defined.

An implied decimal does not use a storage position; instead, it identifies its location in the body of a field by a "tagging" process. A comprehensive discussion of the definition, editing, and processing of numeric fields is included in Chapters 4 and 5.

Field Name (columns 53–58).   For a program-defined physical file, the programmer must create his or her own field names. Externally defined files have their field names defined in the *Data Description Specifications*. In either case, the rules for creating field names are summarized in Figure 3-17.

Relationship of the *Input Specifications* instructions to the *Output Specifications* is shown in Figure 3-18. Note that the *Record Identifying Indicator* **01** is specified on the output form in one field of the *Output Indicator* area. When a data record is read from the physical file, **01** is turned on. *Conditioning* output with the **01** indicator controls printing of the output record. If the **01** indicator is omitted on the output form, the program would execute successfully. However, the following two conditions would result:

1. Because the first processing cycle of RPG occurs before a record is read, any output <u>not</u> conditioned by an indicator will be executed. For the example program, this would cause two extra blank lines to be printed (note the **2** in the *Space Before* field) before the data in the first record was processed.

2. A *warning error* would be generated during program compilation, identifying that the **01** indicator defined on input was **UNREFERENCED.**

Any of the available **01** to **99** indicators could have been specified on the *input specifications*. However, informal standards followed by many programmers have led to the functional assignment of indicator usage. Often **01** to **20** are reserved for input, and **21** to **99** are grouped for calculations and other program control. Also, notice in Figure 3-18 that

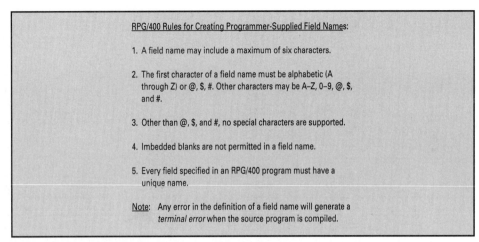

Figure 3-17 RPG/400 rules for creating field names.

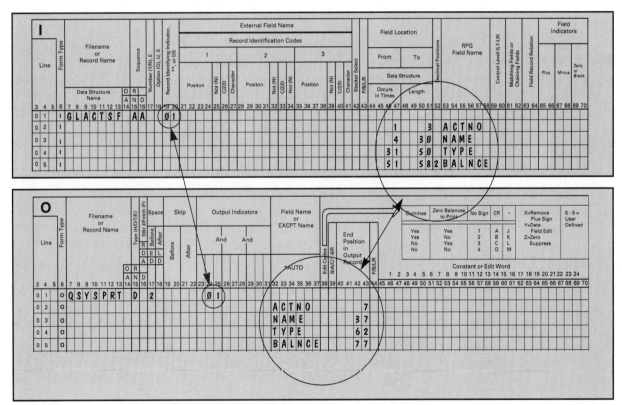

Figure 3-18 Relationship of the Record Identifying Indicator and fields defined on the Input Specifications to the output specifications.

the fields defined on the input specifications are identical to those specified on output. Any difference in a related field name results in two compilation errors: a *warning error* identifying an **UNREFERENCED** input field and a *terminal error* for the **UNDEFINED** output field.

An explanation of the processing logic associated with *Record Identifying Indicators* is detailed in the example program's source listing in Figure 3-19.

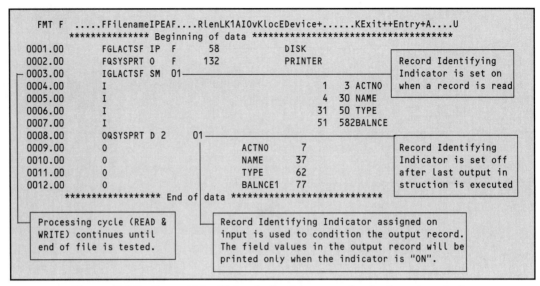

Figure 3-19 Record Identifying Indicator processing logic and control.

THE RPG/400 LOGIC CYCLE

During execution, an RPG/400 program automatically follows a sequence of operations for each record that is processed. This built-in program cycle includes the following logical steps:

1. reading input (READ)
2. processing calculations (PROCESS)
3. writing output (WRITE)

A flowchart that illustrates the *General RPG/400 Program Logic Cycle* is presented in Figure 3-20. The numbers (1–7) to the left of the flowchart symbol identify the following processing sequence:

1. RPG/400 processes all *Heading* and *Detail* lines (**H** or **D** in position 15 of the *Output Specifications*). **D** *(Detail)* lines were used in the two example programs discussed in this chapter; **H** *(Heading)* lines will be introduced in Chapter 4.
2. RPG/400 reads the next input record and sets on the *Record Identifying* and *Control Level Indicators. Control Level Indicators* will be discussed in Chapter 8.
3. RPG/400 processes *total* calculations, which are conditioned by an **L1** through **L9** or **LR** indicator, or an **L0** entry. All of these indicator types will be explained in Chapter 8.
4. RPG/400 processes all *total output lines* (identified by a **T** in position 15 of an *Output Specifications* instruction).
5. RPG/400 determines if the **LR** indicator is ON. If it is ON, the program is ended and control is returned back to the operating system.
6. The fields of the selected input records are moved from the record to a processing area. RPG/400 sets on *Field Indicators,* which will be discussed later in the text.

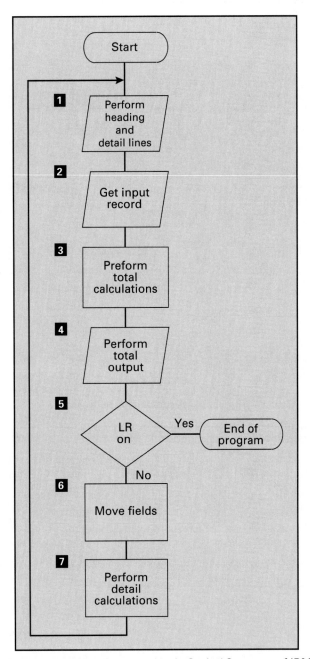

Figure 3-20   General RPG/400 Program Logic Cycle (*Courtesy of IBM*).

    7.   RPG/400 processes all *detail calculations* (those not conditioned by *Control Level Indicators* in positions 7 and 8 of the *Calculation Specifications*) on the data from the record read at the beginning of the cycle.

For a *detailed* flowchart and explanation of the complete *RPG/400 Logic Cycle,* refer to IBM's RPG/400 User's Guide.

    Figure 3-21 shows the relationship of the example RPG/400 program to the steps in the *RPG/400 Logic Cycle.* Because the program does not include total calculations, total output, or detail calculations, steps 3, 4, and 7 are not relevant. All of these processing functions will be discussed in subsequent chapters.

    The report generated by the example program that processes a *program-defined* physical file is identical to the output for the *externally defined* file shown in Figure 3-13.

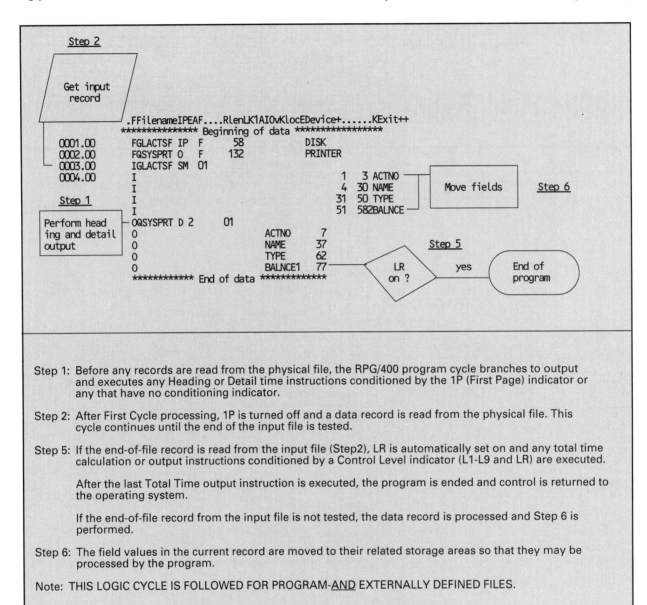

Figure 3-21   Example program's processing cycle.

Step 1: Before any records are read from the physical file, the RPG/400 program cycle branches to output and executes any Heading or Detail time instructions conditioned by the 1P (First Page) indicator or any that have no conditioning indicator.

Step 2: After First Cycle processing, 1P is turned off and a data record is read from the physical file. This cycle continues until the end of the input file is tested.

Step 5: If the end-of-file record is read from the input file (Step2), LR is automatically set on and any total time calculation or output instructions conditioned by a Control Level indicator (L1-L9 and LR) are executed.

After the last Total Time output instruction is executed, the program is ended and control is returned to the operating system.

If the end-of-file record from the input file is not tested, the data record is processed and Step 6 is performed.

Step 6: The field values in the current record are moved to their related storage areas so that they may be processed by the program.

Note: THIS LOGIC CYCLE IS FOLLOWED FOR PROGRAM-AND EXTERNALLY DEFINED FILES.

SUMMARY

The function of the seven RPG specification forms *(Control, File Description, Extension, Line Counter, Input, Calculations, and Output)* were discussed in this chapter. For RPG/400 programs that process an ***externally defined*** physical file and generate a report not requiring calculations, only the *File Description* and *Output Specifications* instructions are required. Programs that process physical files that do not have a DDS format ***(program-defined)*** must define the attributes of the fields in the *Input Specifications*.

The development of an RPG/400 program includes the *compilation* and *execution* phases. The *compilation* phase, which is controlled by the **CRTRPGPGM** command, identifies syntax errors that prevent an object from being created. After successful compilation of a program, the *execution* phase generates the required output if there are no logic errors.

The RPG logic cycle automatically controls the opening of files, reading and writing of records, closing of files, and end of file processing. These functions may be explicitly specified in a program with **OPEN, READ, WRITE,** and **CLOSE** operations.

RPG/400 program instructions are entered via SEU which has *format* or *prompt lines* for the complete or section of each specifications type. Any attempt to enter invalid syntax for an instruction will be identified by SEU.

Field names supported by RPG/400 may be specified with a maximum of six characters. Numeric fields may be defined with a maximum size of 30 digits and include no more than 9 decimal positions. Alphanumeric (character) fields may be defined with no more than 256 characters.

When an RPG/400 program is executed, the logic cycle causes heading and detail output to occur first. Any input or calculation instructions (when included) are ignored for this *first cycle* processing. Consequently, when output is **program defined,** it is important that it is conditioned with one or more indicators to prevent uncertain results from occurring.

QUESTIONS

3-1. Explain the steps involved in the development of an RPG/400 program.

3-2. Name the AS/400 utility that supports the entry of an RPG/400 program's source code. What two methods of entering instructions are available?

3-3. What *Control Language command* compiles an RPG/400 program?

3-4. Name the error types that may be generated in the compilation of an RPG/400 program. Which will prevent compilation of the program?

3-5. Briefly explain the information included in the listing generated when an RPG/400 program is compiled.

3-6. Name all of the RPG/400 specification forms.

3-7. Refer to Question 3-6 and explain the function of each specification.

3-8. What is the compilation order of an RPG/400 program? What happens if the compilation order is not followed?

3-9. Refer to the specification type that defines the files processed by an RPG/400 program, and indicate the minimum entries needed to process an *externally defined* physical file.

3-10. Refer to the specification type that defines the files processed by an RPG/400 program, and indicate the minimum entries needed to process a *program-defined* physical file.

3-11. Identify any syntax errors on the following form.

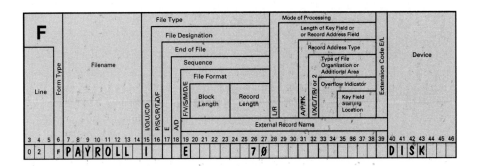

3-12. Identify the minimum specification types required in an RPG/400 program that processes an *externally defined* physical file and generates a report.

3-13. Whan are *Input Specification* instructions required in RPG/400 programs?

3-14. What are *Record Identifying Indicators?* What is their function in an RPG/400 program? Where are they defined and specified? When are they set on? When do they turn off?

3-15. Explain the term *conditioning an instruction.*

3-16. Explain the following entries. When are they necessary?

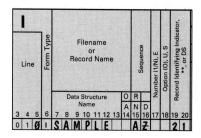

3-17. Identify any syntax errors in the following *Input Specifications*.

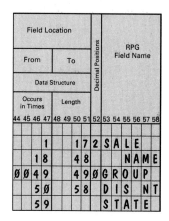

3-18. Identify and explain any syntax errors in the following form.

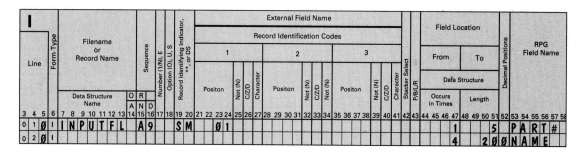

3-19. When does the **LR** indicator turn on in the program cycle?

3-20. Explain the function of the *Output Specifications* form.

3-21. Refer to an *Output Specifications* form: identify the logical areas and explain their processing functions.

3-22. What entries may be specified in column 15 of the *Output Specifications* form?

3-23. If a **3** was specified in the *Before* field (column 17) in the output form, how many blanks spaces would be provided between two print lines?

3-24. When is the **N1P** indicator used on the output form?

3-25. If a **01** to **99** indicator is used on the output form, where was it defined? What compilation error is generated if the indicator is not defined? What compilation error is generated if the indicator is defined but not used in an output instruction?

3-26. Do RPG/400 programs that process *externally defined* or *program-defined* physical files require *Record Identifying Indicators?* Explain your answer.

3-27. What does **QSYSPRT** define?

3-28. What does the entry in the field *End Position in Output Record* indicate? What is the source of this entry?

3-29. Examine the following output form and explain the function of each entry.

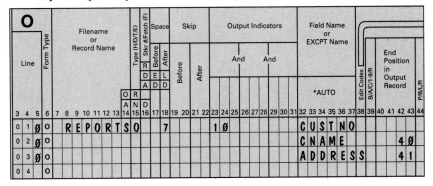

Line	Form Type	Filename or Record Name	Type (H/D/T/E)	Stkr #/Fetch (F)	Space Before R D A E D N D	Space After L D	Skip Before	Skip After	Output Indicators And	Output Indicators And	Field Name or EXCPT Name *AUTO	Edit Codes	B/A/C/1-9/R	End Position in Output Record	P/B/L/R
0 1	O	Q S Y S P R T	D		3	3			N 1	P					
0 2	O										E M P N O			1 0	
0 3	O										N A M E			4 5	

3-30. Identify and explain any errors in the following output form.

Line	Form Type	Filename or Record Name	Type (H/D/T/E)	Stkr #/Fetch (F)	Space Before R D A E D N D	Space After L D	Skip Before	Skip After	Output Indicators And	Output Indicators And	Field Name or EXCPT Name *AUTO	Edit Codes	B/A/C/1-9/R	End Position in Output Record	P/B/L/R
0 1 Ø	O	R E P O R T S O			7				1 Ø		C U S T N O				
0 2 Ø	O										C N A M E			4 Ø	
0 3 Ø	O										A D D R E S S			4 1	
0 4	O														

3-31. Explain the processing steps in the *General RPG/400 Logic Cycle*.

PROGRAMMING ASSIGNMENTS

Before any RPG/400 programs for the following assignments can be completed, the related physical file must have been compiled and loaded with data. The attributes of the physical file for each assignment are included in the Programming Assignments for Chapter 2. The related physical file may have been created by your instructor, or you may have to reference the related assignment in Chapter 2 and create and load the file. See your professor for instructions.

Your completed assignments must include:

1. The compilation listing of your RPG/400 program
2. A copy of the report

Programming Assignment 3-1: ACTIVE EMPLOYEE LISTING

From the following Printer Spacing Chart, write an RPG/400 program to generate the report format shown.

	0	1	2	3	4	5	6
1	XXXX	X X X		X	X X		
2							
3	XXXX	X X X		X	X X		
4	(EMP#) (FINIT) (SINIT)	(LNAME)			(SSNO)		
5							

Reference *Programming Assignment 2-1* for the attributes of the physical file that this program will process.

Programming Assignment 3-2: EASTERN STATE REPORT LISTING

From the following information, write an RPG/400 program to generate the required report.

Refer to *Programming Assignment 2-2* for the attributes of the physical file. Complete a Printer Spacing Chart based on the following information. Indicate that the report is to be double-spaced.

Field	Print Positions
State letter	6–7
State name	16–35
State capital	46–70
Largest city	81–105

Programming Assignment 3-3: CUSTOMER MAILING LIST

Refer to *Programming Assignment 2-3* for the attributes of the physical file that this program will process. Then, from the following Printer Spacing Chart, write an RPG/400 program to generate the required report. Notice that three different output lines are printed for each record processed. Consequently, three separately formatted detail lines must be included in the program's output coding.

	0	1	2	3	4
	1234567890	1234567890	1234567890	1234567890	123456789
1	X	X		(NAME)	
2	X	X		(STREET)	
3	X	X	XX	XXXXX	
4					
5		(CITY)	(STATE)	(ZIP)	
6					

Note:

Triple-space between customer groups.

chapter 4

Report Headings
and Editing

Chapter 3 presented the RPG/400 syntax and procedures required to print a report without headings, numeric data, or editing. Generally, however, reports do have headings and include numeric values that require editing for readability. This chapter discusses the RPG/400 syntax and processing logic needed to provide for these important features.

Examine the report shown in Figure 4-1 and notice the following:

1. The first heading line includes a date, constants, and page number.
2. The second heading line contains all constants.
3. The variable data (detail lines) is printed below the second heading line.
4. The variable spacing (triple, double, and single) is included in the body of the report.

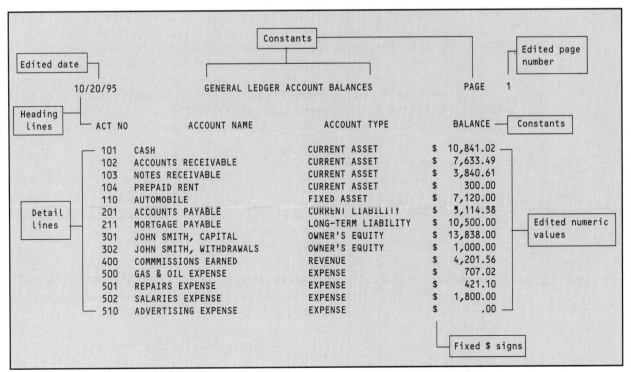

Figure 4-1 Printed report with two heading lines and edited numeric values.

5. All numeric fields (date, page number, and balance) are edited. Editing refers to zero suppression and the insertion of special characters in the body of a numeric value.

6. A fixed dollar sign ($) is printed before every edited balance value.

The printer spacing chart related to the report (Figure 4–1) is detailed in Figure 4-2. Notice that the first heading line contains the variable field **UDATE,** the constant GENERAL LEDGER ACCOUNT BALANCES, the constant **PAGE,** and the variable field for the page number, shown as XXØX.

	0	1	2	3	4	5	6	7
1	ØX/XX/XX		GENERAL LEDGER ACCOUNT BALANCES					PAGE XXØX
2	(UDATE)							
3								
4	ACT NO		ACCOUNT NAME		ACCOUNT TYPE			BALANCE
5								
6	XXX	X		X	X		X	$ XXX,XXØ.XX
7	XXX	X		X	X		X	$ XXX,XXØ.XX
8								
9								
10	NOTES:							
11								
12	1. HEADINGS ON TOP OF EVERY PAGE							
13								
14	2. DATE IS SYSTEM-SUPPLIED							
15								

Figure 4-2 Printer spacing chart format with headings and numeric field editing requirements.

The variable field, identified as **UDATE** (positions 1-8), indicates that the system-supplied date is to be used for the report. Editing requirements for this field are indicated by the ØX/XX/XX format.

The XXØX after the constant **PAGE** is another RPG/400 control feature that supplies an ascending page number on every page of a report. Page numbering starts at 0001 and increments to 9999.

The constants for the headings lines are coded in the RPG/400 program to print every time the related instruction is executed. Variable field items are identified by the name enclosed in parentheses or by a related column heading.

In the RPG/400 environment, alphanumeric and numeric field values are represented on a print chart with Xs. Editing requirements for a numeric field are indicated by the placement of insertion characters (e.g., decimal point, commas) in the body of the field. The extent of zero suppression in a numeric field is identified by a Ø (zero) in the appropriate field location, as shown in the following example.

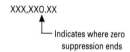

Examine Figure 4-2 and notice that the **UDATE** and page number fields also include a Ø (zero) to represent the control of zero suppression. Included in the editing of the detail lines is a fixed dollar sign printed before each balance value.

Finally, required line spacing—triple after the first heading line, double after the second heading line, and single for the detail lines—is indicated on the print chart by the location of the related lines. Notice that the two identically formatted detail lines represent single spacing and *not* that the values from every input record are to be printed twice.

The specific types of lines that may be included in a printed report are classified as follows:

1. **Heading lines.** Print lines that include only constants and/or a combination of constants and variables. Depending on the report requirements, any number of

heading lines may be specified in a program. They are designated in an RPG/400 program by the letter **H** in column 15 of the *Output Specifications*.

2. **Detail lines.** Print lines that include values input into or generated by the program. Constants are often included in this type of line. A detail line is specified in an RPG/400 program by the letter **D** in column 15 of the output form.

3. **Final total lines.** Print lines that are generated in an RPG/400 program after the end of the data file is sensed. Referred to as *total time output processing,* which is controlled in an RPG/400 program by specifying the letter **T** in column 15 of the output form. The syntax and logic associated with this line type will be discussed in Chapter 5.

4. **Control total lines.** Group totals that are printed in the body of a report. A comprehensive discussion of this type of line is presented in Chapter 8.

5. **Exception lines.** The **EXCPT** operation, a Calculation Specification instruction, controls the processing of this line type. Related output is identified by the letter **E** in column 15 of the output form. The syntax and logic for this output will be discussed in Chapter 7.

Notice that the use of **H** and **D** lines is only for documentation. Any line specified as **H** (heading) in an RPG/400 program may be coded as **D** (detail), or vice versa, without generating a syntax error. However, the output records must be assigned in an **H, D,** and **T** order. **E** *(Exception)* lines may be included anywhere on output without regard to the **H, D, T** order.

RPG SYNTAX FOR PAGE AND HEADING CONTROL

When a report extends to more than one page (most of them do), control must be included in an RPG/400 program for this output processing. This is referred to as *page overflow,* which is performed in an RPG/400 program by *skip* control. The logic for page overflow control is shown in Figure 4-3.

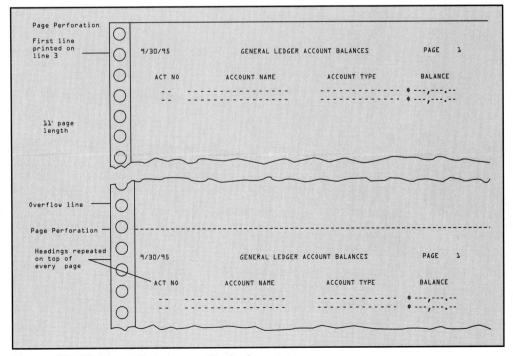

Figure 4-3   Page overflow processing logic.

Note on Types of Printers

The page control shown in Figure 4-3 assumes that a *line printer* is used with continuous forms of paper. Line printers print a complete line in one stroke. The standard carriage width is 132 characters. Wider models are available, however.

Other popular types include the *serial* and *laser* printers. *Serial* printers, which are commonly used with microcomputers, print one character at a time across a line. They are usually multidirectional in that they print a line from left to right and then on the following line, print right to left. Like line printers, serial printers will also support printing on continuous forms.

Laser printers differ from line and serial types of printers in that they format an entire page before printing. They are the fastest, have the best type quality, and offer a multitude of print types. Continuous forms paper, however, is not supported with laser printers; the output is printed on individual sheets.

Regardless of the type of printer used, the syntax and control of page overflow and spacing in the body of a report remain the same in an RPG/400 program.

On most computer systems, the standard form length and the overflow line are set when the system is configured. For line printers, the standard size of continuous forms paper is usually $14\frac{1}{2}$ by 11 inches.

FILE DESCRIPTION AND OUTPUT SPECIFICATIONS CODING FOR PAGE CONTROL

Top-of-Page Control

For printer- and workstation-supported output files, *spacing* refers to the advancing of one, two, or three lines at a time. *Skipping* refers to jumping from one print line to another. Examine the output form in Figure 4-4 and notice that the number **03** is entered in the *Skip Before* field (columns 19 and 20) of the first output instruction. During program execution, this entry will cause the paper to advance to the top of a new page and then begin printing on line 3. Any number from **01** to **99** may be entered in the *Skip Before* or *After* fields. For line numbers greater than 99, entries **A0** to **A9** will control skipping to

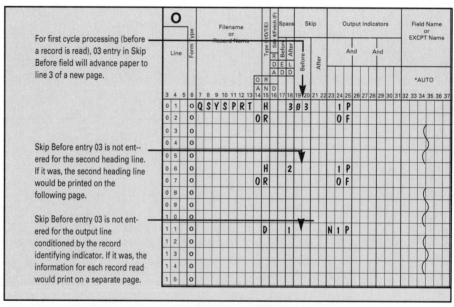

Figure 4-4 Output Specifications skipping control entry.

lines 100 to 109; and entries **B0** to **B9,** for skip control to lines 110 to 112, respectively. Notice that *Skip Before* controls skipping to the designated line *before* printing the record. Conversely, *Skip After* performs the skipping function *after* the current output record is printed.

Also, observe in Figure 4-4 that the **03** *Skip Before* entry is not made in the second heading or detail lines. If the entries had been specified, the second heading line would be printed on a separate page after the first heading line, and the information for every record read and processed would be printed on individual pages.

First Page Control

A section of the RPG/400 program logic flowchart is illustrated at the top of Figure 4-5. Notice that the heading (first cycle) processing is executed before the first record is read

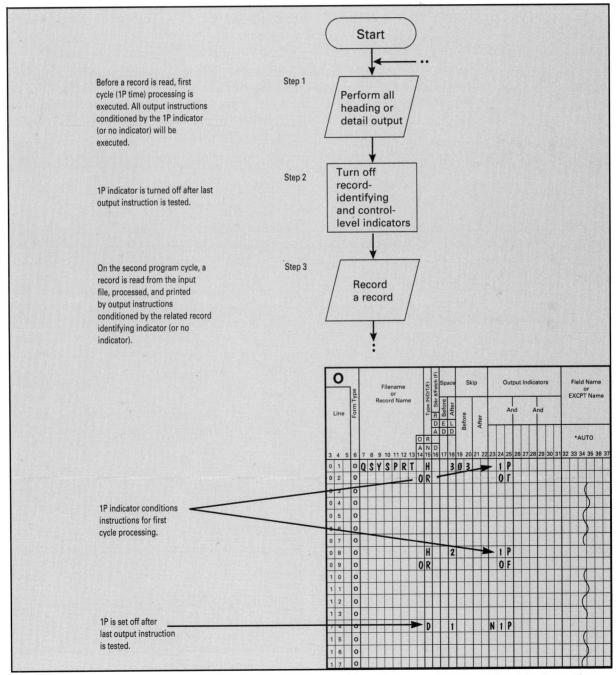

Figure 4-5 First cycle (1P time) processing logic and Output Specifications syntax.

from an input file. Consequently, no *Record Identifying Indicator* has been turned on to condition output instructions. Because of this built-in processing cycle, RPG/400 has provided a **1P** (first page) indicator to control first cycle output. *After the last output instruction is tested, the 1P indicator is automatically set off and will never turn on again during program execution.*

The output form included in Figure 4-5 shows that the two heading lines are conditioned by a **1P** indicator. Because **UDATE** and **PAGE** are RPG/400 reserved words, their values are supplied by the system or job and are available at **1P** time. Understand, however, that any field values from the data records will not be loaded in their related storage areas at first page time.

Furthermore, the detail line conditioned by the **N1P** indicator will not be executed during this first cycle processing. During the second cycle, when the first data record is read, the **1P** lines are ignored, and the detail line conditioned with the **N1P** indicator will be executed. This processing logic continues until the end of the input file is sensed.

Page Overflow Control

Indicators **OA** through **OG** and **OV** are preassigned indicators that control the page overflow function. *Overflow indicators* are automatically turned on when the overflow line for the type of form is sensed. For standard size paper, the line number on which page overflow is to execute is assigned when the system is generated. However, it may be modified by the *Line Counter Specifications* discussed at the end of this chapter.

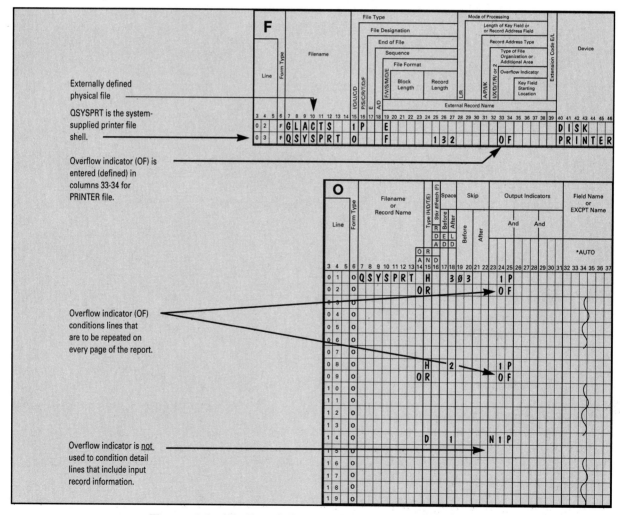

Figure 4-6 File Description and Output Specifications entries for control of page overflow.

Overflow indicators may not be used in an RPG/400 program for any other processing function. The reason there are eight overflow indicators is that a program may support more than one printer file and each must be assigned to a different overflow indicator.

Examine the *File Description Specifications* in Figure 4-6, and notice that the **OF** indicator has been specified in the *Overflow Indicator* field (columns 33–34). This is where the overflow indicator is defined. If it is not entered here and specified in the output form, a terminal error (**UNDEFINED INDICATOR**) will be generated in compilation of the source program. Any of the other overflow indicators could have been used; the one selected is at the option of the programmer.

The *Output Specifications* shown in Figure 4-6 shows how the overflow indicator (**OF**) is used. Notice that it is included as an **OR** instruction that immediately follows the related **1P** line. The **OR** entered in columns 14 and 15, on the same line with the **OF** indicator, specifies that the overflow instruction is in an "or" relationship with the **1P** (or other indicator) instruction. If one of the two conditions is *true*, page overflow processing will be executed.

Skipping to the top of a new page (page overflow) is controlled by the sensing of the overflow line, which turns on the overflow indicator specified in the program. When this condition occurs, the overflow line is printed, the paper advances to the top of the next page, and the first heading line is printed. Notice that the *Skip Before* or *After* entry assigned to the related **1P** instruction determines the line to which the paper advances on page overflow.

Further examination of Figure 4-6 indicates that an overflow instruction is not assigned to the detail line conditioned by the **N1P** indicator. If it were, a detail line printed at the bottom of a page (overflow line) would be repeated on the following page. This repetition of information for a variable record on every overflow page would be confusing to the user and should be avoided.

RPG Syntax for Headings

A constant is defined in an RPG/400 program in columns 45 to 70 of the *Output Specifications* by enclosing it in apostrophes. Figure 4-7 gives examples of valid and invalid entries for the definition of constants.

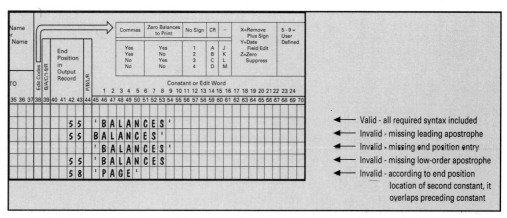

Figure 4-7 Examples of valid and invalid entries for the definition of constants.

The relationship of the constants and variable fields formatted in the printer spacing chart to the *Output Specifications* coding is illustrated in Figure 4-8. Locate the heading constant, GENERAL LEDGER ACCOUNT BALANCES, included in the first line of the print chart. Notice that the letter **T** is entered in column 46 of the constant ACCOUNT. Now follow the arrowed line to the output form and observe that **46** is entered in columns 42 and 43 of the *End Position in Output Record* field. This entry refers to the position in which the low-order character of a constant or field value will be placed (printed for this

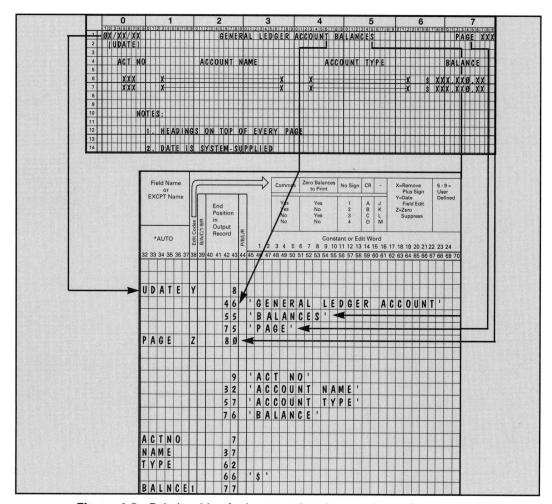

Figure 4-8 Relationship of printer spacing chart entries to Output Specifications.

example). The high-order characters in the constant or field value are located accordingly in the preceding positions. The constant GENERAL LEDGER ACCOUNT will be printed as follows:

Refer to the print chart in Figure 4-8, and notice that the constant BALANCES ends in column 55. Trace the line that connects it to the *Output Specifications* and observe that **55** is entered in the end position field. This entry will place the low-order S in BALANCES in print position 55 on output. Even though the space between ACCOUNT and BALANCES has not been included in either constant, the end position entry (55) for BALANCES places this constant so that it begins one space after ACCOUNT. The result of this coding is as follows:

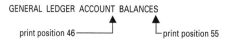

If the end position for BALANCES had been specified as 53, a space would not be included after ACCOUNT; if 53, the B in BALANCES would overlap the T in ACCOUNT, and the constant would print as follows:

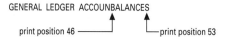

Because the constants in the first heading line could not be entered on one line of output coding, BALANCES is included on a separate line. The end position references place a constant in its required horizontal location.

Included in this example are the RPG/400 reserved field names for **UDATE** and **PAGE.** The values for these items are also positioned on output by their end position entries. This composite of instructions completes the output record (first heading line), which is controlled during processing by the related *Record Description* entries in columns 7 to 31.

The second heading line, which includes all constants, is coded on the *Output Specifications* by enclosing each constant in apostrophes and specifying the related end positions entry.

The example shown in Figure 4-8 is not to be construed as the only approach for the coding of headings in a program. Providing that the constants are enclosed in apostrophes, the end position is specified, and the items do not overlap, any coding style is acceptable. The format followed is at the option of the programmer.

System or Job Date (UDATE)

The system date is initially entered when the computer is installed. Its value is usually stored in a default **MMDDYY** format; however, it may be changed by an entry in column 19 of the *Control Specifications* (**H** statement) of an RPG/400 program. If column 19 is blank (default) or includes an **M,** an **MMDDYY** format is generated; if a **D** is specified, a **DDMMYY** format will be supported; and a **Y** will generate a **YYMMDD** format. A job date may be created to override the system date. The job date is entered in a prompt in one of the displays for the **CHGJOB** *(Change Job)* command and will be available for that job.

RPG/400 provides the reserved word **UDATE** for accessing the system or job date value, which may be used as a field in input, calculations, or output. Because **UDATE** is a reserved word, it does not have to be defined in the program. During program execution, the system or job date is available at first cycle (**1P**) processing before a data record is read. This feature enables the **UDATE** value to be included in heading lines conditioned by the **1P** indicator.

UDATE may be separated into individual month, day, and year values by the reserved words **UMONTH, UDAY,** and **UYEAR,** respectively. Figure 4-9 illustrates *Output Specification* entries for **UDATE, UMONTH, UDAY, UYEAR,** and their related values. **UDATE** (or any date value) is usually edited so that slashes (/) are included in the printed or displayed value with the leading zero for months 01 through 09 suppressed. The function and syntax of edit codes and edit words will be discussed in a separate section of this chapter.

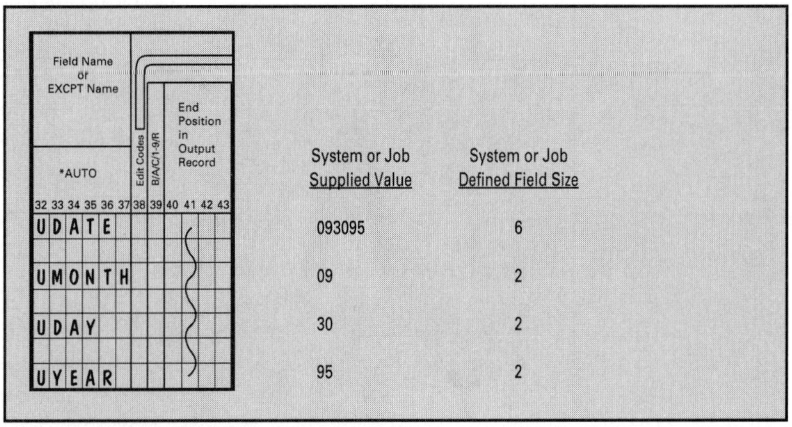

Figure 4-9 System or job date values provided by the RPG/400 reserved words **UDATE, UMONTH, UDAY,** and **UYEAR.**

Page Numbering (PAGE)

PAGE is an RPG/400 reserved word that controls the numbering of report pages. It is predefined as a four-byte numeric field with zero decimal positions (integer) that starts page numbering at 0001 and is automatically incremented by 1 for each subsequent page.

PAGE may also be defined from 1 to 15 bytes in input or calculations and may be initialized to a starting page number minus one. The incrementation of the page numbers will still be controlled automatically. Reserved RPG/400 words, **PAGE1** through **PAGE7,** are also provided so that pages of a report may be numbered differently, or so that they can be used in a program that supports more than one PRINTER file.

Figure 4-10 illustrates how **PAGE** is used in the example program and the values in the field for the first and second pages of the report. Use of the constant **PAGE** is optional and has no effect on the function of the reserved word **PAGE.**

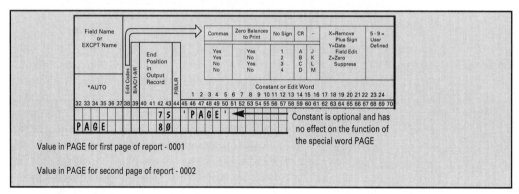

Figure 4-10 Syntax and processing results of the reserved word **PAGE.**

SUMMARY OF THIS SECTION

The example program source listing and related notes shown in Figure 4-11 summarize the syntax and control for headings, page overflow, constants, and the reserved RPG/400 words discussed in the previous paragraphs.

```
SEQNBR*...+... 1 ...+... 2 ...+... 3 ...+... 4 ...+... 5 ...+... 6 ...+... 7 ...+.
   100    * PROGRAM PROCESSES A PF IN ARRIVAL SEQUENCE & GENERATES A REPORT
   200    * WITH HEADINGS AND NUMERIC FIELD EDITING....
   300    FGLACTS  IP  E                    DISK
   400    FQSYSPRT O   F    132       OF    PRINTER
   500    OQSYSPRT H  301   1P— 3                             1
   600    O         OR       OF
   700    O                          UDATE Y    8
   800    O              4   2               46 'GENERAL LEDGER ACCOUNT'
   900    O                        6          55 'BALANCES'                    5
  1000    O                                   75 'PAGE'
  1100    O                          PAGE  Z   80
  1200    O         H  2    1P— 3
  1300    O         OR       OF       7
  1400    O                                    9 'ACT NO'
  1500    O              2                     32 'ACCOUNT NAME'               5
  1600    O                                    57 'ACCOUNT TYPE'
  1700    O                                    76 'BALANCE'
  1800    O         D  1    N1P
  1900    O                          ACTNO     7
  2000    O                          NAME     37
  2100    O                          TYPE     62
  2200    O                                   66 '$'
  2300    O                          BALNCE1  77
```

Figure 4-11 Example program summarization for the syntax and control of headings, page overflow, constants, and reserved RPG/400 words.

1. Overflow indicator **(OF)** is defined in columns 33–34 for the **PRINTER** file.

2. Overflow indicator **(OF)** is specified on two heading lines. When the overflow line is sensed, the overflow indicator is set on, line printed, and paper advanced to the top of the next page. Any heading line conditioned with the **OF** indicator is printed.

3. First page indicator **(1P)** controls the printing of headings on the first report page. Because a record has not been read from the input file, any field values related to input records are not available at this time. Input and calculation instructions are ignored in first cycle processing.

4. Entry in the *Skip Before* field (columns 19–20) advances paper to the line specified (3 for this program) before printing the related line. An entry in the *Skip After* field (columns 21–22) will advance paper to the designated line after printing. Either of these controls also applies to overflow pages.

5. Constants are defined on the *Output Specifications* in columns 45–70 and must be enclosed in apostrophes. End position entry refers to the low-order character in constants, not the low-order apostrophe.

6. UDATE is an RPG/400 reserved word that extracts the system or job date from the computer as a six-byte integer in an **MMDDYY** default format. The date value may be accessed at **1P** (first cycle) time.

7. **PAGE** is an RPG/400 reserved word that provides automatic page numbering for a report. It is predefined as a four-byte integer with a starting value of 0001. Incrementation is automatic and may be specified at **1P** (first cycle) time.

Figure 4-11 Example program summarization for the syntax and control of headings, page overflow, constants, and reserved RPG/400 words. (Continued)

NUMERIC FIELDS

Input Specifications Definition (Program-defined File)

Fields may be defined as numeric in the *Input* or *Calculation Specifications*. A field is defined as numeric on input by specifying a number from 0 through 9 in the *Decimal Positions* field (column 52). The decimal position entry *cannot be larger* than the field size specified in the *FROM* and *TO* fields in the *Input Specifications*. In addition, *the maximum size of a numeric field in RPG/400 is 30 digits, and no more than 9 decimal positions may be assigned.*

A **0** entered in column 52 defines the field as an *integer,* and any digit from **1** to **9** defines it as a *decimal* number with the specified number of *implied* decimal positions. Decimal points are not included in a numeric field value stored on disk, diskette, tape, or display (*explicit* decimal), but they are *implied* in memory during program execution by the related decimal position entry assigned in the program. Figure 4-12 illustrates the effect of decimal position entry assignments on numeric values during program execution.

On the AS/400, if a field is defined as numeric but contains nonnumeric characters, program execution will halt. When processing halts, the operator has the option of ending the job or ignoring the record that caused the condition and continue to process.

Signed Numeric Values

In the RPG/400 environment, an unsigned numeric value is processed as positive, and negative numbers must be explicitly signed as negative. When entering a negative number using an IBM workstation keyboard, a field minus (**FIELD** -) key is provided that will define the value as negative. On the extended keyboard for microcomputers, the nu-

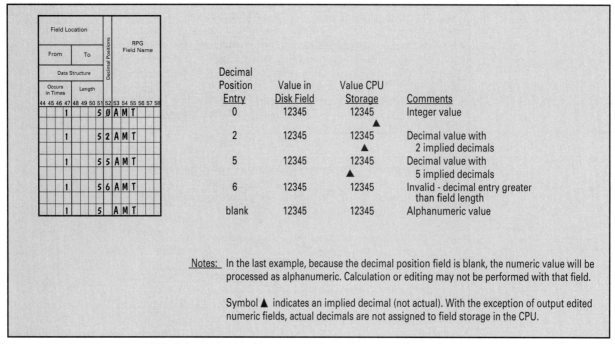

Figure 4-12 Effects of the decimal position assignments on numeric values during program execution.

meric keypad (right side of keyboard) includes a minus key (-) which supplies the negative sign to the numeric value. On disk or in memory, the minus sign is stored over the *low-order* byte in the field value, which <u>does not</u> increase the field size or consume one of the digit positions.

Numeric Field Editing

Only fields that have been defined as numeric may be edited. *Editing* refers to the insertion, suppression, or replacement of characters within the body of a numeric value that is printed or displayed. Editing numeric fields is performed in RPG/400 by *Edit Codes* and *Edit Words*. Each method is discussed separately in the following paragraphs.

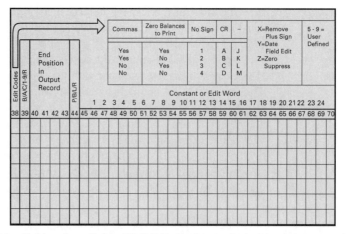

Figure 4-13 Table of available RPG Edit Codes included in the upper right side of all Output Specifications.

Edit Codes—Simple and Combination. All the available RPG/400 *Edit Codes* are conveniently included in a table in the upper right side of the *Output Specifications* form as shown in Figure 4-13. The heavy arrowed line from the *Edit Codes* field to the boxed-in edit code area indicates that the codes are entered in column 38. An examination of the table shows that Edit Codes 1, 2, 3, 4, A, B, C, D, J, K, L, M, X, Y, and Z are provided by RPG/400. With the exception of X, which is not used, each *Edit Code* provides a slightly different pattern. Edit Codes may be classified into two types: simple and combination.

Simple Edit Codes (Y and Z): Simple Edit Codes, which include Y and Z, perform functions unique to the combination class of edit codes. *Edit Code* Y is usually used only to edit date fields (as suggested by the table notation) and performs the editing functions detailed in Figure 4-14.

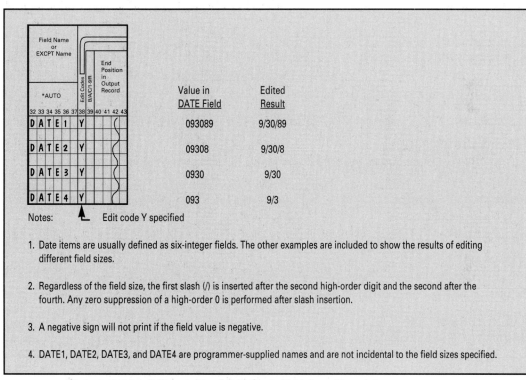

Figure 4-14   Edit results of Edit Code Y (date edit code).

As shown in Figure 4-14, the default insertion characters for *Edit Code* Y are slashes. This may be changed to blanks by specifying an ampersand in column 20 of the *Control Specifications* (**H** statement). Any other character may be specified as the separator by entering it in column 20.

Edit Code Z performs only the suppression of leading zeros in a numeric field value. Any implied decimals defined for the related field are ignored when this *Edit Code* is specified, and the value is printed as an integer. The Z *Edit Code* is typically used with fields defined as integers (e.g., page numbers) that do not require commas and/or a decimal point for readability. Figure 4-15 illustrates the results of editing when *Edit Code* Z is specified with a field.

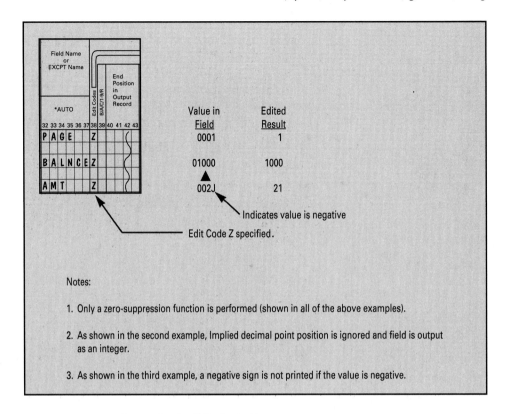

Figure 4-15   Edit results for Edit Code Z.

Combination Edit Codes: The *combination Edit Codes* include 1, 2, 3, 4, A, B, C, D, J, K, L, and M. Because they each perform a different edit function, they are listed as three separate groups in the *Output Specifications* table. *Edit Codes* 1, 2, 3, and 4 are listed as a No-Sign group; A, B, C, and D as a CR group; and J, K, L, and M as the minus group. In addition, the columns for commas and for Zero Balances to Print identify some of the basic edit functions provided by each of the *Edit Codes.* All the combination *Edit Codes* will insert a decimal point in the edited output for decimal values, but not after the low-order digit for integers.

Figure 4-16 details the functions performed by each *Edit Code.*

The processing results of the various *Edit Codes* are illustrated in Figure 4-17. Notice that the unedited value for each column is included horizontally on the first line, *Unedited.*

Edit Code	Commas	Decimal Point	Sign for Negative Balance	Entry in Column 21 of Control Specification			Zero Suppress
				D or Blank	I	J	
1	Yes	Yes	No Sign	.00 or 0	,00 or 0	0,00 or 0	Yes
2	Yes	Yes	No Sign	Blanks	Blanks	Blanks	Yes
3		Yes	No Sign	.00 or 0	,00 or 0	0,00 or 0	Yes
4		Yes	No Sign	Blanks	Blanks	Blanks	Yes
5-9[1]							
A	Yes	Yes	CR	.00 or 0	,00 or 0	0,00 or 0	Yes
B	Yes	Yes	CR	Blanks	Blanks	Blanks	Yes
C		Yes	CR	.00 or 0	,00 or 0	0,00 or 0	Yes
D		Yes	CR	Blanks	Blanks	Blanks	Yes
J	Yes	Yes	- (minus)	.00 or 0	,00 or 0	0,00 or 0	Yes
K	Yes	Yes	- (minus)	Blanks	Blanks	Blanks	Yes
L		Yes	- (minus)	.00 or 0	,00 or 0	0,00 or 0	Yes
M		Yes	- (minus)	Blanks	Blanks	Blanks	Yes
N	Yes	Yes	- (floating minus)	.00 or 0	,00 or 0	0,00 or 0	Yes
O	Yes	Yes	- (floating minus)	Blanks	Blanks	Blanks	Yes
P		Yes	- (floating minus)	.00 or 0	,00 or 0	0,00 or 0	Yes

[1]These are the user-defined edit codes.

[2]The X edit code ensures a hexadecimal F sign for positive values. Because the system does this for you, normally you do not have to specify this code.

[3]The Y edit code suppresses the leftmost zero of a date field that is 3- to 6-digits long and it suppresses the two leftmost zeros of a field that is seven positions long. The Y edit code also inserts slashes (/) between the month, day, and year according to the following pattern:

nn/n
nn/nn
nn/nn/n
nn/nn/nn
nnnn/nn/nn

[4]The Z edit code removes the sign (plus or minus) from a numeric field and suppresses leading zeros of a numeric field.

Figure 4-16   Edit Codes 1, 2, 3, 4, A, B, C, D, J, K, L, and M functions. (*Courtesy of IBM*)

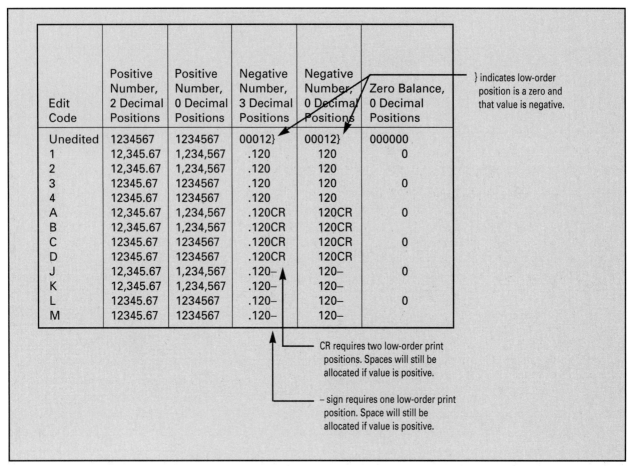

Edit Code	Positive Number, 2 Decimal Positions	Positive Number, 0 Decimal Positions	Negative Number, 3 Decimal Positions	Negative Number, 0 Decimal Positions	Zero Balance, 0 Decimal Positions
Unedited	1234567	1234567	00012}	00012}	000000
1	12,345.67	1,234,567	.120	120	0
2	12,345.67	1,234,567	.120	120	
3	12345.67	1234567	.120	120	0
4	12345.67	1234567	.120	120	
A	12,345.67	1,234,567	.120CR	120CR	0
B	12,345.67	1,234,567	.120CR	120CR	
C	12345.67	1234567	.120CR	120CR	0
D	12345.67	1234567	.120CR	120CR	
J	12,345.67	1,234,567	.120–	120–	0
K	12,345.67	1,234,567	.120–	120–	
L	12345.67	1234567	.120–	120–	0
M	12345.67	1234567	.120–	120–	

} indicates low-order position is a zero and that value is negative.

CR requires two low-order print positions. Spaces will still be allocated if value is positive.

– sign requires one low-order print position. Space will still be allocated if value is positive.

Figure 4-17 Processing results of the 1, 2, 3, 4, A, B, C, D, J, K, L, and M Edit Codes. (*Courtesy of IBM*)

Dollar Signs ($) with Edit Codes: A dollar sign may be coded as floating or fixed. Figure 4-18 illustrates the syntax for each option when the dollar sign is used with an *Edit Code*. If a floating dollar sign is assigned and an *Edit Code* is not specified for the field, a terminal error is generated during program compilation.

Edit Words.   Because *Edit Codes* are simple to use and their editing results are predetermined, they should be used whenever possible. Sometimes, however, they may not satisfy all editing requirements and an *Edit Word* must be specified. For example, the standard printed format of a social security number is 011-11-1111, in which the leading zero is not suppressed and hyphens are inserted in the body of the value. Because none of the *Edit Codes* provide for this pattern, an *Edit Word* must be used. Other special editing functions, such as the insertion of blanks in the print pattern, or the addition of words at the end of the edited value, may be required. The syntax rules for forming *Edit Words* are detailed in Figure 4-19. Notice that rules 1, 2, and 4 are applicable to all *Edit Word* patterns and are not individually shown, but they are included in the coding examples in Figure 4-19.

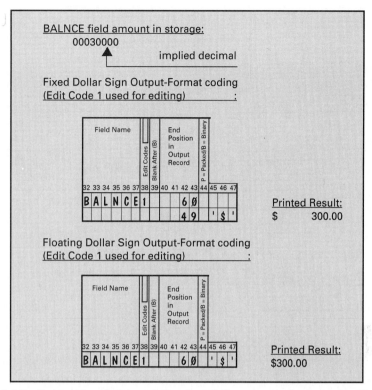

Figure 4-18 Syntax for fixed and floating dollar signs when used with an Edit Code.

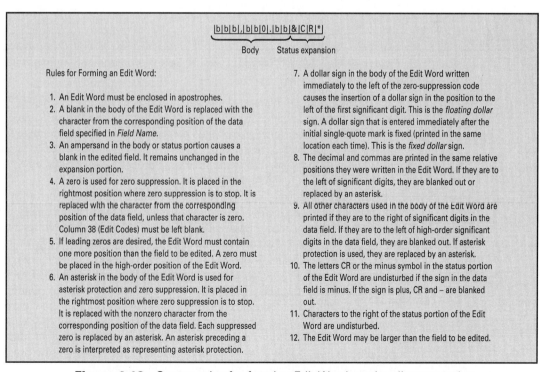

Figure 4-19 Syntax rules for forming Edit Words and coding examples.

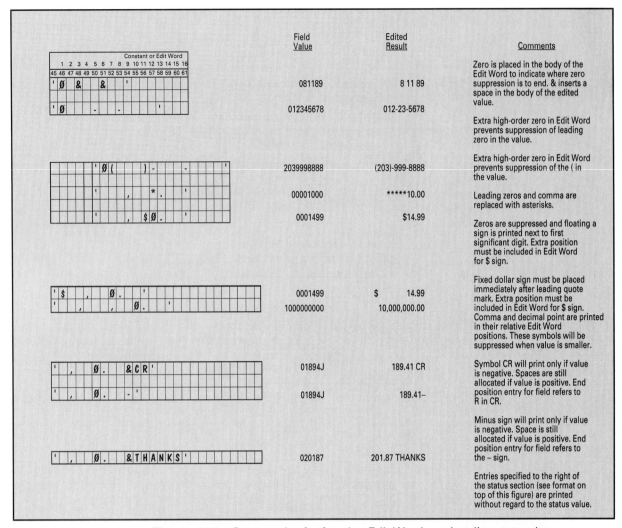

	Field Value	Edited Result	Comments
'∅ & & '	081189	8 11 89	Zero is placed in the body of the Edit Word to indicate where zero suppression is to end. & inserts a space in the body of the edited value.
'∅ - - '	012345678	012-23-5678	Extra high-order zero in Edit Word prevents suppression of leading zero in the value.
'∅ ( ) - - '	2039998888	(203)-999-8888	Extra high-order zero in Edit Word prevents suppression of the (in the value.
', * . '	00001000	*****10.00	Leading zeros and comma are replaced with asterisks.
'$∅. '	0001499	$14.99	Zeros are suppressed and floating a sign is printed next to first significant digit. Extra position must be included in Edit Word for $ sign.
'$, ∅. '	0001499	$ 14.99	Fixed dollar sign must be placed immediately after leading quote mark. Extra position must be included in Edit Word for $ sign. Comma and decimal point are printed in their relative Edit Word positions. These symbols will be suppressed when value is smaller.
', , ∅. '	1000000000	10,000,000.00	
', ∅.&CR'	01894J	189.41 CR	Symbol CR will print only if value is negative. Spaces are still allocated if value is positive. End position entry for field refers to R in CR.
', ∅.-'	01894J	189.41–	Minus sign will print only if value is negative. Space is still allocated if value is positive. End position entry for field refers to the – sign.
', ∅.&THANKS'	020187	201.87 THANKS	Entries specified to the right of the status section (see format on top of this figure) are printed without regard to the status value.

Figure 4-19   Syntax rules for forming Edit Words and coding examples. (Continued)

Data Entry of Numeric Values.   It was explained in Chapter 3 that numeric data must be stored right-justified in its related field position when entered. Because this concept cannot be overemphasized, it is presented again as a timely review. Examine the top section of Figure 4-20 and observe what processing results occur if a numeric value is not stored right-justified. The value should be processed as 123.45, but if entered incorrectly, as shown in the figure, it will be processed as 12345.00.

In an environment that does not support a data entry or screen utility, numeric values smaller than the field size are usually entered with the required leading zeros. However, as illustrated in Figure 4-20, the entry of numeric data in an interactive environment is simplified. Two optional methods are shown. Option 1 places the CRT cursor at the high-order position of the field; as digits are entered, the cursor moves to the right. After all the numbers are entered, pressing the ENTER or FIELD EXIT key will automatically right-justify the value in its related storage area in memory. Option 2 places the CRT cursor at the low-order position of the field; as digits are entered, the number previously stored in the low-order position moves one space to the left. For either option, any unused high-order positions do not have to be filled with zeros. Zeros are automatically included when the value is moved from the screen field to the storage area. Today, most of the screen and data entry utilities support both options.

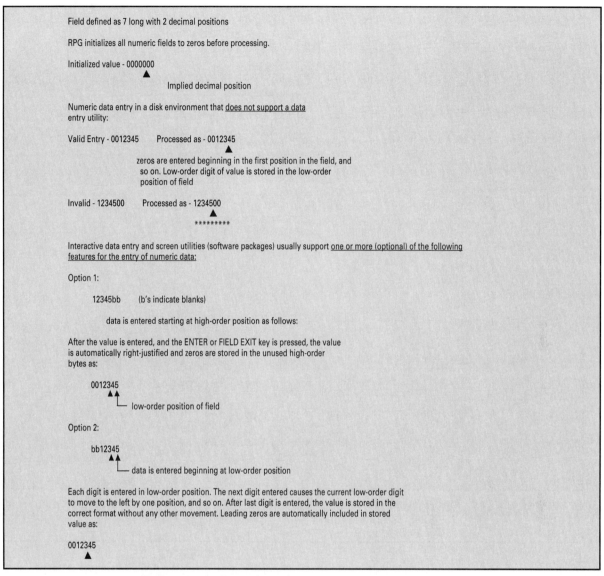

Figure 4-20   Procedures for valid numeric data entry.

Numeric Field Definition and Editing in the Example Program. A source listing of the example program and its relationship to the printed report are shown in Figure 4-21. Notice the following:

1. The field BALNCE, defined as numeric in the physical file, is edited on output by the *Edit Code* 1 entry in column 38.

2. The system date (**UDATE**) is edited by *Edit Code* Y, which suppresses the leading zero and inserts two slashes.

3. The special word **PAGE** is edited by *Edit Code* Z, which suppresses leading zeros in the page number.

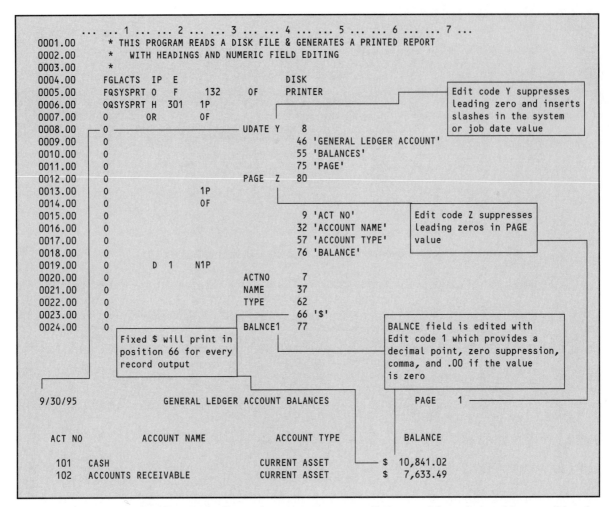

Figure 4-21 Example program source listing and its relationship to editing included in the printed report.

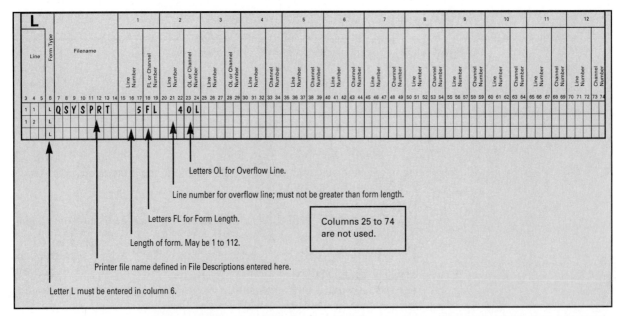

Figure 4-22 Line Counter Specifications and example entries for printers that use line (not channel) references.

RPG CONTROL FOR MODIFICATION OF FORM LENGTHS

The standard form length that is specified when the computer is configured is usually defined with a default length of 66 lines (printing at 6 lines per inch) with the default overflow on line 60. Printer adjustment at the top of the form will, however, determine the exact location of the page overflow line in the body of a printed report.

Special forms, such as labels, checks, invoices, transcripts, and so forth, are not often the standard paper length supported by a system. Consequently, procedures have been included in the RPG/400 environment to modify a form length when needed. Two methods are available on most systems to modify the length of a form. One includes control by the command language (e.g., CL). The other method controls variable form lengths directly in an RPG/400 program by *Line Counter Specification* instructions.

A *Line Counter Specifications* form is detailed in Figure 4-22. Note that this form is included at the bottom of the *Extension Specifications* and that the "L" instructions must be stored in the compilation order (H, F, E, L, I, C, O) required for all RPG/400 programs.

The documentation and RPG/400 syntax for an application program that generates customer mailing labels is presented to illustrate how the *Line Counter Specifications* form is used to modify the standard page length and overflow line location.

APPLICATION PROGRAM: CUSTOMER MAILING LABELS

Documentation

The specifications presented in Figure 4-23 describe the processing requirements for an RPG/400 program that generates mailing labels.

PROGRAM SPECIFICATIONS   Page 1 of 1

Program Name: Customer Mailing Labels   Program ID: CLABELS   Written by: SM

Purpose: Print customer mailing labels   Approved by: CM

Input files: CUSTMRS _____   _____   _____   _____

Output files: QSYSPRT _____   _____   _____   _____

Processing Requirements:

Write an RPG/400 program to print customer mailing labels on pre-glued continuous form labels.

Input to the program:

The externally defined physical file, CUSTMRS, contains customer names and addresses in the format shown in the attached record layout form.

Processing:

Read the physical file in arrival sequence until end of file. For every record processed, print three detail lines on a mailing label form.

Output:

A Printer Spacing Chart is attached which shows the output format for the mailing labels. Pages of continuous forms labels are used.

The following must be included in the program to control the printing of the labels:

1. Line Counter Specifications must be included with a form length defined as 5 lines and overflow on line 4.
2. Printer must be set at 6 lines per inch.
3. One label per form is to be printed in the format detailed in the print chart.

Figure 4-23 Specifications for customer mailing label program.

A system flowchart indicating the files processed by the program is shown in Figure 4-24.

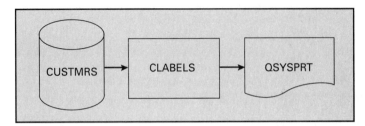

Figure 4-24   System flowchart for customer mailing label program.

The format of the records in the input file, CUSTMRS, is presented in Figure 4-25. A listing of the data file is also included at the bottom of the figure.

```
                    PHYSICAL FILE DESCRIPTION

    SYSTEM: AS/400                           DATE: 4/10/95
    FILE NAME: CUSTMRS                       REV NO: 0
    RECORD NAME: CUSTMRSR                    KEY LENGTH: None
    SEQUENCE: Non-keyed                      RECORD SIZE: 65

                     FIELD DEFINITIONS

    FIELD    FIELD NAME    SIZE   TYPE     POSITION     COMMENTS
     NO                                   FROM    TO


      1      NAME          20     C         1      20
      2      ADDRES        20     C        21      40
      3      CITY          20     C        41      60
      4      STATE          2     C        61      62
      5      ZIP            5     P        63      65

Physical File Listing:


    PAUL CEZANNE        44 RUE PIGALLE      STAMFORD       CT06518
    EDGAR DEGAS         10 ROSE TERRACE     WESTPORT       PA07777
    BUCKMINISTER FULLER 999 PARK AVENUE     GREENWICH      CT06444
```

Figure 4-25   Record layout form and listing of the input file processed by the customer mailing label program.

The print format of the continuous form labels is shown in Figure 4-26. Notice that the individual label forms are 5 lines in length, printing is to begin on line 2 of each label, and page overflow occurs on line 4.

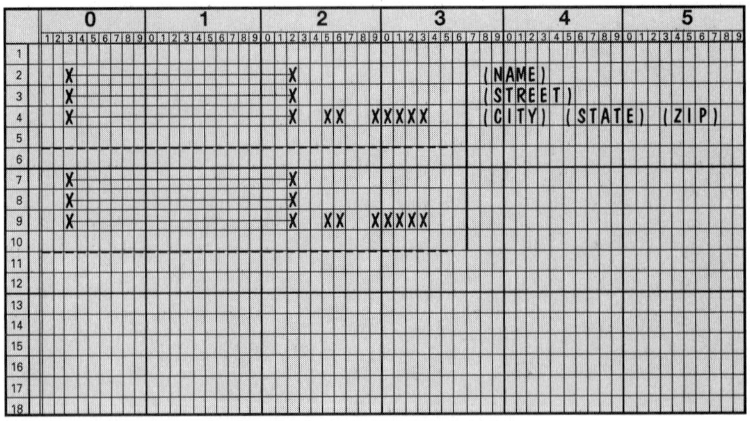

Figure 4-26   Printer spacing chart for customer label program.

Source Program Coding for Customer Labels Program

The source program listing in Figure 4-27 identifies the syntax that controls the size and processing of the labels. Also included at the bottom of the figure is a listing of the labels with comments documenting the line references included in the *Line Counter Specifications* and *Skip Before* entries in the program.

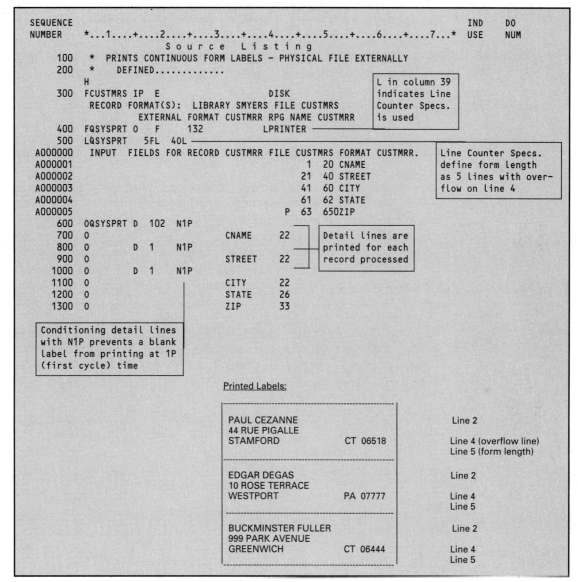

Figure 4-27 Compiled program listing and printed labels with program-related line reference comments.

SUMMARY

Headings (constants) in an RPG/400 program are defined in columns 45 to 70 of the *Output Specifications* and must be enclosed in apostrophes (single quotation marks). A printer spacing chart is usually referenced to determine end position locations for a constant or group of constants. The programmer has unlimited flexibility as to how constants are coded in a program.

First page output is controlled during the first cycle of program execution by the **1P** *(First Page)* indicator. Because a record has not been read from a file, *Input* and

Calculation Specification instructions are ignored in first cycle processing. The **1P** indicator is automatically set off after the last output instruction is executed.

Reserved RPG/400 words that access the system or job date are **UDATE, UMONTH, UDAY,** and **UYEAR. UDATE** is accessed in a default **MMDDYY** format unless changed by an entry in column 19 of the *Control Specifications* (**H** statement). The individual elements of **UDATE** are accessed in their two-byte values.

PAGE is another RPG/400 reserved word that provides for automatic page numbering in a report. **UDATE, UMONTH, UDAY, UYEAR,** and **PAGE** are available at **1P** *(First Page)* time before any data records are read.

Top-of-page control is included in a program by a *Skip Before* or *Skip After* entry on the *Output Specifications.* The entry refers to the line number that the paper will advance to before or after printing.

The repetition of headings on every page of a report is controlled by the *overflow indicators* **OA** to **OG** and **OV.** An overflow indicator is defined in the *File Description Specifications* (columns 33–34) for a PRINTER specified file. They are included on the *Output Specifications,* often in an **OR** relationship with the **1P** indicator to condition the related output.

Fields in an *externally defined* physical file are defined as numeric in the related DDS. Numeric fields are defined in a *program-defined* file by entering a related number for decimal positions in column 52 of the *Input Specifications* field description. Integers are defined with a zero and decimal values with 1 to 9. The maximum size of a numeric field in the RPG/400 is 30 digits with a maximum of 9 decimal positions.

Only fields defined as numeric may be edited in RPG/400. Editing is performed by *Edit Codes* or *Edit Words.* The function of *Edit Codes* is predetermined, and they are, therefore, easier to use. *Edit Words,* however, offer additional features and must be used when an *Edit Code* will not meet the editing requirements.

For line printers, the standard form length is 66 lines with overflow set on line 60. This standard form length may be modified in an RPG/400 program by the *Line Counter Specifications.* Any form size may be controlled by this RPG/400 syntax. Statements in a Control Language Program (CLP) may also be used to control form lengths.

QUESTIONS

4-1. Where are report headings defined in an RPG/400 program?

4-2. On a blank output form define the following report heading:
SALARIED EMPLOYEE PAYROLL INFORMATION

4-3. When does the **1P** indicator turn on in an RPG/400 program? What function does it perform? What variables are available at **1P** (first cycle) time?

4-4. What is the function of the *Skip Before* and *Skip After* entries in an RPG/400 program? How does skipping control differ from spacing?

4-5. Is skipping specified for every output record type? Explain your answer.

4-6. Explain the page overflow function.

4-7. What overflow indicators are provided by RPG/400? Where is an overflow indicator defined? Where is it specified? Is it assigned to every output record type?

4-8. What, if anything, is wrong with the following source program coding for a heading line? Note **10** is a *Record Identifying Indicator.*

O		Filename or Record Name	Type (H/D/T/E)	Stkr #/Fetch (F)	Space		Skip		Output Indicators			
					Before	After	Before	After		And	And	
Line	Form Type			R	E	L						
				D	D	D						
				A	D	D						
			O	R								
			A	N	D							
3 4 5	6	7 8 9 10 11 12 13	14 15	16	17 18	19 20	21 22	23	24 25	26 27 28	29 30 31	
0 1	O	BALANCE	H		7 1 2				1 Ø			
0 2	O		OR						O V			

4-9. What is the RPG/400 reserved word for the system date? In what format is it stored? Into what elements may it be subdivided? Are these values available for processing at **1P** (first cycle) time?

4-10. Explain how page numbering is provided for in an RPG/400 program that generates a report.

4-11. What, if anything, is wrong with the following partial *Output Specifications* coding for a heading line?

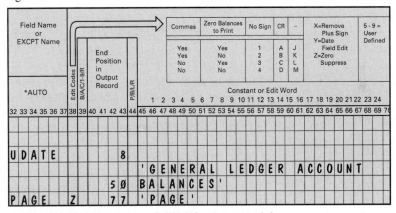

4-12. How and on which coding form are fields defined as numeric?

4-13. What is the maximum length of a numeric field supported by RPG/400? What is the maximum number of decimal positions that may be assigned to a numeric field? May the number of decimal positions assigned exceed the related field length?

4-14. Explain the alternative processing results that may occur when an alphanumeric field (value includes nonnumeric characters) is defined as numeric.

4-15. Define the term *implied decimal position*. What function does it perform in an RPG/400 program?

4-16. Define the term *explicit decimal position*. Where is it specified in an RPG/400 program?

4-17. Other than the physical file, where else may fields be defined as numeric?

4-18. If editing is specified for a field that is not defined as numeric, what is the result during program compilation? What is the result during program execution?

4-19. Explain the editing function. By what methods may it be controlled in an RPG/400 program? How does syntax for the methods differ? What field types may be edited?

4-20. Determine the edited results for the following integers if the Y *Edit Code* is specified:

Value in Storage	Edited Result
081195	
0811	
08	
000000	
123195	

4-21. Determine the edited results for the following values when the *Edit Code* specified is assigned:

Value In Storage	Edit Code Specified	Edited Result
.		
0000000 ▲	1	
0000000 ▲	2	
0123456 ▲	1	
1000000 ▲	3	
0000099 ▲	4	
200000J ▲	A	
0200000 ▲	B	
0001000 ▲	Z	
012459} ▲	K	

▲ Indicates implied decimal position

4-22. On the basis of the values in storage, format the *Edit Words* to generate the indicated edited results. For all *monetary* values, the format .00 is to be printed for decimal values and 0 for integers if the value is zero. In addition, for monetary values, include commas in the Edit Word if the size suggests them. Field sizes are indicated by the values in storage (first column).

Value In Storage	Edited Result	Required Edit Word (format on a blank output form)
012223456 ▲	012-22-3456	
010290 ▲	1/02/90	
00001000 ▲	****10.00	
00009944 ▲	$99.44	
2033334444 ▲	(203) 333 4444	
00500000 ▲	$ 5,000.00	
000187N ▲	18.75 CR	
0213500J ▲	$ 2,135,001–	
0015000 ▲	150.00 DEBIT	

▲ Indicates implied decimal position in storage

4-23. Do the blank positions in an *Edit Word* pattern have to be *equal* to the related field size? Explain your answer.

4-24. When an *Edit Code* is used, how is a fixed dollar sign specified? How is a floating dollar sign specified? If an *Edit Word* is used, how is a fixed dollar sign specified? How is a floating dollar sign specified?

4-25. For line printers, what is the standard paper length for forms expressed in lines? On what line is page overflow set?

4-26. Which specifications are required to modify the standard paper length? Refer to the form(s), and identify the entries required.

PROGRAMMING ASSIGNMENTS

For each of the following programming assignments, a physical file must have been created and loaded with the related data records. Your instructor will inform you as to whether you have to create the physical file and load it or if it has been prepared for the assignment.

Programming Assignment 4-1: SALARIED EMPLOYEE REPORT

From the following documentation, write an RPG/400 program to generate the report formatted in the printer spacing chart.

Physical File Format:

```
                    PHYSICAL FILE DESCRIPTION

        SYSTEM: AS/400                    DATE: Yours
        FILE NAME: Yours                  REV NO: 0
        RECORD NAME: Yours                KEY LENGTH: None
        SEQUENCE: Non-keyed               RECORD SIZE: 36

                         FIELD DEFINITIONS

        FIELD    FIELD NAME    SIZE   TYPE    POSITION      COMMENTS
        NO                                   FROM    TO

          1      EMPNO          4      C       1      4
          2      LNAME         16      C       5     20
          3      FINIT          1      C      21     21
          4      SINIT          1      C      22     22
          5      SSNO           9      P      23     27
          6      WEKSRY         6      P      28     31   2 decimals
          7      YTDSRY         8      P      32     36   2 decimals
```

Physical File Data:

Employee Number	Last Name	Initials 1st	2nd	SS Number	Weekly Salary	YTD Salary
0001	WASHINGTON	G	G	010731799	080000	01600000
0016	LINCOLN	A	T	018091864	110000	00440000
0018	GRANT	U	S	018221885	051599	00051599
0032	ROOSEVELT	F	D	018821945	095000	00950000
0033	TRUMAN	H	S	018841973	099999	02999970
0034	EISENHOWER	D	D	018901971	140000	02940000
0039	CARTER	J		019771981	023000	00920000
0040	REAGAN	R		020111989	200000	02000000
0045	CLINTON	W		030154444	400000	16000000

Report Design:

```
       0         1         2         3         4         5         6         7         8
 1234567890123456789012345678901234567890123456789012345678901234567890123456789012345678901
 1  ØX/XX/XX              SALARIED EMPLOYEE LISTING                              PAGE XXØX
 2
 3
 4      EMP NO        EMPLOYEE NAME              SS NO      SALARY   YTD SALARY
 5
 6      XXXX        X X X            X        XXX-XX-XXXX  X,XXØ.XX  XXX,XXØ.XX
 7
 8      XXXX        X X X            X        XXX-XX-XXXX  X,XXØ.XX  XXX,XXØ.XX
 9
10      NOTES:
11
12        1. DATE IS SYSTEM-SUPPLIED
13
14        2. HEADINGS ON TOP OF EVERY PAGE
```

Programming Assignment 4-2: DATA PERSONNEL SALARY LISTING

Write an RPG/400 program from the following documentation.

Physical File Format:

```
                    PHYSICAL FILE DESCRIPTION

 SYSTEM: AS/400                          DATE: Yours
 FILE NAME: Yours                        REV NO: 0
 RECORD NAME: Yours                      KEY LENGTH: None
 SEQUENCE:Non-keyed                      RECORD SIZE: 30

                      FIELD DEFINITIONS

   FIELD      FIELD NAME    SIZE   TYPE    POSITION     COMMENTS
    NO                                    FROM    TO


     1         TITLE         25     C       1     25
     2         SALARY         5     P      26     28    2 decimals
     3         NOEMP          3     P      29     30
```

Physical File Data:

Job Title	Average Weekly Salary	Number of Employees
APPLICATION PROGRAMMERS	50000	010
SYSTEMS PROGRAMMERS	65000	003
COMPUTER OPERATORS	27500	008
SYSTEMS ANALYST	75000	004
DATA ENTRY CLERKS	25000	010
PROGRAMMER TRAINEES	30000	003
RECORDS CLERKS	22500	002
DATA PROCESSING MANAGER	82500	001
OPERATOR SUPERVISORS	45000	002

Report Design:

```
       0         1         2         3         4         5
 1  ØX/XX/XX                                      PAGE  XXØX
 2
 3  AVERAGE WEEKLY SALARY OF DATA PROCESSING PERSONNEL
 4
 5
 6  NUMBER OF            JOB TITLE              AVERAGE
 7  EMPLOYEES                                   WEEKLY SALARY
 8
 9     XØX      X                        X     $ XXØ.XX
10
11     XØX      X                        X     $ XXØ.XX
12
13    (EMP)          (TITLE)                    (SALARY)
14
15           NOTES:
16
17              1. HEADINGS ON TOP OF EVERY PAGE
18
19              2. DOLLAR SIGNS ARE FIXED
```

Programming Assignment 4-3: AVERAGE ITEMIZED DEDUCTIONS FOR FEDERAL INCOME TAX DETERMINATION

Write an RPG/400 program to generate the report detailed in the printer spacing chart.

Physical File Format:

```
                        PHYSICAL FILE DESCRIPTION

        SYSTEM: AS/400                          DATE: Yours
        FILE NAME: Yours                        REV NO: 0
        RECORD NAME: Yours                      KEY LENGTH: None
        SEQUENCE: Non-keyed                     RECORD SIZE: 30

                          FIELD DEFINITIONS

        FIELD    FIELD NAME   SIZE    TYPE    POSITION       COMMENTS
        NO                                   FROM    TO


         1        NAME         12      C       1      12
         2        IR25          5      P      13      15     0 decimals
         3        IR30          5      P      16      18     0 decimals
         4        IR40          5      P      19      21     0 decimals
         5        IR50          5      P      22      24     0 decimals
         6        IR75          5      P      25      27     0 decimals
         7        IR100         5      P      28      30     0 decimals
```

Physical File Data:

Itemized Deduction	$25,000–30,000	$30,000–40,000	$40,000–50,000	$50,000–75,000	$75,000–100,000	$100,000–200,000
MEDICAL	03306	03137	03612	04002	06003	12087
INTEREST	04662	05011	05667	06595	08847	13324
TAXES	02069	02477	03015	04049	05888	09359
CONTRIBUTIONS	01129	01213	01315	01665	02112	03442

Report Design:

```
         0          1          2          3          4          5          6          7          8
   1234567890123456789012345678901234567890123456789012345678901234567890123456789012345678901234567890123
 1                         AVERAGE ITEMIZED DEDUCTION SCHEDULE                              ØX/XX/XX
 2
 3
 4    ITEMIZED        $25,000-      $30,000-      $40,000-      $50,000-      $ 75,000-      $100,000-
 5    DEDUCTION        30,000        40,000        50,000        75,000        100,000        200,000
 6
 7 X           X     $ØX,XXX       $ØX,XXX       $ØX,XXX       $ØX,XXX       $ ØX,XXX       $ ØX,XXX
 8
 9 X           X      ØX,XXX        ØX,XXX        ØX,XXX        ØX,XXX         ØX,XXX         ØX,XXX
10
11    NOTES:
12          1. USE SYSTEM DATE FOR REPORT
13
14          2. $ ON FIRST DETAIL LINE ONLY
```

Programming Assignment 4-4: STUDENT ENROLLMENT REPORT

Write an RPG/400 program to create the report shown in the printer spacing chart.

Physical File Format:

```
                    PHYSICAL FILE DESCRIPTION

  SYSTEM: AS/400                          DATE: Yours
  FILE NAME: Yours                        REV NO: 0
  RECORD NAME: Yours                      KEY LENGTH: None
  SEQUENCE: Non-keyed                     RECORD SIZE: 59


                       FIELD DEFINITIONS

  FIELD     FIELD NAME    SIZE   TYPE    POSITION      COMMENTS
  NO                                     FROM    TO


    1       SS#            9      P        1      5
    2       SEX            1      C        6      6
    3       SNAME         30      C        7     36
    4       TEL#          10      P       37     42
    5       TECHGY        15      C       43     57
    6       TMARK          3      P       58     59   0 decimals
```

Physical File Data:

SS Number	Sex	Student Name	Telephone Number	Technology	Entrance Test Mark
011223333	M	LAMONT CRANSTON	2037778888	DATA	090
066445432	F	LOIS LANE	2129994322	CHEMISTRY	085
124111235	M	FRANK N STEIN	9142668413	ARCHITECTURAL	078
077889999	M	D R ACULA	9134445555	PREP PROGRAM	060
124111235	F	REDDI WATT	2033777865	MECHANICAL	100

Report Design:

```
        0         1         2         3         4         5         6         7
   12345678901234567890123456789012345678901234567890123456789012345678901234567890
 1 ØX/XX/XX           ENTERING STUDENT ENROLLMENT INFORMATION              PAGE XXØX
 2 (UDATE)
 3
 4             STUDENT NUMBER: XXX-XX-XXXX
 5             STUDENT NAME:   X                              X
 6             TELEPHONE: (XXX)-XXX-XXXX
 7             TECHNOLOGY: X                 X
 8             SEX: X                 ENTRANCE TEST MARK:   ØXX
 9
10
11
12          NOTES:
13
14             1. TRIPLE SPACING BETWEEN STUDENTS.
15
16             2. HEADINGS ON TOP OF EVERY PAGE.
```

chapter 5

RPG/400 Calculations (Arithmetic Functions)

This chapter introduces the syntax and processing logic for RPG/400 calculations and related indicator control. All calculation instructions are included in the *Calculation Specifications*. The logical areas of this form and an explanation of their functions are detailed in Figure 5-1.

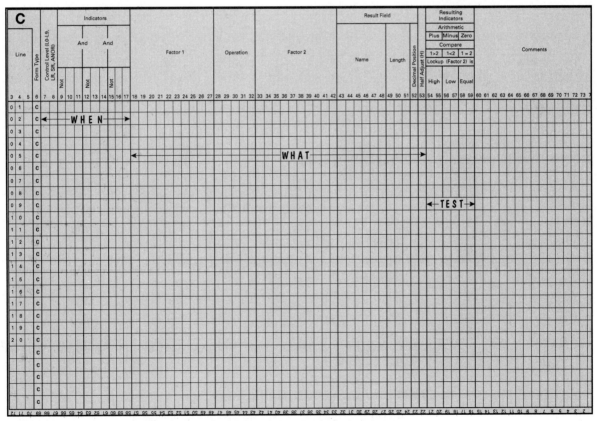

Figure 5-1 RPG/400 Calculation Specifications.

All calculation instructions must have a letter *C* in column 6.

Form Areas:

When (columns 7–17)

Conditioning indicator(s) are specified (only when needed) in this logical area. Columns 7–8 are for the **Control Level Indicators** *L1–L9* that control total time processing; and for the LR indicator that controls last record (end-of-file) time processing. Control level indicator concepts are introduced in Chapter 8 and the *LR* indicator later in this chapter. Any RPG indicators (except *1P* and *LR*) may be specified in columns 9–17 to condition an instruction.

What (columns 18–53)

This area includes fields labeled **Factor 1, Operation, Factor 2, Result Field, Field Length, Decimal Positions,** and **Half Adjust.** Their function is to inform the computer about the operation to be executed. Many operations are supported in the calculation specifications. This chapter only introduces the syntax and processing logic associated with arithmetic operations. Other chapters present the function of other operations.

Test (columns 54–59)

Refer to the form and notice that this area is labeled as **Resulting indicators,** followed by the heading **Arithmetic,** and then the fields for **Plus, Minus,** and **Zero,** Indicators (usually **01–99**) are specified in one or more of these fields to test a result field value for positive, negative, and/or zero. **Resulting indicator(s)** are used to condition other calculations and/or output instructions. The programmer must determine what tests, if any, are to be made.

The heading labeled **Compare** and related fields, **High, Low,** and **Equal,** are used in decision-making instructions which are introduced in the next chapter. The **Lookup** heading and fields are unique to table and array processing, and are discussed in Chapters 9 and 10, respectively.

Comments (columns 60–74)

Comments may be included in this area to support instructions. They do not require an asterisk in column 7 and do not have to be enclosed in apostrophes (quotes).

Figure 5-1 RPG/400 Calculation Specifications. (Continued)

RPG/400 ARITHMETIC OPERATIONS

Regardless of the arithmetic function (addition, subtraction, multiplication, or division), the following must be considered in an RPG/400 programming environment:

1. RPG/400 language formats of arithmetic instructions
2. Optimum size of the result (answer field)
3. Function of the result (answer field)
4. Algebraic rules for addition, subtraction, multiplication, and division
5. Arithmetic signs (positive and negative) of the fields used in an instruction

Each of the foregoing is addressed when the format and rules for writing arithmetic statements for RPG/400 programs are discussed.

RPG/400 Addition (ADD Operation)

All the arithmetic operations in the RPG/400 language follow the laws of algebra. Figure 5-2 explains the algebraic rules for addition. Examine the figure to understand how the sum (answer) is affected by the various combinations of positive and negative signs.

	Rule 1	Rule 2	Rule 3	Rule 3	Rule 3
Addend	+2	−3	+5	+3	+8
Addend	+2	−3	−5	−9	−6
Sum	+4	−6	−0	−6	+2

Explanation of Algebraic Rules:

Rule 1: Addition of two positive values results in a positive value for the sum.

Rule 2: Addition of two negative values results in a negative value for the sum.

Rule 3: Addition of two values with different signs results in the difference in the positive and negative values and the sum carries the sign of the largest value. (see three Rule 3 examples above).

Figure 5-2 Algebraic rules for addition.

The **ADD** operation controls the addition function in RPG/400 programs. Figure 5-3 details the syntax related to this operation.

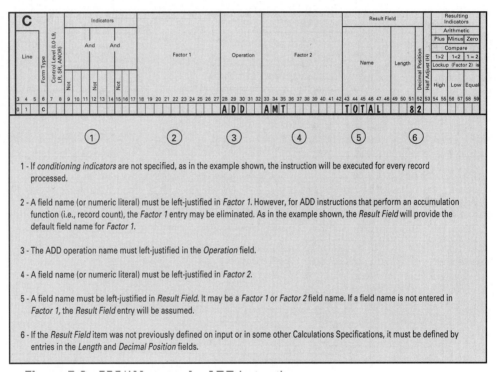

Figure 5-3 RPG/400 syntax for **ADD** instruction.

Four **ADD** instructions are illustrated in Figure 5-4. Notice that the field values *before* and *after* a statement is executed are shown for every example.

After you have examined Figure 5-4, notice the following features for the **ADD** operation:

1. *Factor 1* and *2* entries may be specified in either field.

2. A *Factor 1* or *2* field may be used as the *Result Field*. However, for accumulators it is more efficient to specify the *Factor 1* field entry as the *Result Field*.

3. If a *Factor 1* or *2* field is specified as the *Result Field*, the original value is replaced with the sum.

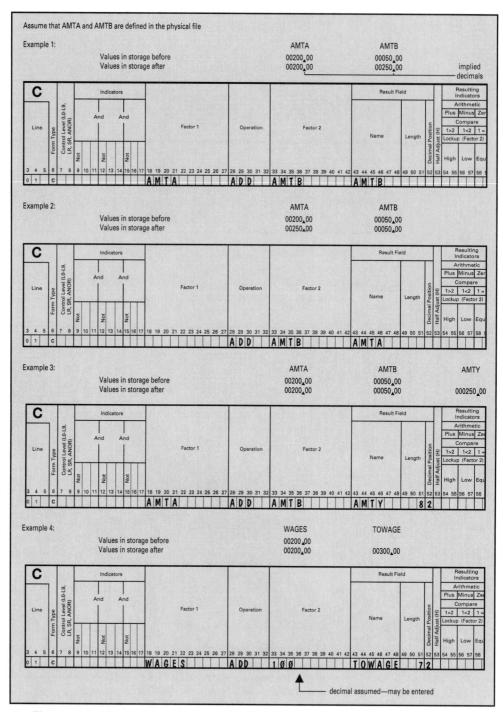

Figure 5-4 Coding examples of **ADD** instructions.

4. Numeric literals may be specified (left-justified) in either *Factor 1* or *2*. A decimal point is required for decimal literals and is optional for integers.
5. Numeric literals may not be specified in the *Result Field*.

The *Result Field* size (sum) should usually be defined at least one byte greater than the largest addend (*Factor 1* or *2* entry). High-order or low-order truncation, depending on the related decimal locations, may result from any sum field that is defined as too small. The data processed will determine the optimum size of a sum field.

RPG Subtraction (SUB Operation)

The algebraic rules for subtraction are explained in Figure 5-5. RPG/400 performs the subtraction function by the **SUB** operation. Unlike the **ADD** operation, it is important which field or numeric literal is specified in *Factors 1* and *2*. The syntax and rules for the **SUB** operation are detailed in Figure 5-6.

	Example 1	Example 2	Example 3	Example 4
Minuend	+7 = +7	+7 = +7	−7 = −7	−7 = −7
Subtrahend	+5 = −5	−5 = +5	−5 = +5	+5 = −5
Difference	+2	+12	−2	−12

General Algebraic Subtraction Rule:

Before subtraction, sign of the subtrahend is changed. Minuend and subtrahend are then added to compute the difference. Finally, the addition sequence follows the algebraic rules for addition explained in Figure 5-2.

Figure 5-5 Algebraic rules for subtraction.

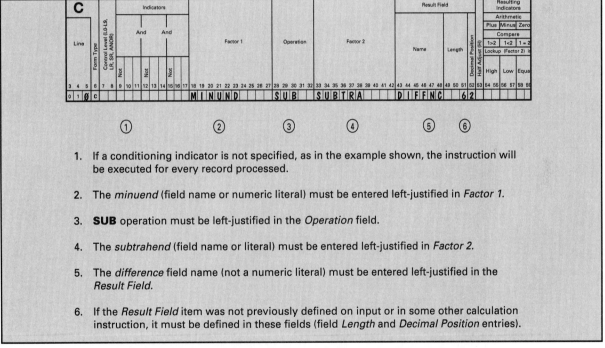

1. If a conditioning indicator is not specified, as in the example shown, the instruction will be executed for every record processed.

2. The *minuend* (field name or numeric literal) must be entered left-justified in *Factor 1*.

3. **SUB** operation must be left-justified in the *Operation* field.

4. The *subtrahend* (field name or literal) must be entered left-justified in *Factor 2*.

5. The *difference* field name (not a numeric literal) must be entered left-justified in the *Result Field*.

6. If the *Result Field* item was not previously defined on input or in some other calculation instruction, it must be defined in these fields (field *Length* and *Decimal Position* entries).

Figure 5-6 RPG/400 syntax for **SUB** (subtraction) instructions.

Four **SUB** instructions are illustrated in Figure 5-7. Observe that the field values *before* and *after* a statement is executed are included for every example.

After you examine Figure 5-7, you should understand the following processing features for the **SUB** operation:

1. The field or literal used as the minuend (top number) must be specified in *Factor 1*.

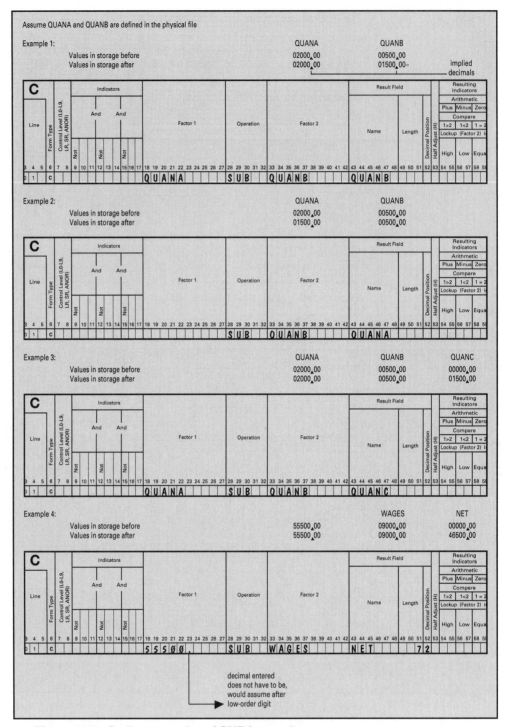

Figure 5-7 Coding examples of **SUB** instructions.

2. A *Factor 1* or *2* field may be used as the *Result Field*. However, to reduce processing time, it is more efficient to specify the *Factor 1* field entry as the *Result Field*.

3. If a *Factor 1* or *2* field is specified as the *Result Field*, the original value of that item is replaced with the value of the difference.

4. Numeric literals may be specified (left-justified) in either *Factor 1* or *2*. A decimal point is required for decimal literals and is optional for integers.

5. Numeric literals may not be specified in the *Result Field*.

The *Result Field* size (difference) should usually be defined as same size as the largest of the *Factor 1* or *2* entries. High-order or low-order truncation, depending on the related decimal locations, may occur if the difference field is not large enough to store the value of the answer.

RPG/400 Multiplication (MULT Operation)

The algebraic rules for multiplication are explained in Figure 5-8. RPG/400 performs the multiplication function by the **MULT** operation. The syntax and rules for this operation are presented in Figure 5-9.

	Rule 1	*Rule 1*	*Rule 2*	*Rule 2*
Multiplicand	+3	–3	+3	–3
Multiplier	+8	–8	–8	+8
Product	+24	+24	–24	–24

Explanation of Rules:

Rule 1: Multiplication of numbers with like signs results in a product with a positive value.

Rule 2: Multiplication of numbers with unlike signs results in a product with a negative value.

Figure 5-8 Algebraic rules for multiplication.

RPG CALCULATION SPECIFICATION

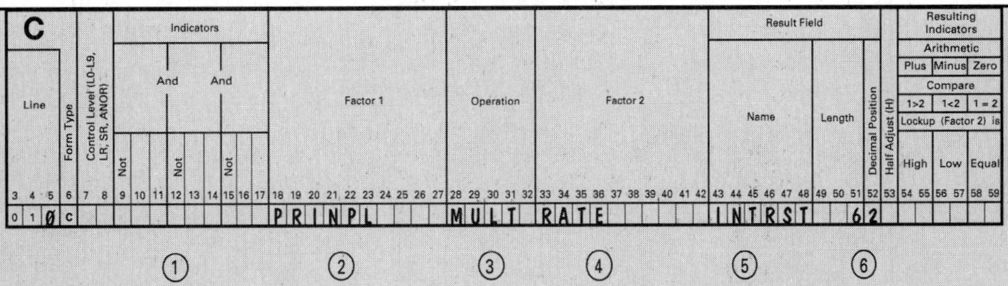

1 - If *conditioning indicators* are not specified, as in the example shown, the instruction will be executed for every record processed.

2 - Either the multiplicand or multiplier may be specified (left-justified) in *Factor 1*. For program efficiency, however, the smaller field (or numeric literal) *should be entered in Factor 1.* If the *Result Field* entry is the same as the *Factor 1* field, the *Factor 1* entry may be eliminated.

3 - The MULT operation name must be left-justified in the *Operation* field.

4 - Either the multiplicand or multiplier field name (or numeric literal) may be specified (left-justified) in *Factor 2.*

5 - A field name for the product (may be a *Factor 1* or *2* field name) must be entered left-justified in the *Result Field.*

6 - If the *Result Field* item was not previously defined on input or in some other calculations instruction, it must be defined by entries in the *Length* and *Decimal Position* fields.

Figure 5-9 RPG/400 syntax for **MULT** (multiplication) instructions.

Coding examples of the **MULT** operation that show before and after values of the *Factor 1*, *Factor 2*, and *Result Field* items are illustrated in Figure 5-10, a study of which shows the following RPG/400 multiplication features:

1. Either *Factor 1* or *Factor 2* may be used for the multiplier or multiplicand. For program efficiency, however, the smaller field or literal should be specified in *Factor 1*.

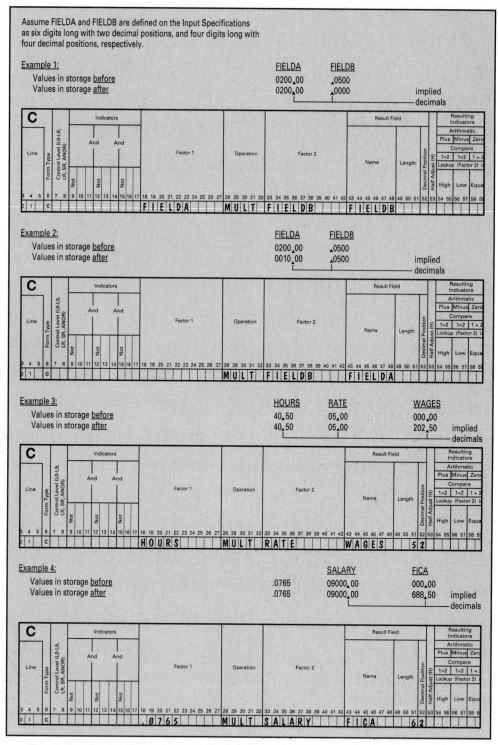

Assume FIELDA and FIELDB are defined on the Input Specifications as six digits long with two decimal positions, and four digits long with four decimal positions, respectively.

Example 1:

	FIELDA	FIELDB
Values in storage before	0200.00	.0500
Values in storage after	0200.00	.0000 — implied decimals

C specification: `FIELDA MULT FIELDB FIELDB`

Example 2:

	FIELDA	FIELDB
Values in storage before	0200.00	.0500
Values in storage after	0010.00	.0500 — implied decimals

C specification: `MULT FIELDB FIELDA`

Example 3:

	HOURS	RATE	WAGES
Values in storage before	40.50	05.00	000.00
Values in storage after	40.50	05.00	202.50 — implied decimals

C specification: `HOURS MULT RATE WAGES 52`

Example 4:

		SALARY	FICA
Values in storage before	.0765	09000.00	000.00
Values in storage after	.0765	09000.00	688.50 — implied decimals

C specification: `.0765 MULT SALARY FICA 62`

Figure 5-10 Coding examples of **MULT** instructions.

2. The *Factor 1* or *Factor 2* field may be used as the *Result Field*. For program efficiency, the *Result Field* should be the same as *Factor 1*.

3. When a *Factor 1* or *2* field is specified as the *Result Field*, the original value of that item is replaced with decimal literals and is optional for integers.

4. Numeric literals may not be specified as a *Result Field*.

For multiplication instructions, the optimum *Result Field* size (product) may be determined by the procedure illustrated in Figure 5-11.

Rule for Field Length Determination:

The maximum field length for the product of multiplication is the sum of the number of digits in the multiplicand and multiplier fields and/or numeric literal.

Rule for Decimal Position Determination:

The number of decimal positions for the product of the multiplication is the sum of the number of decimal positions in the multiplicand and multiplier fields and/or numeric literal.

Computation Routine:

Assume that FLD1, which is 8 digits in length with 2 implied decimals, is multiplied by FLD2 defined as 5 digits long with 5 decimal positions. The maximum size of the product may be determined by the following routine:

Positions	Field or Literal Size	Decimal
FLD1	8	2
FLD2	+5	+5
Maximum product size	13	7

If rounding to zero decimal positions was specified, the product size is computed as follows:

Positions	Field Size	Decimal
Maximum product size	13	7
Less 5	−7	−7
Rounded product size	6	0

Note: 7 must be subtracted from the field size and decimal position values.

Examples: (Assume value shown is related field size)

Size	FLD1	x	FLD2	=	Maximum Product
Values	200▲	x	50▲	=	10000▲
Values	200000▲	x	50		1000000
Values	20000▲	x	50▲	=	1000000▲
Values	20000▲	x	50▲	=	1000000▲

▲ Indicates implied decimal

Figure 5-11 Procedures for the determination of optimum product size for multiplication.

RPG/400 Division (DIV Operation)

The algebraic rules associated with division are explained in Figure 5-12. Division is performed in RPG/400 by the **DIV** operation. The syntax of this operation is explained in

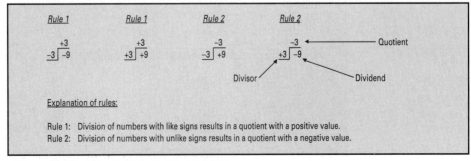

Explanation of rules:

Rule 1: Division of numbers with like signs results in a quotient with a positive value.
Rule 2: Division of numbers with unlike signs results in a quotient with a negative value.

Figure 5-12 Algebraic rules for division.

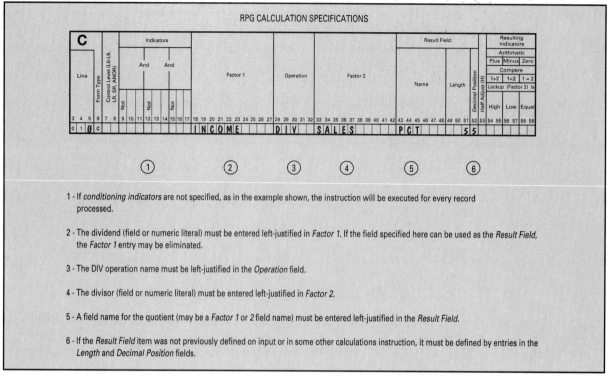

Figure 5-13   RPG/400 syntax for the **DIV** (division) operation.

Figure 5-13. Examples of this operation are shown in Figure 5-14. The following observations should be made from the coding examples in Figure 5-14.

1. A *Factor 1* or *Factor 2* field may be specified for the *Result Field*. However, because the divisor is often smaller than the dividend, its size may not be large enough to store the quotient (answer).
2. When more decimal positions are required than included in either *Factor 1* or *2*, a separate field should be specified for the *Result Field*.
3. Numeric literals may be specified in either *Factor 1* or *2*.

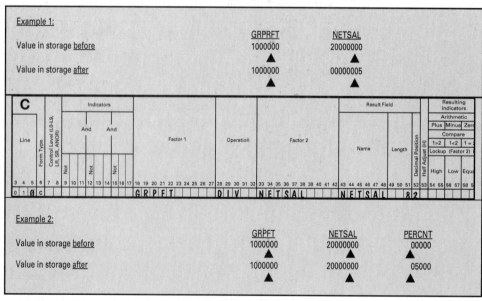

Figure 5-14   Coding examples of the **DIV** operation.

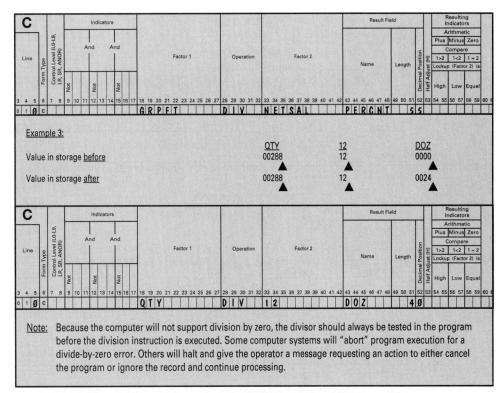

Example 3:

	QTY	12	DOZ
Value in storage before	00288	12	0000
Value in storage after	00288	12	0024

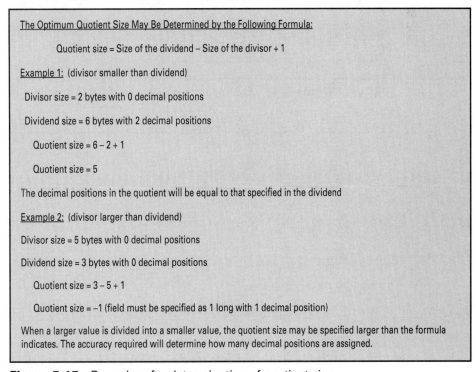

Note: Because the computer will not support division by zero, the divisor should always be tested in the program before the division instruction is executed. Some computer systems will "abort" program execution for a divide-by-zero error. Others will halt and give the operator a message requesting an action to either cancel the program or ignore the record and continue processing.

Figure 5-14   Coding examples of the **DIV** operation. (Continued)

The optimum size of the quotient (answer) for a **DIV** instruction may be determined by the procedure explained in Figure 5-15. It is important to remember that computers will not support division by zero (the divisor cannot have a zero value). Some systems will immediately terminate program execution; others will halt and give the operator some control option.

The Optimum Quotient Size May Be Determined by the Following Formula:

Quotient size = Size of the dividend – Size of the divisor + 1

Example 1: (divisor smaller than dividend)

Divisor size = 2 bytes with 0 decimal positions

Dividend size = 6 bytes with 2 decimal positions

Quotient size = 6 – 2 + 1

Quotient size = 5

The decimal positions in the quotient will be equal to that specified in the dividend

Example 2: (divisor larger than dividend)

Divisor size = 5 bytes with 0 decimal positions

Dividend size = 3 bytes with 0 decimal positions

Quotient size = 3 – 5 + 1

Quotient size = –1 (field must be specified as 1 long with 1 decimal position)

When a larger value is divided into a smaller value, the quotient size may be specified larger than the formula indicates. The accuracy required will determine how many decimal positions are assigned.

Figure 5-15   Procedure for determination of quotient size.

Move Remainder Operation (MVR)

Sometimes it may be necessary to store the remainder of a division instruction for subsequent processing. This function is performed in RPG/400 by the **MVR** operation, which is detailed in Figure 5-16. The size and decimal positions for a remainder field may be determined by the process illustrated in Figure 5-17.

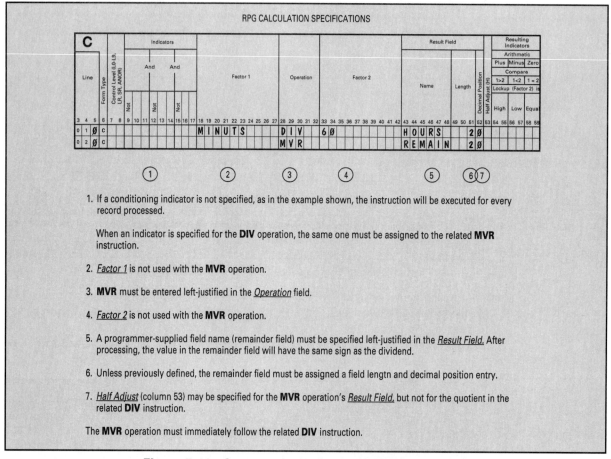

1. If a conditioning indicator is not specified, as in the example shown, the instruction will be executed for every record processed.

   When an indicator is specified for the **DIV** operation, the same one must be assigned to the related **MVR** instruction.

2. *Factor 1* is not used with the **MVR** operation.

3. **MVR** must be entered left-justified in the *Operation* field.

4. *Factor 2* is not used with the **MVR** operation.

5. A programmer-supplied field name (remainder field) must be specified left-justified in the *Result Field.* After processing, the value in the remainder field will have the same sign as the dividend.

6. Unless previously defined, the remainder field must be assigned a field lengtn and decimal position entry.

7. *Half Adjust* (column 53) may be specified for the **MVR** operation's *Result Field,* but not for the quotient in the related **DIV** instruction.

The **MVR** operation must immediately follow the related **DIV** instruction.

Figure 5-16   Syntax and rules for the **MVR** (Move Remainder) operation.

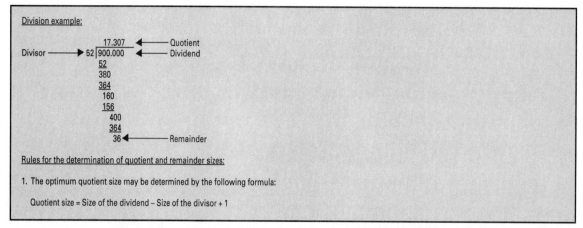

Figure 5-17   Process for determining the size and decimal positions for a remainder field.

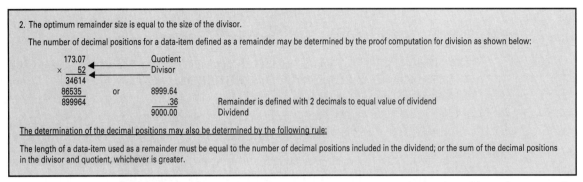

Figure 5-17 Process for determining the size and decimal positions for a remainder field. (Continued)

Half Adjust (Rounding)

The RPG/400 term *half adjust* refers to the mathematical procedure of rounding an answer to a final size. Half adjust may be used with any arithmetic operation and is specified for the instruction by entering the letter **H** in column 53. This function, which is explained in Figure 5-18, is automatically performed by the RPG/400 compiler when it is specified in a statement.

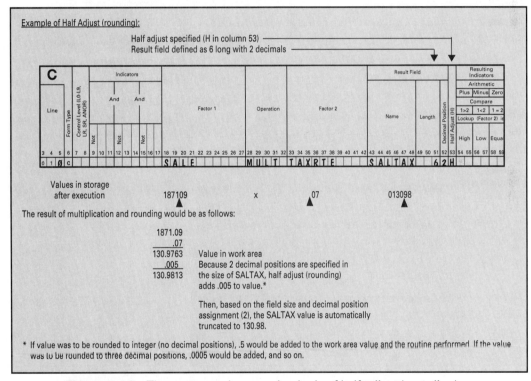

Figure 5-18 The syntax and processing logic of half adjust (rounding).

INITIALIZATION OF NUMERIC FIELDS

A numeric field may be initialized to zeros in an RPG/400 program by the following methods:

1. Subtract the field from itself. Hence, *Factor 1*, *Factor 2*, and the *Result Field* will include the same field name.

2. Multiply the *Factor 1* or *2* field by zero and specify the same field name in the *Result Field*.

3. By the **Z-ADD** or **Z-SUB** operation.
4. By a **MOVE** or **MOVEL** operation.

Because methods 1 and 2 are obvious mathematical procedures, they are not discussed. The **Z-ADD, Z-SUB, MOVE**, and **MOVEL** operations are discussed in the following paragraphs.

The Z-ADD Operation

The **Z-ADD** operation is commonly used in RPG/400 programs to initialize a *Result Field* to zeros or some other value. Figure 5-19 explains the syntax and function of this operation.

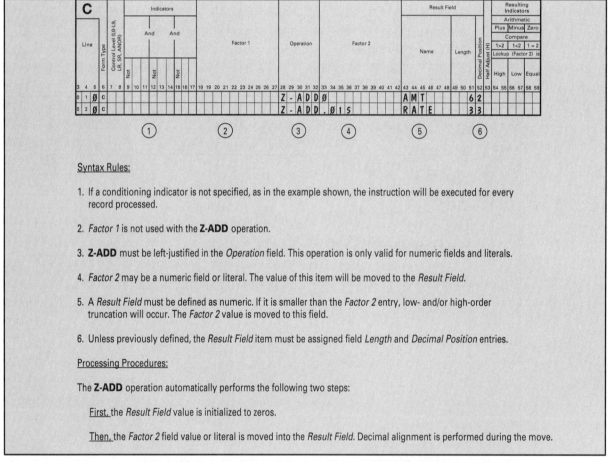

Syntax Rules:

1. If a conditioning indicator is not specified, as in the example shown, the instruction will be executed for every record processed.

2. *Factor 1* is not used with the **Z-ADD** operation.

3. **Z-ADD** must be left-justified in the *Operation* field. This operation is only valid for numeric fields and literals.

4. *Factor 2* may be a numeric field or literal. The value of this item will be moved to the *Result Field*.

5. A *Result Field* must be defined as numeric. If it is smaller than the *Factor 2* entry, low- and/or high-order truncation will occur. The *Factor 2* value is moved to this field.

6. Unless previously defined, the *Result Field* item must be assigned field *Length* and *Decimal Position* entries.

Processing Procedures:

The **Z-ADD** operation automatically performs the following two steps:

First, the *Result Field* value is initialized to zeros.

Then, the *Factor 2* field value or literal is moved into the *Result Field*. Decimal alignment is performed during the move.

Figure 5-19 Syntax and function of the **Z-ADD** operation.

The Z-SUB Operation

The **Z-SUB** operation performs the same processing functions as **Z-ADD** with one exception. The value of the *Factor 2* field or numeric literal value is automatically multiplied by −1 and the product is stored in the result field with a reversed sign. Figure 5-20 explains the syntax and processing logic of this operation.

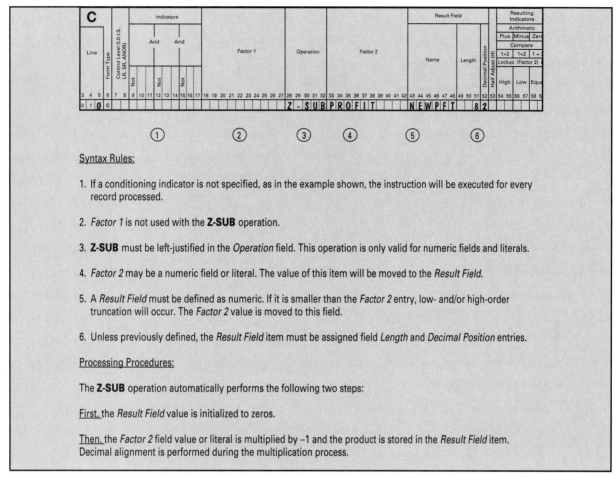

Figure 5-20 Syntax and function of the **Z-SUB** operation.

The MOVE and MOVEL Operations

As was stated previously, the **Z-ADD** and **Z-SUB** operations are limited to numeric fields and literals. The **MOVE** and **MOVEL** operations, however, may also be used with alphanumeric fields and literals. The syntax and processing logic of these operations are explained in Figure 5-21.

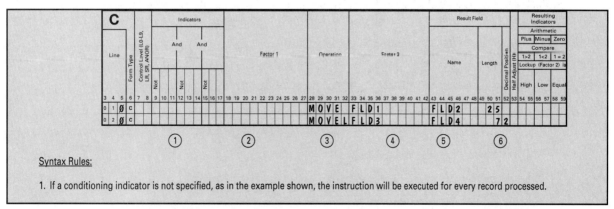

Figure 5-21 Syntax and processing logic of the **MOVE** and **MOVEL** operations.

2. *Factor 1* is not used with the **MOVE** or **MOVEL** operations.

3. **MOVE** or **MOVEL** must be left-justified in the *Operation* field. Either operation may be specified with numeric or alphanumeric fields.

4. *Factor 2* may be a numeric or alphanumeric field or literal.

   (Refer to **MOVE** and **MOVEL** data movement features in item 5)

5. *Result Field* may be defined as a numeric or alphanumeric field.

   For the **MOVE** Operation:

   Movement starts with the low-order bytes of the *Factor 2* field or literal and are moved into the low-order positions of the *Result Field*. **MOVE** stops when all of the bytes from the *Factor 2* item have been moved or when the *Result Field* is full.

   If the *Result Field* is larger than the sending field (*Factor 2*), the excess high-order characters in the *Result Field* are unchanged. On the other hand, if the *Result Field* is smaller, the excess high-order characters from the *Factor 2* item are truncated.

   For the **MOVEL** Operation:

   Movement starts with the high-order bytes of the *Factor 2* field or literal and are moved into the high-order positions of the *Result Field*. **MOVEL** stops when all of the bytes from the *Factor 2* item have been moved or when the *Result Field* is full.

   If the *Result Field* is larger than the sending field (*Factor 2*), the excess low-order characters in the *Result Field* are unchanged. On the other hand, if the *Result Field* is smaller, the excess low-order characters from the *Factor 2* item are truncated.

6. Unless previously defined, the *Result Field* item must be assigned a field length, and if numeric, a decimal position entry.

Notes:

1. Decimal alignment is not performed for **MOVE** or **MOVEL** operations.
2. Numeric field or literals may be moved (**MOVE** or **MOVEL**) to alphanumeric fields, or literals may be moved to numeric fields. However, when an alphanumeric field or literal is moved to a numeric field, only the digit portion of each alphanumeric character is moved. This may cause subsequent execution time errors.

Figure 5-21 Syntax and processing logic of the **MOVE** and **MOVEL** operations. (Continued)

Coding examples and the before and after processing results for the **MOVE** operation are illustrated in Figure 5-22.

Figure 5-23 illustrates coding examples of the **MOVEL** operation supported by the before and after results of processing.

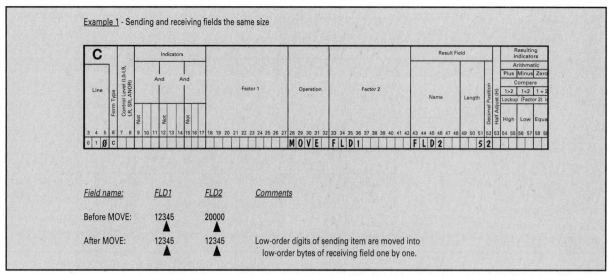

Figure 5-22 Examples of the **MOVE** operation with before and after processing results.

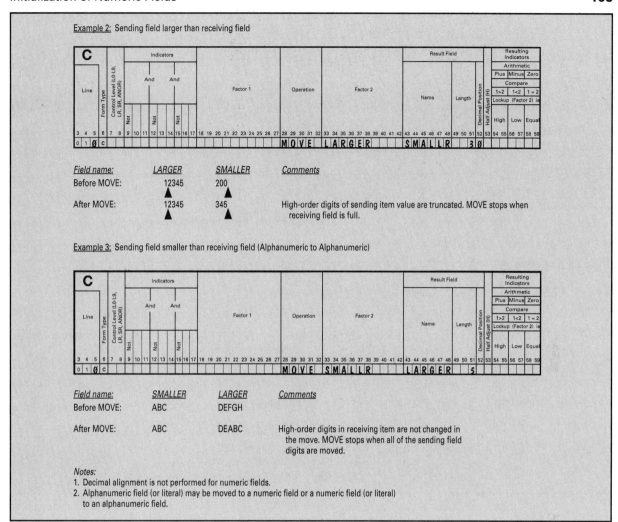

Example 2: Sending field larger than receiving field

Field name:	LARGER	SMALLER	Comments
Before MOVE:	12345	200	
After MOVE:	12345	345	High-order digits of sending item value are truncated. MOVE stops when receiving field is full.

Example 3: Sending field smaller than receiving field (Alphanumeric to Alphanumeric)

Field name:	SMALLER	LARGER	Comments
Before MOVE:	ABC	DEFGH	
After MOVE:	ABC	DEABC	High-order digits in receiving item are not changed in the move. MOVE stops when all of the sending field digits are moved.

Notes:
1. Decimal alignment is not performed for numeric fields.
2. Alphanumeric field (or literal) may be moved to a numeric field or a numeric field (or literal) to an alphanumeric field.

Figure 5-22 Examples of the **MOVE** operation with before and after processing results. (Continued)

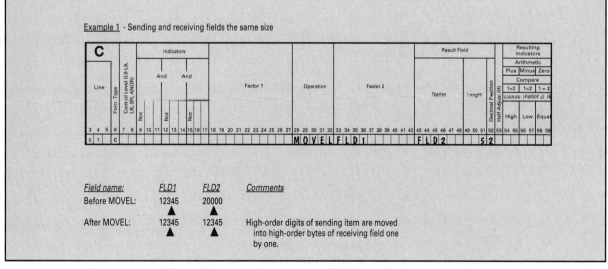

Example 1 - Sending and receiving fields the same size

Field name:	FLD1	FLD2	Comments
Before MOVEL:	12345	20000	
After MOVEL:	12345	12345	High-order digits of sending item are moved into high-order bytes of receiving field one by one.

Figure 5-23 Examples of the **MOVEL** operation with before and after processing results.

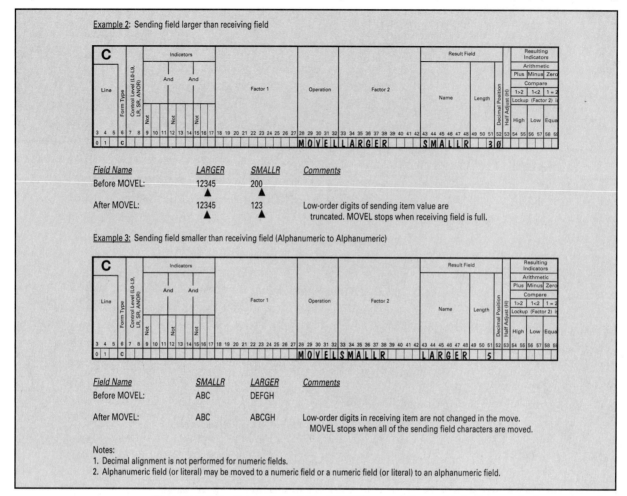

Figure 5-23   Examples of the **MOVEL** operation with before and after processing results. (Continued)

Figurative Constants

Figurative Constants, which include ***BLANK/*BLANKS, *ZERO/*ZEROS, *HIVAL, *LOVAL, *ALL'X . . . .' , *IN, and *OFF,** are *implied literals* that are assigned a predetermined value. They are referenced without regard to length and assume the size of the field to which they relate. An explanation of each Figurative Constant is presented in Figure 5-24.

*BLANK/BLANKS	Indicates the constant contains all blanks (spaces). May only be used with alphanumeric fields.
*ZERO/*ZEROS	Indicates the constant contains all zeros. May be used with any field type.
*HIVAL	Indicates the constant contains the highest character in the collating character set of the computer. If the field in the relational test (or result field) is numeric, *HIVAL defaults to 9s. However, if it is alphanumeric, the constant defaults to hexadecimal FFs.
*LOVAL	Indicates the constant contains the lowest character in the collating character set of the computer. If the field in the relational test (or result field is numeric, *LOVAL is assumed to be negative 9s. However, if it is alphanumeric, the constant defaults to hexadecimal zeros.

Figure 5-24   The processing features of Figurative Constants.

*ALL'X...'	The character string X... etc. is repeated to a length equal to the Factor 1 or Factor 2 field in a relational test or to the Result Field in a mathematical or MOVE, MOVEL, or MOVEA operation. If the relational test or result field item is numeric, all characters in the X string must be numeric. No sign or decimal point may be used in a numeric string.
*ON	Indicates the constant contains all 1s.
*OFF	Indicates the constant contains all 0s.

Figure 5-24 The processing features of Figurative Constants. (Continued)

Examples of how Figurative Constants are used with the **MOVE** instruction are shown in Figure 5-25. Except for ***BLANK/*BLANKS,** each may be specified with a **Z-ADD, Z-SUB,** or any arithmetic operation. Any *Figurative Constant* may be included in a **MOVE** or **MOVEL** instruction.

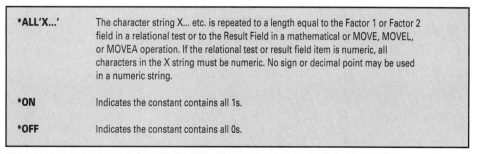

Explanation of Related Instructions:

1. Blanks (spaces) are moved into the 25-byte NAME field.

2. Zeros are moved into the TOTAL field.

3. The string value of . is moved into the DOTS field until it is filled. For this example, 10 periods will be moved into DOTS, resulting in a field value of .... (10 periods). Note that the X included in the syntax (Figure 5-24) is not specified in the figurative constant instruction.

4. If the receiving field is numeric, *HIVAL value is 9s. If alphanumeric, value is hexadecimal FFs. For this example, 9s are moved into the receiving field.

5. If the receiving field is numeric, *LOVAL is assumed to be negative 9s. If alphanumeric, the value is hexadecimal zeros. For this example, negative 9s are moved into the receiving field.

Figure 5-25 Examples of instructions with Figurative Constants.

Resulting Indicators

Refer to the *Calculation Specifications* shown in Figure 5-26, and locate the area (columns 54–59) entitled *Resulting Indicators.* Notice that it includes three headings: *Arithmetic, Compare,* and *Lookup.* This chapter discusses only the *Arithmetic* class of *Resulting Indicators,* reserving discussion of the *Compare* group for Chapter 6 and *Lookup* for Chapters 10 and 11.

Within the *Arithmetic* group of *Resulting Indicators* are three test fields: *Plus, Minus,* and *Zero.* The value of the *Result Field* item from any arithmetic function, **Z-ADD, Z-SUB, MOVE,** OR **MOVEL,** may be tested for one, two, or three of the conditions.

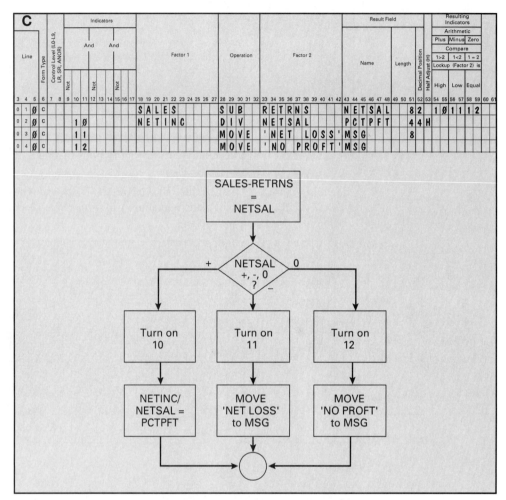

Figure 5-26 Processing logic of the *Arithmetic* class of *Resulting Indicators*.

The flowchart at the bottom of Figure 5-26 explains the processing logic for the *Arithmetic Resulting Indicators* included in the example instruction. Observe that the indicator "turned on" is used to condition a subsequent instruction. In this example, only calculations are conditioned by the related *Resulting Indicator*. Output record formats, fields, and/or constants, however, may also be conditioned by this indicator class. In the example shown in Figure 5-26, the indicators are specified in an ascending 10, 11, 12 order. This is not a requirement; any indicators may be assigned and in any order. However, to avoid uncertain processing results, a *Record Identifying Indicator* should not be specified as a *Resulting Indicator*.

SETON and SETOF Operations

The **SETON** operation is used to turn on the indicator(s) included in the *Resulting Indicators* fields. The indicator(s) is then used to condition one or more calculation and/or output instructions.

The **SETOF** operation is used to turn off the indicators included in the *Resulting Indicators* fields. This operation is often used as a housekeeping function to turn off all *Resulting Indicators* before the next record is processed. Because Record Identifying Indicators turn off automatically after the last output instruction for that processing cycle is tested and executed, they are seldom specified with a **SETOF** operation. Figure 5-27 explains the syntax and features of these operations.

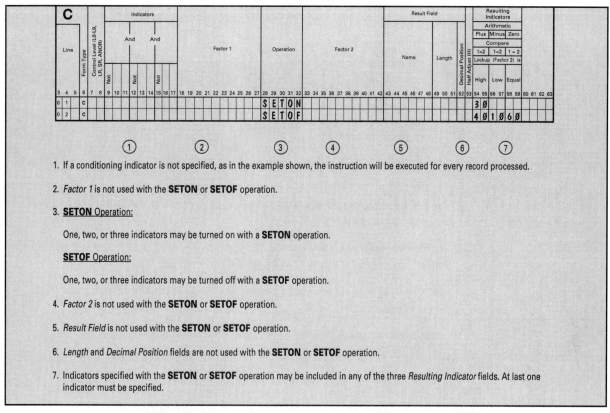

Figure 5-27 Syntax and features of the **SETON** and **SETOF** operations.

RPG/400 Reserved Words *IN and *INxx

RPG/400 indicators may be turned on, turned off, moved, and tested by the reserved words *IN and *INxx. An explanation of their features is included in the following paragraphs.

*IN references a predefined 99 one-position element <u>array</u> defining the indicators **01** through **99**. The format *IN references all 99 elements in the array. One element may be referenced by the format *IN,xx (xx for any one indicator, **01** through **99**).

*INxx is a one-position character <u>field</u> where **xx** represents any RPG/400 indicator except **1P** or **MR.**

Moving (with the **MOVEA** operation discussed in Chapter 11) a <u>character</u> 0 (zero) to *IN will set indicators **01–99** off, whereas moving (with a **MOVE** or **MOVEL** operation) a 0 (zero) to *IN,xx or *INxx will set only the specified indicator off. Conversely, moving the character 1 will set the indicator(s) on. Note that *character* is specified for the 0 and 1 values, *not* number. Hence, the 0 or 1 value must be enclosed in single quotes in the calculation instruction.

In lieu of using '**0**', the binary representation for *"off,"* the *Figurative Constant* *OFF may be used. Conversely, instead of using the binary representation '**1**' for "on," the *Figurative Constant* *ON may be specified.

*IN, IN,xx, or *INxx <u>cannot</u> be used as a subfield in a *data structure,* a *result field* of a **PARM** operation, or in a **SORTA** operation. Each of these topics is discussed in subsequent chapters. Examples of *IN, *IN,xx, and *INxx are shown in Figure 5-28.

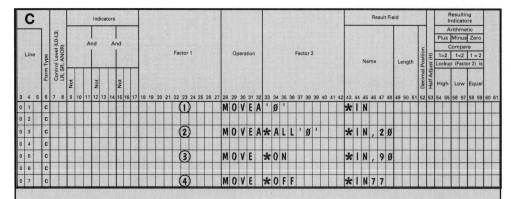

Figure 5-28   Examples of the reserved words **IN, IN,xx,** and ***INxx.**

Recap to Date

The syntax and processing logic of the RPG/400 operations **ADD, SUB, MULT, DIV, MVR, Z-ADD, Z-SUB, MOVE, MOVEL, SETON,** and **SETOF** have been introduced in this chapter. *Figurative Constants* and *Resulting Indicators (Arithmetic)* were also explained. Two reserved words, ***IN** and ***INxx,** were discussed. Most of these RPG/400 features are used in the application programs included in this and subsequent chapters.

APPLICATION PROGRAM: PROFIT ANALYSIS OF SOUP BRANDS

Documentation

The specifications included in Figure 5-29 summarize the processing requirements for this example application program.

The system flowchart in Figure 5-30 indicates that one input disk file and one output printer file are processed by the program.

PROGRAM SPECIFICATIONS   PAGE 1 of 1

Program Name: _Profit Report_   Program-ID: _SOUPS_   Written by: _SM_

Purpose: _Determine profit per case for soups brands_   Approved by: _CM_

Input files: _SOUPMSTR_

Output files: _QSYSPRT_

Processing Requirements:

Write an RPG/400 program to generate a profit report for soup brands.

Input to the program:

The externally defined physical file, SOUPMSTR, contains the selling price and cost per case information for soup brands. The physical file's record format is shown in the supplemental record layout form.

Processing:

Read the physical file in arrival sequence and perform the following for each record processed:

  Detail Calculations:

    Profit per case computation (in $):

      Profit/case = Selling price/case − Cost/case

    Percent of profit per case computation:

    Step 1: Decimal profit = $\dfrac{\text{Profit/Case}}{\text{Cost/case}}$

    Step 2: Percent profit = Decimal profit × 100

    Step 3: Add the Percent profit (step 2) to an accumulator

    Add the number of records processed to an accumulator.

Total time calculations:

Compute the average profit of all soup brands with the following formula:

  Average profit percent = $\dfrac{\text{Total profit percent (Step 3)}}{\text{Record count}}$

Output:

The report design is detailed in a supplemental printer spacing chart.

Figure 5-29   Specifications for profit analysis of soup brands application program.

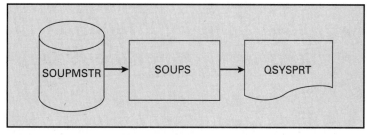

Figure 5-30   System flowchart for soup brand profit report application.

```
            PHYSICAL FILE DESCRIPTION

  SYSTEM: AS/400                    DATE: 11/30/95
  FILE NAME: SOUPMSTR               REV NO: 0
  RECORD NAME: SOUPR                KEY LENGTH: None
  SEQUENCE: Non-keyed               RECORD SIZE: 26

                FIELD DEFINITIONS

  FIELD    FIELD NAME   SIZE   TYPE    POSITION      COMMENTS
   NO                                 FROM    TO

    1      BRAND         20     C       1      20
    2      SPRICE         4     P      21      23   2 decimals
    3      COST           4     P      24      26   2 decimals
```

```
  Physical File Data:
                                       Selling
                    Brand Name          Price      Cost

             CAMPBELL TOMATO SOUP       0648       0504
             LIPTON CHICKEN             1440       1188
             HEINZ VEGETABLE            0792       0576
             PROGRESSO MINESTRONE       1728       1224
             PEPPERIDGE CHOWDER         1404       1116
             STOP & SHOP TOMATO         1476       1044
             A & P CHICKEN RICE         0720       0792
```

Figure 5-31 Input record layout form for soup brand profit report application.

Included with the record layout form in Figure 5-31 is a listing of the physical file. The design of the report is illustrated in the printer spacing chart in Figure 5-32. The report generated from the application program is shown in Figure 5-33.

Source Coding for Soup Brands Profit Report Program

A commented compile listing of the program that generates a soup brands profit report is detailed in Figure 5-34. In addition to the use of the arithmetic functions **ADD, SUB, MULT,** and **DIV,** the following new processing features are introduced:

1. *Detail time* calculations
2. *Total time* (**LR** indicator) calculations
3. *Total time* (**T** in column 15 for output record) output

Figure 5-32 Printer spacing chart for soup brands profit report.

```
11/30/95    CASE LOT PROFIT ANALYSIS OF SOUP BRANDS    PAGE    1


        BRANDS                SP/CASE    COST    PROFIT    % PROFIT

    CAMPBELL TOMATO            6.48      5.04     1.44     28.571 %

    LIPTON CHICKEN           14.40     11.88     2.52     21.212 %

    HEINZ VEGETABLE           7.92      5.76     2.16     37.500 %

    PROGRESSO MINESTRONE     17.28     12.24     5.04     41.176 %

    PEPPERIDGE CHOWDER       14.04     11.16     2.88     25.806 %

    STOP & SHOP TOMATO       14.76     10.44     4.32     41.379 %

    A & P CHICKEN RICE        7.20      7.92      .72-     9.090-%


    AVERAGE PROFIT PERCENT = 26.651 %
```

Figure 5-33 Soup brands profit report listing.

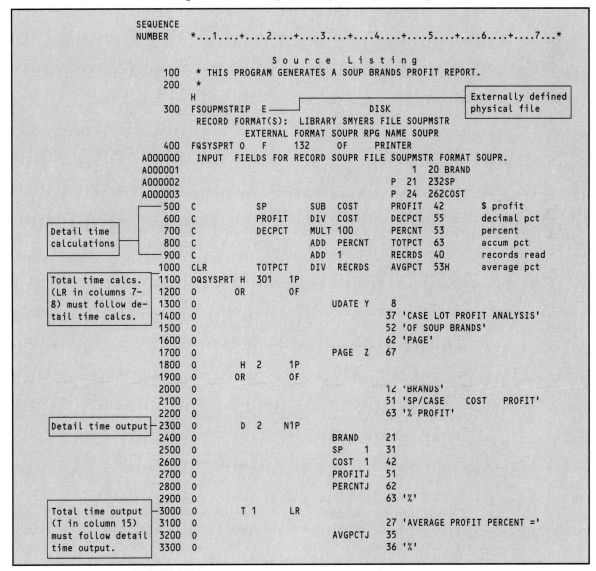

Figure 5-34 Source listing of the soup brands profit report program.

An examination of the compile listing shows that *File Description, Input,* and *Output Specifications* coding are similar to the RPG/400 syntax discussed in the previous chapters. The calculations, which are a new topic, are explained in the following paragraphs.

Calculation Specifications Coding

The Calculation Specifications included in the soup brand profit report program are shown in Figure 5-35. Notice that calculations are performed at *detail* and *total times. Detail time* calculations must be specified first and must include those statements either conditioned by an indicator(s) in columns 9 to 17 or not conditioned by any indicator. *Total time* calculations are those conditioned by an **LR** (*Last Record*) or *Control Level Indicator* (discussed in Chapter 8) entered in columns 7 to 8. Any *total time* instructions must follow *detail time,* or a terminal error is generated during compilation processing.

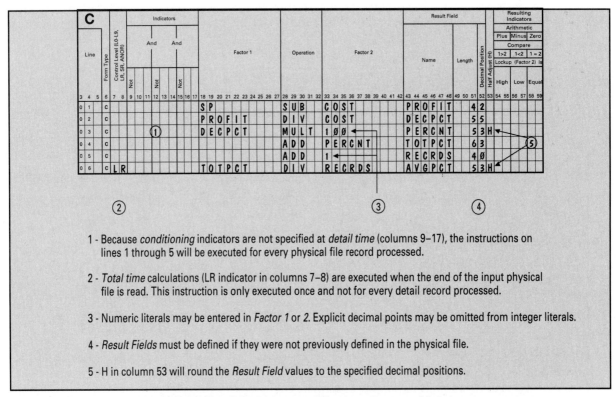

1 - Because *conditioning* indicators are not specified at *detail time* (columns 9–17), the instructions on lines 1 through 5 will be executed for every physical file record processed.

2 - *Total time* calculations (LR indicator in columns 7–8) are executed when the end of the input physical file is read. This instruction is only executed once and not for every detail record processed.

3 - Numeric literals may be entered in *Factor 1* or *2.* Explicit decimal points may be omitted from integer literals.

4 - *Result Fields* must be defined if they were not previously defined in the physical file.

5 - H in column 53 will round the *Result Field* values to the specified decimal positions.

Figure 5-35   Calculation specifications for soup brand report program.

A line-by-line analysis of the results of each calculation instruction for the first data record processed is detailed in Figure 5-36. Observe that the statement conditioned with the **LR** (*Last Record*) indicator is not executed at *detail time.* Instructions conditioned by an **LR** *indicator* are executed only after the end of the input file is sensed.

Last Record (Total Time) Calculations

When the end of an input data file is sensed, RPG/400 automatically turns on the **LR** (*Last Record*) *Indicator,* which is used to condition *Calculation* and *Output Specifications.* The indicator may be specified only with *total time* calculations (**LR** entered in columns 7–8). If **LR** is incorrectly entered in columns 9 to 17 (*detail time* calculations), and error will *not* be generated in program compilation or execution. The instruction will be ignored, however. Figure 5-37 shows the syntax and processing results of *total time* calculations conditioned with an **LR** *indicator.*

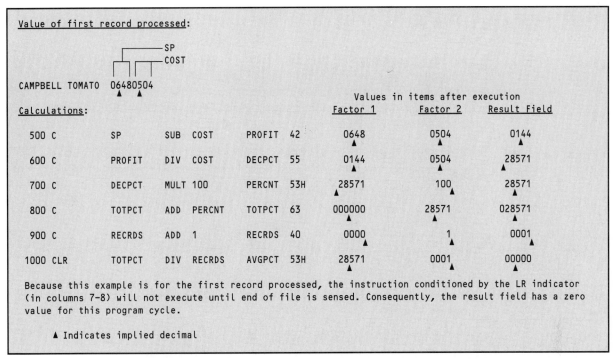

Figure 5-36 Line-by-line analysis of calculation instruction for first input record processed.

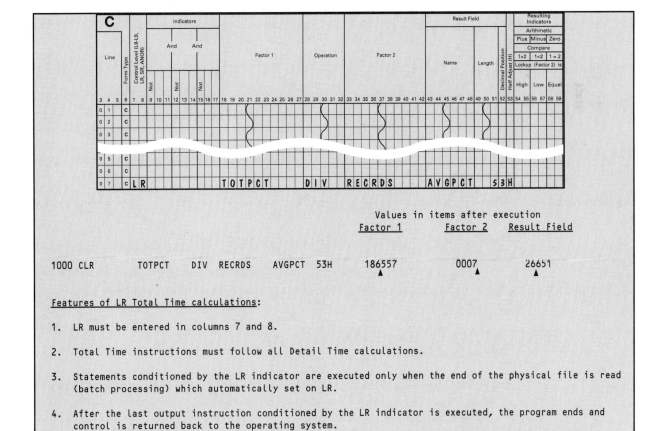

Figure 5-37 *Total time* calculations included in the soup brands profit report program.

Last Record (Total Time Output)

For output control, an **LR** *indicator* may be specified only with *total lines* (letter **T** in column 15). In addition, *total lines* must follow all *heading* and *detail lines* for the related output file (often there is more than one). If an **LR** *indicator* is incorrectly included with an **H** or **D** line, it will be ignored during program execution. No errors will be generated in the compilation or execution phases. Figure 5-38 details the syntax for the *total time* output instructions included in the example program.

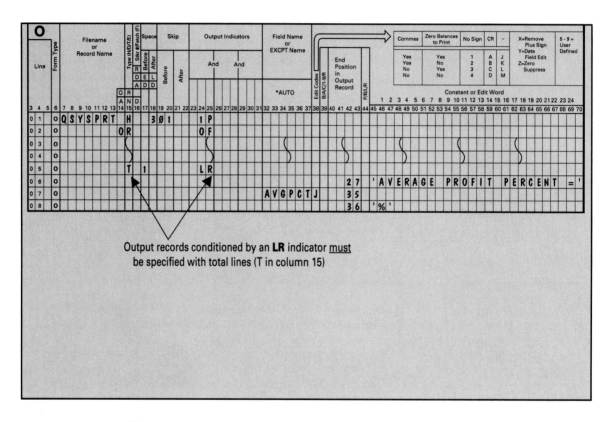

Figure 5-38 *Total time* output coding included in the soup brands profit report program.

RPG/400 Program Cycle for Last Record Time

A subset of the RPG/400 program cycle flowchart identifying the processing steps followed when the end of the file is sensed is presented and explained in Figure 5-39.

Program Summary

The soup brands profit report program introduced the use of the arithmetic functions **ADD, SUB, MULT,** and **DIV**; numeric literals; and half adjust (rounding). In addition, *total time* calculations and output were included in program control. The syntax and processing logic of these new RPG/400 items were explained in separate illustrations.

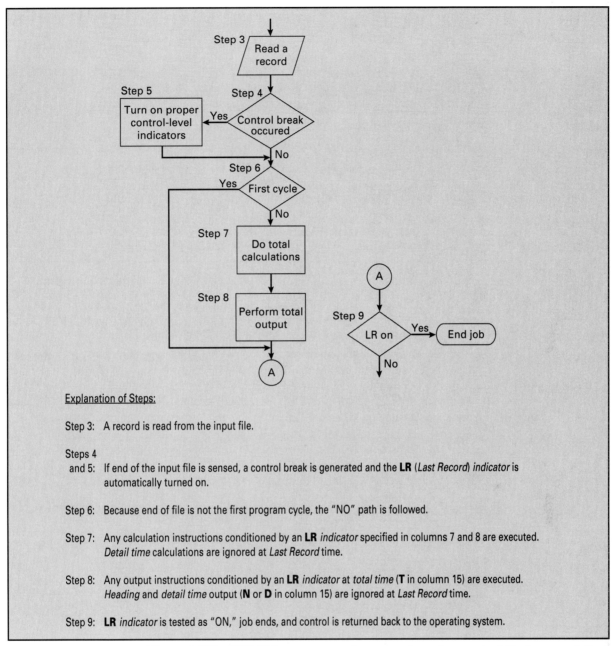

Explanation of Steps:

Step 3:   A record is read from the input file.

Steps 4
  and 5:   If end of the input file is sensed, a control break is generated and the **LR** (*Last Record*) *indicator* is
           automatically turned on.

Step 6:   Because end of file is not the first program cycle, the "NO" path is followed.

Step 7:   Any calculation instructions conditioned by an **LR** *indicator* specified in columns 7 and 8 are executed.
           Detail time calculations are ignored at *Last Record* time.

Step 8:   Any output instructions conditioned by an **LR** *indicator* at *total time* (**T** in column 15) are executed.
           Heading and *detail time* output (**N** or **D** in column 15) are ignored at *Last Record* time.

Step 9:   **LR** *indicator* is tested as "ON," job ends, and control is returned back to the operating system.

Figure 5-39   RPG/400 program cycle processing when end of file is sensed (*Last Record* time). (*Courtesy of IBM.*)

ADDITIONAL RPG/400 FEATURES

Field Indicators

Additional control of calculations and/or output is available to the programmer by the use of *Field Indicators. Field Indicators* are defined in columns 65 to 70 on the *Input Specifications.* Look at Figure 5-40 and notice that this field area is divided into three separate fields: *Plus* (columns 65–66), *Minus* (columns 67–68), and *Zero* (or *Blank*) (columns 69–70). The status of a numeric input field may be tested for *Plus, Minus,* or *Zero,* whereas an alphanumeric field may be tested only for a *blank* condition.

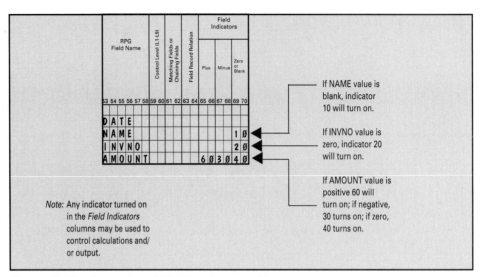

Figure 5-40   Examples of *Field Indicator* coding.

Because indicators in an RPG/400 program require memory and increase processing time, *Field Indicators* should be assigned only when some subsequent calculation or output instruction(s) requires conditioning by the related indicator(s).

Figure 5-41 illustrates the syntax required in the *Record Description* section of the *Input Specifications* to access fields from an **externally defined** physical file for *Field Indicator* testing. Only the fields that require *Field Indicator* testing have to be specified on the input form, and not every field from the related physical file. Note that the physical file's record name must be specified in the *Record Name* field (columns 7–14), and *Field Location* fields are <u>not</u> included.

At the bottom of Figure 5-41 is the *Input Specifications* syntax (*Record Description* section) to support a **program-defined** physical file. Note that the file name is specified in the *Filename* field (columns 7–14), and the *Field Locations* <u>are</u> included.

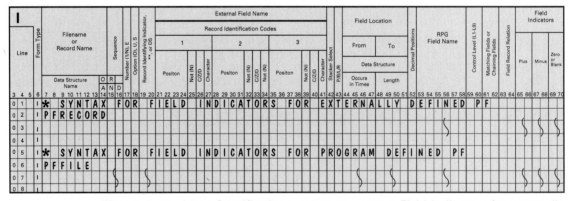

Figure 5-41   Input Specifications syntax to support Field Indicators for externally and program-defined files.

The Square Root Operation (SQRT)

The square root of a number may be computed in an RPG/400 program by the **SQRT** operation. Figure 5-42 explains the syntax associated with this function.

Example Program Using the SQRT Operation and Field Indicators

An example RPG/400 program that includes the **SQRT** operation and *Field Indicators* is detailed in Figure 5-43 with the report that it generated.

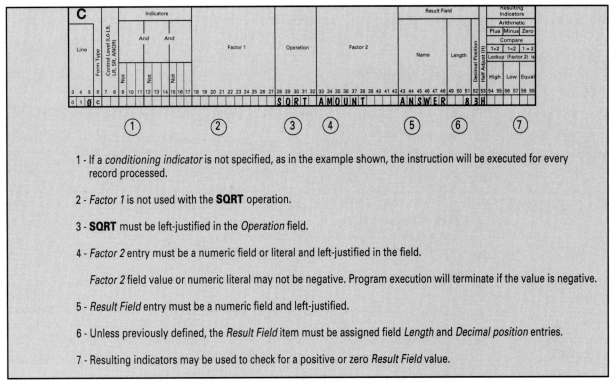

1 - If a *conditioning indicator* is not specified, as in the example shown, the instruction will be executed for every record processed.

2 - *Factor 1* is not used with the **SQRT** operation.

3 - **SQRT** must be left-justified in the *Operation* field.

4 - *Factor 2* entry must be a numeric field or literal and left-justified in the field.

   Factor 2 field value or numeric literal may not be negative. Program execution will terminate if the value is negative.

5 - *Result Field* entry must be a numeric field and left-justified.

6 - Unless previously defined, the *Result Field* item must be assigned field *Length* and *Decimal position* entries.

7 - Resulting indicators may be used to check for a positive or zero *Result Field* value.

Figure 5-42   Syntax for the **SQRT** (square root) operation.

```
SEQUENCE                                                              IND    DO
NUMBER   *...1....+....2....+....3....+....4....+....5....+....6....+....7...*  USE   NUM
                       S o u r c e   L i s t i n g
    100  * THIS PROGRAM CALCULATES THE SQUARE ROOT OF INPUT NUMBERS.
    200  * FIELD INDICATORS ARE USED TO VALIDATE THE INPUT NUMBER VALUE
    300  * FOR PLUS, MINUS, AND ZERO.  THE SQRT STATEMENT AND OUTPUT MSGS
    400  * ARE CONDITIONED BY THE FIELD INDICATORS
    500  * PHYSICAL FILE IS PROGRAM DEFINED
         H
    600  FNUMBERS IP  E              DISK              Physical file's
         RECORD FORMAT(S): LIBRARY SMYERS FILE NUMBERS. record name must
                 EXTERNAL FORMAT NUMREC RPG NAME NUMREC be specified
    700  FQSYSPRT O   F  132    OF    PRINTER
    800  INUMREC
    900  I                                    NUMBER    202122        Field indicators
    900   INPUT  FIELDS FOR RECORD NUMREC FILE NUMBERS FORMAT NUMREC.  20, 21, 22 test
 A000001                               P  1  30NUMBER   202122        for +, -, and 0
   1000  *                                                            respectively
   1100  * If NUMBER is positive (indicator 20 on), execute SQRT instruction
   1200  C   20           SQRT NUMBER   ROOT   83H
   1300  OQSYSPRT H 201 1P
   1400  O       OR      OF
   1500  O                      47 'SQUARE ROOT OF NUMBERS'
   1600  O       H  1  1P
   1700  O       OR      OF
   1800  O                      47 'NUMBER       SQUARE'
   1900  O       H  2  1P
   2000  O       OR      OF
   2100  O                      46 'ROOT'
   2200  O       D  2  N1P
   2300  O              NUMBERJ  30
   2400  O          20  ROOT  3  46          Field indicators
   2500  O          21          55 'NUMBER NEGATIVE CHECK'  condition related
   2600  O          21          60 'DATA'    output value or
   2700  O          22          56 'NUMBER ZERO CHECK DATA' constant
```

Figure 5-43   Program and report listings for the Square Root example program.

```
              SQUARE ROOT OF NUMBERS

              NUMBER              SQUARE
                                   ROOT

               144               12.000

               746-      NUMBER NEGATIVE CHECK DATA

            60,000             244.949

            92,000             303.315

                 0       NUMBER ZERO CHECK DATA

            87,411             295.654
```

Figure 5-43 Program and report listings for the Square Root example program. (Continued)

The *LIKE DEFN *(Field Definition)* Declarative Operation

The program examples presented in this chapter have defined the *Result Field* items either in the related physical file or in a calculation statement. Other than the fields previously defined in the physical file(s) processed by an RPG/400 program, it is more efficient to define any new fields with ***LIKE DEFN** statements. The **DEFN** operation is a declarative operation that defines a *Result Field* item based on the attributes of another field. Figure 5-44 explains the syntax of the ***LIKE DEFN** statement.

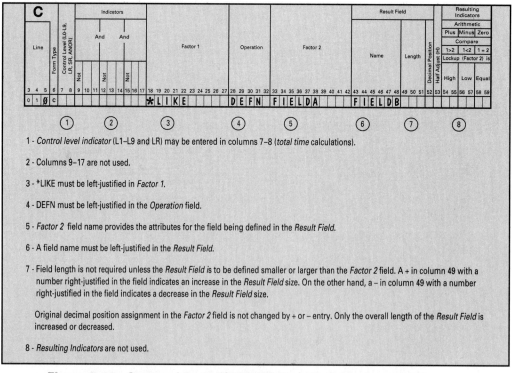

1 - *Control level indicator* (L1–L9 and LR) may be entered in columns 7–8 (*total time* calculations).

2 - Columns 9–17 are not used.

3 - *LIKE must be left-justified in *Factor 1.*

4 - DEFN must be left-justified in the *Operation* field.

5 - *Factor 2* field name provides the attributes for the field being defined in the *Result Field.*

6 - A field name must be left-justified in the *Result Field.*

7 - Field length is not required unless the *Result Field* is to be defined smaller or larger than the *Factor 2* field. A + in column 49 with a number right-justified in the field indicates an increase in the *Result Field* size. On the other hand, a – in column 49 with a number right-justified in the field indicates a decrease in the *Result Field* size.

Original decimal position assignment in the *Factor 2* field is not changed by + or – entry. Only the overall length of the *Result Field* is increased or decreased.

8 - *Resulting Indicators* are not used.

Figure 5-44 Syntax of the ***LIKE DEFN** (Field Definition) statement.

Examples of ***LIKE DEFN** statements are shown in Figure 5-45.

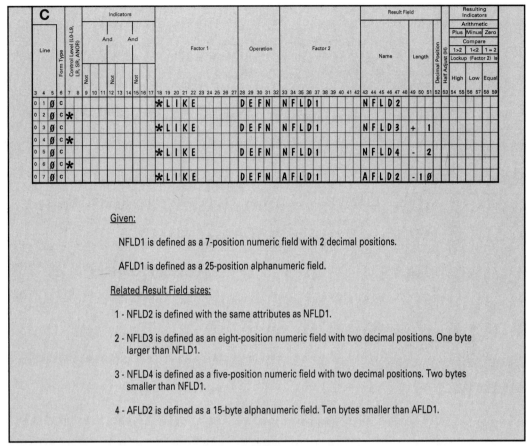

Figure 5-45   Examples of ***LIKE DEFN** statements.

Given:

NFLD1 is defined as a 7-position numeric field with 2 decimal positions.

AFLD1 is defined as a 25-position alphanumeric field.

Related Result Field sizes:

1 - NFLD2 is defined with the same attributes as NFLD1.

2 - NFLD3 is defined as an eight-position numeric field with two decimal positions. One byte larger than NFLD1.

3 - NFLD4 is defined as a five-position numeric field with two decimal positions. Two bytes smaller than NFLD1.

4 - AFLD2 is defined as a 15-byte alphanumeric field. Ten bytes smaller than AFLD1.

SUMMARY

All calculations are performed in RPG/400 by instructions included in the *Calculation Specifications.* The arithmetic operations are **ADD, SUB, MULT,** and **DIV.** *Result Fields* not previously defined may be defined when the related calculation instruction is initially specified. *Field Length* and *Decimal Position* entries define *Result Fields* not previously defined in the physical file.

The **MVR** *(Move Remainder)* operation may be used with a **DIV** *(Divide)* statement to save the remainder when needed.

Numeric field values may be initialized by **Z-ADD, Z-SUB, MOVE,** and **MOVEL** instructions. The **Z-ADD** and **Z-SUB** operations move zeros into the *Result Field* before moving in the *Factor 2* value. However, the **Z-SUB** operation <u>reverses</u> the sign of the *Factor 2* value in the *Result Field* value. The **MOVE** and **MOVEL** operations do not initialize the *Result Field* before the movement of the *Factor 2* item value.

The **LR** *(Last Record) indicator* is automatically turned on during program execution when the end of the input file is read. **LR** is used to condition calculation and output instructions at *total time* only.

Indicators may be turned on in an RPG/400 program by the **SETON** operation and turned off by **SETOF.** In addition, indicator on and off control may be executed by the reserved words ***IN** and ***INxx.** ***IN** defines a one-position element array defining indicators 01–99. ***INxx** is a one-position character field where **xx** may represent any indicator except **1P** and **MR.**

Resulting Indicators (arithmetic—columns 54–59) are used to test a *Result Field* value for *Positive, Minus,* or *Zero* by including one, two, or three indicators in the related fields. The indicators are used to condition subsequent calculations and/or output.

The *Figurative Constants* ***BLANK, *BLANKS, *ZERO, *ZEROS, *HIVAL, *LOVAL, *ALLX'.', *ON,** and ***OFF** are unique in that they have predefined values. Each constant assumes the *Result Field* size.

The **SQRT** *(Square Root)* operation computes the square root of a number.

Field Indicators are specified in the *Input Specifications* in columns 65 to 70. An input value may be tested for *Plus, Minus,* or *Zero* (*Blank* for alphanumeric fields) by entering an indicator(s) in one or more of the fields. *Field Indicators* are used to condition related calculations and/or output instructions.

Result Fields that are not defined on input may be more efficiently defined by ***LIKE DEFN** *(Field Definition)* statements than by any other method.

QUESTIONS

5-1. What are the RPG/400 operation names for the following arithmetic functions?

Addition	Division
Subtraction	Remainder
Multiplication	Square Root

5-2. A list of arithmetic terms follows. Identify where they should be specified in the *Calculation Specifications.*

Quotient	Sum	Difference
Subtrahend	Divisor	Dividend
Product	Addend	Multiplier
Multiplicand	Remainder	

5-3. If a five-digit number with two decimals is multiplied by a four-digit number with four decimals, how large should the *Result Field* be and with how many decimals?

5-4. What sign will the *Result Field* carry after the following separate calculation statements?

	Factor 1 Value	Arithmetic Function	Factor 2 Value	Comment
(a)	+25	x	+4	Multiplication
(b)	−19	x	−5	Multiplication
(c)	−100	+	+50	Addition
(d)	+30	−	−35	Subtraction
(e)	+22	/	−2	Division
(f)	+12	x	−10	Multiplication
(g)	−500	/	−20	Division
(h)	−99	−	−9	Subtraction

5-5. Explain the rule for defining the size of the *Result Field* for a division statement.

5-6. What procedure should be followed for defining the size of a remainder?

5-7. Name some of the restrictions for a square root statement.

5-8. What is half adjusting? Where and how is it specified in an RPG/400 program? Should it be included for every instruction?

5-9. Half adjust the following numbers to two decimal positions:

     (a) 45.2891   (c) 99.9959   (e) 73.4444   (g) 26.789

     (b) 18.134   (d) 100.56   (f) .4567   (h) 509.

5-10. For numeric literals that have a decimal value, is an explicit (actual) or implied decimal specified? Must a decimal be included with integer literals?

5-11. On a *Calculation Specifications,* write the instruction to multiply SALES by RATE and store the answer in TAX. The SALES field is defined as 7 digits with 2 decimal positions, and RATE is 3 digits long with 3 decimals. TAX is to be defined in the statement.

5-12. On a *Calculation Specifications,* enter the coding to divide QUANT by 12 and store the answer in DOZENS. QUANT is defined as 6 positions with 0 decimals. DOZENS is to be defined in the statement.

5-13. Refer to Question 5-12 and include an instruction to save the remainder in a field named REMAIN. The size of REMAIN must be determined.

5-14. In an RPG/400 program, when does the **LR** *indicator* turn on? For conditioning of instructions, where is it specified in the *Calculation Specifications?* With which type of line must it be specified on *Output Specifications* coding?

5-15. Examine the following calculations and explain if anything is wrong with the syntax.

C			Indicators						Factor 1	Operation	Factor 2		Result Field			Resulting Indicators				
				And		And							Name	Length	Decimal Position	Plus	Minus	Zero		
																1>2	1<2	1=2		
Line	Form Type	Control Level (L0-L9, LR, SR, AN/OR)	Not		Not		Not									High	Low	Equal		
0 1	C									ADD	SALES		TOTAL	9	2					
0 2	C	LR								ADD	1		COUNT	4	0					
0 3	C		LR						TOTAL	DIV	COUNT		AVG	8	2					

5-16. In an RPG/400 program, where are *Resulting Indicators* specified? What is their function?

5-17. May more than one *Resulting Indicator* condition a calculation or output instruction? May an instruction be conditioned by a *Resulting Indicator* and a *Record Identifying Indicator?*

5-18. What is the function of the **SETON** operation? What is the function of the **SETOF** operation? How many indicators may be controlled by one **SETON** or **SETOF** operation?

5-19. Explain the processing function of the **Z-ADD** operation.

5-20. Determine the *Result Field* value for each of the *Factor 2* values after execution of a **Z-ADD** operation. The size of *Factor 2* and the *Result Field* items are indicated by the beginning values.

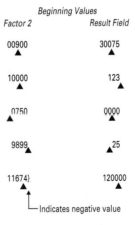

Beginning Values

Factor 2   Result Field

00900▲   30075▲

10000▲   123▲

0750▲   0000▲

9899▲   ▲25

11674}▲   120000▲

└ Indicates negative value

▲ Indicates implied decimal

5-21. How does the **Z-SUB** operation differ from **Z-ADD?** Refer to Question 5-20 and determine the *Result Field* values if a **Z-SUB** operation was specified.

5-22. Explain how the **MOVE** and **MOVEL** operations differ in processing. How do they differ from the function performed by the **Z-ADD** operation?

5-23. Determine the *Result Field* value for each of the **MOVE** statements. The size of the *Factor 2* and *Result Field* items are indicated by the beginning values.

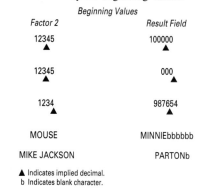

Factor 2	Result Field
Beginning Values	
12345 ▲	100000 ▲
12345 ▲	000 ▲
1234 ▲	987654 ▲
MOUSE	MINNIEbbbbb
MIKE JACKSON	PARTONb

▲ Indicates implied decimal.
b Indicates blank character.

5-24. Refer to Question 5-23, and determine the *Result Field* values for the **MOVEL** operation.

5-25. Name the Figurative Constants and indicate the value supplied by each one. What is their function in an RPG/400 program?

5-26. Where in an RPG/400 program are *Field Indicators* specified? What is their programming function?

5-27. What is the most efficient method to define fields that are not included in an input record?

5-28. On a *Calculation Specifications,* using the method identified in Question 5-27, write the instruction to define TOTAL 1 byte larger than AMOUNT. The AMOUNT field is defined as 7 bytes with 2 decimal positions. How many decimal positions will be defined for the TOTAL field after the operation is executed?

5-29. Write the calculation coding for the following flowchart logic. Use *Resulting Indicators* to test the value of C.

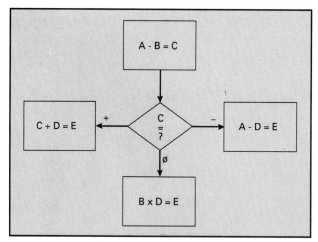

5-30. Complete the *Input Specifications* to test the value of FIELDA for *Plus, Minus,* and *Zero.* Then, from the following flowchart logic, complete the calculation coding.

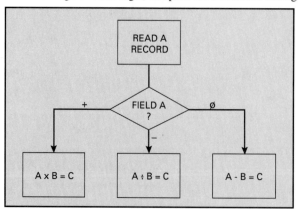

5-31. Write the calculation instructions for the following formula. Include the necessary tests to prevent the program from halting (or aborting on some systems) because of related minus and zero values.

$$\sqrt{\frac{X - Y}{Z}}$$

5-32. Explain the processing result for the following instructions:

Line	Form Type	Control Level (L0-L9, LR, SR, AN/OR)	Not	Indicators And	Not	And	Not	Factor 1	Operation	Factor 2	Result Field Name	Length	Decimal Position	Half Adjust (H)	Plus/High 1>2	Minus/Low 1<2	Zero/Equal 1=2
01	C								MOVE	'1'	*IN40						
02	C																
03	C								MOVE	'0'	*IN						
04	C																
05	C								MOVE	'0'	*IN,20						
06	C																
07	C								MOVE	'0'	*IN,90						

PROGRAMMING ASSIGNMENTS

For each of the following programming assignments, a physical file must have been created and loaded with the related data records. Your instructor will inform you as to whether you have to create the physical file and load it or if it has been prepared for the assignment.

Programming Assignment 5-1: SALES JOURNAL

Write an RPG/400 program to generate a Sales Journal that summarizes all of a month's sales on account.

Processing: Read the input file consecutively, and for every record processed perform the following calculations:

1. Test the Sales Amount field on input for a negative and zero value. If one of those conditions is tested, *do not* perform any calculations for that record. Depending on the error condition, one of the two messages shown in the printer spacing chart that follows is to be printed with the transaction date, customer name, and invoice number from the related record.

For Valid Records:

2. Compute the sales tax by multiplying the sales amount by the numeric literal .0750.
3. Compute the total sale for the record by adding the sales tax to the sales amount.
4. Accumulate the sales amount, sales tax, and total sale into separate total fields.

Physical File Record Format:

```
                    PHYSICAL FILE DESCRIPTION

  SYSTEM: AS/400                              DATE: Yours
  FILE NAME: Yours                            REV NO: 0
  RECORD NAME: Yours                          KEY LENGTH: None
  SEQUENCE:Non-keyed                          RECORD SIZE: 41

                       FIELD DEFINITIONS

  FIELD       FIELD NAME    SIZE  TYPE    POSITION     COMMENTS
   NO                                    FROM    TO


    1         SALDAT         6     P       1      4
    2         CUSNAM        29     C       5     33
    3         INV#           6     P      34     37
    4         SALAMT         7     P      38     41    2 decimals
```

Physical File Data:

Sales Date	Customer Name	Invoice Number	Sales Amount
080196	HUDSON MOTOR CAR COMPANY	40000	081200
080996	PACKARD COMPANY	40001	000000
081196	THE HUPMOBILE COMPANY	40002	857010
081696	THE TUCKER CAR COMPANY	40003	000212
082196	AUBURN INCORPORATED	40004	004500
082796	BRICKLIN LIMITED	40005	106891
083096	THE LOCOMOBILE CAR COMPANY	40006	214000
083196	STUDEBAKER CARS INCORPORATED	40007	005050

Report Design:

Programming Assignment 5-2: COMPUTATION OF SIMPLE INTEREST

Simple interest is the rent paid to a lender for the privilege of borrowing money. It is charged on personal loans, car loans, installment loans, home mortgages, and so forth. The formula for computing simple interest is:

$$I = \frac{P \times R \times T}{365}$$

where I = Dollar amount of simple interest

P = Principal (amount borrowed) on which interest is computed

R = Annual interest rate expressed as a decimal

T = Number of days, months, or years for which the money will be loaned

Note: 365 is used as denominator in above formula if T (time) is in days. If time is in years, denominator may be 1 (or no entry needed).

Processing: Include the formula for computing simple interest in an RPG/400 program. Process the input file consecutively, and generate the report format shown in the supplemental printer spacing chart. Notice that the interest percentage value input must be multiplied by 100 for output.

Physical File Record Format:

```
                    PHYSICAL FILE DESCRIPTION

  SYSTEM: AS/400                          DATE: Yours
  FILE NAME: Yours                        REV NO: 0
  RECORD NAME: Yours                      KEY LENGTH: None
  SEQUENCE: Non-keyed                     RECORD SIZE: 14

                       FIELD DEFINITIONS

  FIELD      FIELD NAME    SIZE   TYPE      POSITION      COMMENTS
   NO                                      FROM    TO


    1        LOAN#           5     P         1      3   0 decimals
    2        PRINPL          8     P         4      8   2 decimals
    3        INTRAT          5     P         9     11   2 decimals
    4        DAYS            4     P        12     14   0 decimals
```

Physical File Data:

Loan #	Principal (P)	Interest Rate (R)	Time of Loan in Days (T)
10000	12000000	08500	0120
10001	00300000	07000	0185
10002	01025000	09100	0730
10003	00047500	10250	0090
10004	00100000	12125	0060

Report Design:

```
          0          1          2          3          4          5          6          7
  1234567890123456789012345678901234567890123456789012345678901234567890123456789
1                         SIMPLE INTEREST LOAN SCHEDULES AS OF ØX/XX/XX
2
3
4       LOAN                    INTEREST RATE    TIME IN      INTEREST            TOTAL
5      NUMBER    PRINCIPAL        /ANNUM          DAYS        ON LOAN         AMOUNT DUE
6
7      XXXXX    $XXX,XXØ.XX      ØX.XXX%         XXØX      $XX,XXØ.XX       $X,XXX,XXØ.XX
8
9      XXXXX    $XXX,XXØ.XX      ØX.XXX%         XXØX      $XX,XXØ.XX       $X,XXX,XXØ.XX
10
11        NOTES:
12
13          1. USE SYSTEM DATE FOR REPORT.
14
15          2. HEADINGS ON TOP OF EVERY PAGE.
```

Programming Assignment 5-3: GROSS PROFIT ANALYSIS REPORT

A computer supply company wants a gross profit report on their best-selling printers. The listed catalog selling prices are subject to trade discounts that range from the series 10%, 5%, 5% to 30%, 10%, 5%.

   Trade discounts are computed as follows:

   Assume a trade discount of 30%, 10%, 5%.

Step 1: Subtract each percentage point from 1.00.

$$1.00 - 0.30 = 0.70$$
$$1.00 - 0.10 = 0.90$$
$$1.00 - 0.05 = 0.95$$

Step 2: Determine equivalent trade discount by multiplying the percentages calculated in Step 1.

$$0.70 \times 0.90 \times 0.95 = 0.5985 \text{ (carry to four decimal places)}$$

Step 3: Multiply the catalog list price by the percentage derived from Step 2.

$$\$1,000 \times 0.5985 = \$598.50 \text{ net selling price (rounded nearest cent)}$$

Step 4: Subtract the net selling price (Step 3) from the catalog list price to determine the trade discount.

Step 5: Determine the item's gross profit by subtracting cost from the net selling price calculated in Step 3.

Step 6: Calculate the percentage of gross profit (decimal expression) by dividing the gross profit (Step 5) by the net selling price (Step 3). *Include the control that prevents a divide-by-zero error.*

Step 7. Multiply the decimal percentage derived from Step 6 by 100 to calculate the percentage expression for printing.

Physical File Record Format:

```
                        PHYSICAL FILE DESCRIPTION

       SYSTEM: AS/400                          DATE: Yours
       FILE NAME: Yours                        REV NO: 0   RECORD
       NAME: Yours                             KEY LENGTH: None
       SEQUENCE:Non-keyed                      RECORD SIZE: 46

                            FIELD DEFINITIONS

          FIELD    FIELD NAME   SIZE  TYPE    POSITION      COMMENTS
          NO                                 FROM    TO

            1       ITEM#         3     P       1     2   0 decimals
            2       DESCRP       30     C       3    32
            3       LISTPR        6     P      33    36   2 decimals
            4       TDISC1        2     P      37    38   2 decimals
            5       TDISC2        2     P      39    40   2 decimals
            6       TDISC3        2     P      41    42   2 decimals
            7       COST          6     P      43    46   2 decimals
```

Physical File Data:

Item Number	Item Description	Catalog List	Trade Discount %			Cost
720	BROTHER JR-35 PRINTER	140000	30	10	05	061000
776	EXP-770 SILVER REED PRINTER	149500	25	10	05	073000
789	JUKI 6100 PRINTER	059900	10	05	05	037500
799	P12 DIABLO SYSTEMS PRINTER	069900	15	05	00	034500
820	H-P LASERJET+ PRINTER	349500	10	10	05	226800

Report Design:

Programming Assignment 5-4: DETERMINATION OF ECONOMIC ORDER QUANTITY

The costs of carrying an item in inventory include deterioration, obsolescence, handling, clerical labor, taxes, insurance, storage, and reasonable return on investment. These costs are weighed against the costs of inadequate inventory, which may lead to loss of sales, loss of customer goodwill, production stoppage, extra purchasing costs, and a higher item cost for small-quantity purchases. Because of these inventory considerations, companies often rely on mathematical models as guidelines for the decision-making process of determining how much to order and when. A useful quantitative tool is the *economic order quantity formula,* which calculates the optimum quantity to order of any one item.

Before an item's *economic order quantity* is calculated, the number of units needed annually, cost per order, unit cost of the item, and its carrying cost must be determined. Then, the following formula may be used.

$$\text{Economic Order Quantity} = \sqrt{\frac{2 \times \text{units needed annually} \times \text{ordering cost}}{\text{item unit cost} \times \text{inventory carrying cost \%}}}$$

$$EOQ = \sqrt{\frac{2 \times U \times OC}{UC \times ICC}}$$

Note: Round EOQ answer to a whole number.

Physical File Record Format:

```
              PHYSICAL FILE DESCRIPTION

    SYSTEM: AS/400                      DATE: Yours
    FILE NAME: Yours                    REV NO: 0
    RECORD NAME: Yours                  KEY LENGTH: None
    SEQUENCE: Non-keyed                 RECORD SIZE: 36

                  FIELD DEFINITIONS

    FIELD    FIELD NAME   SIZE  TYPE    POSITION      COMMENTS
     NO                                FROM    TO


      1      ITEMNM        25    C        1     25
      2      USAGE          5    P       26     28   0 decimals
      3      ORDCST         3    P       29     30   0 decimals
      4      UNTCST         5    P       31     33   2 decimals
      5      CARCST         4    P       34     36   4 decimals
```

Physical File Data:

Item Name	Annual Usage	Order Cost	Unit Cost	Carrying Cost %
LEFT-HAND MONKEY WRENCH	10000	025	01250	0250
MEN'S DIESEL SHAVER	20000	018	01800	1000
ATOMIC TOOTHBRUSH	40000	020	11290	1400
FUEL-INJECTED LAWN MOWER	00200	050	29000	9000
LASER TOOTHPICKS	30000	024	00650	0856

Report Design: Format a printer spacing chart according to the following general format:

```
OX/XX/XX       ECONOMIC ORDER QUANTITIES OF INVENTORY ITEMS       PAGE XXOX


          ITEM NAME                ANNUAL USAGE      EOQ      ORDERS PER YEAR

XXXXXXXXXXXXXXXXXXXXXXXXX            XX,XXO          X,XXO          XXO

XXXXXXXXXXXXXXXXXXXXXXXXX            XX,XXO          X,XXO          XXO

   Note:  Use system date for report.
```

Orders per year is determined by dividing annual usage by the economic order quantity computed. Round to a whole number.

chapter 6

RPG/400 Structured Operations for Decision Making, Branching, and Looping Control

Decision making (without branching) may be controlled in an RPG/400 program by the following:

1. **IF/ELSE** structured operations
2. **SELEC/OTHER** structured operations
3. **COMP** (*Compare*) nonstructured operations

Regardless of the operation used in a decision-making instruction, a *relational* test is made between a *Factor 1* field (or literal) and a *Factor 2* field (or literal). Relational tests with an **IF** or **SELEC** statement include *equal to, less than, greater than, less than or equal to, greater than or equal to,* and *not equal to* conditions without requiring *Resulting Indicators* (columns 54–59). Tests which may be made in a **COMP** instruction include *equal to, less than,* or *greater than* conditions with at least one *Resulting Indicator.*

The test results from the relational comparison of the values in two fields or a field and a literal are controlled by the *collating sequence* of the computer. IBM mainframe and mid-range (AS/400) computer systems support *Extended Binary Coded Decimal Interchange Code* (**EBCDIC**). Others, including IBM's microcomputers, support **ASCII** (*American National Standard Code for Information Interchange*) code structure. Figure 6-1 presents a partial listing of the two code sets. Any character lower in the hierarchy

EBCDIC	ASCII	
(blank)	(blank)	lowest
.	"	
<	$	
(	:	
+	(	
$	)	
*	*	
)	+	
;	,	
-	-	
/	.	
,	/	
>	0 thru 9	
:	;	
=	<	
"	=	
A thru Z	>	
0 thru 9	A thru Z	highest

Figure 6-1 EBCDIC and ASCII code set collating sequences.

than another character will test as *less than* in relational testings. Notice that a blank is the <u>lowest</u> character in both code sets, with 9 being the <u>highest</u> in **EBCDIC** and Z the <u>highest</u> in **ASCII.**

IFxx/ELSE *OPERATIONS*

The **IFxx** *(If/Then),* **ELSE** *(Else/Do),* and **ENDIF** (or **END**) operations are used to control relational condition processing. The **IFxx** statement is used to evaluate a condition, and depending on whether the test is true or false, it will direct program control to a specific instruction within the **IFxx** or **IF/ELSE** group. An **ELSE** statement, which must be related to an **IFxx** instruction, provides for an alternative action if the **IFxx** test is not true. Figure 6-2 explains the syntax associated with the **IFxx, ELSE,** and **ENDIF** (or **END**) operations.

The relational expression tested (**xx** entry) may be *simple* or *complex.* An **IFxx** statement that includes more than one test connected with an **AND** or **OR** relationship is

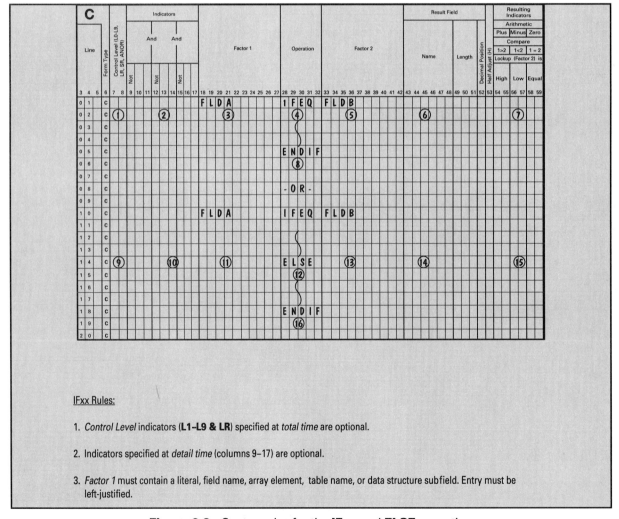

IFxx Rules:

1. *Control Level* indicators (**L1–L9 & LR**) specified at *total time* are optional.

2. Indicators specified at *detail time* (columns 9–17) are optional.

3. *Factor 1* must contain a literal, field name, array element, table name, or data structure subfield. Entry must be left-justified.

Figure 6-2 Syntax rules for the **IFxx** and **ELSE** operations.

4. Operation **IFxx** must be left-justified in the *Operation* field. The **xx** entry may have one of the following values:

xx Option	Relational Test
EQ	Value in *Factor 1* is equal to value in *Factor 2*
GE	Value in *Factor 1* is greater than or equal to value in *Factor 2*
GT	Value in *Factor 1* is greater than value in *Factor 2*
LE	Value in *Factor 1* is less than or equal to value in *Factor 2*
LT	Value in *Factor 1* is less than value in *Factor 2*
NE	Value in *Factor 1* is not equal to value in *Factor 2*

5. Required *Factor 2* entry must be left-justified and may be a literal, field name, array element, table name, or data structure subfield name. The rules for the relational test must be followed, which require that the *Factor 1* and *Factor 2* items be the same type (numeric or alphanumeric).

6. *Result Field* is not used.

7. *Resulting Indicators* are not used.

8. **ENDIF** (or **END**) operation must end the **IFxx** group. A *Control Level* indicator (columns 7–8) may be assigned to this operation to place it within a control group.

ELSE Rules:

9. A *Control Level* indicator (**L1–L9 & LR**) may be assigned at *total time* (columns 7–8) to place the **ELSE** statement within a related control group. The entry has no function and is specified only to meet the RPG/400 sequence rule that *total time* calculations must follow *detail time*.

10. *Detail time* indicators (column 9–17) are not used.

11. *Factor 1* is not used.

12. **ELSE** operation must be left-justified in the *Operation* field.

13. *Factor 2* is not used.

14. *Result Field* is not used.

15. *Resulting Indicators* are not used.

16. An **ENDIF** (or **END**) operation must terminate an **IF/ELSE** group.

Note: An **IFxx** statement may be specified without a related **ELSE** operation. However, an **ELSE** instruction may <u>not</u> be coded without a related IFxx statement.

Figure 6-2 Syntax rules for the **IFxx** and **ELSE** operations. (Continued)

complex. Those that include only one relational test are classified as *simple.* Figure 6-3 shows three flowcharts that detail the processing logic for simple **IFxx** statements that test for *true only, true and false,* and *false only* actions.

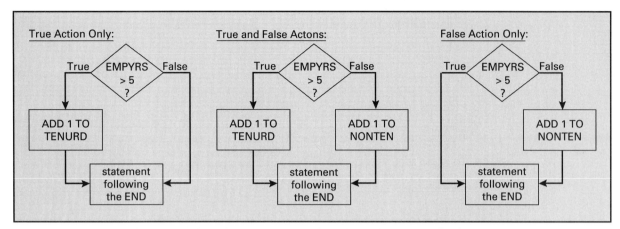

Figure 6-3   Processing logic flowcharts for simple **IFxx** statements.

The RPG/400 **IFxx** statement coding to support the processing logic shown in the flowcharts in Figure 6-3 is detailed in Figure 6-4.

C							Indicators							Factor 1	Operation	Factor 2	Result Field				Resulting Indicators		
Line	Form Type	Control Level (L0-L9, LR, SR, ANOR)		And		And											Name	Length	Decimal Position	Half Adjust (H)	Plus / Minus / Zero (Arithmetic); 1>2 / 1<2 / 1=2 (Compare); High/Low/Equal Lookup		
0 1 Ø	C		*	TRUE ACTION ONLY;																		
0 2 Ø	C		*																			
0 3 Ø	C							EMPYRS	IFGT	5									
0 4 Ø	C								ADD	1	TENURD							
0 5 Ø	C								ENDIF									
0 6 Ø	C		*																			
0 7 Ø	C		*	TRUE AND FALSE ACTIONS																		
0 8 Ø	C		*																			
0 9 Ø	C							EMPYRS	IFGT	5									
1 0 Ø	C								ADD	1	TENURD							
1 1 Ø	C								ELSE									
1 2 Ø	C								ADD	1	NONTEN							
1 3 Ø	C		*						ENDIF									
1 4 Ø	C		*	FALSE ACTION ONLY;																		
1 5 Ø	C		*																			
1 6 Ø	C							EMPYRS	IFGT	5									
1 7 Ø	C								ELSE									
1 8 Ø	C								ADD	1	NONTEN							
1 9 Ø	C								ENDIF									

Figure 6-4   Simple **IFxx/ELSE** statement coding to control true only, true and false, and false only action processing.

Complex IFxx **Statements**

A *complex* **IFxx** statement is one that includes two or more relational tests specified in an **AND** and/or **OR** relationship. When an **AND** relationship is included, <u>all</u> of the conditions must be true to execute the action. For **IFxx** statements in an **OR** relationship, only <u>one</u> of the test conditions has to be true to execute the action. The processing logic and syntax related to a complex **IFxx** statement that includes one **AND** and two **OR** relationships are shown in Figure 6-5.

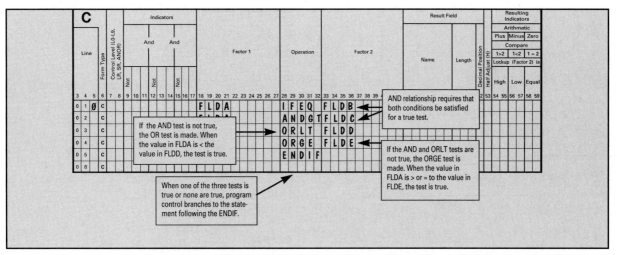

Figure 6-5 Processing logic and syntax related to complex **IFxx** statements.

Nested IFxx **Statements**

Nested **IF** statements are classified as those that pair more than one **IFxx** instruction within an *IF group*. The syntax and processing logic related to this structure are detailed in Figure 6-6.

A weekly payroll report application program that illustrates how **IF/ELSE** operations are used in the decision-making process appears in the following section.

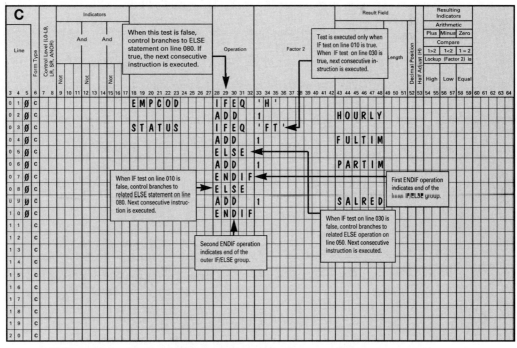

Figure 6-6 Syntax and processing logic for nested **IFxx** statements.

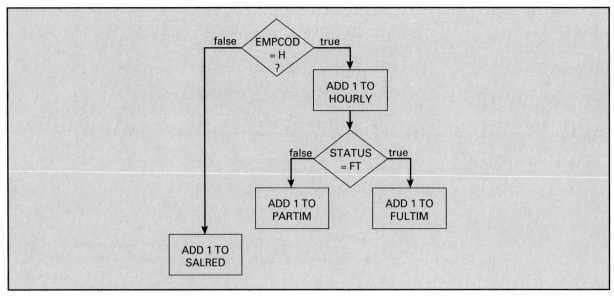

Figure 6-6   Syntax and processing logic for nested **IFxx** statements. (Continued)

APPLICATION PROGRAM: WEEKLY PAYROLL REPORT

Documentation

The specifications in Figure 6-7 summarize the processing requirements for the RPG/400 Weekly Payroll Report program.

PROGRAM SPECIFICATIONS		Page 1 of 1

Program Name: <u>Weekly Payroll Report</u>   Program-ID: <u>PAYROLL</u>   Written by: <u>SM</u>

Purpose: <u>Generate a weekly payroll report</u>   Approved by: <u>CM</u>

Input files: <u>EMPPAYFL</u>   _____   _____   _____

Output files: <u>QSYSPRT</u>   _____   _____   _____

Processing Requirements:

Write a structured RPG/400 program to generate a weekly payroll report for day- and night-shift employees.

<u>Input to the program:</u>

An externally defined physical file, EMPPAYFL, stores the weekly payroll data for each employee. The supplemental record layout form details the record format.

<u>Processing:</u>

Read the Weekly Payroll File, EMPPAYFL, in key value order and perform the following computations:

Step 1:   Test the shift code field to determine if the employee worked the day or night shift. An additional 15% hourly rate bonus is added for the night shift.

Step 2:   Convert minutes to hours. Any remainder less than 30 is considered a 1/2 hour (.5) and if equal to or greater than 30 is processed as 1 hour.

Step 3:   Compute the regular pay as follows:
HOURLY RATE × HOURS WORKED = REGULAR PAY

Figure 6-7   Specifications for Weekly Payroll Report program.

Step 4:   Determine if the employee worked overtime (over 35 hours:
          HOURS WORKED - 35 = OVERTIME HOURS (if greater than 0))

Step 5:   Compute overtime premium as follows:
          HOURLY RATE/2 = OVERTIME PREMIUM RATE (rounded to 2 decimals)
          Then:
          OVERTIME HOURS × OVERTIME PREMIUM RATE = OVERTIME PAY

Step 6:   Compute each employee's total week's pay as follows:
          REGULAR PAY + OVERTIME PAY = TOTAL WEEK'S PAY

Step 7:   Provide totals for the hours worked, regular pay, overtime pay, and total pay.

<u>Output:</u>

Complete the report detailed in the supplemental printer spacing chart.

Figure 6-7   Specifications for Weekly Payroll Report program. (Continued)

The system flowchart in Figure 6-8 indicates that one physical file is processed by an RPG/400 program to generate the report.

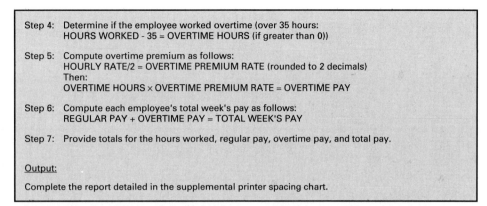

Figure 6-8   System flowchart for Weekly Payroll Report program.

The record format of the physical file is shown in Figure 6-9 with a listing of the stored data.

```
                    PHYSICAL FILE DESCRIPTION

SYSTEM: AS/400                              DATE: 8/11/95
FILE NAME: EMPPAYFL                         REV NO: 0
RECORD NAME: EMPPAYR                        KEY LENGTH: 4
SEQUENCE: Keyed                             RECORD SIZE: 31

                    FIELD DEFINITIONS

FIELD     FIELD NAME    SIZE   TYPE     POSITION      COMMENTS
  NO                                   FROM    TO


   1      EMPNO          4      C        1      4    Key field
   2      EMPNAM        20      C        5     24
   3      SHIFT          1      C       25     25
   4      HRRATE         4      P       26     28    2 decimals
   5      MINUTS         4      P       29     31    0 decimals
```

<u>Physical File Data:</u>

Employee Number	Employee Name	Shift	Hourly Rate	Minutes Worked
1234	LEONARDO DA VINCI	D	2250	2226
2345	ALEXANDER G BELL	N	2000	1800
3456	ROBERT FULTON	D	1275	2450
4567	CHARLES S GOODYEAR	N	1425	2100
5678	MARCHESE MARCONI	D	1500	2130

Figure 6-9   Physical file record format and a listing of the stored data.

The printer spacing chart shown in Figure 6-10 details the design of the report. Also included is a listing of the report generated from execution of the RPG/400 program.

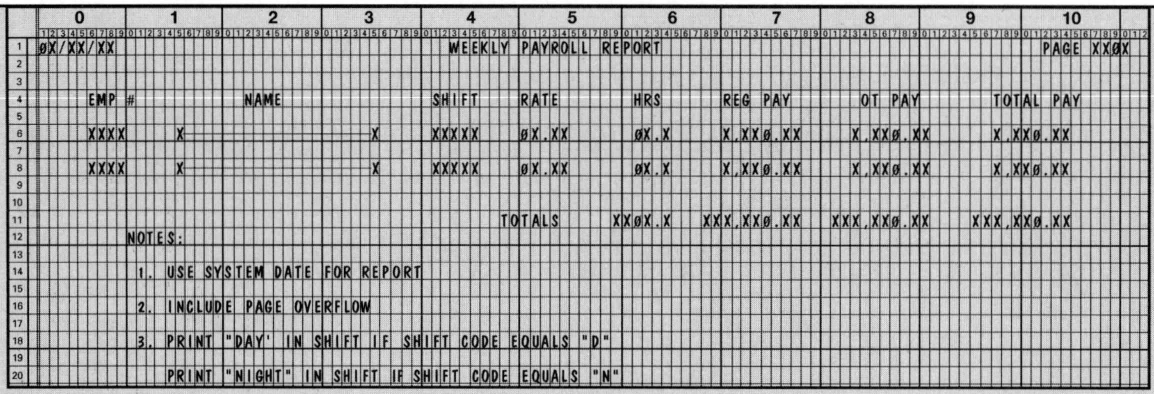

```
10/20/95                      WEEKLY PAYROLL REPORT                        PAGE    1


    EMP #          NAME              SHIFT    RATE      HRS      REG PAY      OT PAY      TOTAL PAY

    1234     LEONARDO DA VINCI        DAY     22.50     37.5      843.75       28.13        871.88

    2345     ALEXANDER G BELL        NIGHT    23.00     30.0      690.00         .00        690.00

    3456     ROBERT FULTON            DAY     12.75     41.0      522.75       38.28        561.03

    4567     CHARLES GOODYEAR        NIGHT    16.38     35.0      573.30         .00        573.30

    5678     MARCHESE MARCONI         DAY     15.00     36.0      540.00        7.50        547.50


                                             TOTALS    179.5    3,169.80       73.91      3,243.71
```

Figure 6-10   Printer spacing chart for Weekly Payroll Report program and report listing.

Source Program for the Weekly Payroll Report

Figure 6-11 contains a compile listing of the RPG/400 program that generates the weekly payroll report.

After examination of the compiled program listing in Figure 6-11, the following should be noted:

1. No *conditioning* indicators are specified in columns 7–8 or 9–17.
2. Instructions are included in clearly defined **IF** groups—one of the coding features that supports *structured* programming.
3. Individual **IF** or **IF/ELSE** statements are ended by **ENDIF** operations. Note that the **END** operation may also be used.
4. *Nested* **IF** statements (two levels in this program) are ended by two **ENDIF** operations.

```
SEQUENCE                                                                        IND   DO
NUMBER    *...1....+....2....+....3....+....4....+....5....+....6....+....7...*  USE   NUM
                            S o u r c e   L i s t i n g
   100    * WEEKLY PAYROLL REPORT FOR HOURLY EMPLOYEES
          H
   200    FEMPPAYFLIP E          K        DISK
          RECORD FORMAT(S): LIBRARY SMYERS FILE EMPPAYFL.
                  EXTERNAL FORMAT EMPPAYR RPG NAME EMPPAYR
   300    FQSYSPRT O  F     132    OF     PRINTER
A000000   INPUT  FIELDS FOR RECORD EMPPAYR FILE EMPPAYFL FORMAT EMPPAYR.
A000001                                    1    4 EMP#
A000002                                    5   24 EMPNAM       ┌──────────────────┐
A000003                                   25   25 SHIFT        │ Compiler supplied │
A000004                                 P 26  282HRRATE        │ IF/ELSE references│
A000005                                 P 29  310MINUTS        └──────────────────┘
   400    C                Z-ADD0          OTPAY   62    init ot pay
   500    C        SHIFT   IFGT 'D'                      shift test        B001 ─┐ Begin IF
   600    C        HRRATE  MULT 1.15       HRRATE        night rate        001   │
   700    C                MOVE 'NIGHT'    SHIFTO  5     night shift nam   001   │
   800    C                ELSE                                            X001 ─┤ Begin ELSE
   900    C                MOVE 'DAY '     SHIFTO        day shift name     001  │
  1000    C                ENDIF                         end if statmnt    E001 ─┘ End IF
  1100    *
  1200    C        MINUTS  DIV  60         HRS     20    minutes to hrs
  1300    C                MVR             REMAIN  20    save remainder
  1400    *                                                                  ┌──────────────────┐
  1500    C        REMAIN  IFEQ *ZERO                    test for 0     B001 ─┤ Begin outer IF  │
  1600    C                Z-ADDHRS        THRS    31    hrs to thrs    001  │                  │
  1700    C                ELSE                          remain not 0   X001 ─┤ Outer ELSE      │
  1800    C        REMAIN  IFLT 30                       remain < 30    B002 ─┤ Begin nested IF │
  1900    C        HRS     ADD  .5         THRS          add .5 to hrs  002  │                  │
  2000    C                ELSE                          remain = > 0   X002 ─┤ Nested ELSE     │
  2100    C        HRS     ADD  1          THRS          add 1 to hrs   002  │                  │
  2200    C                ENDIF                         end inner IFIF E002 ─┤ End nested IF   │
  2300    C                ENDIF                         end outer IF   E001 ─┘ End outer IF    │
  2400    *                                                              └──────────────────┘
  2500    C        THRS    MULT HRRATE     REGPAY  62    regular pay amt
  2600    *                                                              ┌──────────────┐
  2700    C        THRS    IFGT 35                       hrs > 35?      B001 ─┤ Begin IF │
  2800    C        THRS    SUB  35         OTHRS   31    overtime hrs   001   │          │
  2900    C        HRRATE  DIV  2          OTRATE  42H   overtime rate  001   │          │
  3000    C        OTHRS   MULT OTRATE     OTPAY    H    compute ot pay 001   │          │
  3100    C                ENDIF                         end IF         E001 ─┘ End IF   │
  3200    *                                                              └──────────────┘
  3300    C        REGPAY  ADD  OTPAY      WEKPAY  62    reg + ot amts
  3400    C                ADD  THRS       TOTHRS  51    accum tot hrs
  3500    C                ADD  REGPAY     TOTREG  82    accum reg pay
  3600    C                ADD  OTPAY      TOTOT   82    accum ot pay
  3700    C                ADD  WEKPAY     TOTPAY  82    accum wekpay
  3800    OQSYSPRT H  301        1P
  3900    O        OR            OF
  4000    O                      UDATE Y    8
  4100    O                                64 'WEEKLY PAYROLL REPORT'
  4200    O                               105 'PAGE'
  4300    O                      PAGE Z   110
  4400    O        H  2          1P
  4500    O        OR            OF
  4600    O                                10 'EMP #'
  4700    O                                25 'NAME'
  4800    O                                45 'SHIFT'
  4900    O                                53 'RATE'
  5000    O                                63 'HRS'
  5100    O                                76 'REG PAY'
  5200    O                                89 'OT PAY'
  5300    O                               105 'TOTAL PAY'
  5400    O        D  2          N1P
  5500    O                      EMP#       9
  5600    O                      EMPNAM    34
  5700    O                      SHIFTO    45
  5800    O                      HRRATE1   54
  5900    O                      THRS  1   64
  6000    O                      REGPAY1   77
  6100    O                      OTPAY 1   90
  6200    O                      WEKPAY1  104
  6300    O        T  1          LR
  6400    O                                53 'TOTALS'
  6500    O                      TOTHRS1   64
  6600    O                      TOTREG1   77
  6700    O                      TOTOT 1   90
  6800    O                      TOTPAY1  104
```

Figure 6-11 Compile listing of the Weekly Payroll Report program.

SELEC (Begin a Select Group)

A **SELEC** group conditionally processes a sequence of one or more relational **WHxx** (*When True Then Select*) statements. It may include some or all of the following:

> A **SELEC** statement (required)
> Zero or more **WHxx** statements (optional)
> Optional **OTHER** operation and statement group (optional)
> An **ENDSL** (*End Select*) or **END** statement (required)

The syntax and processing logic of a **SELEC** group are detailed in Figure 6-12.

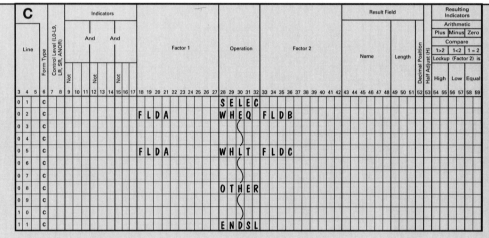

SELEC Operation Syntax Rules:

- *Conditioning indicator(s)* (columns 7–17) may be used.

- *Factor 1* is not used.

- **SELEC** name must be entered in the *Operation* field.

- *Factor 2* is not used.

- *Result Field* is not used.

- *Resulting Indicators* are not used.

- **ENDSL** (or **END**) operation must end a **SELEC** group.

Processing Logic of a **SELEC** Group:

1. Within a **SELEC** group, control passes to the first instruction following the **WHxx** statement that tested as true. After the instructions for the **WHxx** statement are executed, control branches to the instruction following the **ENDSL** (or **END**) operation.

2. If **none** of the **WHxx** statements within the **SELEC** group test as true, instructions following the **OTHER** operation are automatically executed. After the instruction(s) within the **OTHER** group are executed, control will pass to the statement following the **ENDSL** (or **END**) operation.

3. If an **OTHER** operation is not specified and the previous **WHxx** tests are not true, control will branch to the instruction following the **ENDSL** (or **END**) operation.

4. If *conditioning indicator(s)* is/are not on, program control will immediately branch to the statement following the **ENDSL** (or **END**) operation.

Figure 6-12   Syntax and processing logic of a **SELEC** group.

WHxx (When True Then Select)

WHxx statements may only be specified within a **SELEC** group after the **SELEC** operation and before, if included, an **OTHER** operation. Figure 6-13 explains the syntax for the **WHxx** operation.

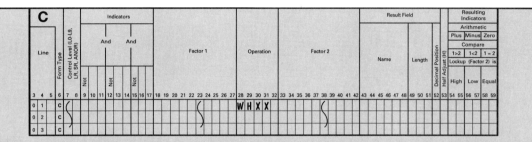

WHxx Operation Syntax Rules

- T*otal time* Control Level indicators (**L1–L9** and **LR**) in columns 7–8 are allowed so that a statement may be placed within a related Control Group. The indicator specified is only for documentation and has no function.

- *Detail time* indicators (columns 9–17) are not permitted.

- A field name or literal must be entered left-justified in *Factor 1*.

- **WHxx** operation must be left-justified in the *Operation* field. The **xx** entry must be an EQ, LT, GT, LE, GE, or NE relational test.

- A field name or literal must be entered left-justified in *Factor 2*.

- *Factor 1* and *Factor 2* items (fields and/or literals) must be the same type (both numeric or alphanumeric).

- *Result Field* is not used.

- *Resulting Indicators* are not used.

- A **WHxx** statement may not be included after an **OTHER** operation.

- **WHxx** statements may be combined with **ANDxx** and **ORxx** test conditions.

Processing Logic of the **WHxx** Operation:

1. When the relational test is true, the instructions following the **WHxx** statement are processed until the next **Whxx, OTHER, ENDSL,** or **END** operation.

2. After the instruction(s) included in the **WHxx** group are executed, control passes to the instruction after the **ENDSL** (or **END**) operation. Any other **WHxx** groups will not be executed.

3. If none of the **WHxx** statements test as true, control will pass to the statement following the **ENDSL** (or **END**) operation. If an **OTHER** operation is included in the **SELEC** group, control will pass to the instruction following the **OTHER**.

4. For **WHxx** statements combined with **ANDxx** conditions, all relational tests must be true to execute the following instructions. However, for **ORxx** conditions, only one of the relational tests must be true. **ANDxx** and **ORxx** tests may be combined in an **WHxx** instruction.

Figure 6-13 Syntax and processing logic of the **WHxx** operation.

OTHER (Otherwise Select)

The **OTHER** operation may optionally be included in a **SELEC** group. If none of the previous **WHxx** conditions are true, control will pass to the first instruction after the **OTHER** statement. Figure 6-14 details the syntax and processing logic of the **OTHER** operation.

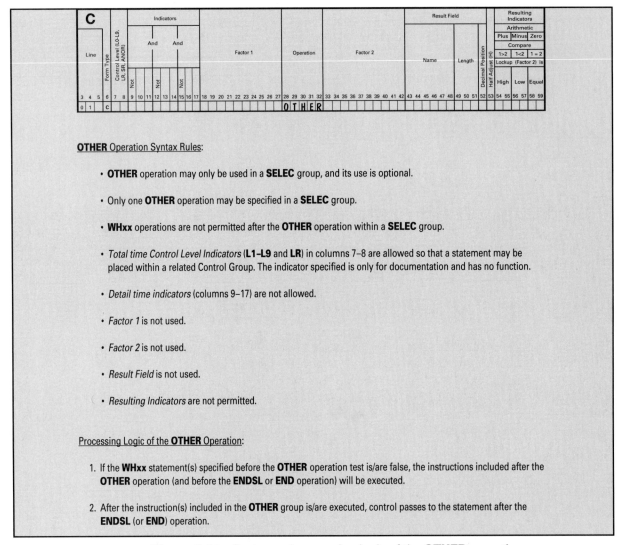

OTHER Operation Syntax Rules:

- **OTHER** operation may only be used in a **SELEC** group, and its use is optional.

- Only one **OTHER** operation may be specified in a **SELEC** group.

- **WHxx** operations are not permitted after the **OTHER** operation within a **SELEC** group.

- *Total time Control Level Indicators* (**L1–L9** and **LR**) in columns 7–8 are allowed so that a statement may be placed within a related Control Group. The indicator specified is only for documentation and has no function.

- *Detail time indicators* (columns 9–17) are not allowed.

- *Factor 1* is not used.

- *Factor 2* is not used.

- *Result Field* is not used.

- *Resulting Indicators* are not permitted.

Processing Logic of the **OTHER** Operation:

1. If the **WHxx** statement(s) specified before the **OTHER** operation test is/are false, the instructions included after the **OTHER** operation (and before the **ENDSL** or **END** operation) will be executed.

2. After the instruction(s) included in the **OTHER** group is/are executed, control passes to the statement after the **ENDSL** (or **END**) operation.

Figure 6-14   Syntax and processing logic of the **OTHER** operation.

RPG/400 Application Program Using a SELEC Group

The Weekly Payroll Report program shown in Figure 6-11 is modified in Figure 6-15 to show use of a **SELEC** group. Note that only the *nested* **IF/ELSE** statements in the original program have been replaced by a **SELEC** group, and not the *simple* **IF** statements.

A comparison of the Weekly Payroll Report program using a nested **IF/ELSE** group with the one that includes a **SELEC** group for the same instruction sequence is presented in Figure 6-16. (see page 144.)

```
SEQUENCE                                                                  IND   DO   LAST      PAGE   PROGR M
NUMBER    *...1....+....2....+....3....+....4....+....5....+....6....+....7...*  USE   NUM
                        S o u r c e   L i s t i n g
    100   * THIS PROGRAM GENERATES A WEEKLY PAYROLL REPORT FOR HOURLY EMPS
    200   *      USING SELEC/WH/OTHER GROUP
          H
    300   FEMPPAYFLIP E          K         DISK
          RECORD FORMAT(S): LIBRARY SMYERS FILE EMPPAYFL.
                    EXTERNAL FORMAT EMPPAYR RPG NAME EMPPAYR
    400   FQSYSPRT O  F     132      OF    PRINTER
A000000   INPUT  FIELDS FOR RECORD EMPPAYR FILE EMPPAYFL FORMAT EMPPAYR.
A000001                                     1    4 EMP#
A000002                                     5   24 EMPNAM
A000003                                    25   25 SHIFT
A000004                                  P 26  282HRRATE
A000005                                  P 29  310MINUTS
    500   C                   Z-ADD0        OTPAY   62    init otpay
    600   C         SHIFT     IFGT 'D'                    shift test          B001
    700   C         HRRATE    MULT 1.15     HRRATE        night rate          001
    800   C                   MOVE 'NIGHT'  SHIFTO  5     night shift         001
    900   C                   ELSE                                            X001
   1000   C                   MOVE 'DAY '   SHIFTO        day shift           001
   1100   C                   ENDIF                                           E001
   1200   *
   1300   C         MINUTS    DIV 60        HRS     20    minutes to hrs
   1400   C                   MVR           REMAIN  20    save remainder
   1500   *
   1600   * SELEC/WH/OTHER GROUP FOR REMAINDER TEST
   1700   C                   SELEC                       begin SELEC grp     B001
   1800   C         REMAIN    WHEQ 0                      test for 0          X001
   1900   C                   Z-ADDHRS      THRS    31    save hrs            001
   2000   C         REMAIN    WHLT 30                     remain < 30?        X001
   2100   C         HRS       ADD .5        THRS          add 1/2 hr          001
   2200   C                   OTHER                       remain => 30        X001
   2300   C         HRS       ADD 1         THRS          add 1 to hrs        001
   2400   C                   ENDSL                       end SELEC group     E001
   2500   *
   2600   C         THRS      MULT HRRATE   REGPAY  62    regular pay amt
   2700   *
   2800   C         THRS      IFGT 35                     hrs > 35?           B001
   2900   C         THRS      SUB 35        OTHRS   31    overtime hrs        001
   3000   C         HRRATE    DIV 2         OTRATE  42H   overtime rate       001
   3100   C         OTHRS     MULT OTRATE   OTPAY   H     ot pay              001
   3200   C                   ENDIF                       end IF              E001
   3300   *
   3400   C         REGPAY    ADD OTPAY     WEKPAY  62    reg + ot amts
   3500   C                   ADD  THRS     TOTHRS  51    accum tot hrs
   3600   C                   ADD  REGPAY   TOTREG  82    accum reg pay
   3700   C                   ADD  OTPAY    TOTOT   82    accum ot pay
   3800   C                   ADD  WEKPAY   TOTPAY  82    accum totla pay
   3900   OQSYSPRT H  301     1P
   4000   O         OR        OF
   4100   O                   UDATE Y    8
   4200   O                            64 'WEEKLY PAYROLL REPORT'
   4300   O                           105 'PAGE'
   4400   O                   PAGE  Z  110
   4500   O         H  2      1P
   4600   O         OR        OF
   4700   O                            10 'EMP #'
   4800   O                            25 'NAME'
   4900   O                            45 'SHIFT'
   5000   O                            53 'RATE'
   5100   O                            63 'HRS'
   5200   O                            76 'REG PAY'
   5300   O                            89 'OT PAY'
   5400   O                           105 'TOTAL PAY'
   5500   O         D  2      N1P
   5600   O                   EMP#      9
   5700   O                   EMPNAM   34
   5800   O                   SHIFTO   45
   5900   O                   HRRATE1  54
   6000   O                   THRS  1  64
   6100   O                   REGPAY1  77
   6200   O                   OTPAY 1  90
   6300   O                   WEKPAY1 104
   6400   O         T  1      LR
   6500   O                            53 'TOTALS'
   6600   O                   TOTHRS1  64
   6700   O                   TOTREG1  77
   6800   O                   TOTOT 1  90
   6900   O                   TOTPAY1 104
```

When a WHxx statement test is true, control is transferred to the statement following the ENDSL operation after the next WHXX, OTHER, or ENDSL statement is encountered

OTHER statement is executed if none of the WHxx statements test true

Figure 6-15 Source listing of the Weekly Payroll Report program modified with a **SELEC** group.

```
              NESTED IF/ELSE GROUP                  |            SELEC/OTHER GROUP

   ... 1 ...+... 2 ...+... 3 ...+... 4 ...+... 5 ...|   ... 1 ...... 2 ...+... 3 ...+... 4 ...+... 5 ...
   * NESTED IF/ELSE STATEMENT GROUP                 |   * SELEC/OTHER GROUP FOR REMAINDER TEST
   C        REMAIN    IFEQ 0                         |   C                  SELEC
   C                  Z-ADDHRS       THRS      31    |   C        REMAIN    WHEQ 0
   C                  ELSE                           |   C                  Z-ADDHRS       THRS      31
   C        REMAIN    IFLT 30                        |   C        REMAIN    WHLT 30
   C        HRS       ADD  .5        THRS            |   C        HRS       ADD  .5        THRS
   C                  ELSE                           |   C                  OTHER
   C        HRS       ADD  1         THRS            |   C        HRS       ADD  1         THRS
   C                  ENDIF                          |   C                  ENDSL
   C                  ENDIF                          |

              Comparison of Nested IF/ELSE Group to SELEC/OTHER Group

      1. SELEC group eliminates the need for nested IF/ELSE groups which may be confusing when three or more
   levels are specified.

      2. Multiple ENDIF (or END) operation are not required with a SELEC group - only one ENDSL (or END) opera-
   tion ends the group.
```

Figure 6-16   Comparison of nested **IF/ELSE** instructions with those in a **SELEC** group, for the Weekly Payroll Report program.

The COMP (*Compare*) Operation

In lieu of using **IFxx** or **WHxx** statements, relational testing (without branching) may be controlled by the **COMP** (*Compare*) operation. It is an unstructured operation that requires the use of indicators for **EQ, LT, GT, GE, LE,** or **NE** relational tests. Hence, the **COMP** operation has limited (if any) use in structured RPG/400 programs.

Figure 6-17 details the syntax related to the **COMP** operation.

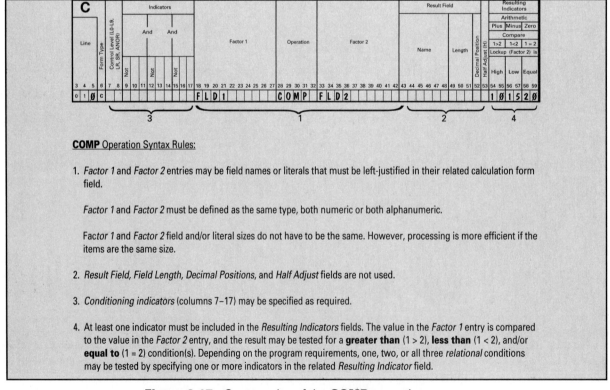

COMP Operation Syntax Rules:

1. *Factor 1* and *Factor 2* entries may be field names or literals that must be left-justified in their related calculation form field.

   Factor 1 and *Factor 2* must be defined as the same type, both numeric or both alphanumeric.

   Factor 1 and *Factor 2* field and/or literal sizes do not have to be the same. However, processing is more efficient if the items are the same size.

2. *Result Field, Field Length, Decimal Positions,* and *Half Adjust* fields are not used.

3. *Conditioning indicators* (columns 7–17) may be specified as required.

4. At least one indicator must be included in the *Resulting Indicators* fields. The value in the *Factor 1* entry is compared to the value in the *Factor 2* entry, and the result may be tested for a **greater than** (1 > 2), **less than** (1 < 2), and/or **equal to** (1 = 2) condition(s). Depending on the program requirements, one, two, or all three *relational* conditions may be tested by specifying one or more indicators in the related *Resulting Indicator* field.

Figure 6-17   Syntax rules of the **COMP** operation.

Examples of **COMP** instructions are shown in Figure 6-18. Note how the use of one or more indicators controls the relational test condition(s).

Line	Form Type	Control Level	Ind (And)	Ind (And)	Factor 1	Operation	Factor 2	Result Name	High	Low	Equal
0 1	C *				EQ TEST......						
0 2	C				FLDA	COMP	FLDG		40		
0 3	C		40		∿INSTRUCTION∿						
0 4	C										
0 5	C *				GT TEST......						
0 6	C				YTDSS	COMP	55500		30		
0 7	C			30	∿INSTRUCTION∿						
0 8	C										
0 9	C *				LT TEST......						
1 0	C				HOURS	COMP	37			29	
1 1	C			29	∿INSTRUCTION∿						
1 2	C										
1 3	C *				GE TEST......						
1 4	C				AMT	COMP	LIMIT		50		50
1 5	C		50		∿INSTRUCTION∿						
1 6	C										
1 7	C *				LE TEST......						
1 8	C				SALE	COMP	BASE			60	60
1 9	C			60	∿INSTRUCTION∿						
2 0	C										
2 1	C *				NE TEST......						
2 2	C				CODE	COMP	TCODE				70
2 3	C		N70		∿INSTRUCTION∿						
2 4	C										
2 5	C *				OR RELATIONSHIP CONTROL......						
2 6	C				FLDC	COMP	FLDE		19		18
2 7	C		18		∿INSTRUCTION∿						
2 8	C		19		∿INSTRUCTION∿						
2 9	C										
3 0	C *				AND RELATIONSHIP CONTROL......						
3 1	C				FLDX	COMP	FLDY		37		32
3 2	C		31	32	∿INSTRUCTION∿						

Processing Logic:

1. The field value (or literal) in *Factor 1* is compared to the field value (or literal) in *Factor 2*. Resulting Indicator(s) determine(s) the relational test made.

2. *Resulting Indicator(s)* turned on as the result of the relational test(s) are use to condition subsequent instructions.

3. *Conditioning* indicator(s) may be entered in any of the *detail time* Indicator fields (columns 9–17).

4. The "OFF" status of an indicator may be specified by including the letter **N** with the indicator (see line 23).

5. An **OR** relationship is controlled by specifying two or three *Resulting Indicators* in the COMP statement and conditioning subsequent instructions with the related indicator (see lines 26–28).

6. An **AND** relationship is controlled by specifying two or three *Resulting Indicators* in the COMP statement and conditioning the related instructions with the two or three indicators (i.e., indicators in columns 10–11, 13–14, and 16–17). See lines 31–32.

Figure 6-18 Examples of **COMP** statements.

To illustrate how the **COMP** operation is used, the Weekly Payroll Report program previously discussed is modified in Figure 6-19. Because *File Description* and *Output Specifications* coding are identical to the **IF** and **SELEC** example programs, only the calculations are shown.

After an examination of Figure 6-19, the following disadvantages of using the **COMP** operation in lieu of the **IF** or **SELEC** operation should be understood:

```
SEQNBR*...+... 1 ...+... 2 ...+... 3 ...+... 4 ...+... 5 ...+... 6 ...+... 7 ...
 500    C                        SETOF                       101120turn off ind.
 600    C                        Z-ADD0      OTPAY   62       init otpay
 700    *
 800    C           SHIFT        COMP 'D'                 10  shift test
 900    C  10       HRRATE       MULT 1.15   HRRATE           night rate
1000    C  10                    MOVE 'NIGHT' SHIFTO  5       output value
1100    C  N10                   MOVE 'DAY ' SHIFTO           output value
1200    *
1300    C           MINUTS       DIV  60     HRS     20       minutes to hrs
1400    C                        MVR         REMAIN  20      11save remainder
1500    *
1600    C  11       Z-ADDHRS     THRS                 31      remain 0
1700    C  N11      REMAIN       COMP 30              20  20remain not 0
1800    C  N20N11   HRS          ADD  .5     THRS             remain >0 & <30
1900    C  20       HRS          ADD  1      THRS             remain > = 30
2000    *
2100    C           THRS         MULT HRRATE REGPAY  62       regualr pay amt
2200    *
2300    C           THRS         COMP 35              20      hrs > 35?
2400    C  20       THRS         SUB  35     OTHRS   31       overtime hrs
2500    C  20       HRRATE       DIV  2      OTRATE  42H      overtime rate
2600    C  20       OTHRS        MULT OTRATE OTPAY    H       compute ot pay
2700    *
2800    C           REGPAY       ADD  OTPAY  WEKPAY  62       reg + ot amts
2900    C                        ADD  THRS   TOTHRS  51       accum tot hrs
3000    C                        ADD  REGPAY TOTREG  82       accum reg pay
3100    C                        ADD  OTPAY  TOTOT   82       accum ot pay
3200    C                        ADD  WEKPAY TOTPAY  82       accum total pay
```

Figure 6-19 Weekly Payroll Report program's calculation instructions using the **COMP** operation.

1. The use of indicators to condition statements may cause difficulty in program debugging and maintenance.

2. Instructions conditioned by one or more indicators take more time to process and utilize more of the computer's memory.

3. False conditions, specified by a Not **"ON"** condition of related indicator (e.g., **N11** and **N20**), are logically more difficult to understand than the **ELSE** alternative for an **IFxx** group or the **WHxx/OTHER** statements in a **SELEC** group.

4. The conditioning of the instruction on line 1800 with two indicators (e.g., **N20** and **N11**) specifying an **AND** relationship is confusing when compared to the **AND** or **OR** statements used in a complex **IFxx** or **WHxx** statement.

BRANCHING CONTROL

Branching may be defined as the transfer of program control to a previous or subsequent instruction not immediately following the one currently executed. Control of branching (without repetitive or iterative processing) is performed by the **GOTO/TAG** or **CABxx/TAG** operation. The syntax for the **GOTO** and **TAG** operations is detailed in Figure 6-20.

More than one **GOTO** statement may reference the same **TAG** operation name (*Factor 2* entry). However, each **TAG** statement must be specified with a <u>different name</u> (*Factor 1* entry) and relate to at least one **GOTO** statement. The program's logic will determine whether the **TAG** statement is placed before or after the related **GOTO** statement(s).

The processing features and restrictions of the **GOTO** operation are explained in Figure 6-21.

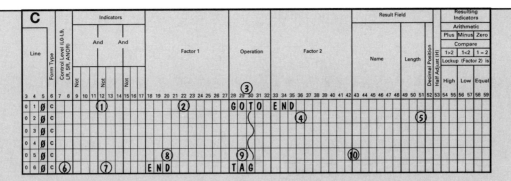

GOTO Operation Syntax Rules:

1. *Total* or *detail time* indicators may be used to condition a **GOTO** operation. If one or more indicators are specified, the instruction is referred to as a *conditional* **GOTO**. If no indicator control is included, the statement is called an *unconditional* **GOTO**.

2. *Factor 1* is not used.

3. **GOTO** operation name must be left-justified in *Operation* field.

4. *Factor 2* entry must be left-justified and a programmer-supplied name that meets RPG/400 field naming convention requirements.

5. Other fields are not used.

TAG Operation Syntax Rules:

6. *Control Level* indicators (**L0–L9** and **LR**), entered in columns 7–8, may be specified with a **TAG** statement.

7. *Detail time* indicators (columns 9–17) are not permitted.

8. *Factor 1* entry must begin in column 18 and be identical to the *Factor 2* entry of the related **GOTO** statement.

9. **TAG** operation name must be left-justified in the *Operation* field.

10. Other fields are not used.

Figure 6-20 RPG/400 syntax for the **GOTO** and **TAG** operations.

A **GOTO** operation may specify a branch:

1. To a previous or following operation.

2. From a *detail time* calculation instruction to another *detail time* calculation instruction.

3. From a *total time* calculation instruction to another *total time* calculation instruction.

4. Within an internal subroutine.

5. From an internal subroutine (not considered a good structured programming practice).

However, a **GOTO** operation may not be specified:

1. From a *detail time* calculation instruction to a *total time* calculation instruction.

2. From *total time* calculations conditioned by **L0–L9** to *total time* calculations conditioned by **LR**.

3. To an internal subroutine.

Figure 6-21 Processing features and restrictions of the **GOTO** operations.

Conditional and Unconditional GOTO Statements

Depending on the program logic, a **GOTO** statement may be *conditional* (controlled by a relational test) or *unconditional* (no test specified). The flowchart and supplemental RPG/400 coding in Figure 6-22 illustrate the processing and syntax of a *conditional* **GOTO** statement.

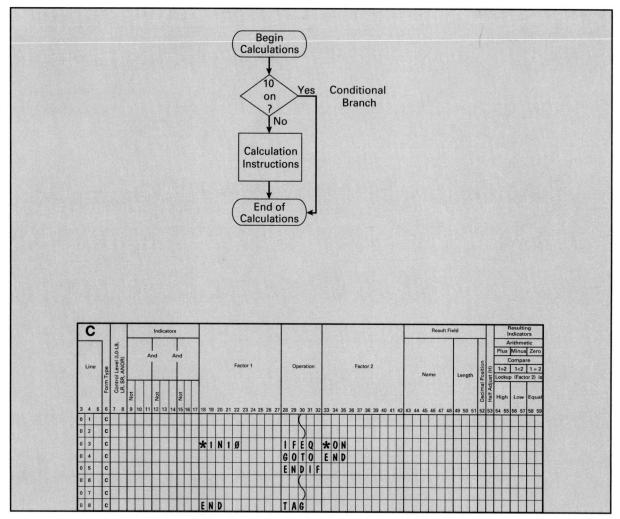

Figure 6-22   Processing logic and related RPG/400 syntax for a conditional **GOTO** statement.

One conditional and one unconditional **GOTO** statement are included in the flowchart and RPG/400 coding in Figure 6-23. Note that execution of the unconditional **GOTO** is not dependent on a relational test. When the **GOTO** statement is read, it immediately passes control to the related **TAG** operation.

The **GOTO** examples shown in Figures 6-22 and 6-23 illustrated the <u>forward</u> branching of program control. **GOTO** statements may also pass control to a previously defined **TAG** statement either to repeat some instruction(s) or to execute one or more that were skipped.

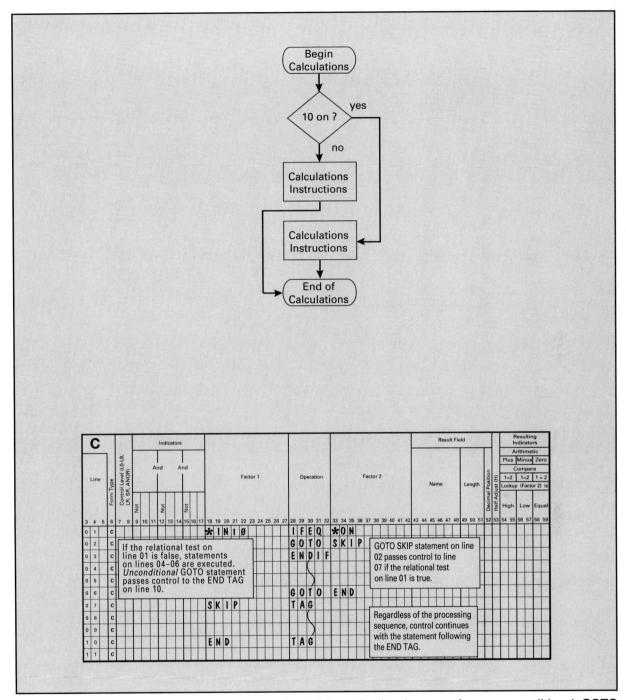

Figure 6-23 Processing logic and related syntax for an unconditional **GOTO** statement.

CABxx (Compare and Branch) Operation

The **CABxx** (*Compare and Branch*) operation includes a relational test (**EQ, GT, LT, GE, LE,** or **NE** for the **xx** entry) and the **GOTO** operation in one statement. The syntax related to the **CABxx** operation is explained in Figure 6-24.

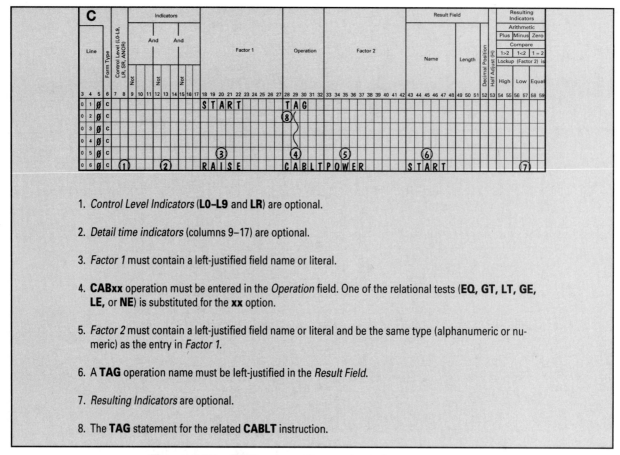

Figure 6-24 **CABxx** operation syntax rules.

1. *Control Level Indicators* (**L0–L9** and **LR**) are optional.

2. *Detail time indicators* (columns 9–17) are optional.

3. *Factor 1* must contain a left-justified field name or literal.

4. **CABxx** operation must be entered in the *Operation* field. One of the relational tests (**EQ, GT, LT, GE, LE,** or **NE**) is substituted for the **xx** option.

5. *Factor 2* must contain a left-justified field name or literal and be the same type (alphanumeric or numeric) as the entry in *Factor 1*.

6. A **TAG** operation name must be left-justified in the *Result Field*.

7. *Resulting Indicators* are optional.

8. The **TAG** statement for the related **CABLT** instruction.

RPG/400 LOOPING CONTROL (ITERATIVE PROCESSING)

Looping in a computer program is defined as the branching of program control to a preceding statement and executing the included instruction(s) one or more times. This process is required for *iterative* calculations where the result is determined after repeating the same instructions a predetermined number of times. Typical business applications that require *iterative* processing are the raising of a number to a power, compound interest computations, mortgage payment calculations, depreciation of an asset over its useful life, and so forth.

RPG/400 supports three structured operations to control looping (*iterative*) processing. Included are the **DO** (*Do*), **DOU** (*Do Until*), and **DOW** (*Do While*) operations, which are discussed individually in the following sections.

The DO (*Do*) Operation

The **DO** operation controls the processing of a group of calculation instructions (within the **DO** group) a predetermined number of times. How many times the group of instructions within the **DO** group are performed is determined by specifying a starting value (or a default value of 1), a limit value, and an index value. The syntax and processing logic of the **DO** operation are explained in Figure 6-25.

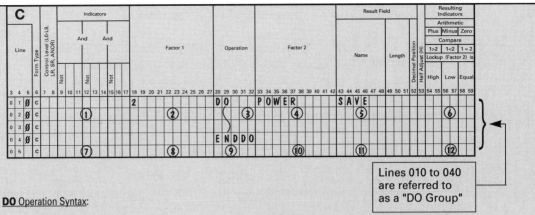

Lines 010 to 040 are referred to as a "DO Group"

DO Operation Syntax:

1. *Conditioning indicators* may be specified at *total time* (columns 7–8) and/or *detail time* (columns 9–17). If the indicator(s) specified is (are) not "**ON**," control will branch to the statement following the **ENDDO** (or **END**) operation. *Conditioning indicators* specified are tested only when the **DO** statement is initially executed. For subsequent loops, the indicator status is ignored.

2. *Factor 1* (starting index value) entry is <u>optional</u>. It may include a numeric literal, field name, array element, table name, or data structure subfield. Any of these numeric items must be defined as an <u>integer</u> (no decimal positions). The value stored in the *Factor 1* entry initializes the index (*Result Field*) to its starting value. If the *Factor 1* entry is omitted, the starting value of the index is a default value of 1.

3. The **DO** operation name must be left-justified in the *Operation* field. It controls automatic looping and exit from the **DO** group when the index value (*Result Field* item) is greater than the limit value (*Factor 2* entry).

4. *Factor 2* (limit value) entry is optional. It may include a numeric literal, field, array name, table name, or data structure subfield. Any of these numeric entries must be defined as an integer. The value stored in the *Factor 2* item specifies the number of times the loop will be executed. If this entry is omitted, the limit value is 1. Note that the limit value must be <u>equal to or greater than</u> the starting value in *Factor 1* (when specified).

5. *Result Field* entry is optional. This entry may be a numeric literal, field, array element, table name, or a data structure subfield. When specified, it defines the index (counter) value, which is automatically incremented by 1, or by the value included in *Factor 2* of the related **ENDDO** (or **END**) statement. If this entry is omitted, the RPG/400 compiler will supply an index.

6. *Resulting Indicators* are not permitted.

END Operation:

7. Optional *conditioning indicators* may be assigned to an **ENDDO** (or **END**) statement which determine if the looping process is to continue. If an indicator is assigned and it is ON, control will pass to the **DO** statement. However, if the indicator is not ON, control will pass to the first executable instruction following the **ENDDO** (or **END**) operation.

8. *Factor 1* is not used.

9. **ENDDO** (or **END**) operation name must be entered left-justified in the *Operation* field.

10. By default, the index will be automatically incremented by 1. It may be incremented with some other value by specifying a numeric literal, field, array element, table name, or data structure subfield in *Factor 2*.

11. *Result Field* is not used.

12. *Resulting Indicators* are not permitted.

Processing Logic:

1. The **DO** operation begins execution by moving the value from *Factor 1* entry (when specified to the index item (*Result Field*). If a *Factor 1* entry is not specified, the index is initialized to 1.

2. When the index value (*Result Field* item if specified is greater than the limit value (*Factor 2* item), control branches to the first statement following the related **ENDDO** (or **END**) operation.

Figure 6-25 **DO** operation syntax and processing logic.

A program example that raises numbers stored in the records of a physical file to a power is illustrated in Figure 6-26. Note that the *index* **RAISE** was initialized to a value of **2** because the first pass through the **DO** group raised the number to the second power. The report generated by the program is also included at the bottom of Figure 6-26.

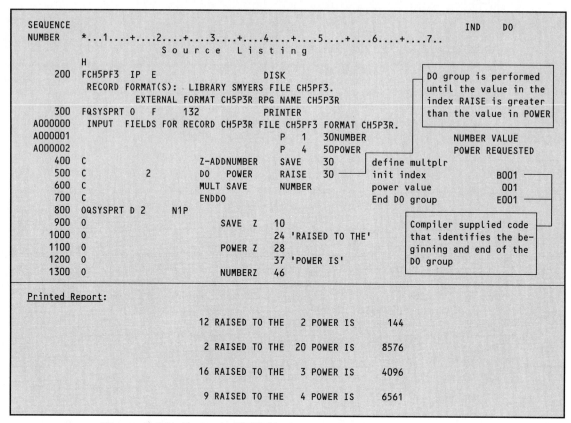

Figure 6-26   Example RPG/400 program that raises a number to a power using **DO** operation control.

The DOUxx (Do Until) Operation

The **DOUxx** operation is another structured RPG/400 instruction that controls *iterative* processing. This operation differs, however, from the **DO** operation in that it requires a *programmer-supplied* counter to control exit from the looping sequence. The syntax and processing logic related to the **DOUxx** operation are detailed in Figure 6-27.

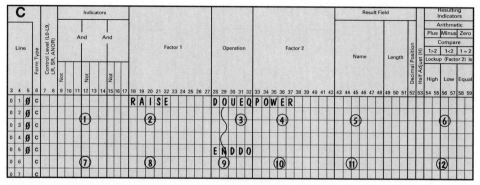

Figure 6-27   **DOUxx** operation syntax and processing logic.

DOUxx Operation Syntax:

1. *Conditioning indicators* may be specified at *total time* (columns 7–8) and/or *detail time*. If the indicator(s) specified is (are) not "ON," control will branch to the statement following the **ENDDO** operation. The status of the indicator(s) is tested every time the **DOUxx** statement is executed.

2. A left-justified *Factor 1* entry is required. It may include a literal, field name, array element, table name, or data structure subfield. The entries in *Factor 1* and *Factor 2* must follow the rules for relational tests in that both must be the same type (numeric or alphanumeric).

3. **DOUxx** operation name must be entered in the *Operation* field. The **xx** relational tests that may be specified in a **DOUxx** statement are **EQ, GT, LT, GE, LE**, and **NE**. Complex tests may be specified in an **OR** or **AND** relationship with the **DOUxx** statement. Note that the **xx** relational test is <u>not</u> made at the **DOUxx** statement, but at the related **ENDDO** (or **END**) operation.

4. A left-justified *Factor 2* entry is required. It may include a literal, field name, array element, table name, or data structure subfield. The entry must be the same type (numeric or alphanumeric) as the *Factor 1* item.

5. The *Result Field* is not used.

6. *Resulting Indicators* are not permitted.

ENDDO (or **END**) Operation:

7. Optional *conditioning indicator(s)* may be assigned to the **ENDDO** (or **END**) operation, which determines if the looping process is to continue. If an indicator is assigned and it is "ON," control will loop back to the **DOUxx** statement. However, if the indicator is <u>not</u> "ON," control will branch to the first executable instructions following the **ENDDO** (or **END**) operation.

8. *Factor 1* is not used.

9. A required **ENDDO** (or **END**) operation marks the end of the **DOUxx** group. The **xx** relational test is made at this statement and not at the **DOUxx** instruction. This processing logic supports the feature that the **DOUxx** group is executed at least once before the relational test is made.

10, 11, 12. *Factor 2, Result Field,* and *Resulting Indicators* are not used.

Processing Logic:

1. The **DOUxx** operation executes the instruction(s) within the group at least once. Subsequent looping depends on the status of the relational test specified in the **DOUxx** statement.

2. Unlike the **DO** operation, a **DOUxx** statement <u>does not</u> include an automatic counter (index). Looping must be controlled by a <u>programmer-supplied</u> counter instruction within the **DOUxx** group.

3. When the condition (**xx**) specified in the **DOUxx** statement, which is tested at the **ENDDO** or (**END**) operation, is true, control will pass to the next executable statement following the related **ENDDO** (or **END**) operation.

Figure 6-27 DOUxx operation syntax and processing logic. (Continued)

The previously discussed application program that raises a number to a power is modified in Figure 6-28 to support the **DOUxx** operation. Note that the relational test is made at the **ENDDO** operation and <u>not</u> at the DOUEQ instruction. Consequently, the **DOUEQ** group will be processed at <u>least once</u>.

The DOWxx (Do While) Operation

The **DOWxx** operation differs from **DOUxx** in that the relational test (e.g., **EQ, GT, LT, GE, LE,** or **NE**) is made at the **DOWxx** statement and not at the related **ENDDO** operation. Consequently, the **DOWxx** group is performed only if the test (**xx**) condition is initially true, and <u>not</u> at least once as with the **DOUxx** operation.

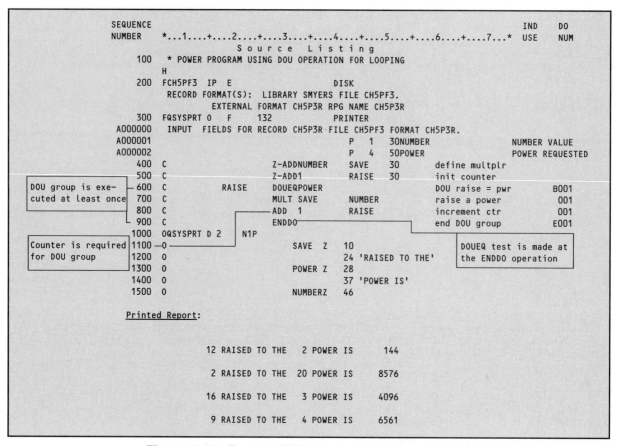

```
                                                                              IND   DO
          SEQUENCE
          NUMBER    *...1....+....2....+....3....+....4....+....5....+....6....+....7...*  USE  NUM
                                          S o u r c e   L i s t i n g
            100     * POWER PROGRAM USING DOU OPERATION FOR LOOPING
                    H
            200     FCH5PF3  IP E                        DISK
                    RECORD FORMAT(S): LIBRARY SMYERS FILE CH5PF3.
                                 EXTERNAL FORMAT CH5P3R RPG NAME CH5P3R
            300     FQSYSPRT O   F   132              PRINTER
          A000000   INPUT  FIELDS FOR RECORD CH5P3R FILE CH5PF3 FORMAT CH5P3R.
          A000001                                       P   1   30NUMBER          NUMBER VALUE
          A000002                                       P   4   50POWER           POWER REQUESTED
            400     C                  Z-ADDNUMBER   SAVE      30      define multplr
            500     C                  Z-ADD1        RAISE     30      init counter
            600     C        RAISE     DOUEQPOWER                      DOU raise = pwr    B001
            700     C                  MULT SAVE     NUMBER            raise a power      001
            800     C                  ADD  1        RAISE             increment ctr      001
            900     C                  ENDDO                          end DOU group      E001
            1000    OQSYSPRT D 2     N1P
            1100    O                              SAVE Z  10
            1200    O                                      24 'RAISED TO THE'
            1300    O                              POWER Z  28
            1400    O                                      37 'POWER IS'
            1500    O                              NUMBERZ  46
```

DOU group is executed at least once — 600 to 900

Counter is required for DOU group — 1000 to 1100

DOUEQ test is made at the ENDDO operation

Printed Report:

```
          12 RAISED TO THE   2 POWER IS      144

           2 RAISED TO THE  20 POWER IS     8576

          16 RAISED TO THE   3 POWER IS     4096

           9 RAISED TO THE   4 POWER IS     6561
```

Figure 6-28 Example RPG/400 program that raises a number to a power using **DOUxx** operation control.

Similar to the **DOUxx** operation, a *programmer-supplied* counter must be included within the group to control exit from the looping sequence. Figure 6-29 details the syntax and processing logic of the **DOWxx** operation.

A compile listing of the example program that raises a number to a power, modified with the **DOWxx** operation, is shown in Figure 6-30.

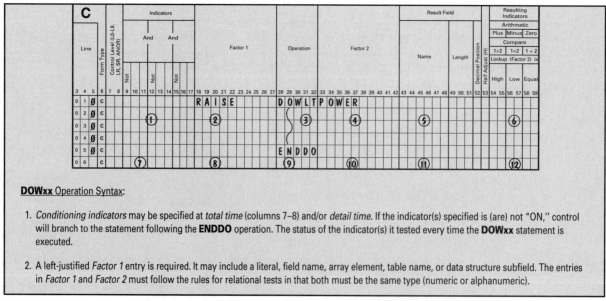

DOWxx Operation Syntax:

1. *Conditioning indicators* may be specified at *total time* (columns 7–8) and/or *detail time*. If the indicator(s) specified is (are) not "ON," control will branch to the statement following the **ENDDO** operation. The status of the indicator(s) it tested every time the **DOWxx** statement is executed.

2. A left-justified *Factor 1* entry is required. It may include a literal, field name, array element, table name, or data structure subfield. The entries in *Factor 1* and *Factor 2* must follow the rules for relational tests in that both must be the same type (numeric or alphanumeric).

Figure 6-29 **DOWxx** operation syntax and processing logic.

3. **DOWxx** operation name must be entered in the *Operation* field. The **xx** relational tests that may be specified in a **DOWxx** statement are **EQ**, **GT**, **LT**, **GE**, **LE**, and **NE**. <u>Complex</u> tests may be specified in an **OR** or **AND** relationship with the **DOWxx** statement. Note that the **xx** relational test is made at the **DOWxx** statement.

4. A left-justified *Factor 2* entry is required. It may include a literal, field name, array element, table name, or data structure subfield. The entry must be the same type (numeric or alphanumeric) as the *Factor 1* item.

5. The *Result Field* is not used.

6. *Resulting Indicators* are not permitted.

<u>**ENDDO** (or **END**) Operation</u>:

7. Optional *conditioning indicator(s)* may be assigned to the **ENDDO** (or **END**) operation, which determines if the looping process is to continue. If an indicator is assigned and it is "ON," control will loop back to the **DOWxx** statement. However, if the indicator is <u>not</u> "ON," control will branch to the first executable instructions following the **ENDDO** (or **END**) operation.

8. *Factor 1* is not used.

9. A required **ENDDO** (or **END**) operation marks the end of the **DOWxx** group.

10, 11, 12. *Factor 2, Result Field,* and *Resulting Indicators* are not used.

<u>Processing Logic</u>:

1. The **DOWxx** operation executes the isntruction(s) within the group if the relational test is initially true.

2. Unlike the **DO** operation, a **DOWxx** statement <u>does not</u> include an automatic counter (index). Looping must be controlled by a programmer-supplied counter instruction within the **DOWxx** group.

3. When the condition (**xx**) specified in the **DOWxx** statement, which is tested at the **DOWxx** statement, is true, control will branch to the next executable statement following the related **ENDDO** (or **END**) operation.

Figure 6-29 **DOWxx** operation syntax and processing logic. (Continued)

```
           SEQUENCE                                                          IND    DO
           NUMBER   *...1....+....2....+....3....+....4....+....5....+....6....+....7...*  USE   NUM
                            S o u r c e   L i s t i n g
               100   * POWER PROGRAM USING DOW OPERATION FOR LOOPING
                     H
               200   FCH5PF3  IP E                   DISK
                       RECORD FORMAT(S): LIBRARY SMYERS FILE CH5PF3.
                              EXTERNAL FORMAT CH5P3R RPG NAME CH5P3R
               300   FQSYSPRT O  F     132           PRINTER
           A000000   INPUT  FIELDS FOR RECORD CH5P3R FILE CH5PF3 FORMAT CH5P3R.
           A000001                                P    1   30NUMBER          NUMBER VALUE
           A000002                                P    4   50POWER           POWER REQUESTED
               400   C            Z-ADDNUMBER   SAVE    30         define multplr
               500   C            Z-ADD1        RAISE   30         init counter
               600   C    RAISE   DOWLTPOWER                       DOW = power ?     B001
               700   C            MULT SAVE     NUMBER             raise a power     001
               800   C            ADD  1        RAISE              increment ctr     001
               900   C            ENDDO                           end DOW group     E001
              1000   OQSYSPRT D 2      N1P
              1100   O                       SAVE  Z  10
              1200   O                                24 'RAISED TO THE'
              1300   O                       POWER Z  28
              1400   O                                37 'POWER IS'
              1500   O                       NUMBERZ  46
```

Test is made at the DOWLT statement

Counter is required for DOW group

ENDDO operation returns control back to the DOW statement where the relational test is made.

<u>Printed Report</u>:

```
          12 RAISED TO THE  2 POWER IS     144

           2 RAISED TO THE 20 POWER IS    8576

          16 RAISED TO THE  3 POWER IS    4096

           9 RAISED TO THE  4 POWER IS    6561
```

Figure 6-30 Example RPG/400 program that raises a number to a power using the **DOWxx** operation.

APPLICATION PROGRAM: COMPOUND INTEREST COMPUTATION

To reinforce the use of the **DO** operation, we present an application program that computes the *daily compound interest of a principal amount.* When interest is computed on the sum of the principal and accumulated interest, it is called *compound interest.* The mathematics of compound interest are illustrated in Figure 6-31.

```
Problem:

Calculate the amount of interest produced by $100 with interest at 6% compounded annually for four years.

Solution:

    $100  ×  .06  =  $     6.00   First year's interest
                     +  100.00    Principal
                        106.00    Balance end of the first year
     106  ×  .06  =  +     6.36   Second year's interest
                        112.36    Balance end of the second year
  112 .36  ×  .06  =  +     6.74   Third year's interest
                        119.10    Balance end of the third year
  119. 10  ×  .06  =  +     7.15   Fourth year's interest
                        126.25    Balance end of the fourth year
                     −  100.00    Principal
                     $   26.25    Amount of compound interest
```

Figure 6-31   Mathematics of compound interest.

Documentation

The specifications included in Figure 6-32 summarize the processing requirements for this example application program.

```
                        PROGRAM SPECIFICATIONS                    Page 1 of 1

Program Name: Compound Interest Report    Program-ID: CDINT      Written by: SM

Purpose:  Print a CD Analysis Report                            Approved by: CM

Input files:  CDACCTS       _____    _____    _____

Output files: QSYSPRT       _____    _____    _____

Processing Requirements:

Write an RPG/400 program to calculate the compound interest earned on depositor's certificate of deposits and
generate the report detailed in the supplemental printer spacing chart.

Input to the program:

The externally defined physical file, CDACCTS, contains the data for certificate of depositor clients in the format
shown in the attached record layout form.
```

Figure 6-32   Specifications for the Compound Interest Report program using the **DO** operation.

Processing:

Read the physical file in arrival sequence until end of file. For every record processed performs the following:

Write the calculations for the following compound interest formula:

$a = (i + 1)^n$ Where: a = Compound amount of \$1
                                                        i = Annual interest rate (must be divided by 365 or 366 for daily rate)
                                                        n = Number of interest periods

Step 1:   Compute the daily rate by dividing the annual rate by 365 (or 366).

Step 2:   Add 1 to the daily rate computed in Step 1.

Step 3:   Save the result from Step 2 by moving it into another field.

Step 4:   Increment a counter and compare it with the number of interest periods input. If the value in the
              counter is <u>not greater than n</u>, multiply the result field from Step 3 by the result field computed in Step 2
              and store in the Step 3 field. Repeat the iterative process until the value in the counter is equal to the
              value of n.

Step 5:   After exit from the **DO** loop, multiply the principal (input) by the compound amount of the factor
              computed in Step 4 to determine the compound amount of the related principal.

Step 6:   Subtract the principal from the compound amount (Step 5) to determine the compound interest
              earned.

Step 7:   Multiply the daily and annual interest rates by 100 for the printing of the percent formats.

Output:

A printer spacing chart, which shows the format of the Certificate of Deposit Analysis report, is attached.

Figure 6-32   Specifications for the Compound Interest Report program using the
DO operation. (Continued)

The system flowchart in Figure 6-33 identifies the input and output files processed by the compound interest report.

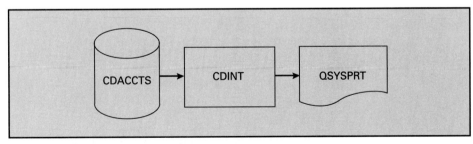

Figure 6-33   System flowchart for the Compound Interest Report program.

The format of the records in the externally defined physical file input to the program and a listing of the stored data are shown in Figure 6-34.

```
                    PHYSICAL FILE DESCRIPTION

        SYSTEM: AS/400                        DATE: Yours
        FILE NAME: Yours                      REV NO: 0
        RECORD NAME: Yours                    KEY LENGTH: None
        SEQUENCE: Non-keyed                   RECORD SIZE: 17

                         FIELD DEFINITIONS

        FIELD    FIELD NAME   SIZE   TYPE     POSITION      COMMENTS
        NO                                   FROM    TO

         1       ACCT#         4     C        1       4
         2       PRINPL        8     P        5       9    2 decimals
         3       IRATE         5     P       10      12    5 decimals
         4       YRDAYS        3     P       13      14    0 decimals
         5       N             5     P       15      17    0 decimals
```

Physical File Data:

```
        Account                  Annual    Interest Periods   Total
        Number     Principal      Rate       Per Annum       Periods

         1000      00100000      10000          365           0365
         2000      00100000      10000          365           0180
         3000      00100000      06500          365           0365
         4000      00100000      06500          365           0180
```

Figure 6-34   Physical file's record format and data listing.

A printer spacing chart that details the report format is presented in Figure 6-35 with the output generated by the program.

```
10/01/95                  CERTIFICATE OF DEPOSIT ANALYSIS               PAGE    1
                           INTEREST COMPOUNDED DAILY


                      ANNUAL      DAILY      INTEREST    COMPOUND    COMPOUND
        ACT NO  PRINCIPAL  RATE    RATE       DAYS       AMOUNT      INTEREST

         1000   1,000.00  10.000%  .0273972%    365     1,105.16     105.16

         2000   1,000.00   7.000%  .0191780%    180     1,035.12      35.12

         3000   1,000.00   4.000%  .0109589%    365     1,040.81      40.81

         4000   1,000.00   2.500%  .0068493%    180     1,012.40      12.40
```

Figure 6-35   Report format and output generated by the Compound Interest Report program.

Compile Listing of the Compound Interest Report Program

A compile listing of the Compound Interest Report program that uses the **DO** operation for iterative control is shown in Figure 6-36.

```
SEQUENCE                                                                          IND   DO
NUMBER    *...1....+....2....+....3....+....4....+....5....+....6....+....7...*    USE   NUM
                            S o u r c e   L i s t i n g
 100    * COMPOUND INTEREST PROGRAM - USING THE DO OPERATION
        H
 200    FCDS     IP E        K        DISK
          RECORD FORMAT(S): LIBRARY SMYERS FILE CDS.
                   EXTERNAL FORMAT CDSR RPG NAME CDSR
 300    FQSYSPRT O  F      132    OF     PRINTER
A000000   INPUT  FIELDS FOR RECORD CDSR FILE CDS FORMAT CDSR.
A000001                                        1    4 ACCT#
A000002    ┌─────────────────────────────┐  P  5   92PRINPL
A000003    │Because first pass through the│  P 10  125IRATE
A000004    │loop raises HOLD to the second│  P 13  140YRDAYS
A000005    │power, CTR (index) is set to 2│  P 15  170N
 400    C  │         IRATE    DIV  YRDAYS│ DARATE  99       daily int rate
 500    C  │         DARATE   ADD  1     │ FACTOR 109       (1 + I)
 600    C  │                  Z-ADDFACTOR│ HOLD   109       save factor
 700    C  └─2              DO  N         CTR      60       > ctr ?            B001
 800    C                   MULT FACTOR   HOLD              X multiplier        001
 900    C                   ENDDO                           end DO group       E001
1000    C         PRINPL    MULT HOLD     CMPAMT  82H       compound amt
1100    C         CMPAMT    SUB  PRINPL   CMPINT  82        compound intrst
1200    C         DARATE    MULT 100      DAYPCT  87        daily percent
1300    C         IRATE     MULT 100      ANPCT   53        annual percent
1400    OQSYSPRT H 101    1P
1500    O        OR        OF
1600    O                         UDATE Y    8
1700    O                                   49 'CERTIFICATE OF DEPOSIT'
1800    O                                   58 'ANALYSIS'
1900    O                                   77 'PAGE'
2000    O                         PAGE  Z  82
2100    O        H 1      1P
2200    O        OR        OF
2300    O                                   48 'INTEREST COMPOUNDED'
2400    O                                   54 'DAILY'
2500    O        H 1      1P
2600    O        OR        OF
2700    O                                   42 'ANNUAL      DAILY'
2800    O                                   67 'INTEREST    COMPOUND'
2900    O                                   79 'COMPOUND'
3000    O        H 2      1P
3100    O        OR        OF
3200    O                                   20 'ACT NO   PRINCIPAL'
3300    O                                   41 'RATE        RATE'
3400    O                                   66 ' DAYS      AMOUNT'
3500    O                                   79 'INTEREST'
3600    O        D 2      N1P
3700    O                         ACCT#      7
3800    O                         PRINPL1   20
3900    O                         ANPCT     31 'O .    %'
4000    O                         DAYPCT    43 'O.        %'
4100    O                         N     Z   52
4200    O                         CMPAMT1   67
4300    O                         CMPINT1   79
```

Figure 6-36   Compile listing of the Compound Interest Report program.

The processing logic for the calculations included in the Compound Interest Report program is detailed in the flowchart in Figure 6-37. Also, the related instructions are included at the bottom of Figure 6-37.

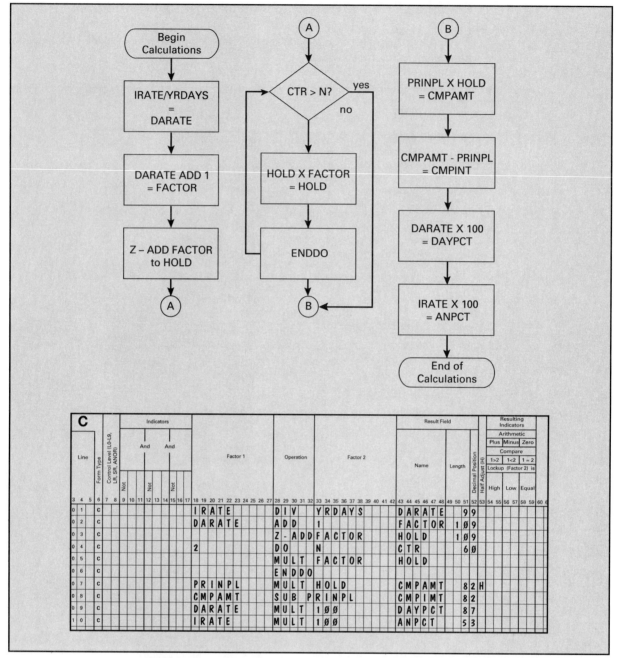

Figure 6-37   Processing logic flowchart and related calculations for the Compound Interest Report program.

Compound Interest Report Program Modified with DOUxx Operation Processing

The calculations for the Compound Interest Report program are modified in Figure 6-38 to support the **DOUxx** operation. Because *File Description* and *Output Specifications* instructions are identical to the **DO** operation example, they have been omitted.

Compound Interest Report Program Modified with DOWxx Operation Processing

Another version of the Compound Interest Report program that uses the **DOWxx** operation is shown in Figure 6-39. Again, because the *File Description* and *Output*

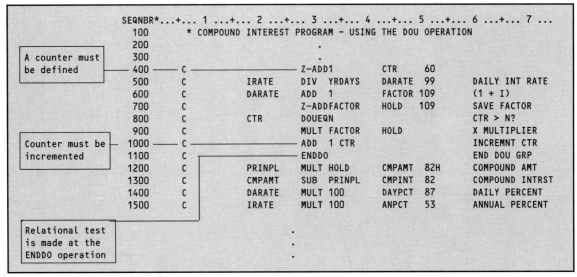

Figure 6-38 Calculations for the Compound Interest Report program modified for **DOUxx** operation processing.

Specifications coding are identical to the original **DO** operation program, only the calculations are presented.

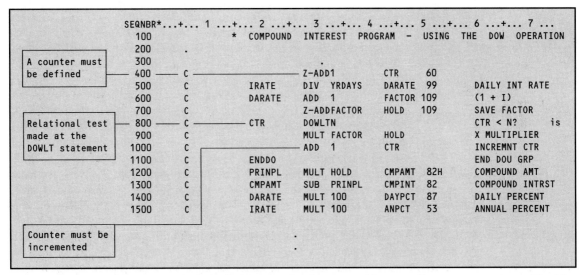

Figure 6-39 Calculations for the Compound Interest Report program modified for **DOWxx** operation processing.

Additional Structured Operations

The **LEAVE** (*Leave a DO Group*) and **ITER** (*Iterate*) operations support additional control within a **DO, DOUxx,** or **DOWxx** group. When a **LEAVE** operation is executed within any of the "Do Groups," control is transferred to the statement <u>following</u> the related **ENDDO** (or **END**) operation. The **ITER** operation passes control <u>to</u> the related **ENDDO** (or **END**) statement and causes the next iteration of the loop to be executed. Figure 6-40 (on page 162) illustrates the use of the **LEAVE** and **ITER** operations. Other than the *Operation* and *conditioning indicator* fields, no other entries are supported for either operation.

```
SEQNBR*...+... 1 ...+... 2 ...+... 3 ...+... 4 ...+... 5 ...+... 6 ...+... 7 ...
  100      * When indicator 04 is on, the ITER operation transfers control to
  200      * the ENDDO operation and the next iteration of the DOWEQ group is
  300      * performed.
  400      * When indicator 05 is on, the LEAVE operation causes an exit from
  500      * the loop by transferring control to the statement following the
  600      * related ENDDO operation.
  700      *
  800    C           *IN03      DOWEQ*OFF
  900    C                       .
 1000    C                       .
 1100    C           *IN04      IFEQ *ON
 1200    C                       ─ITER
 1300    C    ┌──────────────┐  ENDIF
 1400    C    │Control is trans-│  .
 1500    C    │ferred to ENDDO│  .
 1600    C    └──────────────┘  .
 1600    C           *IN05      IFEQ *ON
 1700    C                       LEAVE ────  ┌──────────────────────┐
 1800    C                       ENDIF        │Control is transferred to│
 1900    C                       .            │statement after the ENDDO │
 2000    C                  ──── ENDDO        └──────────────────────┘
 2100    C                       .
```

Figure 6-40   Examples of the **LEAVE** and **ITER** operations.

SUMMARY

The structured RPG/400 operations discussed in this chapter include **IFxx** (*If Then*), **ELSE** (*Else Do*), **ENDIF** (*End If Group*), **SELEC** (*Begin a Select Group*), **ENDSL** (*End Select Group*), **WHxx** (*When True Then Select*), **OTHER** (*Otherwise Select*), **DO** (*Do*), **DOUxx** (*Do Until*), **DOWxx** (*Do While*), and **ENDDO** (*End Do Group*). Any of the special "End" operations (e.g., **ENDDO, ENDIF,** and **ENDSL**) may be substituted with the **END** statement. For any of the **IFxx, DO, DOUxx, DOWxx,** or **SELEC** groups, a related "End" operation must be specified.

An **EQ, GT, LT, GE, LE,** or **NE** *relational* test (the **xx** entry) must be included with the **IFxx, WHxx, DOUxx,** or **DOWxx** operations. The status of the test determines the subsequent processing sequence. Any of the group operations (**IFxx, WHxx, DOUxx,** and **DOWxx**) may be coded as complex statements using an **AND** and/or **OR** relationship(s).

Iterative processing is controlled by the structured operations **DO, DOUxx,** and **DOWxx.** The **DO** operation supports an index (either programmer- or system-defined) that is automatically incremented for every pass through the looping sequence. On the other hand, the **DOUxx** and **DOWxx** operations require a programmer-defined counter that must be incremented by an instruction with the group.

The **DOUxx** operation makes the relational test at the related **ENDDO** (or **END**) operation. Consequently the **DOUxx** group will always be executed at least once. The **DOWxx** operation performs the relational test at the **DOWxx** statement, and instructions within the group are executed only if the specified test is true.

In lieu of the **IFxx** or **WHxx** operations, the **COMP** (*Compare*) statement may be used. Because it requires *Resulting Indicators* and the conditioning of one or more subsequent statements, it is not classified as a structured operation. Hence, its use should be limited or even avoided in RPG/400 programs.

Branching is the passing of program control to a statement other than the one following the one currently being processed. Depending on the program logic, control may be passed forward or backward.

Branching may be performed by the **GOTO** and **CABxx** operations. Both require a related **TAG** statement to identify the label or entry point for the branch. **GOTO** operations conditioned by an indicator or controlled by a relational test in a structured group are classified as *conditional*. Those that are not logically controlled are referred to as *unconditional*.

The **CABxx** operation combines the functions of the **COMP** and **GOTO** operations into one statement. Its primary advantage is that it eliminates the need for the *Resulting Indicators* required for the **COMP** operation and any <u>conditional</u> indicators commonly used with **GOTO** statements.

ITER and **LEAVE** operations may be included in **DO, DOUxx,** or **DOWxx** groups to transfer control. The **ITER** operation transfers control to the related **ENDDO** operation, and the iteration continues. The **LEAVE** operation causes control to exit from the "Do Group" by branching to the first statement following the related **ENDDO.**

QUESTIONS

6-1. Name ten RPG/400 structured operations. What programming advantages do they offer?

6-2. Explain the function of the **IFxx** and **ELSE** operations.

6-3. What variables may be specified in **xx** entry of the **IFxx** operation?

6-4. May an **IFxx** operation be specified without a related **ELSE** statement? May an **ELSE** operation be specified without a related **IFxx** statement?

6-5. What operation flags the end of an **IF** or **IF/ELSE** group?

Examine the following coding and answer Questions 6-6 to 6-9:

```
... ... 1 ... ... 2 ...  ... 3 ... ... 4 ... ... 5

02010C          SEX       IFEQ 'F'
02020C                    ADD  1         FEMALE
02030C                    ELSE
02040C                    ADD 1          MALE
02050C                    ENDIF
```

6-6. When the test on line 02010 is true, what instructions are executed?

6-7. When the test on line 02010 is false, what instructions are executed?

6-8. What is the function of the **ENDIF** statement? Is it required when the **IF** operation is specified without a related **ELSE** statement?

6-9. Name the structure of the **IF/ELSE** statement shown in the foregoing example.

6-10. Name any syntax restrictions related to the *Factor 1* and *Factor 2* entries of an **IF** statement.

6-11. In addition to the operation name, what other entries may be included with an **ELSE** statement?

Examine the following coding and answer Questions 6-12 to 6-16:

```
... ... 1 ... ... 2 ...  ... 3 ... ... 4 ... ... 5

02010C          SEX       IFEQ 'F'
02020C          AGE       ANDLE21
02030C                    ADD  1         GROUP1
02040C                    ELSE
02050C                    ADD 1          GROUP2
02060C                    ENDIF
02070C                     .
```

6-12. When the relational tests on lines 02010 and 02020 are true, which instructions are executed?

6-13. When the test on line 02010 is true and the test on line 02020 is false, which instructions are executed?

6-14. When the test on line 02010 is false and the test on line 02020 is true, which instructions are executed?

6-15. Under what test conditions will the instructions on lines 02040 and 02050 be executed?

6-16. When is the instruction on line 02070 executed?

Examine the following coding and answer Questions 6-17 to 6-21:

```
... ... 1 ... ... 2 ...  ... 3 ... ... 4 ... ... 5

02010C           CODE      IFEQ 'T'
02020C           CODE      OREQ 'X'
02030C                     ADD  1          COUNT1
02040C                     ELSE
02050C                     ADD 1           COUNT2
02060C                     ENDIF
02070C                          .
```

6-17. When the relational tests on lines 02010 and 02020 are true, which instructions are executed?

6-18. When the test on line 02010 is true and the test on line 02020 is false, which instructions are executed?

6-19. When the test on line 02010 is false and the test on line 02020 is true, which instructions are executed?

6-20. Under what test conditions will the instructions on lines 02040 and 02050 be executed?

6-21. When is the instruction on line 02070 executed?

6-22. Name the RPG/400 structured operations that support iterative processing. Identify the one that does not require a programmer-supplied counter for loop control.

Examine the following coding and answer Questions 6-23 to 6-27:

```
... ... 1 ... ... 2 ...  ... 3 ... ... 4 ... ... 5

02010C           2         DO   INTPER    TIMES
02020C                          .
02030C                          .
02040C                     ENDDO2
02050C                          .
```

6-23. Explain the function of the *Factor 1* entry (numeric literal 2).

6-24. What is the function of the *Factor 2* entry (INTPER)?

6-25. Explain the function of the *Result Field* entry (TIMES).

6-26. What is the function of the **ENDDO** operation and the numeric literal specified in *Factor 2?*

6-27. Under what conditions will an exit occur from the **DO** group?

6-28. Are any relational tests included with the **DO** operation?

6-29. How does the processing for the **DOU** (*Do Until*) operation differ from the **DO** operation?

Examine the following coding and answer Questions 6-30 to 6-32:

```
... ... 1 ... ... 2 ...  ... 3 ... ... 4 ... ... 5

02010C           COUNT     DOUEQPERIDS
02020C                          .
02030C                          .
02040C                     ENDDO
02050C                          .
```

6-30. If the value in COUNT is equal to the value in PERIDS, when the **DOUEQ** statement is first tested, where does program control go?

6-31. In which statement is the **xx (EQ)** relational test made?

6-32. How is exit from the **DOUEQ** group controlled?

6-33. How does the processing logic for a **DOWxx** operation differ from a **DOUxx** operation?

Examine the following coding and answer Questions 6-34 to 6-36:

```
... ... 1 ... ... 2 ...   ... 3 ... ... 4 ... ... 5

02010C              COUNT       DOWEQPERIDS
02020C                          .
02030C                          .
02040C                          ENDDO
02050C                          .
```

6-34. If the value in COUNT is equal to the value in PERIDS the first time the **DOWEQ** statement is tested, what statement is tested and what statement will be executed next?

6-35. In which statement is the **xx (EQ)** relational test made?

6-36. How is exit from the **DOWEQ** group controlled?

6-37. What operations are included in a **SELEC** group? Which are required?

6-38. In a **SELEC** group, which operation does relational testing?

Examine the following coding and answer Questions 6-39 to 6-43:

```
... ... 1 ... ... 2 ...   ... 3 ... ... 4 ... ... 5

02010C                          SELEC
02020C              STATUS      WHEQ 'FT'
02030C                          .
02040C                          .
02050C              STATUS      WHEQ 'PT'
02060C                          .
02070C                          .
02080C                          OTHER
02090C                          .
02100C                          .
02110C                          ENDSL
```

6-39. When the relational test on line 02020 is true, which instructions are executed?

6-40. When the relational test on line 02020 is false, which instructions(s) is/are executed?

6-41. When the relational test on line 02050 is true, which instruction(s) is/are executed?

6-42. When the relational test on line 02050 is false, which instruction(s) is/are executed?

6-43. If all of the **WHxx** tests are false, which instruction(s) is/are executed?

6-44. Refer to a *Calculation Specifications* and identify the fields that are used with the **COMP** operation.

6-45. What relational tests may be made in a **COMP** statement?

6-46. What is the function of the **GOTO** operation?

6-47. What fields are used with the **GOTO** operation?

6-48. What is a *conditional* **GOTO** statement? An *unconditional* **GOTO** statement?

6-49. What is the function of the **TAG** operation?

6-50. What operation(s) does the **CABxx** operation replace?

6-51. Refer to a *Calculation Specifications* and identify the fields used with the **CABxx** operation.

6-52. What is the function of the **ITER** and **LEAVE** operations?

PROGRAMMING ASSIGNMENTS

For each of the following programming assignments, a physical file must have been created and loaded with the related data records. Your instructor will inform you as to whether you have to create the physical file and load it or if it has been prepared for the assignment.

Programming Assignment 6-1:
SALESMAN SALARY/COMMISSION REPORT

From the following documentation, write an RPG/400 program to generate the report detailed in the supplemental print chart.

The Happy Sales Company pays its sales employees salary plus a commission on net sales. Payments are based on the following:

1. All sales employees are paid a base salary regardless of their sales. Those with less than two years' employment are paid a $600 monthly base salary. Employees with two or more years are guaranteed a $1,000 monthly salary.
2. Net sales over $2,000 are eligible for a commission that is added to the base salary. In any case, no commission is paid on the first $2,000 of net sales.

The commission amount is determined as follows:

1. Two or More Years' Employment. Twenty percent (0.20) commission is paid on net sales (sales − returns) over $2,000. Any commission sales over $30,000 are paid an additional 5% commission.
2. Less than Two Years' Employment. Twelve percent (0.12) commission is paid on net sales (sales − returns) over $2,000. Any commission sales over $25,000 are paid an additional 2% commission.

Summary:

$$\text{Net Sales} = \text{Monthly Sales} - \text{Sales Return}$$

$$\text{Commission Sales} = \text{Net Sales} - \$2,000$$

All commission computations are based on commission sales.

Physical File Record Format:

```
                     PHYSICAL FILE DESCRIPTION

        SYSTEM: AS/400                       DATE: Yours
        FILE NAME: Yours                     REV NO: 0
        RECORD NAME: Yours                   KEY LENGTH: None
        SEQUENCE:Non-keyed                   RECORD SIZE: 41

                        FIELD DEFINITIONS

        FIELD    FIELD NAME    SIZE   TYPE    POSITION      COMMENTS
         NO                                 FROM    TO


          1      SALMN#          5     C       1      5
          2      SALNAM         25     C       6     30
          3      YRSEMP          2     P      31     32
          4      MTHSAL          8     P      33     37    2 decimals
          5      SALRET          7     P      38     41    2 decimals
```

Physical File Data:

```
        Salesman                         Emp     Sales      Sales
         Number            Name          Yrs     Amount    Returns


          11111   SIEGFRIED HOUNDSTOOTH    4    01125050   0100000
          11112   FELIX GOODGUY            1    02800000   0000000
          22222   OTTO MUTTENJAMMER        6    10000000   0000000
          33333   HANS OFFENHAUSER         1    00250000   0070000
          44444   BARNEY OLDFIELD          3    00190000   0000000
          55555   WILLIAM PETTY            2    02200000   0000000
```

Report Design:

```
        0           1           2           3           4           5           6           7           8           9           10
     1234567890123456789012345678901234567890123456789012345678901234567890123456789012345678901234567890123456789012345678901
 1  ØX/XX/XX                                              COMMISSION REPORT                                              PAGE XXØX
 2
 3
 4                                                                                                                      SALARY/
 5  SALESMAN #          SALESMAN NAME          EMP YRS    GROSS SALES       RETURNS          NET SALES          COMMISSION
 6
 7    XXXXX      X                        X     ØX      XXX,XXØ.XX      XX,XXØ.XX        XXX,XXØ.XX         XXX,XXØ.XX
 8
 9    XXXXX      X                        X     ØX      XXX,XXØ.XX      XX,XXØ.XX        XXX,XXØ.XX         XXX,XXØ.XX
10
11
12                              TOTALS...........X,XXX,XXØ.XX    XXX,XXØ.XX      X,XXX,XXØ.XX       X,XXX,XXØ.XX
13
14
15          NOTES:
16
17            1.  USE SYSTEM DATE FOR REPORT DATE.
18
19            2.  REPORT TOTALS PRINTED ON SAME PAGE AS LAST DETAIL LINE.
```

Programming Assignment 6-2: PAYROLL REGISTER

A payroll register records the year-to-date and weekly payroll information for each employee. Federal income and social security taxes withheld to date and for the current week are included in the report. In addition, the week's gross and net pay amounts are also specified. Other deductions, such as hospitalization, retirement, union dues, and so forth, may also be subtracted from an employee's paycheck. From the record layout form, processing logic flowchart, and printer spacing chart that follows, write a structured RPG/400 program to generate the required report.

Calculations: The logic flowchart that follows details the calculations required for this application. To simplify federal income tax computations, specify a constant rate of 20%.

Processing Logic Flowchart:

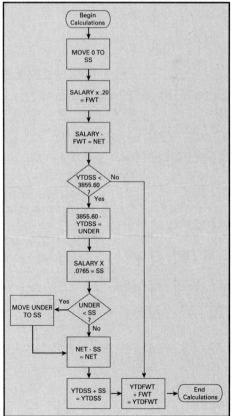

Physical File Record Format:

```
              PHYSICAL FILE DESCRIPTION

   SYSTEM: AS/400                    DATE: Yours
   FILE NAME: Yours                  REV NO: 0
   RECORD NAME: Yours                KEY LENGTH: None
   SEQUENCE: Non-keyed               RECORD SIZE: 41

                  FIELD DEFINITIONS

   FIELD    FIELD NAME    SIZE   TYPE    POSITION      COMMENTS
    NO                                  FROM    TO


     1       SSNO           9     P       1      5
     2       EMPNAM        20     C       6     25
     3       YTDWAG         7     P      26     29    2 decimals
     4       YTDFWT         7     P      30     33    2 decimals
     5       YTDSS          6     P      34     37    2 decimals
     6       WEKSAL         6     P      38     41    2 decimals
```

Physical File Data:

SS Number	Employee Name	Wages	YTD FWT	YTD SS	Week's Salary
050446666	BETTY BURPO	0250000	0050000	019125	050000
001012345	DICK TRACY	4965000	0993000	379823	075000
100709876	SHERLOCK HOLMES	6000000	1200000	385560	100000
020324321	JAMES BOND	5000000	1000000	382500	080000
020400050	INSPECTOR GADGET	5040000	1008000	385560	090000
110889999	PERRY MASON	0011000	0002200	000842	027500

Report Design:

Programming Assignment 6-3: PRESENT VALUE OF A FUTURE AMOUNT

Fixed payment annuities require that a principal amount be invested today to have a specific future amount, considering the current interest rate and the period of the investment. The mathematical steps include the following:

Step 1: Compute the present worth of $1 by dividing 1 by the compound amount of $1, expressed by formula as:

$$PV = \frac{1}{(1+i)^n}$$

where:

PV = present value of $1
i = interest rate per annum
n = number of interest periods

Notes: If interest is compounded more than yearly (i.e., monthly, weekly, or daily), the interest rate *(i)* must be divided by the number of interest periods per year. For accuracy, the answer must be carried to nine decimal positions. The total number of interest periods *(n)* is determined by multiplying the investment years by the interest payments per year.

Step 2: Using the following formula, determine the amount that must be invested today to have the required future annuity amount:

$$P = S \times PV$$

where:

P = amount that must be invested today to have future annuity
S = amount of future annuity
PV = present value of $1

Physical File Record Format:

```
                    PHYSICAL FILE DESCRIPTION

     SYSTEM: AS/400                        DATE: Yours
     FILE NAME: Yours                      REV NO: 0
     RECORD NAME: Yours                    KEY LENGTH: None
     SEQUENCE:Non-keyed                    RECORD SIZE: 11


                       FIELD DEFINITIONS


     FIELD      FIELD NAME    SIZE   TYPE     POSITION      COMMENTS
      NO                                     FROM    TO


       1         FUTAMT         6     P        1      4   0 decimals
       2         YRRATE         5     P        5      7   5 decimals
       3         YEARS          2     P        8      9   0 decimals
       4         YRPRDS         3     P       10     11   0 decimals
```

Physical File Data:

Desired Future Amount	Interest Rate Per Annum	Investment Years	Interest Periods Per Year
10000	08000	10	001
10000	08000	10	012
10000	08000	10	365
10000	10000	10	001
10000	10000	10	012
10000	10000	10	365

Report Design:

Programming Assignment 6-4: STOCKBROKER'S COMMISSION REPORT

Write an RPG/400 program to generate the stockbroker's commission report illustrated in the supplemental printer spacing chart.

Calculations:

Step 1. Multiply the number of shares purchased by the cost per share (input values) to calculate the total dollars of stock purchased.

Step 2. Test the stock exchange input field to determine on which exchange the stock is listed. The stock exchange codes are as follows:

NY New York Stock Exchange
AM American Stock Exchange
OV Over-the-Counter Exchange

Step 3. On the basis of the following individual stock exchange rates compute the broker commission on the total dollars of stock purchased:

NY 5.1%   AM 4.2%   OV 3.5%

Step 4. Accumulate separate totals for the number of transactions related to each stock exchange, and print at LR time.

Step 5. Test the stock exchange input field, and print the related code on each detail line as shown in the printer spacing chart.

Physical File Record Format:

```
                    PHYSICAL FILE DESCRIPTION

        SYSTEM: AS/400                    DATE: Yours
        FILE NAME: Yours                  REV NO: 0
        RECORD NAME: Yours                KEY LENGTH: None
        SEQUENCE: Non-keyed               RECORD SIZE: 35

                       FIELD DEFINITIONS

        FIELD    FIELD NAME   SIZE  TYPE   POSITION      COMMENTS
         NO                                FROM    TO

          1      ACT#          5     C      1      5
          2      STOCK        20     C      6     25
          3      SHARES        6     P     26     29   0 decimals
          4      COSTSH        6     P     30     33   3 decimals
          5      EXCHNG        2     C     34     35
```

Physical File Data:

Acct#	Stock Purchased	Number of Shares	Cost/ Share	Stock Exchange
10000	IBM CORPORATION	001000	057125	NY
12000	ECHLIN MFG	000050	025500	OV
13000	BENQUET INC	010000	004250	NY
14000	BIC CORPORATION	000300	002600	AM
15000	BLACK & DECKER	001500	023750	OV
16000	TRANS-LUX	100000	009125	AM
17000	ALCIDE CORPORATION	025000	003125	OV
18000	PEOPLE'S BANK	004000	009500	OV
19000	XEROX	000100	051375	NY
20000	DU PONT	000300	088125	NY

Report Design:

	0	1	2	3	4	5	6	7	8	9
1	ØX/XX/XX			STOCK	BROKER COMMISSION	REPORT				PAGE XXØX
2										
3				SHARES	PRICE/		PURCHASE IN	STOCK	BROKER	
4	ACT#	STOCK	PURCHASED	PURCHASED	SHARE		DOLLARS	EXCHANGE	COMMISSION	
5										
6	XXXXX	X		X	XXX,XØX	X,XXØ.XX	XX,XXX,XXØ.XX	XX	XX,XXX,XXØ.XX	
7										
8	XXXXX	X		X	XXX,XØX	X,XXØ.XX	XX,XXX,XXØ.XX	XX	XX,XXX,XXØ.XX	
9										
10										
11			NUMBER OF XX	EXCHANGE TRANSACTIONS:	XXØX					
12			NUMBER OF XX	EXCHANGE TRANSACTIONS:	XXØX					
13			NUMBER OF XX	EXCHANGE TRANSACTIONS:	XXØX					

chapter 7

EXCPT Operation, Internal Subroutines, and Calling Programs

The **EXCPT** operation, which adds flexibility to RPG/400 programs, is introduced in this chapter, and its use is shown in two application programs. First, the syntax and processing logic of the **EXCPT** operation are illustrated in an example program that prints the data in a record a predetermined number of times. Second, another example of **EXCPT** operation control is shown in an applications program that generates an electric billing report.

THE EXCPT (EXCEPTION) OPERATION

The syntax of the **EXCPT** operation is detailed in Figure 7-1. The processing logic of the **EXCPT** operation and its control of output are illustrated in Figure 7-2. Notice that the output instructions (*exception output*) controlled by the **EXCPT** operation must be specified with the letter **E** in the Type field (column 15). Any **H** (*heading*), **D** (*detail*), or **T** (*total*) *time* output is ignored when control from an **EXCPT** operation scans the output instructions. Also, **E** (*exception*) type of output may be included in any order and does not have to follow the **H**, **D**, **T** order required for other output types. Furthermore, any number of **EXCPT** operations may be included in a program.

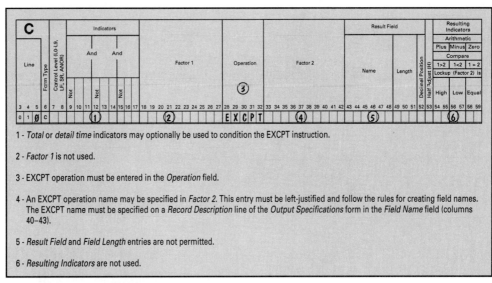

1 - *Total* or *detail time* indicators may optionally be used to condition the EXCPT instruction.

2 - *Factor 1* is not used.

3 - EXCPT operation must be entered in the *Operation* field.

4 - An EXCPT operation name may be specified in *Factor 2*. This entry must be left-justified and follow the rules for creating field names. The EXCPT name must be specified on a *Record Description* line of the *Output Specifications* form in the *Field Name* field (columns 40–43).

5 - *Result Field* and *Field Length* entries are not permitted.

6 - *Resulting Indicators* are not used.

Figure 7-1 **EXCPT** operation syntax.

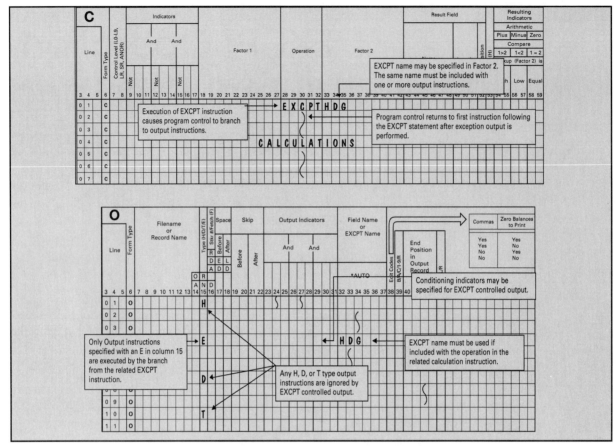

Figure 7-2   Processing logic of the **EXCPT** operation and its control of output.

APPLICATION PROGRAM: PRINTING CUSTOMER SHIPPING LABELS

The specifications for an RPG/400 application program that prints shipping labels are detailed in Figure 7-3. The system flowchart for the Customer Shipping Labels program

PROGRAM SPECIFICATIONS		Page 1 of 1
Program Name: Customer Mailing Labels Program ID: LABELS		Written by: SM
Purpose: Print customer mailing labels		Approved by: CM
Input files: CUSTMRS		
Output files: QSYSPRT		
Processing Requirements:		

Write an RPG/400 program to print customer mailing labels on pre-glued continuous form labels.

Input to the program:

The externally defined physical file, CUSTMRS, contains customer names and addresses in the format shown in the attached record layout form.

Figure 7-3   Specifications for program that prints customer shipping labels.

Processing:

Read the physical file in arrival sequence. For every CUSTMRS record processed, print two labels for the customer.

Provide for a looping sequence, and within the loop include the **EXCPT** operation to control the printing of two labels per customer. After two labels are printed, read another customer record and repeat the process until the end of the physical file is read.

Output:

On the continuous forms pre-glued label paper, print two labels for each CUSTMRS record processed. The attached printer spacing chart shows the format of the labels. Individual labels have a length of 8 lines. Printing on each label form is to begin on line 2 with overflow specified on line 7. Set the line printer at 8 lines per inch.

Figure 7-3 Specifications for program that prints customer shipping labels. (Continued)

shown in Figure 7-4 indicates that one physical file and one printer file are processed by the program. The format of the records in the physical file and a listing of the data are included in Figure 7-5. The design of the report is shown in the printer spacing chart in Figure 7-6 with the report (labels) generated by the program.

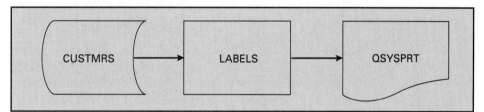

Figure 7-4 System flowchart for program that prints customer shipping labels.

```
              PHYSICAL FILE DESCRIPTION

SYSTEM: AS/400                    DATE: Yours
FILE NAME: CUSTMRS                REV NO: 0
RECORD NAME: CUSTR                KEY LENGTH: 5
SEQUENCE: Keyed                   RECORD SIZE: 78

              FIELD DEFINITIONS

FIELD    FIELD NAME   SIZE  TYPE   POSITION    COMMENTS
NO                                 FROM   TO
  1      CUST#          5    C       1      5  Key field
  2      NAME          20    C       6     25
  3      ADDRS1        15    C      26     40
  4      ADDRS2        15    C      41     54
  5      CITY          19    C      55     73
  6      STATE          2    C      74     75
  7      ZIP            5    P      76     78
```

Physical File Data:

```
Customer
Number    Customer Name   Address One    Address Two   City       State  Zip
10000     ENRICO FERMI    10 NEUTRON LANE              CHICAGO    IL     04010
20000     EDWARD TELLER   ATOMIC LANE    PO BOX 239    LOS ALAMOS NM     08803
```

Figure 7-5 Input file's record format and listing of the data for the Customer Shipping Labels program.

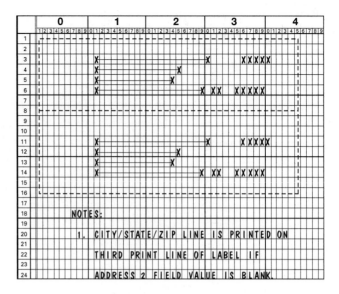

Figure 7-6 Report design and labels generated by the Customer Shipping Labels program.

A compile listing of the Customer Shipping Labels program is presented in Figure 7-7. Notice the following features of this program:

1. Because the labels are a nonstandard forms length, a *Line Counter Specifications* instruction (line 4) is included to define a form (label) length of

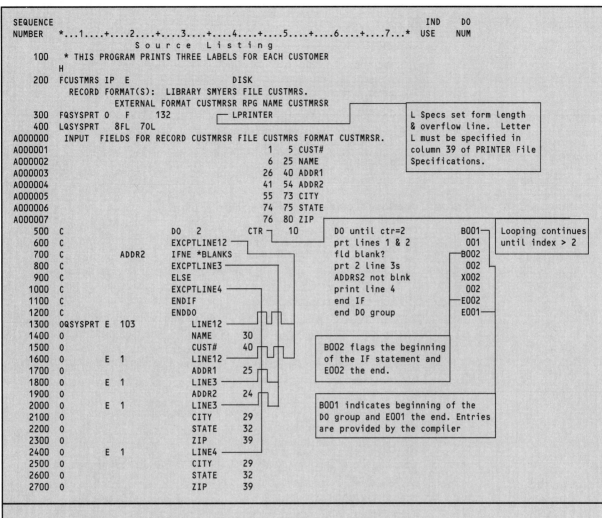

```
SEQUENCE                                                          IND   DO
NUMBER    *...1....+....2....+....3....+....4....+....5....+....6....+....7...*  USE   NUM
                      S o u r c e   L i s t i n g
  100    * THIS PROGRAM PRINTS THREE LABELS FOR EACH CUSTOMER
         H
  200    FCUSTMRS IP E               DISK
           RECORD FORMAT(S): LIBRARY SMYERS FILE CUSTMRS.
                  EXTERNAL FORMAT CUSTMRSR RPG NAME CUSTMRSR
  300    FQSYSPRT O   F    132          ┌─ LPRINTER                    ┌─ L Specs set form length
  400    LQSYSPRT  8FL 70L                                            │  & overflow line. Letter
A000000   INPUT  FIELDS FOR RECORD CUSTMRSR FILE CUSTMRS FORMAT CUSTMRSR.   │  must be specified in
A000001                               1   5 CUST#                     │  column 39 of PRINTER File
A000002                               6  25 NAME                      │  Specifications.
A000003                              26  40 ADDR1                     └─
A000004                              41  54 ADDR2
A000005                              55  73 CITY
A000006                              74  75 STATE
A000007                              76  80 ZIP
  500    C               DO    2    CTR   10      DO until ctr=2      B001┐  ┌─ Looping continues
  600    C               EXCPTLINE12                prt lines 1 & 2   001 │  │  until index > 2
  700    C      ADDR2    IFNE *BLANKS               fld blank?        B002 │  └─
  800    C               EXCPTLINE3                 prt 2 line 3s     002 │
  900    C               ELSE                       ADDRS2 not blnk   X002 │
 1000    C               EXCPTLINE4                 print line 4      002 │
 1100    C               ENDIF                      end IF            E002 │
 1200    C               ENDDO                      end DO group      E001┘
 1300    OQSYSPRT E 103        LINE12
 1400    O                     NAME     30                            ┌──────────────────────────┐
 1500    O                     CUST#    40                            │ B002 flags the beginning  │
 1600    O         E 1         LINE12                                 │ of the IF statement and   │
 1700    O                     ADDR1    25                            │ E002 the end.             │
 1800    O         E 1         LINE3                                  └──────────────────────────┘
 1900    O                     ADDR2    24
 2000    O         E 1         LINE3                                  ┌──────────────────────────┐
 2100    O                     CITY     29                            │ B001 indicates beginning  │
 2200    O                     STATE    32                            │ of the DO group and E001  │
 2300    O                     ZIP      39                            │ the end. Entries          │
 2400    O         E 1         LINE4                                  │ are provided by the       │
 2500    O                     CITY     29                            │ compiler                  │
 2600    O                     STATE    32                            └──────────────────────────┘
 2700    O                     ZIP      39
```

Line #

200 The externally defined physical file CUSTMRS is processed in arrival sequence.

300 QSYSPRT is the system name for the program-defined printer file. The statement includes an **L** in column 39 indicating that form length is controlled by the program and not the default values supplied by the system.

400 *Line Counter Specifications* statement defines the form length **(FL)** as 8 with page overflow **(OL)** on line 7.

500 The 2 in *Factor 2* of the **DO** statement determines when the loop will end. When the counter (CTR), which is automatically incremented by 1, is greater than 2, control will pass to the statement following the **ENDDO** statement on line 1200.

600 **EXCPT LINE 12** statement transfers control to exception line 1300, which advances the forms to the top of a label. The NAME and CUST# values are printed by these statements. Line 1600 controls the printing of another LINE 12 exception line after advancing 1 line. The value in ADDRS1 is printed with this output.

700-
800 The **IFNE** statement tests the value in ADDRS2 for blanks. If ADDRS2 is not blank, **EXCPT LINE3** will be executed, passing control to exception line 1800 where the value in ADDRS2 is printed. Then, exception line 2000 (also named LINE3), which controls the printing of the values in CITY, STATE, and ZIP, will be executed.

900-
1000 When the **IFNE** statement test is false, control will execute the **EXCPT LINE4** statement, which passes control to line 2400 where the values in CITY, STATE, and ZIP are printed immediately after the ADDRS1 value. This coding prevents a blank line from being inserted between the ADDRS1 value and the values in CITY, STATE, and ZIP when ADDRS2 is blank.

1200 The ENDDO operations ends the **DO** group and passes control back to the **DO** statement on line 500, where the test is made to end the loop or continue the iterative process.

Figure 7-7   Compile listing of the Customer Shipping Labels program.

eight lines and page overflow on line 7. If necessary, refer to Chapter 4 for a review of the syntax related to this RPG/400 specifications.

2. The RPG/400 processing cycle is altered by the **EXCPT** operation.

3. The number of labels (two) to print for each customer is "hard-coded" in the program. In practice, however, the number of labels to print for each customer would be input interactively by a *display file* or the value stored in a *Data Area*. Both would be accessed by the RPG/400 program.

4. Only **E** (*Exception*) type lines are specified for output. Before each label is printed, program control advances the printer to line 3 of the next continuous forms label (see line 1300).

Page Overflow Control for Exception Output

Fetch Overflow Feature. When page overflow is sensed during the program cycle, detail, total, and exception lines are printed on the page even after overflow has occurred. A problem may occur if a number of different types of lines are printed for which there may not be enough room on the page. This may cause printing over the perforated line on continuous forms paper.

To resolve this problem, the forms may be advanced and the overflow lines printed on a new page immediately after overflow is sensed instead of printing them on the current page. This process is controlled by specifying the letter **F** (*Fetch Overflow*) in column 16 of one or more **H, D, T,** or **E** type output lines. The following processing sequence occurs when *Fetch Overflow* is specified:

1. All total lines conditioned by an overflow indicator are printed.
2. Forms advance to the beginning line number of a new page as specified in the *Skip Before* or *Skip After* fields.
3. Heading lines conditioned by an overflow indicator are printed on the new page.
4. Any detail, total, or exception lines specified with an **F** in column 16 of the record description area are printed.
5. Any remaining detail, exception, or total lines for the page are printed.

The syntax and processing logic of the Fetch Overflow feature are illustrated in Figure 7-8.

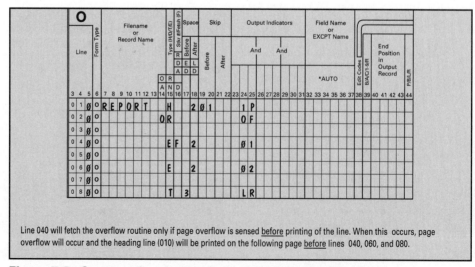

Line 040 will fetch the overflow routine only if page overflow is sensed <u>before</u> printing of the line. When this occurs, page overflow will occur and the heading line (010) will be printed on the following page <u>before</u> lines 040, 060, and 080.

Figure 7-8 Syntax and processing logic of the Fetch Overflow feature.

If, however, the printing of line 040 caused page overflow to occur, lines 040, 060, and 080 (if L1 is on) will be printed on the current page. If printer was near the end of the page, this condition could cause printing on the perforated line which separates the pages of continuous forms paper.

Figure 7-8 Syntax and processing logic of the Fetch Overflow feature. (Continued)

INTERNAL SUBROUTINES

As programs become larger or more complex, they are usually difficult to debug and maintain. One method of keeping any program readable is to separate the calculations into *internal subroutines* (also called *modules*), which may or may not be independent of other coding. Ideally, any instructions related to a select program function should be included in a separate subroutine. The size and number of internal subroutines specified will depend on the program logic, program complexity, and/or the programmer's coding preferences. In addition, internal subroutines support the current trend of structured RPG/400 programming where calculations are modularized and performed in a top–down sequence.

Internal Subroutine Operations

Internal subroutines are specified in the *Calculation Specifications* and include the following operation names:

EXSR—Causes program control to branch to the internal subroutine identified by the programmer-supplied name entered in *Factor 2*. The subroutine name must be formatted according to the syntax related to field names.

BEGSR—Identifies entry point for the subroutine named in *Factor 2* of the **EXSR** operation. The name specified in *Factor 1* must be identical to the related **EXSR** instruction.

ENDSR—Indicates end of the internal subroutine. When this instruction is executed, program control branches to statement immediately following the related **EXSR** operation.

Figure 7-9 details the syntax related to each of the internal subroutine operations. Notice that an internal subroutine begins with a **BEGSR** instruction and ends with an **ENDSR**

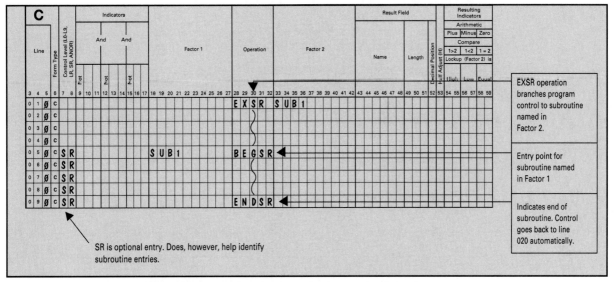

Figure 7-9 RPG/400 syntax for internal subroutines.

statement. Internal subroutines must follow all *detail* and *total time* calculations and may be assigned in any order. Furthermore, subroutines do not have to be specified in the same sequence as their related **EXSR** operations.

Other than conditioning indicators at *total* or *detail time*, the entries shown are the only ones permitted for each operation. The **SR** entry that may be included in columns 7 and 8 with each subroutine instruction is optional. They may be omitted and/or replaced with Control Level Indicators when required.

The rules related to the use of internal subroutines are listed in Figure 7-10.

INTERNAL SUBROUTINE RULES

1. Internal subroutine instructions must follow all *detail* and *total time* calculations.

2. Each subroutine must have a unique name.

3. The operation codes **EXSR** (or **CASxx**), **BEGSR**, and **ENDSR** must be used with each internal subroutine.

4. Any RPG/400 operation may be used within an internal subroutine.

5. Fields specified in a subroutine may be defined in the routine or outside of it.

6. Any RPG/400 indicators (Except **1P**) may be entered in columns 7–17 (*total* and *detail times*) to condition instructions in the subroutine.

7. A subroutine may branch to another subroutine by the **EXSR** (or **CASxx**) operation. Program control will return back to the instruction following the related **EXSR** (or **CASxx**) statement.

8. **GOTO** operations may be used in an internal subroutine. However, a **GOTO** statement cannot be used to enter a subroutine. It is not considered good structured programming, but a **GOTO** statement may be used to exit from an internal subroutine.

9. The **ENDSR** operation (in lieu of a **TAG** statement) may be used as the entry point for a **GOTO** operation included in the subroutine.

Figure 7-10   Internal subroutine rules.

The syntax for rules 1, 6, 7, 8, and 9 is applied in the statements shown in Figure 7-11.

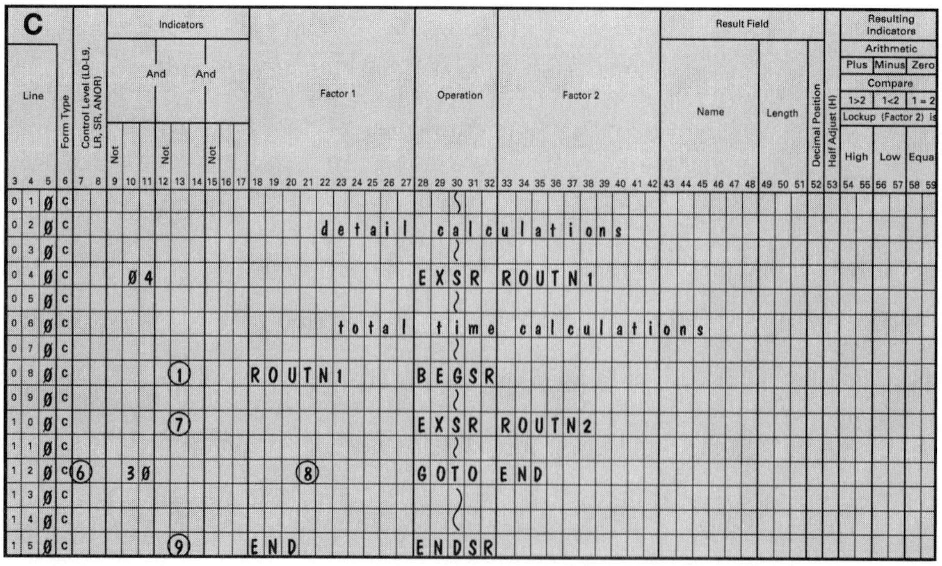

Figure 7-11   Coding examples for syntax rules 1, 6, 7, 8, and 9

THE CASxx OPERATION

When a *relational* test is required before exiting to an internal subroutine, the **CASxx** operation should be used. The functions provided by the **COMP** and **EXSR** operations are included in a **CASxx** instruction. Because of its functions, the **CASxx** operation eliminates the need for *Resulting Indicators* required in a **COMP** statement and their use in conditioning a related **EXSR** statement. The syntax for the **CASxx** operation is detailed in Figure 7-12.

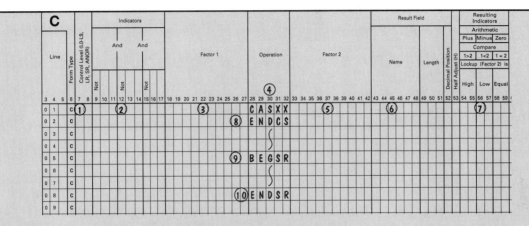

1. A *total time* indicator may condition a **CASxx** instruction.

2. *Detail time* indicators may condition a CASxx instruction.

3. Unless the xx entry in the CASxx operation is blank, a field name or literal must be entered in *Factor 1*. The item entered in this field must be the same type as the entry in *Factor 2*.

4. The CASxx operation name is entered in the *Operation* field. Entries for the xx value may be GT, LT, EQ, NE, GE, LE, or blanks (*Factor 1* not compared to *Factor 2*).

5. *Factor 2* must include a literal or field name and be defined as the same type as the *Factor 1* field or literal. If the xx entry in the CASxx operation is blank, an entry in the field is not required.

6. A programmer-supplied internal subroutine name must be entered in the *Result Field*.

7. One or more *Resulting Indicators* are required if the CASxx operation is specified without a relational test condition and the *Factor 1 and 2* entries are included. Otherwise, the indicator(s) is (are) optional.

8. A required ENDCS (or END) operation indicates the end of a single CASxx statement or group.

9. A BEGSR operation indicates the beginning of an internal subroutine. The name specified in the *Result Field* of the related CASxx statement must be entered left-justified in *Factor 1*. Internal subroutines must follow all *detail* and *total time* calculations.

10. An ENDSR operation indicates the end of the internal subroutine. It may be used as a TAG operation for a GOTO or CABxx statement within the internal subroutine.

Notes:

1. After a CASxx statement is executed, control returns to the statement following the related ENDCS (or END) operation. Consequently, when a CASxx instruction is executed, any subsequent CASxx statements within the group will be ignored.

2. Only CASxx statements may be included in a CASxx group.

3. The normal placement of a CASbb (**b = blanks**) instruction (no relational test specified) is after any other CASxx statements within the group.

Figure 7-12 Syntax for the **CASxx** operation.

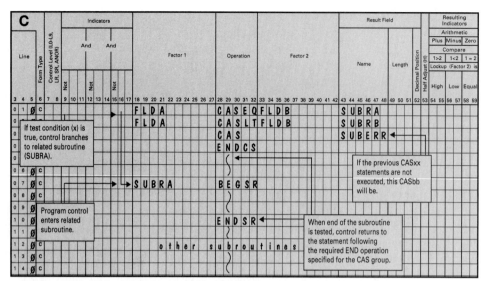

Figure 7-13 Processing logic of a **CASxx** group.

The processing logic related to a **CASxx** group is detailed in Figure 7-13. When a **CASxx** instruction within a *Case Group* is executed, any following **CASxx** statements will be ignored. Program control returns to the statement following the related **ENDCS** (or **END**) operation, which must always terminate <u>one</u> or <u>more</u> **CASxx** instructions. This processing logic differs from the **EXSR** operation, where program control returns to the statement immediately following the related **EXSR** instruction.

Identical to all of the RPG/400 structured operations, a **CASxx** statement may be complex by including one or more **AND** and/or **OR** conditions in the relational test.

NAMED CONSTANTS

Programmer-defined literal values that are too long for a *Factor 1* or *Factor 2* entry, each having only 10 available positions, may be specified by *Named Constants*. The literal value (numeric or alphanumeric) is assigned a name on the *Input Specifications* which may be subsequently referenced in calculations and/or output instruction(s). Figure 7-14 details the syntax related to *Named Constants*.

<u>NAMED CONSTANTS RULES</u>

1. Named Constants are defined on the *Input Specifications* form, columns 21–41.

2. The letter C must be entered in column 43 on the same line as the value. If the value is too long to fit in columns 21–41 and continues to the next line, the C is permitted only on the first line of the Named Constant definition.

3. Alphanumeric values must be enclosed within single quotes. If the value will not fit on one line, continuation is indicated by a – (minus sign), without a single quote, after the last character of the named constant. A single quote must be specified as the first character on the next continuation line. Location of the minus sign indicates the end of the value for the line. The maximum size of an alphanumeric Named Constant value is 256.

4. Numeric values are specified <u>without</u> quotes. If the value will not fit on one line, continuation is indicated by a – (minus sign) <u>immediately</u> after the last digit. *Negative values* are defined by a leading – (minus sign). The maximum size of a numeric Named Constant is 30 digits. No more than nine decimal positions may be defined.

5. Programmer-supplied Named Constant field names must be specified in the *Field Name* field (columns 53–58) on the first line of a Named Constant.

Figure 7-14 Syntax rules for Named Constants.

Examples of how numeric and alphanumeric *Named Constants* are defined are detailed in Figure 7-15.

The input specification form (Figure 7-15) contains the following entries:

Line	Record Identification Codes / Constant	P/B/L/R	RPG Field Name
01	-12345.67	C	SIGNED
03	12345.67	C	ZONED
05	1234567891234567891-	C	LNGNO
06	23456.78		
08	'ALPHANUMERIC VALUE'	C	SHORTA
10	'EXAMPLE OF A LONG -	C	LONGA
11	'ALPHANUMERIC CONSTA-		
12	NT'		

Figure 7-15 Examples of numeric and alphanumeric Named Constants.

Numeric Named Constants may be used in calculations as a *Factor 1 or 2* entry with any RPG/400 operation that supports numeric fields or literals. *Alphanumeric Named Constants* may also be used as a *Factor 1 or 2* entry with any RPG/400 operation that supports alphanumeric fields or literals. A *numeric or alphanumeric Named Constant* may be specified as a field or constant on the output form.

System Time

Unlike other RPG/400 reserved words, such as **PAGE, UDATE, UDAY, UMONTH,** and **UYEAR,** the value for the system time is not available at **1P** (*First Page*) time. Instead, **TIME** (stored in an **HHMMSS** format) must be accessed by a calculation statement and output with indicator or exception control. Figure 7-16 illustrates one method of controlling the access and output of System Time using *exception* time output.

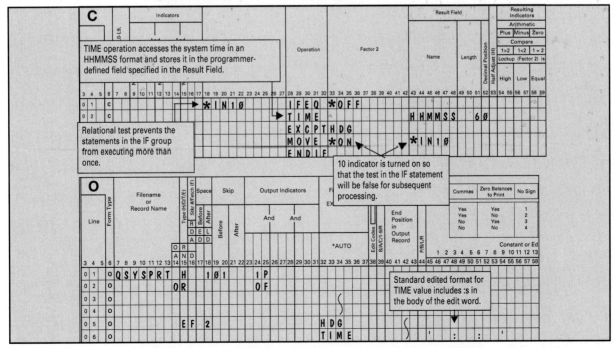

Figure 7-16 RPG/400 coding to access *System Time* **(TIME)** and control its output.

An application program that illustrates how internal subroutines and Named Constants are used in an RPG/400 program is discussed in the following paragraphs. Understand, however, that internal subroutines are not a coding requirement but are used only to enhance the readability of a program and support and encourage structured design.

APPLICATION PROGRAM: ELECTRIC BILLING REPORT

The specifications for an RPG/400 program that generates a billing report for an electric company are presented in Figure 7-17. Other program documentation is supported by the system flowchart in Figure 7-18.

PROGRAM SPECIFICATIONS   Page _1_ of _1_

Program Name: Electric Bill Report   Program-ID: ELBILLS   Written by: SM

Purpose: Generate an electric bill report   Approved by: CM

Input files: _ELCUSTRS_

Output files: _QSYSPRT_

Processing Requirements:

Write an RPG/400 program to generate a billing report for an electric company's customers.

Input to the program:

The externally defined physical file, ELCUSTRS, includes the record format shown in the supplemental record layout form. The file is to be processed in arrival sequence.

Processing:

The company has different base and usage rates for industrial and home-owners which are detailed below:

   Rates for Homeowners:
     Base usaged = 1000 kilowatt hours
     Base charge = $40
     Additional rate for usage over 1000 kwh = $.042/kwh

   Rates for Industrial:
     Base usage = 5000 kilowatt hours
     Base charge = $175
     Additional rate for usage over 5000 kwh = $.035/kwh

Test the user code field in each record processed. If the value is H, branch to an internal subroutine for homeowners's calculations. If the value is I, branch to a separate routine for industrial users.

For either user, if the kilowatt hours used is equal to or less than the base usage (1000 or 5000), the related base charge (40 or 175) is billed for the month.

If more than the base amount is used, then the excess usage over the base amount is multiplied by the applicable additional rate (.042 or .035). The base charge and additional amount are added to determine the amount billed.

In addition, all users are subject to a tax based on $.015 per 100 kwh used. The tax is added to the amount billed. Add the total amount billed to an accumulator.

Figure 7-17 Specifications for an RPG/400 program that generates an electric billing report.

Complete the report format detailed in the supplemental print chart.

Figure 7-17   Specifications for an RPG/400 program that generates an electric billing report. (Continued)

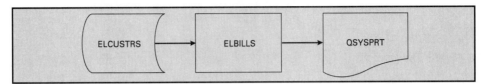

Figure 7-18   System flowchart for an RPG/400 program that generates an electric billing report.

The physical file's record format and data listing are shown in Figure 7-19.

The report design is detailed in the printer spacing chart in Figure 7-20 with a report listing.

```
                    PHYSICAL FILE DESCRIPTION

SYSTEM: AS/400                        DATE: 9/20/95
FILE NAME: ELCUSTRS                   REV NO: 0
RECORD NAME: ELCUSTR                  KEY LENGTH: None
SEQUENCE: Non-keyed                   RECORD SIZE: 25

                    FIELD DEFINITIONS

FIELD      FIELD NAME    SIZE   TYPE     POSITION      COMMENTS
NO                                     FROM      TO


  1        CNAME          20     C        1       20
  2        KWH             6     P       21       24    0 decimals
  3        USER            1     C       25       25    H - Home
                                                        I - Indust
```

Physical File Data:

```
                              Kilowatt
          Customer Name      Hours Used   User


          IVAN PATZIK          000945       H
          MANAGEMENT COMPANY   011000       I
          CHRIS LENTZ          001400       H
          TAYCO INCORPORATED   004500       I
          FRANZ ECKART         001050       H
          COMPUTER SERVICES CO 150000       I
```

Figure 7-19   Physical file's record format and data listing for the Electric Billing Report program.

```
        0          1          2          3          4          5
1  ØX/XX/XX          EDISON ELECTRIC COMPANY            PAGE XXØX
2  XX:XX:XX      CUSTOMER USAGE AND BILLING REPORT
3
4         NAME              USER TYPE    KWH HRS      TOTAL BILL
5
6  X                 X   INDUSTRIAL    XXX,XØX      XX,XXØ.XX
7
8  X                 X      HOME       XXX,XØX      XX,XXØ.XX
9
10
11                TOTAL BILLINGS                   XXX,XXØ.XX
12
13 NOTES:
14
15   1. HEADINGS ON TOP OF EVERY PAGE.
16
17   2. USE SYSTEM DATE FOR REPORT.
```

Figure 7-20   Print spacing chart and report generated by the Electric Billing Report Program.

```
10/01/95              EDISON ELECTRIC COMPANY          PAGE    1
13:26:47          CUSTOMER USAGE AND BILLING REPORT

          NAME            USER TYPE   KWH HRS    TOTAL BILL

   IVAN PATZIK              HOME         945          40.14

   MANAGEMENT COMPANY     INDUSTRIAL   11,000       386.65

   CHRIS LENTZ             HOME        1,400         57.01

   TAYCO INCORPORATED     INDUSTRIAL   4,500        175.68

   FRANZ ECKART            HOME        1,050         42.25

   COMPUTER SERVICES CO   INDUSTRIAL  150,000      5,272.50


                        TOTAL BILLINGS             5,974.23
```

Figure 7-20   Print spacing chart and report generated by the Electric Billing Report Program. (Continued)

The flowchart in Figure 7-21 details the processing logic for the Electric Billing Report program.

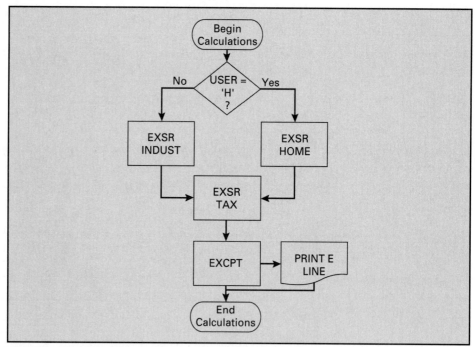

Figure 7-21   Processing logic for internal subroutines included in the Electric Billing Report program.

Compile Program Listing

Examine the compile listing in Figure 7-22, and observe that two *Named Constants,* four internal subroutines, system time, and *exception* time output—all RPG/400 functions introduced in this chapter—are included in the program.

```
                              S o u r c e   L i s t i n g
        100   * THIS PROGRAM COMPUTES AND GENERATES A BILLING REPORT FOR AN
        200   * ELECTRIC COMPANY'S HOMEOWNER AND INDUSTRIAL CUSTOMERS
              H
        300   FELCUSTRSIP E                        DISK
              RECORD FORMAT(S): LIBRARY SMYERS FILE ELCUSTRS.
                EXTERNAL FORMAT ELCUSTR RPG NAME ELCUSTR
        400   FQSYSPRT O   F    132      OF     PRINTER
        500   I            'INDUSTRIAL'          C        INDTRY
        600   I            '  HOME  '            C        HOME
        700   *
      A000000   INPUT  FIELDS FOR RECORD ELCUSTR FILE ELCUSTRS FORMAT ELCUSTR.
      A000001                                      1   20 CNAME
      A000002                                    P 21  240KWH
      A000003                                       25  25 USER
        800   C            *IN10     CASEQ*OFF     HOUSEK           exit to SR
        900   C                      ENDCS                          end CAS
       1000   *
       1100   C            USER      CASEQ'H'      HOMESR           exit to SR
       1200   C                      CAS           INDSR            indust user SR
       1300   C                      ENDCS                          end CAS group
       1400   C                      EXSR TAXSR                     tax & totals SR
       1500   C                      EXCPTPLINE                     print E line
       1600   *
       1700   C            HOUSEK    BEGSR                          begin HOUSEK SR
       1800   C                      TIME          HHMMSS 60        access sys time
       1900   C                      MOVE *ON      *IN10            turn on ind 10
       2000   C                      MOVE *ON      *INOF            turn on ind OF
       2100   C                      ENDSR                          end HOUSEK SR
       2200   *
       2300   C            HOMESR    BEGSR                          begin HOME SR
       2400   C                      MOVE HOME     TYPE   10        to output field
       2500   C                      Z-ADD40       BILL   72        base amount
       2600   C            KWH       CABLE1000     ENDHOM           <= 1000 kwh?
       2700   C            KWH       SUB  1000     EXCESS 60        kwh > 1000
       2800   C            EXCESS    MULT .042     EXTRA  72        extra amt
       2900   C                      ADD  EXTRA    BILL             base + extra
       3000   C            ENDHOM    ENDSR                          end HOME SR
       3100   *
       3200   C            INDSR     BEGSR                          begin INDSR SR
       3300   C                      MOVE INDTRY   TYPE             to output field
       3400   C                      Z-ADD175      BILL             base amt
       3500   C            KWH       CABLE5000     ENDIND           <= 5000 kwh?
       3600   C            KWH       SUB  5000     EXCESS           kwh > 5000
       3700   C            EXCESS    MULT .035     EXTRA            extra amt
       3800   C                      ADD  EXTRA    BILL             base + extra
       3900   C            ENDIND    ENDSR                          end INDUST SR
       4000   *
       4100   C            TAXSR     BEGSR                          begin TAXSR SR
       4200   C            KWH       DIV  100      TKWH   40        kwh for tax
       4300   C            TKWH      MULT .015     TAX    62H       compute tax
       4400   C                      ADD  TAX      BILL             add tax to bill
       4500   C                      ADD  BILL     TOTALB 82        accum bills
       4600   C                      ENDSR                          end TAX SR
       4700   OQSYSPRT H 101     OF
       4800   O                      UDATE Y    8
       4900   O                                51 'PAGE'
       5000   O                      PAGE  Z   56
       5100   O                                40 'EDISON ELECTRIC COMPANY'
       5200   O         H 2     OF
       5300   O                      HHMMSS     8 '  :  :  '
       5400   O                                30 'CUSTOMER USAGE AND'
       5500   O                                45 'BILLING REPORT'
       5600   O         H 2     OF
       5700   O                                11 'NAME'
       5800   O                                31 'USER TYPE'
       5900   O                                41 'KWH HRS'
       6000   O                                56 'TOTAL BILL'
       6100   O         EF 2          PLINE
       6200   O                       CNAME    20
       6300   O                       TYPE     32
       6400   O                       KWH    2 41
       6500   O                       BILL   1 56
       6600   O         TF1    LR
       6700   O                                28 'TOTAL BILLINGS'
       6800   O                       TOTALB1  56
```

Annotation boxes (left margin):

- Name Constants → (lines 500, 600)
- After the first record is processed, SR will never be excuted again
- OF is set on so output occurs at OF time instead of at 1P time
- All H lines are conditioned with an OF indicator
- System time output
- Exception time output. F in col 16 fetches OF lines when overflow is sensed

Figure 7-22   Compile listing of the Electric Billing Report program.

Line #

300 -
400   Externally defined physical file is processed in arrival sequence. Output is assigned to the system printer
       QSYSPRT.

500 -
600   Because INDUSTRIAL is 10 characters, it cannot be entered in *Factor 2*, which supports only 8 alphanumeric
       character and 2 apostrophes. Consequently, two **Named Constants** are used for this control. Depending on the
       user type (**H** or **I**), the value in INDTRY or HOME will be moved into the output field TYPE (see lines 2400 & 3300).

800 -
900   When indicator **10** is off, which is only for the first record read, control branches to the HOUSEK subroutine.
       System time is accessed and indicators **10** and **OF** turned on. Indicator **10** is turned on so that this statement will
       never test as true again, preventing the subroutine from being executed for every record processed. The required
       ENDCS operation ends the CASEQ statement.

1100 - The value in the input field USER is tested for **H** (homeowner). If the test is true, an exit is made to the HOMESR
       subroutine, where computations are performed for a homeowner user.

1200 - If the CASEQ test on line 1100 is false, this CAS statement will exit to the INDSR routine, where computations are
       performed for the industrial user.

1300 - The ENDCS operation ends the CAS group.

1400 - After computations are performed in the HOMESR or INDSR routine, an exit is made to the TAXSR routine, where
       the sales tax is computed.

1500 - The EXCPT statement passes control to output line 6100, which controls the printing of the customer name, user
       type, kilowatt hours used, and the amount of the bill.

Beginning of
subroutines

1700 - Begins the HOUSEK subroutine.

1800 - The system time is accessed by the TIME statement and stored unedited in the **HHMMSS** field.

1900 - Indicator 10, which is used in the CASEQ statement on line 800, is turned on. This prevents the HOUSEK
       subroutine from being executed again after the first record from the physical file is processed.

2000 - Indicator **OF** is turned on, which causes the heading output on lines 4700–6000 to occur when the first record is
       read instead of at 1P time. Because the value in the *System Time* field is not available at 1P (first cycle) time, its
       output must be controlled by another indicator. After printing the headings on the first page of the report, OF is
       turned off automatically until the overflow line is detected again.

2100 - The ENDSR operation ends the HOUSEK subroutine.

2300 - Begins the HOMESR subroutine.

2400 - The HOME field value, in which the Named Constant HOME is stored, is moved into the output field TYPE.

2500 - The base (40) amount for a homeowner user is moved to the BILL field.

2600 - The CABLE statement determines if the kilowatt hours used are less than or equal to the base amount. If the test
       is true, control will branch to the ENDHOM ENDSR statement, which is used as the TAG operation for the CABLE
       statement.

2700 - If the kilowatt hours used are greater than 1000, the 1000 base amount is subtracted from the input field KWH to
       determine the EXCESS usage.

2800 - The EXCESS kilowatt hours are multiplied by the user's rate to determine the EXTRA amount.

2900 - The EXTRA amount is added to BILL, which will now include the base amount of 40 and the EXCESS amount.

3000 - The ENDSR statement ends the HOMESR subroutine. Note that the ENDHOM entry in *Factor 1* is the label for the
       CABLE statement on line 2600.

3200 - Begins the INDSR subroutine.

3300 - The INDTRY field value, in which the Named Constant INDUSTRY is stored, is moved into the output field TYPE.

3400 - The base (175) amount for an industrial user is moved to the BILL field.

3500 - The CABLE statement determines if the kilowatt hours used are less than or equal to the base amount. If the test
       is true, control will branch to the ENDIND ENDSR statement, which is used as a TAG operation for the CABLE
       statement.

3600 - If the kilowatt hours used are greater than 5000, the 5000 base amount is subtracted from the input field KWH to
       determine the EXCESS usage.

Figure 7-22   Compile listing of the Electric Billing Report program. (Continued)

3700 - The EXCESS kilowatt hours is multiplied by the user's rate to determine the EXTRA amount.

3800 - The EXTRA amount is added to BILL which will now include the base amount of 175 and the EXCESS amount.

3900 - The ENDSR statement ends the INDSR subroutine. Note that the ENDIND entry in *Factor 1* is the label for the CABLE statement on line 3500.

4100 - Begins the TAXSR subroutine.

4200 - KWH is divided by 100 to determine the taxable kilowatt hours (TKWH).

4300 - The taxable amount, TKWH, is multiplied by the tax amount to determine the tax (TAX).

4400 - The TAX amount is added to the BILL for the total bill.

4500 - The value in BILL is added to the total bill accumulator, TOTALB, which is printed at LR time.

Output:

4700 -
6000   Heading output is controlled by the OF indicator which was turned on at line 2000 after the first record was read from the physical file. Lines 4700–5100 could have been conditioned by a 1P indicator and printed at first cycle time. However, because the system time is accessed by the **TIME** operation in calculations, its output must be conditioned by an indicator other than 1P. After this output is executed for the first record processed, OF is turned off until the overflow line is detected on the bottom of every page.

6100 -
6500   *Exception* time output is executed by the EXCPT statement on line 1500. The F in column 16 in the line 6100 statement fetches the output conditioned by the OF indicator when the overflow line is detected and before this line is printed.

6600 -
6800   *Total time* output is conditioned by the LR indicator which is turned on automatically when the end of the physical file is read. Line 6600 also includes an F in column 16, which will fetch overflow before this output is printed.

Figure 7-22   Compile listing of the Electric Billing Report program. (Continued)

CALLING OTHER PROGRAMS

Any RPG/400 program may receive and send values from or to a *Control Language* program (**CLP**) or another RPG/400 program. The passing of values to and from an RPG/400 or *Control Language* program requires the three operation codes **PLIST, PARM,** and **CALL.** The syntax of each is explained in the following sections.

The PLIST Operation

The declarative **PLIST** operation identifies a parameter list (one or more **PARM** statements) that immediately follows. Figure 7-23 details the syntax related to the **PLIST** operation.

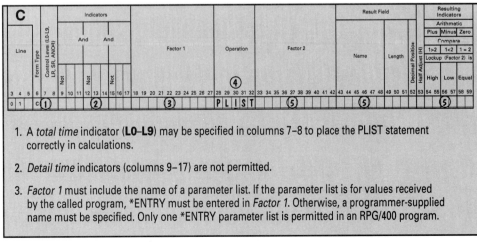

1. A *total time* indicator (**L0–L9**) may be specified in columns 7–8 to place the PLIST statement correctly in calculations.

2. *Detail time* indicators (columns 9–17) are not permitted.

3. *Factor 1* must include the name of a parameter list. If the parameter list is for values received by the called program, *ENTRY must be entered in *Factor 1*. Otherwise, a programmer-supplied name must be specified. Only one *ENTRY parameter list is permitted in an RPG/400 program.

Figure 7-23   Syntax of the **PLIST** operation.

4. The PLIST operation name must be specified in the *Operation* field and may be included anywhere in calculations.

5. *Factor 2, Result Field, and Resulting Indicators* are not used.

6. At least one PARM statement must be specified immediately after a PLIST operation.

Figure 7-23   Syntax of the **PLIST** operation. (Continued)

The PARM Operation

The declarative **PARM** operation defines the parameters that are included in the **PLIST** (parameter) list. **PARM** statements may be placed anywhere in calculations and must immediately follow a **PLIST** operation. Values are transferred to and from a *called* program by fields or literals included in **PARM** statements. The syntax for the **PARM** operation is explained in Figure 7-24.

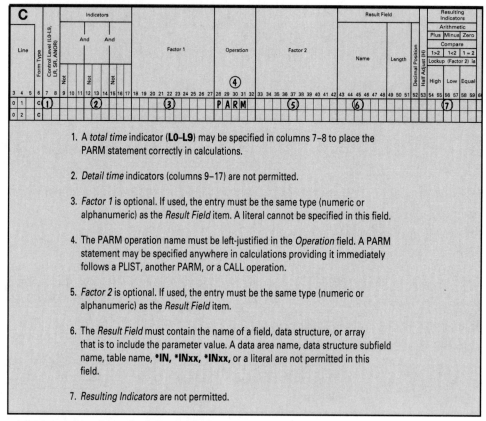

1. A *total time* indicator (**L0–L9**) may be specified in columns 7–8 to place the PARM statement correctly in calculations.

2. *Detail time* indicators (columns 9–17) are not permitted.

3. *Factor 1* is optional. If used, the entry must be the same type (numeric or alphanumeric) as the *Result Field* item. A literal cannot be specified in this field.

4. The PARM operation name must be left-justified in the *Operation* field. A PARM statement may be specified anywhere in calculations providing it immediately follows a PLIST, another PARM, or a CALL operation.

5. *Factor 2* is optional. If used, the entry must be the same type (numeric or alphanumeric) as the *Result Field* item.

6. The *Result Field* must contain the name of a field, data structure, or array that is to include the parameter value. A data area name, data structure subfield name, table name, ***IN, *INxx, *INxx,** or a literal are not permitted in this field.

7. *Resulting Indicators* are not permitted.

Figure 7-24   Syntax of the **PARM** operation.

The CALL Operation

The **CALL** operation passes control to the program specified in *Factor 2*. Any values included in **PARM** statements are passed to and are available for processing by the *called* program. Figure 7-25 details the syntax related to the **CALL** operation.

Figure 7-25   Syntax of the **CALL** operation.

1. A *total time* indicator (**L0–L9**) or *detail time* indicator may be specified.

2. *Factor 1* is not used.

3. The CALL operation name must left-justified in the *Operation* field.

4. *Factor 2* must include a field name, literal, or array name that contains the name of the program to be called. When a literal is used and a library name is included, the library name must be specified first followed by a / (slash) and then the program name. The total length of the literal cannot exceed 8 characters. The maximum length of a field is 21 characters.

5. The *Result Field* may be blank if the PARM statements directly follow the CALL operation or if the called program does not access parameters.

6. *Resulting Indicator* columns 54–55 must be blank. An indicator may be specified in columns 56–57 to identify an error return from the *called* program. In addition, an indicator may be specified in columns 58–59, which turn on if the RPG/400 program called returns with **LR** on.

Figure 7-25   Syntax of the **CALL** operation. (Continued)

Coding Example for CALLing a Program

Figure 7-26 illustrates an example of how the **CALL, PLIST,** and **PARM** operations are used in a *calling* program, and the **ENTRY* parameter and **PLIST** and **PARM** operations in the *called* program. The processing logic is also explained.

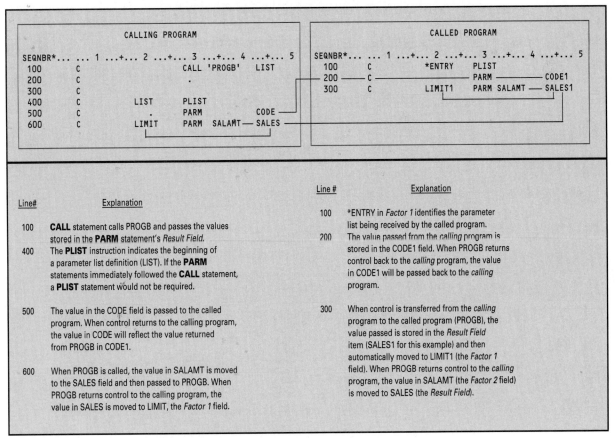

Figure 7-26   Coding example for calling a program.

Notes:

1. Coding examples assume fields are previously defined.
2. Related field names in calling and called programs may be the same. However, for clarity it may be expedient to use different names in each program.
3. Field values are passed to and from the calling and called programs positionally. Hence, the first **PARM** field specified in the calling program must be specified in the first **PARM** statement of the called program.
4. Parameter lists are <u>ended</u> when a statement other than a **PARM** is encountered.
5. From the called program, values are <u>passed back</u> to the calling program when the **RETRN** operation (if specified) is encountered or when **LR** turns on.

Figure 7-26   Coding example for calling a program. (Continued)

APPLICATION PROGRAM: CALLING A PROGRAM

This section presents an application program that passes the individual fields **LNAME** (last name), **FNAME** (first name), **MIDINT** (middle initial), **CITY** (city), **STATE** (state code), and **ZIP** (zip code) from a calling program to a called program for concatenation. After concatenation is performed (e.g., STANLEY E MYERS and NORWALK, CT 06854) by the called program, and the values are passed back to the calling program, a report line is printed.

Program Documentation

The specifications for this application are detailed in Figure 7-27.

PROGRAM SPECIFICATIONS   Page <u>1</u> of <u>1</u>

Program Name: <u>Customer Address List</u>   Program-ID: <u>CUSTLIST</u>   Written by: <u>SM</u>

Purpose: <u>Print customer address listing</u>   Approved by: <u>CM</u>

Input files: <u>CADDRS</u>

Output files: <u>QSYSPRT</u>

Processing Requirements:

Write an RPG/400 program to print a customer address listing.

<u>Input to the program:</u>

The externally defined physical file, CADDRS, contains customer names and addresses in the format shown in the attached record layout form.

<u>Processing:</u>

Read the physical file in keyed sequence until end of file. For every record processed, pass the LNAME, MIDINT, FNAME, CITY, STATE, and ZIP parameters to the RPG/400 program, CATENATE. The called program is written to concatenate the FNAME, MIDINT, and LNAME with one space between the field values. In addition, the called program also provides for concatenation of CITY, STATE, and ZIP so that one space is included between those separate elements.

The CATENATE program is stored as an object in a library in your library list.

Output:

A supplemental printer spacing chart shows the report design.

Figure 7-27   Specifications for an application program that calls a program.

Figure 7-28 illustrates a system flowchart that identifies the files processed by this application program.

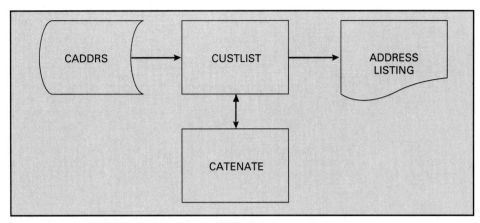

Figure 7-28   System flowchart for an applications program that calls a program.

The record format of the physical file and listing of the stored data are presented in Figure 7-29.

```
                        PHYSICAL FILE DESCRIPTION

        SYSTEM: AS/400                        DATE: 9/11/94
        FILE NAME: CADDRS                     REV NO: 0
        RECORD NAME: CADDRSR                  KEY LENGTH: 5
        SEQUENCE: Keyed                       RECORD SIZE: 71


                        FIELD DEFINITIONS

        FIELD     FIELD NAME    SIZE   TYPE    POSITION      COMMENTS
        NO                                    FROM     TO


          1       CUST#          5      C       1       5    Key Field
          2       LNAME         15      C       6      20
          3       MIDINT         1      C      21      21
          4       FNAME         12      C      22      33
          5       STREET        18      C      34      51
          6       CITY          15      C      52      66
          7       STATE          2      C      67      68
          8       ZIP            5      P      69      71
```

Physical File Data:

Customer Number	Last Name	Initial	First Name	Street	City	State	Zip
10000	APPEL	E	KAREL	20 AMSTERDAM AVE	NEW YORK	NY	07450
11000	BRAQUE	F	GEORGES	300 ST CLAIR ST	TRENTON	NJ	05501
12000	CEZANNE	C	PAUL	44 RUE PIGALLE	STAMFORD	CT	06518
13000	CHAGALL	W	MARC	222 QUAIL AVENUE	BRIDGEPORT	CT	06666
14000	DEGAS	T	EDGAR	10 ROSE TERRACE	WESTPORT	PA	07777
15000	ERNST	S	MAX	1 FRANKFURT DRIVE	FRANKFURT	KY	05551
16000	FULLER	H	BUCKMINSTER	999 PARK AVE	NEW YORK	NY	07550
17000	GONZALEZ	G	JULIO	101 SMITH LANE	GREENWICH	CT	06444
18000	HYPPOLITE	H	HECTOR	888 PEACHTREE AVE	ATLANTA	GA	03332
19000	JEANERET	R	PIERRE	90 CHATEAU DRIVE	GENEVA	NY	07777
20000	KANDINSKY	F	WASSILY	13 WARSAW LANE	LOS ANGELES	CA	09990
21000	CORBUSIER	C	CHARLES	10 PARIS PLACE	ENGELWOOD	NJ	07632

Figure 7-29   Physical file record format and data listing.

The report design is detailed in the printer spacing chart in Figure 7-30. Also included is the printed report generated by the program. Note that as a result of the called

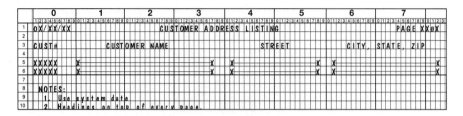

```
        0         1         2         3         4         5         6         7
     123456789012345678901234567890123456789012345678901234567890123456789012 3
 1  0X/XX/XX                    CUSTOMER ADDRESS LISTING                PAGE XXøX
 2
 3  CUST#          CUSTOMER NAME              STREET             CITY, STATE, ZIP
 4
 5  XXXXX      X                              X   X            X   X            X
 6  XXXXX      X                              X   X            X   X            X
 7
 8  NOTES:
 9   1. Use system date
10   2. Headings on top of every page.
```

```
10/01/95                    CUSTOMER ADDRESS LISTING                    PAGE    1

CUST#          CUSTOMER NAME              STREET             CITY, STATE, ZIP

10000     KAREL K APPEL             20 AMSTERDAM AVE    NEW YORK, NY 07450
11000     GEORGES F BRAQUE          300 ST CLAIR ST     TRENTON, NJ 05501
12000     PAUL C CEZANNE            44 RUE PIGALLE      STAMFORD, CT 06518
13000     MARC W CHAGALL            222 QUAIL AVENUE    BRIDGEPORT, CT 06666
14000     EDGAR T DEGAS             10 ROSE TERRACE     WESTPORT, PA 07777
15000     MAX S ERNST               1 FRANKFURT DRIVE   FRANKFORT, KY 05551
16000     BUCKMINSTER H FULLER      999 PARK AVENUE     NEW YORK, NY 07550
17000     JULIO G GONZALEZ          101 SMITH LANE      GREENWICH, CT 06444
18000     HECTOR H HYPPOLITE        888 PEACHTREE AVE   ATLANTA, GA 03332
19000     PIERRE R JEANERET         90 CHATEAU DRIVE    GENEVA, NY 07777
20000     WASSILY F KANDINSKY       13 WARSAW LANE      LOG ANGELES, CA 09990
21000     CHARLES C CORBUSIER       10 PARIS PLACE      ENGLEWOOD, NJ 07632
```

Figure 7-30   Report design and printed output.

program's concatenation process, the three name elements and city, state, and zip code values have only one space separating each of them.

Compile Listing of the Calling Program

A compile listing of the calling program is presented in Figure 7-31.

```
SEQUENCE                                                          IND   DO
NUMBER    *...1....+....2....+....3....+....4....+....5....+....6....+....7...*  USE   NUM
                       S o u r c e   L i s t i n g
   100    * THIS CALLING PROGRAM PASSES PARAMETERS TO A CALLED PROGRAM
   200    * WHICH CONCATENATES NAME AND ADDRESS ELEMENTS FOR A REPORT
          H
   300    FCADDRS IP E           K        DISK
          RECORD FORMAT(S): LIBRARY SMYERS FILE CADDRS.
                   EXTERNAL FORMAT CADDRSR RPG NAME CADDRSR
   400    FQSYSPRT O   F   132     OF      PRINTER
A000000   INPUT  FIELDS FOR RECORD CADDRSR FILE CADDRS FORMAT CADDRSR.
A000001                                    1   5 CUST#
A000002                                    6  17 FNAME
A000003                                   18  18 MIDINT
A000004                                   19  33 LNAME
A000005                                   34  51 STREET
A000006                                   52  66 CITY
A000007                                   67  68 STATE
A000008                                   69  73 ZIP
   500    I          DS
   600    I                               1  28 NAME
   700    I                              29  50 CSZIP
   800    C              CALL 'CATENATE'              call program
   900    *
  1000    * Store NAME value in left-justified in NAME field.
  1100    * Store CITY value left-justified in CSZIP field.
  1200    * PARM operations pass related result field values
  1300    * positionally to the called program (CATENATE)..
  1400    *
```

Figure 7-31   Compile listing of the calling program.

```
1500  C                    PARM FNAME     NAME
1600  C                    PARM           MIDINT
1700  C                    PARM           LNAME
1800  C                    PARM CITY      CSZIP
1900  C                    PARM           STATE
2000  C                    PARM           ZIP
2100  OQSYSPRT H  206   1P
2200  O       OR        OF
2300  O                        UDATE Y    8
2400  O                                  50 'CUSTOMER ADDRESS LISTING'
2500  O                                  77 'PAGE'
2600  O                        PAGE  Z   82
2700  O        H   2    1P
2800  O       OR        OF
2900  O                                   5 'CUST#'
3000  O                                  28 'CUSTOMER NAME'
3100  O                                  52 'STREET'
3200  O                                  79 'CITY, STATE, ZIP'
3300  O        D   1    N1P
3400  O                        CUST#      5
3500  O                        NAME      37
3600  O                        STREET    58
3700  O                        CSZIP     82
```

Line #

300 -
400   Externally defined physical file is processed in keyed sequence and printed output is to the system printer QSYSPRT.

500 -
700   The DS in columns 19–20 of the first *Input Specifications* statement define a data structure. NAME, which will store the catenated elements of the FNAME, MIDINIT, and LNAME values, and CSZIP, which will store the catenated elements of the CITY, STATE, and ZIP values, are defined as data structure fields. Both NAME and CSZIP are defined to support their related field elements and required spaces.

800 -   The CALL statement calls the "*called*" program CATENATE so that the values specified in the following PARM statements can be passed to it.

1500 - The PARM statement stores the FNAME value left-justified in the NAME field, which was defined in the data structure on line 600, and passes the value to the "called" program.

1600 -
1700   The PARM statements on lines 1600 and 1700 pass the values in MIDINT and LNAME to the "called" program.

1800 - The PARM statement stores the CITY value left-justified in the CSZIP field which was defined in the data structure on line 700 and passes the value to the "called" program.

1900 -
2000   The PARM statements on lines 1900 and 2000 pass the values in STATE and ZIP to the "called" program.

2100 -
3700   Headings are printed at **1P** and **OF** time. Detail output includes CUST#, the catenated value in NAME, STREET, and the catenated value in CSZIP.

Note: A PARM group ends when the first statement that is not a PARM is encountered.

Figure 7-31   Compile listing of the calling program. (Continued)

Compile Listing of the Called Program

An examination of the compile listing for the called program in Figure 7-32 indicates that a new operation (**CAT**) has been introduced to control concatenation. FNAME, MIDINT, and LNAME (all passed from the calling program) are concatenated in the NAME field.

```
SEQUENCE                                                                    IND  DO
NUMBER    *...1....+....2....+....3....+....4....+....5....+....6....+....7...*  USE  NUM
                          S o u r c e   L i s t i n g
    100   * THIS CALLED PROGRAM CONCATENATES NAME AND ADDRESS ELEMENTS
    200   * RECEIVED FROM A CALLING PROGRAM.......
          H
    300   C           *ENTRY    PLIST
    400   C                     PARM              NAME   28
    500   C                     PARM              MIDINT  1
    600   C                     PARM              LNAME  15
    700   C                     PARM              CSZIP  22
    800   C                     PARM              STATE   2
    900   C                     PARM              ZIP     5
   1000   * CONCATENATE NAME FIELDS........
   1100   C           NAME      CAT  MIDINT:1  NAME
   1200   C           NAME      CAT  LNAME:1   NAME       P
   1300   * CONCATENATE CITY, STATE, & ZIP CODE FIELDS
   1400   C           CSZIP     CAT  ',':0     CSZIP
   1500   C           CSZIP     CAT  STATE:1   CSZIP
   1600   C           CSZIP     CAT  ZIP:1     CSZIP      P
   1700   C                     RETRN
```

Line #

300 - The *ENTRY in *Factor 1* of the PLIST statement indicates that PARM field values are being received from a calling program.

400 - This **PARM** statement receives the first **PARM** value passed from the calling program. The FNAME value was stored left-justified in the NAME field before it was passed to the called program.

500 -
600   The two **PARM** statements receive the MIDINT and LNAME field values passed from the calling program.

700 - This **PARM** statement receives the fourth **PARM** value passed from the calling program. The CITY value was stored left-justified in the CSZIP field before it was passed to the called program.

800 -
900   The two **PARM** statements receive the STATE and ZIP field values passed from the calling program.

1100 - The value in MIDINT is concatenated one space after the FNAME value that was stored left-justified in the NAME field in the calling program.

1200 - The value in LNAME is concatenated one space after the previously concatenated MIDINT value.

The result of lines 1100 and 1200 CAT statements for the NAME field is shown below:

KAREL K APPEL   NAME field

CAT statements store field values with one space between them.

1400 - A comma is concatenated after the last low-order character in the CITY value previously stored in CSZIP and passed from the calling program.

1500 - The value in STATE is concatenated one space after the previously concatenated comma.

1600 - The value in ZIP is concatenated one space after the previously concatenated STATE value.

The result of lines 1400–1600 **CAT** statements in the CSZIP field is shown below:

NEW YORK, NY 07450   CSZIP field

concatenated comma — | — concatenated space

1700 - The RETRN operation returns control and the previously passed fields back to the calling program.

Figure 7-32 Compile listing of the called program.

Note that no input or output files are defined in the **called** program. A program is syntactically correct if only one or more calculation statements are specified.

The **called** program in Figure 7-32 uses the **CAT**, which is explained in Figure 7-33, to concatenate FNAME, MIDINT, and LNAME values in the NAME field. In addition, CITY, STATE, and ZIP values are concatenated and stored in CSZIP. Program control automatically returns the values back to the calling program when a **RETRN** operation or a statement that turns **LR** on is executed in the **called** program.

Note that the values passed from the **calling** program are passed positionally to the **called** program. The first field specified in the **calling** program is the first accessed in the **called** program, and so forth. Because of this positional processing feature, the related field names do not have to be the same in the **calling** and **called** programs.

The CAT (Concatenate Two Character Strings) Operation

The *called* program in Figure 7-32 introduced the **CAT** operation, which controlled the *concatenation* of the values (strings) in the NAME and CSZIP fields. Figure 7-33 explains the syntax and processing logic of the **CAT** operation.

The **CAT** operation concatenates the character string (field name, array element, data structure name, table name, or literal) specified in *Factor 2* to the end of the character string (field value, array element, data structure name, table name, or literal) entered in *Factor 1*. The concatenated string (value in *Factors 1 and 2*) is stored left-justified in the *Result Field*. An example is shown below:

```
*.. 1 ...+... 2 ...+... 3 ...+... 4 ...+... 5 ...+...
CLON01N02N03Factor1+++OpcdeFactor2+++ResultLenDHHHiLoEqComments+++++
C                   MOVE 'Dr.'    TITLE  3
C                   MOVE 'Watson' LNAME  6
C           TITLE   CAT  LNAME    NAME   9

Result: No blank between Dr. and Watson

        Dr.Watson
```

Factor 2 may include the number of blanks to be inserted between the concatenated strings. When this is required, the string name (or literal) is specified first followed by a colon and then the number of blanks to insert. The number of blanks element must be defined as a numeric integer. It may be a literal, field name, named constant, array name, or a table name. An example is shown below.

```
*.. 1 ...+... 2 ...+... 3 ...+... 4 ...+... 5 ...+...
CLON01N01N03Factor1+++OpcdeFactor2+++ResultLenDHHHiLoEqComments+++++
C                   MOVE 'Dr.'     TITLE  3
C                   MOVE 'Watson'  LNAME  6
C           TITLE   CAT  LNAME:1   NAME   10
                              └─ Specifies number of blanks to insert between the
                                 Factor 1 and 2 strings

Result: Blank inserted between Dr. and Watson
```

Figure 7-33 Syntax and processing logic of the **CAT** operation.

```
              Dr.bWatson        (Note b indicates blank value)
Any leading or trailing blanks included in the Factor 1 and/or Factor 2 strings are included in the concatenated
string in the Result Field.  An example is shown below.

    *.. 1 ...+... 2 ...+... 3 ...+... 4 ...+... 5 ...+...
    CLON01N01N03Factor1+++OpcdeFactor2+++ResultLenDHHHiLoEqComments+++++
    C                   MOVE 'Dr.'     TITLE   3
    C                   MOVE 'bbWatson'LNAME   8
    C           TITLE   CAT  LNAME:1   NAME   12

    Result: Blank inserted between Dr. and bbWatson

            Dr.bbbWatson  (leading blanks in the Factor 2 string are part of the
                          concatenated value)
```

If the number of blanks is not specified, any leading and trailing blanks in the Factor 1 and 2 item are not affected. An example is shown below.

```
    *.. 1 ...+... 2 ...+... 3 ...+... 4 ...+... 5 ...+...
    CLON01N01N03Factor1+++OpcdeFactor2+++ResultLenDHHHiLoEqComments+++++
    C                   MOVE 'bDr.b'   TITLE   5
    C                   MOVE 'bbWatson'LNAME   8
    C           TITLE   CAT  LNAME     NAME   13

    Result: Three blanks are inserted between bbDr.b and bbWatson-one stored in the
            low-order position of the TITLE value and two stored in the high-order
            position of the LNAME value.

            bDr.bbbWatson  (leading blanks in the Factor 2 string are part of the
                           concatenated value)
```

The Result Field must be defined as alphanumeric and may include a field name, array element, data structure
name, or table name. Its length must be large enough to include the Factor 1 and 2 values plus any inserted
blanks. right truncation will occur is the Result Field is not large enough. An example is shown below.

```
    *.. 1 ...+... 2 ...+... 3 ...+... 4 ...+... 5 ...+...
    CLON01N01N03Factor1+++OpcdeFactor2+++ResultLenDHHHiLoEqComments+++++
    C                   MOVE 'bDr.b'   TITLE   5
    C                   MOVE 'bbWatson'LNAME   8
    C           TITLE   CAT  LNAME     NAME   12  (Result Field too small)

    Result: Low-order n of the Factor 2 string is truncated

            bDr.bbbWatso
```

A P in column 53 of the CAT statement pads the low-order positions of the Result Field value
with blanks after concatenation is performed.

Figurative constants _cannot_ be used in any of the field items.

Figure 7-33   Syntax and processing logic of the **CAT** operation. (Continued)

SUMMARY

The **EXCPT** (*Exception*) operation modifies the regular RPG/400 logic cycle and causes output to be performed directly from calculations. **Output Specification** lines that support *Exception* output must be defined with an **E** in column 15. Traditional RPG coding requires conditioning *exception* time output with one or more indicators. With RPG/400, a programmer-supplied *exception line name* may be used. The name is entered in *Factor 2* of the **EXCPT** statement and in the *EXCPT Name* field of the related output **Record Description**.

Internal subroutines logically group calculation statements into separate modules. They are specified in an RPG/400 program by three operations: **EXSR** (*Exit to internal subroutine*), **BEGSR** (*Begin internal subroutine*), and **ENDSR** (*End internal subroutine*). When the end of an *internal subroutine* is encountered, program control returns to the statement <u>following</u> the related **EXSR** operation and any *detail* or *total time* processing continues. Then, within the sequence of instructions, when the first **BEGSR** statement is read without an **EXSR** controlled branch, all of the subroutines are ignored and program control "falls through" to the first **implied** or **explicit** output instruction.

The instructions for each *internal subroutine* must follow all *detail* and *total time* calculations. The order of the subroutines does not indicate the processing sequence; that is controlled by the order of the **EXSR** operations.

The **CASxx** operation combines the functions of the **COMP** and **EXSR** operations. One or more **CASxx** statements in a consecutive order are referred to as a *Case Group*, which must be ended by an **ENDCS** or **END** operation. If more than one **CASxx** statement is included in a *Case Group*, and one is executed, any subsequent ones are ignored. After a subroutine is executed, program control returns to the statement following the related **ENDCS** (or **END**) operation.

Programmer-defined literal values that are too large to be entered in *Factor 1 or Factor 2* may be defined by **Named Constants. Named Constants** are entered in the *Input Specifications* in columns 21–41 with a **C** in column 43. Alphanumeric value may contain 256 characters, and numeric may have 30 digits with a maximum of 9 decimal positions. **Named Constants** too long to fit on one input line are continued by entering a dash (-) after the last character (or digit) on the current line.

The *Fetch Overflow* feature adds additional control to the automatic page overflow cycle included in the RPG/400 compiler. It resolves the problem that occurs when overflow is sensed and more lines are specified for a page. Under that condition, without Fetch Overflow control, a line may be printed on the page perforation on continuous forms paper. Fetch Overflow is specified by entering the letter **F** in column 16 in one or more **H, D, T,** or **E** type lines.

Unlike the *System Date* value, *System Time* is not available at First Cycle (**1P** time) processing. It is accessed in calculations by the **TIME** operation in an HHMMSS format. An Edit Word must be used to print or display the value as HH:MM:SS.

An RPG/400 program may send and receive values from another RPG/400 program by the **CALL** operation and the **PLIST** and **PARM** declaratives. The program that sends values is referred to as the *calling* program and the one that receives the values, the *called* program. In addition to the **PLIST** and **PARM** declaratives, the *called* program must include ***ENTRY** as a *Factor 1* entry of the **PLIST** instruction. A **PLIST** group ends when a statement other than a **PARM** is encountered. The called program must include a **RETRN** operation or turn on **LR** to return control and pass the values back to the calling program.

QUESTIONS

7-1. Explain how the **EXCPT** operation processing differs from the regular RPG/400 logic cycle.

7-2. What coding forms and entries are used to control *exception time* processing?

7-3. After an **EXCPT** statement is executed and *exception output* performed, what processing occurs next?

7-4. How many **EXCPT** statements are permitted in an RPG/400 program?

7-5. What is an *exception name?*

7-6. When *exception output* occurs, are *heading, detail,* or *total time* output executed if they are conditioned by the same indicators? Explain the processing procedure.

7-7. Define *internal subroutines.* When should they be included in an RPG/400 program?

7-8. What operations control the processing of an *internal subroutine?* Explain the function of each.

7-9. Where in the sequence of calculation statements are *internal subroutines* located?

7-10. If more than one *internal subroutine* is included in a program, what controls the order in which they will be processed?

7-11. What is the sequence of processing after an *internal subroutine* is executed?

7-12. What RPG/400 operations and indicators may be included in an *internal subroutine?*

7-13. Explain the function of the **CASxx** operation. What does the **xx** entry represent?

7-14. What is a *Case Group?* How is it ended?

Examine the following coding and answer Questions 7-15 through 7-17.

Line	Form Type	Control Level	Indicators And Not	And Not	And Not	Factor 1	Operation	Factor 2	Result Field Name	Length	Dec Pos	H Adj	Arith Plus	Minus	Zero	Compare 1>2	1<2	1=2
0 1 0	C					FLDA	CASEQ	FLB	SUBR1									
0 2 0	C					FLDA	CASGT	FLC	SUBR2									
0 3 0	C						CAS		SUBR3									
0 4 0	C						ENDCS											

7-15. If the statement on line 010 tests as true, where does the program branch and where does it return?

7-16. If the statement on line 010 is false, what processing occurs?

7-17. When is the **CAS** statement on line 030 executed? Where does program control return after processing?

7-18. What is the function of the *Fetch Overflow* feature? When should it be included in a program?

7-19. What coding form(s) and field(s) are used to specify *Fetch Overflow?*

7-20. Define *Named Constants.* When are they used?

7-21. What coding form(s) and fields are used to specify a *Named Constant?*

7-22. In an RPG/400 program, how is the system time accessed?

7-23. When is an RPG/400 program a *calling* program? A *called* program?

7-24. To pass parameters to a *called* program, what RPG/400 operations are required in the *calling* program?

7-25. What RPG/400 operations are required in the *called* program to receive parameters from a *calling* program?

7-26. When are the values in the *called* program passed back to the *calling* program?

Examine the following coding included in a calling program and answer Questions 7-27 through 7-32.

Line	Form Type	Control Level	Indicators And Not	And Not	And Not	Factor 1	Operation	Factor 2	Result Field Name	Length	Dec Pos	H Adj	Arith Plus	Minus	Zero	Compare 1>2	1<2	1=2
0 1	C						CALL	'PROG2'	PASS									
0 2	C						.											
0 3	C						.											
0 4	C					PASS	PLIST											
0 5	C						PARM		VALUE									
0 6	C					RATING	PARM	CHARGE	AMT									

7-27. What is the function of the **CALL** statement on line 010?

7-28. Other than a literal, what may be specified in *Factor 2* of a **CALL** statement?

7-29. When is a *Result Field* entry not required for a **CALL** statement?

7-30. What is the function of the **PLIST** statement on line 040? When is it not required?

7-31. What is the function of the **PARM** statement on line 050?

7-32. What is the function of the *Factor 1 and 2* entries in the **PARM** statement on line 060?

Examine the following coding included in a called program and answer Questions 7-33 through 7-36.

```
Line  Form Type  Indicators          Factor 1      Operation   Factor 2      Result Field
010   C                              *ENTRY        PLIST
020   C                                            PARM                      VALUE1
030   C                              RATING        PARM        CHARGE        AMT1
040   C                                            .
050   C                                            .
060   C                                            .
070   C                                            RETRN
```

7-33. What is the function of the statement on line 010?

7-34. What is the function of the statement on line 020?

7-35. Explain the function of the *Factor 1, Factor 2, and Result Field* entries in the statement on line 030.

7-36. What is the function of the **RETRN** operation on line 070?

7-37. If a **RETRN** operation is not included in a *called* program, when does the processing explained for Question 7-36 occur?

7-38. On a blank *Calculation Specifications* form, write the statements to concatenate **MONTH** (month name), **UDAY** (system day), the literal 19, and **UYEAR** (system year). Specify a space after the **MONTH** value, a comma and a space after the **UDAY** value, and no space between 19 and the **UYEAR** value.

PROGRAMMING ASSIGNMENTS

For each of the following programming assignments, a physical file must have been created and loaded with the related data records. Your instructor will inform you as to whether you have to create the physical file and load it or if it has been prepared for the assignment.

Programming Assignment 7-1: STRAIGHT-LINE DEPRECIATION SCHEDULE

Write an RPG/400 program to generate a report that details a depreciation schedule for a company's fixed assets. Depreciation is a tax-deductible expense for assets that are used in the production of income. It may be defined as the "allocation of the cost of an asset over its useful life." Because of its simplicity and acceptance by the Internal Revenue Service, one of the most popular determinations of annual depreciation expense is the straight-line method, which is computed by the following formula:

$$\text{Annual Depreciation} = \frac{\text{Cost} - \text{Salvage (Trade-In)}}{\text{Estimated Useful Life}}$$

where:

Annual Depreciation = the amount of depreciation expense computed for each year of the asset's life.
Cost = the original cost of the asset plus any capital improvements.
Salvage Value (also called Trade-In) = the amount the asset will realize as scrap or trade-in at the end of its estimated useful life.
Estimated Useful Life = the expected life of the asset based on its estimated productivity. The tax laws have established useful life by general categories of assets. For example, autos and light-duty trucks are assigned a three-year life, whereas all other capital goods (machinery, equipment, and so forth) have a five-year life.

Physical File Record Format:

```
                    PHYSICAL FILE DESCRIPTION

      SYSTEM: AS/400                         DATE: Yours
      FILE NAME: Yours                       REV NO: 0
      RECORD NAME: Yours                     KEY LENGTH: None
      SEQUENCE: Non-keyed                    RECORD SIZE: 40

                        FIELD DEFINITIONS

      FIELD     FIELD NAME    SIZE  TYPE    POSITION       COMMENTS
       NO                                  FROM    TO


        1       ASSET          25    C        1     25
        2       PDATE           6    P       26     29
        3       COST            9    P       30     34    2 decimals
        4       EUL             2    P       35     36    0 decimals
        5       SALVGE          6    P       37     40    0 decimals

      Physical File Data:
                              Date of                    Salvage
           Asset Name         Purchase      Cost    EUL   Value


      BPT MILLING MACHINE     051495   001500000    07   003000
      IBM AS/400 - MODEL E    021095   037500000    05   020000
      IBM MICRO - 426         011195   000280000    03   000400
      OFFICE FURNITURE        100195   000900000    10   000600
      FACTORY BUILDING        061595   120000000    18   000000
```

Processing: Read the physical file and for every record processed compute the annual depreciation expense for the asset based on the formula that has been given. Notice that the accumulated depreciation and book value must be computed each year for the life of the asset. The printer spacing chart indicates the field sizes for these items. The annual depreciation, accumulated depreciation, and book value amounts are rounded to the nearest dollar. Because of rounding, the book value after the last year's depreciation as calculated may not equal the cost of the asset. Any dollar difference must be added to the last year's annual depreciation amount, so the book value is zero for the last year.

Report Design: Page overflow is to be specified in the report for the two heading lines for the columns (i.e., YEAR, ANNUAL, ACCUMULATED, BOOK, and so forth) only and not for the first four report lines.

```
       0          1          2          3          4          5         6
    1234567890123456789012345678901234567890123456789012345678901234567890123456789012345
 1  ØX/XX/XX          DEPRECIATION SCHEDULE                        PAGE XXØX
 2                    STRAIGHT-LINE METHOD
 3
 4
 5      ASSET: X                        X   PURCHASE DATE: ØX/XX/XX
 6
 7      COST: X,XXX,XXØ.XX        EHL: ØX       SALVAGE VALUE: XX,XØX
 8
 9                    ANNUAL          ACCUMULATED       BOOK
10           YEAR     DEPRECIATION    DEPRECIATION      VALUE
11
12           ØX       X,XXX,XØX       X,XXX,XØX       X,XXX,XØX
13
14           ØX       X,XXX,XØX       X,XXX,XØX       X,XXX,XØX
15
16      NOTES:
17
18        1. USE SYSTEM DATE FOR REPORT.
19
20        2. PRINT OUTPUT FOR EACH ASSET ON SEPARATE PAGE.
21
22        3. ONLY HEADING LINES 9 AND 1Ø ARE TO BE PRINTED
23
24           ON OVERFLOW PAGES.
```

The depreciation schedule is complete when the accumulated depreciation value is equal to the depreciable amount (i.e., when the remainder is zero).

Programming Assignment 7-2: ACRS AUTOMOBILE DEPRECIATION SCHEDULE

Beginning with the 1987 tax year, the federal tax laws require that special rates (referred to as ACRS rates) must be applied to automobiles used 50% or more for business purposes. The maximum depreciation deduction allowed each year for the life of an automobile is as follows:

```
Year 1    $2,560
Year 2     4,000
Year 3     2,450
Year 4     1,475 (this last amount is taken until
                  the asset is fully depreciated)
```

Under this method, a full year's depreciation may be taken regardless of when the asset was purchased. Also, salvage or trade-in value is ignored in the computations.

Physical File Record Format:

```
                    PHYSICAL FILE DESCRIPTION

SYSTEM: AS/400                         DATE: Yours
FILE NAME: Yours                       REV NO: 0
RECORD NAME: Yours                     KEY LENGTH: None
SEQUENCE: Non-keyed                    RECORD SIZE: 34

                     FIELD DEFINITIONS

FIELD    FIELD NAME    SIZE   TYPE    POSITION      COMMENTS
NO                                   FROM     TO


  1      ASSET          25     C        1      25
  2      PDATE           6     P       26      29
  3      COST            5     P       30      32    0 decimals
  4      USE             3     P       33      34    2 decimals
```

Physical File Data:

Asset Name	Date of Purchase	Cost	USE
MERCURY SABLE WAGON	032095	19250	100
MITSUBISHI 3000 GT	041895	38900	030
SATURN COUPE	011195	16490	090
FIREBIRD FIREHAWK	060195	21760	020
MUSTANG GT	081195	18230	070

Processing: For each record processed, compute the annual depreciation using the statutory amounts given above. For assets used less than 100% for business, the annual limit must be multiplied by the related percentage of business use to compute the deductible depreciation expense for the year. The depreciation schedule for each asset must include all the years needed to fully depreciate the automobile to its allowable depreciable amount. The steps related to the determination of annual depreciation, accumulated depreciation, and remaining amount follow:

Step 1:   Compute the depreciable amount:

Cost × Business Percentage = Depreciable Amount

Step 2:   Initialize a remainder field with the depreciable amount value.

Step 3:   Determine each year's depreciation by multiplying the year's factor (e.g., $2,560) by the business percentage.

Factor × Business Percentage = Year's Depreciation

Step 4:   Determine if the remainder (Step 1) is less than the current year's depreciation (Step 3). If it is, move the remainder value to the year's depreciation field.

Step 5:   Accumulate the current year's depreciation:

Accumulated Depreciation + Year's Depreciation = Accumulated Depreciation

Step 6:   Subtract accumulated depreciation from the depreciable amount.

Depreciable Amount − Accumulated Depreciation = Remaining Amount

Round the annual depreciation, accumulated depreciation, and remaining values to the nearest dollar.

Report Design:

```
        0         1         2         3         4         5         6         7
   1234567890123456789012345678901234567890123456789012345678901234567890123456789 01
 1 0X/XX/XX                    AUTOMOBILE DEPRECIATION SCHEDULE              PAGE XX0X
 2                                   ACRS METHOD
 3
 4
 5     ASSET NAME: X                       X       DATE PURCHASED: 0X/XX/XX
 6
 7     COST: XX,X0X        BUSINESS USE: 0XX%      DEPRECIABLE AMT: XX,X0X
 8
 9                         ANNUAL           ACCUMULATED        REMAINING
10       YEAR      FACTOR   DEPRECIATION     DEPRECIATION     DEPRECIABLE AMT
11
12       0X       X,XXX        X,XXX           XX,XXX           XX,XXX
13
14       0X       X,XXX        X,XXX           XX,XXX           XX,XXX
15
16     NOTES:
17
18       1. USE SYSTEM DATE FOR REPORT.
19
20       2. PRINT EACH ASSET ON A SEPARATE PAGE.
```

Programming Assignment 7-3: HOSPITAL BILLING REPORT

Write an RPG/400 program to generate a billing report for a hospital based on the following information.

Physical File Record Format:

```
                       PHYSICAL FILE DESCRIPTION

         SYSTEM: AS/400                        DATE: Yours
         FILE NAME: Yours                      REV NO: 0
         RECORD NAME: Yours                    KEY LENGTH: 5
         SEQUENCE: Keyed                       RECORD SIZE: 40


                          FIELD DEFINITIONS


         FIELD     FIELD NAME   SIZE   TYPE    POSITION      COMMENTS
          NO                                   FROM   TO


           1       PATNT#        5      C        1     5  Key field
           2       PNAME        20      C        6    25
           3       ADMIT         6      P       26    29  Admit date
           4       CHKOUT        6      P       30    33  Out date
           5       DAYS          3      P       34    35
           6       RMTYPE        1      C       36    36  I, P, S
           7       NURSE         1      C       37    37  N
           8       TV            1      C       38    38  T
           9       OXY           1      C       39    39  O
          10       IV            1      C       40    40  V
```

```
Physical File Data:

                                Admit    Out            Room    Private
        Patient#  Patient Name  Date     Date   Days    Type    Nurse     TV   Oxygen   IV

          10000   WALTER WINCHELL  010595  011595  10     P                 T
          11000   EDGAR BERGEN     010895  011395   5     S                 T
          12000   ZAZU PITTS       010295  011995  17     I                           O
          13000   LON CHANEY       010695  011595   9     I      N                          V
          14000   FANNY BRICE      011095  011495   4     P                 T
          15000   W.C. FIELDS      012095  013195  11     S                 T
          16000   JACK BENNY       012295  013095   8     I      N          T       O       V
```

Processing: The following steps are required to determine a patient's bill:

Step 1: Include the following rate information in the calculations:

Room Type	Input Code	Daily Rate
Intensive care	I	$400
Private room	P	$300
Semi-private room	S	$200

Extra Services	Input Code	Daily Rate
Private nurse	N	$110
Oxygen	O	$250
I.V. Feeding	V	$105
Television	T	$ 10

Step 2: Test the room type code (**I, P, S**) and multiply the related rate by the number of days the patient was in the hospital. Accumulate each room-type billing amount to a separate total field.

Step 3: Test the extra service code (**N, T, O, V**) and multiply the related rate by the number of days the services were rendered. Add the services charges to a total field.

Step 4: Add the number of intensive care, private room, and semi-private patients to three accumulators.

Step 5: Accumulate a total for the number of patients and extra services amount.

Report Design:

```
          0         1         2         3         4         5         6         7         8         9         10
    1234567890123456789012345678901234567890123456789012345678901234567890123456789012345678901234567890123456789012345
 1                                          GET WELL HOSPITAL                                              PAGE XXØX
 2                                          ROOM BILLING REPORT
 3                                             AS OF ØX/XX/XX
 4
 5
 6   PATIENT                         ADMIT      CHECKOUT     BILLING                        ROOM       EXTRA SERVICES
 7   NUMBER        PATIENT NAME       DATE        DATE        DAYS       ROOM TYPE          CHARGE         CHARGE
 8
 9   XXXXX    X                  X   ØX/XX/XX   ØX/XX/XX     XØX    X              X   XXX,XXØ.XX   XXX,XXØ.XX
10
11   XXXXX    X                  X   ØX/XX/XX   ØX/XX/XX     XØX    X              X   XXX,XXØ.XX   XXX,XXØ.XX
12
13        TOTALS:
14
15            NUMBER OF PATIENTS:............X,XØX
16            PRIVATE ROOM BILLING:.........$X,XXX,XXØ.XX
17            INTENSIVE CARE ROOM BILLING:..$X,XXX,XXØ.XX
18            SEMI-PRIVATE ROOM BILLING:....$X,XXX,XXØ.XX
19            EXTRA SERVICES BILLING:.......$X,XXX,XXØ.XX
20
21   NOTE: Use system date for this report.
22
```

For the room type output, print INTENSIVE CARE, PRIVATE, or SEMI-PRIVATE. Because two of the room constants are too long to fit in *Factor 2* of a **MOVE** operation, define them as Named Constants. Depending on the room type, move the related field value to <u>one</u> output field defined for room type.

Programming Assignment 7-4: MORTGAGE AMORTIZATION SCHEDULE

Banks and other lending institutions often provide the mortgagor with an amortization schedule of the monthly payments. For fixed-rate mortgages, the payments are the same for the life of the mortgage. Included in the schedule are details related to the amount of the payment and what part of it applies separately to the principal and interest. A new principal balance is computed after each payment, and the interest for the next period is calculated on that amount.

Physical File Record Format:

```
                    PHYSICAL FILE DESCRIPTION

SYSTEM: AS/400                          DATE: Yours
FILE NAME: Yours                        REV NO: 0
RECORD NAME: Yours                      KEY LENGTH: 5
SEQUENCE:Keyed                          RECORD SIZE: 36

                    FIELD DEFINITIONS

FIELD    FIELD NAME    SIZE  TYPE    POSITION      COMMENTS
  NO                                 FROM   TO

  1      LOAN#          5     C        1     5   Key field
  2      MORTGR        20     C        6    25
  3      TIME           2     P       26    27   0 decimals
  4      RATE           5     P       28    30   5 decimals
  5      PRINPL         6     P       31    34   0 decimals
  6      PAYPYR         2     P       35    36   0 decimals
```

Physical File Data:

Loan#	Mortgagor	Time In Yrs	Rate	Principal	Payments Per Year
12345	HENRY W. LONGFELLOW	05	12500	020000	04
13333	EDGAR A. POE	30	12000	056000	12
22222	GOEFFREY CHAUCER	10	10000	060000	12
22333	JOHN MILTON	15	07250	200000	24

Calculations:

Step 1: Determine the constant fixed monthly payment from the following formula:

$$\text{Monthly Payment} = \left(\frac{P}{1 - \frac{1}{(1+i)^n}}{i} \right)$$

where:

i = annual mortgage rate. Must be divided by number of interest payments per year to determine application's interest rate period month.
n = total number of payment periods for the year.
P = balance of the mortgage principal.

Step 2: Calculate the interest amount of the monthly payment using the following formula for simple interest:

$$I = \frac{P \times R \times T}{12}$$

where:

I = simple interest amount.

P = principal amount. The balance of the principal will decline after each monthly payment.

R = annual interest rate.

T = time for the life of the mortgage. If payments are monthly, time is expressed as total number of months for the mortgage loan.

12 = Because payments are monthly, 12 is used as a denominator in formula.

Step 3: The amount of the monthly payment applicable to the payment of the principal (reduces the principal) is determined as follows:

$$\text{Principal Payment} = \text{Monthly Payment} - \text{Interest Amount}$$

Step 4: The end-of-month principal balance is determined by subtracting the monthly principal payment (Step 3) amount from the previous principal balance. The new balance is used for the next month's computation of the principal and interest parts of the monthly payment.

Report Design:

```
   0         1         2         3         4         5         6         7         8
 1 ØX/XX/XX                    MORTGAGE AMORTIZATION SCHEDULE                      PAGE XXØX
 2
 3
 4 LOAN NUMBER: XXXXX          MORTGAGOR: X                X          RATE/YR: ØX.XXX %
 5
 6  PAYMENT        BEGINNING        MORTGAGE        PRINCIPAL       INTEREST    ENDING PRINCIPAL
 7  NUMBER         PRINCIPAL        PAYMENT         AMOUNT          AMOUNT          BALANCE
 8
 9    XØX         XXX,XXØ.XX       XXX,XXØ.XX      XXX,XXØ.XX      XXX,XXØ.XX     XXX,XXØ.XX
10
11    XØX         XXX,XXØ.XX       XXX,XXØ.XX      XXX,XXØ.XX      XXX,XXØ.XX     XXX,XXØ.XX
12
13
14 NOTES:
15
16  1. PRINT HEADING LINES 6 AND 7 ON OVERFLOW PAGES.
17
18  2. BEGIN EACH LOAN ON A SEPARATE PAGE.
19
20  3. DATE IS SYSTEM SUPPLIED.
21
22  4. MULTIPLY RATE BY 1ØØ FOR PRINTING.
```

Programming Assignment 7-5: CREDIT SALES REPORT

This assignment requires the completion of <u>two</u> RPG/400 programs. One will be a *calling* program that generates a Credit Sales Report after passing values to and receiving values from a *called* program. The processing steps include the following:

1. The calling program must pass the UMONTH, UYEAR, and SALE AMOUNT values to the *called* program.

2. The called program must test the UMONTH value and move the related month name to a field that must be defined large enough to include the month name, the constant 19, and the UYEAR value. To access the month name, nested IF statements or a SELEC group must be specified in the *called* program.

3. The month name, the constant 19, and the UYEAR value are to be concatenated in the *called* program. One space is to be included after the month name with no space between 19 and the UYEAR value as shown below:

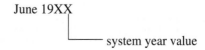

June 19XX

— system year value

4. The sales amount value passed from the *calling* program is to be tested in the called program to determine the applicable sales discount. Sales discounts are determined as follows:

Sales Amount Range	Sales Discount Percent
5000 to 10000	1.5%
10001 to 30000	2.5%
30001 to 50000	4%
50001 and over	5%

5. After the date elements have been concatenated and the sales discount computed in the called program, the values are to be passed back to the calling program.
6. The calling program must generate the report shown in the supplemental printer spacing chart.

Physical File Record Format:

```
                  PHYSICAL FILE DESCRIPTION

SYSTEM: AS/400                        DATE: Yours
FILE NAME: Yours                      REV NO: 0
RECORD NAME: Yours                    KEY LENGTH: 4
SEQUENCE: Non-keyed                   RECORD SIZE: 41

                    FIELD DEFINITIONS

FIELD      FIELD NAME    SIZE   TYPE    POSITION       COMMENTS
  NO                                  FROM     TO


   1        ACTNO          4     C       1       4    Key field
   2        ACTNAM        25     C       5      29
   3        SALDAT         6     P      30      33
   4        INVNO          5     P      34      36
   5        SALAMT         8     P      37      41    2 decimals
```

Physical File Data:

```
                                                      Sales
Acct#     Account Name      Sale Date   Invoice#     Amount

1000     IVAN SNODSMITH       0103??      13568      00620099
1200     THERESA PIRES        0105??      13569      07098014
1300     RALPH SCADDED        0108??      13570      04574026
1400     HENRY CARLSON        0115??      13571      02990089
1500     JUAN HERNANDEZ       0122??      13572      10032415
1600     IRA FINKELSTEIN      0128??      13573      00462018
```

└───── Replace ?? with your
system or job year

Report Design:

chapter 8

Control Level Break Processing

THE CONTROL LEVEL BREAK PROCESSING ENVIRONMENT

Record Identifying (**01–99**), *Resulting, First Page* (**1P**), *Overflow* (**OA–OG** and **OV**), *Field,* and *Last Record* (**LR**) indicators have been introduced and used in previous chapters. Another class of indicators, called *Control Level* (**L1–L9**), are included in the repertoire of indicators supplied by RPG/400. These indicators are commonly used for applications requiring subtotals within the body of reports. The previously discussed *Last Record* indicator (**LR**), which turns on automatically when end of file is sensed, is a control level indicator. However, **LR** provides for final totals only and does not control (except at last record time) the processing of subtotal calculations and/or output.

Detail Report with Subtotals

Figure 8-1 shows a report that includes subtotals for salesperson groups. Notice that when the salesperson number changes (from 1000 to 1100; 1100 to 1200; and so forth), a total

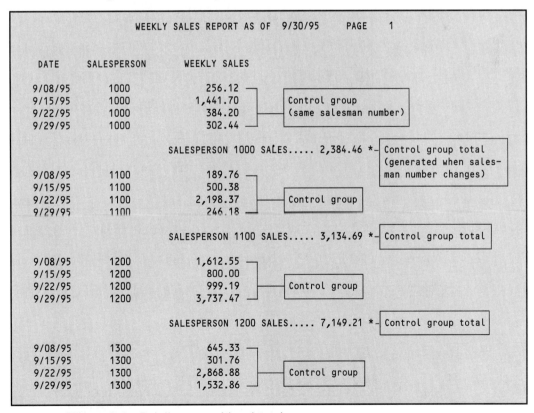

Figure 8-1 Detail report with subtotals.

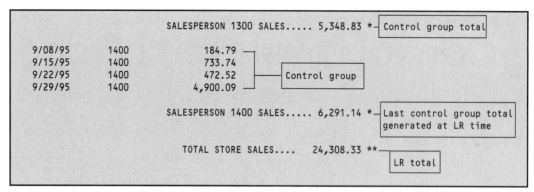

Figure 8-1   Detail report with subtotals. (Continued)

line for the related salesperson is printed. In addition, at end of file (**LR** time) the total for the last salesperson group is printed before the TOTAL STORE SALES sum. An examination of the report shows that the data is in ascending order by date (minor field), which is within the ascending salesperson number (major field) order. The logic of *Control Level Break* processing requires that the data file defined as input be sorted in ascending or descending order by control field(s) before processing.

Structure of the Data File

Figure 8-2 shows the data file that was processed for the report in Figure 8-1. Comments identify new terms associated with this environment including *Control Field, Control Break, Control Group Totals,* and *total time.*

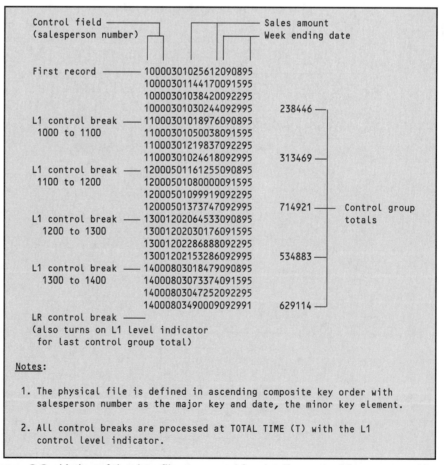

Figure 8-2   Listing of the data file processed for detail report with one control level break (subtotal).

Source Program Coding

A listing of the program that processed the file in Figure 8-2 and generated the report in Figure 8-1 is presented in Figure 8-3. Notice that input, calculations, and output coding include instructions unique to *Control Level Break* processing. The syntax and processing logic of each entry will be explained by separate illustrations.

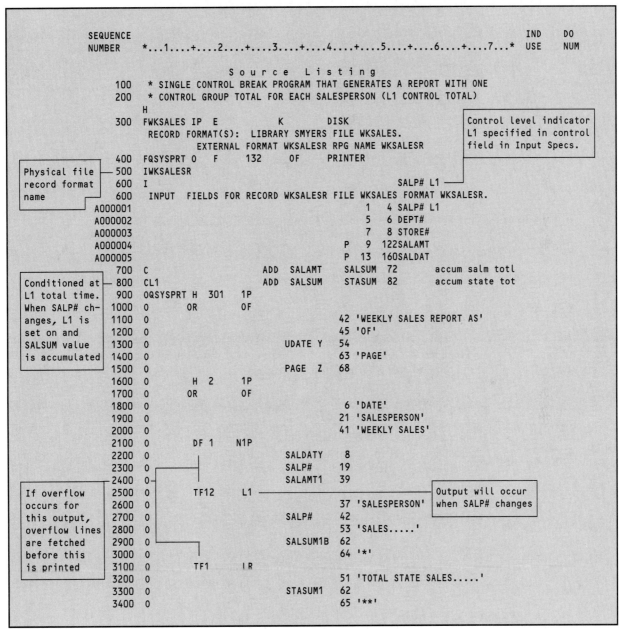

Figure 8-3   Compile listing of the program that generates a report with one control group total.

Input Specifications Coding

Detailed in the *Input Specifications* shown in Figure 8-4 are the syntax and logic related to Control Level Break processing. Because the SALP# field has a *Control Level Indicator (L1)* entered in columns 59 to 60, it is referred to as a *Control Field*. When the value in this field for the record currently being processed is different from the value in the field for the previous record, the L1 Control Level indicator is automatically turned

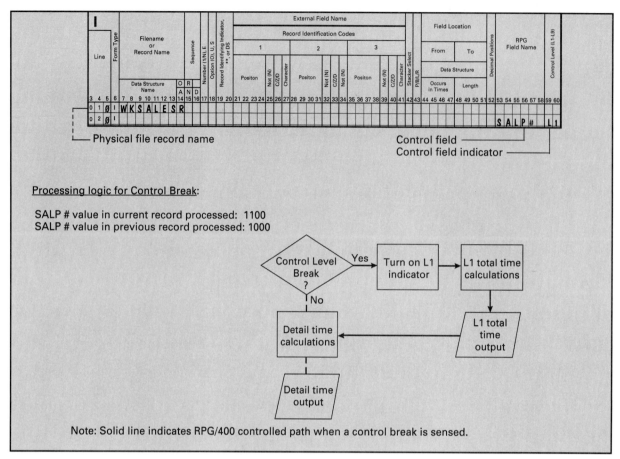

Figure 8-4   Input specifications coding for program that generates a report with one control group total.

on by RPG/400 control. *Any calculations and output instructions conditioned by the **L1** indicator are immediately executed, temporarily skipping any detail processing.* Detail calculations, followed by detail output, are returned to after all related level break processing is executed. Comparison of the current and previous record *Control Field* values is controlled by RPG/400; the programmer does not have to include this processing in the program.

Control Fields and Control Level Indicators

Control fields are specified on input by including a *Control Level* indicator in columns 59 and 60 of the input form. The features of *Control Fields* and *Control Level* indicators are outlined in Figure 8-5. "Split" control field concepts are not included; they will be introduced later in this chapter.

<u>Single Control Field Features</u>:

1. Must be located in the same columns within a physical file's record format.

2. May be located in different columns within the record formats of two or more physical files.

Figure 8-5   Control field and Control Level indicator processing features.

3. May be defined numeric or alphanumeric. Maximum numeric *control field* size is 30 bytes and alphanumeric 256.

4. If the same *control field* has been assigned the same *control level* in the record formats of two or more physical files, they must be defined as the same type (numeric or alphanumeric) and length. The same *control field* name may be specified in each record format.

5. Decimal positions are ignored when *control field* values are compared. All numeric fields are considered integers.

6. Signs are ignored when *control field* values are compared. All numeric fields are considered positive for control break testing.

<u>Control Level Indicator (**L1-L9**) Features:</u>

1. Nine *control level* indicators (**L1-L9**) are available in RPG/400.

2. A higher-level indicator turns on all lower-level indicators. For example, if **L3** is turned on by program control, **L2** and **L1** will automatically be set on.

3. At end of file, when **LR** is turned on, all lower-level indicators used in the program are automatically set on.

4. **L1** is commonly assigned to the lowest *control field* and **L2**, **L3**, etc., assigned in order as needed. For example, **L1** would be assigned to employee number, **L2** to department number, **L3** to store, and so forth.

5. **L1-L9** may be assigned to *control fields* in any order providing the logic specified in item 4 (above) is followed.

6. A *control level* indicator turned on in calculations by the SETON or other operation does not set on any lower-level indicator. For example, if **L2** was turned on by a SETON statement, **L1** would not automatically be turned on.

Figure 8-5 Control field and Control Level indicator processing features. (Continued)

Calculation Specifications Coding

Calculation statements that are conditioned by a *Control Level* indicator entered in columns 7 and 8 are executed at total time. Instructions conditioned by **L1** to **L9** in columns 10 to 11, or 13 to 14, or 16 to 17 are executed at detail time. The significance of these processing "times" is explained in the example program's calculations illustrated in Figure 8-6.

The processing logic shown in Figure 8-6 identifies the following four important features when a control break is sensed:

    1. *Detail time* calculation is automatically skipped, and **L1** *total time* calculation is executed.

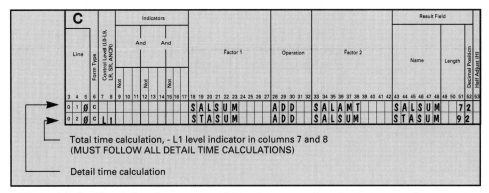

Figure 8-6 Example of one control break program's calculations and processing logic when a control break is sensed.

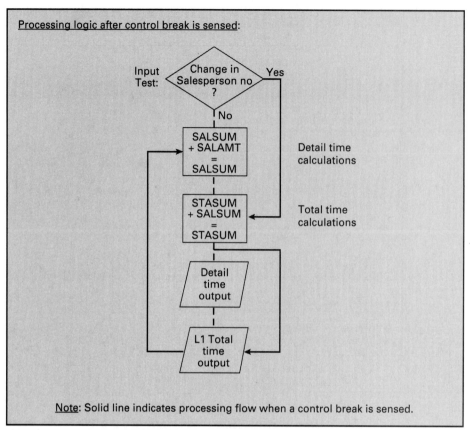

Processing logic after control break is sensed:

Input Test: Change in Salesperson no ? — Yes

No

SALSUM + SALAMT = SALSUM — Detail time calculations

STASUM + SALSUM = STASUM — Total time calculations

Detail time output

L1 Total time output

Note: Solid line indicates processing flow when a control break is sensed.

Figure 8-6 Example of one control break program's calculations and processing logic when a control break is sensed. (Continued)

2. Then, *detail time* output is skipped, and *total time* output is executed.
3. Program control returns to the *detail time* calculation after *total time* output is executed.
4. After *detail time* calculation is executed, program control skips the *total time* calculation and executes *detail time* output.

The total time calculation statements must follow all detail time calculations, and total time output instructions must follow detail time output coding. A terminal error will result during program compilation if this rule is not followed.

Output Specifications Coding

Examine the partial output coding for the one control break example program in Figure 8-7 and notice the following:

1. **L1** *total time* output follows *detail time* output.
2. The function of the letter **B,** entered in column 39, is to initialize the SALSUM field to zeros after output and before the next salesperson group is accumulated.

L1 Detail Time Processing—Calculation Control. All control break processing discussed has been addressed to *total time* calculations and output. Sometimes program logic requires that it be performed at *detail time.* For example, in the example

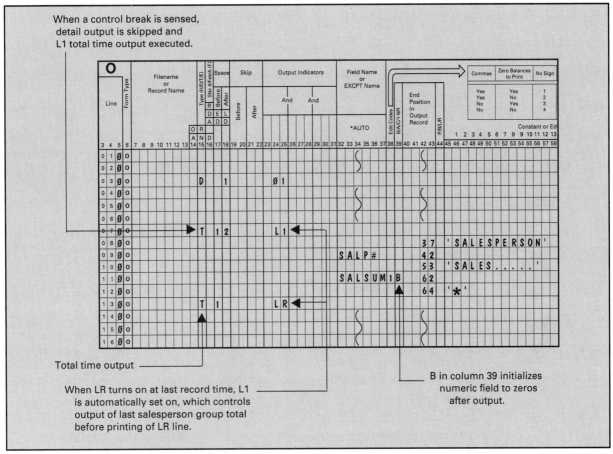

When a control break is sensed, detail output is skipped and L1 total time output executed.

Total time output —

When LR turns on at last record time, L1 is automatically set on, which controls output of last salesperson group total before printing of LR line.

B in column 39 initializes numeric field to zeros after output.

Figure 8-7 Example of one control break program's output coding for **L1** control group total.

program, **B** was specified in column 39 on the *Output Specifications* to initialize the accumulator, SALSUM, to zeros after printing. An alternative approach to clearing an accumulator requires the use of a calculation instruction that is conditioned with a related *control level* indicator at detail time. Figure 8-8 illustrates the coding for this method and the corresponding processing logic.

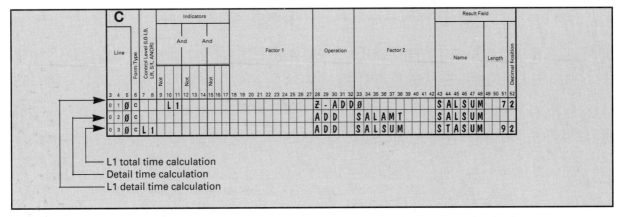

— L1 total time calculation
— Detail time calculation
— L1 detail time calculation

Figure 8-8 *Detail* and *total time* calculations and processing logic.

Processing Logic of L1 Detail and Total Times:

Salesperson number:

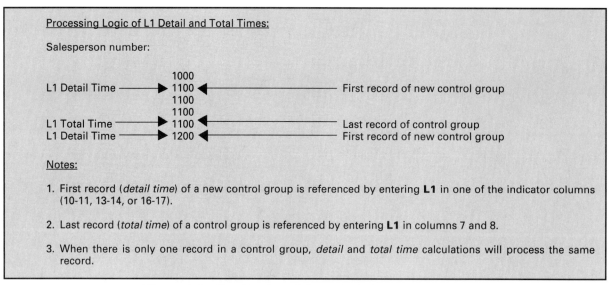

```
                                  1000
        L1 Detail Time ─────────► 1100 ◄────────────── First record of new control group
                                  1100
                                  1100
        L1 Total Time ──────────► 1100 ◄────────────── Last record of control group
        L1 Detail Time ─────────► 1200 ◄────────────── First record of new control group
```

Notes:

1. First record (*detail time*) of a new control group is referenced by entering **L1** in one of the indicator columns (10-11, 13-14, or 16-17).

2. Last record (*total time*) of a control group is referenced by entering **L1** in columns 7 and 8.

3. When there is only one record in a control group, *detail* and *total time* calculations will process the same record.

Figure 8-8   *Detail* and *total time* calculations and processing logic. (Continued)

L1 Detail Time Processing—Output Control.   A reexamination of the detail report in Figure 8-1 will show that more than one salesperson group is included on a page. If, however, the application required that each salesperson group be printed on a separate page, **L1** *detail time* output control would be necessary. Figure 8-9 illustrates a report that prints salesperson groups on separate pages.

```
                    WEEKLY SALES REPORT AS OF  9/30/95       PAGE    1


        DATE      SALESPERSON      WEEKLY SALES

      9/08/95        1000             256.12
      9/15/95        1000           1,441.70
      9/22/95        1000             384.20
      9/29/95        1000             302.44

                            SALESPERSON 1000 SALES..... 2,384.46

    - - - - - - - - - - - - - - - - - - - - - - - - - - - - - - - -

                    WEEKLY SALES REPORT AS OF  9/30/95       PAGE    2


        DATE      SALESPERSON      WEEKLY SALES


      9/08/95        1100             189.76
      9/15/95        1100             500.38
      9/22/95        1100           2,198.37
      9/29/95        1100             246.18

                            SALESPERSON 1100 SALES..... 3,134.69
```

Figure 8-9   Modified report with salesperson groups on separate pages.

Changes needed to the original program (Figure 8-3) are shown in the partial source listing in Figure 8-10. Only the output coding has to be modified to support the new report requirements.

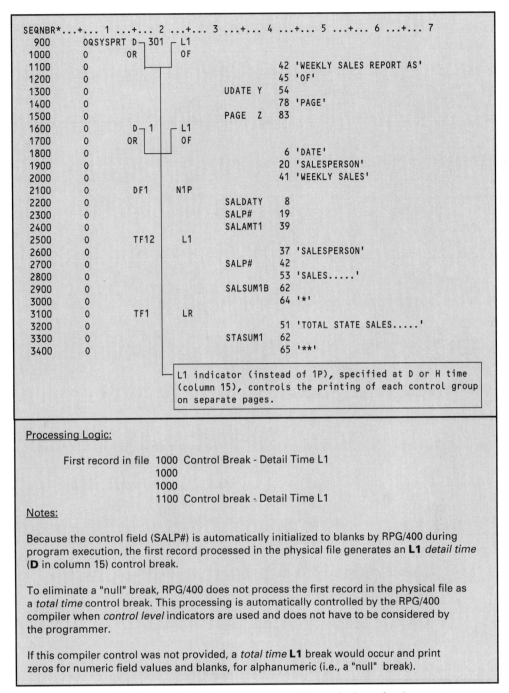

```
SEQNBR*...+... 1 ...+... 2 ...+... 3 ...+... 4 ...+... 5 ...+... 6 ...+... 7
  900    OQSYSPRT D  301   L1
 1000    O        OR       OF
 1100    O                              42 'WEEKLY SALES REPORT AS'
 1200    O                              45 'OF'
 1300    O                    UDATE Y   54
 1400    O                              78 'PAGE'
 1500    O                    PAGE  Z   83
 1600    O        D  1     L1
 1700    O        OR       OF
 1800    O                               6 'DATE'
 1900    O                              20 'SALESPERSON'
 2000    O                              41 'WEEKLY SALES'
 2100    O        DF1      N1P
 2200    O                    SALDATY    8
 2300    O                    SALP#     19
 2400    O                    SALAMT1   39
 2500    O        TF12     L1
 2600    O                              37 'SALESPERSON'
 2700    O                    SALP#     42
 2800    O                              53 'SALES.....'
 2900    O                    SALSUM1B  62
 3000    O                              64 '*'
 3100    O        TF1      LR
 3200    O                              51 'TOTAL STATE SALES.....'
 3300    O                    STASUM1   62
 3400    O                              65 '**'
```

> L1 indicator (instead of 1P), specified at D or H time
> (column 15), controls the printing of each control group
> on separate pages.

Processing Logic:

First record in file 1000 Control Break - Detail Time L1
                      1000
                      1000
                      1100 Control break - Detail Time L1

Notes:

Because the control field (SALP#) is automatically initialized to blanks by RPG/400 during program execution, the first record processed in the physical file generates an **L1** *detail time* (**D** in column 15) control break.

To eliminate a "null" break, RPG/400 does not process the first record in the physical file as a *total time* control break. This processing is automatically controlled by the RPG/400 compiler when *control level* indicators are used and does not have to be considered by the programmer.

If this compiler control was not provided, a *total time* **L1** break would occur and print zeros for numeric field values and blanks, for alphanumeric (i.e., a "null" break).

Figure 8-10   Modified program coding to control the printing of salesperson groups on separate pages. (Continued)

MULTIPLE CONTROL BREAK PROCESSING

The previous program examples have illustrated the processing logic and RPG/400 syntax for single control breaks. Reports, however, often include more than one control break. An example of a report with three control breaks is illustrated in Figure 8-11. Each subtotal is identified with the appropriate *Control Level* indicator used in the program to condition the print line. Notice that SALESMAN SALES is an **L1** total; DEPT SALES, an **L2** total; and STORE SALES, an **L3** total. Also, understand that when **LR** turns on,

```
                WEEKLY SALES REPORT AS OF  9/30/95                    PAGE   1


   DATE      SALESPERSON  DEPT    STORE      WEEKLY SALES

  9/08/95       1000       03      01           256.12
  9/15/95       1000       03      01         1,441.70
  9/22/95       1000       03      01           384.20
  9/29/95       1000       03      01           302.44

                                    SALESPERSON 1000 SALES.. 2,384.46 *————— L1 total

  9/08/95       1100       03      01           189.76
  9/15/95       1100       03      01           500.38
  9/22/95       1100       03      01         2,198.37
  9/29/95       1100       03      01           246.18

                                    SALESPERSON 1100 SALES.. 3,134.69 *————— L1 total
                                    DEPT 03   SALES.........  5,519.15 **———— L2 total

  9/08/95       1200       05      01         1,612.55
  9/15/95       1200       05      01           800.00
  9/22/95       1200       05      01           999.19
  9/29/95       1200       05      01         3,737.47

                                    SALESPERSON 1200 SALES.. 7,149.21 *————— L1 total
                                    DEPT 05   SALES.........  7,149.21 **———— L2 total
                                    STORE 01  SALES........ 12,668.36 ***——— L3 total

  9/08/95       1300       12      02           645.33
  9/15/95       1300       12      02           301.76
  9/22/95       1300       12      02         2,868.88
  9/29/95       1300       12      02         1,532.86

                                    SALESPERSON 1300 SALES.. 5,348.83 *————— L1 total
                                    DEPT 12   SALES.........  5,348.83 **———— L2 total
                                    STORE 02  SALES........  5,348.83 ***——— L3 total

  9/08/95       1400       08      03           184.79
  9/15/95       1400       08      03           733.74
  9/22/95       1400       08      03           472.52
  9/29/95       1400       08      03         4,900.09

                                    SALESPERSON 1400 SALES.. 6,291.14 *————— L1 total
                                    DEPT 08   SALES.........  6,291.14 **———— L2 total
                                    STORE 03  SALES........  6,291.14 ***——— L3 total

                                    TOTAL SALES...........  24,308.33 ****    LR total
```

Figure 8-11 Detail report with multiple control groups.

any *Control Level* indicators included in the program are automatically set ON. This RPG/400 feature provides for the output of the last control group before the TOTAL SALES line is printed.

A compile listing of the program that generated the multiple control group report in Figure 8-11 is detailed in Figure 8-12.

```
SEQUENCE                                                                   IND  DO
NUMBER    *...1....+....2....+....3....+....4....+....5....+....6....+....7...* USE NUM
                           S o u r c e   L i s t i n g

   100    * MULTIPLE CONTROL BREAK PROGRAM THAT GENERATES A REPORT WITH
   200    * THREE CONTROL GROUP TOTALS—L1 SALESPERSON, L2 DEPT, & L3 STORE
```

Figure 8-12 Compile listing of multiple control break program.

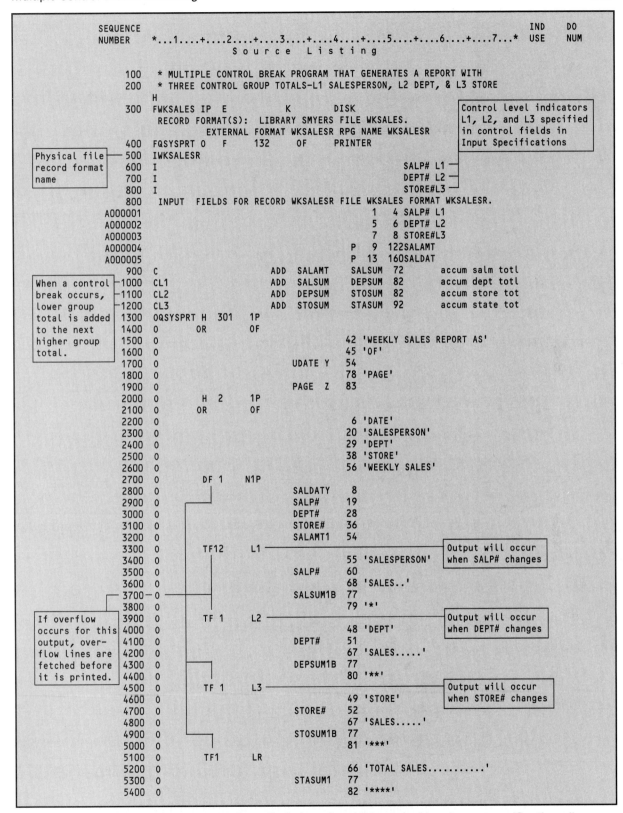

Figure 8-12 Compile listing of multiple control break program. (Continued)

The data in the file listing in Figure 8-13 is identical to the one presented in Figure 8-1. However, now DEPT# and STORE# are used as additional *control fields* to generate subtotals for departments and stores. The file is in a composite key order with STORE# (the primary key element), DEPT# (second key element), SALP# (third key element), and SALDAT (fourth key element). If the physical file was not created with the required

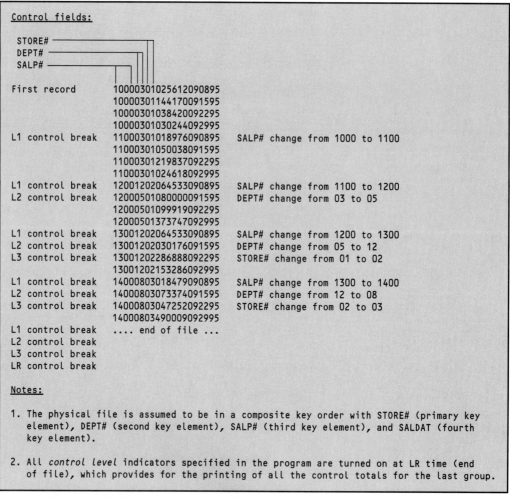

```
Control fields:

   STORE# ──────────────────────────┐ │
    DEPT# ───────────────────────┐ │ │
    SALP# ──────────────────┐ │ │ │ │

First record        10000301025612090895
                    10000301144170091595
                    10000301038420092295
                    10000301030244092995
L1 control break    11000301018976090895      SALP# change from 1000 to 1100
                    11000301050038091595
                    11000301219837092295
                    11000301024618092995
L1 control break    12001202064533090895      SALP# change from 1100 to 1200
L2 control break    12000501080000091595      DEPT# change form 03 to 05
                    12000501099919092295
                    12000501373747092995
L1 control break    13001202064533090895      SALP# change from 1200 to 1300
L2 control break    13001202030176091595      DEPT# change from 05 to 12
L3 control break    13001202286888092295      STORE# change from 01 to 02
                    13001202153286092995
L1 control break    14000803018479090895      SALP# change from 1300 to 1400
L2 control break    14000803073374091595      DEPT# change from 12 to 08
L3 control break    14000803047252092295      STORE# change from 02 to 03
                    14000803490009092995
L1 control break    .... end of file ...
L2 control break
L3 control break
LR control break

Notes:

1. The physical file is assumed to be in a composite key order with STORE# (primary key
   element), DEPT# (second key element), SALP# (third key element), and SALDAT (fourth
   key element).

2. All control level indicators specified in the program are turned on at LR time (end
   of file), which provides for the printing of all the control totals for the last group.
```

Figure 8-13   Listing of the data file processed for a detail report with three *control level* breaks (subtotals).

composite keys, a *logical file* may be created to access the data in the required *control field* order. This topic is discussed in Chapter 16.

Multiple Control Break Example Program

Input Specification. The *Input Specifications* coding for the multiple control break program and the processing logic are detailed in Figure 8-14.

The following input control is provided by the RPG/400 compiler:

1. Creation of a holding area where the first record of a control group is stored.
2. Comparison of the current record's *control field* value with the previous record processed (in holding area).
3. Automatic set ON of *control level* indicators when a control break (change in *control field* value) is sensed.
4. Execution of related control break calculation and output instructions.
5. Return to *detail time* processing (calculations and output) of the record that generated the control break.

Each of these features would have to be provided by the programmer in other high-level languages such as COBOL, BASIC, and FORTRAN.

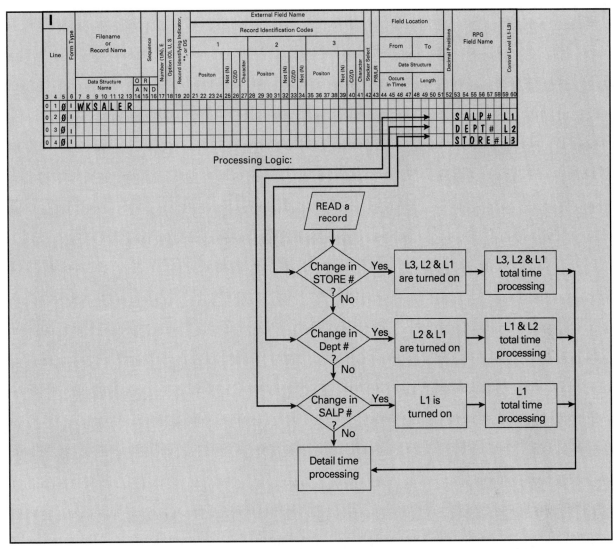

Figure 8-14 Input Specifications coding for multiple control break program.

Further examination of Figure 8-14 indicates that the *control level* indicators were assigned in ascending order (i.e., **L1, L2, L3**). The location of the related *control field* in a record format determines the order in which the indicators are specified. RPG/400 does not require that any designated order be followed.

Calculation Specifications. The calculation specifications coding for the multiple control break program and related processing logic are presented in Figure 8-15.

Figure 8-15 Calculation Specifications for multiple control break program.

Processing logic:

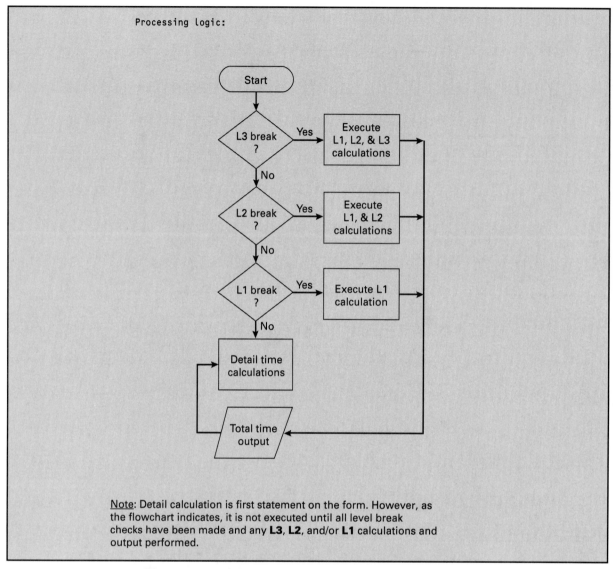

Figure 8-15 Calculation Specifications for multiple control break program. (Continued)

Remember, when *control level* indicators are entered in columns 7 and 8 of the calculation specifications, the related statement is executed at *total time*. Statements conditioned by a level indicator entered in the other conditioning columns (10–11, 13–14, and 16–17) are performed at *detail time*. Also, any statement conditioned at *total time* (columns 7 and 8) must follow any detail calculations. This error will be identified as terminal in compilation of the source program.

With AS/400 computers, the level indicators may be assigned in any order on the *Calculation Specifications.*

Figure 8-16 illustrates the calculation steps generated by the RPG/400 compiler when an **L2** control break is sensed. It is important to understand that on the basis of the illustrated calculations, all control totals are saved in the next higher subtotal before output. Otherwise, because of the necessary "blanking out" of the field after output to prevent incorrect accumulation of different control group totals, the value would be lost.

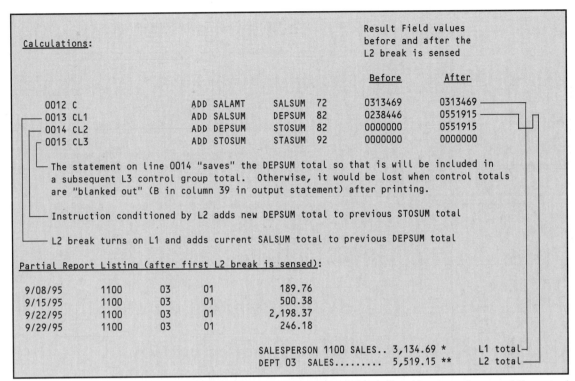

Figure 8-16 Relationship of calculations with printed report when an **L2** control break program is sensed.

Output Specifications. A partial *Output Specifications* (heading line coding is not shown) for the multiple control break program is illustrated in Figure 8-17.

Line	Type	Output Indicators	Field Name or EXCPT Name	End Position	P/B	Constant or Edit Word
01						
02						
03	TF21	L1				
04				52		'SALESPERSON'
05			SALP#	57		
06				68		'SALES......'
07			SALSUM	77	1B	
08				79		'*'
09	TF 1	L2				
10				48		'DEPT'
11			DEPT#	51		
12				67		'SALES........'
13			DEPSUM	77	1B	
14				80		'**'
15	TF11	L3				
16				49		'STORE'
17			STORE#	52		
18				67		'SALES.........'
19			STOSUM	77	1B	
20				81		'***'
21	TF1	LR				
22				66		'TOTAL SALES'............
23			STASUM	77	1B	
24				82		'****'

Figure 8-17 Output Specifications for multiple control break program.

The processing logic for the *Output Specifications* is detailed in the flowchart in Figure 8-18.

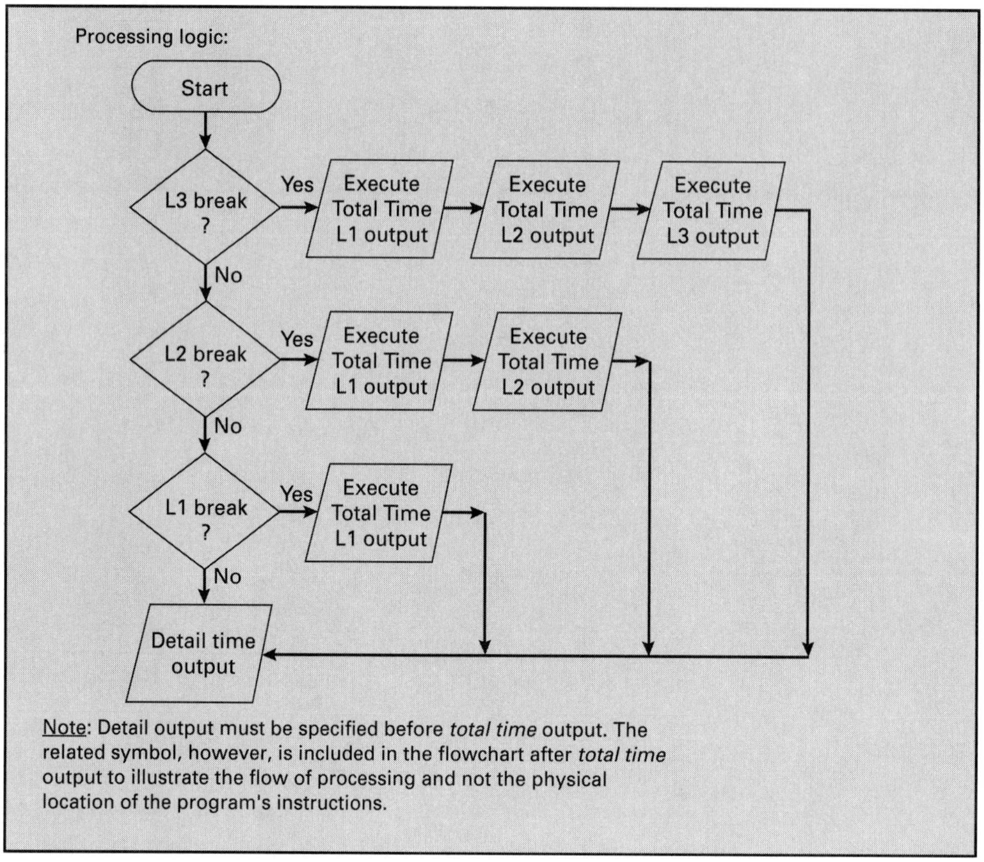

Figure 8-18 RPG/400 controlled processing logic for output coding for multiple control break program.

Group Reports

The reports shown in Figures 8-1 and 8-11 are referred to as *Detail Reports* because the control field information is printed for every detail record within a group. Readability may be enhanced by including less information. Reports of this type are broadly classified as *Group and Summary*.

Figure 8-19 illustrates the report from Figure 8-11 modified as a *Group Report*. Notice that the control field information is printed for only the first record in a group when a control break is sensed, and not for every detail record.

```
                 WEEKLY SALES REPORT AS OF  9/30/95                     PAGE   1


 DATE       SALESPERSON  DEPT    STORE      WEEKLY SALES

9/08/95       1000        03      01           256.12
9/15/95                                      1,441.70
9/22/95                                        384.20
9/29/95                                        302.44

                                        SALESPERSON 1000 SALES.. 2,384.46 *——— L1 total
```

Figure 8-19 Group report generated by modified multiple control break program.

```
9/08/95        1100                          189.76
9/15/95        1100                          500.38
9/22/95        1100                        2,198.37
9/29/95        1100                          246.18

                                SALESPERSON 1100 SALES.. 3,134.69 *——— L1 total
                                DEPT 03   SALES.........  5,519.15 **——— L2 total


9/08/95        1200          05            1,612.55
9/15/95        1200          05              800.00
9/22/95        1200          05              999.19
9/29/95        1200          05            3,737.47

                                SALESPERSON 1200 SALES.. 7,149.21 *——— L1 total
                                DEPT 05   SALES.........  7,149.21 **——— L2 total
                                STORE 01  SALES........ 12,668.36 ***——— L3 total


9/08/95        1300          12      02      645.33
9/15/95                                      301.76
9/22/95                                    2,868.88
9/29/95                                    1,532.86

                                SALESPERSON 1300 SALES.. 5,348.83 *——— L1 total
                                DEPT 12   SALES.........  5,348.83 **——— L2 total
                                STORE 02  SALES........   5,348.83 ***——— L3 total


9/08/95        1400          08      03      184.79
9/15/95                                      733.74
9/22/95                                      472.52
9/29/95                                    4,900.09

                                SALESPERSON 1400 SALES.. 6,291.14 *——— L1 total
                                DEPT 08   SALES.........  6,291.14 **——— L2 total
                                STORE 03  SALES.........  6,291.14 ***——— L3 total


                                TOTAL SALES..........   24,308.33 ****  LR total
```

Control field values are _not_ printed
in every detail record.

Figure 8-19 Group report generated by modified multiple control break program. (Continued)

The changes needed in the example program to generate a group instead of a detail report are shown in the partial output form in Figure 8-20.

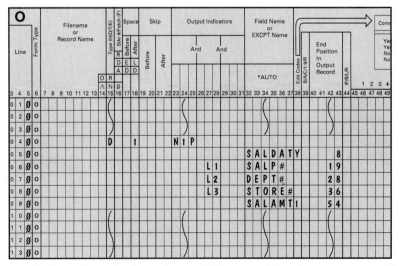

Figure 8-20 Partial output form for multiple control break program modified for group report format.

> Specifying any control level indicator at detail time restricts printing of values to the first record in the control group. The level indicators in columns 27 and 28 are in an "AND" relationship with NIP indicator.
>
> Output indicator columns 24-25 or 30-31 could have been used for the level indicators. Indentation does enhance readability and understanding of the program's syntax.

Figure 8-20 Partial output form for multiple control break program modified for group report format. (Continued)

Summary Reports

Reports directed to higher levels of management usually include less detail information than those to lower management. In fact, the reports often include only group totals. In the RPG/400 environment, these are called *Summary Reports*. Figure 8-21 illustrates a *Summary Report* generated from the same data file used for the other report formats previously discussed. Notice the absence of any detail lines and that each salesperson, department, and store control group totals are summarized for easy reference.

```
WEEKLY SALES REPORT AS OF  9/30/95                          PAGE    1


              SALESPERSON 1000 SALES.. 2,384.46 *

              SALESPERSON 1100 SALES.. 3,134.69 *
              DEPT 03   SALES.........  5,519.15 **

              SALESPERSON 1200 SALES.. 7,149.21 *
              DEPT 05   SALES.........  7,149.21 **
              STORE 01  SALES........ 12,668.36 ***

              SALESPERSON 1300 SALES.. 5,348.83 *
              DEPT 12   SALES.........  5,348.83 **
              STORE 02  SALES........  5,348.83 ***

              SALESPERSON 1400 SALES.. 6,291.14 *
              DEPT 08   SALES.........  6,291.14 **
              STORE 03  SALES........  6,291.14 ***

              TOTAL SALES...........   24,308.33 ****
```

Figure 8-21 Summary report generated by modified multiple control break program.

An examination of a partial source listing of the modified control break program in Figure 8-22 indicates that the *detail time* coding lines have been deleted to support the *Summary Report* format. All other coding in the program is unchanged.

```
SEQNBR*...+... 1 ...+... 2 ...+... 3 ...+... 4 ...+... 5 ...+... 6 ...+... 7
 1300     OQSYSPRT H  301    1P
 1400   . O          OR      OF
 1500     O                              42 'WEEKLY SALES REPORT AS'
 1600     O                              45 'OF'
 1700     O                    UDATE Y   54
 1800     O                              78 'PAGE'
```

Figure 8-22 Partial output coding from multiple control break program modified for *Summary Report* format.

```
1900        0                          PAGE  Z    83
2000        0         TF21    L1                          ┌─────────────────────┐
2100        0                              55  'SALESPERSON'   │ Column headings and │
2200        0                  SALP#       60            │ Detail Time instruc-│
2300        0                              68  'SALES..'  │ tions deleted       │
2400        0                  SALSUM1B    77            └─────────────────────┘
2500        0                              79  '*'
2600        0         TF 1    L2
2700        0                              48  'DEPT'
2800        0                  DEPT#       51
2900        0                              67  'SALES.........'
3000        0                  DEPSUM1B    77
3100        0                              80  '**'
3200        0         TF 1    L3
3300        0                              49  'STORE'
3400        0                  STORE#      52
3500        0                              67  'SALES........'
3600        0                  STOSUM1B    77
3700        0                              81  '***'
3800        0         TF1     LR
3900        0                              66  'TOTAL SALES...........'
4000        0                  STASUM1     77
4100        0                              82  '****'
```

Figure 8-22   Partial output coding from multiple control break program modified for *Summary Report* format. (Continued)

Split Control Fields

A control field that includes more than one field in a record is called a *Split Control Field*. It is defined by specifying the same control level indicator with two or more of a record's fields. An example of a *Split Control Field* is shown in the input form in Figure 8-23. Refer to the notes at the bottom of the figure for the rules associated with split control field usage.

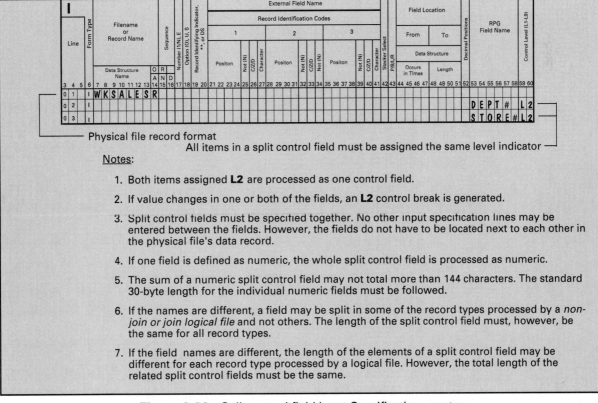

Notes:

1. Both items assigned **L2** are processed as one control field.

2. If value changes in one or both of the fields, an **L2** control break is generated.

3. Split control fields must be specified together. No other input specification lines may be entered between the fields. However, the fields do not have to be located next to each other in the physical file's data record.

4. If one field is defined as numeric, the whole split control field is processed as numeric.

5. The sum of a numeric split control field may not total more than 144 characters. The standard 30-byte length for the individual numeric fields must be followed.

6. If the names are different, a field may be split in some of the record types processed by a *non-join or join logical file* and not others. The length of the split control field must, however, be the same for all record types.

7. If the field names are different, the length of the elements of a split control field may be different for each record type processed by a logical file. However, the total length of the related split control fields must be the same.

Figure 8-23   Split control field Input Specifications syntax.

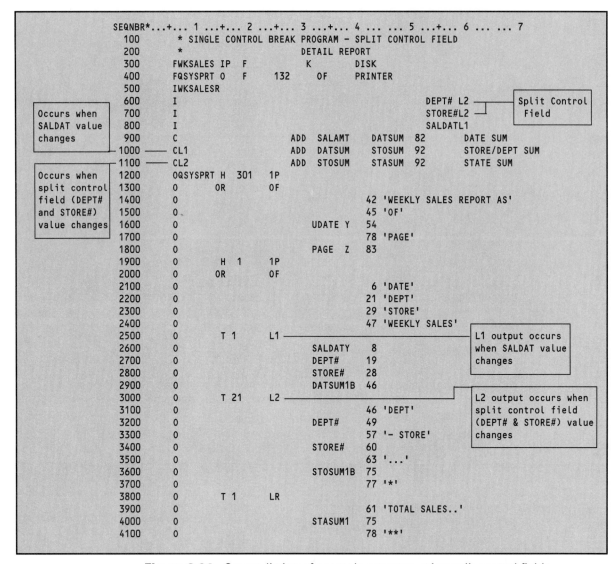

Figure 8-24 Source listing of example program using split control fields.

A listing of a modified version of the previous control break programs that includes *split control field* processing is presented in Figure 8-24. The following changes have been included in this modified program:

1. The same data file used in this chapter's other program examples is specified as input. However, it has been resorted in a STORE# (major field), DEPT# (first minor), and SALDAT (second minor) order.

2. The input form defines STORE# and DEPT# as the elements of a *Split Control Field*.

3. Weekly sales amount for the same date (salespersons within the STORE/DEPT group) are added and are output when the date changes (**L1** control break).

4. Control Total for Store/Department is accumulated and output when the *split control field* value changes (**L2** control break).

5. The report format shown in Figure 8-25 is modified with the following changes:
   a. Salesperson headings, detail, and total output deleted.
   b. **L1** control group total is sum for week ending date within the STORE/DEPT *split field control* group.
   c. **L2** group total line for STORE#/DEPT# total.

```
                       WEEKLY SALES REPORT AS OF  9/30/95                    PAGE   1


      DATE           DEPT    STORE      WEEKLY SALES

     9/08/95          03      01           445.88
     9/15/95          03      01         1,942.08          ┌─────────────────────────┐
     9/22/95          03      01         2,582.57          │ Composite DEPT#/STORE#   │
     9/29/95          03      01           548.62──────────│ L2 control break         │
                                                           └─────────────────────────┘
                                       DEPT 03 - STORE 01...     5,519.15 *

     9/08/95          05      01         1,612.55
     9/15/95          05      01           800.00
     9/22/95          05      01           999.19
     9/29/95          05      01         3,737.47

                                       DEPT 05 - STORE 01...     7,149.21 *

     9/08/95          12      02           645.33
     9/15/95          12      02           301.76
     9/22/95          12      02         2,868.88
     9/29/95          12      02         1,532.86

                                       DEPT 12 - STORE 02...     5,348.83 *

     9/08/95          08      03           184.79
     9/15/95          08      03           733.74
     9/22/95          08      03           472.52
     9/29/95          08      03         4,900.09

                                       DEPT 08 - STORE 03...     6,291.14 *

                                       TOTAL SALES..           24,308.33 **
```

Figure 8-25   Report generated by split control field program.

PROGRAMMER-DEFINED CONTROL BREAK PROCESSING

Single Control Group

In lieu of using the RPG/400 logic cycle and *Control Level* indicators, the programmer may prefer to use his or her own logic and syntax. The current trend in the RPG/400 environment is to avoid traditional RPG coding (i.e., indicators and the logic cycle) and write programs similar to the logic used in COBOL, C, PL-1, BASIC, and so forth.

The traditional single control group program previously shown in Figure 8-3 has been modified in Figure 8-26 to support programmer-defined control breaks and processing. Examine the listing and note the following coding features:

1. Because a *Control Level* indicator (**L1**) is not specified, *Input Specifications* statements are not required.
2. **DEFN** statements are used to define fields needed in the program that are not included in the physical file.
3. Three *internal subroutines* are specified.
4. Output for headings is controlled at **OF** time instead of at first cycle processing (**1P**) time.
5. Detail, control group, and last record output are all specified as *exception time* output, and not *detail or total time* output.

A line-by-line explanation of the program's instructions is included at the end of the compiled listing.

```
SEQUENCE
NUMBER    *...1....+....2....+....3....+....4....+....5....+....6....+....7...*
                       S o u r c e   L i s t i n g
   100    * THIS PROGRAM GENERATES A REPORT WITH ONE CONTROL GROUP TOTAL
   200    * USING PROGRAMMER-SPECIFIED CONTROL LEVEL BREAK PROCESSING
          H
   300    FWKSALES IP E          K        DISK
          RECORD FORMAT(S): LIBRARY SMYERS FILE WKSALES.
                     EXTERNAL FORMAT WKSALESR RPG NAME WKSALESR
   400    FQSYSPRT O  F     132    OF    PRINTER
A000000   INPUT  FIELDS FOR RECORD WKSALESR FILE WKSALES FORMAT WKSALESR.
A000001                                        1    4 SALP#
A000002                                        5    6 DEPT#
A000003                                        7    8 STORE#
A000004                                      P  9  122SALAMT
A000005                                      P 13  160SALDAT
   500    C          *LIKE     DEFN SALP#     HSALP#        Move to hold fd
   600    C          *LIKE     DEFN SALAMT    SALSUM+ 1     Define L1 accum
   700    C          *LIKE     DEFN SALAMT    STASUM+ 3     Define LR accum
   800    *
   900    C          *IN10     CASEQ*OFF      HOUSEK        Brch if 10 off
  1000    C          SALP#     CASNEHSALP#    L1SR          Change in SALP#
  1100    C                    ENDCS                        End case group
  1200    C                    ADD  SALAMT    SALSUM        Accum SALP# amt
  1300    C                    EXCPTDETOUT                  Detail output
  1400    CLR                  EXSR LRSR                    Brch to LRSR sr
  1500    *
  1600    C          HOUSEK    BEGSR                        Begin HOUSEK sr
  1700    C                    MOVE SALP#     HSALP#        Move to hold fd
  1800    C                    MOVE *ON       *IN10         Set on 10
  1900    C                    MOVE *ON       *INOF         Set on OF
  2000    C                    ENDSR                        End HOUSEK sr
  2100    *
  2200    C          L1SR      BEGSR                        Begin L1SR sr
  2300    C                    ADD  SALSUM    STASUM        Add to state tl
  2400    C                    EXCPTL1OUT                   print SALP# tot
  2500    C                    MOVE SALP#     HSALP#        Move to hold fd
  2600    C                    Z-ADD0         SALSUM        Intial. accum
  2700    C                    ENDSR                        End L1SR sr
  2800    *
  2900    C          LRSR      BEGSR                        Begin LRSR sr
  3000    C                    EXSR L1SR                    Brch to L1SR sr
  3100    C                    EXCPTLROUT                   Print state tot
  3200    C                    ENDSR                        End LRSR sr
  3300    OQSYSPRT H  301   OF
  3400    O                                     42 'WEEKLY SALES REPORT AS'
  3500    O                                     45 'OF'
  3600    O                    UDATE Y          54
  3700    O                                     63 'PAGE'
  3800    O                    PAGE  Z          68
  3900    O          H  2    OF
  4000    O                                      6 'DATE'
  4100    O                                     20 'SALESPERSON'
  4200    O                                     41 'WEEKLY SALES'
  4300    O          EF 1      DETOUT
  4400    O                    SALDATY          8
  4500    O                    SALP#           19
  4600    O                    SALAMT1         39
  4700    O          EF12      L1OUT
  4800    O                                     37 'SALESPERSON'
  4900    O                    SALP#           42
  5000    O                                     53 'SALES.....'
  5100    O                    SALSUM1         62
  5200    O                                     64 '*'
  5300    O          EF1       LROUT
  5400    O                                     51 'TOTAL STATE SALES.....'
  5500    O                    STASUM1         62
  5600    O                                     65 '**'
```

Figure 8-26   Single control group program with programmer-controlled control break processing.

Line#	Explanation
500	The holding field HSALP# is defined with the same field attributes as the physical file field SALP#.
600	SALSUM is defined one integer larger than the physical file field SALAMT.
700	STASUM is defined 3 integers larger than the physical file field SALAMT.
900	The HOUSEK subroutine is performed if indicator 10 is off. Indicator 10 is set on in the HOUSEK subroutine so that it will be executed only for the first data record processed and not for every record in the file.
1000	The value in SALP# is compared to the value in the holding field HSALP#. If the values are not equal, the L1SR subroutine is executed. When the first data record is processed, statement (1700) in the HOUSEK routine moves the value in SALP# to HSALP#. Then, for subsequent processing, when the values are not equal, a control break will be sensed, the statements in the L1SR routine performed, and the related output executed.
1100	ENDCS ends the CAS group.
1200	The value in the SALAMT field is added to the SALSUM accumulator.
1300	The values for the current record are output at exception time.
1400	When end of the input file is read, LR is seton which passes control to the LRSR internal subroutine for LR processing.
1600	Begins the internal subroutine HOUSEK which is branched to from the CASEQ test on line 900.
1700	SALP# (input from physical file record) value is moved the holding field HSALP#.
1800	Indicator 10 is set on so that this subroutine will not be executed again (see line 900 for this control).
1900	Indicator OF is set to control output after the first detail record is read instead of at 1P (First Page time).
2000	ENDSR ends the HOUSEK subroutine.
2200	Begins the internal subroutine L1SR which is branched to from the control break test on line 1000.
2300	Value in the accumulator SALSUM is added to STASUM.
2400	EXCPT statement causes program control to branch to line 4700 (E line) and print the control group items for the previous salesperson.
2500	SALP# value in the current record processed (one that caused the control break) is moved to the holding field HSALP#.
2600	The accumulator SALSUM is initialized to zero before the next salesperson total is accumulated.
2700	ENDSR ends the L1SR subroutine.
2900	Begins the internal subroutine LRSR which is branched to when LR turns as the end of file is read in the physical file.
3000	The L1SR subroutine is branched to so that the last salesperson group total is output before the state total (STASUM).
3100	EXCPT statement causes program control to branch to line 5300 (E line) and print the items related to the state total.

Figure 8-26 Single control group program with programmer-controlled control break processing. (Continued)

A processing logic flowchart for the programmer-controlled single control group program is detailed in Figure 8-27. The line numbers to the side of the symbols relate to the statement number in the program.

The report generated by the program in Figure 8-26 is identical to the one previously shown in Figure 8-1.

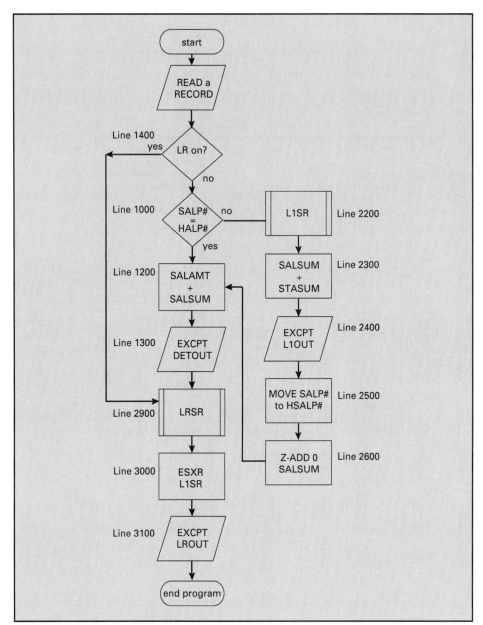

Figure 8-27 Processing logic flowchart for the programmer-controlled single control break program.

Programmer-Controlled Multiple Control Groups

The source listing for a programmer-controlled multiple control group program is detailed in Figure 8-28. Examine the syntax, and note the following structure:

1. For the first data record processed, the programmer-defined control fields (SALP#, DEPT#, and STORE#) are moved to their related holding fields in the HOUSEK subroutine (lines 3300–3500).

2. The largest control field (STORE#) is tested first (line 1800). If a change in STORE# is detected, the subroutine (L1SR) for the salesperson group is processed, followed by the department (L2SR), and then the store (L3SR).

```
        SEQUENCE
        NUMBER    *...1....+....2....+....3....+....4....+....5....+....6....+....7...*
                                    S o u r c e   L i s t i n g
          100     * MULTIPLE CONTROL GROUP PROGRAM THAT GENERATES A REPORT WITH
          200     * THREE PROGRAMMER-DEFINED CONTROL BREAKS
                  H
          300     FWKSALES IP  E           K        DISK
                  RECORD FORMAT(S): LIBRARY SMYERS FILE WKSALES.
                           EXTERNAL FORMAT WKSALESR RPG NAME WKSALESR
          400     FQSYSPRT O  F    132    OF    PRINTER
          500     *
          600     * DEFINE HOLDING AND GROUP TOTAL FIELDS....
        A000000   INPUT  FIELDS FOR RECORD WKSALESR FILE WKSALES FORMAT WKSALESR.
        A000001                                        1    4 SALP#
        A000002                                        5    6 DEPT#
        A000003                                        7    8 STORE#
        A000004                                     P  9  122SALAMT
        A000005                                     P 13  160SALDAT
          700     C          *LIKE     DEFN SALP#      HSALP#         holding field
          800     C          *LIKE     DEFN DEPT#      HDEPT#         holding field
          900     C          *LIKE     DEFN STORE#     HSTOR#         holding field
         1000     C          *LIKE     DEFN SALAMT     SALSUM+ 1      salesperson tot
         1100     C          *LIKE     DEFN SALAMT     DEPSUM+ 2      department tot
         1200     C          *LIKE     DEFN SALAMT     STOSUM+ 2      store total
         1300     C          *LIKE     DEFN SALAMT     STASUM+ 3      state total
         1400     *
         1500     C          *IN10     CASEQ*OFF       HOUSEK         EXSR if 10 off
         1600     C                    ENDCS
         1700     C                    SELEC                          begin SELEC grp
         1800     C          STORE#    WHNE HSTOR#                     chg in STORE#?
         1900     C                    EXSR L1SR                      brch-sales sr
         2000     C                    EXSR L2SR                      brch-dept sr
         2100     C                    EXSR L3SR                      brch-store sr
         2200     C          DEPT#     WHNE HDEPT#                     chg in DEPT#?
         2300     C                    EXSR L1SR                      brch-sales sr
         2400     C                    EXSR L2SR                      brch-dept sr
         2500     C          SALP#     WHNE HSALP#                     chg in SALP#?
         2600     C                    EXSR L1SR                      brch-sales sr
         2700     C                    ENDSL                          end SELEC grp
         2800     C                    ADD  SALAMT     SALSUM         accum sales amt
         2900     C                    EXCPTDETOUT                    detail output
         3000     CLR                  EXSR LRSR                      brch-state sr
         3100     *
         3200     C          HOUSEK    BEGSR                          begin HOUSEK sr
         3300     C                    MOVE SALP#      HSALP#         SALP# to hold
         3400     C                    MOVE DEPT#      HDEPT#         DEPT# to hold
         3500     C                    MOVE STORE#     HSTOR#         STORE# to hold
         3600     C                    MOVE *ON        *IN10          set on 10
         3700     C                    MOVE *ON        *INOF          set on OF
         3800     C                    ENDSR                          end HOUSEK sr
         3900     *
         4000     C          L1SR      BEGSR                          begin SALP# sr
         4100     C                    ADD  SALSUM     DEPSUM         add to dept acc
         4200     C                    EXCPTL10OUT                    sales total out
         4300     C                    MOVE SALP#      HSALP#         move to hold fd
         4400     C                    Z-ADD0          SALSUM         init. sales tot
         4500     C                    ENDSR                          end sales sr
         4600     *
         4700     C          L2SR      BEGSR                          begin DEPT# sr
         4800     C                    ADD  DEPSUM     STOSUM         add STORE total
         4900     C                    EXCPTL20OUT                    dept total out
         5000     C                    MOVE DEPT#      HDEPT#         move to hold fd
         5100     C                    Z-ADD0          DEPSUM         init. dept total
         5200     C                    ENDSR                          end dept sr
         5300     *
         5400     C          L3SR      BEGSR                          begin STORE# sr
         5500     C                    ADD  STOSUM     STASUM         add to state tl
         5600     C                    EXCPTL30OUT                    store total out
         5700     C                    MOVE STORE#     HSTOR#         move to hold fd
         5800     C                    Z-ADD0          STOSUM         init. store tot
         5900     C                    ENDSR                          end store sr
```

Figure 8-28   Multiple control group program with programmer-controlled control break processing.

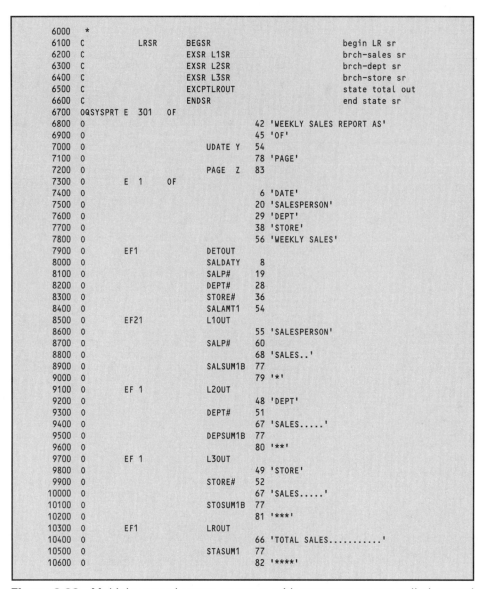

```
6000   *
6100   C           LRSR        BEGSR                        begin LR sr
6200   C                       EXSR L1SR                    brch-sales sr
6300   C                       EXSR L2SR                    brch-dept sr
6400   C                       EXSR L3SR                    brch-store sr
6500   C                       EXCPTLROUT                   state total out
6600   C                       ENDSR                        end state sr
6700   OQSYSPRT E  301    OF
6800   O                                        42 'WEEKLY SALES REPORT AS'
6900   O                                        45 'OF'
7000   O                       UDATE Y          54
7100   O                                        78 'PAGE'
7200   O                       PAGE  Z          83
7300   O       E  1      OF
7400   O                                         6 'DATE'
7500   O                                        20 'SALESPERSON'
7600   O                                        29 'DEPT'
7700   O                                        38 'STORE'
7800   O                                        56 'WEEKLY SALES'
7900   O       EF1         DETOUT
8000   O                       SALDATY     8
8100   O                       SALP#      19
8200   O                       DEPT#      28
8300   O                       STORE#     36
8400   O                       SALAMT1    54
8500   O       EF21        L1OUT
8600   O                                        55 'SALESPERSON'
8700   O                       SALP#      60
8800   O                                        68 'SALES..'
8900   O                       SALSUM1B   77
9000   O                                        79 '*'
9100   O       EF 1        L2OUT
9200   O                                        48 'DEPT'
9300   O                       DEPT#      51
9400   O                                        67 'SALES.....'
9500   O                       DEPSUM1B   77
9600   O                                        80 '**'
9700   O       EF 1        L3OUT
9800   O                                        49 'STORE'
9900   O                       STORE#     52
10000  O                                        67 'SALES.....'
10100  O                       STOSUM1B   77
10200  O                                        81 '***'
10300  O       EF1         LROUT
10400  O                                        66 'TOTAL SALES...........'
10500  O                       STASUM1    77
10600  O                                        82 '****'
```

Figure 8-28 Multiple control group program with programmer-controlled control break processing. (Continued)

3. If a change in STORE# is not detected, the next lower control field (DEPT#) is tested (line 2200). If a change in the DEPT## value is sensed, the internal subroutine (L1SR) for the salesperson group is processed, followed by department (L2SR) subroutine.

4. If a change is not tested in DEPT#, the internal subroutine for the lowest control field (SALP#) is tested (line 2500). If a change in the SALP# value is detected, the internal subroutine (L1SR) for the salesperson group is processed.

5. At last record time **(LR),** the LRSR internal subroutine is executed, from which the L1SR, L2SR, and L3SR routines are consecutively processed before the state total is output. This syntax prints all of the totals for the last control group before the state total is output.

6. Output for each control group total (lines 4200, 4900, and 5600) and detail record (2900) is processed at *exception time*.

7. After a control group is processed, the current record processed is printed at *exception time* (line 2900).

A flowchart that indicates the processing sequence of the program's internal subroutines for the multiple control group totals is presented in Figure 8-29. Note two important aspects of this coding:

1. Control break tests are made in a *higher-to-lower* order. For this program, the control break for store is tested first, department second, and salesperson last.
2. Within the L3SR and L2SR subroutines, control break output is performed in *lowest-to-highest* order.

The report generated by the programmer-controlled multiple control group program is identical to that shown previously in Figure 8-11.

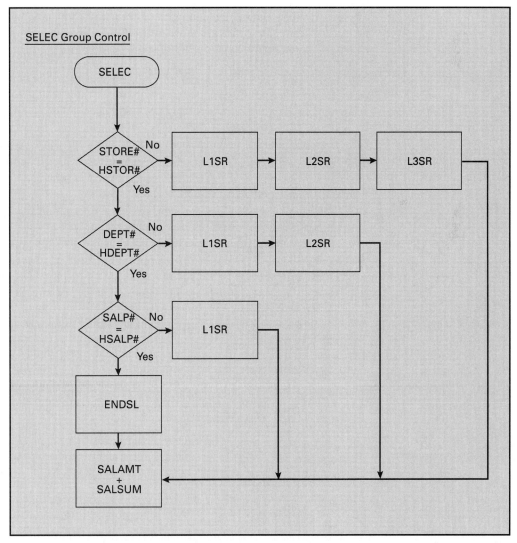

Figure 8–29   Flowchart for the programmer-defined multiple control break program's internal subroutine processing sequence.

SUMMARY

In addition to end-of-file totals, many reports require subtotals. The RPG/400 compiler supports control group processing by *Control Level* indicators **L1–L9.** Depending on the subtotal requirements, one or more Control Level indicators are assigned to an input field. Consequently, for an externally defined physical file, the record format and related *control fields* must be specified on the *Input Specifications*. A *control field* is defined by entering the appropriate control level indicator **(L1–L9)** in columns 59–60 with the related field. When the value in a control field changes, a *control break* is sensed, and the calculations and output for that break are processed.

When <u>multiple</u> control fields are specified, calculation and output processing is executed from the <u>lowest</u> to the <u>highest</u> Control Group (i.e., **L1** to **L3**).

When the end of file is read and **LR** is automatically turned on, any <u>lower</u> control group processing (**L1** through **L9**) is executed before last record **(LR)** calculations and output.

Total time calculations (Control Level indicator in columns 7–8) must follow all *detail time. Total time* output (**T** in column 15) must follow all heading and detail time output.

Programmer-controlled control group processing eliminates the need for indicators and results in programs that are more efficient. Ideally, RPG/400 programs should be written with no indicators or as few as logically possible.

QUESTIONS

8-1. In a traditional RPG/400 program, how are subtotals controlled in the body of a report?

8-2. What are the *Control Level* indicators? Where are they defined in an RPG/400 program? On what specifications may they be used to condition instructions?

8-3. What are *Control Fields? Control Groups?*

8-4. How should a physical file that is processed by an RPG/400 program that includes *Control Level Breaks* be organized?

8-5. What is generated when a *control field* value changes?

8-6. If **L1, L2,** and **L3** are used in a program and **L3** is turned on, what other *control level* indicators are set on?

8-7. Refer to Question 8-6. When **LR** is turned on at the end of a physical file, what other *Control Level* indicators are set on?

8-8. A *Control Level* indicator entered in columns 7 and 8 of a calculation instruction processes the statement at _____ time.

8-9. A *Control Level* Indicator entered in columns 10 and 11, 13 and 14, or 16 and 17 of a calculation instruction processes the statement at _____ time.

8-10. Examine the following data file and indicate where *detail time* and *total time* **L1** processing are executed. Answer by placing a **DL1** and/or **TL1,** and/or **TLR** alongside the related control field value. Only *control field* values are shown.

1000	first record
1000	
1000	
2000	
2000	
3000	

8-11. When a *control break* is sensed, *detail time* processing for the current record is executed before *total time* calculations are performed. Answer TRUE or FALSE.

8-12. If only one record is included in a *Control Group, detail time* and *total time* processing are performed on the same record. Answer TRUE or FALSE.

8-13. *Control Level* indicators must be assigned in ascending order in the *Input Specifications.* Answer TRUE or FALSE.

8-14. *Control Level* indicators must be assigned in ascending order in the *Calculation Specifications.* Answer TRUE or FALSE.

8-15. A *Record Identifying Indicator* may be on at the same time as a *Control Break* indicator **(L1–L9).** Answer TRUE or FALSE.

8-16. A *Record Identifying Indicator* may be on at the same time as **LR.** Answer TRUE or FALSE.

8-17. What, if anything, is wrong with the following related lines of input coding for the control fields assignments? EMPNO is the lowest control field and DIVISN the highest.

RPG Field Name	Control Level (L1-L9)	Matching Fields or Chaining Fields	Field Record Relation	Field Indicators		
				Plus	Minus	Zero or Blank
53 54 55 56 57 58	59 60	61 62	63 64	65 66	67 68	69 70
E M P N O	L 5					
S E C T O N	L 4					
D E P T	L 2					
D I V I S N	L 3					

8-18. What, if anything, is wrong with the related lines of coding in the following calculation form? VOTERS is an input field and VOTOTL, COUNTY, DISTCT, and STATE are control group total fields.

Line	Form Type	Control Level (L0-L9, LR, SR, ANOR)	Indicators						Factor 1	Operation	Factor 2	Result Field		
				And		And						Name	Length	Decimal Position
			Not		Not		Not							
3 4 5	6	7 8	9 10 11	12 13	14 15 16 17	18 19 20 21 22 23 24 25 26 27	28 29 30 31 32	33 34 35 36 37 38 39 40 41 42	43 44 45 46 47 48	49 50 51	52
0 1 0	c	L 1				V O T E R S	A D D	V O T O T L	V O T O T L		
0 2 0	c	L 3				V O T O T L	A D D	C O U N T Y	C O U N T Y		
0 3 0	c	L 4				C O U N T Y	A D D	D I S T C T	D I S T C T		
0 4 0	c	L 2				D I S T C T	A D D	S T A T E	S T A T E		

8-19. What, if anything, is wrong with the following calculation coding?

Line	Form Type	Control Level (L0-9, LR, SR, ANOR)	Indicators						Factor 1	Operation	Factor 2	Result Field		
				And		And						Name	Length	Decimal Position
			Not		Not		Not							
3 4 5	6	7 8	9 10 11	12 13	14 15 16 17	18 19 20 21 22 23 24 25 26 27	28 29 30 31 32	33 34 35 36 37 38 39 40 41 42	43 44 45 46 47 48	49 50 51	52
0 1 0	c					S E C T O N	A D D	W A G E S	S E C T O N		
0 2 0	c	L 1				D E P T	A D D	S E C T O N	D E P T		
0 3 0	c	L 2				D I V I S N	A D D	D E P T	D I V I S N		
0 4 0	c	L R				P L A N T	A D D	D I V I S N	P L A N T		

8-20. Name three classifications of reports. Explain their differences.

8-21. Examine the following partial output coding and determine what class of report will be generated.

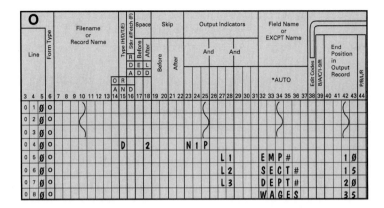

8-22. If the ouput coding includes no detail time output, the report is classified as a _____ report.

8-23. Define a *Split control field*.

8-24. *Split control fields* must be entered in the input form next to each other. Answer TRUE or FALSE.

8-25. *Split control fields* defined on input do not have to be physically next to each other in the logical record. Answer TRUE or FALSE.

8-26. The fields included in the *Split control field* group must all be defined as the same type. Answer TRUE or FALSE.

8-27. What are programmer-controlled breaks? What is their advantage over the traditional indicator method?

8-28. When the first record is read from the physical file, what housekeeping is necessary for a programmer-controlled group report program?

8-29. In a programmer-controlled group report program that supports two control groups (department and division), which control field would be tested first? Which will be processed first?

PROGRAMMING ASSIGNMENTS

For each of the following programming assignments, a physical file must have been created and loaded with the related data records. Your instructor will inform you as to whether you have to create the physical file and load it or if it has been prepared for the assignment.

Programming Assignment 8-1: VOTER REPORT BY TOWN AND STATE TOTALS

Write an RPG/400 program to generate the report detailed in the supplemental printer spacing chart.

Physical File Record Format:

```
                    PHYSICAL FILE DESCRIPTION

        SYSTEM: AS/400                          DATE: Yours
        FILE NAME: Yours                        REV NO: 0
        RECORD NAME: Yours                      KEY LENGTH: 9
        SEQUENCE: Keyed                         RECORD SIZE: 13
```

```
┌─────────────────────────────────────────────────────────────────┐
│                        FIELD DEFINITIONS                          │
│                                                                   │
│      FIELD     FIELD NAME    SIZE   TYPE     POSITION    COMMENTS  │
│       NO                                    FROM    TO            │
│                                                                   │
│        1       DIST#          4      C        1      4   3rd key  │
│        2       TOWN#          3      C        5      7   2nd key  │
│        3       CONTY#         2      C        8      9   1st key  │
│        4       VOTERS         6      P       10     13   0 decimals│
└─────────────────────────────────────────────────────────────────┘
```

Physical File Data:

District Number	Town Number	County Number	Number of Voters In District
1000	100	10	215625
1010	100	10	082784
1020	100	10	104716
1030	100	10	012899
1040	100	10	267004
2000	200	10	057800
2010	200	10	014111
2020	200	10	118923
2030	200	10	073807
3000	300	30	200749
3010	300	30	111111
4000	400	40	067242
4010	400	40	104338
4020	400	40	099917
4030	400	40	178615
4040	400	40	222234
4050	400	40	033845
4060	400	40	117871
4070	400	40	064899
4080	400	40	045348
4090	400	40	888888

Note: A field is included for county number that is not referenced for this assignment. It is, however, required for the multiple control group report for Assignment 8-3.

Processing: Process the input file consecutively, and accumulate the number of voters in each district into a control total. Also, maintain a total for all the voters in the state that is to be printed after end of file is tested. Refer to the following printer spacing chart result field sizes. Print the report in a *detail* format.

Report Design:

```
      0         1         2         3         4         5         6         7         8
      1234567890123456789012345678901234567890123456789012345678901234567890123456789012345678
 1   ØX/XX/XX                        STATE OF CONFUSION                         PAGE XXØX
 2
 3
 4                     DISTRICT      TOWN                        VOTERS
 5
 6                       XXXX        XXX                        XXX,XXØ
 7                       XXXX        XXX                        XXX,XXØ
 8
 9                 TOTAL VOTERS FOR TOWN XXX                  X,XXX,XXØ *
10
11
12                 TOTAL VOTERS FOR STATE                   XXX,XXX,XXØ
13
14         NOTES:
15
16           1. HEADINGS ON TOP OF EVERY PAGE.
17
18           2. REPORT DATE IS SYSTEM-SUPPLIED.
19
20           3. PAGE OVERFLOW ON LINE 2Ø
```

Because of the limited number of data records, page overflow control will not be tested. Therefore, with permission and procedures from the instructor, use the Line

Counter form to change the page length to line 22 with page overflow on line 20. Printer type will determine whether line numbers or channel numbers are referenced.

Programming Assignment 8-2: VOTER REPORT BY TOWN, COUNTY, AND STATE TOTALS

If Assignment 8-1 was previously completed, supplement it to include the changes in the modified printer spacing chart shown below. On the other hand, if Assignment 8-1 was not completed, refer to that assignment for input record format and data.

Physical File Record Format: Refer to the record format in Assignment 8-1. Define town number and county number as the two control fields.

Processing: Read the file consecutively and accumulate a town total. When the town number changes (**L1** *control break*), add the accumulated town total to a county total field. Then, when the county number changes (**L2** *control break*), add the accumulated county total to a state total. Print related output according to the report format detailed in the print chart.

Report Design*:*

Programming Assignment 8-3: VOTER REPORT BY TOWN AND STATE TOTALS—PROGRAMMER-CONTROLLED CONTROL BREAKS

Refer to the documentation for Assignment 8-1 and write an RPG/400 program using a programmer-controlled control break.

Programming Assignment 8-4: VOTER REPORT BY TOWN, COUNTY, AND STATE TOTALS—PROGRAMMER-CONTROLLED CONTROL BREAKS

Refer to the documentation for Assignment 8-2 and write an RPG/400 program using programmer-controlled control breaks.

Programming Assignment 8-5: PLANT RAW MATERIALS REPORT

From the following information, write an RPG/400 program (either traditional or programmer-controlled) to generate the detail report shown in the supplemental printer spacing chart.

Physical File Record Format:

```
                    PHYSICAL FILE DESCRIPTION

      SYSTEM: AS/400                        DATE: Yours
      FILE NAME: Yours                      REV NO: 0
      RECORD NAME: Yours                    KEY LENGTH: 11
      SEQUENCE: Keyed                       RECORD SIZE: 37

                        FIELD DEFINITIONS

        FIELD    FIELD NAME   SIZE   TYPE    POSITION      COMMENTS
        NO                                  FROM    TO

          1       PART#        4      C       1      4   4th key
          2       JOB#         3      C       5      7   3rd key
          3       SECT#        2      C       8      9   2nd key
          4       DEPT#        2      C      10     11   1st key
          5       DESCRP      20      C      12     31
          6       USED         4      P      32     34   0 decimals
          7       COST         5      P      35     37   2 decimals
```

Physical File Data:

Part#	Job#	Section#	Dept#	Part Description	Qty Used	Cost/Item
6278	100	200	10	CLOSER-WHITE	0024	00550
6280	100	200	10	JAMB BRACKET-WHITE	0024	00073
6284	100	200	10	DOOR BRACKET-WHITE	0024	00049
6349	101	200	10	PHILP 12 X 1 SCREWS	0192	00008
6350	101	200	10	PHILP 8 X 1 SCREWS	0144	00006
6355	101	200	10	PHILP 6 X 1/2 SCREWS	0096	00050
6364	101	200	10	THUMB SCREW	0384	00117
6461	102	210	20	36" SCREEN-WHITE	0012	02999
6462	102	210	20	36" SCREEN-BLACK	0024	02999
6463	102	210	20	32" SCREEN-ALMOND	0010	03299
6573	103	300	20	INSIDE HANDLE	0024	00320
6574	103	300	20	OUTSIDE HANDLE	0024	00305
6576	103	300	20	LATCH ASSEMBLY	0024	01244

For each detail record processed, the quantity used is multiplied by the cost per item to obtain the total cost for the part. Three control fields must be specified with job number the lowest; section number, second; and department, third. The plant total, which must include the cost of all the parts, is to be printed at last record time.

Report Design:

	0	1	2	3	4	5	6	7
1	ØX/XX/XX		PART USAGE REPORT		PAGE XXØX			
2		BY JOB, SECTION, & DEPT						
3								
4								
5	PART NO	DESCRIPTION		TOTAL COST				
6								
7	XXXX X		X	X,XXX,XXØ.XX				
8	XXXX X		X	X,XXX,XXØ.XX				
9								
10								
11		JOB NO XXX TOTAL		XX,XXX,XXØ.XX *				
12								
13		SECTION XX TOTAL		XXX,XXX,XXØ.XX **				
14								
15		DEPT XX TOTAL		X,XXX,XXX,XXØ.XX ***				
16								
17		PLANT TOTAL		XX,XXX,XXX,XXØ.XX				
18								
19								
20		NOTE: HEADINGS ON TOP OF EVERY PAGE.						

chapter 9

Data Structures and Data Areas

Data structures, which are specified in the **Input Specifications** of an RPG/400 program, define an area in storage and the layout of related subfields. Data structures may be used to:

1. Divide a field into subfields.
2. Change the format of a field.
3. Group noncontiguous data in a contiguous format.
4. Define an area of storage in more than one format.
5. Define multiple occurrences of a data structure (discussed in Chapter 11).

The following three special-purpose **data structures** may also be included in an RPG/400 program:

1. *Data Area Data Structure*
2. *File Information Data Structure* (**INFDS**)
3. *Program Status Data Structure*

Data structures may be <u>program-</u> or <u>externally</u> defined and must include two parts: the *data structure statement* and at least one related *subfield*. Figure 9-1 details the syntax for all of the data structure types.

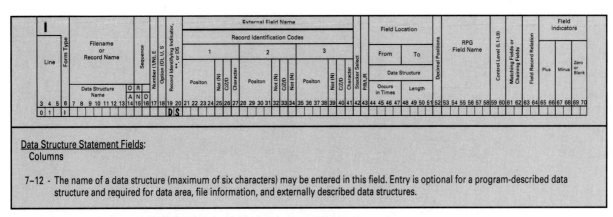

Figure 9-1 Data structure coding rules.

13–16 - Not used.

17   - **Blank** for all program-described data structures, and **E** for externally described.

18   - **Blank** for program described data structure; **U** for data area data structure; and **S** for program status data structure.

19–20 - **DS** must be entered for all data structures.

21–30 - **Blank** for program-described data structure. For externally described data structure, the name of the physical file whose record format contains the field descriptions used as the subfields in the data structure must be entered.

31–43 - Not used.

44–47 - **Blank** for single occurrence, data area, file information, and program status data structures. Multiple occurrence data structures require a numeric integer entry (from 1 to 9999) right-justified in this field indicating the number of occurrences.

48–51 - The length of the data structure may optionally be included right-justified in this field.

52–74 - Not used.

Subfields:

43   - Entries in this field for a program-described data structure are:

Blank - Indicates character data if a decimal poisition entry is not included in column 52. If **0–9** is entered in column 52, the field is defined as zoned decimal format.

P   - Subfield is in packed decimal format.

B   - Subfield is in binary format.

The RPG/400 compiler converts the data to the format specified when a record is read, at detail or total calculation time, or at detail or output time.

All of the subfields in a data structure are considered to be character, and any numeric subfields must be initialized with numeric data before they are used in an arithmetic or editing operation.

Individual subfield length is determined the same as the packed, zoned decimal, or binary fields in a physical file. The maximum length of a data structure is 9,999. Subfields defined as character may be 256 bytes, and numeric 30 with a maximum of 9 decimal positions.

44–47 - Entry must be right-justified indicating the beginning position of the subfield in the body of the data structure.

48–51 - Entry must be right-justified indicating the ending position of the subfield in the body of the data structure.

52   - A **0** through **9** entry in this field defines the subfield as numeric. **Blank** defines the subfield as character.

53–58 - Subfield names must begin on a coding line immediately following the data structure statement and must be defined according to the rules for RPG/400 field names. A subfield cannot have the same name as the data structure name specified in columns 7–12 of the data structure statement.

59–74 - Not used.

Figure 9-1   Data structure coding rules. (Continued)

Subfield Coding Rules

The rules that must be followed when defining the subfields in a **data structure** are detailed in Figure 9-2.

DATA STRUCTURE SUBFIELD RULES

1. An input field name cannot
   • Be specified as a subfield name and a data structure name
   • Be used more than once in a data structure

2. If a subfield is defined with a different length or decimal position than the original defintion, the attributes of the first definition are used.

Figure 9-2   Data structure subfield rules.

> 3. Subfield name cannot be larger than the length of the related input field or larger than the length of the data structure (when specified in columns 48–51).
>
> 4. Overlapping subfields cannot be used as the elements of a calculation statement.
>
> 5. One-byte subfields must have the same entry in the *FROM* and *TO* fields.
>
> 6. One subfield may redefine another subfield.
>
> 7. Numeric subfields must be initialized with numeric data before they are used in calculations.
>
> 8. When an array or array element is specified in calculations, the entire array is checked for an overlap condition.

Figure 9-2   Data structure subfield rules. (Continued)

Examples of each of the **data structure** types will be discussed in the following paragraphs.

Data Structure to Separate a Field into Subfields

Parts of a field (subfields) may be defined by traditional input coding, by the **MOVEL** and **MOVE** operations, or by a **data structure**. Figure 9-3 illustrates two coding examples of this data structure type. The first example specifies a **data structure** name in columns 7–12 with the subfields defined in the subfield area (columns 44–58). A limitation of this method is that the **data structure** name (ACT#) is automatically defined as character and cannot be used as a field in calculations. However, the composite field ACTNO, which redefines the elements of ACT#, may be used as a numeric field. The second example in Figure 9-3 does not include an entry in the **data structure name** field (columns 7–12). Instead, the input field name is specified as a subfield and then redefined into its related elements.

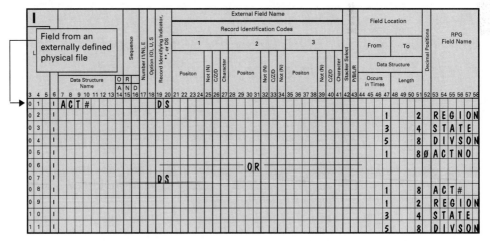

Figure 9-3   Defining subfields within a field with a data structure.

Data Structure to Reorganize the Fields in an Input Record

Figure 9-4 shows the coding for a **data structure** that is used to reorganize a field from a program-defined physical file. The input DATE field is an MMDDYY format, but processing logic requires that it be rearranged into a YYMMDD format. First, the input field is subdivided into its related elements (MM, DD, YY). Then, the **data structure** re-

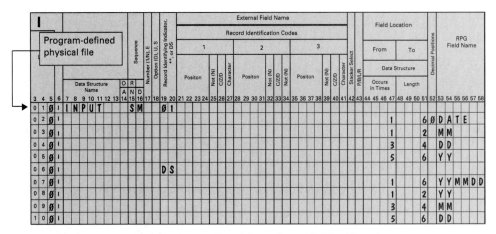

Figure 9-4   Reorganizing the subfields in an input field with a data structure.

arranges the MM, DD, YY elements into a YY, MM, DD order and stores their values in the YYMMDD field. This is a more efficient approach than using a mathematical formula or **MOVE** or **MOVEL** operation to separate and reorganize the data elements.

Data Structure to Group Fields

Input fields may be grouped for subsequent processing by a **data structure**. The building of a *composite key* field to access records randomly from a keyed physical file is one example for which this **data structure** format may be required. Figure 9-5 illustrates the coding for a **data structure** that groups fields.

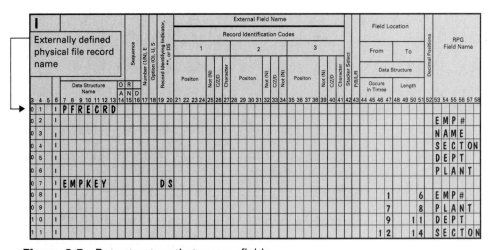

Figure 9-5   Data structure that groups fields.

Data Structure That Defines a Storage Area in More Than One Format

An example of defining an area of storage for more than one record format is illustrated in Figure 9-6. For the input coding shown, the file name, *Record Identifying Indicators, Record Identification Codes,* and *TO* and *FROM* field locations indicate that the physical file is program-defined. Recall that physical files that are formatted with *Data Description Specification* entries support only one record format. Consequently, to illus-

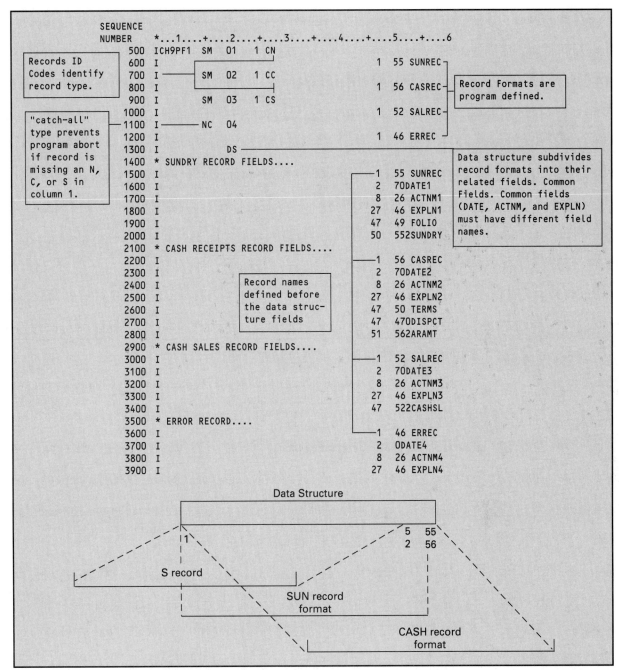

Figure 9-6 Data structure that defines an area of storage in three record formats.

trate the function of this **data structure,** the data is stored in a physical file that does not have a DDS record format.

Instead of defining multiple record formats in a program-defined physical file with traditional input coding, a **data structure** will save storage during program execution. In the coding shown on lines 500 through 1200 of Figure 9-6, three record types are identified by the *Record Identification Codes* N, C, or S entered in column 1 of their related records. The fourth record type (lines 1100–1200), with no code specified, is a "catch-all" that prevents program execution from halting if a record is read that does not include an **N, C,** or **S** in column 1.

The **data structure** included on lines 1300–3900 subdivides each of the previously defined record types into their field elements.

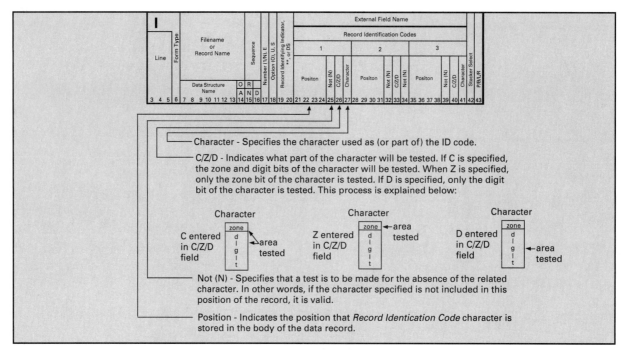

Figure 9-7   Record Identification Code syntax.

Figure 9-7 explains the syntax related to *Record Identification Codes*. Any number of positions in a record format may be allocated for a code, and any characters may be specified.

Data Area Data Structures

A *data area* is an object that may exist permanently or temporarily in any library on the system. It may have been created by the **CRTDTAARA** (*Create Data Area*) command and loaded in a permanent library or by execution of an RPG/400 program and loaded in the job's temporary library (QTEMP). A *data area data structure* in an RPG/400 program and the related data area must have the same name.

Data areas may be *implicitly or explicitly* retrieved and written. When the data area is defined in an RPG/400 program as a data area data structure, its data is *implicitly* retrieved for processing and written back (updated) at the end of the program. The *explicit* processing of data area data structures will be discussed later in this chapter. Figure 9-8 details the syntax for data area data structures.

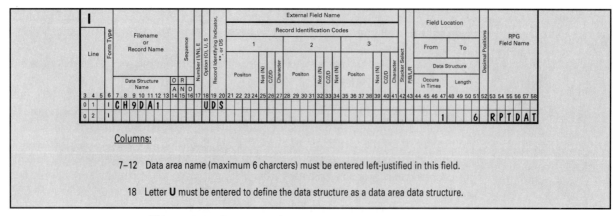

Columns:

7–12   Data area name (maximum 6 charcters) must be entered left-justified in this field.

18   Letter **U** must be entered to define the data structure as a data area data structure.

Figure 9-8   Data area data structure syntax.

19-20 DS must be entered to specify a data structure.

44-47 Subfield names must begin on a new line. The beginning poisition of the related data item must
       be specified. If the data area already exists, the fields specified must relate to the posi-
       tions in which the data is stored.

48-51 The ending position of the subfield. Character subfields may be 256 bytes, and numeric 30.
       Because the data in the data area is stored in one contiguous area, it must be subdivided in
       the RPG/400 to access the applicable values.

   52 Decimal position entry (**0-9**) defines the subfield as numeric.

53-58 Subfield name must be entered left-justified and be a maximum of six characters. Unlike an externally
       defined physical file, data areas have no DDS definition and the subfield must be program-defined.

Figure 9-8   Data area data structure syntax. (Continued)

DATA STRUCTURES FOR EXCEPTION/ERROR CONTROL

Exception errors that cause program execution to cancel are not uncommon in the programming environment. Routines may be included in an RPG/400 program to identify
and control *exception/errors* and prevent program execution "aborts." *File Information
Data Structures and Program Status Data Structures* are two RPG/400 run-time methods
to control exception/error processing.

File Information Data Structure (INFDS)

A *File Information Data Structure* provides exception/error information that may have
occurred when processing a file during program execution. This type of **data structure**
contains predefined subfields that identify:

1. The name of the file for which the error occurred
2. The record processed when the error occurred
3. The operation being processed when the error occurred
4. The status code number
5. The RPG/400 routine in which the error occurred

Specifically, keywords including ***FILE, *INP, *MODE, *OUT, *OPCODE, *SIZE,
*STATUS, *RECORD,** and ***ROUTINE** provide the previously named information for
any file processed by the program. For a comprehensive discussion of the nine error routines, consult IBM's *RPG/400 User's Guide.*

Many RPG/400 operations (e.g., **CHAIN, WRITE, UPDAT, DELET, SETLL,**
and **SETGT**) identify processing errors by specifying an indicator in columns 56–57 of
the related calculation instruction. Exception errors can be controlled, thus preventing
cancellation of program execution by testing the status of the indicator. However, if an
operation does not support an error indicator (such as **DIV, MULT, SUB, ADD,** and
SORT) or if it is not specified, exception errors may be controlled by testing for an error
code in the ***STATUS** field which is included in a *File Information Data Structure* or
Program Status Data Structure. ***STATUS** code errors that may be identified in a *File
Information Data Structure* are listed in Figure 9-9.

Table 7 (Page 1 of 2). Exception/Error Codes			
Code	Device[1]	RC[2]	Condition
01011	W,D,SQ	n/a	Undefined record type (input record does not match record identifying indicator).
01021	W,D,SQ	n/a	Tried to write a record that already exists (file being used has unique keys and key is duplicate, or attempted to write duplicate relative record number to a subfile).
01031	W,D,SQ	n/a	Match field out of sequence.
01041	n/a	n/a	Array/table load sequence error.
01051	n/a	n/a	Excess entries in array/table file.
01052	n/a	n/a	Clearing of table prior to dump of data failed.
01071	W,D,SQ	n/a	Numeric sequence error.
01121[4]	W	n/a	No indicator on the DDS keyword for Print key.
01122[4]	W	n/a	No indicator on the DDS keyword for Roll Up key.
01123[4]	W	n/a	No indicator on the DDS keyword for Roll Down key.
01124[4]	W	n/a	No indicator on the DDS keyword for Clear key.
01125[4]	W	n/a	No indicator on the DDS keyword for Help key.
01126[4]	W	n/a	No indicator on the DDS keyword for Home key.
01201	W	34xx	Record mismatch detected on input.
01211	all	n/a	I/O operation to a closed file.
01215	all	n/a	OPEN issued to a file already opened.
01216[3]	all	yes	Error on an implicit OPEN/CLOSE operation.
01217[3]	all	yes	Error on an explicit OPEN/CLOSE operation.
01218	D,SQ	n/a	Record already locked.
01221	D,SQ	na	Update operation attempted without a prior read.
01231	SP	n/a	Error on SPECIAL file.
01235	P	n/a	Error in PRTCTL space or skip entries.
01241	D,SQ	n/a	Record number not found (Record number specified in record address file is not present in file being processed.)
01251	W	80xx 81xx	Permanent I/O error occurred.
01255	W	82xx 83xx	Session or device error occurred. Recovery may be possible.
01261	W	n/a	Attempt to exceed maximum number of acquired devices.
01281	W	n/a	Operation to unacquired device.
01282	W	0309	Job ending with controlled option.
01285	W	0800	Attempt to acquire a device already acquired.
01286	W	n/a	Attempt to open shared file with SAVDS or IND options.
01287	W	n/a	Response indicators overlap IND indicators.
01299	W,D,SQ	yes	Other I/O error detected.
01331	W	0310	Wait time exceeded for READ from WORKSTN file.

Note: "Device" refers to the devices for which the condition applies. The following abbreviations are used: P = PRINTER; D = DISK; W = WORKSTN; SP = SPECIAL; SQ = Sequential. The major/minor return codes under column RC apply only to WORKSTN files. [2]The formula mmnn is used to described major/minor return codes: mm is the major and nn the minor. [3]Any errors that occur during an open or close operation will result in a *STATUS value of 1216 or 1217 regardless of the major/minor return code value.

Figure 9-9   RPG/400 run-time file status (INFDS) code errors (*Courtesy of IBM*).

The RPG/400 *File Description* and *Input Specifications* coding to support a *File Information Data Structure* (**INFDS**) is detailed in Figure 9-10. Note that a *File Exception/Error Subroutine* (**INFSR**) is specified on a second continuation statement which accesses the RPG/400-supplied ***PSSR** routine. When an error is detected, control will pass to this subroutine automatically. Based on the error type, programmer-supplied statements in the ***PSSR** routine will determine the action to be taken (i.e., end the job or ignore the error and continue processing).

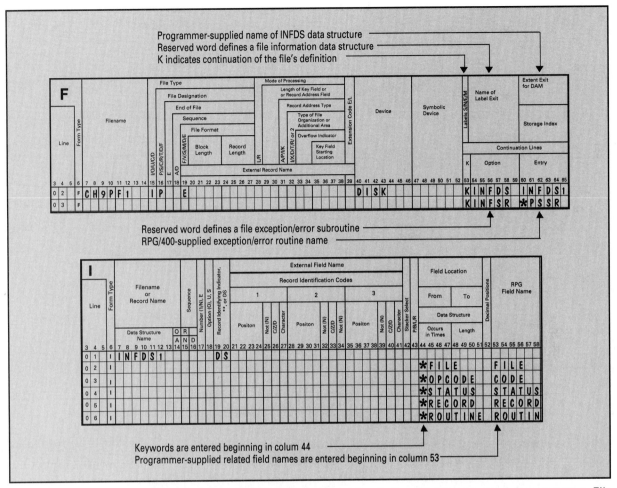

Figure 9-10 File Description and Input Specifications syntax to support a File Information Data Structure (INFDS).

The *Input Specifications* in Figure 9-10 define the keyword information that is to be accessed if an exception/error occurs. One or all nine of the available keywords may be included to identify information about the error condition. The ***PSSR** routine will be accessed only if the ***STATUS** code value is greater than 00099. All files, or select files only, processed by an RPG/400 program may be assigned a *File Information Data Structure*. If this control is not included in an RPG/400 program, the system will generate a message on the user's screen which provides cancel, go, dump, or system dump options. This system-supplied exception/error control is not advisable in a batch environment.

A partial listing of the chapter's example program in Figure 9-11 illustrates the use of a *File Information Data Structure*.

The output generated in the ***PSSR** routine may be directed to any output device and include **INFDS** keyword values and/or programmer-supplied code. Some errors may require that execution of the program be cancelled. Under those circumstances, ***CANCL** would be moved to the READAG field (line 8500) and the program would end. In any case, **INFDS** exception/error control prevents the display of system-supplied errors which could utilize system resources if a user response was not timely.

Note that the exception/error information for the keywords is only generated if the ***STATUS** keyword value is greater than 00099.

All or select files only processed by an RPG/400 program may be assigned a *File Information Data Structure*. Furthermore, the **dump** option which appears on the screen when an exception/error occurs will provide the same information as this data structure

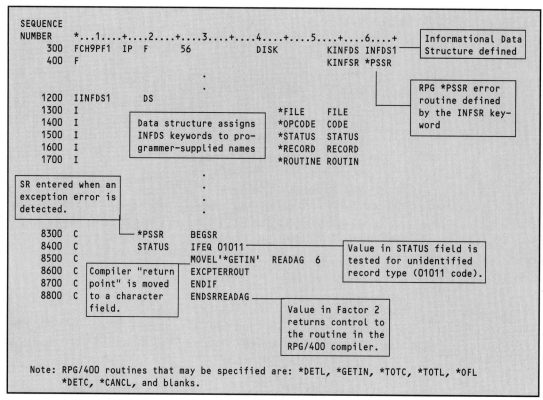

```
SEQUENCE
NUMBER      *...1....+....2....+....3....+....4....+....5....+....6....+      ┌─────────────────┐
     300  FCH9PF1 IP  F    56           DISK          KINFDS INFDS1          │ Informational Data│
     400  F                                           KINFSR *PSSR           │ Structure defined │
                                                                            └─────────────────┘
                                 .
                                 .                                          ┌─────────────────┐
    1200  IINFDS1      DS                                                    │ RPG *PSSR error   │
    1300  I          ┌─────────────────────┐          *FILE    FILE         │ routine defined   │
    1400  I          │ Data structure assigns│         *OPCODE  CODE         │ by the INFSR key- │
    1500  I          │ INFDS keywords to pro-│         *STATUS  STATUS       │ word              │
    1600  I          │ grammer-supplied names│         *RECORD  RECORD       └─────────────────┘
    1700  I          └─────────────────────┘          *ROUTINE ROUTIN
 ┌─────────────────┐                         .
 │ SR entered when an│                        .
 │ exception error is│                        .
 │ detected.        │                         .
 └─────────────────┘
    8300  C           ┌─ *PSSR      BEGSR
    8400  C              STATUS      IFEQ 01011 ───────      ┌─────────────────────┐
    8500  C                          MOVEL'*GETIN'  READAG 6 │ Value in STATUS field is│
    8600  C           ┌─────────────┐ EXCPTERROUT            │ tested for unidentified │
    8700  C           │Compiler "return│ ENDIF                │ record type (01011 code).│
    8800  C           │point" is moved │ ENDSRREADAG ──┐      └─────────────────────┘
                      │to a character  │               │  ┌─────────────────────┐
                      │field.          │               └─│ Value in Factor 2      │
                      └─────────────┘                   │ returns control to     │
                                                        │ the routine in the     │
                                                        │ RPG/400 compiler.      │
                                                        └─────────────────────┘

 Note: RPG/400 routines that may be specified are: *DETL, *GETIN, *TOTC, *TOTL, *OFL
       *DETC, *CANCL, and blanks.
```

Figure 9-11   Partial listing of an RPG/400 program with INFDS control.

type. However, *File Information Data Structures* allow the programmer to select the file(s) that he or she wants to check, access the keyword information desired, and prevent cancellation of program execution.

Program Status Data Structure

As has been previously discussed, a *File Information Data Structure* identifies exception/errors associated with file processing and includes its own set of ***STATUS** code er-

Status Code	Condition
00100	String error message
00101	Negative square root
00102	Divide by zero
00121	Array index not valid
00122	OCUR outside of range
00123	Reset attempted during initialization step of program
00202	Called program failed; halt indicator (H1 through H9 not on)
00211	Program specified on CALL or FREE not found
00221	Called program tried to use a parameter that was not passed to it
00231	Called program returned with halt indicator on
00232	Halt indicator on in this program
00233	Halt indicator on when RETRN operation run
00299	RPG/400-formatted dump failed
00333	Error on DSPLY operation

Figure 9-12   Program Status Data Structure codes (*Courtesy of IBM*).

rors. *Program Status Data Structures,* however, identify exceptions/errors that are generated in the program by RPG/400 operations and not by a file. The five-digit ***STATUS** codes that may be identified in a *Program Status Data Structure* are summarized in Figure 9-12. Note that any code greater than 00099 is flagged as an exception/error.

Four keywords—***STATUS, *ROUTINE, *PARMS,** and ***PROGRAM**—are supported by a *Program Status Data Structure.*

The eight-character ***ROUTINE** keyword contains the name of the RPG/400 routine (e.g., ***INIT, *GETIN, *DETL, *DETC, *TOTC, *TOTL, *DETC, *OFL, *TERM, SR name, PGM name**) in which the exception/error occurred. ***PARMS** is a three-digit numeric keyword that stores the number of parameters passed to the program from a **calling** program. ***PROGRAM** is a 10-position character field that stores the name of the program in which the *Program Status Data Structure* is specified.

Figure 9-13 details the *File Description* and *Input Specifications* syntax for a *Program Status Data Structure.* Instead of the RPG/400 ***PSSR** routine, a programmer-named routine may be specified.

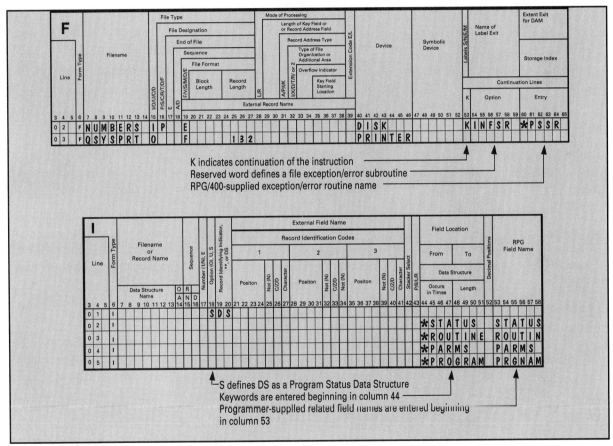

Figure 9-13 File Description and Input Specifications syntax for a Program Status Data Structure.

The Square Root program from Chapter 4 has been modified in Figure 9-14 to include a *Program Status Data Structure.* Note that any of the RPG/400 routines previously mentioned could have been used in lieu of ***GETIN.** The error(s) tested will determine which routine should be accessed. In the event of a negative value for NUMBER, this exception/error control will prevent cancellation of program execution and identify the error condition.

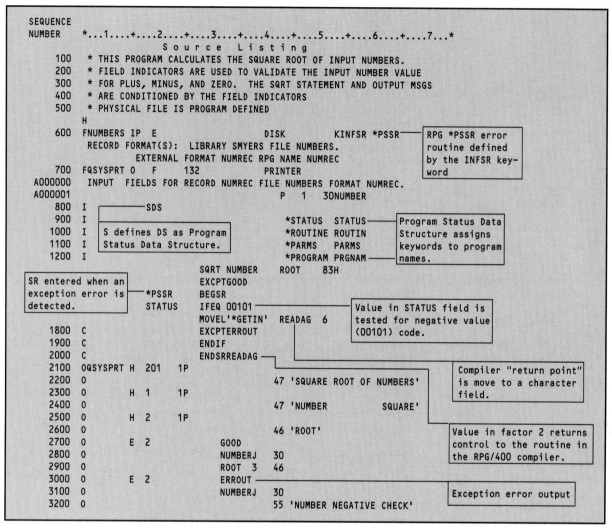

Figure 9-14 Example Square Root program with Program Status Data Structure control.

DATA AREAS

Data areas, which were previously defined when *Data Area Data Structures* were discussed in this chapter, are objects used to transfer data to one or more programs within a job or between jobs. A data area may be considered as a one-record storage area whose value is extracted for processing by an RPG/400 or CL program.

Data areas may be created by the **CRTDTAARA** command, their values updated by the **CHGDTAARA** command, and viewed by the **DSPDTAARA** command. Figure 9-15 shows the display generated by entering **CRTDTAARA** on a command line and pressing **F4**.

The **CRTDTARRRA** display in Figure 9-15 named the data area CH9DA1, which will be stored in the current library (***CURLIB**) and defined as a ***DEC** type with a length of six digits and zero decimal positions. The value 123194 is entered on the *Initial value* line. If character (***CHAR**) type was specified, the value must be enclosed in single quotes.

A *data area* defined with a ***DEC** type parameter may be 24 digits with a maximum of 9 decimal positions. ***CHAR** type may store a maximum character string of

```
                         Create Data Area (CRTDTAARA)

 Type choices, press Enter.

 Data area . . . . . . . . . . > CH9DA1——        Name
   Library . . . . . . . . . . >   *CURLIB——     Name, *CURLIB
 Type . . . . . . . . . . . . . > *DEC           *DEC, *CHAR, *LGL
 Length:
   Length . . . . . . . . . . > 6——             1-2000
   Decimal positions . . . . . > 0——             0-9
 Initial value . . . . . . . . > 123194 _____
 Text 'description' . . . . . . > ch9 - first data area example_____
   ___

                                                                     Bottom
 F3=Exit   F4=Prompt   F5=Refresh   F10=Additional parameters   F12=Cancel
 F13=How to use this display       F24=More keys
```

Figure 9-15   CRTDTAARA (*Create Data Area*) display.

2,000 characters. ***LGL** (logical) may contain a 1 or 0 indicating an on/off, true/false, or yes/no condition, respectively. For a comprehensive discussion of all the parameters, refer to the appropriate IBM Control Language Reference manual.

The value of a data area may be changed by an RPG/400 program, a CL program, or by the **CHGDTAARA** command. Identical to any other CL command, **CHGDTAARA** is entered on a command line and **F4** pressed to access the display shown in Figure 9-16.

```
                         Change Data Area (CHGDTAARA)

 Type choices, press Enter.

 Data area specification:

   Data area . . . . . . . . . > CH9DA1_____ Name, *LDA, *GDA, *PDA
     Library . . . . . . . . . >   SMYERS_____ Name, *LIBL, *CURLIB
   Substring specifications:
   Substring starting position .  *ALL__        1-2000, *ALL
   Substring length . . . . . .   ____          1-2000
   New value . . . . . . . . . .  123194_____

                                                                     Bottom
 F3=Exit    F4=Prompt   F5=Refresh   F12=Cancel   F13=How to use this display
 F24=More keys
```

Figure 9-16   CHGDTAARA (*Change Data Area*) display.

The old value may be replaced with a new value entirely, or it may be partially changed, by entering a value in the *Substring starting position*. The ***ALL** default indicates that all of the current value will be changed. If the new value is larger, the new length must be entered for the *Substring length* parameter.

The value stored in a *data area* may be reviewed by the **DSPDTAARA** command shown in Figure 9-17.

```
                        Display Data Area
                                                    System:   AS/400

Data area . . . . . . . :   CH9DA1
   Library . . . . . . . :     SMYERS
Type  . . . . . . . . . :   *DEC
Length  . . . . . . . . :   6 0
Text  . . . . . . . . . :   ch9 - first data area example
Value . . . . . . . . . :   123194




Press Enter to continue.

F3=Exit    F12=Cancel
```

Figure 9-17   DSPDTAARA (*Display Data Area*) display.

Processing of Data Areas

The *Data Area Data Structure* previously explained illustrated how the data in a *data area* may be *implicitly* retrieved and written by an RPG/400 program. *Data areas* may be *explicitly* retrieved and written with **IN** and **OUT** operations in an RPG/400 program. The operations and reserved words related to the *explicit* processing of *data areas* are summarized in Figure 9-18.

RPG/400 OPERATIONS AND RESERVED WORDS
FOR DATA AREA PROCESSING

Operation	Function
IN (Retrieve a Data Area)	Explicitly retrieves a data area and optionally allows the programmer to "lock" it so that it cannot be updated by another program during execution of the controlling program.
OUT (Write a Data Area)	Explicitly updates the data area specified in *Factor 2* of the **OUT** statement and unlocks it so that it may be used by other programs.
DEFN (Field Definition)	When used with a ***NAMVAR** reserved word in *Factor 1,* it specifies that the entry in *Factor 2* is a data area.
UNLCK (Unlock a Data Area)	Releases (unlocks) one or all of the data areas locked by the controlling program. This operation is only applicable if a ***NAMVAR DEFN** statement defined the data area. When ***NAMVAR** is specified in *Factor 2* of an **UNLCK** statement, all data areas locked by the program are unlocked. If a data area name is specified in *Factor 2,* only that data area will be unlocked.

Reserved Words	Function
*LOCK	When used as a *Factor 1* entry with the **IN** operation, this reserved word places an object-lock on the specified data area. When used as a *Factor 1* entry with the **OUT** operation, the data area is written to but retains its object-lock.
*NAMVAR	When used as a *Factor 1* entry in a **DEFN** statement, it declares the entry in *Factor 2* as a data area. If a *Factor 2* entry is not specified, the field name in the *Result Field* is used as the data area name.
	When used as a *Factor 2* entry in an **IN** statement, all of the data areas included in the program are accessed.

Figure 9-18   RPG/400 operations and reserved words for the explicit processing of data areas.

RPG/400 EXPLICIT ACCESS OF DATA AREAS

Data Area Assigned to a Field

The RPG/400 program in Figure 9-19 illustrates the syntax required to access the value from a data area *when the* data area *is assigned to a field.* Note the following features of the example program:

1. An input file is not specified. This has nothing to do with the processing of a data area. The program is simplified to emphasize data area processing rather than other RPG/400 syntax.
2. Because no input file is defined, end-of-program processing is controlled by the **MOVE *ON *INLR** statement on line 600.
3. The value in the data area, **CKINFO,** is assigned to the field **CHECKS.**
4. The **IN** statement accesses the value stored in **CHECKS.**
5. The **MOVEL** and **MOVE** statements on lines 400 and 500 separate the *data area value* into its logical field values.

The printed output is included only to show that the value stored in the data area was accessed by the program.

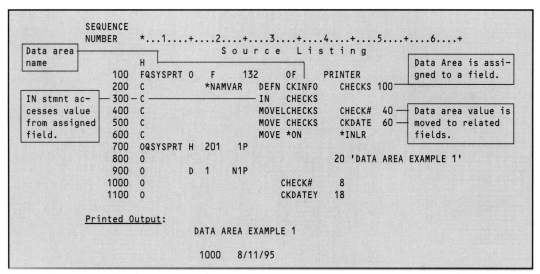

Figure 9-19 Example program that assigns a data area to a field with resulting printed output.

Data Area Assigned to a Data Structure

The RPG/400 program in Figure 9-19 is modified in Figure 9-20 to assign a data area to a data structure name. Note that the data structure name is specified in the *Result Field* of the ***NAMVAR DEFN** statement on line 500.

The two methods shown here for accessing a data area in an RPG/400 program are just two examples of the many other coding alternatives.

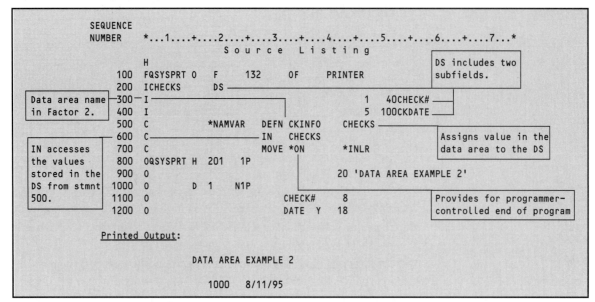

Figure 9-20 Example program that assigns a data area to a data structure with resulting printed output.

RPG/400 Control to Change the Value in a Data Area

The two previous program examples that accessed a data area did not change its value. To change the value in a data area, the **OUT** operation is required. The program in Figure 9-21 details the syntax needed for such a change. A data area previously <u>locked</u> by an **IN** statement is automatically <u>released</u> from the locked state after the **OUT** statement is executed. If more than one data area is supported by the program, specifying an **UNLCK** statement with ***NAMVAR** in *Factor 2* will unlock all of them at one time. On the other hand, if only a select data area is to be unlocked, the *data area name* must be entered in *Factor 2*.

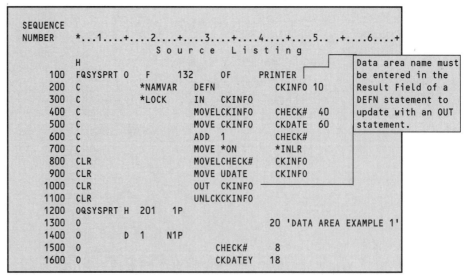

Figure 9-21 Example program that changes the value in a data area.

Two **DSPDTAARA** (*Display Data Area*) displays are presented in Figure 9-22, which shows the data area value *before* and *after* execution of the program in Figure 9-21.

```
┌──────────────────────────────────────────────────────────────────────────┐
│ Before:                                                                    │
│                              Display Data Area                             │
│                                                          System:   AS/400  │
│ Data area . . . . . . . . :   CKINFO                                       │
│   Library . . . . . . . . :     SMYERS                                     │
│ Type . . . . . . . . . . :   *CHAR                                         │
│ Length . . . . . . . . . :   10                                            │
│ Text . . . . . . . . . . :   ch9 data area example 1                       │
│                                                                            │
│             Value                                                          │
│ Offset      *...+....1....+....2....+....3....+....4....+....5              │
│             '1000081195'                                                   │
│                                                                            │
│                                                                    Bottom  │
│ Press Enter to continue.                                                   │
│                                                                            │
│ F3=Exit    F12=Cancel                                                      │
└──────────────────────────────────────────────────────────────────────────┘
```

```
┌──────────────────────────────────────────────────────────────────────────┐
│ After:                                                                     │
│                              Display Data Area                             │
│                                                          System:   AS/400  │
│ Data area . . . . . . . . :   CKINFO                                       │
│   Library . . . . . . . . :     SMYERS                                     │
│ Type . . . . . . . . . . :   *CHAR                                         │
│ Length . . . . . . . . . :   10                                            │
│ Text . . . . . . . . . . :   ch9 data area example 1                       │
│                                                                            │
│             Value                                                          │
│ Offset      *...+....1....+....2....+....3....+....4....+....5              │
│             '1001083195'                                                   │
│                                                                            │
│                                                                    Bottom  │
│ Press Enter to continue.                                                   │
│                                                                            │
│ F3=Exit    F12=Cancel                                                      │
└──────────────────────────────────────────────────────────────────────────┘
```

Figure 9-22 DSPDTAARA displays showing the data area value before and after execution of the change program.

SUMMARY

Data structures, which are defined in the *Input Specifications* of an RPG/400 program, define a temporary storage area with a layout of one or more subfields. They are commonly used to divide a field into subfields, change the format of a field, group noncontiguous data in a contiguous format, define an area of storage in more than one format, define multiple occurrences of a data structure.

Data Area Data Structure, File Information Data Structure (INFDS), and *Program Status Data Structures* are special-purpose data structures. *Data Area Data Structures* assign a data area to an RPG/400 and *implicitly* input the stored value and output the original or changed value from and to the data area. *File Information Data Structures* identify a class of exception/error codes, and when coded accordingly, prevent cancellation of program execution. *Program Status Data Structures* also identify a different class of exception/error codes and prevent the "abort" of program execution.

Data Areas are objects used to transfer data to one or more programs within a job or between jobs. A *Data Area* may be considered a one record storage area whose value must be extracted for processing by an RPG/400 or CL program. A beginning check number, a report date, a batch total are some of the many data items that may be stored in a *Data Area.*

Data Areas are created by the **CRTDTAARA** command, value changed by the **CHGDTAARA** command, and viewed by the **DSPDTAARA** command. In an RPG/400 program, *Data Areas* may be assigned as a *Data Structure,* which *implicitly* controls the access and change of its value. *Data Areas* are *explicitly* accessed in an RPG/400 program by assigning it to a data structure or field with an ***NAMVAR DEFN** statement. Its value is then accessed by an **IN** statement and changed with an **OUT** instruction.

QUESTIONS

9-1. What are the functions of a **data structure** in an RPG/400 program? May more than one data structure be included in a program?

9-2. Where in an RPG/400 program are **data structures** defined?

9-3. Explain some of the syntax rules that must be followed when defining a **data structure** in an RPG/400 program.

9-4. Name three special-purpose **data structures.** What is the function of each?

9-5. Write the coding required to define a **data structure** to separate CUSTNO into its STATE, COUNTY, and CITY elements.

9-6. Using a different coding method, modify Question 9-5 to accomplish the same results.

9-7. Write a **data structure** to format a DATE field stored in the physical file INVMSTR from its YYYYMMDD format to an MMDDYYYY format. Remember the physical field entries!

9-8. Write a **data structure** to format CUSTNO, STATE, COUNTY, and CITY fields from the physical file record format CUSTRCD into the field CUSKEY for processing. Remember the physical file's record entries!

9-9. In an RPG/400 program, what is the function of *Record Identification Codes*? Where are they specified in the program? Where are they included in a physical file record format?

9-10. How many characters may be used as *Record Identification Codes* in a physical file record format?

9-11. In the coding for *Record Identification Codes*, what does the letter **C** entered in the **C/Z/D** field(s) indicate? What does **Z** indicate? What does **D** indicate?

9-12. Explain the advantage of a **data structure** that defines an area of storage into more than one record format.

9-13. If a physical file stores data in more than one record format, how is it defined in the RPG/400 program?

9-14. Write the coding needed to access a **data area data structure named** TERMDT to extract the term date (six-byte field) for student records processing.

9-15. What ***STATUS** error codes indicate an exception/error?

9-16. By what methods may exception/errors be controlled in an RPG/400 program?

9-17. Write the required coding to define a **File Information Data Structure** for the physical file STUMSTR. Only the value stored in ***STATUS** is to be accessed. Include the coding that will transfer control to the RPG/400 routine ***PSSR** if an exception/error is detected.

9-18. Name some of the ***STATUS** codes identified by a **Program Status Data Structure.**

9-19. Write the required coding to define a **Program Status Data Structure** for the physical file ACTMSTR. The values in all of the keywords are to be accessed. Include the coding that will transfer control to the RPG/400 routine ***PSSR** if an exception/error is detected.

9-20. Define a **data area.**

9-21. What CL command creates a **data area?** What entries must be made on the display to create the data area?

9-22. Which CL command supports changes to a **data area?** What command displays the stored value?

9-23. What RPG/400 statement explicitly assigns a **data area** to a field or data structure? Which RPG/400 operation accesses the value from the **data area?** Which operation changes the value in a **data area?**

9-24. Which RPG/400 operation explicitly prevents other programs from using the **data area** after it has been accessed by a program? What operation explicitly releases the **data area?**

9-25. Write the required RPG/400 coding to assign the **data area** RPTDAT to the field DATE, access the value for processing, and change the **data area** value with **UDATE.** Explicitly lock the **data area** and release it after processing.

PROGRAMMING ASSIGNMENTS

For each of the following programming assignments, a physical file and a data area must have been created and loaded with the related data. Your instructor will inform you as to whether you have to create the physical file(s) and load it/them or if they have been prepared for the assignment.

Programming Assignment 9-1: Schedule of Accounts Receivable

Write an RPG/400 program to generate the report shown in the supplemental printer spacing chart.

Physical File Record Format:

```
                    PHYSICAL FILE DESCRIPTION

SYSTEM: AS/400                          DATE: Yours
FILE NAME: Yours                        REV NO: 0
RECORD NAME: Yours                      KEY LENGTH: 5
SEQUENCE: Keyed                         RECORD SIZE: 42

                      FIELD DEFINITIONS

FIELD     FIELD NAME    SIZE   TYPE    POSITION      COMMENTS
  NO                                   FROM    TO

   1      IDCODE          2    C         1      2    AR
   2      CUSTNO          5    C         3      7    key field
   3      NAME           30    C         8     37
   4      BALNCE          8    P        38     42    2 decimals
```

Physical file data:

Record ID Code	Customer Number	Customer Name	Acct Balance
AR	11111	ALWAYS ABLE	00219215
AR	11121	MARY BEST	00051322
AF	11444	I. M. CURRENT	00020010
AR	12345	LARS DEFICIT	00797788
AR	12356	HUGH DENT	00011154
AR	13344	NEVER EARLY	00485673
AR	14455	ONA TIME	00061487
AT	15376	I. C. GUNN	01065936
AR	16443	Y. HOLD	00004128
AR	17777	I. ITCH	00613366
AR	18123	H. I. JUMP	00032446
AR	19996	E. Z. KIDD	00444444
AR	20019	I. M. A. LUMOX	00056784

In addition, create another physical file with exactly the same record format to store unidentified record types.

Processing: Create a **data area** and define its size as 11 characters. Store the report date value 123195 in the first six characters of the data area, and in the other five positions, load the total number of records processed by the program at **LR** time. Also, change the report date value in the data area to 033196.

Process the input file to end of file and accumulate the account balance from each record and the number of records processed.

Report Design: The format of the report is detailed in the printer spacing chart. Note that the dollar sign is specified only on the first detail line and the total line. As shown on lines 9 and 11, underlining is to be included.

Programming Assignment 9-2: CASH DISBURSEMENTS JOURNAL

A Cash Disbursements Journal is used in an accounting system to record all cash disbursements. Special columns are included in the journal for the elements of each transaction. Write an RPG/400 program to generate the journal format shown in the supplemental printer spacing chart.

Physical File Record Format:

```
                    PHYSICAL FILE DESCRIPTION

      SYSTEM: AS/400                      DATE: Yours
      FILE NAME: Yours                    REV NO: 0
      RECORD NAME: Yours                  KEY LENGTH: 3
      SEQUENCE: Keyed                     RECORD SIZE: 53

                      FIELD DEFINITIONS
```

FIELD NO	FIELD NAME	SIZE	TYPE	POSITION FROM	TO	COMMENTS
1	TRCODE	1	C	1	1	S or P
2	CKDATE	6	P	2	5	
3	CHECK#	3	P	6	7	key field
4	PAYEE	20	C	8	27	
5	ACTDEB	20	C	28	47	
6	FOLPCT	3	P	48	49	3 decimals
7	TRAMT	6	P	50	53	2 decimals

Physical file data:

Record ID	Check Date	Check#	Payee	Account Debited	Dis Pct or Folio	Acts Pay or Sundry Amount
S	010295	100	APEX REALTY	RENT EXPENSE	503	250000
P	010395	101	EAST SALES CO	EAST SALES CO	020	100000
S	010495	102	SAVO AND SONS	OFFICE EQUIPMENT	110	050000
S	010595	103	JERRY HALE	SALARIES EXPENSE	505	066000
P	011095	104	ACME MFG CO	ACME MFG CO	020	200000
S	011495	105	ELSIE TRUCKING CO	DELIVERY EXPENSES	590	005798
P	011895	106	SMITH AND SONS	SMITH AND SONS	025	030000
P	012295	107	ARIZONA SUPPLY CO	ARIZONA SUPPLY CO	015	095010
D	012395	108	ABC REPAIR SERVICE	OFFICE REPAIRS	508	007825
P	012595	109	WESTERN SUPPLY CO	WESTERN SUPPLY CO	010	089045
S	012995	110	SHELTON FORD	CAR EXPENSE	511	045093
P	013195	111	MATCHLESS TOOL CO	MATCHLESS TOOL CO	030	060000
A	013195	112	STAPLES SUPPLY	OFFICE SUPPLIES	100	034967

Note that the two record formats are logically supported by the physical file. They are identical in field sizes but differ for the related **S** or **P** type transaction. Record type **S** uses the FOLPCT field for a Folio value and TRAMT for a Sundry value. Record type **P** uses the FOLPCT field for a discount percent value and TRAMT for an Accounts Payable value.

For this assignment, define the data file in the RPG/400 program as *program-defined* (**F** in column 19 of the *File Description* statement) and define the **S** and **P** record formats in the *Input Specifications*. Use *Record Identification Codes* to identify the **S** and **P** record types.

Processing: Include a File Information Data Structure in the program to identify and process unidentified record types (without an **S** or **P**) and prevent cancellation of program execution.

Because the FOLPCT field is defined in the record format as three bytes with three decimal positions, it must be redefined as an integer for the Folio value in **S** type records. Consequently, multiply the FOLPCT field by 1000 and store the value in a three-byte integer field for printing. Note that for **S** records the TRAMT field value is printed in two columns in the report.

For **P** type records, multiply the discount TRAMT field by the FOLPCT field to determine the purchase discount. Then subtract the purchase discount from the TRAMT field to determine the cash credit value (last column in printer spacing chart).

Accumulate totals for the sundry, accounts payable, purchase discount, and cash credit columns, and print them at **LR** time.

Report Design:

chapter 10

Table Processing

In the RPG/400 environment, a *table* may be defined as a list of data stored in memory. The storage positions for a table are built and loaded during program execution before any other input files are read and processed. Tables include relatively *fixed* data that is referenced by other data. Tax rates, transaction codes, pay grades, pay rates, month names, and so forth are examples of data commonly included in tables.

TABLE STRUCTURE

Argument and Function Tables

Figure 10-1 illustrates six examples of table structures. A single table is referred to in

Illustration 1		Illustration 2		Illustration 3	
Pay Code	Hourly Rate	Item Number	Price	SS No.	Name
A	500	1234	00056	040000009	DROPOUT A
B	550	5678	00188	222222222	FAIL Y
C	610	9123	00239	789665555	HONORS HI
D	675	8321	00751	820801234	SUCCEED I
E	735	1789	01051	934202601	TOPP ON
F	800				
Argument Table	Function Table	Argument Table	Function Table	Argument Table	Function Table

Related tables sorted in ascending order.

Smaller numeric table entries must be padded with high-order zeros. Both tables are in an unordered sequence.

Smaller alphabetic (or alphanumeric) entries are padded with low-order blanks. SS No table is in ascending order and related Name table in unordered sequence.

Illustration 4			Illustration 5		Illustration 6
Taxable Amount	Fixed Amount	Tax Percent	Item #	Brand	Special Characters
			300	COCA COLA	&
035	0336	18	500	SPRITE	*
073	1020	21	400	7-UP	#
202	3729	23	550	SLICE	:
231	4396	27	600	FRESCA	∂
2C0	5422	31	900	HIRE3 ROOT BEER	?
333	7406	35	100	WELCH'S GRAPE	/
Argument Table	Function Table 1	Function Table 2	Argument Table	Function Table	Argument Table

Three tables that relate to each other. All sorted in ascending order.

Items table arranged in a "frequency" of processing order.

Single table of special characters in unordered sequence

Notes:

1. Decimal points are not included in numeric table data, but implied in program (Extension form) when the table is defined.

2. Depending on the application, any table (when two or more are related) may be procesed as an argument or function table.

3. Sorted order (ascending or dscending) of any table processed as an argument table will control an "early exit" if the search argument value is not found.

4. Argument tables may be intentionally structured in an unordered sequence to place items that are more frequently accessed at the beginning of the table.

Figure 10-1   Examples of table structures.

RPG/400 as a *Simple Table.* A table may be processed as a standalone table or used to relate to one or more other *Simple Tables.*

Two new terms, *argument* and *function,* are introduced in Figure 10-1. An *argument table* is the one that is "looked up" by a data item called the *search argument.* A *function table* relates physically and logically to an *argument table.* For example, the first entry in an *argument table* relates to the first entry in a corresponding *function table.* Any number of *function tables* may relate to an *argument table;* and, depending on the application, any table may be referenced as an *argument* or *function table.*

LOADING TABLES

Loading a table refers to the time in the program cycle when data is read, moved, and stored in the memory positions defined and built by an RPG/400 program. Tables may be loaded at *Compile Time* or at *Prerun Time.* Figure 10-2 details the processing logic associated with loading a table at each time in the program cycle.

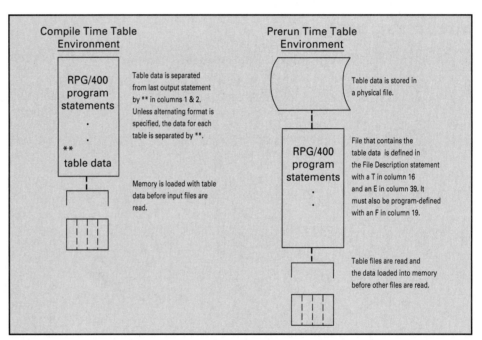

Figure 10-2 Processing logic for loading tables at Compile and Prerun Times.

TABLE DESCRIPTION

The number of table entries, size of an entry, type, and sequence (referred to as attributes) are specified in the *Extension Specifications.* This form allocates the table's total storage area before the loading of data. Refer to Figure 10-3 for an explanation of the fields used

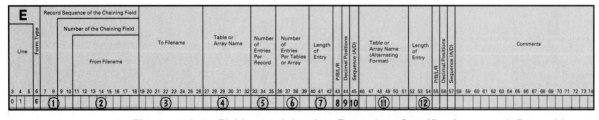

Figure 10-3 Fields used in the *Extension Specifications* to define tables at Compile and Prerun Times.

* All *Extension Specification* instructions must include an **E** in column 6 and immediately follow the last *File Description* statement.

1 Columns 7–10 - not used.

2 **From Filename** (columns 11–18) - Required for *Prerun Time* tables. File name, defined in a *File Description* statement, must be entered left-justified in this field.

3 **To Filename** (columns 19–26) - Optional for *Prerun Time* tables. If the table data is to be written to an output device at the end of the program, the name of the output file must be entered left-justified in this field.

4 **Table Name** (columns 27–32) - All table names must begin with the letters **TAB**. The one, two, or three additional characters must be programmer-supplied.

5 **Number of Entries Per Record** (columns 33–35) - Specifies how many individual table elements are stored on a record.

6 **Number of Entries Per Table** (columns 36–39) - Specifies how many table elements are stored in the table.

7 **Length of Entry** (columns 40–42) - Specifies the size of the table entries. All elements of a table must be the same size. Elements in character tables may be defined from 1 to 256 bytes. Numeric table elements may be defined from 1 to 30 bytes.

8 **P/B/L/R** (column 43) - If the numeric data in a *Prerun Time* table is stored in packed decimal format, the letter **P** must be specified in this field. If the data is stored in binary format, a **B** must be specified. If no entry is specified, the numeric table data is stored as zoned decimal. *Compile Time* table data is entered in a zoned decimal format. An **L** entered in this field indicates that a separate sign is stored to the left of the value and an **R** to the right.

9 **Decimal Positions** (columns 44) - A blank in this field indicates that the table is character. A number from 0 to 9 defines the table elements as numeric with the indicated implied decimal positions. The entry cannot be larger than the *Length of Entry* size.

10 **Sequence (A/D)** (column 45) - If the table is not in a sorted order, this field must be blank. If the data is in an ascending order, an **A** may be entered. On the other hand, if the table data is in a descending order, a **D** may be specified. If sequence is specified, an "early exit" is provided for an unsuccessful equal lookup condition, reducing run times.

11 **Table Name (Alternating Format)** (columns 46–51) - A table name entered in this field indicates that two or more entries from two related tables are stored in each record, for example, data for a TAB1 element followed by the data for a TAB2 element. *Number of Entries Per Record* specifies how many "pairs" are included on a record.

12 Columns 52–57 - These four fields relate to the attributes of the alternating table. Refer to items 7, 8, 9, and 10 for an explanation of these fields.

Figure 10-3 Fields used in the *Extension Specifications* to define tables at Compile and Prerun Times. (Continued)

to define a table at *Compile* and *Prerun* Times. *Notice that all table names must begin with the letters TAB* with one, two, or three additional programmer-supplied characters.

RPG SYNTAX FOR COMPILE TIME TABLES

Figure 10-2 indicated that *Compile Time* table data is an integral (hard-coded) part of an RPG/400 program. The table data is included after a ** control statement entered in columns 1 and 2, and follows the last output (**O**) statement in the program. Unless an al-

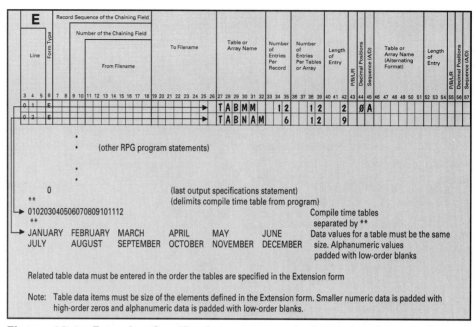

Figure 10-4 *Extension Specifications* syntax and related data for two Compile Time tables.

ternating sequence is specified, the data for two or more tables must also be separated by a ** statement. Figure 10-4 shows the relationship of the *Extension Specifications* coding and the data for two *Compile Time* tables.

RPG/400 SYNTAX FOR COMPILE TIME TABLES STORED IN AN ALTERNATING FORMAT

Figure 10-5 shows the table data from Figure 10-4 rearranged in an alternating format with the modifed *Extension Specifications* coding.

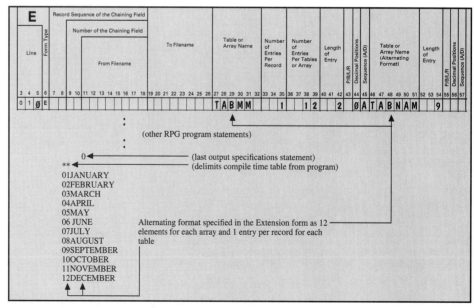

Figure 10-5 *Extension Specifications* syntax and related data for two Compile Time tables arranged in an alternating format.

RPG SYNTAX FOR PRERUN TIME TABLES

Data for *Prerun Time* tables is stored externally from the program in a physical file. The table is formatted and loaded with data before any other data files are read. Tables remain in storage for the complete program cycle and, unless updated by the program, are not changed.

Figure 10-6 illustrates the syntax required in an RPG/400 program to define *Prerun Time* tables when the data is stored in a physical file. The example assumes the same month number and name table data as in Figure 10-5. The *File Description Specifications* must define the file that contains the table data. However, in addition to the usual entries (**I** in column 15, etc.), the letter **T** is entered in column 16 and **E** in column 39. **T** indicates to the program that the file is to be processed as a table file and that the tables are to be loaded before other input files are read. **E** specifies that the attributes of the table are defined in the *Extension Specifications* instead of in the *Input Specifications*.

A limitation of table files is that a maximum of two tables (if an alternating format is used) may be included in one file. Additional files would need to be created and loaded if more than two tables were required.

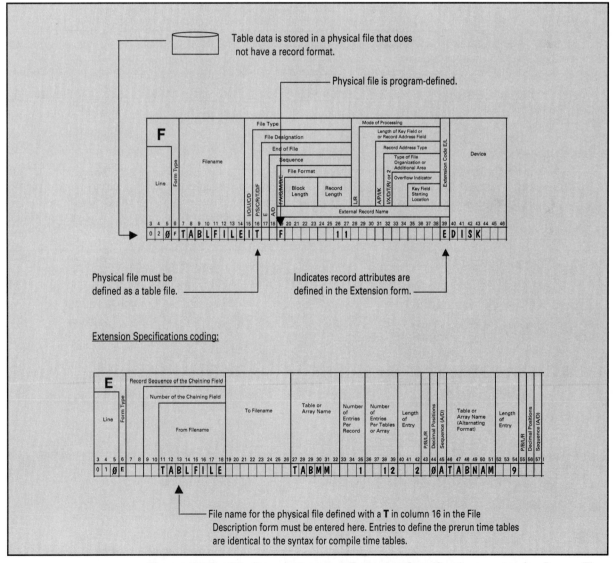

Figure 10-6 *File Descriptions* and *Extension Specifications* syntax for *Prerun Time* tables. Data is arranged in an alternating format.

FORMAT OF TABLE DATA

The records that store the data for *Compile* and *Prerun Time* tables must be formatted according to the rules explained in Figure 10-7. The decision on whether to use a *Compile* or *Prerun Time* table in a program generally depends on the following:

1. *Compile Time* tables are used when the table contains few entries, data is not likely to change, and/or data is not shared by other programs. The month/name tables previously shown are examples of the program data included in this type of table.

2. *Prerun Time* tables are used when tables contain many entries, data is frequently updated, and/or data is used by other programs.

---

1. Data must begin in first position of each record.

2. Entries for a table must be the same size.

3. Smaller numeric elements must be padded with high-order zeros, and smaller alphanumeric elements must be padded with low-order blanks.

4. When alternating sequence is used for the data for two tables, the values for the tables must be included on a record based on the Number of **Entries Per Record** entry in the *Extension Specifications*. Values may <u>not</u> be separated on two records.

5. Order of the data in a **Compile Time** table must relate to the *Extension Specification* entry. The first table defined must have its data specified first at the end the program (after a ** statement), and so forth.

Figure 10-7 Rules for formatting the table data records for *Compile* and *Prerun Times*.

PROCESSING TABLES

So far the RPG/400 syntax to define tables has been explained without discussion of how tables are processed. A table is searched consecutively by the **LOKUP** operation, and depending on the table's structure, until an equal, high-range, or low-range test condition is satisfied.

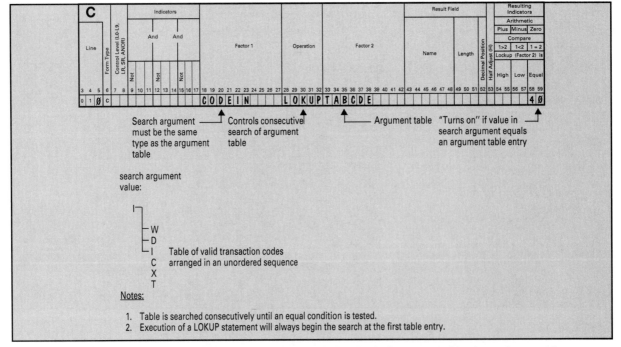

Figure 10-8 Syntax and processing logic for an equal lookup of one table.

Single (Standalone) Table Processing

An *argument* table may be processed by a program without any relationship to other tables, or it may be related to one or more *function* tables. Single table processing is commonly used in data validation functions. An example is shown in Figure 10-8 where an input code value is checked with a table of acceptable codes. When an input value is not found in the table, some alternative action is usually provided. This concept will be fully covered in Chapter 12, where data validation procedures are discussed in detail.

The ***search argument*** (*Factor 1* entry) must be defined as the *same type* (numeric or alphanumeric) as the *argument* table (*Factor 2* entry).

Related Table Processing

In addition to single table processing, two or more tables may relate to each other. An *argument* table is searched, and when the lookup condition is satisfied, the related value from a function table is accessed. Figure 10-9 details the syntax and logic associated with the processing of three related tables.

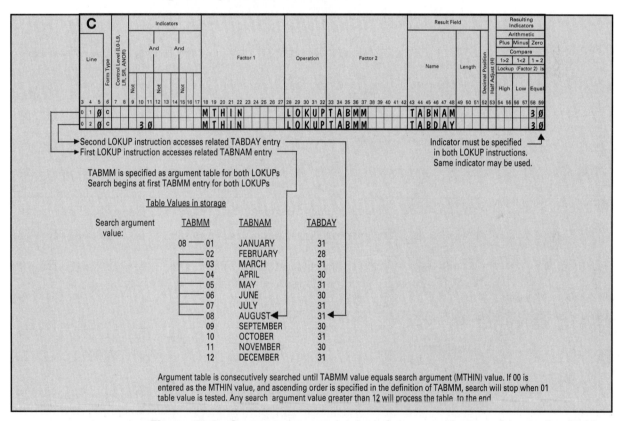

Figure 10-9　Syntax and processing logic for an equal lookup of three related tables.

"EARLY EXIT" CONTROL OF TABLE LOOKUP

For an unsuccessful search, an unordered sequence of the table data will cause program control to process to the end of the table. For small tables this is not significant. It is, however, for large tables. More efficient processing is provided if the *argument* table data is sorted in either an ascending or descending order. A sorted order supports an "early exit" for an unsuccessful "equal" table lookup condition. Figure 10-10 details the processing logic of an "early exit." If the table was sorted in a descending order, early exit would be executed when a lower table value was tested.

When a *Compile Time* table is specified in the *Extension Specifications* as sorted (either **A** or **D**) and the table data is unordered, a terminal error will be generated during

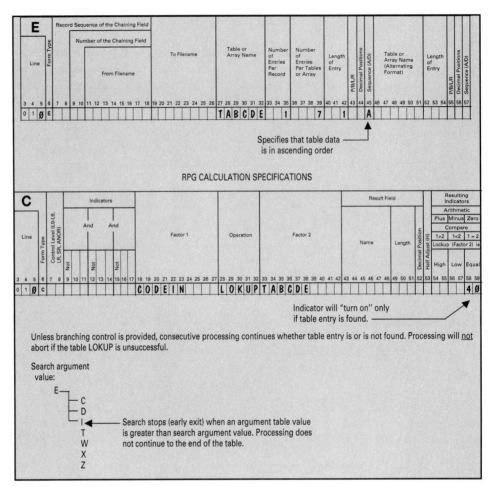

Figure 10-10 Syntax and processing logic for "early exit" control.

compilation of the program. For *Prerun Time* tables, however, sequence errors are "flagged" during program execution.

An application program that incorporates most of the table syntax and processing concepts introduced in the previous paragraphs will now be discussed.

APPLICATION PROGRAM: WEEKLY PAYROLL REPORT

Documentation

The specifications presented in Figure 10-11 explain the processing requirements for an application program that generates a weekly payroll report. The system flowchart in

---

PROGRAM SPECIFICATIONS		Page 1 of 1
Program Name: Weekly Payroll Report	Program - ID: CH1OP1	Written by: SM
Purpose: Weekly payroll report for hourly employees		Approved by: CM
Input files: PAYROLL		
Output files: QSYSPRT		

Figure 10-11 Specifications for an application program using tables that generates a weekly payroll report.

Processing Requirements:

Write an RPG/400 program to generate a weekly payroll report for day- and night-shift employees.

Input to the program:

The externally defined physical file, PAYROLL, contains the weekly payroll data for day- and night-shift hourly employees. A supplemental record layout form details the physical file's record format.

Processing:

Include the following compile time tables in the RPG/400 program:
1. A table for month numbers and a related table for month names.
2. Tables for labor grades, day-shift rates, and night-shift rates with the following values:

Labor Grade	Day Rate	Night Rate
A	0800	0900
B	1000	1150
C	1275	1525
D	1600	1800
E	1950	2300

Look up the month number table with the month value from WKDATE field in the first record processed to access the month name from the related month name table. Include the month name on the second heading line. Use the month and year values from the WKDATE field for the third heading line.

For each input record, test the shift field for a D or N and look up the labor grade table to access the related shift rate. Two LOKUP statements must be provided, one to access the day rates table and the other to access the night rates table.

For a successful search of the grade table, compute the week's pay for an employee by multiplying the hours worked by the accessed rate table value. If the search is unsuccessful, print the error message ....LABOR GRADE NOT VALID.... Refer to the print chart for the location of this message.

Add each employee's wages to an accumulator and print the value at LR time.

Output:

Refer to the supplemental printer spacing chart and code the output accordingly.

Figure 10-11 Specifications for an application program using tables that generates a weekly payroll report. (Continued)

Figure 10-12 indicates that one physical file and one output printer file are processed by the program. Figure 10-13 details the record format of the input file. The *Labor Grade* field will be used as the *search argument* in the **LOKUP** operations. The design of the Weekly Payroll Report is shown in Figure 10-14, and the report generated by it is shown in Figure 10-15.

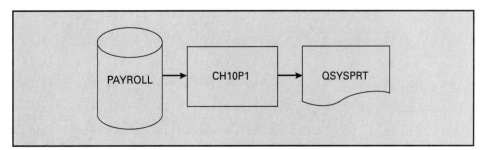

Figure 10-12 System flowchart for Weekly Payroll Report program.

```
┌─────────────────────────────────────────────────────────┐
│                PHYSICAL FILE DESCRIPTION                  │
│                                                           │
│  SYSTEM: AS/400                         DATE: 8/01/95     │
│  FILE NAME: PAYROLL                     REV NO: 0         │
│  RECORD NAME: PAYROLLR                  KEY LENGTH: 9     │
│  SEQUENCE: Keyed                        RECORD SIZE: 33   │
│                                                           │
│                   FIELD DEFINITIONS                       │
│                                                           │
│    FIELD    FIELD NAME   SIZE   TYPE   POSITION   COMMENTS│
│     NO                                 FROM   TO          │
│                                                           │
│      1      SS#            9     P      1     5   Key field│
│      2      NAME          20     C      6    25           │
│      3      LGRADE         1     C     26    26           │
│      4      SHIFT          1     C     27    27           │
│      5      WEKHRS         3     P     28    29   0 decimals│
│      6      WKDATE         6     P     30    33           │
│                                                           │
│  Physical file data:                                      │
│                                                           │
│                                                   Week    │
│                                      Labor        Ending  │
│    SS Number   Employee Name         Grade  Shift Hours Date│
│                                                           │
│    011111111   DONALD DRAKE            E      D    40  091595│
│    022222222   LAMONT CRANSTON         A      N    32  091595│
│    033333333   MICKEY MOUSE            C      D    37  091595│
│    044444444   RICHARD TRACY           F      N    40  091595│
│    055555555   PAUL VALIANT            D      N    35  091595│
│    066666666   MORTIMER SNERD          B      D    30  091595│
│    077777777   ANDREW GUMP             E      N    40  091595│
└─────────────────────────────────────────────────────────┘
```

Figure 10-13   Physical file record format and data listing.

Figure 10-14   Design of Weekly Payroll Report.

```
┌─────────────────────────────────────────────────────────────────┐
│              WEEKLY PAYROLL REPORT                      PAGE    1  │
│                   FOR SEPTEMBER                                    │
│                WEEK ENDING  9/15/95                                │
│                                                                   │
│                            LABOR          HOURLY   HOURS    WEEK   │
│      SS#          NAME      GRADE  SHIFT    RATE    WORKED   WAGES  │
│                                                                   │
│  011-11-1111  DONALD DRAKE    E      D     19.50     40     780.00 │
│                                                                   │
│  022-22-2222  LAMONT CRANSTON A      N      9.00     32     288.00 │
│                                                                   │
│  033-33-3333  MICKEY MOUSE    C      D     12.75     37     471.75 │
│                                                                   │
│  044-44-4444  RICHARD TRACY   F    ....LABOR GRADE NOT VALID....   │
└─────────────────────────────────────────────────────────────────┘
```

Figure 10-15   Report generated by Weekly Payroll Report program.

```
055-55-5555   PAUL VALIANT         D        N       18.00      35       630.00

066-66-6666   MORTIMER SNERD       B        D       10.00      30       300.00

077-77-7777   ANDREW GUMP          E        N       23.00      40       920.00


                                           TOTAL WAGES FOR WEEK       3,389.75
```

Figure 10-15   Report generated by Weekly Payroll Report program. (Continued)

Source Program Coding

A compile listing of the Weekly Payroll Report program is detailed in Figure 10-16.

```
SEQUENCE
NUMBER      *...1....+....2....+....3....+....4....+....5....+....6....+....7...*
                            S o u r c e   L i s t i n g
   100    *         WEEKLY PAYROLL REPORT FOR HOURLY EMPLOYEES
   200    *  PROGRAM INCLUDES THE FOLLOWING COMPILE TIME TABLES:
   300    *     1. TABLE OF MONTH NUMBERS AND RELATED TABLE OF MONTH NAMES.
   400    *     2. TABLE OF LABOR GRADE CODES.
   500    *     3. RELATED TABLES FOR HOURLY DAY AND NIGHT SHIFT RATES.
   600    *  LABOR GRADE CODE IS SEARCH ARGUMENT FOR LOKUP OF GRADE TABLE
          H
   700    FPAYROLL IP  E          K         DISK
             RECORD FORMAT(S): LIBRARY SMYERS FILE PAYROLL.
                    EXTERNAL FORMAT PAYROLLR RPG NAME PAYROLLR
   800    FQSYSPRT O   F        132      OF       PRINTER
   900    E                        TABMM#  2  12  2 0ATABNAM  9   mth#'s & names
  1000    E                        TABGRD  5   5  1 A             labor grades
  1100    E                        TABDAY  5   5  4 2A            day rates
  1200    E                        TABNIT  5   5  4 2A            night rates
A000000   INPUT  FIELDS FOR RECORD PAYROLLR FILE PAYROLL FORMAT PAYROLLR.
A000001                                       P   1   50SS#
A000002                                           6   25 NAME
A000003                                          26   26 LGRADE
A000004                                          27   27 SHIFT
A000005                                       P  28   290WEKHRS
A000006                                       P  30   330WKDATE
  1300    C           *IN10    CASEQ'O'       HDG            brch to HDG sr
  1400    C                    ENDCS                         end CASE group
  1500    C                    EXSR PROCES                   brch-PROCES sr
  1600    CLR                  EXCPTLROUT                    LR output
  1700    *
  1800    C           HDG      BEGSR                         begin HDG sr
  1900    C                    MOVELWKDATE    MM      20     access mth no
  2000    C           MM       LOKUPTABMM#    TABNAM  20 get mth name
  2100    C                    MOVE *ON       *INOF          set on OF
  2200    C                    MOVE *ON       *IN10          set on 10
  2300    C                    ENDSR                         end HDG sr
  2400    *
  2500    C           PROCES   BEGSR                         bgn PROCES sr
  2600    C                    SELEC                         bgn SELECT grp
  2700    C           SHIFT    WHEQ 'D'                      day shift?
  2800    C           LGRADE   LOKUPTABGRD    TABDAY  20 get day rate
  2900    *
  3000    C           *IN20    IFEQ *ON                      LOKUP ok?
  3100    C           TABDAY   MULT WEKHRS    PAY     62     day pay
  3200    C                    ADD  PAY       TOTPAY  82     accum pay
  3300    C                    Z-ADDTABDAY    RATE    42     output fld
  3400    C                    EXCPTGOOD                     print record
  3500    C                    ELSE                          bad LOKUP
  3600    C                    EXCPTERROR                    print err msg
  3700    C                    ENDIF                         end IF group
  3800    *
```

Figure 10-16   Compile listing of the Weekly Payroll Report program.

```
3900 C                       OTHER                              night shift
4000 C            LGRADE      LOKUPTABGRD    TABNIT          20 get nht rate
4100   *
4200 C            *IN20       IFEQ *ON                           LOKUP ok?
4300 C            TABNIT      MULT WEKHRS    PAY                  night pay
4400 C                       ADD  PAY       TOTPAY 82            accum pay
4500 C                       Z-ADDTABNIT    RATE                 output fld
4600 C                       EXCPTGOOD                           print record
4700 C                       ELSE                                bad LOKUP
4800 C                       EXCPTERROR                          print err msg
4900 C                       ENDIF                               end IF group
5000   *
5100 C                       ENDSL                               end SELECT grp
5200 C                       ENDSR                               end PROCES sr
5300 OQSYSPRT E  101    OF
5400 O                                      50 'WEEKLY PAYROLL REPORT'
5500 O                                      75 'PAGE'
5600 O                              PAGE  Z  80
5700 O          E 1     OF
5800 O                                      36 'FOR'
5900 O                              TABNAM  46
6000 O          E 2     OF
6100 O                                      41 'WEEK ENDING'
6200 O                              WKDATEY 50
6300 O          E 1     OF
6400 O                                      42 'LABOR'
6500 O                                      76 'HOURLY    HOURS      WEEK'
6600 O          E 2     OF
6700 O                                       7 'SS#'
6800 O                                      26 'NAME'
6900 O                                      59 'GRADE     SHIFT      RATE'
7000 O                                      77 'WORKED    WAGES'
7100 O          EF 2           GOOD
7200 O                              SS#     12 'O  -  -  '
7300 O                              NAME    34
7400 O                              LGRADE  40
7500 O                              SHIFT   49
7600 O                              RATE  1 59
7700 O                              WEKHRS2 67
7800 O                              PAY   2 78
7900 O          EF 2           ERROR
8000 O                              SS#     12 'O  -  -  '
8100 O                              NAME    34
8200 O                              LGRADE  40
8300 O                                      62 '....LABOR GRADE NOT '
8400 O                                      72 'VALID....'
8500 O          EF1            LROUT
8600 O                                      66 'TOTAL WAGES FOR WEEK'
8700 O                              TOTPAY1 78
     * * * * *  E N D   O F   S O U R C E   * * * * *

5738RG1 V2R1M1  920327           IBM SAA RPG/400                    SMYERS/CH10P1
SEQUENCE
NUMBER    *...+....1....+....2....+....3....+....4....+....5....+....6....+....7....+
         A d d i t i o n a l   D i a g n o s t i c   M e s s a g e s
 7086       700   RPG PROVIDES BLOCK OR UNBLOCK SUPPORT FOR FILE PAYROLL.
5738RG1 V2R1M1  920327           IBM SAA RPG/400                    SMYERS/CH10P1
SEQUENCE
NUMBER    *...+....1....+....2....+....3....+....4....+....5....+....6....+....7....+
            C o m p i l e - T i m e   T a b l e s
Table/Array . . . . . . :  TABMM#
Table/Array . . . . . . :  TABNAM
   8900  01JANUARY  02FEBRUARY
   9000  03MARCH    04APRIL
   9100  05MAY      06JUNE
   9200  07JULY     08AUGUST
   9300  09SEPTEMBER100CTOBER
   9400  11NOVEMBER 12DECEMBER
Table/Array . . . . . . :  TABGRD
   9600  ABCDE
Table/Array . . . . . . :  TABDAY
   9800  08001000127516001950
Table/Array . . . . . . :  TABNIT
  10000  09001150152518002300
```

Figure 10-16 Compile listing of the Weekly Payroll Report program. (Continued)

700 -
800   The physical file PAYROLL is defined as input keyed. Output is assigned to the system printer QSYSPRT.

900   *TABMM#,* which contains month numbers, is defined as a compile time table with its data stored in an alternating format with the data in the *TABNAM* (month name) table. Two elements of each table are included on six records.

1000 -
1200   *TABGRD* (labor grade) is defined as the third compile time table. *TABDAY* (day rates) specified as the fourth compile time table, and *TABNIT* (night rates) as the fifth. The data for each compile time table is separated from the others at the end of the program by ** in columns 1 and 2.

1300 -
1400   When indicator **10** is off, the **CASEQ** statement will pass control to the HDG subroutine. Because indicator **10** is turned on in the HDG subroutine, this statement will test true only for the first record read. This prevents the subroutine from being executed for each record processed. The **ENDCS** operation ends the **CASEQ** statement.

1500   For all records processed, a branch is made to the PROCES subroutine where the computations are included to determine the week's wages for each employee and accumulate the amounts.

1600   When end of the physical file is read and **LR** is set on automatically, this EXCPT statement, conditioned by **LR** at total time, branches control to exception output line 8500 where the TOTPAY value and a constant are printed. Because there are no additional calculation or output statements conditioned by the **LR** indicator, the job is ended after control returns from this exception output.

1800   Begins the HDG subroutine.

1900   The first two bytes (month value) of the WKDATE field are moved to an MM field. The MM field is used to look up the *TABMM#* table (line 2000) to extract the related month name from the *TABNAM* table.

2000   This **LOKUP** statement uses the MM value from statement 1900 as the *search argument* to look up the *TABMM#* table and extract the related month name from the *TABNAM* table.

2100 -
2300   Indicator **10,** which is used in the **CASEQ** statement line 1300 to prevent the subroutine from being executed for each record processed, is set on. The overflow indicator OF is set on so that the heading lines will print for the first record processed.

2500   Begins the PROCES subroutine.

2600   Begins the **SELEC** group.

2700   The **WHEQ** statement tests the SHIFT field value for D.

2800   If the test on line 2700 is true, the LGRADE field value is used as the *search argument* to look up *TABGRD* (labor grades table) to extract the related hourly rate from *TABDAY* (day rates table). Indicator **20,** specified in the *Resulting Indicator* equal field, turns on if the value in LGRADE is equal to a value in *TABGRD. TABGRD* is searched sequentially until an equal condition results or end of the table is tested.

3000   If the **LOKUP** on line 2800 is successful (indicator **20** is on), the statements included within the **IFEQ** group will be executed.

3100   The value in the *TABDAY* table (accessed in statement 2800) is multiplied by WEKHRS to determine the week's pay, which is stored in PAY.

3200   The value in PAY is added to the accumulator TOTPAY, which is printed at **LR** time.

3300   The **Z-ADD** statement stores the value in *TABDAY* in the RATE field. Using the same output field for day and night rates reduces output coding.

Figure 10-16 Compile listing of the Weekly Payroll Report program. (Continued)

3400	The current employees record, table, and computed values are exception output beginning on exception line 7100.
3500 - 3600	When the **IFEQ** statement test on line 3000 is not true (indicator **20** not set on by a successful table lookup), the **ELSE** (false) action is performed which executes the **EXCPT** statement on line 3600. Control passes to the exception line 7900, where variables and an error message are printed.
3700	The **ENDIF** operation ends the **IFEQ** group that began on line 3000.
3900	The **OTHER** operation begins the false action if the **WHEQ** statement on line 2700 does not test true.
4000 - 4900	The explanation for these statements is identical to those discussed for statements 2800–3700 except the table (*TABNIT*) for a night-shift employee is accessed.
5100	The **ENDSL** operation ends the **SELEC** group that began with the **SELEC** operation on line 2600.
5200	The **ENDSR** operation ends the PROCES subroutine that began on line 2500.
5300 - 7000	This output is executed when the **OF** indicator is "on." In the HDG routine, indicator **OF** was set on for the first record processed from the physical file. This initially controlled the first printing of the headings. For subsequent pages of the report, **OF** will be set on automatically when the overflow line is detected and set off after printing.
7100 - 7800	This exception output is executed when a successful *TABGRD* look up results (line 2800 or 4000). *EXCPT* statements on line 3400 or 4600 control this output.
7900 - 8400	This exception output is executed when an unsuccessful *TABGRD* look up results (line 2800 or 4000). **EXCPT** statements on lines 3600 and 4800 control this output.
8500 - 8700	This exception output is executed when **LR** is automatically turned on at end of file and the **EXCPT** statement on line 1600 executed.

Figure 10-16   Compile listing of the Weekly Payroll Report program. (Continued)

TABLE RANGE LOOKUP

The examples and application program presented have all used an *equal* test condition for table processing. Some tables, however, are structured in a format that requires a *range* **LOKUP**. Federal and state income tax tables are generally accessed by this processing method.

Figure 10-17 illustrates a state's tax tables used to determine the tax liability on dividends and interest income. The taxpayer's Adjusted Gross Income (AGI) determines the percentage of tax on dividends and interest income. No tax is applied to this income for any AGI below $54,000.

The tables shown in Figure 10-17 require processing by *range* **LOKUP** control. Table format restrictions to support this processing method are as follows:

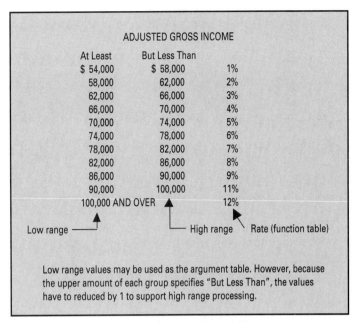

Figure 10-17 Tax tables for a state's dividends and interest income.

1. *Argument* table data must be sorted in an ascending or descending order. *Compile Time* tables that are unordered will be flagged by a terminal error in compilation. Unordered *Prerun Time* tables will not be identified until program execution, which will then cause processing to abort.

2. The letter **A** (or **D**) should be specified in the sequence column of the *Extension Specifications* for the related table. If sequence is not specified, an ascending order of the table data is assumed. A warning error will be generated if the entry is omitted and the data is in ascending order. However, if the table data is arranged in a descending order and sequence is not specified, a terminal error during compilation will result for *Compile Time* tables, and execution time error will occur for *Prerun Time* tables.

Low-Range LOKUP Control

In Figure 10-18, the data from Figure 10-17 has been formatted into two tables for processing. Notice that the At Least values (low range) have been used as the *argument* table data and the related percentages used for the *function* table entries. When low-range processing is specified, the high-range (But Less Than) values are not needed.

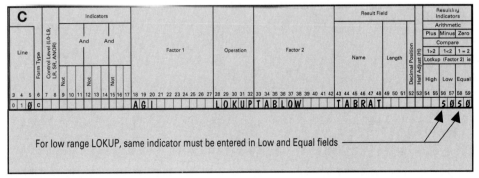

Figure 10-18 Structure of tables and processing logic for Low-Range **LOKUP** control.

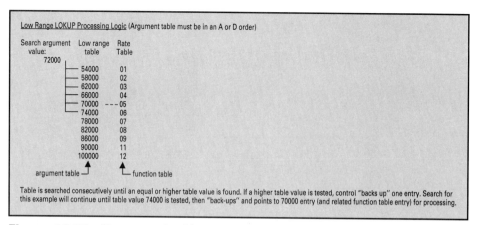

Figure 10-18 Structure of tables and processing logic for Low-Range **LOKUP** control. (Continued)

High-Range LOKUP Control

An examination of Figure 10-19 shows that the data from Figure 10-17 has been reformatted for high-range table **LOKUP** processing. Notice that the But Less Than values have been reduced by 1 for each entry. Because the high amount of a range relates to values less than those specified in Figure 10-17, the original table amounts must be reduced accordingly.

Range **LOKUP** processing will be discussed further in the following application program that determines a taxpayer's federal income tax liability.

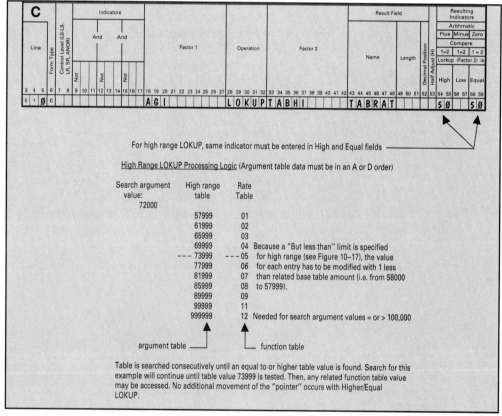

Figure 10-19 Structure of tables and processing logic for High-Range **LOKUP** control.

APPLICATION PROGRAM: FEDERAL INCOME TAX COMPUTATION

Documentation

The specifications shown in Figure 10-20 detail the processing requirements for an application program that computes the federal income tax liability for taxpayers who have a filing status of Single, Married–Filing Jointly, Married–Filing Separately, or Head of Household. Input and output files processed by the program are identified in the system

PROGRAM SPECIFICATIONS		Page 1 of 1
Program Name: Federal Tax Report Program - ID: CH1OP2		Written by: SM
Purpose: Federal Income Tax Liability Report		Approved by: CM

Input files: INCOME

Output files: QSYSPRT

Processing Requirements:

Write an RPG/400 program to generate a Federal Income Tax Liability Report for individual taxpayers.

Input to the program:

The externally defined physical file, INCOME, contains records with the information for individual taxpayers. The attached record layout form identifies the fields in the physical file's record format. Note that the taxable income amount was previously computed and is not a function of this program.

Processing:

Format the following four Rate Schedules into nine Compile Time tables. Because the range of percents is the same for all filing classifications (i.e., 15% 28%, 31%), only one percent table has to be specified. Use the Over amount as the argument table with the related fixed and percent values as the related function tables.

Table values:

Schudule X – Use if your filing status is Single

If the amount on Form 1040, line 37, Is: Over —	But not over—	Enter on Form 1040, line 38	of the amount over—
$0	$21,450	.... 15%	$0
21,450	51,900	$3,217.50 + 28%	21,450
51,900		11,743.50 + 31%	51,900

Schudule Y-1 – Use if your filing status is Married filing jointly or Qualifying widow(er)

If the amount on Form 1040, line 37, Is: Over —	But not over—	Enter on Form 1040, line 38	of the amount over—
$0	$35,800	.... 15%	$0
35,800	86,500	$5,370.00 + 28%	35,850
86,500	....	19,566.00 + 31%	86,500

Figure 10-20 Specifications for the Federal Income Tax Liability Report program.

Schedule Y-2 – Use if your filing status is Married filing separately

If the amount on Form 1040, line 37, Is: Over —	But not over—	Enter on Form 1040, line 38	of the amount over—
$0	$17,900	. . . . 15%	$0
17,900	43,250	$2,685.00 + 28%	17,900
43,250	. . . .	9,783.00 + 31%	43,250

Schudule Z – Use if your filing status is Head of household

If the amount on Form 1040, line 37, Is: Over —	But not over—	Enter on Form 1040, line 38	of the amount over—
$0	$28,750	. . . . 15%	$0
28,750	74,150	$4,312.50 + 28%	28,750
74,150	. . . .	17,024.50 + 31%	74,150

Test the input filing status field (STATUS) for S (single), J (married—filing jointly), M (married—filing separately), and H (head of household), and execute the related internal subroutine to look up the argument table with the TAXINC field.

The following calculations are required:

1. Look up the appropriate low-range table (Over—amounts) with the taxable income field (TAXINC), and extract the fixed amount from the related function table.

2. Look up the same low-range (Over–) argument table, and extract the percent value from the common percent table.

3. Subtract the "of the amount over—" (same as Over– table value) from the taxable income field (TAXINC), and store the difference in a work field.

4. Multiply the difference in Step 3 by the table percent from Step 2 and store in an output field for the tax due.

5. Add the fixed table amount (Step 1) to the tax due field (Step 4) to compute the total Federal Income Tax due for the taxpayer.

With the exception of the different tables, the five steps detailed are identical for each filing status.

Output:

Generate the report shown in the attached printer spacing chart. Note that the tax year is accessed from the first data record processed.

Figure 10-20 Specifications for the Federal Income Tax Liability Report program. (Continued)

flowchart shown in Figure 10-21. The format of the records in the physical file and a listing of the data are detailed in Figure 10-22. The printer spacing chart in Figure 10-23 details the design of the report. A listing of the printed report generated by the program is shown in Figure 10-24.

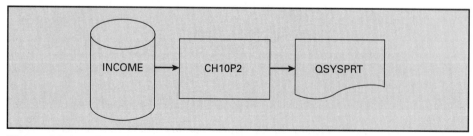

Figure 10-21 System flowchart for Federal Income Tax Liability Report program.

```
                    PHYSICAL FILE DESCRIPTION

    SYSTEM: AS/400                          DATE: 1/32/95
    FILE NAME:INCOME                        REV NO: 0
    RECORD NAME: INCOMER                    KEY LENGTH: 9
    SEQUENCE: Keyed                         RECORD SIZE: 32

                       FIELD DEFINITIONS

      FIELD    FIELD NAME    SIZE  TYPE   POSITION      COMMENTS
       NO                                FROM    TO

        1      SS#            9     P      1      5    Key field
        2      NAME          20     C      6     25
        3      TAXINC         6     P     26     29    0 decimals
        4      STATUS         1     C     30     30    S, J, M, H
        5      TAXYR          2     C     31     32
```

Physical file data:

| | | Taxable | Filing | Tax |
SS#	Taxpayer's Name	Income	Status	Year
011111111	DONALD & DAISY DRAKE	050000	J	95
022222222	LAMONT CRANSTON	080000	H	95
033333333	MIKE & MINA MOUSE	200000	J	95
044444444	RICHARD TRACY	010000	M	95
055555555	PAUL VALIANT	023901	H	95
066666666	MORTIMER SNERD	014875	M	95
077777777	ANDREW GUMP	100000	S	95

Figure 10-22 Record layout and listing of input file data processed by the Federal Income Tax Liability Report program.

```
                         FEDERAL INCOME TAX REPORT           PAGE XX0X
                        FOR INDIVIDUALS-TAX YEAR 19XX


                                   FILING    TAXABLE     FEDERAL
     SS#            TAXPAYER NAME   STATUS    INCOME      INCOME TAX

 XXX-XX-XXXX X                 X    X         XXX,XX0     XXX,XX0.XX

 XXX-XX-XXXX X                 X    X         XXX,XX0     XXX,XX0.XX

     NOTES:

        1. HEADINGS ON TOP OF EVERY PAGE.

        2. OBTAIN TAX YEAR ENTRY FOR HEADING LINE 2 FROM
           FIRST RECORD.
```

Figure 10-23 Design of the Federal Income Tax Liability Report program.

```
                    FEDERAL INCOME TAX REPORT         PAGE    1
                   FOR INDIVIDUALS-TAX YEAR 1995


                               FILING    TAXABLE    FEDERAL
     SS#          TAXPAYER NAME STATUS    INCOME     INCOME TAX

 011-11-1111  DONALD & DAISY DRAKE   J     50,000      9,346.00

 022-22-2222  LAMONT CRANSTON        H     80,000     18,838.00

 033-33-3333  MIKE & MINA MOUSE      J    200,000     54,751.00

 044-44-4444  RICHARD TRACY          S     10,000      1,500.00

 055-55-5555  PAUL VALIANT           H     23,901      3,585.15

 066-66-6666  MORTIMER SNERD         H     14,875      2,231.25

 077-77-7777  ANDREW GUMP            S    100,000     26,654.50
```

Figure 10-24 Report generated by Federal Income Tax Liability Report program.

283

Source Program Coding

A commented compile listing of the federal income tax report application program is presented in Figure 10-25.

```
SEQUENCE
 NUMBER    *...1....+....2....+....3....+....4....+....5....+....6....+....7...*
                             S o u r c e   L i s t i n g
   100    *                 FEDERAL INCOME TAX REPORT
   200    *      FOR INDIVIDUAL TAXPAYERS - FOR EVERY FILING STATUS
   300    *      9 COMPILE TIME TABLES ARE DEFINED, WHICH INCLUDE:
   400    *         1. TWO TABLES FOR SINGLE STATUS-LOW RANGE, FIXED AMT
   500    *         2. TWO TABLES FOR MARRIED FILING JOINTLY-LOW-RANGE & FIXED AMT
   600    *         3. TWO TABLES FOR MARRIED FILING SEPARATELY-LOW RANGE & FIXED AMT
   700    *         4. TWO TABLES FOR HEAD OF HOUSEHOLD STATUS-LOW RANGE & FIXED AMT
   800    *         5. ONE PERCENT TABLE (COMMON TO EACH FILING STATUS)
   900    *
  1000    *
  1100    *
          H
  1200    FINCOME  IP  E           K         DISK
          RECORD FORMAT(S): LIBRARY SMYERS FILE INCOME.
                   EXTERNAL FORMAT INCOMER RPG NAME INCOMER
  1300    FQSYSPRT O  F      132     OF      PRINTER
  1400    E                         TABSL  1   3  6 0ATABSF   7 2 single low & fIXd
  1500    E                         TABJL  1   3  6 0ATABJF   7 2 joint low & fixed
  1600    E                         TABML  1   3  6 0ATABMF   7 2 sep low & fixed
  1700    E                         TABHL  1   3  6 0ATABHF   7 2 house low & fixed
  1800    E                         TABPCT 3   3  2 2             percent table ent
A000000   INPUT  FIELDS FOR RECORD INCOMER FILE INCOME FORMAT INCOMER.
A000001                                       P  1    50SS#
A000002                                          6   25 NAME
A000003                                       P 26   290TAXINC
A000004                                         30   30 STATUS
A000005                                         31   32 TAXYR
  1900    C          *IN11     CASEQ*OFF     HDG           11 off EXSR sr
  2000    C                    ENDCS                       end case group
  2100    C          TAXINC    CASNE*ZEROS   PROCES        10 off EXSR sr
  2200    C                    ENDCS                       end case group
  2300    *
  2400    C          HDG       BEGSR                       begin HDG sr
  2500    C                    MOVE *ON      *IN11         set on 11 ind.
  2600    C                    MOVE *ON      *INOF         set on OF ind.
  2700    C                    ENDSR                       end HDG sr
  2800    *
  2900    C          PROCES    BEGSR                       begin PROCES sr
  3000    C          STATUS    CASEQ'S'      SSUB          single status?
  3100    C          STATUS    CASEQ'J'      JSUB          joint status?
  3200    C          STATUS    CASEQ'M'      MSUB          sep status?
  3300    C          STATUS    CASEQ'H'      HSUB          house status?
  3400    C                    ENDCS                       end case group
  3500    C                    EXCPTDETOUT                 print line
  3600    C                    ENDSR                       end PROCES sr
  3700    *
  3800    C          SSUB      BEGSR
  3900    C          TAXINC    LOKUPTABSL    TABSF      5050get fixed amt
  4000    C          *IN50     IFEQ *ON                  range found?
  4100    C          TAXINC    LOKUPTABSL    TABPCT     5050get percent
  4200    C          TAXINC    SUB  TABSL    NET     82
  4300    C          TABPCT    MULT NET      TAX     82     extra amt
  4400    C                    ADD  TABSF    TAX            single tax due
  4500    C                    ENDIF                       end IF group
  4600    C                    ENDSR                       end single sr
  4700    *
  4800    C          JSUB      BEGSR
  4900    C          TAXINC    LOKUPTABJL    TABJF      5050get fixed amt
  5000    C          *IN50     IFEQ *ON                  range found?
  5100    C          TAXINC    LOKUPTABJL    TABPCT     5050get percent
  5200    C          TAXINC    SUB  TABJL    NET     82
```

Figure 10-25 Compile listing of the Federal Income Tax Liability Report program.

```
5300  C           TABPCT    MULT NET     TAX      82      extra amt
5400  C                     ADD  TABJF   TAX              joint tax due
5500  C                     ENDIF                         end IF
5600  C                     ENDSR                         end joint sr
5700  *
5800  C           MSUB      BEGSR
5900  C           TAXINC    LOKUPTABML   TABMF    5050get fixed amt
6000  C           *IN50     IFEQ *ON                      range found?
6100  C           TAXINC    LOKUPTABML   TABPCT   5050get percent
6200  C           TAXINC    SUB  TABML   NET      82
6300  C           TABPCT    MULT NET     TAX      82      extra amt
6400  C                     ADD  TABMF   TAX              sep tax due
6500  C                     ENDIF                         end IF
6600  C                     ENDSR                         end separate sr
6700  *
6800  C           HSUB      BEGSR
6900  C           TAXINC    LOKUPTABHL   TABHF    5050get fixed amt
7000  C           *IN50     IFEQ *ON                      range found?
7100  C           TAXINC    LOKUPTABHL   TABPCT   5050get percent
7200  C           TAXINC    SUB  TABHL   NET      82
7300  C           TABPCT    MULT NET     TAX      82      extra amt
7400  C                     ADD  TABHF   TAX              house tax due
7500  C                     ENDIF                         end if
7600  C                     ENDSR
7700  OQSYSPRT H 101   OF
7800  O                                        42 'FEDERAL INCOME TAX'
7900  O                                        49 'REPORT'
8000  O                                        65 'PAGE'
8100  O                           PAGE  Z      70
8200  O         H 3     OF
8300  O                                        37 'FOR INDIVIDUALS-'
8400  O                                        48 'TAX YEAR 19'
8500  O                           TAXYR        50
8600  O         H 1     OF
8700  O                                        53 'FILING     TAXABLE'
8800  O                                        65 'FEDERAL'
8900  O         H 2     OF
9000  O                                         6 'SS#'
9100  O                                        30 'TAXPAYER NAME'
9200  O                                        42 'STATUS'
9300  O                                        52 'INCOME'
9400  O                                        67 'INCOME TAX'
9500  O         EF 2          DETOUT
9600  O                           SS#          12 'O - - '
9700  O                           NAME         34
9800  O                           STATUS       39
9900  O                           TAXINC2      53
10000 O                           TAX  1       67
      * * * * *   E N D   O F   S O U R C E   * * * * *
      A d d i t i o n a l   D i a g n o s t i c   M e s s a g e s
      7086      1200  RPG PROVIDES BLOCK OR UNBLOCK SUPPORT FOR FILE INCOME.
5738RG1 V2R1M1  920327              IBM SAA RPG/400                SMYERS/CH10P2
SEQUENCE
NUMBER    *...+....1....+....2....+....3....+....4....+....5....+....6....+....7....+
              C o m p i l e - T i m e   T a b l e s
Table/Array . . . . . . :    TABSL
Table/Array . . . . . . :    TABSF
  10200  0000000000000
  10300  0214500321750
  10400  0519001174350
Table/Array . . . . . . :    TABJL
Table/Array . . . . . . :    TABJF
  10600  0000000000000
  10700  0358000537000
  10800  0865001956600
Table/Array . . . . . . :    TABML
Table/Array . . . . . . :    TABMF
  11000  0000000000000
  11100  0179000268500
  11200  0432500978300
```

Figure 10-25 Compile listing of the Federal Income Tax Liability Report program. (Continued)

```
Table/Array  . . . . . . :    TABHL
Table/Array  . . . . . . :    TABHF
   11400  0000000000000
   11500  0287500431250
   11600  0741501702450
Table/Array  . . . . . . :    TABPCT
   11800  152831
```

Line #

1200 -
1300   The physical file INCOME is defined as an externally defined keyed file that will be
       processed in an ascending key value order. Output is assigned to the system printer
       QSYSPRT.

1400 -
1800   The low-range values for each filing status is assigned to TABSL (single), TABJL (married
       jointly), TABML (married separately), and TABHL (head of household), tables. One table
       element is included on each *Compile Time* record. There are three elements per table, and
       the elements are all defined as six-byte integers.

       The fixed-amount values for each filing status is assigned to TABSF (single), TABJF
       (married jointly), TABMF (married separately), TABHF (head of household). Note that the
       tables are specified in an alternating format with their related low-range table values. All of
       the elements are defined for the related tables as seven-bytes with two decimal poistions.

       The TABPCT (percent) table has values common to each filing status. Consequently, a
       separate table is not required for each. The table data is stored with three elements per
       record with a length of two bytes with two decimal positions.

       All of the tables are defined as **Compile Time.**

1900 -
2000   When indicator **11** is off, the **CASEQ** statement will pass control to the HDG subroutine.
       Because indicator **11** is turned on in the HDG subroutine, this statement will test true only
       for the first record read. This prevents the subroutine from being executed for every record
       processed. The **ENDCS** operation on line 2000 ends the **CASEQ** statement.

2100 -
2200   The TAXINC field value from the physical file is tested in the **CASNE** statement for zero. If
       the value is not zero, control will pass to the PROCES subroutine. The **ENDCS** operation on
       line 2200 ends the **CASNE** statement.

2400 -
2700   Line 2400 begins the HDG subroutine. Indicator **11** is set on line 2500, which is used in the
       CASEQ statement on line 1900 to prevent the subroutine from being executed for each
       record processed. The overflow indicator **OF** is set on so that the heading lines will print for
       the first record processed instead of at **1P** time. The **ENDSR** operation on line 2700 ends
       the subroutine.

2900 -
3400   Line 2900 begins the PROCES subroutine. The **CASEQ** statements on lines 3000–3300 test
       the STATUS field from the physical file for the taxpayer's filing status. The STATUS value
       tested will pass control to the related subroutine (SSUB, JSUB, MSUB, or HSUB). The
       ENDCS operation on line 3400 ends the **CASEQ** group.

3500   After control returns from one of the subroutines where the taxpayer's tax liability was
       computed, the **EXCPT** statement passes control to exception output on lines 9500–10000.
       This statement completes the processing for a taxpayer's record.

3600   The **ENDSR** operation ends the PROCES subroutine.

Figure 10-25   Compile listing of the Federal Income Tax Liability Report program.
(Continued)

3800 -
3900   Line 3800 begins the SSUB subroutine. The **LOKUP** statement on line 3900 uses the TAXINC field from the physical file as the *search argument* to look up TABSL (single low-range) table and extracts the related fixed value from the TABSF table. Indicator **50,** which is specified in *Resulting indicator* low and equal fields for a low- range look up, will turn on if the **LOKUP** operation is successful.

4000 -
4500   The **IFEQ** statement tests the status of indicator **50.** If it is "on," indicating a successful table lookup on line 3900, statement on lines 4100–4500 will be executed.

The **LOKUP** statement on line 4100 uses the TAXINC field again to look up TABSL and extract the related percent value from the TABPCT table. Indicator **50** specified in *Resulting Indicator* low and equal fields will turn on for a successful lookup.

On line 4200, the TABSF table value (fixed amount) extracted in the **LOKUP** statement on line 3900 is subtracted from TAXINC and the difference stored in NET.

On line 4300, the NET value, computed on line 4200, is multiplied by the TABPCT value extracted by the **LOKUP** statement on line 4100 and the value stored in TAX.

On line 4400, the value in table TABSF, extracted in the **LOKUP** statement on line 3900, is added to the TAX value computed on line 4300. This is the final step for computing the taxpayer's tax.

The **ENDIF** statement on line 4500 ends the **IFEQ** group.

4600   The **ENDSR** operation ends the SSUB subroutine.

4800 -
5600   The statements in the JSUB subroutine follow the same sequence of instructions discussed for the single taxpayer on lines 4000–4500. The only difference is that the tables (TABJL and TABJF) for the married filing jointly taxpayer are used in the computations.

5800 -
6600   The statements in the MSUB subroutine follow the same sequence of instructions discussed for the single taxpayer on lines 4000–4500. The only difference is that the tables (TABML and TABMF) for the married filing separately taxpayer are used in the computations.

6800 -
7600   The statements in the HSUB subroutine follow the same sequence of instructions discussed for the single taxpayer on lines 4000–4500. The only difference is that the tables (TABHL and TABHF) for the head of household taxpayer are used in the computations.

7700 -
9400   This output is executed when the **OF** indicator is "on." On line 2600 of the HDG subroutine, indicator **OF** was set on to control the printing of the heading lines after the first record is read. For subsequent pages of the report, **OF** will be set on automatically when the overflow line is detected, and off after it is printed.

9500 -
10000 This exception output is performed for every record processed by the **EXCPT** statement on line 3500.

Figure 10-25   Compile listing of the Federal Income Tax Liability Report program. (Continued)

Processing Logic for the Federal Income Tax Liability Report Program (Low-Range LOKUP)

A listing of the two tables related to the married filing jointly status and the common percent table for all filing categories with the mathematical steps to compute the tax liability

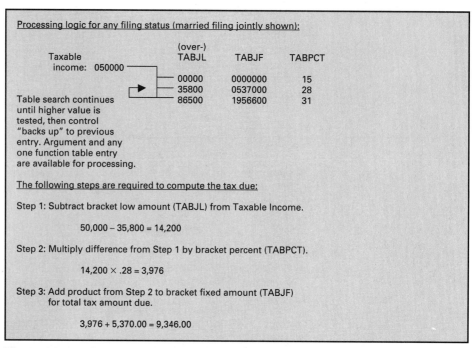

Figure 10-26 Processing logic for Federal Income Tax Liability Report program using low-range table **LOKUP** and mathematical steps to compute the tax due.

are shown in Figure 10-26. With the exception of the different table values, the other three filing statuses follow the same lookup logic and calculations.

Calculations for the Federal Income Tax Liability Report Program (Married Filing Jointly Status)

The calculations included in the program for the married filing jointly status routine are shown in Figure 10-27. Included at the right side are the field values after the related

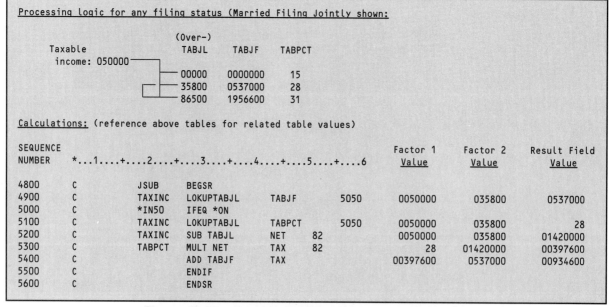

Figure 10-27 Calculations for Federal Income Tax Liability Report program using low-range table LOKUP for married filing jointly status.

statement is executed. Because the same sequence of calculations is followed for every filing status, an understanding of the mathematics for one will apply to the others. Refer back to Figure 10-24 for a review of the report generated by the Federal Income Tax Liability Report program.

SUMMARY

In the programming environment, *tables* are lists of data stored in a computer's memory. A table may stand alone or relate to one or more other tables.

Tables are defined in *Extension Specifications* instructions, which are entered in the program after the *File Description* statements. Tables may be defined as *Compile Time* or *Prerun Time*. The data for *Compile Time* tables is stored in the program after the last output instruction and the delineating control statement **. *Prerun Time* table data is stored in a data file and requires that a table file be defined in the *File Description Specifications* by identifying it with the letter **T** in column 16.

Tables are always processed consecutively and are accessed by a **LOKUP** operation. The entry (literal or field name) in *Factor 1*, referred to as the search argument, must be the same type as the *argument* table entry in *Factor 2*. One related *function* table may be specified in the *Result Field*. If more than one *function* table is required for the application, additional **LOKUP** instructions must be provided.

For an equal **LOKUP** condition, an indicator must be specified in the equal field (columns 58–59) of the calculation instruction. When the value in the search argument (*Factor 1*) equals the value in the *argument* table (*Factor 2*), the indicator will be set on. A low-range table condition may be tested by including the same indicator in the *Low* and *Equal* fields. High-range conditions may be controlled by specifying the same indicator in the *High* and *Equal* fields. In either case, an *argument* table value is found even though an equal condition is not tested.

For processing efficiency, an early exit from an equal table **LOKUP** may be controlled by storing the table data in an ascending or descending order. Then, when a *search argument* is not found in a related *argument* table, table **LOKUP** is terminated before the table is searched to the end.

QUESTIONS

10-1. When should tables be included in an RPG/400 program?

10-2. Name two business applications that require the use of tables.

10-3. On which RPG/400 specifications are tables defined? Where are these instructions placed in the source program?

10-4. How is a table stored in memory?

10-5. When in the program cycle may tables be loaded with data? Where is the data stored (before processing) for each loading method?

10-6. Reference a blank *Extension Specifications*. Identify and explain the function of the fields used to define a table. Indicate the fields used (and not used) for each loading method.

10-7. What new entries are needed in the *File Descriptions* to support each loading method? What new entries are needed on the input form to define and/or process tables?

10-8. What are some of the syntax rules regarding the assignment of a table name?

10-9. Define the following table terms:

SEARCH ARGUMENT   ARGUMENT TABLE
FUNCTION TABLE   LOKUP

10-10. Reference a *Calculation Specifications,* and answer the following:
   a. Entry in *Factor 1* is referred to as the _____ .
   b. Entry in *Factor 2* is referred to as the _____ .
   c. Entry in the *Result Field* is referred to as the _____ .
   d. What are the minimum entries that must be specified with a **LOKUP** operation?
   e. How many tables may be accessed in one **LOKUP** operation?

10-11. Explain the rules for formatting table data.

10-12. What are alternating tables? How many tables may be defined in an alternating format?

10-13. Answer the following questions about table processing:
   a. Where in a table does a search begin?
   b. Does the search begin at the same table entry for successive **LOKUP** operations?
   c. Are tables consecutively or randomly processed?
   d. If the table data is in an unordered sequence and a search is unsuccessful, at which entry in the table does processing stop? Does this cancel program execution?

10-14. Explain the table processing term *early exit.* How is it provided for in an RPG/400 program?

10-15. If a table is defined as sorted and the data is not in the required sequence, when is this error identified?

10-16. Explain the following table processing terms:

EQUAL lookup   **HIGH RANGE**
          LOW RANGE

10-17. What additional entries are needed in the *Extension* and *Calculation Specifications* to support low-range table processing? High-range table processing?

10-18. If a low-range **LOKUP** is specified, which table entry will be accessed if the *search argument* value is 07000? What table entry will be accessed if a high-range **LOKUP** is specified and the *search argument* value is 07000?

00000
02480
03670
04750
07010
09170

10-19. Following are three simple tables that relate to one another. Format the TABCDE and TABSTA entries in an alternating format with one entry per record. Include all the related percentages on one record. Assuming they are *Compile Time,* format the tables (with required control statement(s)) as they would be entered in a program.

TABCDE	TABSTA	TABTAX
NJ	NEW JERSEY	6.0%
CT	CONNECTICUT	7.5%
NY	NEW YORK	7.0%
MA	MASSACHUSETTS	6.0%
VT	VERMONT	5.0%
NH	NEW HAMPSHIRE	3.0%

Note: TABCDE data must be sorted in ascending order.

10-20. Refer to Question 10-19, and complete the *Extension* and *Calculation Specifications* coding to define and access the three tables. Assume that the search argument STATE is defined as a two-byte alphanumeric input field.

10-21. Refer to Questions 10-19 and 10-20, and include and/or make any additional changes to define and process the tables as *Prerun Time.*

10-22. Given below are a state's sales tax percentage tables. All sales over $1.07 are subject to a 7% sales tax. If the sales amount is:

Over:	But Not Over:	The Tax Is:
$ .00	$ .07	$ .00
.07	.21	.01
.21	.35	.02
.35	.49	.03
.49	.64	.04
.64	.78	.05
.78	.92	.06
.92	1.07	.07

Format the table entries so that all the entries for a table are included on one record. Assume that the tables are to be loaded at *Compile Time*. Use *low-range* processing for the amount of sales (argument) table.

10-23. Refer to Question 10-22, and complete the *Extension* and *Calculations Specifications* to define and process the tables. Assume SALES is the *search argument* item.

10-24. Refer to Question 10-22, and format the table data for *high-range* processing. Complete the *Extension* and *Calculation Specifications* to define and process the tables. Assume that the *search argument* is SALES.

PROGRAMMING ASSIGNMENTS

For each of the following programming assignments, a physical file must have been created and loaded with the related data records. Your instructor will inform you as to whether you have to create the physical file and load it or if it has been prepared for the assignment.

Programming Assignment 10-1:   REAL PROPERTY TAX REPORT

A county wants a report of selected real property owners in some of the cities within its jurisdiction.

Physical File Record Format:

```
                    PHYSICAL FILE DESCRIPTION

  SYSTEM: AS/400                          DATE: Yours
  FILE NAME: Yours                        REV NO: 0
  RECORD NAME: Yours                      KEY LENGTH: None
  SEQUENCE: Non-keyed                     RECORD SIZE: 28

                     FIELD DEFINITIONS

   FIELD    FIELD NAME   SIZE  TYPE    POSITION      COMMENTS
    NO                                FROM    TO

     1       CTYCDE        2    C       1     2
     2       TAXPYR       20    C       3    22
     3       ASMAMT        8    P      23    27    0 decimals
     4       VETERN        1    C      28    28    V or blank
```

Physical file data:

City Code	Taxpayer Name	Assessed Amount	Vet Code
NL	W.C. FIELDS	00125000	V
SD	CLARK GABLE	01050000	
ST	MARILYN MONROE	12495000	
GH	CHARLIE CHAPLIN	09896500	V
BT	STANLEY LAUREL	00700590	
MN	BETTY BOOP	10456330	V
NK	JOHN WAYNE	15000000	
NH	JAYNE MANSFIELD	08750900	
HD	TYRONE POWELL	00500788	V
ST	ERROL FLYNN	20598500	

Table Data: (Include as Compile Time *tables)*

City Code	City Name	Mill Rate
GH	GREENWICH	57.2
SD	STAMFORD	52.1
NK	NORWALK	50.7
BT	BRIDGEPORT	48.8
ST	STRATFORD	46.5
NH	NEW HAVEN	47.0
MN	MIDDLETOWN	39.6
HD	HARTFORD	42.3
NL	NEW LONDON	38.4

Processing: The following steps are required:

1. Look up the City Code table with the code field from each input record, and access the City Name table for the related city's name.
2. Look up the City Code table again to get the related value from the Mill Rate table.
3. Divide the assessed amount by 1,000 to determine the multiples of $1,000.

Example:

$$\text{Assessed amount } \frac{\$60,000}{1,000} = 60 \text{ multiples of } \$1,000$$

Veterans are allowed a $1,000 tax exemption that is subtracted from the assessed amount before the multiple is computed. A **V** in the Veteran Status field of a physical file record indicates that the taxpayer is a veteran.

4. Multiply the related Mill Rate table value from Step 2 by the multiple computed in Step 3 to determine the property tax liability for the taxpayer.

Report Design: Format the report shown in the printer spacing chart. Note that a YES or NO is printed by testing the Veteran Status field for a **V** and moving a YES or NO literal to an output field.

```
      0         1         2         3         4         5         6         7         8
 1  0X/XX/XX              REAL PROPERTY TAX REPORT BY CITIES                    PAGE XX0X
 2  HH:MM:SS
 3
 4                                                    MILL/              TAX
 5       TAXPAYER          CITY        ASSESSMENT     RATE    VET     LIABILITY
 6
 7   X          X      X          X   $XX,XXX,X0X    XX.X    YES    $ X,XXX,XX0.XX
 8                                                           (NO)
 9   X          X      X          X    XX,XXX,X0X    XX.X    YES      X,XXX,XX0.XX
10                                                           (NO)
11  NOTES:
12
13    (1) Use system date for report.
14
15    (2) Headings on top of every page.
16
17    (3) $ only on first detail line.
18
19    (4) Print YES or NO for vet value.
```

Programming Assignment 10-2: WEEKLY SHIPPING REPORT

A company needs a weekly report of the shipping charges it incurs. All deliveries are made FOB destination (seller pays shipping cost).

Physical File Record Format: A physical file of customers is maintained with the following attributes:

```
              PHYSICAL FILE DESCRIPTION

SYSTEM: AS/400                        DATE: Yours
FILE NAME: Yours                      REV NO: 0
RECORD NAME: Yours                    KEY LENGTH: 4
SEQUENCE: Keyed                       RECORD SIZE: 32

                  FIELD DEFINITIONS

FIELD    FIELD NAME    SIZE   TYPE    POSITION      COMMENTS
NO                                   FROM    TO


  1      CUSTNM         20     C       1      20
  2      INVNO           4     P      21      23   Key field
  3      INVAMT          6     P      24      27   2 decimals
  4      PDS             2     P      28      29   0 decimals
  5      OZS             2     P      30      31   0 decimals
  6      COD             1     C      32      32   Y or blank
```

Physical file data:

| | | | Invoice Weight | | |
Customer Name	Invoice Number	Invoice Amount	PDS	OZ	COD
HENRY JACKSON	1244	002400	05	08	
DOROTHY PARTON	1235	010000	20	00	
ROBERT WARFIELD	1236	004500	08	09	Y
MARIO LANZA	1237	120000	70	00	Y
ENZIO PINZA	1238	245000	82	12	
NELSON EDDY	1239	001000	01	00	

Table Data: Include the following as *Compile Time* tables in the program:

Weight (PDS)	Rate (2 decimal positions)
01	129
02	137
03	146
04	154
05	163
06	171
07	180
08	188
09	197
10	205
11	214
12	222
13	231
14	239
15	248
16	256
17	265
18	273
19	282
20	290

Processing: Use the invoice shipping weight field as the *search argument,* and look up the weight table to access the related shipping charge. For weights that contain any ounces over a pound, round to the next higher pound. All shipments over 20 pounds are charged the table amount for that weight plus an additional 6 cents for each pound over 20.

A maximum shipping limit of 70 pounds is imposed by the parcel delivery firm. Identify this condition on the report by the message OVER WEIGHT, and skip any additional calculations.

For invoice amounts under $25, the shipping charge is absorbed by the buyer and added to the invoice total. Identify these transactions on the report by asterisks in place of the shipping charge amount.

For COD sales, a flat charge of $1.50 is added to the invoice on all invoices under $50. COD shipments are identified by the letter **Y** in the related input field.

Report Design:

```
        0         1         2         3         4         5         6         7
ØX/XX/XX              FOB DESTINATION SHIPMENT REPORT                    PAGE XXØX

                                                  WEIGHT           SHIPPING
     CUSTOMER NAME        INVOICE   INVOICE AMT    PDS OZS   COD    CHARGE
   X               X      XXXX      X,XXØ.XX       ØX  ØX   YES     XXØ.XX
   X               X      XXXX      X,XXØ.XX       ØX  ØX           ******
   X               X      XXXX      X,XXØ.XX       ØX  ØX           OVER WEIGHT

        NOTES:

        1. HEADINGS ON TOP OF EVERY PAGE.

        2. REPORT DATE IS SYSTEM SUPPLIED.

        3. PRINT ASTERISKS IN SHIPPING CHARGE COLUMN IF CUSTOMER PAYS.

        4. PRINT OVER WEIGHT IN SHIPPING CHARGE COLUMN IF INVOICE
           WEIGHT OVER 7Ø POUNDS.
```

Programming Assignment 10-3: FLEXIBLE BUDGET REPORT

A company has a flexible budget formula for its factory overhead expenses. Each expense item has a fixed dollar amount plus a variable rate based on the standard direct labor hours (hours budgeted for the level of production attained). The formula is expressed as:

Budget amount for
overhead expense = Fixed $ amount + (variable rate × std direct hrs)
item

At the end of each accounting period, the company wants to determine the flexible budget amount for each expense item and compare it with the actual dollars incurred to identify a *favorable* or *unfavorable variance.* A favorable variance occurs when the actual costs incurred for the expense are less than the budget allowance. An unfavorable variance results when the actual costs are more than the budget amount.

Physical File Record Format:

```
                    PHYSICAL FILE DESCRIPTION

SYSTEM: AS/400                           DATE: Yours
FILE NAME: Yours                         REV NO: 0
RECORD NAME: Yours                       KEY LENGTH: 3
SEQUENCE: Keyed                          RECORD SIZE: 8

                     FIELD DEFINITIONS

  FIELD    FIELD NAME   SIZE  TYPE   POSITION      COMMENTS
   NO                                FROM   TO

    1      ACTNO         3     C      1      3   Key field
    2      ACTCST        8     P      4      8   0 decimals
```

Physical file data:

Account Number	Actual Cost Incurred
600	03000090
601	05100010
602	00550068
603	00840000
604	01500025
605	00850010
606	01000005
607	00950000
608	00705078
609	00420015

Data Area Requirements: Create a data area that includes the accounting period date—113095--and 50,000 for standard direct labor hours. The date is to be used as the report date and the standard direct labor hours in the computation of the total budget amount.

Table Data: Include the following data in *Compile Time* tables:

Account Number	Account Name	Fixed Amount	Variable Rate Per Direct Labor Hours (2 decimals)
600	INDIRECT LABOR	20000	015
601	FACTORY SUPPLIES	02000	100
602	FACTORY ELECTRICITY	03000	006
603	MACHINE REPAIRS	01000	010
604	PLANT MAINTENANCE	04000	020
605	FACTORY HEATING OIL	02700	004
606	FACTORY CUSTODIAL	05000	010
607	TOOL CRIB LABOR	04500	011
608	COST CLERKS	04000	008

Processing: Use the Account Number field from the input records as the *search argument,* and look up the related Account Number table for an equal condition. Provide for an early exit if the account number is not found in the table.

If the table search is successful, multiply the standard direct labor hours input by the related variable rate table entry. Add this amount to the fixed amount table entry for the item for the total flexible budget amount allowed for the level of activity (standard direct labor hours input).

The favorable or unfavorable variance for each expense item is determined by subtracting the total flexible budget amount from the actual cost incurred. A positive difference indicates an unfavorable variance; a negative, favorable.

Examine the printer spacing chart, and notice that the letter **F** (favorable) or **U** (unfavorable) is printed alongside the variance amount. *Do not print a negative sign.*

Report Design:

Programming Assignment 10-4: WEEKLY PAYROLL CHECKS

The XYZ Company needs an RPG/400 program to print the weekly payroll checks (with stubs) on preprinted check forms for its employees.

General Information: By federal law all employee wages are subject to federal withholding tax (FWT) and Social Security/Medicare Tax (FICA) deductions. There are many acceptable methods to compute the federal tax that must be withheld under the pay-as-you-earn system. The percentage method, which requires the use of tables, is popular for computerized systems and will be used for this program.

Earnings, number of exemptions, marital status, and payroll period (weekly, biweekly, and so forth) determine the amount of federal income tax withheld. Based on the company's payroll, this program requires computations only for a weekly payroll period for single and married wage earners.

Processing: The steps needed to compute the Federal Withholding Tax (FWT) to be withheld from an employee's weekly pay using the percentage method are detailed below. Note that the value determined in Step 1 is used as the search argument to look up the low-range table.

Assume the following
    Weekly Salary: $ 450.00
    Exemptions: 1
    Marital Status: Single

Computations to determine Federal Income to withhold:

Step 1:   The number of exemptions is multiplied by a statutory allowance of $ 38.46 (for single/weekly payroll period) and product subtracted from the week's wages.

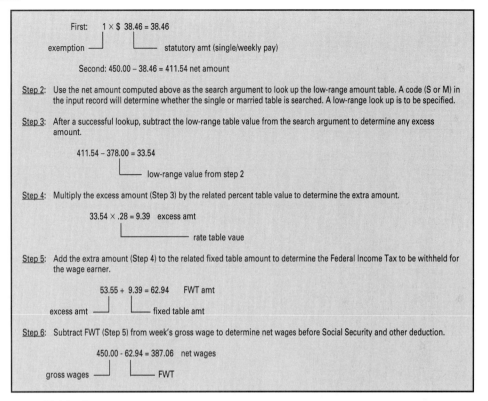

Table Data:

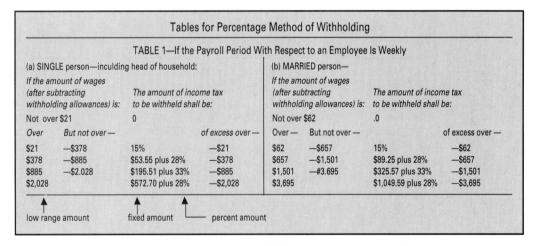

As of 1994, the *Social Security Tax* (**FICA**) is computed at 7.65% on the first $60,600 paid to an employee. A *Medicare Tax* of 1.45%, which is not limited by amount of income, is included in the 7.65%. The following must be considered in the computation of the *Social Security/Medicare Tax:*

1. If the year-to-date wages (before adding the current week) are greater than $60,600, no **FICA** is computed. However, the *Medicare Tax* deduction of 1.45% continues on all additional earnings.

2. If the year-to-date wages are not $60,600 or greater, then it must be determined if all, or only part, of the current week's pay is subject to the Social Security part (6.20%) of the 7.65% total tax. For example, if the year-to-date wages are $60,400 and the current week's pay is $600, only $200 will be subject to the FICA 7.65% rate. However, any additional amounts and future pay will continue to be reduced by the 1.45% Medicare Tax rate.

3. Note that there is no limit on the *Federal Withholding Tax* (**FWT**) withheld.

Physical File Record Format:

```
                    PHYSICAL FILE DESCRIPTION

        SYSTEM: AS/400                    DATE: Yours
        FILE NAME: Yours                  REV NO: 0
        RECORD NAME: Yours                KEY LENGTH: 3
        SEQUENCE: Keyed                   RECORD SIZE: 50

                        FIELD DEFINITIONS

        FIELD    FIELD NAME   SIZE  TYPE    POSITION      COMMENTS
        NO                                FROM    TO

          1      EMP#           3    C       1      3   Key field
          2      NAME          22    C       4     25
          3      SS#            9    P      26     30
          4      YTDWAG         9    P      31     35   2 decimals
          5      YTDFWT         7    P      36     39   2 decimals
          6      YTDSS          6    P      40     43   2 decimals
          7      WKWAGE         6    P      44     47   2 decimals
          8      EXEMPT         2    P      48     49   0 decimals
          9      STATUS         1    C      50     50
```

<u>Physical file data</u>:

Employee Number	Employee Name	SS Number	YTD Wages	YTD FWT	YTD SS	Week's Wages	Exemptions	Marital Status
111	ROBERT FULTON	040503871	06040000	1280000	462060	120000	2	M
222	THOMAS EDISON	030216532	03000000	0600000	229500	058000	1	S
333	ALEXANDER BELL	020315555	13470000	2694000	571035	260000	4	M
444	HENRY FORD	060548754	06500000	1300000	497250	145500	1	S
555	WALTER CHRYSLER	050703302	06000000	1200000	459000	320000	2	M

Create a data area to store the week ending date and the beginning check number. Use 091094 for the date value and 1000 as the beginning check number.

Report Design: Output is to be printed on simulated preprinted check forms. Assume that all of the *constants* shown in the printer spacing chart are preprinted. The RPG/400 program is to output only the variable data (shown with the **X's**). Control page overflow so that only one check and stub will print per page (***see your instructor, however, before you execute your program and change the standard form length***).

```
          0          1          2          3          4          5          6
    1234567890123456789012345678901234567890123456789012345678901234567890123456789
 1  XXX-XX-XXXX                    XYZ COMPANY                            XXXX
 2                                 ALCATRAZ,CA
 3                                                   WEEK ENDING  0X/XX/XX
 4  PAY TO THE
 5  ORDER OF      X                          X              EMP NO   XXX
 6
 7           PAY EXACTLY  $ *,***.XX
 8
 9                ALWAYS ACCURATE BANK
10                     HOPE, CA
11                                              JOHN DIDIT JR
12                                              CONTROLLER
13
14  DO NOT CASH - CHECK STUB                                        XXXX
15  XXX-XX-XXXX
16                                                    EMP NO   XXX
17
18  GROSS PAY    FWT         FICA      NET PAY    YTD EARNINGS
19
20  X,XX0.XX    X,XX0.XX    XX0.XX    X,XX0.XX    XX,XX0.XX
21
22               YTD FWT    YTD FICA
23
24               XX,XX0.XX   X,XX0.XX
```

Correct alignment of the variables may be determined by a transparency master of the report supplied by the instructor or with a forms ruler.

chapter 11

Array Processing

COMPARISON OF ARRAYS TO TABLES

Because *arrays* and *tables* are similar, you may be confused about when to use an array instead of a table, or vice versa. Two broad considerations may help you to determine whether to use an array or a table in an RPG/400 program:

1. The way the data for loading the array or table is arranged in the records
2. The way the array or table will be processed

The structural and processing differences of arrays and tables are explained in the comparison detailed in Figure 11-1.

Array Features	Table Features
1. Data used to load a run time array may be stored anywhere in the body of the records and need not be stored contiguously.	1. Data used to load tables must be stored beginning in the first byte of the input records. The data must be stored consecutively.
2. Arrays may be searched randomly by indexing. A specific element may be accessed without starting the search from the beginning of the array.	2. Tables must be consecutively searched, beginning with the first table entry for every lookup. Indexing is not supported for table processing.
3. All the elements in an array may be accessed at one time by specifying only the array name.	3. Only one table element may be accessed at a time. Reference to other entries requires additional lookups.
4. During processing, elements in related arrays may be cross-referenced by indexing.	4. Three or more tables are related by successive lookups.

Figure 11-1 Comparison of the structural and processing features of arrays and tables.

ARRAY STRUCTURE

As related to computers, an *array* may be defined as an arrangement of computer memory positions in one (or multiple) dimension with each position having the same attributes. Figure 11-2 illustrates the structures of one- and two-dimensional arrays.

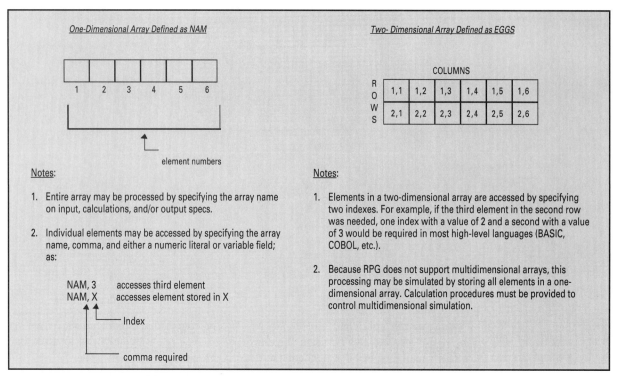

Figure 11-2 Structure of one- and two-dimensional arrays.

One-Dimensional Arrays

The storage positions built for an array are referred to as *elements*. The array NAM, shown in Figure 11-2, was built with six *elements*. All *elements* may be accessed at one time by specifying only the array name. Individual *elements* may be accessed by including a comma and a literal or variable field index with the array name. Program requirements will determine how the array is processed.

Multidimensional Arrays

Refer to Figure 11-2 for an example of a two- (multi-) dimensional array. This structure may be better understood if the array shown is thought of as an egg carton with two rows of six eggs each. In languages such as COBOL and BASIC, the third egg (column 3) from row 2 would be accessed by specifying two indexes. For example, the coding in COBOL would be:

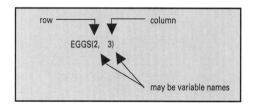

RPG/400 does not directly support multidimensional arrays. However, they may be simulated by defining one or more *Multiple Occurrence Data Structures* in a program and processing them with one or more **OCUR** statements. An example program that includes these features is discussed later in this chapter.

LOADING AN ARRAY

Loading an array refers to the time in the program cycle during which data is read, moved, and stored in the array elements built by the attributes defined in the *Extension Specifications*. Similar to tables, arrays may be loaded at *Compile* and *Prerun Times*. They may also be loaded by input and calculation as *Run Time* arrays. Figure 11-3 details the processing logic associated with loading an array at various times in the program cycle.

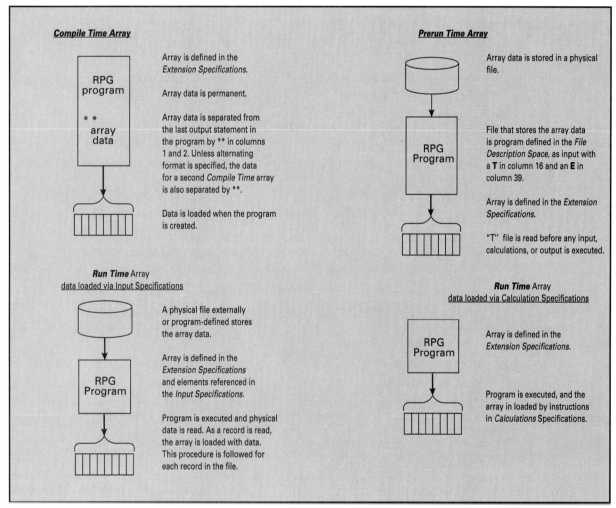

Figure 11-3 Processing logic for loading arrays at *Compile, Prerun,* and *Run Times.*

ARRAY DESCRIPTION

The number of elements, size of the elements, type, and sequence (referred to as attributes) are specified in the *Extension Specifications*. This form allocates the array's total storage area before the loading of data. Refer to Figure 11-4 for an explanation of the fields used to define and load an array at *Compile, Prerun,* and *Run Times.*

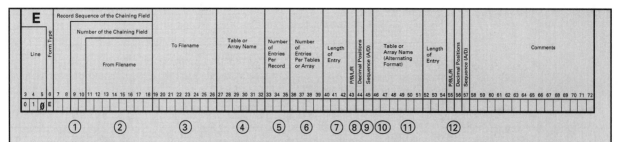

* All *Extension Specification* instructions must include an **E** in column 6 and immediately follow the last *File Description* statement.

1   Columns 7–10 - not used.

2   **From Filename** (columns 11–18) - Required for **Prerun Time** arrays. File name, specified in a *File Description* statement (**T** in column 16) as program-defined (**F** in column 19) must be entered left-justified in this field.

3   **To Filename** (columns 19–26) - Optional for **Prerun Time** arrays. If the array data is to be written to an output device at the end of the program, the name of the output file must be entered left-justified in this field.

4   **Array Name** (columns 27–32) - Programmer-supplied array name must be entered in this field. If the array is to be indexed, the required comma and index name or literal must be considered in the arrays specified in the program.

5   **Number of Entries Per Record** (columns 33–35) - Specifies how many individual array elements are stored on a record. Entry is only for **Compile** and **Prerun Time** arrays.

6   **Number of Entries Per Array** (columns 36–39) - Specifies how many array elements are stored in the array. Required for all array types.

7   **Length of Entry** (columns 40–42) - Specifies the size of the array elements. All elements of an array must be the same size. Elements in character arrays may be defined from 1 to 256 bytes. Numeric array elements may be defined from 1 to 30 bytes.

8   **P/B/L/R** (column 43) - If the numeric data in a **Prerun** or **Run Time** array is stored in packed decimal format, the letter P must be specified in this field. If the data is stored in binary format, a **B** must be specified. If no entry is specified, the numeric array data is stored as zoned decimal. *Compile Time* array data is entered in a zoned decimal format. An **L** entered in this field indicates that a separate sign is stored to the left of the value and an **R** to the right.

9   **Decimal Positions** (column 44) - A blank in this field indicates that the array is character. A number from 0 to 9 defines the array elements as numeric with the indicated implied decimal positions. The entry cannot be larger than the Length of Entry size.

10 **Sequence (A/D)** (column 45) - If the array is not in a sorted order, this field must be blank. If the data is in an ascending order, an **A** may be entered. On the other hand, if the array data is in a descending order, a **D** may be specified. If sequence is specified, an "early exit" is provided for an unsuccessful equal lookup condition, reducing run times.

11 **Array Name (Alternating Format)** (columns 46–51). An array name entered in this field indicates that two or more entries from two related arrays are stored in each record, for example, data for an SSNO element followed by the data for a NAME element. Number of Entries Per Record specifies how many "pairs" are included on a record. Only valid for **Compile** and **Prerun Time** arrays.

12 Columns 52–57 - These four fields relate to the attributes of the alternating array. Refer to items 7, 8, 9, and 10 for an explanation of these fields.

Figure 11-4   Fields used in the *Extension Specifications* to define arrays at *Compile, Prerun,* and *Run Times.*

RPG/400 SYNTAX FOR COMPILE TIME ARRAYS

It was previously indicated that *Compile Time* array data is an integral ("hard-coded") part of an RPG/400 program. It must be included after a ** control statement entered in columns 1 and 2 and follow the last output (**O**) statement in the program. Unless alternating sequence is specified, the data for two or more arrays must also be separated by a ** control statement. Figure 11-5 shows the relationship of the *Extension Specifications* coding and the data for two *Compile Time* arrays.

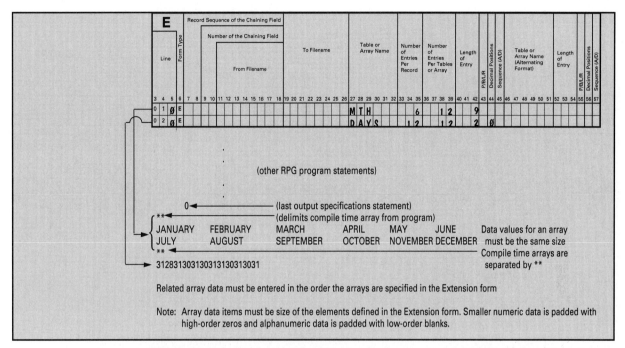

Figure 11-5   *Extension Specifications* syntax and related data for two *Compile Time* arrays.

RPG/400 SYNTAX FOR COMPILE TIME ARRAYS STORED IN AN ALTERNATING FORMAT

Figure 11-6 shows the array data from Figure 11-5 rearranged in an alternating format with the modified *Extension Specifications* coding.

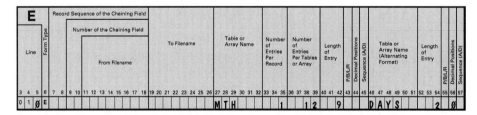

Figure 11-6   *Extension Specifications* syntax and related data for two *Compile Time* arrays arranged in an alternating format.

RPG/400 SYNTAX FOR PRERUN TIME ARRAYS

Data for *Prerun Time* arrays is stored externally from the program in a physical file. When processed, the array is created and loaded with data from the physical file before any other files are processed. The array data remains in storage for the complete program cycle.

Figure 11-7 illustrates the syntax required in an RPG/400 program to support a *Prerun Time* array. In the *File Description Specifications*, the physical file must be program-defined (**F** in column 19) and coded as an input (**I** in column 15) table file (**T** in

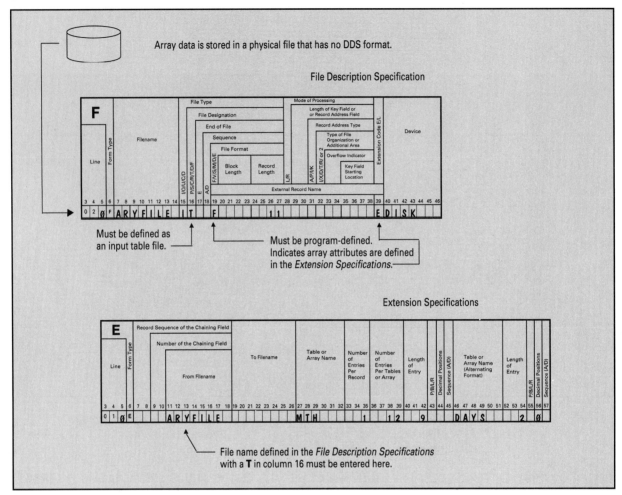

Figure 11-7   *File Description* and *Extension Specifications* syntax for *Prerun Time* arrays.

column 16). The **E** in column 39 indicates that the attributes for the arrays are defined in the *Extension Specifications*. Also, notice that the physical file's name must be entered in the *From Filename* field (columns 11–18) in the *Extension Specifications*.

FORMAT OF DATA FOR COMPILE AND PRERUN TIME ARRAYS

Data for the *Compile* and *Prerun Time* arrays must be formatted according to the rules explained in Figure 11-8.

1. Data must begin in first column of each record.

2. Elements for an array must be the same size.

3. Smaller numeric elements must be padded with high-order zeros, and smaller alphanumeric elements must be padded with low-order blanks.

4. When alternating sequence is used for the data for two arrays, the values for the two arrays must be included on a record based on the Number of Entries Per Record entry in the *Extension Specifications* form. Values may <u>not</u> be separated on two records.

5. Order of the data in a *Compile Time* array must relate to the *Extension* entry. The first array defined must have its data included first at the end of the program (after a **), and so forth.

Figure 11-8   Rules for formatting the data records for *Compile* and *Prerun Time* arrays.

The decision to use a *Compile* or *Prerun Time* array in a program usually depends on the following:

1. *Compile Time* arrays are used when the array is small (i.e., having few elements), the data is not likely to change, and/or the data is not shared by other programs. The month name and the day arrays previously shown are an example of the type of information that may be included in this array classification.
2. *Prerun Time* arrays are used when an array is large (i.e., having many elements), the data is frequently updated, and/or the data is used by other programs.

RPG/400 SYNTAX FOR RUN TIME ARRAYS (LOADED IN INPUT SPECIFICATIONS)

Like *Prerun Time,* the data for *Run Time* arrays (loaded in *Input Specifications*) is stored in a physical file. However, there are significant storage and processing differences, which are identified in the comparison in Figure 11-9.

Run Time Array (Load in Input Specifications)	Prerun Time Array Features
1. Data for the array may be stored in any field (or fields) in the body of a physical file record.	1. Data for the array must begin in column 1 of the input records unless the elements relate to the data for a second array formatted in an alternating sequence.
2. Any number of arrays may be specified for an externally or program-defined physical file defined as input.	2. A maximum of two arrays (alternating format) may be included in a program-defined physical table file (**T** in column 16 of *File Specs.*).
3. Other fields in the record not defined as arrays may be accessed and processed.	3. Any data following array value(s) is ignored and not available for processing.
4. Array is built and loaded with data after the program is executed and first data record is read from a related physical file.	4. Array is loaded with data from the physical file before input, calculations, or output is executed.
5. Array data is changed for every record processed.	5. Array data remains unchanged (unless updated) for the complete program cycle.

Figure 11-9 Comparison of storage and processing logic for *Run Time* and *Prerun Time* arrays.

Run Time arrays are usually used when the data is loaded into an array from one or more input records and/or when the data is stored in one or more fields in the body of a physical file's record format.

Run Time Array (Loaded in Input Specifications)—Data Stored in an Externally Defined Physical File

When the data for a *Run Time* array is stored in an externally defined physical file in contiguous or noncontiguous fields, the data may be loaded into the array elements in the *Input Specifications* by the method shown in Figure 11-10.

Note the following two syntax features in Figure 11-10:

1. Physical file record format name (not the file name) is specified in the *Record Name* field of the *Input Specifications*.
2. *Indexing* (discussed in detail later in the chapter) is used to define the related array element in which the data from the related physical file's field is to be stored. A comma must be included after the array name followed by numeric

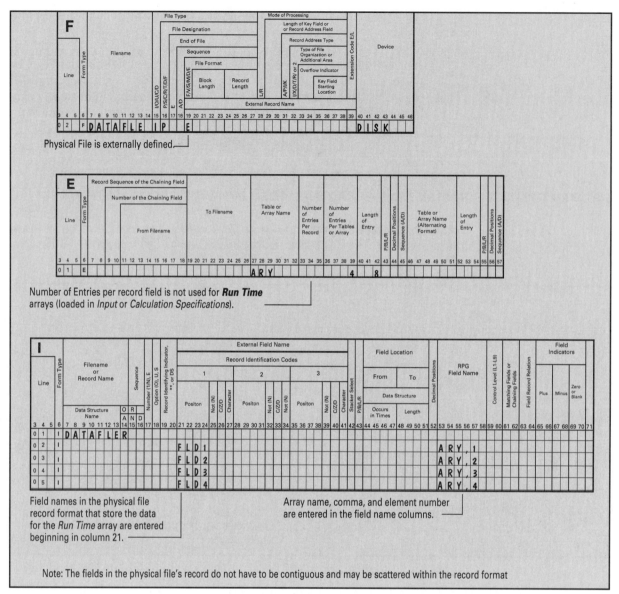

Figure 11-10 Loading data into a *Run Time* array in *Input Specifications* from an externally defined physical file.

literal or index name. When defining an array for which indexing is required, the maximum field length of six bytes must be considered.

Run Time Array Loaded in Input Specifications from the Data Stored in a Program-Defined Physical File

If a physical file was created without a DDS definition, and contiguous data is to be processed in a *Run Time* array, the file must be program-defined. The location of the array elements must be specified in the *From* and *To* fields in the *Input Specifications*. Figure 11-11 details the *File, Extension,* and *Input Specifications* syntax.

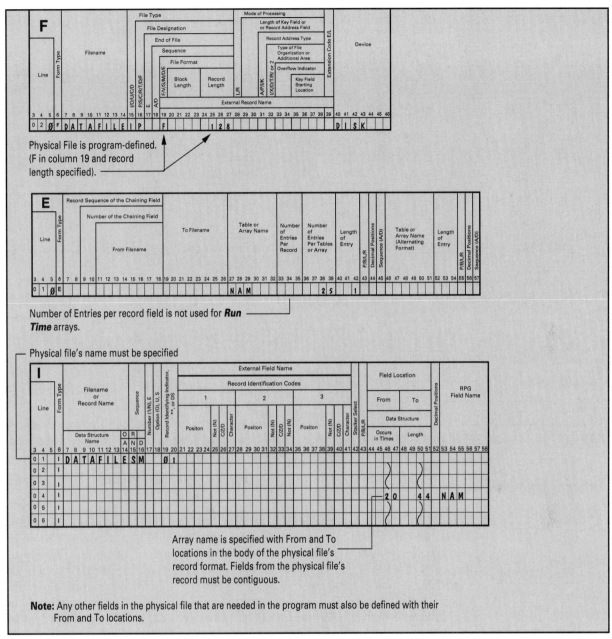

Figure 11-11 Loading a *Run Time* array in *Input Specifications* from the data stored in a program-defined physical file.

Run Time Array (Loaded in *Calculation Specifications*)

Run Time arrays loaded by one or more calculation statements are defined in the *Extension Specifications* without a *Number of Entries Per Record* field entry. Any arithmetic and **Z-ADD, Z-SUB, SQRT, MOVE, MOVEL, MOVEA** (discussed later) operations may be used to load a *Run Time* array in calculations. Figure 11-12 details the syntax for loading a *Run Time* array in calculations with the data from another *Run Time* array that is loaded from the *Input Specifications*.

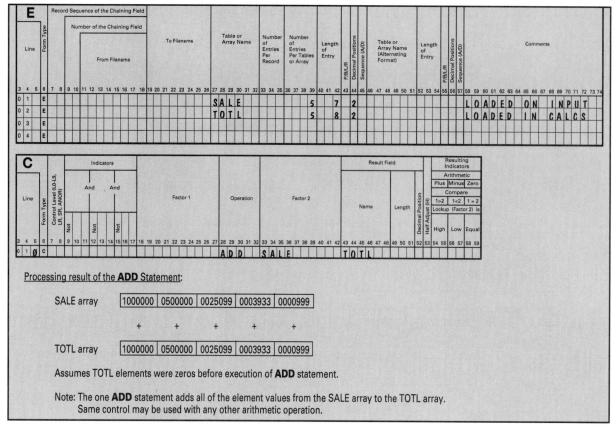

Figure 11-12 *Extension* and *Calculation Specifications* syntax to process and load a *Run Time* array with an **ADD** statement.

PROCESSING ARRAYS

The RPG/400 syntax used to define all the array types has been explained in the preceding paragraphs without any discussion of how they are processed. *Compile, Prerun,* or *Run Time* arrays may be processed consecutively or randomly. An entire array may be processed at one time, or individual elements may be randomly accessed. Extracting select elements from an array requires the use of indexes. This and other processing methods are explained in the following text and program examples. The first example of an application program illustrates the consecutive processing of two *Run Time* arrays.

APPLICATION PROGRAM: SALESPERSON MONTHLY PERFORMANCE REPORT

Documentation

The specifications presented in Figure 11-13 explain the processing requirements for the first application program that generates a Monthly Sales Performance Report by salesperson.

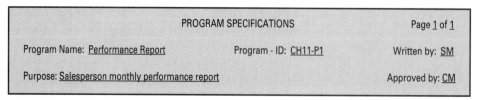

Figure 11-13 Specifications for the monthly sales performance report program that processes two *Run Time* arrays.

Input files: DAT11P1 ____ _____ _____ _____

Output files: QSYSPRT ____ _____ _____ _____

Processing Requirements:

Write an RPG/400 program to generate a salesperson monthly performance report.

Input to the program:

The externally defined monthly sales file (DAT11P1) contains the sales transactions for the company's salespersons for one month of the current year. A supplemental record layout form details the format of the physical record.

Processing:

Define a *Run Time* array that will be loaded in the *Input Specifications* from the data stored in the externally defined physical file. Also, define a second *Run Time* array that will be loaded in calculations from the data loaded in the *Run Time* input array.

For every record processed, cross-foot the five salesperson elements to accumulate the total sales for the week. Add the five salesperson amounts (loaded for each record read in the *Run Time* input array) to the five elements in the *Run Time* calculation array. At **LR** time, cross-foot the *Run Time* calculation array for the total company's monthly sales.

Output:

Generate the report detailed in the attached printer spacing chart.

Figure 11-13 Specifications for the monthly sales performance report program that processes two *Run Time* arrays. (Continued)

The system flowchart in Figure 11-14 indicates that one physical file and one program-defined printer file are processed by the program.

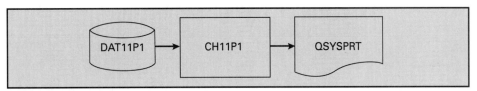

Figure 11-14 System flowchart for monthly sales performance report program.

Figure 11-15 details the physical file's record format. The five salesperson fields will be loaded into the five-element SALS array for each record processed.

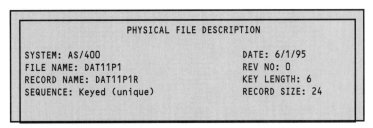

Figure 11-15 Physical file record format and data listing for the monthly sales performance report program.

```
                        FIELD DEFINITIONS

        FIELD    FIELD NAME   SIZE TYPE   POSITION    COMMENTS
         NO                               FROM    TO


          1      WEDATE         6    P     1     4    Key field
          2      SALSP1         7    P     5     8    2 decimals
          3      SALSP2         7    P     9    12    2 decimals
          4      SALSP3         7    P    13    16    2 decimals
          5      SALSP4         7    P    17    20    2 decimals
          6      SALSP5         7    P    21    24    2 decimals
```

Physical file data:

```
   Week
   Ending   Sales-     Sales-     Sales-     Sales-     Sales-
   Date     Person 1   Person 2   Person 3   Person 4   Person 5


   060495   0008000    0014530    0035140    0012400    0005224
   061195   0054300    0057000    0580001    0058500    0063000
   061895   0009000    0040000    0052500    0053500    0754000
   062595   0050000    0045300    0012099    0085000    0086000
   063195   0012000    0012300    0014000    0150800    0003000
```

Figure 11-15   Physical file record format and data listing for the monthly sales performance report program. (Continued)

The design of the sales performance report and the listing generated by the RPG/400 program are shown in Figure 11-16.

```
6/30/95              MONTHLY SALES PERFORMANCE REPORT              PAGE    1
                          BY SALESPERSON


 WEEK        SALESPERSON  SALESPERSON  SALESPERSON  SALESPERSON  SALESPERSON    WEEKLY
 ENDING          #1           #2           #3           #4           #5         TOTAL

 6/04/95        80.00       145.30       351.40       124.00        52.24      752.94

 6/11/95       543.00       570.00     5,800.01       585.00       630.00    8,128.01

 6/18/95        90.00       400.00       525.00       535.00     7,540.00    9,090.00

 6/25/95       500.00       453.00       120.99       850.00       860.00    2,783.99

 6/31/95       120.00       123.00       140.00     1,508.00        30.00    1,921.00


 TOTALS      1,333.00     1,691.30     6,937.40     3,602.00     9,112.24   22,675.94
```

Figure 11-16   Report design and generated report for the monthly sales performance report program.

Source Program Coding

A compile listing of the Monthly Sales Performance Report program is presented in Figure 11-17. The syntax related to the processing of the two *Run Time* arrays is discussed in separate figures.

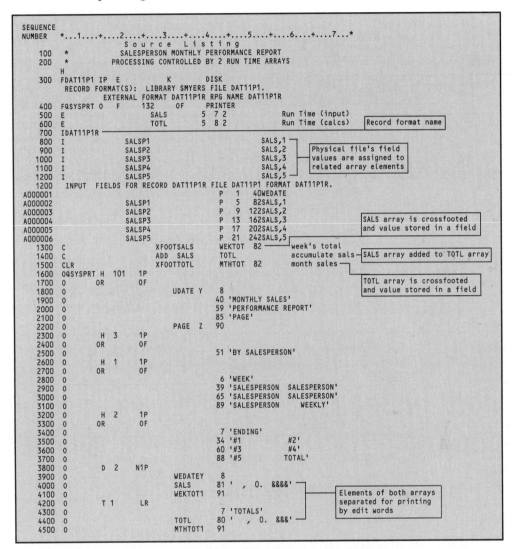

```
SEQUENCE
NUMBER    *...1....+....2....+....3....+....4....+....5....+....6....+....7...*
                        S o u r c e   L i s t i n g
  100    *          SALESPERSON MONTHLY PERFORMANCE REPORT
  200    *          PROCESSING CONTROLLED BY 2 RUN TIME ARRAYS
         H
  300    FDAT11P1 IP  E          K          DISK
         RECORD FORMAT(S): LIBRARY SMYERS FILE DAT11P1.
              EXTERNAL FORMAT DAT11P1R RPG NAME DAT11P1R
  400    FQSYSPRT O   F      132     OF      PRINTER
  500    E                  SALS        5 7 2               Run Time (input)
  600    E                  TOTL        5 8 2               Run Time (calcs)       Record format name
  700    IDAT11P1R
  800    I                  SALSP1                   SALS,1
  900    I                  SALSP2                   SALS,2       Physical file's field
 1000    I                  SALSP3                   SALS,3       values are assigned to
 1100    I                  SALSP4                   SALS,4       related array elements
 1200    I                  SALSP5                   SALS,5
 1200    INPUT  FIELDS FOR RECORD DAT11P1R FILE DAT11P1 FORMAT DAT11P1R.
A000001                                         P  1  40WEDATE
A000002                  SALSP1                 P  5  82SALS,1
A000003                  SALSP2                 P  9 122SALS,2
A000004                  SALSP3                 P 13 162SALS,3     SALS array is crossfooted
A000005                  SALSP4                 P 17 202SALS,4     and value stored in a field
A000006                  SALSP5                 P 21 242SALS,5
 1300    C                  XFOOTSALS      WEKTOT   82     week's total
 1400    C             ADD  SALS           TOTL           accumulate sals   SALS array added to TOTL array
 1500    CLR                XFOOTTOTL      MTHTOT   82     month sales
 1600    OQSYSPRT H   101     1P                                      TOTL array is crossfooted
 1700    O        OR          OF                                      and value stored in a field
 1800    O                           UDATE Y    8
 1900    O                                      40 'MONTHLY SALES'
 2000    O                                      59 'PERFORMANCE REPORT'
 2100    O                                      85 'PAGE'
 2200    O                           PAGE  Z   90
 2300    O        H   3     1P
 2400    O        OR          OF
 2500    O                                      51 'BY SALESPERSON'
 2600    O        H   1     1P
 2700    O        OR          OF
 2800    O                                       6 'WEEK'
 2900    O                                      39 'SALESPERSON   SALESPERSON'
 3000    O                                      65 'SALESPERSON   SALESPERSON'
 3100    O                                      89 'SALESPERSON      WEEKLY'
 3200    O        H   2     1P
 3300    O        OR          OF
 3400    O                                       7 'ENDING'
 3500    O                                      34 '#1          #2'
 3600    O                                      60 '#3          #4'
 3700    O                                      88 '#5        TOTAL'
 3800    O        D   2     N1P
 3900    O                           WEDATEY    8
 4000    O                           SALS      81 ' ,  0. &&&&'      Elements of both arrays
 4100    O                           WEKTOT1   91                    separated for printing
 4200    O        T   1     LR                                       by edit words
 4300    O                                       7 'TOTALS'
 4400    O                           TOTL      80 ' ,  0. &&&'
 4500    O                           MTHTOT1   91
```

Figure 11-17   Compile listing of the monthly sales performance report program.

File Description and *Extension Specifications* Syntax

Because *Run Time* arrays do not require any entries in the *File Description Specifications*, we do not discuss this topic. The syntax for the program's *Extension Specifications* is shown in Figure 11-18.

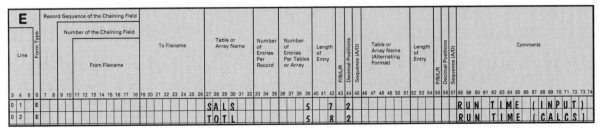

Figure 11-18   *Extension Specifications* syntax for the monthly sales performance report program.

Input Specifications **Syntax**

The syntax in Figure 11-19 shows how the data from a physical file record is loaded on input into the elements of a *Run Time* array.

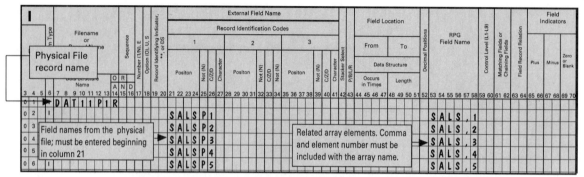

Figure 11-19 *Input Specifications* syntax for the sales performance report program.

Calculation Specifications **Syntax**

The **XFOOT** (*Summing the elements of an array*) operation, which is unique to numeric array processing, crossfoots (adds) the values in the elements of an array in one operation. Figure 11-20 explains the syntax of the **XFOOT** operation.

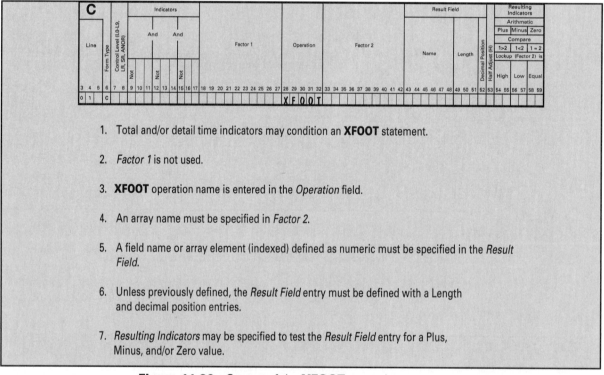

1. Total and/or detail time indicators may condition an **XFOOT** statement.

2. *Factor 1* is not used.

3. **XFOOT** operation name is entered in the *Operation* field.

4. An array name must be specified in *Factor 2*.

5. A field name or array element (indexed) defined as numeric must be specified in the *Result Field*.

6. Unless previously defined, the *Result Field* entry must be defined with a Length and decimal position entries.

7. *Resulting Indicators* may be specified to test the *Result Field* entry for a Plus, Minus, and/or Zero value.

Figure 11-20 Syntax of the **XFOOT** operation.

Use of the **XFOOT** operation and the results of processing are detailed in Figure 11-21. The **XFOOT** statement on line 010 adds (crossfoots) the five elements of the SALS array and stores the sum in the WEKTOT field. Also, the **ADD** statement on line 020 adds the five elements in the SALS array to the five elements in the TOTL array. The **XFOOT**

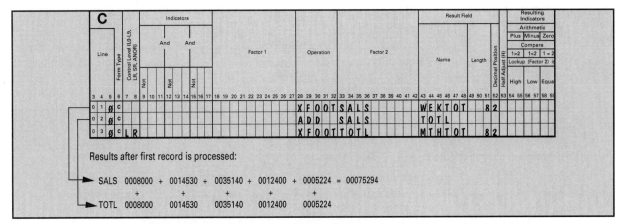

Figure 11-21 Calculations for the sales performance report program.

statement on line 030 adds (crossfoots) the TOTL array elements at **LR** time and stores the sum in the MTHTOT field.

Output Specifications Syntax

An examination of the compile listing in Figure 11-17 reveals that familiar syntax is used for the output coding. However, the method of editing numeric arrays requires some discussion. The following two considerations must be given to the editing of arrays:

1. Separation of elements for printing (or display)
2. Spacing and editing requirements for each element

Numeric array elements may be separated and edited by *Edit Words*, *Edit Codes*, or *Indexing*. The separation of alphanumeric arrays into individual elements is controlled only by *indexing*. However, because RPG/400 does not support the editing of alphanumeric fields, this function cannot be included for arrays defined in this class. Each of these separation and editing functions is discussed in the following paragraphs.

Editing of Numeric Arrays by Edit Words. The coding to edit the SALS array using an Edit Word and processing results are shown in the partial output form in Figure 11-22. If a review of the syntax for Edit Words is needed, refer to Chapter 4, pages 75-76.

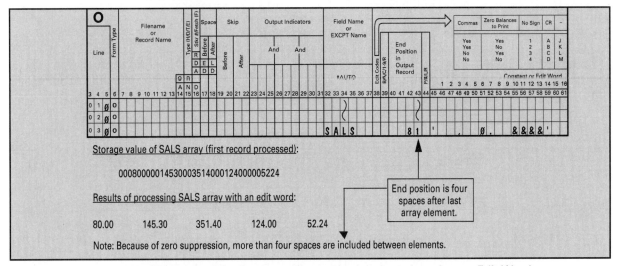

Figure 11-22 Output coding and printed results using an *Edit Word*.

Editing of Numeric Arrays by Edit Codes. Less flexibility in report designs is provided when Edit Codes are used because only two spaces are provided between edit elements. Figure 11-23 gives the results of using an *Edit Code* to separate and edit the elements of the SALS array. Any of the available *Edit Codes* may be used to edit a numeric array.

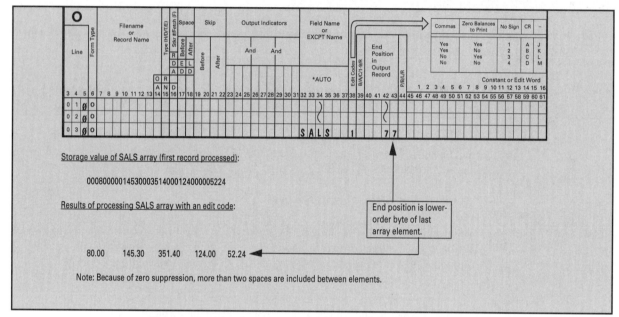

Storage value of SALS array (first record processed):

00080000014530003514000124000005224

Results of processing SALS array with an edit code:

End position is lower-order byte of last array element.

80.00   145.30   351.40   124.00   52.24

Note: Because of zero suppression, more than two spaces are included between elements.

Figure 11-23 Output coding and printed results using an *Edit Code*.

Editing of Numeric and Alphanumeric Arrays by Indexing. The most flexibility in array element separation and editing is provided by the use of *indexing*. As related to array processing, indexing is the method by which individual array elements are randomly accessed. An *index* may be a numeric literal or field and must be used with an array name and comma, as shown in Figure 11-24.

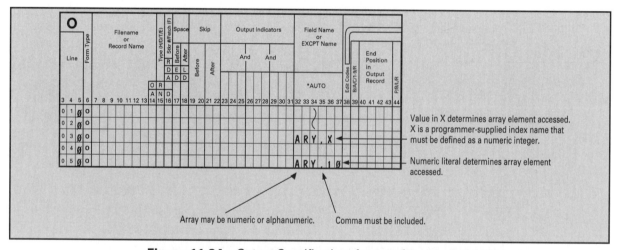

Value in X determines array element accessed. X is a programmer-supplied index name that must be defined as a numeric integer.

Numeric literal determines array element accessed.

Array may be numeric or alphanumeric.

Comma must be included.

Figure 11-24 *Output Specifications* formats for array indexing.

An examination of Figure 11-25 shows how indexing is used to separate the five SALS array elements so they may be individually edited and printed. With indexing, each array element is processed and controlled as a separate data-item.

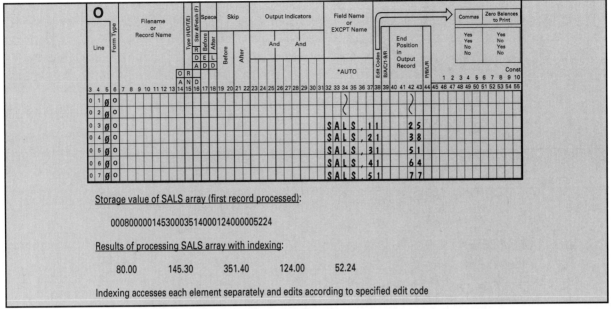

Storage value of SALS array (first record processed):

000800000145300035140001240000005224

Results of processing SALS array with indexing:

80.00   145.30   351.40   124.00   52.24

Indexing accesses each element separately and edits according to specified edit code

Figure 11-25 Output coding and printed results using indexing.

Loading Arrays from More Than One Input Record

The data for loading an array may not always be conveniently stored on one data record, as shown in the previous program example. Data may be scattered within or included on more than one record. For example, the input file in Figure 11-26 shows that the sales data for the five salespersons for each week is now stored in five separate records. Hence, the data for the entire month is stored on 25 records instead of 5, as in the file for the previous program. Also, notice that the record format has been modified to include a sales-

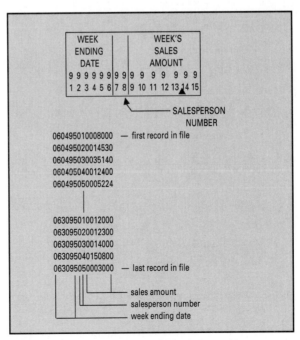

Figure 11-26 Modified record format and file listing of input array data stored on separate records.

person number field. This addition is needed to determine which record for a related week belongs to which salesperson. Furthermore, if the physical file was not in the required week ending date/salesperson number order, a logical file (or a sort) would have to be created to access the data in the sequence needed for the report. For this program, the data is stored in an externally defined keyed physical file with WEDATE (week ending date) the major key and SALPR# (salesperson number) the minor. A detailed compile listing of the modified program is presented in Figure 11-27.

```
SEQUENCE
NUMBER    *...1....+....2....+....3....+....4....+....5....+....6....+....7...*
                             S o u r c e   L i s t i n g
   100    *           SALESPERSON MONTHLY PERFORMANCE REPORT
   200    *           PROCESSING CONTROLLED BY 2 RUN TIME ARRAYS
   300    *      BOTH LOADED IN CALCULATIONS FROM SEPARATE INPUT RECORDS
          H
   400    FDAT11P2 IP  E           K       DISK
          RECORD FORMAT(S): LIBRARY SMYERS FILE DAT11P2.
                 EXTERNAL FORMAT DAT11P2R RPG NAME DAT11P2R
   500    FQSYSPRT O   F    132    OF      PRINTER
   600    E                 SALS       5 7 2          Run Time array
   700    E                 TOTL       5 8 2          Run Time array
   800    IDAT11P2R
   900    I                                   SALPR#L1
  1000    *
   900    INPUT  FIELDS FOR RECORD DAT11P2R FILE DAT11P2 FORMAT DAT11P2R.
A000001                               P   1   40WEDATE
A000002                               P   5   60SALPR#L1
A000003                               P   7  102WEKSAL
  1100    C               ADD  1      X        10      init. index
  1200    C               MOVE WEKSAL  SALS,X          load array
  1300    C          X    IFEQ 5                       array loaded?
  1400    C               XFOOTSALS    WEKTOT  82      week's total
  1500    C               ADD  SALS    TOTL            accum salp tot
  1600    C   L1          MOVE WEDATE  DATE    60      move to print
  1700    C               EXCPTDETAIL                  print line
  1800    C               Z-ADD0       X               init. index
  1900    C               ENDIF                        end if group
  2000    CLR             XFOOTTOTL    MTHTOT  82      mth total
  2100    OQSYSPRT H  101    1P
  2200    O        OR      OF
  2300    O                     UDATE Y   8
  2400    O                            40 'MONTHLY SALES'
  2500    O                            59 'PERFORMANCE REPORT'
  2600    O                            85 'PAGE'
  2700    O                     PAGE Z  90
  2800    O        H  3    1P
  2900    O        OR      OF
  3000    O                            51 'BY SALESPERSON'
  3100    O        H  1    1P
  3200    O        OR      OF
  3300    O                             6 'WEEK'
  3400    O                            39 'SALESPERSON   SALESPERSON'
  3500    O                            65 'SALESPERSON   SALESPERSON'
  3600    O                            89 'SALESPERSON      WEEKLY'
  3700    O        H  2    1P
  3800    O        OR      OF
  3900    O                             7 'ENDING'
  4000    O                            34 '#1          #2'
  4100    O                            60 '#3          #4'
  4200    O                            88 '#5         TOTAL'
  4300    O        E  2          DETAIL
  4400    O                     DATE Y   8
  4500    O                     SALS    81 '  ,   0.  &&&&'
  4600    O                     WEKTOT1 91
  4700    O        T  1    LR
```

> SALPR# specified as control field for execution of statement 1600

> Date from the first record of every salesperson group is moved to an output field

Figure 11-27 Compile listing of the modified sales performance report program.

```
4800  O                               7 'TOTALS'
4900  O                     TOTL     80 '  ,  0. &&&'
5000  O                     MTHTOT1  91
      * * * * *   E N D   O F   S O U R C E   * * * * *
```

Processing result of statement 1200 after first record is processed:

Value in index X: 1

Data record value: 060495010008000   SALS array element 1 loaded

0008000	0000000	0000000	0000000	0000000

Note: SALS array is built in storage according to attributes defined in the Extension form. Numeric array elements are automatically initialized to zeros by the RPG/400 compiler before first record is read.

Line #

400 -
500 The externally defined physical file is processed in composite key (WEDATE and SALPR#) order, and output is assigned to the system printer QSYSPRT.

600 -
700 SALS is defined as a *Run Time* array. Unlike the previous program, the array will be loaded in calculations (line 1200). The TOTL array is defined as a *Run Time* array and like the other program is loaded in calculations.

800 -
900 Because a field from the physical file is accessed on the *Input Specifications*, the physical file's record format name is entered on line 800. On line 900, the SALPR# field is specified as a control field by the **L1** control level indicator. **L1** is specified at *detail time* (columns 10–11) on line 1600 to save the WEDATE value in the DATE field for the first record processed in a WEDATE group. The DATE value is output on line 4400.

1100 **X**, which is used as the array index on line 1200, is defined and incremented by 1. For every record processed from the physical file, **X** will be incremented by 1.

1200 The value in WEKSAL is moved to the related array element as determined by the value in **X**. The WEKSAL value for the first record processed in a WEDATE group is moved to the first array element; the second record processed will move the WEKSAL value to the second array element; and so forth. This loading process will be repeated until the value in **X** is equal to 5. Then, the loaded array will be exception output and **X** is initialized to zero for the next WEDATE group.

1300 When the value in **X** is equal to 5, the statements in the **IFEQ** group will be executed.

1400 The **XFOOT** statement adds the five element values in the SALS array to the WEKTOT field.

1500 The value in the five elements of the SALS array are added to the five elements in the TOTL array.

1600 At **L1** *detail time*, which is executed when the first record in a WEDATE group is processed, the value in WEDATE is moved to the DATE field. If this statement was conditioned by the **L1** indicator at *total time*, the previous WEDATE value would be saved: not the value required.

1700 The DETAIL line is exception output, printing a line that includes the DATE, five SALS array element values, and the WEKTOT values. A new SALPR# value will cause an **L1** control break and generate another output line in the report.

1800 The **X** counter/index is initialized to zero before the next WEDATE group is processed.

Figure 11-27 Compile listing of the modified sales performance report program. (Continued)

1900   The **ENDIF** operation ends the **IFEQ** group that began on line 1300.

2000   The **XFOOT** statement, conditioned at **LR** *total time* (columns 7–8), adds the element values in the TOTL array and stores the sum in the MTHTOT field.

2100 -

4200   Heading output is controlled at **1P** time and will be repeated on every overflow page by the **OF** statements.

4300 -

4600   The **EXCPT** statement on line 1700 controls the printing of this exception output. The **EXCPT** statement on line 1700 is executed after the five elements in the SALS array are loaded from five records in the physical file.

4700 -

5000 - This output is executed at **LR** total time after the end of the physical file is read.

Figure 11-27   Compile listing of the modified sales performance report program. (Continued)

RANDOM PROCESSING OF ARRAYS

Similar to tables, the access to individual array elements may be controlled by the **LOKUP** operation. However, there are major differences between array and table lookup processing, which are summarized in Figure 11-28. Array lookup may be performed *with* or *without* an index. The processing logic and syntax of each method are discussed in the following paragraphs.

Array **LOKUP** Features

1. Element values may be accessed positionally without a LOKUP operation.

2. Any number of arrays may be related by a common index. Result field is not used in array **LOKUP** operations.

3. Arrays may be randomly processed by using an index. Value is extracted directy.

4. Relative location of an element may be determined by indexing.

5. Multidimensional array processing may be simulated.

6. Binary search of arrays may be programmer-coded.

7. An equal or range condition **LOKUP** may be specified.

8. Search argument (*Factor 1*) must be defined the same type as the argument array (*Factor 2*).

Table **LOKUP** Features

1. Table values may be accessed only by a **LOKUP** operation.

2. Two tables may be related by entering second table name in the *Result Field*. Access to other related tables requires additional **LOKUP** operations.

3. Only consecutive table **LOKUP** is supported. Execution of a **LOKUP** operation starts processing at first entry in the table.

4. Relative location of any table entry cannot be determined.

5. Only one-dimensional table processing may be performed.

6. Binary search is not available.

7. Same as arrays.

8. Same as arrays.

Figure 11-28   Comparison of array and table **LOKUP** processing.

ARRAY LOOKUP WITHOUT INDEXING

An array is processed without using an index when an element value does not have to be processed after it is found. Checking of a transaction code from an input record by a search of a *Compile Time* array of valid codes is one example of array lookup that does not require indexing. Figure 11-29 details the syntax and process logic of this type of array lookup.

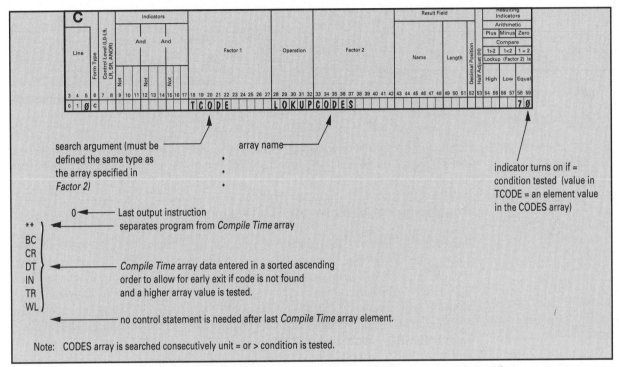

Figure 11-29 Syntax and processing logic of array **LOKUP** without indexing.

ARRAY LOOKUP BY INDEXING

Positional Processing without the LOKUP **Operation**

Indexing must be used in an array lookup if an element value is to be extracted and used in subsequent processing. Access of an element is controlled by indexing with or without the **LOKUP** operation (positional processing). An example of the processing of an array by the position of its elements (no **LOKUP** operation) is shown in Figure 11-30. A

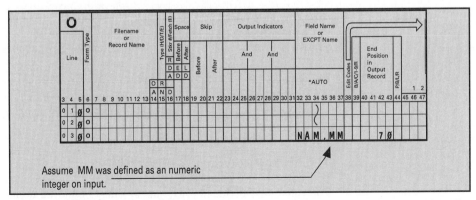

Figure 11-30 Syntax and processing logic to access an array element positionally.

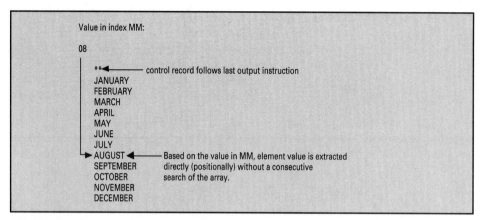

Figure 11-30   Syntax and processing logic to access an array element positionally. (Continued)

month name from the array is accessed for printing by specifying the array and index name. Assume for this example that the index name was previously defined as an input field.

Processing an Array by the LOKUP Operation

Processing an array by indexing with the **LOKUP** operation is often used to extract an element (when its position is not known) or to relate the values from two or more arrays. Remember, in table lookup, a *function table* name may be entered in the *Result Field*, and the value is automatically extracted in a successful *argument table* **LOKUP**. Array **LOKUP** does not support this processing feature (see Figure 11-28), and any relationship between arrays must be controlled by a common index. The processing logic unique to array **LOKUP** is summarized in Figure 11-31.

               Array **LOKUP** Operation with Indexing Features

1. Index must be defined as a numeric integer.

2. Index must be initialized before the **LOKUP** operation is executed.

3. Search of an array begins at the element specified as the value in the index.

4. Index is automatically incremented as the array is consecutively searched for an equal or range condition.

5. End-of-array control is automatically provided.

6. An array element found is not retained from **LOKUP**, but may be accessed by specifying the array and index name after the lookup condition is satisfied.

Figure 11-31   Array **LOKUP** operation with index processing features.

Illustrated in Figure 11-32 are the syntax and control for processing two related arrays by the **LOKUP** operation with indexing. Item numbers are stored in one *Compile Time* array, and the related item name is stored in a second *Compile Time* array in an alternating format.

The Move Array (MOVEA) Operation

The values of individual array elements may be moved to another array element or to a field, or from a field to an array element by the **MOVE** and **MOVEL** operations. However, if a select *group* of array element values has to be moved or loaded, neither of

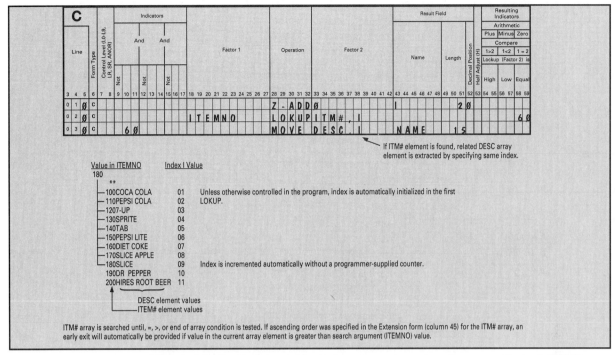

Figure 11-32 Syntax and logic for processing related arrays with the **LOKUP** operation and index control.

these previously discussed operations will provide the necessary control. The **MOVEA** operation, which may be used only if *Factor 2* and/or the *Result Field* is an array(s), is provided in RPG/400 for this processing. Figure 11-33 gives the rules, syntax, and examples of the **MOVEA** operation.

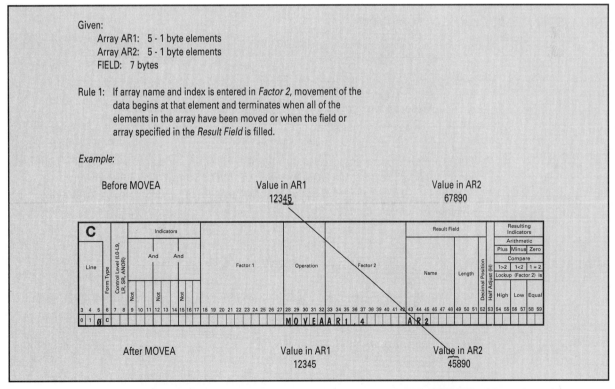

Figure 11-33 Rules, syntax, and examples of the **MOVEA** *(Move Array)* operation.

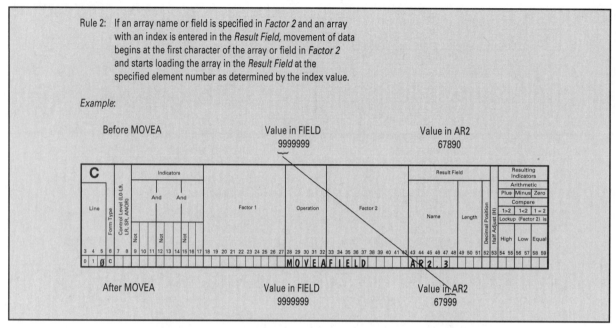

Figure 11-33 Rules, syntax, and examples of the **MOVEA** *(Move Array)* operation. (Continued)

Identical to the **MOVE** and **MOVEL** operations, the **MOVEA** operation does *not* provide a decimal alignment relationship between the sending (*Factor 2*) and receiving fields (*Result Field*). The data is moved from an array to a field (or array), or from a field to an array according to the rules specified in Figure 11-33.

ERRORS IN ARRAY EXECUTION TIME

Execution (run-time) errors that are common to array processing are the following:

1. Index value zero
2. Index value greater than number of elements in the array
3. Index value negative

Depending on the computer system, any of these array index errors is usually identified by an **ARRAY INDEX ERROR** or **ARRAY INDEX OUT OF RANGE** error message. The specific error (one of the three) may have to be determined by debugging. See Chapter 21 for debugging methods.

APPLICATION PROGRAM: CANNED SODA INVENTORY REPORT

Many of the array features discussed in the previous paragraphs, such as **LOKUP**, indexing, related array access, and positional processing, are included in this application program.

The specifications detailed in Figure 11-34 explain the processing requirements for this application program.

PROGRAM SPECIFICATIONS   Page 1 of 1

Program Name: Soda Inventory Report   Program - ID: CH11P3   Written by: SM

Purpose: Generate a canned soda inventory report   Approved by: CM

Input files: DAT11P3 _____   _____   _____   _____

Output files: QSYSPRT _____   _____   _____   _____

Processing Requirements:

Write an RPG/400 program to generate a canned soda inventory report

Input to the program:

A canned soda inventory physical file includes a field for soda numbers and the related quantity of cans on hand. A supplemental layout form details the record format.

Table Data:

Include the following three **Compile Time** array data in the program:

Item#	Description	Cost/Can (2 decimals)
100	COCA COLA	45
110	PEPSI COLA	47
120	7-UP	41
130	SPRITE	49
140	TAB	51
150	PEPSI LITE	50
160	DIET COKE	44
170	SLICE APPLE	48
180	SLICE	43
190	DR PEPPER	63
200	HIRES ROOT BEER	56

Also include an error message array with the following value:

.. ITEM NOT FOUND ..

Processing:

Use the ITEMNO field from the physical file's records as the search argument to "look up (with indexing) the item number array. For a successful search, use the same index value to access the related values from the description and cost per can arrays. Then, multiply the input quantity (QTY) by the cost per can array value to determine the dollar amount on hand.

If an item number from the input record is not found in the item number array, print the error message in the location shown on the printer spacing chart.

Output:

Generate the report detailed in the attached printer spacing chart.

Figure 11-34 Specifications for the Canned Soda Inventory Report program.

A system flowchart in Figure 11-35 indicates that one physical file is processed by the program to generate the Canned Soda Inventory Report.

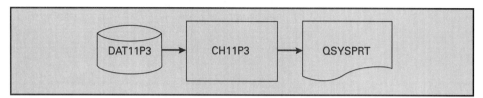

Figure 11-35   System flowchart for the Canned Soda Inventory Report program.

The format of the records in the physical file is presented in Figure 11-36 with a listing of the stored data.

```
                        PHYSICAL FILE DESCRIPTION

     SYSTEM: AS/400                        DATE: 5/19/95
     FILE NAME: DAT11P3                    REV NO: 0
     RECORD NAME: DAT11P3R                 KEY LENGTH: None
     SEQUENCE: Non-keyed                   RECORD SIZE: 6


                           FIELD DEFINITIONS

     FIELD     FIELD NAME    SIZE   TYPE     POSITION      COMMENTS
      NO                                    FROM    TO


       1       ITEMNO         3      C        1      3
       2       QTY            4      P        4      6

     Physical file data:


                       Item Number    Qty On Hand

                           150           2400
                           210           0000
                           100           2000
                           200           0600
                           155           0000
```

Figure 11-36   Record layout form and listing of the input file processed by the Canned Soda Inventory Report program.

The design of the Canned Soda Inventory Report is detailed in the printer spacing chart in Figure 11-37 with a listing of the report generated by the program.

```
        0         1         2         3         4         5         6
   1234567890123456789012345678901234567890123456789012345678901234567890
 1 ØX/XX/XX            CANNED SODA INVENTORY REPORT          PAGE XXØX
 2
 3
 4     ITM#      DESCRIPTION      COST/CAN    AMT ON HAND    DOLLAR AMT
 5
 6   XXX      X             X    XX         XXØX         X,XXØ.XX
 7
 8   XXX      ..ITEM NOT FOUND..
 9
10      NOTES:
11
12          1. HEADINGS ON TOP OF EVERY PAGE
13
14          2. REPORT DATE IS SYSTEM SUPPLIED
```

Figure 11-37   Design of the Canned Soda Inventory Report and generated report listing.

```
        6/09/95                 CANNED SODA INVENTORY REPORT              PAGE    1


          ITM#      DESCRIPTION      COST/CAN      AMT ON HAND      DOLLAR AMT

          150     PEPSI LITE          .50            2,400          1,200.00

          210     ..ITEM NOT FOUND..

          100     COCA COLA           .45            3,000          1,350.00

          200     HIRES ROOT BEER     .56              600            336.00

          155     ..ITEM NOT FOUND..
```

Figure 11-37   Design of the Canned Soda Inventory Report and generated report
listing. (Continued)

Figure 11-38 shows a compile listing of the Canned Soda Inventory Report program.
The *Extension* and *Calculation Specifications* syntaxes for the program are explained separately in the following text and figures.

```
SEQUENCE
NUMBER     *...1....+....2....+....3....+....4....+....5....+....6....+....7...*
                          S o u r c e   L i s t i n g
    100    *            CANNED SODA INVENTORY REPORT
    200    * THREE RELATED COMPILE TIME ARRAYS ARE INCLUDED FOR ITEM#, COST,
    300    * AND DESCRIPTION.  ONE ERROR MSG ARRAY IS SPECIFIED.
           H
    400    FDAT11P3 IP  E              DISK
           RECORD FORMAT(S): LIBRARY SMYERS FILE DAT11P3.
                     EXTERNAL FORMAT DAT11P3R RPG NAME DAT11P3R    ┌──────────────┐
    500    FQSYSPRT O   F    132    OF    PRINTER                   │ Four compile time│
    600    E                 ITM#  1  11  3   DESC  15─── item#/description
    700    E                 COST  11 11  2 2─────── cost per can
    800    E                 MSG   1   1 18 ──────── error msg
    900    *
A000000   INPUT  FIELDS FOR RECORD DAT11P3R FILE DAT11P3 FORMAT DAT11P3R.
A000001                                       1    3 ITEMNO
A000002                                    P  4   60QTY
   1000   C                 Z-ADD1         X      20       init. index
   1100   C       ITEMNO    LOKUPITM#,X               50find item#
   1200   C       *IN50     IFEQ *ON                     item# found?
   1300   C       QTY       MULT COST,X    AMT    72      total $ amount
   1400   C                 EXCPTDETAIL
   1500   C                 ELSE
   1600   C                 EXCPTERROR
   1700   C                 ENDIF
   1800   OQSYSPRT H  301    1P
   1900   O        OR        OF
   2000   O                  UDATE Y    8
   2100   O                             40 'CANNED SODA INVENTORY'
   2200   O                             47 'REPORT'
   2300   O                             60 'PAGE'
   2400   O                  PAGE  Z    65
   2500   O        H  2      1P
   2600   O        OR        OF
   2700   O                             22 'ITM#     DESCRIPTION'
   2800   O                             34 'COST/CAN'
   2900   O                             49 'AMT ON HAND'
   3000   O                             63 'DOLLAR AMT'
   3100   O        E  2      DETAIL
   3200   O                  ITEMNO   5
```

Figure 11-38   Compile listing of the Canned Soda Inventory Report program.

```
    3300   0                     DESC,X    24
    3400   0                     COST,X1   31
    3500   0                     QTY    2  45
    3600   0                     AMT    1  61
    3700   0         E  2        ERROR
    3800   0                     ITEMNO    5
    3900   0                     MSG       27
           * * * * *  E N D   O F   S O U R C E  * * * * *
               A d d i t i o n a l   D i a g n o s t i c   M e s s a g e s
    * 7086     400   RPG PROVIDES BLOCK OR UNBLOCK SUPPORT FOR FILE DAT11P3.
    5738RG1 V2R2M0  920925           IBM SAA RPG/400                  SMYERS/CH11P3
    SEQUENCE
    NUMBER    *...+....1....+....2....+....3....+....4....+....5....+....6....+....7....+
                       C o m p i l e - T i m e   T a b l e s
    Table/Array . . . . . . :  ITM#
    Table/Array . . . . . . :  DESC
        4100   100COCA COLA ─────┐
        4200   110PEPSI COLA     │
        4300   1207-UP           │
        4400   130SPRITE         │
        4500   140TAB            │     ┌──────────────────────────┐
        4600   150PEPSI LITE     ├─────┤ ITM# array and DESC array data│
        4700   160DIET COKE      │     │ stored in alternating format  │
        4800   170SLICE APPLE    │     └──────────────────────────┘
        4900   180SLICE          │
        5000   190DR PEPPER      │
        5100   200HIRES ROOT BEER┘
    Table/Array . . . . . . :  COST
        5300   4547414951504448436356
    Table/Array . . . . . . :  MSG
        5500   ..ITEM NOT FOUND..
```

Figure 11-38 Compile listing of the Canned Soda Inventory Report program. (Continued)

Extension Specifications Syntax

The *Extension Specifications* syntax and its relationship to the data in the four *Compile Time* arrays are illustrated in Figure 11-39. In a batch processing environment it is common programming practice to include program-controlled (not system-supplied) error

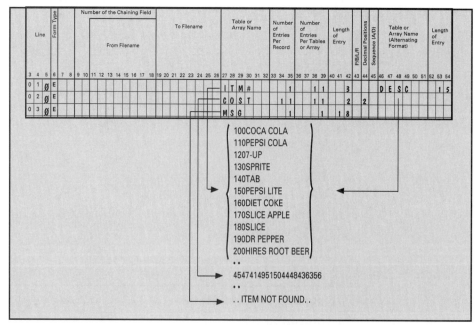

Figure 11-39 Extension coding for the Canned Soda Inventory Report program and its relationship to the data in the four *Compile Time* arrays.

messages in a *Compile Time* array. A one-element array defined as MSG is included in this program to flag an ITEMNO (search argument) value that is not found in the ITM# array. As shown in the compile listing in Figure 11-38, the MSG array element value is printed when an unsuccessful array lookup is determined (indicator **50** *not* set on by the **LOKUP** instruction on line 1100) and the **EXCPT** statement on line 1600 executed.

Calculation Specifications Syntax

An explanation of the calculation instructions in the Canned Soda Inventory Report program after a successful lookup of the ITM# array and the access of related array elements is detailed in Figure 11-40.

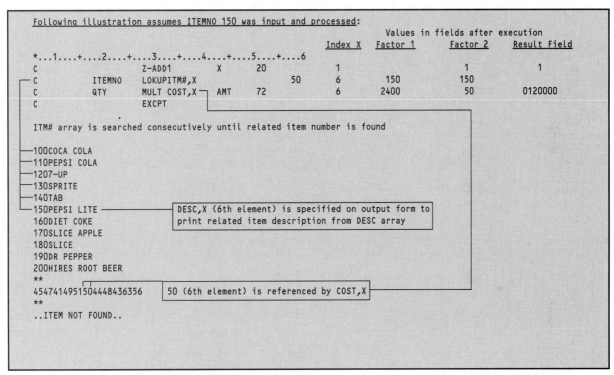

Figure 11-40 Calculation instructions and the result of array processing after a successful **LOKUP**.

MULTIDIMENSIONAL PROCESSING WITH MULTIPLE OCCURRENCE DATA STRUCTURES

OCUR (SET/GET Occurrence of a Data Structure)

It was emphasized at the beginning of this chapter that RPG/400 does not directly support multidimensional array processing. When needed, however, it may be simulated by a combination of *multiple occurrence data structures* and one or more **OCUR** operations. The *data structures* build the *occurrences* (relative positions) of the data in storage, and **OCUR** instructions access the values of select *occurrences*.

All the data for *multiple occurrence data structures* must be loaded into memory before an **OCUR** instruction is executed. The data for a *multiple occurrence data structure* may be stored externally in a physical file. Or, if a small number of records with fixed values are required, the data may be hard-coded in a program's calculations. For simplicity, the hard-coded method is used in the example program discussed later in this chapter.

Input Specifications Syntax for a Multiple Occurrence Data Structure

Figure 11-41 details the input coding required to define 2 *multiple occurrence data structures* that support 20 occurrences each. Also shown are the storage results from building the data structures.

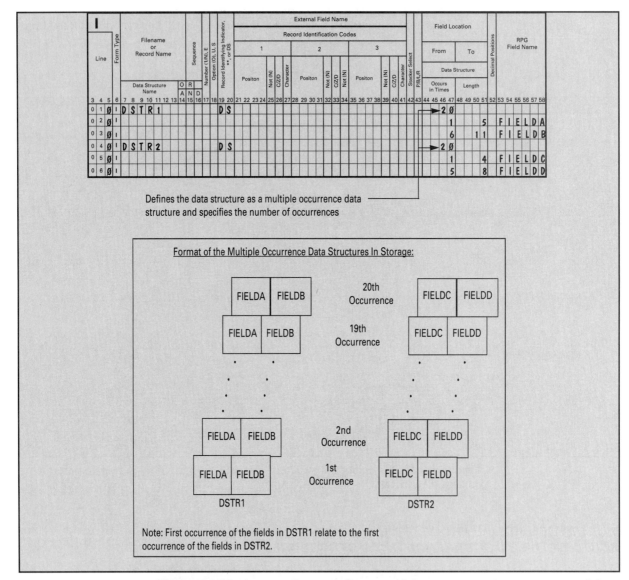

Figure 11-41   Input coding to define a multiple occurrence data structure and the memory results.

OCUR (SET/GET OCCURRENCE OF A DATA STRUCTURE) SYNTAX

The syntax related to the **OCUR** operation is explained in Figure 11-42.

Calculation instructions detailing some of the methods by which the *multiple occurrence data structures* previously defined in Figure 11-41 may be processed with **OCUR** operations are shown in Figure 11-43.

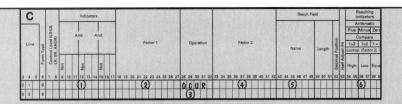

1 - *Total or Detail Time Indicators* may be used to condition an **OCUR** instruction.

2 - *Factor 1* is an optional entry. If specified, its value must be a numeric literal or field with zero decimal positions; or a data structure name. This entry is used to set (point to) the occurrence of the data structure specified in *Factor 2*.

3 - The **OCUR** operation must be left-justified in the *Operation* field.

4 - A *Factor 2* entry is required and must include the name of a multiple occurrence data structure.

5 - A *Result Field* entry is optional. When used, it must be a numeric field defined with zero decimal positions. This field will contain the value of the current occurrence of the data structure referenced in *Factor 2*. For example, if control points to the 15th occurrence, 15 will be stored in the *Result Field* entry.

6 - A *Resulting Indicator* may be specified in columns 56–57. The indicator is set on if the occurrence specified is outside of the range (number of occurrences defined on the input form) established by the data structure included in *Factor 2*.

Figure 11-42 Syntax rules for the **OCUR** operation.

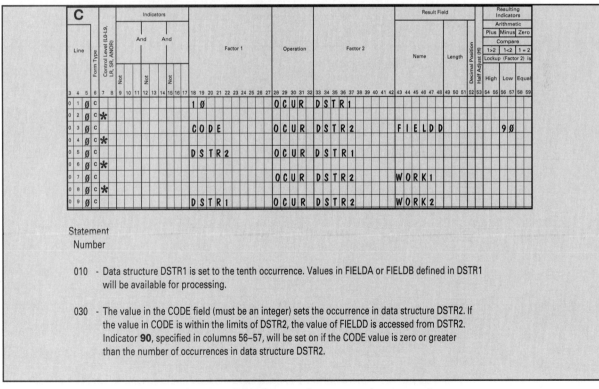

Statement
Number

010 - Data structure DSTR1 is set to the tenth occurrence. Values in FIELDA or FIELDB defined in DSTR1 will be available for processing.

030 - The value in the CODE field (must be an integer) sets the occurrence in data structure DSTR2. If the value in CODE is within the limits of DSTR2, the value of FIELDD is accessed from DSTR2. Indicator **90**, specified in columns 56–57, will be set on if the CODE value is zero or greater than the number of occurrences in data structure DSTR2.

Figure 11-43 **OCUR** operation processing examples.

050 - Data structure DSTR1 is set to the current occurrence of DSTR2. If DSTR2 had been previously set to the eighteenth occurrence, DSTR1 would also be set to the same occurrence.

070 - The current occurrence of DSTR2 is stored in WORK1. Any field specified in the *Result Field* of an**OCUR** instruction must be defined as an integer (zero decimal positions).

090 - Data structure DSTR2 is set to the current occurrence of DSTR1. If DSTR1 had been previously set to the twelfth occurrence, DSTR2 would also be set to the same occurrence. The numeric value of the DSTR2 occurrence is stored in WORK2.

Figure 11-43   OCUR operation processing examples. (Continued)

APPLICATION RPG/400 PROGRAM THAT PROCESSES A MULTIPLE OCCURRENCE DATA STRUCTURE

The specifications for an RPG/400 program that processes a *multiple occurrence data structure* to access the data in a two-dimensional format are detailed in Figure 11-44.

PROGRAM SPECIFICATIONS   Page 1 of 1

Program Name: Weekly Payroll Report   Program - ID: CH11-P4   Written by: SM

Purpose: Weekly payroll report of day/night employees   Approved by: CM

Input files: DAT11P4

Output files: QSYSPRT

Processing Requirements:

Write an RPG/400 program to print a weekly payroll report of day- and night-shift employees.

Input to the program:

The externally defined physical file, DAT11P4, contains the information shown in the attached record layout form.

Processing:

Define a multiple occurrence data structure in the program that includes three occurrences with the following values:

	Day	Night
Grade	Rate	Rate
1	2000	2300
2	1700	1950
3	1400	1600

Occurrence —┘   └   ┘ └── Values in multiple occurrence data structure (day and night rate fields)

Figure 11-44   Specifications for an RPG/400 program that processes a multiple occurrence data structure.

Hard-code the day and night rate data for multiple occurrence data structure in the program and load it into the three occurrences before any other processing functions are executed. Use the GRADE field (values of 1, 2, or 3) from each physical file record read to position the OCUR statement at the related occurrence in the data structure. After data structure is "set" to the related occurrence (by the value in the GRADE field), test SHIFT field (**D** or **N**) in the physical file's record to determine whether a day- or night-shift employee is being processed. Access the related field from the multiple occurrence data structure to extract the day- or night-shift employee's hourly rate.

Output:

A supplemental printer spacing chart details the report requirements.

Figure 11-44 Specifications for an RPG/400 program that processes a multiple occurrence data structure. (Continued)

The system flowchart in Figure 11-45 indicates that one physical file is processed to generate a report.

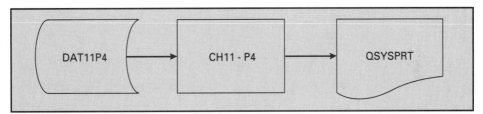

Figure 11-45 System flowchart for an RPG/400 program that processes a multiple occurrence data structure.

The record layout form in Figure 11-46 shows the field structure of the physical file. A listing of the data is also included in the figure.

```
                    PHYSICAL FILE DESCRIPTION

   SYSTEM: AS/400                          DATE: 5/20/95
   FILE NAME: DAT11P4                      REV NO: 0
   RECORD NAME: DAT11P4R                   KEY LENGTH: 9
   SEQUENCE: Keyed (Unique)                RECORD SIZE: 9

                      FIELD DEFINITIONS

   FIELD    FIELD NAME    SIZE  TYPE   POSITION    COMMENTS
   NO                                  FROM   TO


     1      SS#             9    P      1      5   Key field
     2      GRADE           1    P      6      6   0 decimals
     3      SHIFT           1    C      7      7
     4      HRS             3    P      8      9   0 decimals

   Physical file data:

                 SSNO      Grade    Shift    Hours

                 011111111   3        N       40
                 022222222   1        D       35
                 033333333   2        D       50
                 044444444   3        D       30
                 055555555   1        N       40
                 066666666   2        N       25
```

Figure 11-46 Record layout form and data listing of the physical file read by the program that processes a multiple occurrence data structure.

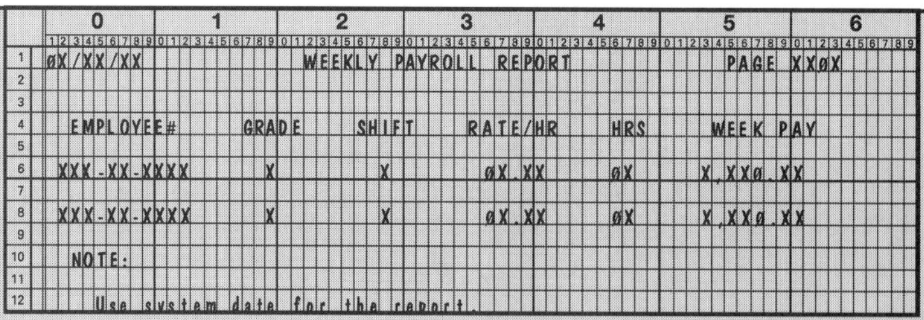


```
6/09/95              WEEKLY PAYROLL REPORT                PAGE    1

 EMPLOYEE#     GRADE    SHIFT    RATE/HR     HRS      WEEK PAY

011-11-1111      3        N        16.00      40        640.00

022-22-2222      1        D        20.00      35        700.00

033-33-3333      2        D        17.00      50        850.00

044-44-4444      3        D        14.00      30        420.00

055-55-5555      1        N        23.00      40        920.00

066-66-6666      2        N        19.50      25        487.50
```

Figure 11-47 Report design and listing generated by the multiple occurrence data structure program.

Figure 11-47 includes a printer spacing chart showing the design of the report and the output generated by the program.

A compile listing of the RPG/400 program that processes a *multiple occurrence data structure* is presented in Figure 11-48.

```
SEQUENCE
NUMBER   *...1....+....2....+....3....+....4....+....5....+....6....+....7...*
                   S o u r c e   L i s t i n g
    100   *                  WEEKLY PAYROLL REPORT
    200   *          WITH A MULTIPLE OCCURRENCE DATA STRUCTURE
    300   *
          H
    400  FDAT11P4 IP  E           K        DISK
          RECORD FORMAT(S):  LIBRARY SMYERS FILE DAT11P4.
                  EXTERNAL FORMAT DAT11P4R RPG NAME DAT11P4R
    500  FQSYSPRT O   F     132            PRINTER
A000000   INPUT  FIELDS FOR RECORD DAT11P4R FILE DAT11P4 FORMAT DAT11P4R.
A000001                                        P   1   50SS#
A000002                                        P   6   60GRADE
A000003                                            7   7 SHIFT
A000004                                        P   8   90HRS
    600  IRATES       DS                           3 ------- Defines a multiple occurrence
    700  I                                         1   42DAYRAT  data structure and the number
    800  I                                         5   82NITRAT  of occurrences
    900   *
   1000  C           *IN10     CASEQ*OFF     LOAD              10 off? branch
   1100  C                     ENDCS                           end CAS group
   1200  C           GRADE     OCUR RATES                      get shift data
   1300  C           SHIFT     IFEQ 'D'                        day shift?
   1400  C                     Z-ADDDAYRAT   RATE    42        access day rate
   1500  C                     ELSE                            not day shift
   1600  C                     Z-ADDNITRAT   RATE              access nit rate
   1700  C                     ENDIF                           end if group
   1800  C           HRS       MULT RATE     PAY     62        compute pay
```

Figure 11-48 Compile listing of the multiple occurrence data structure program.

```
1900    *
2000    C           LOAD      BEGSR                        begin sr
2100    C           1         OCUR RATES                   find 1st occurn
2200    C                     MOVE 20002300  RATES         load 1st occurn
2300    C           2         OCUR RATES                   find 2nd occurn
2400    C                     MOVE 17001950  RATES         load 2nd occurn
2500    C           3         OCUR RATES                   find 3rd occurn
2600    C                     MOVE 14001600  RATES         load 3rd occurn
2700    C                     MOVE *ON       *IN10         set on 10
2800    C                     ENDSR                        end load sr
2900    OQSYSPRT H  201       1P
3000    O                            UDATE Y   8
3100    O                                     42 'WEEKLY PAYROLL REPORT'
3200    O                                     58 'PAGE'
3300    O                            PAGE  Z  63
3400    O           H 2       1P
3500    O                                     11 'EMPLOYEE '
3600    O                                     30 'GRADE    SHIFT'
3700    O                                     48 'RATE/HR    HRS'
3800    O                                     61 'WEEK PAY
3900    O           D 2       N1P
4000    O                            SS#      12 '0  -  -  '
4100    O                            GRADE    19
4200    O                            SHIFT    28
4300    O                            RATE  1  40
4400    O                            HRS   2  47
4500    O                            PAY   1  60
        * * * * *   E N D   O F   S O U R C E   * * * * *

        Processing results for first record processed — GRADE value 3 and
        SHIFT value N:

        Data stored in the multiple occurrence data structure RATES

                DAYRAT    NITRAT

                2000      2300
                1700      1950
```
└─3rd occurrence────────1400────────1600────────Night Shift Rate─┘

Line #

400 -
500   Externally defined physical file DAT11P4 is processed in key order, and output is assigned to the system printer QSYSPRT.

600 -
800   RATES is defined in the *Input Specifications* as a multiple occurrence data structure by the letters **DS** in columns 19–20 and the three right-justified in the *From Field* (indicating the number of occurrences). Two fields, DAYRAT and NITRAT, are defined in the data structure. The fields will be loaded with hard-coded data in the LOAD subroutine that begins on line 2000.

1000 -
1100   The **CASEQ** statement tests the status of indicator **10**. If it is "off," control will branch to the LOAD subroutine. The **MOVE** statement on ine 2700 sets on the **10** indicator so that the subroutine will only be executed for the first record processed. The **ENDCS** operation on line 1100 ends the **CASEQ** statement.

1200   This **OCUR** statement accesses an occurrence of the data structure determined by the value in the GRADE field. The program example indicates that GRADE has a value of **3** which accesses the third occurrence of the data structure. A GRADE value of **1** would access the first occurrence and **2**, the second occurrence.

1300 -
1700   The value in the SHIFT field is tested for **D** with the **IFEQ** statement. If the relational test is true, the **Z-ADD** statement on line 1400 moves the value in the multiple occurrence data structure's DAYRAT field to RATE.

        When the **IFEQ** statement on line 1300 test is false, the **Z-ADD** statement on line 1600 moves the data structure's NITRAT field value to RATE. The **ENDIF** operation on line 1700 ends the IFEQ group.

Figure 11-48   Compile listing of the multiple occurrence data structure program. (Continued)

1800	The input field HRS is multiplied by RATE (loaded with a DAYRAT or NITRAT value) and stores the product in PAY.
2000	Begins the LOAD subroutine which includes the statements that load the hard-coded data into the occurrences of the multiple occurrence data structure RATES. The subroutine was accessed by the **CASEQ** statement on line 1000.
2100 - 2200	The **1** specified in *Factor 1* for this **OCUR** statement accesses the <u>first</u> occurrence of the multiple occurrence data structure RATES. The **MOVE** statement on line 2200 moves the hard-coded data into the <u>first</u> occurrence.
2300 - 2400	The **2** specified in *Factor 1* for this **OCUR** statement accesses the <u>second</u> occurrence of the multiple occurrence data structure RATES. The **MOVE** statement on line 2400 moves the hard-coded data into the <u>second</u> occurrence.
2500 - 2600	The **3** specified in *Factor 1* for this **OCUR** statement accesses the <u>third</u> occurrence of the multiple occurrence data structure RATES. The **MOVE** statement on line 2600 moves the hard-coded data into the <u>third</u> occurrence. After statements 2100 through 2600 are completed, the three occurrences of the multiple occurrence data structure RATES are loaded with data.
2700	The **MOVE** statement sets on indicator **10,** which prevents the LOAD subroutine from being executed again by the **CASEQ** statement on line 1000.
2800	The **ENDSR** operation ends the LOAD subroutine.
2900 - 3800	Heading lines are conditioned by the **1P** indicator with no overflow control specified.
3900 - 4500	Detail line output, conditioned by the **N1P** indicator (executed when **1P** is off), is executed for every physical file record processed. Included with the SS#, GRADE, SHIFT, and HRS values input from a record, the RATE value, extracted from the multiple occurrence data structure, and the computed PAY value are also printed.

Figure 11-48   Compile listing of the multiple occurrence data structure program. (Continued)

ARRAY SORTING

The data in the elements of an array may be sorted by the following methods:

Prerun and Run Time (loaded on input) arrays

1. External from the program by a **logical file** or **sort utility**
2. Internal in the program by the **SORTA** operation

Compile and Run Time (loaded in calculations) arrays

1. Internal in the program by the **SORTA** operation

Only the *internal* sorting of arrays with the **SORTA** operation is discussed in this chapter. For the procedures and syntax related to *external* sorting, refer to Chapter 20.

The SORTA **Operation**

During program execution, arrays may be sorted in either an ascending or descending order by the **SORTA** operation. Figure 11-49 details the *Extension* and *Calculation Specifications* coding for the **SORTA** operation.

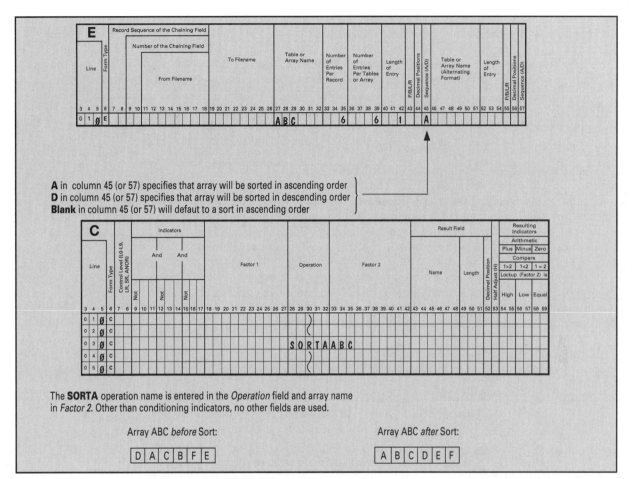

A in column 45 (or 57) specifies that array will be sorted in ascending order
D in column 45 (or 57) specifies that array will be sorted in descending order
Blank in column 45 (or 57) will defaut to a sort in ascending order

The **SORTA** operation name is entered in the *Operation* field and array name in *Factor 2*. Other than conditioning indicators, no other fields are used.

Array ABC *before* Sort:

| D | A | C | B | F | E |

Array ABC *after* Sort:

| A | B | C | D | E | F |

Figure 11-49 Extension and calculation syntax for the **SORTA** operation.

The SCAN (Scan Character String) Operation

The **SCAN** operation scans the character (base string) specified in *Factor 2* for the characters stored in *Factor 1*. When the **SCAN** condition is satisfied, the <u>location</u> of the *Factor 1* item value in the character string in *Factor 2* is stored in the *Result Field*. If an array name (defined with one-byte elements in a size equal to or greater than the *Factor 2* string) is entered in the *Result Field*, every incidence of the *Factor 1* value in the *Factor 2* string will be stored in the array elements. Figure 11-50 explains the syntax of the **SCAN** operation.

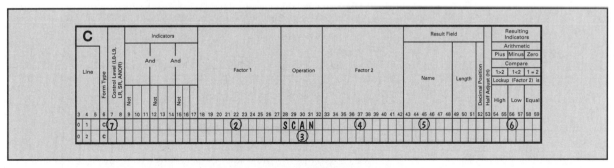

Figure 11-50 Syntax of the **SCAN** operation.

1. *Total* or *detail time* indicators may condition a SCAN statement.

2. *Factor 1* must contain a character string (not numeric) defined as a field name, array element, named constant, data structure name, literal, or table name. The *Factor 1* item may be specified with or without a low-order colon (:). When the item is specified without the colon, the full value stored in the *Factor 1* entry is compared to the *Factor 2* character string. If the colon is included at the end of the *Factor 1* entry, followed by an item defined as a numeric integer, the compare will begin at the first character in the *Factor 1* item and compare only the number of characters specified. Thus, if the *Factor 1* entry is 10 characters in length, and a 5 is specified after the colon, only the first 5 characters will be used to scan the *Factor 2* item.

3. The **SCAN** operation must be left-justified in the *Operation* field.

4. *Factor 2* must contain a base string entry or a base string entry followed by a colon (:) and the start location for the **SCAN**. The base string entry must be defined as character and may be a field name, array element, named constant, data structure name, literal, or table name. If no start location is specified, the **SCAN** begins at the <u>first</u> character in the base string. When a colon follows the entry and an item defined as a numeric integer, the start location begins at that value.

5. The *Result Field* may contain a field name, array element, array name, or table name defined as a numeric integer. If a *Result Field* is not specified, a *Resulting Indicator* in positions 58–59 must be included. When the *Result Field* contains an array, the location of each occurrence is stored in the array beginning with the leftmost occurrence in element 1 of the array. The array should be defined with one-byte elements in a size equal to the base string.

6. A *Resulting Indicator* may be included in columns 58–59 and may be set on if the string scanned for is found in the base string. An indicator may also be specified in columns 56–57 and will be set on if an error occurs during execution of the **SCAN** operation.

Figure 11-50 Syntax of the **SCAN** operation. (Continued)

Coding examples of the **SCAN** operation are detailed in Figure 11-51.

```
*...1....+....2....+....3....+....4....+....5....+....6....+....7...*
CLON01N02N03Factor1+++OpcdeFactor2+++ResultLenDHHiLoEqComments++++++
*
* The SCAN operation searches the base string in Factor 2 (beginning
* with the first character for the value in Factor 1.  XYZ is found
* in the Factor 2 string beginning in position 3.  The integer 3 will
* be stored in HOLD.  Because the scan is successful, indicator 70 is
* set on.
C           'XYZ'       SCAN 'ABXYZCD' HOLD              70
*
*
* The SCAN operation searches the string stored in Factor 2 (FIELD1)
* starting in position 1 for the value stored in Factor 1 (FIELD2).
* Because the Result Field of the SCAN instruction is an array, 2 and
* 3, the positions of G in the Factor 2 entry, are stored in the first
* and second elements of the array (ARRAY).  Indicator 70 will be set
* on if the scan is successful.
C                       MOVE 'EGGS'    FIELD1
C                       MOVE 'G'       FIELD2
C           FIELD2      SCAN FIELD1    ARRAY            70
*
*
* The SCAN operation searches the string in Factor 2, starting in posi-
* tion 2, for an occurrence of the string in Factor 1 for a length of
* 3 characters.  Because the scan is not successful, HOLD is set to
* zero and indicator 70 is turned off.
C                       MOVE 'ANYTHING'FIELD1
C                       MOVE 'NYG'     FIELD2
C           FIELD2:3    SCAN FIELD2:2  HOLD             70
```

Figure 11-51 Coding examples of the **SCAN** operation.

The SUBST (Substring) Operation

The **SUBST** operation extracts characters included in the substring in *Factor 2*, starting at the location specified in *Factor 2*, and moves the specified number of characters to the *Result Field* based on the value in the *Factor 1* entry. Figure 11-52 explains the syntax of the **SUBST** operation.

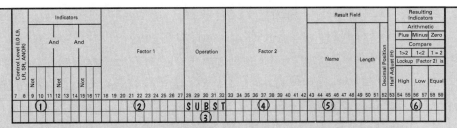

1. *Total* or *detail time* indicators may condition a **SUBST** statement.

2. *Factor 1* must include the length of the string to be extracted from the string specified in *Factor 2*. The entry may be a literal, field name, named constant, array element, or table name defined as a numeric integer.

3. The **SUBST** operation name must be entered in the *Operation* field.

4. *Factor 2* must include a base character string with or without a following colon (:) and a starting location. The base string *must be defined as character and may contain a literal*, field name, table name, named constant, data structure name, or an array element.

   When specified, the entry following the colon must be defined as a numeric integer and have a value greater than zero and not greater than the length of the base string. The start location may be a literal, field name, named constant, array element, or table name. If the starting location is omitted, execution of a **SUBST** instruction begins in position 1 of the *Factor 2* base string.

5. The *Result Field* must be defined as character and may contain a field name, table name, array element, or data structure. The substring passed from the *Factor 2* entry is left-justified in the *Result Field* item. Its length should be no less than that specified in *Factor 1*. If the substring passed is longer than the *Result Field* entry, low-order characters in the string will be truncated.

   If the *Factor 1* entry is shorter than the *Result Field* item, a **P** entered in the operation extender position (column 53) will pad the low-order positions in the *Result Field* entry with blanks.

6. An indicator may be entered in columns 56–57 which will set on if an error occurs when the **SUBST** statement is executed. An error may occur if the start position is greater than the length of the *Factor 2* entry, or if the *Factor 1* entry is larger than the *Result Field* item.

<u>Processing Logic:</u>

The **SUBST** operation moves the string value entered in *Factor 2* to the *Result Field* item. If a colon and numeric integer item are not included after the string entry, movement begins at the first character in the *Factor 2* string. If a colon and a numeric integer item are included, movement begins at that position in the *Factor 2* string. The number of characters moved from the *Factor 2* string to the *Result Field* item is controlled by the *Factor 1* entry.

A **P** in column 53 of a **SUBST** statement will pad any low-order positions in the *Result Field* when the characters moved from the *Factor 2* string are less than the size of the *Result Field* entry.

Figure 11-52 Syntax of the **SUBST** operation.

Coding examples of the **SUBST** operation are shown in Figure 11-53.

```
*...1....+....2....+....3....+....4....+....5....+....6....+....7...*
CLON01N02N03Factor1+++OpcdeFactor2+++ResultLenDHHiLoEqComments++++++
*
* The SUBST operation extracts the substring from Factor 2 beginning at
* position 3.  The 5 in Factor 1 indicates that five characters from
* the Factor 2 string (BASE) will be moved into LAST. Because the
* move is successful, indicator 70 will not be set on.  LAST will cont-
* ain MOUSE after the SUBST is executed.
C                      MOVEL'M MOUSE' BASE     7
C           5          SUBSTBASE:3    LAST      5      70
```

Figure 11-53 Coding examples of the **SUBST** operation.

```
*
*
* The SUBST operation extracts the substring from Factor 2 (YY) begin-
* ning at default position 1.  The 2 in Factor 1 indicates that two
* characters starting in position 1 of YY will be moved left-justified
* into YYMMDD.  The Result Field YYMMDD will have value of 200930 after
* the SUBST statement is executed.  Because the operation is successful,
* indicator 70 will not be set on.  Example assumes DATE value is 093099
C                    MOVE '20'      YY      2
C                    MOVELDATE      MMDD    4
C                    MOVE MMDD      YYMMDD  6
C          2         SUBSTYY        YYMMDD      70
*
*
* The SUBST operation moves the value in the YY substring to the high-
* order two positions in YYMMDD.  The P entry in column 53 stores blanks
* in the four low-order positions.  YYMMDD will have a value of 20bbbb
* (b = blank) after the SUBST statement is executed.
C                    MOVE '20'      YY      2
C          2         SUBSTYY        YYMMDD  6 P 70
```

Figure 11-53 Coding examples of the **SUBST** operation. (Continued)

Application Program Using the SCAN and SUBST Operations

An RPG/400 application program that extracts the state code from a city/state field from the records in a physical file is detailed in Figure 11-54. The example assumes that the state code is one space after the city name in all of the data records. Note that the **SCAN** operation (line 700) locates the space after the city name and stores its position in X. Then, after incrementing the index by 1 (line 900), the **SUBST** operation (line 1000) extracts the two-byte state code from the CITST field and stores it in STATE.

```
SEQUENCE
NUMBER   *...1....+....2....+....3....+....4....+....5....+....6....+....7...*
                         S o u r c e   L i s t i n g
   100   *      THIS PROGRAM GENERATES A CUSTOMER LISTING AND EXTRACTS
   200   *      THE STATE CODE FROM THE CITST FIELD WITH THE SCAN AND
   300   *                     SUBST OPERATIONS
   400   *
         H
   500   FDAT11P5 IP  E                  DISK
         RECORD FORMAT(S): LIBRARY SMYERS FILE DAT11P5.
                   EXTERNAL FORMAT DAT11P5R RPG NAME DAT11P5R
   600   FQSYSPRT O   F     132    OF    PRINTER
A000000  INPUT  FIELDS FOR RECORD DAT11P5R FILE DAT11P5 FORMAT DAT11P5R.
A000001                                    1    4 CUST#
A000002                                    5   24 NAME
A000003                                   25   44 STREET
A000004                                   45   59 CITST
A000005                                 P 60   62 ZIP
   700   C           ' '       SCAN CITST:5  X     20    60 blank search
   800   C           *IN60     IFEQ *ON                    blank found?
   900   C                     ADD  1        X             incrmnt index
  1000   C           2         SUBSTCITST:X  STATE  2       move to field
  1100   C           STATE     IFNE *BLANKS                 blank value?
  1200   C                     EXCPTGOOD                    not blank outp
  1300   C                     ELSE                         blank value
  1400   C                     EXCPTBAD                     blank output
  1500   C                     ENDIF                        end 1100 IF
  1600   C                     ENDIF                        end 800 IF
  1700   OQSYSPRT H  301    1P
  1800   O         OR         OF
  1900   O                    UDATE Y   26
```

Figure 11-54 Compile listing of an example program that uses the **SCAN** and **SUBST** operations to extract a state code from a city/state field.

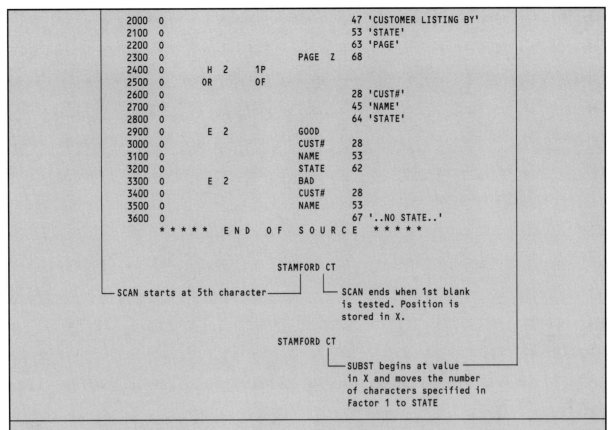

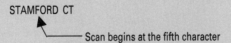

Line #

500 -
600 The physical file, DAT11P5, is defined as an externally defined keyed file. Output is assigned to the system printer QSYSPRT.

700 The blank specified in *Factor 1* is used as the value to **SCAN** the CITST field for an equal condition. The 5 included after the colon in the *Factor 2* entry indicates that the **SCAN** will begin at the fifth position in the CITST field as shown below:

STAMFORD CT

— Scan begins at the fifth character

To provide for CITST values such as NEW YORK NY or NEW HAVEN CT, which include an extra embedded blank, the **SCAN** statement is coded to begin in position 5 for this example. Otherwise, the first blank found would not extract the state code from the value.

Indicator **60** in the *Resulting Indicator* equal field (columns 58–59) will be set on if execution of the **SCAN** statement is successful.

800 -
1000 This **IFEQ** statement tests the status of indicator **60**. If it is "on" (**SCAN** successful), the statements in this **IFEQ** group will be executed.

The **ADD** statement on line 900 increments the index X by 1 to provide for the blank after the city value in the CITST field and extract the two-letter state code.

The **SUBST** statement on line 1000 extracts the two-letter state code value from the CITST field beginning at the character position specified in X and stores it in STATE. The literal 2 in *Factor 1* specifies that two characters are to be moved from the CITST field to STATE. This example assumes that the data in the CITST field is correctly entered with one space after the city value.

Figure 11-54 Compile listing of an example program that uses the **SCAN** and **SUBST** operations to extract a state code from a city/state field. (Continued)

1100 -
1500   This **IFNE** statement test the status of the STATE field, loaded by the **SUBST** statement on line 1000. If it is not equal to blanks, indicating that a state code was found in the CITST field, the **EXCPT** statement on line 1200 is executed, which passes control to exception line 2900.

If the **IFNE** test on line 1100 is false, the **EXCPT** statement on line 1400 is executed, which passes control to exception line 3300, where an error message is included. The **ENDIF** operation on line 1500 ends the **IFNE** group that began on ine 1100.

1600   This **ENDIF** operation ends the **IFEQ** group that began on line 800.

1700 -
2800   Heading output is controlled at **1P** and **OF** times.

2900 -
3200   This exception output is performed when the **EXCPT** statement on line 1200 is executed.

3300 -
3600   This exception output is performed when the **EXCPT** statement on line 1400 is executed.

Figure 11-54   Compile listing of an example program that uses the **SCAN** and **SUBST** operations to extract a state code from a city/state field. (Continued)

The report generated by the example **SCAN/SUBST** program is shown in Figure 11-55.

```
6/09/95   CUSTOMER LISTING BY STATE        PAGE    1

    CUST#             NAME             STATE
    1110      HARRY FORD                CT
    1120      BETTY STRIESAND           NY
    1130      WILLIAM MATHIS            PA
    1140      GEORGE SINATRA            KY
    1150      MICHAEL CAMPBELL          CA
    1160      JOSEPH JACKSON          ..NO STATE..
```

Figure 11-55   Report generated by example **SCAN/SUBST** program.

SUMMARY

Arrays may be defined as *Compile, Prerun,* and *Run Time* in an RPG/400 program. As with tables, an array element may be accessed by a **LOKUP** operation. However, a related array cannot be specified in the *Result Field.* If related arrays are to be processed together, an *index* from a previous **LOKUP** must be used to extract an element value from the other array(s). Array values may be accessed *positionally* or randomly by *indexing.*

Arrays are defined in an RPG/400 program in the *Extension Specifications.* If the *Entries Per Record* entry is omitted, the array is defined as a *Run Time* array loaded on input or in calculations. When the entry is specified, the array is defined as *Compile* or *Prerun Time.*

Individual elements of a numeric array may be edited by *Edit Codes, Edit Words,* or *indexing.* Alphanumeric array elements may be edited (separated) only by *indexing.* RPG/400 does not directly support multidimensional array processing; however, it may be simulated with one or more *multiple occurrence data structures* with one or more **OCUR** statements.

After an array is loaded with data, it may be *sorted* in ascending or descending order in the RPG/400 program by the **SORTA** operation.

The **SCAN** operation locates the position of a value in *Factor 1* in the string specified in *Factor 2* and stores the related position in the *Result Field* item. If an array is included in the *Result Field,* all occurrences of the *Factor 1* value in the *Factor 2* string will be stored in the array elements.

The **SUBST** operation extracts the number of characters from the *Factor 2* string based on the value in the *Factor 1* item. When a colon and numeric integer immediately follow the *Factor 2* string, the characters are extracted beginning with that position.

QUESTIONS

11-1. What is an array in the RPG/400 programming environment?

11-2. Describe the logical structure of a one-dimensional array and, then, of a two-dimensional array. How many dimensions does RPG/400 support for arrays?

11-3. What factors should be considered in deciding whether to use arrays or tables in a program?

11-4. Compare the processing features of arrays to those of tables.

11-5. On which RPG/400 coding form are arrays defined? Where are these instructions placed in an RPG/400 program?

11-6. When may arrays be loaded in the program cycle?

11-7. Refer to Question 11-6, and explain where the array data is stored and the loading process for each method.

11-8. Refer to Question 11-6, and explain under what conditions each loading method should be used.

11-9. Reference a blank *Extension Specifications.* Identify and explain the function of the fields used to define an array. Indicate the fields used (and not used) with each loading method.

11-10. Do array names have to begin with special letters? What should be considered when specifying the length of an array name?

11-11. What is the function of the ** control statement in the format of array data? With which array type is it used?

11-12. By what methods may the elements of a numeric array be separated and edited for printed output? How may the elements of an alphanumeric array be separated for output?

11-13. How may an array be processed?

11-14. What is the function of the **XFOOT** operation? May it be used to control all the arithmetic functions?

Examine the following calculation instruction and answer Questions 11-15 and 11-16:

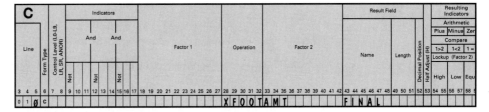

11-15. The *Factor 2* entry must be: (a) a field name; (b) an array name; (c) either a field or an array name.

11-16. The *Result Field* entry must be: (a) a field name; (b) an array name; (c) either a field or an array name.

11-17. What arithmetic operations may be used with numeric arrays? Are all the elements accessed in one instruction, or does each element have to be individually processed?

11-18. As related to array processing, what is an index? How must an index be defined? Where may an index be defined?

11-19. Name and explain the common (execution time) processing errors associated with the processing of arrays by indexes.

11-20. Explain the meaning of the following field name entry on the output form: NAME,X.

11-21. What is the function of the **LOKUP** operation for arrays? How does it differ from table **LOKUP** processing?

11-22. Define positional array processing. Does this type of array access require a **LOKUP** operation?

11-23. When an array is processed with the **LOKUP** operation, how is the index incremented?

11-24. If three arrays, MTH, NAM, and DAYS, are related for processing and X is specified as the index, how many **LOKUP** instructions are needed for control? If MTH is the argument array, how are the related values from NAM and DAYS accessed?

11-25. How does **MOVEA** operation processing differ from the **MOVE** and **MOVEL** operations?

11-26. Refer to the following **MOVEA** instructions and determine the value in the *Result Field* item after the move is executed. Array or field sizes are indicated by values in *Factor 2* and *Result Field*.

Entries		Values in		
	Result	Factor 1	Result Field	Result Field
Factor 2	*Field*	*before MOVEA*	*before MOVEA*	*after MOVEA*
ARY1	ARY2	123456	789000	_____
FIELD	LAST, 6	DONALD	DUCK, bbbbbb	_____
STAT, 3	NAM, 7	CTNYNJ	DEVONbbb	_____
AMT	FIELD	010000	9999999	_____
AMT,3	FIELD	001400	88	_____

Note: Items defined as a field (not an array) are specified as FIELD.

11-27. What is the function of a *multiple occurrence data structure?* What coding is necessary to define this data type of data structure?

11-28. What RPG/400 operation is required to process a *multiple occurrence data structure?*

11-29. Refer to data given below and complete the coding needed to define it as a *multiple occurrence data structure*. Use **D** and **S** as the required field names.

MODEL	D	S
1	1200	1000
2	1350	1175
3	1600	1450
4	1200	1790

11-30. Refer to Question 11-29 and complete the coding needed to hard-code and process the *multiple occurrence data structure* data.

11-31. What is the function of the **SCAN** operation?

Refer to the statement shown below and answer Questions 11-32 through 11-34.

11-32. What is the function of the *Factor 1* entry? Other than a character literal, what other entries may be specified?

11-33. What is the function of the *Factor 2* entry? In this example, where will the search begin? How may the search be modified to begin at some other character than the first?

11-34. What is stored in the *Result Field* entry? If the entry was an array, what would be stored in the element(s)?

Examine the statement shown below and answer Questions 11-35 through 11-38 for the statement on line 020.

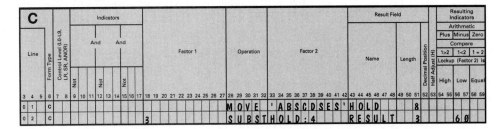

11-35. What is the function of the *Factor 1* entry? Other than a numeric literal, what other entries may be specified?

11-36. What is the function of the *Factor 2* entry? In this example, where will access begin? If the colon and integer were omitted, at which position will the **SUBST** operation begin?

11-37. What is stored in the *Result Field* entry?

11-38. When will the indicator specified in columns 56–57 turn on?

PROGRAMMING ASSIGNMENTS

For each of the following programming assignments, a physical file must have been created and loaded with the related data records. Your instructor will inform you as to whether you have to create the physical file and load it or if it has been prepared for the assignment.

Programming Assignment 11-1: FACTORY OVERHEAD BUDGET

Write an RPG/400 program using arrays to generate the report shown in the printer spacing chart.

Physical File Record Format: (Define the fields QTR1 through QTR4 as the four elements of a Run Time array.)

```
                    PHYSICAL FILE DESCRIPTION

        SYSTEM: AS/400                      DATE: Yours
        FILE NAME: Yours                    REV NO: 0
        RECORD NAME: Yours                  KEY LENGTH: None
        SEQUENCE: Non-keyed                 RECORD SIZE: 40

                      FIELD DEFINITIONS

        FIELD     FIELD NAME   SIZE   TYPE    POSITION        COMMENTS
        NO                                   FROM     TO


          1       ACTNAM        24     C       1       24
          2       QTR1           6     P      25       28     0 decimals
          3       QTR2           6     P      29       32     0 decimals
          4       QTR3           6     P      33       36     0 decimals
          5       QTR4           6     P      37       40     0 decimals
```

```
Physical file data:

                    1st Quarter   2nd Quarter   3rd Quarter   4th Quarter
      Account Name    Sales         Sales         Sales         Sales

  INDIRECT LABOR      250000        190000        201910        186750
  FACTORY SUPPLIES    086000        070000        103480        093100
  HEAT, LIGHT, POWER  067440        079000        080500        071330
  SUPERVISION         150000        150000        165000        167000
  MAINTENANCE         090000        087000        089000        077900
  TAXES AND INSURANCE 110000        110000        110000        110000
  DEPRECIATION        125000        125000        125000        125000
```

Calculations: For every record processed, each expense account's quarterly amounts are to be crossfooted to calculate the sum for the year. In addition, the quarterly amounts are added to calculate the sum for each quarter. At end of file, the quarter totals are to be crossfooted for the year's total.

Report Design:

Programming Assignment 11-2:   INCOME STATEMENT BY QUARTERS

Write an RPG/400 program to generate the income statement shown in the printer spacing chart.

Define <u>one</u> four-element *Run Time* array that will be loaded in the *Input Specifications* with the four quarterly amounts for each input record processed. Also define <u>seven</u> other four-element *Run Time* arrays—one each for Sales, Cost of Goods Sold, Gross Profit, Operating Expenses, Net Income, Decimal Percentage of Net Income to Sales, and Percentage of Net Income to Sales—that will be loaded in calculations.

Physical File Record Format:

```
                    PHYSICAL FILE DESCRIPTION

    SYSTEM: AS/400                         DATE: Yours
    FILE NAME: Yours                       REV NO: 0
    RECORD NAME: Yours                     KEY LENGTH: None
    SEQUENCE: Non-keyed                    RECORD SIZE: 19

                         FIELD DEFINITIONS

    FIELD     FIELD NAME    SIZE   TYPE     POSITION        COMMENTS
     NO                                    FROM     TO

      1        ACTCOD        1      C        1        1    S, C, E
      2        YEAR          2      P        2        3
      3        QR1AMT        6      P        4        7    0 decimals
      4        QR2AMT        6      P        8       11    0 decimals
      5        QR3AMT        6      P       12       15    0 decimals
      6        QR4AMT        6      P       16       19    0 decimals
```

```
Physical file data:

  ID
  Code   Year    1Q        2Q        3Q        4Q

   S      95    200000    175000    210000    309000
   C      95    100000    092000    120000    209000
   E      95    070000    052000    089000    105000
```

The *Run Time* array loaded on input and the Sales, Cost of Sales, Gross Profit, Operating Expenses, and Net Income arrays must be defined with four six-byte elements with no decimal positions.

The Decimal Percentage of Net Income to Sales array must be defined with four five-byte elements with five decimal positions. The Percentage of Net Income to Sales array must be defined with four four-byte elements with two decimal positions.

Processing: For each record read from the physical file, the *Run Time* array will automatically be loaded. In calculations, test the ACTCOD field and load the related array. For the "S" record, load the Sales array; for the "C" record, load the Cost of Sales array; and for the "E" record, load the Operating Expenses array.

*A*fter the three records from the physical file are read and the three arrays loaded, complete the following steps at **LR** time:

1. Subtract the Cost of Sales array from the Sales array, and store the differences in the Gross Profit array.

2. Subtract the Operating Expenses array from the Gross Profit array, and store the differences in the Net Income array.

3. Divide the Net Income array by the Sales array, and store the quotients in the Decimal Percentage of Net Income to Sales array.

4. Multiply the Decimal Percentage of Net Income to Sales array by 100, and store the products in the Percentage of Net Income to Sales array.

5. Crossfoot the Sales, Cost of Sales, Gross Profit, Operating Expenses, and Net Income arrays to compute the totals for the four quarters.

6. The Percentage of Net Income <u>total</u> cannot be calculated by crossfooting. The value must be determined by dividing the total for the Net Income array by the total for the Sales array.

7. Print the entire report at LR time.

Report Design:

```
                                        DAGWOOD COMPANY
                                        INCOME STATEMENT
                                     FOR YEAR ENDING 12/31/XX

                           1Q           2Q           3Q           4Q          TOTAL

SALES                $ XXX,XX0   $ XXX,XX0   $ XXX,XX0   $ XXX,XX0   $ X,XXX,XX0
LESS COST OF SALES     XXX,XX0     XXX,XX0     XXX,XX0     XXX,XX0     X,XXX,XX0
   GROSS PROFIT      $ XXX,XX0   $ XXX,XX0   $ XXX,XX0   $ XXX,XX0   $ X,XXX,XX0
LESS OPERATING EXPENSE XXX,XX0     XXX,XX0     XXX,XX0     XXX,XX0     X,XXX,XX0
   NET INCOME (LOSS--) $ XXX,XX0 $ XXX,XX0   $ XXX,XX0   $ XXX,XX0   $ X,XXX,XX0

PCT OF NET INCOME TO SALES  X0.XX       X0.XX       X0.XX       X0.XX       X0.XX

   NOTES:

      1. PERCENT DECIMAL COMPUTED IN CALCULATIONS IS MULTIPLIED BY 100
         FOR PRINTING.

      2. DOLLAR SIGNS ARE ALL FIXED.
```

Programming Assignment 11-3:   CUSTOMER LISTING IN LAST NAME ORDER

Write an RPG/400 program to generate the report shown in the attached printer spacing chart.

Physical File Record Format:

```
                    PHYSICAL FILE DESCRIPTION

      SYSTEM: AS/400                        DATE: Yours
      FILE NAME: Yours                      REV NO: 0
      RECORD NAME: Yours                    KEY LENGTH: None
      SEQUENCE: Non-keyed                   RECORD SIZE: 63


                       FIELD DEFINITIONS

      FIELD    FIELD NAME   SIZE   TYPE    POSITION      COMMENTS
       NO                                 FROM    TO


        1      NAME          20     C       1      20
        2      STREET        25     C      21      45
        3      CITYST        15     C      46      60
        4      ZIP            5     P      61      63
```

Physical file data:

Name	Street	City/State	Zip
ALEXANDER HAMILTON	10 RESERVE STREET	NEW YORK, NY	07701
THOMAS JEFFERSON	30 SKYLINE DRIVE	MONTICELLO, VA	05555
JOHN JAY	44 CONSTITUTION PLACE	RYE, NY	07744
GEORGE WASHINGTON	1 APPLE TREE LANE	MT VERNON, VA	04444
FRANKLIN ROOSEVELT	1 FDR BOULEVARD	HYDE PARK, NY	06000
ANN KENSINGTON	1 DISNEY STREET	ORLANDO, FL	09000

Processing: Read the physical file in arrival sequence, and for each record processed, extract the customer's <u>last</u> name from the NAME field and the state code from the CITYST field. Store the last name left-justified into an array element and the state code right-justified. Define the array with 15 byte elements and specify 7 elements.

At end of file, sort the array in ascending order. Extract the last name and state code values from the sorted array, and exception-output the values for each array element. A **DO, DOU,** or **DOW** group will have to be included in the program to access and print the array's elements.

Elements that have a blank value are not to be printed.

Report Design:

```
        0         1         2         3         4         5
   1234567890123456789012345678901234567890123456789012345678 9
 1 HH:MM:SS   CUSTOMER LISTING IN LAST NAME ORDER    PAGE XX0X
 2                    AS OF 0X/XX/XX
 3
 4
 5            CUSTOMER NAME                    STATE
 6
 7       X-              X              XX
 8
 9       X-              X              XX
10
11
12     NUMBER OF CUSTOMERS: X,X0X
13
14 NOTES:
15
16    1. USE SYSTEM DATE.
17
18    2. HEADINGS ON TOP OF EVERY PAGE.
```

Programming Assignment 11-4:   SHIPPING CHARGE REPORT (Multiple Occurrence Data Structure)

Write an RPG/400 program to generate the report shown in the supplemental printer spacing chart.

Physical File Record Format:

```
          PHYSICAL FILE DESCRIPTION

SYSTEM: AS/400                      DATE: Yours
FILE NAME: Yours                    REV NO: 0
RECORD NAME: Yours                  KEY LENGTH: 4
SEQUENCE: Keyed                     RECORD SIZE: 33


              FIELD DEFINITIONS

FIELD   FIELD NAME   SIZE  TYPE   POSITION      COMMENTS
  NO                                FROM   TO


   1      NAME        20    C       1     20
   2      INVNO        4    C      21     24    Key field
   3      INVAMT       6    P      25     28    2 decimals
   4      PDS          2    P      29     30    0 decimals
   5      OZS          2    P      31     32    2 decimals
   6      DELDAY       1    P      33     33    0 decimals
```

Physical file data:

Customer Name	Invoice Number	Invoice Amount	Shipping Weight PDS	OZS	1 or 2 Day Delivery
HENRY JACKSON	1234	002400	05	08	1
DOROTHY PARTNER	1235	010000	10	00	2
ROBERT WARFIELD	1236	004500	09	09	1
MARIO LANZA	1237	120000	20	00	1
ENZIO PINZA	1238	245000	20	12	2
NELSON EDDY	1239	001000	01	00	2

Processing: Load the following as hard-coded data into a *multiple occurrence data structure:*

Weight in Lbs.	1-day Rate	2-day Rate
01	129	161
02	137	171
03	146	183
04	154	192
05	163	204
06	171	213
07	180	225
08	188	235
09	197	246
10	205	257

2 decimal positions

Use the invoice shipping pounds to access the related *multiple occurrence data structure's* field entries. Increase any shipping weights over a pound to the next higher pound. Test the delivery field in each physical file record for 1 or 2. An entry of **1** indicates one-day delivery and a **2**, two- or more day delivery. Extract the 1- or 2-day delivery rate from the related *multiple occurrence data structure's* field.

Any package weighing over 10 pounds is charged the 1- or 2-day delivery amount for 10 pounds plus an additional 6 cents for each pound over 10.

A maximum shipping weight limit of 20 pounds is imposed by the parcel delivery firm. Any packages over 20 pounds cannot be shipped. Identify this on the report by the message OVER WEIGHT in the position shown on the printer spacing chart.

For any invoice amounts under $25, the shipping charge is added to the invoice amount. Print asterisks in place of the shipping charge.

Report Design:

	0	1	2	3	4	5	6	7	8
1	ØX/XX/XX		FOB DESTINATION SHIPMENT REPORT					PAGE XXØX	
3			INVOICE			WEIGHT	1 OR 2	SHIPPING	
4	CUSTOMER NAME		NUMBER	INVOICE AMOUNT		PDS OZS	DAY	CHARGE	
6	X	X	XXXX	X,XXØ.XX		ØX ØX	X	XXØ.XX	
8	X	X	XXXX	X,XXØ.XX		ØX ØX	X	OVER WEIGHT	
10	X	X	XXXX	X,XXØ.XX		ØX ØX	X	******	
12	NOTES:								
14	1. USE SYSTEM DATE.								
16	2. HEADINGS ON TOP OF EVERY PAGE.								
18	3. CONSTANT OVER WEIGHT IS PRINTED FOR PACKAGES OVER 2Ø PDS.								
20	4. ASTERISKS ARE PRINTED FOR INVOICE AMTS UNDER $25.								

Programming Assignment 11-5:   MAILING LABELS

A mail-order company needs a program written to generate mailing labels for the shipment of goods to their customers. The labels are gummed and mounted on standard size ($14\frac{1}{2}$ inch x 11 inch) continuous forms paper in the format shown in the printer spacing chart ahead.

Processing: Define four-element arrays for the following input fields:

1.   CUSTOMER NAME
2.   STREET
3.   APARTMENT NUMBER (or other second address information)
4.   CITY/STATE/ZIP (all items in one array)

After an input record is read, move the field values into their related arrays. A counter must be incremented for use as an index to load the input record values into their individual array elements. When the counter is equal to 4 (four elements in each array loaded), output a detail line of labels and initialize the counter back to 0 before the next group of four customer records is processed. Because the counter may not always be equal to 4 when the end of file is sensed, the printing of the last line of labels must be separately controlled.

Notice in the following record layout form that there are two address fields. ADDRS2 is for supplemental information such as apartment number, office number, blank value, and the like. If the input value for this field is blank, the CITY/STATE/ZIP line will be printed on the third line so that a blank line will not be included after the ADDRS1 value. If the ADDRS2 field is not blank, all four lines are to be printed for the label.

Physical File Record Format:

```
                    PHYSICAL FILE DESCRIPTION

SYSTEM: AS/400                        DATE: Yours
FILE NAME: Yours                      REV NO: 0
RECORD NAME: Yours                    KEY LENGTH: None
SEQUENCE: Non-keyed                   RECORD SIZE: 78
```

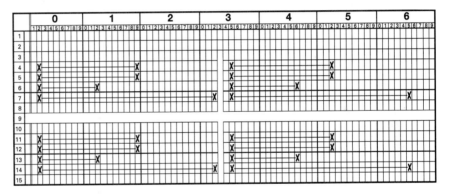

```
                        FIELD DEFINITIONS

          FIELD    FIELD NAME   SIZE  TYPE    POSITION      COMMENTS
          NO                                  FROM    TO

          1        NAME          18    C        1      18
          2        ADDRS1        18    C       19      36
          3        ADDRS2        11    C       37      47
          4        CTSTZP        31    C       48      78
```

Physical File Data:

```
     Name              Address 1      Address 2    City/State/Zip

   KAREL APPEL       20 AMSTERDAM AVE   APT 35    NEW YORK, NY  074500000
   GEORGES BRAQUE    300 ST CLAIR ST              NEW JERSEY, NJ  055011234
   PAUL CEZANNE      44 RUE PIGALLE     BLDG 10   STAMFORD, CT  065180010
   MARC CHAGALL      222 QUAIL AVENUE             BRIDGEPORT, CT  066661000
   EDGAR DEGAS       10 ROSE TERRACE              WESTPORT, PA  077770000
   MAX ERNST         1 FRANKFURT DRIVE  LOT 14    FRANKFORT, KY  055510111
   BUCKMINSTER FULLER 999 PARK AVENUE   APT 201   NEW YORK, NY  075500000
   JULIO GONZALEZ    101 SMITH LANE               GREENWICH, CT  064440000
   HECTOR HYPPOLITE  888 PEACHTREE AVE            ATLANTA, GA  033322200
   PIERRE JEANERET   90 CHATEAU DRIVE             GENEVA, NY  077774000
   WASSILY KANDINSKY 13 WARSAW LANE               LOS ANGELES, CA  099900000
   CHARLES CORBUSIER 10 PARIS PLACE               ENGLEWOOD CLIFFS, NJ  076320000
   PABLO PICASSO     1784 BASTILLE BLD            FRANCE, KY  088800000
```

Format of the Labels:

Note: Four labels are printed per line (one label per customer).

chapter 12

Data Validation (Batch Mode)

One of the most important functions associated with the data processing environment is ensuring the accuracy of the data. Regardless of how well structured or efficient application programs are, if the input data is not accurate, the end results will usually be unacceptable. Once "bad" data is loaded in a file, it is often difficult to correct. For example, if invalid data was included in a daily transaction file used to update a master file, it would ultimately filter throughout the system, thus making subsequent corrections difficult.

DATA VALIDATION METHODS

The procedures for maintaining the accuracy of data are referred to as *data validation*. Whether the data entry environment is batch or interactive will determine how data is validated on input. Validation functions may be implemented by one or a combination of the procedures described in the following paragraphs.

Batch Procedures External to a Data Entry Program

Data is entered from source documents directly onto such storage media as diskettes, disks, or magnetic tape by a related hardware unit. Most of these recording machines also support a separate verification function. Verification in this environment requires that an operator reference the source documents and duplicate the keying process. In this mode, the machine does not record data but compares what is already stored with what is currently being keyed. The machine locks to indicate any differences found. Then, the value is checked to determine whether the original data or the currently keyed value is incorrect.

Batch Procedures Internal to a Data Entry Program

Data is entered from source documents directly onto the storage medium by the related hardware device. The file created and loaded is then processed by an RPG/400 entry program to validate the data. Controls are included in the program to load records with errors to an error *rejection* or *abeyance* file. An *error rejection* file stores the record information for identification only, whereas the records loaded to an *error abeyance* file may be subsequently corrected by an update program or system utility.

Interactive Procedures Internal to a Data Entry Program

Data is entered via a workstation controlled by an RPG/400 program. Some validation procedures may be supported by the screen generator software, whereas others are in the program. Popular software utilities are available, such as **SDA** and **SEU**, that provide for the design, syntax, and control of interactive screens. The standalone screens are interfaced with an RPG/400 program with syntax and procedures unique to the computer system. See Chapters 15 and 16 for interactive processing methods.

Often, not every data entry error can be identified by the procedures just discussed. Additional validation may be provided by batch total checks, edit listings, and feedback from users.

Internal Data Validation in a Batch Environment

The following procedures are commonly included in an RPG/400 data validation program in a batch processing environment:

1. Data type testing
   a. Numeric or alphabetic
   b. Arithmetic signs or zeros
2. Data field checking
   a. Presence or absence of data
   b. Justification of data
   c. Acceptability of data
   d. Relationship to other data
   e. Structure of the data

Each of these validation processes is separately explained and supported by standalone programs, and is then integrated into a single comprehensive data validation program.

DATA TYPE TESTING

Input data may be tested for numeric or alphabetic class but not for alphanumeric class because all characters supported by a computer may be considered alphanumeric. Numeric testing and alphabetic testing are individually discussed in the following paragraphs.

Numeric Field Testing

In the AS/400 environment when **DFU** or a *display file* record format is used to enter data into a field defined as numeric, only the digits **(0–9)** may be entered. Any attempt to enter a character other than **0** through **9** will cause an entry error. Consequently, in that scenario numeric validation is performed when the data is entered. However, data may be input from files loaded by another computer system which may include invalid numeric data and require numeric validation to prevent run-time halts or aborts. Refer to Figure 12-1 for examples of valid and invalid numeric data.

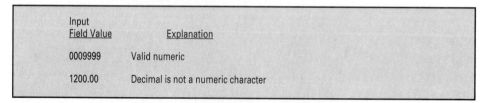

Figure 12-1 Examples of valid and invalid numeric values.

A345000	Letter is not a numeric character
123	Blank is not a numeric character
002400J	Valid numeric (low order letter represents -1)

Note: Field is defined as 7 bytes with 2 implied decimals.

Figure 12-1 Examples of valid and invalid numeric values. (Continued)

TESTN **Operation**

In a batch processing environment, numeric field validation may be controlled in an RPG/400 program by the **TESTN** operation. Figure 12-2 explains the syntax of this operation. Notice that the field specified in the *Result Field* must be defined as alphanumeric. If the value passes the numeric test (**TESTN**), then it may be moved to a numeric field. If the field tested is defined on input, it may be specified as alphanumeric with one name and then redefined as numeric with another.

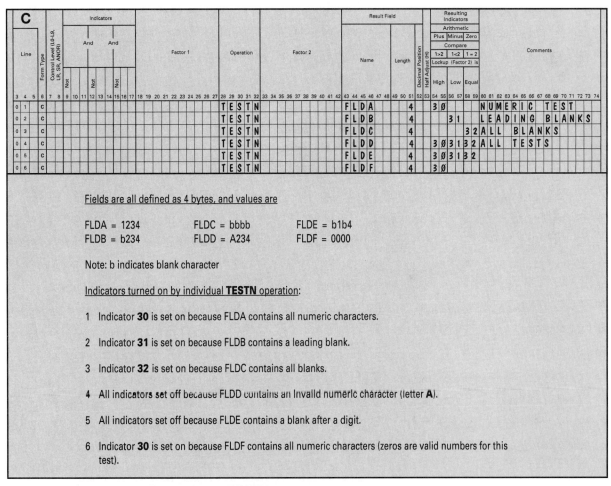

Fields are all defined as 4 bytes, and values are

FLDA = 1234   FLDC = bbbb   FLDE = b1b4
FLDB = b234   FLDD = A234   FLDF = 0000

Note: b indicates blank character

Indicators turned on by individual **TESTN** operation:

1   Indicator **30** is set on because FLDA contains all numeric characters.

2   Indicator **31** is set on because FLDB contains a leading blank.

3   Indicator **32** is set on because FLDC contains all blanks.

4   All indicators set off because FLDD contains an invalid numeric character (letter **A**).

5   All indicators set off because FLDE contains a blank after a digit.

6   Indicator **30** is set on because FLDF contains all numeric characters (zeros are valid numbers for this test).

Figure 12-2 **TESTN** operation syntax.

The example program in Figure 12-3 shows how the **TESTN** operation is used as a data validation function. Notice that all three tests (numeric, leading blanks, and all blanks) are included in the program. An application, however, may require that only one or two of the tests be specified.

A copy of the data file processed by the example numeric validation program and related report are presented in Figure 12-4.

```
SEQUENCE                                                                        IND   DO
NUMBER      *...1....+....2....+....3....+....4....+....5....+....6....+....7...* USE   NUM
                          S o u r c e   L i s t i n g
    100     *  EXAMPLE NUMERIC VALIDATION PROGRAM
    200     *
            H
    300     FC12DATP1IP E                    DISK
            RECORD FORMAT(S): LIBRARY SMYERS FILE C12DATP1.
                      EXTERNAL FORMAT C12DAT1R RPG NAME C12DAT1R
    400     FQSYSPRT O  F     132    OF    PRINTER
    500     E                  MSG    1   3 22               error msgs
 A000000    INPUT  FIELDS FOR RECORD C12DAT1R FILE C12DATP1 FORMAT C12DAT1R.
 A000001                                      1    8 ALPQTY
    600     C                  TESTN      ALPQTY    101112numeric test   1 2 3
    700     C                  SELEC                                           B001
    800     C        *IN10     WHEQ *OFF                  not numeric          X001
    900     C        *IN11     ANDEQ*OFF                                       001
   1000     C        *IN12     ANDEQ*OFF                                       001
   1100     C                  MOVE 1     X        10     not numeric          001
   1200     C                  EXCPTERROR                                      001
   1300     C        *IN11     WHEQ *ON                   leading blanks       X001
   1400     C                  MOVE 2     X                                    001
   1500     C                  EXCPTERROR                                      001
   1600     C        *IN12     WHEQ *ON                   all blanks           X001
   1700     C                  MOVE 3     X                                    001
   1800     C                  EXCPTERROR                                      001
   1900     C                  OTHER                      value numeric        X001
   2000     C                  MOVE ALPQTY   NUMQTY 82    move to num fld      001
   2100     C                  EXCPTGOOD                                       001
   2200     C                  ENDSL                                          E001
   2300     OQSYSPRT H  301    1P
   2400     O       OR         OF
   2500     O                                   45 'NUMERIC VALIDATION'
   2600     O        E  2             ERROR
   2700     O                         ALPQTY    30
   2800     O                         MSG,X     55
   2900     O        E  2             GOOD
   3000     O                         NUMQTY    30
         * * * * *  E N D   O F   S O U R C E  * * * * *
          A d d i t i o n a l   D i a g n o s t i c   M e s s a g e s
    7086      300   RPG PROVIDES BLOCK OR UNBLOCK SUPPORT FOR FILE C12DATP1.
   5738RG1 V2R2M0  920925          IBM SAA RPG/400               SMYERS/C12RPG1
SEQUENCE
NUMBER      *...+....1....+....2....+....3....+....4....+....5....+....6....+....7....+....8
               C o m p i l e - T i m e   T a b l e s
Table/Array . . . . . . :  MSG
   3300  QTY NOT NUMERIC
   3400  QTY HAS LEADING BLANKS
   3500  QTY IS BLANK
```

Figure 12-3 Example numeric data validation program.

```
Data File Listing          Printed Report

                         NUMERIC VALIDATION

   01450000          01450000

   j1234500          j1234500   QTY NOT NUMERIC

    100000            100000    QTY HAS LEADING BLANKS

   00099.99          00099.99   QTY NOT NUMERIC

   12500000          12500000

                               QTY IS BLANK
```

Figure 12-4 Data file listing and report for the numeric validation program.

Alphabetic Value Testing

Valid alphabetic characters include the character blank and the letters A through Z. Few field values are purely alphabetic. For example, names of individuals, places, and things often include nonalphabetic characters (e.g., the apostrophe in O'Brien). The two-letter state code abbreviations (e.g., NY, CT, PA) are, however, one example of a field value that should always test as alphabetic.

Examples of valid and invalid alphabetic values are presented in Figure 12-5.

```
          Input
        Field Value        Explanation

            CT          Valid alphabetic value

            Y           Blank is valid alphabetic value

            12          Digits are not alphabetic

           `M.          Special characters are not alphabetic

        Note: Field is defined as a two byte alphanumeric
```

Figure 12-5   Examples of valid and invalid alphabetic values.

The RPG/400 language does not provide a method for defining alphabetic values; fields are specified as either numeric or alphanumeric. Also, because a separate operation is not available for the testing of alphabetic values, other controls must be used. One method for testing alphabetic values in an RPG/400 program is by array processing, which is detailed in the program example in Figure 12-6. A listing of the data file and printed output generated by the program are shown in Figure 12-7.

```
SEQUENCE                                                                      IND   DO
NUMBER    *...1....+....2....+....3....+....4....+....5....+....6....+....7...* USE   NUM
                          S o u r c e   L i s t i n g
   100    *  EXAMPLE ALPHABETIC VALIDATION PROGRAM
   200    *
          H
   300    FC12PFP2 IP  E                    DISK
              RECORD FORMAT(S): LIBRARY SMYERS FILE C12PFP2.
                      EXTERNAL FORMAT C12PFP2R RPG NAME C12PFP2R
   400    FQSYSPRT O  F     132    OF      PRINTER
   500    E                 NAM     20  1              name array
   600    E                 CHAR    27  27  1          alpha chars array
   700    E                 MSG      1   1 20          error msg array
A000000    INPUT  FIELDS FOR RECORD C12PFP2R FILE C12PFP2 FORMAT C12PFP2R.
A000001                                     1  20 NAME
   800    C               MOVEANAME    NAM             field to array
   900    C               DO  20       X        20                         B001
  1000    C      NAM,X    LOKUPCHAR             60look up array      3     001
  1100    C      *IN60    IFEQ *OFF             char not found?            B002
  1200    C               EXCPTERROR            print error                002
  1300    C               LEAVE                 exit DO group              002
  1400    C               ENDIF                 end IF group         E002
  1500    C               ENDDO                 end DO group         E001
  1600    C      *IN60    IFEQ *ON              good test?                 B001
  1700    C               EXCPTGOOD             print good rcd             001
  1800    C               ENDIF                 end IF group         E001
  1900    OQSYSPRT H  301    1P
  2000    O        OR        OF
```

Figure 12-6   Example of an alphabetic data validation program.

```
      2100  O                                    40 'ALPHABETIC VALIDATION'
      2200  O          E   2            ERROR
      2300  O                           NAME   30
      2400  O                           MSG    55
      2500  O          E   2            GOOD
      2600  O                           NAME   30
           * * * *  E N D   O F   S O U R C E  * * * * *
            A d d i t i o n a l   D i a g n o s t i c   M e s s a g e s
    * 7086       300   RPG PROVIDES BLOCK OR UNBLOCK SUPPORT FOR FILE C12PFP2.
    5738RG1 V2R2M0 920925            IBM SAA RPG/400                    SMYERS/C12RPG2
    SEQUENCE
    NUMBER     *...+....1....+....2....+....3....+....4....+....5....+....6....+....7....+....8
                     C o m p i l e - T i m e   T a b l e s
    Table/Array . . . . . . :  CHAR
        2800  ABCDEFGHIJKLMNOPQRSTUVWXYZ
    Table/Array . . . . . . :  MSG
        3000  VALUE NOT ALPHABETIC
```

Figure 12-6 Example of an alphabetic data validation program. (Continued)

```
    Data File Listing                    Report Listing

                                        ALPHABETIC VALIDATION

    SEAN O'BRIEN              SEAN O'BRIEN              VALUE NOT ALPHABETIC

    DOCTOR FRANKENSTEIN       DOCTOR FRANKENSTEIN

    KING HENRY THE 5         KING HENRY THE 5          VALUE NOT ALPHABETIC

    COUNT VON-LUCKNER        COUNT VON-LUCKNER         VALUE NOT ALPHABETIC

    JOSE' GONZALEZ           JOSE' GONZALEZ            VALUE NOT ALPHABETIC

    SIDNEY GREENSTREET       SIDNEY GREENSTREET
```

Figure 12-7 Data file listing and printed report for the alphabetic validation program.

Sign Testing

Sign testing is a data validation function that checks a numeric field for *positive* or *negative* value. This test is important to assure that data is correctly signed before being used in file maintenance or report generation. For example, if a master file was updated by the addition of daily transactions, any transaction amount that was incorrectly specified as negative would cause the value to be subtracted from the related master record field value rather than added.

Also included in this validation function is testing numeric field values for zero. If a field is used as a divisor and its value is *zero*, an exception error will occur that may cancel program execution (unless an error routine is included in the program).

Sign testing may be controlled by any of the following methods:

1. Specifying one or more indicators in the *Field Indicators Plus, Minus,* and *Zero* fields for a field in the *Input Specifications*. Then, using the indicator(s) to condition subsequent calculation and/or output instructions.

2. Testing a *Result Field* item in a calculation instruction by specifying one or more indicators in the *Plus, Minus,* and *Zeros* fields. Then, using the indicator(s) to condition subsequent calculation and/or output instructions.

3. Using one or more of the RPG/400 structured operations (i.e., **IFxx, WHxx, DOUxx, DOWxx, CASxx**) in instructions that use a relational test to determine if a field value is positive, negative, or zero.

The third method (using structured operations) is included in the sign testing validation program shown in Figure 12-8.

```
SEQUENCE                                                                           IND   DO
NUMBER    *...1....+....2....+....3....+....4....+....5....+....6....+....7...*   USE   NUM
                         S o u r c e   L i s t i n g
    100   *  EXAMPLE SIGN TESTING VALIDATION PROGRAM
    200   *
          H
    300   FC12PFP3 IP  E                 DISK
          RECORD FORMAT(S):  LIBRARY SMYERS FILE C12PFP3.
                         EXTERNAL FORMAT C12PFP3R RPG NAME C12PFP3R
    400   FQSYSPRT O   F       132     OF      PRINTER
    500   E                        MSG     1   3 22            error msg array
A000000   INPUT  FIELDS FOR RECORD C12PFP3R FILE C12PFP3 FORMAT C12PFP3R.
A000001                                       P   1   30QTY
    600   C                    SELEC                        begin SELEC grp      B001
    700   C          QTY       WHGT 0                        qty positive?       X001
    800   C                    MOVE 1         X       10     access msg 1         001
    900   C          QTY       WHLT 0                        qty negative?       X001
   1000   C                    MOVE 2         X              access msg 2         001
   1100   C                    OTHER                         qty zero?           X001
   1200   C                    MOVE 3         X              access msg 3         001
   1300   C                    ENDSL                         end SELEC grp       E001
   1400   OQSYSPRT H  301     1P
   1500   O         OR         OF
   1600   O                                     45 'SIGN TEST VALIDATION'
   1700   O         D  2      N1P
   1800   O                            QTY   J   30
   1900   O                            MSG,X     55
          * * * * *  E N D   O F   S O U R C E  * * * * *
          A d d i t i o n a l   D i a g n o s t i c   M e s s a g e s
* 7086       300   RPG PROVIDES BLOCK OR UNBLOCK SUPPORT FOR FILE C12PFP3.
5738RG1 V2R2M0  920925           IBM SAA RPG/400                    SMYERS/C12RPG3
SEQUENCE
NUMBER    *...+....1....+....2....+....3....+....4....+....5....+....6....+....7....+....8
                         C o m p i l e - T i m e   T a b l e s
Table/Array . . . . . . :   MSG
   2100  VALUE POSITIVE
   2200  VALUE NEGATIVE
   2300  VALUE ZERO
```

Figure 12-8 Example sign testing data validation program.

The data file processed by the sign testing validation program and the report generated are detailed in Figure 12-9.

Data File Listing	Printed Report
	SIGN TEST VALIDATION
00000	0 VALUE ZERO
00144	144 VALUE POSITIVE
00012-	12- VALUE NEGATIVE

Figure 12-9 Data file listing and report generated by sign validation program.

CHECKING DATA FIELDS

Included in data testing are procedures for the validation of data for *presence, absence, justification, acceptability, relationship,* and *structure.*

Presence of Data

This data validation function is performed to ensure that a value other than all zeros (for numeric items) or all blanks (for alphanumeric items) is stored in the field. Presence testing checks that all data for the record has been entered into the related fields. This function is used only to validate that something has been entered in the assigned field positions; it does not check the accuracy of the data.

Absence of Data

Unused fields are sometimes included in a record format to allow for uncertainties about the format's size when it was designed. These field positions may be used in validation programs to check for the justification of any field values that are located before and/or after the unused area. For example, if an unused record area did not test as blank, that would indicate that the preceding, or following, or both field values were incorrectly justified.

When an RPG/400 program is executed, zeros are stored in all numeric fields before any data record is processed. Consequently, a justification test for numeric fields is not valid. If, however, an unused area exists before or after a numeric field, an absence test of the area may provide for a justification test for the numeric field.

Justification Checking

Alphanumeric (and alphabetic) data is usually left-justified in a related field, and any subsequent processing assumes this positioning. The justification of data is typically performed only on the high-order byte(s) of alphanumeric fields. For the reasons stated previously, numeric fields are not justification-tested.

Figure 12-10 shows a record format and stored data that include *presence, absence,* and *justification* errors.

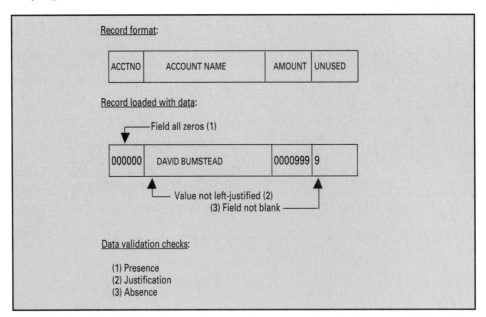

Figure 12-10 An example record that includes presence, absence, and justification validation errors.

The CHECK Operation

The **CHECK** operation verifies that each character in the *Factor 2* string is included in

C	Line	Form Type	Control Level (L0-L9, LR, SR, AN/OR)	Indicators					Factor 1	Operation	Factor 2	Result Field				Resulting Indicators		
				And		And						Name	Length	Decimal Position	Half Adjust (H)	Arithmetic: Plus / Minus / Zero; Compare: 1>2 / 1<2 / 1=2; Lookup (Factor 2) is High / Low / Equal		
				Not		Not		Not								High	Low	Equal
0 1		C		①					②	CHECK	④	⑤					⑥	⑤
0 2		C								③								
0 3		C																

1 *Total* and/or *Detail Time Indicators* may condition a **CHECK** statement.

2 The *Factor 1* item must be defined as <u>character</u> (not numeric) and may include a field name, array element, named constant, data structure name, table name, or literal.

3 The **CHECK** operation name must be specified in the *Operation* field.

4 *Factor 2* must include the name of the string to be checked. The entry may be a field name, array element, named constant, data structure name, table name, or literal dfined as character. The entry may be specified with or without a colon and start location. The start location, which must be defined as an integer, indicates where checking for the *Factor 1* characters is to begin in the *Factor 2* string. The entry may be a field name, array element, name constant, table name, or literal. If no start location is specified (colon and entry omitted after the string item), checking will begin at the first character in the *Factor 2* value.

5 The optional *Result Field* entry must be defined as an integer and may be a field, array element, array name, or table name. If it is not specified, a *Resulting Indicator* in the *Equal* field (columns 58–59) must be included.

   If the *Result Field* contains an array name, the location of every *Factor 2* character that does not equal a *Factor 1* character will be stored in the array elements. If the *Result Field* is not an array, only the location of the first invalid character is stored in the *Result Field* item.

6 A *Resulting Indicator* may be specified in the *Low* field (columns 56–57), which will be set on if an execution error occurs.

   Figurative Constants cannot be used in *Factor 1*, *Factor 2*, or the *Result Field*.

   <u>Processing Logic</u>:

   Each character in the *Factor 1* item checks the *Factor 2* string for an invalid character (not equal to the character or characters in *Factor 1*). If an invalid character is found in the *Factor 2* string, its location is stored in the *Result Field* item. If the *Result Field* is not specified, the *Resulting Indicator* in the *Equal* Field (columns 58–59) will be set on when the first invalid character is found in the *Factor 2* string.

   The **CHECK** operation begins at the leftmost character (or the starting position specified) in the *Factor 2* string and continues character by character from left to right until a character not equal to a *Factor 1* character is found or the end of the *Factor 2* string is encountered. If the *Factor 1* character(s) is (are) found in the *Factor 2* string, the *Result Field* item is set to zero.

   If an array name is specified in the *Result Field*, the checking will continue and store the location of every invalid character in the *Factor 2* string. If the *Factor 1* characters are found in the *Factor 2* string, the array elements are all set to zero.

Figure 12-11 Syntax of the **CHECK** operation.

the character(s) in the *Factor 1* item. Figure 12-11 details the syntax for the **CHECK** operation.

Coding examples of the **CHECK** operation are shown in Figure 12-12.

```
*...1....+....2....+....3....+....4....+....5....+....6....+....7...*
CLON01N02N03Factor1+++OpcdeFactor2+++ResultLenDHHiLoEqComments++++++
 *
 * The CHECK operation checks the Factor 2 string for invalid characters
 * with characters from the Factor 1 value.  In the example shown below,
 * 'bMOUSE' is stored in the Factor 2 string (NAME). The string will be
 * checked from left to right with the blank literal in Factor 1. The
 * position (2), of the first non-blank character (M) will be stored in
 * the Result Field X.
C           ' '         CHECKNAME      X         10
 *
 *
 * When an array is specified in the Result Field, the position of every
 * invalid character in the Factor 2 string will be stored in the elements.
 * In the example shown below, 0123456789 is stored in the Named
 * Constant NUMBRS.  The DATE field specified as the Factor 2 string
 * has a value of b8/11/95.  After execution of the statement, 1, 3, 6
 * (the location of b, /, and / will be stored in the elements of the array.
C           NUMBRS      CHECKDATE      ARRAY
 *
 *
 * When a starting location is specified with the Factor 2 string, check-
 * ing for the characters in the Factor 1 value will begin at that position
 * in the Factor 2 string.  For the example shown below, the 26 letters
 * of the alphabetic and a blank are stored in the Named Constant ALPHA.
 * The CITYST string in Factor 2 has a value of NEW YORK, NY.  After
 * execution of the statement, 9 (the location of the comma) will be
 * stored in the Result Field N.
C           ALPHA       CHECKCITYST:3  N         10

 Note: b indicates a blank character
```

Figure 12-12   Coding examples of the **CHECK** operation.

A compile listing of an RPG/400 program that validates the *presence, absence,* and *justification* of data is shown in Figure 12-13. Note that the **CHECK** operation on line 1400 checks the NAME field for the first invalid character (not a blank). When the first nonblank character is found, its position in the NAME string is stored in LOCATN. If the value in LOCATN is greater than 1 (line 1500 **IF** statement test), a left-justification error in the NAME string is indicated.

```
SEQUENCE                                                                    IND    DO
NUMBER    *...1....+....2....+....3....+....4....+....5....+....6....+....7...*  USE    NUM
                        S o u r c e   L i s t i n g
    100   *  EXAMPLE PRESENCE, ABSENCE, & JUSTIFICATION VALIDATION PROGRAM
    200   *
          H
    300   FC12PFP4 IP  E                    DISK
          RECORD FORMAT(S): LIBRARY SMYERS FILE C12PFP4.
                   EXTERNAL FORMAT C12PFP4R RPG NAME C12PFP4R
    400   FQSYSPRT O   F     132     OF     PRINTER
    500   E                  MSG     1   3 23              error msg array
A000000   INPUT  FIELDS FOR RECORD C12PFP4R FILE C12PFP4 FORMAT C12PFP4R.
A000001                                         1    50ACCTNO
A000002                                         6   25 NAME
```

Figure 12-13   Example program for presence, absence, and justification validation tests.

```
    A000003                                        P  26  292AMT
    A000004                                           30  37 UNUSED
      600  C                    MOVE *OFF      *IN60           set off 60
      700  * Test account number for presence of data
      800  C          ACCTNO    IFEQ *ZEROS                    acctno zeros?       B001
      900  C                    MOVE 1         X        10     1st error msg       001
     1000  C                    EXSR ERROR                     exit to SR          001
     1100  C                    ENDIF                          end IF stmnt        E001
     1200  *
     1300  * Test name for left-justification
     1400  C          ' '       CHECKNAME      LOCATN   20     non-blank char
     1500  C          LOCATN    IFGT 1                         non-blank posit     B001
     1600  C                    MOVE 2         X               access msg 2        001
     1700  C                    EXSR ERROR                     exit to SR          001
     1800  C                    ENDIF                          end IF stmnt        E001
     1900  *
     2000  * Test unused field for absence of data
     2100  C          ' '       CHECKUNUSED    POSITN   20     non-blank char
     2200  C          POSITN    IFGT 0                         non-blank postn     B001
     2300  C                    MOVE 3         X               access msg 3        001
     2400  C                    EXSR ERROR                     exit to SR          001
     2500  C                    ENDIF                          end IF stmnt        E001
     2600  *
     2700  C          ERROR     BEGSR                          begin SR
     2800  C          *IN60     IFEQ *OFF                      60 off?             B001
     2900  C                    EXCPTPRINT1                    print output        001
     3000  C                    MOVE *ON       *IN60           set on 60           001
     3100  C                    ELSE                           60 on               X001
     3200  C                    EXCPTPRINT2                    print output        001
     3300  C                    ENDIF                          end IF stmnt        E001
     3400  C                    ENDSR                          end SR
     3500  OQSYSPRT H  301    1P
     3600  O       OR        OF
     3700  O                              56 'PRESENCE, ABSENCE, AND'
     3800  O                              75 'JUSTIFY VALIDATION'
     3900  O       E 21            PRINT1
     4000  O                       ACCTNO  15
     4100  O                       NAME    35
     4200  O                       AMT     42
     4300  O                       UNUSED  50
     4400  O                       MSG,X   93
     4500  O       E  1            PRINT2
     4600  O                       MSG,X   93
          * * * * *  E N D   O F   S O U R C E  * * * * *
            A d d i t i o n a l   D i a g n o s t i c   M e s s a g e s
  * 7086      300   RPG PROVIDES BLOCK OR UNBLOCK SUPPORT FOR FILE C12PFP4.
  5738RG1 V2R2M0  920925          IBM SAA RPG/400              SMYERS/C12RPG4
  SEQUENCE
  NUMBER    *...+....1....+....2....+....3....+....4....+....5....+....6....+....7....+....8
              C o m p i l e - T i m e   T a b l e s
  Table/Array . . . . . . :   MSG
     4800  ACCT NO IS ZERO
     4900  NAME NOT LEFT-JUSTIFIED
     5000  UNUSED AREA NOT BLANK
```

Figure 12-13 Example program for presence, absence, and justification validation tests. (Continued)

The **CHECK** operation is also used on line 2100. The UNUSED field is validated for the presence of blanks. If a nonblank character is found, its position in UNUSED is stored in POSITN. When the value on POSITN is greater than 0 (line 2200 **IF** statement), an absence error is indicated.

A listing of the data file and the report generated by the program in Figure 12-13 are presented in Figure 12-14.

```
Data File Listing:

00000 DAVID BUMSTEAD      00009999
20000LAMONT CRANSTON      0010000
30000 HOMER GOMEZ         0450000
40000RENE RENAULT         70000000
00000LORD SMEDLEY         1234000


Printed Report:
                              PRESENCE, ABSENCE, AND JUSTIFY VALIDATION


00000 DAVID BUMSTEAD      00009999                              ACCT NO IS ZERO
                                                                NAME IS NOT LEFT-JUSTIFIED
                                                                UNUSED AREA NOT BLANK


30000 HOMER GOMEZ         0450000                               NAME NOT LEFT-JUSTIFIED


40000RENE RENAULT         70000000                              UNUSED AREA NOT BLANK


00000 LORD SMEDLEY        1234000                               ACCT NO IS ZERO
                                                                NAME NOT LEFT-JUSTIFIED
```

Figure 12-14 Data file processed and report generated by validation program that tests for presence, absence, and justification of data.

ACCEPTABILITY OF DATA

Range Checking

The verification of month, day, and year values in a transaction date is a common function of *range check* validation. A customer's eligibility for a cash discount as in terms 2/10, N/30 (2% discount if paid for within 10 days after the invoice date), determination of delinquent accounts, and so forth are some of the applications that require date testing. The program listing in Figure 12-15 controls month, day, year, and leap year validation. Date element processing includes the following procedures:

1. The transaction month number is checked to ensure that it is not 0 or greater than 12.
2. If the month number is valid, the transaction day value is checked with a *Compile Time* array of valid days for a related month. Because this routine will not be executed if the month number is invalid, error messages will not print for invalid month and day tests.
3. The transaction year is valid if it is equal to the current (**UYEAR**) or following year.
4. A routine executed only for February (02) is included for leap year computations.

```
SEQUENCE                                                        IND   DO
NUMBER    *...1....+....2....+....3....+....4....+....5....+....6....+....7...*  USE   NUM
                    S o u r c e   L i s t i n g
   100   * RANGE VALIDATION OF TRANSACTION DATE ELEMENTS (MM DD YY)
   200   * 1. MONTH (MM) IS TESTED FOR > 00 AND < 13.
   300   * 2. DAY (DD) IS TESTED BY INDEXING AN ARRAY OF VALID MAXIMUM NUMBE
   400   *    OF DAYS IN A MONTH.  LEAP YEAR TEST & ADJUSTMENT INCLUDED.
   500   * 3. YEAR (YY) IS VALID IF CURRENT OR FOLLOWING YEAR.
   600   *
```

Figure 12-15 Example program for range validation of date elements.

```
        H
   700  FC12PFP5 IP E                  DISK
        RECORD FORMAT(S): LIBRARY SMYERS FILE C12PFP5.
                EXTERNAL FORMAT C12PFP5R RPG NAME C12PFP5R
   800  FQSYSPRT O  F     132     OF    PRINTER
   900  E                  DAY  12 12  2 0            days array
  1000  E                  MSG   1  3 13              error msg array
A000000  INPUT FIELDS FOR RECORD C12PFP5R FILE C12PFP5 FORMAT C12PFP5R.
A000001                               P  1  40DATE
  1100  I         DS
  1200  I                          1  60DATE
  1300  I                          1  20MM      ┐  Data structure subdivides
  1400  I                          3  40DD      ├  DATE value into separate
  1500  I                          5  60YY      ┘  fields
  1600  C                 SETOF                2030  set off 20 & 30   1 2
  1700  C                 EXSR MMTEST                exit to SR
  1800  C        *IN20    CASEQ*OFF   DDTEST         month valid? ─┐ DDTEST subroutine
  1900  C                 ENDCS                      end CAS group │ is executed only
  2000  C                 EXSR YYTEST                exit to SR    │ if MM is valid
  2100  C *
  2200  C * valid month number test - > 00 and < 12
  2300  C        MMTEST   BEGSR                      begin MM SR
  2400  C        MM       IFEQ 00                    MM = 0?           B001
  2500  C        MM       ORGT 12                    MM > 12?          001
  2600  C                 MOVE 1      X    10        error msg index   001
  2700  C                 EXSR ERRSR                 exit to SR        001
  2800  C                 MOVE *ON     *IN20         set on 20         001
  2900  C                 ENDIF                      end IF stmnt      E001
  3000  C                 ENDSR                      end MM SR
  3100  C *
  3200  C * Day validation test: Leap year & non-leap year control
  3300  C        DDTEST   BEGSR                      begin DD SR
  3400  C                 Z-ADDDAY,MM  MDAYS  20     move arry value
  3500  C        MM       CASEQ02     LEPSUB         leap yr?
  3600  C                 ENDCS                      end CAS group
  3700  C        DD       IFGT MDAYS                 DD > valid days   B001
  3800  C                 MOVE 2      X              access msg 2      001
  3900  C                 EXSR ERRSR                 exit to SR        001
  4000  C                 ENDIF                      end IF stmnt      E001
  4100  C                 ENDSR                      end DD SR
  4200  C *
  4300  C * Leap year test subroutine
  4400  C        LEPSUB   BEGSR                      begin SR
  4500  C        YY       DIV  4      QUOT  11       leap yr comp
  4600  C        QUOT     IFEQ 0                     leap year test    B001
  4700  C                 ADD  1      MDAYS          leap yr + 1       001
  4800  C                 ENDIF                      end IF stmnt      E001
  4900  C                 ENDSR                      end SR
  5000  C *
  5100  C * Year test: must be = or no more than 1 > UYEAR
  5200  C        YYTEST   BEGSR                      begin SR
  5300  C        YY       IFLT UYEAR                 YY > UYEAR?       B001
  5400  C                 MOVE 3      X              access msg 3      001
  5500  C                 EXSR ERRSR                 exit to SR        001
  5600  C                 ELSE                       false action      X001
  5700  C        UYEAR    ADD  1      NYR   20       incrment UYEAR    001
  5800  C        YY       IFGT NYR                   > ?               B002
  5900  C                 MOVE 3      X              access msg 3      002
  6000  C                 EXSR ERRSR                 exit to SR        002
  6100  C                 ENDIF                      end line 58 IF    E002
  6200  C                 ENDIF                      end line 53 IF    E001
  6300  C                 ENDSR                      end YY SR
  6400  C *
  6500  C * Error msg control - date is only printed on 1st error msg line
  6600  C        ERRSR    BEGSR                      begin SR
  6700  C        *IN30    IFEQ *OFF                  30 off?           B001
  6800  C                 EXCPTPRINT1                print 1st line    001
  6900  C                 MOVE *ON     *IN30 ─┐      set on 30         001
  7000  C                 ELSE                │      false action      X001
  7100  C                 EXCPTPRINT2 ────────┘           print line 2       001
  7200  C                 ENDIF                      end IF stmnt      E001
  7300  C                 ENDSR                      end SR
```

Figure 12-15 Example program for range validation of date elements. (Continued)

```
   7400  OQSYSPRT H  301      1P
   7500  O        OR          OF
   7600  O                              30 'DATE ELEMENT VALIDATION'     Indicator 30 is set on
   7700  O        E 21           PRINT1                                  after the first exception
   7800  O                       DATE  Y    20                          line (PRINT1) is printed
   7900  O                       MSG,X      34                          to control the printing of
   8000  O        E  1           PRINT2                                  the PRINT2 exception line
   8100  O                       MSG,X      34                          for additional error messages
         * * * * *  E N D   O F   S O U R C E  * * * * *
             A d d i t i o n a l   D i a g n o s t i c   M e s s a g e s
   * 7086      700  RPG PROVIDES BLOCK OR UNBLOCK SUPPORT FOR FILE C12PFP5.
   5738RG1 V2R2M0  920925            IBM SAA RPG/400              SMYERS/C12RPG5
   SEQUENCE
   NUMBER    *...+....1....+....2....+....3....+....4....+....5....+....6....+....7....+....8
                     C o m p i l e - T i m e   T a b l e s
   Table/Array . . . . . . :  DAY
     8300  3128313031303131303313031
   Table/Array . . . . . . :  MSG
     8500  INVALID MONTH
     8600  INVALID DAY
     8700  INVALID YEAR
```

Figure 12-15 Example program for range validation of date elements. (Continued)

The data file processed by the date validation program and report listings generated are shown in Figure 12-16. Notice that transaction dates that pass the three validation tests (month, day, and year) are not printed. In addition, if a date includes errors for month and day, an error message will not print for the invalid day because that routine is not executed if the month value is incorrect.

```
Data File Listing          Printed Report


                           DATE ELEMENT VALIDATION      1/01/96

    013294                 1/32/94 INVALID DAY
                                   INVALID YEAR


    023096                 2/30/96 INVALID DAY


    133097                 13/30/97 INVALID MONTH


    013199                 1/31/99 INVALID YEAR


    003095                 0/30/95 INVALID MONTH
                                   INVALID YEAR
```

Figure 12-16 Data file processed and report generated by date element validation program.

Check Digits

Many account or customer numbers are large (for example, MasterCard has 16 digits), which often causes transposition or substitution errors on data entry. This problem may be controlled by including a *check digit* in the body of the number. Common methods used to develop and validate check digits are Modulus-10 and Modulus-11. Because

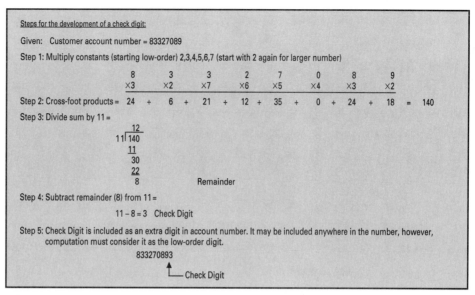

Figure 12-17 Mathematical steps for the development of a check digit by the Modulus-11 method.

Modulus-11 provides more control over transposition and substitution errors (it identifies over 95 percent of such errors), it is the method discussed.

The mathematical steps for the development of a check digit are detailed in Figure 12-17. The program that creates a check digit by the mathematical procedures outlined in Figure 12-17 and builds a new account number with the digit included in the low-order-byte is shown in Figure 12-18.

```
SEQUENCE                                                                                IND   DO
NUMBER     *...1....+....2....+....3....+....4....+....5....+....6....+....7...*         USE   NUM
                        S o u r c e   L i s t i n g
     100    *  THIS PROGRAM DEVELOPS CHECK DIGITS FOR ACCT NUMBERS & BUILDS
     200    *  A NEW ACCOUNT NUMBER WITH A CHECK DIGIT IN THE LOW-ORDER BYTE
     300    *
            H
     400    FC12PFP6 IP  E              DISK
            RECORD FORMAT(S): LIBRARY SMYERS FILE C12PFP6.
                   EXTERNAL FORMAT C12PFP6R RPG NAME C12PFP6R
     500    FQSYSPRT O   F     132      OF    PRINTER
     600    E              NUM      5 1 0          actno array
     700    E              SUM      5 2 0          product array
     800    *
     900    * Data structure redefines array as a field
A000000    INPUT  FIELDS FOR RECORD C12PFP6R FILE C12PFP6 FORMAT C12PFP6R.
A000001                                   P   1   30ACT#
    1000    I         D3                                            Data structure
    1100    I                          1   5 NUM                    defines two work
    1200    I                          1   50HOLD                   fields
    1300    C                  Z-ADDACT#   HOLD          fld to fld
    1400    C                  EXSR TOTSR                exit to SR   30
    1500    C                  EXSR BLDSR                exit to SR
    1600    C       TOTSR      BEGSR                     begin Sr
    1700    C                  Z-ADD5     X      10      init. counter
    1800    C                  Z-ADD2     N      10      init. multipler
    1900    *
    2000    * Step #'s in comment area relate to math steps in fig 12-17
    2100    C       X          DOUEQ0                    begin DOU group      B001
    2200    C       NUM,X      MULT N     SUM,X          Step 1               001
    2300    C                  SUB  1     X              decremnt index       001
```

Figure 12-18 An example program that creates a check digit by the Modulus-11 method.

```
2400  C              X         IFNE  0                       X not = zero?        B002
2500  C                        ADD   1       N               incrment multpr       002
2600  C                        ENDIF                         end IF stmnt         E002
2700  C                        ENDDO                         end DOU group        E001
2800  *
2900  C                        XFOOTSUM      TOTAL   40       Step 2
3000  *
3100  C              TOTAL     DIV   11      QUOT    30       Step 3
3200  C                        MVR           REMAIN  30       Step 3
3300  C              11        SUB   REMAIN  DIGIT   10       Step 4
3400  C                        ENDSR                         end SR
3500  *
3600  C              BLDSR     BEGSR                          begin SR
3700  * New ACT# is built - old loaded in 5 high-order bytes & check
3800  * digit loaded to the low-order byte..........................
3900  C                        MOVELACT#     NEWACT  60       5 hi-ordr bytes
4000  C                        MOVE DIGIT    NEWACT           low-order byte
4100  C                        EXCPTPRINT                     print E line
4200  C                        ENDSR                          end SR
4300  *
4400  OQSYSPRT H    301        1P
4500  O        OR             OF
4600  O                                      29 'MODULUS-11 CHECK DIGIT'
4700  O                                      41 'COMPUTATION'
4800  O        H    2          1P
4900  O        OR             OF
5000  O                                      15 'OLD ACCT#'
5100  O                                      29 'CHECK DIGIT'
5200  O                                      42 'NEW ACCT#'
5300  O        E    2          PRINT
5400  O                        ACT#          13
5500  O                        DIGIT         24
5600  O                        NEWACT        41
```

Figure 12-18 An example program that creates a check digit by the Modulus-11 method. (Continued)

Examine the report in Figure 12-19, and notice that the old account number, the computed check digit, and the new composite number are separately shown. The length of the new number is six bytes.

MODULUS-11 CHECK DIGIT COMPUTATION		
OLD ACCT#	CHECK DIGIT	NEW ACCT#
12000	6	120006
13000	1	130001
14000	7	140007
15000	2	150002
21000	5	210005
30000	4	300004
40000	9	400009

Figure 12-19 Report generated by check digit creation program.

The mathematical steps to validate an account number that includes a check digit in the low-order byte is detailed in Figure 12-20.

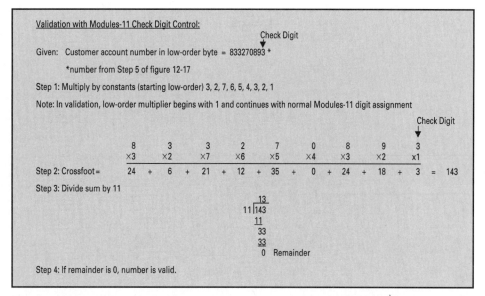

Figure 12-20 Mathematical steps to validate a number that includes a check digit in the low-order byte.

Figure 12-21 shows a program that validates account numbers by the Modulus-11 method. To expedite an understanding of the calculations, the steps from Figure 12-20 are included on the right side of the related instructions.

```
SEQUENCE                                                              IND  DO
NUMBER    *...1....+....2....+....3....+....4....+....5....+....6....+....7...*  USE  NUM
                           S o u r c e   L i s t i n g
  100   *  THIS PROGRAM VALIDATES ACCT NUMBERS BY THE MODULUS-11 METHOD
        H
  200   FC12PFP7 IP  E              DISK
          RECORD FORMAT(S): LIBRARY SMYERS FILE C12PFP7.
                  EXTERNAL FORMAT C12PFP7R RPG NAME C12PFP7R
  300   FQSYSPRT O   F     132    OF    PRINTER
  400   E              NUM       6 1 0              actno array
  500   E              SUM       6 2 0              product array
  600   E              MSG     1 1 13              msg array
A000000   INPUT  FIELDS FOR RECORD C12PFP7R FILE C12PFP7 FORMAT C12PFP7R.
A000001                               P   1   40ACT#
  800   * DS to redefine NUM array as a field....          Loading HOLD with ACT#
  700   I         DS                                       value will also load the
  800   I                         1   6 NUM —              NUM array with the same
  900   I                         1   60HOLD—              value.  NUM is redefined
 1000   * Load ACT# value to HOLD field and NUM array....  as HOLD in data structure
 1100   C               Z-ADDACT#    HOLD ——
 1200   C               Z-ADD6       X     10              init. index
 1300   C               Z-ADD1       N     10              init. multplr
 1400   *
 1500   C        X      DOWGTO                             begin DOU group     B001
 1600   C        NUM,X  MULT N       SUM,X                 Step 1              001
 1700   C               SUB 1        X                     decrment index      001
 1800   C               ADD 1        N                     incrmnt multplr     001
 1900   C               ENDDO                                                  E001
 2000   *
 2100   C               XFOOTSUM     TOTAL 40              Step 2
 2200   *
 2300   C        TOTAL  DIV 11       QUOT  30              Step 3
 2400   C               MVR          REMAIN 30             save remainder
```

Figure 12-21 An example program that validates account numbers by the Modulus-11 check digit method.

```
2500  C          REMAIN    IFGT 0                        Step 4          B001
2600  C                    EXCPTPRINT                    print error      001
2700  C                    ENDIF                         end IF group    E001
2800  *
2900  OQSYSPRT H  301   1P
3000  O        OR       OF
3100  O                              33 'MODULUS-11 CHECK DIGIT'
3200  O                              44 'VALIDATION'
3300  O        E  2      PRINT
3400  O                  ACT#     18
3500  O                  MSG      43


5738RG1 V2R2M0  920925        IBM SAA RPG/400              SMYERS/C12RPG7
EQUENCE
NUMBER    *...+....1....+....2....+....3....+....4....+....5....+....6....+....7....+....8
                Additional  Diagnostic  Messages
* 7086    200  RPG PROVIDES BLOCK OR UNBLOCK SUPPORT FOR FILE C12PFP7.
5738RG1 V2R2M0  920925        IBM SAA RPG/400              SMYERS/C12RPG7
SEQUENCE
NUMBER    *...+....1....+....2....+....3....+....4....+....5....+....6....+....7....+....8
                  Compile-Time  Tables
Table/Array ......:   MSG
    3700  ACCT# INVALID
```

Figure 12-21 An example program that validates account numbers by the Modulus-11 check digit method. (Continued)

The report generated in Figure 12-22 identifies the account numbers that did not pass the Modulus-11 test. An examination of the data file listing in Figure 12-22 shows that 130001 and 150002 were the only valid numbers processed. For convenience, the same account numbers developed in Figure 12-19 are used. Obviously, five of them were modified with incorrect check digits to test the function of the program in Figure 12-21.

```
Data File Listing           Printed Report

                       MODULUS-11 CHECK DIGIT VALIDATION

     120005            120005        ACCT# INVALID
     130001
     140009            140009        ACCT# INVALID
     150002
     200001            200001        ACCT# INVALID
     300005
     400000            300005        ACCT# INVALID

                       400000        ACCT# INVALID
```

Figure 12-22 Data file listing and error report generated by the Modulus-11 validation program.

Limit Checking

Limit checking is a validation function that controls a maximum (and sometimes minimum) value for a variable item. The maximum credit allowed to a customer or maximum sales amount for a department are examples of this test. If this function was included as a validation procedure, any customer who attempted to charge a purchase would have the transaction rejected if his or her credit limit had been reached. This process would be better controlled in an interactive environment, where decisions may be made at the time of the purchase. In a batch processing mode, the information would be available only after the fact.

Relationship of Data

When possible, additional validation of data may be made by relating it to other data. For example, if a hospital charged maternity fees to a male patient, this would obviously indicate that the relationship of the service to the individual's sex had not been checked. Another application might require that some transaction codes relate to positive amounts and others to negative.

```
Data File Listing                          Printed Report

    112000}S  (} = negative 0)    TRANSACTION CODE & SALES AMOUNT LIMIT VALIDATION
    225000JC  (J = negative 1)
    4330000C
    1000999X                      1   S   1,200.00-   SIGN NOT VALID FOR CODE
    3025000S
                                  4   C   3,300.00    SIGN NOT VALID FOR CODE
Note: 225000JC is a valid record                      INVALID DEPT NUMBER

                                  1   X      9.99     CODE NOT VALID

                                  3   S    250.00     SALES AMT OVER DEPT LIMIT
```

Figure 12-23 Data file processed and report generated by example limits/relationship validation program.

The data file and report listings in Figure 12-23 show the result of following *limits* and *relationship* validation tests included in the example program in Figure 12-24.

```
SEQUENCE                                                              IND  DO
NUMBER   *...1....+....2....+....3....+....4....+....5....+....6....+....7...*  USE  NUM
                           S o u r c e   L i s t i n g
   100   * RANGE CHECK OF AMT & CODE/SIGN RELATIONSHIP VALIDATION
   200   * VALID CODES ARE S AND C
   300   *   IF CODE = S, TRANSACTION AMT MUST BE POSITIVE
   400   *   IF CODE = C, TRANSACTION AMT MUST BE NEGATIVE
   500   * VALID DEPT#'S ARE 1, 2, AND 3
   600   *   IF DEPT# IS NOT VALID, LIMIT CHECK IS NOT PERFORMED
   700   *
         H
   800   FC12PFP8 IP  E                    DISK
         RECORD FORMAT(S): LIBRARY SMYERS FILE C12PFP8.
                   EXTERNAL FORMAT C12PFP8R RPG NAME C12PFP8R
   900   FQSYSPRT O   F     132     OF     PRINTER
  1000   E                     CODES   2   2 1              code array
  1100   E                     DEPT    3   3 1 0            dept# array
  1200   E.                    LIMT    3   3 6 2            limit array
  1300   E                     MSG     1   4 25             msg array
A000000  INPUT  FIELDS FOR RECORD C12PFP8R FILE C12PFP8 FORMAT C12PFP8R.
A000001                                    P   1  10DEPT#
A000002                                    P   2  52AMT
A000003                                        6   6 CODE
  1400   C                     MOVE *OFF     *IN20          set off 20
  1500   C                     EXSR CODESR                  exit to SR
  1600   C                     EXSR SALESR                  exit to SR
  1700   *
  1800   C          CODESR     BEGSR                        begin SR
  1900   C          CODE       LOKUPCODES                   22find valid code    3
  2000   *
  2100   C                     SELEC                        begin SELEC grp      B001
  2200   C          *IN22      WHEQ *OFF                    code not found?      X001
  2300   C                     MOVE 1        X    10        error msg 1          001
```

Figure 12-24 An example program that controls limits and relationship validation functions.

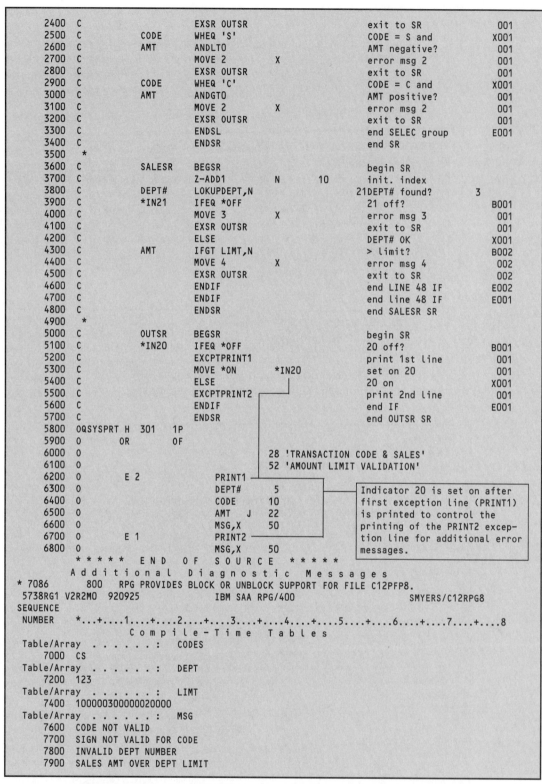

```
2400  C                           EXSR OUTSR                        exit to SR              001
2500  C              CODE         WHEQ 'S'                          CODE = S and            X001
2600  C              AMT          ANDLTO                            AMT negative?           001
2700  C                           MOVE 2            X               error msg 2             001
2800  C                           EXSR OUTSR                        exit to SR              001
2900  C              CODE         WHEQ 'C'                          CODE = C and            X001
3000  C              AMT          ANDGTO                            AMT positive?           001
3100  C                           MOVE 2            X               error msg 2             001
3200  C                           EXSR OUTSR                        exit to SR              001
3300  C                           ENDSL                             end SELEC group         E001
3400  C                           ENDSR                             end SR
3500     *
3600  C              SALESR       BEGSR                             begin SR
3700  C                           Z-ADD1            N       10      init. index
3800  C              DEPT#        LOKUPDEPT,N                     21DEPT# found?          3
3900  C              *IN21        IFEQ *OFF                         21 off?                 B001
4000  C                           MOVE 3            X               error msg 3             001
4100  C                           EXSR OUTSR                        exit to SR              001
4200  C                           ELSE                              DEPT# OK                X001
4300  C              AMT          IFGT LIMT,N                       > limit?                B002
4400  C                           MOVE 4            X               error msg 4             002
4500  C                           EXSR OUTSR                        exit to SR              002
4600  C                           ENDIF                             end LINE 48 IF          E002
4700  C                           ENDIF                             end line 48 IF          E001
4800  C                           ENDSR                             end SALESR SR
4900     *
5000  C              OUTSR        BEGSR                             begin SR
5100  C              *IN20        IFEQ *OFF                         20 off?                 B001
5200  C                           EXCPTPRINT1                       print 1st line          001
5300  C                           MOVE *ON          *IN20           set on 20               001
5400  C                           ELSE                              20 on                   X001
5500  C                           EXCPTPRINT2                       print 2nd line          001
5600  C                           ENDIF                             end IF                  E001
5700  C                           ENDSR                             end OUTSR SR
5800  OQSYSPRT H  301       1P
5900  O         OR            OF
6000  O                                      28 'TRANSACTION CODE & SALES'
6100  O                                      52 'AMOUNT LIMIT VALIDATION'
6200  O          E 2          PRINT1
6300  O                       DEPT#       5
6400  O                       CODE       10
6500  O                       AMT  J     22
6600  O                       MSG,X      50
6700  O          E 1          PRINT2
6800  O                       MSG,X      50
```

Indicator 20 is set on after first exception line (PRINT1) is printed to control the printing of the PRINT2 exception line for additional error messages.

```
* * * * *  E N D   O F   S O U R C E  * * * * *
            A d d i t i o n a l   D i a g n o s t i c   M e s s a g e s
* 7086       800    RPG PROVIDES BLOCK OR UNBLOCK SUPPORT FOR FILE C12PFP8.
5738RG1 V2R2M0  920925            IBM SAA RPG/400               SMYERS/C12RPG8
SEQUENCE
NUMBER      *...+....1....+....2....+....3....+....4....+....5....+....6....+....7....+....8
                C o m p i l e - T i m e   T a b l e s
Table/Array . . . . . . :  CODES
   7000  CS
Table/Array . . . . . . :  DEPT
   7200  123
Table/Array . . . . . . :  LIMT
   7400  100000300000020000
Table/Array . . . . . . :  MSG
   7600  CODE NOT VALID
   7700  SIGN NOT VALID FOR CODE
   7800  INVALID DEPT NUMBER
   7900  SALES AMT OVER DEPT LIMIT
```

Figure 12-24 An example program that controls limits and relationship validation functions. (Continued)

1. Valid department numbers are 1 2 3.

2. Individual department sales have the following limits:

Dept #	Maximum Sale Allowed
1	1,000.00
2	3,000.00
3	200.00

3. Valid transaction codes and their functions are:

Code	Function	Valid Sign for Code
S	Sale	+
C	Credit	−

Note: If code is S, value must be positive; if code is C, value must be negative to be acceptable as a valid transaction.

The limits/relationship validation program listing is detailed in Figure 12-24. Comments in the beginning of the program and at the right side of the calculation form explain the processing logic.

Correspondence Checking

In inquiry or update maintenance, key fields are used to find a select record from a master file. If the corresponding key value is found in the master file, the required processing is performed. However, processing a record based on one field value may not provide enough control. Sometimes another field must be used to ensure that the correct record is accessed. For example, a wrong social security number may be assigned to a payroll transaction. It may be a valid social security number but not related to the correct employee. Consequently, subsequent processing of that record would access the wrong payroll account. Errors of this type can be reduced through the use of *correspondence checking*. In addition to the social security number, another field value from the transaction record may be used to check with a related field from a master file (or table).

An example of correspondence checking is detailed in Figure 12-25. A *Prerun Time* table includes valid social security numbers, and a second table contains the first five characters of employee names. The records in the data file include the social security number and the complete employee name. As records from the data file are processed, the social security number is used to look up the related *argument* table. If the lookup is successful, the *function* table and first five bytes of the transaction record's name field are compared. When an equal condition is indicated, the transaction corresponds to the related employee.

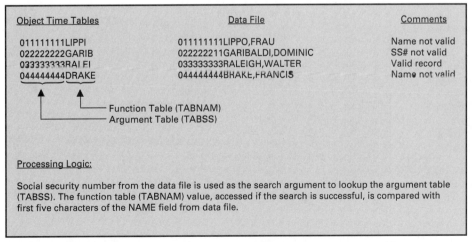

Figure 12-25 *Prerun Time* table values and data records processed by correspondence checking program.

The report generated by the example *correspondence checking* program is shown in Figure 12-26. Program control performs *correspondence checking* only for records for which the social security number was found in the argument table. Any others are identified on the report by the following error message: SS# NOT FOUND IN TABLE.

```
                    SS#/NAME CORRESPONDENCE VALIDATION


     011-11-1111    LIPPO,FRAU           NAME DOES NOT CORRESPOND WITH SS#

     022-22-2111    GARIBALDI,DOMINIC    SS# NOT FOUND IN TABLE

     044-44-4444    BRAKE,FRANCIS        NAME DOES NOT CORRESPOND WITH SS#
```

Figure 12-26 Report generated by correspondence checking program.

A detailed source listing of the example *correspondence checking* program is presented in Figure 12-27.

```
SEQUENCE                                                                          IND   DO
NUMBER     *...1....+....2....+....3....+....4....+....5....+....6....+....7...*    USE   NUM
                             S o u r c e   L i s t i n g
   100     * SS#/NAME CORRESPONDENCE VALIDATION.  SS# & FIRST 5 CHARACTERS
   200     * OF LAST NAME FROM TRANSACTION FILE ARE CHECKED WITH OBJECT TIME
   300     * TABLES.  TABSS CONTAINS SS#'S & TABNAM THE FIRST 5 CHARACTERS
   400     * OF LAST NAMES.  IF SS# IS NOT FOUND IN THE ARGUMENT TABLE (TABSS)
   500     * NAME COMPARISON IS NOT EXECUTED....
   600     *
           H
   700     FC12NAMESIT F      14           EDISK
   800     FC12PFP9 IP  E                  DISK
           RECORD FORMAT(S): LIBRARY SMYERS FILE C12PFP9.
                    EXTERNAL FORMAT C12PFP9R RPG NAME C12PFP9R
   900     FQSYSPRT O   F     132     OF   PRINTER
  1000     E   C12NAMES       TABSS   1   4  9 0ATABNAM  5    ss# & name tables
  1100     E                  MSG     1   2 33               error msg array
A000000    INPUT  FIELDS FOR RECORD C12PFP9R FILE C12PFP9 FORMAT C12PFP9R.
A000001                                     P   1   50SS#
A000002                                         6  25 NAME
  1200     C         SS#        LOKUPTABSS   TABNAM      20find SS#              3
  1300     C         *IN20      IFEQ *OFF                SS not fnd?         B001
  1400     C                    MOVE 1     X       10    error msg 1         001
  1500     C                    EXCPTPRINT                print error        001
  1600     C                    ELSE                     SS# found          X001
  1700     C                    MOVELNAME  FIRST5  5     high 5 chars        001
  1800     C         FIRST5     IFNE TABNAM                not = table?      B002
  1900     C                    MOVE 2     X             error msg 2         002
  2000     C                    EXCPTPRINT                print error        002
  2100     C                    ENDIF                    line 1800 IF       E002
  2200     C                    ENDIF                    line 1300 IF       E001
  2300     *
  2400     OQSYSPRT H  301     1P
  2500     O          OR      OF
  2600     O                                   43 'SS#/NAME CORRESPONDENCE'
  2700     O                                   54 'VALIDATION'
  2800     O          E 2               PRINT
  2900     O                            SS#     15 '0  -  -   '
  3000     O                            NAME    38
  3100     O                            MSG,X   75
           * * * * *  E N D   O F   S O U R C E  * * * * *
           A d d i t i o n a l   D i a g n o s t i c   M e s s a g e s
           5738RG1 V2R2M0  920925        IBM SAA RPG/400           SMYERS/C12RPG9
```

Figure 12-27 Example correspondence checking program listing.

```
SEQUENCE
NUMBER    *...+....1....+....2....+....3....+....4....+....5....+....6....+....7....+....8
* 7086      700   RPG PROVIDES BLOCK OR UNBLOCK SUPPORT FOR FILE C12NAMES.
* 7086      800   RPG PROVIDES BLOCK OR UNBLOCK SUPPORT FOR FILE C12PFP9.
5738RG1 V2R2M0  920925              IBM SAA RPG/400                    SMYERS/C12RPG9
SEQUENCE
NUMBER    *...+....1....+....2....+....3....+....4....+....5....+....6....+....7....+....8
                         C o m p i l e - T i m e   T a b l e s
Table/Array . . . . . . :    MSG
   3300  SS# NOT FOUND IN TABLE
   3400  NAME DOES NOT CORRESPOND WITH SS#
```

Figure 12-27 Example correspondence checking program listing. (Continued)

Batch Total Validation

Batch totals, which indicate a total amount for a group of source documents, are usually developed by a user department such as sales, payroll, accounting, and so forth. The batch total is entered when the program that processes the related transaction file is executed. Transaction amounts in the file are accumulated, and at end of file the batch total previously entered is compared with the transaction file total. If the totals are equal, the transaction amounts entered are considered correct. However, if they are not equal, either the batch total and/or the transaction file data is incorrect.

Batch totals may be entered into an RPG/400 program by any of the following methods:

1. Via a *data area* that is *implicitly* or *explicitly* accessed by an RPG/400 program (discussed in Chapter 9).
2. Via a physical file that is input to an RPG/400 program.
3. Via an interactive program that supports a display file (introduced in Chapter 14).
4. Via a **CL** program that passes the *batch total* parameter to an RPG/400 program (introduced in Chapter 19).

The first method, which accesses a data area, is used in the example RPG/400 program that controls batch total validation. Refer to the compile listing in Figure 12-28, and note that a data area data structure (discussed in Chapter 9) is defined by the letter U in column 18 (line 600). The data from the data area data structure will be *implicitly* accessed when the program is executed. At the end of the program, the data in the data structure will automatically be updated regardless of whether it has changed.

```
SEQUENCE                                                                IND  DO
NUMBER    *...1....+....2....+....3....+....4....+....5....+....6....+....7...*  USE  NUM
                        S o u r c e   L i s t i n g
   100  * BATCH TOTAL ENTERED VIA A DATA AREA AND VALUE CHECKED WITH THE
   200  * TOTAL OF TRANSACTION AMOUNTS IN THE RECORDS OF THE INPUT FILE
   300  *
        H
   400  FC12PFP10IP  E                     DISK
        RECORD FORMAT(S): LIBRARY SMYERS FILE C12PFP10.
              EXTERNAL FORMAT C12PF10R RPG NAME C12PF10R
   500  FQSYSPRT O   F      132      OF    PRINTER
A000000  INPUT  FIELDS FOR RECORD C12PF10R FILE C12PFP10 FORMAT C12PF10R.
A000001                                      1   5 CUST#
A000002                                      6  25 NAME
```

Figure 12-28 Example program that accesses a batch number and total stored in a data area.

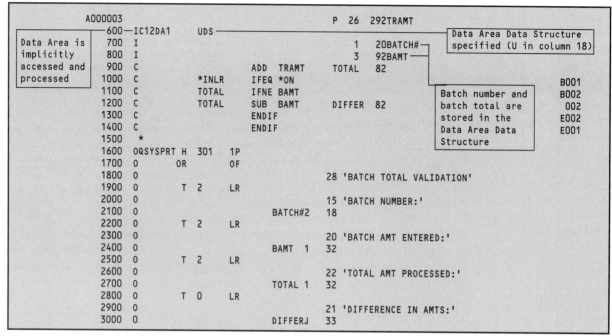

Figure 12-28 Example program that accesses a batch number and total stored in a data area. (Continued)

The report generated by the example batch validation program and a listing of the data file are shown in Figure 12-29.

```
        Data File Listing                    │        Printed Report

                                             │      BATCH TOTAL VALIDATION

    11111MORTIMER SNORD      0500000         │    BATCH NUMBER:  1
    22222DAFFY MOOSE         0002299         │
    33333BUGS RABBIT         1200000         │    BATCH AMT ENTERED:    17,868.44
    44444SYLVESTER D DOG     0084545         │
                                             │    TOTAL AMT PROCESSED: 17,868.44
    Note: Record amounts total 17,868.44     │    DIFFERENCE IN AMTS:        .00
```

Figure 12-29 Report generated by the example batch validation program and the data file listing.

Other Batch Validation Functions

Many other functions, procedures, and combinations may be included in RPG/400 programs that control batch validation. *Record Identification Codes* and *sequence checking* are a few of the other validation processes available. However, because *externally defined* physical files only support one record type, Record Identification codes and sequence checking are seldom used.

The **CHAIN** operation, which will be introduced in Chapter 13, may be used to verify that an account number, customer number, and related data are valid. This could eliminate the need for check digits for existing accounts; however, the random access of a physical file with the **CHAIN** operation requires more processing time than calculation instructions.

Data Validation in an Interactive Environment

In the AS/400 environment, many of the data validation functions introduced in this chapter as program-controlled are, instead, supported by interactive processing. Specifically, procedures such as *numeric field testing, justification, mandatory entry, mandatory fill, check digits, range testing, value testing,* and so forth are controlled by the syntax in one or more display files processed by an RPG/400 program. This topic will be introduced in Chapter 14.

APPLICATION RPG/400 PROGRAM: BATCH VALIDATION OF AN ACCOUNTS RECEIVABLE TRANSACTION FILE

To illustrate how the batch validation functions introduced in this chapter are integrated, we discuss an application RPG/400 program that incorporates many of them. The program specifications shown in Figure 12-30 detail the batch validation procedures that must be tested with the example program. Because of the complexity of the program, the instructions related to each validation function are included in separate internal subroutines.

PROGRAM SPECIFICATIONS		Page 1 of 2
Program Name: Validation Report Program - ID: CH12VAL		Written by: SM
Purpose: Customer transactions validation report		Approved by: CM

Input files: TRANFILE

Output files: QSYSPRT

Processing Requirements:

Write an RPG/400 program to generate a validation report for the customer transaction file.

Input to the program:

The sales transactions for customers are stored in the externally defined physical file TRANFILE. A supplemental description form details the attributes of the record format.

Include a data structure to redefine the record format as a field, separate the elements of the transaction date (DATE) into MM, DD, YY fields, redefine the account number field (ACT#) as an array, and redefine the first byte in the customer name field (NAME).

Processing:

All of the following validation functions are to be performed for every input record processed:

1. Account number (ACT#) by the Modulus-11 check digit method. Hint: redefine the ACT# field in a data structure as an array.

2. Customer name (NAME) for left-justification and valid alphabetic characters. Include A through Z, blank, and ' (apostrophe) in a Compile Time array. Move the NAME field value into a Run Time array and look up the Compile Time array of valid characters with each

Figure 12-30 Specifications for a batch edit program.

character in the NAME array. If the value is not left-justified, do not check for valid characters.

3. a. Check that the month value is not less than 1 or greater than 12.

   b. Include the maximum number of days in each month in a Compile Time array. If the month test is valid, look up the array with the day value. When the day value from the input record is greater than the related array value, a validation error is indicated.

   c. When the transaction month value is 2 (February), a leap year test must be made. Instead of the 28 days, leap years support 29 as the maximum number of days in February.

     To test for leap year, divide the transaction year by 4. If the remainder is zero, a leap year is indicated. Add 1 to the array element before the transaction day value is tested. Hint: move the array element value to a field before adding 1 so that it will not be incremented for each 02 month transaction.

   d. The transaction year must not be less than UYEAR or greater than the following year (UYEAR +1). Note: for the date to generate the report for this assignment, store 011095 in a data area or change the job date before executing the program.

4. Check the transaction amount (AMT) for an invalid negative value.

5. Include the following error messages in a Compile Time array.

> ACCOUNT NUMBER NOT VALID
> NAME NOT LEFT-JUSTIFIED
> NAME CONTAINS INVALID CHARACTER
> INVALID MONTH
> INVALID DAY
> INVALID YEAR
> AMOUNT NEGATIVE

Access the error message array positionally.

Output:

A report in the format detailed in the supplemental printer spacing chart is to be generated. Only records that have validation errors are to be printed. Note that the data for a record is printed only on the line with the <u>first</u> error message and is not repeated for any other errors for the record. Also note that the entire record is printed, not just the individual fields.

Figure 12-30   Specifications for a batch edit program. (Continued)

System Flowchart

The system flowchart in Figure 12-31 indicates that a physical file in which transaction data is stored is input to the batch edit program which generates a printed report. Instead of printing, output is often written to one or more physical files that are subsequently processed. This topic will be introduced when physical file maintenance is discussed in Chapter 13.

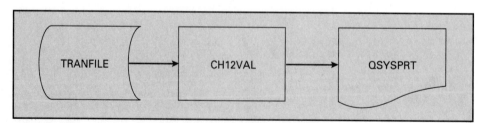

Figure 12-31   System flowchart for batch edit program.

Physical File Attributes

Figure 12-32 shows the record format of the physical file and a listing of the transaction data.

```
                        PHYSICAL FILE DESCRIPTION

      SYSTEM: AS/400                          DATE: 1/10/94
      FILE NAME: TRANFILE                     REV NO: 0
      RECORD NAME: TRANSR                     KEY LENGTH: 6
      SEQUENCE: Keyed (not unique)            RECORD SIZE: 32

                          FIELD DEFINITIONS

      FIELD    FIELD NAME    SIZE   TYPE    POSITION      COMMENTS
      NO                                   FROM    TO


        1       ACT#           6     P       1      4    Key field
        2       NAME          20     C       5     24
        3       DATE           6     P      25     28
        4       AMT            7     P      29     32    2 decimals
```

Physical file data:

Account Number	Account Name	Transaction Date	Transaction Amount
120006	ALEXANDER DUMAS	003097	0002500
130000	HAROLD ROBBINS	022996	0023900-
140007	GEOFREY CHAUCE4	033295	0789000
210005	WILLIAM SHAKESPEARE	022896	0010000
300004	JACQUELINE SUSAN	013194	0056007

Figure 12-32 Physical file record format and data listing processed by the batch edit program.

The report design shown in the printer spacing chart and listing are shown in Figure 12-33. Note that the record image is printed, not the individual fields. Also observe that the data for an error record is not repeated when there is more than one validation error.

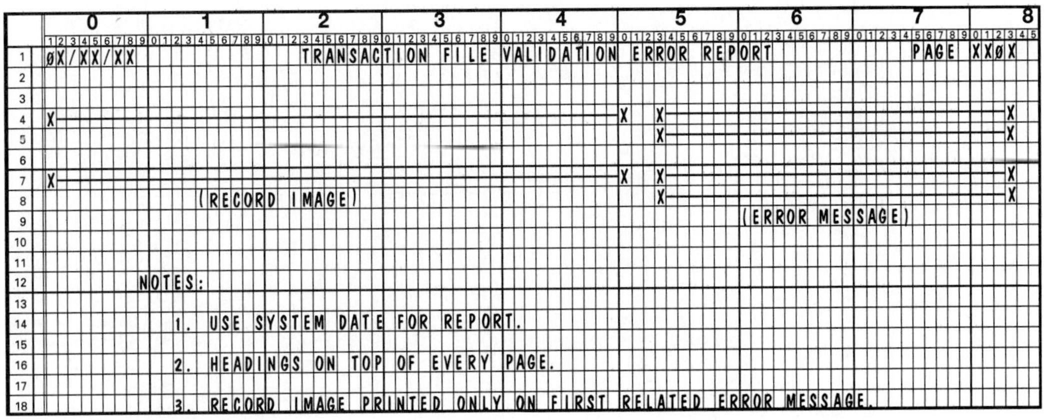

Figure 12-33 Report design and listing generated by the batch edit application program.

```
3/31/95              TRANSACTION FILE VALIDATION ERROR REPORT           PAGE    1


    120006 ALEXANDER DUMAS      0030970002500        NAME NOT LEFT-JUSTIFIED
                                                     INVALID MONTH
                                                     INVALID YEAR

    130000HAROLD ROBBINS        022996002390}        ACCOUNT NUMBER NOT VALID
                                                     AMOUNT NEGATIVE

    140007GEOFREY CHAUCE4       0332950789000        NAME CONTAINS INVALID CHARACTER
                                                     INVALID DAY

    300004JACQUELINE SUSAN      0131940056007        INVALID YEAR
```

Figure 12-33 Report design and listing generated by the batch edit application program. (Continued)

The detailed compile listing of the batch edit application program is presented in Figure 12-34.

```
SEQUENCE                                                               IND    DO
NUMBER     *...1....+....2....+....3....+....4....+....5....+....6....+....7...*  USE   NUM
                        S o u r c e   L i s t i n g
   100    *          **** TRANSACTION FILE FIELD VALIDATION ****
   200    * VALIDATION FUNCTIONS PERFORMED:
   300    *     1. ACCT# VALIDATION BY MODULUS-11 METHOD
   400    *     2. NAME JUSTIFICATION
   500    *     3. VALID ALPHABETIC CHARACTERS (AND ') IN NAME FIELD
   600    *     4. VALID MONTH
   700    *     5. VALID DAY (TEST IS MADE ONLY IF MONTH IS VALID)
   800    *     6. VALID YEAR (MUST NOT BE < CURRENT YEAR OR > NEXT YEAR)
   900    *     7. VALID POSITIVE AMOUNT
  1000    *
  1100    *
          H
  1200    FTRANFILEIP E           K        DISK
          RECORD FORMAT(S): LIBRARY SMYERS FILE TRANFILE.
                    EXTERNAL FORMAT TRANSR RPG NAME TRANSR
  1300    FQSYSPRT O  F    132    OF     PRINTER
  1400    E             AARY       6  1 0            Acct# array
  1500    E             MSG     1  7 31             Error msg array
  1600    E             DAY    12 12  2 0           Max days in mths
  1700    E             SUM        6  2 0           for M-11 compute
  1800    E             NAM       20  1             NAME array
  1900    E             ALPHA  28 28  1             Alpha char array
A000000   INPUT  FIELDS FOR RECORD TRANSR FILE TRANFILE FORMAT TRANSR.
A000001                                 P   1   40ACT#
A000002                                     5   24 NAME
A000003                                 P  25   28ØDATE
A000004                                 P  29   322AMT
  2000    I      DS
  2100    I                              1    60ACT#
  2200    I                              1    60AARY
  2300    I                              7   26 NAME
  2400    I                              7    7 FIRST
  2500    I                             27   32ØDATE
  2600    I                             27   28ØMM
  2700    I                             29   30ØDD
  2800    I                             31   32ØYY
  2900    I                              1   39 RECORD
  3000    *
  3100    C              EXSR HOUSEK                 Exit HOUSEK SR
  3200    C              EXSR ACTSR                  Exit to ACT SR
  3300    C              EXSR NAMESR                 Exit to NAME SR
```

Data structure for loading the ACT# value into the run-time array AARY. Redefines the first byte of the NAME field and separates DATE into MM, DD, YY fields.

Record format is redefined without fields for output

Figure 12-34 Compile listing of the batch edit program.

```
3400  C                         EXSR MTHSR                      Mth test SR
3500  C            *IN20        CASEQ*OFF         DAYSR         Only if vald MM
3600  C                         ENDCS                           End CAS
3700  C                         EXSR YEARSR                     YY test SR
3800  C                         EXSR SIGNSR
3900  *
4000  * Housekeeping routine......
4100  *
4200  C            HOUSEK       BEGSR                           Begin SR
4300  C                         MOVEA*OFF         *IN,20        Set off indctrs
4400  C                         ENDSR                           End SR
4500  *
4600  * Acct# test by Modulus-11 check digit method......
4700  *
4800  C            ACTSR        BEGSR                           Begin Sr
4900  C                         Z-ADD6            X      20     Array index
5000  C                         Z-ADD1            N      10     Multiplier
5100  *
5200  * Multiply AARY element by N (incremented for every loop) and store in
5300  * an element of the SUM array.  Continue until the value of X = 0.
5400  C            X            DOWGT*ZERO                      DOW > = to 1         B001
5500  C            AARY,X       MULT N            SUM,X         Compute SUM          001
5600  C            X            SUB  1            X             decrease index       001
5700  C            X            IFEQ *ZERO                                           B002
5800  C                         LEAVE                                                002
5900  C                         ENDIF                                                E002
6000  C            N            ADD  1            N             Incrmnt multplr      001
6100  C                         ENDDO                           End DOW              E001
6200  *
6300  * Crossfoot SUM array......
6400  *
6500  C                         XFOOTSUM          TOTAL  40     Crossfoot array
6600  *
6700  C            TOTAL        DIV  11           QUOT   30
6800  C                         MVR               REMAIN 30     Test remainder
6900  C            REMAIN       IFGT *ZERO                      Remainder > 0?       B001
7000  C                         MOVE 1            Y      10     MSG arry elmt 1      001
7100  C                         EXSR OUTSR                                           001
7200  C                         ENDIF                           End IF               E001
7300  C                         ENDSR                           End SR
7400  *
7500  * NAME validation - Justification & valid characters..........
7600  * Justification check (first byte of NAME field blank?)........
7700  *
7800  C            NAMESR       BEGSR                           Begin SR
7900  C            FIRST        IFEQ *BLANK                     NAME justified?      B001
8000  C                         MOVE 2            Y             MSG 2                001
8100  C                         EXSR OUTSR                      Print error msg      001
8200  C                         ELSE                            NAME justified       X001
8300  *
8400  * If justified, check for valid characters with Compile Time CODE array......
8500  *
8600  C                         MOVEANAME         NAM           Load NAM array       001
8700  C                         DO   20           X             Begin DO group       B002
8800  C            NAM,X        LOKUPALPHA                      20Array lookup     3 002
8900  C            *IN20        IFEQ *OFF                       Invalid char?        B003
9000  C                         MOVE 3            Y             MSG 3                003
9100  C                         EXSR OUTSR                      Print error msg      003
9200  C                         LEAVE                           Exit DO group        003
9300  C                         ENDIF                           End line 82 IF       E003
9400  C                         ENDDO                           End DO group         E002
9500  C                         ENDIF                           End line 73 IF       E001
9600  C                         ENDSR                           End sr
9700  *
9800  * Valid month number test - > 00 and < 13......
9900  *
10000 C            MTHSR        BEGSR                           Begin MTH sr
10100 C            MM           IFEQ *ZERO                      MM = 0?              B001
10200 C            MM           ORGT 12                         or > 12?             001
```

Figure 12-34 Compile listing of the batch edit program. (Continued)

```
10300  C                      MOVE 4          Y              MSG 4                    001
10400  C                      EXSR OUTSR                     Print error msg          001
10500  C                      MOVE *ON        *IN20          Set on 20                001
10600  C                      ENDIF                                                   E001
10700  C                      ENDSR                          End MTHSR
10800  *
10900  * If month is valid, validate days......
11000  *
11100  C         DAYSR        BEGSR                          Begin DAYSR
11200  C                      Z-ADDDAY,MM     MDAYS   20      Move arry value
11300  C         MM           CASEQ02         LEPSR          Feb? Exit to SR
11400  C                      ENDCS                          End case group
11500  C         DD           IFGT MDAYS                     Days > array?            B001
11600  C                      MOVE 5          Y              Invalid days             001
11700  C                      EXSR OUTSR                     Print error msg          001
11800  C                      ENDIF                          End line IF              E001
11900  C                      ENDSR                          End DAYSR
12000  *
12100  * Leap year test......
12200  *
12300  C         LEPSR        BEGSR                          Begin LEPSR
12400  C         YY           DIV 4           QUOTNT  11      Leap math
12500  C         QUOTNT       IFEQ *ZERO                     Leap year test           B001
12600  C                      ADD 1           MDAYS          + 1 if leap yr           001
12700  C                      ENDIF                                                   E001
12800  C                      ENDSR                          End LEPSR
12900  *
13000  * Year test: Must be = or no more than 1 > UYEAR......
13100  *
13200  C         YEARSR       BEGSR                          Begin YEARSR
13300  C                      Z-ADD0          NYR
13400  C         UYEAR        ADD 1           NYR     20      Add 1 to UYEAR
13500  C         YY           IFLT UYEAR                     > bad year               B001
13600  C         YY           ORGT NYR                       > bad year               001
13700  C                      MOVE 6          Y              MSG 6                    001
13800  C                      EXSR OUTSR                     Print error msg          001
13900  C                      ENDIF                                                   E001
14000  C                      ENDSR                          End YEAR SR
14100  *
14200  * Test for negative AMT value....
14300  *
14400  C         SIGNSR       BEGSR                          Begin SIGNSR
14500  C         AMT          IFLT *ZERO                     AMT negative?            B001
14600  C                      MOVE 7          Y              Msg 8                    001
14700  C                      EXSR OUTSR                     Print error msg          001
14800  C                      ENDIF                                                   E001
14900  C                      ENDSR                          End SIGNSR sr
15000  *
15100  * Print record values & first error on first line and other
15200  * error messages on the following lines......
15300  *
15400  C         OUTSR        BEGSR                          Begin SR
15500  C         *IN60        IFEQ *OFF                      Ind. 60 off?             B001
15600  C                      EXCPTLINE1                     Print 1st msg            001
15700  C                      MOVE *ON        *IN60          Set on 60                001
15800  C                      ELSE                           Other error msg          X001
15900  C                      EXCPTLINES                     Print other msg          001
16000  C                      ENDIF                                                   E001
16100  C                      ENDSR                          End OUTSR sr
16200  *
16300  OQSYSPRT H  101    1P
16400  O          OR         OF
16500  O                          UDATE Y    8
16600  O                                    38 'TRANSACTION FILE'
16700  O                                    62 'VALIDATION ERROR REPORT'
16800  O                                    78 'PAGE'
16900  O                          PAGE  Z   83
17000  O          E 11            LINE1
17100  O                          RECORD    50
```

Figure 12-34 Compile listing of the batch edit program. (Continued)

```
17200  O                    MSG,Y    83
17300  O        E  1         LINES
17400  O                    MSG,Y    83
       * * * * *  E N D   O F   S O U R C E  * * * * *
             A d d i t i o n a l   D i a g n o s t i c   M e s s a g e s
   7086     1200   RPG PROVIDES BLOCK OR UNBLOCK SUPPORT FOR FILE TRANFILE.
 5738RG1 V2R2M0 920925            IBM SAA RPG/400              SMYERS/CH12DVD
 EQUENCE
 NUMBER    *...+....1....+....2....+....3....+....4....+....5....+....6....+....7....+....8
                 C o m p i l e - T i m e   T a b l e s
 Table/Array . . . . . . . :   MSG
   17600   ACCOUNT NUMBER NOT VALID
   17700   NAME NOT LEFT-JUSTIFIED
   17800   NAME CONTAINS INVALID CHARACTERS
   17900   INVALID MONTH
   18000   INVALID DAY
   18100   INVALID YEAR
   18200   AMOUNT NEGATIVE
 Table/Array . . . . . . . :   DAY
   18400   3128313031303131313030313031
 Table/Array . . . . . . . :   ALPHA
   18600   'ABCDEFGHIJKLMNOPQRSTUVWXYZ
```

1200 -
1300   The transaction file TRANFILE is defined as an input, primary, externally defined, keyed physical file. Output is assigned to the system printer file, QSYSPRT.

1400 - AARY is defined as a *Run Time* array. It elements are loaded by the value in the ACT# field, which is referenced in a data structure.

1500 -
1600   MSG is a *Compile Time* array that includes the seven error messages. DAY is a *Compile Time* array that includes the maximum number of days for each month.

1700 - SUM is a *Run Time* array loaded in calculations from a step for the Modulus-11 method.

1800 - NAM is a *Run Time* array loaded in calculations with the NAME field value.

1900 - ALPHA is a *Compile Time* array in which valid alphabetic characters (specified in the specifications) are stored. **Blank**, single apostrophe ('), and **A** through **Z** are considered alphabetic.

2000 -
2900   A *data structure* is specified that includes the fields explained below.

        On line 2100 the input field ACT# is defined followed by the AARY array name on line 2200. Notice that the FROM and TO references for both entries are the same. This coding loads the *Run Time* array AARY from the value in ACT#.

        The input field NAMF is defined on line 2300 followed by the FIRST field, which redefines the first position of NAME. FIRST is used in left-justification validation of the NAME field.

        The input field DATA is defined on line 2500 and redefined into its MM, DD, YY values on lines 2600 through 2800. The redefined fields are used to validate the transaction date.

        The physical file's record format of 39 characters is redefined on line 2900 with the RECORD field. The report format requires that the input record's "image" be printed instead of the individual fields separated by spaces.

3100 -
3800 - The **EXSR** statement on line 3100 passes control to the HOUSEK subroutine where all indicators used in the program are set off. The **EXSR** statement on line 3200 transfers control to the ACTSR subroutine where the ACT# value is validated with the Modulus-11 check digit method.

Figure 12-34   Compile listing of the batch edit program. (Continued)

The **EXSR** branches to the NAMESR subroutine where the NAME field value is validated for left-justification and valid characters. The **EXSR** statement on line 3400 transfers control to the MTHSR subroutine where the MM value of the DATE field is validated.

The **CASEQ** statement on line 3500 tests that the MM value is valid (indicaotr **20** off). If it is valid, control is passed to the DAYSR subroutine where a test is made for the maximum number of days in a month. The **ENDCS** operation on line 3600 ends the CASEQ statement.

The **EXSR** statement on line 3700 transfers control to the YEARSR where the YY value in DATE is validated. The **EXSR** statement on line 3800 transfers control to the SIGNSR subroutine where a sign test is made for the AMT field.

Begin Subroutines:

4200 -
4400   The **MOVEA** statement on line 4300 turns off all the indicators in the indicator array built automatically for every program by the RPG/400 compiler. The ***IN,20** *Factor 2* entry turns off (from "1s" to "0s") the indicators beginning with **20** (element 20 in the array). This coding technique provides a method of turning off many indicators with one statement instead of with multiple **MOVE** or **SETOF** instructions. The **ENDSR** operation on ine 4400 ends the subroutine.

4800 -
7300   The ACTSR subroutine includes the arithmetic instructions for the Modulus-11 check digit method. The **Z-ADD** statements on lines 4900 and 5000 define and initialize the index for the AARY array and the multiplier N.

        Statement 5400 begins the **DOWGT** group, which is repeated while the value in X (array index) is greater than zero. For the first pass through the **DOW** group, the MULT statement on line 5500 multiplies the sixth digit in ACT# by 1 (the Modulus-11 low-order starting digit). The product is stored in the sixth element of the SUM array, which is crossfooted on line 6500. Within the **DOW** group, X is decremented on line 5600, N is incremented on line 6000, and the multiplication continued until X is equal to zero (all of the digits in ACT# individually multiplied by their related Modulus-11 digit).

        The **IFEQ** statement on line 5700 tests X for a zero value. If X is zero, the **LEAVE** operation on line 5800 transfers control out of the DOW group to line 6500. The **ENDIF** operation ends the **IFEQ** group. The ADD statement on line 6000 increments N by 1. The **ENDDO** operation on line 6100 ends the **DOWGT** group.

6500   The products stored in the elements of the SUM array are crossfooted by the **XFOOT** operation and the sum stored in the TOTAL field.

6700   TOTAL is divided by the Modulus-11 constant 11.

6800 - The **MVR** statement saves the remainder value from the **DIV** statement on line 6700 and stores it in the REMAIN field.

6900 - The **IFGT** statement tests the remainder for a value greater than zero. If REMAIN is greater than zero, it indicates that the ACT# value did not pass the Modulus-11 validation test.

7000 -
7100 - When the **IFGT** test on line 6900 is true (error condition), 1 is moved to Y, which is the index for the MSG array. The **EXSR** statement on line 7100 transfers control to the OUTSR subroutine, which controls the exception output of the record's values and messages.

7200 -
7300   The **ENDIF** operation ends the **IFGT** group and the **ENDSR** ends the ACTSR subroutine.

7800 -
8100   The **BEGSR** operation on line 7800 begins the NAMESR. The **IFEQ** statement on line 7900 tests the first field (defined in the data structure) for blank. If the test is true, a left-justification error is indicated. The **MOVE** statement on line

Figure 12-34   Compile listing of the batch edit program. (Continued)

8000 moves 2 to the MSG index Y. The **EXSR** statement on line 8100 transfers control to the OUTSR subroutine, where printed ouput is controlled.

8200   If the value in NAME passes the justification check (FIRST not equal to blank), it is checked for valid alphabetic characters.

8600 - The **MOVEA** statement moves the value in the NAME field to the NAM array.

8700 - The statements within the **DO** group are repeated until the value in X is greater than 20 (*Factor 2* entry). X is automatically initialized to 1 when the **DO** statement is executed for the first time.

8800 - The value in X determines which NAM element is tested against the valid characters stored in the ALPHA array. The first pass in the loop tests the first character in the array; the second pass, the second character; and so forth. When a valid character is tested, indicator **20** is set on.

8900
9100 - The **IFEQ** statement tests the status of the **20** indicator. When it is "off," an invalid character in the NAM array is indicated. The literal 3 is moved to the MSG array's index Y and an exit executed to the OUTSR subroutine, where the error message is output.

9200 - The **LEAVE** operation transfer control out of the **DO** group to line 9500.

9300 -
9600   The **ENDIF** operation on line 9300 ends the **IFEQ** statement on line 8900. The **ENDDO** operation on line 9400 ends the **DO** statement on line 8700. The **ENDIF** operation on line 9500 ends the **IFEQ** statement on line 8900. The **ENDSR** operation on line 9600 ends the NAMESR subroutine.

10000 - Begins the MTHSR subroutine.

10100 -
10400   The value in MM (defined in the data structure as the first two characters of DATE) is tested in the compound **IF** statement for a value equal to zero or greater than 12. If either test is true, 4 is moved to the MSG index Y, and control branches to the OUTSR subroutine, where the error message will be exception output.

10500 - The **MOVE** statement turns on indicator **20** which conditions the **CASEQ** statement on line 3500, which is executed when the indicator is "off" (value in MM valid).

10600 -
10700   The **ENDIF** operation ends the **IFEQ** statement on line 10100. **ENDDO** ends the MTHSR subroutine.

11100 - Begins the DAYSR subroutine which is executed only if MM passes its validation test.

11200 - An element value in the DAY array is accessed positionally using MM as the index and its value stored in MDAYS by the **Z-ADD** operation.

11300 - The **CASEQ** statement tests the value in MM for 02 (February). If the test is true, control passes to the LEPSR subroutine, where the leap year test is made.

11400 - The **ENDCS** operation ends the **CASEQ** statement on line 11300.

11500 -
11900   The **IFGT** statement tests the value in DD with the value in MDAYS. If the test is true, the **MOVE** statement on line 11600 moves 5 to the MSG index Y, and a branch is made to the OUTSR subroutine. The **ENDIF** operation on line 11800 ends the **IFGT** statement on line 11500, and the **ENDSR** operation ends the DAYSR subroutine.

12300 - The **BEGSR** statement begins the LEPSR subroutine, which is accessed only if the **CASEQ** test on line 11300 is true (MM = 02).

12400 - YY is divided by 4 and the quotient stored in QUOTNT.

Figure 12-34   Compile listing of the batch edit program. (Continued)

12500 - The **IFEQ** statement tests the value in QUOTNT for zero. If the test is true, 1 is added to MDAYS, increasing the
         maximum number of days for February from 28 to 29. The **ENDIF** operation on line 12700 ends the **IFEQ** statement
         on line 12500. The **ENDSR** operation ends the LEPSR subroutine.

13200 - The **BEGSR** statement begins the YEARSR.

13300 - The **Z-ADD** statement initializes the NYR field to zero.

13400 - Because a transaction year that is one year greater than UYEAR is considered valid (see specifications), 1 is added to
         UYEAR.

13500 -
13800 - The compound **IF** statement tests the value in YY to determine if it is less than UYEAR or greater than UYEAR + 1. If
         either of these tests is true, 6 is moved to the Y and a branch is made to the OUTSR subroutine.

13900 -
14000   The **ENDIF** operation ends the compound **IF** statement on lines 13500 and 13600. The **ENDDO** operation ends the
         YEARSR subroutine.

14400 - The **BEGSR** statement begins the SIGNSR.

14500 - The **IFLT** statement tests AMT for a value less than zero (indicating a negative value). If the test is true, 7 is moved
         to the Y and control is transferred to the OUTSR subroutine.

14800 -
14900   The **ENDIF** operation ends the **IFEQ** statement on line 14500, and the **ENDSR** operation ends the SIGNSR
         subroutine.

15400 - The **BEGSR** statement begins the OUTSR subroutine, which controls the printing of all error messages.

15500 -
15600   The **IFEQ** statement tests the status of indicator **60**, which is set on by the **MOVE** statement on line 157000 after
         the first error message and record values are exception-output. When the test is false, the **EXCPT LINE1** statement
         on line 15600 transfers control to line 17000 where the value in RECORD (defined in the *data structure*) and the first
         error message for the current record are printed.

15700 - The **MOVE** statement turns on indicator **60** so that **LINE1** cannot be exception-output for any additional validation
         errors.

15800 - After the first error message is printed and indicators **60** set on, any other validation errors will execute the **EXCPT**
         LINES statement on line 15900 transfer control to line 17300, where a message is printed. After the first error
         message is printed, this output controls the printing of any other messages for the current record.

16000 -
16100   The **ENDIF** operation ends the **IFEQ** statement on line 15500. The **ENDSR** operation ends the OUTSR subroutine.

16300 -
16900   The constants, UDATE, and PAGE values are printed at **1P** time and on every overflow page.

17000 -
17200   The first error message (Y = 1) in the MSG array and the value in RECORD (defined in the *data structure*) are printed
         by this exception line.

17300 -
17400   Any additional error messages for the current record are printed without the RECORD value by this exception
         output.

Figure 12-34 Compile listing of the batch edit program. (Continued)

SUMMARY

Data validation is important in the *batch* and/or *interactive* mode to ensure that data entered into a computerized system is accurate. The hardware and software restrictions of the computer installation usually determine when and how data is validated. Data may be validated by *batch* procedures external to a program, by batch procedures internal to a program, or by *interactive* procedures internal to a program.

Validation procedures may be broadly classified as *data type testing* and *data field checking*.

Data type testing includes the testing of numeric fields for valid numeric characters (**0–9**) and may be supported in a *batch* program by the **TESTN** operation or interactively by screen control. Because RPG/400 does not have syntax unique to alphabetic testing, it may be supported by including a *Compile Time* array of valid alphabetic characters in the program. Then, any characters that are not usually considered alphabetic (the single quote mark, for example) may be included as valid in the testing procedure. *Sign testing* may be controlled by testing input fields with *Field Indicators* (columns 65–70) or *Result Fields* in calculations with *Resulting Indicators* (columns 54–59). Included in sign testing is the check of a numeric field for a zero value. This is an important test for fields that are used as a divisor in a divide instruction. Any attempt to divide a value by zero will cause either a termination of or a halt of program execution.

Data field checking includes the *presence* or *absence*, *justification*, *acceptabiltiy*, *relationship*, and *structure* of data. The *presence* of data check assures that something has been entered in the related field. On the other hand, the *absence* of data check determines if nothing is entered into the field area. *Justification* validation is usually performed only on alphanumeric fields to test if the value is entered beginning in the high-order position. The *acceptability* of data includes *range checking, testing of a check digit, limit checking, correspondence checking,* and the *validation of a batch total.*

QUESTIONS

12-1. Define data validation.

12-2. How may data validation procedures be implemented in a computer environment?

12-3. Explain how each of the data validation procedures named in Question 12-2 may be controlled in a computer environment?

12-4. What is the purpose of an error rejection or abeyance file?

12-5. Name and explain the validation functions included in data type testing.

12-6. By what coding methods may input data be validated as numeric?

12-7. What characters in a computer's character set are considered numeric?

12-8. Examine the following instruction and explain the function of each *Resulting Indicator*:

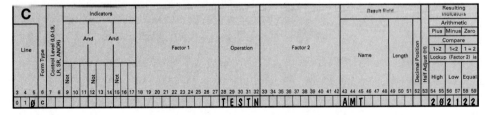

12-9. How must the *Result Field* specified in the **TESTN** operation in Question 12-8 be defined?

12-10. Explain the validation procedure(s) that may be included in an RPG/400 program for testing a field value as alphabetic.

12-11. Name the methods by which *sign testing* may be implemented in an RPG/400 program.

12-12. During processing, where is the sign of a number stored in a computer's memory? In a hexadecimal copy listing (over-and-under format) generated in an IBM mainframe or minicomputer environment, where is the sign identified?

12-13. When is it important to check a field value for zero?

12-14. What are some of the data validation functions that may be included in data field checking?

12-15. How is the *presence* of data checking implemented in an RPG/400 program?

12-16. How is the *absence* of data checking supported in an RPG/400 program?

12-17. Is *justification* checking usually performed on numeric or alphanumeric data (or both)? Explain your answer.

12-18. What data validation functions are related to the *acceptability of data* testing?

12-19. Identify an application in which *range* checking is applicable.

12-20. Refer to Question 12-19, and explain how the application may be controlled in an RPG/400 program.

12-21. Explain the function of a *check digit*. Where is it usually stored in the related field value?

12-22. Use the Modulus-11 method to create a *check digit* for account numbers 12000 and 123456.

12-23. Use the Modulus-11 *check digit* method to determine if account numbers 130003 and 77003 are valid.

12-24. Name an application in which *limit* checking may be used. How is it implemented in an RPG/400 program?

12-25. Give an example of *correspondence* checking. How may it be controlled in an RPG/400 program?

12-26. What is a *batch total?* How may it be controlled in an RPG/400 program?

12-27. Explain the function of the **CHECK** operation.

Refer to the statement below and answer Questions 12-28 through 12-34.

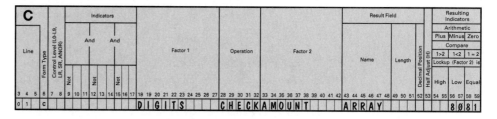

12-28. What entries may be specified in *Factor 1?*

12-29. What entries may be specified in *Factor 2?*

12-30. What entries may be specified in the *Result Field?*

12-31. In the example shown above, what will be stored in ARRAY?

12-32. Where does the checking of the characters in DIGITS begin in ACCOUNT? How could this control be modified to begin checking at some other character?

12-33. When is indicator **80** set on?

12-34. When is indicator **81** set on? When must an indicator be specified in columns 58–59?

PROGRAMMING ASSIGNMENTS

For each of the following programming assignments, a physical file must have been created and loaded with the related data records. Your instructor will inform you as to whether you have to create the physical file and load it or if it has been prepared for the assignment.

Programming Assignment 12-1: BATCH VALIDATION OF SAVINGS ACCOUNT TRANSACTIONS

A bank wants a program created that will ensure the accuracy of all daily savings account transactions before updating a depositor's account. The program is to perform the following validation checks on the input data:

1. Transaction code
2. Transaction amount
3. Transaction date

Details related to each of these are explained in the following paragraphs. When a validation error is found, no further checks are to be performed, and any subsequent processing for that record is to be discontinued. The related error message is to be printed on the report with the record information.

Transaction Code Validation.   The valid transactions codes are

D - Deposit   W - Withdrawal   I - Interest Credit

A - Debit Adjustment   C - Credit Adjustment

Any other code value is to be considered invalid.

Transaction Amount Validation.   The following tests are to be performed on the transaction amount:

1. Invalid zero value.
2. If transaction code is D, I, or C, the amount must be positive.
3. If transaction code is W or A, the amount must be negative.

Transaction Date Validation.   The following functions are to be performed, in the sequence presented, for transaction date validation.

Valid Month Number Test:

1. Test the transaction month number to determine if it is greater than 0 and less than 13.

Days in a Month Test:

1. If the transaction month test is passed, look up an array for the maximum number of days for the related month.
2. If the transaction month is equal to 02 (Feb.), divide the year element of the date by 4 and test the remainder value. If the remainder is zero (indicates a leap year), add 1 to the array value 28. (*Note:* Move the array value to a work field. Changing the array value will store the new value for the entire run.)
3. If transactions days is not zero, compare it with the array value from step 1 or 2. Transactions days is invalid if it is either zero or greater than the related array value.

Transaction Year Validation.   The year value in the transaction date must be equal to the report year.

Array Data

Days in a Month Array. Processed positionally with the transaction month value as the index.

312831303130313130313031

Error Message Array. Processed positionally with the related error number as the index value.

INVALID TRANSACTION CODE
TRANSACTION AMOUNT ZERO
CODE INDICATES AMOUNT MUST BE POSITIVE
CODE INDICATES AMOUNT MUST BE NEGATIVE
TRANSACTION MONTH INVALID
TRANSACTION DAYS INVALID
TRANSACTION YEAR INVALID

Input of Report Date: Create a *data area* and load it with a report date value of 022996. Input it to the program *implicitly* with a *data area data structure* or *explicitly* with calculation statements.

Physical File Record Format:

PHYSICAL FILE DESCRIPTION

SYSTEM: AS/400	DATE: Yours
FILE NAME: Yours	REV NO: 0
RECORD NAME: Yours	KEY LENGTH: 6
SEQUENCE: Keyed	RECORD SIZE: 15

FIELD DEFINITIONS

FIELD NO	FIELD NAME	SIZE	TYPE	POSITION FROM	TO	COMMENTS
1	TRCODE	1	C	1	1	D,W,I,A,C
2	ACCT#	6	C	2	7	Key field
3	TRDATE	6	P	8	11	
4	TRAMT	7	P	12	15	2 decimals

Physical file data:

Transaction Code	Account Number	Transaction Date	Transaction Amount
D	100000	020195	0084000
W	200000	023196	1250000
T	300000	021096	0009250
A	400000	023096	0024567-
I	500000	021596	090000Y
C	600000	020196	0067899
D	700000	021196	0000000
W	800000	023096	0012094-
D	900000	022896	0002500-
D	910000	130896	0100000
C	980000	022997	0070000-

Report Design:

```
        0              1              2              3              4              5              6              7              8
   1234567890123456789012345678901234567890123456789012345678901234567890123456789012345678901234567890
 1                          QUARTERLY  SAVINGS  ACCOUNT  TRANSACTIONS                          PAGE XXØX
 2                               FOR  QUARTER  ENDING  ØX/XX/XX
 3
 4
 5   ACCOUNT NO     DATE        CODE       AMOUNT                        ERROR  MESSAGES
 6
 7     XXXXXX    ØX/XX/XX        X      XX,XXØ.XX    X-------------------------------------------X
 8
 9     XXXXXX    ØX/XX/XX        X      XX,XXØ.XX    X-------------------------------------------X
10
11        NOTES:
12
13           1.  HEADINGS ON TOP OF EVERY PAGE.
14
15           2.  SINGLE SPACE ERROR MESSAGES.  DOUBLE SPACE AFTER LAST ERROR
16
17               MESSAGE FOR TRANSACTION.
```

Programming Assignment 12-2:   BATCH VALIDATION OF ITEM PURCHASES

A company requests a program to batch validate item purchases before accounts payable and general ledger accounts are updated.

Processing: The following validation functions must be included in the RPG/400 program:

Item Number Validation: Use the Modulus-11 check digit method to validate that the item number is correct.

Item Name Validation:

1. Test that the name value is alphabetic. Blank, hyphen, and A through Z are to be considered alphabetic characters. ***Hint: store these characters in a Named Constant and use the CHECK operation to check the NAME field for an invalid character.***
2. Test the NAME value for left-justification.

Vendor Number Validation: Include the following valid vendor numbers in a *Compile Time* table defined with six one-byte elements: **124568.** Using VENDR# as the search argument, look up the table for a valid vendor number.

Cost Validation: Multiply QTY by UCOST to determine the cost of the purchase. Validate that the purchase cost does not exceed $2,000.

Error Identification: Include the following error messages in a *Compile Time* array:

ITEM NUMBER DOES NOT CHECK
ITEM NAME NOT ALPHABETIC
ITEM NAME NOT LEFT-JUSTIFIED
VENDOR NUMBER NOT VALID
COST EXCEEDS $2,000

The program is to be written so that every test is made.

Physical File Record Format:

```
                            PHYSICAL FILE DESCRIPTION

         SYSTEM: AS/400                              DATE: Yours
         FILE NAME: Yours                            REV NO: 0
         RECORD NAME: Yours                          KEY LENGTH: 5
         SEQUENCE: Keyed                             RECORD SIZE: 48

                              FIELD DEFINITIONS

         FIELD      FIELD NAME    SIZE   TYPE    POSITION        COMMENTS
          NO                                    FROM    TO

           1        ITEMNO         5      C        1      5   Key field
           2        NAME          26      C        6     31
           3        PDATE          6      P       32     35
           4        VENDR#         1      P       36     36
           5        QTY            3      P       37     38   0 decimals
           6        UCOST          6      P       39     42   2 decimals
           7        UMEASR         6      C       43     48
```

Physical file data:

Item Number	Item Name	Purchase Date	Vendor Number	Quantity	Cost Per Item	Unit of Measure
11184	BLACK TRUFFLES	040195	7	024	008500	JAR/OZ
11206	SHARK FIN SOUP	040595	4	120	001000	CAN/OZ
11304	PICKLED TRIPE	041095	3	036	000400	JAR/OZ
11509	SMOKED PHEASANT	041595	8	012	001200	CAN/PK
11607	BLACK CAVIAR	041895	5	060	003900	CAN/OZ
11703	CHOCOLATE-COVERED ANTS	042095	6	048	000650	CAN/OZ
11800	SEA WATER KEL9 SPROUTS	042895	2	144	002000	JAR/OZ
T2009	REINDEER MILK YOGURT	043095	9	010	000700	JAR/QT

Report Design: Examine the printer spacing chart and notice that the values for a record's fields are only printed on the line for the first error message. Any other error messages for the related record are to be printed without the field values. Only the records that have validation errors are to be printed.

```
ØX/XX/XX                    ITEM PURCHASES VALIDATION REPORT                    PAGE XXØX

ITEM        ITEM NAME        DATE    VENDOR   QTY     COST/ITEM   UNIT OR MEAS.  ERROR MESSAGES

XXXXX  X---------------X  ØX/XX/XX   X      XØX   X,XXØ.XX     XXXXXX       X-----------------X
                                                                           X-----------------X

XXXXX  X---------------X  ØX/XX/XX   X      XØX   X,XXØ.XX     XXXXXX       X-----------------X
                                                                           X-----------------X

       NOTES:

          1. USE SYSTEM DATE FOR REPORT.

          2. PAGE OVERFLOW ON LINE 18.

          3. DOUBLE SPACE AFTER LAST ERROR MESSAGE FOR RELATED RECORD.
```

chapter 13
Physical File Maintenance (Batch Mode)

The *Data Description Specifications* syntax to create physical files was discussed in Chapter 2. Recall that a physical file may be created as **keyed** or **nonkeyed** and may be defined with the following additional attributes:

1. *Keyed* file with records that have *unique* keys (duplicate keys not supported).
2. *Keyed* file that supports records with duplicate keys.
3. *Keyed* file defined so that the records are processed in a descending key order instead of the default ascending key order.
4. *Keyed* file that processes the records in a *LIFO* (last-in-first-out) key group order instead of the default *FIFO* (first-in-first-out) order.
5. *Keyed* file defined with a *composite* key which includes more than one field from the physical file record format. The file may be processed by the composite key or a partial key.
6. Other keywords support editing, relational tests, validation, referencing the record or field attributes from other files, and numerous other functions.

PHYSICAL FILE PROCESSING

Keyed and *nonkeyed* physical files may be processed by the following methods:

Keyed Physical Files:

1. In a *keyed* sequence by the RPG/400 logic cycle, or sequentially retrieve records in a keyed order with a **READ** (*Read from a file*), **READE** (*Read next record with an equal key*), **READP** (*Read prior record from a data file*), or **REDPE** (*Read prior record with an equal key*) operation.
2. Randomly, by a full or partial key value with the **CHAIN** operation.
3. By lower and upper key limits with the records processed sequentially forward or backward by one of the **READ** operations.

Nonkeyed Physical Files:

1. In *arrival sequence* (first-in-first-out order).
2. By *relative record number* (record's position in the physical file) by a **READ** or **READP** operation.

PHYSICAL FILE MAINTENANCE

The maintenance of physical files includes the following functions:

1. *Addition* of records
2. *Update* of existing records
3. *Logical deletion* of existing records
4. *Tagging* of records for deletion (an update function)
5. *Reorganization*

Each of these maintenance functions will be discussed, and standalone program examples will be shown in the following sections.

Addition of Records to a Physical File

After a physical file is created, the process of loading it with data records is an add function. Under the control of an RPG/400 program, records may be added to a physical file by the **WRITE** operation or with the compiler's logic cycle.

Record Addition with the WRITE Operation

The addition of records to an externally defined physical file with the **WRITE** operation does not require that *Output Specifications* be included in the program. When the **WRITE** statement is executed, the record format for the current record processed is written to the physical file after the last record stored. The syntax of the **WRITE** operation is detailed in Figure 13-1.

WRITE Operation Syntax:

1. Any *total or detail time* indicator(s) may be specified in columns 7–17 to condition a WRITE statement.

2. The WRITE operation name is entered in the *Operation* field.

3. *Factor 2* must contain the name of a record format for externally defined physical files. For program-described physical files, the related file name must be specified in *Factor 2*.

4. If *Factor 2* includes a record format name, the *Result Field* must be blank. When a physical file name is specified in *Factor 2*, the *Result Field* must contain a *data structure name*.

5. An indicator may be specified in columns 56–57 of the *Resulting Indicators* field. The indicator will be set on if an error condition is detected when the WRITE statement is executed. A file full, duplicate key, or device error will cause the indicator to turn on. With this indicator option, program control can control the error and prevent cancellation of the program.

6. On a WRITE to a *subfile* (discussed in Chapter 17), an indicator may be specified in *Resulting Indicator* columns 58–59, which is set on if the subfile is full.

Figure 13-1 Syntax of the **WRITE** operation.

Processing Features:

• When *Factor 2* contains a record format name, the current value of all the fields in the record format is written to the file.

• When records are added to a nonkeyed file, the *relative record number* must be specified. The record number field must be updated so that the record contains the relative record number of the record written to the file.

Figure 13-1 Syntax of the **WRITE** operation. (Continued)

File Description Syntax for Record Addition

The *File Description* syntax to add records to a physical file is detailed in Figure 13-2. Two examples are shown, one which defines the file as **output** and the other which defines output as *update/full-procedural.*

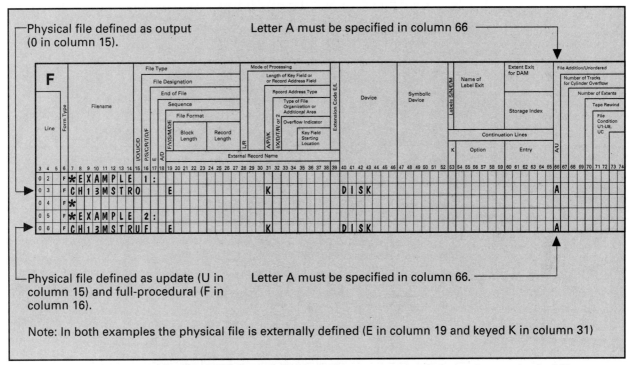

Figure 13-2 RPG/400 *File Description* syntax to add records to a physical file.

RPG/400 Example Batch Adds Program

The specifications for the RPG/400 program that adds transaction records to a master file are detailed in Figure 13-3.

PROGRAM SPECIFICATIONS		Page 1 of 1
Program Name: Master Field Addition	Program - ID: CH13P1	Written by: SM
Purpose: Add records to a customer master file		Approved by: CM

Figure 13-3 Specifications for an RPG/400 program that adds records to a physical file.

Input files: CH13ADDS _____ (nonkeyed) _____ _____

Output files: CH13MSTR _____ (keyed/unique)   CH13ERRS _____ (nonkeyed)

Processing Requirements:

Write an RPG/400 program to add transaction records to a customer master file and detect and store records that generate duplicate key errors.

Input to the program:

The externally defined nonkeyed physical file CH13ADDS contains data records for new customers.

Processing:

Read the transaction file (CH13ADDS) in arrival sequence until end of file. For every record processed, add it to the customer master file CH13MSTR. Because CH13MSTR is defined to support only unique keys, any attempt to add a record that has a key already stored in the file will result in a duplicate key error. Records with duplicate keys are to be added to the error file CH13ERRS.

Output:

Move the field values from the transaction file to the customer master fields and write the master record to the customer master file. For records that flag a duplicate key error, move the field values from the transaction file to the error record's fields and write the error record to the error file.

Figure 13-3 Specifications for an RPG/400 program that adds records to a physical file. (Continued)

The system flowchart in Figure 13-4 indicates that three physical files are processed by the "adds" program. A transaction file (CH13ADDS) includes the "add" records, a master file (CH13MSTR) to which the records are to be added, and an error file (CH13ERRS) to which transaction records that have key values already stored in the master file (*duplicate key error*) are written.

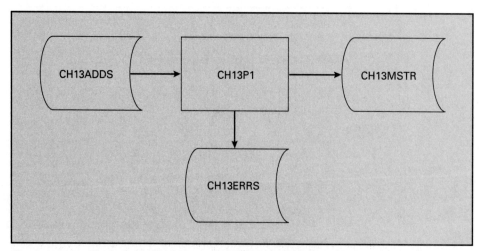

Figure 13-4 System flowchart for the "adds" program.

A listing of the transaction ("adds") file's record format and a **CPYF** (*Copy File*) utility listing of the data in *hexadecimal* format are shown in Figure 13-5.

```
                        Data Description Source
SEQNBR  *...+....1....+....2....+....3....+....4....+....5....+....6....+
  100   A           R ADDSRCD
  200   A             TCODE      1
  300   A             TACT#      5
  400   A             TNAME     30 │ P or blank in column 35
  500   A             TDATE      6│ 0    defines packed decimal
  600   A             TAMT       7  2
```

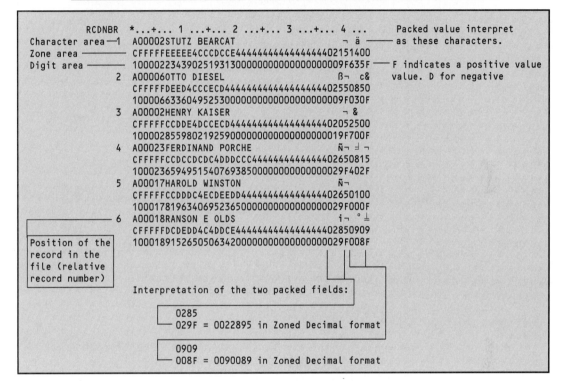

Figure 13-5 Partial source listing of the transaction file's DDS and "hexadecimal" listing of the data.

A listing of the master file's record format to which the transaction data is to be added and a **CPYF** listing of the data in *hexadecimal* format *before* the transaction records are added are detailed in Figure 13-6.

Because the error file's (CH13ERRS) record format is identical to the transaction file (CH13ADDS) and the master file (CH13MSTR), its format is not shown. Also, before execution of the "adds" program, this file contains no data.

```
                        Data Description Source
SEQNBR  *...+....1....+....2....+....3....+....4....+....5....+....6....+
  100   A                                            UNIQUE
  200   A           R MSTRRCD
  300   A             MCODE      1
  400   A             MACT#      5
  500   A             MNAME     30
  600   A             MDATE      6  0
  700   A             MBAL       7  2
  800   A           K MACT#
```

Figure 13-6 Partial source listing of the master file's DDS and "hexadecimal" listing of the data <u>before</u> adding records.

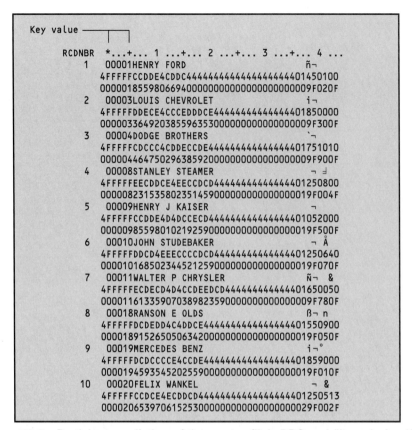

```
         Key value
                    
          RCDNBR  *...+... 1 ...+... 2 ...+... 3 ...+... 4 ...
               1    00001HENRY FORD                      ñ¬
                    4FFFFFCCDDE4CDDC4444444444444444444401450100
                    0000018559806694000000000000000000009F020F
               2    00003LOUIS CHEVROLET                 i¬
                    4FFFFFDDECE4CCCEDDDCE44444444444444401850000
                    0000033649203855963530000000000000009F300F
               3    00004DODGE BROTHERS                  ¬
                    4FFFFFCDCCC4CDDECCDE44444444444444444401751010
                    0000044647502963859200000000000000009F900F
               4    00008STANLEY STEAMER                 ¬  ⌐
                    4FFFFFEECDDCE4EECCDCD44444444444444401250800
                    0000082315358023514590000000000000019F004F
               5    00009HENRY J KAISER                  ¬
                    4FFFFFCCDDE4D4DCCECD44444444444444444401052000
                    0000098559801021925900000000000000019F500F
               6    00010JOHN STUDEBAKER                 ¬  Å
                    4FFFFFDDCD4EEECCCCDCD44444444444444401250640
                    0000101685023445212590000000000000019F070F
               7    00011WALTER P CHRYSLER               Ñ¬  &
                    4FFFFFECDECD4D4CCDEEDCD4444444444444401650050
                    0000116133590703898235900000000000009F780F
               8    00018RANSON E OLDS                   ß¬  n
                    4FFFFFDCDEDD4C4DDCE44444444444444444401550900
                    0000189152650506342000000000000000019F050F
               9    00019MERCEDES BENZ                   i¬°
                    4FFFFFDCDCCCCE4CCDE44444444444444444401859000
                    0000194593545202559000000000000000019F010F
              10    00020FELIX WANKEL                    ¬  &
                    4FFFFFCCDCE4ECDDCD44444444444444444401250513
                    0000206539706152530000000000000000029F002F
```

Figure 13-6 Partial source listing of the master file's DDS and "hexadecimal" listing of the data <u>before</u> adding records. (Continued)

Source Program Coding

A compile listing of the RPG/400 program that "adds" transaction records to a master file is presented in Figure 13-7. Recall that the six-digit numbers preceded by an **A, B,** or **C** are inserted in the original source code and represent the input and output fields from the record formats of three physical files. The **A** numbers relate to the input transaction file (CH13ADDS), the **B** numbers to the output master file (CH13MSTR), and the **C** numbers to the output error file (CH13ERRS).

```
SEQUENCE                                                              IND   DO
NUMBER   *...1....+....2....+....3....+....4....+....5....+....6....+....7...*  USE   NUM
                        S o u r c e   L i s t i n g
    100   * THIS PROGRAM ADDS RECORDS TO A PHYSICAL FILE WITH RECORDS
    200   * FROM A TRANSACTION PHYSICAL FILE DEFINED AS NONKEYED
    300   * DUPLICATE ADDS ARE LOADED TO A PHYSICAL FILE WITH A DDS
    400   * FORMAT IN THE INPUT RECORD IMAGE.....
    500   *
          H
    600   FCH13ADDSIP E                    DISK ─────────────────┐ Transaction file
          RECORD FORMAT(S): LIBRARY SMYERS FILE CH13ADDS.
                EXTERNAL FORMAT ADDSRCD RPG NAME ADDSRCD
    700   FCH13MSTRO  E         K          DISK             A ───┤ Master file
          RECORD FORMAT(S): LIBRARY SMYERS FILE CH13MSTR.
                EXTERNAL FORMAT MSTRRCD RPG NAME MSTRRCD
    800   FCH13ERRSO  E                    DISK             A ───┤ Error File
          RECORD FORMAT(S): LIBRARY SMYERS FILE CH13ERRS.
                EXTERNAL FORMAT ERRRCD RPG NAME ERRRCD
```

Figure 13-7 Compile listing of the "adds" program.

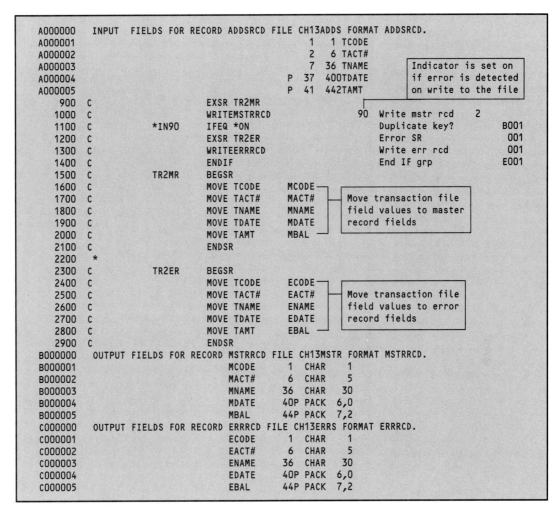

```
A000000  INPUT FIELDS FOR RECORD ADDSRCD FILE CH13ADDS FORMAT ADDSRCD.
A000001                                        1   1 TCODE
A000002                                        2   6 TACT#
A000003                                        7  36 TNAME        ┌─────────────────────┐
A000004                                      P 37 400TDATE        │ Indicator is set on │
A000005                                      P 41 442TAMT         │ if error is detected│
   900  C                 EXSR TR2MR                              │ on write to the file│
  1000  C                 WRITEMSTRRCD            90  Write mstr rcd  2 └──────────────┘
  1100  C       *IN90     IFEQ *ON                   Duplicate key?       B001
  1200  C                 EXSR TR2ER                  Error SR             001
  1300  C                 WRITEERRRCD                 Write err rcd        001
  1400  C                 ENDIF                       End IF grp          E001
  1500  C       TR2MR     BEGSR
  1600  C                 MOVE TCODE     MCODE ─┐
  1700  C                 MOVE TACT#     MACT#  │  ┌────────────────────┐
  1800  C                 MOVE TNAME     MNAME  │  │ Move transaction file│
  1900  C                 MOVE TDATE     MDATE  │  │ field values to master│
  2000  C                 MOVE TAMT      MBAL ─┘  │ record fields        │
  2100  C                 ENDSR                    └────────────────────┘
  2200  *
  2300  C       TR2ER     BEGSR
  2400  C                 MOVE TCODE     ECODE ─┐
  2500  C                 MOVE TACT#     EACT#  │  ┌────────────────────┐
  2600  C                 MOVE TNAME     ENAME  │  │ Move transaction file│
  2700  C                 MOVE TDATE     EDATE  │  │ field values to error│
  2800  C                 MOVE TAMT      EBAL ─┘  │ record fields        │
  2900  C                 ENDSR                    └────────────────────┘
B000000  OUTPUT FIELDS FOR RECORD MSTRRCD FILE CH13MSTR FORMAT MSTRRCD.
B000001                           MCODE    1 CHAR    1
B000002                           MACT#    6 CHAR    5
B000003                           MNAME   36 CHAR   30
B000004                           MDATE  40P PACK  6,0
B000005                           MBAL   44P PACK  7,2
C000000  OUTPUT FIELDS FOR RECORD ERRRCD FILE CH13ERRS FORMAT ERRRCD.
C000001                           ECODE    1 CHAR    1
C000002                           EACT#    6 CHAR    5
C000003                           ENAME   36 CHAR   30
C000004                           EDATE  40P PACK  6,0
C000005                           EBAL   44P PACK  7,2
```

Figure 13-7 Compile listing of the "adds" program. (Continued)

A **CPYF** listing of the master file (CH13MSTR) *after* the "adds" program is executed is shown in Figure 13-8.

Two transaction file (CH13ADDS) records, with keys 00002 and 00018, had the same key value as records already stored in the master file (CH13MSTR). Because the master file was defined with **UNIQUE** keys, records with the same key value are not supported. Indicator **90** in columns 56–57 of the **WRITE** statement flagged this error condition, and program control, for this example, wrote the duplicate records to a nonkeyed physical file (CH13ERRS).

```
     Key value ─┐
               ┌┴┐
     RCDNBR   *...+... 1 ...+... 2 ...+... 3 ...+... 4 ...
          1    00001HENRY FORD                  ñ¬
               4FFFFFCCDDE4CDDC4444444444444444444401450100
               000000185598066940000000000000000000009F020F
       ┌─ 11   A00002STUTZ BEARCAT                  ¬ ä
       │       CFFFFFEEEEE4CCCDCCE44444444444444444402151400
       │       1000022343902519313000000000000000000009F635F
       │    2  00003LOUIS CHEVROLET                 ¡¬
       │       4FFFFFDDECE4CCCEDDDCE44444444444444444401850000
       └─      000003364920385596353000000000000000000009F300F
```

Figure 13-8 **CPYF** utility listing in hexadecimal format of the master file <u>after</u> execution of the "adds" program.

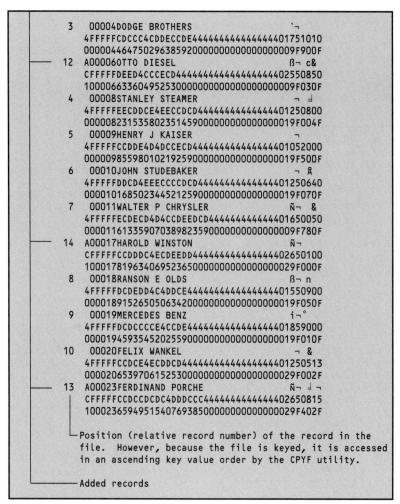

Figure 13-8 **CPYF** utility listing in hexadecimal format of the master file <u>after</u> execution of the "adds" program. (Continued)

Update of Records in a Physical File

After records have been added to a physical file, a common maintenance function is to modify field values. With the exception of key fields, any other field in a *keyed* physical file may be changed. For *nonkeyed* files, the value in any field may be updated.

Before "update" maintenance is introduced, the **SETLL, CHAIN,** and **UPDAT** operations will be discussed. The syntax of the **SETLL** operation is explained in Figure 13-9.

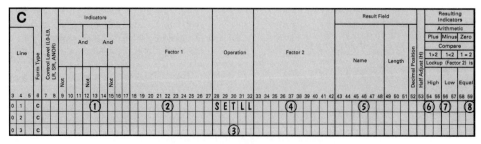

Figure 13-9 Syntax of the **SETLL** operation.

1. *Total or Detail Time* indicators may condition a **SETLL** statement.

2. If the file is accessed by key value, *Factor 1* must contain a field name, Named Constant, Figurative Constant, a literal, or **KLIST** name.

   If the file is accessed by relative record number (position in the file), *Factor 1* must contain a numeric field, integer literal, or Named Constant with no decimal positions.

3. **SETLL** must be specified in the *Operation* field.

4. *Factor 2* must contain either a file name or, for *externally defined* files, a record name.

5. The *Result Field* is not used.

6. An optional indicator may be specified in *Resulting Indicator* columns 54–55 which is set on if the key value or relative record number in *Factor 1* is greater than that stored in the file.

7. If an indicator is specified in *Resulting Indicator* columns 56–57, it is set on if an error occurs when the operation is executed.

8. If an indicator is specified in *Resulting Indicator* columns 58–59, it is set on when the *Factor 1* entry is equal to a key value or relative record number in the file.

Processing Features:

- The **SETLL** operation positions the file at a record that has a key value or relative record number equal to or greater than the value stored in the *Factor 1* item.

- The file accessed must be defined as a *full procedural* file (F in column 16 of the *File Description* statement in the RPG/400 program).

- A **SETLL** statement does not access the record for processing, it only positions the file at a record. **CHAIN** or one of the **READ** operations must access the record for processing.

- If the **SETLL** operation is not successful, the file is positioned at the end. The file, however, may be repositioned by executing the same or another **SETLL** statement.

Figure 13-9   Syntax of the **SETLL** operation. (Continued)

An example and the processing logic of the **SETLL** operation are shown in Figure 13-10.

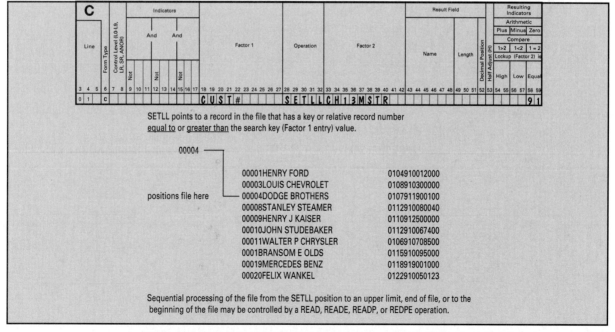

Figure 13-10   Coding example and processing logic of the **SETLL** operation.

The **CHAIN** operation *randomly* retrieves a record from a file based on a key value or relative record number stored in the item specified in *Factor 1* of the statement. Figure 13-11 details the syntax of the **CHAIN** operation.

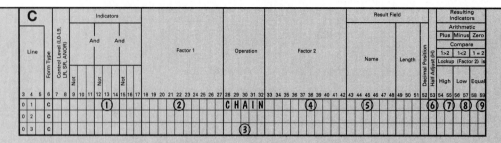

1. *Total or Detail Time* indicators may condition a CHAIN statement.

2. If the file is accessed by key value, *Factor 1* must contain a field name, Named Constant, Figurative Constant, a literal, or KLIST name.

   If the file is accessed by relative record number (position in the file), *Factor 1* must contain a numeric field, integer literal, or Named Constant with no decimal positions.

3. CHAIN must be specified in the *Operation* field.

4. *Factor 2* must contain either a file name or, for *externally defined* files, a record name.

5. A *data structure* name may be specified in the *Result Field* only if *Factor 2* is a program- described file (**F** in column 19 of the *File Description Specifications* statement for the file).

6. An **N** may be specified in column 53, which will prevent a record lock from occurring when update processing is performed on the file. If the file is defined as input (**I** in column 15 of the *File Description Specifications* statement), all records are read without *locks* and the **N** must be omitted in this field.

7. An indicator must be specified in *Resulting Indicator* columns 54–55, which is set on if no record in the file matches the search argument (Factor 1 entry).

8. If an indicator is specified in *Resulting Indicator* columns 56–57, it is set on if an error occurs when the CHAIN operation is executed.

9. Positions 58–59 are not used.

Processing Features:

• The CHAIN operation retrieves a record from a full procedural file (**F** in column 16 of the *File Description Specifications* for the file) and stores the data from the record into its fields.

• When a CHAIN is successful, the file specified in *Factor 2* is positioned so that a subsequent read will retrieve the next sequential record.

• When a CHAIN is not successful, the file must be repositioned by a CHAIN or SETLL statement before any subsequent reads are executed.

• If an update is performed on a file after a successful CHAIN, the last record retrieved is updated.

Figure 13-11 Syntax of the **CHAIN** operation.

A coding example of the **CHAIN** operation is shown in Figure 13-12.

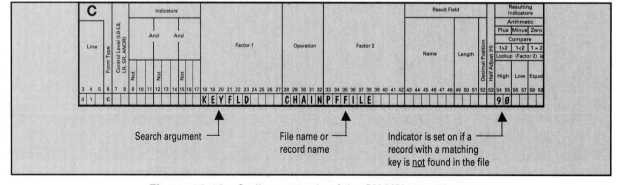

Figure 13-12 Coding example of the **CHAIN** operation.

The **UPDAT** operation modifies the last record retrieved for processing from a file defined as an *update* file (**U** in column 15 of the related *File Description Specifications statement*). A successful **CHAIN** (or **READ, READE, READP, REDPE, READC**) statement must have been executed and a record retrieved before an **UPDAT** to the record is issued. Figure 13-13 explains the syntax of the **UPDAT** operation.

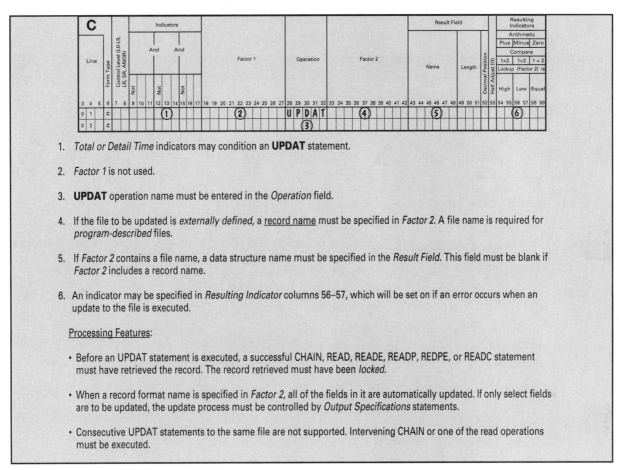

1. *Total or Detail Time* indicators may condition an **UPDAT** statement.

2. *Factor 1* is not used.

3. **UPDAT** operation name must be entered in the *Operation* field.

4. If the file to be updated is *externally defined,* a <u>record name</u> must be specified in *Factor 2.* A file name is required for *program-described* files.

5. If *Factor 2* contains a file name, a data structure name must be specified in the *Result Field.* This field must be blank if *Factor 2* includes a record name.

6. An indicator may be specified in *Resulting Indicator* columns 56–57, which will be set on if an error occurs when an update to the file is executed.

<u>Processing Features</u>:

• Before an UPDAT statement is executed, a successful CHAIN, READ, READE, READP, REDPE, or READC statement must have retrieved the record. The record retrieved must have been *locked.*

• When a record format name is specified in *Factor 2,* all of the fields in it are automatically updated. If only select fields are to be updated, the update process must be controlled by *Output Specifications* statements.

• Consecutive UPDAT statements to the same file are not supported. Intervening CHAIN or one of the read operations must be executed.

Figure 13-13 Syntax of the **UPDAT** operation.

An example **UPDAT** instruction is shown in Figure 13-14.

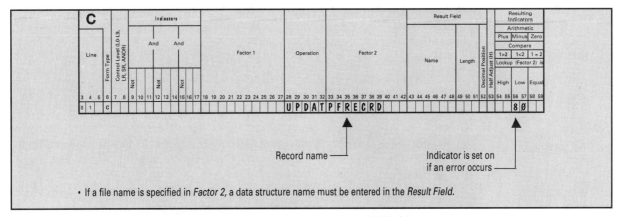

• If a file name is specified in *Factor 2,* a data structure name must be entered in the *Result Field.*

Figure 13-14 Coding example of the **UPDAT** operation.

RPG/400 Example Update Program

The specifications for an RPG/400 program that updates records in a physical file are presented in Figure 13-15.

PROGRAM SPECIFICATIONS   Page 1 of 1

Program Name: Master File Update   Program - ID: CH13P2   Written by: SM

Purpose: Update records in a customer master file   Approved by: CM

Input files: CH13UPS   (nonkeyed)   CH13MSTR   (keyed/unique)

Output files: CH13MSTR   (keyed/unique)   CH13ERRS   (nonkeyed)

Processing Requirements:

Write an RPG/400 program to update records in a customer master file and add transaction records that do not have a matching master record to an error file.

Input to the program:

An externally defined nonkeyed phsyical file CH13UPS contains data records with update information. Because the master file (CH13MSTR) must be defined as an update file, the file is automatically processed as both input and output.

Processing:

Read the transaction file (CH13UPS) in arrival sequence until end of file. For every record processed, CHAIN to the customer master file CH13MSTR with the customer number field (UACT#) from the transaction file.

For a successful CHAIN, move the transaction field values in UCODE, UNAME, and UAMT to their related master record fields. Before the UNAME field value is moved, however, test it for blanks. If it tests as blank, do not move the value to the master record field. Also, move the value in UDATE to the related master record field.

In the event of an unsuccessful CHAIN, move all of the transaction record field values to the related fields in the error file (CH13ERRS) and add the record to the error file.

Output:

Update the master file with the updated record. Add error records to the error file.

Figure 13-15 Specifications for an RPG/400 program that updates records in a physical file.

The system flowchart in Figure 13-16 shows that three physical files are processed by the "update" program: a transaction file (CH13UPS) that contains the "update" data, a master file (CH13MSTR) in which the records are updated, and an error file (CH13ERRS) where transaction records that do not have a matching master file record are written. Note that the double-headed arrow from the RPG/400 program to the CH13MSTR file indicates that the file is input to the program and also output (a file defined as update).

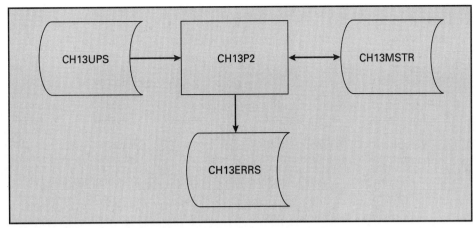

Figure 13-16   System flowchart for the "update" program.

A listing of the transaction ("updates") and a **CPYF** (*Copy File*) utility listing of the data in *hexadecimal* format are shown in Figure 13-17.

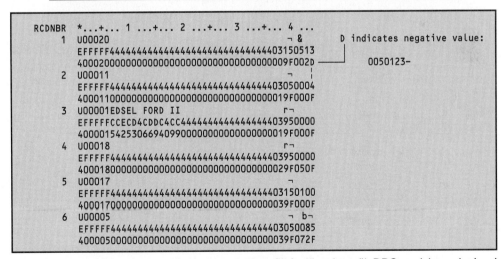

Figure 13-17   Listing of the transaction file's ("updates") DDS and hexadecimal listing of the data.

Hexadecimal listings of the customer master file (CH13MSTR) before and after updating are presented in Figure 13-18. Because the record format for CH13MSTR is identical to the "adds" program, it is not repeated here.

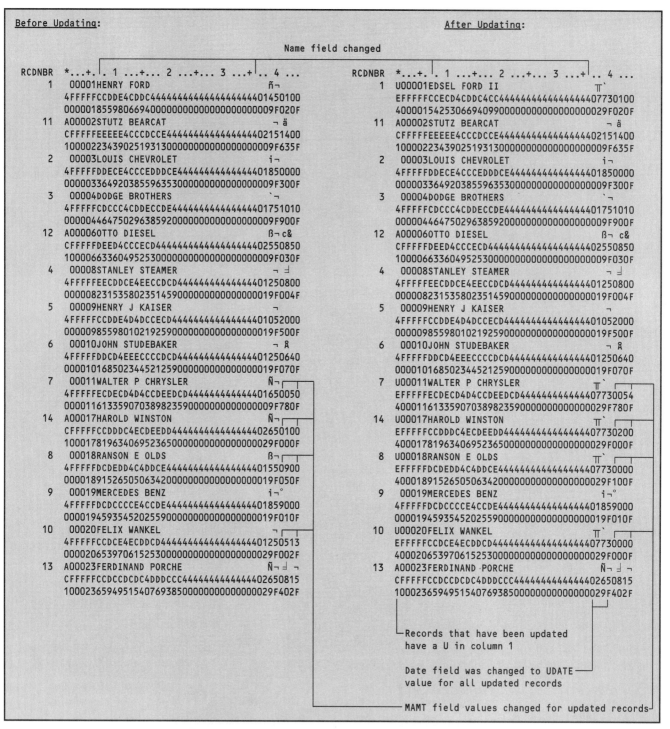

Figure 13-18 CPYF utility listings in hexadecimal format of the CH13MSTR file Before and After updating.

A **CPYF** listing in hexadecimal format of the error file (CH13ERRS) is presented in Figure 13-19. Note that only one update transaction record has been added (00005). The other two records were added by the previously discussed "adds" program.

```
RCDNBR   *...+... 1 ...+... 2 ...+... 3 ...+... 4 ...
     1   A00002HENRY KAISER                        ¬ &  ──── Error records (duplicate keys)
         CFFFFFCCDDE4DCCECD4444444444444444402052500        previously added by the "adds"
         10000285598021925900000000000000000019F700F        program
     2   A00018RANSON E OLDS
         CFFFFFDCDEDD4C4DDCE4444444444444444402850909
         10001891526505063420000000000000000029F008F
     3   U00005                                    ¬ b¬  ──── Error record (master record not
         EFFFFF44444444444444444444444444444403050085        found) added by the "update"
         40000500000000000000000000000000000039F072F        program
```

Figure 13-19 **CPYF** utility listing in hexadecimal format of the CH13ERRS file after execution of the "update" program.

RPG/400 Syntax for the Update Program

The *File Description Specifications* coding for the example "*update*" program is shown in Figure 13-20. Note that CH13MSTR is defined as an *update* (**U** in column 15), *full procedural* (**F** in column 16), *externally defined* (**E** in column 19), and *keyed* (**K** in column 31) file.

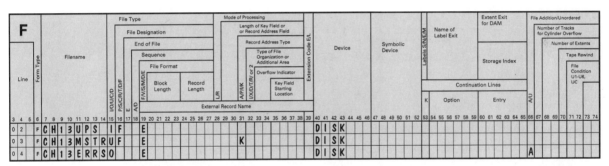

Figure 13-20 *File Description Specifications* coding for the example "update" program.

Defining a file as *update* indicates that it is *both* input and output. A file defined as *full procedural* specifies that it may be processed by any valid file processing operation. The transaction file, CH13UPS, is defined as *nonkeyed* (column 31 blank), *input* (**I** in column 15), *primary* (**P** in column 16), and *externally described* (**E** in column 19). CH13ERRS is defined as a *nonkeyed* (column 31 blank), *output* (**O** in column 15), *externally described* (**E** in column 19), *adds* (**A** in column 66) file.

A compile listing of the program is detailed in Figure 13-21.

Examine the calculations, and note the following syntax:

- The **SETLL** instruction on line 800 determines if a master file key matches the transaction file's search key (UACT#) value. **SETLL** is more efficient than the **CHAIN** operation for initially determining if the record is stored in the file.

- The **CHAIN** instruction on line 1400 accesses the master file record for processing. Within the internal subroutine, transaction file field values are moved to their related master file fields. If UNAME is blank, its value is not moved to the master file field MNAME.

- The **UPDAT** instruction on line 2100 writes the currently retrieved (by the **CHAIN** instruction) and updated record back to its location in CH13MSTR.

- If the **SETLL** instruction on line 800 did not find an equal key value in

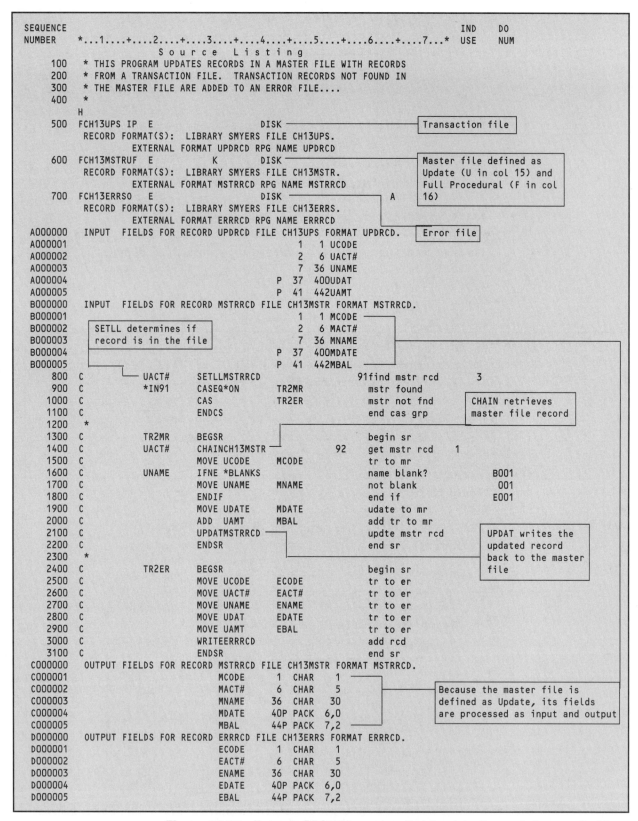

```
SEQUENCE                                                           IND  DO
NUMBER     *...1....+....2....+....3....+....4....+....5....+....6....+....7...*  USE  NUM
                        S o u r c e   L i s t i n g
    100    * THIS PROGRAM UPDATES RECORDS IN A MASTER FILE WITH RECORDS
    200    * FROM A TRANSACTION FILE.  TRANSACTION RECORDS NOT FOUND IN
    300    * THE MASTER FILE ARE ADDED TO AN ERROR FILE....
    400    *
           H
    500    FCH13UPS IP  E              DISK ──────────────────────┤ Transaction file │
           RECORD FORMAT(S): LIBRARY SMYERS FILE CH13UPS.
                    EXTERNAL FORMAT UPDRCD RPG NAME UPDRCD        ┌──────────────────────┐
    600    FCH13MSTRUF  E         K    DISK ───────────────────── │ Master file defined as │
           RECORD FORMAT(S): LIBRARY SMYERS FILE CH13MSTR.        │ Update (U in col 15) and│
                    EXTERNAL FORMAT MSTRRCD RPG NAME MSTRRCD      │ Full Procedural (F in col│
    700    FCH13ERRSO   E              DISK ─────────────────── A │ 16)                     │
           RECORD FORMAT(S): LIBRARY SMYERS FILE CH13ERRS.        └──────────────────────┘
                    EXTERNAL FORMAT ERRRCD RPG NAME ERRRCD
A000000    INPUT   FIELDS FOR RECORD UPDRCD FILE CH13UPS FORMAT UPDRCD.   │ Error file │
A000001                                     1    1 UCODE
A000002                                     2    6 UACT#
A000003                                     7   36 UNAME
A000004                                   P 37  400UDAT
A000005                                   P 41  442UAMT
B000000    INPUT   FIELDS FOR RECORD MSTRRCD FILE CH13MSTR FORMAT MSTRRCD.
B000001                                     1    1 MCODE
B000002    ┌──────────────────┐            2    6 MACT#
B000003    │ SETLL determines if│          7   36 MNAME
           │ record is in the file│       P 37  400MDATE
B000004    └──────────────────┘          P 41  442MBAL
B000005
    800    C      ┌─ UACT#    SETLLMSTRRCD                91find mstr rcd      3
    900    C          *IN91   CASEQ*ON   TR2MR               mstr found
   1000    C                  CAS        TR2ER               mstr not fnd      ┌─────────────────┐
   1100    C                  ENDCS                          end cas grp       │ CHAIN retrieves  │
   1200    *                                                                   │ master file record│
   1300    C          TR2MR   BEGSR                          begin sr          └─────────────────┘
   1400    C          UACT#   CHAINCH13MSTR ─┐               92  get mstr rcd      1
   1500    C                  MOVE UCODE     MCODE            tr to mr
   1600    C          UNAME   IFNE *BLANKS                    name blank?         B001
   1700    C                  MOVE UNAME     MNAME            not blank           001
   1800    C                  ENDIF                           end if              E001
   1900    C                  MOVE UDATE     MDATE            udate to mr
   2000    C                  ADD  UAMT      MBAL             add tr to mr        ┌─────────────────┐
   2100    C                  UPDATMSTRRCD ─┐                 updte mstr rcd      │ UPDAT writes the │
   2200    C                  ENDSR          │                end sr             │ updated record   │
   2300    *                                 │                                   │ back to the master│
   2400    C          TR2ER   BEGSR          │                begin sr           │ file             │
   2500    C                  MOVE UCODE     ECODE            tr to er           └─────────────────┘
   2600    C                  MOVE UACT#     EACT#            tr to er
   2700    C                  MOVE UNAME     ENAME            tr to er
   2800    C                  MOVE UDAT      EDATE            tr to er
   2900    C                  MOVE UAMT      EBAL             tr to er
   3000    C                  WRITEERRRCD                     add rcd
   3100    C                  ENDSR                           end sr
C000000    OUTPUT FIELDS FOR RECORD MSTRRCD FILE CH13MSTR FORMAT MSTRRCD.
C000001                       MCODE      1   CHAR    1 ─┐
C000002                       MACT#      6   CHAR    5  │          ┌─────────────────────┐
C000003                       MNAME     36   CHAR   30  │          │ Because the master file is│
C000004                       MDATE     40P  PACK   6,0 │          │ defined as Update, its fields│
C000005                       MBAL      44P  PACK   7,2 ┘          │ are processed as input and output│
D000000    OUTPUT FIELDS FOR RECORD ERRRCD FILE CH13ERRS FORMAT ERRRCD.  └─────────────────────┘
D000001                       ECODE      1   CHAR    1
D000002                       EACT#      6   CHAR    5
D000003                       ENAME     36   CHAR   30
D000004                       EDATE     40P  PACK   6,0
D000005                       EBAL      44P  PACK   7,2
```

Figure 13-21   Example RPG/400 program that "updates" records in a master file.

CH13MSTR, the TR2ER routine is executed. TR2ER moves the transaction record field values to the error file's fields. The error record is then added to CH13ERRS by the **WRITE** instruction on line 3000.

DELETION OF RECORDS IN A PHYSICAL FILE

Tagging Records for Deletion

Tagging records for deletion is an "update" process that stores a character in a field in the body of a record. Identical to updating, the record must be retrieved by a **CHAIN** or one of the **READ** operations, a character moved into the delete field, and the record written back to its original storage position in the file. Programs that access the file usually test the related field for the delete character to avoid processing (or sometimes, to process) records *tagged* as deleted. Refer to the previously discussed "update" program for the syntax needed to *tag* records in a physical file as deleted.

Logical Deletion of Records

Unlike the *tagging* method, *logical deletion* permanently removes the record from a physical file. The syntax of the **DELET** operation, which is used to delete records *logically,* is explained in Figure 13-22.

1. *Total or Detail Time* indicators may condition a DELET statement.

2. *Factor 1* may have no entry or, for <u>keyed</u> files, may include a field, data structure name, constant, or KLIST name that contains a key value. For file processed by <u>relative record number</u>, *Factor 1* may have no entry, field defined as a numeric integer (no decimal positions), or integer constant.

3. The DELET operation name must be entered in the *Operation* field.

4. *Factor 2* must contain the name of a file or name of a record format in the file from which the record is to be deleted. A record format name may only be used for files that are externally defined.

   Result Field is not used.

5. If *Factor 1* has an entry, an indicator must be specified in *Resulting Indicator* columns 54–55, which will be set on if the record to be deleted is not found in the file.

6. An indicator may be entered in columns 56–57 if the operation does not complete successfully (e.g., user does not have authority to delete records).

<u>Processing Features</u>:

- If *Factor 1* does not have an entry, a successful CHAIN, READ, READE, READP, REDPE, or READC statement must have retrieved the record. The record retrieved must have been *locked*.

- If *Factor 1* has an entry, the record accessed by the DELET statement is deleted.

- If a read operation is immediately executed on the file in which a DELET statement was successfully completed, the next record is accessed.

- File in which records are to be *logically* deleted (or tagged for deletion) must be defined as an <u>update</u> file (**U** in column 15 of the related *File Description Specifications* statement).

Figure 13-22 Syntax of the **DELET** operation.

A coding example of the **DELET** operation is shown in Figure 13-23. Because an externally defined file was specified, *Factor 1* is not used and the file's record format name is specified in *Factor 2*.

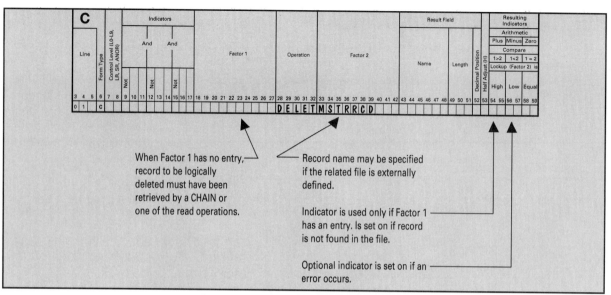

When Factor 1 has no entry, record to be logically deleted must have been retrieved by a CHAIN or one of the read operations.

Record name may be specified if the related file is externally defined.

Indicator is used only if Factor 1 has an entry. Is set on if record is not found in the file.

Optional indicator is set on if an error occurs.

Figure 13-23 Coding example of the **DELET** operation.

RPG/400 Example Logical Delete Program

The specifications for a program that logically deletes records in a physical file are presented in Figure 13-24.

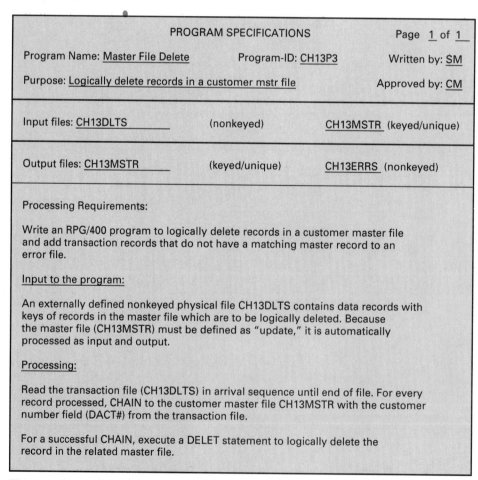

Figure 13-24 Specifications for an RPG/400 program that logically deletes records in a physical file.

In the event of an unsuccessful CHAIN, move all of the transaction record field values to the related fields in the error file (CH13ERRS) and add the record to the error file.

Output:

Logically delete the master file record based on the key value in the transaction file. Add any transaction records without a matching master file record to the error file (CH13ERRS).

Figure 13-24 Specifications for an RPG/400 program that logically deletes records in a physical file. (Continued)

The system flowchart in Figure 13-25 indicates that three physical files are processed by the example program: a transaction file (CH13DLTS) that includes keys for the records to be logically deleted, the master file (CH13MSTR) in which records are to be logically deleted, and an error file (CH13ERRS) where transaction records that do not have a matching master record are added.

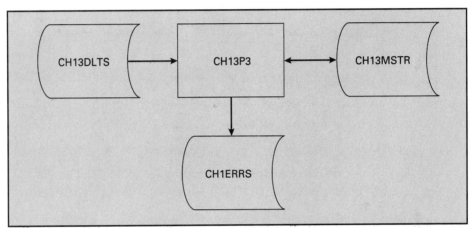

Figure 13-25 System flowchart for the program that logically deletes records from a master file.

The record format of the transaction file (CH13DLTS) and a listing of the stored data are shown in Figure 13-26.

```
                                          Data Description Source
   SEQNBR  *...+....1....+....2....+....3....+....4....+....5....+....6....+
     100      A          R DLTRCD
     200      A            DCODE          1
     300      A            DACT#          5
```

```
RCDNBR  *...+.
     1  D00020
        CFFFFF
        400020
     2  D00001
        CFFFFF
        400001
     3  D00014
        CFFFFF
        400014
```

Figure 13-26 Listing of the transaction file's record format and hexadecimal listing of the data (key values).

Because the record formats of the customer master file (CH13MSTR) and the error file (CH13ERRS) were discussed for the "adds" and "update" programs, they are not repeated again.

RPG/400 Syntax for the Logical Delete Program

A detailed compile listing of the logical delete program is presented in Figure 13-27. Examine the instructions, and note the following:

- To support logical deletion of records from CH13MSTR, the externally described file is defined as "update" (**U** in column 15 of the related *File Description* statement, line 600) and *full procedural* (**F** in column 16).
- The **SETLL** instruction on line 800 determines if the key value in DACT# has a matching key in CH13MSTR.

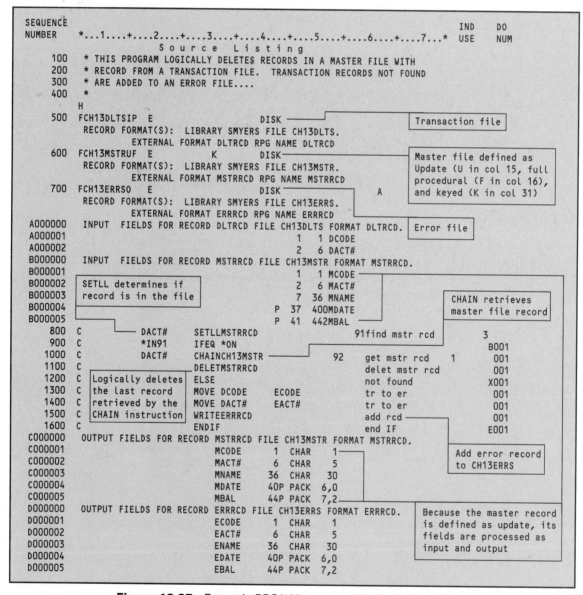

Figure 13-27 Example RPG/400 program that logically deletes records in a master file.

- If the record is found in CH13MSTR, the **CHAIN** statement on line 1000 accesses the record for processing.
- The **DELET** statement on line 1100 *logically deletes* the record previously retrieved by the **CHAIN** statement on line 1000.
- Transaction records that do not have a matching key in CH13MSTR are added to CH13ERRS.

Figure 13-28 shows a **CPYF** hexadecimal listing of CH13MSTR before and after records are logically deleted.

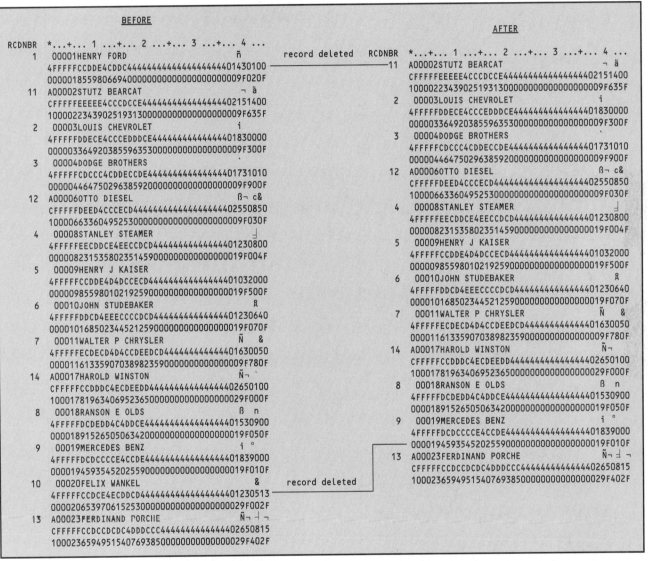

Figure 13-28 **CPYF** hexadecimal listing of CH13MSTR Before and After records are logically deleted.

THE *READ, READE, READP,* **AND** *REDPE* **OPERATIONS**

The *read* operations supported by the RPG/400 compiler include **READ, READE, READP,** and **REDPE.** Each operation reads one record from a data file and stores it for processing. If more than one record is to be sequentially processed (but not the entire file), the read statement must be executed again, usually within a **DO, DOU,** or **DOW** group. Unlike the **CHAIN** operation, read statements do not randomly access records from a file. After a file is **OPEN**ed (by either the RPG/400 logic cycle or the **OPEN** statement), and a **READ** or **READE** statement is executed, the first record in the file is accessed. If, however, the file "pointer" is set to a select key or relative record number by a **SETLL** or **SETGT** statement, any of the *read* statements will access that record.

Syntax of the *READ* Operation

The RPG/400 syntax for the **READ** operation is detailed in Figure 13-29.

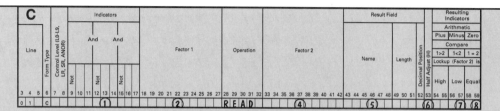

1. *Total or Detail Time* Indicators may condition a READ statement.

2. *Factor 1* is not used.

3. The **READ** operation name must be entered in the *Operation* field.

4. *Factor 2* must contain the name of a file or name of a record format in the file which is to be read. A record format name may only be used for files that are externally defined (**E** in column 19 of the related *File Description* statement).

5. The *Result Field* may contain the name of a data structure into which the record is read only if the file specified in *Factor 2* is program-defined (**F** in column 19 of the related *File Description* statement).

6. If the file processed is defined as an <u>update</u> file, a letter **N** entered in column 53 will prevent the record from being "locked" when it is read.

7. An indicator may be specified in columns 56–57. It is set on when the **READ** statement does not complete successfully.

8. An indicator that indicates whether end of file is detected <u>must</u> be entered in columns 58–59. A file cannot be read beyond the end-of-file record.

<u>Processing Features:</u>

- A file processed by a **READ** statement must be defined as *full procedural* (**F** in column 19 of the related *File Description* statement).

- When a file is opened by the RPG/400 logic cycle or the **OPEN** operation, the file is positioned at the first record. A **READ** statement will begin reading at that record.

- If a **SETLL**, **SETGT**, or **CHAIN** statement positions the "pointer" in the file, a **READ** statement will begin the read at that record, not the first record in the file.

- If a **READ** statement is successful, the file is positioned at the next record that satisfies the read condition.

- When an end-of-file condition is tested, the indicator specified in columns 58–59 will be set on. Subsequent reads of the file must only be executed if the end-of-file condition is not tested. Any attempt to read a file after end-of-file is sensed will cause an exception error and cancel program execution.

Figure 13-29   Syntax of the **READ** operation.

An example of a **READ** statement and its processing logic are shown in Figure 13-30.

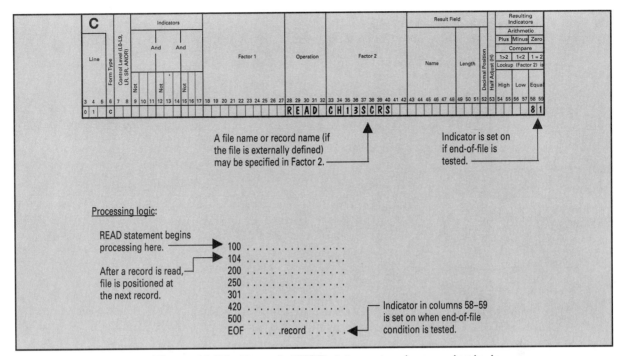

Figure 13-30 Example **READ** statement and processing logic.

Syntax of the *READE* (Real Equal Key) Operation

The **READE** operation is similar to the **READ** operation. However, it accesses a record only if the *search argument* value (*Factor 1* entry) matches a record in the file. From its current position in the file, and if executed within a **DO, DOU,** or **DOW** group, a **READE** statement searches a file sequentially until the equal condition or end of file is tested. If a match does <u>not</u> occur or if the end of file is detected, the <u>required</u> indicator in columns 58–59 is set on. The syntax of the **READE** operation is explained in Figure 13-31.

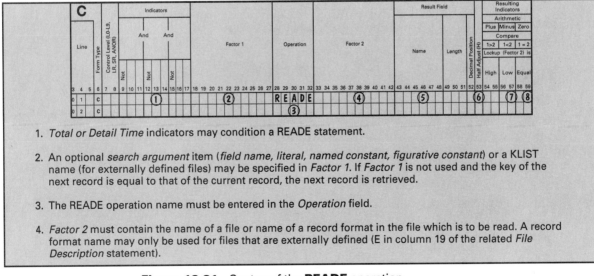

1. *Total or Detail Time* indicators may condition a READE statement.

2. An optional *search argument* item (*field name, literal, named constant, figurative constant*) or a KLIST name (for externally defined files) may be specified in *Factor 1*. If *Factor 1* is not used and the key of the next record is equal to that of the current record, the next record is retrieved.

3. The READE operation name must be entered in the *Operation* field.

4. *Factor 2* must contain the name of a file or name of a record format in the file which is to be read. A record format name may only be used for files that are externally defined (E in column 19 of the related *File Description* statement).

Figure 13-31 Syntax of the **READE** operation.

5. The *Result Field* may contain the name of a data structure into which the record is read only if the file specified in *Factor 2* is program-defined (**F** in column 19 of the related *File Description* statement).

6. If the file processed is defined as an <u>update</u> file, a letter **N** entered in column 53 will prevent the record from being "locked" when it is read.

7. An indicator may be specified in columns 56–57. It is set on when the READE statement does not complete successfully.

8. An indicator <u>must</u> be entered in columns 58–59, which is set on if either the search argument (*Factor 1* entry) value does not equal a key in the file; or if an end-of-file condition occurs.

<u>Processing Features:</u>

• A file processed by a READE statement must be defined as *full procedural* (**F** in column 19 of the related *File Description* statement).

• If a SETLL, SETGT, or CHAIN statement positions the "pointer" in the file, a READE statement will begin the search at that record, not at the first record in the file.

• If a READE statement is specified <u>without</u> a *Factor 1* entry and immediately follows an OPEN statement, an error will occur. The file must be repositioned by a SETLL, SETGT, or CHAIN operation.

• If a READE statement is specified <u>with</u> a *Factor 1* entry (search argument) and immediately follows an OPEN statement, the first record that matches the search argument value is retrieved.

Figure 13-31   Syntax of the **READE** operation. (Continued)

An example of a **READE** statement and its processing logic are shown in Figure 13-32.

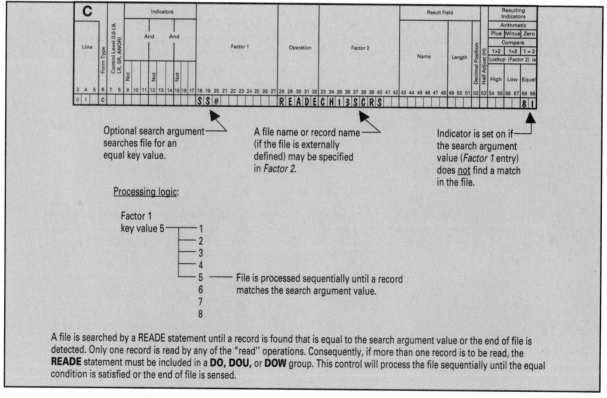

Figure 13-32   Example **READE** statement and processing logic.

The *READP* (Read Prior Record) Operation

The **READP** operation reads the <u>prior</u> record from a file defined as *full procedural* (**F** in column 16 of the related *File Description* statement). Identical to any of the "read" operations, the **READP** statement must be included within a **DO, DOU,** or **DOW** group to access more than one record from the file. The syntax of the **READP** operation is explained in Figure 13-33.

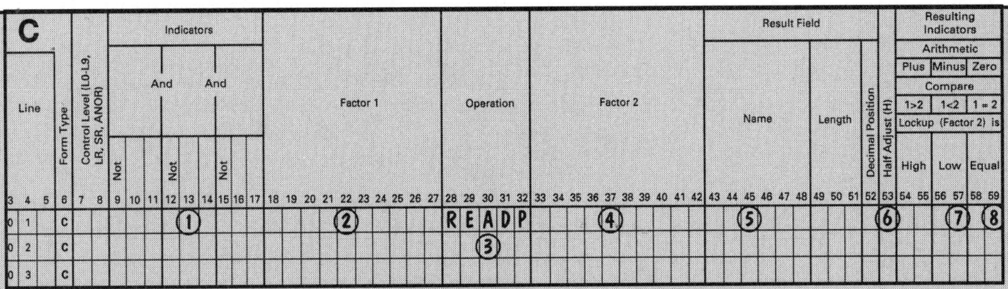

1. *Total or Detail Time* indicators may condition a **READP** statement.

2. *Factor 1* is not used.

3. The **READP** operation name must be entered in the *Operation* field.

4. *Factor 2* must contain the name of a file or name of a record format in the file which is to be read. A record format name may only be used for files that are externally defined (E in column 19 of the related *File Description* statement).

5. The *Result Field* may contain the name of a data structure into which the record is read only if the file specified in *Factor 2* is program-defined (**F** in column 19 of the related *File Description* statement).

6. If the file processed is defined as an <u>update</u> file, a letter **N** entered in column 53 will prevent the record from being "locked" when it is read.

7. An indicator may be specified in columns 56–57. It is set on when the **READP** statement does not complete successfully.

8. An indicator <u>must</u> be entered in columns 58–59 that indicates whether the beginning of the file is detected. A file cannot be read above the beginning of the file. In the event of this condition, the file must be repositioned by a SETLL, SETGT, or CHAIN statement.

<u>Processing Features:</u>

- A file processed by a **READP** statement must be defined as *full procedural* (**F** in column 19 of the related *File Description* statement).

- When a file is opened by the RPG/400 logic cycle or the **OPEN** operation, the file is positioned at the first record. If a **READP** statement was immediately executed, the beginning of the file would be detected and indicator in columns 58–59 set on flagging an error condition. Consequently, the file must be repositioned by a **SETLL, SETGT,** or **CHAIN** statement to some other record in the file before a **READP** statement is executed.

- If a **READ** statement is successful, the file is positioned at the next record that satisfies the read condition.

- When the beginnning-of-file condition is tested, the indicator specified in columns 58–59 will be set on. Subsequent reads of the file must only be executed if the beginning-of-file condition is not tested.

Figure 13-33   Syntax of the **READP** operation.

An example **READP** statement and its processing logic are detailed in Figure 13-34.

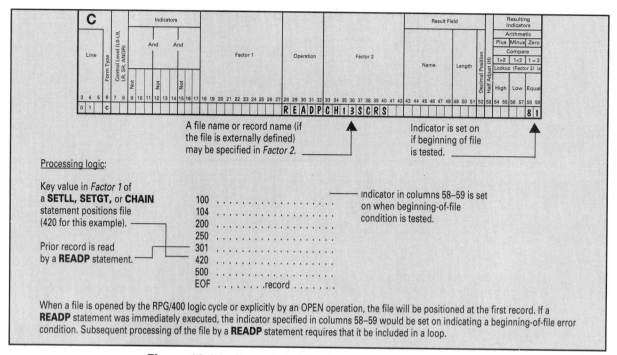

A file name or record name (if the file is externally defined) may be specified in *Factor 2.*

Indicator is set on if beginning of file is tested.

Processing logic:

Key value in *Factor 1* of a **SETLL, SETGT,** or **CHAIN** statement positions file (420 for this example).

Prior record is read by a **READP** statement.

```
100  . . . . . . . . . . . . . . . . . .
104  . . . . . . . . . . . . . . . . . .
200  . . . . . . . . . . . . . . . . . .
250  . . . . . . . . . . . . . . . . . .
301  . . . . . . . . . . . . . . . . . .
420  . . . . . . . . . . . . . . . . . .
500  . . . . . . . . . . . . . . . . . .
EOF  . . . . . . . .record . . . . . . .
```

indicator in columns 58–59 is set on when beginning-of-file condition is tested.

When a file is opened by the RPG/400 logic cycle or explicitly by an OPEN operation, the file will be positioned at the first record. If a **READP** statement was immediately executed, the indicator specified in columns 58–59 would be set on indicating a beginning-of-file error condition. Subsequent processing of the file by a **READP** statement requires that it be included in a loop.

Figure 13-34   Example **READP** statement and processing logic.

The *REDPE* (Read Prior Equal) Operation

The **REDPE** operation retrieves the <u>next prior</u> record sequentially from a *full procedural* file (**F** in column 16 of the related *File Description* statement) if the key of the file's record matches the search argument value (*Factor 1* entry). Identical to all of the read operations, continued sequential processing of the file is controlled by including the **REDPE** statement within a **DO, DOU,** or **DOW** group. The syntax of the **REDPE** operation is explained in Figure 13-35.

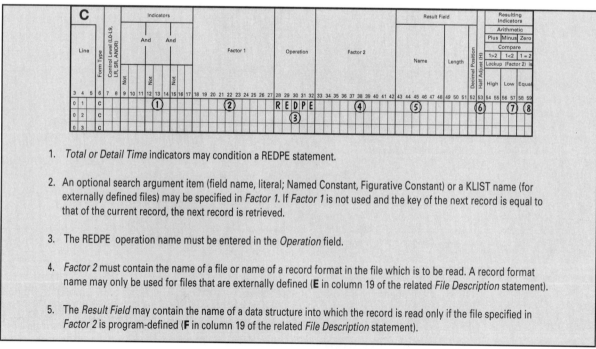

1. *Total or Detail Time* indicators may condition a REDPE statement.

2. An optional search argument item (field name, literal; Named Constant, Figurative Constant) or a KLIST name (for externally defined files) may be specified in *Factor 1*. If *Factor 1* is not used and the key of the next record is equal to that of the current record, the next record is retrieved.

3. The REDPE operation name must be entered in the *Operation* field.

4. *Factor 2* must contain the name of a file or name of a record format in the file which is to be read. A record format name may only be used for files that are externally defined (**E** in column 19 of the related *File Description* statement).

5. The *Result Field* may contain the name of a data structure into which the record is read only if the file specified in *Factor 2* is program-defined (**F** in column 19 of the related *File Description* statement).

Figure 13-35   Syntax of the **REDPE** operation.

6. If the file processed is defined as an <u>update</u> file, a letter **N** entered in column 53 will prevent the record from being "locked" when it is read.

7. An indicator may be specified in columns 56–57. It is set on when the **REDPE** statement does not complete successfully.

8. An indicator <u>must</u> be entered in columns 58–59, which is set on if the search argument (*Factor 1* entry) value does not equal a key in the file or if a beginning-of-file condition occurs.

<u>Processing Features:</u>

- A file processed by a **REDPE** statement must be defined as *full procedural* (**F** in column 19 of the related *File Description* statement).

- If a **SETLL SETGT,** or **CHAIN** statement positions the "pointer" in the file, a **REDPE** statement will begin the search at that record, not at the first record in the file.

- If a **REDPE** statement is specified <u>without</u> a *Factor 1* entry and immediately follows an **OPEN** statement, an error will occur. The file must be repositioned by a **SETLL, SETGT,** or **CHAIN** operation.

- If a **REDPE** statement is specified <u>with</u> a *Factor 1* entry (search argument) and immediately follows an **OPEN** statement, the first record that matches the search argument value is retrieved.

- If a **REDPE** statement is not successful, the file must be repositioned by a **SETLL, SETGT,** or **CHAIN** operation.

Figure 13-35   Syntax of the **REDPE** operation. (Continued)

An example **REDPE** statement and its processing logic are detailed in Figure 13-36.

The syntax, coding examples, and the processing logic of the **READ, READE, READP,** and **REDPE** operations have been discussed in detail in the previous sections of this chapter. Now, an application program that uses the **READE** operation will be introduced.

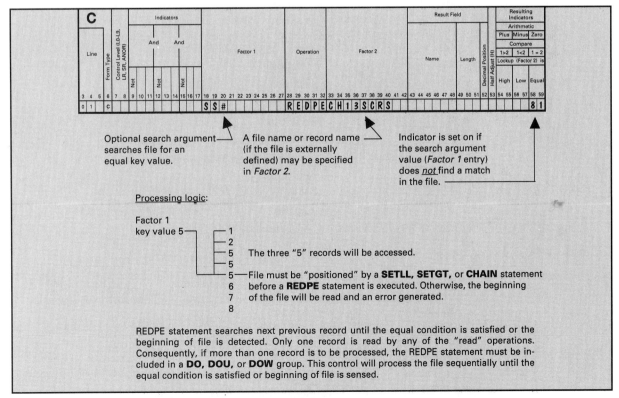

Figure 13-36   Example **REDPE** statement and processing logic.

RPG/400 APPLICATION PROGRAM: STUDENT TRANSCRIPTS

The specifications for an RPG/400 application program that generates student transcripts are detailed in Figure 13-37.

PROGRAM SPECIFICATIONS   Page 1 of 1

Program Name: Student Transcripts   Program - ID: CH13P4   Written by: SM

Purpose: Generate temporary student transcripts   Approved by: CM

Input files: CH13SMST   (keyed)   CH13SCRS   (keyed)

Output files: QSYSPRT   (printer)

Processing Requirements:

Write an RPG/400 program to generate temporary student transcripts for all of the students stored in the master file CH13SMST.

Input to the program:

An externally defined keyed physical file, CH13SMST contains general student data (i.e., name, address, major, etc.), and the keyed file, CH13SCRS, includes year-to-date course records.

Processing:

Read the student master file (CH13SMST) in arrival sequence until end of file. For each master record accessed, read the related records from the course file (CH13SCRS). A student may have no, one, or more course records. Consequently, a "do" loop must be coded to access all of the course records related to a student. The student master and course files are matched by the student's social security number.

Compute each student's cumulative point average based on the following:

   A = 4 points, B = 3 points, C = 2 points, D = 1 point, F = 0 points

Step 1:   Multiply the course credits (CREDIT) by the points for the letter grade. For example,
          a 3-credit course that earned an A would result in 12 points (3 credits × 4
          points).

Step 2:   For each student accumulate the total points and total credits.

Step 3:   After the last course record for a student is processed, divide the total points by the total credits to
          determine the student's cumulative point average.

Convert term date from its stored YYMMDD format to an MMDDYY format by multiplying it by 100.0001.

Output:

Generate a temporary transcript for each student in the master file in the format shown in the attached printer spacing chart. For students who have no course records, print a transcript and include the error message **NO COURSE RECORDS FOUND**

Figure 13-37 Specifications for Student Transcripts program.

The system flowchart shown in Figure 13-38 indicates that two input files as well as printer output are processed by the program.

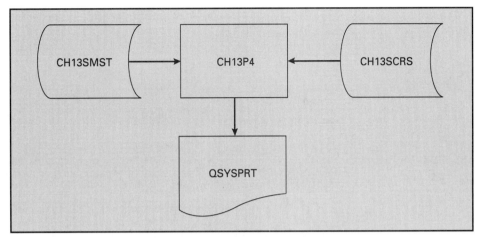

Figure 13-38 System flowchart for Student Transcripts program.

A listing of the student master file's (CH13SMST) record format and a **CPYF** utility listing of the data in hexadecimal format are shown in Figure 13-39.

```
                                            Data Description Source
       SEQNBR   *...+....1....+....2....+....3....+....4....+....5....+
         100    A                                                 UNIQUE
         200    A          R SMSTRRCD
         300    A            SS#            9 0
         400    A            SNAME         20
         500    A            SADD1         20
         600    A            SADD2         15
         700    A            SCITY         20
         800    A            SSTATE         2
         900    A            SZIP           5 0
        1000    A            SMAJOR        20
        1100    A          K SS#
```

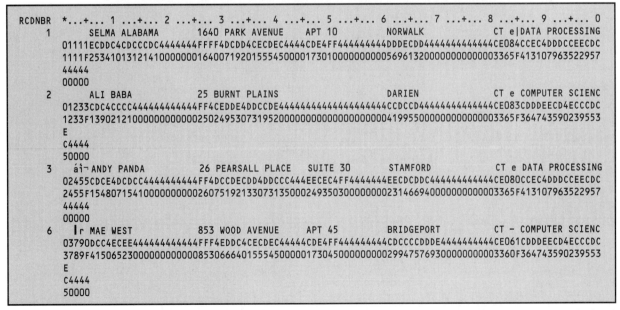

Figure 13-39 Listing of the student master file's record format and hexadecimal listing of the data.

```
4    Çh±TOM THUMB             102 VIRGINIA AVENUE            GREENWICH          CT ⊢ COMPUTER SCIENC
     01688EDD4ECEDC4444444444FFF4ECDCDCC4CECDEC444444444444444CDCCDECCC4444444444CE07OCDDDEECD4ECCCDC
     4688F3640384420000000000010205997959101555450000000000000007955569380000000000003364F364743590239553
     E
     C4444
     50000
5    é r⊥CLARK KENT             7 BOOT SHOP LANE             NEW CANNAN         CT î|DATA PROCESSING
     05199CDCDD4DCDE4444444444F4CDDE4ECDD4DCDC44444444444444444DCE4CCDDCD4444444444CE054CCEC4DDDCCEECDC
     5199F331920255300000000007026630286703155000000000000000000005560315515000000000003365F413107963522957
     44444
     00000
```

Figure 13-39 Listing of the student master file's record format and hexadecimal listing of the data. (Continued)

A listing of the student course file's (CH13SCRS) record format and a hexadecimal listing of the data are shown in Figure 13-40. Note that the data is in a *composite key* (CSS#, CDATE, CNO) order.

```
                                    Data Description Source
         SEQNBR   *:...+....1....+....2....+....3....+....4....+....5....+
          100     A                                        UNIQUE
          200     A           R SCRRECRD
          300     A             CSS#           9 0
          400     A             CNAME         20
          500     A             CNO            6
          600     A             CDATE          6 0
          700     A             CINST#         3 0
          800     A             CMARK          1
          900     A             CREDIT         1
         1000     A           K CSS#
         1100     A           K CDATE        ┌─────────────────────────────┐
         1200     A           K CN           │ Composite key. Records may be │
                                             │ accessed by the three key fields│
                                             │ or by CSS#, or by CSS# and CDATE│
                                             └─────────────────────────────┘
```

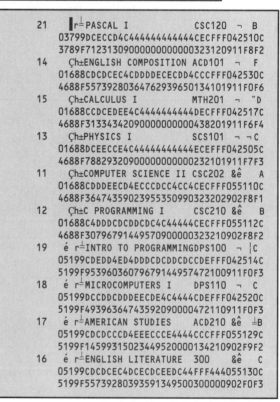

```
RCDNBR  *...+... 1 ...+... 2 ...+... 3 ...+...
    4      ENGLISH COMPOSITION ACD10  ¬  C
         01111CDCDCEC4CDDDDECECDD4CCCFFF042530C
         1111F557392803647629396501341019 11F0F3
    3      INTRO TO PROGRAMMINGDPS100  ¬ |A
         01111CDEDD4ED4DDDCDCDDCDCCDEFFF042514C
         1111F953960360796791449574721009 11F0F1
    5      COLLEGE ALGEBRA I  MTH100  ¬  C
         01111CDDDCCC4CDCCCDC4C444DECFFF042511C
         1111F363357501375291090004381009 11F6F3
    1      INTRO TO RPG/400    DPS200 &ē  A
         01111CDEDD4ED4DDC6FFF4444CDEFFF055121C
         1111F953960360977140000004722009 02F2F1
    2      COBOL I             DPS210 &ē  B
         01111CDCDD4C4444444444444CDEFFF055121C
         1111F362630900000000000004722109 02F2F2
    6      COMPUTER SCIENCE I  CSC101  ¬  B
         01233CDDDEECD4ECCCDCC4C44CECFFF042510C
         1233F364743590239553509003231019 11F9F2
    7      COMPUTER SCIENCE II CSC202 &ē  C
         01233CDDDEECD4ECCCDCC4CC4CECFFF055110C
         1233F364743590239553509903232029 02F8F3
    8      CALCULUS I          MTH201 &ē  "B
         01233CCDCEDEE4C4444444444DECFFF055117C
         1233F313343420900000000004382019 02F6F2
    9    á¡¬INTRO TO PROGRAMMINGDPS100  ¬ |B
         02455CDEDD4ED4DDDCDCDDCDCCDEFFF042514C
         2455F953960360796791449574721009 11F0F2
   10    á¡¬MICROCOMPUTERS I   DPS110  ¬  A
         02455DCCDDCDDDEECDE4C4444CDEFFF042520C
         2455F493963647435920900004721109 11F0F1
   20     ⏋r⊥COMPUTER SCIENCE I  CSC101  ¬  A
         03799CDDDEECD4ECCCDCC4C44CECFFF042510C
         3789F364743590239553509003231019 11F9F1
```

```
   21    ⏋r⊥PASCAL I            CSC120  ¬  B
         03799DCECCD4C44444444444CECFFF042510C
         3789F712313090000000000003231209 11F8F2
   14    Çh±ENGLISH COMPOSITION ACD101  ¬  F
         01688CDCDCEC4CDDDDECECDD4CCCFFF042530C
         4688F557392803647629396501341019 11F0F6
   15    Çh±CALCULUS I          MTH201  ¬  "D
         01688CCDCEDEE4C4444444444DECFFF042517C
         4688F313343420900000000004382019 11F6F4
   13    Çh±PHYSICS I           SCS101  ¬ ¬C
         01688DCEECCE4C4444444444ECEFFF042505C
         4688F788293209000000000002321019 11F7F3
   11    Çh±COMPUTER SCIENCE II CSC202 &ē  A
         01688CDDDEECD4ECCCDCC4CC4CECFFF055110C
         4688F364743590239553509903232029 02F8F1
   12    Çh±C PROGRAMMING I     CSC210 &ē  B
         01688C4DDDCDCDDCDC4C44444CECFFF055112C
         4688F307967914495709000003232109 02F8F2
   19    é r⊥INTRO TO PROGRAMMINGDPS100  ¬ |C
         05199CDEDD4ED4DDDCDCDDCDCCDEFFF042514C
         5199F953960360796791449574721009 11F0F3
   18    é r⊥MICROCOMPUTERS I   DPS110  ¬  C
         05199DCCDDCDDDEECDE4C4444CDEFFF042520C
         5199F493963647435920900004721109 11F0F3
   17    é r⊥AMERICAN STUDIES   ACD210 &ē ⊥B
         05199CDCDCCCD4EEECCCE4444CCCFFF055129C
         5199F145993150234495200001342109 02F9F2
   16    é r⊥ENGLISH LITERATURE 300    &ē  C
         05199CDCDCEC4DCECDCEEDC44FFF444055130C
         5199F557392803935913495003000000 902F0F3
```

Figure 13-40 Listing of the student course file's record format and hexadecimal listing of the data.

The design of the report is detailed in the printer spacing chart shown in Figure 13-41.

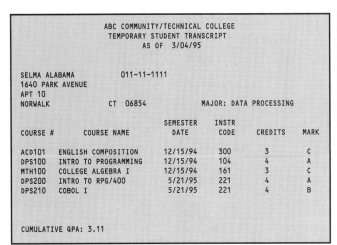

Editor's note: the printer spacing chart shows the report layout:

```
                0         1         2         3         4         5         6
     1234567890123456789012345678901234567890123456789012345678901234567890112
  1                        ABC COMMUNITY/TECHNICAL COLLEGE
  2                        TEMPORARY STUDENT TRANSCRIPT
  3                              AS OF ØX/XX/XX
  4
  5
  6  X                    X      XXX-XX-XXXX
  7  X                    X
  8  X               X
  9  X                    X XX  XXXXX                    MAJOR: X                    X
 10
 11                                          SEMESTER   INSTR
 12  COURSE #        COURSE NAME              DATE       CODE      CREDITS    MARK
 13
 14  XXXXX   X                          X    XX/XX/XX    XX        X          X
 15  XXXXX   X                          X    XX/XX/XX    XX        X          X
 16                  **NO COURSE RECORDS FOUND**
 17
 18
 19
 20  CUMULATIVE QPA: X.XX
 21
 22  NOTE: PRINT EACH STUDENT'S TRANSCRIPT ON A SEPARATE PAGE.
 23        USE SYSTEM DATE FOR THE TRANSCRIPTS.
```

Figure 13-41　Report design for the Student Transcripts program.

The transcript program is written to process all six students in the master file (CH13SMST). However, because of space limitations, only two transcripts are presented in Figure 13-42: one for a student with course records and the other for a student with no course records.

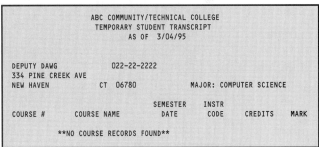

Figure 13-42　One good and one error transcript generated by the Student Transcripts program.

RPG/400 Syntax for the Student Transcripts Program

Examine the compile listing of the Student Transcripts program in Figure 13-43, and note the following coding features:

```
SEQUENCE                                                               IND   DO
NUMBER     *...1....+....2....+....3....+....4....+....5....+....6....+....7...*  USE   NUM
                        S o u r c e   L i s t i n g
   100    * THIS PROGRAM GENERATES STUDENT TRANSCRIPTS - INPUT FROM A
   200    * STUDENT MASTER FILE AND A COURSE FILE - PROCESSED BY THE READE
   300    * OPERATION....
          H
   400    FCH13SMSTIP E           K         DISK
            RECORD FORMAT(S): LIBRARY SMYERS FILE CH13SMST.
                 EXTERNAL FORMAT SMSTRRCD RPG NAME SMSTRRCD
   500    FCH13SCRSIF E           K         DISK
            RECORD FORMAT(S): LIBRARY SMYERS FILE CH13SCRS.
                 EXTERNAL FORMAT SCRRECRD RPG NAME SCRRECRD
   600    FQSYSPRT O   F    132            PRINTER
   700    *
   800    *
   900    * Housekeeping.......
A000000    INPUT  FIELDS FOR RECORD SMSTRRCD FILE CH13SMST FORMAT SMSTRRCD.
A000001                                      P   1   50SS#
A000002                                          6   25 SNAME
A000003                                         26   45 SADD1
A000004                                         46   60 SADD2
A000005                                         61   80 SCITY
A000006                                         81   82 SSTATE
A000007                                      P  83  850SZIP
A000008                                         86  105 SMAJOR
B000000    INPUT  FIELDS FOR RECORD SCRRECRD FILE CH13SCRS FORMAT SCRRECRD.
B000001                                      P   1   50CSS#
B000002                                          6   25 CNAME
B000003                                         26   31 CNO
B000004                                      P  32  350CDATE
B000005                                      P  36  370CINST#
B000006                                         38  38 CMARK
B000007                                      P  39  390CREDIT
  1000    C                   Z-ADD0     TOTCRD              init. to zero
  1100    C                   Z-ADD0     TOTPTS              init. to zero
  1200    *
  1300    C                   EXCPTHDGS                      print hdgs
  1400    C        SS#        SETLLCH13SCRS                  80key in file?      3
  1500    C        *IN80      IFEQ *OFF                      no key found            B001
  1600    C                   EXCPTERROR                     error output            001
  1700    C                   ELSE                           key found           X001
  1800    *
  1900    * Read first course record for a student....
  2000    C        SS#        READECH13SCRS                  81equal key?        3   001
  2100    C        *IN81      DOWEQ*OFF                      get courses             B002
  2200    *
  2300    * Compute cumulative QPA........
  2400    C                   SELEC                          begin SELEC             B003
  2500    C        CMARK      WHEQ 'A'                                           X003
  2600    C        CREDIT     MULT 4       POINTS    20      A points            003
  2700    C        CMARK      WHEQ 'B'                                           X003
  2800    C        CREDIT     MULT 3       POINTS            B points            003
  2900    C        CMARK      WHEQ 'C'                                           X003
  3000    C        CREDIT     MULT 2       POINTS            C points            003
  3100    C        CMARK      WHEQ 'D'                                           X003
  3200    C        CREDIT     MULT 1       POINTS            D points            003
  3300    C                   OTHER                                              X003
  3400    C                   Z-ADD0       POINTS            F points            003
  3500    C                   ENDSL                          end SELEC group     E003
  3600    *
  3700    C        CDATE      MULT 100.0001 MMDDYY   60      convert date        002
  3800    C                   EXCPTCOURSE                    print course        002
  3900    C                   ADD  CREDIT  TOTCRD    40      total credits       002
  4000    C                   ADD  POINTS  TOTPTS    40      total points        002
  4100    *
  4200    * Read another course record for the student....
  4300    C        SS#        READECH13SCRS                  81equal key? ?      3   002
  4400    C                   ENDDO                          end DO group        E002
  4500    C        TOTPTS     DIV  TOTCRD   QPA      32      cum pt average      001
  4600    C                   EXCPTQAVG                      print QPA           001
```

Course file is defined as full-procedural to support SETLL and READE operations

Figure 13-43 Detailed compile listing of the Student Transcripts program.

```
4700 C                       ENDIF                        end IF group        E001
4800 OQSYSPRT E  101         HDGS
4900 O                                         43 'ABC COMMUNITY/TECHNICAL'
5000 O                                         51 'COLLEGE'
5100 O        E  1           HDGS
5200 O                                         38 'TEMPORARY STUDENT'
5300 O                                         49 'TRANSCRIPT'
5400 O        E  3           HDGS
5500 O                                         34 'AS OF'
5600 O                       UDATE Y           43
5700 O        E  1           HDGS
5800 O                       SNAME             20
5900 O                       SS#               35 '0   -   -    '
6000 O        E  1           HDGS
6100 O                       SADD1             20
6200 O        E  1           HDGS
6300 O                       SADD2             15
6400 O        E  2           HDGS
6500 O                       SCITY             20
6600 O                       SSTATE            23
6700 O                       SZIP              30
6800 O                                         49 'MAJOR:'
6900 O                       SMAJOR            70
7000 O        E  1           HDGS
7100 O                                         43 'SEMESTER'
7200 O                                         52 'INSTR'
7300 O        E  2           HDGS
7400 O                                          8 'COURSE #'
7500 O                                         26 'COURSE NAME'
7600 O                                         40 'DATE'
7700 O                                         51 'CODE'
7800 O                                         63 'CREDITS'
7900 O                                         71 'MARK'
8000 O        E  1           COURSE
8100 O                       CNO                7
8200 O                       CNAME             30
8300 O                       MMDDYYY           43
8400 O                       CINST#            51
8500 O                       CREDIT            60
8600 O                       CMARK             70
8700 O        E  2           ERROR
8800 O                                         31 '**NO COURSE RECORDS'
8900 O                                         39 'FOUND**'
9000 O        E  3           QAVG
9100 O                                         16 'CUMULATIVE QPA:'
9200 O                       QPA          1    21
```

Line #		Explanation
1000 -		
1100		Accumulators, TOTCRD and TOTPTS, are initialized to zeros before any records are read from the student course file (CH13SCRS).
1300		Nine HDGS lines (4800–7900) are exception output. Field values from the student master file (CH13SMST) and heading constants are printed.
1400		The **SETLL** instruction points to a record in the student course file that has a social security number equal to the value in SS# from the current record in the student master file (CH13SMST). Indicator **80** will be set on if a match occurs.
1500 -		
1600		If indicator **80** is <u>not</u> turned on (equal SS# <u>not</u> found in the student course file), an exception line is printed (8700–8900) indicating **NO COURSE RECORDS FOUND**. No other calculations or output will occur, and another record is read automatically from the student master file (CH13SMST).
2000		If a matching record is found in the student course file by the **SETLL** statement, a record with the same SS# is read from the student course file by the READE statement. Indicator **81** will be set on if a matching record is not found or an end-of-file condition tested.

Figure 13-43 Detailed compile listing of the Student Transcripts program. (Continued)

2100 If a matching record is found (indicator **81** OFF), the **DOWEQ** group is performed, related
student course record processed, and the QPA totals accumulated until a matching record is
not found in the student course file or end of CH13SCRS file is encountered (**81** will be ON for
both conditions).

2400 -
3500 The statements within the **SELEC** group compute the value for POINTS based on the
equivalent letter grade mark.

3700 The YYMMDD format in CDATE (semester date in the course records) is converted to an
MMDDYY format for printing by multiplying the YYMMDD field value by 100.0001 and storing
the result in a six-byte field (MMDDYY).

 If a date value was to be changed from an MMDDYY to a YYMMDD format, the MMDDYY field
must be multiplied by 10000.01 and the product stored in a six-byte field.

3800 The field values from the student course record and converted date are exception output.

3900 The CREDIT field value from the student course record is added to the accumulator TOTCRD.

4000 The computed POINTS field value is added to the accumulator TOTPTS.

4300 The READE statement reads another record from the student course file (CH13SCRS).
Indicator **81** will be set on if a matching record is not found or end of file tested.

4400 The **ENDDO** statement transfers control back to the **DOWEQ** statement on line 2100, where
the test is made to exit from the **DOW** group or continue processing. This "looping" process
will continue until a matching record is _not_ found in the student course file or the end of
CH13SCRS is read.

4500 After exit from the **DOW** group (all of the current student's course records read), the QPA is
computed by dividing the total points (TOTPTS) by the total credits (TOTCRD).

4600 The print lines for the CUMULATIVE QPA are exception output.

4700 The ENDIF statement ends the IFEQ instruction on line 1500.

 The calculation instructions (lines 1000–4700) will be repeated for every record in the student
master file. If select student transcripts were to be printed, the social security numbers would
be loaded in another input data file, or more likely, input via a _display file_. Interactive
processing using _display files_ will be discussed in Chapter 14.

Figure 13-43 Detailed compile listing of the Student Transcripts program.
(Continued)

- The student master file (CH13SMST) is defined as _input, primary, and keyed._ It
will be processed by the RPG/400 logic cycle until end of file is detected.
- The student course file (CH13SCRS), defined as _input, full procedural_ (**F** in column 16), and _keyed,_ will be processed by the **READE** operation.
- The social security number (SS#) from each student master file record accesses
the related records from the course file by processing of a **READE** statement
within a **DOWEQ** group.

A line-by-line explanation of the program's calculation instructions supplements the
listing.

OTHER RPG/400 FILE CONTROL OPERATIONS

Some of the other RPG/400 file control operations that will be discussed in this chapter
are **OPEN, CLOSE, SETGT,** and **KLIST.**

The _OPEN_ (Open File for Processing) Operation

Instead of files automatically **OPEN**ing under the control of the RPG/400 logic cycle,
files may be explicitly **OPEN**ed by an **OPEN** operation. Figure 13-44 details the syntax
related to this operation.

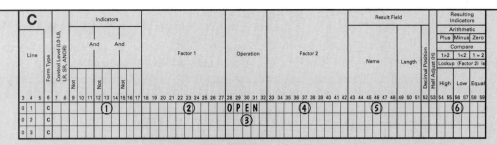

1. *Total or Detail Time* indicators may condition an OPEN statement.

2. *Factor 1* is not used.

3. **OPEN** operation name must be left-justified in the *Operation Field*.

4. A file name <u>must</u> be specified in *Factor 2*. However, it <u>cannot</u> be defined as a *primary, secondary,* or *table* file. Only f*ull procedural* and *combined* files are supported by the **OPEN** operation.

5. *Result Field* is not used.

6. A *Resulting Indicator* may be specified in columns 56–57, which is set on if the **OPEN** statement is <u>not</u> completed successfully.

<u>Processing Logic:</u>

* If a file is to be opened for the <u>first</u> time in a program, UC must be entered in columns 71–72 of the related *File Description* statement. However, if a file is opened automatically by the RPG/400 logic cycle and later closed by a **CLOSE** statement, it may be reopened by an **OPEN** instruction without the **UC** entry.

* Multiple **OPEN** statements are valid providing the file is closed by a **CLOSE** operation before it is reopened.

Figure 13-44   Syntax of the **OPEN** operation.

An example **OPEN** statement and its related *File Description* coding are presented in Figure 13-45.

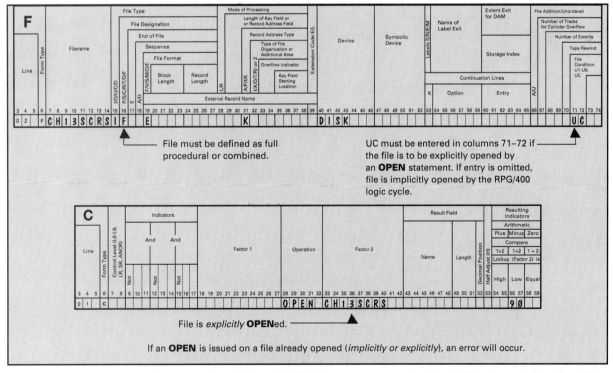

Figure 13-45   Example **OPEN** statement and related *File Description Specifications* coding.

The *CLOSE* (Close Files) Operation

The **CLOSE** operation closes one or more files or devices and disconnects them from the related program. Once a file is closed with a **CLOSE** statement, it cannot be referenced again in the program unless an explicit **OPEN** statement for the file is executed. One file or all of the files specified in the program may be closed by one **CLOSE** operation. To close all of the files at one time, the keyword ***ALL** must be entered in *Factor 2* of the **CLOSE** statement. Figure 13-46 details the syntax of the **CLOSE** operation.

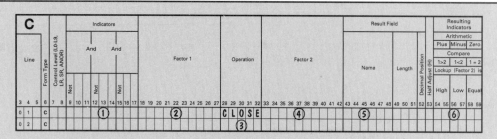

1. *Total or Detail Time* indicators may condition a CLOSE statement.

2. *Factor 1* is not used.

3. **CLOSE** operation name must be entered in the *Operation Field*.

4. A file name <u>must</u> be specified in *Factor 2*. However, an array or table file (defined with a **T** in column 16 of the related *File Description* statement) <u>cannot</u> be specified in *Factor 2*.

   If more than one file is to be closed at one time, the keyword *ALL must be specified in *Factor 2*. This will close all of the files referenced by the program whether *implicitly* or *explicitly* opened.

5. *Result Field* is not used.

6. A *Resulting Indicator* may be specified in columns 56–57, which will be set on if an error occurs when the **CLOSE** statement is executed.

<u>Processing Logic:</u>

- A **CLOSE** statement executed on a file already closed will <u>not</u> cause an error condition.

- A **CLOSE** statement may be specified for a file *implicitly* or *explicitly* opened.

Figure 13-46   Syntax of the **CLOSE** operation.

An example **CLOSE** statement that closes all of the files defined in the RPG/400 program and another that closes only one file are shown in Figure 13-47.

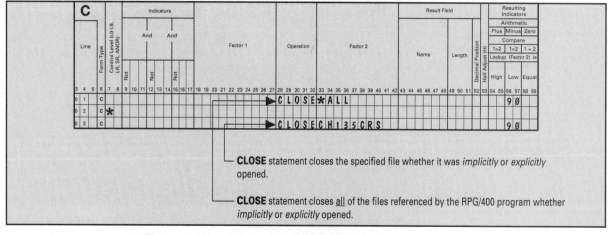

Figure 13-47   Examples of **CLOSE** statements.

The *SETGT* (Set Greater Than) Operation

The **SETGT** operation positions a file at a record with a key or relative record number that is <u>greater than</u> the value of the key or relative record number specified in the item in *Factor 1*. Figure 13-48 explains the syntax of the **SETGT** operation.

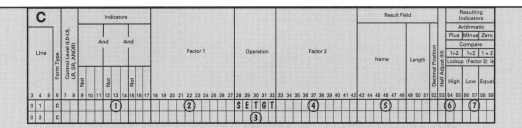

1. *Total or Detail Time* indicators may condition a **SETGT** statement.

2. If the file is accessed by key value, *Factor 1* must contain a field name, Named Constant, Figurative Constant, a literal, or **KLIST** name.

   If the file is accessed by relative record number (position in the file), *Factor 1* must contain a numeric field, integer literal, or named constant with no decimal positions.

3. SETGT must be specified in the *Operation* field.

4. *Factor 2* must contain either a file name or, for *externally defined* files, a record name.

5. The *Result Field* is not used.

6. An optional indicator may be specified in *Resulting Indicator* columns 54–55, which is set on if <u>no</u> record is found with a key or relative record number that is <u>greater than</u> the *Factor 1* value.

7. If an indicator is specified in *Resulting Indicator* columns 56–57, it is set on if an error occurs when the operation is executed.

<u>Processing Features</u>:

- The **SETGT** operation positions the file at a record that has a key value or relative record number <u>greater than</u> the value stored in the *Factor 1* item.

- The file accessed must be defined as a *full procedural* file (F in column 16 of the *File Description* statement in the RPG/400 program).

- A **SETGT** statement does not access the record for processing, it only positions the file at a record. **CHAIN** or one of the **READ** operations must access the record for processing.

- If the **SETGT** operation is not successful, the file is positioned at the end. The file, however, may be repositioned by executing the same or another **SETGT** statement with a different *Factor 1* key or relative record number value.

Figure 13-48 Syntax of the **SETGT** operation.

An example **SETGT** statement and its processing logic are detailed in Figure 13-49.

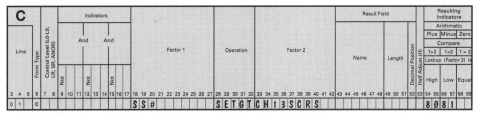

Figure 13-49 Example **SETGT** statement and processing logic.

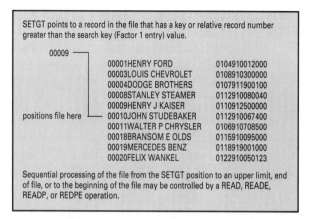

Figure 13-49 Example **SETGT** statement and processing logic. (Continued)

The *KLIST* (Define a Composite Key) and *KFLD* (Define Parts of a Key) Operations

The **KLIST** *Operation.* **KLIST** is a *declarative* operation that names a list of **KFLDs.** The **KLIST** name may be used as the *search argument* (*Factor 1* entry) to retrieve records from files defined with *composite* keys. Figure 13-50 explains the syntax of the **KLIST** operation.

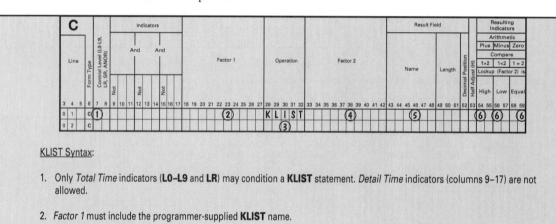

KLIST Syntax:

1. Only *Total Time* indicators (**L0–L9** and **LR**) may condition a **KLIST** statement. *Detail Time* indicators (columns 9–17) are not allowed.

2. *Factor 1* must include the programmer-supplied **KLIST** name.

3. The **KLIST** operation name must be entered in the *Operation* Field.

4. *Factor 2* is not used.

5. *Result Field* is not used.

6. *Resulting Indicators* are not used.

Processing Features:

• A **KLIST** name may only be specified as the search argument (*Factor 1* entry) for *externally defined* files.

• A **KLIST** statement must be immediately followed by at least one **KFLD** statement.

• A **KLIST** is ended when a non-**KFLD** statement is encountered.

• A **KLIST** name may be used as the search argument (*Factor 1* entry) in a **CHAIN, DELET, READE, REDPE, SETLL,** or **SETGT** operation.

Figure 13-50 Syntax of the **KLIST** operation.

The **KFLD** *Operation.* **KFLD** is also a *declarative* operation that identifies that the field is part of the *search argument* specified in *Factor 1* of the related **KLIST** statement. The **KLIST** and **KFLD** operations must be used together; neither is valid if used without the other one. The syntax of the **KFLD** operation is discussed in Figure 13-51.

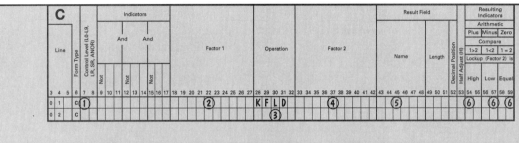

1. Only *Total Time* indicators (**L0–L9** and **LR**) may condition a **KFLD** statement. *Detail Time* indicators are not supported.

2. *Factor 1* is not used.

3. The **KFLD** operation name must be left-justified in the *Operation* field.

4. *Factor 2* is not used.

5. The *Result Field* must contain the name of a field that is part of the search argument (*Factor 1* entry of the related **KLIST** statement). An array or table name is not permitted.

6. *Resulting Indicators* are not used.

<u>Processing Features</u>:

- The field specified in a **KFLD** statement must be defined exactly the same as the related field in the composite key of the record or file. However, the field names do <u>not</u> have to be the same.

- The **KFLD** fields must be in the same order as the composite key in the corresponding record or file. Hence, the first **KFLD** statement relates to the first (high-order) key in the record format.

Figure 13-51   Syntax of the **KFLD** operation.

An example of a **KLIST/KFLD** group is shown in Figure 13-52.

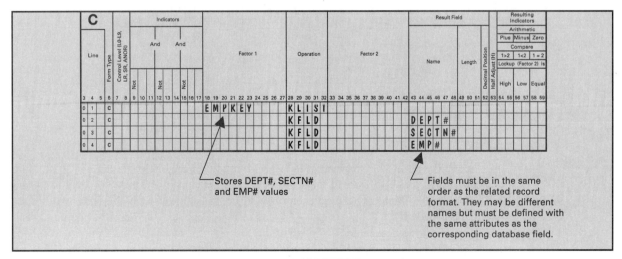

Figure 13-52   Example **KLIST/KFLD** statement group.

REORGANIZING DATA IN PHYSICAL FILE MEMBERS

The **RGZPFM** (*Reorganize Physical File Member*) command performs the following functions:

- Removes deleted records and compresses the file, which changes the following relative record numbers (record positions in file).
- Records are added to a physical file after the last record and are usually loaded in a random key order. The **RGZPFM** command resequences the file in a key value order. The **KEYFILE** parameter of the command must be used for this control.
- A physical file member can be reorganized in the following ways:

1. By key fields of the physical file
2. By key fields of a logical file based on a physical file

An **RGZPFM** display is shown in Figure 13-53. Note that the only user-entered parameters for this example are CH13MSTR and SMYERS; the others are defaults. For a comprehensive discussion of this command, refer to IBM's related *Control Language Manual*.

```
            Reorganize Physical File Mbr (RGZPFM)

 Type choices, press Enter.
 Data base file . . . . . . . . .   CH13MSTR     Name
   Library  . . . . . . . . . .     SMYERS       Name, *LIBL, *CURLIB
 Member . . . . . . . . . . . .     *FIRST       Name, *FIRST, *LAST
 Source update options  . . . . .   *SAME        *SAME, *SEQNBR, *DATE
 Source sequence numbering:
   Starting sequence number . . .   1.00         0.01-9999.99
   Increment number . . . . . . .   1.00         0.01-9999.99
 Key file:
   Logical file . . . . . . . . .   *FILE        Name, *NONE, *FILE
     Library  . . . . . . . . . .                Name, *LIBL, *CURLIB
   Member . . . . . . . . . . . .                Name
   Record format  . . . . . . . .   *ONLY        Name, *ONLY

                                                             Bottom


 F3=Exit   F4=Prompt   F5=Refresh   F12=Cancel   F13=How to use this display
 F24=More keys
```

Figure 13-53   RGZPFM (Reorganize Physical File Member) display.

The results of executing a **RGZPFM** command are shown in Figure 13-54. Note that the *before* and *after* listings are generated by using the **DSPPFM** command and pressing the Print key to print each display. Because a hexadecimal format was not selected, the **DSPPFM** utility displayed "unreadable characters" in the right margin of each display for the packed fields. Copies of the *before* and *after* displays are presented only to show how the **RGZPFM** command reorganized the physical file in an ascending key value order.

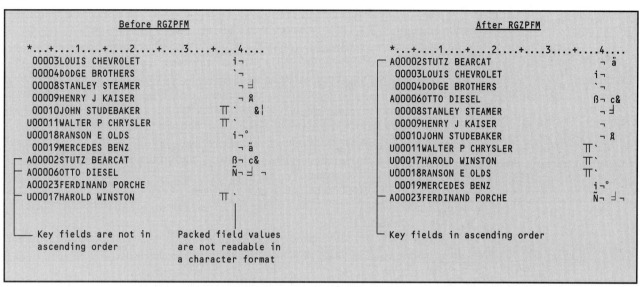

Figure 13-54 *Before* and *after* **DSPPFM** command displays showing the result of executing the **RGZPFM** command.

SUMMARY

Physical file maintenance includes

1. Adding records
2. Updating (changing) field values in the body of a record
3. Deleting records (logical and tagging methods)
4. Reorganizing files

Adding records to a physical file requires use of the **WRITE** operation and defining the file as output or update. *Keyed* physical files defined as unique will not support the addition of records with the same key value (duplicate key error). However, keyed physical files not defined as unique will support records that are added with the same key value.

In *update* maintenance, one or more field values of a record are changed. Except for key fields, any field values may be changed. The physical file to be updated must be defined as an *update* file (**U** in column 15) and *full procedural* (**F** in column 16) of the related *File Description* statement. Update processing requires use of the **UPDAT** operation.

Deletion of records in a physical file may be done by the *tagging* or *logical* method. The tagging method is an update process in which a record is accessed, a character is moved to a designated field, and the record is written back to its storage area. Logical deletion requires use of the **DELET** operation, which logically deletes a record from the file. Any subsequent processing of the file will not read records that are deleted by the **DELET** operation.

The **CHAIN** operation randomly retrieves a record from a physical file. The *Factor 1* entry (*search argument*) must contain either a key field value or a relative record number.

A **SETLL** operation "points" to a record in the file with a key value or relative record number value equal to or greater than the *Factor 1* entry of the statement. The **SETGT** operation "points" to a record in the file greater than the key or relative number value in the *Factor 1* item.

The **READ** operation reads one record in a physical file from the current record location <u>forward</u>. A **READE** operation also reads one record in a file but searches for a record with a key or relative record number equal to the key or relative number value in the *Factor 1* entry of the statement. The **READP** operation reads a record from the current record location <u>backward</u>. A **REDPE** operation reads backward and searches for a record with a key or relative record number equal to the *Factor 1* entry of the statement. Sequential processing of the file with a **READ, READE, READP,** or **REDPE** operation is controlled by a **DO, DOU,** or **DOW** group and/or multiple "read" statements.

Physical files are usually opened and closed automatically by the RPG/400 logic cycle. However, they may be *explicitly* opened by the **OPEN** operation and *explicitly* closed by the **CLOSE** operation.

The **KLIST** operation defines a group of fields specified in **KFLD** statements to build a composite key field. Values in the **KFLD** statements are stored in the *Factor 1* item of the related **KLIST** operation.

Physical files are reorganized by the **RGZPFM** command. This command removes deleted records from a file and sequences the file in a key value order.

QUESTIONS

13-1. Name the maintenance functions for physical files.

13-2. How must the physical file be defined in an RPG/400 program to support each maintenance function?

13-3. Name the RPG/400 operations to perform each maintenance function.
Examine the following calculation statement and answer Questions 13-4 through 13-6.

```
+...1....+....2....+....3....+....4....+....5....+....6
                WRITEABC                    80
```

13-4. What maintenance function does the **WRITE** operation support?

13-5. What is the ABC (*Factor 2*) entry?

13-6. When does the *Resulting Indicator* specified in columns 56–57 turn on? Name the specific conditions that may set the indicator on.

13-7. How must a physical file be defined in an RPG/400 program to support a **WRITE** statement?

13-8. After execution of a **WRITE** statement, where are the records stored in the physical file?

13-9. What CL command will generate a listing of a file? What CL command will display the records in a data file?

13-10. How does a hexadecimal (***HEX**) display or listing differ from a character (***CHAR**) display?
Examine the following calculation statement and answer Questions 13-11 through 13-15.

```
+...1....+....2....+....3....+....4....+....5....+....6
        AAA       SETLLXYZ                  8081
```

13-11. Explain the function of the **SETLL** operation.

13-12. What is stored in the AAA (*Factor 1*) entry?

13-13. What is the XYZ (*Factor 2*) entry?

13-14. When is *Resulting Indicator* **80** set on?

13-15. When is *Resulting Indicator* **81** set on?

13-16. What record will be "pointed to" by a **SETLL** statement?
Examine the following calculation statement and answer Questions 13-17 through 13-20.

```
+...1....+....2....+....3....+....4....+....5....+....6
        EMP#      CHAINZYX                  90
```

13-17. Explain the function of the **CHAIN** operation.

13-18. What is stored in the EMP# (*Factor 1*) entry?

13-19. What is the ZYX (*Factor 2*) entry?

13-20. When does *Resulting Indicator* **90** turn on?

13-21. How must a physical file be defined to support a **CHAIN** statement?

Examine the following calculation statement and answer Questions 13-22 through 13-24.

```
+...1....+....2....+....3....+....4....+....5....+....6
          UPDATABCDE                      85
```

13-22. Explain the function of the **UPDAT** operation.

13-23. What must be specified in the *Factor 2* (ABCDE) entry?

13-24. When does *Resulting Indicator* **85** (columns 56–57) turn on?

13-25. How must a physical file be defined to support an **UPDAT** statement?

13-26. Before an **UPDAT** statement is executed, what other function(s) have to be performed in the RPG/400 program?

Examine the following calculation statement and answer Questions 13-27 through 13-29.

```
+...1....+....2....+....3....+....4....+....5....+....6
          DELETCDEFG                      80
```

13-27. Explain the function of the **DELET** operation.

13-28. What must be specified in the *Factor 2* (CDEFG) entry?

13-29. When does *Resulting Indicator* **80** (columns 56–57) turn on?

13-30. How must a physical file be defined to support an **UPDAT** statement?

13-31. Before a **DELET** statement is executed, what other function(s) have to be performed in the RPG/400 program?

13-32. Explain the processing features of the **READ** and **READE** operations.

Examine the following calculation statement and answer Questions 13-33 through 13-35.

```
+...1....+....2....+....3....+....4....+....5....+....6
   SSNO        READEABCDE                      81
```

13-33. What is entered in the *Factor 1* (SSNO) entry?

13-34. What is specified in the *Factor 2* (ABCDE) entry?

13-35. Under what conditions will *Resulting Indicator* **81** (columns 58–59) be set on?

Examine the following calculation statement and answer Questions 13-36 through 13-38.

```
+...1....+....2....+....3....+....4....+....5....+....6
   ACCT#       REDPECDEFG                      80
```

13-36. What is entered in the *Factor 1* (ACCT#) entry?

13-37. What is specified in the *Factor 2* (CDEFG) entry?

13-38. Under what conditions will *Resulting Indicator* **80** (columns 58–59) be set on?

13-39. What RPG/400 operation explicitly opens a file? Which operation explicitly closes a file?

13-40. If the open and close functions for a file are to be explicitly controlled in a program, what additional coding is required in the RPG/400 program?

13-41. How does the processing controlled by a **SETGT** operation differ from the **SETLL** operation?

Examine the following calculation statement and answer Questions 13-42 through 13-45.

```
+...1....+....2....+....3....+....4....+....5....+....6
   PART#       KLIST
               KFLD            PLANT#
               KFLD            BIN#
               KFLD            ITEM#
```

13-42. What is the function of the **KLIST** and **KFLD** operations?

13-43. After execution of the **KLIST** statement, what is stored in PART#?

13-44. Where are **PLANT#**, **BIN#**, and **ITEM#** defined?

13-45. What "ends" a **KLIST** group?

13-46. Which Control Language command reorganizes a physical file?

13-47. Name some of the functions performed by execution of the CL command answered for Question 13-46.

PROGRAMMING ASSIGNMENTS

For each of the following programming assignments, more than one physical file must have been created. Two must be loaded with the related data records. Your instructor will inform you as to whether you have to create the physical files and load them or if they have been prepared for the assignment.

Programming Assignment 13-1: SAVINGS ACCOUNT MASTER FILE ADDITION

Write an RPG/400 program to add records to a Savings Account Master file. Three physical files are required for this assignment: a Savings Account Master file, a transaction file, and a file for error records. The File/Record attributes of each file and the related data for the Savings Account Master and transaction (Adds) files are detailed in the following sections.

Savings Account Master File/Record Format:

```
                        PHYSICAL FILE DESCRIPTION

        SYSTEM: AS/400                          DATE: Yours
        FILE NAME: Yours                        REV NO: 0
        RECORD NAME: Yours                      KEY LENGTH: 5
        SEQUENCE: Keyed (Unique)                RECORD SIZE: 82

                          FIELD DEFINITIONS

        FIELD     FIELD NAME    SIZE   TYPE     POSITION      COMMENTS
        NO                                     FROM    TO

          1       DECODE         1     C        1      1      D=deleted
          2       ACCTNO         5     C        2      6      Key field
          3       NAME          31     C        7     37
          4       STREET        20     C       38     57
          5       CITY          16     C       58     73
          6       STATE          2     C       74     75
          7       ZIP            5     P       76     78      0 decimals
          8       BALNCE         6     P       79     82      2 decimals
```

Savings Account Master Data:

Acct#	Account Name	Street	City	State	Zip	Deposit Amount
21345	JOHN DOE	212 ELM STREET	BRIDGEPORT	CT	06610	120000
31121	LOUISE LESSER	12 APPLES ROAD	BAHA	CA	92100	081299
48891	JUDY JOHNSON	114 EASY DRIVE	RALEIGH	NC	44410	006017
50000	DAVE HOOTEN	8 STRIKE LANE	LOS ANGELES	CA	90000	064111
51540	MARIE BLAKE	GREEN PASTURE RD	NEWARK	NJ	07733	940013
63141	JOSEPH WELCH	110 DILL STREET	NEW YORK	NY	10000	077777
71510	JOHN HINES	220 HIGH DRIVE	KEENE	ND	58847	000940

Transaction (Adds) File/Record Format:

```
                        PHYSICAL FILE DESCRIPTION

        SYSTEM: AS/400                          DATE: Yours
        FILE NAME: Yours                        REV NO: 0
        RECORD NAME: Yours                      KEY LENGTH: 5
        SEQUENCE: Keyed (Unique)                RECORD SIZE: 81
```

```
                          FIELD DEFINITIONS

          FIELD    FIELD NAME   SIZE  TYPE    POSITION      COMMENTS
          NO                                 FROM    TO

           1       ACCTNO         5    C       1      5   Key field
           2       NAME          31    C       6     36
           3       STREET        20    C      37     56
           4       CITY          16    C      57     72
           5       STATE          2    C      73     74
           6       ZIP            5    P      75     77   0 decimals
           7       DEPOST         6    P      78     81   2 decimals
```

Transaction File (Adds) Data:

Acct#	Account Name	Street	City	State	Zip	Amount
80000	SIDNEY GREENSTREET	10 CASTLE LANE	ALCATRAZ	CA	92220	100000
10000	PETER LORRE	9 DREARY DRIVE	HUNGRY	AL	99999	004500
71510	JOHN HINES	220 HIGH DRIVE	KEENE	ND	58847	075950
60000	BORIS KARLOFF	1 INNER SANCTUM	MISERABLE	AK	10000	549000

Error File: The error file, where transaction records that have key equal to records already stored in the Savings Account Master (duplicate key error) are written, must be created with the same record format as the transaction file.

After the program is executed, generate hexadecimal listings of the Savings Account Master and error files with the **CPYF** command.

Programming Assignment 13-2: SAVINGS ACCOUNT MASTER FILE UPDATE AND LOGICAL DELETION OF RECORDS

Programming Assignment 13-1 must have been completed, or the master file previously created and loaded with data, before this assignment is started.

Write an RPG/400 program to *update* and *logically delete* records in the Savings Account Master file with data from a transaction file. In addition, generate the edit report shown in the supplemental printer spacing chart. *Before* the program is executed, print a **CPYF** listing of the Savings Account Master file in hexadecimal format.

Transaction File/Record Format:

```
                        PHYSICAL FILE DESCRIPTION

   SYSTEM: AS/400                              DATE: Yours
   FILE NAME: Yours                            REV NO: 0
   RECORD NAME: Yours                          KEY LENGTH: 5
   SEQUENCE: Keyed (not unique)                RECORD SIZE: 82

                          FIELD DEFINITIONS

          FIELD    FIELD NAME   SIZE  TYPE    POSITION      COMMENTS
          NO                                 FROM    TO

           1       TRCODE         1    C       1      1   U or D
           2       ACT#           5    C       2      6   Key field
           3       TNAME         31    C       7     37
           4       TSTRET        20    C      38     57
           5       TCITY         16    C      58     73
           6       TSTATE         2    C      74     75
           7       TZIP           5    P      76     78   0 decimals
           8       TAMT           6    P      79     82   2 decimals
```

```
Transaction File Data:

Trans                                                                      Trans
Code   Acct#      Account Name        Street          City      State  Zip   Amount

D     61000
U     80000                                                                 200000
U     21345    JOHN DOEST         10 ROSE TERRACE    TRUMBULL    VT   07779
U     40000                                                                 015000
U     63141                                                                 077777-
D     48891


Note: Blank field values are not to be used to update the related field(s) in the
      Savings Account Master file
```

Records that include a **U** in the transaction code field contain update data and those with a **D** indicate that the record is to be logically deleted. Update records that have a blank value in a field are not to change the related master record field!

Report Design:

```
          0         1         2         3         4         5         6         7         8         9        10
    1234567890123456789012345678901234567890123456789012345678901234567890123456789012345678901234567890123456
 1  ØX/XX/XX                              SAVING ACCOUNTS EDIT REPORT                                PAGE XXØX
 2
 3
 4  BEFORE UPDATING:
 5
 6  X   XXXXX X                            X X            X X              X XX XXXXX X,XXØ.XX
 7
 8  X   XXXXX .....ACCOUNT NOT FOUND.....
 9
10
11  AFTER UPDATING:
12
13  X   XXXXX X                            X X            X X              X XX XXXXX X,XXØ.XX
14
15
16     NOTES:
17
18       1. HEADINGS ON TOP OF EVERY PAGE.
19
20       2. USE SYSTEM DATE FOR REPORT.
21
22       3. WHEN AN ACCOUNT IS NOT FOUND DO NOT PRINT AFTER UPDATE OUTPUT LINES.
```

Print a **CPYF** listing in hexadecimal format after the program is executed and compare the before and after listings for the update and delete results.

Programming Assignment 13-3: CEREAL BRANDS MASTER FILE ADDITION

Write an RPG/400 program to add records to a Cereal Brands Master file. Two physical files are required for this assignment: the Cereal Brands Master file and a transaction (adds) file. A printed report is also to be generated. The File/Record attributes of each file and the related data for the Cereal Brands Master and transaction (Adds) files are detailed in the following sections.

Cereal Brands Master Record Format:

```
                        PHYSICAL FILE DESCRIPTION

        SYSTEM: AS/400                      DATE: Yours
        FILE NAME: Yours                    REV NO: 0
        RECORD NAME: Yours                  KEY LENGTH: 5
        SEQUENCE: Keyed (Unique)            RECORD SIZE: 63
```

```
                          FIELD DEFINITIONS

           FIELD    FIELD NAME    SIZE   TYPE    POSITION      COMMENTS
           NO                                   FROM    TO

            1       DECODE         1      C       1      1     D=deleted
            2       BRAND#         5      C       2      6     Key field
            3       BRAND         20      C       7     26
            4       SIZE           3      P      27     28
            5       UNIT           2      C      29     30
            6       MFGR          15      C      31     45
            7       LPDATE         6      P      46     49
            8       UNITCT         6      P      50     53     4 decimals
            9       QTYHND         5      P      54     56     0 decimals
           10       AVGCST         6      P      57     60     4 decimals
           11       UNITSP         4      P      61     63     2 decimals
```

Cereal Brands Master File Data:

						Unit		Average	Unit
Brand#	Brand Name	Size	Measure	Manufacturer	Date	Cost	On Hand	Cost	SP
C1100	TOTAL	012	OZ	GENERAL MILLS	060795	016111	00360	016111	0183
C1134	KIX	014	OZ	GENERAL MILLS	060795	019990	00480	019990	0239
C4889	BRAN CHEX	014	OZ	RALSTON	071195	012899	00840	012899	0149
C5150	RICE CHEX	012	OZ	RALSTON	051195	014550	01200	014550	0169
C6314	RAISIN BRAN	020	OZ	KELLOGG	071295	018840	00960	018840	0209
C6550	CORN FLAKES	018	OZ	KELLOGG	061595	010000	02400	010000	0118
C6900	FROSTED FRAKES	010	OZ	KELLOGG	061595	010910	01800	010910	0129
C7000	GRAPE-NUT FLAKES	012	OZ	POST	061695	012788	02400	012788	0139
C7100	FRUIT & FIBER	014	OZ	POST	051895	016220	01200	016220	0189
C7440	ALPHA-BITS	015	OZ	POST	052095	017050	04800	017050	0195
C8000	CAP'N CRUNCH	016	OZ	QUAKER	072195	017233	06000	017233	0199
C8100	PUFFED WHEAT	006	OZ	QUAKER	062295	010000	12000	010000	0119

Transaction (Adds) File Record Format:

```
                    PHYSICAL FILE DESCRIPTION

      SYSTEM: AS/400                       DATE: Yours
      FILE NAME: Yours                     REV NO: 0
      RECORD NAME: Yours                   KEY LENGTH: 5
      SEQUENCE: Keyed (Unique)             RECORD SIZE: 62

                      FIELD DEFINITIONS

           FIELD    FIELD NAME    SIZE   TYPE    POSITION      COMMENTS
           NO                                   FROM    TO

            1       ABRAND         5      C       1      5     Key field
            2       ANAME         20      C       6     25
            3       ASIZE          3      P      26     27
            4       AMEAS          2      C      28     29
            5       AMFGR         15      C      30     44
            6       APDATE         6      P      45     48
            7       APCOST         6      P      49     52     4 decimals
            8       AQTYHD         5      P      53     55     0 decimals
            9       AVCOST         6      P      56     59     4 decimals
           10       ASPRCE         4      P      60     62     2 decimals
```

Physical File Data:

					Last Purchase Date	Last Purchase Price	Amount On Hand	Avg Cost/ Unit	SP Price/ Unit
Brand#	Brand Name	Size	Measure	Manufacturer					
C5200	SUN FLAKES	015	OZ	RALSTON	082295	019900	00600	019900	0219
C1134	CHEERIOS	020	OZ	GENERAL MILLS	082195	025500	12000	025500	0279
C9000	SHREDDED WHEAT SS	012	OZ	NABISCO	082495	011500	01080	011500	0125
C8100	PAC-MAN	013	OZ	GENERAL MILLS	082595	017899	24000	017899	0199
C1200	TREATS	014	OZ	KELLOGG'S	083095	028895	07200	028895	0349

Report Design:

```
      |    0    |    1    |    2    |    3    |    4    |
      |1234567890|1234567890|1234567890|1234567890|1234567890|
    1 |ØX/XX/XX  |         |DUPLICATE RECORDS|        |PAGE XØX|
    2 |          |         |         |         |         |
    3 |          |         |         |         |         |
    4 |          |         |  XXXXX  (BRAND#) |         |
    5 |          |         |         |         |         |
    6 |          |         |  XXXXX  |         |         |
    7 |          |         |         |         |         |
    8 |          |         |         |         |         |
    9 |RECORDS LOADED X.XØX| ERROR RECORDS X.XØX|         |
```

Programming Assignment 13-4: CEREAL BRANDS MASTER FILE UPDATE AND LOGICAL DELETION OF RECORDS

Programming Assignment 13-3 must have been completed, or the master file previously created and loaded with data, before this assignment is started.

Write an RPG/400 program to *update* and *logically delete* records in the Cereal Brands Master file with data from two transaction files. One file includes purchase and sales transactions, and the other contains "change" data and the key values of records that are to be logically deleted.

The following update functions are to be performed:

From the purchase/sales transaction file, a record with a **P** code indicates a purchase transaction that requires the following moving average computations:

Step 1: Determine Total Quantity and Cost after Purchase:

	Avg. Price Unit	*	Qty. on Hand	–	Total
Values in master record	1.0000	*	12000	–	12000
Values in transaction record	1.1000	*	08000	–	08800
Totals			20000		20800

Step 2: Determine New Average Cost Per Unit:

Total Cost/Total Qty. = 20800/20000 = 1.0400 (new avg. cost)

In addition to changing the average cost for purchase transactions, the last purchase date, last purchase price, and quantity on hand in the related master records are to be updated with the transaction file data.

Transaction records coded with an **S** indicate sales transactions which require that the related master record quantity on hand field be reduced by the quantity field value of the sale. No other computations are needed.

*Sales and Purchases (**S** and **P**) Transaction File/Record Format:*

```
                    PHYSICAL FILE DESCRIPTION

     SYSTEM: AS/400                        DATE:Yours
     FILE NAME: Yours                      REV NO: 0
     RECORD NAME: Yours                    KEY LENGTH: 5
     SEQUENCE: Keyed (non-unique)          RECORD SIZE: 17

                      FIELD DEFINITIONS

       FIELD   FIELD NAME   SIZE  TYPE   POSITION      COMMENTS
        NO                                FROM   TO

         1     SPCODE        1     C       1     1    P or S
         2     SPBND#        5     C       2     6    Key field
         3     SPQTY         5     P       7     9    0 decimals
         4     PCOST         6     P      10    13    2 decimals
         5     PDATE         6     P      14    17

     Note: S (sales records) must have zeros stored in the PCOST
           and PDATE fields.
```

```
Physical File Data:

         Trans                                Transaction    Purchase
         Code    Brand#    Quantity           Amount         Date

          P      C2121     00400              019000         091595
          P      C8000     02000              017000         092195
          S      C6550     00500
          S      C8900     10000
          S      C7440     00800
          S      C1200     07600
```

The second transaction file stores **C** type records that contain data that will "change" one or more fields in a related master file record. Because the transaction record format includes all of the fields in the master record, each field in the transaction record must be tested for the presence of a value (blank for alphanumeric or zero for numeric). Otherwise, master record fields that are not to be changed will be updated with blanks and zeros.

In addition, this file stores the key value of master file records that are to be logically deleted. The records are identified with a **D** in the transaction code field.

Changes (*C*)/Deletes (*D*) Transaction File/Record Format:

```
                    PHYSICAL FILE DESCRIPTION

    SYSTEM: AS/400                     DATE: Yours
    FILE NAME: Yours                   REV NO: 0
    RECORD NAME: Yours                 KEY LENGTH: 5
    SEQUENCE: Keyed (not unique)       RECORD SIZE: 63

                        FIELD DEFINITIONS

    FIELD     FIELD NAME    SIZE   TYPE    POSITION        COMMENTS
     NO                                    FROM    TO

      1       CCODE           1     C        1      1     C
      2       CBRND#          5     C        2      6     Key field
      3       CNAME          20     C        7     26
      4       CSIZE           3     P       27     28
      5       CUNIT           2     C       29     30
      6       CMFGR          15     C       31     45
      7       CLPDAT          6     P       46     49
      8       CUITCT          6     P       50     53     4 decimals
      9       CQTHND          5     P       54     56     0 decimals
     10       CAVCST          6     P       57     60     4 decimal
     11       CUITSP          4     P       61     63     2 decimals
```

Trans Code	Brand#	Brand Name	Size	Measure	Manufacturer	Last Purchase Date	Last Purchase Price	Amount On Hand	Avg Cost/ Unit	SP Price/ Unit
C	C1100						017000			0190
D	C7100									
C	C4889		012			081595				
C	C8100	PUFFED RICE								
C	C1300									
D	C7440								020000	

In addition, generate an edit report in the following format of transaction records not found in the master file.

Report Design:

```
        0              1              2              3              4
  1234567890123456789012345678901234567890123456789012345678901234567890123
 1 ØX/XX/XX        UPDATE/DELETE TRANSACTIONS        HH:MM:SS
 2                 WITH NO MASTER FILE KEY
 3
 4                 CODE              KEY
 5                                   VALUE
 6
 7                   X              XXXXX
 8                   X              XXXXX
 9
10
11 TRANSACTIONS PROCESSED:  XXØX
12
13 MASTER RECORDS UPDATED:  XXØX
14
15 ERROR RECORDS:  XXØX
16
17
18 NOTES:  USE SYSTEM DATE & TIME.
```

Before the program is executed, print a **CPYF** listing of the Cereal Brands Master file in hexadecimal format and a listing *after* the program is run. Compare the listings for the results of the update/delete transaction processing.

chapter 14

Display Files

A *display file* defines the format of one or more records that will be shown on a display device. The record format usually includes fields, constants, indicators, and keywords. Display files are initially developed in source code and then compiled to create an object. A display file may contain a maximum of 1,024 record formats with no more than 32, 763 characters in each format. They may include entries at the *File, Record, Field,* and *Help Levels.*

The record format(s) in a display file (**DSPF**) may be created by the following two methods:

1. Design a screen format on a form, complete the DDS coding, enter the code via **SEU,** and compile with the **CRTDSPF** command.
2. Design and code a screen format using the *Screen Design Aid* (**SDA**) utility.

The procedures and syntax for creating display files using the *Screen Design Aid* (**SDA**) utility are detailed in Appendix D. This chapter will follow the familiar **SEU** method for creating display files.

CREATING A DISPLAY FILE RECORD

The steps required to create a display file using the **SEU** method are as follows:

1. Design the record format on a CRT layout form (or print chart).
2. Code the record format on DDS forms (may be skipped).
3. Enter the DDS instructions via **SEU.**
4. Save, compile (**CRTDSPF** command), debug, and optionally test with the **SDA** test utility.

Each of the steps is detailed in upcoming sections.

Designing the Record Format

The **DSPF** record design shown in Figure 14-1 will be used as the input/output medium to add, update, inquiry, and logically delete records from a physical file.

```
 1
 2   0X/XX/XX                                                    HH:MM:SS
 3              CUSTOMER NAME & ADDRESS
 4
 5              CUSTOMER NUMBER: XXXXX
 6
 7          NAME:              X_____X
 8
 9        STREET:              X_____X
10
11          CITY:              X_____X
12
13         STATE:              XX
14
15           ZIP:              XXXXX
16
17        BALANCE:             XXXXXXXXX
18
19
20          F3 - EOJ      F2 - ENTER      F5 - REDISPLAY
```

Figure 14-1 Display file record design.

Coding the Record Format on DDS Forms

Similar to the coding for physical files, the DDS form is also used to code display file (**DSPF**) record formats. Figure 14-2 presents the completed DDS form for the record design in Figure 14-1. *Note that the column 1 row 1 position cannot be used; it is reserved for a system-supplied Record Identification Code.*

The *File, Record,* and *Field Levels* for the example **DSPF** record format are discussed separately in the following sections.

Seq	Form Type	AndOr	Condition Name	Name Type	Name	Ref (R)	Length	Data Type	Dec	Usage	Line	Pos	Functions
1	A												REF(SMYERS/GLMASTER)
2	A												PRINT
3	A												CA03(03 'EOJ')
4	A												CF02(02 'ENTER')
5	A												CA05(05 'REDISPLAY')
6	A			R	GLDFR1								CHGINPDFT(CS)
7	A										2	6	DATE EDTCDE(Y)
8	A										2	69	TIME
9	A										3	30	'CUSTOMER NAME & ADDRESS'
10	A										5	20	'CUSTOMER NUMBER:'
11	A				CUST#	R				Y B	5	40	EDTCDE(Z)
12	A		99										ERRMSG('DUPLICATE RECORD' 99)
13	A										7	20	'NAME:'
14	A				NAME	R				B	7	40	
15	A										9	20	'STREET:'
16	A				STREET	R				B	9	40	
17	A										11	20	'CITY:'
18	A				CITY	R				B	11	40	
19	A										13	20	'STATE:'
20	A				STATE	R				B	13	40	
21	A										15	20	'ZIP:'
22	A				ZIP	R			Y	B	15	40	
23	A										17	20	'BALANCE'
24	A				BALANC	R				B	17	40	
25	A										20	16	'F3 - EOJ CK2 - ENTER F3-
26	A												- REDISPLAY'

Figure 14-2 DDS coding for example **DSPF** record format.

File Level Syntax

The *File Level* entries for the example **DSPF** record format are shown and explained in Figure 14-3.

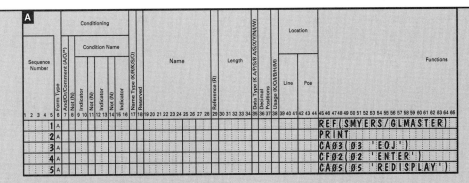

File Level (Lines 1 to 5):

Line#   Functions (Columns 45–80)

1 The keyword **REF** (Reference) retrieves the field descriptions from a previously described record format. Its format is shown below:

        REF([library-name]/data-base-file-name/ [record name])

   As indicated by the brackets [ ], the library-name and record-name entries are optional. The library-name entry is only needed if the database file referenced is not in a library included in your library list. The record-name entry is required if the referenced database file has more than one record format, which is not relevant for physical files.

2 The keyword **PRINT** controls the printing of a displayed screen when the print key is pressed on the keyboard. Without this entry the screen image could not be printed at the operator's discretion. Its format is shown below:

   PRINT [(response-indicator ['text']) | (*PGM) | (*PGM) | ([library-name/]printer-file name)]

   The following examples indicate ways to format the **PRINT** keyword:

   PRINT - Stores the screen image to the user's output queue. The Reset key must be pressed to continue.

   PRINT (01 "Press print key') - Tells the operator what to do and passes control to the program which determines the action to be taken.

   PRINT (*PGM) - Control is automatically returned to your program after the Print key is pressed.

   PRINT(library-name/printer-file-name) - Spools output to the specified printer file.

3 The keyword **CA03** (Command Attention key) assigns the Command Key 3 to some display file function and turns on an optional response-indicator. Command Attention keys 01 through 24 may be assigned at the *file* or *record level*. They do not, however, provide for the transmission of input data from display file to an RPG/400 program. The format of the **CA** keyword is shown below:

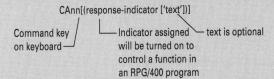

   Note that the response-indicator specified does not have to be the same as the **CA** key.

   When a **CA** key is pressed during program execution, all other command keys are turned off.

   CA03(03 'EOJ') will be used to control end-of-job processing and **CA05(05 'REDISPLAY')** for redisplay in an example RPG/400 program discussed in Chapter 15.

4 The keyword **CF02** (Command Function key) assigns the Command Key 2 to some screen control function and turns on an optional response-indicator. Command function keys 01 through 24 may be assigned at the *file* or *record level*. The Command Function keyword **(CF)** differs from the Command Attention keyword **(CA)** in that it does provide for the transmission of data from a display file to a program. The format of a **CF** keyword is shown below:

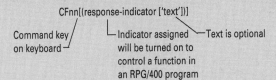

   Note that the response-indicator specified does not have to be the same assigned to the **CF** key.

Figure 14-3 *File Level* syntax for the example **DSPF** record format.

When a **CF** key is pressed during program execution, all other command keys are turned off.

CF02(02 'ENTER') will be used to control the writing of records to a physical file in an RPG/400 program introduced in Chapter 15.

5   See the explanation of the **CA** keyword for line 3.

Figure 14-3   *File Level* syntax for the example **DSPF** record format. (Continued)

A list of other *File Level* keywords is presented in Figure 14-4. Note that those that are both *File* and *Record Levels* are identified with an asterisk, and those that are functional at the *File, Record,* and *Field Levels* are marked with two asterisks.

Not all of the keywords listed in Figure 14-4 are used or defined in this chapter. For a comprehensive discussion of each keyword, refer to the *AS/400 Data Specifications Reference* manual.

```
  * ALWGPH  (Allow Graphics)              ** INDTXT  (Indicator Text)
  * CAnn    (Command Attention)            * INVITE
  * CFnn    (Command Function)               MSGLOC  (Message Location)
 ** CHGINPTDFT (Change Input Default)        OPENPRT (Open Printer File)
  * CLEAR                                     PASSRCD (Passed Record)
    DSPSIZ  (Display Size)                 * PRINT
  * HELP                                     REF     (Reference)
  * HLPRTN  (Help Return)                 ** ROLLUP/ROLLDOWN
  * HOME                                    U SRDSPMGT (User Display Management)
    INDARA  (Indicator Area)               * VLDCMDKEY (Valid Command Key)


  * Indicates File and Record Level keyword
 ** Indicates File Record and Field Level keyword
```

Figure 14-4   *File Level* keywords for display files.

Record Level Syntax

The *Record Level* entries specified in the example display file are detailed in Figure 14-5.

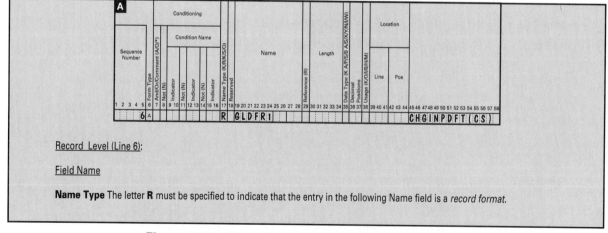

Record Level (Line 6):

Field Name

Name Type The letter **R** must be specified to indicate that the entry in the following Name field is a *record format.*

Figure 14-5   *Record Level* syntax for the example **DSPF** record format.

Name

Columns 19–28   Programmer-supplied record name must be entered left-justified in this field. The record name may be a maximum of 10 characters and begin with an alphabetic letter (A–Z), or @, $, or #. All other characters may be A through Z, 0 through 9, @, $, #, and _ (underscore). Embedded blanks are not permitted.

Function

Columns 45–80   The **CHGINPDFT** (*Change Input Default*) keyword changes the default attribute for input and input/output capable fields. Without this keyword, all variable fields in the file and/or record format will be displayed with underlining. The **CHGINPDFT(CS)** keyword used in the example changes all of the input/output capable fields (not constants) from the underline default to column separators (dots).

The format of this keyword is

CHGINPDFT[(input-default 1 input-default 2 . . .]

The valid entries (input-default1, etc.) are

Value	Equivalent DDS Keyword	Function
none	none	Remove underlining
BL	DSPATR (BL)	Blinking field
CS	DSPATR (CS)	Column separators (dots)
HI	DSPATR (HI)	High intensity
RI	DSPATR (RI)	Reverse image
UL	DSPATR (UL)	Underline
FE	CHECK (FE)	Field Exit
LC	CHECK (LC)	Lowercase
ME	CHECK (ME)	Mandatory enter
MF	CHECK (MF)	Mandatory fill

A *File Level* **CHGINPDFT** changes all of the input and input/output capable fields in all of the record formats to the designated parameter value. **CHGINPDFT** keywords at the *Record Level* will override any specified at the *File Level*. Similarly, *Field Level* **CHGINPDFT** entries will override those previously specified at the *File* and *Record Levels*. In other words, any lower-level **CHGINPDFT** keyword will override any specified at a higher level.

Figure 14-5   *Record Level* syntax for the example **DSPF** record format. (Continued)

Keywords that may be specified at the *Record Level* are listed in Figure 14-6. Note that keywords that may be specified at the *File Level* are identified with an asterisk; those that may also be used at the *Field Level,* with double asterisks; and those that may also be specified at the *File* and *Field Levels,* with triple asterisks.

```
    ALARM (Audible Alarm)                HLPSEQ (Help Sequencing)             SFL (Subfile)
    ALTNAME (Alternative Record Name)  * HOME                                 SFLCLR (Subfile Clear)
  * ALWGPH (Allow Graphics)          *** INDTXT (Indicator Text)             SFLCTL (Subfile Control)
    ALWROL (Allow Roll)               * INVITE                                SFLDLT (Subfile Delete)
    ASSUME                              INZINP (Initialize Input)             SFLDROP (Subfile Drop)
    BLINK                              INZRCD (Initialize Record)            SFLDSP (Subfile Display)
  * CAnn (Command Attention)           KEEP                                  SFLDSPCTL (Subfile Display Control)
  * CFnn (Command Function)            LOCK                                  SFLEND (Subfile End)
 ** CHANGE                             LOGINP (Log Input)                    SFLENTER (Subfile Enter)
*** CHGINPDFT (Change Input Default)   LOGOUT                                SFLINZ (Subfile Initialize)
  * CLEAR                              MDTOFF (Modified Data Tag OFF)        SFLLIN (Subfile Line)
    CLRL (Clear Line)                  OVERLAY                               SFLMSG (Subfile Message)
    CSRLOC (Cursor Location)           PROTECT                               SFLMSGID (Subfile Message ID)
    DSPMOD (Display Mode)              PUTOVR (Put with Explicit Override)   SFLMSGRCD (Subfile Message Record)
    ERASE                           ** PUTRETAIN (Put-Retain)                SFLNXTCHG (Subfile Next Changed)
    ERASEINP (Erase Input)             RETKEY (Retain Function Keys)         SFLPAG (Subfile Page)
    FRCDTA (Force Data)                RETCMDKEY (Retain Command Keys)       SFLRNA (Subfile Records Not Active)
    GETRETAIN (Get Retain)          * ROLLUP/ROLLDOWN                        SFLSIZ (Subfile Size)
  * HELP                               RTNDTA (Return Data)                  SLNO (Starting Line Number)
  * HLPRTN (Help Return)               SETOFF (Set Off)                   ** TEXT
                                                                             UNLOCK
     *  Indicates File and Record Level keyword                              USRDFN (User-Defined)
    **  Indicates Record and Field Level keyword                          * VLDCMDKEY (Valid Command Key)
   ***  Indicates File, Record, and Field Level keyword
```

Figure 14-6   *Record Level* keywords for display files.

Field Level **Keywords and Entries**

Because of the number of new syntax concepts related to display files at the *Field Level*, the entries are detailed in separate sections.

System Date and Time (DATE/TIME Keywords)

The **DATE** keyword accesses the system date in an MMDDYY format. Standard date editing (i.e., MM/DD/YY) is not included and must be separately specified with an **EDTCDE** (*Edit Code*) or **EDTWRD** (*Edit Word*) keyword.

Sytem time, which is accessed by the **TIME** keyword, displays in an HH:MM:SS format with the colons automatically inserted. An explanation of how these keywords are used in the example display file is detailed in Figure 14-7.

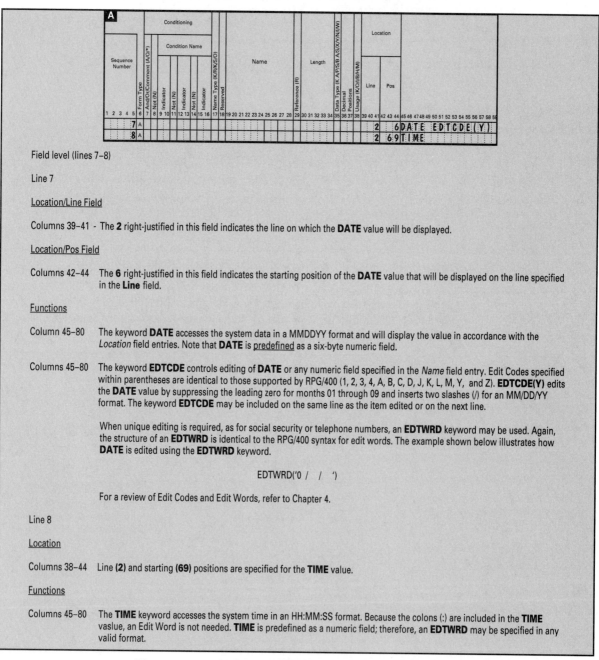

Field level (lines 7–8)

Line 7

Location/Line Field

Columns 39–41 - The **2** right-justified in this field indicates the line on which the **DATE** value will be displayed.

Location/Pos Field

Columns 42–44   The **6** right-justified in this field indicates the starting position of the **DATE** value that will be displayed on the line specified in the **Line** field.

Functions

Column 45–80   The keyword **DATE** accesses the system data in a MMDDYY format and will display the value in accordance with the *Location* field entries. Note that **DATE** is <u>predefined</u> as a six-byte numeric field.

Columns 45–80   The keyword **EDTCDE** controls editing of **DATE** or any numeric field specified in the *Name* field entry. Edit Codes specified within parentheses are identical to those supported by RPG/400 (1, 2, 3, 4, A, B, C, D, J, K, L, M, Y, and Z). **EDTCDE(Y)** edits the **DATE** value by suppressing the leading zero for months 01 through 09 and inserts two slashes (/) for an MM/DD/YY format. The keyword **EDTCDE** may be included on the same line as the item edited or on the next line.

When unique editing is required, as for social security or telephone numbers, an **EDTWRD** keyword may be used. Again, the structure of an **EDTWRD** is identical to the RPG/400 syntax for edit words. The example shown below illustrates how **DATE** is edited using the **EDTWRD** keyword.

EDTWRD('0 /   /   ')

For a review of Edit Codes and Edit Words, refer to Chapter 4.

Line 8

Location

Columns 38–44   Line **(2)** and starting **(69)** positions are specified for the **TIME** value.

Functions

Columns 45–80   The **TIME** keyword accesses the system time in an HH:MM:SS format. Because the colons (:) are included in the **TIME** vaslue, an Edit Word is not needed. **TIME** is predefined as a numeric field; therefore, an **EDTWRD** may be specified in any valid format.

Figure 14-7   **DATE** and **TIME** keyword entries in the example display file.

The other *Field Level* keywords, constants, and fields used in the example display file record format are explained in Figure 14-8.

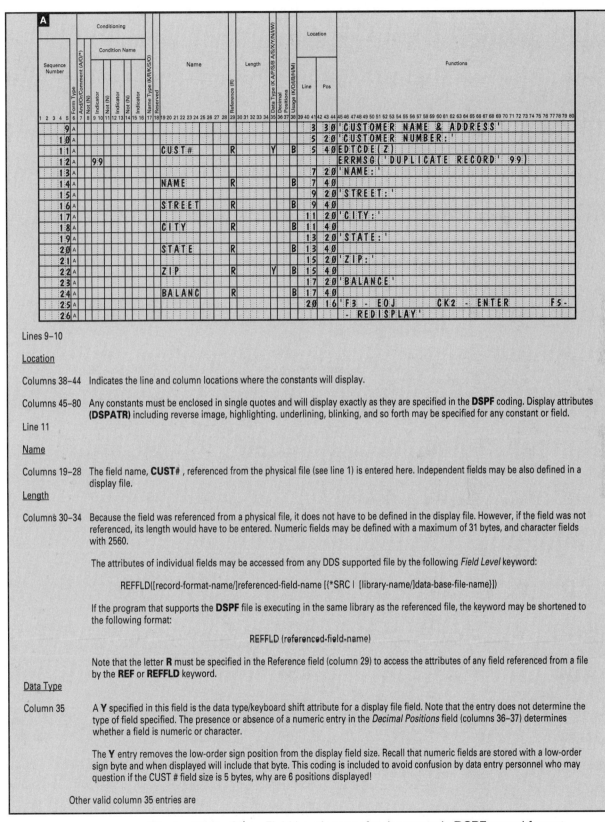

Lines 9–10

Location

Columns 38–44 Indicates the line and column locations where the constants will display.

Columns 45–80 Any constants must be enclosed in single quotes and will display exactly as they are specified in the **DSPF** coding. Display attributes **(DSPATR)** including reverse image, highlighting, underlining, blinking, and so forth may be specified for any constant or field.

Line 11

Name

Columns 19–28 The field name, **CUST#** , referenced from the physical file (see line 1) is entered here. Independent fields may be also defined in a display file.

Length

Columns 30–34 Because the field was referenced from a physical file, it does not have to be defined in the display file. However, if the field was not referenced, its length would have to be entered. Numeric fields may be defined with a maximum of 31 bytes, and character fields with 2560.

The attributes of individual fields may be accessed from any DDS supported file by the following *Field Level* keyword:

REFFLD([record-format-name/]referenced-field-name [{*SRC | [library-name/]data-base-file-name}])

If the program that supports the **DSPF** file is executing in the same library as the referenced file, the keyword may be shortened to the following format:

REFFLD (referenced-field-name)

Note that the letter **R** must be specified in the Reference field (column 29) to access the attributes of any field referenced from a file by the **REF** or **REFFLD** keyword.

Data Type

Column 35 A **Y** specified in this field is the data type/keyboard shift attribute for a display file field. Note that the entry does not determine the type of field specified. The presence or absence of a numeric entry in the *Decimal Positions* field (columns 36–37) determines whether a field is numeric or character.

The **Y** entry removes the low-order sign position from the display field size. Recall that numeric fields are stored with a low-order sign byte and when displayed will include that byte. This coding is included to avoid confusion by data entry personnel who may question if the CUST # field size is 5 bytes, why are 6 positions displayed!

Other valid column 35 entries are

Figure 14-8 Other *Field Level* syntax for the example **DSPF** record format.

Entry	Meaning	Valid Data Type
Blank	Default	
X	Alphabetic only	Character
A	Alphanmumeric shift	Character
N	Numeric shift	Character or numeric
S	Signed numeric	Numeric
Y	Numeric only	Numeric
W	Katakana (Japanese)	Character
I	Inhibit keyboard entry	Character or numeric
D	Digits only	Character or numeric
M	Numeric only character	Character
F	Floating point	Numeric

Refer to the *Data Description Specifications* Manual (Display File chapter) for an explanation of these entries.

**Decimal
Positions**

Columns 36–37 Because all of the field attributes are referenced from the GLMASTER physical file, no entry has to be specified. When a numeric field is defined in the display file, the number of related decimal positions must be included in this field. Recall that the number of decimal positions for a numeric field processed by an RPG/400 program is limited to 9. For character fields this area must be blank.

Usage

Column 38 The **B** specified indicates that the field is defined both as an input and an output field. Values may be input from the screen to a program or output from a program to a screen as required in update or deletion processing.

Other options include:

O - Output from a program to the screen as required by inquiry processing.

I - Input from the screen to a program as required by data entry processing or adding records to an existing file.

Location

Columns 39–44 *Line* and *Pos* entries define the line and starting positions respectively, of the field value.

Functions

Columns 45–80 The **EDTCDE(Z)** keyword suppresses all leading zeros in the displayed field. Without this keyword, zeros will be included when the display file's record format is displayed.

Line 12

Functions

Columns 45–80 The **ERRMSG** keyword controls the display of the error text specified within the parentheses and single quotes. A conditioning indicator(s) must be specified in columns 8 through 16, which is turned on when the related error condition is flagged during execution of an RPG/400 program; controls the display of the error message.

The format of the **ERRMSG** keyword is illustrated below:

ERRMSG ('message-text' [response-indicator])

Programmer-supplied ⟵   ⟶ Conditioning indicator (columns 8 through 16) is specified here
and will turn off when the Reset key is pressed.

In the example shown, indicator **99** will be turned on in an RPG/400 program if an attempt is made to **WRITE** a record to a physical file defined with unique keys with a key already stored in the file. When the related error occurs, the programmer-supplied text in the body of the **ERRMSG** keyword will display in reverse image at the bottom (line 24) of the screen and the cursor will move to the input field that generated the error. The Reset key must be pressed to continue.

If more than one **ERRMSG** keyword is specified and the errors tested occur at the same time, only the first **ERRMSG** text will be displayed.

Lines 13–24

The constant and field entries on these lines follow the syntax previously explained above. Note that the ZIP field also includes a **Y** in the *Data Type* field, which will eliminate the low-order sign position from this packed numeric item.

Lines 25–26

The constant entered on line 25 differs from the others in that it continues to another line. Continuation of an entry is controlled by including a minus sign (-) or plus sign (+) at the end of the item. The entry is continued on the next line without any leading quote. Note that **SEU** will indicate an error (reverse-image display) for line 25 when the ENTER Key is pressed. Completing the statement on line 26 will correct the syntax error.

Figure 14-8 Other *Field Level* syntax for the example **DSPF** record format. (Continued)

SEU Entry and Compilation of Display Files

If the *Programmer Menu* is used to access **SEU, 8** must be entered in the *Selection* field, the display file name in the **Parm** field, and **DSPF** for the member type. To compile the display file, **3** must be entered in the *Selection* field of the Programmer Menu with the **Parm** and *Type* entries. If any of the default parameters are to be changed, the **CRTDSPF** command has to be entered on the command line of any display and **F4** pressed. The programmer can then select the parameters to be changed.

If **PDM** is used to develop a display file, refer to Appendix B for the procedures that must be followed.

Figure 14-9 shows the listing generated from compilation of the example display file. Note that the Expanded Source listing, which provides supplemental information, is not shown.

```
5738SS1 V2R2M0  920925              Data Description         SMYERS/GLDF1
File name . . . . . . . . . . . . . . . . . . . :  GLDF1
   Library name  . . . . . . . . . . . . . . . :  SMYERS
File attribute  . . . . . . . . . . . . . . . . :  Display
Source file containing DDS  . . . . . . . . . . :  QDDSSRC
   Library name  . . . . . . . . . . . . . . . :  SMYERS
Source member containing DDS  . . . . . . . . . :  GLDF1
Source member last changed  . . . . . . . . . . :  09/07/95  12:43:01
Source listing options  . . . . . . . . . . . . :  *SOURCE    *LIST      *NOSECLVL
DDS generation severity level . . . . . . . . . :  20
DDS flagging severity level . . . . . . . . . . :  00
Authority . . . . . . . . . . . . . . . . . . . :  *LIBCRTAUT
Replace file  . . . . . . . . . . . . . . . . . :  *YES
Text  . . . . . . . . . . . . . . . . . . . . . :  ch14 - example 1 - display file
Compiler  . . . . . . . . . . . . . . . . . . . :  IBM AS/400 Data Description Processor
                              Data Description Source
SEQNBR  *...+....1....+....2....+....3....+....4....+....5....+....6....+....7....+....8  Date
  100    A                                    REF(SMYERS/GLMASTER)           09/07/95
  200    A                                    PRINT                          09/07/95
  300    A                                    CA03(03 'EOJ')                 09/07/95
  400    A                                    CF02(02 'ENTER')               09/07/95
  500    A                                    CA05(05 'REDISPLAY')           09/07/95
  600    A          R GLDFR1                   CHGINPDFT(CS)                  09/07/95
  700    A                               2  6DATE EDTCDE(Y)                  09/07/95
  800    A                               2 69TIME                           09/07/95
  900    A                               3 30'CUSTOMER NAME & ADDRESS'       09/07/95
 1000    A                               5 20'CUSTOMER NUMBER:'              09/07/95
 1100    A          CUST#   R   Y B     5 40EDTCDE(Z)                        09/07/95
 1200    A 99                               ERRMSG('DUPLICATE RECORD' 99)    09/07/95
 1300    A                               7 20'NAME:'                         09/07/95
 1400    A          NAME    R     B     7 40                                 09/07/95
 1500    A                               9 20'STREET'                        09/07/95
 1600    A          STREET  R     B     9 40                                 09/07/95
 1700    A                              11 20'CITY:'                         09/07/95
 1800    A          CITY    R     B    11 40                                 09/07/95
 1900    A                              13 20'STATE:'                        09/07/95
 2000    A          STATE   R     B    13 40                                 09/07/95
 2100    A                              15 20'ZIP:'                          09/07/95
 2200    A          ZIP     R   Y B    15 40EDTCDE(Z)                        09/07/95
 2300    A                              17 20'BALANCE:'                      09/07/95
 2400    A          BALANC  R     B    17 40                                 09/07/95
 2500    A                              20 16'F3 - EOJ      F2 - ENTER    F5- 09/07/95
 2600    A                                 - REDISPLAY'                      09/07/95
```

Figure 14-9 Listing generated from compilation of the example display file.

A Print key listing of the display file's record format displayed by the *Test* function of **SDA** (see Appendix D for the required steps) is shown in Figure 14-10. If the *Test* function of **SDA** was not used to review the displayed record format, it could not be tested until the related RPG/400 program was written, compiled, debugged, and tested.

In the **SDA** *Test* mode, the **Bs** indicate that the variable field is defined as character

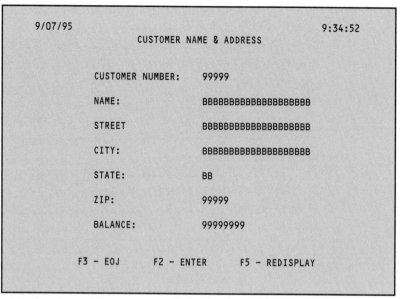

Figure 14-10   Display of the example **DSPF** record format.

with **B Usage** (input and output) . The **9s** indicate that the field is defined as numeric with **B Usage.**

Character fields defined with **I Usage** (input) will display with one or more **Is** indicating the field size and type. Input numeric fields would be identified by one or more **3s.**

On the other hand, character fields defined with **O Usage** (output) will display one or more **Os** indicating the field size and type. Output numeric fields are displayed with one or more **6s.**

DISPLAY FILE ENHANCEMENTS

A modified version of the previous display file example is shown in Figure 14-11 and includes the following changes:

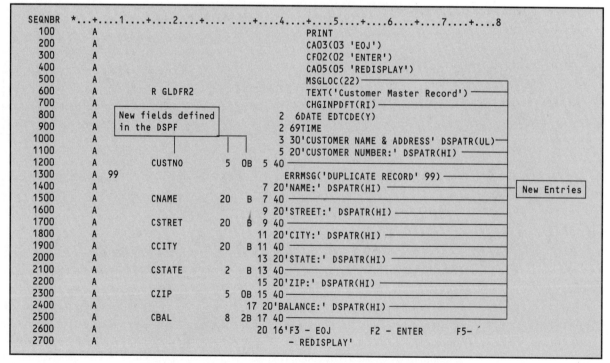

Figure 14-11   Display file syntax for modified example.

1. The **REF (MYERS/GLMASTER)** keyword and related **R** in column 29 have been deleted for every field. This required that the fields be defined in the display file with entries in the *Length* and *Decimal Positions* (when numeric) fields.

2. The **MSGLOC** (*Message Location*) keyword is specified to display the **ERRMSG** text on line 22 instead of default line 24.

3. The **CHGINPDFT(CS)** keyword has been changed to **CHGINPDFT(RI)** so that the field sizes are displayed in reverse image (light background with dark foreground letters) instead of with the default underline attribute.

4. **DSPATR** (*Display Attribute*) keywords are used to assign display attributes to selected constants.

Each of these changes will be discussed in the following paragraphs.

CHGINPDFT (Change Input Default) Keyword

As was mentioned before, the **CHGINPDFT** keyword changes input (**I Usage**) and input/output (**B Usage**) fields from the default underline display to the attribute(s) specified. The **CHGINPDFT(RI)** on line 700 of Figure 14-11 changes the default underline attribute for *all* of the fields (CUSTNO through CBAL) to reverse image.

The *TEXT* Keyword

The **TEXT** keyword is only specified for program documentation in that it supplies a descriptive comment for a record format or field. All of the record formats and fields in any DDS file type may be supplemented with a **TEXT** keyword. The text (included between the single quotes) appears only on a source or compiled source listing and is not displayed in the record format. Upper- or lower- (or both) case letters and any other valid characters may be specified in the text. Figure 14-12 shows how the **TEXT** keyword is used in the example **DSPF.**

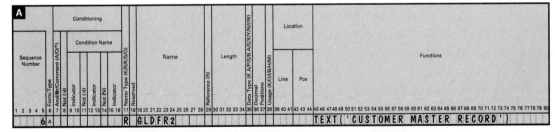

Figure 14-12 **TEXT** keyword used in the example **DSPF.**

The *DSPATR* (Display Attribute) Keyword

Display attributes are controlled in a display file by the **DSPATR** and **CHGINPDFT** keywords. The functions controlled by the *Field Level* **DSPATR** keyword for *all* fields include *blinking* (**BL**), *column separators* (**CS**), *high intensity* (**HI**), *nondisplay* (**ND**), *position cursor* (**PC**), *reverse image* (**RI**), and *underline* (**UL**). In addition, input-capable fields also support **MDT** (*set changed data tag*), **OID** (*operator identification*), **PR** (*protect field value from input*), and **SP** (*select by light pen*). Figure 14-13 explains the features of each attribute.

For All Fields:

Display Attribute	Meaning	Explanation
* BL	Blinking Field	Field (or constant) will blink when displayed.
CS	Column Separator	Display dots equal to the size of the field.
* HI	High Intensity	Highlights the field (or constant) when it is displayed.
* ND	Nondisplay	Prevents field (or constant) from being displayed. Often used for passwords and other security-sensitive data.
PC	Position Cursor	Positions the cursor at the first (high-order) position of the related field. If specified for more than one field, the cursor will position at the first field defined with this attribute.
* RI	Reverse Image	Reverses the image of this field (or constant) from the screen's image. For example, if the screen is light-on-dark, the field will display as dark-on-light, or vice versa.
* UL	Underline	Underlines a field or constant. All input-capable fields (**I** or **B Usage**) default to underlining. This default may be overridden with a **CHGINPDFT** keyword specified at the *File or Record* Level or with individual **DSPATR** keywords.

For Input-Capable Fields Only:

MDT	Set Modified Data Tag	Ensures that a field value is read from the screen.
OID	Operator Identification	Allows magnetic strip reader OID in the field.
PR	Protect	Prevents the workstation user from entering data into an input-capable field (**I** or **B Usage**).
SP	Select by Light Pen	Allows this field to be selected by light pen.

* Indicates that the attribute may be used with constants.

Figure 14-13   **DSPATR** and **CHGINPDFT** keyword display attributes.

CHGINPDFT display attribute functions are limited to blinking, column separators, high intensity, reverse image, and underline at the *File, Record,* or *Field Level.*

Figure 14-14 illustrates the displayed results for select constants and fields in the modified display file example. Note that the **CHGINPDFT** keyword on line 700 globally changes all of the input/output fields from the default **UL** (*underline*) attribute to **RI** (*reverse image*). The constants for the fields (lines 1100, 1400, etc.) are specified with the **HI** (*high intensity*) attribute by individual **DSPATR** keywords. Underlining (**UL**) is specified for the constant on line 1000.

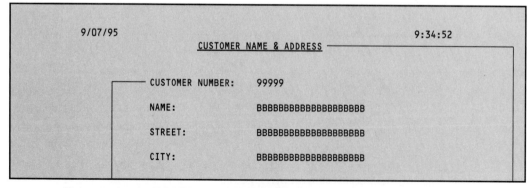

Figure 14-14   **DSPATR** and **CHGINPDFT** attribute results in the modified example display file.

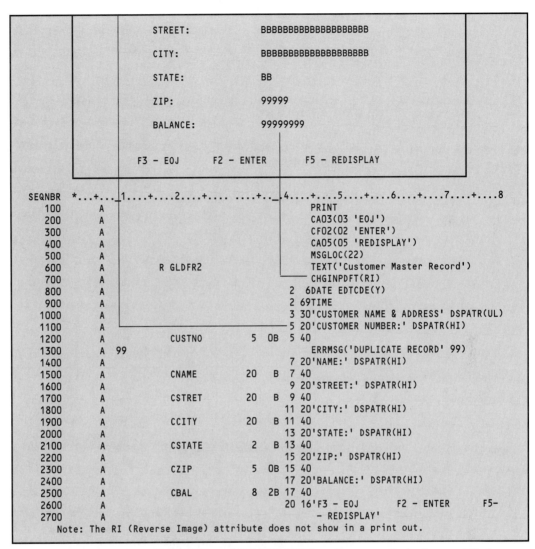

```
                              STREET:            BBBBBBBBBBBBBBBBBBBB

                              CITY:              BBBBBBBBBBBBBBBBBBBBBB

                              STATE:             BB

                              ZIP:               99999

                              BALANCE:           99999999


                        F3 - EOJ     F2 - ENTER      F5 - REDISPLAY


SEQNBR  *...+....1....+....2....+.... ....+...4....+....5....+....6....+....7....+....8
  100   A                                            PRINT
  200   A                                            CAO3(03 'EOJ')
  300   A                                            CFO2(02 'ENTER')
  400   A                                            CAO5(05 'REDISPLAY')
  500   A                                            MSGLOC(22)
  600   A             R GLDFR2                        TEXT('Customer Master Record')
  700   A                                            CHGINPDFT(RI)
  800   A                                          2  6DATE EDTCDE(Y)
  900   A                                          2 69TIME
 1000   A                                          3 30'CUSTOMER NAME & ADDRESS' DSPATR(UL)
 1100   A                                          5 20'CUSTOMER NUMBER:' DSPATR(HI)
 1200   A               CUSTNO        5   0B  5 40
 1300   A  99                                        ERRMSG('DUPLICATE RECORD' 99)
 1400   A                                          7 20'NAME:' DSPATR(HI)
 1500   A               CNAME        20    B  7 40
 1600   A                                          9 20'STREET:' DSPATR(HI)
 1700   A               CSTRET       20    B  9 40
 1800   A                                         11 20'CITY:' DSPATR(HI)
 1900   A               CCITY        20    B 11 40
 2000   A                                         13 20'STATE:' DSPATR(HI)
 2100   A               CSTATE        2    B 13 40
 2200   A                                         15 20'ZIP:' DSPATR(HI)
 2300   A               CZIP          5   0B 15 40
 2400   A                                         17 20'BALANCE:' DSPATR(HI)
 2500   A               CBAL          8   2B 17 40
 2600   A                                         20 16'F3 - EOJ        F2 - ENTER        F5-
 2700   A                                            - REDISPLAY'
        Note: The RI (Reverse Image) attribute does not show in a print out.
```

Figure 14-14 **DSPATR** and **CHGINPDFT** attribute results in the modified example display file. (Continued)

A list of all the keywords for display files is presented in Figure 14-15.

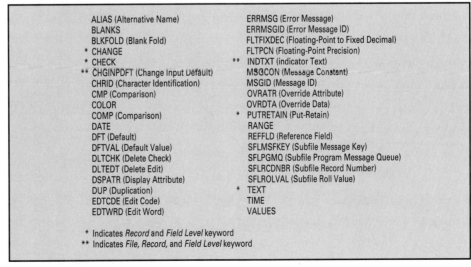

Figure 14-15 *Field Level* keywords for display files.

DATA VALIDATION KEYWORDS

Display file keywords that support *data validation* interactively include **CHECK, COMP, RANGE,** and **VALUES.** The syntax of each keyword will be discussed in the following sections.

The *CHECK* Keyword

For validity checking, the codes that may be specified with the **CHECK** keyword are detailed in Figure 14-16.

```
CHECK
Code        Meaning

AB          Allow blanks
ME          Mandatory enter
MF          Mandatory fill
M10         IBM Modulus-10 self-check algorithm
M11         IBM Modulus-11 self-check algorithm
VN          Validate name
VNE         Validate name extended
```

Figure 14-16   CHECK keyword edit codes for validity checking.

The function of each edit code is explained in the following paragraphs.

AB **(Allow Blanks) CHECK Keyword Code**

This code usually supplements another so that blanks will be allowed as an alternative value to satisfy the validity check. For example, if an account number field is validated with the **M11** (*Modulus-11*) Code and the data entered does not pass the test, the user may enter blanks to satisfy the validity check and continue to the next field or exit from the screen. Without the **AB** code any further action would not be possible and the user would have to press the Shift and System Req keys to exit from the screen and program. An example of how the **CHECK** keyword Code is specified is shown in Figure 14-17.

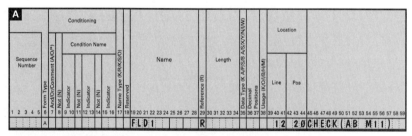

Figure 14-17   CHECK(AB) keyword coding example.

In addition to validity checking, the **CHECK** keyword may be used for *keyboard and cursor* control. Refer to IBM's *Data Description Reference* Manual for an explanation of those functions.

ME **(Mandatory Enter) CHECK Keyword Code**

When specified, the **CHECK** keyword's **ME** code requires that at least one character (a blank is valid) be entered in the field. Note that when none of the fields in the current display have been changed, the *mandatory entry* function is not enforced. If all of the fields in the record format are to support mandatory entry, **DSPATR (MDT)** must be specified for at least one field, or a **CHECK** keyword would have to be specified for each field. Figure 14-18 illustrates the syntax for the **CHECK(ME)** keyword.

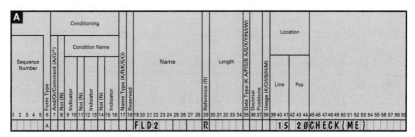

Figure 14-18   CHECK(ME) keyword coding example.

The *MF* (Mandatory Fill) *CHECK* Keyword Code

The **CHECK** keyword's **MF** code requires that if any character(s) in the field is changed, each position in the field must include a character. In other words, if the field is defined as five positions, five characters must be entered. Figure 14-19 shows the syntax for the **CHECK(MF)** keyword.

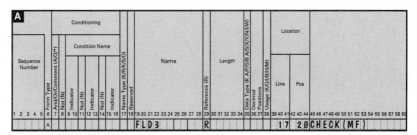

Figure 14-19   CHECK(MF) keyword coding example.

M10 (Modulus-10) and *M11* (Modulus-11) CHECK Keyword Codes

Chapter 12 introduced and explained the mathematics of the Modulus-11 method (see Figure 12-18) for validating numeric fields that include a check digit in the low-order byte. Because the Modulus-11 method provides for a greater percent of error detection (transpositional and substitution errors) than the Modulus-10 method, it is discussed in this text. Specifying the **CHECK(M11)** keyword with a numeric field that has a check digit included in its value will automatically compute the mathematical steps previously shown in Figure 12-18. To control any values that do not pass the **M11** test, the **AB** (*Allow Blanks*) code should be included in the keyword. An example **CHECK(AB M11)** statement is illustrated in Figure 14-20.

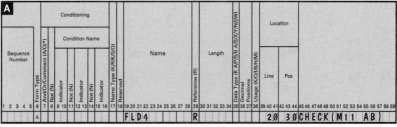

Figure 14-20   CHECK(M11) keyword coding example.

The *VN* (Validate Name) *CHECK* **Keyword Code**

Validates that the first character of a field defined as character is a **$, #, @,** or **A** through **Z** with a *keyboard shift* (column 35) of **A, N, X, W,** or **I.** Any remaining field entries may be **$, #, @, A** through **Z, 0** through **9,** or **underscore (_)** with no embedded blanks. Figure 14-21 illustrates an example **CHECK(VN)** keyword.

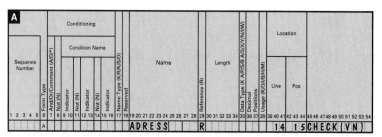

Figure 14-21   CHECK(VN) keyword coding example.

The *VNE* (Validate Name Extended) *CHECK* **Keyword Code**

The **VNE** code validates that the first byte in a character field (keyboard shift of **A, N, X, W,** or **I**) is **A** through **Z, a** through **z, #, $,** or **@.** Any remaining characters must be **A** through **Z, a** through **z, , $, _ ,** or a period. The size of the related character field is limited to 10 characters. In the validation process, lowercase letters will be converted to upper case. An example of the **CHECK(VNE)** keyword is shown in Figure 14-22.

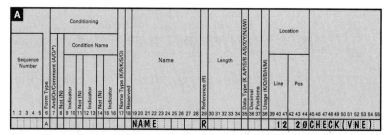

Figure 14-22   CHECK(VNE) coding example.

The *COMP* (Comparison) **Keyword**

The **COMP** keyword, which may also be specified as **CMP,** validates that the value specified is **EQ** (*Equal*), **NE** (*Not equal*), **LT** (*Less than*), **NL** (*Not less than*), **GT** (*Greater than*), **NG** (*Not greater than),* **LE** (*Less than or equal*), or **GE** (*Greater than or equal*) to the related field value. Depending on whether the field is defined as numeric or character, the value in the **COMP** keyword must be the same type (numeric or character). Character values must be enclosed in single quotes. Valid numeric values include **0** through **9** and a leading sign (+ or −). Numeric values that do not include a sign are compared as positive. Figure 14-23 illustrates two coding examples of the **COMP** keyword.

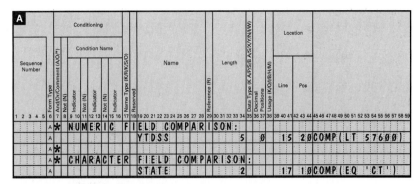

Figure 14-23   COMP (*Comparison*) keyword coding examples.

The *RANGE* Keyword

The **RANGE** keyword validates that the data in a field value is *equal to or greater than the lower value and less than or equal to the higher value* specified in the **RANGE** keyword. The format of the keyword is

RANGE (low-value high-value)

When the related field is defined as character, the low and high values must both be enclosed in single quotes. The quotes are omitted for numeric fields. Figure 14-24 details two examples of the **RANGE** keyword.

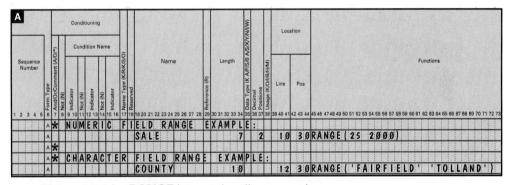

Figure 14-24   RANGE keyword coding examples.

The *VALUES* Keyword

The **VALUES** keyword validates that a field value is equal to one of the values included in the specified list. It is similar to the **COMP** keyword in that a relational test is made. However, the **VALUES** keyword only performs an *equal* test on a *list* of values, whereas the **COMP** keyword may include any of the relational tests, but only for one value. The format of the keyword is

VALUES (value-1 [value-2 ... [value-100]])

One hundred values may be specified, each separated by at least one blank. A **VALUES** keyword specified with character fields must have each value in the list enclosed in single quotes. Numeric values are specified without quotes. Identical to any relational comparison function, the value list must be the same type as the related field. Figure 14-25 shows two coding examples of the **VALUES** keyword.

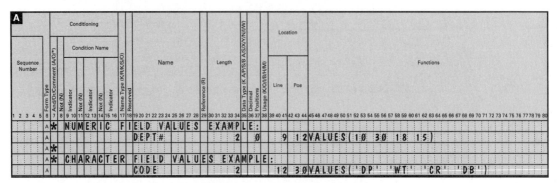

Figure 14-25 **VALUES** keyword coding examples.

Example Display File Modified with Validation Keywords

A source listing of the example display file modified with validation keywords and a supplemental explanation of the processing that occurs when a validation error is detected are detailed in Figure 14-26.

```
                           Data Description Source
SEQNBR  *...+....1....+....2....+....3....+....4....+....5....+....6....+....7....+....8
  100        * Display file for validation control.....
  200     A                                REF(SMYERS/GLMASTER)
  300     A                                PRINT
  400     A                                CA03(03 'EOJ')
  500     A                                CF02(02 'ENTER')
  600     A                                CA05(05 'REDISPLAY')
  700     A          R GLDFR3              CHGINPDFT(RI)
  800     A                              2  6DATE EDTCDE(Y)
  900     A                              2 69TIME
 1000     A                              3 30'CUSTOMER NAME & ADDRESS' DSPATR(UL)
 1100     A                              5 20'CUSTOMER NUMBER:'
 1200     A          CUST#   R     Y B   5 40CHECK(AB M11) EDTCDE(Z)─┐
 1300     A 99                             ERRMSG('DUPLICATE RECORD' 99)
 1400     A                              7 20'NAME:' DSPATR(HI)
 1500     A          NAME    R     X B   7 40CHECK(ME)───────────────┤
 1600     A                              9 20'STREET' DSPATR(HI)
 1700     A          STREET  R       B   9 40CHECK(ME)───────────────┤
 1800     A                             11 20'CITY:' DSPATR(HI)                    ┌──────────┐
 1900     A          CITY    R     X B  11 40CHECK(ME)───────────────┤            │Validation│
 2000     A                             13 20'STATE:' DSPATR(HI)                   │keywords  │
 2100     A          STATE   R       B  13 40CHECK(MF)───────────────┤            └──────────┘
 2200     A                                VALUES('ME' 'NH' 'VT' 'MA' 'RI'─┤
 2300     A                                'CT' 'NY' 'NJ')
 2400     A                             15 20'ZIP:' DSPATR(HI)
 2500     A          ZIP     R     D B  15 40CHECK(MF) EDTCDE(Z)──────┤
 2600     A                             17 20'BALANCE:' DSPATR(HI)
 2700     A          BALANC  R       B  17 40RANGE(10.00 99999.99)────┘
 2800     A                             20 16'F3 - EOJ       F2 - ENTER       F5-
 2900     A                              - REDISPLAY'
                           Data Type──┘
```

Figure 14-26 Example display file modified with validation keywords.

Line #	Keyword	Function and Error Identification
1200	**CHECK(AB M11)**	The Modulus-11 check digit method (code **M11**) validates the numeric field for transpositional and/or substitution errors. If the correct value is not known, the operator must enter blanks (code **AB**) to advance to the next field, redisplay the screen, or end the job.
		Usually all of the field values in the display are entered before the related function or ENTER key is pressed and any validation errors identified. Every field that is specified with a validation keyword will be validated sequentially beginning with the first field.
		The system-supplied message generated on line 24 for an **M11** error is
		The value for the field does not meet modulus 10 or 11 check.
1500	**CHECK(ME)**	The mandatory entry code (ME) for this character field requires that at least one character be entered to pass the validation criteria. *Note that if nothing is entered in the field, the mandatory entry function will not be enforced.* Supplemental to this keyword, Keyboard Shift **X** is entered in the *Data Type* field (column 35) which allows only the characters **A** through **Z**, **a** through **z**, comma, period, dash, or space to be entered.
		When an error is detected, a system-supplied error number 0021 is displayed on line 24. Pressing the Help key will display the following message on line 24:
		Mandatory enter field must have data entered.
1700 & 1900	**CHECK(ME)**	The mandatory entry code **(ME)** is entered for these fields, requiring that at least one valid character be entered. Because the STREET value usually includes numbers, the *Keyboard Shift* **X** is omitted in the *Data Type* field (column 35). However, it is specified with the CITY field.
2100 2200	**CHECK(MF)** & **VALUES(...)**	The mandatory fill keyword, **CHECK(MF),** specified with this field requires that every position in the field must include a character. *Note that if no character is entered in this field, the mandatory fill function will not be enforced.* When an error is detected, the message number 0021 displays on line 24. Pressing the Help key will display the following error message on line 24:
		The field must be filled before exiting. Key used not valid.
		The **VALUES** keyword requires that either ME, NH, VT, MA, RI, CT, NY, or NJ be entered in this field. Any other value will generate the following system-supplied message on line 24:
		Value for field is not valid.
		The operator may access the valid values by pressing the Help key.
2500	**CHECK(MF)**	The mandatory fill code specified with this field requires that a character be entered in all of the field positions. The *Keyboard Shift* **D** in the *Data Type* field (column 35) restricts the characters entered to 0 through 9.
2700	**RANGE(10.00 99999.99)**	
		This keyword requires that the data entered must be greater than or equal to the lower value (10.00) and less than or equal to the greater value (99999.99). When an error is detected, the following system supplied message will be displayed:
		Valid range for the field is 1000 to 9999999.

Figure 14-26 Example display file modified with validation keywords. (Continued)

SUMMARY

Display files define the format of one or more records that will be shown on a display device. The instructions for display files may be entered via **SEU,** or the record formats may be "painted" on the screen using the **SDA** utility. With either method the source member must be compiled to generate an object. A display file may include 1,024 record formats and include entries at the *File, Record,* and *Field Levels.*

The display of <u>constants</u> may be changed from their default *low-intensity* image by the **DSPATR** keyword and the *underline* default for <u>variables</u> with the **CHGINPDFT** keyword. Attributes included with the **DSPATR** keyword may be specified for any constant or variable. However, the **CHGINPDFT** keyword is functional only with input- or input/output-capable fields.

The display attributes supported are **BL** (blinking field), **CS** (column separators), **HI** (high intensity), **ND** (nondisplay), **PC** (position cursor), **RI** (reverse image), **UL** (underline), **MDT** (set modified data tag), **PR** (protect), **OID** (operator identification), and **SP** (select by light pen).

Command attention (**CAnn**) and *Command Function* (**CFnn**) keywords provide programmer-supplied end of job and other controls between the display file and an RPG/400 or CL program. Function keys assigned with **CAnn** <u>do not</u> support the passing of data from the display file to the RPG/400 or CL program, whereas those specified with **CFnn** <u>do</u>.

The keywords that support data validation include **CHECK, COMP** (or **CMP**), **VALUES,** and **RANGE.** Each has its own syntax and related controls. In addition to these keywords, a *Keyboard Shift* entry in the *Data Type* field (column 35) can restrict the type of data entered. System-supplied error messages (or error numbers) are displayed on line 24 of the screen if a validation error is detected after the related function key or the ENTER key is pressed. Additional information may be accessed about the error by pressing the Help key. To exit from the error condition and correct or ignore the validation error, the Reset key must be pressed.

QUESTIONS

14-1. What are display files? For what processing functions are they used?

14-2. By what methods may display files be created?

14-3. How many record formats may be included in a display file?

14-4. Explain the procedures for entering the DDS coding for a display file using the Programmer Menu.

14-5. Explain the function of the following display file keywords:

PRINT	DSPATR	EDTWRD	DATE
CAnn	ERRMSG	REF	TIME
CFnn	EDTCDE	REFFLD	CHGINPDFT

14-6. How does the processing controlled by the **CAnn** and **CFnn** keywords differ?

14-7. Explain the function of each part of the following keyword:

CF04(04 'update record')

14-8. Is the following entry valid for the maintenance function specified?

CA02(02 'add record')

14-9. Where may the fields specified in a display file be defined?

14-10. In what format is the **DATE** value accessed? The **TIME** value?

14-11. What is the default display attribute for input and input/output fields? How may this default attribute be globally changed?

14-12. What is the default display attribute for constants? How is this attribute globally changed?

14-13. Name the available display attributes. Explain the function of each one.

14-14. Write the keyword to change the default attribute for *all* of the input/output fields in a display file's record format to reverse image.

14-15. Write the keyword to position the cursor at the related field when the screen is displayed and to provide blinking.

14-16. Refer to a DDS specification and explain the **O, I,** and **B** values that may be entered in the *Usage* field (column 38).

14-17. Refer to Question 14-16 and relate a physical file maintenance function to the **O, I,** and **B** entries for the *Usage* field.

14-18. Refer to a DDS form and explain the function of the following *Data Type* (column 35) entries: **A, P, S, X, D, Y.**

14-19. What is the function of the **Line** and **Pos** field entries on the form for display files?

14-20. What levels of coding may be specified in a display file?

14-21. Write the keyword to access the field attributes of all the fields in the record format of the physical file INVENTRY stored in the PARTS library.

14-22. Write the keyword to access the attributes of the PTNAME field defined in the record format of the INVENTRY physical file stored in the PARTS library.

14-23. With the keywords specified for Questions 14-21 and 14-22, what must be entered in column 29?

Questions 14-24 through 14-26 relate to the following instruction:

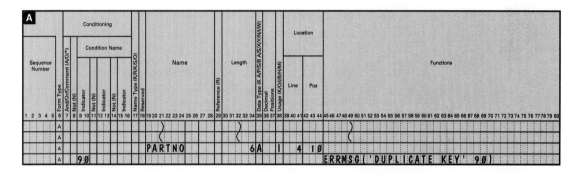

14-24. What is the function of the indicator specified in columns 9 and 10? Where and under what conditions is it set on?

14-25. What happens if indicator **90** is set on?

14-26. How is indicator **90** turned off?

14-27. May more than one **ERRMSG** be included in a record format of a display file?

14-28. What is the default line for the **ERRMSG** text? What keyword is used to change the line on which the text will display?

14-29. Name the display file keywords used for data validation.

14-30. Write the keyword to validate that the field value passes the Modulus-11 test and to provide for exit from the field if the value is incorrect and the correct entry is unknown.

14-31. Write the keyword to test that a SALES field value is not less than 25.00 and not greater than 3000.00.

14-32. Write the keyword to validate that a COURS# field has all of its characters entered.

14-33. Write the keyword to validate that the value in DEPT# is equal to 10, 15, 20, or 25.

14-34. Write the keyword to validate that the value in LGRADE is not greater than 8.

PROGRAMMING ASSIGNMENTS

For each of the following programming assignments, a physical file must have been created (but not loaded with data). Your instructor will inform you as to whether you have to create the physical file or if it has already been created.

Programming Assignment 14-1: VALIDATION OF NEW CUSTOMER ACCOUNTS

From the following CRT layout form, create a display file record format. Include the following validation functions:

1. Modulus-11 validation for the CUSTNO field.
2. Mandatory entry for the NAME field and test that the data type is alphabetic.
3. Mandatory entry for the STREET field.
4. Mandatory entry for the CITY field and test that the data type is alphabetic.
5. Values entered for the STATE field are OH, MI, NY, IL, PA, NY, and CA.
6. Mandatory fill for the ZIP field.
7. Test that the data entered for the LIMIT field is from 500 to 5000.
8. Test that the values entered in the RATING field are A, A−, B, B−, C.
9. Specify **B** (input and output) for the *Usage* field (column 38) for all of the fields.
10. Reference the field attributes of the physical file created for this assignment (see format below).

```
 1  MM/DD/YY                              CUSTOMER ENTRY                           HH:MM:SS
 2
 3
 4     CUSTOMER NUMBER: XXXXX        NAME: X_____X
 5
 6     STREET: X_____X
 7
 8     CITY: X_____X      STATE: XX       ZIP: XXXXX
 9
10     CREDIT LIMIT: XXXXXXX                              CREDIT RATING: XX
11
12
13        CMD KEY 3 - EOJ          CMD KEY 2 - ENTER          CMD KEY 5 - IGNORE
14
15     NOTES:
16        1. HIGHLIGHT ALL CONSTANTS.
17        2. UNDERLINE CONSTANT ON LINE 1.
18        3. REVERSE IMAGE ALL VARIABLE FIELDS.
19        4. INCLUDE THE ERRMSG 'RECORD ALREADY EXISTS' FOR THE CUSTOMER NO. FIELD.
```

A physical file with the following attributes must be created before the display file is compiled:

```
                    PHYSICAL FILE DESCRIPTION

        SYSTEM: AS/400                      DATE: Yours
        FILE NAME: Yours                    REV NO: 0
        RECORD NAME: Yours                  KEY LENGTH: 5
        SEQUENCE: Keyed  (Unique)           RECORD SIZE: 71

                        FIELD DEFINITIONS

        FIELD    FIELD NAME   SIZE   TYPE    POSITION       COMMENTS
         NO                                 FROM     TO


          1      CUSTNO         5    P         1       3   Key field
          2      NAME          24    C         4      27
          3      STREET        20    C        28      47
          4      CITY          20    C        48      57
          5      STATE          2    C        58      59
          6      ZIP            5    P        60      62
          7      LIMIT          7    P        66      69   0 decimals
          8      RATING         2    C        70      71
```

Use **SDA** to test your compiled display file record format.

Programming Assignment 14-2: STUDENT COURSE FILE ADDITION

From the following CRT layout form, create a display file record format. Include the following validation functions.

1. Mandatory fill for the SSNO field and suppress the low-order sign position in the displayed field.
2. Mandatory entry for the COURS# field.
3. Mandatory entry for the CRSNAM field and test that the data entered is alphabetic.
4. Mandatory fill for the TDATE field and suppress the low-order sign position in the displayed field.
5. Mandatory fill for the INSTCD field and suppress the low-order sign position in the displayed field.
6. Test that the CREDIT field is from 0 through 5. Suppress the low-order sign.
7. Validate that the data entered for the MARK field is **A, B, C, D, F, I,** or **W.**
8. Specify display file field names different from those in the related physical file.
9. The semester date value on line 2 will be accessed from a data area. Define an output-only field for this value.

```
 1  ØX/XX/XX                    STUDENT COURSES - FINAL GRADES                  HH:MM:SS
 2                              FOR SEMESTER ENDING XX/XX/XX
 3
 4
 5          STUDENT NO: XXXXXXXXX                  COURSE NO: XXXXXX
 6
 7          COURSE NAME: X_____X        TERM DATE: XXXXXX
 8
 9          INSTRUCTOR CODE: XXX         CREDITS: X              MARK: X
10
11
12                  CK3 - EOJ       CK2 - ENTER        CK5 - IGNORE
13     NOTES:
14        1. HIGHLIGHT ALL CONSTANTS.
15        2. UNDERLINE CONSTANTS ON LINE 1.
16        3. REVERSE IMAGE THE CONSTANTS ON LINE 12.
17        4. USE DEFAULT ATTRIBUTE FOR VARIABLE FIELDS.
18        5. LOCATE ERRMSG 'DUPLICATE KEY' ON LINE 15, WILL DISPLAY IF
19           A STUDENT NUMBER IS ENTERED THAT ALREADY EXISTS IN THE FILE.
```

A physical file with the following attributes must be created before the *display file* is compiled:

```
                    PHYSICAL FILE DESCRIPTION

        SYSTEM: AS/400                        DATE: Yours
        FILE NAME: Yours                      REV NO: Ø
        RECORD NAME: Yours                    KEY LENGTH: 21
        SEQUENCE: Keyed (Unique)              RECORD SIZE: 39

                        FIELD DEFINITIONS

        FIELD    FIELD NAME    SIZE  TYPE   POSITION      COMMENTS
         NO                                 FROM    TO


          1      SSNO           9     P      1      5    Key fld 1
          2      COURS#         6     C      6      11   Key fld 2
          3      COURNM        20     C     12      31
          4      TDATE          6     P     32      35   Key fld 3
          5      INSTCD         3     P     36      37
          6      CREDIT         1     P     38      38
          7      MARK           1     C     39      39
```

Use **SDA** to test your display file record format.

Programming Assignment 14-3: INTERACTIVE LOADING OF A PARTS MASTER INVENTORY FILE

From the following CRT layout form, create a *Display File* record format. Include the following validation functions:

```
     01...10........20........30........40........50........60........70......80
 1        MM/DD/YY                    PARTS INVENTORY                HH:MM:SS
 2                                        ENTRY
 3
 4
 5          PART NUMBER: XXXXX
 6
 7          PART NAME: X_____X
 8
 9          AMT-ON-HAND: XXXXXX              AVG COST: XXXXXXX
10
11          AMT-ON-ORDER: XXXXXX            AMT ALLOCATED: XXXXXX
12
13          EOQ: XXXXXX                     SAFETY STOCK: XXXXXX
14
15          LEAD TIME: XXX DAYS             WAREHOUSE LOCATION: XXX
16
17
18            CMD KEY 3 - EOJ                  CMD KEY 5 - IGNORE
19                          CMD KEY 2 - ENTER
20  NOTES:
21    1. DATE AND TIME ARE SYSTEM SUPPLIED.
22    2. HIGHLIGHT ALL CONSTANTS.
23    3. UNDERLINE HEADING AND REVERSE IMAGE VARIABLE FIELDS.
```

1. Mandatory entry for the PNAME field.
2. Suppress the low-order sign in the AVGCST field.
3. Mandatory entry for the EOQ field and suppress the low-order sign position.
4. Mandatory entry for the SAFSTK field and suppress the low-order sign position.
5. Mandatory entry for the LEDTIM field and suppress the low-order sign position.
6. Mandatory fill for the WAREHL field and validate that the characters entered are alphabetic.
7. Use the default line for the **ERRMSG** text 'DUPLICATE KEY—CANNOT ADD RECORD'.
8. Reference the field attributes of the physical file created for this assignment (see format below).

```
                    PHYSICAL FILE DESCRIPTION

     SYSTEM: AS/400                      DATE: Yours
     FILE NAME: Yours                    REV NO: 0
     RECORD NAME: Yours                  KEY LENGTH: 5
     SEQUENCE: Keyed  (Unique)           RECORD SIZE: 54

                       FIELD DEFINITIONS

     FIELD    FIELD NAME   SIZE  TYPE    POSITION      COMMENTS
      NO                                FROM   TO

       1       PART#        5     C       1     5    Key field
       2       PNAME       20     C       6    25
       3       AMTHND       6     P      26    29
```

4	AMTORD	6	P	30	33
5	AVGCST	7	P	34	37 2 decimals
6	AMTALL	6	P	38	41
7	EOQ	6	P	42	45
8	SAFSTK	6	P	46	49
9	LEDTIM	3	P	50	51
10	WAREHL	3	C	52	54

Programming Assignment 14-4: MODIFICATION OF ASSIGNMENT 14-1, 14-2, OR 14-3

Modify any Chapter 14 programming assignment you have completed to include a second record format in the display file. The coding for the second record format may be specified *before* or *after* the existing one. Depending on the programming assignment (14-1, 14-2, or 14-3) previously completed, the *generic format* of the new record shown below must be modified accordingly.

You must supply your own constants and variable. Note, however, the only variable specified is the key field for the related physical file. Specify the end-of-job *Command Attention* keyword at the *Record Level.*

```
 1  ØX/XX/XX        YOUR LAB 14-1, 14-2, OR 14-3 RELATED HEADING HERE              HH:MM:SS
 2
 3          YOUR RELATED KEY CONSTANT & VARIABLE HERE.
 4
 5
 6
 7
 8          CK3 - EOJ              ENTER - TO DISPLAY ENTRY SCREEN
 9
10  NOTES:
11      1. HIGHLIGHT ALL CONSTANTS AND DATE AND TIME.
12      2. REVERSE IMAGE ALL VARIABLE FIELDS.
13      3. LOCATE ERRMSG 'DUPLICATE EXISTS' ON LINE 5.
```

In addition, modify the original record format completed for assignment 14-1, 14-2, or 14-3 as follows:

1. Remove the *Command Attention* keyword for end-of-job control and the related constant and include it in the new record format. Reformat the other two command key constants as needed to maintain a balanced screen design.

2. The *Command Function* key for adding a record and the *Command Attention* key to ignore the entry and return to the first display (new record format) are to be moved from the *File Level* (if specified there) to the format's *Record Level.*

chapter 15

Interactive Processing

An RPG/400 program is *interactive* when it processes one or more display files and one or more physical and/or logical files. Interactive programs that control physical file maintenance and inquiry use the same **WRITE, CHAIN, UPDAT, DELET,** and **SETLL** operations previously introduced in Chapter 13 for batch maintenance.

The following syntax must be considered when coding an interactive RPG/400 program:

1. All display files accessed must be defined as *workstation* (**WORKSTN**) files.
2. The **EXFMT** (*Write/Then Read Format*) operation (or separate **WRITE** and **READ** statements) must be specified to process any display file's record format.
3. Usually one or more **DOU** or **DOW** groups are included to control the interactive (looping) control needed with interactive processing.
4. The indicators assigned to the *Command Attention* (**CAnn**) and *Command Function* (**CFnn**) keys in a display file are tested for an ***ON** or ***OFF** condition in the RPG/400 program to control a specific processing function (i.e., end-of-job, redisplay, file addition, file inquiry, record deletion, and record update).

The RPG/400 syntax required to process display files and access their record formats for physical file maintenance will be discussed in the following sections.

File Description Syntax for Workstation Files

Any display file defined in an RPG/400 program must be assigned to a **WORKSTN** (*Workstation*) file. The *File Description* syntax for a **WORKSTN** file is explained in Figure 15-1.

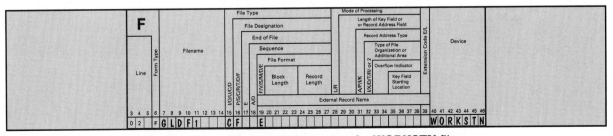

Figure 15-1 *File Description* syntax for **WORKSTN** files.

1. The display file name must be left-justified in the *Filename* field positions 7–14.

2. A **C** (for combined input and output), **I** (for input), or **O** (for output) file may be specified in position 15.

3. An **F** (full procedural), **P** (primary), **S** (secondary), and a **blank** (for a file that has **O** in column 15) may be entered in position 16.

4. An **E** (externally defined) or an **F** (program-described) may be entered in position 19.

5. **WORKSTN** must be entered in the *Device* field (positions 40–46).

Notes:

1. The entries for the example shown define the display file as combined (supports input and output processing), full procedural, and externally defined.

2. The **EXFMT** operation is valid only with externally defined Display Files.

Figure 15-1 *File Description* syntax for **WORKSTN** files. (Continued)

The EXFMT (Write/Then Read Format) Operation

The RPG/400 **EXFMT** operation is valid only for **WORKSTN** files defined in a *File Description* statement as *combined* (**C** in column 15), *full procedural* (**F** in column 16), and *externally defined* (**E** in column 19). An **EXFMT** instruction is a combined **WRITE** (to the CRT) followed by a **READ** (from the CRT). Separate **WRITE** and **READ** statements may be specified in lieu of an **EXFMT** statement. A unique feature of the **EXFMT** operation is that it holds the display on the CRT after it has been written. The operator must press either a function or the ENTER key to continue. Figure 15-2 details the syntax of this operation.

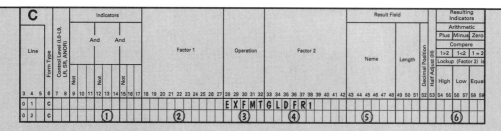

1. *Control Level* or *Detail Time* indicators may condition an **EXFMT** statement.

2. *Factor 1* is not used.

3. **EXFMT** operation name must be entered in the *Operation* field.

4. A display file record format name must be entered left-justified in *Factor 2*.

5. *Result Field* is not used.

6. An optional indicator may be specified in the *Resulting Indicator Low* field (columns 56–57). When used, the indicator will be set on if an error occurs during the **WRITE** cycle of the **EXFMT** statement. Other *Resulting Indicator* fields (*High* and *Equal*) are not used.

Figure 15-2 Syntax of the **EXFMT** operation.

Other RPG/400 operations that are valid for **WORKSTN** files are detailed in Figure 15-3 with their required *File Description Specifications* column 15 and 16 entries.

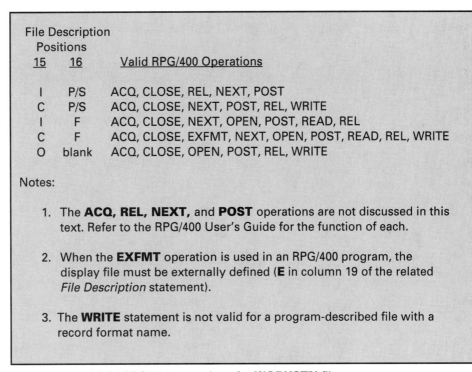

Figure 15-3 Valid RPG/400 operations for **WORKSTN** files.

The CLEAR Operation

When fields in a display file's record format are defined with a *Usage* (column 38 of the DDS form) of **O** (output) or **B** (input/output), they are not initialized to blanks or zeros after a display. This would be confusing to a user doing inquiry, update, or deletion processing when some or all of the previous record's values are redisplayed.

The **CLEAR** operation clears the fields or elements in a record format, data structure, array, table, or subfield to blanks (for character fields) or zeros (for numeric fields). Indicators are automatically set to "O" (off). Depending how the statement is formatted, it clears fields, elements, and indicators individually or globally (all fields, elements, and indicators) at one time. Figure 15-4 displays the syntax of the **CLEAR** operation.

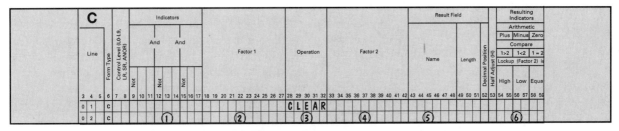

Figure 15-4 CLEAR operation syntax.

1. *Control* or *Detail Time* indicators may condition a **CLEAR** statement.

2. *Factor 1* must be blank unless *Factor 2* contains a record format name from a physical or logical file. Then, ***NOKEY** may be specified so that all fields except the key field is cleared.

3. The operation name **CLEAR** must be entered in the *Operation* field.

4. *Factor 2* may contain a record format name, data structure name, array name, table name, field name, subfield, array element, or indicator name. In any case, character fields are initialized to blanks, numeric fields to zeros, and indicators set to 'O' (off).

   If a record format or data structure name is specified, the fields are cleared in the order they are defined in the element. When a table name is specified, the current table element is cleared. For arrays, all of its elements are cleared. However, if an array element is specified (name with index), only that element is cleared.

5. *Result Field* is not used.

6. *Resulting Indicators* are not used.

- Only fields that are defined with an **O** (output) or **B** (input/output) *Usage* in the display file's record format are cleared with the **CLEAR** operation. Because it is assumed that new values are to be entered, input only (**I** *Usage*) is not cleared.

Figure 15-4   CLEAR operation syntax. (Continued)

Six RPG/400 programs that support interactive processing will be discussed in the remainder of this chapter in the following order:

1. Addition of records to a physical file
2. Inquiry of records in a physical file
3. Update of records in a physical file
4. Logical deletion of records in a physical file
5. Combined addition, update, and deletion maintenance
6. Data validation

RPG/400 PROGRAM: INTERACTIVE ADDITION OF RECORDS

The display file that is processed by the program that adds records to a physical file defined with unique keys is shown in Figure 15-5. Note that it includes the following features:

1. Two record formats are coded. One is a prompt record in which a customer number is entered to determine if the key value already exists. Error identification (i.e., **DUPLICATE RECORD**) is controlled in this record format. The prompt screen is used to identify duplicate keys before the second record format is displayed, data entered, and then the record rejected because of a duplicate key condition. If the physical file supported duplicate keys, this record format would not be needed for add maintenance.

```
                                   Data Description Source
SEQNBR  *...+....1....+....2....+....3....+....4....+....5....+....6....+....7....+
  100          * PROMPT SCREEN........
  200        A                                      MSGLOC(05)
  300        A                                      REF(SMYERS/GLMASTER)
  400        A                                      PRINT
  500        A          R PROMPT
  600        A                                      CA03(03 'END OF JOB')
  700        A                                    1  3DATE EDTCDE(Y)
  800        A                                    1 32'CUSTOMER FILE ADDITION'
  900        A                                    1 71TIME
 1000        A                                    3 10'ENTER CUSTOMER NO:'
 1100        A          CUSTNO         5Y OI      3 29DSPATR(RI)
 1200        A 90                                   ERRMSG('DUPLICATE RECORD' 90)
 1300        A                                    9 18'F3 - EOJ'
 1400        A                                    9 50'ENTER KEY - ENTRY SCREEN'
 1500        *
 1600        * ENTRY SCREEN......
 1700        A          R ADDRCD                     CHGINPDFT(CS)
 1800        A                                      CA12(12 'DO NOT ADD RECORD')
 1900        A                                    1  3DATE EDTCDE(Y)
 2000        A                                    1 30'CUSTOMER FILE ADDITION'
 2100        A                                      DSPATR(UL)
 2200        A                                    3 20'CUSTOMER NUMBER:' DSPATR(HI)
 2300        A          CUST#       R   Y B       3 40DSPATR(PR) ┐
 2400        A                                    5 20'NAME:' DSPATR(HI)       │
 2500        A          NAME        R     I       5 40DSPATR(PC) ┐             │
 2600        A                                    7 20'STREET' DSPATR(HI)  │   │
 2700        A          STREET      R     I       7 40                     │   │
 2800        A                                    9 20'CITY:' DSPATR(HI)   │   │
 2900        A          CITY        R     I       9 40                     │   │
 3000        A                                   11 20'STATE:' DSPATR(HI)  │   │
 3100        A          STATE       R     I      11 40                     │   │
 3200        A                                   13 20'ZIP:' DSPATR(HI)    │   │
 3300        A          ZIP         R   Y I      13 40                     │   │
 3400        A                                   15 20'BALANCE:' DSPATR(HI)│   │
 3500        A          BALANC      R     I      15 40                     │   │
 3600        A                                   20 10'PRESS ENTER TO ADD RECORD' │
 3700        A                                   20 50'PRESS F12 TO NOT ENTER' │

        Cursor is positioned at this field ─────────────────────┘   │

        Value in the CUSTNO field in the PROMPT format
        is moved to this field in the RPG/400 progran.
        DSPATR(PR) keyword protects the field so that
        its value cannot be changed. ──────────────────────────────────┘
```

Figure 15-5 Display file for "adds" maintenance.

2. With the exception of the CUST# field in the second record format, all of the
    fields are defined with an **I** *Usage,* which supports input only (from the screen
    to the program). Because the CUSTNO value from the prompt screen is moved
    into the CUST# field in the entry screen, the CUST# field is defined with a **B**
    Usage. This will display the value when the entry screen displays. To prevent
    the CUST# value from being changed, the field is protected with the
    DSPATR(PR) keyword and the cursor is positioned at the NAME field with
    the **DSPATR(PC)** keyword.

3. *Command Attention* (CA) and *Command Function* (CF) keys are specified at
    the *Record Level,* which limits a specific function to each record type. End-of-
    job control and access of the second record format is controlled in the prompt
    screen. The decision to write the current record to the physical file or ignore the
    entry is controlled in the second format.

A Print key copy of the displays generated from execution of the related RPG/400 program is shown in Figure 15-6 with data included.

```
9/16/95                    CUSTOMER FILE ADDITION              13:28:27

     ENTER CUSTOMER NO: 20000                                          PROMPT
                                                                       Display




         F3 - EOJ                          ENTER KEY - ENTRY SCREEN
```

```
9/16/95                    CUSTOMER FILE ADDITION

           CUSTOMER NUMBER:    20000

           NAME:               EDGAR POE

           STREET              10 DREARY LANE

           CITY:               HOPELESS                                ADDRCD
                                                                       Display
           STATE:              CA

           ZIP:                09901

           BALANCE:            35000



     PRESS ENTER TO ADD RECORD          PRESS F12 TO NOT ENTER
```

Figure 15-6 Print key copy of the display file's two record formats for "adds" maintenance.

The RPG/400 program that adds records to a physical file includes the following operations:

DOUEQ group	**SETLL statement**
EXFMT statement	**IFEQ statement**
CASEQ statement	**WRITE statement**

A compile listing of the program and supplemental line-by-line explanation of the instructions are presented in Figure 15-7.

```
SEQUENCE
NUMBER    *...1....+....2....+....3....+....4....+....5....+....6....+....7...*
                    S o u r c e   L i s t i n g
   100    * THIS PROGRAM PERFORMS PF (GLMASTER) INTERACTIVE RECORD ADDITION...
   200    *
          H
   300    FGLDFADD CF  E                   WORKSTN
          RECORD FORMAT(S):  LIBRARY SMYERS FILE GLDFADD.
                  EXTERNAL FORMAT PROMPT RPG NAME PROMPT
                  EXTERNAL FORMAT ADDRCD RPG NAME ADDRCD
   400    FGLMASTERUF E        K          DISK                         A
          RECORD FORMAT(S):  LIBRARY SMYERS FILE GLMASTER.
                  EXTERNAL FORMAT GLRCRD RPG NAME GLRCRD
A000000   INPUT  FIELDS FOR RECORD PROMPT FILE GLDFADD FORMAT PROMPT.
A000001                                    1    1 *IN03         END OF JOB
A000002                                    2    2 *IN90         DUPLICATE RECORD
A000003                                    3   70CUSTNO
B000000   INPUT  FIELDS FOR RECORD ADDRCD FILE GLDFADD FORMAT ADDRCD.
B000001                                    1    1 *IN12         DO NOT ADD RECORD
```

Figure 15-7 Detailed compile listing of the "adds" program.

```
B000002                                    2   60CUST#
B000003                                    7   26 NAME
B000004                                   27   46 STREET
B000005                                   47   66 CITY
B000006                                   67   68 STATE
B000007                                   69   730ZIP
B000008                                   74   812BALANC
C000000    INPUT  FIELDS FOR RECORD GLRCRD FILE GLMASTER FORMAT GLRCRD.
C000001                              P    1   30CUST#
C000002                                    4   23 NAME
C000003    ┌─────────────────────┐        24   43 STREET
C000004    │ Entry process continues│      44   63 CITY
C000005    │ until F3 is pressed when│     64   65 STATE
C000006    │ in the PROMPT screen    │ P  66   680ZIP
C000007    └─────────────────────┘   P  69   732BALANC
    500  C─────────┘  *IN03      DOUEQ*ON                     do until eoj        B001
    600  C                       EXFMTPROMPT                  dsp prompt scrn       001
    700  C            *IN03      CASEQ*OFF    ADDSR           not eoj?              001
    800  C                       ENDCS                        end CAS group         001
    900  C                       ENDDO                        end DOU group       E001
   1000  C                       MOVE *ON     *INLR           end job
   1100     *
   1200  C            ADDSR      BEGSR                         begin sr
   1300  C            CUSTNO     SETLLGLMASTER             90record exists?      3
   1400  C            *IN90      IFEQ *OFF                    no dup record       B001
   1500  C                       Z-ADDCUSTNO  CUST#          df fld to pf fd       001
   1600  C                       EXFMTADDRCD                  dsply screen          001
   1700  C            *IN12      IFEQ *OFF                    ignore entry?       B002
   1800  C                       WRITEGLRCRD              90  add recd to pf   2   002
   1900  C                       ENDIF                        end lne 1700 IF     E002
   2000  C                       ENDIF                        end lne 1400 IF     E001
   2100  C                       ENDSR                        end add sr
   D000000   OUTPUT FIELDS FOR RECORD PROMPT FILE GLDFADD FORMAT PROMPT.
   D000001                       *IN90        1   CHAR   1              DUPLICATE RECORD
   E000000   OUTPUT FIELDS FOR RECORD ADDRCD FILE GLDFADD FORMAT ADDRCD.
   E000001                       CUST#        5   ZONE  5,0
   F000000   OUTPUT FIELDS FOR RECORD GLRCRD FILE GLMASTER FORMAT GLRCRD.
   F000001                       CUST#       3P   PACK  5,0
   F000002                       NAME        23   CHAR  20
   F000003                       STREET      43   CHAR  20
   F000004                       CITY        63   CHAR  20
   F000005                       STATE       65   CHAR   2
   F000006                       ZIP         68P  PACK  5,0
   F000007                       BALANC      73P  PACK  8,2
```

Line #	Explanation
300	**WORKSTN** file (GLDFADD) is defined as combined (**C** in column 15), full-procedural (**F** in column 16), and externally defined (**E** in column 19).
400	Physical file is defined as update (**U** in column 15), full procedural (**F** in column 16), externally defined (**E** in column 19), and keyed (**K** in column 31). The **A** in column 66 indicates that records may be added. Because the **SETLL** statement on line 1300 determines if the current record exists before attempting to add it, the physical file must be defined as update to support this operation. Without the **SETLL** statement, the file could have been defined as output (**O** in column 15).
500	The **DOUEQ** group controls the display of the PROMPT and ADDRCD formats and the addition of records to the physical file. The iterative processing (looping) continues until the operator presses F3, which sets on indicator **03,** when in the PROMPT display to end the job. The relational test for the **DOUEQ** statement is made at the related **ENDDO** statement on line 900. Consequently, the **DOUEQ** group will be executed at least once.
600	The **EXFMT** statement <u>writes</u> the PROMPT record to the screen and holds it there. After the operator enters a customer number and presses the ENTER key, the variable is <u>read</u> and the ADDRCD screen or a **DUPLICATE RECORD** error message will display on line 5. The operator may end the job by pressing F3.

Figure 15-7 Detailed compile listing of the "adds" program. (Continued)

700   If indicator **03** is "off," control branches to the **ADDSR** subroutine where a duplicate key condition is tested, ADDRCD screen displayed, and the record written to the physical file.

800   The **ENDCS** operation ends the **CASEQ** statement.

900   The **ENDDO** operation ends the **DOUEQ** group. Recall that the relational test is made here and <u>not</u> at the **DOUEQ** statement on line 500. When indicator **03** is on, control will exit from the **DOUEQ** group and execute the statement on line 1000 to end the job.

1000 The **MOVE** statement sets on the **LR** indicator to end the job. However, control will execute any calculation and/or output instructions conditioned by the **LR** indicator before the job is ended.

1200 Beginning of the ADDSR subroutine.

1300 The CUSTNO value from the PROMPT screen is specified in the **SETLL** statement to search the GLMASTER file for a duplicate key condition. If a duplicate key is found, *Resulting Indicator* **90** will be set on.

1400 The **IFEQ** statement tests the status of indicator **90.** If it is "off," which indicates that a duplicate key is <u>not</u> stored in the file, the statements on lines 1500 and 1600 will be executed. Otherwise, control will branch to the **ENDIF** operation on line 2000.

1500 The **Z-ADD** statement moves the CUSTNO value from the PROMPT screen into the CUST# value in the ADDRCD screen. This assures that the entered customer number will be included in the physical file's record format when it is written to the file.

1600 The **EXFMT** statement writes the ADDRCD display on the screen and holds it so that data may be entered. After entering the data, the operator may press the ENTER key to read the display and write the record to the physical file, or press F12 at any time <u>not</u> to enter the data. In either case, program control will redisplay the PROMPT screen.

1700 This **IFEQ** statement tests the status of indicator **12.** When it is "off," the current record will be written to the physical file, the nested **IF** group ended, and control returned back to the **DOUEQ** statement on line 500. However, when indicator **12** is "on," statement 1800 will not be executed and the record will <u>not</u> be written to the physical file.

1800 The **WRITE** statement writes the ADDRCD screen record to the physical file.

1900 This **ENDIF** statement ends the **IF** statement on line 1700.

2000 This **ENDIF** statement ends the **IF** statement on line 1400.

2100 The **ENDSR** statement ends the ADDSR internal subroutine.

Figure 15-7   Detailed compile listing of the "adds" program. (Continued)

A **DSPPFM** (*Display Physical File Member*) command display of the physical file will show that the "add" records are stored at the end of the file. However, because the physical file is keyed, a **CPYF** (*Copy File*) listing will place the "add" records in their key sequence location(s).

RPG/400 PROGRAM: INTERACTIVE INQUIRY OF RECORDS

A source listing of the display file processed by a program that inquiries records in a physical file defined with unique keys is shown in Figure 15-8.

```
                                    Data Description Source
SEQNBR   *...+....1....+....2....+....3....+....4....+....5....+....6....+....7....+..
  100        * PROMPT SCREEN........
  200      A                                          MSGLOC(05)
  300      A                                          REF(SMYERS/GLMASTER)
  400      A                                          PRINT
  500      A         R PROMPT
  600      A                                          CA03(03 'END OF JOB')
  700      A                               1  3DATE EDTCDE(Y)
  800      A                               1 32'CUSTOMER FILE INQUIRY'
  900      A                               1 71TIME
 1000      A                               3 10'ENTER CUSTOMER NO:'
 1100      A          CUSTNO        5Y 0I  3 29DSPATR(RI)
 1200      A 91                                        ERRMSG('RECORD NOT FOUND' 91)
 1300      A                               9 18'F3 - EOJ'
 1400      A                               9 50'ENTER KEY - INQUIRY'
 1500      *
 1600      * INQUIRY SCREEN......
 1700      A         R INQRCD                          PRINT
 1800      A                               1  3DATE EDTCDE(Y)
 1900      A                               1 30'CUSTOMER FILE INQUIRY'
 2000      A                                          DSPATR(UL)
 2100      A                               3 20'CUSTOMER NUMBER:' DSPATR(HI)
 2200      A          CUST#         R     0 3 40DSPATR(PR)
 2300      A                               5 20'NAME:' DSPATR(HI)
 2400      A          NAME          R     0 5 40DSPATR(PC)
 2500      A                               7 20'STREET' DSPATR(HI)
 2600      A          STREET        R     0 7 40
 2700      A                               9 20'CITY:' DSPATR(HI)
 2800      A          CITY          R     0 9 40
 2900      A                              11 20'STATE:' DSPATR(HI)
 3000      A          STATE         R     0 11 40
 3100      A                              13 20'ZIP:' DSPATR(HI)
 3200      A          ZIP           R     0 13 40
 3300      A                              15 20'BALANCE:' DSPATR(HI)
 3400      A          BALANC        R     0 15 40
 3500      A                              20 10'PRESS ENTER TO CONTINUE'
```

O Usage supports output only: from the program to the display record

Figure 15-8 Display file inquiry processing.

Note that the following features are included:

1. Two record formats are coded. One is a PROMPT record in which a customer number is entered to determine if a record with that key value is stored in the physical file. Error identification (i.e., **RECORD NOT FOUND**) is controlled in this record format.
2. The *Command Attention* key, **CA03,** is defined at the *Record Level* in the PROMPT record, to control end-of-job processing. The job is continued when a CUSTNO value is entered and the ENTER key pressed.
3. The second (INQRCD) record format defines all of the fields with **O** *Usage,* which supports the display of values from the program to this record format. Control is returned to the PROMPT display by pressing the ENTER key.

A Print key copy of the displays generated from execution of the RPG/400 inquiry program is shown in Figure 15-9.

The RPG/400 inquiry program includes the following operations:

DOUEQ group   CHAIN statement
EXFMT statement   IFEQ statement
          CASEQ statement

```
 9/28/95                    CUSTOMER FILE INQUIRY                    14:30:00

        ENTER CUSTOMER NO: 12345                                              PROMPT
                                                                              Display




           F3 - EOJ                              ENTER KEY - INQUIRY
```

```
 9/28/95                    CUSTOMER FILE INQUIRY

                CUSTOMER NUMBER:    12345

                NAME:               KAREL APPEL

                STREET              20 AMSTERDAM AVENUE

                CITY:               NEW YORK                                   INQRCD
                                                                              Display
                STATE:              NY

                ZIP:                07450

                BALANCE:            00125000




      PRESS ENTER TO CONTINUE
```

Figure 15-9 Print key copy of the display file's two record formats for file inquiry.

A compile listing of the inquiry program and a supplemental line-by-line explanation of the instructions are detailed in Figure 15-10.

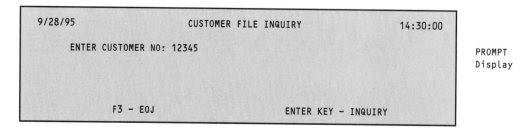

```
SEQUENCE                                                                   IND   DO
NUMBER     *...1....+....2....+....3....+....4....+....5....+....6....+....7...*  USE   NUM
                          S o u r c e   L i s t i n g
   100     * THIS PROGRAM PERFORMS PF (GLMASTER) INTERACTIVE INQUIRY......
   200     *
           H
   300     FGLDFINQ CF  E                     WORKSTN
           RECORD FORMAT(S):  LIBRARY SMYERS FILE GLDFINQ.
                   EXTERNAL FORMAT PROMPT RPG NAME PROMPT
                   EXTERNAL FORMAT INQRCD RPG NAME INQRCD
   400     FGLMASTERIF E          K          DISK
           RECORD FORMAT(S):  LIBRARY SMYERS FILE GLMASTER.
                   EXTERNAL FORMAT GLRCRD RPG NAME GLRCRD
A000000    INPUT  FIELDS FOR RECORD PROMPT FILE GLDFINQ FORMAT PROMPT.
A000001                                          1   1 *IN03              END OF JOB
A000002                                          2   2 *IN91              RECORD NOT FOUND
A000003                                          3   70CUSTNO
B000000    INPUT  FIELDS FOR RECORD INQRCD FILE GLDFINQ FORMAT INQRCD.
C000000    INPUT  FIELDS FOR RECORD GLRCRD FILE GLMASTER FORMAT GLRCRD.
C000001                                       P  1   30CUST#
C000002                                          4  23 NAME
C000003      ┌──────────────────────┐           24  43 STREET
C000004      │ Inquiry continues until │         44  63 CITY
C000005      │ F3 is pressed in PROMPT │         64  65 STATE
C000006      │ screen                 │       P 66  68ZIP
C000007      └──────────────────────┐       P 69  732BALANC
   500     C └──────*IN03    DOUEQ*ON                     do until eoj         B001
   600     C                 EXFMTPROMPT                  dsp prompt scrn      001
```

Figure 15-10 Detailed compile listing of the "inquiry" program.

```
       700   C              *IN03      CASEQ*OFF      INQSR          not eoj?              001
       800   C                         ENDCS                         end CAS stmnt         001
       900   C                         ENDDO                         end DO group          E001
      1000   C                         MOVE *ON       *INLR          end job
      1100   *
      1200   C              INQSR      BEGSR                         begin sr
      1300   C              CUSTNO     CHAINGLMASTER          91      get pf record   1
      1400   C              *IN91      IFEQ *OFF                      record found?         B001
      1500   C                         EXFMTINQRCD                    dsply inq scrn        001
      1600   C                         ENDIF                          end IF stmnt          E001
      1700   C                         ENDSR                          end sr
   D000000   OUTPUT FIELDS FOR RECORD PROMPT FILE GLDFINQ FORMAT PROMPT.
   D000001                             *IN91      1   CHAR    1                  RECORD NOT FOUND
   E000000   OUTPUT FIELDS FOR RECORD INQRCD FILE GLDFINQ FORMAT INQRCD.
   E000001                             CUST#      5   ZONE    5,0
   E000002                             NAME      25   CHAR   20
   E000003                             STREET    45   CHAR   20
   E000004                             CITY      65   CHAR   20
   E000005                             STATE     67   CHAR    2
   E000006                             ZIP       72   ZONE    5,0
   E000007                             BALANC    80   ZONE    8,2
```

Line #	Explanation

<u>Line #</u>   <u>Explanation</u>

300   **WORKSTN** file (GLDFINQ) is defined as combined (**C** in column 15), full-procedural (**F** in column 16), and externally defined (**E** in column 19).

400   Physical file is defined as input (**I** in column 15), full procedural (**F** in column 16), externally defined (**E** in column 19), and keyed (**K** in column 31). Because the file is randomly accessed with the **CHAIN** operation, the file must be defined as full-procedural.

500   The **DOUEQ** group controls the display of the PROMPT and INQRCD formats and the inquiry of records in the physical file. The iterative processing (looping) continues until the operator presses F3, which sets on indicator **03,** when in the PROMPT display to end the job. The relational test for the **DOUEQ** statement is made at the related **ENDDO** statement on line 900. Consequently, the **DOUEQ** group will be executed at least once.

600   The **EXFMT** statement <u>writes</u> the PROMPT record to the screen and holds it there. After the operator enters a customer number and presses the ENTER key, the variable is <u>read</u> and the "filled-in" INQRCD screen or the **RECORD NOT FOUND** error message on line 5 displayed. The operator ends the job from the PROMPT display by pressing F3.

700   If indicator **03** is "off," control branches to the INQSR subroutine, where a record with the previously entered CUSTNO is accessed from the physical file by a **CHAIN** instruction.

800   The **ENDCS** operation ends the **CASEQ** statement.

900   The **ENDDO** operation ends the **DOUEQ** group. Recall that the relational test is made here and <u>not</u> at the **DOUEQ** statement on line 500. When indicator **03** is on, control will exit from the **DOUEQ** group and execute the statement on line 1000 to end the job.

1000   The **MOVE** statement sets on the **LR** indicator to end the job. However, control will execute any calculation and/or output instructions conditioned by the **LR** indicator before the job is ended,

1200   Beginning of the INQSR subroutine.

1300   The CUSTNO value from the PROMPT screen is specified in the **CHAIN** statement to access the record from the GLMASTER file. If the record is not found, the required indicator will be set on. The **CHAIN** operation requires that an indicator be specified in the *Resulting Indicator High* field (columns 54–55).

1400   The **IFEQ** statement tests the status of indicator **91**. If it is "off," it indicates that the record was found by the **CHAIN** statement, and line 1500 will be executed. If the indicator is "on," a record not found condition, control will branch to the **ENDSR**

Figure 15-10   Detailed compile listing of the "inquiry" program. (Continued)

statement on line 1700. For either condition, control will branch back to line 800 and then to 500 to repeat the processing cycle or end the job.

1500   The **EXFMT** statement writes the "filled-in" INQRCD record with the physical file's field values to the screen. The operator must press ENTER to continue processing, which passes control to the **ENDSR** statement on line 1700 and then to line 800 and 500 to repeat the inquiry process or end the job.

1600   The **ENDIF** statement ends the **IFEQ** statement on line 1400.

1700   The **ENDSR** statement ends the internal subroutine and passes control back to line 800 and then to line 500.

Figure 15-10   Detailed compile listing of the "inquiry" program. (Continued)

Instead of using the **DSPPFM** or **CPYF** command to view the records in a physical file, which may be difficult for the user to read, an inquiry program is usually more "user-friendly." However, the **DSPPFM** and **CPYF** commands are generic and may be used with any physical file, whereas an inquiry program is applicable only for one file.

RPG/400 PROGRAM: INTERACTIVE UPDATE OF RECORDS

The display file processed by a program that updates records in a physical file defined with *unique* keys is shown in Figure 15-11.

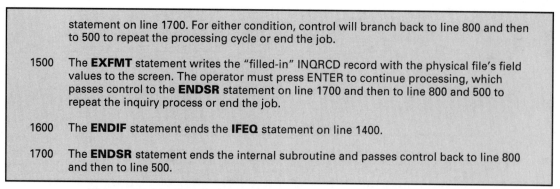

```
                                        Data Description Source
       SEQNBR *...+....1....+....2....+....3....+....4....+....5....+....6....+....7....+
         100    A                                          PRINT
         200    A                                          MSGLOC(05)
         300    A                                          REF(SMYERS/GLMASTER)
         400    * PROMPT SCREEN........
         500    A            R PROMPT
         600    A                                          CA03(03 'END OF JOB')
         700    A                                      1   3DATE EDTCDE(Y)
         800    A                                      1 32'CUSTOMER FILE UPDATE'
         900    A                                      1 71TIME
        1000    A                                      3 10'ENTER CUSTOMER NO:'
        1100    A            CUSTNO        5Y 0I       3 29DSPATR(RI)
        1200    A 91                                     ERRMSG('RECORD NOT FOUND' 91)
        1300    A                                      9 18'F3 - EOJ'
        1400    A                                      9 50'ENTER KEY - UPDATE'
        1500    * UPDATE SCREEN......
        1600    A            R UPDRCD
        1700    A                                        CA12(12 'DO NOT UPDATE')
        1800    A                                        CHGINPDFT(RI)
        1900    A                                      1   3DATE EDTCDE(Y)
        2000    A                                      1 30'CUSTOMER FILE UPDATE'
        2100    A                                        DSPATR(UL)
        2200    A                                      3 20'CUSTOMER NUMBER:' DSPATR(HI)
        2300    A            CCUST#        5Y 0B       3 40
        2400    A                                      5 20'NAME:' DSPATR(HI)
```

Figure 15-11   Display file for update maintenance.

```
2500    A              CNAME      20   B  5 40
2600    A                              7 20'STREET' DSPATR(HI)
2700    A              CSTRET     20   B  7 40
2800    A                              9 20'CITY:' DSPATR(HI)
2900    A              CCITY      20   B  9 40
3000    A                             11 20'STATE:' DSPATR(HI)
3100    A              CSTATE      2   B 11 40
3200    A                             13 20'ZIP:' DSPATR(HI)
3300    A              CZIP       5Y  OB 13 40
3400    A                             15 20'BALANCE:' DSPATR(HI)
3500    A              CBAL        8  2B 15 40
3600    A                             20 10'PRESS ENTER TO UPDATE'
3700    A                             20 50'PRESS F12 TO NOT UPDATE'


          B supports output and input:
          from and to the program
```

Figure 15-11   Display file for update maintenance. (Continued)

Note that the figure includes the following features:

1.   Two record formats are coded. One is a PROMPT record in which a customer number is entered to determine if a record with that key value is stored in the physical file. Error identification (i.e., **RECORD NOT FOUND**) is controlled in this record format.

2.   The *Command Attention* key **CA03,** defined at the *Record Level* in the PROMPT record, controls end-of-job processing. The job is continued when a CUSTNO value is entered and the ENTER key is pressed.

3.   The second (UPDRCD) record format defines all of the fields with **B** *Usage,* which supports the input and output of values to and from this display to the program. In an interactive update process, a record must be retrieved, displayed (output), values changed, display read (input), and the screen record written back to the same record location in the physical file.

     The record is updated when the operator presses the ENTER key. If the decision is made not to update, the operator presses **F12.** For either case, control redisplays the PROMPT screen and the operator decides whether to end the job or continue the update process.

4.   Instead of referencing the field attributes from the physical file, new field names are defined in the UPDRCD format. This is important in update maintenance to ensure that the changed data is written back to the file. In the RPG/400 program, the field values from the retrieved physical file record are moved to the related display record fields. Then, after the data is changed, the display record's field values are moved back to the fields in the physical file's record format.

A Print key copy of the PROMPT and UPDRCD displays generated from execution of the RPG/400 update program is shown in Figure 15-12. Note that two UPDRCD displays are shown, one *before* values are changed and the other *after* they have been changed. When the operator presses the ENTER key, the physical file's record will be updated with the new values.

The RPG/400 update program includes the following operations:

DOUEQ group	**CHAIN statement**
EXFMT statements	**IFEQ statements**
CASEQ statement	**UPDAT statement**
EXSR statements	

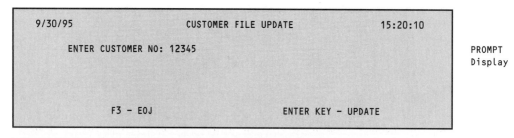

```
 9/30/95                    CUSTOMER FILE UPDATE                15:20:10

       ENTER CUSTOMER NO: 12345                                               PROMPT
                                                                              Display



              F3 - EOJ                          ENTER KEY - UPDATE
```

```
 9/28/95                    CUSTOMER FILE UPDATE

               CUSTOMER NUMBER:    12345

               NAME:               KAREL APPEL

               STREET              20 AMSTERDAM AVENUE

               CITY:               NEW YORK
                                                                              UPDRCD Display
               STATE:              NY                                         before values
                                                                              are changed
               ZIP:                07450

               BALANCE:            00125000



 PRESS ENTER TO CONTINUE                    PRESS F12 - TO NOT UPDATE
```

```
     9/28/95                    CUSTOMER FILE UPDATE

                   CUSTOMER NUMBER:    12345

                   NAME:               KAREL APPEL

                   STREET              9 SECOND HILL LANE

                   CITY:               TRENTON
                                                                              UPDRCD Display
                   STATE:              NJ                                     after values
                                                                              are changed
                   ZIP:                08330

                   BALANCE:            00125000



     PRESS ENTER TO UPDATE                  PRESS F12 TO NOT UPDATE
```

Figure 15-12 Print key copy of the display file's PROMPT display and two UPDRCD displays showing before and after screen values are changed for update program.

A compile listing of the update program and a supplemental line-by-line explanation of the instructions are detailed in Figure 15-13.

The update result may be checked by recalling the record and viewing the newly stored values.

```
SEQUENCE                                                                      IND   DO
NUMBER      *...1....+....2....+....3....+....4....+....5....+....6....+....7...*  USE   NUM
                          S o u r c e   L i s t i n g
  100     * THIS PROGRAM PERFORMS PF (GLMASTER) INTERACTIVE UPDATE......
  200     *
          H
  300     FGLDFUPD CF  E                    WORKSTN
          RECORD FORMAT(S):  LIBRARY SMYERS FILE GLDFUPD.
                   EXTERNAL FORMAT PROMPT RPG NAME PROMPT
                   EXTERNAL FORMAT UPDRCD RPG NAME UPDRCD
  400     FGLMASTERUF E          K          DISK
          RECORD FORMAT(S):  LIBRARY SMYERS FILE GLMASTER.
                   EXTERNAL FORMAT GLRCRD RPG NAME GLRCRD.
A000000     INPUT  FIELDS FOR RECORD PROMPT FILE GLDFUPD FORMAT PROMPT.
A000001                                        1    1 *IN03              END OF JOB
A000002                                        2    2 *IN91              RECORD NOT FOUND
A000003                                        3    70CUSTNO
B000000     INPUT  FIELDS FOR RECORD UPDRCD FILE GLDFUPD FORMAT UPDRCD.
B000001                                        1    1 *IN12              DO NOT UPDATE
B000002                                        2   60CCUST#
B000003                                        7   26 CNAME
B000004                                       27   46 CSTRET
B000005                                       47   66 CCITY
B000006                                       67   68 CSTATE
B000007                                       69  730CZIP
B000008                                       74  812CBAL
C000000     INPUT  FIELDS FOR RECORD GLRCRD FILE GLMASTER FORMAT GLRCRD.
C000001                                     P  1   30CUST#
C000002                                        4   23 NAME
C000003     ┌─────────────────────┐        24   43 STREET
C000004     │ Updating continues until │    44   63 CITY
C000005     │ F3 is pressed when in the │   64   65 STATE
C000006     │ PROMPT display       │     P 66  680ZIP
C000007     └─────────────────────┘     P 69  732BALANC
  500     C      ┌──── *IN03     DOUEQ*ON                 do until eoj          B001
  600     C      │               EXFMTPROMPT              dsp prompt scrn       001
  700     C      │     *IN03      CASEQ*OFF     UPDSR      not eoj?              001
  800     C      │               ENDCS                    end CAS group         001
  900     C      │               ENDDO                    end DO group          E001
 1000     C      │               MOVE *ON       *INLR     end job
 1100     *      │
 1200     C      │     UPDSR      BEGSR                    begin upd sr
 1300     C      └──── CUSTNO     CHAINGLMASTER         91 get pf record    1
 1400     C            *IN91      IFEQ *OFF                record found          B001
 1500     C                       EXSR PFTODF              pf to df sr           001
 1600     C                       EXFMTUPDRCD              dsply screen          001
 1700     C            *IN12      IFEQ *OFF                do not update?        B002
 1800     C                       EXSR DFTOPF              df to pf sr           002
 1900     C                       UPDATGLRCRD           90 update pf recrd  2   002
 2000     C                       ENDIF                    end ln 1700 IF        E002
 2100     C                       ENDIF                    end ln 1400 IF        E001
 2200     C                       ENDSR                    end update sr
 2300     *
 2400     * Move pf field values to df fields....
 2500     C            PFTODF     BEGSR                    beg pf to df sr
 2600     C                       MOVE CU3T#     CCU3T#
 2700     C                       MOVE NAME      CNAME
 2800     C                       MOVE STREET    CSTRET
 2900     C                       MOVE CITY      CCITY
 3000     C                       MOVE STATE     CSTATE
 3100     C                       MOVE ZIP       CZIP
 3200     C                       MOVE BALANC    CBAL
 3300     C                       ENDSR                    end pf to df sr
 3400     *
 3500     * Move df field values to pf fields....
 3600     C            DFTOPF     BEGSR                    beg df to pf sr
 3700     C                       MOVE CCUST#    CUST#
```

Figure 15-13 Compile listing of the update maintenance program.

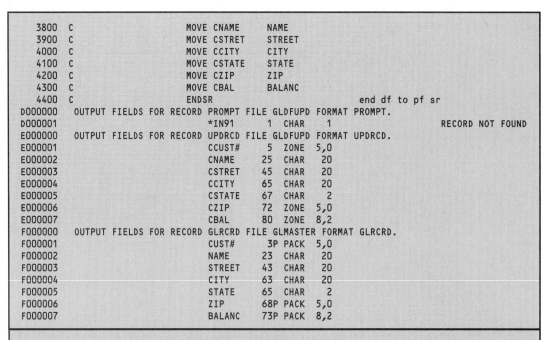

```
3800   C                           MOVE  CNAME      NAME
3900   C                           MOVE  CSTRET     STREET
4000   C                           MOVE  CCITY      CITY
4100   C                           MOVE  CSTATE     STATE
4200   C                           MOVE  CZIP       ZIP
4300   C                           MOVE  CBAL       BALANC
4400   C                           ENDSR                      end df to pf sr
D000000     OUTPUT FIELDS FOR RECORD PROMPT FILE GLDFUPD FORMAT PROMPT.
D000001                       *IN91      1  CHAR   1                  RECORD NOT FOUND
E000000     OUTPUT FIELDS FOR RECORD UPDRCD FILE GLDFUPD FORMAT UPDRCD.
E000001                       CCUST#     5  ZONE  5,0
E000002                       CNAME     25  CHAR   20
E000003                       CSTRET    45  CHAR   20
E000004                       CCITY     65  CHAR   20
E000005                       CSTATE    67  CHAR    2
E000006                       CZIP      72  ZONE  5,0
E000007                       CBAL      80  ZONE  8,2
F000000     OUTPUT FIELDS FOR RECORD GLRCRD FILE GLMASTER FORMAT GLRCRD.
F000001                       CUST#      3P PACK  5,0
F000002                       NAME      23  CHAR   20
F000003                       STREET    43  CHAR   20
F000004                       CITY      63  CHAR   20
F000005                       STATE     65  CHAR    2
F000006                       ZIP       68P PACK  5,0
F000007                       BALANC    73P PACK  8,2
```

Line #	Explanation
300	**WORKSTN** file (GLDFUPD) is defined as combined (**C** in column 15), full procedural (**F** in column 16), and externally defined (**E** in column 19).
400	Physical file is defined as update (**U** in column 15), full procedural (**F** in column 16), externally defined (**E** in column 19), and keyed (**K** in column 31). Because records are read from and to the physical file, it must be defined as update. In addition, because file processing operations are used (i.e, **CHAIN** and **UPDAT**), the file must be defined as full procedural.
500	The **DOUEQ** group controls the display of the PROMPT and UPDRCD formats and the update of records in the physical file. The iterative processing (looping) continues until the operator presses F3, which sets on indicator **03**, when in the PROMPT display to end the job. The relational test for the **DOUEQ** statement is made at the related **ENDDO** statement on line 900. Consequently, the **DOUEQ** group will be executed at least once.
600	The **EXFMT** statement <u>writes</u> the PROMPT record to the screen and holds it there. After the operator enters a customer number and presses the ENTER key, the variable is <u>read</u> and the "filled-in" UPDRCD screen or the **RECORD NOT FOUND** error message on line 5 displayed. The operator ends the job from the PROMPT display by pressing F3.
700	If indicator **03** is "off," control branches to the UPDSR subroutine where a record with the previously entered CUSTNO is accessed from the physical file by a **CHAIN** instruction.
800	The **ENDCS** operation ends the **CASEQ** statement.
900	The **ENDDO** operation ends the **DOUEQ** group. Recall that the relational test is made here and <u>not</u> at the **DOUEQ** statement on line 500. When indicator **03** is on, control will exit from the **DOUEQ** group and execute the statement on line 1000 to end the job.
1000	The **MOVE** statement sets on the **LR** indicator to end the job. However, control will execute any calculation and/or output instructions conditioned by the **LR** indicator before the job is ended.
1200	Beginning of the UPDSR subroutine.
1300	The CUSTNO value from the PROMPT screen is specified in the **CHAIN** statement to access the record from the GLMASTER file. If the record is not found, the required indicator will be set on. The **CHAIN** operation requires that an indicator be specified in the *Resulting Indicator High* field (columns 54–55).

Figure 15-13 Compile listing of the update maintenance program. (Continued)

1400   The **IFEQ** statement tests the status of indicator **91.** If it is "off," it indicates that the record was found by the **CHAIN** statement, and line 1500 will be executed. If the indicator is "on," a record-not-found condition, control will branch to the **ENDSR** statement on line 2200. For either condition, control will then branch back to line 900 and then to 500 to repeat the processing cycle or end the job.

1500   If the record is found (indicator **91** is "off"), the **EXSR** statement is executed, passing control to the PFTODF subroutine beginning on line 2500. The statement in this subroutine moves the retrieved record's field values to the related UPDRCD record's fields.

1600   The **EXFMT** statement writes the "filled-in" UPDRCD record with the physical file's field values to the screen. When in this display, the operator may change any field value except the key value (customer number). Then, the option either to update the physical file's record by pressing the ENTER key or not to update by pressing F12 may be made.

1700   The **IFEQ** statement tests the status of Indicator **12.**

1800   When the **IFEQ** statement test on line 1700 is true (indicator "off"), program control will branch to the DFTOPF beginning on line 3600.

1900   The **UPDAT** statement writes the displayed record back to the physical file with the changed values.

2000   This **ENDIF** operation ends the **IF** statement on line 1700.

2100   This **ENDIF** operation ends the **IF** statement on line 1400.

2200   The **ENDSR** operation ends the UPDSR internal subroutine, which passes control back to the **ENDDO** operation on line 900 and then to line 500 to repeat the processing cycle or end the job.

2500   The **BEGSR** statement is the entry point for the PFTODF subroutine.

2600 -
3200   The field values from the physical file are moved to their related fields in the UPDRCD format in the display file *before* the record is displayed. This is necessary because the physical file's field names were *not* used in the UPDRCD format.

3300   The **ENDSR** operation ends the PFTODF subroutine, which passes control back to the **EXFMT** statement on line 1600 which displays the UPDRCD record format "filled in" with field values.

3600   The **BEGSR** statement is the entry point for the DFTOPF subroutine.

3700 -
4300   The field values from the UPDRCD display are moved into the related physical file's fields before the record is updated (written back to the file). Again, this is necessary because the physical file's field names were not specified in the display file's UPDRCD format.

4400   The **ENDSR** operation ends the DFTOPF subroutine, which passes control back to line 1900 where the physical file's record is updated.

Figure 15-13   Compile listing of the update maintenance program. (Continued)

RPG/400 PROGRAM: INTERACTIVE LOGICAL DELETION OF RECORDS

The display file processed by a program that logically deletes records in a physical file defined with unique keys is shown in Figure 15-14.

Note that the following features are included:

1.   Two record formats are coded. One is a PROMPT record in which a customer number is entered to determine if a record with that key value is stored in the physical file. Error identification (i.e., **RECORD NOT FOUND**) is controlled in this record format.

```
                              Data Description Source
SEQNBR  *...+....1....+....2....+....3....+....4....+....5....+....6....+....7....+....8
  100    A                                              MSGLOC(05)
  200    A                                              REF(SMYERS/GLMASTER)
  300    A                                              PRINT
  400     * PROMPT SCREEN........
  500    A           R PROMPT
  600    A                                              CA03(03 'END OF JOB')
  700    A                                          1  3DATE EDTCDE(Y)
  800    A                                          1 32'CUSTOMER FILE DELETES'
  900    A                                          1 71TIME
 1000    A                                          3 10'ENTER CUSTOMER NO:'
 1100    A           CUSTNO        5Y OI            3 29DSPATR(RI)
 1200    A 91                                         ERRMSG('RECORD NOT FOUND' 91)
 1300    A                                          9 18'F3 - EOJ'
 1400    A                                          9 50'ENTER KEY - DELETE'
 1500     *
 1600     * DELETE SCREEN......
 1700    A           R DLTRCD                          CA12(12 'DO NOT DELETE RECORD')
 1800    A                                              CHGINPDFT
 1900    A                                          1  3DATE EDTCDE(Y)
 2000    A                                          1 30'CUSTOMER FILE DELETES'
 2100    A                                              DSPATR(UL)                CUST# field is
 2200    A                                          3 20'CUSTOMER NUMBER:' DSPATR(HI)  defined with B
 2300    A           CUST#      R      B            3 40─────                     Usage
 2400    A                                          5 20'NAME:' DSPATR(HI)
 2500    A           NAME       R      O            5 40─────
 2600    A                                          7 20'STREET' DSPATR(HI)
 2700    A           STREET     R      O            7 40─────
 2800    A                                          9 20'CITY:' DSPATR(HI)        Other fields are
 2900    A           CITY       R      O            9 40─────                     defined with O
 3000    A                                         11 20'STATE:' DSPATR(HI)       usage
 3100    A           STATE      R      O           11 40─────
 3200    A                                         13 20'ZIP:' DSPATR(HI)
 3300    A           ZIP        R      O           13 40─────
 3400    A                                         15 20'BALANCE:' DSPATR(HI)
 3500    A           BALANC     R      O           15 40─────
 3600    A                                         20 10'PRESS ENTER TO DELETE RECORD'
 3700    A                                         20 50'PRESS F12 TO NOT DELETE'
```

Figure 15-14   Display file for logical deletion maintenance.

2. The *Command Attention* key **CA03,** defined at the *Record Level* in the PROMPT record, controls end-of-job processing. The job is continued when a CUSTNO value is entered and the ENTER key is pressed.

3. The second (DLTRCD) record format defines the CUST# field with **B** *Usage,* which supports the input and output of its value so that the key value may be written to the screen and then read, to logically delete the retrieved record. All of the other fields are defined with an **O** *Usage* (output only) so that their values may be displayed but not changed. There is no reason for changing field values when the record is to be logically deleted. The record is logically deleted when the operator presses the ENTER key. If the decision is made not to delete the record, **F12** is pressed. In either case, control redisplays the PROMPT screen, and the operator decides whether to end the job or continue the deletion process.

A Print key copy of the PROMPT and DLTRCD displays generated from execution of the RPG/400 update program is shown in Figure 15-15.

The RPG/400 program that logically deletes records from a physical file includes the following operations:

DOUEQ group   CHAIN statement
EXFMT statements   IFEQ statements
CASEQ statement   DELET statement
EXSR statements

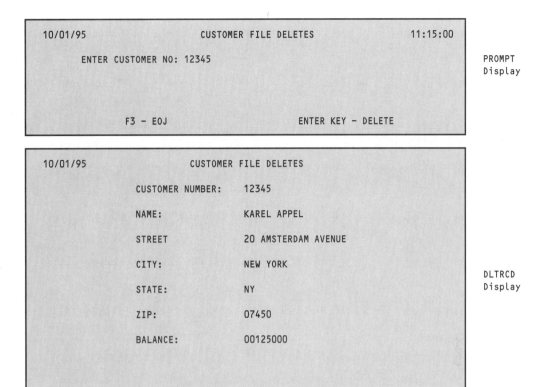

```
10/01/95                    CUSTOMER FILE DELETES                   11:15:00

         ENTER CUSTOMER NO: 12345                                             PROMPT
                                                                              Display




              F3 - EOJ                             ENTER KEY - DELETE
```

```
10/01/95                    CUSTOMER FILE DELETES

                  CUSTOMER NUMBER:    12345

                  NAME:               KAREL APPEL

                  STREET              20 AMSTERDAM AVENUE

                  CITY:               NEW YORK

                  STATE:              NY                                      DLTRCD
                                                                              Display
                  ZIP:                07450

                  BALANCE:            00125000




         PRESS ENTER TO DELETE RECORD              PRESS F12 TO NOT DELETE
```

Figure 15-15   Print key copy of the display file's PROMPT and DLTRCD displays.

A compile listing of the deletion program and a supplemental line-by-line explanation of the instructions are detailed in Figure 15-16.

```
SEQUENCE                                                              IND    DO
NUMBER     *...1....+....2....+....3....+....4....+....5....+....6....+....7...*  USE    NUM
                  S o u r c e   L i s t i n g
     100   * THIS PROGRAM PERFORMS PF (GLMASTER) INTERACTIVE LOGICAL DELETION
     200   *
           H
     300   FGLDFDLT  CF  E                    WORKSTN
           RECORD FORMAT(S):  LIBRARY SMYERS FILE GLDFDLT.
                     EXTERNAL FORMAT PROMPT RPG NAME PROMPT
                     EXTERNAL FORMAT INQRCD RPG NAME INQRCD
     400   FGLMASTERUF  E          K          DISK
           RECORD FORMAT(S):  LIBRARY SMYERS FILE GLMASTER.
                     EXTERNAL FORMAT GLRCRD RPG NAME GLRCRD
  A000000  INPUT  FIELDS FOR RECORD PROMPT FILE GLDFDLT FORMAT PROMPT.
  A000001                                  1    1 IN03         END OF JOB
  A000002                                  2    2 *IN91        RECORD NOT FOUND
  A000003                                  3   70CUSTNO
  B000000  INPUT  FIELDS FOR RECORD DLTRCD FILE GLDFDLT FORMAT DLTRCD.
  C000000  INPUT  FIELDS FOR RECORD GLRCRD FILE GLMASTER FORMAT GLRCRD.
  C000001                              P   1   30CUST#
  C000002                                  4   23 NAME
  C000003     Delete processing continues  24   43 STREET
  C000004     until F3 is pressed when in  44   63 CITY
  C000005     the PROMPT display           64   65 STATE
  C000006                              P  66  680ZIP
  C000007                              P  69  732BALANC
     500   C           *IN03     DOUEQ*ON                     do until eoj          B001
```

Figure 15-16   Compile listing of the deletion maintenance program.

```
 600  C                    EXFMTPROMPT                       dsp prompt scrn        001
 700  C         *IN03      CASEQ*OFF         DLTSR           not eoj?               001
 800  C                    ENDCS                             end CAS stmnt          001
 900  C                    ENDDO                             end DO group          E001
1000  C                    MOVE *ON          *INLR           end job
1100  *
1200  C         DLTSR      BEGSR                             begin sr
1300  C         CUSTNO     CHAINGLMASTER               91    get pf record    1
1400  C         *IN91      IFEQ *OFF                         record found?         B001
1500  C                    EXFMTDLTRCD                       dsply dlt scrn         001
1600  C         *IN12      IFEQ *OFF                         delete record?        B002
1700  C                    DELETGLRCD                        delete record          002
1800  C                    ENDIF                             end ln 1600 IF        E002
1900  C                    ENDIF                             end ln 1400 IF        E001
2000  C                    ENDSR                             end sr
D000000    OUTPUT FIELDS FOR RECORD PROMPT FILE GLDFDLT FORMAT PROMPT.
D000001                    *IN91      1    CHAR    1                   RECORD NOT FOUND
E000000    OUTPUT FIELDS FOR RECORD DLTRCD FILE GLDFDLT FORMAT DLTRCD.
E000001                    CUST#      5    ZONE    5,0
E000002                    NAME      25    CHAR   20
E000003                    STREET    45    CHAR   20
E000004                    CITY      65    CHAR   20
E000005                    STATE     67    CHAR    2
E000006                    ZIP       72    ZONE    5,0
E000007                    BALANC    80    ZONE    8,2
```

Line #	Explanation
300	**WORKSTN** file (GLDFDLT) is defined as combined (**C** in column 15), full procedural (**F** in column 16), and externally defined (**E** in column 19).
400	Physical file is defined as update (**U** in column 15), full procedural (**F** in column 16), externally defined (**E** in column 19), and keyed (**K** in column 31). Because records are read from and to the physical file, it must be defined as update. In addition, because file processing operations are used (i.e., **CHAIN** and **DELET**), the file must be defined as full procedural.
500	The **DOUEQ** group controls the display of the PROMPT and DLTRCD formats and the update of records in the physical file. The iterative processing (looping) continues until the operator presses F3, which sets on indicator **03**, when in the PROMPT display to end the job. The relational test for the **DOUEQ** statement is made at the related **ENDDO** statement on line 900. Consequently, the **DOUEQ** group will be executed at least once.
600	The **EXFMT** statement *writes* the PROMPT record to the screen and holds it there. After the operator enters a customer number and presses the ENTER key, the variable is *read* and the "filled-in" DLTRCD screen or the **RECORD NOT FOUND** error message on line 5 displayed. The operator ends the job from the PROMPT display by pressing F3.
700	If indicator **03** is "off," control branches to the DLTSR subroutine where a record with the previously entered CUSTNO is accessed from the physical file by a **CHAIN** instruction.
800	The **ENDCS** operation ends the **CASEQ** statement.
900	The **ENDDO** operation ends the **DOUEQ** group. Recall that the relational test is made here and *not* at the **DOUEQ** statement on line 500. When indicator **03** is on, control will exit from the **DOUEQ** group and execute the statement on line 1000 to end the job.
1000	The **MOVE** statement sets on the **LR** indicator to end the job. However, control will execute any calculation and/or output instructions conditioned by the **LR** indicator before the job is ended.
1200	Beginning of the DLTSR subroutine.
1300	The CUSTNO value from the PROMPT screen is specified in the **CHAIN** statement to access the record from the GLMASTER file. If the record is not found, the required indicator will be set on.

Figure 15-16 Compile listing of the deletion maintenance program. (Continued)

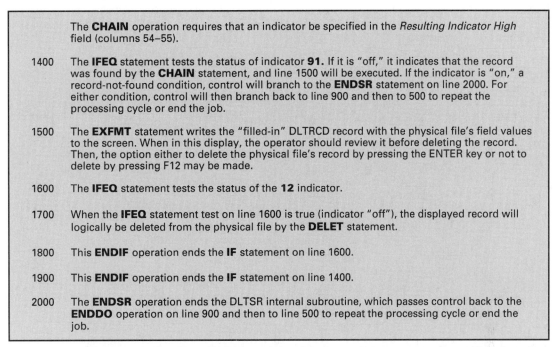

The **CHAIN** operation requires that an indicator be specified in the *Resulting Indicator High* field (columns 54–55).

1400   The **IFEQ** statement tests the status of indicator **91**. If it is "off," it indicates that the record was found by the **CHAIN** statement, and line 1500 will be executed. If the indicator is "on," a record-not-found condition, control will branch to the **ENDSR** statement on line 2000. For either condition, control will then branch back to line 900 and then to 500 to repeat the processing cycle or end the job.

1500   The **EXFMT** statement writes the "filled-in" DLTRCD record with the physical file's field values to the screen. When in this display, the operator should review it before deleting the record. Then, the option either to delete the physical file's record by pressing the ENTER key or not to delete by pressing F12 may be made.

1600   The **IFEQ** statement tests the status of the **12** indicator.

1700   When the **IFEQ** statement test on line 1600 is true (indicator "off"), the displayed record will logically be deleted from the physical file by the **DELET** statement.

1800   This **ENDIF** operation ends the **IF** statement on line 1600.

1900   This **ENDIF** operation ends the **IF** statement on line 1400.

2000   The **ENDSR** operation ends the DLTSR internal subroutine, which passes control back to the **ENDDO** operation on line 900 and then to line 500 to repeat the processing cycle or end the job.

Figure 15-16   Compile listing of the deletion maintenance program. (Continued)

As shown in Figure 15-17, the result of logically deleting the example record may be tested by entering the customer number (12345 in this case) and observing that the error message **RECORD NOT FOUND** is displayed on line 5 of the PROMPT screen. The Reset key must be pressed to continue processing and enter another customer number or end the job.

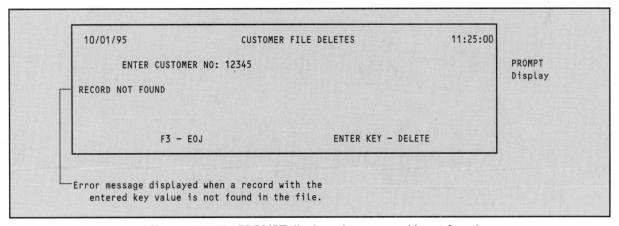

Figure 15-17   PROMPT display when a record is not found.

RPG/400 PROGRAM: COMBINED MAINTENANCE

The previous program examples in this chapter each supported only one maintenance function. Sometimes it may be advantageous to combine record addition, update, and deletion maintenance in one program. The changes needed in the display file and RPG/400 program to support the three maintenance functions are discussed in the following sections.

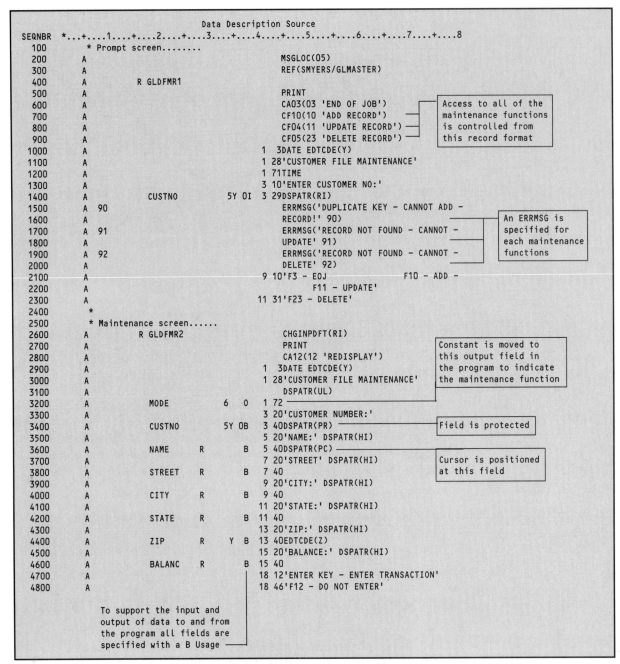

```
                              Data Description Source
 SEQNBR  *...+....1....+....2....+....3....+....4....+....5....+....6....+....7....+....8
  100       * Prompt screen........
  200       A                                    MSGLOC(05)
  300       A                                    REF(SMYERS/GLMASTER)
  400       A          R GLDFMR1
  500       A                                    PRINT
  600       A                                    CA03(03 'END OF JOB')
  700       A                                    CF10(10 'ADD RECORD')
  800       A                                    CF04(11 'UPDATE RECORD')
  900       A                                    CF05(23 'DELETE RECORD')
 1000       A                              1  3DATE EDTCDE(Y)
 1100       A                              1 28'CUSTOMER FILE MAINTENANCE'
 1200       A                              1 71TIME
 1300       A                              3 10'ENTER CUSTOMER NO:'
 1400       A            CUSTNO      5Y 0I  3 29DSPATR(RI)
 1500       A 90                            ERRMSG('DUPLICATE KEY - CANNOT ADD -
 1600       A                               RECORD!' 90)
 1700       A 91                            ERRMSG('RECORD NOT FOUND - CANNOT -
 1800       A                               UPDATE' 91)
 1900       A 92                            ERRMSG('RECORD NOT FOUND - CANNOT -
 2000       A                               DELETE' 92)
 2100       A                              9 10'F3 - EOJ               F10 - ADD -
 2200       A                                 F11 - UPDATE'
 2300       A                             11 31'F23 - DELETE'
 2400       *
 2500       * Maintenance screen......
 2600       A          R GLDFMR2                  CHGINPDFT(RI)
 2700       A                                    PRINT
 2800       A                                    CA12(12 'REDISPLAY')
 2900       A                              1  3DATE EDTCDE(Y)
 3000       A                              1 28'CUSTOMER FILE MAINTENANCE'
 3100       A                                 DSPATR(UL)
 3200       A            MODE        6  0   1 72
 3300       A                              3 20'CUSTOMER NUMBER:'
 3400       A            CUSTNO      5Y 0B  3 40DSPATR(PR)
 3500       A                              5 20'NAME:' DSPATR(HI)
 3600       A            NAME     R     B   5 40DSPATR(PC)
 3700       A                              7 20'STREET' DSPATR(HI)
 3800       A            STREET   R     B   7 40
 3900       A                              9 20'CITY:' DSPATR(HI)
 4000       A            CITY     R     B   9 40
 4100       A                             11 20'STATE:' DSPATR(HI)
 4200       A            STATE    R     B  11 40
 4300       A                             13 20'ZIP:' DSPATR(HI)
 4400       A            ZIP      R   Y B  13 40EDTCDE(Z)
 4500       A                             15 20'BALANCE:' DSPATR(HI)
 4600       A            BALANC   R     B  15 40
 4700       A                             18 12'ENTER KEY - ENTER TRANSACTION'
 4800       A                             18 46'F12 - DO NOT ENTER'
```

Access to all of the maintenance functions is controlled from this record format

An ERRMSG is specified for each maintenance functions

Constant is moved to this output field in the program to indicate the maintenance function

Field is protected

Cursor is positioned at this field

To support the input and output of data to and from the program all fields are specified with a B Usage

Figure 15-18 Display file that supports addition, update, and deletion maintenance.

Examine Figure 15-18, and note that the following syntax is included in the display file to support all of the maintenance functions:

1. Additional *Command Function Keys* are specified in the GLDFMR1 prompt screen including **CF10** (*ADD RECORD*), **CF11** (*UPDATE RECORD*), and **CF23** (*DELETE RECORD*). End-of-job processing is controlled by *Command Attention Key* **03.**

   Three **ERRMSG** statements are specified to identify the error generated by each maintenance function. Additional constants are included at the bottom of the screen indicating the key action the operator must take to perform the selected function or end the job.

2. A MODE field is defined in the GLDFMR2 record format to which a maintenance function constant is moved in the RPG/400 program. The constant **ADD,**

UPDATE, or **DELETE** will display on line 1 beginning in position 72 of the GLDMR2 screen.

With the exception of the MODE and CUSTNO fields, the others are referenced from the physical file, GLMASTER.

Because the MODE field value is only to be displayed (output), it is defined with an **O** *Usage*. The CUSTNO field is the same as that defined in the GLDFMR1 format and will display the value entered in the GLDFMR1 prompt screen. To prevent the value from being changed, a **DSPATR(PR)** keyword is assigned, and the cursor is positioned at the NAME field with the **DSPATR(PC)** keyword.

A maintenance transaction is completed by the operator pressing the ENTER key. The transaction may be ignored by pressing **F12.**

A Print key listing of the GLDFMR1 (prompt) and GLDFMR2 (maintenance) displays is shown in Figure 15-19. When the operator presses one of the maintenance function keys (**F11** for this example), the same screen GLDFMR2 format will display for all of them. The user is reminded of the maintenance mode he or she is currently in by the **UPDATE, ADD,** or **DELETE** constant in the upper-right corner of the GLDFM2R display. The application could have been developed by including a different record format for each maintenance function, each with its own display attributes.

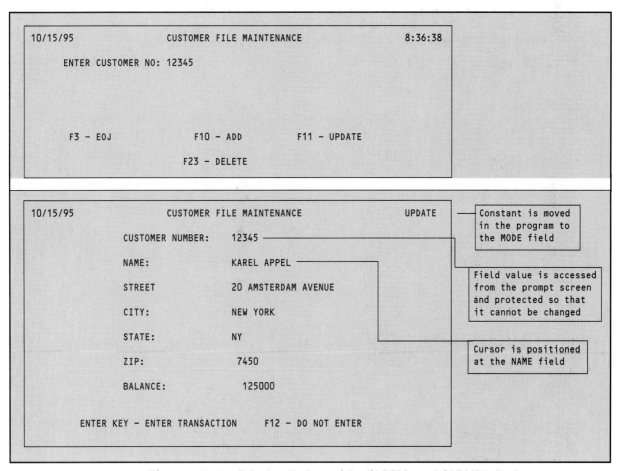

Figure 15-19 Print key listings of the GLDFM1 and GLDMR2 displays.

A compile listing of the RPG/400 program that includes adds, update, and deletion maintenance, supplemented with a line-by-line explanation of the syntax, is presented in Figure 15-20.

```
SEQUENCE                                                              IND  DO
NUMBER   *...1....+....2....+....3....+....4....+....5....+....6....+....7...*  USE  NUM
                         S o u r c e   L i s t i n g
    100  * THIS PROGRAM CONTROLS PF MAINTENANCE FUNCTIONS (ADDS, UPDATES,
    200  * AND LOGICAL DELETION) FOR THE GLMASTER FILE
    300  *
         H
    400  FGLDF1M  CF  E                   WORKSTN
         RECORD FORMAT(S): LIBRARY SMYERS FILE GLDF1M.
                   EXTERNAL FORMAT GLDFMR1 RPG NAME GLDFMR1
                   EXTERNAL FORMAT GLDFMR2 RPG NAME GLDFMR2
    500  FGLMASTERUF E          K      DISK                  A
         RECORD FORMAT(S): LIBRARY SMYERS FILE GLMASTER.
                   EXTERNAL FORMAT GLRCRD RPG NAME GLRCRD
A000000  INPUT  FIELDS FOR RECORD GLDFMR1 FILE GLDF1M FORMAT GLDFMR1.
A000001                                  1   1 *IN03              END OF JOB
A000002                                  2   2 *IN10              ADD RECORD
A000003                                  3   3 *IN11              UPDATE RECORD
A000004                                  4   4 *IN23              DELETE RECORD
A000005                                  5   5 *IN90              DUPLICATE KEY - CANNOT ADD RECORD!
A000006                                  6   6 *IN91              RECORD NOT FOUND - CANNOT UPDATE
A000007                                  7   7 *IN92              RECORD NOT FOUND - CANNOT DELETE
A000008                                  8  120CUSTNO
B000000  INPUT  FIELDS FOR RECORD GLDFMR2 FILE GLDF1M FORMAT GLDFMR2.
B000001                                  1   1 *IN03              REDISPLAY
B000002                                  2   60CUSTNO
B000003                                  7  26 NAME
B000004                                 27  46 STREET
B000005                                 47  66 CITY
B000006                                 67  68 STATE
B000007                                 69  730ZIP
B000008                                 74  812BALANC
C000000  INPUT  FIELDS FOR RECORD GLRCRD FILE GLMASTER FORMAT GLRCRD.
C000001                               P  1   30CUST#
C000002                                  4  23 NAME
C000003                                 24  43 STREET
C000004                                 44  63 CITY
C000005                                 64  65 STATE
C000006                               P 66  680ZIP
C000007                               P 69  732BALANC
    600  IDFFLDS    DS
    700  I                               1   50CUSTNO
    800  I                               6  25 NAME
    900  I                              26  45 STREET
   1000  I                              46  65 CITY
   1100  I                              66  67 STATE
   1200  I                            P 68  700ZIP
   1300  I                            P 71  752BALANC
   1400  C        *IN03     DOUEQ*ON                    do until eoj      B001
   1500  C                  CLEARDFFLDS                 clear df fields   001
   1600  C                  EXFMTGLDFMR1                dsp screen        001
   1700  C        *IN03     CABEQ*ON    SKIP            eoj control       001
   1800  C        *IN10     CASEQ*ON    ADDSR           adds sr           001
   1900  C        *IN11     CASEQ*ON    UPSR            update sr         001
   2000  C        *IN23     CASEQ*ON    DELSR           delete sr         001
   2100  C                  ENDCS                       end cas group     001
   2200  C        SKIP      TAG                         cab label         001
   2300  C                  ENDDO                       end DO group      E001
   2400  C                  MOVE *ON    *INLR           end job
   2500  *
   2600  C        ADDSR     BEGSR                       begin add sr
   2700  C        CUSTNO    SETLLGLMASTER             90check for dup    3
   2800  C        *IN90     IFEQ *OFF                                     B001
   2900  C                  MOVE 'ADD  ' MODE           dsply mode        001
   3000  C                  EXFMTGLDFMR2                display screen    001
   3100  C        *IN12     CABEQ*ON    SKIP1           do not add rcd    001
   3200  C                  Z-ADDCUSTNO CUST#           move to pf fld    001
   3300  C                  WRITEGLRCRD             99  write PF record 2 001
   3400  C                  ENDIF                       end IF            E001
   3500  C        SKIP1     ENDSR                       end SR
   3600  *
   3700  C        UPSR      BEGSR                       begin update sr
   3800  C        CUSTNO    CHAINGLMASTER           91  get pf record  1
   3900  C        *IN91     IFEQ *OFF                   record found      B001
   4000  C                  MOVE 'UPDATE' MODE          dsply mode        001
```

Data Structure defined so that fields may be cleared to blanks & zeros by the CLEAR statement on line 1500

Figure 15-20 Compile listing of the program that includes all of the maintenance functions.

490

```
        4100   C                        EXFMTGLDFMR2                      dsply screen         001
        4200   C             *IN12      CABEQ*ON       SKIP2              do not update        001
        4300   C                        UPDATGLRCRD                       update record        001
        4400   C                        ENDIF                             end IF             E001
        4500   C             SKIP2      ENDSR                             end update sr
        4600   *
        4700   C             DELSR      BEGSR                             begin del sr
        4800   C             CUSTNO     CHAINGLRCRD                92     get pf record     1
        4900   C             *IN92      IFEQ *OFF                         record found       B001
        5000   C                        MOVE 'DELETE'  MODE               dsply mode           001
        5100   C                        EXFMTGLDFMR2                      dsply screen         001
        5200   C             *IN12      CABEQ*ON       SKIP3              do not delete        001
        5300   C                        DELETGLRCRD                       delete record        001
        5400   C                        ENDIF                             end IF             E001
        5500   C             SKIP3      ENDSR                             end delete sr
        D000000      OUTPUT FIELDS FOR RECORD GLDFMR1 FILE GLDF1M FORMAT GLDFMR1.
        D000001                         *IN90      1  CHAR     1          DUPLICATE KEY - CANNOT ADD RECORD!
        D000002                         *IN91      2  CHAR     1          RECORD NOT FOUND - CANNOT UPDATE
        D000003                         *IN92      3  CHAR     1          RECORD NOT FOUND - CANNOT DELETE
        E000000      OUTPUT FIELDS FOR RECORD GLDFMR2 FILE GLDF1M FORMAT GLDFMR2.
        E000001                         MODE       6  CHAR     6
        E000002                         CUSTNO    11  ZONE   5,0
        E000003                         NAME      31  CHAR    20
        E000004                         STREET    51  CHAR    20
        E000005                         CITY      71  CHAR    20
        E000006                         STATE     73  CHAR     2
        E000007                         ZIP       78  ZONE   5,0
        E000008                         BALANC    86  ZONE   8,2
        F000000      OUTPUT FIELDS FOR RECORD GLRCRD FILE GLMASTER FORMAT GLRCRD.
        F000001                         CUST#      3P PACK   5,0
        F000002                         NAME      23  CHAR    20
        F000003                         STREET    43  CHAR    20
        F000004                         CITY      63  CHAR    20
        F000005                         STATE     65  CHAR     2
        F000006                         ZIP       68P PACK   5,0
        F000007                         BALANC    73P PACK   8,2
```

Line #	Explanation
400	**WORKSTN** file **(GLDF1M)** is defined as combined (**C** in column 15), full procedural (**F** in column 16), and externally defined (**E** in column 19).
500	Physical file is defined as update (**U** in column 15), full procedural (**F** in column 16), externally defined (**E** in column 19), and keyed (**K** in column 31). The **A** in column 66 is needed to support adds to the file. Because update and delete maintenance requires that records be read from and to the physical file, it must be defined as update. In addition, because file processing operations are used (i.e., **CHAIN, SETLL, UPDAT, DELET,** and **WRITE**), the file must be defined as full procedural.
600 - 1300	The data structure, DFFLDS, defines the GLDFMR2 format's fields that are to be initialized to blanks and zeros by the **CLEAR** operation before it is displayed again. If the GLDFMR2 record format in the display file was specified in lieu of a data structure, all indicators would be set off, a condition not wanted for this application.
1400	The **DOUEQ** group controls the display of the GLDFMR1 and GLDFMR2 formats and the maintenance function selected. The iterative processing (looping) continues until the operator presses F3, which sets on indicator **03**, when in the GLDFMR1 display to end the job. The relational test for the **DOUEQ** statement is made at the related **ENDDO** statement on line 2300. Consequently, the **DOUEQ** group will be executed at least once.
1500	The **CLEAR** statement clears all of the fields defined in the data structure specified in *Factor 2* to blanks (for character fields) and zeros (for numeric fields).
1600	The **EXFMT** statement <u>writes</u> the GLDFMR1 (prompt) record to the screen and holds it there. After the operator enters a customer number and presses one of the designated command keys, the variable is <u>read</u> and the GLDFMR2 screen or one of the error messages on line 5 displayed. The operator ends the job from the GLDFMR1 display by pressing F3.
1700 -	When the operator presses F3, which sets on indicator 03, the **CABEQ** statement branches program control to the **TAG** statement on line 2200, tests the status of the **03** indicator in the **ENDDO** statement, and ends the job with the **MOVE** statement on line 2400.

Figure 15-20 Compile listing of the program that includes all of the maintenance functions. (Continued)

1800 - 2100	The **CASnn** group includes the control to branch to three different internal subroutines and add, update, or delete records in the GLMASTER physical file. The *Command Key* pressed in the GLDFMR1 display determines which subroutine is executed. After exit from a subroutine, control returns to the statement following the **ENDCS** operation on line 2100.
2200	This **TAG** statement is the label for the **CABEQ** statement on line 1700.
2300	The **ENDDO** operation ends the **DOUEQ** group. Recall that the relational test is made here and <u>not</u> at the **DOUEQ** statement on line 1400. When indicator **03** is on, control will exit from the **DOUEQ** group and execute the statement on line 2400 to end the job.
2400	The **MOVE** statement sets on the **LR** indicator to end the job. However, control will execute any calculation and/or output instructions conditioned by the **LR** indicator before the job is ended.
2600	Beginning of the ADDSR subroutine which is branched to by the **CASEQ** statement on line 1800.
2700	The CUSTNO value from the GLDFMR1 prompt display is specified in the **SETLL** statement to determine if the "add" record is already stored in the physical file. If it is stored, indicator **90** will be set on.
2800	The status of the **90** indicator (specified with the **SETLL** statement) is tested in this **IFEQ** statement. If it is "off," the instructions to add a record to the file will be executed. If **90** is "on," control will skip to the **ENDSR** statement on line 3500.
2900	The literal 'ADD ' is moved to the MODE field defined in the GLDFMR2 record format.
3000	This **EXFMT** statement displays a blank GLDFMR2 screen.
3100	The status of the **12** indicator is tested with the **CABEQ** statement, which allows the operator to either complete the adds process or abort it by branching to the **ENDSR.**
3200	The CUSTNO value from the PROMPT screen is moved to the physical file field CUST#.
3300	The physical file's record format is written to the physical file with the **WRITE** statement.
3400	The **ENDIF** operation ends the **IFEQ** statement on line 2800.
3500	The **ENDSR** statement ends the ADDSR routine and is the SKIP1 label for the **CABEQ** statement on line 3100.
3700	This **BEGSR** statement is branched to by the **CASEQ** statement on line 1900.
3800	The CUSTNO value entered in the GLDFMR1 prompt display is used in the **CHAIN** statement to access the record to be updated. If the record (same key value) <u>is</u> found, indicator **91** will <u>not</u> be set on.
3900	When this **IFEQ** statement tests as "true," statements on lines 4000–4300 will be executed.
4000	The literal 'UPDATE' is moved to the MODE field defined in the GLDFMR2 record format.
4100	This **EXFMT** statement displays the GLDFMR2 screen "filled in" with field values from the accessed physical file record.
4200	The status of the **12** indicator is tested with a **CABEQ** statement. If it is "on," the operator pressed F12 <u>not</u> to update the current record, which branches control to the **ENDSR** statement on line 4500.
4300	The **UPDAT** statement writes the changed physical file record back to its storage location.
4400	The **ENDIF** operation ends the **IFEQ** statement on line 3900.
4500	The **ENDSR** statement ends the UPSR routine and is the SKIP2 label for the **CABEQ** statement on line 4200.
4700	This **BEGSR** statement is branched to by the **CASEQ** statement on line 2000.
4800	The CUSTNO value entered in the GLDFMR1 prompt display is used in the **CHAIN** statement to access the record to be deleted. If the record (same key value) <u>is</u> found, indicator **92** will <u>not</u> be set on.

Figure 15-20 Compile listing of the program that includes all of the maintenance functions. (Continued)

4900	When this **IFEQ** statement tests as "true," statements on lines 5000–5300 will be executed.
5000	The literal 'DELETE' is moved to the MODE field defined in the GLDFMR2 record format.
5100	This **EXFMT** statement displays the GLDFMR2 screen "filled in" with field values from the accessed physical file record.
5200	The status of the 12 indicator is tested with a **CABEQ** statement. If it is "on," the operator pressed F12 <u>not</u> to delete the current record, which transfers control to the **ENDSR** statement on line 5500.
5300	The **DELET** statement logically deletes the current record from the physical file.
5400	The **ENDIF** operation ends the **IFEQ** statement on line 4900.
5500	The **ENDSR** statement ends the DELSR routine and is the SKIP3 label for the **CABEQ** statement on line 5200.

Figure 15-20   Compile listing of the program that includes all of the maintenance functions. (Continued)

RPG/400 PROGRAM: INTERACTIVE DATA VALIDATION

Chapter 14 introduced and explained the syntax of the keywords that may be specified in a display file to support interactive data validation. A source listing of the example display file shown in Figure 15-21 includes the **CHECK, VALUES,** and **RANGE** keywords to control the required validation functions.

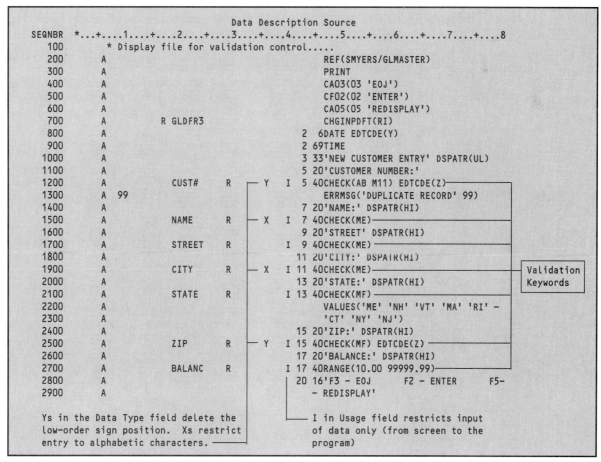

```
                              Data Description Source
  SEQNBR *...+....1....+....2....+....3....+....4....+....5....+....6....+....7....+....8
    100         * Display file for validation control.....
    200       A                                    REF(SMYERS/GLMASTER)
    300       A                                    PRINT
    400       A                                    CA03(03 'EOJ')
    500       A                                    CF02(02 'ENTER')
    600       A                                    CA05(05 'REDISPLAY')
    700       A          R GLDFR3                   CHGINPDFT(RI)
    800       A                                 2  6DATE EDTCDE(Y)
    900       A                                 2 69TIME
   1000       A                                 3 33'NEW CUSTOMER ENTRY' DSPATR(UL)
   1100       A                                 5 20'CUSTOMER NUMBER:'
   1200       A            CUST#     R   ─ Y   I 5 40CHECK(AB M11) EDTCDE(Z)──┐
   1300       A  99                                 ERRMSG('DUPLICATE RECORD' 99)
   1400       A                                 7 20'NAME:' DSPATR(HI)
   1500       A            NAME      R   ─ X   I 7 40CHECK(ME)────────────────┤
   1600       A                                 9 20'STREET' DSPATR(HI)
   1700       A            STREET    R         I 9 40CHECK(ME)────────────────┤
   1800       A                                11 20'CITY:' DSPATR(HI)
   1900       A            CITY      R   ─ X   I 11 40CHECK(ME)───────────────┤  ┌──────────┐
   2000       A                                13 20'STATE:' DSPATR(HI)          │Validation│
   2100       A            STATE     R         I 13 40CHECK(MF)───────────────┤  │Keywords  │
   2200       A                                   VALUES('ME' 'NH' 'VT' 'MA' 'RI' ─ └──────────┘
   2300       A                                   'CT' 'NY' 'NJ')
   2400       A                                15 20'ZIP:' DSPATR(HI)
   2500       A            ZIP       R   ─ Y   I 15 40CHECK(MF) EDTCDE(Z)──────┤
   2600       A                                17 20'BALANCE:' DSPATR(HI)
   2700       A            BALANC    R         I 17 40RANGE(10.00 99999.99)────┘
   2800       A                                20 16'F3 - EOJ      F2 - ENTER      F5-
   2900       A                                  - REDISPLAY'
```

    Ys in the Data Type field delete the   I in Usage field restricts input
    low-order sign position. Xs restrict   of data only (from screen to the
    entry to alphabetic characters. ─────   program)

Figure 15-21   Display file with data validation keywords.

A Print key listing of the screen image is shown in Figure 15-22. Note that only one record format is included in the display file instead of two as in the other examples in this chapter.

```
 10/26/95                                                        9:46:06
                            NEW CUSTOMER ENTRY

                CUSTOMER NUMBER:    40000

                    NAME:           SALVATORE DALI

                    STREET          2 CUBIST LANE

                    CITY:           WESTPORT

                    STATE:          CT

                    ZIP:            06498

                    BALANCE:            80000


              F3 - EOJ      F2 - ENTER      F5 - REDISPLAY
```

Figure 15-22 Print key copy of the display file's record format that validates new customer accounts.

An examination of the compile listing of the program that supports interactive validation for data entry in Figure 15-23 will indicate that it is identical to one that supports the addition of records to a physical file without validation. As compared to the batch validation program discussed in Chapter 12 (see Figure 12-34), interactive data validation significantly simplifies the program's syntax. Now all of the validation functions are included in the display file, and not in the RPG/400 program.

After each system-supplied validation error message or number is displayed, the operator may press the Help key to access supplemental information about the error. The Reset key must be pressed after each error to continue processing.

```
SEQUENCE                                                                 IND   DO
NUMBER    *...1....+....2....+....3....+....4....+....5....+....6....+....7...*  USE   NUM
                      S o u r c e   L i s t i n g
     100  * THIS PROGRAM PROCESSES A DSPF FILE TO INPUT DATA TO A PF.
     200  * VALIDATION FUNCTIONS SPECIFIED IN THE DISPLAY FILE
          H
     300  FGLDF3   CF  E               WORKSTN
          RECORD FORMAT(S):  LIBRARY SMYERS FILE GLDF3.
                    EXTERNAL FORMAT GLDFR3 RPG NAME GLDFR3
     400  FGLMASTERO   E       K       DISK                        A
          RECORD FORMAT(S):  LIBRARY SMYERS FILE GLMASTER.
                    EXTERNAL FORMAT GLRCRD RPG NAME GLRCRD
 A000000  INPUT   FIELDS FOR RECORD GLDF3 FILE GLDF3 FORMAT GLDFR3.
 A000001                              1   1 *IN03               EOJ
 A000002                              2   2 *IN02               ENTER
 A000003                              3   3 *IN05               REDISPLAY
 A000004                              4   4 *IN99               DUPLICATE RECORD
 A000005                              5    90CUST#
 A000006                             10  29 NAME
 A000007                             30  49 STREET
 A000008                             50  69 CITY
 A000009                             70  71 STATE
```

Figure 15-23 RPG/400 program that supports interactive validation for the entry of data.

```
A000010                                              72  760ZIP
A000011                                              77  842BALANC
 500  C           *IN03     DOUEQ*ON                       do until eoj        B001
 600  C                     EXFMTGLDFR3                     dsp entry scrn       001
 700  C           *IN03     CABEQ*ON    SKIP               eoj control          001
 800  C           *IN05     CABEQ*ON    SKIP               redisplay            001
 900  C           *IN02     CASEQ*ON    ENTER              exit to sr           001
1000  C                     ENDCS                          end cas group        001
1100  C           SKIP      TAG                            cab label            001
1200  C                     ENDDO                          end DO group        E001
1300  C                     MOVE *ON    *INLR              end job
1400  *
1500  C           ENTER     BEGSR                          begin SR
1600  C                     WRITEGLRCRD            99       write PF record   2
1700  C                     ENDSR                          end SR
B000000  OUTPUT FIELDS FOR RECORD GLRCRD FILE GLMASTER FORMAT GLRCRD.
B000001                     CUST#    3P PACK  5,0
B000002                     NAME    23  CHAR  20
B000003                     STREET  43  CHAR  20
B000004                     CITY    63  CHAR  20
B000005                     STATE   65  CHAR   2
B000006                     ZIP     68P PACK  5,0
B000007                     BALANC  73P PACK  8,2
```

Line #	Explanation
300	**WORKSTN** file (GLDF3) is defined as combined (**C** in column 15), full procedural (**F** in column 16), and externally defined (**E** in column 19).
400	Physical file is defined as output (**O** in column 15), externally defined (**E** in column 19), and keyed (**K** in column 31). The **A** in column 66 supports the addition of records to the file.
500	The **DOUEQ** group controls the display of the GLDFR3 format, the entry of data, and the addition of records to the physical file. The iterative processing (looping) continues until the operator presses F3, which sets on indicator **03**, to end the job. The relational test for the **DOUEQ** statement is made at the **ENDDO** statement on line 1200. Consequently, the **DOUEQ** group will be executed at least once.
600	The **EXFMT** statement writes the GLDFR3 record to the screen and holds it there until the operator presses one of the command keys.
700	*Command Attention Key 3* was assigned in the display file to indicator **03**. When F3 is pressed and indicator **03** set on, the **CABEQ** statement will pass control to the **TAG** statement on line 1100, execute the **DOUEQ** test at the **ENDDO** operation, and end the job with the **MOVE** statement on line 1300.
800	*Command Attention Key 5* was assigned in the display file to indicator **05**. When F5 is pressed and indicator **05** set on, the **CABEQ** statement will pass control to the **TAG** statement on line 1100, the **ENDDO** statement will test the status of indicator **03** and pass control back to the **DOUEQ** statement on line 500 without adding the record to the physical file.
900	*Command Function Key 2* was assigned in the display file to indicator **02**. When F2 is pressed and indicator **02** set on, the **CASEQ** statement will pass control to the **BEGSR** statement on line 1500 where a record is added to the physical file by the **WRITE** statement on line 1600. If a duplicate record (same key value) is detected, the **99** indicator assigned to the **WRITE** statement will be set on and the **ERRMSG** text in the display file's record format displayed on line 24 (default line) of the screen.
1000	The **ENDCS** operation ends the **CASEQ** statement.
1100	The **TAG** statement is the label for the **CABEQ** statements on lines 700 and 800.
1200	The **ENDDO** operation ends the **DOUEQ** group. Recall that the relational test is made here and <u>not</u> at the **DOUEQ** statement on line 500. When indicator **03** is on, control will exit from the **DOUEQ** group and execute the statement on line 1300 to end the job.
1300	The **MOVE** statement sets on the **LR** indicator to end the job.

Figure 15-23 RPG/400 program that supports interactive validation for the entry of data. (Continued)

1500	The **BEGSR** statement is the label for the **CASEQ** statement on line 900.
1600	The **WRITE** statement writes the field values from the display file's record format to the physical file. If a duplicate record is tested (same key value), indicator **99** will be set on and the **ERRMSG** text (specified in the display file) displayed on default line 24 of the screen.
1700	The **ENDSR** statement ends the ENTER subroutine and returns control back to line 1000. The processing cycle is continued until the operator presses F3 to end the job.

Figure 15-23 RPG/400 program that supports interactive validation for the entry of data. (Continued)

SUMMARY

Unlike batch processing, *interactive processing* connects the user directly with database file(s) and facilitates immediate access to authorized data. The creation (source and object) of display files is necessary to support *interactive processing* in the AS/400 environment.

Any display file processed by an RPG/400 program must be defined in a *File Description Specifications* statement as a full procedural, externally described **WORKSTN** (workstation) file.

The record formats in a display file are accessed in an RPG/400 program by an **EXFMT** operation, which controls the writing of a format by the program to the screen and then the reading from the screen to the program. In lieu of the **EXFMT** operation, separate **WRITE** and **READ** statements may be specified to write and read a display file's record format.

Error identification is controlled and displayed by one or more **ERRMSG** keywords specified at the *Field Level* in the record format of a display file. The conditioning indicator specified with the **ERRMSG** keyword will control the display of the text. Indicators included in **WRITE, CHAIN,** and **SETLL** statements are set on when an error occurs. The indicators are specified with their related **ERRMSG** keyword to control the display of the error message text.

The first four programs discussed in the chapter separately support addition, update, logical deletion maintenance, and inquiry processing. A fifth program combines addition, update, and deletion maintenance. The sixth program controls the interactive validation of data.

In an RPG/400 program, addition maintenance is performed with the **WRITE** operation, update with the **CHAIN** and **UPDAT** operations, and logical deletion with the **CHAIN** and **DELET** operations. Inquiry processing is executed with the **CHAIN** operation.

When the fields in a display file's record format are defined with an **O** or **B** *Usage,* they usually have to be initialized to blanks and zeros before the format is redisplayed. This prevents the previously entered values from appearing when the format is displayed again. The **CLEAR** operation, which may be specified with a field, record, data structure, array name, array element, or table name, will initialize character fields to blanks and numeric fields to zeros.

QUESTIONS

Examine the following statement and answer Questions 15-1 through 15-5.

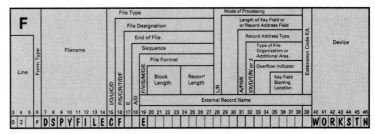

15-1. What is the function of the letter **C** in column 15?

15-2. In lieu of the **C** in column 15, what other entries may be specified? Explain their functions.

15-3. What control is supported by the **F** in column 16? May any other entry be specified for display files?

15-4. What is the function of the letter **E** in column 19? May any other entry be specified for display files?

15-5. What physical device is supported by the **WORKSTN** device name?

Examine the following statement and answer Questions 15-6 through 15-9.

```
    +...1....+....2....+....3....+....4....+....5....+....6
                    EXFMTDFR1                         80
```

15-6. What is the function of the **EXFMT** operation? May any other RPG/400 operations be specified to provide the same control?

15-7. What does the DFR1 entry in *Factor 2* refer to? May any other entry be specified?

15-8. When does the indicator (**80**) specified in columns 56–57 turn on? What does this indicator usually control?

15-9. What occurs if the **EXFMT** statement is executed successfully?

15-10. How should a physical file that supports "adds-only" processing be defined? Under what conditions would the file be defined as an update file?

15-11. What RPG/400 operation supports the addition of records to a physical file? Identify the processing errors that may occur when the statement is executed. How may these errors be identified in the related display file?

15-12. What is specified in *Factor 2* of the operation named in Question 15-11?

15-13. How should a physical file that supports "update" processing be defined?

15-14. What RPG/400 operations support the update of records in a physical file? Identify the processing errors that may occur when these statements are executed. Which operation is coordinated with an **ERRMSG** keyword in a display file's record format?

15-15. What is specified in *Factor 2* of the operations named in Question 15-14?

15-16. How should a physical file that supports "logical deletion" processing be defined?

15-17. What RPG/400 operations support the logical deletion of records in a physical file? Identify the processing errors that may occur when these statements are executed. Which operation is coordinated with an **ERRMSG** keyword in a display file's record format?

15-18. What is specified in *Factor 2* of the operations named in Question 15-17?

15-19. How should a physical file that supports "inquiry" processing be defined?

15-20. What RPG/400 operation supports physical file inquiry? Identify the processing errors that may occur when this statement is executed.

15-21. What is specified in *Factor 2* of the operation named in Question 15-20?

15-22. What is the function of the **CLEAR** operation? With what file type(s) may it be specified?

15-23. What may be specified in *Factor 2* of a **CLEAR** statement?

PROGRAMMING ASSIGNMENTS

Before any of these assignments are started, the related physical and display files from the assignments for Chapter 14 must be completed.

The following record format is to be added to the display file completed in Assignment 14-1 for Assignments 15-1, 15-2, 15-3, and 15-4:

```
        01 02 03 04 05 06 07 08 09 10 11 12 13 14 15 16 17 18 19 20 21 22 23 24 25 26 27 28 29 30 31 32 33 34 35 36 37 38 39 40 41 42 43 44 45 46 47 48 49 50 51 52 53 54 55 56 57 58 59 60 61 62 63 64 65 66 67 68 69 70 71 72 73 74 75 76 77 78 79 80
   1    H H : M M : S S                              C U S T O M E R   M A I N T E N A N C E                                M M / D D / Y Y
   2
   3              E N T E R   C U S T O M E R   N U M B E R :   X X X X X
   4
   5
   6
   7                         F 3   -   E O J                              F 2   -   E N T E R
   8    N O T E S :
   9        1 .   H I G H   I N T E N S I T Y   A L L   C O N S T A N T S
  10        2 .   R E V E R S E   I M A G E   T H E   V A R I A B L E .
  11        3 .   D I S P L A Y   O N E   O F   T H E   F O L L O W I N G   E R R M S G   O N   L I N E   5 :
  12              D U P L I C A T E   K E Y
  13              R E C O R D   N O T   F O U N D
```

The following additional changes are required in the display file completed for Assignment 14-1:

1. Change the constant CUSTOMER ENTRY to CUSTOMER MAINTENANCE.
2. Include a seven-character MODE field on line 2 and center it under the CUSTOMER MAINTENANCE constant.
3. Delete the F3—**EOJ** constant and move the F2—**ENTER** constant to its position.
4. Delete the *Command Key 3* keyword.
5. Delete the **ERRMSG** keyword.
6. For Assignment 15-1, change the *Usage* to **I,** for 15-2 to **O,** 15-3 to **B,** and 15-4 to **I** and **O.**

Programming Assignment 15-1:   VALIDATION OF NEW CUSTOMER ACCOUNTS

Complete an RPG/400 program to add records interactively to the physical file created in Assignment 14-1. The error message **DUPLICATE KEY** is to be displayed on line 5 of the prompt screen when a key is entered that is already stored in the file. If the add record is not stored, move the customer number entered from the prompt screen field to the related entry screen field. Also, move the literal ADD to the MODE field in the entry screen.

Enter all of the data for a record, then press *Command Key 2* to check each field for its validation test. If the customer number does not pass the Modulus-11 test, enter blanks to continue validation of the other fields. Correct the other fields with your own data so that all of the fields will be validated. However, *do not* add a corrected record to the physical file.

Physical File Data:

Customer Number	Name	Street	City	State	Zip	Limit	Rating
12343	JOHN FIRESTONE	20 TYRE LANE	AKRON	OH	05456	2000	B
13005	WILLIAM GOODYEAR	19 TUBE ROAD	DETROIT	MI	06606	5000	A
14100	JOHN KELLY	100 PATCH PLACE	FRANKFORT	KY	07701	7000	A+
21008	JAMES GOODRICH	81 VALVE TERRACE	CHICAGO	IL	04404	3000	B
35009	CLAUDE MICHELIN	1 PARIS PLACE	FRANCE	PA	05500	6000	C
44008	ANTHONY PIRELLI	33 FIAT BOULEVARD	ROME	NY	06608	4000	A-
47104	TOYO KOGO THE 2ND	12 HIROSHIMA ROAD	TOKYO2	CA	09900	0100	D
50008	JAMES COOPER	55 FLAT STREET	COOPERSTOWN	NY	06620	0500	C
60003	WILLIAM BRIDGESTONE	80 WHEEL DRIVE	AGOURA	CA	09940	2000	B-
65005	HENRY ATLAS	210 LUG AVENUE	GREENWICH	CT	06649	3000	B

Programming Assignment 15-2: CUSTOMER FILE INQUIRY

Assignment 15-1 must be completed, or the data loaded to the physical file with **DFU,** before this assignment is started.

Complete an RPG/400 program to inquiry the physical file interactively. The error message **RECORD NOT FOUND** is to be displayed on line 5 of the prompt screen if the key entered is not stored in the file. When a record is found, its values are to be displayed in the inquiry record format. Also, move the literal INQUIRY to the MODE field in the inquiry screen.

Inquiry records with key values **12343, 14000, 44008,** and **65005.**

Programming Assignment 15-3: CUSTOMER FILE UPDATE

Assignment 15-1 must be completed, or the data loaded to the physical file with **DFU,** before this assignment is started.

Further modify the update format to *protect* the customer number and *position* the cursor at the NAME field. Also, change all of the fields in the update format to **B** *Usage.*

Complete an RPG/400 program to update the physical file interactively. The error message **RECORD NOT FOUND** is to be displayed on line 5 of the prompt screen if the key entered is not stored in the file. When a record is found, its values are to be displayed in the update record format. Except for the customer number, every other field value may be changed. Also, move the literal UPDATE to the MODE field in the update screen.

Update Data:

	Record 1	Record 2	Record 3	Record 4
CUSTNO	65005	20000	13005	60003
NAME				
STREET	150 TREAD PLACE		WALTER DUNLOP	99 BALANCE LANE
CITY	ORLANDO			PITTSBURGH
STATE	FL			PA
ZIP	08801			07701
LIMIT		2000		3000
RATING		B		A-

* If the data for a field is blank, the original values are not to be changed!

Programming Assignment 15-4: CUSTOMER FILE RECORD DELETION

Assignment 15-1 must be completed, or the data loaded to the physical file with **DFU,** before this assignment is started.

Further modify the delete format to *protect* the customer number field. The customer number field must be defined with an **B** *Usage* and the other fields with an **O** *Usage.*

Complete an RPG/400 program to interactively delete records logically in the physical file. The error message **RECORD NOT FOUND** is to be displayed on line 5 of the prompt screen if the key entered is not stored in the file. When a record is found, its values are to be displayed in the delete record format. Also, move the literal DELETE to the MODE field in the delete screen.

Delete records with key value **50008** and **14000** from the physical file.

Programming Assignment 15-5: STUDENT COURSE FILE MAINTENANCE

Before this assignment is started, Assignment 14-2 must have been completed.

The following changes are required in the display file for Assignment 14-2:

1. Change the constant on line 1 to COURSE FILE MAINTENANCE.
2. Delete the constant on line 2 and center a seven-character MODE under the line 1 constant.
3. Delete the F3—**EOJ** constant and move an F2—**ENTER** constant to its position.
4. Delete the *Command Key 3* keyword.
5. Delete the **ERRMSG** keyword.
6. Define all of the fields with **B** *Usage.*

The following record format is to be added to the display file completed for Assignment 14-2:

1	HH:MM:SS .... MM/DD/YY
2	STUDENT COURSE FILE MAINTENANCE
3	
4	ENTER COMPOSITE KEY -
5	
6	STUDENT NUMBER: XXXXXXXXX COURSE NUMBER: XXXXX TERM DATE: XXXXXX
7	
8	
9	F3 - EOJ F2 - ADD F11 - UPDATE
10	F23 - DELETE F6 - INQUIRY
11	NOTES:
12	1. HIGHLIGHT ALL CONSTANTS.
13	2. UNDERLINE CONSTANT ON LINE 2.
14	3. REVERSE IMAGE THE VARIABLE FIELDS.
15	4. INCLUDE THE FOLLOWING ERRMSG FOR LINE 5:
16	DUPLICATE RECORD
17	RECORD NOT FOUND
18	5. DELETE THE SIGN IN THE STUDENT NUMBER & TERM DATE FIELDS.

Write an RPG/400 program that includes adds, update, and logical deletion maintenance and inquiry processing. The command key pressed in the prompt screen will determine the maintenance function or end-of-job routine executed.

Adds Maintenance: For *adds* maintenance, the physical file must be checked for a duplicate key (SSNO, COURS#, and TDATE composite) before the entry screen is displayed. If the record is already stored in the file, the **ERRMSG** text **DUPLICATE RECORD** must be displayed in the prompt screen.

Add Data:

SSNO	COURS#	COURNM	TDATE	INSTCD	CREDIT	MARK
011111111	ACD101	ENGLISH COMPOSITION	052295	300	3	B
011111111	DPS100	INTRO TO PROGRAMMING	121595	104	4	I
011111111	MTH100	ALGEBRA I	121595	161	3	C
011223333	DPS200	INTRO TO RPG/400	052295	221	4	A
011223333	DPS210	COBOL I	121595	221	4	B
022334444	CSC101	COMPUTER SCIENCE I	052295	190	4	B
022334444	CSC202	COMPUTER SCIENCE II	121595	189	4	F
033445555	MTH201	CALCULUS I	052295	167	5	D
044556666	CSC210	INTRO TO C	052295	200	4	A
044556666	CSC310	ADVANCED C	121595	200	4	B
055667777	DPS110	MICROCOMPUTERS I	121595	100	4	A
066778888	CSC101	COMPUTER SCIENCE I	052295	190	4	X

Update Maintenance: For *update* maintenance, the composite SSNO/ COURS#/TDATE entered from the prompt screen randomly accesses the physical file for the stored record. If it is found, the entry screen must be displayed with the related physical file's field values included. When the record is not found, the error message **RECORD NOT FOUND** must be displayed on line 5 of the prompt screen. With the exception of SSNO, COURS#, and TDATE, the user may change the value of any other field in the entry screen. Consequently, the SSNO, COURS#, and TDATE fields must be protected and the cursor positioned at the NAME field.

Update Data:

	Record 1	Record 2	Record 3	Record 4
SSNO	011111111	011233333	011111111	066778888
COURS#	DPS100	DSP200	ACD101	CSC101
COURNM			ENGLISH I	
TDATE	121595	121095	052295	
INSTCD				221
CREDIT				
MARK	C	B		F

Deletion Maintenance: For *deletion* maintenance, the composite SSNO, COURS#, and TDATE key value entered from the prompt screen randomly accesses the physical file for the stored record. If it is found, the entry screen must be displayed with the related physical file's field values included. When the record is not found, the error message **RECORD NOT FOUND** must be displayed on line 5 of the prompt screen. The SSNO, COURS#, and TDATE fields must be protected. Logically delete the records with the following composite key values:

033445555	MTH201	052295
	-and-	
044556666	CSC202	052595
SSNO	**COURS#**	**TDATE**

Inquiry Processing: For *inquiry* processing, the composite SSNO/COURS/ TDATE key must be entered in the prompt screen to access randomly the physical file for the stored record. If it is found, the second screen must be displayed with the related record's field value included. When a record is not found, the error message **RECORD NOT FOUND** must be displayed on line 5 of the prompt screen. Inquiry records with the following composite key values:

055667777	DPS110	121595
	-and-	
011111111	ACD102	052295
SSNO	**COURS#**	**TDATE**

Where indicated above, **DSPATR** keywords (i.e., protect and position cursor) must be conditioned to provide the required display result for the selected maintenance function.

Programming Assignment 15-6: PARTS INVENTORY MASTER FILE MAINTENANCE

Before this assignment is started, Assignment 14-3 must have been completed.

The following changes are required in the display file for Assignment 14-3:

1. Change the constant on line 1 to PARTS MAINTENANCE.
2. Delete the line 2 constant, and include a seven-character MODE field and center it under the line 1 constant.
2. Delete the F3—**EOJ** constant and move the F2—**ENTER** constant to its position.
3. Delete the *Command Key 3* keyword.
4. Delete the **ERRMSG** keyword.
5. Define all of the fields with **B** *Usage*.

The following record format is to be added to the display file completed for Assignment 14-3.

1	MM/DD/YY PARTS INVENTORY MAINTENANCE HH:MM:SS
2	
3	
4	ENTER PART NUMBER: XXXXX
5	
6	
7	PART NUMBER NOT FOUND
8	DUPLICATE RECORD
9	
10	
11	
12	CK3 - EOJ CK10 - ADD CK11 - UPDATE
13	
14	CK16 - INQUIRY CK23 - DELETE
15	
16	NOTES:
17	1. HIGHLIGHT ALL CONSTANTS.
18	2. REVERSE IMAGE VARIABLE.

Write an RPG/400 program that includes adds, update, and logical deletion maintenance and inquiry processing. The command key pressed in the prompt screen will determine the maintenance function or end-of-job routine executed.

Adds Maintenance: For *adds* maintenance, the physical file must be checked for a duplicate PART# key before the entry screen is displayed. If the record is already stored in the file, the **ERRMSG** text **DUPLICATE RECORD** must be displayed in the prompt screen on line 7.

Adds Data:

Part#	Part Name	Amount On Hand	Amount On Order	Avg Cost /Unit	Amount Allocated	EOQ	Safety Stock	Lead Time	Warehouse Location
A2345	AC SPARK PLUG	000000	012000	0000075	005000	001440	002000	014	ABC
B6789	FRAM OIL FILTERS	004000	001200	0000324	001875	001875	000500	031	DEF
C5555	POINT SETS	000500	000000	0000227	000000	001000	002000	015	AAA
D9876	LOCKING GAS CAP	000325	001000	0000455	000400	002400	000400	090	GHI
E3459	LIQUID CAR WASH	010224	000000	0000125	050000	004000	003000	015	BBB
C5555	ARMOR-ALL	036000	001200	0000325	004800	003000	005000	010	EFG

Update Maintenance: For *update* maintenance, the PART# entered from the prompt screen randomly accesses the physical file for the stored record. If it is found, the entry screen must be displayed with the related physical file's field values included. When the record is not found, the error message **PART NUMBER NOT FOUND** must be displayed on line 7 of the prompt screen. With the exception of PART#, the user may change all of the field values in the entry screen. Consequently, the PART# field must be protected and the cursor positioned at the PNAME field.

Update Data:

	Record 1	Record 2	Record 3
PART#	E3459	A2345	F6666
PNAME		AC SPARK PLUGS	
AMTHND		500	
AMTORD		4500	
AVGCST			
AMTALL		0	
EOQ			
SAFSTK			
LEDTIM	30		
WAREHL		CCC	DDD

Deletion Maintenance: For *deletion* maintenance, the part number key value entered from the prompt screen randomly accesses the physical file for the stored record. If it is found, the entry screen must be displayed with the related physical file's field values included. When the record is not found, the error message **PART NUMBER NOT FOUND** must be displayed on line 7 of the prompt screen. The PART# field must be protected and the cursor positioned at the PNAME field. Logically delete the records with key values **D9876** and **E4448.**

Inquiry Processing: For *inquiry* processing, the part number entered from the prompt screen randomly accesses the physical file for the stored record. If it is found, the entry screen must be displayed with the related physical file's field value included. When the record is not found, the error message **PART NUMBER NOT FOUND** must be displayed on line 7 of the prompt screen. Inquiry records with key values **B6789** and **C6666.**

Where indicated above, **DSPATR** keywords (i.e., protect and position cursor) must be conditioned to provide the required display result for the selected maintenance function.

chapter 16

Logical Files

A *logical file* is a database file used to access the data stored in one or more physical files. The features unique to logical files include the following:

1. Logical files do not contain data.
2. Access paths (indexes) may be built by logical files to process the data stored in one or more physical files in an arrival sequence or in any single or multiple field (key) value order.
3. Any physical file may be processed by any number of logical files.
4. Two or more logical files may share the same access path.
5. Omit and select criteria may be specified in a logical file to process only the required physical file data.
6. A logical file may include multiple record formats. Each format, however, must relate to one or more physical files and include at least one key field.
7. Any one logical file with multiple record formats may process the data from more than one physical file as though all the data were stored in the same physical file.
8. A logical file with multiple record formats may be used to process the data from more than one physical file. The physical file record formats accessed may be of different lengths.
9. During processing, a physical file's field attributes may be changed by a logical file. However, the data stored in the physical file will not be modified.

Logical files may be specified as either *nonjoin* or *join*. A *nonjoin* logical file processes each record individually from one or more physical files. *Join* logical files, however, create a single record from the selected fields from two or more physical files.

The type of logical file (*nonjoin* or *join*) specified is determined in the related DDS coding. In the following text, the processing logic and DDS syntax for *nonjoin* logical files are introduced first, followed by the coding requirements associated with *join* logical files.

NONJOIN LOGICAL FILES (ONE-RECORD FORMAT)

All logical files are formatted and defined by DDS coding. The DDS coding for nonjoin logical files is specified in the following order:

1. *File level* entries (optional)
2. *Record level* entries
3. *Field level* entries (optional)
4. *Key field level* entries (optional)
5. *Select/omit level* entries (optional)

Accessing One Physical File by a Logical File

Processing Logic. In the traditional computer environment, keyed files are processed in an order different from the base index either by sorting the file with a Sort/Merge utility or by specifying alternate indexes when the file is initially created. Logical files eliminate the restrictions imposed by those methods by building access paths that process a physical file(s) by any select field or fields included in the physical file's record format.

Figure 16-1 illustrates the logic associated with processing of a physical file (created with CUST# as the key) by a logical file that will process it in a STATE code order. The term *access path* refers to a separate index built and maintained by the related logical file.

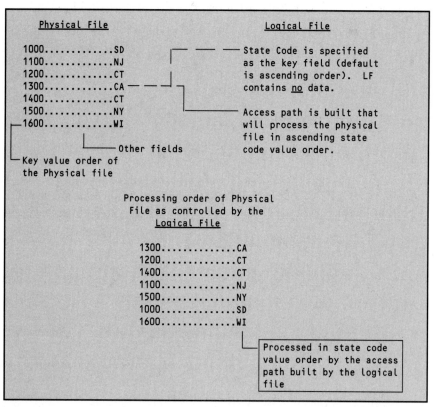

Figure 16-1 Processing logic of the access path created by a logical file (one-record format).

Data Description Specifications Coding (Nonjoin Logical File)

Logical files (**LF**) are created according to DDS syntax that is entered and stored via **SEU**. **LF** must be entered in the TYPE field on the Programmer Menu to initiate the required **SEU** format. Similar to physical and display files, logical files must be compiled and an object created. Figure 16-2 details the syntax to control the processing shown in Figure 16-1.

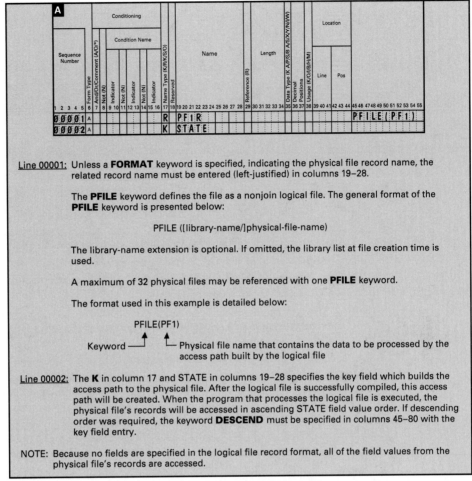

Line 00001: Unless a **FORMAT** keyword is specified, indicating the physical file record name, the related record name must be entered (left-justified) in columns 19–28.

The **PFILE** keyword defines the file as a nonjoin logical file. The general format of the **PFILE** keyword is presented below:

PFILE ([library-name/]physical-file-name)

The library-name extension is optional. If omitted, the library list at file creation time is used.

A maximum of 32 physical files may be referenced with one **PFILE** keyword.

The format used in this example is detailed below:

PFILE(PF1)

Keyword ⎯⎯⎯⎯⎯┘   └⎯ Physical file name that contains the data to be processed by the access path built by the logical file

Line 00002: The **K** in column 17 and STATE in columns 19–28 specifies the key field which builds the access path to the physical file. After the logical file is successfully compiled, this access path will be created. When the program that processes the logical file is executed, the physical file's records will be accessed in ascending STATE field value order. If descending order was required, the keyword **DESCEND** must be specified in columns 45–80 with the key field entry.

NOTE: Because no fields are specified in the logical file record format, all of the field values from the physical file's records are accessed.

Figure 16-2 DDS syntax for a logical file that processes one physical file in a STATE code order.

RPG Program Control of a Nonjoin Logical File

An RPG/400 program that processes the logical file shown in Figure 16-2 is detailed in Figure 16-3. Because the logical file is designated as a primary (**P** in column 16) of the *File Descriptions* instruction (line 100), it will access the related physical file consecutively in an ascending key value (STATE code) order.

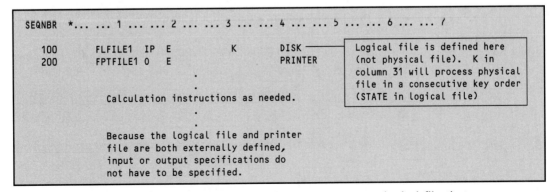

Figure 16-3 RPG/400 program that processes one logical file that accesses one physical file consecutively.

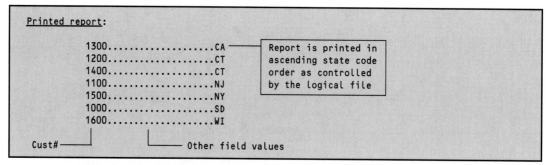

Figure 16-3 RPG/400 program that processes one logical file that accesses one physical file consecutively. (Continued)

If the physical file were to be randomly processed, the letter **P** must be replaced by an **F** (full procedural file). Then, operations including **CHAIN, READ, READE, READP, SETLL, SETGT, DELET,** and **WRITE** could be supported by the program. Because the logical and printer files are externally defined, no input or output instructions are required in the program. Calculations must include instructions to control page over-flow and any report computations.

Accessing More Than One Physical File with a Nonjoin Logical File

More than one physical file may be accessed with one logical file. If the record formats are not common to all the physical files, separate **PFILE** keywords must be specified. Figure 16-4 details the processing logic that supports the access of two physical files that have differing record formats. The records are merged for processing in the order that the physical files are specified in the logical file.

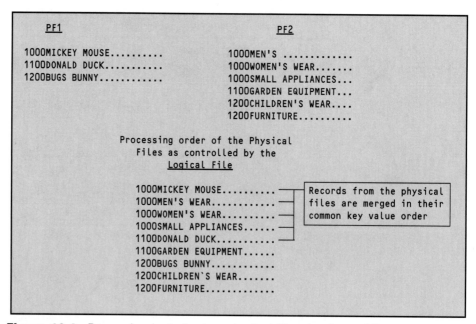

Figure 16-4 Processing logic for two physical files that have different record formats with one logical file.

The DDS coding for the logical file that controls the processing of the two physical files is presented in Figure 16-5.

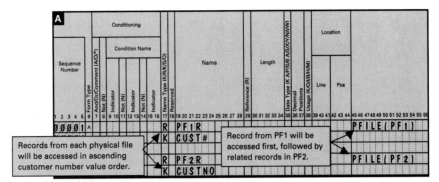

Figure 16-5 DDS coding for a logical file that processes two physical files that have different record formats.

A partial listing of the RPG/400 program that processes the logical file that accesses two physical files with different record formats is shown in Figure 16-6. The coding is identical to that explained for the processing of one physical file. The merging of the records from the two physical files is controlled by the logical file and not by the program.

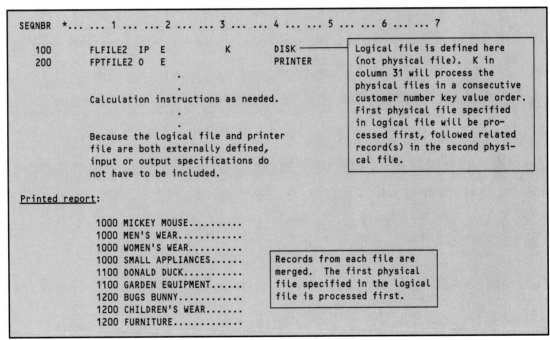

Figure 16-6 RPG/400 program that processes one logical file that accesses two physical files.

Merging Records from Two Physical Files and Resequencing One Physical File

The example illustrated in Figure 16-7 details the processing logic for a nonjoin logical file that accesses two physical files by a common key and then resequences the records in the second physical file.

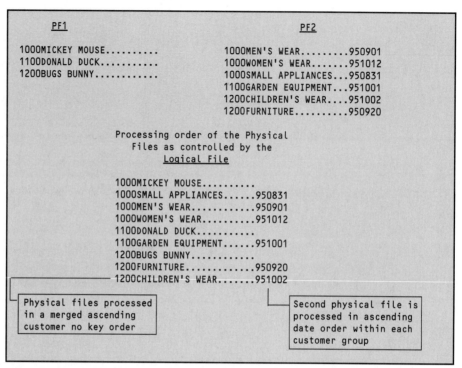

Figure 16-7 Processing logic for a logical file that processes two physical files by a common key field and then resequences the second physical file within the group.

The DDS coding for the logical file that controls the processing explained in Figure 16-7 is presented in Figure 16-8. Because the physical file PF1 does not include a date field in its record format, a ***NONE** word must be specified to offset the related **DATE** field in the record format of PF2. Then the merging process will be executed with a PF1 record first, followed by any number of related records (with the same customer number) from the PF2 file in an ascending date order.

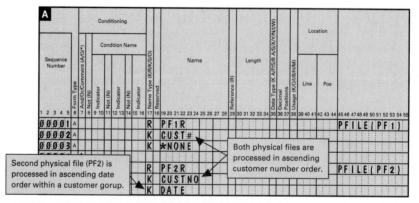

Figure 16-8 DDS coding for a logical file that processes two physical files by a common key and then resequences the records in the second physical file by a second key.

Merging Records from Two Physical Files and Resequencing Both Files within Two Groups

Figure 16-9 details the processing logic associated with the processing of two physical files and the resequencing of both files within two groups. Notice that STATE is related only to PF1, CUST# to both files, and DATE only to PF2.

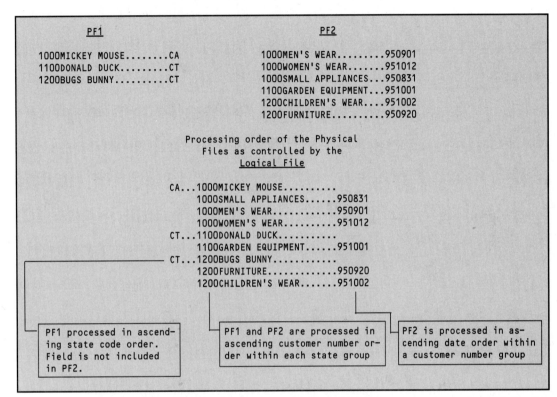

Figure 16-9 Processing logic for a logical file that processes two physical files by three key fields.

The DDS coding that supports the processing shown in Figure 16-9 is detailed in Figure 16-10. When a related key field is missing in one of the physical files, the special

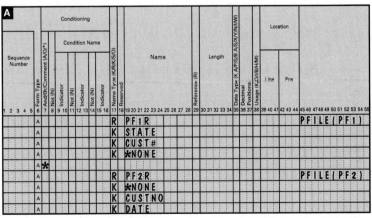

Figure 16-10 DDS coding for a logical file that processes two physical files by three key fields.

word ***NONE** is included in that position. The effect of this coding on the order of processing is as follows:

		Key Position in DDS	
Physical File		**Coding**	
	1	**2**	**3**
PF1	STATE	CUST#	*NONE
PF2	*NONE	CUSTNO	DATE

The processing sequence may be parallel to that of sorting, with STATE/*NONE as the major field level, CUST#/CUSTNO as the intermediate field level, and *NONE/DATE as the minor field level.

Multiple Physical Files Accessed with One Logical File Record

When a logical file record accesses more than one physical file in a single **PFILE** keyword, the record formats must be identical to each physical file. In the example shown in Figure 16-11, two physical files that include transaction records for two separate weeks are merged and processed in an ascending customer number order and in a descending date order within a customer group.

```
            WEEK1                                    WEEK2

1100JEWELRY.........950825          1000MEN'S WEAR ........950901
1000MEN'S SHOES.....950826          1000WOMEN'S WEAR.......950912
1200CARPETING.......950827          1000SMALL APPLIANCES...950930
1000COSMETICS.......950828          1100GARDEN EQUIPMENT...950902
                                    1200CHILDREN'S WEAR....950905
                                    1200FURNITURE.........950920

               Processing order of the Physical
                   Files as controlled by the
                          Logical File

              1000SMALL APPLIANCES......950930
              1000WOMEN'S WEAR..........950912
              1000MEN'S WEAR...........950901
              1000COSMETICS............950828
              1000MEN'S SHOES..........950826
              1100GARDEN EQUIPMENT......950902
              1100JEWELRY..............950825
              1200FURNITURE............950920
              1200CHILDREN'S WEAR.......950905
              1200CARPETING............950827

  Physical files are processed in      Physical files are pro-
  a merged ascending customer          cessed in a descending
  number order (major field)           date order (minor field)
                                       within each merged cust-
                                       omer number group
```

Figure 16-11 Processing logic for the access of two physical files with identical record formats by a logical file that includes one **PFILE** keyword.

The syntax included in a logical file to support the merging of two physical files that have identical record formats is detailed in Figure 16-12. The first file specified in the **PFILE** keyword will be processed first.

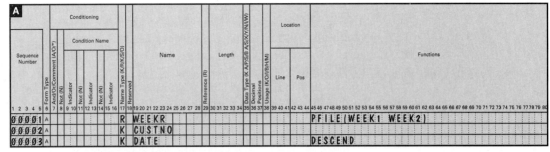

Figure 16-12 DDS coding for a logical file that processes two physical files that have identical record formats with one **PFILE** keyword.

Selecting Fields from a Physical File

The previous examples of logical files have assumed that all the fields from the physical files are accessed. This default action may be changed by specifying only select fields from the physical file in the related logical file record format. The DDS syntax for a logical file with this control is shown in Figure 16-13.

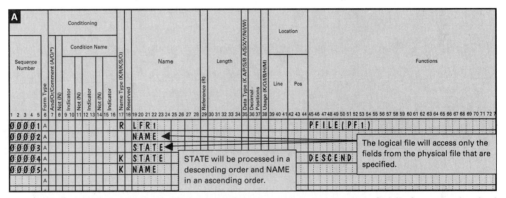

Figure 16-13 Logical file syntax for accessing only select fields from a physical file and not the complete record format.

The syntax in the RPG/400 program to process a logical file that accesses select fields from a physical file is identical to the examples previously shown.

Nonjoin Logical File Summary

Logical files do not include data. Their function is to build access paths to one or more related physical files that will process the data in an order different from that specified by the physical file(s).

The processing of one physical file by a logical file may be compared to that of sorting. Any field(s) included in the physical file may be specified as a key (or keys) in the logical file. This control will process the physical file in any required order by any field or field values.

In addition, the base key sequence of a physical file may be ignored and the file processed in an arrival sequence by a logical file. This processing is controlled by not specifying any key field in the related logical file.

Unless otherwise controlled in an RPG/400 program, the records from two or more physical files are sorted and merged in an order controlled by fields referenced as keys in the logical file.

Nonjoin logical files may specify more than one record format. If two or more physical files with *different* record formats are to be accessed by a logical file, separate **PFILE** keywords must be specified. When the record formats are the same, only one **PFILE** keyword is required. A maximum of 32 physical files may be referenced in one **PFILE** keyword.

When two or more physical files with different record formats are accessed by a logical file, ***NONE** may be specified as a key field substitute for any of the following conditions:

1. The related key fields from the physical files do not have the same attributes.
2. The key fields from the physical files have the same attributes, but they are not to be merged and sequenced together.

APPLICATION PROGRAM: PROCESSING THREE PHYSICAL FILES WITH A NONJOIN LOGICAL FILE

The specifications presented in Figure 16-14 detail the processing requirements for an RPG/400 program that reads a logical file that accesses three physical files.

PROGRAM SPECIFICATIONS — Page 1 of 1

Program Name: Credit card report — Program-ID: CH22P1 — Written By: S. Myers

Purpose: Generate a credit card activity report — Approved By: The Boss

Input files (directory names):
Physical Files CUSMAST, CUSTRAN, and CUSPAID
Logical File CUSHIST

Output files (directory names):
QSYSPRT

Processing Narrative:

Create a logical file that will access the three physical files, CUSMAST, CUSTRAN, and CUSPAID, in an ascending order by customer number and transaction date. Complete an RPG/400 program to process the logical file and generate a report that includes information from all of the physical files.

Input:

An access path is to be built by a logical file that processes the three physical files in a customer number/transaction date composite key order. Because the CUSMAST record format does not include a transaction date field, the keyword ***NONE** is to be substituted in the composite key for that file.

Customer number and transaction date are to be used as the keys for the CUSTRAN file, and customer number and payment date for the CUSPAID file.

For all of the composite keys, customer number is the major key element (specified first) and date the minor.

The CUSMAST file includes address, credit limit, and beginning balance for each account. CUSTRAN contains records for charge transactions that have occurred for each account. CUSPAID includes records that store information for payments on account.

Include each physical file's record format name in the input specifications (columns 7–14). Assign a unique record identifying indicator to each record format and specify the related customer number field with the control level indicator **L1**.

Processing:

Define the logical file in a *File Description* statement as an input, primary, and externally defined keyed file. The logical file is to be processed by the normal RPG/400 cycle (not with a **READ** operation). Include separate internal subroutines in the program for charge and payment processing. Determine the ending balance for each account by adding charge amounts to the beginning balance and subtracting payments.

Output:

Generate the report format shown in the supplemental printer spacing chart. The printing of each customer group is to be controlled at **L1** time.

Figure 16-14 Specifications for an RPG/400 program that processes a logical file that accesses three physical files.

The system flow chart in Figure 16-15 shows that three physical files, CUSMAST, CUSTRAN, and CUSPAID, are accessed by the logical file CUSHIST, which is read by the program CH22P1.

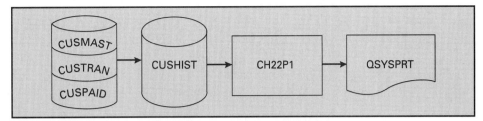

Figure 16-15 System flowchart for an RPG/400 program that processes a logical file that accesses three physical files.

Figure 16-16 shows the record formats for the three physical files (CUSMAST, CUSTRAN, and CUSPAID) accessed by the logical file CUSHIST. Because the *Data Description* (top section) is identical for all the physical files (except for the file name), it has been omitted from all of the listings. Observe that all the files have the customer number as the *major* key field, with CUSTRAN and CUSPAID defined with transaction date as a *minor* key field.

A printer chart that details the format of the report and a listing generated by the program that processes a nonjoin logical file are presented in Figure 16-17.

```
CUSMAST Physical File Description:

                            Data Description Source

SEQNBR  *...+....1....+....2....+....3....+....4....+....5....+....6....+....7....+....8  Date

  100    A* CUSMAST FILE                                                      08/11/95
  200    A        R MASTR                                                     08/11/95
  300    A          CUST#      5                                             08/11/95
  400    A          NAME      15                                             08/11/95
  500    A          ADDR      20                                             08/11/95
  600    A          CITY      10                                             08/11/95
  700    A          STATE      2                                             08/11/95
  800    A          ZIP        5 0                                           08/11/95
  900    A          LIMIT      5 0                                           08/11/95
 1000    A          BEGBAL     7 2                                           08/11/95
 1100    A        K CUST#                                                    08/11/95


CUSTRAN Physical File Description:

SEQNBR  *...+....1....+....2....+....3....+....4....+....5....+....6....+....7....+....8  Date

  100    A* CUSTRAN FILE                                                     08/11/95
  200    A        R CHARGR                                                   08/11/95
  300    A          CUSTNO     5                                             08/11/95
  400    A          NAME      15                                             08/11/95
  500    A          PAYEE     12                                             08/11/95
  600    A          PADDR     15                                             08/11/95
  700    A          PCITY     12                                             08/11/95
  800    A          PSTAT      2                                             08/11/95
  900    A          PZIP       5 0                                           08/11/95
 1000    A          AMT        7 2                                           08/11/95
 1100    A          CDATE      6 0                                           08/11/95
 1200    A        K CUSTNO                                                   08/11/95
 1300    A        K CDATE                                                    08/11/95


CUSPAID Physical File Description:

SEQNBR  *...+....1....+....2....+....3....+....4....+....5....+....6....+....7....+....8  Date

  100* CUSPAID FILE                                                          08/11/95
  200         R PAIDR                                                        08/11/95
  300           CUSTN      5                                                 08/11/95
  400           NAME      15                                                 08/11/95
  500           PAMT       7 2                                               08/11/95
  600           PDATE      6 0                                               08/11/95
  700         K CUSTN                                                        08/11/95
  800         K PDATE                                                        08/11/95
```

Figure 16-16 Record formats of the physical files accessed by the logical file CUSHIST.

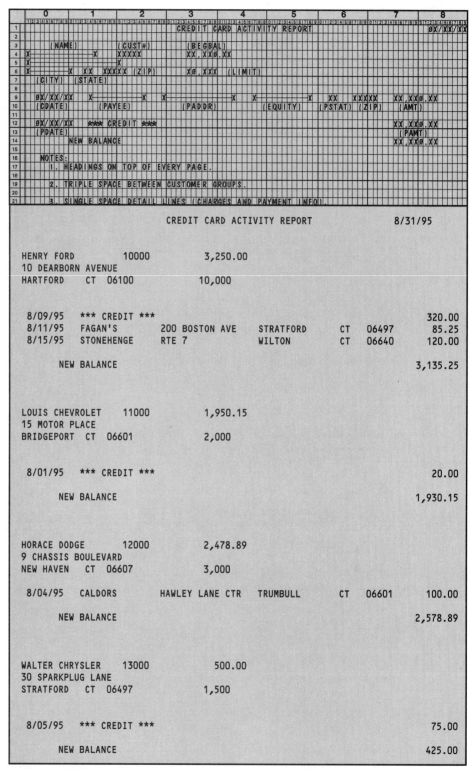

Figure 16-17 Printer spacing chart and report generated by the program that processes a nonjoin logical file.

Nonjoin Logical File Syntax

The syntax for the nonjoin logical file that accesses three physical files is explained in Figure 16-18.

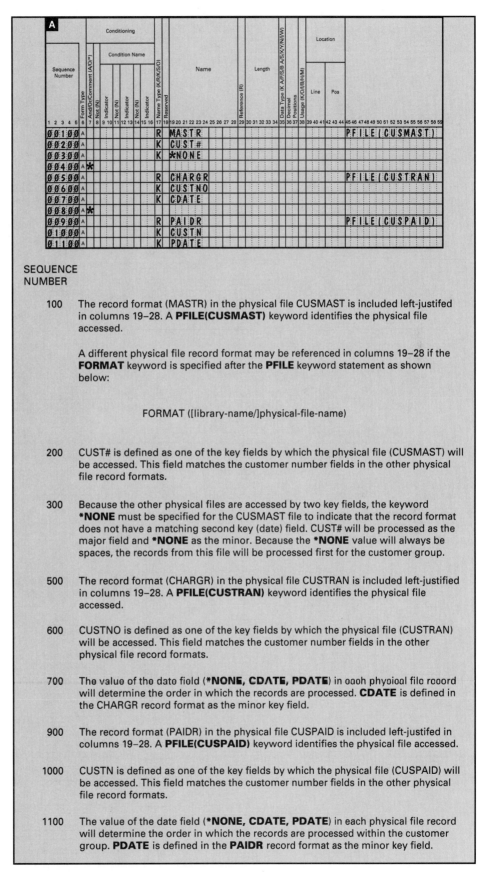

SEQUENCE
NUMBER

100 The record format (MASTR) in the physical file CUSMAST is included left-justifed in columns 19–28. A **PFILE(CUSMAST)** keyword identifies the physical file accessed.

A different physical file record format may be referenced in columns 19–28 if the **FORMAT** keyword is specified after the **PFILE** keyword statement as shown below:

FORMAT ([library-name/]physical-file-name)

200 CUST# is defined as one of the key fields by which the physical file (CUSMAST) will be accessed. This field matches the customer number fields in the other physical file record formats.

300 Because the other physical files are accessed by two key fields, the keyword ***NONE** must be specified for the CUSMAST file to indicate that the record format does not have a matching second key (date) field. CUST# will be processed as the major field and ***NONE** as the minor. Because the ***NONE** value will always be spaces, the records from this file will be processed first for the customer group.

500 The record format (CHARGR) in the physical file CUSTRAN is included left-justifed in columns 19–28. A **PFILE(CUSTRAN)** keyword identifies the physical file accessed.

600 CUSTNO is defined as one of the key fields by which the physical file (CUSTRAN) will be accessed. This field matches the customer number fields in the other physical file record formats.

700 The value of the date field (***NONE, CDATE, PDATE**) in each physical file record will determine the order in which the records are processed. **CDATE** is defined in the CHARGR record format as the minor key field.

900 The record format (PAIDR) in the physical file CUSPAID is included left-justifed in columns 19–28. A **PFILE(CUSPAID)** keyword identifies the physical file accessed.

1000 CUSTN is defined as one of the key fields by which the physical file (CUSPAID) will be accessed. This field matches the customer number fields in the other physical file record formats.

1100 The value of the date field (***NONE, CDATE, PDATE**) in each physical file record will determine the order in which the records are processed within the customer group. **PDATE** is defined in the **PAIDR** record format as the minor key field.

Figure 16-18 Syntax for a nonjoin logical file that accesses three physical files.

The first listing (Expanded Listing not shown) generated from compilation of the nonjoin logical file processed by the application program is presented in Figure 16-19.

```
File name . . . . . . . . . . . . . . . . . . . . . :  CUSHIST
   Library name  . . . . . . . . . . . . . . . . . :  SMYERS
File attribute  . . . . . . . . . . . . . . . . . . :  Logical
Source file containing DDS  . . . . . . . . . . . . :  QDDSSRC
   Library name  . . . . . . . . . . . . . . . . . :  SMYERS
Source member containing DDS  . . . . . . . . . . . :  CUSHIST
Source member last changed  . . . . . . . . . . . . :  10/11/95  10:30:33
Source listing options  . . . . . . . . . . . . . . :  *SOURCE    *LIST     *NOSECLVL
DDS generation severity level . . . . . . . . . . . :  20
DDS flagging severity level . . . . . . . . . . . . :  00
File type . . . . . . . . . . . . . . . . . . . . . :  *DATA
Authority . . . . . . . . . . . . . . . . . . . . . :  *LIBCRTAUT
Replace file  . . . . . . . . . . . . . . . . . . . :  *NO
Text  . . . . . . . . . . . . . . . . . . . . . . . :  ch 16 - logical file - nonjoin
Compiler  . . . . . . . . . . . . . . . . . . . . . :  IBM AS/400 Data Description Processor


                              Data Description Source


SEQNBR  *...+....1....+....2....+....3....+....4....+....5....+....6....+....7....+....8  Date

    100    A      R MASTR                PFILE(CUSMAST)                          10/11/95
    200    A      K CUST#                                                        10/11/95
    300    A      K *NONE                                                        10/11/95
    400    *                                                                     10/11/95
    500    A      R CHARGR               PFILE(CUSTRAN)                          10/11/95
    600    A      K CUSTNO                                                       10/11/95
    700    A      K TDATE                                                        10/11/95
    800    *                                                                     10/11/95
    900    A      R PAIDR                PFILE(CUSPAID)                          10/11/95
   1000    A      K CUSTN                                                        10/11/95
   1100    A      K DATE                                                         10/11/95
```

Figure 16-19 First listing (expanded not shown) generated from compilation of the nonjoin logical file.

The processing logic controlled by the nonjoin logical file read by the application program is presented in Figure 16-20.

```
     CUSMAST              CUSTRAN                 CUSPAID

     10000..........      10000.......081195      10000.......080995
     11000..........      12000.......080495      11000.......080195
     12000..........      10000.......081595      13000.......080595
     13000..........


               Order the records are processed


             10000            -  CUSMAST record
             10000080995      -  CUSPAID record
             10000081195      -  CUSTRAN record
             10000081595      -  CUSTRAN record
             11000            -  CUSMAST record
             11000080195      -  CUSPAID record
             12000            -  CUSMAST record
             12000080495      -  CUSTRAN record
             13000            -  CUSMAST record
             13000080595      -  CUSPAID record


     The logical file controls the processing of three physical
     files in ascending customer number order and in an ascending
     date order within each customer group.  Because the value of
     the *NONE field for the CUSMAST record is spaces, a record from
     the master file is processed first for each customer group.
     Then, the records from the other two physical files are
     selected for processing in an ascending date value order.
```

Figure 16-20 Processing logic for the application program that accesses a nonjoin logical file.

Source Program Coding

A compile listing of the application program that reads a logical file that accesses three physical files is detailed in Figure 16-21.

```
SEQUENCE                                                                        IND  DO
NUMBER    *...1....+....2....+....3....+....4....+....5....+....6....+....7...*  USE  NUM
                          S o u r c e   L i s t i n g
   100    * This program processes three physical files accessed by a
   200    * non-join logical file......
          H
   300    FCUSHIST IP  E           K           DISK
          RECORD FORMAT(S): LIBRARY SMYERS FILE CUSHIST.
                  EXTERNAL FORMAT MASTR RPG NAME MASTR
                  EXTERNAL FORMAT CHARGR RPG NAME CHARGR
                  EXTERNAL FORMAT PAIDR RPG NAME PAIDR
   400    FQSYSPRT O   F         132     OF      PRINTER
   500    IMASTR        01
   600    I                                            CUST# L1
   600    INPUT  FIELDS FOR RECORD MASTR FILE CUSHIST FORMAT MASTR.
A000001                                      P   1   30CUST# L1
A000002                                          4   18 NAME
A000003                                         19   38 ADDR
A000004                                         39   48 CITY
A000005                                         49   50 STATE
A000006                                      P  51  530ZIP
A000007                                      P  54  560LIMIT
A000008                                      P  57  602BEGBAL
   700    ICHARGR       02
   800    I                                            CUSTNOL1
   800    INPUT  FIELDS FOR RECORD CHARGR FILE CUSHIST FORMAT CHARGR.
B000001                                      P   1   30CUSTNOL1
B000002                                          4   18 NAME
B000003                                         19   30 PAYEE
B000004                                         31   45 PADDR
B000005                                         46   57 PCITY
B000006                                         58   59 PSTATE
B000007                                      P  60  620PZIP
B000008                                      P  63  662PAMT
B000009                                      P  67  700TDATE
   900    IPAIDR        03
  1000    I                                            CUSTN L1
  1000    INPUT  FIELDS FOR RECORD PAIDR FILE CUSHIST FORMAT PAIDR.
C000001                                      P   1   30CUSTN L1
C000002                                          4   18 NAME
C000003                                      P  19  222AMT
C000004                                      P  23  260DATE
  1100    C       *INL1       IFEQ *ON                ctrl break?         B001
  1200    C                   Z-ADDBEGBAL  OWED    72 store begbal        001
  1300    C                   EXCPTHDGING             print headings       001
  1400    C                   ENDIF                  end IF statment      E001
  1500    C       *INO2       CASEQ*ON     CHARSR     SR branch if on
  1600    C       *INO3       CASEQ*ON     PAYTSR     SR branch if on
  1700    C                   ENDCS                  end CA3 group
  1800    *
  1900    C       CHARSR      BEGSR                  begin SR
  2000    C                   EXCPTCHARGE            print chrg line
  2100    C                   ADD  PAMT     OWED      add to beg bal
  2200    C                   ENDSR                  end charsr SR
  2300    *
  2400    C       PAYTSR      BEGSR                  begin SR
  2500    C                   EXCPTPAYMT             print payt line
  2600    C                   SUB  AMT      OWED      reduce beg bal
  2700    C                   ENDSR                  end paytsr SR
  2800    OQSYSPRT H  301      1P
  2900    O       OR          OF
  3000    O                                    51 'CREDIT CARD ACTIVITY'
  3100    O                                    58 'REPORT'
```

Figure 16-21   Compile listing of an RPG/400 program that reads a nonjoin logical file that accesses three physical files.

```
3200  0                              UDATE Y   80
3300  0            E  1               HDGING
3400  0                               NAME     15
3500  0                               CUST#    24
3600  0                               BEGBAL1  42
3700  0            E  1               HDGING
3800  0                               ADDR     20
3900  0            E  3               HDGING
4000  0                               CITY     10
4100  0                               STATE    14
4200  0                               ZIP      21
4300  0                               LIMIT 1  39
4400  0            E  1               CHARGE
4500  0                               TDATE Y   10
4600  0                               PAYEE     25
4700  0                               PADDR     43
4800  0                               PCITY     58
4900  0                               PSTATE    63
5000  0                               PZIP      71
5100  0                               PAMT  1   83
5200  0            E  1               PAYMT
5300  0                               DATE  Y   10
5400  0                                         27 '*** CREDIT ***'
5500  0                               AMT   1   83
5600  0            T 13      L1
5700  0                                         20 'NEW BALANCE'
5800  0                               OWED  1   83
```

SEQUENCE
NUMBER

300 -
400   The logical file (CUSHIST) is defined as processed by the normal RPG/400 logic cycle (**P** in column
       16) and externally defined (**E** in column 19). In addition, the letter **K** in column 31 defines the logi-
       cal file as keyed. Printed output is program-defined.

500 -
1000   Entries in the File/Record Name field (colums 7–14) reference the related physical file record
       names (MASTR, CHARGR, and PAIDR). The field names specified (CUST#, CUSTNO, and CUSTN)
       are included for **L1** control level break processing.

1100   The status of the **L1** control level indicator is tested by this **IF** statement. If true, the heading lines
       (HDGING) for the next customer group is output by the **EXCPT** operation on line 1100.

1200   The BEGBAL value is saved by moving it into the new field OWED which is incremented by
       charges and decremented by paid transactions.

1300   The **EXCPT** instruction controls the printing of the HDGING lines for statements 3300–4300.

1400   This **ENDIF** operation indicates end of the **IF** statement on line 1100.

1500   The status of *Record Identifying Indicator* (**02**) is tested. If it is "ON", the internal subroutine
       CHARSR is branched to where charge transactions are processed.

1600   The status of *Record Identifying Indicator* (**03**) is tested. If it is "ON", the internal subroutine
       PAYTSR is branched to where payment transactions are processed.

1700   A required **ENDCS** operation indicates the end of the **CAS** group.

1900-
2200   The CHARGR subroutine, which is executed when a CHARGR record is processed (**02** indicator is
       set on by input control), controls the printing of a CHARGE record at exception time. The ADD in-
       struction on line 2100 increments the beginning balance (OWED) by the transaction amount.

2400-
2700   The PAYTSR subroutine, which is executed when a PAIDR record is processed (**03** indicator is set
       on by input control), controls the printing of a PAYMT record at exception time. The **SUB** instruc-
       tion on line 2600 decreases the beginning balance (OWED) by the transaction amount.

Figure 16-21 Compile listing of an RPG/400 program that reads a nonjoin logical
file that accesses three physical files. (Continued)

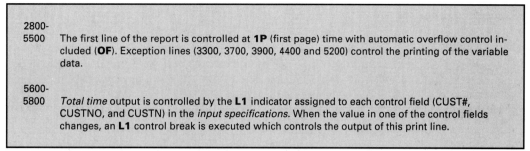

2800- 5500	The first line of the report is controlled at **1P** (first page) time with automatic overflow control included (**OF**). Exception lines (3300, 3700, 3900, 4400 and 5200) control the printing of the variable data.
5600- 5800	*Total time* output is controlled by the **L1** indicator assigned to each control field (CUST#, CUSTNO, and CUSTN) in the *input specifications.* When the value in one of the control fields changes, an **L1** control break is executed which controls the output of this print line.

Figure 16-21   Compile listing of an RPG/400 program that reads a nonjoin logical file that accesses three physical files. (Continued)

JOIN LOGICAL FILES

Join logical files concatenate the fields from the records in two or more physical files and process them as one record. The advantages of *join logical files* include the following:

1. *Increased productivity.* Because multiple **READ** operations are not required with join logical files, the coding in RPG/400 programs is simplified.

2. *Improved performance.* Because a join logical file builds only one record for processing, program performance is improved. Only one **READ** (or **CHAIN**) operation has to be specified instead of the multiple **READs** (or **CHAINs**) required for nonjoin logical file processing. Furthermore, if a program has fewer open data paths, the job's **PAG** (*Process Access Group*) size is reduced. This saves main storage and facilitates faster program loading.

3. *More flexible database.* As compared to nonjoin logical files, join logical files parallel the design and processing features related to a true database structure. Hence, more complex accesses may be built around the existing database.

Features of Join Logical Files.   The features unique to join logical files supported by IBM's AS/400 computer are the following:

1. Join logical files are **READ** only files and may not be used in update processing.

2. Join logical files support only *inner* and *left outer joins. Outer join processing* is not supported.

3. They may reference from 2 to 32 physical files. The physical files specified may be in key or arrival sequence. A common key (or keys) is not required to link the files. In addition, because the same physical file may be specified as the base file more than once, it may be joined to itself.

4. Any key field specified must be included in the primary file.

5. *Select/omit* criteria may be specified for any field in a join logical file.

Join Logical File Keywords.   The steps in building a join logical file include the following:

1. Name all the physical files that will be accessed by the join logical file.

2. Specify the fields that will relate the physical files to each other.

3. Define all the fields from each physical file that will be included in the join logical file's record format.

The creation of a join logical file depends on a knowledge of the seven keywords:

JFILE, JOIN, JFLD, JREF, JDUPDEQ, JDFTVAL, and **DYNSLT.** The function and syntax of each of these keywords are explained in the following paragraphs.

JFILE Keyword (Record Level):   This record level (which requires the letter **R** in column 17 of the *Data Description* statement) keyword is used to identify the physical files to be accessed in a join logical file. At least 2 physical files and no more than 32 may be specified in one **JFILE** keyword.

The general format of the **JFILE** keyword follows:

JFILE([library-name/]physical-file-name [..32])

The first file included in a **JFILE** keyword is called the primary file, and it is this file from which the join processing starts.

When a user formats a **JFILE** keyword, the physical file that has the smallest number of data records should be specified first (as the primary file). The sequence in which the physical files are specified in the **JFILE** keyword can affect both performance and the results of join logical file processing.

JOIN Keyword (Join Level):   The **JOIN** keyword is required in the coding for a join logical file to join two physical files for processing. If three physical files are accessed by the join logical file, two **JOIN** keywords must be specified; if four physical files are accessed, three **JOIN** statements must be included, and so forth. The general format of a **JOIN** keyword is as follows:

JOIN(from-file to-file)

The from-file and to-file entries may be the names or relative numbers of two physical files that were included in the **JFILE** keyword. In the first example that follows, relative numbers 1 and 2 are used in the alternative coding in the **JOIN** keyword. To join the third file to the master file, the second example uses 1 and 3.

JFILE(CUSMAST CUSTRAN CUSPAID)

The **JOIN** keyword may be formatted as:

JOIN(CUSMAST CUSTRAN) -or- JOIN(1 2)

and

JOIN(CUSMAST CUSPAID) -or- JOIN(1 3)

When duplicate physical file names are specified in a **JFILE** keyword, the **JOIN** keyword must use the relative number format. Definition of the **JOIN** keyword requires that the letter **J** be included in column 17 of the DDS statement.

JFLD Keyword (Join Level):   A **JFLD** keyword identifies the *from* field and the *to* field that will join two physical files. The related fields must have the same attributes (type, size, and decimal positions), but they do not need to have the same name. Any from field and to field that does not have the same attributes may be redefined in the join logical file. Any fields specified in a **JFLD** keyword must have been defined in the related physical file. Consequently, join fields do not have to be defined in the join logical file. The general format of the **JFLD** keyword is

JFLD(from-field-name to-field-name)

Notice that only two fields may be specified in a **JFLD** keyword. If the physical files are to be joined by other fields, then additional **JFLD** keywords must be defined.

JREF Keyword (Field Level):   The **JREF** keyword is used when the physical files accessed by the join logical file have some or all of the same field names. **JREF** is used to identify the physical file in which the field is related. The general format of the **JREF** keyword is

JREF(file-name|relative-file-number)

A file name or the relative position of the file's name in the **JFILE** keyword may be included in the **JREF** statement. The related field name must be entered in the Name field (columns 19–28) of the DDS statement.

JDUPSEQ Keyword (Join Level):   A **JDUPSEQ** keyword specifies the order in which the records from physical files that have duplicate join fields will be processed. The general format of the **JDUPSEQ** keyword is

JDUPSEQ(sequencing-file-name[*DESCEND])

If ***DESCEND** is included in the keyword, the duplicate records (same field value) will be retrieved in a descending order instead of an ascending default order.

JDFTVAL Keyword (File Level):   The **JDFTVAL** keyword enables primary file records that do not have matching secondary file records to be included in the join. Without the **JDFTVAL** keyword, any primary file record that did not have a matching secondary file record would be skipped. The general format of the **JDFTVAL** keyword is

JDFTVAL

DYNSLT Keyword (File Level):   The **DYNSLT** keyword is required when the **JDFTVAL** keyword is specified in a join logical file. When specified, it causes record selection to occur when a record is read instead of after it is stored. The general format of the **DYNSLT** keyword is

DYNSLT

JOIN Logical File Coding Examples

The DDS coding for the first join logical file example is shown in Figure 16-22. Two physical files (HISTORY and COURSES) are accessed by the join logical file and joined by student number fields that are common to both files. The processing result indicates that the physical files are retrieved in an ascending student number order. Multiple records from the COURSES file are grouped within their related student number.

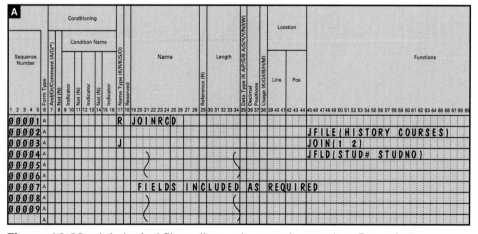

Figure 16-22   Join logical file coding and processing results—Example 1.

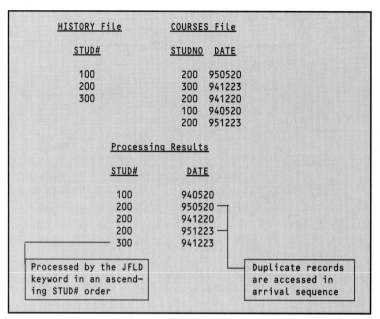

Figure 16-22 Join logical file coding and processing results—Example 1. (Continued)

The processing results in Figure 16-22 do not indicate a printed report but rather the order in which the records from the physical files are retrieved by the join logical file. Only one record will be read from the HISTORY (primary) file and stored. Then, one or more records will be retrieved from the COURSES file in an arrival sequence until the student number changes.

The DDS coding for the second join logical file example is shown in Figure 16-23. Two physical files (HISTORY and COURSES) are accessed by the join logical file and joined by student number fields that are common to both files. In addition, the **JDUPSEQ(DATE)** statement accesses the records from the COURSES file in an ascending date order within a student group as shown in the processing results in Figure 16-23.

As shown in Figure 16-23, the only change in the join logical file syntax from example 1 is the addition of a **JDUPSEQ** keyword. When more than one record for a student is retrieved from the COURSES file, the **JDUPSEQ(DATE)** keyword indicates that the records from that file are to be processed in an ascending date order within the related student number group.

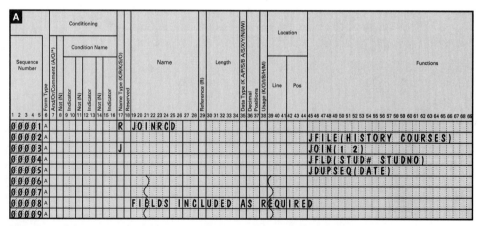

Figure 16-23 Join logical file coding and processing results—Example 2.

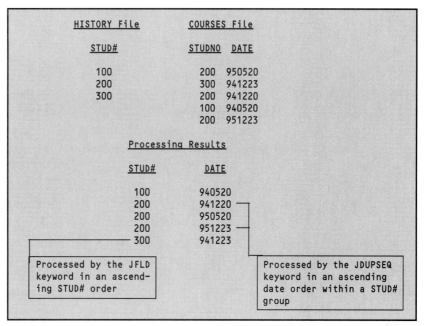

Figure 16-23 Join logical file coding and processing results—Example 2. (Continued)

If you will relate the HISTORY file record to the miles digit on an automobile's speedometer and regard the COURSES records as incrementations of tenths of a mile, you may have a clearer understanding of join logical file processing.

APPLICATION PROGRAM: PROCESSING TWO PHYSICAL FILES WITH A JOIN LOGICAL FILE

An application program that processes two physical files with a join logical file is presented in the following paragraphs. Except for only one transaction file, the documentation for this application is identical to that of the previously discussed nonjoin logical file program. Consequently, only the format of the transaction (TRANS) physical file is presented in the source listing in Figure 16-24.

```
                                     Data Description Source
SEQNBR  *...+....1....+....2....+....3....+....4....+....5....+....6....+....7....+....8
  100     A          R CHARGR
  200     A            CUSTNO        5 0
  300     A            NAME         15
  400     A            PAYEE        12
  500     A            PADDR        15
  600     A            PCITY        12
  700     A            PSTAT         2
  800     A            PZIP          5 0
  900     A            AMT           7 2
 1000     A            DATE          6 0
 1100     A            CODE          1
 1200     A          K CUSTNO
 1300     A          K DATE
```

Figure 16-24 Format of the transaction file.

Join Logical File Syntax

Figure 16-25 details the syntax for the join logical file processed by the application program. Notice the sequence in which the join logical file keywords are specified. Syntax errors will result in compilation if the keywords are not specified in the indicated order.

```
Seq #    Form  Name      Name Type  Name      Functions
         Type            (col 17)
00001    A                          JDFTVAL
00002    A               R          CHISTR
00003    A                          JFILE(CUSMAST TRANS)
00004    A               J          JOIN(CUSMAST TRANS)
00005    A                          JFLD(CUST# CUSTNO)
00006    A                          JDUPSEQ(DATE)
00007    A                          NAME      JREF(1)
00008    A                          CUST#
00009    A                          BEGBAL
00010    A                          ADDR
00011    A                          CITY
00012    A                          STATE
00013    A                          ZIP
00014    A                          LIMIT
00015    A                          DATE
00016    A                          PAYEE
00017    A                          PADDR
00018    A                          PCITY
00019    A                          PSTAT
00020    A                          PZIP
00021    A                          AMT
00022    A                          CODE
00023    A               K          CUST#
```

SEQUENCE NUMBER

00001   The **JDFTVAL** statement controls the processing of a primary (physical) file record when the secondary (physical) file does not have a related record (same key field value(s)).

00002   The letter **R** in column 17 identifies this entry as the join logical file's record format. Unlike nonjoin logical files, this entry cannot be a record name from one of the physical files.

Only _one_ record format name may be specified for a join logical file.

00003   The **JFILE** keyword joins CUSMAST and TRANS for access by the join logical file. This entry must be made at the record level on the same line as the record name or as a separate entry on the next coding line.

The first file specified in the **JFILE** keyword is the primary file and the other file, the secondary.

00004   The letter **J** must be entered in column 17 with a **JOIN** keyword. This entry identifies which pair of physical files are to be joined for processing. At least one **JOIN** keyword is required in a join logical file.

00005   The **JFLD** keyword joins the two files specified in the preceding **JOIN** statement by common fields (CUST# and CUSTNO). This entry must immediately follow a related **JOIN** keyword.

00006   The **JDUPSEQ(DATE)** controls the processing of records from the TRANS file in an ascending transaction date order within the customer group.

00007 to 00022   Because the NAME field is included in the record formats of the CUSMAST and TRANS files, a **JREF(1)** keyword must be specified to indicate from which physical file the value is to be used. The **1** entry included with the **JREF** keyword indicates the file referenced by its relative position in the **JFILE** keyword.

Figure 16-25   Syntax for a join logical file that accesses two physical files.

The fields to be included in the join logical file processing are specified in these entries. Lines 00007 through 00014 include fields from the CUSMAST file with the remaining fields from the TRANS file.

00023 CUST# is defined as the key field which will cause the join logical file to process both files in ascending customer number order. However, because of the **JDUPSEQ** keyword, transaction records will be accessed in an ascending date order within the customer group.

Figure 16-25 Syntax for a join logical file that accesses two physical files. (Continued)

The first listing (expanded not shown) generated from compilation of the join logical file is presented in Figure 16-26.

```
5738SS1 V2R2M0  920925              Data Description            SMYERS/CH16LF2
 File name . . . . . . . . . . . . . . . . . . . . . :  CH16LF2
   Library name  . . . . . . . . . . . . . . . . . . :  SMYERS
 File attribute  . . . . . . . . . . . . . . . . . . :  Logical
 Source file containing DDS  . . . . . . . . . . . . :  QDDSSRC
   Library name  . . . . . . . . . . . . . . . . . . :  SMYERS
 Source member containing DDS  . . . . . . . . . . . :  CH16LF2
 Source member last changed  . . . . . . . . . . . . :  10/11/95  13:03:20
 Source listing options  . . . . . . . . . . . . . . :  *SOURCE    *LIST     *NOSECLVL
 DDS generation severity level . . . . . . . . . . . :  20
 DDS flagging severity level . . . . . . . . . . . . :  00
 File type . . . . . . . . . . . . . . . . . . . . . :  *DATA
 Authority . . . . . . . . . . . . . . . . . . . . . :  *LIBCRTAUT
 Replace file  . . . . . . . . . . . . . . . . . . . :  *NO
 Text  . . . . . . . . . . . . . . . . . . . . . . . :  ch16 - join logical file
 Compiler  . . . . . . . . . . . . . . . . . . . . . :  IBM AS/400 Data Description Processor

                              Data Description Source

SEQNBR  *...+....1....+....2....+....3....+....4....+....5....+....6....+....7....+....8  Date
  100    A                              JDFTVAL                              10/11/95
  200    A       R CHISTR                                                    10/11/95
  300    A                              JFILE(CUSMAST TRANS)                 10/11/95
  400    A       J                      JOIN(CUSMAST TRANS)                  10/11/95
  500    A                              JFLD(CUST# CUSTNO)                   10/11/95
  600    A                              JDUPSEQ(DATE)                        10/11/95
  700    A         NAME ─┐              JREF(1)                              10/11/95
  800    A         CUST#  │                                                  10/11/95
  900    A         BEGBAL │                                                  10/11/95
 1000    A         ADDR   │                                                  10/11/95
 1100    A         CITY   ├─ CUSMAST fields                                  10/11/95
 1200    A         STATE  │                                                  10/11/95
 1300    A         ZIP    │                                                  10/11/95
 1400    A         LIMIT ─┘                                                  10/11/95
 1500    A         DATE ─┐                                                   10/11/95
 16UU    A         PAYEE  │                                                  10/11/95
 1700    A         PADDR  │                                                  10/11/95
 1800    A         PCITY  ├─ TRANS fields                                    10/11/95
 1900    A         PSTAT  │                                                  10/11/95
 2000    A         PZIP   │                                                  10/11/95
 2100    A         AMT    │                                                  10/11/95
 2200    A         CODE ─┘                                                   10/11/95
 2300    A       K CUST#                                                     10/11/95
```

Figure 16-26 First listing (expanded not shown) generated from compilation of the join logical file.

The processing logic controlled by the join logical file read by the application program is detailed in Figure 16-27.

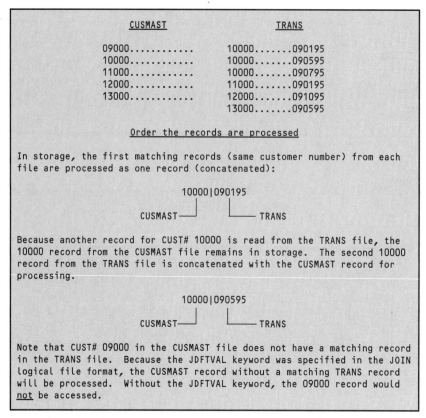

Figure 16-27   Processing logic that accesses two physical files.

Source Program Coding

The source listing of the RPG/400 program that reads a join logical file that processes two physical files is detailed in Figure 16-28.

The report generated by the RPG/400 program that processes the join logical file is identical to that shown in Figure 16-17.

```
SEQUENCE                                                                      IND  DO
NUMBER    *...1....+....2....+....3....+....4....+....5....+....6....+....7...* USE  NUM
                        S o u r c e   L i s t i n g
   100    * This program processes two physical files with a join LF
          H
   200    FCH16LF2 IP  E          K          DISK
          RECORD FORMAT(S):  LIBRARY SMYERS FILE CH16LF2.
                    EXTERNAL FORMAT CHISTR RPG NAME CHISTR
   300    FQSYSPRT O   F     132    OF    PRINTER
   400    ICHISTR      01
   500    I                                      CUST# L1
   500    INPUT  FIELDS FOR RECORD CHISTR FILE CH16LF2 FORMAT CHISTR.
 A000001                                    1  15 NAME
 A000002                                  P 16  180CUST# L1
 A000003                                  P 19  222BEGBAL
 A000004                                    23  42 ADDR
 A000005                                    43  52 CITY
 A000006                                    53  54 STATE
 A000007                                  P 55  570ZIP
 A000008                                  P 58  600LIMIT
 A000009                                  P 61  640DATE
```

Figure 16-28   RPG/400 program that processes a join logical file that accesses two physical files.

```
A000010                                    65   76 PAYEE
A000011                                    77   91 PADDR
A000012                                    92  103 PCITY
A000013                                   104  105 PSTAT
A000014                                 P 106 1080PZIP
A000015                                 P 109 1122AMT
A000016                                   113  113 CODE
   600 C           *INL1    IFEQ *ON                    ctrl break?         B001
   700 C                    Z-ADDBEGBAL    OWED   72     store begbal        001
   800 C                    EXCPTHDGING                  print headings      001
   900 C                    ENDIF                        end IF statment    E001
  1000 C           CODE     CASEQ'C'       CHARSR        SR branch if on
  1100 C    ·      CODE     CASEQ'P'       PAYTSR        SR branch if on
  1200 C                    ENDCS                        end CAS group
  1300 *
  1400 C           CHARSR   BEGSR                        begin SR
  1500 C                    EXCPTCHARGE                  print chrg line
  1600 C                    ADD  AMT       OWED          add to beg bal
  1700 C                    ENDSR                        end charsr SR
  1800 *
  1900 C           PAYTSR   BEGSR                        begin SR
  2000 C                    EXCPTPAYMT                   print payt line
  2100 C                    SUB  AMT       OWED          reduce beg bal
  2200 C                    ENDSR                        end paytsr SR
  2300 OQSYSPRT H  301      1P
  2400 O       OR           OF
  2500 O                                    51 'CREDIT CARD ACTIVITY'
  2600 O                                    58 'REPORT'
  2700 O                       UDATE Y      80
  2800 O       E  1            HDGING
  2900 O                       NAME         15
  3000 O                       CUST#        24
  3100 O                       BEGBAL1      42
  3200 O       E  1            HDGING
  3300 O                       ADDR         20
  3400 O       E  3            HDGING
  3500 O                       CITY         10
  3600 O                       STATE        14
  3700 O                       ZIP          21
  3800 O                       LIMIT 1      39
  3900 O       E  1            CHARGE
  4000 O                       DATE  Y      10
  4100 O                       PAYEE        25
  4200 O                       PADDR        43
  4300 O                       PCITY        58
  4400 O                       PSTAT        63
  4500 O                       PZIP         71
  4600 O                       AMT   1      83
  4700 O       E  1            PAYMT
  4800 O                       DATE  Y      10
  4900 O                                    27 '*** CREDIT ***'
  5000 O                       AMT   1      83
  5100 O       T  13          L1
  5200 O                                    20 'NEW BALANCE'
  5300 O                       OWED  1      83
```

Line #

200 -
300   The logical file (CH16LF2) is defined as processed by the RPG/400 logic cycle (**P** in column 16). It is also specified as an externally defined (**E** in column 19) keyed (**K** in column 31) file that will process the related physical files in the specified key order.

400   The CHISTR entry in the *File/Record Name* field (columns 7–14) references the record format from the join logical file. Because a concatenated record is created in memory, only one record format has to be specified.

Figure 16-28   RPG/400 program that processes a join logical file that accesses two physical files. (Continued)

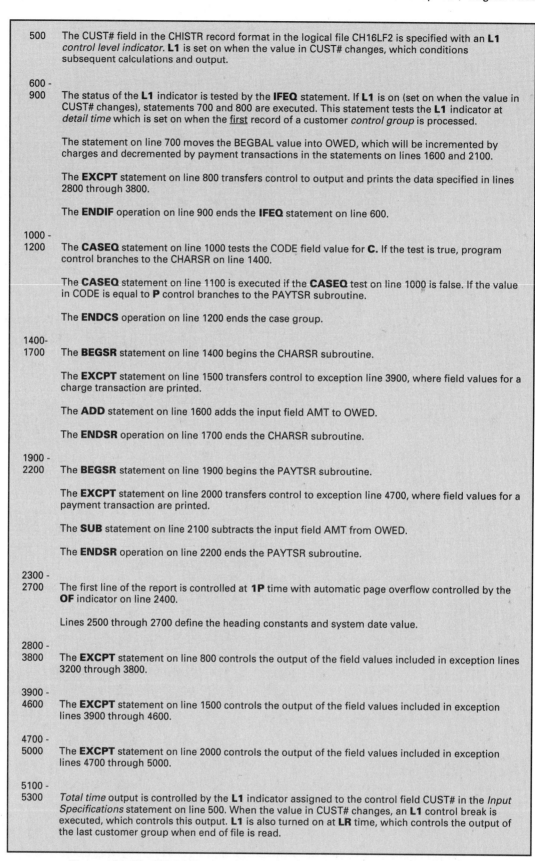

500   The CUST# field in the CHISTR record format in the logical file CH16LF2 is specified with an **L1** *control level indicator*. **L1** is set on when the value in CUST# changes, which conditions subsequent calculations and output.

600 -
900   The status of the **L1** indicator is tested by the **IFEQ** statement. If **L1** is on (set on when the value in CUST# changes), statements 700 and 800 are executed. This statement tests the **L1** indicator at *detail time* which is set on when the <u>first</u> record of a customer *control group* is processed.

      The statement on line 700 moves the BEGBAL value into OWED, which will be incremented by charges and decremented by payment transactions in the statements on lines 1600 and 2100.

      The **EXCPT** statement on line 800 transfers control to output and prints the data specified in lines 2800 through 3800.

      The **ENDIF** operation on line 900 ends the **IFEQ** statement on line 600.

1000 -
1200   The **CASEQ** statement on line 1000 tests the CODE field value for **C.** If the test is true, program control branches to the CHARSR on line 1400.

      The **CASEQ** statement on line 1100 is executed if the **CASEQ** test on line 1000 is false. If the value in CODE is equal to **P** control branches to the PAYTSR subroutine.

      The **ENDCS** operation on line 1200 ends the case group.

1400-
1700   The **BEGSR** statement on line 1400 begins the CHARSR subroutine.

      The **EXCPT** statement on line 1500 transfers control to exception line 3900, where field values for a charge transaction are printed.

      The **ADD** statement on line 1600 adds the input field AMT to OWED.

      The **ENDSR** operation on line 1700 ends the CHARSR subroutine.

1900 -
2200   The **BEGSR** statement on line 1900 begins the PAYTSR subroutine.

      The **EXCPT** statement on line 2000 transfers control to exception line 4700, where field values for a payment transaction are printed.

      The **SUB** statement on line 2100 subtracts the input field AMT from OWED.

      The **ENDSR** operation on line 2200 ends the PAYTSR subroutine.

2300 -
2700   The first line of the report is controlled at **1P** time with automatic page overflow controlled by the **OF** indicator on line 2400.

      Lines 2500 through 2700 define the heading constants and system date value.

2800 -
3800   The **EXCPT** statement on line 800 controls the output of the field values included in exception lines 3200 through 3800.

3900 -
4600   The **EXCPT** statement on line 1500 controls the output of the field values included in exception lines 3900 through 4600.

4700 -
5000   The **EXCPT** statement on line 2000 controls the output of the field values included in exception lines 4700 through 5000.

5100 -
5300   *Total time* output is controlled by the **L1** indicator assigned to the control field CUST# in the *Input Specifications* statement on line 500. When the value in CUST# changes, an **L1** control break is executed, which controls this output. **L1** is also turned on at **LR** time, which controls the output of the last customer group when end of file is read.

Figure 16-28   RPG/400 program that processes a join logical file that accesses two physical files. (Continued)

SELECT/OMIT FIELD NAMES

Records in a physical file may be selected or omitted for processing by a nonjoin or join logical file that includes one or more *select* and/or *omit* fields. The rules related to this control are explained in Figure 16-29.

1. Select fields are identified in a logical file's record format by an **S** in position 17 and omit fields by an **O**. Select and omit fields must follow all field and key field level entries.

2. Select and omit fields may only be specified if key fields are defined for the logical file's record format or if the **DYNSLT** (*Dynamic Select*) keyword is assigned at the file level. If the application does not require a key field, ***NONE** may be specified to satisfy the key field requirement.

3. A blank in position 17 of the statement immediately following a select or omit field indicates that the field is in an **AND** relationship with the previous **S** or **O** field. A following field with an **S** or **O** indicates that it is in an **OR** relationship.

4. If both **S** or **O** fields are included in a logical record, the order in which they are specified is important. Select and omit statements are processed in the order that they are coded. A record is either selected or omitted as specified and any remaining select/omit statements are ignored.

5. If both select and omit statements are included in a logical file's record format, records not meeting the selection tests may be selected or omitted by the **ALL** keyword.

6. If the **ALL** keyword is not specified, records that do not meet the selection criteria are omitted and records that do not meet the omission criteria are selected.

7. A field name may not be included in an **All** statement. However, as appropriate, an **S** or **O** must be specified in position 17.

8. Valid keywords that may be used with **S** or **O** fields are **COMP, RANGE,** and **VALUES.**

Figure 16-29 Rules for logical file select/omit fields.

Examples that explain the syntax and processing logic of select and omit fields for logical files are illustrated in Figure 16-30.

For logical file control, **COMP, RANGE,** and **VALUES** keywords may be used only with select/omit statements. When specified with a standalone field, they will only control validity checking for a related display file field and *not* for a field from a physical file. To access the validity keyword, the logical file's field must be referenced (letter **R** in column 29) in the display file's record format.

```
Example 1:

SEQNBR *...+....1....+....2....+....3....+....4....+....5....+....6....+....7....+....8

            * Select statement on line 300, processes only the physical file (TRANS)
            * records that have a C stored in the CODE field.   All other records are
            * ignored.
    100     A          R CHARGR                    PFILE(TRANS)
    200     A          K CUSTNO
    300     A          S CODE                      COMP(EQ 'C')
```

Figure 16-30 Syntax and processing logic of select and omit fields.

Example 2:

```
SEQNBR *...+....1....+....2....+....3....+....4....+....5....+....6....+....7....+....8

              * Select statement on line 300, processes only the physical file (TRANS)
              * records that have a C or P stored in the CODE field.   All other records
              * are ignored.
   100      A       R CHARGR               PFILE(TRANS)
   200      A       K CUSTNO
   300      A       S CODE                 (VALUES 'C' 'P')
```

Example 3:

```
SEQNBR *...+....1....+....2....+....3....+....4....+....5....+....6....+....7....+....8

              * Select statement on line 300 is in an AND relationship with the implied
              * select statement on line 400.  Physical file records will be processed
              * that have a C or P stored in the CODE field and have an AMT value from
              * 100.00 to 500.00.   All other records are ignored.
   100      A       R CHARGR               PFILE(TRANS)
   200      A       K CUSTNO
   300      A       S CODE                 VALUES('C' 'P')
   400      A         AMT                  RANGE(100.00 500.00)
```

Example 4:

```
SEQNBR *...+....1....+....2....+....3....+....4....+....5....+....6....+....7....+....8

              * Omit statement on line 300 is in an OR relationship with the omit state-
              * ment on line 400.  Physical file records will not be processed that have
              * a C stored in the CODE field or have an AMT value less than 100.00.  All
              * other records will be selected for processing.
   100      A       R CHARGR               PFILE(TRANS)
   200      A       K CUSTNO
   300      A       O CODE                 COMP(EQ 'C')
   40       A ┌───── O AMT                 COMP(LT 100.00)
          ┌──┘
   └── OR relationship is indicated for two or more select/omit statements when an S
       and/or O entry is included in position 17.
```

Example 5:

```
SEQNBR *...+....1....+....2....+....3....+....4....+....5....+....6....+....7....+....8

              * Omit statement on line 300 is in an AND relationship with the omit state-
              * ment on line 400.  Physical file records will not be processed that have
              * a P stored in the CODE field and an AMT value greater than 101.00.  The
              * ALL statement on line 500 explicitly specifies that all other records
              * will be selected for processing.
   100      A       R CHARGR               PFILE(TRANS)
   200      A       K CUSTNO
   300      A       O CODE                 COMP(EQ 'P')
   400      A ┌─────   AMT                 COMP(GT 101.00)
   500      A │     S                      ALL
          ┌──┘
   └── AND relationship is indicated for two or more select/omit statements when an S
       and/or O entry is not included in position 17.
```

Figure 16-30   Syntax and processing logic of select and omit fields. (Continued)

SUMMARY

A *logical file* is a database file that accesses the data stored in one or more physical files. When created over a physical file, an *access path,* which includes the processing criteria, is built. Logical files do not contain data and, unlike physical files, may include more than one record format.

Two types of logical files supported by the AS/400 are *nonjoin* and *join*. *Nonjoin logical files* may process either one physical file or two or more by merging the records. *Join logical files* support only one record format and are used only when two or more physical files are to be processed together. A join logical file creates one record in storage from two or more matched records (same key values) from the physical files. Join logical files are "read-only." Consequently, they may not be used to update the related physical files.

The code for a logical file is included in *Data Description Specifications* and is entered via **SEU.** Identical to other DDS file types, the logical file source must be compiled to generate an object. Once a logical file is created over a physical file, the physical file cannot be deleted unless the logical file is deleted first.

Records from one or more physical files may be selected or omitted from processing by a nonjoin or join logical file's *select/omit* control. Select and omit fields must follow all field and key field entries and are identified by an **S** (for *select*) or **O** (for *omit*) in column 17 of the DDS statement(s). Select/omit criteria are controlled by **COMP, RANGE,** and **VALUES** keywords, which may be specified individually or in an **AND** or **OR** relationship.

An RPG/400 program that processes a logical file must include its name in columns 7–14 of the *File Description* statement and define it as externally defined (**E** in column 19). If the logical file is keyed, a **K** must be entered in column 31, or the related physical file(s) will be processed in arrival sequence.

QUESTIONS

16-1. Name some of the processing functions for which logical files are used.

16-2. As compared to the sorting of files, what are the advantages of logical files?

16-3. Is data stored in a logical file? On what specifications form is the syntax for a logical file included? Does the compilation of a logical file delete the data in the related physical file(s)?

16-4. Name the two types of logical files. How do they differ in processing logic?

16-5. When a logical file references one or more physical files, what is automatically built by each logical file to control processing?

16-6. What is the function of a **PFILE** keyword?

Examine the following DDS coding and answer Questions 16-7 through 16-12.

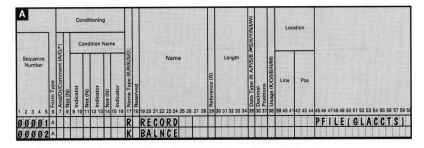

16-7. What is the function of the letter **R** in column 17 of line 1?

16-8. What does the entry in the *Name* field (columns 19–28) reference?

16-9. What does the entry GLACCTS in the **PFILE** keyword reference?

16-10. Explain the function of the entry on line 2.

16-11. In what order will the physical file be processed?

16-12. What fields will be accessed in the record format of the physical file?

Examine the following DDS coding and answer Questions 16-13 through 16-16.

Sequence Number	Form Type	A/O/*	Name Type	Name	Location / Keywords
00001	A		R	PF2R	PFILE(PF1)
00002	A				FORMAT(PF2)
00003	A		K	ACCT#	DESCEND
00004	A	*			
00005	A		R	PF3R	PFILE(PF3)
00006	A				FORMAT(PF2)
00007	A		K	ACCT#	DESCEND

16-13. How many physical files will be accessed by the nonjoin logical file?

16-14. What is the function of the **FORMAT** keyword?

16-15. Where are the field names in columns 19 to 28 defined?

16-16. What is the function of the **DESCEND** keyword?

Examine the following DDS coding and answer Questions 16-17 through 16-19.

Sequence Number	Form Type	A/O/*	Name Type	Name	Location / Keywords
00001	A		R	GLRECD	PFILE(GLEDER)
00002	A		K	ACCT#	
00003	A		K	*NONE	
00004	A	*			
00005	A		R	TRRECD	PFILE(GLTRAN)
00006	A		K	ACTNO	
00007	A		K	TDATE	

16-17. How many physical files are accessed by the nonjoin logical file?

16-18. What is the function of the *NONE keyword on line 3?

16-19. Within an account group, which of the physical files will be processed first, second, and third? What controls this processing?

16-20. Explain the function of the following join logical file keywords:

JFILE	**JFLD**	**JDUPSEQ**
JOIN	**JREF**	**DYNSLT**

16-21. Identify the level of the join logical file keywords listed in Question 16-20—*file, record, field, or join.*

Examine the following DDS coding and answer Questions 16-22 through 16-24.

Sequence Number	Form Type	Name Type	Name	Functions
00001	A	R	JRECRD	JFILE(SUMMARY ITEMS)
00002	A	J		JOIN(SUMMARY ITEMS)
00003	A			JFLD(INV# INV#)
00004	A		CUST#	
00005	A		INV#	JREF(1)
00006	A		DESCRP	
00007	A		QTY	
00008	A		UCOST	

16-22. How many record formats are being joined into one record? Which physical file is considered primary?

16-23. By what value and order will the physical files be processed?

16-24. What is the function of the **JREF(1)** keyword?

16-25. How would a **JDFTVAL** keyword control change the processing of the physical files?

16-26. What is the function of select/omit control for logical files?

16-27. Name the keywords supported with logical file select/omit control.

16-28. Explain the function of each of the keywords named in Question 16-27.

16-29. How is an **OR** relationship between two or more select/omit statements specified? How is an **AND** relationship indicated?

16-30. *Examine the following related statements and explain the processing logic:*

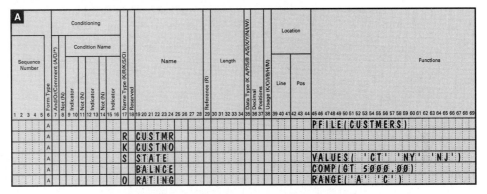

PROGRAMMING ASSIGNMENTS

For each of the following programming assignments, more than one physical file must have been created and loaded with data. Your instructor will inform you as to whether you have to create the physical files and load them or if they have been prepared for the assignment.

Programming Assignment 16-1: STUDENT TRANSCRIPTS (USING A NONJOIN LOGICAL FILE)

Write an RPG/400 program to process a student master file and a student course file to generate temporary transcripts. A nonjoin logical file is to be created to access the two physical files.

Student Master File Record Format:

```
                        PHYSICAL FILE DESCRIPTION

  SYSTEM: AS/400                              DATE: Yours
  FILE NAME: Yours                           REV NO: 0
  RECORD NAME: Yours                         KEY LENGTH: 9
  SEQUENCE: Keyed (Unique)                   RECORD SIZE: 105

                        FIELD DEFINITIONS

  FIELD      FIELD NAME    SIZE    TYPE    POSITION       COMMENTS
  NO                                       FROM    TO

   1         SS#            9       P       1       5    Key field
   2         SNAME         20       C       6      25
   3         SADD1         20       C      26      45
   4         SADD2         15       C      46      60
   5         SCITY         20       C      61      80
   6         SSTATE         2       C      81      82
   7         SZIP           5       P      83      85
   8         SMAJOR        20       C      86     105
```

SS#	SNAME	SADDR	SADD2	SCITY	SSTATE	SZIP	SMAJOR
011111111	HENRY CHURCHILL	1640 PARK AVENUE	APT 10	NORWALK	CT	06854	DATA PROCESSING
011223333	GEORGE ROOSEVELT	25 BURNT PLAINS		DARIEN	CT	06853	COMPUTER SCIENCE
022445555	NELSON FORD	26 PEARSALL PLACE	SUITE 30	STAMFORD	CT	06850	DATA PROCESSING
033778990	WILLIAM CARTER	853 WOOD AVENUE	APT 45	BRIDGEPORT	CT	06601	COMPUTER SCIENCE
041668888	PHILIP BUSH	102 VIRGINIA AVENUE		GREENWICH	CT	06740	COMPUTER SCIENCE
055119999	FRANK TRUMAN	7 BOOT SHOP LANE		NEW HAVEN	CT	06554	DATA PROCESSING
066227777	FREDERICK GRANT	14 GETTSBURG PLACE		BRISTOL	CT	06770	DATA PROCESSING

Student Course File Record Format:

```
                    PHYSICAL FILE DESCRIPTION

      SYSTEM: AS/400                          DATE: Yours
      FILE NAME: Yours                        REV NO: 0
      RECORD NAME: Yours                      KEY LENGTH: 21
      SEQUENCE: Keyed (Unique)                RECORD SIZE: 53

                     FIELD DEFINITIONS

      FIELD      FIELD NAME    SIZE   TYPE    POSITION       COMMENTS
      NO                                      FROM    TO


       1         CSS#           9      P       1       5  Major key
       2         CNAME         20      C       6      25
       3         CNO            6      C      26      45  Minor key 2
       4         CDATE          6      P      46      49  Minor key 1
       5         CINST#         3      P      50      51
       6         CMARK          1      C      52      52
       7         CREDIT         1      P      53      53
```

Physical File Data:

CSS#	CNAME	CNO	CDATE	CINST#	CMARK	CREDIT
011111111	ENGLISH COMPOSITION	ACD101	941215	300	C	3
011111111	INTRO TO PROGRAMMING	DPS100	941215	104	A	4
011111111	COLLEGE ALGEBRA I	MTH100	951215	161	C	3
011111111	INTRO TO RPG/400	DPS200	950521	221	A	4
011111111	COBOL I	DPS210	950521	221	A	4
011223333	COMPUTER SCIENCE I	CSC101	941215	190	B	4
011223333	COMPUTER SCIENCE II	CSC202	950521	180	C	4
011223333	CALCULUS I	MTH201	950521	167	B	3
022445555	INTRO TO PROGRAMMING	DPS100	941215	104	C	4
022445555	MICROCOMPUTERS I	DPS110	941215	200	A	4
033778999	COMPUTER SCIENCE I	CSC101	942115	190	C	4
033778999	PASCAL I	CSC120	941215	180	A	4
041668888	ENGLISH COMPOSITION	ACD101	941215	300	F	3
041668888	CALCULUS I	MTH201	941215	167	D	3
041668888	PHYSICS I	SCS101	941215	075	C	4
041668888	COMPUTER SCIENCE II	CSC202	950521	180	C	4
041668888	C PROGRAMMING I	CSC210	950521	182	B	4
055119999	MICROCOMPUTERS I	DPS110	941215	200	A	4
055119999	AMERICAN STUDIES	ACD210	950521	299	A	3
055119999	ENGLISH LITERATURE	ACD210	950521	300	B	3

Processing: A nonjoin logical file must be created to merge the student master file in an ascending student number order with the course file in ascending student number and ascending term date order. For each student a temporary transcript is to be printed.

Compute each student's cumulative point average based on the following:

A = 4 points, B = 3 points, C = 2 points, D = 1 point, F = 0 points

Step 1: Multiply the course credits by the points for the letter grade. For example, a 3-credit course that earned an A would result in 12 points (3 credits × 4 points).

Step 2: For each student accumulate the total points and total credits.

Step 3: After the last course record for a student is processed, divide the total points by the total credits to determine the student's cumulative point average.

Because the term date is stored in a YYMMDD format, it must be converted to an MMD-DYY format before printing. A data structure should be used for this conversion.

Output: Generate a temporary transcript for each student in the master file in the format shown in the attached printer spacing chart. For students that have no course records, print a transcript and include the error message ****NO COURSE RECORDS FOUND**** in the course section.

Report Design:

```
            0         1         2         3         4         5         6
   1234567890123456789012345678901234567890123456789012345678901234567890 12
 1                        ABC COMMUNITY TECHNICAL COLLEGE
 2                        TEMPORARY STUDENT TRANSCRIPT
 3                             AS OF 0X/XX/XX
 4
 5
 6  X                    X      XXX-XX-XXXX
 7  X                    X
 8  X              X
 9  X                    X XX   XXXXX                      MAJOR: X              X
10
11                                          SEMESTER      INSTR
12  COURSE #        COURSE NAME             DATE          CODE      CREDITS     MARK
13
14  XXXXXX   X                        X     XX/XX/XX      XX       X           X
15  XXXXXX   X                        X     XX/XX/XX      XX       X           X
16              **NO COURSE RECORDS FOUND**
17
18
19
20  CUMULATIVE GPA: X.XX
21
22  NOTE:   PRINT EACH STUDENT'S TRANSCRIPT ON A SEPARATE PAGE.
23          USE SYSTEM DATE FOR THE TRANSCRIPTS.
```

Programming Assignment 16-2: STUDENT TRANSCRIPTS (USING A JOIN LOGICAL FILE)

If Programming Assignment 16-1 was completed, modify it to process the physical files with a join logical file. On the other hand, if the assignment was not completed, refer to the specifications in Assignment 16-1 and process the physical files using a join logical file instead of with a nonjoin logical file.

Programming Assignment 16-3: MONTHLY SALES REPORT (USING A NONJOIN LOGICAL FILE)

Write an RPG/400 program to generate the monthly sales report detailed in the attached printer spacing chart. Two physical files with the following record formats are to be processed by a nonjoin logical file.

Salesperson Master File Record Format:

```
PHYSICAL FILE DESCRIPTION

SYSTEM: AS/400                              DATE: Yours
FILE NAME: Yours                           REV NO: 0
RECORD NAME: Yours                         KEY LENGTH: 3
SEQUENCE: Keyed (Unique)                   RECORD SIZE: 29

                     FIELD DEFINITIONS

FIELD    FIELD NAME    SIZE   TYPE    POSITION        COMMENTS
NO                                   FROM    TO

  1      SALP#          3      P       1      2    Key field
  2      BRNCH#         2      P       3      4
  3      SPNAME        20      C       5     24
  4      MHTODT         9      P      25     29    2 decimals
```

Physical File Data:

SALP#	BRNCH#	SPNAME	MHTODT
123	10	RICHARD H MACY	001232415
234	10	JOHN GIMBEL	000863579
345	10	JOHN WANAMAKER	001000000
456	20	BERT ALTMAN	000080000
567	20	ROGER PEET	003200000
678	30	JOHN PENNEY	010856700

Salesperson Transaction File Record Format:

```
PHYSICAL FILE DESCRIPTION

SYSTEM: AS/400                              DATE: Yours
FILE NAME: Yours                           REV NO: 0
RECORD NAME: Yours                         KEY LENGTH: 3
SEQUENCE: Keyed (not unique)               RECORD SIZE: 13

                     FIELD DEFINITIONS

FIELD    FIELD NAME    SIZE   TYPE    POSITION        COMMENTS
NO                                   FROM    TO

  1      SALPNO         3      P       1      2    Key field
  2      BRNHNO         2      P       3      4
  3      UNITSP         5      P       5      7    2 decimals
  4      QTYSLD         3      P       8      9    0 decimals
  5      SALDAT         6      P      10     13    0 decimals
```

Physical File Data:

SALPNO	BRNHNO	UNITSP	QTYSLD	SALDAT
345	10	01200	500	110195
123	10	10000	020	110195
678	30	01850	240	110195
234	10	09000	100	110295
456	20	02800	050	110295
567	20	35000	006	110395
123	10	00500	200	110395
123	10	60000	002	110495
345	10	50000	010	110495
678	30	09999	050	110495
456	20	14000	012	110695
678	30	01999	360	110695

Processing:

Step 1: Create a nonjoin logical file that will access the records from the two physical files in an ascending branch (major key) and salesperson (minor key) number order.

Step 2: For each transaction record, multiply the selling price per unit by the quantity sold to determine the daily sales dollar amount. Add this dollar sales amount to a weekly sales accumulator.

Step 3: When the salesperson number changes (**L1** control break), add the accumulated week's total for the salesperson to the month-to-date value from the master record and print the line that includes the salesperson number, name, weekly sales amount, and the accumulated monthly total.

Step 4: When an **L1** control break is tested, add the accumulated weekly sales and monthly sales for a salesperson to their related branch totals (see print chart).

Step 5: When the branch number changes (**L2** control break), the branch's weekly and monthly totals are to be added to the related company accumulators (see print chart) and the total branch sales line printed. The company totals are to be printed at **LR** time on a separate page.

Step 6: Create a data area into which the report date value **110695** is to be stored. Access the data area to extract the date for line 2 of the report (see print chart).

Report Design:

Programming Assignment 16-4: MONTHLY SALES REPORT (USING A JOIN LOGICAL FILE)

If Programming Assignment 16-3 was completed, modify it to process the physical files with a join logical file. On the other hand, if the assignment was not completed, refer to the specifications in Assignment 16-3 and process the physical files using a join logical file instead of using a nonjoin logical file.

chapter 17

Subfiles

A *subfile* is a group of records that is loaded and read from or written to a display device file. Examples of subfile applications follow:

1. For inquiry processing, a subfile may be created to which a group of records read from a physical file are loaded.

2. For update processing, a subfile may be used to store a group of records read from a physical file. All or select records may be updated. Under control of an RPG/400 program (**READC** operation), only the changed records are written back to the physical file.

3. For adds processing, a subfile may be built to load the new records that may be edited before adding them to an existing physical file.

4. For deletion processing, a subfile may be created to load a group of records that may be logically deleted or tagged for deletion.

The processing logic for subfiles included in RPG/400 programs that control inquiry, update, or deletion maintenance is detailed in Figure 17-1.

Similar to any display file, subfiles are coded as DDS specifications using either **SEU** (Source Entry Utility) or **SDA** (Screen Design Aid). All subfiles must include a *subfile record format* and a related *subfile control record format* in the DDS coding. The function of each format is explained in the next paragraph.

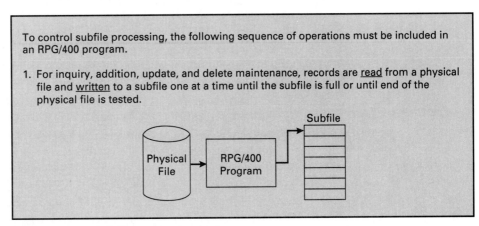

To control subfile processing, the following sequence of operations must be included in an RPG/400 program.

1. For inquiry, addition, update, and delete maintenance, records are <u>read</u> from a physical file and <u>written</u> to a subfile one at a time until the subfile is full or until end of the physical file is tested.

Figure 17-1 Subfile processing logic.

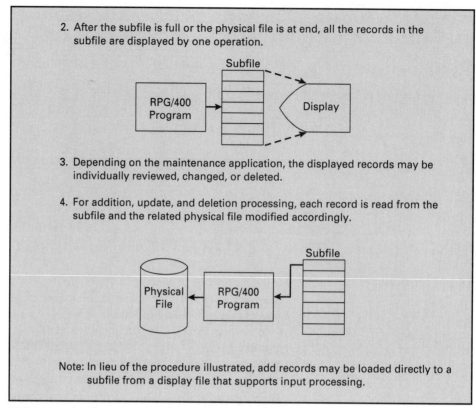

2. After the subfile is full or the physical file is at end, all the records in the subfile are displayed by one operation.

3. Depending on the maintenance application, the displayed records may be individually reviewed, changed, or deleted.

4. For addition, update, and deletion processing, each record is read from the subfile and the related physical file modified accordingly.

Note: In lieu of the procedure illustrated, add records may be loaded directly to a subfile from a display file that supports input processing.

Figure 17-1   Subfile processing logic. (Continued)

The *subfile record format* defines the fields in the subfile record. RPG/400 programs that control subfile processing use the *subfile record format* to read the subfile (input), write records to the subfile (output), and perform update operations to the subfile. Processing of the *subfile record format* is performed between the subfile and the RPG/400 program. The display is not changed on operations to a *subfile record format.*

The *subfile control record format* describes any heading syntax and controls unique subfile functions such as size, clearing, and initialization. DDS coding requires that the *subfile record format* description precede the *control record format* instructions. An RPG/400 program must access the *control record format* in order to write the complete subfile to the display unit and to read the subfile from the display unit.

The minimum *Data Description Specification* (DDS) keywords required in the definition of a subfile are **SFL, SFLCTL, SFLSIZ, SFLPAG,** and **SFLDSP.** The function of each is explained in the following paragraphs.

- **SFL:** A *record level* keyword that specifies the *subfile record format,* which consists of variable data items. The instructions for this format must immediately precede the *subfile control record format.*
- **SFLCTL:** A *record level* keyword that specifies the *subfile control record format* in which display, clearing, and initialization functions are controlled.
- **SFLSIZ:** A *record level* control record keyword that specifies the number of records that may be loaded in the subfile. The maximum allowed for a subfile is 9,999.
- **SFLPAG:** A *record level* control record keyword that specifies the number of records that may be displayed on the CRT at the same time.

- **SFLDSP:** A *record level* control record keyword that displays the subfile when the RPG/400 program issues an output operation to the *control record format.* The **SFLDSP** instruction must be conditioned by one or more indicators set on in the RPG/400 program at the appropriate time in the processing cycle.

Other special-purpose DDS keywords for subfiles that must be specified at the *record level* in the control record format include the following:

- **SFLCLR:** Clears a subfile of all records before new records are loaded. The subfile is *not* deleted by execution of this keyword, only cleared.
- **SFLINZ:** Initializes all records in a subfile. Alphanumeric fields are initialized with blanks and numeric fields with zeros.
- **SFLDLT:** Deletes a subfile. It is used when more than one subfile is controlled by an RPG/400 program and one or more are no longer needed. Because the number of subfiles that may be active at any time is limited to 24, this keyword may be specified to delete subfiles so that others may be included in the processing cycle.
- **SFLDSPCTL:** Displays constants and fields defined within the control record instruction format. This keyword is usually conditioned by an indicator that is turned on in an RPG/400 program at the appropriate time in the processing cycle.
- **SFLEND:** A *record level* control record keyword that displays a plus sign in the lower-right area of the screen. The plus sign indicates that more records are stored in the subfile than can display at one time on the screen. Pressing the Roll Up key displays the next group of records in the subfile. A plus sign will not display if there are no more records in the subfile. Recall that the number of records displayed on the screen is controlled by the value included with the **SFLPAG** keyword. **SFLEND** is usually conditioned by an indicator.
- **SFLRNA:** This keyword is used with **SFLINZ** for program-controlled initialization of a subfile with no active records. A workstation user may key data into the related blank subfile records. **SFLRNA** must be specified when the **SFLINZ** keyword is included in the coding of a subfile.
- **SFLMSG:** Specifies a subfile record error that is included in the control record format and displays on the error message line (default 24) unless the location is changed by an **MSGLOC** keyword.
- **SFLDROP:** Controls the folding of records when they are too long to display at one time on the screen. This keyword is used with a command key that the workstation operator may press to display the folded format of the subfile record.

For an explanation of the function of other subfile keywords, **SFLROLVAL, SFLNXTCHG, SFLRCDNBR, SFLLIN, SFLMSGRCD, SFLPGMO, SFLMSGID, SFLMSGKEY,** and **SFLENTER,** refer to the system's DDS Manual. Use of many of these keywords will be seen in the presentation of three application programs that include subfiles for inquiry, update, and the adds maintenance of a physical file.

SUBFILE APPLICATION PROGRAM: INQUIRY PROCESSING

The specifications for a program that processes a subfile for the inquiry of a physical file are detailed in Figure 17-2.

PROGRAM SPECIFICATIONS   Page ___1___ of ___1___

Program Name: Customer File Inquiry   Program-ID: CH17INQ   Written by: SM

Purpose: Inquiry of the customer file using a subfile   Approved by: CM

Input files: _P1PF1_   (keyed)   SFLINQ (display file)

Output files: SFLINQ   (display file)

Processing Requirements:

Write an RPG/400 program to inquiry records from the customer master file utilizing a subfile.

Input to the program:

Create a display file that includes a prompt screen, a subfile record, a subfile control record, and a command line record. The designs of the prompt screen and subfile are included in supplemental forms. Define the subfile to store 10 records with 8 per page.

The prompt screen, which will be executed first, is included for the entering of a customer number. The entry (key value) specifies the record at which the reading of the physical file is to begin.

The subfile must be coded with the subfile record statements first, followed by the subfile control record and then the command line format.

Processing:

Read the physical file (beginning at the student number entered) and sequentially write the records to the subfile. The loading process is to continue until the subfile is full or the physical file is "at end."

Output:

Display the three subfile record formats on the screen and provide control to return to the prompts screen to continue inquiry or end the job.

Figure 17-2 Specifications for an application program that controls the inquiry file with a subfile.

The system flowchart shown in Figure 17-3 indicates that the program accesses records from a physical file and stores them in a subfile for review.

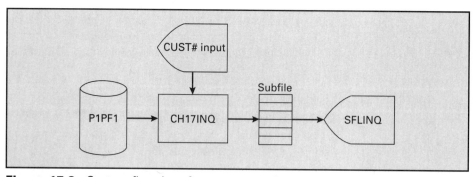

Figure 17-3 System flowchart for a program that accesses records from a physical file for inquiry with subfile control.

The structure of the physical file (P1PF1) processed by the subfile inquiry application program is shown in Figure 17-4. Also included is a listing of the data stored in the file.

```
                        PHYSICAL FILE DESCRIPTION

        SYSTEM: AS/400                          DATE: Yours
        FILE NAME: Yours                        REV NO: 0
        RECORD NAME: Yours                      KEY LENGTH: 5
        SEQUENCE: Keyed (Unique)                RECORD SIZE: 75

                          FIELD DEFINITIONS

        FIELD    FIELD NAME    SIZE   TYPE    POSITION      COMMENTS
         NO                                  FROM    TO

          1      CUST#           5     C       1      5   Key field
          2      NAME           20     C       6     25
          3      STREET         20     C      26     45
          4      CITY           20     C      46     65
          5      STATE           2     C      66     67
          6      ZIP             5     P      68     70
          7      BALANC          8     P      71     75  2 decimals
```

```
12345KAREL APPEL          20 AMSTERDAM AVENUE NEW YORK       NY0745000125000
23456GEORGES BRAQUE       300 ST CLAIR STREET TRENTON        NJ0550100010000
34567PAUL CEZANNE         44 RUE PIGALLE      STAMFORD       CT0651808190000
45678MARC CHAGALL         222 QUAIL AVENUE    BRIDGEPORT     CT0666600092600
56789EDGAR DEGAS          10 ROSE TERRACE     WESTPORT       PA0777700784599
67890MAX ERNST            1 FRANKFURT DRIVE   FRANKFORT      KY0555100050000
78900BUCKMINSTER FULLER   999 PARK AVENUE     NEW YORK       NY0755503300010
89000JULIO GONZALEZ       101 SMITH LANE      GREENWICH      CT0644400065478
90000HECTOR HYPPOLITE     888 PEACHTREE AVENUEATLANTA        GA0333212000000
91000PIERRE JEANERET      90 CHATEAU DRIVE    GENEVA         NY0777700000945
```

Figure 17-4 Physical file (P1PF1) structure and listing of the stored data processed by the subfile inquiry program.

The design of the prompt screen included in the display file is shown in Figure 17-5.

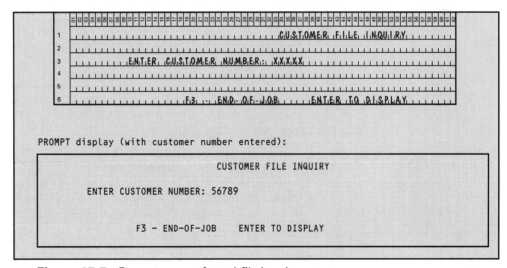

Figure 17-5 Prompt screen for subfile inquiry program.

The format of the subfile, which is displayed when the inquiry program is executed, is illustrated in Figure 17-6. Notice that Xs represent the size and location of the variable

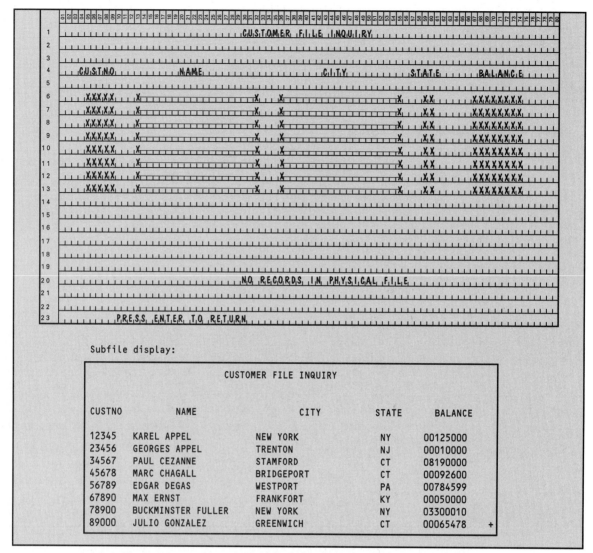

Figure 17-6 Display format of the subfile controlled by the inquiry program.

field data. As shown in the last section of Figure 17-6, the Xs are replaced with field values when the subfile is executed under program control.

Subfile DDS Syntax—Inquiry Program

The instructions for a subfile may be explicitly entered with **SEU** (Source Entry Utility) or be generated by **SDA** (Screen Design Aid) through a series of prompt screens. In any case, the structure of the subfile and the function of its keywords are the same. Common to the method used in the previous chapters, the entering of DDS source code via **SEU** will be followed.

A listing of the display file (SFINQ), which includes record formats for the prompt screen (PROMPT), subfile record (SM01SFR), subfile control record (SM01CTL), and command message record (CMDLINE), is presented in Figure 17-7. An explanation of the function of each instruction is also included.

Notice the following two important coding features in the syntax of the subfile:

1. The keyword **OVERLAY** is included in the subfile control record format so that the subfile's variables and constants will not erase the message lines (CMDLINE format) after they are displayed. In the RPG/400 pro-

```
SEQNBR*...+... 1 ...+... 2 ...+... 3 ...+... 4 ...+... 5 ...+... 6 ...+... 7 ...
  100    A                                            PRINT
  200    A                                            REF(SMYERS/P1PF1)
  300       * Prompt screen........
  400    A        R PROMPT
  500    A                                            CA03(03 'END OF JOB')
  600    A                                          1 34'CUSTOMER FILE INQUIRY'
  700    A                                          3 10'ENTER CUSTOMER NUMBER:'
  800    A          CUSTNO        5   I  3 33
  900    A                                          6 18'F3 - END-OF-JOB'
 1000    A                                          6 38'ENTER TO DISPLAY'
 1100       * Subfile record definition........
 1200    A        R SM01SFR                         SFL
 1300    A          CUST#         R      0  6  5
 1400    A          NAME          R      0  6 13
 1500    A          CITY          R      0  6 36
 1600    A          STATE         R      0  6 59
 1700    A          BALANC        R      0  6 67
 1800       * Subfile control record........
 1900    A        R SM01CTL                         SFLCTL(SM01SFR)
 2000    A                                          SFLSIZ(10)
 2100    A                                          SFLPAG(8)
 2200    A 80                                       SFLCLR
 2300    A 81                                       SFLDSP
 2400    A 81                                       SFLDSPCTL
 2500    A 81                                       SFLEND
 2600    A                                          OVERLAY
 2700    A                                        1 30'CUSTOMER FILE INQUIRY'
 2800    A                                        4  4'CUSTNO'
 2900    A                                        4 20'NAME'
 3000    A                                        4 43'CITY'
 3100    A                                        4 57'STATE'
 3200    A                                        4 68'BALANCE'
 3300       * Command record........
 3400    A        R CMDLINE
 3500    A 70                                      20 30'NO RECORDS IN PHYSICAL FILE'
 3600    A                                         23 10'PRESS ENTER TO RETURN'
```

Line #

100   The keyword **PRINT** allows use of the Print key to print a copy of the screen image.

200   The keyword **REF** references the field attributes in the physical file P1PF1.

400 -
1000   The instructions included in this group relate to a prompt screen in which the operator enters a customer number to begin an inquiry of the physical file or end the job.

1200   The letter **R** in column 17, the programmer-supplied record name SM01SFR (columns 19–28), and the **SFL** keyword define this statement as the subfile record format.

1300 -
1700   The physical file (P1PF1) field attributes included in the subfile record format are referenced by the letter **R** in column 29. Individual field line (columns 39–41) and column locations (columns 42–44) are specified for each field entry. The **6** entry for line number indicates the beginning line on which the first record will be displayed. Subsequent records will automatically be displayed on the following lines. Because this subfile only supports inquiry processing, the letter **O** (output from the program to the screen) is specified in the *Usage* field (column 38) for all of the data items.

1900   The letter **R** in column 17, the programmer-supplied name SM01CTL (columns 19–28), and supporting keywords define this entry as the subfile control record format.

        The **SFLCTL(SM01SFR)** keyword defines the record format as the control record for the subfile record SM01SFR specified on line 1200.

2000   The **SFLSIZ(10)** keyword defines the size of the subfile. For this example, the file will store 10 records. A subfile may store a maximum of 9,999 records.

Figure 17-7 Syntax for display file (SFLINQ), including record formats for PROMPT, SM01SFR, SM01CTL, and CMDLINE.

2100 The **SFLPAG(8)** keyword specifies how many subfile records are to be displayed at one time on the screen. This number specified does not include the constants or variables that may be described in the subfile control record.

2200 The **SFLCLR** keyword clears the subfile before it is loaded. Indicator **80** is turned on in the RPG/400 program, and the clearing function is performed when the control record is executed by an **EXFMT SM01CTL** instruction.

2300 The **SFLDSP** keyword displays the subfile record values when indicator **81** is set on in the RPG/400 program and an **EXFMT SM01CTL** statement executed. The number of records displayed on the screen is determined by the **SFLPAG(8)** keyword.

2400 **SFLDSPCTL** displays the constants included in the subfile control record (SM01CTL) when indicator **81** is set on in the RPG/400 program and an **EXFMT SM01CTL** statement executed.

2500 **SFLEND** controls the display of a + (plus sign) to the right of the last subfile record displayed on the screen. The + sign indicates that more records are included on the following page. When there are no more records in the subfile, the + sign does not display. This keyword is accessed when indicator **81** is set on in the RPG/400 program and the control record executed by an **EXFMT SM01CTL** statement.

2600 The **OVERLAY** keyword prevents the CMDLINE constants from being cleared when the control record (SM01CTL) is displayed. Each record format will automatically display 24 lines unless the **OVERLAY** keyword is specified. Overlaying formats must begin on lines not used by a previously displayed record.

2700 -
3200 The constants included in these statements are displayed when an **EXFMT SM01CTL** statement that controls the display of the subfile control record is executed in the RPG/400 program.

3400 - Display of the constants included in the CMDLINE record format are controlled with a **WRITE CMDLINE** statement in the RPG/400 program. This record format is displayed <u>before</u> the subfile control record.

3500 - Indicator **70,** set on in the RPG/400 program by a **READ** statement when no records are stored in the physical file, conditions the constant NO RECORDS IN PHYSICAL FILE. Display of this constant is controlled by the **WRITE CMDLINE** statement in the RPG/400 program. If **70** is on, the statement will be executed.

3600 - The constant PRESS ENTER TO RETURN display is controlled by the **WRITE CMDLINE** statement in the RPG/400 program. As coded, it will display beginning in column 10, line 23 of the screen.

Figure 17-7 Syntax for display file (SFLINQ), including record formats for PROMPT, SM01SFR, SM01CTL, and CMDLINE. (Continued)

gram, the message line(s) is (are) displayed by a **WRITE** statement before the subfile control record format (SM01CTL) is executed by an **EXFMT** operation. Because processing is so fast, the sequence of the record displays will not be seen by the operator. All the variables in the subfile record (one page) and constants in the subfile control record and command line appear to display simultaneously.

2. A separate record format (CMDLINE) must be included for the command line constants (error and action messages) and is displayed before the other subfile record formats.

The relationship of the subfile record, control record, and command line record formats are illustrated in Figure 17-8. The subfile control record (SM01CTL) includes the constants (two heading lines) and control keywords; the subfile record (SM01SFR) defines variable fields and stores the data; and the command record (CMDLINE) file defines the

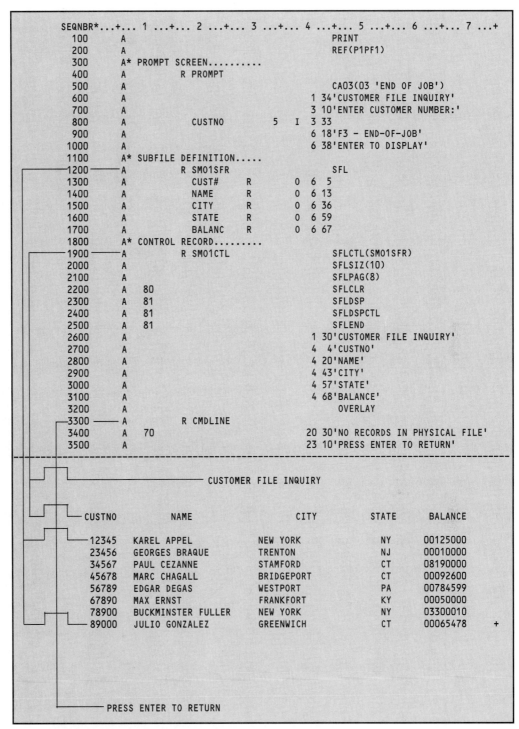

```
SEQNBR*...+... 1 ...+... 2 ...+... 3 ...+... 4 ...+... 5 ...+... 6 ...+... 7 ...+
   100     A                                        PRINT
   200     A                                        REF(P1PF1)
   300     A* PROMPT SCREEN..........
   400     A         R PROMPT
   500     A                                        CA03(03 'END OF JOB')
   600     A                                      1 34'CUSTOMER FILE INQUIRY'
   700     A                                      3 10'ENTER CUSTOMER NUMBER:'
   800     A           CUSTNO        5  I  3 33
   900     A                                      6 18'F3 - END-OF-JOB'
  1000     A                                      6 38'ENTER TO DISPLAY'
  1100     A* SUBFILE DEFINITION.....
  1200     A         R SM01SFR              SFL
  1300     A           CUST#      R       0 6  5
  1400     A           NAME       R       0 6 13
  1500     A           CITY       R       0 6 36
  1600     A           STATE      R       0 6 59
  1700     A           BALANC     R       0 6 67
  1800     A* CONTROL RECORD.........
  1900     A         R SM01CTL              SFLCTL(SM01SFR)
  2000     A                                SFLSIZ(10)
  2100     A                                SFLPAG(8)
  2200     A  80                            SFLCLR
  2300     A  81                            SFLDSP
  2400     A  81                            SFLDSPCTL
  2500     A  81                            SFLEND
  2600     A                                      1 30'CUSTOMER FILE INQUIRY'
  2700     A                                      4  4'CUSTNO'
  2800     A                                      4 20'NAME'
  2900     A                                      4 43'CITY'
  3000     A                                      4 57'STATE'
  3100     A                                      4 68'BALANCE'
  3200     A                                        OVERLAY
  3300     A         R CMDLINE
  3400     A  70                                   20 30'NO RECORDS IN PHYSICAL FILE'
  3500     A                                       23 10'PRESS ENTER TO RETURN'
```

```
                        CUSTOMER FILE INQUIRY


      CUSTNO        NAME                CITY          STATE     BALANCE

      12345   KAREL APPEL          NEW YORK            NY      00125000
      23456   GEORGES BRAQUE       TRENTON             NJ      00010000
      34567   PAUL CEZANNE         STAMFORD            CT      08190000
      45678   MARC CHAGALL         BRIDGEPORT          CT      00092600
      56789   EDGAR DEGAS          WESTPORT            PA      00784599
      67890   MAX ERNST            FRANKFORT           KY      00050000
      78900   BUCKMINSTER FULLER   NEW YORK            NY      03300010
      89000   JULIO GONZALEZ       GREENWICH           CT      00065478    +




      PRESS ENTER TO RETURN
```

Figure 17-8   Relationship of subfile coding to subfile display.

message lines. All these subfile components are displayed simultaneously in the RPG/400 program by either a **WRITE** or **EXFMT** operation.

Subfile RPG Source Coding—Subfile Inquiry Program

A line-by-line explanation of the function of each instruction supplements the RPG/400 source listing in Figure 17-9.

```
SEQUENCE                                                                      IND    DO
NUMBER    *...1....+....2....+....3....+....4....+....5....+....6....+....7...* USE    NUM
                        S o u r c e   L i s t i n g
   100    * Customer master inquiry with a subfile....
   200    *
          H
   300    FSFLINQ  CF  E                    WORKSTN
   400    F                                SFRRN1KSFILE SM01SFR
          RECORD FORMAT(S): LIBRARY SMYERS FILE CH17INQ.
                 EXTERNAL FORMAT PROMPT RPG NAME PROMPT
                 EXTERNAL FORMAT SM01SFR RPG NAME SM01SFR
                 EXTERNAL FORMAT SM01CTL RPG NAME SM01CTL
                 EXTERNAL FORMAT CMDLINE RPG NAME CMDLINE
   500    FP1PF1   IF  E         K        DISK
          RECORD FORMAT(S): LIBRARY SMYERS FILE P1PF1.
                 EXTERNAL FORMAT P1PF1R RPG NAME P1PF1R
A000000   INPUT  FIELDS FOR RECORD PROMPT FILE CH17INQ FORMAT PROMPT.
A000001                                      1    1 *IN01             END OF JOB
A000002                                      2    6 CUSTNO
B000000   INPUT  FIELDS FOR RECORD SM01SFR FILE CH17INQ FORMAT SM01SFR.
B000001                                      1    5 CUST#             CUSTOMER NO
B000002                                      6   25 NAME              CUSTOMER NAME
B000003                                     26   45 CITY              CITY ADDRESS
B000004                                     46   47 STATE             STATE ADDRESS
B000005                                     48  552BALANC             CUSTOMER BALANCE
C000000   INPUT  FIELDS FOR RECORD SM01CTL FILE CH17INQ FORMAT SM01CTL.
D000000   INPUT  FIELDS FOR RECORD CMDLINE FILE CH17INQ FORMAT CMDLINE.
E000000   INPUT  FIELDS FOR RECORD P1PF1R FILE P1PF1 FORMAT P1PF1R.
E000001                                      1    5 CUST#             CUSTOMER NO
E000002                                      6   25 NAME              CUSTOMER NAME
E000003                                     26   45 STREET            STREET ADDRESS
E000004                                     46   65 CITY              CITY ADDRESS
E000005                                     66   67 STATE             STATE ADDRESS
E000006                                    P 68   70 ZIP              ZIP CODE
E000007                                    P 71  752BALANC            CUSTOMER BALANCE
   600    C                   EXFMTPROMPT                dspf prompt rcd
   700    C         *IN03     DOWEQ*OFF                                          B001
   800    C                   MOVE *ON   *IN80           sfl clear ctrl          001
   900    C                   WRITESM01CTL               xeq sfl clear           001
  1000    C                   MOVE *OFF  *IN80           set off 80              001
  1100    C                   Z-ADD0     SFRRN1  40      init rcd ctr            001
  1200    C                   SETOF                7071  set off 70 & 71 1 2     001
  1300    C         CUSTNO    SETLLP1PF1                 set PF pointer          001
  1400    C                   READ P1PF1                70read a pf rcd        3 001
  1500    C         *IN70     IFEQ *OFF                  no records test         B002
  1600    *
  1700    * If one or more crecords are stored in the physical file, load the
  1800    * subfile until end of physical file or subfile is full....
  1900    *
  2000    C         *IN71     DOWEQ*OFF                  pf load control         B003
  2100    C                   ADD  1     SFRRN1          increment ctr           003
  2200    C                   WRITESM01SFR              71 write sfl rcd       3 003
  2300    C         *IN71     IFEQ *OFF                  sfl full test           B004
  2400    C                   READ P1PF1                71 read a pf rcd       3 004
  2500    C                   ENDIF                      end line 23 IF          E004
  2600    C                   ENDDO                      end line 20 dow         E003
  2700    C                   ENDIF                      end line 15 IF          E002
  2800    *
  2900    * Display subfile on screen or msg if no records in physical file
  3000    *
  3100    C                   WRITECMDLINE               dsp cmd constns         001
  3200    C                   MOVE *ON   *IN81           sfl dsp indictr         001
  3300    C                   EXFMTSM01CTL               dsp subfile             001
  3400    C                   MOVE *OFF  *IN81           set off 81              001
  3500    C                   EXFMTPROMPT                dsp prompt scrn         001
  3600    C                   ENDDO                      end line 7 dow          E001
```

Figure 17-9 Detailed source listing of an RPG/400 program that processes a sub-file for inquiry of a physical file.

```
 3700 C                      MOVE *ON      *INLR           eoj control
F000000  OUTPUT FIELDS FOR RECORD PROMPT FILE CH17INQ FORMAT PROMPT.
G000000  OUTPUT FIELDS FOR RECORD SM01SFR FILE CH17INQ FORMAT SM01SFR.
G000001                      CUST#     5   CHAR   5             CUSTOMER NO
G000002                      NAME     25   CHAR  20             CUSTOMER NAME
G000003                      CITY     45   CHAR  20             CITY ADDRESS
G000004                      STATE    47   CHAR   2             STATE ADDRESS
G000005                      BALANC   55   ZONE  8,2            CUSTOMER BALANCE
H000000  OUTPUT FIELDS FOR RECORD SM01CTL FILE CH17INQ FORMAT SM01CTL.
H000001                      *IN80     1   CHAR   1
H000002                      *IN81     2   CHAR   1
I000000  OUTPUT FIELDS FOR RECORD CMDLINE FILE CH17INQ FORMAT CMDLINE.
I000001                      *IN70     1   CHAR   1
```

Line #

300 The display file, which includes formats for the PROMPT screen, subfile record format, and subfile control record, is specified as a combined, full procedural, externally defined workstation file.

400 The **K** in column 53 indicates that this instruction is a continuation of the previous one.

The SFRRN1 entry in columns 47–52 specifies a programmer-defined field in which relative record numbers of records written to the subfile are stored and incremented.

The **SFILE** keyword in columns 54–59 specifies that this statement is related to a subfile.

The SM01SFR entry in columns 60–65 specifies the name of the subfile record format, included in the display file SFLINQ, processed by this program.

500 The physical file, P1PF1, is specified as an input, full procedural, externally defined, keyed disk file.

600 The **EXFMT** statement displays the PROMPT screen record for entry of a customer number or the end to the job.

700 If **F3** (EOJ control) is not pressed as a response to the PROMPT screen (indicator **03** not turned on), the **DOWEQ** statement will control execution of statements 700 through 3600. Additional inquiries may be made to the physical file until the operator pressses **F3** to end the job.

800 Indicator **80,** specified with the **SFLCLR** keyword in the subfile control record, is set on to clear the subfile when the statement on line 900 is executed.

900 The subfile control record, SM01CTL, is written by a **WRITE** statement to clear the subfile.

1000 Indicator **80,** which controls clearing of the subfile, is set off.

1100 The relative record number counter, specified in the *File Description* statement for the display file on line 400, is defined and initialized to zero.

1200 The **SETOF** instruction turns off all *Resulting Indicators.*

1300 The **SETLL** positions the file pointer at the customer number value entered via the PROMPT screen. If the customer number is not found in the physical file, the pointer is positioned at the next highest key value.

1400 The **READ** statement reads the first record from the physical file, P1PF1. Indicator **70** will be set on if no records are stored in the disk file.

1500 The **IFEQ** statement tests the status of indicator **70,** which was specified with the **READ** statement on line 1400. If the indicator is "on," program control will branch over the following **DOWEQ** group to line 3100 and display the subfile with the error message **FILE CONTAINS NO RECORDS,** indicating that the physical file has no records.

Figure 17-9 Detailed source listing of an RPG/400 program that processes a subfile for inquiry of a physical file. (Continued)

2000   Within the **DOWEQ** group, indicator **71** is turned on if the subfile is full or if the physical file is at its end. This iterative process, which controls loading of the subfile, continues until indicator **71** is turned on by one of the described conditions.

2100   The relative record number counter, SFRRN1, specified in the *File Description* statement for the subfile (line 400) is incremented by 1 when a physical file record is loaded to the subfile. When this counter is greater than the number of records specified in the **SFLSIZ** keyword in DDS coding for the subfile, loading of the subfile will stop and the subsequent statements executed.

2200   The **WRITE** statement writes a record to the subfile in the relative record position as determined by the value in SFRNN1. If the value in SFRNN1 is 1, the current record is written to the first record position in the subfile. When the value in SFRNN1 is 2, the record is written to the second record position in the subfile; and so forth. Indicator **71,** specified in columns 58–59, will turn on when the subfile is full.

2300-   The **IFEQ** statement tests the status of the indicator assigned to the **WRITE** statement on line
2400   2200 (subfile full test). When the **71** is "off," another record will be read from the physical file. When **71** is on, control will branch to the **ENDIF** on line 2700.

2600   The **ENDDO** operation ends the **DOWEQ** group (lines 2000–2600).

2700   This **ENDIF** statement ends the **IFEQ** instruction on line 1500.

3100   The **WRITE CMDLINE** instruction displays the constants included in the display file's record format CMDLINE. Note that the error message **NO RECORD IN PHYSICAL FILE** included in this format will only display if indicator **70** is on.

3200   Indicator **81,** which conditions the **SFLDSP, SFLDSPCTL,** and **SFLEND** keywords in the subfile's DDS coding, is set on. When the **EXFMT** statement on line 3300 is executed, the subfile control record constants, the subfile record field values, and the continuation symbol will be displayed simultaneously.

3300   The **EXFMT** statement displays the subfile record values, the constants in the subfile control record, and the continuation symbol. If indicator **81** was not previously set on (line 3200), nothing would display.

3400   Indicator **81** is set off.

3500   The PROMPT screen is displayed again so that the operator may continue processing of the physical file for another inquiry or end the job.

3600   The **ENDDO** statement ends the **DOWEQ** group beginning on line 700.

3700   The **MOVE** statement sets on indicator **LR,** which ends the job and returns control back to the operating system.

Figure 17-9   Detailed source listing of an RPG/400 program that processes a subfile for inquiry of a physical file. (Continued)

The processing logic of the RPG/400 program that executes a subfile for inquiry of a physical file is detailed in the flowchart shown in Figure 17-10.

An examination of the source listing in Figure 17-9 and the related line-by-line explanation show that previously discussed RPG/400 syntax unique to interactive processing has been included. Other than the **WRITE** and **EXFMT** statements that control the display of the subfile components, the only unfamiliar coding is included in a *continuation line* for the *File Description* entries for the WORKSTN file. An explanation of this instruction segment is presented in Figure 17-11.

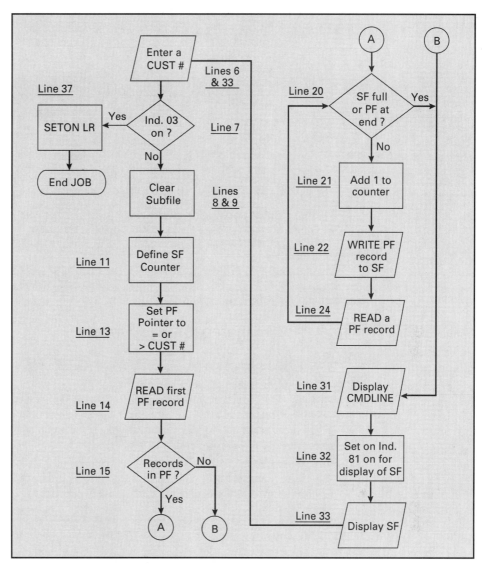

Figure 17-10 Processing logic flowchart for subfile inquiry program.

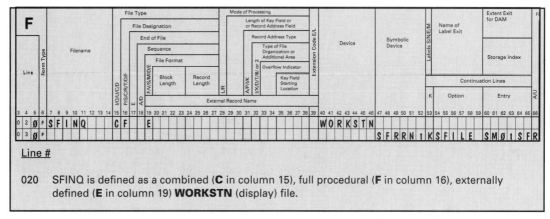

Figure 17-11 *File Description* entries that define a WORKSTN (display) file that includes a subfile.

030 A programmer-supplied entry (SFRRN1), which is used as a record counter to indicate in
what location the record is to be stored in the subfile and "flags" when the subfile is full, is
specified in the *Symbolic Device* field (columns 47–52). Note that this entry must be defined
as a numeric integer field in the RPG/400 program.

The letter **K** in column 53 identifies this instruction as a continuation of line 020.

The keyword **SFILE** must be entered in the *Option* field (columns 54–59) to specify that the
WORKSTN (display) file includes a subfile and that the entries in this instruction are related
to its definition and processing.

The programmer-supplied entry, SMO1SFR, in the *Entry* field (columns 60–66) is the name
of the subfile record defined in the DDS coding for the subfile.

THE FIELD NAMES ON THE CONTINUATION LINE (i.e., *Symbolic Device, Labels, Option,*
and so forth) HAVE NO DIRECT MEANING TO THE DEFINITION OF A SUBFILE. THE
LOCATION OF THE ENTRIES DETERMINES THEIR FUNCTION AND IS INTERPRETED BY THE
RPG/400 COMPILER ACCORDINGLY.

Figure 17-11 *File Description* entries that define a WORKSTN (display) file that includes a subfile. (Continued)

SUBFILE APPLICATION PROGRAM: UPDATE PROCESSING

Instead of accessing and updating one physical file record at a time, subfiles may be used effectively to access a group of records for selective changes. The processing is similar to functions supported by some third-party utilities, such as REVUE, except that it is controlled by a user RPG/400 program. Perhaps more important, however, is that the displayed records are in a format specifically designed for and familiar to the end user, who is not typically a programmer.

The system flowchart illustrated in Figure 17-12 details the processing sequence controlled by an RPG program that updates a physical file via a subfile. An explanation of the processing steps are detailed in the following paragraphs:

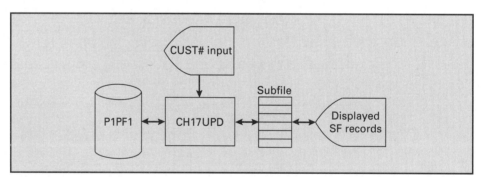

Figure 17-12 System flowchart for an RPG program that updates a physical file with subfile control.

1. Records are read from the physical file in the RPG/400 program by a **READ** statement and written to the subfile by a **WRITE** instruction.
2. After the subfile is loaded (or the physical file is at its end), it is displayed by an **EXFMT** instruction.
3. The user scans the records and makes necessary changes.
4. Only the records that have been changed are processed by the RPG/400 program with a **READC** (*Read Change*) operation. When any byte in the body of a record is changed, a *Modified Data Tag* (**MDT**) is automatically turned on by the system to identify the record for update processing. Therefore, if only one

record is changed in the subfile, that record is processed in the update of the physical file, and not every record in the subfile. This feature saves both input and output resources and processing time.

5. The SCUST# field from each record read by the **READC** instruction is used to **CHAIN** to the physical file and locate the address of the record before it is updated by an **UPDAT** operation.

DDS Coding—Subfile Update Program

Modifications to the DDS coding for the subfile inquiry application to support update processing are identified in Figure 17-13 and explained in the following paragraphs.

Instead of specifying the physical file's field names that were used in the inquiry program, new fields have been defined in the *subfile's record format*. This is a necessary change because once the physical file's records are accessed and loaded to the subfile, their storage addresses have been lost and the records must be randomly accessed again before updating.

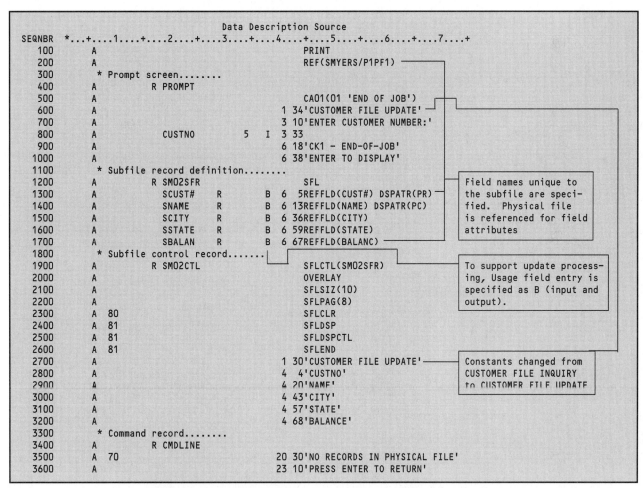

```
                              Data Description Source
SEQNBR  *...+....1....+....2....+....3....+....4....+....5....+....6....+....7....+
  100   A                                          PRINT
  200   A                                          REF(SMYERS/P1PF1)
  300      * Prompt screen........
  400   A           R PROMPT
  500   A                                          CA01(01 'END OF JOB')
  600   A                                        1 34'CUSTOMER FILE UPDATE'
  700   A                                        3 10'ENTER CUSTOMER NUMBER:'
  800   A             CUSTNO       5   I  3 33
  900   A                                        6 18'CK1 - END-OF-JOB'
 1000   A                                        6 38'ENTER TO DISPLAY'
 1100      * Subfile record definition........
 1200   A           R SMO2SFR                       SFL
 1300   A             SCUST#     R     B  6  5REFFLD(CUST#) DSPATR(PR)
 1400   A             SNAME      R     B  6 13REFFLD(NAME) DSPATR(PC)
 1500   A             SCITY      R     B  6 36REFFLD(CITY)
 1600   A             SSTATE     R     B  6 59REFFLD(STATE)
 1700   A             SBALAN     R     B  6 67REFFLD(BALANC)
 1800      * Subfile control record.......
 1900   A           R SMO2CTL                       SFLCTL(SMO2SFR)
 2000   A                                          OVERLAY
 2100   A                                          SFLSIZ(10)
 2200   A                                          SFLPAG(8)
 2300   A 80                                        SFLCLR
 2400   A 81                                        SFLDSP
 2500   A 81                                        SFLDSPCTL
 2600   A 81                                        SFLEND
 2700   A                                        1 30'CUSTOMER FILE UPDATE'
 2800   A                                        4  4'CUSTNO'
 2900   A                                        4 20'NAME'
 3000   A                                        4 43'CITY'
 3100   A                                        4 57'STATE'
 3200   A                                        4 68'BALANCE'
 3300      * Command record........
 3400   A           R CMDLINE
 3500   A 70                                      20 30'NO RECORDS IN PHYSICAL FILE'
 3600   A                                         23 10'PRESS ENTER TO RETURN'
```

Field names unique to the subfile are specified. Physical file is referenced for field attributes

To support update processing, Usage field entry is specified as B (input and output).

Constants changed from CUSTOMER FILE INQUIRY to CUSTOMER FILE UPDATE

Figure 17-13 DDS subfile coding to support the update processing of a physical file.

If the same field names were used in both the physical file and subfile definitions, the second access of the physical file's records would replace any changed subfile values and the physical file's records would be updated with their original field values.

Consequently, it is necessary to move the physical file's field values to the subfile fields before loading the subfile and, then, after modifying records in the subfile, move the subfile field values to their related physical file fields before updating the physical file.

Another change needed in the DDS coding to support update processing is in the *Usage* (column 38) field for the subfile record data items in which **B** (both input and output) is specified instead of **O** (output only). This entry controls both the output of field values from the program to the screen and the input from the screen to the program.

The last change in the DDS coding replaces the constants on lines 600 and 2700 from CUSTOMER FILE INQUIRY to CUSTOMER FILE UPDATE.

RPG/400 Source Coding—Subfile Update Program

An examination of the RPG/400 program in Figure 17-14 indicates that coding for the update processing of a physical file via subfile control is similar to the previously discussed inquiry application. Any changes and additions to convert the inquiry program to support update processing are identified in comments included on the right side of the figure.

```
SEQUENCE                                                            IND   DO
NUMBER    *...1....+....2....+....3....+....4....+....5....+....6....+....7...*  USE   NUM
                          S o u r c e   L i s t i n g
     100  * Customer master update with a subfile....
     200  *
          H
     300  FCH17UPD CF  E                      WORKSTN
     400  F                                   SFRRN1KSFILE SMO2SFR
          RECORD FORMAT(S): LIBRARY SMYERS FILE CH17UPD.
                      EXTERNAL FORMAT PROMPT RPG NAME PROMPT
                      EXTERNAL FORMAT SMO2SFR RPG NAME SMO2SFR
                      EXTERNAL FORMAT SMO2CTL RPG NAME SMO2CTL
                      EXTERNAL FORMAT CMDLINE RPG NAME CMDLINE
     500  FP1PF1  UF  E           K       DISK ─────────── Physical file defined
          RECORD FORMAT(S): LIBRARY SMYERS FILE P1PF1.          as update (U in col 15)
                      EXTERNAL FORMAT P1PF1R RPG NAME P1PF1R
A000000   INPUT  FIELDS FOR RECORD PROMPT FILE CH17UPD FORMAT PROMPT.
A000001                                    1    1 *IN01            END OF JOB
A000002                                    2    6 CUSTNO
B000000   INPUT  FIELDS FOR RECORD SMO2SFR FILE CH17UPD FORMAT SMO2SFR.
B000001                                    1    5 SCUST#           CUSTOMER NO
B000002                                    6   25 SNAME            CUSTOMER NAME
B000003                                   26   45 SCITY            CITY ADDRESS
B000004                                   46   47 SSTATE           STATE ADDRESS
B000005                                   48  552SBALAN            CUSTOMER BALANCE
C000000   INPUT  FIELDS FOR RECORD SMO2CTL FILE CH17UPD FORMAT SMO2CTL.
D000000   INPUT  FIELDS FOR RECORD CMDLINE FILE CH17UPD FORMAT CMDLINE.
E000000   INPUT  FIELDS FOR RECORD P1PF1R FILE P1PF1 FORMAT P1PF1R.
E000001                                    1    5 CUST#            CUSTOMER NO
E000002                                    6   25 NAME             CUSTOMER NAME
E000003                                   26   45 STREET           STREET ADDRESS
E000004                                   46   65 CITY             CITY ADDRESS
E000005                                   66   67 STATE            STATE ADDRESS
E000006                                  P 68  700ZIP              ZIP CODE
E000007                                  P 71  752BALANC           CUSTOMER BALANCE
     600  C                  EXFMTPROMPT           dspf prompt rcd
     700  C        *IN03     DOWEQ*OFF             Do until EOJ         B001 ┐   DOW group deter-
     800  C                  MOVE *ON    *IN80     sfl clear ctrl        001 │   mines when to end
     900  C                  WRITESMO2CTL          xeq sfl clear         001 │   the program
    1000  C                  MOVE *OFF   *IN80     set off 80            001 │
    1100  C                  Z-ADD0      SFRRN1 40 init rcd ctr          001 ┘
    1200  C                  SETOF            7071 set off 70 & 71 1 2   001
    1300  C        CUSTNO    SETLLP1PF1            set PF pointer        001
    1400  C                  READ P1PF1        70read a pf rcd       3   001
    1500  C        *IN70     IFEQ *OFF             no records test      B002
    1600  *
    1700  * If one or more crecords are stored in the physical file, load the
    1800  * subfile until end of physical file or subfile is full....
```

Figure 17-14 Source listing of an RPG/400 program that processes a subfile for the update of a physical file.

```
1900  *
2000  C           *IN71      DOWEQ*OFF                    pf load control          B003───┐ DOW group that
2100  C                      EXSR PF2SF                   sr for pf tp sf            003   │ controls loading
2200  C                      ADD  1        SFRRN1         increment ctr              003   │ of the subfile
2300  C                      WRITESM02SFR              71 write sfl rcd        3     003   │
2400  C           *IN71      IFEQ *OFF                    sfl full test            B004   │
2500  C                      READ P1PF1                71 read a pf rcd        3     004   │
2600  C                      ENDIF                        end line 23 IF           E004   │
2700  C                      ENDDO                        end line 20 dow          E003───┘
2800  C                      ENDIF                        end line 15 IF           E002
2900  *
3000  * Display subfile on screen or msg if no records in physical file
3100  *
3200  C                      WRITECMDLINE                 dsp cmd constns           001
3300  C                      MOVE *ON      *IN81          sfl dsp indictr           001
3400  C                      EXFMTSM02CTL                 dsp subfile               001
3500  C                      MOVE *OFF     *IN81          set off 81                001
3600  *
3700  * Update of physical file with modified subfile records
3800  *
3900  C           *IN72      DOWEQ*OFF                    update group             B002───┐
4000  C           *IN70      ANDEQ*OFF                    records in pf?             002   │
4100  C                      READCSM02SFR              72 read sf record       3     002   │
4200  C           *IN72      IFEQ *ON                     sfl at end?              B003   │
4300  C                      LEAVE                        brch to line 52            003   │
4400  C                      ENDIF                        end line 42 if           E003   │ DOW group that
4500  C           SCUST#     CHAINP1PF1                99 get pf record        1     002   │ controls update
4600  C           *IN99      IFEQ *ON                     rcd not found?           B003   │ of the PF with
4700  C                      LEAVE                        brch to line 52            003   │ modified SF rcds
4800  C                      ENDIF                        end line 46 if           E003   │
4900  C                      EXSR SF2PF                   sr for sf to pf            002   │
5000  C                      UPDATP1PF1R                  update pf rcd             002   │
5100  C                      ENDDO                        end line 39 dow          E002───┘
5200  C                      EXFMTPROMPT                  dsp prompt rcd            001
5300  C                      ENDDO                        end line 7 dow           E001
5400  C                      MOVE *ON      *INLR          eoj control
5500  *
5600  * Move pf field values to sf fields before display
5700  *
5800  C           PF2SF      BEGSR
5900  C                      MOVE CUST#    SCUST#───┐     SR statements move
6000  C                      MOVE NAME     SNAME    │     PF field values to
6100  C                      MOVE CITY     SCITY    │     related SF fields
6200  C                      MOVE STATE    SSTATE   │     before SF is dis-
6300  C                      MOVE BALANC   SBALAN───┘     played
6400  C                      ENDSR
6500  *
6600  * Move sf field values to pf fields before update
6700  *
6800  C           SF2PF      BEGSR
6900  C                      MOVE SCUST#   CUST#────┐     SR statements move
7000  C                      MOVE SNAME    NAME     │     SF field values to
7100  C                      MOVE SCITY    CITY     │     related PF fields
7200  C                      MOVE SSTATE   STATE    │     before the PF record
7300  C                      MOVE SBALAN   BALANC───┘     is updated
7400  C                      ENDSR
F000000  OUTPUT FIELDS FOR RECORD PROMPT FILE CH17UPD FORMAT PROMPT.
G000000  OUTPUT FIELDS FOR RECORD SM02SFR FILE CH17UPD FORMAT SM02SFR.
G000001                      SCUST#     5  CHAR    5                  CUSTOMER NO
G000002                      SNAME     25  CHAR   20                  CUSTOMER NAME
G000003                      SCITY     45  CHAR   20                  CITY ADDRESS
G000004                      SSTATE    47  CHAR    2                  STATE ADDRE33
G000005                      SBALAN    55  ZONE  8,2                  CUSTOMER BALANCE
H000000  OUTPUT FIELDS FOR RECORD SM02CTL FILE CH17UPD FORMAT SM02CTL.
H000001                      *IN80      1  CHAR    1
H000002                      *IN81      2  CHAR    1
I000000  OUTPUT FIELDS FOR RECORD CMDLINE FILE CH17UPD FORMAT CMDLINE.
I000001                      *IN70      1  CHAR    1
J000000  OUTPUT FIELDS FOR RECORD P1PF1R FILE P1PF1 FORMAT P1PF1R.
J000001                      CUST#      5  CHAR    5                  CUSTOMER NO
J000002                      NAME      25  CHAR   20                  CUSTOMER NAME
J000003                      STREET    45  CHAR   20                  STREET ADDRESS
J000004                      CITY      65  CHAR   20                  CITY ADDRESS
J000005                      STATE     67  CHAR    2                  STATE ADDRESS
J000006                      ZIP       70P PACK  5,0                  ZIP CODE
J000007                      BALANC    75P PACK  8,2                  CUSTOMER BALANCE
```

Figure 17-14 Source listing of an RPG/400 program that processes a subfile for the update of a physical file. (Continued)

The instructions (lines 3900–5100) that control the update processing of the physical file are detailed separately in Figure 17-15.

```
3700    * Update of physical file with modified subfile records
3800    *
3900  C        *IN72    DOWEQ*OFF                     update group        B002
4000  C        *IN70    ANDEQ*OFF                     records in pf?       002
4100  C                 READCSMO2SFR                  72 read sf record  3 002
4200  C        *IN72    IFEQ *ON                      sfl at end?         B003
4300  C                 LEAVE                         brch to line 52      003
4400  C                 ENDIF                         end line 42 if      E003
4500  C        SCUST#   CHAINP1PF1         99         get pf record    1  002
4600  C        *IN99    IFEQ *ON                      rcd not found?      B003
4700  C                 LEAVE                         brch to line 52      003
4800  C                 ENDIF                         end line 46 if      E003
4900  C                 EXSR SF2PF                    sr for sf to pf      002
5000  C                 UPDATP1PF1R                   update pf rcd        002
5100  C                 ENDDO                         end line 39 dow     E002
```

Line #

3900 -
4000   The **DOWEQ** group is performed while there are "changed" records in the subfile (indicator **72** off—assigned to the **READC** instruction on line 4100), and if the **READ** statement on line 1400 tested that at least one record is stored in the physical file (indicator 70 "off")

4100   The **READC** operation reads only the subfile records that have been "changed." When processing determines that there are no more "changed" records in the subfile, indicator **72,** specified in the *Equal* field (columns 58–59), will automatically be set on. Any subfile records <u>not</u> changed are <u>not</u> processed by the **READC** operation.

4200   This **IFEQ** statement tests the status of indicator **72,** which is set on in the **READC** statement on line 4100 if the subfile does not have any more "changed" records.

4300   When the **IFEQ** test on line 4200 is true (**72** "on"), the **LEAVE** operation transfers control to line 5200 (first statement after the **ENDDO** operation on line 5100).

4400   **ENDIF** operation ends the **IFEQ** statement on line 4200.

4500   The customer number value of a "changed" subfile record is used to **CHAIN** to the physical file to find the related record so it may be updated. Processing of the subfile automatically begins at the first "changed" record.

4600   This **IFEQ** statement tests the status of indicator **99** specified with the **CHAIN** operation on line 4500. When the **CHAIN** is <u>not</u> successful (record not found), indicator **99** is set "on."

4700   When the **IFEQ** test on line 4600 is "true" (record not found), the **LEAVE** operation will transfer control to line 5200 (first statement after the **ENDDO** operation on line 5100).

4800   **ENDIF** operation ends the **IFEQ** statement on line 4600.

4900   When the **IFEQ** test on line 4600 is false (record found), control is transferred to the SF2PF subroutine where subfile field values in the "changed" record are moved to their related physical file fields.

5000   After control returns from the SF2PF routine, the **UPDAT** statement writes the "changed" physical file record to its original location in the file.

5100   **ENDDO** operation ends the **DOWEQ** group that began on line 3900.

Figure 17-15 DOWEQ group that controls the update of a physical file from changed subfile records.

READC (Read Next Modified Record)

The syntax of the **READC** (*Read Next Modified Record*) operation is explained in Figure 17-16.

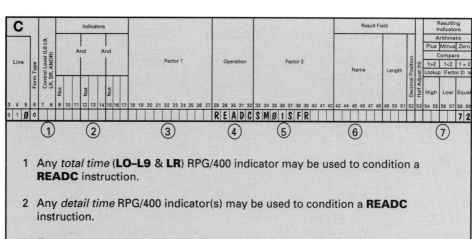

1 Any *total time* (**LO–L9** & **LR**) RPG/400 indicator may be used to condition a **READC** instruction.

2 Any *detail time* RPG/400 indicator(s) may be used to condition a **READC** instruction.

3 *Factor 1* must be blank (not used).

4 **READC** operation name must be specified in the *Operation* field.

5 The subfile record format name that was specified in the *Entry* field (columns 60–65) of the continuation line for the *File Description* definition of the WORKSTN file must be entered in left-justified in *Factor 2.*

6 *Result Field* must be blank (not used).

7 *Resulting indicator* > field (columns 54–55) must be blank (not used).

An <u>optional</u> indicator may be entered in the *Resulting Indicator* < field (columns 56–57) to test for an error condition when the operation is executed.

A <u>required</u> indicator must be entered in the *Resulting Indicator* = field (columns 58–59) that is set on when there are no more "changed" records in the subfile.

Note: The **READC** operation may only be specified for WORKSTN files that process a display file that includes a subfile, identified by the **SFILE** keyword in the *Option* field (columns 54–60) of the *File Description* statement.

Figure 17-16 Syntax of the **READC** (Read Next Modified Record) operation.

Results of the subfile update processing are shown in Figure 17-17. The top section shows that two subfile records have been changed; the bottom section is a redisplay of the

```
Display of Subfile Before Update of Physical File:

                        CUSTOMER FILE UPDATE


     CUSTNO        NAME            CITY        STATE    BALANCE

     12345    KAREL APPEL       NEW YORK        NY     00125000
     23456    GEORGES BRAQUE    TRENTON         NJ     00010000 - Changed from 10000
     34567    PAUL CEZANNE      STAMFORD        CT     08190000      to 20000
```

Figure 17-17 Before and after results of updating a physical file with a subfile.

```
      45678    MARC CHAGALL          BRIDGEPORT          CT      00092600
      56789    EDGAR DEGAS           WESTPORT            PA      00784599
      67890    MAX ERNST             FRANKFORT           KY      00050000 - Changed from 50000
      78900    BUCKMINSTER FULLER    NEW YORK            NY      03300010      to 69000
      89000    JULIO GONZALEZ        GREENWICH           CT      00065478      +


   Re-display of Subfile After Physical File Records Are Updated:

                              CUSTOMER FILE UPDATE


      CUSTNO        NAME               CITY          STATE     BALANCE

      12345    KAREL APPEL           NEW YORK            NY      00125000
      23456    GEORGES BRAQUE        TRENTON             NJ      00020000 - Record changed
      34567    PAUL CEZANNE          STAMFORD            CT      08190000
      45678    MARC CHAGALL          BRIDGEPORT          CT      00092600
      56789    EDGAR DEGAS           WESTPORT            PA      00784599
      67890    MAX ERNST             FRANKFORT           KY      00069000 - Record changed
      78900    BUCKMINSTER FULLER    NEW YORK            NY      03300010
      89000    JULIO GONZALEZ        GREENWICH           CT      00065478      +
```

Figure 17-17   Before and after results of updating a physical file with a subfile. (Continued)

same data after the physical file record is updated. Again, the only physical file records updated are the two changed in the subfile; the others are ignored by the **READC** instruction in the update process.

SUBFILE APPLICATION PROGRAM: ADDITION PROCESSING

Interactive data validation procedures may be enhanced by first loading the input data to a subfile. Then, the user may review the records for errors before they are added to a physical file. The system flowchart shown in Figure 17-18 details the file processing associated with the addition of records to a physical file via a subfile. The sequence of processing steps shown in Figure 17-18 are controlled by the RPG/400 program and include the following:

1. Records are input via a separate display file record format and loaded to the subfile.
2. The subfile is displayed and the records are reviewed by the user. Any necessary changes are made.
3. The subfile records are added to the physical file.

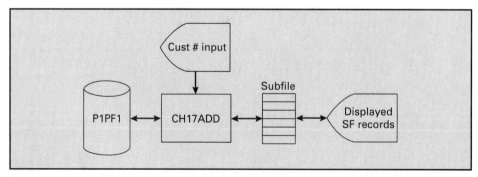

Figure 17-18   System flowchart for an RPG/400 program that adds records to a physical file via a subfile.

DDS Coding—Subfile Adds Program

Formats of the four records, ENTRY, SM03SFR, SM03CTL, and CMDLINE, included in the display file SFLADD are shown in Figure 17-19. The constants defined on line 23 of the subfile are defined as the fourth record format in the display file.

Entry Record Format:

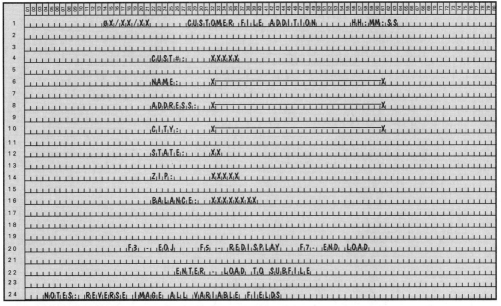

Subfile Record Formats:

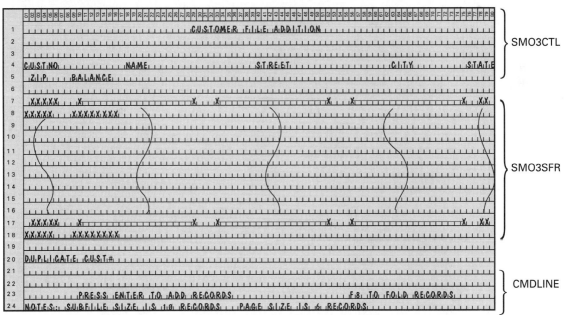

Figure 17-19 Record formats defined in the display file SFLADD.

A source listing and a line-by-line explanation of the DDS coding of the display file SFADD processed by the subfile addition program is detailed in Figure 17-20. Notice that three keywords not used in the previous subfile programs have been specified in this application. Included is the subfile record keyword, **SFLNXTCHG,** and the subfile control record keywords **SFLNRA** and **SFLINZ.** The function of each is explained in the text that supplements Figure 17-20.

```
   ... ... 1 ... ... 2 ... ... 3 ... ... 4 ... ... 5 ... ... 6 ... ... 7 ...
0001 A                                        PRINT
0002 A                                        MSGLOC(20)
0003 A                                        REF(P1PF1)
0004 A* Entry screen..........
0005 A        R ENTRY                         CA03(03 'END OF JOB')
0006 A                                        CF05(05 'REDISPLAY')
0007 A                                        CA07(07 'END SF LOAD')
0008 A                                       1 14DATE EDTCDE(Y)
0009 A                                       1 56TIME
0010 A                                       1 28'CUSTOMER FILE ADDITION'
0011 A                                       4 22'CUST#:'
0012 A          CUST#      R      I   4 32DSPATR(RI)
0013 A                                       6 22'NAME:'
0014 A          NAME       R      I   6 32DSPATR(RI)
0015 A                                       8 22'STREET:'
0016 A          STREET     R      I   8 32DSPATR(RI)
0017 A                                      10 22'CITY:'
0018 A          CITY       R      I  10 32DSPATR(RI)
0019 A                                      12 22'STATE:'
0020 A          STATE      R      I  12 32DSPATR(RI)
0021 A                                      14 22'ZIP:'
0022 A          ZIP        R      I  14 32DSPATR(RI)
0023 A                                      16 22'BALANCE:'
0024 A          BALANC     R      I  16 32DSPATR(RI)
0025 A                                      20 17'F3 -EOJ     F5 - REDISPLAY
0026 A                                           F7 - END LOAD'
0027 A                                      22 26'ENTER - LOAD TO SUBFILE'
0028 A* Subfile record definition.....
0029 A        R SM03SFR                       SFL
0030 A                                        SFLNXTCHG
0031 A          CUST#      R      B   7  2
0032 A   99                                   DSPATR(RI)
0033 A          NAME       R      B   7 10
0034 A          STREET     R      B   7 33
0035 A          CITY       R      B   7 56
0036 A          STATE      R      B   7 78
0037 A          ZIP        R      B   8  1
0038 A          BALANC     R      B   8  9
0039 A* Control record definition......
0040 A        R SM03CTL                       SFLCTL(SM03SFR)
0041 A                                        OVERLAY
0042 A                                        SFLRNA
0043 A                                        SFLSIZ(10)
0044 A                                        SFLPAG(6)
0045 A   80                                   SFLCLR
0046 A   80                                   SFLINZ
0047 A   81                                   SFLDSP
0048 A   81                                   SFLDSPCTL
0049 A   81                                   SFLEND
0050 A                                        SFLDROP(CF08)
0051 A   99                                   SFLMSG('DUPLICATE CUST#' 99)
0052 A                                       1 29'CUSTOMER FILE ADDITION'
0053 A                                       4  1'CUSTNO'
0054 A                                       4 18'NAME'
0055 A                                       4 40'STREET'
0056 A                                       4 63'CITY'
0057 A                                       4 76'STATE'
0058 A                                       5  2'ZIP'
0059 A                                       5  9'BALANCE'
0060 A        R CMDLINE
0061 A                                      23 10'PRESS ENTER TO ADD RECORDS'
0062 A                                      23 55'F8 TO FOLD RECORDS'
```

Figure 17-20 DDS coding for the display file that supports the subfile addition program.

Line #

0001   **PRINT** keyword supports printing of a screen image when the Print key is pressed.

0002   **MSGLOC(20)** keyword specifies that **SFLMSG** text, DUPLICATE CUST# (line 0051), is to display on line 20 instead of on default line 24.

0005   The field attributes of the physical file P1PF1 are referenced by the **REF(P1PF1)** keyword.

0005 -
0007   The entry screen record, ENTRY, is defined with its related controlling command keys. **CA03** controls end of job in the RPG/400 program; **CF05** redisplays this screen without adding the record to the subfile; and **CA07** allows the operator to stop loading the subfile. As specified in a constant, the **ENTER** key will add the record to the subfile

0008 -
0027   These instruction define the screen record that supports the entry of data and subsequent loading to the subfile.

0029   The record SM03SFR is defined as a subfile record format by the **SFL** keyword.

0030   The keyword **SFLNXTCHG** enables a **READC** instruction in an RPG/400 program to process all of the subfile records as "changed."

0031 -
0038   Physical file fields are referenced in these instructions. Because the physical file was defined as supporting only **UNIQUE** keys, any attempt to add a record with a duplicate key will cause a **WRITE** error. Indicator **99,** assigned to the **WRITE** instruction (columns 56–57) in the RPG/400 program, identifies this error by turning on, which is used here to display the CUST# value in reverse image when the subfile record values are displayed.

0040   The **SFLCTL(SM03SFR)** keyword defines record format SM03CTL as the subfile control record related to the subfile record SM03SFR.

0041   **OVERLAY** prevents the previously displayed record format (CMDLINE) from being written over when this record format is output. Because the processing of the subfile control record, subfile record, and command record are so fast, it will appear as if they display simultaneously. However, the constants in the CMDLINE are displayed first by the RPG/400 program.

0042   The keyword **SFLRNA** initializes the subfile with no active records. This keyword is used in conjunction with **SFLINZ,** which actually performs the initialization function.

0043   **SFLSIZ(10)** specifies that the subfile is to store a maximum of 10 records.

0044   **SFLPAG(6)** specifies that six records are to be displayed on each page of the subfile.

0045   **SFLCLR** clears the subfile area before the subfile is created. This action is performed in the RPG/400 program when indicator **80** is turned on and the subfile control record is executed by a **WRITE** statement.

0046   **SFLINZ** initializes alphanumeric fields to blanks and numeric fields to zeros in all of the subfile records with one operation when indicator **80** is set on in the RPG/400 program and the subfile control record is executed.

        Because the **READC** operation is used to read records from a subfile, the records must be changed to support this function. When the input records are added to a subfile initialized by an **SFLINZ** operation, they are flagged as "changed" and may then be processed by a **READC** instruction. For this program example, all of the subfile records are added to a physical file.

        Without the **SFLRNA/SFLINZ** keywords, none of the subfile records would be "flagged" as changed. Consequently, no records would be read by a **READC** operation and none added to the physical file.

0047 -
0049   Indicator **81,** turned on in the RPG/400 program, conditions the following subfile functions:

Figure 17-20 DDS coding for the display file that supports the subfile addition program. (Continued)

SFLDSP   - Displays the subfile records.
SFLDSPCTL - Displays the constants and any variables specied in the subfile control record format.
SFLEND   - Displays a + (plus sign) to the right of the last subfile record on the current page, indicating that another page of records is stored in the subfile.

0050   The **SFLDROP(CF08)** keyword controls the folding of subfile control and record formats when the constants and/or variables require a display of more than 80 columns on a standard CRT. The command function or attention key specified with this keyword (**CF08** for this example) must be pressed to cause the subfile records to change from a truncated to a folded format (continued on next line specified). Note that the constants in the control record format will automatically wrap to the line specified. However, a command key <u>must</u> be pressed to continue the subfile record field values on another line.

Notice in the control record format, lines 0058 and 0059, that the constants ZIP and BALANCE are defined on line 5 immediately below the other constants on line 4. This coding places these constants on the following line when F8 is pressed and the **SFLDROP** function executed.

Refer to the subfile record format, lines 0037 and 0038, and notice that the variables ZIP and BALANC are defined to display on line 8 below the other related field variables on line 7. This coding places these variables on the following line when F8 is pressed and the **SFLDROP** function executed.

The line location in the subfile record identifies the location of the first record. Other records are sequentially displayed on subsequent lines of the screen as defined by the **SFLPAG** keyword.

0051   **SFLMSG** performs the same function as an **ERRMSG** keyword. When the **WRITE** statement in the RPG/400 program attempts to add a record that has a key value already stored in the physical file, indicator **99** specified in columns 56–57 of the **WRITE** statement will be turned on. Because this keyword is conditioned by indicator **99,** the message DUPLICATE CUST# will be displayed on line 20 as specified by the **MSGLOC(20)** keyword. Indicator **99,** which is included in the parentheses of the **SFLMSG** keyword, turns off the indicator when any key is subsequently pressed.

0052 -
0059   Column headings are defined in these instructions. When the subfile control record format is executed by an **EXFMT** instruction, the headings will be displayed in their specified locations.

0060 -
0062   Record format CMDLINE includes constants that are displayed at the bottom of the subfile to inform the operator what actions to take to add the subfile records to the physical file or fold the truncated field values on to the next display line.

Figure 17-20   DDS coding for the display file that supports the subfile addition program. (Continued)

RPG/400 Source Coding—Subfile Addition Program

A detailed source listing of the RPG/400 program that controls addition to a physical file via a subfile is presented in Figure 17-21.

```
SEQUENCE                                                                                     IND   DO
NUMBER     *...1....+....2....+....3....+....4....+....5....+....6....+....7...*  USE   NUM
                            S o u r c e   L i s t i n g
       100   * Customer master adds with a subfile....
       200   *
             H
```

Figure 17-21   Source listing of an RPG/400 program that processes a subfile for the addition of records to a physical file.

```
 300   FCH17ADD CF  E                    WORKSTN
 400   F                                       SFRRN1KSFILE SMO3SFR
         RECORD FORMAT(S): LIBRARY SMYERS FILE CH17ADD.
                 EXTERNAL FORMAT ENTRY RPG NAME ENTRY
                 EXTERNAL FORMAT SMO3SFR RPG NAME SMO3SFR
                 EXTERNAL FORMAT SMO3CTL RPG NAME SMO3CTL
                 EXTERNAL FORMAT CMDLINE RPG NAME CMDLINE
 500   FP1PF1   O   E         K          DISK                          A
         RECORD FORMAT(S): LIBRARY SMYERS FILE P1PF1.
                 EXTERNAL FORMAT P1PF1R RPG NAME P1PF1R
A000000   INPUT  FIELDS FOR RECORD ENTRY FILE CH17ADD FORMAT ENTRY.
A000001                                    2   2 *IN01              END OF JOB
A000002                                    1   1 *IN03              REDISPLAY
A000003                                    3   3 *IN04              END SF LOAD
A000004                                    4   8 CUST#              CUSTOMER NO
A000005                                    9  28 NAME               CUSTOMER NAME
A000006                                   29  48 STREET             STREET ADDRESS
A000007                                   49  68 CITY               CITY ADDRESS
A000008                                   69  70 STATE              STATE ADDRESS
A000009                                   71  75 ZIP                ZIP CODE
A000010                                   76  83 BALANC             CUSTOMER BALANCE
B000000   INPUT  FIELDS FOR RECORD SMO3SFR FILE CH17ADD FORMAT SMO3SFR.
B000001                                    1   5 CUST#              CUSTOMER NO
B000002                                    6  25 NAME               CUSTOMER NAME
B000003                                   26  45 STREET             STREET ADDRESS
B000004                                   46  65 CITY               CITY ADDRESS
B000005                                   66  67 STATE              STATE ADDRESS
B000006                                   68  72 ZIP                ZIP CODE
B000007                                   73  80 BALANC             CUSTOMER BALANCE
C000000   INPUT  FIELDS FOR RECORD SMO3CTL FILE CH17ADD FORMAT SMO3CTL.
C000001                                    1   1 *IN99              DUPLICATE CUST#
D000000   INPUT  FIELDS FOR RECORD CMDLINE FILE CH17ADD FORMAT CMDLINE.
 600   C           *IN03      DOUEQ*ON                                     B001
 700   C                      CLEARENTRY               clear screen        002
 800   *
 900   * Load subfile with records entered via ENTRY display......
1000   *
1100   C           *IN71      DOUEQ*ON             dou sfl is full         B002
1200   C                      EXFMTENTRY           dsp entry rcd           002
1300   C           *IN03      CABEQ*ON     EOJ     eoj test                002
1400   C           *IN05      CABEQ*ON     SKIP    redisplay               002
1500   C           *IN07      IFEQ *ON             op ends sf load         B003
1600   C                      LEAVE                brch to line 24         003
1700   C                      ENDIF                end line 16 if          E003
1800   C                      ADD  1       SFRRN1  incrmnt sfl ctr         002
1900   C                      WRITESMO3SFR      71 load rcd to sfl         002
2000   C           SKIP       TAG                  for line 15 cab         002
2100   C                      ENDDO                end line 10 dou         E002
2200   *
2300   * Display subfile and command records......
2400   *
2500   C                      WRITECMDLINE         dsp cmd constns         001
2600   C                      MOVE *ON     *IN81   sfl dsp indictr         001
2700   C                      EXFMTSMO3CTL         dsp subfile             001
2800   C                      MOVE *OFF    *IN81   set off 81              001
2900   *
3000   * Add subfile records to physical file......
3100   *
3200   C                      Z-ADD1       SFRRN1  init. sfl ctr           001
3300   C                      READCSMO3SFR      72 read 1st sf rcd    3    001
3400   C           *IN72      DOWEQ*OFF            dow not end sfl         B002
3500   C                      WRITEP1PF1R       99 add rcd to pf      2    002
3600   C                      ADD  1       SFRRN1  incrmnt sf ctr          002
3700   C                      READCSMO3SFR      72 read a sf rcd      3    002
3800   C                      ENDDO                end line               E002
3900   C                      EXSR CLEAR           brch to sr              001
4000   C           EOJ        TAG                  for lne 14 cab          001
4100   C                      ENDDO                line 10 dou             E001
4200   C                      MOVE *ON     *INLR   end of job est
4300   *
```

Figure 17-21   Source listing of an RPG/400program that processes a subfile for the addition of records to a physical file. (Continued)

```
 4400   * Subroutine to clear subfile & initialize record counter......
 4500   *
 4600   C           CLEAR       BEGSR                       begin sr
 4700   C                       MOVE *ON      *IN80         set on clear in
 4800   C                       WRITESMO3CTL                clear subfile
 4900   C                       MOVE *OFF     *IN80         set 80 off
 5000   C                       Z-ADD0        SFRRN1  40    init. rcd ctr
 5100   C                       SETOF                 7172  set off ind    1 2
 5200   C                       ENDSR                       end sr
E000000   OUTPUT FIELDS FOR RECORD ENTRY FILE CH17ADD FORMAT ENTRY.
F000000   OUTPUT FIELDS FOR RECORD SMO3SFR FILE CH17ADD FORMAT SMO3SFR.
F000001                     *IN99     1   CHAR     1
F000002                     CUST#     6   CHAR     5            CUSTOMER NO
F000003                     NAME     26   CHAR    20            CUSTOMER NAME
F000004                     STREET   46   CHAR    20            STREET ADDRESS
F000005                     CITY     66   CHAR    20            CITY ADDRESS
F000006                     STATE    68   CHAR     2            STATE ADDRESS
F000007                     ZIP      73   ZONE   5,0            ZIP CODE
F000008                     BALANC   81   ZONE   8,2            CUSTOMER BALANCE
G000000   OUTPUT FIELDS FOR RECORD SMO3CTL FILE CH17ADD FORMAT SMO3CTL.
G000001                     *IN80     1   CHAR     1
G000002                     *IN81     2   CHAR     1
G000003                     *IN99     3   CHAR     1            DUPLICATE CUST#
H000000   OUTPUT FIELDS FOR RECORD CMDLINE FILE CH17ADD FORMAT CMDLINE.
H000001                     *IN70     1   CHAR     1
I000000   OUTPUT FIELDS FOR RECORD P1PF1R FILE P1PF1 FORMAT P1PF1R.
I000001                     CUST#     5   CHAR     5            CUSTOMER NO
I000002                     NAME     25   CHAR    20            CUSTOMER NAME
I000003                     STREET   45   CHAR    20            STREET ADDRESS
I000004                     CITY     65   CHAR    20            CITY ADDRESS
I000005                     STATE    67   CHAR     2            STATE ADDRESS
I000006                     ZIP      70P  PACK   5,0            ZIP CODE
I000007                     BALANC   75P  PACK   8,2            CUSTOMER BALANCE
```

Line #

300   The display file which includes the ENTRY screen, subfile record format, subfile control record, and command line record is defined as a combined, full procedural, externally defined workstation file.

400   The **K** in column 53 indicates that this instruction is a continuation of line 300.

The SFRRN1 entry in columns 47–52 specifies a programmer-defined field in which relative record numbers of records written to the subfile are stored and incremented.

The **SFILE** keyword in columns 54–59 specifies that this statement is related to a subfile.

The SM03SFR entry in columns 60–65 specifies the name of the subfile record format,

500   The physical file, P1PF1, is defined as an externally described output file that supports record addition (**A** in column 66).

600   The **DOUEQ** group is performed until the operator presses F3 to end the job by passing control to line 4200, where **LR** is set on.

700   The **CLEAR** statement clears the ENTRY screen before the data for the next record is entered.

1100   **DOUEQ** group of instructions are performed until the subfile is full (indicator **71** on).

1200   **EXFMT** instruction displays record format ENTRY so data may be entered, or the job ended (F3), or redisplay the screen (F5), or display the subfile (F7).

1300   If F3 is pressed, control is passed to line 4000, the **DOUEQ** test made at the **ENDDO** on line 4100, and the job ended by the **MOVE** statement on line 4200.

Figure 17-21   Source listing of an RPG/400 program that processes a subfile for the addition of records to a physical file. (Continued)

1400 If the operator changes his/her mind about entering the current record, F5 must be pressed, which will pass control to the **TAG** operation line 2000 and then to 1100 to continue the entry of new data or end the job.

1500-
1600 The operator may end the addition of records to the subfile at any time (instead of filling the subfile) by pressing F7. When the **IFEQ** test is true (indicator **07** on), the **LEAVE** operation on line 1600 will exit the **DOUEQ** group to line 2500.

1700 This **ENDIF** statement ends the **IFEQ** statement on line 1500.

1800 The subfile record counter, SFRRN1, is incremented by 1.

1900 The **WRITE** statement controls loading of the current screen record to a subfile record position as determined by the current value in the SFRRN1 counter. Indicator **71**, entered in the *equal* field (columns 58–59), will turn on when the subfile is full. The indicator is specified in the **DOUEQ** statement on line 1100 as one of the conditions that determines when loading of the subfile is to be stopped.

2000 This **TAG** statement is the label for the **CABEQ** statement on line 1400.

2100 The **ENDDO** operation ends the **DOUEQ** group (lines 1100 through 2100). The equal test specified in the **DOUEQ** statement on line 1100 is made at this **ENDDO** operation.

2500 The constants in the CMDLINE record format are displayed by this **WRITE** statement.

2600 Indicator **81,** which controls the display of the subfile record and control record formats, is set on.

2700 The **EXFMT** statement displays the subfile control record constants and subfile record variables. Indicator **81,** which was turned on in line 2600, conditioned the subfile's keywords (**SFLDSP, SFLDSPCTL,** and **SFLEND**) in the DDS coding for this control.

2800 Indicator **81** is set off.

3300 This **READC** statement reads the first "changed" record from the subfile record format (SM03SFR). If no records are stored in the subfile, indicator **72,** specified in the equal field (columns 58–59) will turn on. Indicator **72** is included in the test for the following **DOWEQ** statement (line 3400) to determine when the subfile is at its end and to stop the writing of records to the physical file. Note that the **SFLNXTCHG** keyword must be specified in the subfile record format for the **READC** operation to identify all of the subfile records as "changed."

Note that only the **READC** operation may be used to read the "changed" subfile records, and not one of the other **READ** operations.

3400 The **DOWEQ** group controls the reading of subfile records and loading of the physical file with them until end of the subfile is tested (indicator **72** is on). Execution of the **SFLRNA** and **SFLINZ** keywords in the subfile control record cleared the subfile and initialized its relative record positions to a "changed" mode.

3500 The **WRITE** statement adds the current subfile record to the physical file.

3700 Another "changed" record is read from the subfile by the **READC** statement.

3800 The **ENDDO** operation ends the **DOWEQ** group (lines 3400–3800). When this statement is executed, control is passed back to the **DOWEQ** statement on line 3400, where the end-of-subfile test is made.

4000 This **TAG** statement is the label for the **CABEQ** statement on line 1300, which was executed when the operator pressed F3 in the ENTRY screen to end the job.

4100 The **DOUEQ** test on line 600 is made at this **ENDDO** operation. If the operator presses F3, the **DOUEQ** test on line 600 will be true and control will pass to the statement on line 4200 to end the job.

If F3 was not pressed to end the job, control will return back to the **DOUEQ** statement on line 600 and the processing cycle continued.

Figure 17-21 Source listing of an RPG/400 program that processes a subfile for the addition of records to a physical file. (Continued)

4200 **MOVE LR** statement ends the job and returns control back to the operating system.

4600 -

5200 This subroutine includes instructions that clear the subfile (lines 4700–4800), initialize the subfile relative record counter (line 5000), and set off the *Resulting Indicators* (line 5100).

Figure 17-21 Source listing of an RPG/400 program that processes a subfile for the addition of records to a physical file. (Continued)

Execution of the subfile addition program generates the screen displays illustrated in Figure 17-22. The first screen shown (ENTRY) supports the entry of data to load the

```
Displayed ENTRY Record Format:

      12/01/95        CUSTOMER FILE ADDITION        11:15:00


                    CUST#:   20000

                    NAME:    PAUL GAUGUIN

                    STREET:  12 TAHITI PLACE

                    CITY:    PACIFIC

                    STATE:   CA

                    ZIP:     09900

                    BALANCE:    10012



            CK1 - EOJ  CK3 - REDISPLAY  CK4 - END LOAD

                   ENTER - LOAD TO SUBFILE
```

```
Displayed SM03CTL, SM03SFR, and CMDLINE Subfile Record Formats:

                       CUSTOMER FILE ADDITION

    CUSTNO         NAME              STREET          CITY        STATE
      ZIP     BALANCE

     20000   PAUL GAUGUIN       12 TAHITI PLACE    PACIFIC        CA
    09900  00010012
     35000   EDWARD MONET       4 IMPRESSIONIST ROAD  MILAN       PA
    04444  00089500
     40000   HENRI MATISSE      44 RUE PIGALLE     FRANCE         KY
    07777  00034910
     90000   PIERRE RENOIR      96 MONTCLAIR DRIVE  PARIS         NY
    01111  00100000                                                  +




    PRESS ENTER TO ADD RECORDS              CK5 TO FOLD RECORDS
```

Figure 17-22 Displays of the ENTRY and subfile's SM03SFR, SM03CTL, and CMDLINE formats.

subfile, and the second shows a display of the subfile after it is loaded. Under control of the subfile display, the user has the option to move the cursor to any record and modify one or all of the field values. To see the truncated subfile record values (ZIP and BAL-ANC), the operator must press command key 5. This action folds the two hidden field values onto the next line for review and/or change. As was previously explained in Figure 17-20, folding the subfile record values is controlled by the **SFLDROP** keyword in the subfile's control record format (SM03CTL).

A display of the physical file (P1PF1) generated by the **DSPPFM** (*Display Physical File Member*) command will show that the "add" records are stored at the end of the file in the order they were loaded.

WINDOWS

Windowing is the superimposing of one or more displays within the body of one or more existing displays. Figure 17-23 illustrates a window format displayed in the body of an existing display.

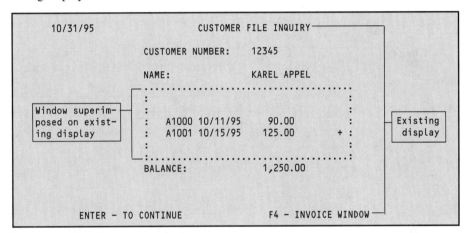

Figure 17-23 Window example.

The syntax for windows may be defined by the programmer or with special keywords supplied by DDS for display files. All of the examples shown will apply the DDS keywords.

Window Keywords

Display file keywords unique to windows are **WINDOW, WDWBORDER, RMVWDW,** and **USRRSTDSP.** The function of each keyword is explained in Figure 17-24.

Keyword	Function
WINDOW	Defines the display record as a window format. Row, column, width, and height of the window are defined with this keyword.
WDWBORDER	Defines the window's border attributes including *CHAR, *DSPATR, and *COLOR. Supplies the top and bottom lines and left and right border characters.
RMVWDW	Clears all window formats from the display. Then, the window format that includes this keyword is displayed.
USRRSTDSP	Reduces blanking and blinking when the displays overlap each other.

Figure 17-24 DDS keywords for windows.

The WINDOW Keyword

The syntax for the two formats of the **WINDOW** keyword and its parameters and functions are detailed in Figure 17-25.

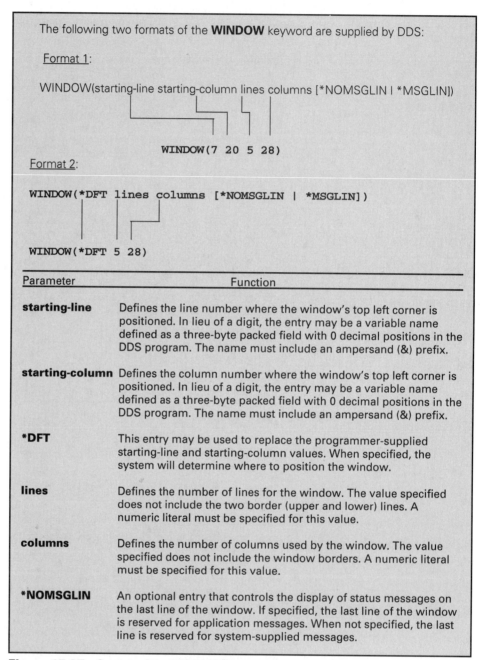

Figure 17-25   Syntax of the **WINDOW** keyword.

Figure 17-26 shows the relationship of the entries in a **WINDOW** keyword to its related display.

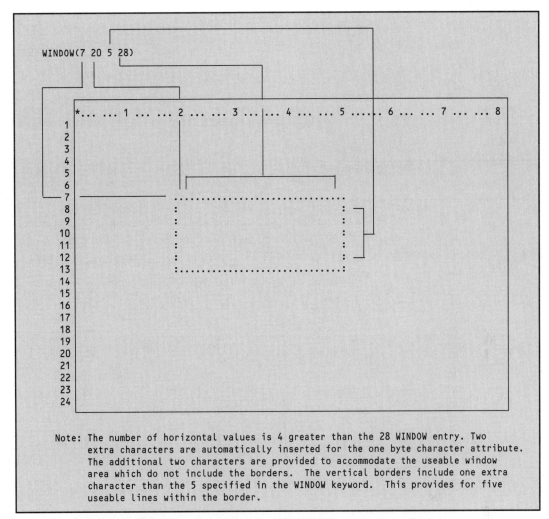

Figure 17-26   Relationship of the **WINDOW** keyword to a display.

The WDWBORDER Keyword

The syntax and parameters of the **WDWBORDER** keyword are explained in Figure
17-27.

WDWBORDER Format:

WDWBORDER((ctrl-parm1 options) (ctrl-parm2 options) (ortl-parm3 options))

Parameter	Options	Function
*CHAR	any 8 characters	A window border must include 8 characters that have the following functions in the indicated order:
		1. Top left corner
		2. Top row border
		3. Top right corner
		4. Left column border
		5. Right column border

Figure 17-27   WDWBORDER parameters and options.

		6. Bottom left corner 7. Bottom row border 8. Bottom right corner
		<u>Example:</u>　WDWBORDER((*CHAR'+ - + | | + - + '))
*DSPATR	BL, CS, HI, ND, RI, UL	Only one display attribute may be specified for a window border. All are valid for monochrome or color displays. HI (highlight) is the default for monochrome displays and normal for color.
		<u>Example:</u>　WDWBORDER((*DSPATR RI))
*COLOR	BLU, GRN, PNK, RED, TRQ, WHT, YLW	Only one color may be specified for a window border. The color parameter is ignored by monochrome displays. <u>Example:</u>　WDWBORDER((*COLOR GRN))

Figure 17-27 **WDWBORDER** parameters and options. (Continued)

The relationship of the **WDWBORDER** keyword and its related display is shown in Figure 17-28.

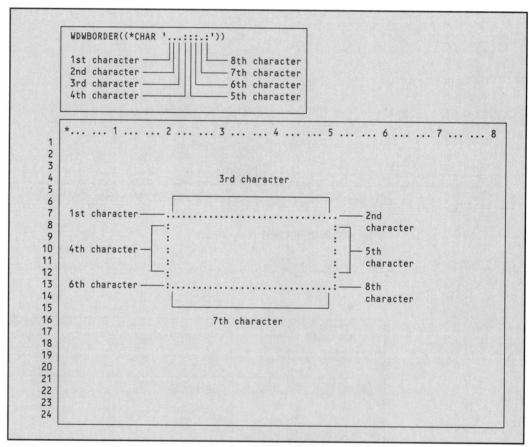

Figure 17-28　Relationship of the **WDWBORDER** keyword to a display.

The format, **WDWBORDER ((*CHAR '...::..:'))**, is only one of any number of ***CHAR** parameter options that may be used. A programmer may specify any combination of characters that he or she finds acceptable for the window borders. Figure 17-29 illustrates a few other window border patterns that are often used.

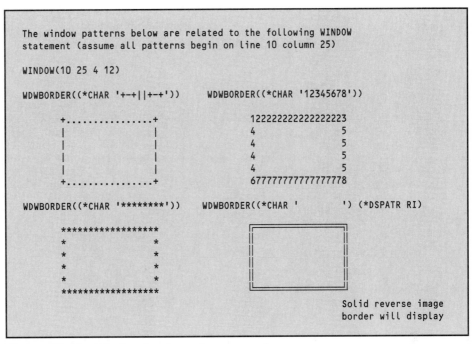

Figure 17-29 Window border pattern examples.

EXAMPLE SUBFILE PROGRAM USING WINDOWING

A source listing of a display file that includes five record formats is shown in Figure 17-30.

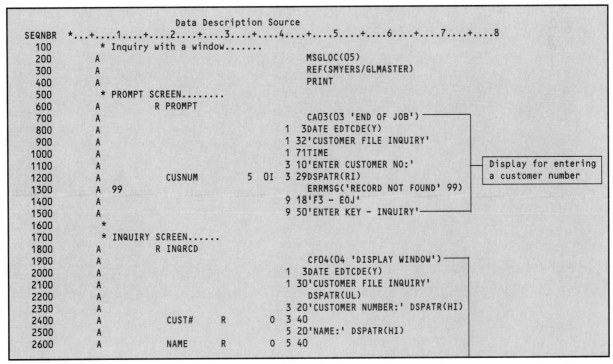

Figure 17-30 Display file that controls the processing of a subfile that includes windowing.

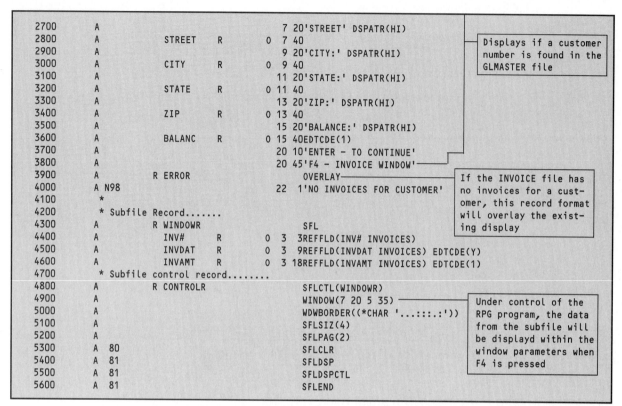

```
2700    A                            7 20'STREET' DSPATR(HI)
2800    A        STREET   R      0   7 40                              ┌─── Displays if a customer
2900    A                            9 20'CITY:' DSPATR(HI)            │    number is found in the
3000    A        CITY     R      0   9 40                              │    GLMASTER file
3100    A                           11 20'STATE:' DSPATR(HI)           │
3200    A        STATE    R      0  11 40                              │
3300    A                           13 20'ZIP:' DSPATR(HI)             │
3400    A        ZIP      R      0  13 40                              │
3500    A                           15 20'BALANCE:' DSPATR(HI)         │
3600    A        BALANC   R      0  15 40EDTCDE(1)                     │
3700    A                           20 10'ENTER - TO CONTINUE'         │
3800    A                           20 45'F4 - INVOICE WINDOW'─────────┘
3900    A        R ERROR                OVERLAY──────────────┐  If the INVOICE file has
4000    A N98                       22  1'NO INVOICES FOR CUSTOMER'    no invoices for a cust-
4100    *                                                              omer, this record format
4200    * Subfile Record.......                                        will overlay the exist-
4300    A        R WINDOWR              SFL                            ing display
4400    A        INV#     R      0   3  3REFFLD(INV# INVOICES)
4500    A        INVDAT   R      0   3  9REFFLD(INVDAT INVOICES) EDTCDE(Y)
4600    A        INVAMT   R      0   3 18REFFLD(INVAMT INVOICES) EDTCDE(1)
4700    * Subfile control record........
4800    A        R CONTROLR             SFLCTL(WINDOWR)
4900    A                               WINDOW(7 20 5 35)─────────┐  Under control of the
5000    A                               WDWBORDER((*CHAR '...::..:')) │  RPG program, the data
5100    A                               SFLSIZ(4)                     │  from the subfile will
5200    A                               SFLPAG(2)                     │  be displayd within the
5300    A 80                            SFLCLR                        │  window parameters when
5400    A 81                            SFLDSP                        │  F4 is pressed
5500    A 81                            SFLDSPCTL
5600    A 81                            SFLEND
```

Figure 17-30 Display file that controls the processing of a subfile that includes windowing. (Continued)

The function of the record formats included in the display file are explained in the following paragraphs.

- **PROMPT record**—First record displayed. Provides for the entry of a customer number, error message display (**RECORD NOT FOUND**), and end-of-job control.

- **INQRCD record**—Second record displayed after customer number is entered via the PROMPT screen accesses the related record in the physical file. This display writes over the PROMPT screen. Error message on line 4000 is displayed when the user presses F4 to display subfile window and no records for the customer are stored in INVOICES. If records are stored in INVOICES, the subfile window will display with two records shown. User may roll to examine any other invoices stored in the subfile for the customer.

- **WINDOWR record**—Defines the subfile record format. Because only one **REF** keyword may be included in a display file, **REFFLD** keywords must reference the field attributes of INVOICES, the second physical file processed by the program. The data from INVOICES is the input to the subfile window.

- **CONTROLR record**—Defines the subfile control record which references the subfile record WINDOWR and controls the display of the window and the subfile's data; both within the INQRCD display.

The display images are shown in Figure 17-31.

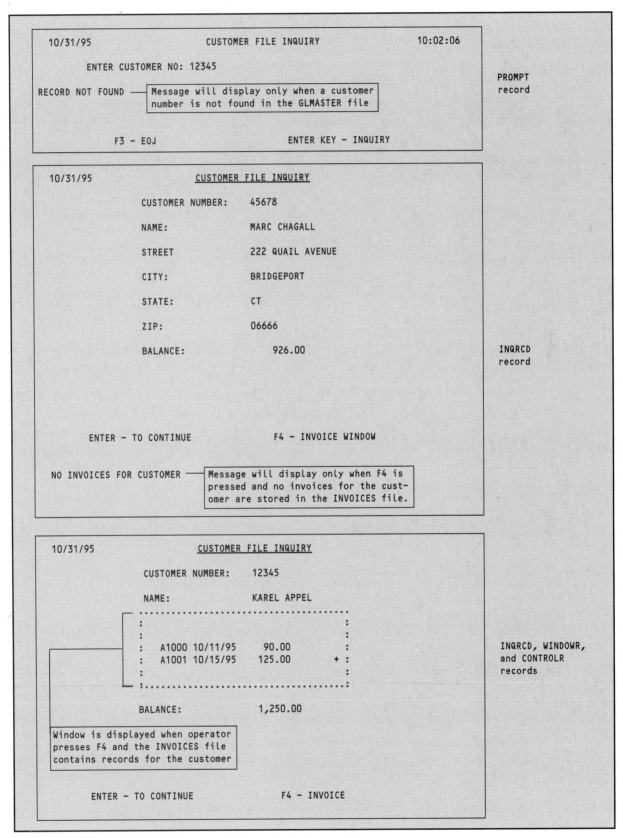

Figure 17-31 Display file's record images.

A detailed compile listing of the RPG/400 program that processes all of the display file's record formats is presented in Figure 17-32.

The windowing example discussed used a window to support a subfile. Note, however, that windows may be specified without a subfile and a display file may include more than one.

```
SEQUENCE                                                                              IND   DO
NUMBER      *...1....+....2....+....3....+....4....+....5....+....6....+....7...*      USE   NUM

                     S o u r c e   L i s t i n g
    100     * Customer master inquiry with a subfile window........
    200     *
            H

    300     FCH17WND CF  E                        WORKSTN
    400     F                                              SFRRN1KSFILE WINDOWR
            RECORD FORMAT(S): LIBRARY SMYERS FILE CH17WND.
                    EXTERNAL FORMAT PROMPT RPG NAME PROMPT
                    EXTERNAL FORMAT INQRCD RPG NAME INQRCD
                    EXTERNAL FORMAT ERROR RPG NAME ERROR
                    EXTERNAL FORMAT WINDOWR RPG NAME WINDOWR
                    EXTERNAL FORMAT CONTROLR RPG NAME CONTROLR

    500     FGLMASTERIF  E       K        DISK
            RECORD FORMAT(S): LIBRARY SMYERS FILE GLMASTER.
                    EXTERNAL FORMAT GLRCRD RPG NAME GLRCRD

    600     FINVOICESIF  E       K        DISK
    700     *
    800     * Display PROMPT screen to enter customer number........
            RECORD FORMAT(S): LIBRARY SMYERS FILE INVOICES.
                    EXTERNAL FORMAT INVRCD RPG NAME INVRCD

A000000     INPUT  FIELDS FOR RECORD PROMPT FILE CH17WND FORMAT PROMPT.
A000001                                      1    1 *IN03              END OF JOB
A000002                                      2    2 *IN91              RECORD NOT FOUND
A000003                                      3   70CUSNUM
B000000     INPUT  FIELDS FOR RECORD INQRCD FILE CH17WND FORMAT INQRCD.
B000001                                      1    1 *IN04              DISPLAY WINDOW
C000000     INPUT  FIELDS FOR RECORD ERROR FILE CH17WND FORMAT ERROR.
D000000     INPUT  FIELDS FOR RECORD WINDOWR FILE CH17WND FORMAT WINDOWR.
D000001                                      1    5 INV#
D000002                                      6  110INVDAT
D000003                                     12  182INVAMT
E000000     INPUT  FIELDS FOR RECORD CONTROLR FILE CH17WND FORMAT CONTROLR.
F000000     INPUT  FIELDS FOR RECORD GLRCRD FILE GLMASTER FORMAT GLRCRD.
F000001                                    P  1   30CUST#
F000002                                       4   23 NAME
F000003                                      24   43 STREET
F000004                                      44   63 CITY
F000005                                      64   65 STATE
F000006                                    P 66  680ZIP
F000007                                    P 69  732BALANC
G000000     INPUT  FIELDS FOR RECORD INVRCD FILE INVOICES FORMAT INVRCD.
G000001                                    P  1   30CUSTNO
G000002                                       4    8 INV#
G000003                                    P  9  120INVDAT
G000004                                    P 13  162INVAMT
    900     C                   EXFMTPROMPT              dsp prompt rcd
   1000     C         *IN03     DOWEQ*OFF                end of job?              B001
   1100     C         CUSNUM    CHAINGLMASTER       99   find rcd        1        001
   1200     C         *IN99     IFEQ *OFF                rcd found?               B002
   1300     *
   1400     * Display inquiry screen with customer data........
   1500     C                   EXFMTINQRCD              dsp inqrcd rcd           002
   1600     C         MOVE *ON          *IN80            sfl clear ind.           002
   1700     C                   WRITECONTROLR            xeq sfl clear            002
   1800     C         MOVE *OFF         *IN80            set off 80               002
```

Figure 17-32 Compile listing of an RPG/400 program that processes a subfile that supports windowing.

```
 1900 C                     Z-ADD0         SFRRN1  40      init. rcd ctr           002
 2000 C                     SETOF                      71  set off ind.       2    002
 2100 *
 2200 * If no records in INVOICES for customer and F4 pressed
 2300 * (window requested), display error msg at bottom of screen.
 2400 C          CUSNUM      SETLLINVOICES              98  find rcd         3    002
 2500 C          *IN98       IFEQ *OFF                      rcd not found         B003
 2600 C          *IN04       ANDEQ*ON                       & F4 pressed          003
 2700 C                      EXFMTERROR                     dsp error msg         003
 2800 C                      ENDIF                          end 2500 IFEQ         E003
 2900 *
 3000 * If rcds for customer in INVOICES & sfl not at end and
 3100 * INVOICES not at end, load sfl with a record........
 3200 C          *IN98       DOWEQ*ON                       rcd found and         B003
 3300 C          *IN71       ANDEQ*OFF                      file not at end       003
 3400 C          CUSNUM      READEINVOICES              71  read a pf rcd    3    003
 3500 C                      ADD  1         SFRRN1          increment ctr         003
 3600 C          *IN71       IFEQ *OFF                      eof test              B004
 3700 C                      WRITEWINDOWR               71  write to sfl     3    004
 3800 C                      ENDIF                          end 3600 IFEQ         E004
 3900 C                      ENDDO                          end 3200 DOW          E003
 4000 *
 4100 * If records are found in invoices and F4 pressed, display sfl
 4200 C          *IN98       IFEQ *ON                       rcd found and         B003
 4300 C          *IN04       ANDEQ*ON                       F4 pressed            003
 4400 C                      MOVE *ON       *IN81           sfl dsp indictr       003
 4500 C                      EXFMTCONTROLR                  dsp sfl window        003
 4600 C                      MOVE *OFF      *IN81           set off 81            003
 4700 C                      ENDIF                          end 4200 IFEQ         E003
 4800 C                      ENDIF                          end 1200 IFEQ         E002
 4900 *
 5000 * Display PROMPT screen to continue inquiry or end job......
 5100 C                      EXFMTPROMPT                    dsp prompt scrn       001
 5200 C                      ENDDO                          end 1000 DOW          E001
 5300 C                      MOVE *ON       *INLR           eoj control
```

Line #

300   The display file, which includes the PROMPT screen, inquiry screen (INQRCD), subfile record format (WINDOWR), and subfile control record (CONTROLR), is defined as a combined, full procedural, externally defined workstation file.

400   The **K** in column 53 indicates that this instruction is a continuation of line 300.

      The SFRRN1 entry in columns 47–52 specifies a programmer-defined field in which relative record numbers of records written to the subfile are stored and incremented.

      The **SFILE** keyword in columns 54–59 specifies that this statement is related to a subfile.

      The **WINDOWR** entry in columns 60–65 specifies the name of the subfile record format,

500   The physical file, GLMASTER, is defined as externally described, full procedural, and keyed. Information related to the customers is stored in this file.

600   The physical file, INVOICES, is defined as externally described, full procedural, and keyed. Information related to invoices for each customer is stored in this file.

900   The **EXFMT** statement displays the PROMPT screen in which a customer number is entered.

1000 The **DOWEQ** group is performed until the operator presses F3 to end the job by passing control to line 5300 where **LR** is set on to end the program.

1100 The **CHAIN** statement uses the CUSNUM value, entered from the PROMPT display, to search the GLMASTER file for an equal key. If the record is found, indicator **99**, entered in the *Resulting Indicator High* field (columns 54–55) will not be set on.

Figure 17-32   Compile listing of an RPG/400 program that processes a subfile that supports windowing. (Continued)

1200 The **IFEQ** statement tests the status of indicator **99** specified with the **CHAIN** statement on line 1100. An "off" condition indicates that the record was found and an "on" condition that the record was not found in the file. When **99** is set on, the error message (**RECORD NOT FOUND**) coded in the PROMPT record will display.

1500 When the **IFEQ** test on line 1200 is true, the **EXFMT** statement displays the INQRCD screen "filled in" with field values from the related GLMASTER record.

1600 The **MOVE** statement turns on indicator **80,** which is specified in the subfile control record (CONTROLR) to clear the subfile before records from the INVOICES file are loaded.

1700 The **WRITE** statement executes the subfile control record CONTROLR, which clears the subfile.

1800 The **MOVE** statement turns off indicator **80.**

1900 The subfile's record counter (SFRRN1), specified on line 400, is initialized to zero.

2000 Indicator **71** is used with the **READE** statement on line 3400, and the **WRITE** statement on line 3700 is set off.

2400 The **SETLL** statement uses the CUSNUM, input from the PROMPT screen, as the search argument to position the "pointer" at the first record in the INVOICES file for the customer.

2500 -
2600 The compound **IFEQ** statement tests the status of indicator **98** (specified with the **SETLL** statement on line 2400) and indicator **04** (set on by the operator pressing F4 from the INQRCD display). When **98** is "off" and **04** "on," an error condition indicating that no records were found in the INVOICES file for the current customer, F4 is pressed to display the subfile window.

2700 The display file's ERROR record, which contains the constant NO INVOICES FOR CUSTOMER, is displayed when this **IFEQ** test on lines 2500–2600 is true. This control prevents the subfile window from being displayed when no INVOICES records are found for the customer.

2800 The **ENDIF** operation ends the **IFEQ** statement on lines 2500–2600.

3200 -
3300 The **DOWEQ** group is executed if a record was found in the INVOICES file (**98** set on by the **SETLL** statement on line 2400) and INVOICES is not at end, or the subfile is not full (**71** set on for either condition).

3400 The **READE** statement reads a record from the INVOICES file equal to the CUSNUM key value. Indicator **71** is set on when an equal key is <u>not</u> found or when an end-of-file condition occurs.

3500 The subfile record counter, SFRRN1, is incremented by 1 so that the next record will be loaded into the related subfile's record position.

3600 The **IFEQ** statement tests the status of indicator **71**. If it is off, the **READE** statement on line 3400 was successful (a record found condition or end of the INVOICES file not read).

3700 The **WRITE** statement adds an INVOICES record to the subfile WINDOWR.

3800 The **ENDIF** operation ends the **IFEQ** statement on line 3600.

3900 The **ENDDO** operation ends the **DOWEQ** group that began on line 3200.

4200 -
4300 The compound **IFEQ** statement tests the status of indicator **98** (specified with the **SETLL** statement on line 2400) and the status of indicator **04,** set on by the operator pressing F4 from the INQRCD display. When **98** is "on," indicating at least one record was found and loaded to the subfile from INVOICES, and **04** "on," the subfile window is displayed.

4400 The **MOVE** statement sets on indicator **81,** which conditions the keywords **SFLDSP, SFLDSPCTL,** and **SFLEND** in the subfile control record. The keywords control the display of the subfile records and the constants in the subfile.

Figure 17-32 Compile listing of an RPG/400 program that processes a subfile that supports windowing. (Continued)

4500 The **EXFMT** statement executes the subfile control record, which displays two subfile records and the window border on the screen.

4600 The **MOVE** statement sets off indicator **81**.

4700 The **ENDIF** operation ends the **IFEQ** statement on lines 4200–4300.

4800 The **ENDIF** operation ends the **IFEQ** statement on line 1200.

5100 The **EXFMT** statement displays the PROMPT record. The user may enter another customer number and continue the inquiry process by pressing ENTER, or end the job by pressing F3.

5200 The **ENDDO** operation flags the end of the **DOWEQ** group and passes control back to the **DOWEQ** statement on line 1000, where the end-of-job test is made.

5300 The **MOVE** statement sets on indicator **LR,** which ends the program. This statement is branched to when the **DOWEQ** statement on line 1000 tests a false condition (indicator **03** "on" by the operator pressing F3 to end the program).

Figure 17-32   Compile listing of an RPG/400 program that processes a subfile that supports windowing. (Continued)

SUMMARY

A *subfile* is a temporary area in memory which records may be written to and read from a display file device. They may be used for any of the physical file maintenance functions when more than one record is to be displayed at one time.

Subfiles are created like any display file, with **SEU** or **SDA.** However, they must include special keywords that control their loading, display, and processing functions. At least *two* record formats must be specified in the display file that supports a subfile. The *subfile record,* which must be coded first in the DDS, defines the areas where the data is stored, and the *subfile control record* defines the processing functions. Subfile functions, including the number of records to display on the screen, number of records to be stored in the subfile, clearing of the screen, display of the subfile's data, display of constants, display of page continuation symbol, and overlay of an existing screen, are some of the functions that may be specified in the *subfile control record.*

An RPG/400 program that processes a subfile must define it in the *File Description* statement for the related display file. A field for a record counter, the continuation symbol, the keyword **SFILE,** and the *subfile record* name must be specified in the definition of the display file. In the program, the *control record format* is usually executed first to clear the subfile area. Then, the subfile is loaded and the *control record format* displayed again. Indicators that were assigned to select keywords in the *subfile control record* must be set on in the RPG/400 program before the control record is executed.

Windowing is supported on the AS/400 by the keywords **WDWBORDER, WINDOW, USRRSTDSP,** and **RMVWDW.** Windows have horizontal and vertical borders that are superimposed on an existing display. The RPG/400 program coding for windows follows standard display and, when specified, subfile processing logic.

QUESTIONS

17-1. Define a subfile as related to the AS/400 environment.

17-2. For what processing functions may a subfile be used?

17-3. How may a subfile be created?

17-4. Name the minimum number of record formats that must be included in the definition of a subfile. In what order must they be specified?

17-5. Refer to Question 17-4 and explain the function of each record format.

17-6. What is the minimum number of keywords that must be included in the definition of a subfile?

The following subfile terms relate to Questions 17-7 through 17-21.

Match the following keywords to their related definition:

a. SFL	**e. SFLDSP**	**i. SFLRNA**	**m. SFLMSG**
b. SFLCTL	**f. SFLCLR**	**j. SFLDSPCTL**	**n. SFLDROP**
c. SFLSIZ	**g. SFLINZ**	**k. SFLEND**	**o. SFLNXTCHG**
d. SFLPAG	**h. SFLDLT**	**l. SFLLIN**	

17-7. ___ Deletes a subfile from the current processing environment.

17-8. ___ Used in conjunction with another keyword that actually performs the initialization of a subfile's field values.

17-9. ___ Specifies the number of spaces between columns of subfile records when the subfile is displayed horizontally.

17-10. ___ Determines the number of records that may be stored in the subfile.

17-11. ___ Indicates the number of subfile records that may be displayed on the screen at one time.

17-12. ___ Specifies that the record format defined is a subfile control record format.

17-13. ___ Controls display of the records stored in the subfile record format.

17-14. ___ Initializes alphanumeric fields in the subfile to blanks and numeric fields to zeros.

17-15. ___ Supports the folding of truncated subfile record format field values.

17-16. ___ Identifies the subfile record format.

17-17. ___ Controls display of the constants and variables defined in the subfile control record format.

17-18. ___ Identifies on the CRT that more records are included in the subfile.

17-19. ___ Is the control record format keyword that supports the display of an error message.

17-20. ___ Enables RPG/400 program to identify subfile records that have been modified.

17-21. ___ Clears the subfile of all records.

17-22. For inquiry processing, what *Usage* must be assigned to the subfile record's fields? What *Usage* is specified for update and for addition processing?

17-23. What RPG/400 operation is used to read records from a subfile? In what resulting indicator field(s) must the indicator(s) be specified? What is the function of the indicator(s)?

Examine the following File Description Specifications and answer Questions 17-24 through 17-27.

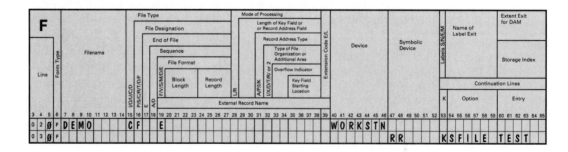

17-24. Explain the function of the **RR** entry in the *Symbolic Device* field in an RPG/400 program.

17-25. What is the purpose of the letter **K** in column 53?

17-26. The **SFILE** entry in the *Option* field (columns 54–59) indicates what?

17-27. What does the **TEST** entry in the *Entry* field (columns 60–65) represent?

17-28. When a subfile is cleared, is the control record format or the subfile record format included in the **WRITE** statement?

17-29. When a subfile is displayed, is the control record format or the subfile record format included in the **EXFMT** statement?

17-30. Name the RPG/400 operation that loads records to a subfile. What is the function of the indicator(s) that must be specified in the resulting indicator field(s)? In which resulting indicator field(s) must it be included?

17-31. As related to display files, define windowing.

17-32. What DDS keywords support windowing? Explain the functions of each.

17-33. Explain the function of each entry in the following statement:

WINDOW(10 30 8 40)

17-34. Explain the function of each entry in the following statement:

WDWBORDER ((*CHAR '12345678') (*DSPATR RI))

17-35. Refer to Question 17-34 and draw how the window will display.

17-36. What special RPG/400 operations are required to process a window? May a window only be specified with subfiles?

PROGRAMMING ASSIGNMENTS

Before the assignments are started for this chapter, create a physical file with the following attributes:

```
                    PHYSICAL FILE DESCRIPTION

SYSTEM: AS/400                      DATE: Yours
FILE NAME: Yours                    REV NO: 0
RECORD NAME: Yours                  KEY LENGTH: 5
SEQUENCE: Keyed (Unique)            RECORD SIZE: 54

                     FIELD DEFINITIONS

  FIELD     FIELD NAME    SIZE   TYPE     POSITION      COMMENTS
  NO                                     FROM    TO

    1       PART#          5      C        1      5    Key field
    2       NAME          20      C        6     25
    3       AMTHND         6      P       26     29    0 decimals
    4       AMTORD         6      P       30     33    0 decimals
    5       AVGCST         7      P       34     37    2 decimals
    6       AMTALL         6      P       38     41    0 decimals
    7       EOQ            6      P       42     45    0 decimals
    8       SAFSTK         6      P       46     49    0 decimals
    9       LEADTM         3      P       50     51    0 decimals
   10       WARELO         3      C       52     54
```

Programming Assignment 17-1: INQUIRY PROCESSING WITH A SUBFILE

Create a subfile to *inquiry* process the physical file described above. The record formats for the display file are detailed below.

Physical File Data:

Part#	Part Name	Amount On Hand	Amount On Order	Avg Cost/ Unit	Amount Allocated	Economic Order Qty	Safety Stock	Lead Time	Warehouse Location
A2345	AC SPARK PLUGS	000000	018000	0000075	005000	000150	002000	014	ABC
B6789	FRAM OIL FILTRS	004000	001200	0000325	000480	001200	000500	031	DEF
C5555	POINT SETS	000600	000000	0000850	000000	000100	000100	015	AAA
D9876	LOCKING GAS CAP	000024	000012	0000499	000012	000012	000012	090	GHI
E3459	LIQUID CAR WASH	000360	000120	0000179	000480	000072	000200	016	BBB
E4555	TURTLE WAX	001200	000480	0000236	000900	000240	000500	030	BBC
F6666	CHAMOIS (LARGE)	000600	000120	0000397	000240	000048	000100	120	BBD
G7800	ARMOR ALL	002800	000840	0000219	001400	000240	000700	025	CCC
H1000	NO TOUCH FOAM	001350	000360	0000275	000800	000120	000300	030	CCD
H2100	GAS LINE AF	004000	001200	0000051	003000	000480	001000	020	DDD
I3120	NU FINISH WAX	001300	000600	0000419	001000	000240	000240	010	DEG
J4000	WD-40 (SMALL)	002500	001200	0000181	000900	000120	000300	015	EFG

Prompt Screen Format:

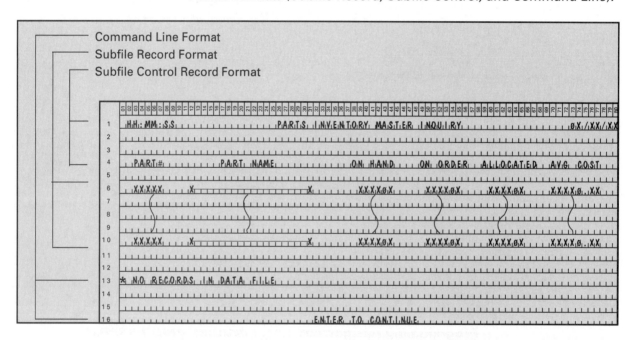

Subfile Formats (Subfile Record, Subfile Control, and Command Line):

The key value entered in the Prompt screen is the starting key and does *not* have to be one stored in the file. Hence, code the RPG/400 program with this control.

Programming Assignment 17-2: UPDATE PROCESSING WITH A SUBFILE

The physical file, display file, and subfile formats for this assignment are identical to those in Assignment 17-1. If Assignment 17-1 was completed, it must be modified to support update processing. However, if the assignment was not completed, refer to the specifications for Assignment 17-1.

In either case, the following changes must be made to Assignment 17-1 to support update processing:

1. Change the constant on line 1 in both screens to:
    PARTS INVENTORY MASTER UPDATE
2. Move the constant ENTER TO CONTINUE on line 16 from starting position 33 to 20 and change to ENTER TO UPDATE.
3. Add the constant F5—IGNORE UPDATE to line 16 beginning in position 49.
4. Fields in the subfile record must be defined with a **B** *Usage* (input/output).

Update Data:

Field	Record 1	Record 2	Record 3	Record 4
PART#......	E3459	B6789	C5500	A2345
NAME.......		FRAM OIL FILTERS		CHAMPION SPARK PLUGS
AMTHND.....	000480			018000
AMTORD.....	000000		004000	004800
AVGCST.....		0000370		
AMTALL.....				002000

Note: Fields in the transaction records that <u>do not</u> have a value are <u>not</u> to be updated!

The key value entered in the Prompt screen is the starting key and does not have to be one stored in the file. Hence, code the RPG/400 program with this control.

Programming Assignment 17-3: LOGICAL DELETION WITH A SUBFILE

Assignment 17-2 must be completed before this program is started. The following modifications must be made to Assignment 17-2 to support the logical deletion of records in the physical file:

1. Change the constant on line 1 in both screens to:
    PARTS INVENTORY MASTER DELETION
2. Move the constant ENTER TO CONTINUE on line 16 from starting position 33 to 20 and change to ENTER TO DELETE.
3. Add the constant F5—IGNORE DELETE to line 16 beginning in position 49.

Delete records with key values **C5500, D9876,** and **J4000.**

Programming Assignment 17-4: ADDITION PROCESSING WITH A SUBFILE

Refer to completed Assignment 17-1, 17-2, or 17-3, and modify the display file, subfile, and RPG/400 program to support the addition of records to a physical file with subfile control. Replace the prompt screen in Assignment 17-1, 17-2, or 17-3 with an entry display in the following format:

```
        MM/DD/YY                  PARTS INVENTORY                    HH:MM:SS
                                      ENTRY


           PART NUMBER: XXXXX

           PART NAME: X                        X

           AMT-ON-HAND: XXXXXX          AVG COST: XXXXXXX

           AMT-ON-ORDER: XXXXXX           AMT ALLOCATED: XXXXXX

           EOQ: XXXXXX                    SAFETY STOCK: XXXXXX

           LEAD TIME: XXX DAYS          WAREHOUSE LOCATION: XXX

          CMD KEY 3 - EOJ                  CMD KEY 5 - IGNORE
                               CMD KEY 2 - ENTER

NOTES:
   1. DATE AND TIME ARE SYSTEM SUPPLIED
   2. HIGHLIGHT ALL CONSTANTS
   3. UNDERLINE HEADING AND REVERSE IMAGE VARIABLE FIELDS
```

Modify the *subfile record* and *control formats* in one of the previously completed assignments for this chapter to include all of the fields in the physical file. Unless the workstation supports a screen that is 132 columns wide, the **SFLDROP** keyword will have to be specified in the subfile control record to display the truncated constants and fields in a folded (next line) format. Define the subfile so that it will store 10 records, with 5 records per page.

In order for the **READC** statement in the RPG/400 program to recognize all of the records in the subfile as "changed," the **SFLNXTCHG** keyword must be specified in the subfile record format. In addition, the **SFLRNA** and **SFLINZ** keywords must be included in the subfile control record.

Subfile Record, Control, and Command Line Formats:

```
HH:MM:SS               PARTS INVENTORY MASTER ADDITION


PART#    PART NAME          ON HAND  ON ORDER  ALLOCATED AVG COST
         EOQ      SAFETY STOCK        LEAD TIME          LOCATION

XXXXX    X             X    XXXX0X    XXXX0X    XXXX0X    XXXX0.XX
         XXXX0X          XXXX0X          X0X          XXX







XXXXX    X             X    XXXX0X    XXXX0X    XXXX0X    XXXX0.XX
         XXXX0X          XXXX0X          X0X          XXX



* DUPLICATE RECORD
                                                       CK 8 TO FOLD
                            ENTER TO ADD RECORDS
NOTES:  1. HIGHLIGHT ALL CONSTANTS AND REVERSE IMAGE ALL VARIABLE FIELDS.
```

Add Data:

```
Field              Record 1              Record 2              Record 3

Part#..........    A1000 .............. C5000 ............. D9876
Part Name......    PRESTONE DE-ICER.... CHAMOIS (LARGE).... LOCKING GAS CAP
Amt-on-hand....    000000 ............. 000000 ............ 000000
Amt-on-order...    000144 ............. 000120 ............ 000144
Avg-cost/unit..    0000259 ........... 0000675 ........... 0000115
Amt-allocated..    000000 ............. 000012 ............ 000000
EOQ............    000144 ............. 000120 ............ 000024
Safety Stock...    000100 ............. 000024 ............ 000012
Lead time......    010 ................ 015 ............... 090
```

Programming Assignment 17-5: WINDOWING WITH A SUBFILE

Create the following physical file of vendor information and load it with the data indicated. The data from this file will be input to the subfile for display in the window.

Physical File Record Format:

```
                    PHYSICAL FILE DESCRIPTION

         SYSTEM: AS/400                    DATE: Yours
         FILE NAME: Yours                  REV NO: 0
         RECORD NAME: Yours                KEY LENGTH: 5
         SEQUENCE: Keyed (not unique)      RECORD SIZE: 61

                       FIELD DEFINITIONS

         FIELD    FIELD NAME   SIZE  TYPE    POSITION     COMMENTS
          NO                                FROM    TO

           1      PARTNO         5    C       1      5  Key field
           2      VNAME         15    C       6     20
           3      VADDRS        15    C      21     35
           4      VCITY         15    C      36     50
           5      VSTATE         2    C      51     52
           6      VZIP           5    P      53     55
           7      VTEL#         10    P      56     61
```

Physical File Data:

Part Number	Vendor Name	Address	City	State	Zip	Telephone Number
A2345	GENERAL MOTORS	1 PLUG LANE	DETROIT	MI	07702	3133334444
A2345	GM-AC DIVISION	2 SPARK PLACE	LANSING	MI	07704	5171234567
A2345	GM-PARTS SUPPLY	9 GOODWRENCH ST	MOUNT VERNON	NY	09901	9144569876
X9999	JOHNSON & SONS	2 FIXUM BLVD	RACINE	WI	04400	4146785432
H1000	ARMOR ALL CO	7 FOAM DRIVE	FRESNO	CA	05500	2099990090

Modify the display file completed for Assignment 17-1 to include a window that supports a subfile. Define the window to begin on line 11, column 22, with 6 lines and 35 columns. Use a border design of your choice. The subfile must store three records, with two records per page. Include only the VNAME and VTEL# field values from the vendor file in the subfile. Edit the VTEL# value as '0( )- - '.

If a vendor is not found for a part number, display NO VENDOR FOR PART on line 24, column 31 of inquiry screen, and prevent the window from displaying.

Indicate in the inquiry screen that the window may be displayed if the user presses **F8**.

chapter 18

Printer Files

All of the previously discussed programs that included printed output have specified the system-supplied printer file shell **QSYSPRT** (**QPRINT** may also be used) as the output file. Use of the "print shell" required that the syntax for a report be included by the traditional method, in the *Output Specifications* of the RPG/400 program.

Instead of hard-coding the syntax for report formats in an RPG/400 program, they may be externally described by a programmer-defined *printer file*. The syntax for printer files is entered, debugged, and compiled by exactly the same procedures followed for the other DDS file types. If the Programmer Menu is used to access **SEU, PRTF** must be entered as the selection type. As compared to the traditional method of coding report formats, printer files offer the following advantages:

1. RPG/400 programs include less coding and are therefore easier to maintain.
2. If more than one program uses the same report format, the coding does not have to be duplicated in each program.
3. Modifications have to be made to only one source member and not to every program that references the report format.
4. Because the RPG/400 built-in processing cycle for output control cannot be followed, page overflow, line count, and page numbering must be controlled by programmer-supplied statements. This requirement eliminates many of the problems associated with RPG/400 controlled printed output. For example, overflow lines cannot be specified with exception lines (**E** in column 15) for standard RPG/400 controlled output. In addition, programmer-controlled output parallels the logic familiar to procedure-oriented languages such as COBOL, BASIC, and so forth.

Printer File Keywords

The keywords valid for printer files (**PRTF**) are listed in Figure 18-1. For a comprehensive discussion of all the valid **PRTF** keywords, refer to the *Data Description Specifications* manual. Only those specified in the example printer file are summarized in the following paragraphs.

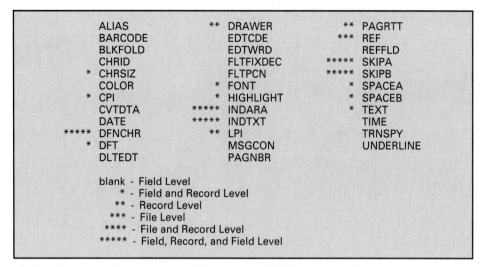

ALIAS		**	DRAWER	**	PAGRTT
BARCODE			EDTCDE	***	REF
BLKFOLD			EDTWRD		REFFLD
CHRID			FLTFIXDEC	*****	SKIPA
*	CHRSIZ		FLTPCN	*****	SKIPB
COLOR		*	FONT	*	SPACEA
*	CPI	*	HIGHLIGHT	*	SPACEB
CVTDTA		*****	INDARA	*	TEXT
DATE		*****	INDTXT		TIME
*****	DFNCHR	**	LPI		TRNSPY
*	DFT		MSGCON		UNDERLINE
DLTEDT			PAGNBR		

```
        blank -  Field Level
            *  -  Field and Record Level
           **  -  Record Level
          ***  -  File Level
         ****  -  File and Record Level
        *****  -  Field, Record, and Field Level
```

Figure 18-1   Valid keywords for printer files (**PRTF**).

DATE *Keyword.*   **DATE** is a *Field Level* keyword that accesses and prints the current job date. The standard format is MMDDYY, which may be edited by an **EDTCDE** (*Edit Code*) or **EDTWRD** (*Edit Word*) keyword.

EDTCDE *Keyword.*   **EDTCDE** (*Edit Code*) is a *Field Level* keyword that controls the editing of output capable numeric fields. The Edit Code options, which are identical to those available in RPG/400, include 1, 2, 3, 4, A, B, C, D, J, K, L, M, Y, and Z. Examples of the syntax and edited results for three **EDTCDE** keywords are shown in Figure 18-2.

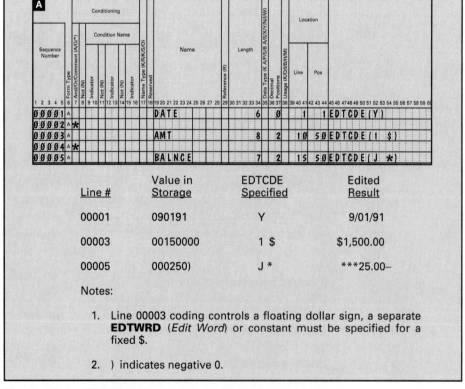

Line #	Value in Storage	EDTCDE Specified	Edited Result
00001	090191	Y	9/01/91
00003	00150000	1 $	$1,500.00
00005	000250)	J *	***25.00−

Notes:

1. Line 00003 coding controls a floating dollar sign, a separate **EDTWRD** (*Edit Word*) or constant must be specified for a fixed $.

2.) indicates negative 0.

Figure 18-2   **EDTCDE** keyword and edited result examples.

The table presented in Figure 18-3 summarizes all the valid **EDTCDE** (*Edit Code*) keyword options and their editing functions. An **EDTCDE** (or **EDTWRD**) is valid only for numeric fields specified as a *Data Type* **S** (signed) or **P** (packed) in position 35 of the DDS form.

Edit Code	Commas	Decimal Point	Sign for Negative Balance	Entry in Column 21 of Control Specification			Zero Suppress
				D or Blank	I	J	
1	Yes	Yes	No sign	.00 or 0	,00 or 0	0,00 or 0	Yes
2	Yes	Yes	No sign	Blanks	Blanks	Blanks	Yes
3		Yes	No sign	.00 or 0	,00 or 0	0,00 or 0	Yes
4		Yes	No sign	Blanks	Blanks	Blanks	Yes
5-9[1]							
A	Yes	Yes	CR	.00 or 0	0,00 or 0	Yes	
B	Yes	Yes	CR	Blanks	Blanks	Blanks	Yes
C		Yes	CR	.00 or 0	,00 or 0	0,00 or 0	Yes
D		Yes	CR	Blanks	Blanks	Blanks	Yes
J	Yes	Yes	– (minus)	.00 or 0	,00 or 0	0,00 or 0	Yes
K	Yes	Yes	– (minus)	Blanks	Blanks	Blanks	Yes
L		Yes	– (minus)	.00 or 0	,00 or 0	0,00 or 0	Yes
M		Yes	– (minus)	Blanks -	Blanks	Blanks	Yes
X[2]							
Y[3]							Yes
Z[4]							Yes

1 These are the user-defined edit codes.

2 The X edit code ensures a hexidecimal F sign for positive values. Because the system does this for you, normally you do not have to specify this code.

3 The Y edit code suppresses the leftmost zero of a date field that is 3- to 6-digits long and it suppresses the two leftmost zeros of a field that is seven positions long. The Y edit code also inserts slashes(/) between athe month, day, and year according to the following pattern:
    nn/n
    nn/nn
    nn/nn/n
    nn/nn/nn
    nnnn/nn/nn

4 The Z edit code removes the sign (plus or minus) from a numeric field and suppresses leading zeros of a numeric field.

Figure 18-3 Summary of all valid **EDTCDE** codes and editing functions (*Courtesy of IBM*).

EDTWRD *Keyword.* When the edit requirements cannot be satisfied by an **EDTCDE**, an **EDTWRD** must be specified. An **EDTWRD** is a *Field Level* keyword that may be specified with numeric fields defined as *Data Type* **S** or **P**.

An **EDTWRD** (*Edit Word*) consists of three parts: the body, the status, and the expansion, as shown in the following format.

The *body* of an **EDTWRD** is the area that allocates space for the digits from the sending field. It must be formatted equal to or greater than the size of the field to be edited. When floating dollar signs are included, the body of the *Edit Word* must be one space larger than the related numeric field. The body of the *Edit Word* ends with the low-order position that may be replaced by a digit.

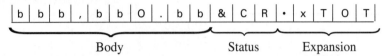

The *status* is an optional part of an **EDTWRD** that immediately follows the body and supports a minus sign or a CR (credit) symbol. If the numeric field value is negative and a minus sign is included in this area, a minus sign will print (or display) after the low-order digit. On the other hand, if CR is specified and the value is negative, CR will print or display in the area. When the field value is positive (a plus sign), blanks will print in the positions allocated to the status section. If a minus sign or credit symbol is not specified, a status entry is not part of an **EDTWRD.**

The *expansion* area of an **EDTWRD** begins after the status section, or after the body if the status is not specified. The characters included in this area will print or display every time the instruction is executed; it does not depend on the field value. Blanks are not permitted in the expansion area. If blanks are required, they must be specified by ampersands (&). Examples of **EDTWRD** formats and their edited results are shown in Figure 18-4. In addition to the parentheses, **EDTWRD**s must also be enclosed in single quotes.

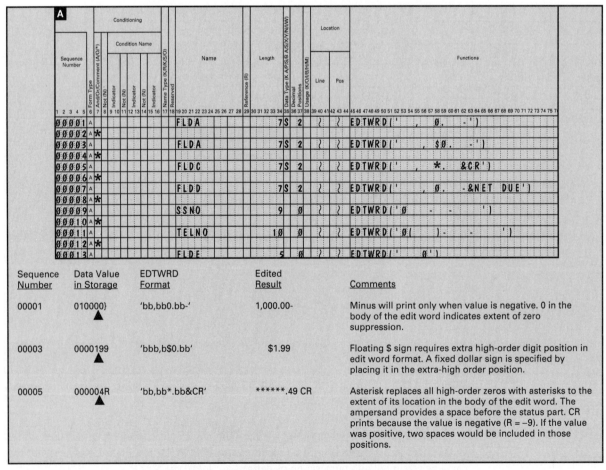

Figure 18-4   EDTWRD formats and editing example.

00007	1250000 ▲	'bb,bb0.bb-&NET&DUE'	12,500.00 NET DUE	Because the value is positive, the minus sign does not print. The space after the status and in the expansion part are controlled by ampersands. NET DUE, which is in the expansion area, follows the status for this example. If a status was not specified, the expansion value would follow the body. Regardless of the value of the edited item, the expansion entry will print.
00009	011223333	'0bbb-bb-bbbb'	011-22-3333	To prevent suppression of the leading zero in the social security number, a 0 must be specified in an extra high-order position in the body of the edit word.
00011	2039998888	'0(bbb)•bbb•bbbb'	(203)-999-8888	To prevent suppression of the leading parenthesis, a 0 must be specified in an extra high-order position in the body of the edit word.
00012	00000 ▲	'bbbb0'		Complete zero suppression may be specified by placing a 0 in the low-order position in the body of an edit word.

b's in body part of edit word indicate spaces.

▲ Indicates implied decimal position in stored value

Figure 18-4   **EDTWRD** formats and editing example. (Continued)

PAGNBR *(Page Number) Keyword.*   The **PAGNBR** keyword predefines a four-byte numeric integer field. Its value is automatically initialized to zeros when the program is executed and is incremented by 1 before printing a page. Page numbers are not incremented beyond 9999, but **PAGNBR** may be reset to 1 by conditioning the related instruction with an indicator. Figure 18-5 illustrates two coding examples of the **PAGNBR** keyword.

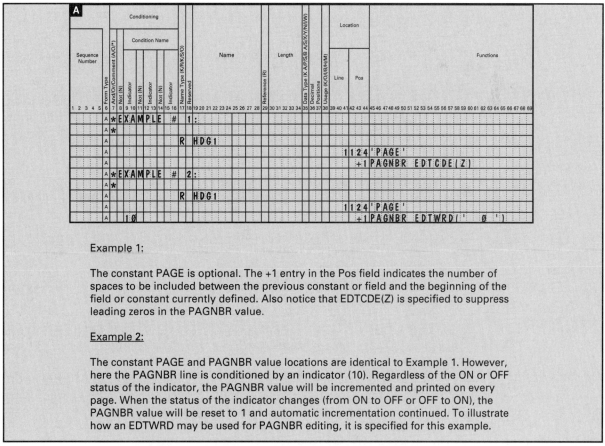

Example 1:

The constant PAGE is optional. The +1 entry in the Pos field indicates the number of spaces to be included between the previous constant or field and the beginning of the field or constant currently defined. Also notice that EDTCDE(Z) is specified to suppress leading zeros in the PAGNBR value.

Example 2:

The constant PAGE and PAGNBR value locations are identical to Example 1. However, here the PAGNBR line is conditioned by an indicator (10). Regardless of the ON or OFF status of the indicator, the PAGNBR value will be incremented and printed on every page. When the status of the indicator changes (from ON to OFF or OFF to ON), the PAGNBR value will be reset to 1 and automatic incrementation continued. To illustrate how an EDTWRD may be used for PAGNBR editing, it is specified for this example.

Figure 18-5   Examples of the **PAGNBR** keyword.

***SKIPA** (Skip After) Keyword.*   The **SKIPA** (*Skip After*) keyword, which may be specified at the *File, Record,* or *Field Level,* controls skipping to a specific line *after* one or more lines are printed. If the specified line number has been passed, control will advance the paper to the next page and begin printing on the line indicated. When **SKIPA** is specified at the *File Level,* skipping will be performed *after* all the records defined in the PRTF have been printed. If **SKIPA** is assigned at the *Record Level,* skipping will be performed *after* all the lines related to the record format are printed. Finally, when **SKIPA** is included at the *Field Level,* skipping will be executed *after* the related field value is printed.

***SKIPB** (Skip Before) Keyword.*   The **SKIPB** (*Skip Before*) keyword may be specified at the *File, Record,* or *Field Level.* It controls skipping to a specified line *before* the next line is printed. If the designated line has been passed, control will advance the paper to the next page and begin printing on the specified line. When **SKIPB** is specified at the *File Level,* skipping will be performed *before* all the records defined in the PRTF have been output. If **SKIPB** is assigned at the *Record Level,* skipping will be performed *before* any of the lines related to the record format are printed. Finally, when **SKIPB** is included at the *Field Level,* skipping will be executed *before* the related field value is printed.

***SPACEA** (Space After) Keyword.*   The **SPACEA** keyword controls line spacing *after* a record or line is printed. It may be specified only at the *Record* or *Field Level.* The valid parameters for this keyword are as follows:

- 0 No spacing
- 1 Space one line
- 2 Space two lines
- 3 Space three lines

If **SPACEA** is specified at the *Record Level,* spacing occurs *after* all the lines related to that record have been printed. When used at the *Field Level,* spacing is performed *after* the field value is printed.

A line number assignment (positions 39–41) cannot be specified along with a **SPACEA** keyword. If they are used together, the compilation of the **PRTF** will flag the line numbers as errors. If a line number or a **SPACEA** keyword is not used, overprinting will result.

***SPACEB** (Space Before) Keyword.*   The **SPACEB** keyword controls line spacing *before* a record or line is printed. It may be specified only at the *Record* or *Field Level.* The valid parameters for this keyword are as follows:

- 0 No spacing
- 1 Space one line
- 2 Space two lines
- 3 Space three lines

If **SPACEB** is specified at the *Record Level,* spacing occurs before the first line related to that record is printed. When used at the *Field Level,* spacing is performed before the field value is printed.

A line number assignment (positions 39–41) cannot be specified along with a **SPACEB** keyword. If they are used together, the compilation of the **PRTF** will flag line numbers as errors. If a line number or the **SPACEB** keyword is not specified, overprinting will result.

Examples of SKIPA, SKIPB, SPACEA, SPACEB Keywords Control

The parameter included with a **SKIPA, SKIPB, SPACEA,** or **SPACEB** keyword is coded in the following general format:

Keyword ————
Line number ————

SKIPB(n)   SPACEA(n)

———— Spacing value (0, 1, 2, 3)
———— Keyword

Coding examples and the processing functions of the **SKIPB** and **SPACEA** keywords are illustrated in Figure 18-6.

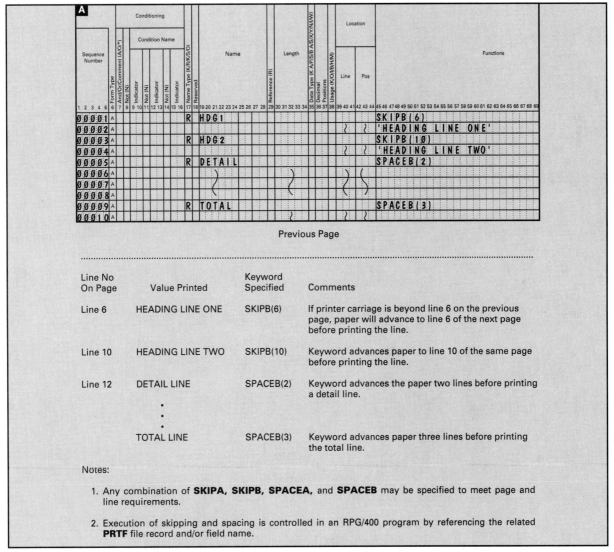

Previous Page

Line No On Page	Value Printed	Keyword Specified	Comments
Line 6	HEADING LINE ONE	SKIPB(6)	If printer carriage is beyond line 6 on the previous page, paper will advance to line 6 of the next page before printing the line.
Line 10	HEADING LINE TWO	SKIPB(10)	Keyword advances paper to line 10 of the same page before printing the line.
Line 12	DETAIL LINE	SPACEB(2)	Keyword advances the paper two lines before printing a detail line.
	TOTAL LINE	SPACEB(3)	Keyword advances paper three lines before printing the total line.

Notes:

1. Any combination of **SKIPA, SKIPB, SPACEA,** and **SPACEB** may be specified to meet page and line requirements.

2. Execution of skipping and spacing is controlled in an RPG/400 program by referencing the related **PRTF** file record and/or field name.

Figure 18-6 **SKIPB** and **SPACEB** syntax and processing functions.

TIME (Current System Time)

TIME is a *Field-Level*–only keyword that prints the current system time as a constant in an edited **HH:MM:SS** format. Other edited formats may be specified by an **EDTWRD**

or user-defined *Edit Code.* Conditioning indicators may be used to control the printing of a specific **TIME** value format. Figure 18-7 shows two examples of the syntax and processing results for this keyword. An application program that accesses a *Printer File* (**PRTF**) instead of including Output Specifications to generate a report is introduced in the following sections.

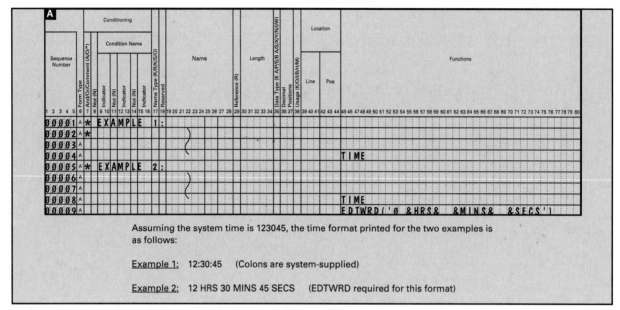

Figure 18-7 Two examples of the syntax and processing results for **TIME** keyword.

Example Printer File

The report design in Figure 18-8 will be used to illustrate the syntax for a Printer File (**PRTF**).

Figure 18-8 Report design for a printer file.

The *Data Description Specifications* statements for the report design are shown in Figure 18-9.

An examination of the DDS coding in Figure 18-9 will indicate the following features:

```
     Sequence  Form  A/O/*  Condition                Name        Ref Length Dec Usage  Line Pos   Functions
     Number    Type         Name
  A  *                 Example PRTF FILE.....
  A                                                                                          REF(SMYERS/GLMASTER)
  A          R HDGS                                                                          SKIPB(6)
  A                                                                                      1   TIME
  A                                                                                     24   'EVERYBODY COMPANY'
  A                                                                                     61   'PAGE'
  A                                                                                     +1   PAGNBR EDTCDE(Z) SPACEA(1)
  A                                                                                     18   'SCHEDULE OF ACCOUNTS RECEIVABLE'
  A                                                                                          SPACEA(1)
  A                                                                                     29   DATE EDTCDE(Y) SPACEA(3)
  A                                                                                      4   'CUSTOMER'
  A                                                                                     28   'CUSTOMER NAME'
  A                                                                                     56   'BALANCE' SPACEA(2)
  A                                                                                     52   '$' SPACEA(Ø)
  A          R DETAIL
  A            CUST#              R                                                      6
  A            NAME               R                                                     2Ø
  A            BALANC             R                                                     56   EDTCDE(J) SPACEA(1)
  A          R TOTALS
  A                                                                                          SPACEB(1)
  A            TOTAL                      9    2                                        52   EDTWRD('$&  ,    .  Ø .   -')
  A                                                                                          SPACEB(3)
  A                                                                                     1Ø   'RECORDS PROCESSED'
  A            RECRDS                     6    Ø                                        29   EDTCDE(1)
```

Figure 18-9 *Data Description Specifications* statements for example printer file (**PRTF**).

1. Three record formats, HDGS, DETAIL, and TOTALS, are defined. The HDGS format includes top-of-page control and line spacing. The DETAIL and TOTALS record formats include line spacing only.

2. The **SPACE(0)** keyword on line 1400 prevents spacing after the $ is printed so that the first DETAIL record will print on the same line (see Figure 18-10).

3. Because line spacing is controlled with the **SPACEA** and **SPACEB** keywords, the Line reference (columns 39–41) does not have to be specified. In any case, however, the *Pos* entry (columns 42–44) must be included.

4. Field attributes are referenced from the related physical file. Two non-database fields, *TOTAL* and *RECRDS,* are defined in the DDS coding for the printer file.

A source listing of the example printer file and its relationship to the printed report are illustrated in Figure 18-10.

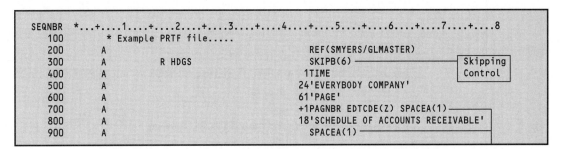

Figure 18-10 Relationship of **SKIPB, SPACEA,** and **SPACEB** line control to the printed report.

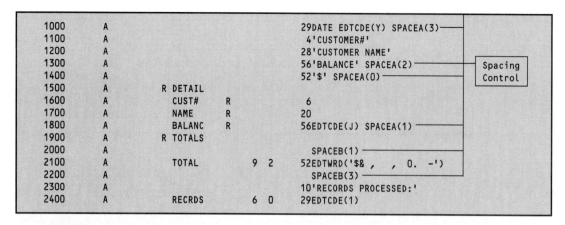

```
1000    A                                      29DATE EDTCDE(Y) SPACEA(3)
1100    A                                       4'CUSTOMER#'                      ┐
1200    A                                      28'CUSTOMER NAME'                  │
1300    A                                      56'BALANCE' SPACEA(2)              │  Spacing
1400    A                                      52'$' SPACEA(0)                    │  Control
1500    A            R DETAIL                                                     │
1600    A              CUST#      R              6                                │
1700    A              NAME       R             20                                │
1800    A              BALANC     R             56EDTCDE(J) SPACEA(1)             │
1900    A            R TOTALS                                                     │
2000    A                                         SPACEB(1)                       │
2100    A              TOTAL      9 2           52EDTWRD('$&  ,    , 0. -')        │
2200    A                                         SPACEB(3)                       │
2300    A                                      10'RECORDS PROCESSED:'             │
2400    A              RECRDS     6 0           29EDTCDE(1)                        ┘
```

```
Printed Report:                                           Keyword/PRTF Line Ref

    13:32:54            EVERYBODY COMPANY              PAGE    1  SKIPB(6)  Line 300
                SCHEDULE OF ACCOUNTS RECEIVABLE                   SPACEA(1) Line 700
                        9/20/95                                   SPACEA(1) Line 900


    CUSTOMER#              CUSTOMER NAME          BALANCE         SPACEA(3) Line 1000
                                                                 SPACEA(2) Line 1300
      12345          KAREL APPEL          $     1,250.00         SPACEA(0) Line 1400
      23456          GEORGES BRAQUE              100.00          SPACEA(1) Line 1800
      34567          PAUL CEZANNE              81,900.00            "         "
      45678          MARC CHAGALL                926.00            "         "
      56789          EDGAR DEGAS               7,854.99            "         "
      67890          MAX ERNST                   500.00            "         "
      78900          BUCKMINSTER FULLER        33,000.10           "         "
      89000          JULIO GONZALEZ              654.78            "         "
    - - - - - - - - - - - - - - - - - - - - - - - - - - - - - - - - - -

    13:32:54            EVERYBODY COMPANY              PAGE    2  SKIPB(6)  Line 300
                SCHEDULE OF ACCOUNTS RECEIVABLE                   SPACEA(1) Line 700
                        9/20/95                                   SPACE(1)  Line 900


    CUSTOMER#              CUSTOMER NAME          BALANCE         SPACEA(3) Line 1000
                                                                 SPACEA(2) Line 1300
      90000          HECTOR HYPPOLITE     $   120,000.00         SPACEA(0) Line 1400
      91000          PIERRE JEANERET                9.45         SPACEA(1) Line 1800
      92000          WASSILY KANDINSKY        375,000.00           "         "
      93000          CHARLES CORBUSIER           250.00            "         "

                                          $   621,445.32         SPACEB(1) Line 2000

    RECORDS PROCESSED:       12                                  SPACEB(3) Line 2200
```

Note: The keyword/line references indicate position of printer carriage <u>after</u> related statement is executed.

Figure 18-10 Relationship of **SKIPB, SPACEA,** and **SPACEB** line control to the printed report. (Continued)

Example RPG/400 Printer File Program

Page overflow *cannot* be controlled by an overflow indicator in columns 33–34 of the *File Description Specifications* statement in the definition of a printer file. Consequently, page overflow control must be programmer-defined in calculation statements in the RPG/400 program. The page overflow and line control items needed include:

1. An independent field that includes a value for the number of lines per page
2. An independent field for a line counter
3. **WRITE** statements to control the output of the printer file's record formats.

The processing logic for programmer-controlled page overflow and line type (headings, detail, and total) control is illustrated in the flowchart in Figure 18-11.

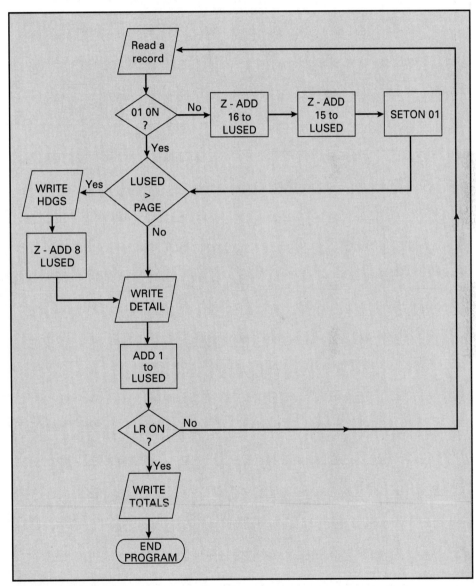

Figure 18-11 Processing logic flowchart for programmer-controlled page overflow and line type output.

A compile listing of the RPG/400 program that processes a printer file and a line-by-line explanation of the instructions are detailed in Figure 18-12.

Refer back to Figure 18-10 to review the report generated by execution of the RPG/400 program.

```
SEQUENCE                                                                    IND   DO
NUMBER  *...1....+....2....+....3....+....4....+....5....+....6....+....7...*  USE   NUM
                          S o u r c e   L i s t i n g
          H
   200   FGLMASTERIP E           K           DISK
          RECORD FORMAT(S):  LIBRARY SMYERS FILE GLMASTER.
                    EXTERNAL FORMAT GLRCRD RPG NAME GLRCRD
   300   FCH18PRF10  E                       PRINTER
   400   *
          RECORD FORMAT(S):  LIBRARY SMYERS FILE CH18PRF1.
                    EXTERNAL FORMAT HDGS RPG NAME HDGS
                    EXTERNAL FORMAT DETAIL RPG NAME DETAIL
                    EXTERNAL FORMAT TOTALS RPG NAME TOTALS
A000000   INPUT  FIELDS FOR RECORD GLRCRD FILE GLMASTER FORMAT GLRCRD.
A000001                                   P   1   30CUST#
A000002                                       4   23 NAME
A000003                                      24   43 STREET
A000004                                      44   63 CITY
A000005                                      64   65 STATE
A000006                                   P 66   680ZIP
A000007                                   P 69   732BALANC
   500   * Initialize line counter and page length fields......
   600   C          *IN01     IFEQ *OFF                  ind off?        B001
   700   C                    Z-ADD16   LUSED   20       line counter    001
   800   C                    Z-ADD15   LPAGE   20       lines/page      001
   900   C                    MOVE *ON  *IN01            set on ind 01   001
  1000   C                    ENDIF                      end line 4 IF   E001
  1100   *
  1200   * Test for page overflow and initialize line counter if true......
  1300   C          LUSED     IFGT LPAGE                 page ovflw test B001
  1400   C                    WRITEHDGS                  write hdg lines 001
  1500   C                    Z-ADD8    LUSED            init. line ctr  001
  1600   C                    ENDIF                      end line 9 IF   E001
  1700   *
  1800   * Write detail line. Increment line ctr, total rcrds, & BALANC total
  1900   C                    WRITEDETAIL                write detl rcrd
  2000   C                    ADD  1    LUSED            increment ctr
  2100   C                    ADD  1    RECRDS           rcrds processed
  2200   C                    ADD  BALANC   TOTAL        accum total
  2300   *
  2400   * Write total line after end of file is read......
  2500   CLR                  WRITETOTALS                write at eof
B000000   OUTPUT FIELDS FOR RECORD HDGS FILE CH18PRF1 FORMAT HDGS.
C000000   OUTPUT FIELDS FOR RECORD DETAIL FILE CH18PRF1 FORMAT DETAIL.
C000001                       CUST#    5   ZONE  5,0
C000002                       NAME    25   CHAR  20
C000003                       BALANC  33   ZONE  8,2
D000000   OUTPUT FIELDS FOR RECORD TOTALS FILE CH18PRF1 FORMAT TOTALS.
D000001                       TOTAL    9   ZONE  9,2
D000002                       RECRDS  15   ZONE  6,0
```

Line #	Explanation
200	GLMASTER is defined as an input (**I** in column 15), primary (**P** in column 16), externally described (**E** in column 19), keyed (**K** in column 31) physical file. The records in the file will be processed in a batch mode in ascending key value (CUST#) order.
300	CH18PRTF is defined as an output (**O** in column 15), externally described (**E** in column 19) *printer file.*
600	The **IFEQ** statement controls the initialization of the line counter (LUSED) and lines per page (LPAGE) fields. Statements in the **IFEQ** group will only be executed <u>once</u> when the first record is read from the physical file. The **MOVE** statement on line 900 sets on the **01** indicator, which will prevent the statements within the **IFEQ** group from being executed again.

Figure 18-12   Example RPG/400 program that processes a printer file.

700	The **Z-ADD** statement initializes the line counter field (LUSED) to 16, one larger than the 15 lines per page field (LPAGE). This coding will cause page overflow to occur when the first detail record is read from the physical file.
800	This **Z-ADD** statement initializes the lines per page field (LPAGE) to 15. Depending on the paper used, the lines per page can be modified simply by changing this value.
900	The **MOVE** statement sets on the **01** indicator, which is specified in the **IFEQ** test on line 600. This causes the **IFEQ** test on line 600 to be false after the first detail record is processed.
1000	This **ENDIF** operation ends the **IFEQ** statement on line 600.
1300	The **IFGT** test determines if the line counter (LUSED) value is <u>greater than</u> the lines per page (LPAGE) value. Note that this will cause page overflow to occur after 15 lines (heading and detail) are printed.
1400	When the **IFGT** test on line 1300 is true, the HDGS record in the *printer file* is printed. Note that the HDGS record includes all of the heading lines and line spacing for a total of eight lines.
1500	The **Z-ADD** statement initializes the line counter (LUSED) to 8, the number of lines used in the HDGS record.
1600	This **ENDIF** operation ends the **IFGT** statement on line 1300.
1900	Regardless of the result of the **IFGT** test on line 1300, the current detail record will be printed by the **WRITE** statement. The *Factor 2* entry (DETAIL) in the **WRITE** statement is the second record format in the *printer file*.
2000	The number of lines used (1) for each DETAIL record printed is added to the line counter (LUSED). Detail lines are single-spaces; hence, 1 is added to LUSED. If double spacing was required, 2 would be added; triple spacing, 3; and so forth. Unlike the 3 space-before and space-after maximums for RPG/400 line spacing control, there is no restriction when line spacing is controlled by a programmer-defined routine.
2100	The number of physical file records read is accumulated in the RECRDS counter.
2200	The BALANC field value from every detail record read is added to the TOTAL accumulator.
2500	When end of the physical file is read, which sets on the **LR** indicator, the third record format (TOTALS) in the *printer file* is printed. This record format includes the TOTAL value, constant and RECRDS value, and related line spacing.

Figure 18-12   Example RPG/400 program that processes a printer file. (Continued)

Printer File (PRTF) Command Parameters

External parameters for printer files are assigned by the **CRTPRTF** (*Create Printer File*) command. Controls, including form size, lines per inch, characters per inch, page overflow, forms alignment, print quality, font type, and so forth, may be specified by a series of prompt screens generated when **CRTPRTF** is entered on a command line and F4 is pressed. Displays 1 and 2 of the seven accessed by the **CRTPRTF** command are shown in Figure 18-13. Some of the parameters are only valid for select printers. Most of them, however, are valid for laser printers, some for serial printers, and a few for line printers.

```
                        Create Printer File (CRTPRTF)

Type choices, press Enter.

    File . . . . . . . . . . . . .   CH18PRF1     Name
      Library  . . . . . . . . . .     *CURLIB    Name, *CURLIB
    Source file  . . . . . . . . .   *NONE        Name, *NONE
      Library  . . . . . . . . . .                Name, *LIBL, *CURLIB
    Source member  . . . . . . . .   *FILE        Name, *FILE
    Generation severity level  . . . 20           0-30
    Flagging severity level  . . . . 0            0-30
    Device specification:
      Printer  . . . . . . . . . .   *JOB         Name, *JOB, *SYSVAL
    Printer device type  . . . . . . *SCS         *SCS, *IPDS, *USERASCII...
    Text 'description' . . . . . . . ch 18 - printer file 1




                                                                   Bottom
F3=Exit   F4=Prompt   F5=Refresh   F10=Additional parameters   F12=Cancel
F13=How to use this display       F24=More keys

- - - - - - - - - - - - - - - - - - - - - - - - - - - - - - - - - - - - - -
                        Create Printer File (CRTPRTF)

Type choices, press Enter.


                        Additional Parameters
Source listing options . . . . .                 *SRC, *NOSRC, *SOURCE...
               + for more values
Page size:
    Lengthñlines per page  . . . .   66           .001-255.000
    Widthñpositions per line  . .    132          .001-378.000
    Measurement method . . . . . .   *ROWCOL      *ROWCOL, *UOM
Lines per inch . . . . . . . .       6            6, 3, 4, 7.5, 7,5, 8, 9, 12
Characters per inch . . . . . .      10           10, 5, 12, 13.3, 13,3, 15...
Front margin:
    Offset down  . . . . . . . . .   *DEVD        0-57.790, *DEVD
    Offset across  . . . . . . . .                0-57.790


                                                                   More...
F3=Exit   F4=Prompt   F5=Refresh   F12=Cancel   F13=How to use this display
F24=More keys
```

Figure 18-13 **CRTPRTF** (Create Printer File) command displays 1 and 2.

Printer File (PRTF) Shells

In lieu of including the syntax for a report in a printer file, programmers may prefer to follow traditional *Output Specifications* coding procedures. Normally, this would prevent many of the options available in the **CRTPRTF** command from being specified. The problem may be resolved by creating a printer file "shell" with the **CRTPRTF** command and include no DDS source code in the member. The coding for the report would be included in the *Output Specifications* of the RPG/400 program. A compile listing of an example program that supports this method is shown in Figure 18-14.

SUMMARY

In the AS/400 environment, the syntax for printed reports may be specified by the following methods:

```
SEQUENCE                                                                  IND  DO
NUMBER    *...1....+....2....+....3....+....4....+....5....+....6....+....7...*  USE  NUM
                          S o u r c e   L i s t i n g
    100   * RPG/400 program that processes a PRTF "shell"
          H
    200   FGLMASTERIP E           K        DISK
          RECORD FORMAT(S): LIBRARY SMYERS FILE GLMASTER.
              EXTERNAL FORMAT GLRCRD RPG NAME GLRCRD
    300   FCH18PRF20  F      132    OF    PRINTER
A000000   INPUT  FIELDS FOR RECORD GLRCRD FILE GLMASTER FORMAT GLRCRD.
A000001                                        P    1   30CUST#
A000002                                             4   23 NAME
A000003                                            24   43 STREET
A000004                                            44   63 CITY
A000005                                            64   65 STATE
A000006                                        P  66   680ZIP
A000007                                        P  69   732BALANC
    400   C           *IN01      CASEQ*OFF     TIMSUB
    500   C                      END
    600   C                      ADD  BALANC   TOTAL   92
    700   C                      ADD  1        RECRDS  60
    800   C           TIMSUB     BEGSR
    900   C                      MOVE *ON      *IN01
   1000   C                      MOVE *ON      *INOF
   1100   C                      TIME          HHMMSS  60
   1200   C                      ENDSR
   1300   OCH18PRF2H  106    OF
   1400   O                             HHMMSS    8 ' : : '
   1500   O                                      40 'EVERYBODY COMPANY'
   1600   O                                      64 'PAGE'
   1700   O                             PAGE  Z  69
   1800   O           H  1     OF
   1900   O                                      37 'SCHEDULE OF ACCOUNTS'
   2000   O                                      48 'RECEIVABLE'
   2100   O           H  3     OF
   2200   O                             UDATE Y  36
   2300   O           H  2     OF
   2400   O                                      12 'CUSTOMER#'
   2500   O                                      40 'CUSTOMER NAME'
   2600   O                                      62 'BALANCE'
   2700   O           H  0     OF
   2800   O                                      52 '$'
   2900   O           DF 1     N1P
   3000   O                             CUST#    10
   3100   O                             NAME     44
   3200   O                             BALANCJ  66
   3300   O           T  1     LR
   3400   O                                      52 '$'
   3500   O                             TOTAL J  66
   3600   O           T  2     LR
   3700   O                                      27 'RECORDS PROCESSED:'
   3800   O                             RECRDS2  35
```

Because PRTF is a shell (no DDS format), it must be program-defined (F in column 19) and record length (132 in columns 24-27).

System time is accessed by the TIME operation

Overflow is supported for PRTF shell

When overflow line is tested, fetch overflow (F in column 16) will print overflow lines before the current detail output.

Figure 18-14   Example RPG/400 program that processes a printer file shell.

1. Included in the RPG/400 program's *Output Specifications*
2. Included in a printer file using unique DDS syntax
3. Create a printer file "shell" to support select printer features (e.g., print quality, font type, and so forth) not accessible in standard RPG/400 coding. The syntax for the report is coded in the program's *Output Specifications*.

The *Data Description Specifications* for printer files include special keywords. Skipping and line spacing are controlled by the **SKIPA, SKIPB, SPACEA,** and **SPACEB** keywords. Constants are defined exactly the same as those for display files. Fields may be defined in the DDS, or their attributes may be referenced from a file by the **REF** or **REFFLD** keyword. Usually more than one record format is included in a printer file for heading, detail, and total lines. Because page overflow indicators (**OA–OG, OV**) are *not* supported by printer files, this control must be included in calculation statements in the RPG/400 program. Furthermore, headings, detail, and total lines are printed by **WRITE** statements with the select printer file's record format specified in *Factor 2*.

QUESTIONS

18-1.   What are printer files?

18-2.   As compared to standard RPG/400 *Output Specifications* coding for reports, what are the advantages of printer files? Are there any disadvantages?

18-3.   How are printer files created?

18-4.   Where and how are printer files defined in an RPG/400 program?

18-5.   What is the function of each of the following printer file keywords?

DATE	**EDTWRD**	**SPACEB**
SPACEA	**SKIPA**	**SKIPB**
TIME	**PAGNBR**	**EDTCDE**

18-6.   Where in the DDS form are the keywords in Question 18-5 specified?

18-7.   In what format is the **DATE** value accessed?

18-8.   In what format is the **TIME** value accessed?

18-9.   What is the maximum value that may be specified with the **SPACEA** and **SPACEB** keywords?

18-10.   What is the result of processing if **SKIPB(06)** is specified and the printer carriage is on line 1? On line 10?

18-11.   Format **EDTCDE** keywords to generate the indicated edited result for the following examples:

	Value in Storage	Edited Output	EDTCDE Format
a.	0000000 ▲	.00	
b.	092291	9/22/91	
c.	1250000) ▲	125,000.00–	
d.	00000000 ▲		

▲ Indicates implied decimal position

18-12.   Format **EDTWRD** keywords to generate the indicated edited result for the following examples:

	Value in Storage	Edited Output	EDTWRD Format
a.	0015000 ▲	$ 150.00	
b.	0015000 ▲	$150.00	
c.	011223333	011-22-3333	
d.	011223333	011 22 3333	
e.	2038380601	(203)-838-0601	
f.	00000900 ▲	*****9.00 CREDIT	
g.	00001	1	
h.	093091	9/30/91	
i.	25000) ▲	2,500.00–	

▲ Indicates implied decimal position

Assume all dollar values are to include commas in the EDTWRD when large enough

18-13.   How is page overflow controlled in an RPG/400 program when printer files are used for report formats?

18-14. Explain the processing logic of the following calculation instructions:

```
*... ... 1 ... ... 2 ... ... 3 ... ... 4 ... ... 5 ... ... 6
     C          *IN10     IFNE *ON
     C                    Z-ADD55        LCOUNT  20
     C                    Z-ADD54        PAGLEN  20
     C                    MOVE *ON       *IN10
     C                    ENDIF
```

18-15. Explain the processing logic of the following calculation instructions:

```
*... ... 1 ... ... 2 ... ... 3 ... ... 4 ... ... 5 ... ... 6
     C          LCOUNT    IFGE PAGLEN
     C                    WRITEHDINGS
     C                    MOVE 06        LCOUNT
     C                    ENDIF
     C                    WRITEDETLIN
     C                    ADD  2         LCOUNT
     CLR                  WRITETOLINE
```

18-16. Refer to Question 18-15 and explain where HDINGS, DETLIN, and TOLINE are defined. How are they defined? What general syntax is included in each?

18-17. What is the function of the **CRTPRTF** command? Name some of the controls that may be specified by this command.

18-18. Under what conditions may the syntax for a report be included in the *Output Specifications* and a related printer file be specified in the *File Description Specifications?*

PROGRAMMING ASSIGNMENTS

The programming assignments for this chapter will require you refer to assignments in other chapters. If the referenced assignment was not previously completed, create the physical file, load the data, create a printer file from the report design, and write the RPG/400 program to generate the report. If the assignment had been completed, create a printer file for the report design and modify the program accordingly.

Programming Assignment 18-1: SALES JOURNAL

Refer to Programming Assignment 5-1 for the specifications.

Programming Assignment 18-2: SALESPERSON SALARY/COMMISSION REPORT

Refer to Programming Assignment 6-1 for the specifications.

Programming Assignment 18-3: VOTER REPORT BY TOWN, COUNTY, AND STATE TOTALS

Refer to Programming Assignment 8-2 for the specifications.

Programming Assignment 18-4: INCOME STATEMENT BY QUARTERS

Refer to Programming Assignment 11-2 for the specifications.

chapter 19

Control Language Programming

The AS/400 Control Language allows the programmer to communicate with OS/400, the AS/400 operating system. There are well over a thousand commands for the programmer to select from. To simplify command usage, IBM adopted standard naming conventions. These naming conventions were briefly discussed in Chapter 1.

All commands begin with a three-letter *verb* indicating the type of action the programmer wants to take. Examples of verbs are as follows:

STR	Start	END	End
EDT	Edit	CHG	Change
WRK	Work with	ADD	Add
DSP	Display	CRT	Create
DLT	Delete	CLR	Clear

Verbs such as those listed above are combined with a *subject* to create a command. Subjects are generally represented by three or four letters, although they may be shorter or longer. A few example subjects are listed below:

OUTQ	Output Queue	WTR	Writer
PGM	Program	OBJ	Object
LIB	Library	LIBL	Library List
PFM	Physical File Member	MSG	Message
JOB	Job	F	File

The combination of verbs with subjects produces commands similar to those that follow:

WRKOUTQ	Work with Output Queue
SNDMSG	Send Message
EDTLIBL	Edit Library List
DLTF	Delete File
CLRPFM	Clear Physical File Member
DSPPGM	Display Program

Sometimes, additional information is needed to make the command meaningful. *Modifiers* may be added to the subject to clarify the meaning of the command. For example:

WRKACTJOB	**Work with Active Jobs**
CRTCLPGM	**Create CL Program**
STRPRTWTR	**Start a Print Writer**
SNDBRKMSG	**Send a Break Message**

Most commands have additional parameters which provide the operating system with specific information (such as *which* CL program to create or *where* to send the break message). Some parameters, known as *required parameters,* must have a value entered. Other parameters, known as *optional parameters,* contain default values that the programmer may choose to use or override. Each command has a specific order in which it expects to receive parameter values, thus each command's parameters may be entered in a *positional* format. When using *positional* format to enter a command, a space is used as the parameter delimiter, and each of the command's parameters is assigned a value based on that value's position in the command string (see Figure 19-1).

```
Positional Format

    COMMAND    PARM1  PARM2  PARM3 . . .

    DSPJOBD    SMYERS/PGM1    *PRINT


Keyword Format

    COMMAND    KEYWORD1(PARM1)  KEYWORD2(PARM2)  KEYWORD3(PARM3) . . .

    DSPJOBD    JOBD(SMYERS/PGM1)  OUTPUT(*PRINT)
```

Figure 19-1 Command syntax formats.

If a command has a large number of parameters, using the positional format to enter the command may become confusing. Another method of specifying parameter values (also shown in Figure 19-1) identifies each parameter by *keyword.* Keywords may be thought of as parameter names. By specifying a keyword with an associated value, the programmer may enter the parameter values in any order. Also, the programmer may choose to enter only the parameters for which values must be specified, and accept the default values for the remaining parameters.

CL PROGRAMMING

Many commands may be entered on the command line and run interactively. However, the AS/400's Control Language is a flexible programming language that allows the programmer to combine commands into programs, store them in source files, and compile them into system objects.

The programmer uses **SEU** (the *Source Entry Utility*) to enter the Control Language Program (*CLP*). Programs are stored as source-type CLP and, although the IBM default source file for CL programs is QCLSRC, programs may be stored in any source file. While entering the CL commands, the programmer may request the command prompt screens by pressing **F4.** This simplifies the program entry and allows the programmer to verify command parameters. The resulting source code may then be used to create a CLP object using the **CRTCLPGM** (*Create CL Program*) command (or option 3 of the Programmer Menu) or selecting option 14 from a **PDM** source member display.

Figure 19-2 illustrates the basic CLP structure. Comments may appear anywhere within the program, even spanning several lines, and are denoted by the slash-asterisk (/*) and the asterisk-slash (*/) that surround the comment text.

The **PGM** (*Program*) statement is required and indicates the beginning of a CLP. It may or may not include a list of parameters that are passed into the program upon execu-

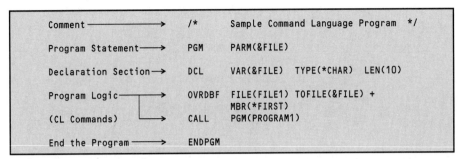

Figure 19-2 Basic structure of a CL program.

tion. These parameters are positional, and any variables listed must be defined in the *Declaration Section* of the program.

All program variables must be declared in the Declaration Section of the program using the **DCL** (*Declare Variable*) statement. Variable names begin with an ampersand (**&**) and may be up to 10 characters in length. Variables may be character (***CHAR**), decimal (***DEC**), or Boolean logical (***LOG**) data type. A **VALUE** clause may be added to the **DCL** statement to assign an initial value to the variable.

The programmer may also declare *one* externally defined file (a display file, physical file, or logical file) using the **DCLF** (*Declare File*) statement for processing by the program.

Almost any Control Language command may be used to form the *Program Logic* portion of the CLP. Commands may be specified as either positional or keyword syntax. A plus sign (+), as shown in the **OVRDBF** command in Figure 19-2, indicates that the command continues on the next line.

The optional **ENDPGM** (*End Program*) command indicates that all program processing is complete.

CALLING MULTIPLE PROGRAMS

CL programs are often used to execute consecutive programs. When the processing of one program is dependent upon another program having been run, a CLP that executes the programs in the appropriate order may prove useful. Figure 19-3 illustrates this concept.

```
100-   PGM
200-   CLRPFM    FILE(WORKFILE) MBR(*FIRST)
300-   CALL      PGM(BLDFILE) /* BUILD WORK FILE */
400-   CALL      PGM(PRTRPT)  /* PRINT WORK FILE */
500-   ENDPGM
```

Figure 19-3 CLP to execute two programs.

Like the skeleton program shown in Figure 19-2, the example CLP shown in Figure 19-3 begins with a **PGM** statement (at line 100). However, unlike the skeleton program, the program in Figure 19-3 has no variable declarations. This program does not require any variables, so none have been defined.

The first command issued by the program is **CLRPFM** (*Clear Physical File Member*) (line 200). This command removes all data from the specified member (in this case *FIRST, the first member) of a physical file (in this example, WORKFILE).

Next, the first program is executed by the **CALL** command at line 300. The comment on line 300 indicates that this program will output records to WORKFILE. Once the first program, BLDFILE, has completed, the second program will be executed. Again a **CALL** command on line 400 is issued, this time to run the program PRTRPT, which reads the WORKFILE and prints a report.

By creating the example CL program, the programmer has ensured that the programs will be executed in the appropriate order. If, as in this example, none of the programs require operator interaction, the CLP may be submitted to the batch subsystem (QBATCH) for execution in batch mode. To submit the previous program (PRTRPTCL), a **SBMJOB** (*Submit Job*) command such as the following would be used:

SBMJOB JOB(BATCH _ JOB) CMD(CALL PGM(PRTRPTCL)) JOBD(QBATCH)

PASSING PARAMETERS

CL programs are frequently used to retrieve and pass parameters between programs. Figure 19-4 contains a simple Control Language program that retrieves a date range from a data area and passes the dates as parameters to a report program. Three program variables have been defined. The first, *&DATES,* will hold the 12 characters of data found in the data area DATES. The remaining two variables, *&FROM* and *&TO,* will each eventually hold a date value in numeric format.

```
  1-    /* PASS DATES FROM DATA AREA TO PROGRAM */
100-    PGM
200-    DCL        VAR(&DATES) TYPE(*CHAR) LEN(12)
300-    DCL        VAR(&FROM)  TYPE(*DEC)  LEN(6 0)
400-    DCL        VAR(&TO)    TYPE(*DEC)  LEN(6 0)
500-    RTVDTAARA  DTAARA(DATES)  RTNVAR(&DATES)
600-    CHGVAR     VAR(&FROM) VALUE(%SST(&DATES 1 6))
700-    CHGVAR     VAR(&TO)   VALUE(%SST(&DATES 7 6))
800-    CALL       PGM(RPTPGM1) PARM(&FROM &TO)
900-    ENDPGM
```

Figure 19-4   CLP to pass parameters.

Information stored in the data area DATES is retrieved by using the **RTVD-TAARA** (*Retrieve Data Area*) command. The retrieved information is stored in a specified variable field, in this example, *&DATES.*

The **CHGVAR** (*Change Variable*) command is used to move data from one variable to another and to convert the data from character to numeric format. The receiving field is specified in the **VAR** parameter, and a sending field or constant is specified in the **VALUE** parameter. Because the *&DATES* field is defined as character data, it is possible to use the *substring* function (**%SST**) to extract the individual date elements. The format of the *substring* function and its use are depicted in Figure 19-5.

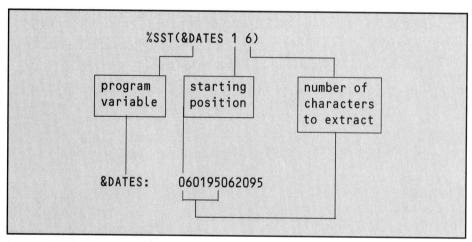

Figure 19-5   The substring function.

Once the dates have been separated into the variables *&FROM* and *&TO* (at lines 600 and 700), they are available for passing as parameters when the program RPTPGM1 is called. Parameters passed to a program via the **CALL** statement are positional, with a space as the delimiter. In the example shown in Figure 19-6, the called program

```
            H
     100   FDAT1OP1 IP  E                      DISK
            RECORD FORMAT(S): LIBRARY JANELIB FILE DAT1OP1.
                  EXTERNAL FORMAT DAT1OP1R RPG NAME DAT1OP1R
     200   FQSYSPRT O   F      132    OF      PRINTER
     300   E                   SALS       5 7 2          INPUT TIME ARRAY
     400   E                   TOTL       5 8 2          CALC TIME ARRAY
     500   IDAT1OP1R
     600   I              SALSP1                      SALS,1
     700   I              SALSP2                      SALS,2
     800   I              SALSP3                      SALS,3
     900   I              SALSP4                      SALS,4
    1000   I              SALSP5                      SALS,5
    1000     INPUT  FIELDS FOR RECORD DAT1OP1R FILE DAT1OP1 FORMAT DAT1OP1R.
  A000001                               P   1   40WEDATE
  A000002          SALSP1               P   5   82SALS,1
  A000003          SALSP2               P   9  122SALS,2
  A000004          SALSP3               P  13  162SALS,3
  A000005          SALSP4               P  17  202SALS,4
  A000006          SALSP5               P  21  242SALS,5
    1100   C       *IN10    IFEQ *OFF
    1200   C       *ENTRY   PLIST
    1300   C                PARM           $FROM   60
    1400   C                PARM           $TO     60
    1500   C                MOVE *ON       *INOF
    1600   C                MOVE *ON       *IN10
    1700   C                ENDIF
    1800   C       WEDATE   IFGE $FROM
    1900   C       WEDATE   ANDLE$TO
    2000   C                XFOOTSALS      WEKTOT 82     week's total
    2100   C                ADD  SALS      TOTL          accumulate sals
    2200   C                EXCPT@PRINT
    2300   C                ENDIF
    2400   CLR              XFOOTTOTL      MTHTOT 82     month sales
    2500   OQSYSPRT H 101    OF
    2600   O                      UDATE Y  8
    2700   O                               40 'SALES PERFORMANCE'
    2800   O                               59 'REPORT BY SALESPER'
    2900   O                               62 'SON'
    3000   O                               85 'PAGE'
    3100   O                      PAGE  Z  90
    3200   O        H  3    OF
    3300   O                               30 'FOR'
    3400   O                      $FROM Y  40
    3500   O                               44 'TO'
    3600   O                      $TO   Y  53
    3700   O        H  1    OF
    3800   O                                6 'WEEK'
    3900   O                               39 'SALESPERSON  SALESPERSON'
    4000   O                               65 'SALESPERSON  SALESPERSON'
    4100   O                               89 'SALESPERSON     WEEKLY'
    4200   O        H  2    OF
    4300   O                                7 'ENDING'
    4400   O                               34 '#1        #2'
    4500   O                               60 '#3        #4'
    4600   O                               88 '#5        TOTAL'
    4700   O        EF 2            @PRINT
    4800   O                      WEDATEY  8
    4900   O                      SALS     81 '  , 0. &&&&'
    5000   O                      WEKTOT1  91
    5100   O        TF1     LR
    5200   O                                7 'TOTALS'
    5300   O                      TOTL     80 '  , 0. &&&'
    5400   O                      MTHTOT1  91
           * * * * *  E N D   O F   S O U R C E  * * * * *
```

Figure 19-6 RPG/400 program that received date parameters.

Report Generated by RPG/400 Program RPTPGM1

10/29/95	SALES PERFORMANCE REPORT BY SALESPERSON						PAGE 1
	FOR 6/01/95 TO 6/20/95						
WEEK ENDING	SALESPERSON #1	SALESPERSON #2	SALESPERSON #3	SALESPERSON #4	SALESPERSON #5	WEEKLY TOTAL
6/04/95	80.00	145.30	351.40	124.00	52.24	752.94
6/11/95	543.00	570.00	5,800.01	585.00	630.00	8,128.01
6/18/95	90.00	400.00	525.00	535.00	7,540.00	9,090.00
TOTALS	713.00	1,115.30	6,676.41	1,244.00	8,222.24	17,970.95

Figure 19-6   RPG/400 program that received date parameters. (Continued)

RPTPGM1 will first receive the *&FROM* date, and then the *&TO* date value, as two six-position numeric data fields.

As can be seen in Figure 19-6, the RPG/400 coding necessary to receive the parameters passed by the CL program is the same as that required to receive parameters from another RPG/400 program. A *parameter list* (**PLIST**) is defined at line 1200 to receive the parameters upon program initialization (***ENTRY**). Data fields to receive the data are defined as parameter fields using the **PARM** operation at lines 1300 and 1400. The length and type of data specified for these fields must match the CLP definition of the fields being passed. Once received, the data in the parameter fields may be processed like any other data by the program. Upon completion of the called program (when the **LR** indicator is turned on or a **RETRN** operation is encountered), the values in the parameter data fields are returned to the calling CLP.

Once the called program RPTPGM1 has finished executing, processing is complete. An **ENDPGM** statement indicates the end of the CL program (see Figure 19-4).

PROCESSING A DISPLAY FILE

As mentioned before, Control Language programs may be used to process one externally defined file. Figure 19-7 shows a CLP that presents a display screen (also shown in Figure 19-7) from which the user may select a batch of orders to be processed. Each day's orders are stored in a separate member of the ORDERS physical file. Based on the day of the week chosen, the appropriate orders will be selected for processing.

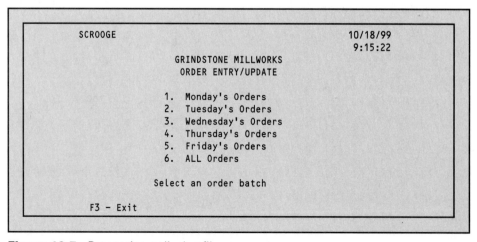

Figure 19-7   Processing a display file.

```
 100-        PGM
 200-        DCLF    FILE(BATCHES) RCDFMT(SELECT)
A00001-      DCL     VAR(&IN03)   TYPE(*CHAR) LEN(1)
A00002-      DCL     VAR(&CHOICE) TYPE(*CHAR) LEN(1)
 400-        /* DISPLAY & READ THE SCREEN */
 500- DSPLY: SNDRCVF RCDFMT(SELECT)
 600-        IF      COND(&IN03 *EQ '1') THEN(GOTO EXIT)
 700-        /* PROCESS SELECTION */
 800-        IF      COND(&CHOICE *EQ '1')  THEN(+
 900                 OVRDBF FILE(ORDERS) TOFILE(*FILE) MBR(MONDAY))
1000-        IF      COND(&CHOICE *EQ '2')  THEN(+
1100                 OVRDBF FILE(ORDERS) TOFILE(*FILE) MBR(TUESDAY))
1200-        IF      COND(&CHOICE *EQ '3')  THEN(+
1300                 OVRDBF FILE(ORDERS) TOFILE(*FILE) MBR(WEDNESDAY))
1400-        IF      COND(&CHOICE *EQ '4')  THEN(+
1500                 OVRDBF FILE(ORDERS) TOFILE(*FILE) MBR(THURSDAY))
1600-        IF      COND(&CHOICE *EQ '5')  THEN(+
1700                 OVRDBF FILE(ORDERS) TOFILE(*FILE) MBR(FRIDAY))
1800-        IF      COND(&CHOICE *EQ '6')  THEN(+
1900                 OVRDBF FILE(ORDERS) TOFILE(*FILE) MBR(*ALL))
2000-        /* EXECUTE PROGRAM */
2100-        CALL    PGM(EDITORDS)
2200-        DLTOVR  FILE(ORDERS)
2300-        GOTO    CMDLBL(DSPLY)
2400- EXIT:  ENDPGM
```

Figure 19-7   Processing a display file. (Continued)

The CLP begins with the **PGM** statement, indicating that this is a program, followed by the declaration of the display file with the **DCLF** (*Declare File*) statement. Only one file may be defined in a Control Language program, and its declaration must be placed after the **PGM** statement and before any other command statements. The **DCLF** command shown in Figure 19-7 indicates that the program will use the record format SELECT in the BATCHES file. The record contains the variables *&IN03* (associated with F3 to end processing) and *&CHOICE* (which contains the selected option). The display file has been coded with a **VALUES** clause, which will edit the *&CHOICE* field and prevent an invalid value from being entered.

The **SNDRCVF** (*Send/Receive File*) command on line 500 is used to display, and then read, the SELECT screen. A *label,* **DSPLY**, allows processing to loop back up and redisplay the screen.

Seven **IF** statements are used to test for specific conditions and take appropriate action. The general format of the **IF** command is illustrated in Figure 19-8. Alphanumeric constants used for comparison must be enclosed in apostrophes, while numeric constants are entered without them. Note that various relationships may be tested:

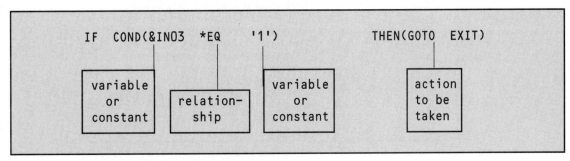

Figure 19-8   The **IF** command.

*EQ	Equal to	*NE	Not Equal to
*GT	Greater Than	*GE	Greater Than or Equal to
*LT	Less than	*LE	Less Than or Equal to

Although not shown in this example, compound **IF** statements are possible. Multiple conditions may be joined using ***AND** and ***OR** to produce more sophisticated testing.

The first **IF** statement, located at line 600, tests *&IN03* to determine if the user has requested that the program end. If the indicator is *ON* (the condition is true), control is passed to the statement labeled **EXIT** (the **ENDPGM** statement). The remaining **IF** statements determine the value entered in *&CHOICE* and, using the **OVRDBF** (*Override Data Base File*) command, direct the ORDERS file to access the appropriate physical file member (i.e., Monday through Friday, or all members).

Finally, the edit program EDITORDS is called on line 2100. Then, the file override is removed using the **DLTOVR** (*Delete Override*) command (line 2200), and control is returned to the **SNDRCVF** (*Send/Receive File*) command at line 500 to display the selection screen again. Only when **F3** is pressed and *&IN03* is set ON will control pass to the **ENDPGM** (*End Program*) statement and end the program.

PROCESSING A DATABASE FILE

Database files may also be processed by CL programs. Figure 19-9 shows a CLP that se-

```
100      **------------------------------------------------------------
200      ** REPORTS - REPORTS TO BE RUN BY CL PROGRAM
300      **------------------------------------------------------------
400      A        R PGMREC
500      A          PGM          10
600      A          TITLE        35
700      A          PARMS        80
800      A        K PGM
         * * * * *  E N D   O F   S O U R C E  * * * * *
```

```
 100-          PGM
 200-          DCLF     FILE(REPORTS) RCDFMT(PGMREC)
A00001-        DCL      VAR(&PGM)    TYPE(*CHAR) LEN(10)
A00002-        DCL      VAR(&TITLE) TYPE(*CHAR) LEN(35)
A00003-        DCL      VAR(&PARMS) TYPE(*CHAR) LEN(80)
 300-          DCL      VAR(&MSG)    TYPE(*CHAR) LEN(80)
 400-          DCL      VAR(&CMD)    TYPE(*CHAR) LEN(80)
 500-          DCL      VAR(&COUNT) TYPE(*DEC)  LEN(3 0)
 600-          DCL      VAR(&NUMBR) TYPE(*CHAR) LEN(3)
 700-          /*  READ FILE  */
 800-          OVRDBF   FILE(REPORTS) TOFILE(*FILE) NBRRCDS(1) SEQONLY(*YES 1)
 900- READ:    RCVF     RCDFMT(*FILE)
1000-          MONMSG   MSGID(CPF0864)  EXEC(DO)
1100-          CHGVAR  VAR(&NUMBR) VALUE(&COUNT)
1200-          GOTO CMDLBL(EXIT)
1300-          ENDDO
1400-          /*  SUBMIT REPORT PROGRAM  */
1500-          IF       COND(&PARMS *EQ '          ') THEN(+
1600-          CHGVAR VAR(&CMD) VALUE('CALL' *BCAT &PGM)
1700-          ELSE     CHGVAR VAR(&CMD) VALUE('CALL ' *CAT &PGM *CAT +
1800-                   ' PARM(''' *CAT &PARMS *CAT ''')')
1900-          SBMJOB   JOB(&PGM) CMD(&CMD) JOBD(QBATCH)
2000-          CHGVAR   VAR(&COUNT) VALUE(&COUNT + 1)
2100-          GOTO     CMDLBL(READ)
2200- EXIT:    CHGVAR   VAR(&MSG) VALUE('Processing complete. ' *CAT &NUMBR +
2300                       *CAT ' programs executed.')
2300-          SNDPGMMSG MSG(&MSG)  TOPGMQ(QSYSOPR) MSGTYPE(*INFO)
2400-          ENDPGM
```

Figure 19-9 Processing a database file.

quentially reads the REPORTS file. Records in the file contain a program name, a brief description of the program, and a list of parameters necessary to execute the program. As each record is read, the report program is submitted to run in batch mode. When all records in the REPORTS file have been read and an end-of-file condition is sensed, a message indicating how many programs were processed is sent to the system operator's message queue.

Similar to the other example programs shown in this chapter, the program in Figure 19-9 begins with a **PGM** statement and a declarative section. Within the declarative section, the file REPORTS is defined using the **DCLF** (*Declare File*) statement specifying record format PGMREC. The physical file's record format PGMREC contains three fields (*&PGM, &TITLE,* and *&PARMS*) which, when the CL program is compiled, generate variable declaration (**DCL**) statements. Four additional variables (*&MSG, &CMD, &COUNT,* and *&NUMBR*) have been added for use by the program (lines 300 to 600).

An **OVRDBF** (*Override Data Base File*) command is issued on line 800 for the REPORTS file to itself. The **NBRRCDS** (*Number Records*) parameter of the **OVRDBF** command specifies that one record at a time is to be moved from auxiliary storage (disk) into main storage for processing. The **SEQONLY** (*Sequential Only*) parameter shown in the example indicates that the file will be processed sequentially and that one record at a time will be transferred from the database to the program's internal buffer.

It is the **RCVF** (*Receive File*) command on line 900 which reads the database file. Data is placed into the appropriate variables based on the record format specified in the **RCDFMT** (*Record Format*) parameter. In the example, **FILE* has been specified as the record format to be used. This is a special entry that indicates that there is only one record format in the specified database file and that, whatever its name, it is the format that is to be used.

If an end-of-file condition is experienced when the program executes the **RCVF** (*Receive File*) command, the system issues an error message. The program monitors for this message, CPF0864, using the **MONMSG** (*Monitor Message*) command. When the system issues the CPF0864 message, the **MONMSG** command will execute the command specified in the **EXEC** (*Execute*) parameter. In the example shown in Figure 19-9, the command specified in the **EXEC** parameter is a **DO** command. This allows several commands to be performed. All of the commands listed between the **DO** and the **ENDDO** statements will be executed. In this instance, the value in the variable *&COUNT* will be converted from numeric format to character format and stored in the variable *&NUMBR* by the **CHGVAR** (*Change Variable*) command. Then the **GOTO** command will cause program control to branch to the statement labeled **EXIT** (statement number 2200) before processing continues.

If a record was found (that is, the end-of-file does not occur), processing continues with the formatting of a message. The **BCAT* (*Concatenate with a Leading Blank*) function, as illustrated in Figure 19-10, allows literal values to be joined with program variables to produce a desired character string. Note in Figure 19-10 that although the variable *&PGM* is 10 characters long, only the portion of the variable that contains data is used. Notice also that the value of each variable or literal value which was preceded by a

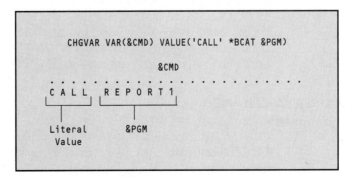

Figure 19-10 The ***BCAT** (Concatenate with Leading Blank) function.

*BCAT in the **VALUE** clause of the **CHGVAR** command is preceded by a blank in the *&CMD* variable. Using the concatenate function in the **VALUE** clause of the **CHGVAR** (*Change Variable*) command results in the entire character string being stored in the variable *&CMD*.

An **IF** command checks to see whether parameters have been specified. If no parameters were specified, a simple **CALL** command is constructed using the ***BCAT** function and stored in the *&CMD* variable. Otherwise, if parameters are to be included, the list of parameters contained in the variable *&PARMS* is included in the **CALL** command. The ***CAT** function (illustrated in Figure 19-11) is used to construct the command string. Notice in Figure 19-11 that some of the literal values specified contain spaces intended to separate them from the value stored in the *&PGM* variable. However, when constructing the parameter list, no spaces are included.

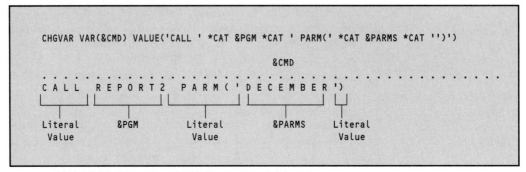

Figure 19-11   The ***CAT** (Concatenate) function.

Other than the inclusion of a leading blank, the ***CAT** and ***BCAT** functions process data in the same way, and either one may be used to concatenate program variables and literal values into character strings. Also note that where a single apostrophe would normally be placed within the character string, two apostrophes have been keyed. This indicates to OS/400 that the apostrophe is to be included as part of the character string and not to be confused with the apostrophes surrounding the character data.

An **SBMJOB** (*Submit Job*) command is issued at line 1900 of the program (Figure 19-9) to submit the program specified in the *&PGM* variable for processing in batch mode.

Next the *&COUNT* variable is incremented using the **CHGVAR** command, and the **GOTO** command transfers control back to the **READ** label (at statement 900) to read the next record.

Only when an end-of-file condition is encountered will the program execute statements 2200 through 2400. Recall that when an end-of-file condition is sensed by the **MONMSG** (*Monitor Message*) command at statement 1000, the value in the *&COUNT* variable is converted from numeric to character format and stored in the variable *&NUMBR*. Then, the program branches to statement 2200 as a result of the **GOTO** command on line 1200.

Once again, the **CHGVAR** command is used to create a character string. This time the ***CAT** (*Concatenate*) function is used to include the value currently in the *&NUMBR* variable in the message text stored in *&MSG*. The message is then sent to the system operator's message queue by the **SNDPGMMSG** (*Send Program Message*) command on line 2300, and the program ends with the **ENDPGM** statement.

CREATING USER COMMANDS

CL programs may be used to create commands similar to the OS/400 commands. The **CRTTESTF** (*Create Test File*) command (shown in Figure 19-12) is a user-defined command that copies 25 records from a specified file into a file by the same name in the pro-

```
100-          CMD        PROMPT('Create Test File')
200-          PARM       KWD(LIVEFILE)  TYPE(*CHAR) LEN(10) +      ·
300                      MIN(1) PROMPT('Live File to Copy:')
```

Figure 19-12   Source for **CRTTESTF** (Create Test File) command.

grammer's current library. It can be very useful when creating small files for testing programs.

Command parameters are defined in a command source (source type CMD) similar to the example shown in Figure 19-12 and are entered via **SEU.** Six types of command definition statements exist:

Statement	Function
CMD	Defines the prompt text to be used for the command. Only one CMD statement per command definition is allowed.
PARM	Defines the parameter to be passed to the command processing program (CPP). Several (to a maximum of 75) parameters may be defined, and the order in which they appear within the command source is the order in which they will appear on the command prompt.
ELEM	Defines the elements of a list of values which may be entered for a parameter (for example, the command may require that a list of library names be entered).
QUAL	Defines a qualifier for a parameter (for example, an object's library name).
DEP	Defines a dependency (for example, if PARM1 is equal to *YES then PARM1 must also be specified).
PMTCTL	Allows control of prompting based on a variety of criteria (for example, display additional prompts when CF10 is pressed).

The example shown in Figure 19-12 contains only the **CMD** statement and one **PARM** statement. The **CMD** statement indicates that the prompt text "Create Test File" (defined by the keyword **PROMPT**) will appear at the top of the command prompt screen. The **PARM** statement contains several keywords. **KWD** stands for *keyword* and indicates that the word LIVEFILE will be used to indicate this parameter when entering the command parameters in keyword format. The **TYPE** keyword defines the type of data being defined for this parameter, in this case *CHAR or character data. **LEN** specifies the length of the parameter (10 positions in this example). The LIVEFILE parameter will be a required parameter because a minimum entry, **MIN(1),** has been specified. And finally, "Live File to Copy" has been specified as the prompt text for the parameter (**PROMPT**). Later, when the **CRTCMD** (*Create Command*) command is executed, the command source shown in Figure 19-12 will be used to generate a command object called **CRTTESTF.**

The CLP **CRTTESTFC** (shown in Figure 19-13) is used to process the **CRTTESTF** command. **CRTTESTFC** was created in the same way that any other con-

```
100-          PGM        PARM(&FILE)
200-          CPYF       FROMFILE(&FILE) TOFILE(*CURLIB/&FILE) +
300                      MBROPT(*REPLACE) CRTFILE(*YES) TORCD(25)
400-          ENDPGM
```

Figure 19-13   CLP **CRTTESTFC** (CPP for **CRTTESTF**) command.

trol language program is created. However, as can be seen in Figure 19-14, when the **CRTCMD** (*Create Command*) command was executed to create the **CRTTESTF** command, **CRTTESTFC** was specified as the **CPP** (*Command Processing Program*) in the *Program to process command* prompt.

Figure 19-14 contains all of the **CRTCMD** (*Create Command*) command prompts. Only the *Command, Program to process the command, Source file,* and *Source member* parameters are required parameters. The remaining parameters may be defaulted. Many of the prompt responses displayed contain default values. However, the programmer has elected to change a few of these parameters.

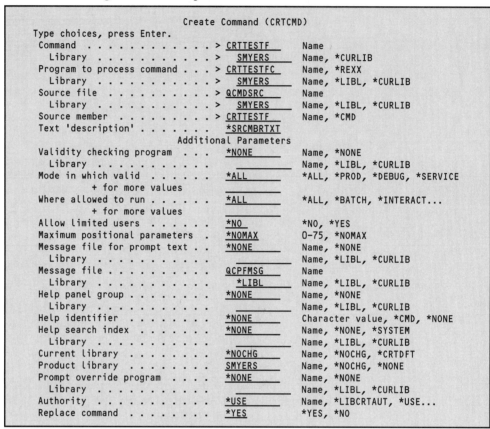

```
                         Create Command (CRTCMD)
          Type choices, press Enter.
            Command . . . . . . . . . . . . > CRTTESTF     Name
              Library . . . . . . . . . . . > SMYERS       Name, *CURLIB
            Program to process command . . . > CRTTESTFC   Name, *REXX
              Library . . . . . . . . . . . > SMYERS       Name, *LIBL, *CURLIB
            Source file . . . . . . . . . . > QCMDSRC      Name
              Library . . . . . . . . . . . > SMYERS       Name, *LIBL, *CURLIB
            Source member . . . . . . . . . > CRTTESTF     Name, *CMD
            Text 'description' . . . . . . . *SRCMBRTXT
                              Additional Parameters
            Validity checking program . . . *NONE          Name, *NONE
              Library . . . . . . . . . . .                Name, *LIBL, *CURLIB
            Mode in which valid . . . . . . *ALL           *ALL, *PROD, *DEBUG, *SERVICE
                    + for more values
            Where allowed to run . . . . . . *ALL          *ALL, *BATCH, *INTERACT...
                    + for more values
            Allow limited users . . . . . . *NO            *NO, *YES
            Maximum positional parameters . *NOMAX         0-75, *NOMAX
            Message file for prompt text . . *NONE         Name, *NONE
              Library . . . . . . . . . . .                Name, *LIBL, *CURLIB
            Message file . . . . . . . . . . QCPFMSG       Name
              Library . . . . . . . . . . .  *LIBL         Name, *LIBL, *CURLIB
            Help panel group . . . . . . . . *NONE         Name, *NONE
              Library . . . . . . . . . . .                Name, *LIBL, *CURLIB
            Help identifier . . . . . . . . *NONE          Character value, *CMD, *NONE
            Help search index . . . . . . . *NONE          Name, *NONE, *SYSTEM
              Library . . . . . . . . . . .                Name, *LIBL, *CURLIB
            Current library . . . . . . . . *NOCHG         Name, *NOCHG, *CRTDFT
            Product library . . . . . . . . SMYERS         Name, *NOCHG, *NONE
            Prompt override program . . . . *NONE          Name, *NONE
              Library . . . . . . . . . . .                Name, *LIBL, *CURLIB
            Authority . . . . . . . . . . . *USE           Name, *LIBCRTAUT, *USE...
            Replace command . . . . . . . . *YES           *YES, *NO
```

Figure 19-14 The **CRTCMD** (Create Command) command.

In this example the programmer chose not to include a *validity checking* program. Had the programmer chosen to do so, a validity checking program could have been specified at the *Validity checking program* prompt. OS/400 will verify that all required parameters are entered for the command, that each parameter is of the data type and length specified in the command definition, that each parameter value meets any defined optional requirements (such as a list of valid values, a range of values, or a relational comparison to a value), and that conflicting parameters are not entered. Beyond this, any parameter verification must be done in either a validity checking program or within the CPP. Verifying that the command prompt entries are logically valid (such as checking the validity of a date entry) is frequently done in a validity checking program to ensure that only valid entries are passed to the CPP. Validity checking programs may be written in CL or in another language (like RPG/400).

Users will be able to execute the **CRTTESTF** command regardless of the processing mode they are currently in because the programmer specified ***ALL** to the *Mode in which valid* prompt. This means, for example, that even if the programmer is in debug mode (has issued the **STRDBG** (*Start Debug*) command) the command may be executed. The programmer has also specified that the **CRTTESTF** command may be executed interactively, in batch, or in a CL program by entering ***ALL** to the *Where allowed to run* prompt.

Users whom the Security Officer has indicated as being limited on their user profiles are not allowed to execute certain commands. The programmer's response of ***NO** to the *Allow limited users* prompt will prevent these users from executing the **CRTTESTF** command.

The *Maximum positional parameters* prompt allows the programmer to specify the maximum number of parameters that may be entered positionally for the command. The default is ***NOMAX** (*no maximum*), which allows all command parameters to be entered positionally. The **CRTTESTF** command has only one parameter, so the programmer may enter either **1** or ***NOMAX** for this prompt.

Prompt text may be stored in a message file. The **CRTTESTF** command prompt text is stored in the command source member, so the programmer has accepted the default value of ***NONE** for the *Message file for prompt text* parameter.

The QCPFMSG file contains all of the messages used by OS/400. If an error occurs, a message is retrieved from this file and displayed. Other *message files* exist for various AS/400 products, and programmers may define their own message files to be used with their programs. The *Message file* parameter allows the programmer to specify which message file is to be used should an error occur while processing the **CRTTESTF** command. In the example, the programmer has chosen to accept the default value and use the QCPFMSG file.

The *Help panel group, Help identifier,* and *Help search index* parameters contain information used by OS/400 to identify help text screens for the command. The example **CRTTESTF** command has no associated help text, therefore the programmer has allowed the default value of ***NONE** to remain for all three of these parameters.

A command may need a different current library while processing, so the programmer has the option of specifying the desired current library for the command. Any library on the system may be specified. In the example, the **CRTTESTF** command expects the current library to be the programmer's development library and no change is desired, so the programmer has specified ***NOCHG** (*no change*) in response to the *Current library* prompt.

Note that a product library was specified in the *Product library* prompt. As you will recall from the discussion of library lists in Chapter 1, a product library is placed before the user portion of the library list. Specifying a product library ensures that the library containing the objects needed by the CPP will be included in the individual's library list.

The *prompt override program* replaces the default values for selected parameters on the prompt display with current actual values. The program name may be specified in the *Prompt override program* parameter. However, the example does not have a prompt override program, so the programmer has responded to the prompt with ***NONE.**

The value specified in the *Authority* parameter defines the authority the programmer is granting to other people who wish to use the **CRTTESTF** command. Specifying ***USE** allows others to use the command but not make changes to it.

Specifying ***YES** to the *Replace command* parameter allows the system to replace an older version of the **CRTTESTF** command with the most current version.

Figure 19-15 shows the resulting **CRTTESTF** command. OS/400 does not differentiate between the user-defined command and the Control Language command. Both

```
                        Create Test File (CRTTESTF)
  Type choices, press Enter.
  Live File to Copy: . . . . . . .    ORDERS       Character value




                                                                  Bottom
  F3=Exit   F4=Prompt   F5=Refresh   F12=Cancel   F13=How to use this display
  F24=More keys
```

Figure 19-15   CRTTESTF (Create Test File) command prompt screen.

recognize **F3** as a cancel request, and typing either command and pressing **F4** will result in a prompt screen. No additional coding to process the command keys is required. Thus, user-defined commands are useful as user interfaces to Control Language programs.

Additional information about creating user-defined commands may be found in IBM's *Programming: Control Language Programming Guide* manual.

SUMMARY

AS/400 Control Language allows the programmer to interface with OS/400, the AS/400 operating system. IBM developed naming conventions that make control language easy to use. Command names are a combination of three-letter *verbs* and *subjects* (and occasionally *modifiers*) which produce meaningful commands such as **CRTCLPGM** (*Create CL Program*) or **WRKOUTQ** (*Work with Output Queue*).

Commands generally have associated parameters that provide the operating system with additional information for processing the command. *Required parameters* must have a value entered in order for the command to process. Other parameters, known as *optional parameters,* contain default values which the programmer may choose to use or override.

Each command expects to receive its parameter values in a specific order. Parameters may be entered in the specified order, separated by spaces, in what is known as *positional format.* An alternative method of specifying command parameters identifies each parameter by name, or *keyword.* Specifying a *keyword,* with an associated value in parentheses, allows the programmer to enter command parameters in any order.

CL commands may be combined to create programs. CL programs have a basic structure, which includes a *Program Statement,* a *Declaration* section, a *Program Logic* section, and an *End of Program* section. The *Program Statement,* or **PGM** command, is required and indicates the beginning of a CLP. The **DCL** (*Declare Variable*) and **DCLF** (*Declare File*) statements are used to define variables and files within the Declaration section. The program logic section may contain almost any CL command and its appropriate parameters. The **ENDPGM** (*End Program*) command is used to indicate that program processing is complete. Comments may appear anywhere throughout the program.

CL programs may be used for a variety of purposes. Examples within the chapter illustrate using a **CLP** to execute a series of programs in a specific order, to pass parameters into a program, to process a display file, and to read and process a database file. The *Substring* (**%SST**) and *Concatenate* (***CAT** and ***BCAT**) functions were detailed, and several new commands (and their associated parameters) were introduced.

User-defined commands may use **CLP**s as **CPP**s (*Command Processing Programs*). Because OS/400 does not differentiate between user-defined commands and Control Language commands, user-defined commands are useful as user interfaces to control language programs.

QUESTIONS

19-1. Explain the IBM naming conventions for AS/400 commands.
19-2. What is the difference between *required* and *optional* parameters?
19-3. What are the two methods of formatting a command and its parameters?
19-4. Which command is required at the beginning of every CL program?
19-5. Write the declaration statement for a program variable for a date field which is six numeric positions (no decimal positions) with an initial value of 063095.
19-6. What symbol is used to indicate that a command's parameters continue on the next line of a program?

19-7. Which command indicates the end of a CL program?

19-8. Write the command to extract the value stored in the sixth position of a 10-byte character variable called *&TEN* and store it in a variable named *&SIX*.

19-9. Which command is used to display, and then read, a display file format?

19-10. Write the **IF** command to determine if the value in *&COST* is greater than 100.00, and if so, to call program TOOMUCH.

19-11. Which command reads a database file?

19-12. When reading a database file in a CLP, how is an end-of-file condition sensed?

19-13. Use the ***BCAT** function to create a *VALUE* parameter for a **CHGVAR** command that will join the value stored in *&DAY* with the literal 'Today is'.

19-14. Change the *VALUE* parameter defined in Question 19-13 to use the ***CAT** function.

19-15. Which command is used to close a file?

19-16. Write the command to convert the value in a numeric field *&SUM* to character data and store it in a variable called *&TOTAL*.

19-17. Which parameter on the **CRTCMD** command links the user-defined command to the CL program which will process the command?

PROGRAMMING ASSIGNMENTS

The following programming assignments require the use of three programs that the student has already written. We recommend using the Sales Journal from either Programming Assignment 5-1 or 18-1, the Salesperson Salary/Commission Report from either Programming Assignment 6-1 or 18-2, and the Income Statement from either Programming Assignment 11-2 or 18-4. However, any RPG/400 programs the student has already created may be used.

Programming Assignment 19-1: CONSECUTIVE PROGRAM PROCESSING

Select three programs from previous programming assignments. Write a CLP to consecutively execute the three selected programs.

Programming Assignment 19-2: THE SALES DEPARTMENT REPORT MENU

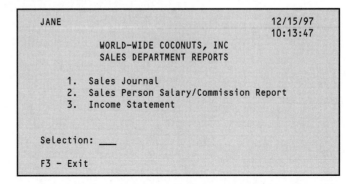

Design a display file similar to the one shown above. Use **F3** as the "exit" key. Allow the user to enter an option 1 through 3. Then write the CL program to output the display file, read the user's selected option, and execute the appropriate program.

Programming Assignment 19-3: THE PROGRAM FILE

```
              PHYSICAL FILE DESCRIPTION

SYSTEM: AS/400                          DATE: Yours
FILE NAME: PGMS                         REV NO: 0
RECORD NAME: Yours                      KEY LENGTH: 10
SEQUENCE: Keyed                         RECORD SIZE: 35


                   FIELD DEFINITIONS


FIELD    FIELD NAME   SIZE  TYPE   POSITION      COMMENTS
  NO                                FROM   TO

   1     ZPGM          10    C       1     10   Program
   2     ZDESC         25    C      11     35   Description
```

Define and create the physical file PGMS (shown above). Use **DFU** to load the names and descriptions of three RPG/400 programs. Then write a CLP to read the file PGMS and execute the program specified in the program name field.

Programming Assignment 19-4: THE RUNPGMS COMMAND

Write the command source to create a command **RUNPGMS** (*Run Programs*). The command will have no parameters. Use the CLP created in Programming Assignment 19-3 as the command processing program (CPP).

chapter 20

Sort and Open Query File

Logical files allow the programmer to select records and/or process a file in a specific order. Why then would a programmer need an alternative method in order to process a file in a specific sequence? The following paragraphs each offer possible answers to this question.

Sometimes it is a performance issue. Maintaining the access path associated with each logical file requires system overhead. Every change made to a physical file must be reflected in all of its associated logical files. If a physical file has too many associated logical files, performance problems may occur (the number of logical files that can be associated with a physical file without causing performance problems depends on the individual AS/400's configuration and workload).

Some applications require that the software have the ability to select records and process them in a specific order based on parameters entered interactively by the user. Logical files are generally created to be permanent database files and lack this degree of flexibility.

Perhaps the application will be run infrequently (such as annually), thereby not justifying the system overhead involved in maintaining a permanent logical file.

Or, as often happens, an application may have to be converted from an existing system to run on the AS/400. Here the goal is to replicate the existing software, not rewrite it. If the existing software sorts a file before processing, then the AS/400 version will also need to sort the file before processing.

SORT UTILITY

The AS/400 *Sort Utility* allows the programmer to merge and sort a maximum of eight input files into a single output file. The AS/400 can perform three different types of sorting. A *regular sort* produces output records that contain detail data in the format specified in the sort specifications. A *summary sort* generates output records that contain summary data. In this type of sort, data from selected numeric fields are added together and records are output based on changes in control field values (similar in concept to level breaks). The third type of sort produces records containing a four-byte binary record address. The output file is known as an *addrout* (*address output*) file and is the result of the *record address* sort.

Sort specifications are stored in a source file member. They indicate the type of sort to perform, which records are to be included or omitted, in what order to store the sorted records, and the format of the sorted output record. Figure 20-1 shows the sort specifica-

```
                         Order Master File

                    PHYSICAL FILE DESCRIPTION

        SYSTEM: AS/400                      DATE: 1/17/93
        FILE NAME: ORDMST                   REV NO: 0
        RECORD NAME: ORDREC                 KEY LENGTH: 4
        SEQUENCE: Keyed                     RECORD SIZE: 45

                       FIELD DEFINITIONS

        FIELD    FIELD NAME   SIZE  TYPE    POSITION    COMMENTS
         NO                                FROM   TO
          1      OCODE          1    C       1     1    Status
          2      OITEM          4    C       2     5    Item# (key)
          3      OINAME        25    C       6    30    Description
          4      OVENDR         1    C      31    31    Vendor Code
          5      ODATE          6    Z      32    37    Order Dt
          6      OQTY           3    Z      38    40    Order Qty
          7      OCOST          5    Z      41    45    Order Cost
                                                        2 decimals
```

```
   Columns . . . :   1  71        Edit                  SMYERS/QTXTSRC
   SEU==>_____        SORT1
   FMT **  ...+... 1 ...+... 2 ...+... 3 ...+... 4 ...+... 5 ...+... 6 ...+... 7
        *************** Beginning of data ***************************
   0001.00     HSORTA  026A       X           SORT ORDER MASTER
   0002.00   O C00010001NECA                  OMIT INACTIVE RECORDS
   0003.00   00C00360037NEKUYEAR              OR IF NOT CURRENT YEAR
   0004.00   I                                INCLUDE ALL OTHERS
   0005.00     FNC00310031                    SORT BY VENDOR CODE
   0006.00     FNC00060030                    SORT BY ITEM NAME
        *************** End of data ***********************************




   F3=Exit      F4=Prompt   F5=Refresh   F9=Retrieve   F10=Cursor
   F16=Repeat find          F17=Repeat change          F24=More keys
```

Figure 20-1   Example record address sort specifications.

tions necessary to create a record address sort to sort an Order Master File in Item Name within Vendor sequence. The sort specifications were entered via **SEU** (the *Source Entry Utility*) and are stored in the source file member SORT1 as type **TXT.**

Figure 20-2 details the completed **SEU** *Sort Header Specification* prompt (prompt type **RH**) from the example sort specifications. Use of the **RH** prompt will place an **H** in column 6 of the record to indicate that the record is a *Sort Header Specification.*

```
   Prompt type . . .  RH    Sequence number . . .   0001.00

     Job    (SORTR,  Control Field      Collating          Alternate
     SORTRS, SORTA)  Length           Sequence (A,D)      Sequence (F,S)
      SORTA              026                A                  _
   Output                                         Statement
   Option (x)  Comments                           Set Name
      X        SORT ORDER MASTER                   _____
```

Figure 20-2   *Sort Header Specifications* for a record address sort.

<u>Job</u> Denotes the type of sort to be executed (columns 7-12 of the
header specification). An entry of SORTR indicates that a
regular sort is to be performed, while the entry of SORTRS
generates a *summary sort*. In the example, the entry of SORTA
indicates that a *record address sort* is to be performed.

<u>Control Field Length</u> specifies the combined length of all sort control
fields (columns 15-17 of the header specification). Since Vendor
is a one position field, and Item Name is a twenty-five position
field, an entry of 26 has been made.

<u>Collating Sequence</u> The A entered in the example (column 18) indicates
that the sort is to be in ascending sequence (A before B, 1 before 2,
etc.). An entry of D in this position would signify a descending sequence.

<u>Alternate Sequence</u> No entry has been made in this field (column 26). By
default, a blank in this position indicates that the sort is to use the
standard collating sequence. Entering an S in this position would result
in the use of an alternative collating sequence for all control fields.
Entry of an F indicates that an alternative collating sequence is to be
used for specified part(s) of the control fields.

<u>Output Option</u> Entering an X in the Output Option field (column 28)
prevents the control field data from being output to the record.
When processing a *summary* or *regular sort* the programmer may choose to
output control fields at the beginning of the output record. However,
an output file generated by a *record address sort* should contain only
record addresses.

<u>Comments</u> Text information may be entered here (columns 40-72) for
internal documentation purposes.

<u>Statement Set Name</u> Comment area (columns 73-80) used to document sets of
sort records.

Figure 20-2 *Sort Header Specifications* for a record address sort. (Continued)

The next set of sort source records allows the programmer to specify record select
and omit criteria. Any number of *Sort Record Specifications* may be combined using
AND/OR logic to produce sophisticated sets of selection criteria. In Figure 20-3 statement number two of the sample record address sort details a simple *omit* statement.

```
Prompt type . . .   RC      Sequence number . . .    0002.00

Include or  AND/OR    Factor 1   -- Location --              Factor 2
  Omit       Test    Data Type  Start      End   Relation  Data Type
   0          _          C       0001      0001     NE         C
                                                              Statement
Constant                Comments                              Set Name
A                       OMIT INACTIVE RECORDS
```

<u>Include or Omit</u> This field (column 6 of the Record Specification)
indicates the type of specification entry. If records are to be included
based upon the specified criteria, an I is entered in this field. Similarly,
if records are to be omitted based upon the criteria entered, an 0 is entered
in this field. Comment records may be indicated by placing an asterisk (*)
in this field.

<u>AND/OR Text</u> Used to combine selection criteria into selection sets. An A
results in the current record being combined with the previous record in an
AND relationship. An 0 combines the records in an OR relationship. No entry
indicates that an AND/OR relationship does not exist.

Figure 20-3 *Sort Record Specifications* for a record address sort.

```
Factor 1 Data Type  The entry for Factor 1 (column 8) indicates the type of
data found in the first comparison factor.  Data types include:
   C   character data
   Z   character data, use only the zone portion for comparison
   D   character data, use only the digit portion for comparison
   P   signed, packed numeric data
   U   signed, zoned numeric data


Location  The Factor 1 Start and End fields (columns 9-12 and 13-16)
contain the start and end positions of the record field which is to be tested.

Relationship  The relationship between Factor 1 and Factor 2 is defined in
this field (columns 17-18).  Possible relationships are:
   EQ  equal
   NE  not equal
   LT  less than
   GT  greater than
   LE  less than or equal to
   GE  greater than or equal to

Factor 2 Data Type  The entry for Factor 2 (column 19) indicates the type of
field found in Factor 2.  Valid entries are:
   C   a constant
   F   a field in the input record
   K   a keyword (UDATE, UYEAR, UMONTH, or UDAY)
   S   a constant, but shifted one character to the left before comparison

Constant  The constant or keyword (representing a value) which is to be
compared to Factor 1 is specified here (columns 20 - 39).  If Factor 2 is
is also a field on the input record, then prompt type RR should be used and
the Start and End for Factor 2 (columns 20-23 and 24-27) will contain the
starting and ending positions for the second field.

Comments  Comments for documentation purposes may be entered (columns 40-72).

Statement Set Name  A name indicating that this statement belongs to a set of
specifications may be entered (columns 73 - 80
```

Figure 20-3 *Sort Record Specifications* for a record address sort. (Continued)

Line 4 of the example sort specifications in Figure 20-1 is also a *Record Specification*. However, the programmer will note that no conditions have been specified. The only entry on this record is an **I** in column 6, indicating that records are to be included. This is an *include-all specification* which causes all records that were not selected (or in this case omitted) by the previous include/omit selection sets to be selected for processing. A sort may have only one include-all specification, and it must be the last record specification in the sort.

The third type of sort specification is the *Sort Field Specification*. It defines the fields to be used by the sort based on the input record. Three types of fields may be de-

```
Prompt type . . .   RF      Sequence number . . .   0004.00

   Field Type          Data Type      -- Location --
(D,F,N,O,S,*)        (C,D,P,U,V,Z)   Start     End
     N                     C          0031      0031
   Forced              Substitute     Forced Field           Overflow
   Character           Character      Continuation           Field Length

     _                     _                     _              _____
   Comments                             Set Name
   SORT BY VENDOR CODE
```

Figure 20-4 *Sort Field Specifications* for a record address sort.

```
Field Type  Identifies the type of field being defined.  Available types
are:
        D    data field
        N    normal control field
        O    opposite control field
        F    forced control field
        S    summary data field
        *    comment specification
The Vendor Code will be a normal control field and will be sorted according to
the sequence specified in the Sort Header Specification.

Data Type  Specifies the format of the data in the field.  Entries include:
        C    character
        D    character, use only digit portion
        P    signed, packed numeric
        U    signed, zoned numeric
        V    force a single data character into the field
        Z    character, use only zone portion

Location  The starting and ending location of the input field.  The Vendor Code
is found in position 31 of the input record.

Forced Character  The character which, when encountered, is to be forced.
This example does not include forcing a character.

Substitute Character  The character which is to be substituted for the Forced
character when it is encountered.

Forced Field Continuation  Entry of any character in this field causes the
current Sort Field Specification to be combined in an OR relationship with
the previous Field Specifications specifying forced fields.

Overflow Field Length  Used only for summary sorts, this field defines the size
of a summary data field if it needs to be larger than the size of the data
field being summarized.

Comments  Comments for documentation purposes may be entered (columns 40-72).

Statement Set Name  A name indicating that this statement belongs to a set of
specifications may be entered (columns 73 - 80).
```

Figure 20-4 *Sort Field Specifications* for a record address sort. (Continued)

fined: control fields, data fields, and summary data fields. *Control fields* specify the order in which the input records are to be sorted (in the example, Item Name within Vendor was specified).

Data fields are input fields the programmer wishes the sorted output record from a regular sort or summary sort to contain. And *summary data fields* contain summarized data that is output to the sorted output record by a summary sort. Figure 20-4 details the *Sort Field Specification* for line 4 of the sample sort specifications using the **RF** format of **SEU.**

PROCESSING THE SORT

While the command to execute the sort program, **FMTDTA** (*Format Data*), may be executed from the command entry line, it is more commonly found in a Control Language program similar to the one shown in Figure 20-5. Here the **CRTPF** (*Create Physical File*) command is used to build a physical file in the **QTEMP** library to hold the sorted output (because the file is built in **QTEMP** it will be deleted when the job ends). Next the **FMTDTA** (*Format Data*) command is used to sort the Order Master file (ORDMST) based on the sort specifications found in member SORT1 of the QTXTSRC file in library SMYERS. The output is stored in the SORTORD file in library QTEMP. Then an RPG/400 program, ORDPRT1, is called to process the sorted data.

```
SEQNBR *...+... 1 ...+... 2 ...+... 3 ...+... 4 ...+... 5 ...+... 6 ...+... 7
   100- PGM
   200- CRTPF    FILE(QTEMP/SORTORD) RCDLEN(4)
   300- FMTDTA   INFILE(ORDMST) OUTFILE(QTEMP/SORTORD) +
   400             SRCFILE(SMYERS/QTXTSRC) SRCMBR(SORT1)
   500- CALL     PGM(ORDRPT1)
   600- ENDPGM
```

Figure 20-5   Control Language program to sort and process Order Master File.

RPG/400 SYNTAX TO PROCESS AN ADDROUT SORT

Figure 20-6 shows an RPG/400 program that processes the sorted record address file. Note that the *File Description* (line 300) entry for the addrout file, SORTORD, contains

```
SEQUENCE
NUMBER    *...1....+....2....+....3....+....4....+....5....+....6....+....7...*
                        S o u r c e   L i s t i n g
   100   * PROGRAM TO READ AN ADDROUT FILE AND GENERATE A REPORT
   200   *
         H
   300   FSORTORD IR  F       4  4 T      EDISK
   400   FORDMST  IP  E                   DISK
         RECORD FORMAT(S):  LIBRARY SMYERS FILE ORDMST.
                        EXTERNAL FORMAT ORDREC RPG NAME ORDREC
   500   FQSYSPRT O   F     132      OF   PRINTER
   600   E    SORTORD ORDMST
   700   IORDREC      01
   800   I                                        OVENDRL1
   800    INPUT FIELDS FOR RECORD ORDREC FILE ORDMST FORMAT ORDREC.
A000001                                1   1 OCODE              STATUS CODE
A000002                                2   5 OITEM              ITEM NO.
A000003                                6  30 OINAME             ITEM NAME
A000004                               31  31 OVENDRL1           VENDOR CODE
A000005                               32  3700DATE              ORDER DATE
A000006                               38  4000QTY               ODER QTY
A000007                               41  4520COST              ORDER COST
   900   OQSYSPRT H  101     1P
  1000   O       OR          OF
  1100   O                         UDATE Y    8
  1200   O                               49 'ORDER MASTER FILE'
  1300   O                               68 'PAGE'
  1400   O                         PAGE  Z   73
  1500   O       H  2      1P
  1600   O       OR          OF
  1700   O                               51 'ANNUAL REPORT FOR 19'
  1800   O                         UYEAR     53
  1900   O       H  2      1P
  2000   O       OR          OF
  2100   O                                6 'VENDOR'
  2200   O                               17 'ITEM NAME'
  2300   O                               40 'ITEM#'
  2400   O                               49 'ORDER DT'
  2500   O                               54 'QTY'
  2600   O                               62 'COST'
  2700   O       D  1      01
  2800   O                         OVENDR     4
  2900   O                         OINAME    33
  3000   O                         OITEM     40
  3100   O                         ODATE Y   49
  3200   O                         OQTY  Z   54
  3300   O                         OCOST 1   62
  3400   O       T  1      L1
         * * * * *  E N D   O F   S O U R C E  * * * * *
```

Figure 20-6   RPG/400 program to process an addrout file.

several entries specific to record address file processing. Column 16 (*File Designation*) contains an **R**, indicating that the file to be processed is a record address file. The *Record Length*, columns 24 through 27, specifies a length of 4 (each record address is stored as a four-byte binary field, and each record contains one address). Column 31, *Record Address Type*, must be blank for the file to be processed sequentially (remember, the file contains record addresses that have been sorted into the desired sequence). *Type of File Organization*, column 32, contains a **T** to specify that the file both contain only record addresses and be program-described. Finally, column 39 (*Extension Code*) contains an **E**, indicating that an *Extension Specification* exists to define the addrout file further.

The relationship between the addrout file and the Order Master file is further defined in the *Extension Specification* (line 600). Here SORTORD is entered as the *From Filename* (columns 11 through 18), and ORDMST is specified as the *To Filename* (columns 19 through 26). This syntax indicates that the record addresses found in the addrout file records are used to access records in the Order Master file.

All other coding in the program follows standard RPG/400 syntax. There are no special *Input*, *Output*, or *Calculation Specifications* required to process the file.

When executed, the Command Language program (CLP) shown previously in Figure 20-5 calls (at line 500) the RPG/400 program shown in Figure 20-6. Order Master records such as the ones shown at the top of Figure 20-7 are processed using the record address (addrout) file created by the sort. A report, shown at the bottom of Figure 20-7, is produced, listing the items for the current year in alphabetical order by Item Name within Vendor.

Note that records that did not have a OCODE value of A or not a current year (ODATE) value of 95 were omitted in the sort. Consequently, the report includes only 6 records and not all 10 from the file.

```
                    ORDER MASTER FILE CONTENTS


    CODE    ITEM#    ITEM NAME                  VENDOR    DATE     QTY     COST
  (OCODE)(OITEM)    (OINAM)                    (OVENDR)  (ODATE) (OQTY) (OCOST)
     A     Z123     REALLY-YUMMY BUBBLE GUM        X     062295   100     5.00
     A     X341     BLOTTO PAPER TOWELS            R     040195   500   500.00
     D     G870     BINGO CARDS                    R     021095    25     1.00
     A     4X12     PRESTO MAGIC WANDS             G     073094    75    25.00
     A     1238     GIMME-MOR POTATO CHIPS         F     052195    62     5.00
     A     V862     SUPER SOUR CANDY APPLES        F     030194    10     1.20
     A     728B     GRANNY'S LIME SHERBET CUPS     G     101295    50     5.25
     A     2975     MR. FUDGIE SUNDAE CUPS         B     040195    65     7.75
     D     445S     WATERMELON POPCICLES           G     021595    20     5.00
     A     E42Z     CORN SNAX                      F     123094    55     4.50
```

```
  12/31/95                    ORDER MASTER FILE               PAGE    1
                             ANNUAL REPORT FOR 1995


  VENDOR   ITEM NAME                   ITEM# ORDER DT  QTY     COST


     B     MR. FUDGIE SUNDAE CUPS      2975  4/01/95    65     7.75


     F     CORN SNAX                   E42Z  12/30/95   55     4.50
     F     GIMME MOR POTATO CHIPS      1238  5/21/95    62     5.00


     G     GRANNYS LIME SHERBET CUPS   728B  10/10/95   50     5.25


     R     BLOTTO PAPER TOWELS         X341  4/01/95   500   500.00


     X     REALLY-YUMMY BUBBLE GUM     Z123  6/22/95   100     5.00
```

Figure 20-7   Order Master file and Order Report by Item Name within Vendor.

OPEN QUERY FILE PROCESSING

A popular alternative to sorting a database file is to use the **OPNQRYF** (*Open Query File*) command. **OPNQRYF** is a very powerful command that allows the programmer to select records dynamically based on a variety of selection criteria (including field mappings, groupings, and the results of mathematical calculations). Depending on the selection criteria specified, the **OPNQRYF** command may make use of existing file access paths to extract the desired data, or it may construct an access path of its own.

While the **OPNQRYF** command is quite powerful, and is frequently used for applications requiring sophisticated file manipulation, it may also be used for simpler applications. Figure 20-8 shows the CLP to process the example Order Master file using the **OPNQRYF** command.

```
SEQNBR  *...+... 1 ...+... 2 ...+... 3 ...+... 4 ...+... 5 ...+... 6 ...+
  100- PGM
  200- DCL          VAR(&YEAR)  TYPE(*CHAR)  LEN(2)
  300- RTVSYSVAL    SYSVAL(QYEAR)  RTNVAR(&YEAR)
  400- OVRDBF       FILE(ORDMST) TOFILE(JANELIB/ORDMST) SHARE(*YES)
  500- OPNQRYF      FILE((ORDMST)) QRYSLT('(OCODE *NE "D") *AND +
  600-               ("' *CAT &YEAR *CAT '" *EQ %SST(DATE 5 2))') +
  700-               KEYFLD((OVENDR) (OINAME)) +
  800-               MAPFLD((DATE '%DIGITS(ODATE)'))
  900- CALL         PGM(ORDRPT2)
 1000- CLOF         OPNID(ORDMST)
 1100- DLTOVR       FILE(ORDMST)
 1200- ENDPGM
```

Figure 20-8 Control Language program to process with **OPNQRYF** (Open Query File) command.

First the current year is retrieved from the system variable *QYEAR* using the **RTVSYSVAL** (*Retrieve System Value*) command and stored in the program variable *&YEAR* before the file is opened for processing. Then an **OVRBDF** (*Override Data Base File*) command is issued to override the file to itself with a *SHARE(*YES)* parameter. This allows the **OPNQRYF** command to share the file access path (known as the *Open Data Path*, or *ODP*) it uses or creates with the subsequent RPG/400 program (ORDRPT2).

The **OPNQRYF** command specifies that it will be opening the ORDMST file. The *MAPFLD* parameter allows the **OPNQRYF** command to generate a work field, called *DATE*, that uses the **%DIGITS** function to convert the *Order Date* (*ODATE*) field from numeric data to alphanumeric data. The *QRYSLT* (*Query Selection*) parameter, using a concatenate function (***CAT**), incorporates the variable *&YEAR* and compares it to the last two positions of the *DATE* field by using the **%SST** (*substring*) function. Selected records will be made available in the order specified by the *KEYFLD* parameter, Item Name within Vendor.

Once processing has completed, the CLP closes the file using the **CLOF** (*Close File*) command. The override is then deleted by the **DLTOVR** (*Delete Override*) command before the program ends.

Figure 20-9 shows the RPG/400 program called by the CLP shown in Figure 20-8. Note that there is no special coding required to process the file. This is because the RPG/400 program and the **OPNQRYF** command are sharing a common access path (due to the **OVRDBF** with the *SHARE(*YES)* parameter). The selected records are made available to the RPG/400 program in the order specified in the **OPNQRYF** command's *KEYFLD* parameter (in this example, Vendor and Item Name) based on this shared access path.

Figure 20-10 shows the printed report produced when the Control Language program in Figure 20-8 is executed. Note that the resulting Order Report is the same as the one shown in Figure 20-7.

```
SEQUENCE
NUMBER   *...1....+....2....+....3....+....4....+....5....+....6....+....7...*
                        S o u r c e   L i s t i n g
    100  *  PROGRAM TO PROCESS AN OPEN QUERY FILE (OPNQRYF) AND
    200  *  GENERATE  A REPORT
    300  *
         H
    400  FORDMST IP E           K        DISK
         RECORD FORMAT(S): LIBRARY SMYERS FILE ORDMST.
                   EXTERNAL FORMAT ORDREC RPG NAME ORDREC
    500  FQSYSPRT O  F     132    OF    PRINTER
    600  IORDREC      01
    700  I                                    OVENDRL1
    700    INPUT  FIELDS FOR RECORD ORDREC FILE ORDMST FORMAT ORDREC.
A000001                                1    1 OCODE            STAT S CODE
A000002                                2    5 OITEM            ITEM NO.
A000003                                6   30 OINAME           ITEM NAME
A000004                               31   31 OVENDRL1         VENDOR CODE
A000005                               32   37 0DATE            ORDER DATE
A000006                               38   40 0QTY             ODER QTY
A000007                               41   45 20COST           ORDER COST
    800  OQSYSPRT H 101   1P
    900  O     OR         OF
   1000  O                     UDATE Y   8
   1100  O                             49 'ORDER MASTER FILE'
   1200  O                             68 'PAGE'
   1300  O                     PAGE  Z  73
   1400  O     H  2   1P
   1500  O     OR         OF
   1600  O                             51 'ANNUAL REPORT FOR 19'
   1700  O                     UYEAR    53
   1800  O     H  2   1P
   1900  O     OR         OF
   2000  O                              6 'VENDOR'
   2100  O                             17 'ITEM NAME'
   2200  O                             40 'ITEM#'
   2300  O                             49 'ORDER DT'
   2400  O                             54 'QTY'
   2500  O                             62 'COST'
   2600  O     D  1   01
   2700  O                     OVENDR    4
   2800  O                     OINAME   33
   2900  O                     OITEM    40
   3000  O                     ODATE Y  49
   3100  O                     OQTY  Z  54
   3200  O                     OCOST 1  62
   3300  O     T  1   L1
         * * * * *  E N D   O F   S O U R C E  * * * * *
```

Figure 20-9   RPG/400 program to process with **OPNQRYF** (Open Query File) command.

```
12/31/95                  ORDER MASTER FILE          PAGE   1
                          ANNUAL REPORT FOR 1995

     VENDOR  ITEM NAME              ITEM# ORDER DT QTY   COST

       B     MR. FUDGIE SUNDAE CUPS  2975  4/01/95  65   7.75

       F     CORN SNAX               E42Z 12/30/95  55   4.50
       F     GIMME_MOR POTATO CHIPS  1238  5/21/95  62   5.00

       G     GRANNYS LIME SHERBET CUPS 728B 10/10/95 50  5.25

       R     BLOTTO PAPER TOWELS     X341  4/01/95 500 500.00

       X     REALLY-YUMMY BUBBLE GUM Z123  6/22/95 100   5.00
```

Figure 20-10   Order Report created using the **OPNQRYF** (Open Query File) command.

SUMMARY

Although logical files will allow the programmer to select records and/or process a file in a specific order, there may be occasions when an alternative method is more desirable. The AS/400 *Sort Utility* and the **OPNQRYF** (*Open Query File*) command both provide the programmer with alternative means of processing a file.

The AS/400 Sort Utility allows a maximum of eight files to be merged and sorted into a single output file. Three types of sorts are available for the programmer to use: the *regular sort,* the *summary sort,* and the *record address sort.* The regular sort produces output records that contain detail data. The summary sort generates output records that contain summarized numeric data. The *record address sort* produces output records containing four-byte binary record addresses.

Sort specifications, which include the sort statements, are stored in a source file. These specifications are entered using **SEU** (*Source Entry Utility*). Three types of specifications exist. The first of these, the *Sort Header Specifications,* indicates the type of sort to be performed, the collating sequence to be used, and the total length of the *control fields. Sort Record Specifications* specify record select and omit criteria. Any number of *Sort Record Specifications* may be combined using AND/OR logic to create complex sets of selection criteria. The *include-all specification* is a special *Sort Record Specification* which indicates that any records not selected or omitted by previous select/omit groups are to be included. A sort may have only one include-all specification, and it must be the last *Sort Record Specification* in the sort. The third type of specification is the *Sort Field Specification.* Here *control fields, data fields,* and *summary data fields* are defined.

The sort specifications are accessed by the **FMTDTA** (*Format Data*) command. Output is stored in a physical file created prior to the execution of the **FMTDTA** command.

The result of the record address sort is known as an *addrout (address output)* file. Special RPG/400 coding allows the programmer to access the file via the sorted record addresses stored in the addrout file.

OPNQRYF (*Open Query File*) is a powerful command that allows the programmer to select records based on specified criteria and access the selected records in a specified order via a high-level language program. The selection criteria may include CLP variables, which makes the **OPNQRYF** command very versatile.

QUESTIONS

20-1. List the three types of sorting the AS/400 offers.

20-2. Where are sort specifications stored?

20-3. Name the three types of sort specifications.

20-4. What is an include-all specification?

20-5. How many include-all specifications may be used in a sort?

20-6. Where must the include-all specification be placed in the sort specification?

20-7. What is a control field?

20-8. Which Control Language (CL) command executes the sort?

20-9. What size record is created by a Record Address sort?

20-10. What is the name for the file type created by a Record Address sort?

20-11. What special RPG/400 coding is required to access a file processed by the **OPNQRYF** (*Open Query File*) command?

20-12. What allows the RPG/400 program and the **OPNQRYF** command to share an access path?

20-13. Which parameter of the **OPNQRYF** command specifies the order in which records will be accessed by the RPG/400 program?

20-14. Which **OPNQRYF** parameter specifies the record selection criteria?

PROGRAMMING ASSIGNMENT

Programming Assignment 20-1: BROWN COW DAIRY PRODUCT LISTING

Write the DDS specifications to create the Product Master file as defined. Once the file is created, use **DFU** to enter the product data. Then write a record address sort to process the Product Master file in Product Number within Product Group order and an RPG/400 program to produce the Product List shown in the printer spacing chart.

Next, modify the RPG/400 program created in the first step to process the Product Master file using the **OPNQRYF** command. Write the Command Language program (CLP) to execute the **OPNQRYF** command and run the RPG/400 program.

Physical File Record Format:

```
              PHYSICAL FILE DESCRIPTION

SYSTEM: AS/400                        DATE: Yours
FILE NAME: Yours                      REV NO: 0
RECORD NAME: Yours                    KEY LENGTH: 4
SEQUENCE: Keyed                       RECORD SIZE: 36

                 FIELD DEFINITIONS

FIELD     FIELD NAME   SIZE   TYPE     POSITION   COMMENTS
NO                                     FROM   TO

  1       PROD#          4     Z        1     4  key field
  2       DESC          25     C        5    30
  3       OZ             3     Z       31    33
  4       PRICE          4     P       34    36  2 decimals
  5       GROUP          1     C       37    37  C=cheese
                                                 I=ice cream
                                                 M=milk
```

Physical file data:

Prod#	Description	Ounces	Price	Prod Group
0057	AM.CHEESE SLICES	008	0199	C
2500	2% MILK	064	0198	M
1235	SKIM MILK	032	0105	M
2001	COTTAGE CHEESE	016	0145	C
2845	1% MILK	064	0279	M
4261	GOURMET ROCKY ROAD	032	0279	I
0062	SWISS CHEESE	008	0189	C
1234	SKIM MILK	064	0199	M
2205	FRENCH VANILLA	064	0289	I
2012	COTTAGE CHEESE W/FRUIT	016	0188	C
2502	2% MILK	032	0100	M
2675	FUDGE RIPPLE	064	0298	I
2842	1% MILK	032	0105	M
4277	GOURMET BUTTER CRUNCH	032	0279	I

Report Design:

```
       0          1          2          3          4          5          6
  1234567890123456789012345678901234567890123456789012345678901234567890123456789012345678
1  ØX/XX/XX              BROWN COW DAIRY PRODUCT MASTER LIST
2
3  GROUP      PROD#      DESCRIPTION                       OZ      PRICE
4
5      X      XXXX       X                              X  XØX     ØX.XX
6      X      XXXX       X                              X  XØX     ØX.XX
7      X      XXXX       X                              X  XØX     ØX.XX
8
9      X      XXXX       X                              X  XØX     ØX.XX
10     X      XXXX       X                              X  XØX     ØX.XX
```

chapter 21

Program Debugging

Programming errors may be classified into two types: compile-time errors and execution (or run-time) errors. *Compile time errors* are syntax errors that fall into one of the following broad categories:

1. Incorrect syntax, such as placing an entry in the wrong field
2. Undefined and referenced fields
3. Specifying a field in calculations, or as edited output, that was not defined as numeric
4. Undefined and unreferenced indicators
5. Specifying *total time* before *detail time* calculations and/or output

Because these errors are identified on the compile listing, they are easily located.

RUN-TIME ERRORS

Run-time errors, which cause halts or abends (abnormal ends) during execution of a compiled program, are usually logic or data errors that are more difficult to find. Some errors included in this category are the following:

1. Divide by zero
2. Conditioning of an instruction with the wrong indicator
3. Invalid numeric data
4. Neverending (perpetual) loop
5. Unconditional branch
6. Unidentified record type
7. Array index error
8. Incorrect output results

Some run-time errors may be difficult, if not impossible, to locate by standard procedures such as checking the program's syntax, studying the logic, and so forth.

```
                              Display Program Messages
        Job 792069/SMYERS/PROGRMR1 started on 07/22/95 at 15:17:25 in subsystem QINTER
        CH2P2 A000005 decimal-data error in field (C G S D F)




        Type reply, press Enter.
          Reply . . . d




        F3=Exit   F12=Cancel
```

Figure 21-1   Program error message allowing dump action.

PROGRAM DUMP

Often, when a run-time error occurs, the system operator receives a message similar to
the message shown in Figure 21-1, which allows him to produce a program *dump*. Such a
dump may be very useful in the debugging process. It lists both file access information
and the values contained in all program variables at the time of the error. Frequently, the
programmer is able to determine from the system error message and the *dump* what
caused the error and make the appropriate corrections to the program logic. Figure 21-2
shows an example of a program *dump* listing.

The *dump* in Figure 21-2 was caused by a *decimal data error*. **Program status** information such as the *Statement in Error* is listed to help the programmer determine what
may have caused the error. In this example the message **decimal data error in field** indicates that invalid data was found in a numeric field. When we examine the compile listing
of the RPG/400 program CUSTLIST, we see that statement A000005 identifies the field
ZIP in the externally defined file CUSTMAST.

The dump listing shown in Figure 21-3 shows that the program variable *ZIP* contains the value **'404040'X.** The **X** indicates that the value shown is expressed in hexadecimal format, so we can interpret the value found in the *ZIP* field as being spaces.

```
RPG/400 FORMATTED DUMP
Program Status Area:
Program Name . . . . . . . . . . . . . :   SMYERS/CUSTLIST
Program Status . . . . . . . . . . . . :   00907
              decimal-data error in field (C G S D F).
Previous Status . . . . . . . . . . . :    00000
Statement in Error . . . . . . . . . . :   A000005     ←
RPG Routine . . . . . . . . . . . . . :    *OFL
Number of Parameters . . . . . . . . . :   000
Message Type . . . . . . . . . . . . . :   MCH1202
           Decimal data error.
MI Statement Number . . . . . . . . . :    007D
Additional Message Info . . . . . . . :
Message Data . . . . . . . . . . . . . :
Last File Used . . . . . . . . . . . . :   CUSTMAST
Last File Status . . . . . . . . . . . :   00000
Last File Operation . . . . . . . . . :    READ I
Last File Routine . . . . . . . . . . :    *GETIN
Last File Statement . . . . . . . . . :    00000000
Last File Record Name . . . . . . . . :    CUSTREC
Job Name . . . . . . . . . . . . . . . :   PROGRMR1
User Name . . . . . . . . . . . . . . :     SMYERS
```
Statement where error occurred

Figure 21-2   Program dump and associated RPG/400 program.

```
          *...1....+....2....+....3....+....4....+....5....+....6....+....7...*
                                  S o u r c e   L i s t i n g
      100     * THIS PROGRAM LISTS THE CUSTOMER MASTER FILE
      200     *
      300     FCUSTMASTIP E                     DISK
              RECORD FORMAT(S): LIBRARY SMYERS FILE CUSTMAST.
      400     FQSYSPRT O  F    132              PRINTER
      400     INPUT FIELDS FOR RECORD CUSTREC FILE CUSTMAST FORMAT CUSTREC.
  A000001  I                                      1   25 NAME
  A000002  I                                     26   54 STREET
  A000003  I            ┌──────────────┐         55   79 CITY
  A000004  I            │  Statement   │          80   81 STATE
  A000005  I  ◄─────────│  in error    │─────►  P 82  840ZIP
                        └──────────────┘
      500     OQSYSPRT H 201     1P
      600     O                                       50 'CUSTOMER MASTER LIST'
      700     O                         UDATE Y  60
      800     O          D 2    N1P
      900     O                         NAME     25
     1000     O                         STREET   60
     1100     O                         CITY     88
     1200     O                         STATE    92
     1300     O                         ZIP     100
```

Figure 21-2 Program dump and associated RPG/400 program. (Continued)

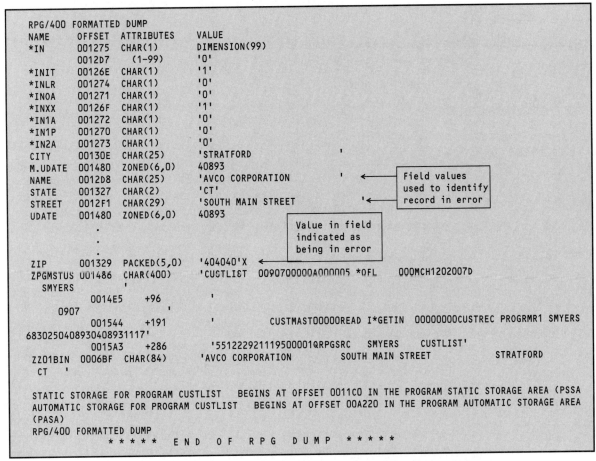

```
RPG/400 FORMATTED DUMP
NAME       OFFSET  ATTRIBUTES    VALUE
*IN        001275  CHAR(1)       DIMENSION(99)
           0012D7  (1-99)        '0'
*INIT      00126E  CHAR(1)       '1'
*INLR      001274  CHAR(1)       '0'
*INOA      001271  CHAR(1)       '0'
*INXX      00126F  CHAR(1)       '1'
*IN1A      001272  CHAR(1)       '0'
*IN1P      001270  CHAR(1)       '0'
*IN2A      001273  CHAR(1)       '0'
CITY       00130E  CHAR(25)      'STRATFORD                '
M.UDATE    001480  ZONED(6,0)    40893
NAME       0012D8  CHAR(25)      'AVCO CORPORATION         '  ◄──┐ Field values
STATE      001327  CHAR(2)       'CT'                            │ used to identify
STREET     0012F1  CHAR(29)      'SOUTH MAIN STREET            '◄┘ record in error
UDATE      001480  ZONED(6,0)    40893
              .                              ┌──────────────────┐
              .                              │ Value in field   │
              .                              │ indicated as     │
                                             │ being in error   │
ZIP        001329  PACKED(5,0)   '404040'X  ◄┴──────────────────┘
ZPGMSTUS   001486  CHAR(400)     'CUSTLIST  0090700000A000005 *OFL   000MCH1202007D
  SMYERS                     '
           0014E5  +96                       '
    0907                     '
           001544  +191                 '           CUSTMAST00000READ I*GETIN  00000000CUSTREC PROGRMR1 SMYERS
6830250408930408931117'
           0015A3  +286          '5512229211195000001QRPGSRC   SMYERS     CUSTLIST'
ZZ01BIN    0006BF  CHAR(84)      'AVCO CORPORATION           SOUTH MAIN STREET              STRATFORD
  CT  '

STATIC STORAGE FOR PROGRAM CUSTLIST   BEGINS AT OFFSET 0011C0 IN THE PROGRAM STATIC STORAGE AREA (PSSA
AUTOMATIC STORAGE FOR PROGRAM CUSTLIST   BEGINS AT OFFSET 00A220 IN THE PROGRAM AUTOMATIC STORAGE AREA
(PASA)
RPG/400 FORMATTED DUMP
            * * * * *  E N D   O F   R P G   D U M P  * * * * *
```

Figure 21-3 Variable field contents listed on the program dump.

To verify this the programmer may choose to produce a *hex listing* of selected records using the **CPYF** (*Copy File*) command. Figure 21-4 shows the hexadecimal listing of the file in an over/under format.

We know from the program dump listing that the record being processed at the time the error occurred had a *NAME* variable equal to AVCO CORPORATION. When we examine the data entered on the record associated with AVCO CORPORATION for the *ZIP* field (positions 82 through 84), we find a value of **404040**. This agrees with the value shown for the *ZIP* field on the dump listing, and we have verified that invalid data exists in the file. The data must be corrected before the file can be processed.

```
5738SS1 V2R1M1  920306       COPY FILE   SMYERS/CUSTMAST CUSTMAST    04/08/93 11:19:52  Page      1
From file . . . . . :  SMYERS/CUSTMAST     Member . . :    CUSTMAST     Record format . . . :  CUSTREC
Record length . . . :  84      To file . . . . . . :  *PRINT
RCDNBR  *...+... 1 ...+... 2 ...+... 3 ...+... 4 ...+... 5 ...+... 6 ...+... 7 ...+... 8 ...+... 9
     1  SIKORSKY AIRCRAFT INC.    RIVER ROAD              STRATFORD              CT ñ
        ECDDDEDE4CCDCDCCE4CDC4444DCECD4DDCC44444444444444444EEDCECDDC44444444444444444CE047
        29269228019939163095 3B00099559909614000000000000000002391366940000000000000003369F
     2  AVCO CORPORATION          SOUTH MAIN STREET      STRATFORD              C        INVALID
        CECD4CDDDDDCECDD44444444EDEEC4DCCD4EEDCCE44444444444EEDCECDDC44444444444444444C|444|<- ZIP
        153603697691396500000000026438041950239553000000000002391366940000000000000003|000|   CODE
     3  PEPPERIDGE FARMS          542 WESTPORT AVENUE    NORWALK                C
        DCDDCDCCCC4CCDDE44444444FFF4ECEEDDDE4CECDEC444444444DDDECDD44444444444444444CE084
        75775994750619420000000005420652376930155545000000000005696132000000000000000003365F
     4  IBM CORPORATION           201 MERRITT SEVEN      NORWALK                CT e|
        CCD4CDDDDDCECDD44444444FFF4DCDDCEE4ECECD444444444DDDECDD44444444444444444CE084
        92403697691396500000000201045999330255550000000000005696132000000000000000003365F
     5  DR. STANLEY E. MYERS      181 RICHARDS AVENUE    NORWALK                CT e|
        CD44EECDDCE4C44DECDE44444FFF4DCCCCDCE4CECDEC444444444DDDECDD44444444444444444CE084
        49B0231535805B048592000001810993819420155545000000000005696132000000000000000003365F
5 records copied to member or label *N in file QSYSPRT in library QSYS. 0 records excluded.
        * * * * *  E N D   O F   C O M P U T E R   P R I N T O U T  * * * * *
```

Figure 21-4 Hexadecimal listing of data records.

THE DEBUG OPERATION

To expedite debugging more complex run-time errors, a **DEBUG** operation is available within RPG/400. Source program coding for the **DEBUG** operation requires additional entries in the *Control* and *Calculation Specifications*. These entries are identified in Figure 21-5. Note that a '1' must be entered in column 15 of the *Control Specifications* to activate the **DEBUG** operation. If the '1' is omitted from column 15, any **DEBUG** operations encountered in the program's *Calculation Specifications* will be processed as comments.

A source listing of a square root program, which has been modified with the **DEBUG** operation, is shown in Figure 21-5. Also included is a partial report listing that shows the output generated by two formats of the **DEBUG** operation. Notice the format specified on line 0900 of the program includes only the indicators that are ON. For the **DEBUG** format on line 01300 of the program, indicators ON and the value of the NUMBER field are printed.

The *Calculation Specifications* for the **DEBUG** operation require that the print file specified in the program's *File Specifications* be entered in *Factor 2* of the Calculation statement. This will cause a list of indicators that are ON when the statement executes to be output to the print file. The programmer has the option of specifying a program variable in the *Result Field* of the Calculation statement which will be included in the listing. The programmer may also specify a literal in *Factor 1* of the Calculation statement to be used as an identifier on the resulting printout. If a literal is not specified, the output will be labeled with the line number of the **DEBUG** operation statement.

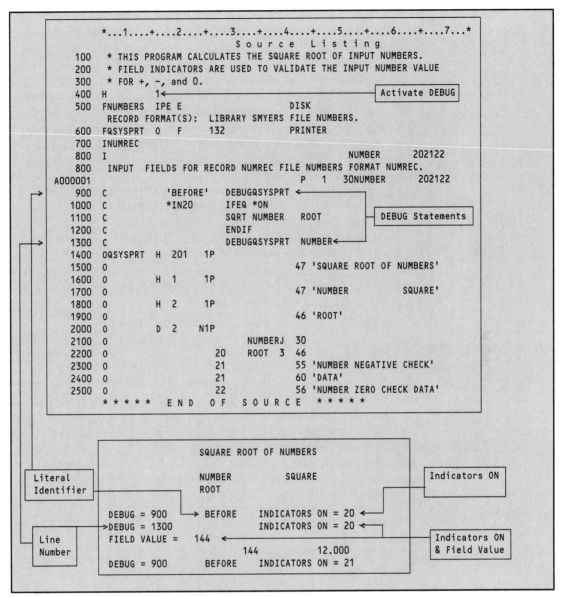

```
      *...1....+....2....+....3....+....4....+....5....+....6....+....7...*
                    S o u r c e   L i s t i n g
100   * THIS PROGRAM CALCULATES THE SQUARE ROOT OF INPUT NUMBERS.
200   * FIELD INDICATORS ARE USED TO VALIDATE THE INPUT NUMBER VALUE
300   * FOR +, -, and 0.
400   H      1                                              Activate DEBUG
500   FNUMBERS IPE E                  DISK
      RECORD FORMAT(S): LIBRARY SMYERS FILE NUMBERS.
600   FQSYSPRT O  F   132             PRINTER
700   INUMREC
800   I                                              NUMBER        202122
800    INPUT  FIELDS FOR RECORD NUMREC FILE NUMBERS FORMAT NUMREC.
A000001                                       P  1  30NUMBER      202122
900   C            'BEFORE'  DEBUGQSYSPRT
1000  C            *IN20     IFEQ *ON
1100  C                      SQRT NUMBER    ROOT              DEBUG Statements
1200  C                      ENDIF
1300  C                      DEBUGQSYSPRT  NUMBER
1400  OQSYSPRT H  201    1P
1500  O                                   47 'SQUARE ROOT OF NUMBERS'
1600  O        H  1      1P
1700  O                                   47 'NUMBER          SQUARE'
1800  O        H  2      1P
1900  O                                   46 'ROOT'
2000  O        D  2     N1P
2100  O                          NUMBERJ  30
2200  O                       20 ROOT  3  46
2300  O                       21          55 'NUMBER NEGATIVE CHECK'
2400  O                       21          60 'DATA'
2500  O                       22          56 'NUMBER ZERO CHECK DATA'
      * * * * *  E N D  O F  S O U R C E  * * * * *
```

```
                     SQUARE ROOT OF NUMBERS

                     NUMBER          SQUARE
                     ROOT
  Literal
  Identifier                                            Indicators ON

 DEBUG = 900    →  BEFORE    INDICATORS ON = 20
→DEBUG = 1300      BEFORE    INDICATORS ON = 20
 FIELD VALUE =   144                              Indicators ON
                           144        12.000      & Field Value
  Line
  Number      DEBUG = 900     BEFORE   INDICATORS ON = 21
```

Figure 21-5 DEBUG example.

External Indicators (U1–U8)

When **DEBUG** operations are included in a program, the program must be recompiled. This can be time consuming in a production environment, especially for large programs A method to eliminate the need to compile a program during or after the debugging process is to condition the **DEBUG** statements using *external indicators* (**U1–U8**). The RPG/400 coding to reference external indicators is the same as that used to reference any other indicator. For example, to condition a **DEBUG** statement, the following coding might be used:

```
*INU1      IFEQ *ON
'BEGIN'    DEBUGQSYSPRT
           ENDIF
```

The ON and OFF status of an *external indicator* is controlled by the programmer's job. If the program to be debugged is submitted for batch processing, the *external indicators* may be specified in the *SWS* (*Switch Setting*) parameter of either the job description used to submit the job or on the **SBMJOB** (*Submit Job*) command itself. If the program is being run interactively, the external indicators may be set using the *SWS* (*Switch Setting*) parameter of the **CHGJOB** (*Change Job*) command.

The *SWS* parameter is specified the same way regardless of the command chosen to set the external indicators. Eight indicators (**U1–U8**) are predefined, and a value of '**1**' for ON or '**0**' for OFF may be assigned. If the programmer does not wish to assign a new value to a particular indicator, an '**X**' may be specified to indicate that no change is to be made. To set ON the first external indicator (**U1**), set OFF the second external indicator (**U2**), and leave the remaining external indicators in whatever state they are currently in, the programmer would issue the following command to change the interactive job:

CHGJOB SWS('10XXXXXX')

By conditioning the **DEBUG** statements (with **U1–U8**) to execute only when an external indicator is ON, and then setting that external indicator ON, the programmer is able to control when the **DEBUG** statements will execute. After the program is debugged, setting the external indicator OFF prevents the **DEBUG** statements from executing and thus eliminates the need to recompile the program.

INTERACTIVE DEBUGGING

Eliminating the need to recompile a program is only one of the reasons that the AS/400's interactive debugging tools are so popular. They may be used to debug both RPG/400 and CL programs. The interactive debugging features allow the programmer to debug even the most complex programs with relative ease.

To begin an interactive debugging session, the programmer must issue the **STRDBG** (*Start Debug*) command. Figure 21-6 shows an example of the **STRDBG** command prompt as it appears when the programmer enters the **STRDBG** command and presses **F4.** As seen in Figure 21-6, the programmer must specify several parameters.

```
                          Start Debug (STRDBG)
   Type choices, press Enter.
     Program . . . . . . . . . .    program1    Name, *NONE
       Library . . . . . . . . .    smyers      Name, *LIBL, *CURLIB
                   + for more values
     Default program . . . . . . .  *PGM        Name, *PGM, *NONE
     Maximum trace statements . . . 200         Number
     Trace full . . . . . . . . . . *STOPTRC    *STOPTRC, *WRAP
     Update production files . . . . *NO        *NO, *YES



                                                                Bottom
   F3=Exit   F4=Prompt   F5=Refresh   F12=Cancel   F13=How to use this display
   F24=More keys
```

Figure 21-6 The **STRDBG** (Start Debug) command.

The program specified in the *Program* parameter is the program(s) against which the debugging processes will be run. A maximum of 10 programs may be included in the debugging process; however, it is rare that more than one program is specified in this parameter.

A default program, for use by the other debugging commands, must be specified in the *Default Program* parameter. The program specified here will be referenced by other debugging commands whenever the programmer specifies *DFTPGM* as a parameter (see Figures 21-10 through 21-12). Any of the programs listed in the *Program* parameter may be selected as the default program. Generally, the program for which the most debugging commands will be entered is selected. The programmer may choose to enter the program name or to reference the first program specified in the *Program* parameter by entering ***PGM** as the default program.

The *Maximum trace statements* parameter limits the number of trace statements stored for review. In the example, 200 statements will be traced before the trace file is full. Once the trace file is full, the decision to stop the tracing activity until the trace data is reviewed (***STOPTRC**) or to overlay trace records until the programmer chooses to review the data (***WRAP**) is determined by the *Trace full* parameter.

Finally, the programmer is asked to specify whether production files should be updated by the program in the *Update production files* parameter. A response of ***NO,** as seen in Figure 21-6, will prevent the program from updating files found in production (***PROD**) libraries. Only files in test libraries (***TEST**) can be updated, thus ensuring that the programmer's testing does not accidentally update the production files.

Sometimes, after starting an interactive debugging session, the programmer finds that he or she needs to change one of the initial debugging parameters. The **CHGDBG** (*Change Debug*) command will allow the programmer to do just that. As shown in Figure 21-7, the **CHGDBG** command allows changes to any of the initial parameters without requiring the programmer to end and restart the debugging session.

```
                       Change Debug (CHGDBG)
 Type choices, press Enter.
 Default program . . . . . . . .    *SAME       Name, *SAME, *NONE
 Maximum trace statements . . . .   500         Number, *SAME
 Trace full . . . . . . . . . . .   *SAME       *SAME, *STOPTRC, *WRAP
 Update production files . . . .    *SAME       *SAME, *NO, *YES




                                                                    Bottom
 F3=Exit    F4=Prompt    F5=Refresh    F12=Cancel    F13=How to use this display
 F24=More keys
```

Figure 21-7 The **CHGDBG** (Change Debug) command.

Trace Control

To trace a range of statements within a program, a *trace request* must be made. The **ADDTRC** (*Add Trace*) command, shown in Figure 21-8, is used to specify the range of statements to be traced. In addition, the programmer may specify program variables whose values are to be displayed when they change and the format in which these values are to be shown.

```
                       Add Trace (ADDTRC)
 Type choices, press Enter.
 Statements to trace:
 Starting statement identifier    2000        Character value, *ALL...
 Ending statement identifier .    5000        Character value
                + for more values_
 Program variables:
    Program variable . . . . . . ._*NONE
    Basing pointer variable  . . ._____
                + for more values_
                + for more values_
 Output format . . . . . . . . .  *CHAR        *CHAR, *HEX
                                                                    More...
    F3=Exit    F4=Prompt    F5=Refresh    F10=Additional parameters    F12=Cancel
    F13=How to use this display    F24=More keys
```

Figure 21-8 The **ADDTRC** (Add Trace) command.

When the program is run, the execution of any statement within the specified range(s) will be recorded. When the trace file is full, or when processing is complete, the programmer may list the statements executed using the **DSPTRCDTA** (*Display Trace Data*) command. As shown in Figure 21-9, the trace output may be viewed on the screen or printed. Also, the programmer may specify whether the trace data is to be retained once it has been displayed or printed.

```
                    Display Trace Data (DSPTRCDTA)
  Type choices, press Enter.
  Output . . . . . . . . . . . . .    *          *, *PRINT
  Clear  . . . . . . . . . . . . .    *NO        *NO, *YES




                                                        Bottom
    F3=Exit   F4=Prompt   F5=Refresh   F12=Cancel   F13=How to use this display
    F24=More keys
```

Figure 21-9   The **DSPTRC** (Display Trace Data) command.

Breakpoint Control

It is sometimes useful to interrupt a program's processing and view the contents of a variable. The AS/400 debugging capabilities allow the programmer to specify program statements where processing is to be interrupted and the contents of selected fields made available for viewing. These interruptions are called *breakpoints* and are specified using the **ADDBKP** (*Add Breakpoint*) command. Figure 21-10 shows the **ADDBKP** command prompt. Note that the programmer is able to specify the statement(s) at which the program is to be interrupted, the program variable(s) to be displayed, the format in which the variable(s) are to be displayed, and the program to be interrupted (generally the default program specified in the **STRDBG** command).

```
                      Add Breakpoint (ADDBKP)
  Type choices, press Enter.
  Statement identifier . . . . . .    2400        Character value
             + for more values       _
  Program variables:
    Program variable . . . . . . .    wfield2
    Basing pointer variable  . . .    _____
             + for more values
             + for more values       _
  Output format  . . . . . . . . .    *CHAR       *CHAR, *HEX
  Program  . . . . . . . . . . . .    *DFTPGM     Name, *DFTPGM
                                                        Bottom
    F3=Exit   F4=Prompt   F5=Refresh   F10=Additional parameters   F12=Cancel
    F13=How to use this display       F24=More keys
```

Figure 21-10   The **ADDBKP** (Add Breakpoint) command.

Program Variables

Any variable within a program may be specified, including indicators, arrays, and array elements. For example, to specify the element of array *AR1* that is being referenced by index *X*, the programmer would enter **AR1** in the *Program variable* parameter and **X** in the *Basing pointer variable* parameter. Indicators may be specified as either ***INxx** (where **xx** represents a specific indicator) or the array **IN* with an indexing variable. To view an entire array, the programmer would specify the array name in the *Program variable* parameter.

Control Language program (CLP) variables may also be specified. Because CLP variable names must begin with an ampersand (&), the variable name must be enclosed in single quotation marks when entered in the *Program variable* parameter. For example, to specify the variable *&DATE,* the programmer would enter **'&DATE'** in the *Program variable* parameter.

Sometimes, when trace data has been reviewed or a value in a specified variable has been displayed, the programmer may want to view the contents of another variable. It is possible to access a command entry screen from either the trace or the breakpoint interrupt screen by pressing **F10.** From the command entry screen the programmer may display additional variables using the **DSPPGMVAR** (*Display Program Variable*) command.

As shown in Figure 21-11, the **DSPPGMVAR** command parameters are similar to those used to specify program variables for the **ADDBKP** and **ADDTRC** commands. Any program variable may be specified for display (including indicators, arrays, array elements, and CLP variables).

```
                      Display Program Variable (DSPPGMVAR)
      Type choices, press Enter.
      Program variables:
        Program variable . . . . . . .   wfield2
        Basing pointer variable  . . .   _____
                    + for more values   _
                    + for more values   _
      Output format  . . . . . . . . .   *CHAR       *CHAR, *HEX
      Output . . . . . . . . . . . . .   *           *, *PRINT
      Program  . . . . . . . . . . . .   *DFTPGM     Name, *DFTPGM
                                                                      Bottom
      F3=Exit   F4=Prompt   F5=Refresh   F10=Additional parameters   F12=Cancel
      F13=How to use this display        F24=More keys
```

Figure 21-11 The **DSPPGMVAR** (Display Program Variable) command.

If, for debugging purposes, it were necessary to change the value stored in a particular variable, the programmer could use the **CHGPGMVAR** (*Change Program Variable*) command. Figure 21-12 shows an example of this command.

```
                      Change Program Variable (CHGPGMVAR)
      Type choices, press Enter.
      Program variables:
        Program variable . . . . . . .   wfield2
        Basing pointer variable  . . .   _____
                    + for more values   _
      New value  . . . . . . . . . . .   'DESK '
      Program  . . . . . . . . . . . .   *DFTPGM     Name, *DFTPGM
                                                                      Bottom
      F3=Exit   F4=Prompt   F5=Refresh   F10=Additional parameters   F12=Cancel
      F13=How to use this display        F24=More keys
```

Figure 21-12 The **CHGPGMVAR** (Change Program Variable) command.

When the **CHGPGMVAR** command shown in Figure 21-12 is executed, the value in variable *WFIELD2* will be changed to **'DESK '.** This will allow the programmer to test the program logic associated with this variable when its value is **'DESK '.**

To return to the trace or breakpoint interrupt screen from the command entry screen press F3.

Ending the Debugging Session

To end an interactive debugging session, the programmer enters the **ENDDBG** (*End*

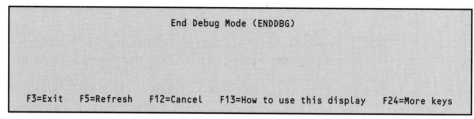

Figure 21-13   The **ENDDBG** (End Debug Mode) command.

Debug Mode) command. As shown in Figure 21-13, the **ENDDBG** command has no additional parameters.

Other debugging techniques were discussed in Chapter 9. *Information Data Structures (INFDS)* and *Program Status Data Structures* are other AS/400 software tools that allow the programmer to identify, correct, and optionally override exception type errors.

SUMMARY

Run-time errors cause halts or abends during program execution and can be difficult to debug. Fortunately, the AS/400 programmer has a number of tools to assist in the debugging process.

Program dumps and *hex listings* of the data files can be used to successfully determine the type of error that occurred, the values contained in the program variables at the time of the error, the file being processed at the time of the error, and the actual data contained in the data file.

The RPG/400 **DEBUG** operation may be used to produce a listing of indicator settings and variable field values when specific statements are executed during program processing. **DEBUG** operations may be coded so that they are controlled by *external indicators* and execute only when the programmer sets the appropriate indicator(s) ON via the *SWS (Switch Setting)* parameter of the job description, the **SBMJOB** (*Submit Job*) command, or the **CHGJOB** (*Change Job*) command.

The AS/400's interactive debugging tools allow the programmer to debug both RPG/400 and CL programs with relative ease. An interactive debugging session begins when the programmer issues the **STRDBG** (*Start Debug*) command, specifying the program(s) to be debugged, the maximum number of trace statements to allow, the action to be taken when the trace file is full, and whether or not to update production files. Any of these processing parameters may be changed without ending and restarting the debugging session by using the **CHGDBG** (*Change Debug*) command. Ranges of statements may be specified for tracing using the **ADDTRC** (*Add Trace*) command. Trace data may be displayed interactively or printed using the **DSPTRCDTA** (*Display Trace Data*) command.

Breakpoints, statements at which the program's processing is to be interrupted, may be specified using the **ADDBKP** (*Add Breakpoint*) command. Program variables, whose contents are to be displayed for viewing, may be specified as parameters of the **ADDBKP** command or displayed via the **DSPPGMVAR** (*Display Program Variable*) command. To change the value contained in a program variable, the programmer may use the **CHGPGMVAR** (*Change Program Variable*) command. To complete the interactive debugging session and end the process, the programmer issues the **ENDDBG** (*End Debug Mode*) command.

QUESTIONS

21-1. What are run-time errors?

21-2. List five examples of possible run-time errors.

21-3. What is a program dump, and what kind of information does it provide for the programmer?

21-4. What is a hex listing, and when would a programmer use it?

21-5. What RPG/400 coding is required to use the RPG/400 **DEBUG** operation?

21-6. What are external indicators, and how may they be used for debugging purposes?

21-7. To prevent production files from being updated while debugging, which parameter on which command(s) should be set to ***NO?**

21-8. What command would the programmer use to specify a range of statements to be traced?

21-9. How would the programmer print a list of traced statements?

21-10. To increase the number of trace statements to be collected from 200 to 400, what command should the programmer use?

21-11. What is a breakpoint?

21-12. How can the programmer view the contents of program variables that were not included in **ADDBKP** or **ADDTRC** commands?

21-13. The programmer would like to test the program logic when the value in FIELD1 of the program is **'GO '.** The breakpoint display shows that FIELD1 contains the value **'STOP'.** How can he or she change the value in FIELD1?

21-14. List the interactive debugging commands that allow the entry of ***DFTPGM** (*Default Program*) to a parameter.

21-15. Which parameters must be specified when issuing the **ENDDBG** (*End Debug Mode*) command?

PROGRAMMING ASSIGNMENT

Programming Assignment 21-1:   PRACTICE PROGRAM DEBUGGING

1. Modify the RPG/400 program created in Programming Assignment 20-1 to process the **OPNQRYF** command to use the **DEBUG** operation. Then rerun the process and produce the Brown Cow Dairy Product List.

2. Begin an interactive debugging session by executing the **STRDBG** command. Specify the RPG/400 program for processing the **OPNQRYF** file as the program to be debugged.

3. Add a breakpoint using the **ADDBKP** command, specifying that the value in the ODATE field be displayed.

4. Define a range of statements to be traced using the **ADDTRC** command.

5. Rerun the CLP to produce the Product List. When the breakpoint occurs, press the *PRINT* key to record the display.

6. When the trace file is full, or when the program finishes processing, print the trace data using the **DSPTRCDTA** command.

7. Use the **CHGDBG** command to add the CLP to the debugging session.

8. Use the **ADDBKP** command to add a breakpoint for the CLP to display the &YEAR field.

9. Rerun the CLP to produce the Product List. When the CLP breakpoint occurs, press the *PRINT* key to record the display.

10. End the debugging session by entering the **ENDDBG** command.

appendix a

Source Entry Utility (SEU)

The *Source Entry Utility* (**SEU**) is a full-screen editor that provides for the entry and update of any source member type. Specifically, when in an edit mode, records may be inserted, deleted, changed, and/or moved. In addition, character strings may be found and/or replaced.

SEU may be accessed by:

- Entering **STRSEU** on any command line and pressing **F4** will access a display where parameter values are entered.
- Option 8 or 5 on the Programmer Menu.
- Option 2 (*Edit*) or 5 (*Display*) on the *Work with Members* display in **PDM.**

EDITING MEMBERS

Upon entering **SEU** by one of the named methods, the Edit screen shown in Figure A-1

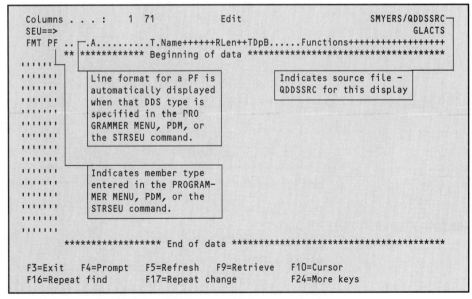

Figure A-1 Edit display for a new physical file member.

645

will display. The syntax supported will depend on the member type entered (i.e., **PF, DSPF, PRTF, LF, CL, CLP, RPG, TXT**) when **SEU** is accessed.

In the Figure A-1 example, **PF** (physical file) was entered as the format for the type prompt in one of the methods to access **SEU**. If a logical file was to be edited, **FMT LF** would be shown; **FMT H** as the first specification type for an RPG/400 program; **FMT DP** for a display file, and so forth. The fields available and the syntax checking supported will depend on the member and/or line type specified.

Entering Source Code

Physical files, display files, logical files, and printer files are all developed as members of a *Data Description Specification* source file. When the source code is entered, the statements for these member types are automatically assigned the letter **A** in column 6. However, the fields supported are not common to all of the member types. For example, physical files do not support the DDS fields related to line and position locations, whereas display and printer files do. The syntax checker will identify any syntactical errors when the source code is entered.

For RPG/400 programs, however, each specifications form has its own *format line* or *prompt* which must be accessed to support the syntax for a specific statement.

Figure A-2 shows the Prompt Selection display, which summarizes the AS/400 member types supported by **SEU.** Entering **P?** or **IP?** in the sequence area of the Edit screen and pressing ENTER will access this display or **F?** or **IF?** for the identical Format Selection display. Entering the type in the Prompt or Format type field and pressing ENTER will display it in the member being edited. Note that RPG/400 has 18 prompt/line types; each is a complete, or a section of a, specification.

```
                          Select Prompt

 Type choice, press Enter.

  Prompt type . . . . . . . . . . .            Values listed below

    RPG/400:        H,F,FC,FK,FX,U,E,L,I,IX,J (I cont),JX,DS,SS,SV,C,O,
                    OD,P (O cont),N,* (Comment)
    COBOL:          CB,C*
    REFORMAT/SORT:  RH,RR,RF,RC
    DDS:            LF (Logical file),PF (Physical file),
                    BC (Interactive Communications Feature file),
                    DP (Display and Printer file),
                    A* (Comment)
    MNU:            MS,MH,MD,MC (MD cont),CC (Comment)
    FORTRAN:        FT, F*
    Other:          NC (No syntax checking),** (Free format)




 F12=Cancel   F23=Select user prompt
```

Figure A-2   Prompt Selection display for AS/400 member types.

FORMAT LINES AND PROMPTS

Format Lines

Source code for any member type may be entered using *format lines* and/or *prompts.* An example of a format line for a physical file is shown in Figure A-3. The format displayed

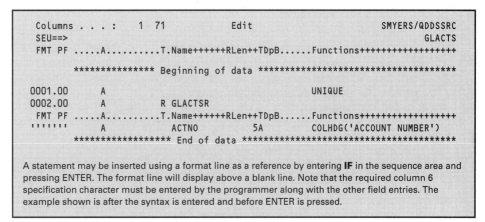

```
    Columns . . . :   1  71              Edit                    SMYERS/QDDSSRC
    SEU==>                                                                GLACTS
    FMT PF .....A..........T.Name++++++RLen++TDpB.....Functions++++++++++++++++++

           *************** Beginning of data ********************************

    0001.00     A                                      UNIQUE
    0002.00     A        R GLACTSR
    FMT PF .....A..........T.Name++++++RLen++TDpB.....Functions++++++++++++++++++
    ''''''''     A          ACTNO        5A            COLHDG('ACCOUNT NUMBER')
           ***************** End of data ***********************************
```

A statement may be inserted using a format line as a reference by entering **IF** in the sequence area and pressing ENTER. The format line will display above a blank line. Note that the required column 6 specification character must be entered by the programmer along with the other field entries. The example shown is after the syntax is entered and before ENTER is pressed.

Figure A-3 Format line for a physical file member.

includes only the fields valid for a physical file. If a display file was edited, only the fields supported by that member type would be included on the format line. Understand that a format line is only a guide to the field locations for the statement. Entries are made on the line under the format.

A format line may be inserted above an existing statement by entering an **F** in the sequence number area of the Edit display and pressing ENTER. However, if a new instruction is inserted using a format line as a reference, **IF** must be entered. After the programmer presses ENTER, the format line will display first followed by a blank line for the instruction. Insertion of blank lines will continue until the ENTER key, without entering a statement, **F5,** or **F12** is pressed.

The format line initially displayed will depend on the member type selected. For example, physical, logical, display, and printer files have only two format line types: **A** for the instructions and * for comments. On the other hand, RPG/400 has 18 line formats. Figure A-4 details the commands to request a format line.

Command	Function
F	Places the format line above for the related statement.
F?	Displays the Prompt Selection screen from which a format line may be selected.
Fff	Places the format line entered for the **ff** entry above the current record.
IF	Inserts a format line for the current record type above the statement.
IF?	Displays the Format Selection screen from which a format line may be selected, and inserts a blank record below the selected format line.
Iff	Places the format line entered for the **ff** entry above a blank record.

Note: All of these commands are entered in the sequence area of the Edit display and executed by pressing the ENTER key.

Figure A-4 Codes for requesting a format line.

Prompts

A *prompt* displays the fields in a line type for *Data Description* members or any of the RPG/400 Specifications after the ********End of data******** delimiter. An example of the prompt for a physical file is shown in Figure A-5. Note that a line is included under each field name, indicating its size.

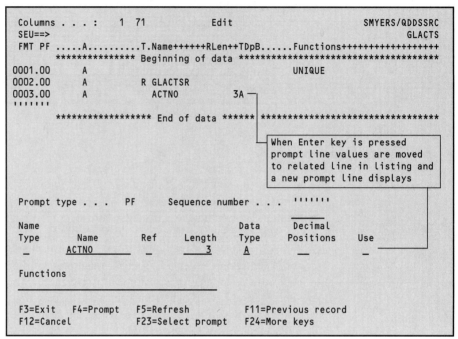

```
Columns . . . :   1  71              Edit                      SMYERS/QDDSSRC
SEU==>                                                             GLACTS
FMT PF .....A..........T.Name++++++RLen++TDpB......Functions++++++++++++++++++
        ************** Beginning of data ***********************************
0001.00     A                                        UNIQUE
0002.00     A          R GLACTSR
0003.00     A            ACTNO        3A ─┐
''''''''
        ***************** End of data ******│***********************************
                                           │
                                      ┌────┴──────────────────────────┐
                                      │ When Enter key is pressed      │
                                      │ prompt line values are moved   │
                                      │ to related line in listing and │
                                      │ a new prompt line displays     │
                                      └────────────────────────────────┤
                                                                        │
 Prompt type . . .   PF    Sequence number . . .   ''''''''            │
                                                                        │
 Name                                   Data    Decimal                │
 Type      Name         Ref   Length    Type    Positions    Use       │
 _         ACTNO        _        3       A        __          _ ───────┘
                                                                        
 Functions
 _____

 F3=Exit   F4=Prompt    F5=Refresh          F11=Previous record
 F12=Cancel             F23=Select prompt   F24=More keys
```

Figure A-5   Prompt example for a physical file member.

A statement may be modified using a prompt by entering a **P** in the sequence number area and pressing ENTER. New statements may be entered by typing **IP** in the sequence number area and pressing ENTER. When the instruction is completed and the ENTER key pressed, it is transferred to its line location in the source member and a *new prompt* is displayed. Exit from the prompt mode is executed by pressing **F5** (*Refresh*) or **F12** (*Previous*). Figure A-6 summarizes the prompt commands. In addition to the commands shown in Figure A-6, a prompt may be requested by pressing **F4.**

The following line commands are used to place an existing record in a prompt:

Command	Function
P	Places the record in a prompt that has the same format as the record.
P?	Displays the Prompt Selection screen for selection of a prompt type. The record is displayed in the selected prompt.
Pff	**ff** specifies the prompt line to be displayed with the record. When editing an RPG/400 program, **PF** will display the prompt for the *File Description*, **PC** for the *Calculation Specifications* prompt, and so forth.

The following line commands insert a blank line and place it in a prompt:

IP	Inserts a blank line after the record and provides for a prompt with the format of the existing record. Related code may be entered in the prompt line(s).

Figure A-6   Prompt commands.

IP?	Displays the Prompt Selection screen for the selection of a prompt type. A blank line is inserted after the existing record with the prompt type selected. Related code may be entered on the prompt line(s).
IPff	**ff** specifies the prompt line to be displayed with the blank record. When editing an RPG/400 program, **IPE** will display the *Extension Specifications* prompt in which the code may be entered.

Figure A-6 Prompt commands. (Continued)

OTHER LINE COMMANDS

Other line commands are used to insert, delete, and move records. Any of the commands must be entered in the sequence number area of the related record(s) and executed by pressing the ENTER key.

COPY Line Commands

COPY line commands are used to copy one or more records to some other location(s) in the source member currently being edited. Figure A-7 summarizes the **COPY** line commands and their target commands.

<u>Copy Commands</u>

<u>Command</u>	<u>Function</u>
C	Copies the record to a target line designated with an A, B, O, or OO.
CC	Copies the group (**CC** placed on first record and last record) beginning on a target line designated with an A, B, O, or OO.
Cn	Copies *n* records, starting with this record, to beginning with a target line designated with an A, B, O, or OO.
CR	Copies this record to target lines specified by multiple A, B, O, or OO lines.
CRn	Copies *n* records, starting with this record, to multiple A, B. O, or OO lines.
CCR	Copies this block of records (identified by two **CCR** commands) to multiple target lines designated by A, B, O, or OO lines.

<u>Target Line Commands</u>

A	Move, copy, or include the specified records after this line.
B	Move, copy, or include the specified records before this line.
An	Move, copy, or include the specified records after this record and repeat the line *n*-1 times.
Bn	Move, copy, or include the specified records before this record and repeat the line *n*-1 times.
O	Overlay this record with the first record specified by the Copy, Copy Repeat, or Move line command.
On	Overlay the specified records on this record, and repeat the lines *n*-1 times.
OO	Overlay all records in this block (defined by two **OO** commands) with the records defined by a Copy, Copy Repeat, or Move line command.

Note: Target commands may be entered <u>before</u> or <u>after</u> their related copy command(s).

Figure A-7 COPY line commands.

An example **COPY** command that copies an instruction to an *after* (**A**) target in a source member is shown in Figure A-8.

```
Before COPY is executed (C entered on line 0002.00 and target A on 0005.00):

FMT **   ...+... 1 ...+... 2 ...+... 3 ...+... 4 ...+... 5 ...+... 6 ...+... 7
         *************** Beginning of data ***************************************
0001.00 Instruction 1
C 02.00 Instruction 2 ─┐  Letter C will copy this record
0003.00 Instruction 3  │  after target A record.
0004.00 Instruction 4  │
A 05.00 Instruction 5 ─┘
0006.00 Instruction 6
         ***************** End of data *****************************************

After COPY is executed:

FMT **   ...+... 1 ...+... 2 ...+... 3 ...+... 4 ...+... 5 ...+... 6 ...+... 7
         *************** Beginning of data ***************************************
0001.00 Instruction 1
0002.00 Instruction 2
0003.00 Instruction 3
0004.00 Instruction 4
0005.00 Instruction 5       Instruction 2 is copied to the inserted record
0005.01 Instruction 2 ───── number 0005.01 immediately after 0005.00.
0007.00 Instruction 6
         ***************** End of data *****************************************
```

Figure A-8 Example **COPY** command that copies an instruction to an *after* (**A**) target.

A **COPY** line command that copies a group of instructions to a *before* (**B**) target is detailed in Figure A-9.

```
Before COPY is executed (CC entered on lines 0001.00 and 0003.00 with target B
on 0006.00):

FMT **   ...+... 1 ...+... 2 ...+... 3 ...+... 4 ...+... 5 ...+... 6 ...+... 7
         *************** Beginning of data *************** **********************
CC 1.00 Instruction 1 ─┐
0002.00 Instruction 2  │  The two CC commands will copy
CC 3.00 Instruction 3  │  the group of records (1-3) be-
0004.00 Instruction 4  │  fore statement 0006.00.
0005.00 Instruction 5  │
B 06.00 Instruction 6 ─┘
         ***************** End of data *****************************************

After COPY is executed:

FMT **   ...+... 1 ...+... 2 ...+... 3 ...+... 4 ...+... 5 ...+... 6 ...+... 7
         *************** Beginning of data ***************************************
0001.00 Instruction 1
0002.00 Instruction 2
0003.00 Instruction 3
0004.00 Instruction 4
0005.00 Instruction 5       Instructions 1-3 are copied to the inserted records
0005.01 Instruction 1 ─┐    0005.01 through 0005.03 immediately before 0006.00
0005.02 Instruction 2  │    which is renumbered 0009.00 because of the insertion
0005.03 Instruction 3 ─┘    of three additional lines.
0009.00 Instruction 6
         ***************** End of data *****************************************
```

Figure A-9 Example **COPY** command that copies a group of instructions to a *before* (**B**) target.

MOVE LINE COMMANDS

MOVE line commands are used to move an instruction or instructions in the source member to a location *before* or *after* one or more target instruction(s). Figure A-10 summarizes the **MOVE** line commands and their target commands, which are identical to those discussed for the **COPY** line command.

```
Move Commands

Command                             Function

  M      Moves the record to a target line designated with an A, B, O, or OO.

  MM     Moves the group (MM placed on first record and last record) beginning on a
         target line designated with an A, B, O, or OO.

  Mn     Moves n records, starting with this record, to beginning with a target line
         designated with an A, B, O, or OO.

Target Line Commands

  A      Move, copy, or include the specified records after this line.

  B      Move, copy, or include the specified records before this line.

  An     Move, copy, or include the specified records after this record and repeat the line
         n-1 times.

  Bn     Move, copy, or include the specified records before this record and repeat the
         line n-1 times.

  O      Overlay this record with the first record specified by the Copy, Copy Repeat, or
         Move line command.

  On     Overlay the specified records on this record, and repeat the lines n-1 times.

  OO     Overlay all records in this block (defined by two OO commands) with the
         records defined by a Copy, Copy Repeat, or Move line command.

Note:  Target commands may be entered before or after their related move
       commands).
```

Figure A-10 **MOVE** line commands.

An example **MOVE** line command that moves an instruction to an *after* (**A**) target in a source member is shown in Figure A-11.

```
Before MOVE is executed (M entered on line 0002.00 and target A on 0005.00):

FMT **  ...+... 1 ...+... 2 ...+... 3 ...+... 4 ...+... 5 ...+... 6 ...+... 7
        *************** Beginning of data *********************************
0001.00 Instruction 1
M 02.00 Instruction 2 ─┐  ┌─────────────────────────────┐
0003.00 Instruction 3  │  │ Letter M will move the record│
0004.00 Instruction 4  │  │ 2 after target A record.     │
A 05.00 Instruction 5 ─┘  └─────────────────────────────┘
0006.00 Instruction 6
        ***************** End of data ***********************************
```

Figure A-11 Example **MOVE** line command that moves an instruction to an *after* (**A**) target.

```
After MOVE is executed:

FMT **  ...+... 1 ...+... 2 ...+... 3 ...+... 4 ...+... 5 ...+... 6 ...+... 7
        *************** Beginning of data ***********************************
0001.00 Instruction 1
0003.00 Instruction 3
0004.00 Instruction 4
0005.00 Instruction 5        ┌─────────────────────────────────────────┐
0005.01 Instruction 2 ───────│ Instruction 2 is moved to the inserted record │
0006.00 Instruction 6        │ number 0005.01 immediately before 0006.00.    │
                             └─────────────────────────────────────────┘
        ***************** End of data ***************************************
```

Figure A-11 Example **MOVE** line command that moves an instruction to an *after*
(**A**) target. (Continued)

A **MOVE** line command that moves a group of instructions to a *before* (**B**) target is
detailed in Figure A-12.

```
Before MOVE is executed (MM entered on lines 0002.00 and 0004.00 and target B
on line 0006.00

FMT **  ...+... 1 ...+... 2 ...+... 3 ...+... 4 ...+... 5 ...+... 6 ...+... 7
        *************** Beginning of data *************** ********************
0001.00 Instruction 1
MM 2.00 Instruction 2 ───┐   ┌─────────────────────────────┐
0003.00 Instruction 3    │   │ The two MM commands will move │
MM 4.00 Instruction 4 ───┤   │ the group of records (2-4) be-│
0005.00 Instruction 5    │   │ fore statement 0006.00        │
B 06.00 Instruction 6 ───┘   └─────────────────────────────┘
        ***************** End of data ***************************************

After MOVE is executed:

FMT **  ...+... 1 ...+... 2 ...+... 3 ...+... 4 ...+... 5 ...+... 6 ...+... 7
        *************** Beginning of data ***********************************
0001.00 Instruction 1
0005.00 Instruction 5
0005.01 Instruction 2 ───┐   ┌──────────────────────────────────────────┐
0005.02 Instruction 3    │   │ Instruction 2-4 are moved to the inserted records │
0005.03 Instruction 4 ───┘   │ 0005.01 through 0005.03 before the 0006.00 line.   │
0006.00 Instruction 6        └──────────────────────────────────────────┘
        ***************** End of data ***************************************
```

Figure A-12 Example **MOVE** command that moves a group of instructions to a
before (**B**) target.

DELETE LINE COMMANDS

Delete line commands delete one or more existing records from a source member. The
commands include **D, DD,** and **Dn. D** deletes the record on which the command is entered. Figure A-13 illustrates the use of the **D** line command.

DD entered on separate records deletes the specified group of records. **Dn** (**n** indicating the number of records) will delete the specified number of records including the
record on which the command is entered. Target line commands are *not* used with delete
commands.

```
Before DELETE is executed (D entered on line 0002.00) :

FMT **   ...+... 1 ...+... 2 ...+... 3 ...+... 4 ...+... 5 ...+... 6 ...+... 7
        ************** Beginning of data ***********************************
0001.00 Instruction 1
D 02.00 Instruction 2 ───┌────────────────────┐
0003.00 Instruction 3    │ D will delete record 2 │
0004.00 Instruction 4    └────────────────────┘
0005.00 Instruction 5
0006.00 Instruction 6
        **************** End of data *************************************

After DELETE is executed:

FMT **   ...+... 1 ...+... 2 ...+... 3 ...+... 4 ...+... 5 ...+... 6 ...+... 7
        ************** Beginning of data ***********************************
0001.00 Instruction 1
0003.00 Instruction 3    ┌────────────────────┐
0004.00 Instruction 4    │ Record 2 is deleted │
0005.00 Instruction 5    └────────────────────┘
0006.00 Instruction 6
        **************** End of data *************************************
```

Figure A-13 Example delete command for deleting one record.

Figure A-14 illustrates use of the **Dn** line command.

```
Before DELETE is executed (D3 entered on line 0002.00):

FMT **   ...+... 1 ...+... 2 ...+... 3 ...+... 4 ...+... 5 ...+... 6 ...+... 7
        ************** Beginning of data ***********************************
0001.00 Instruction 1
D3 2.00 Instruction 2 ───┌───────────────────────────┐
0003.00 Instruction 3    │ D3 will delete records 2-4. At │
0004.00 Instruction 4    │ least one space must follow the │
0005.00 Instruction 5    │ D3 command                 │
0006.00 Instruction 6    └───────────────────────────┘
        **************** End of data *************************************

After DELETE is executed:

FMT **   ...+... 1 ...+... 2 ...+... 3 ...+... 4 ...+... 5 ...+... 6 ...+... 7
        ************** Beginning of data ***********************************
0001.00 Instruction 1
0005.00 Instruction 5    ┌────────────────────┐
0006.00 Instruction 6    │ Records 2-4 are deleted │
        **************** End of data ***** └────────────────────┘ *******
```

Figure A-14 Example of record deletion with the **Dn** command.

WINDOW COMMAND

Different horizontal sections of the Edit display may be viewed by the *Window* command. The command includes **W** and **Wn. W** will show the data beginning in position 1 (default position) of the display, and **Wn,** with **n** as the variable for the first alternative position of the display. For example, if **W10** is entered in the sequence area, the data is moved to the left so that the first position displayed is 10, followed by the other characters. *It is important that at least one blank follow a* **W** *or* **Wn** *command, or the remaining* *sequence numbers will be considered as part of the command.* In lieu of using a Window command, key **F19** (*Scroll left*) will position the records to the left and **F20** (*Scroll right*) will position them to the right.

FINDING/REPLACING CHARACTER STRINGS

The shortcut method of finding a character string in the edit member is to enter the string in the **SEU==>** line and press **F16.** The member will be searched until the first matching string is found. Pressing **F16** again will continue the **Find** function until the next string is found or the **End of data reached** message is displayed.

Strings may also be found and/or replaced with a new value by accessing the Find/Change Services display shown in Figure A-15 from the Edit screen by pressing **F14.** The string to find is entered in the *Find* field and **F16** must be pressed to start the search. When the string is found in the member, **F16** must be pressed again to continue.

```
                            Find/Change Options

     Type choices, press Enter.

         Find . . . . . . . . . . . .   _____
         Change . . . . . . . . . . .   _____
         From column number . . . . .   1__          1-80
         To column number . . . . . .   80_          1-80 or blank
         Occurrences to process . . . .  1            1=Next, 2=All
                                                      3=Previous
         Records to search . . . . . .   1            1=All, 2=Excluded
                                                      3=Non-excluded
         Kind of match . . . . . . . .   2            1=Same case
                                                      2=Ignore case
         Allow data shift . . . . . . .  Y            Y=Yes, N=No
         Search for date . . . . . . .   95/12/12     YY/MM/DD or YYMMDD
            Compare . . . . . . . . . .   _           1=Less than
                                                      2=Equal to
                                                      3=Greater than
     F3=Exit   F5=Refresh      F12=Cancel    F13=Change session defaults
     F15=Browse/Copy options   F16=Find      F17=Change
```

Figure A-15   Find/Change Services display.

Replace is executed by entering the current string in the *Find* field and the new value in the *Change* field and pressing **F17.** To continue to replace the string throughout the document, **F17** must be continually pressed. However, a global replace may be executed by changing the default for the *Occurrences to process* field value from 1 to 2.

EXITING FROM SEU

When in the Edit screen, exit from **SEU** is executed by pressing **F3,** which will display the Exit display in Figure A-16. A detailed explanation of each field is included at the bottom of the figure. From the Exit display, a member is saved by pressing the ENTER key, *not* the **F3** key.

```
                                    Exit
           Type choices, press Enter.

              Change/create member . . . . . . .   Y          Y=Yes, N=No
                 Member . . . . . . . . . . . .    CH17P1     Name, F4 for list
                 File . . . . . . . . . . . . .    QRPGSRC    Name, F4 for list
                    Library . . . . . . . . . .    SMYERS     Name
                 Text . . . . . . . . . . . . .    ch 17 - sfl inquiry program

              Resequence member . . . . . . . .   Y          Y=Yes, N=No
                 Start . . . . . . . . . . . .     0001.00    0000.01-9999.99
                 Increment . . . . . . . . . .     01.00      00.01-99.99

              Print member . . . . . . . . . .    N          Y=Yes, N=No

              Return to editing . . . . . . . .   N          Y=Yes, N=No

              Go to member list . . . . . . . .   N          Y=Yes, N=No


           F3=Exit    F4=Prompt    F5=Refresh    F12=Cancel
```

Change/Create member

Y (Yes) will automatically be specified when any charactor in the edited member has been changed. When a member is accessed and no changes are made, the default is **N.**

Member

The default is the name of the member currently edited. To make a copy of the member, a new name must be entered and **Y** must be specified for the *Change/Create Member* field to save the new member.

File

The default is the source file name specified when entering SEU. Default source file names include **QDDSSRC** for PF, DSPF, LF, PRTF members, **QRPGSRC** for RPG/400 programs, **QCLSRC** for CL programs, and **QCMDSRC** for commands.

Library

The default is the library name specified when the **SEU** session began. It may be changed to store the member in a different library, providing that the programmer has authority to access the referenced library.

Text

Text may be entered to describe the member. If text was entered when the **SEU** session began, it will automatically be included on this line.

Resequence number

The default is **Y,** which will resequence the statements upon exit from this display. Sequence numbers for the statements in the member automatically begin with 0001.00 and increment by 1.00 unless the programmer specifies a different value for each entry. **N** must specified if the statements in the member are <u>not</u> to be resequenced. During the edit process, copy, delete, move, and insert line commands will change the default sequence numbering of statements. Resequencing will reorder the source statements.

Start

If the default **Y** was assumed for the Resequence number, the programmer may change the beginning sequence number. Otherwise, 0001.00 is the beginning default value.

Figure A-16 Exit display.

<u>Increment</u>

If **Y** was entered (or accepted as the default), the 01.00 default value for this field may be changed with a number from 00.01 to 99.99.

<u>Print member</u>

The default for this field is **N.** To print a copy of the member (without compilation), **Y** must be entered.

<u>Return to editing</u>

N is the default for this field. However, if there are syntax errors, control will automatically return to the **SEU** Edit display. Providing that there are no syntax errors, **Y** will save the current version of the member and, in any case, return control to the Edit display.

<u>Go to member list</u>

The default is **N.** A **Y** entry will access the Work with Members Using SEU display, which lists the members of the type currently edited stored in the referenced library.

Figure A-16   Exit display. (Continued)

SPLITTING THE EDIT AND BROWSE DISPLAYS

"Splitting" an Edit display enables the programmer to work with *two* members at the same time. When in the Edit display, pressing **F15** will access the Browse/Copy Options display shown in Figure A-17.

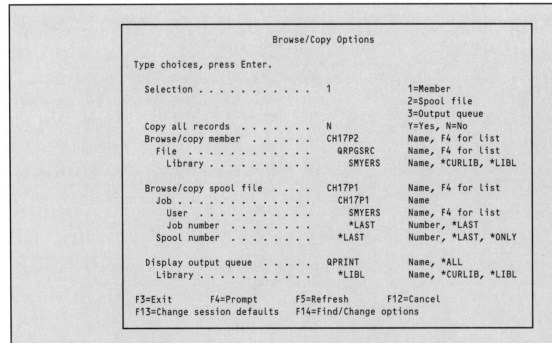

<u>Selection</u>

The default **1** will access a source member, which will be displayed in the lower section of the split Edit display. **2** will access a Spool file, and **3** will view a member in the Output queue.

Figure A-17   Browse/Copy Options display.

Copy all records

The default for this field is **Y** (Yes), which enters **CC** in the <u>first</u> and <u>last</u> record of the browsed member. Specifying **N** (No) gives the programmer the option to select the records to be copied from the browsed member into the edited member.

Browse/Copy member

The name of the member to browse must be entered in this field. If the cursor is in this field, pressing F4 will access the Select Member display to find the member to be browsed.

File

The name of the source file in which the member is stored must be specified in this field. The default is the source file for the member currently being edited or the last value entered for the edit session.

Library

The default for this field is the library that contains the member current edited or the last value entered for the edit session. Otherwise, the library that contains the requested member must be entered.

Browse/copy spool file

The default for this field is the name of the member currently edited. Otherwise, the member name to be viewed must be entered.

Job

The default for this field is the name of the member currently edited. Otherwise, the name of the job that created the spooled file must be entered.

User

The default for this field is the current user's ID. Otherwise, specify the user's profile name.

Job number

The default for this field is ***LAST.** Otherwise, specify the six-digit number of the job that created the spool file.

Spool number

The default for this field is ***LAST.** Otherwise, specify the five-digit number of the spooled file.

Display output queue

The default for this field is **QPRINT.** Otherwise, specify the name of the output queue.

Library

The default for this field is ***LIBL.** Otherwise, specify the name of the library for the output queue.

Figure A-17   Browse/Copy Options display. (Continued)

With the exception of the *Browse/copy member* entry, all other entries may or may not be accepted at their default values. The function of each field is explained in Figure A-17. Pressing the ENTER key will return control back to the Edit display in a "split" format. The number of lines displayed for the edited member in the top section and those for the browsed member in the bottom section will depend on the cursor's location when the Browse/Copy Options display was accessed.

The result of returning back to the Edit display is shown in Figure A-18. **F6** may be used to move the "split line" to the cursor's location and display more or fewer lines for either section.

```
  Columns . . . :    1  71            Edit                    SMYERS/QRPGSRC
  SEU==>                                                              CH17P1
  FMT *  ..... *. 1 ...+... 2 ...+... 3 ...+... 4 ...+... 5 ...+... 6 ...+... 7
         *************** Beginning of data ********************************
  0001.00      * Customer master inquiry with a subfile....
  0002.00      *
  0003.00      FCH17INQ CF  E                  WORKSTN
  0004.00      F                                        SFRRN1KSFILE SM01SFR
  0005.00      FP1PF1   IF  E        K         DISK
  0006.00      C                     EXFMTPROMPT                    dspf prompt

  --------------------------------------------------------------------------
  Columns . . . :    1  71            Browse                  SMYERS/QRPGSRC
  SEU==>                                                              CH17P2
         *************** Beginning of data ********************************
  0001.00      * Customer master update with a subfile....
  0002.00      *
  0003.00      FCH17UPD CF  E                  WORKSTN
  0004.00      F                                        SFRRN1KSFILE SM02SFR
  0005.00      FP1PF1   UF  E        K         DISK
  0006.00      C                     EXFMTPROMPT                    dspf prompt

  F3=Exit     F5=Refresh    F9=Retrieve   F10=Cursor    F12=Cancel
  F16=Repeat find           F17=Repeat change           F24=More keys
```

Figure A-18 "Split" Edit display—edited member in the top and browsed member in the bottom section.

With the exception of prompts, any of the line commands are valid in either section of the Edit display. Roll up and Roll down keys may be used to view records in either section. **F12** will return control to the single format for the edited member.

Change Session Defaults

While in the Edit display, the edit session defaults may be changed by pressing **F13** to access the *Change Session Defaults* display shown in Figure A-19. From this display, the input of uppercase only or both upper- and lowercase characters, syntax checking, sequence numbering of statements, and how many lines the Page keys display may be controlled. An explanation of each prompt is included in Figure A-19.

```
                        Change Session Defaults

  Type choices, press Enter.

       Amount to roll . . . . . . . . . .   H          H=Half, F=Full
                                                        C=Cursor, D=Data
                                                        1-999

       Uppercase input only . . . . . . .   Y          Y=Yes, N=No
       Tabs on  . . . . . . . . . . . . .   N          Y=Yes, N=No
       Increment of insert record . . . .   0.01       0.01-999.99
       Full screen mode . . . . . . . . .   N          Y=Yes, N=No

       Source type  . . . . . . . . . . .   RPG
       Syntax checking:
          When added/modified  . . . . .    Y          Y=Yes, N=No
          From sequence number . . . . . .             0000.00-9999.99
          To sequence number . . . . . . .             0000.00-9999.99
       Set records to date  . . . . . . .      /  /    YY/MM/DD or YYMMDD
                                                                   More...

  F3=Exit      F5=Refresh    F12=Cancel
  F14=Find/Change options    F15=Browse/Copy options
```

Figure A-19 Change Session Defaults display.

<u>Amount to roll</u>

Entry specifies the number of lines to roll up or down when the Page Up or Page Down key is pressed. The default **H** indicates that a half page will roll, and **F** a full page.

<u>Uppercase input only</u>

The default **Y** indicates that only upper case is supported in the Edit session. Entering **N** will support upper and lower case.

<u>Tabs on</u>

The default **N** disables the tab settings. **Y** will enable them.

<u>Increment of insert records</u>

The default .01 will increment inserted records by .01. The incrementation may be changed from 0.01 to 999.99.

<u>Full screen mode</u>

The default **N** indicates that the Edit session is not in a full-screen mode. **Y** will provide for this.

<u>Source type</u>

Indicate the source file type.

<u>When added/modified</u>

The default **Y** indicates that syntax checking related to the source type is supported. **N** will disable syntax checking.

<u>From sequence number</u>

The default is to support syntax checking for all records in the member. When a value is entered, the *When added/modified* entry is ignored and syntax checking will begin at the specified sequence number.

<u>To sequence number</u>

This entry is valid if a statement number was entered for the *From sequence* number field.

<u>Set records to date</u>

A date entered here will include the value in the right margin of each source record and override the default system date.

Figure A-19   Change Session Defaults display. (Continued)

Accessing a List of Members

A list of the members stored in the source file (i.e., QDDSSRC, QRPGSRC, QCLSRC, QCMDSRC, QTXTSRC, or user-named) currently accessed may be displayed by entering **Y** in the *Go to member list* field in the Exit display and pressing ENTER. This action will access the Work with Members Using SEU display shown in Figure A-20.

From this display, the user may edit, delete, browse, or print a member by entering the related number (2, 4, 5, or 6) in the *Opt* field before a member's name.

All of the features of **SEU** have not been covered in this appendix. For a comprehensive review of **SEU,** consult the latest release of IBM's **SEU** manual.

```
                        Work with Members Using SEU

Source file . . . . . .   QRPGSRC                 Library . . . . .   SMYERS
Position to . . . . . . . . . . . . . . . . . . . . . . . . . . . . . . . . .
New member  . . . . . . . . . . . . . . . . . . . . . . . . . . . . . . . . .
  Type for new member . . . . . . . . . . . . . . . . . . . . . . . . .   RPG
  Text  . . . . . . . . .


Type options, press Enter.
  2=Edit        4=Delete       5=Browse          6=Print

Opt Member        Type        Text
    CATENATE      RPG         chapter 7 - called program
    CH10P1        RPG         ch10p1 - sales report program
    CH11P2        RPG         ch11p2 - modified performance report
    CH11P2ID      RPG         ch11p2 - modified for infds
    CH11P3        RPG         ch11p3 - canned soup report
    CH11P4        RPG         ch11p4 - multiple occurrence data structure
    CH11P5        RPG         ch11p5 - customer listing using SCAN & SUBST oper.
    CH11P6        RPG         ch11p5 - customer listing using SCAN & SUBST oper.
                                                                    More...
  F3=Exit          F5=Refresh          F12=Cancel          F14=Display date
  F15=Sort by date                     F17=Subset
```

Figure A-20   Work with Members Using SEU display.

appendix b

Programming Development Manager (PDM)

The *Programming Development Manager,* better known as **PDM,** is a system tool intended to simplify software development and maintenance. To begin using **PDM,** the programmer may enter the command **STRPDM** (*Start Programming Development Manager*) on a command line or select the *Programming* option from the AS/400 Main menu and then select the option to *Start the Programming Development Manager.* A menu similar to the one shown in Figure B-1 is displayed. From this menu, four options are available for selection. Also included are other processes activated by pressing command function keys.

```
            AS/400 Programming Development Manager (PDM)
    Select one of the following:
           1. Work with libraries
           2. Work with objects
           3. Work with members
           9. Work with user-defined options



    Selection or command
    ===> _____
    F3=Exit        F4=Prompt       F9=Retrieve         F10=Command entry
    F12=Cancel     F18=Change defaults
```

Figure B-1   PDM Main menu.

Most of the command function keys are self-explanatory. **F3** allows the programmer to exit the current display. **F4** displays command prompts for any command entered on the command line (or as a standard option on a list display). **F9** will retrieve the previous command entered and display it on the command line. **F10** will begin a command entry (**QCMD**) session. **F12** will cancel the current display and return to the previous display. The meaning of each of these command keys remains consistent throughout all of the **PDM** displays.

The exception is **F18,** *Change Defaults.* Default values for several parameters in frequently used programming commands are stored for each user by **PDM.** These values have been reviewed by the Security Officer and are consistent with the individual company's programming environment. If this is the first time the programmer has used **PDM,** he or she should review these default values and tailor them to his or her specific needs. To review and modify these values, the programmer would press **F18.**

As can be seen in Figure B-2, there are nine parameters to review. First is the *Object library*. This is the default library in which to store objects created via **PDM.** It may be a specific library, the programmer's current library (*CURLIB), or the library containing the source file in which the source member being compiled resides (*SRCLIB). The programmer may also specify whether or not an existing object of the same name and type should be replaced in the *Replace object* parameter, and whether the compile should be submitted to batch or run interactively in the *Compile in batch* parameter.

```
                                Change Defaults
       Type choices, press Enter.
          Object library . . . . . . .   *CURLIB      Name, *CURLIB, *SRCLIB
          Replace object . . . . . . .   Y            Y=Yes, N=No
          Compile in batch . . . . . .   Y            Y=Yes, N=No
          Run in batch . . . . . . . .   N            Y=Yes, N=No
          Job description  . . . . . .   SMYERS       Name, *USRPRF, F4 for list
            Library  . . . . . . . . .     SMYERS     Name, *CURLIB, *LIBL
          Change type and text . . . .   Y            Y=Yes, N=No
          Option file  . . . . . . . .   QAUOOPT      Name
            Library  . . . . . . . . .     QGPL       Name, *CURLIB, *LIBL
          Member . . . . . . . . . . .   QAUOOPT      Name
          Full screen mode . . . . . .   N            Y=Yes, N=No


       F3=Exit      F4=Prompt      F5=Refresh      F12=Cancel
```

Figure B-2   Change Defaults display.

For options other than compiles, the programmer may indicate whether he or she wishes the processes to run interactively or in batch with the *Run in batch* parameter. Jobs submitted for batch processing require a *Job description.* Here the programmer may indicate a particular job description or reference the job description specified in the programmer's user profile (*USRPRF).

The ability of the programmer to modify the type and text description fields of an object or member via the **PDM** displays is controlled by the entry in the *Change type and text* parameter.

The file specified in the *Option file* parameter will be used to interpret the two-position user-defined codes the programmer may enter on the **PDM** displays. The QAUOOPT file in the QGPL library contains the IBM-defined options. If a programmer wishes to modify these options or define new options, it is recommended that he or she copy the QAUOOPT file into his or her own development library. Then modifications may be made to the copy in the development library without affecting other **PDM** users. In such a case, the library specified for the *Option file* parameter should be changed to the programmer's development library. Then the programmer's own version of the file would be accessed as the *Option file.*

Finally, activation of *Full screen mode* produces a display that lists only object or member names and their associated types, without descriptions. This is difficult for the programmer to use and is therefore seldom seen. For our purposes we have chosen not to use this display. As a result, none of the sample screen displays in this appendix are full screen mode displays.

Three types of screen displays are used throughout **PDM:** the *subset definition display,* the *list display,* and the *command specific display.* The subset definition allows the programmer to define selection criteria for the items to be displayed on the list display. The list display presents a list of selected items and allows the programmer to process them using various options. Based on the option specified, a command specific display may appear. Samples of these displays will be presented over the next few pages as the **PDM** Main menu options are discussed in detail.

The next thing a new **PDM** user should do is review the user-defined option file. To do this the programmer would select option 9 from the **PDM** Main menu, Work with

```
                    Specify Option File to Work With
        Type choices, press Enter.
            File . . . . . . . . .    QAUOOPT____   Name
              Library . . . . . . .     QGPL____    *LIBL, *CURLIB, name
            Member  . . . . . . . .    QAUOOPT____  Name




        F3=Exit     F5=Refresh     F12=Cancel
```

Figure B-3 Select User Option File display.

User-Defined Options. A screen similar to Figure B-3 would appear to allow the programmer to specify which option file to work with.

The screen displays the option file specified in the programmer's default values, but this may be overridden. For our example we will be using the IBM default option file, QAUOOPT, in QGPL library.

Pressing the ENTER key brings us to a display similar to the one shown in Figure B-4. Here the User-Defined Options and their associated commands are displayed. Note that some of the commands have variables associated with command parameters. These variables are defined by **PDM.** For example, **&L** represents the library being displayed, **&N** stands for the name of the item (either an object or a file member) being displayed, **&F** refers to the file whose members are currently being displayed, and **&T** represents the object type specified on the display. Several other predefined substitution variables exist. By using these predefined variables, a programmer may construct flexible commands for use with the **PDM** list displays.

```
                    Work with User-Defined Options
    File . . . . . . . :   QAUOOPT____       Member . . . . . . :   QAUOOPT____
      Library . . . . :     QGPL____
    Type options, press Enter.
      2=Change        3=Copy         4=Delete        5=Display
    Opt  Option  Command
    __    C       CALL &O/&N
    __    CC      CHGCURLIB CURLIB(&L)
    __    CL      CHGCURLIB CURLIB(&N)
    __    CD      STRDFU OPTION(2)
    __    CM      STRSDA OPTION(2) SRCFILE(&L/&F) ??SRCMBR()
    __    CS      STRSDA OPTION(1) SRCFILE(&L/&F) ??SRCMBR()
    __    DM      DSPMSG
    __    EA      EDTOBJAUT OBJ(&L/&N) OBJTYPE(&T)
    __    GO      GO &L/&N
                                                              More...
    Parameters or command
    ===> _____
    F3=Exit          F4=Prompt         F5=Refresh       F6=Create
    F9=Retrieve      F10=Command entry                  F24=More keys
```

Figure B-4 Work with User-Defined Options display.

To create a new User-Defined Option, the programmer would press **F6.** A screen similar to the one shown in Figure B-5 would display. The new two-character code would be entered in the *Option* parameter, and the command to be executed would be entered on the *Parameters or command* line. Prompting is available for any command entered in the *Command* parameter to ensure that all appropriate parameters are included.

For example, if the programmer wished to create an option to edit his or her user library list, he or she might enter **EL** as the option and specify **EDTLIBL** (*Edit Library List*) as the command to be executed whenever **EL** is entered. No additional parameters are required for this command, so he or she would not need to specify any variables, and

```
                        Create User-Defined Option

 Type option and command, press Enter.
   Option . . . . . . . . .  ___      Option to create
   Command . . . . . . . .  _____


 _____


 F3=Exit        F4=Prompt        F12=Cancel
```

Figure B-5   Create User-Defined Option display.

prompting is not necessary. Pressing the ENTER key would create the option and return the programmer to the previous screen.

Other options are available from the Work with User-Defined Options display. Entering a **2** next to any of the options on the display will allow the programmer to change that option. A screen such as the one shown in Figure B-6 will be displayed. The programmer may enter the desired modification on this screen. Pressing the ENTER key causes the User-Defined Option to be updated with the specified change and the programmer to then be returned to the previous screen.

```
                        Change User-Defined Option
 Type changes, press Enter.
   Option . . . . . . . . .  _C    Value to change to
   Command . . . . . . . .  CALL &O/&N_____


 _____


 F3=Exit        F4=Prompt        F12=Cancel
```

Figure B-6   Change User-Defined Option display.

To copy an option from one file to another, or to the same file but under a different option name, the programmer would enter a **3** next to the option on the Work with User-Defined Options display. A screen similar to the one shown in Figure B-7 would be displayed.

```
                        Copy User-Defined Options

     From file . . . . . . . :   QAUOOPT
       From library . . . . . :   QGPL
     From member . . . . . . :   QAUOOPT
     Type the file, library, and member to receive copied options.
       To file . . . . . . .   QAUOOPT       Name, F4 for List
         To library . . . . .   SMYERS
       To member . . . . . . .   QAUOOPT
     To rename copied option, type New Option, press Enter.
     Option     New Option
      EL          EL
      __          __
      __          __
                                                              Bottom
     F3=Exit      F5=Refresh      F12=Cancel
```

Figure B-7   Copy User-Defined Options display.

In our example the programmer has selected the user-defined option **EL** to be copied. It is to be copied from the QAUOOPT file in QGPL to the QAUOOPT file in SMYERS, and will retain the code of **EL** to execute the specified command. Once the

ENTER key is pressed, the option will be copied to the specified file and the programmer will be returned to the Work with User-Defined Options display.

Entering a **4** next to an option on the Work with User-Defined Options display indicates that the specified option is to be deleted. A confirmation screen similar to the one shown in Figure B-8 will be displayed. To confirm the deletion, the programmer must press the ENTER key. To cancel the deletion process, the programmer must press **F12.** Either action returns the programmer to the Work with User-Defined Options display.

```
                     Confirm Delete of User-Defined Options
    File . . . . . . . :     QAUOOPT
      Library . . . . . :     QGPL
    Member . . . . . . :     QAUOOPT


    Press Enter to confirm your choices for Delete.
    Press F12=Cancel to return to change your choices.
    Option      Command
      EL          EDTLIBL



                                                                    Bottom
    F12=Cancel
```

Figure B-8   Delete confirmation display.

To display an option in detail, the programmer would enter a **5** next to the option on the Work with User-Defined Options display. A screen similar to the one shown in Figure B-9 would be displayed. The programmer could press **F3, F12,** or the ENTER key to return to the previous screen. From there the programmer would press **F12** to return to the **PDM** Main menu.

```
                         Display User-Defined Option
    Type changes, press Enter.
        Option . . . . . . . . .    C
        Command . . . . . . . . .   CALL &O/&N




    F3=Exit                    F12=Cancel
```

Figure B-9   Display User-Defined Option display.

Having become familiar with the PDM processing defaults assigned to him or her, as well as with the User-Defined Options available for him or her to work with, the programmer is now prepared to utilize the main functions of **PDM.** We will now discuss the more commonly accessed **PDM** functions.

When option 1, *Work with libraries,* is selected from the **PDM** Main menu, a selection screen such as the one shown in Figure B-10 is displayed. This allows the programmer to specify which libraries are to be listed. A variety of subsets is possible. To list all libraries found on the system, the programmer would enter *ALL in the *List type* prompt. Other possible entries include all of the libraries in the programmer's user library list (***USRLIBL**), all libraries except for operating system libraries (***ALLUSR**), the programmer's current library (***CURLIB**), the name of a specific library, a generic name which would display a group of libraries (such as **A***, which would display all libraries with names beginning with the letter **A**), or all libraries in the programmer's library list (***LIBL**).

```
                      Specify Libraries to Work With
     Type choice, press Enter.
        Library . . . . . . . . . .    *LIBL        *LIBL, name, generic*, *ALL,
                                                    *ALLUSR, *USRLIBL, *CURLIB




              F3=Exit      F5=Refresh      F12=Cancel
```

Figure B-10　Library Subset Specification display.

For our example we have requested that the libraries in the programmer's library list be displayed. Figure B-11 shows the Work with Libraries Using PDM display. Note that the libraries listed represent all four parts of the programmer's library list (the system library list (**SYS**), the product library (**PROD**), the current library (**CUR**), and the user library list (**USR**)). From this display, a number of options are possible. Standard options (*Change, Copy, Display,* etc.) are displayed above the list. Any of these options may be entered in an *Opt* field, and the associated process will occur. User-defined options may also be entered in *Opt* fields, adding to the flexibility of the list display. Commands may be entered on the *Parameters or command* line for execution. Or, command function keys may be used to perform any of the functions listed.

```
                         Work with Libraries Using PDM
         List type . . . . . . .    *LIBL
         Type options, press Enter.
           2=Change                  3=Copy         5=Display       7=Rename
           8=Display description     9=Save         10=Restore      12=Work with ...
         Opt  Library    Type      Text
         __   QSYS       *PROD-SYS  System Library
         __   QSYS2      *PROD-SYS  System Library for CPI's
         __   QUSRSYS    *PROD-SYS  SYSTEM LIBRARY FOR USERS
         __   QHLPSYS    *PROD-SYS
         __   QPDA       *PROD-PRD
         __   SMYERS     *TEST-CUR  Stan Myers' development library
         __   FILELIB    *PROD-USR  Production File Library
         __   PROGLIB    *PROD-USR  Production Software Library
         __   QGPL       *PROD-USR  General Purpose Library
                                                                        More...
         Parameters or command
         ===>
         F3=Exit          F4=Prompt          F5=Refresh        F6=Add to list
         F9=Retrieve      F10=Command entry  F23=More options  F24=More keys
```

Figure B-11　Work with Libraries Using PDM display.

The programmer is encouraged to explore the options and command function keys in order to determine just how flexible **PDM** is. In all cases, **F3** will return the programmer to the previous display without executing the command associated with the current display. Eventually the programmer will return to the **PDM** Main menu.

Selection of option 2, *Work with objects,* from the **PDM** Main menu, will display a screen similar to that found in Figure B-12. The programmer has the option of entering a specific library name or selecting the current library (*CURLIB) for the Library parameter. Various entries may be combined in the *Name, Type,* and *Attribute* parameters in order to produce the desired object subset. The example in Figure B-12 requests that all files in the SMYERS library be displayed. The display shown in Figure B-13 is the result of this selection. Note that a variety of files is shown, including logical files (**LF-DTA**), physical files containing data (**PF-DTA**), and physical files containing source code (**PF-SRC**).

```
                      Specify Objects to Work With
Type choices, press Enter.
    Library  . . . . . . . . . .    SMYERS        *CURLIB, name
    Object:
      Name . . . . . . . . . . .    *ALL          *ALL, name, *generic*
      Type . . . . . . . . . . .    *FILE         *ALL, *type
      Attribute  . . . . . . . .    *ALL          *ALL, attribute, *generic*,
                                                           *BLANK


 F3=Exit     F5=Refresh      F12=Cancel
```

Figure B-12   Specify Objects to Work With display.

Again, standard options (*Change, Copy, Display,* etc.) are displayed above the list. Any standard or user-defined option may be entered in an *Opt* field and the associated process will occur. Commands may be entered on the *Parameters or command* line for execution. Or, command function keys may be used to perform any of the functions listed.

```
                      Work with Objects Using PDM
 Library . . . . .    SMYERS             Position to . . . . . . . . _____
                                         Position to type  . . . . . _____

 Type options, press Enter.
    2=Change        3=Copy       4=Delete      5=Display     7=Rename
    8=Display description        9=Save        10=Restore    11=Move ...
 Opt  Object      Type       Attribute   Text
 __   APLVEND     *FILE      LF-DTA      AP Vendor by Vendor Name
 __   APLVEND2    *FILE      LF-DTA      AP Vendor by Vendor Number
 __   APPVEND     *FILE      PF-DTA      AP Vendor Master File
 __   QCLSRC      *FILE      PF-SRC      source for CL programs
 __   QDDSSRC     *FILE      PF-SRC      source for DDS
 __   QRPGSRC     *FILE      PF-SRC      source for RPG programs
 __   WRKFILE     *FILE      PF-DTA      Workfile for report
 __   ZEROBAL     *FILE      PF-DTA      Zero Balance Accounts
                                                                More...

 Parameters or command
 ===> _____
 F3=Exit          F4=Prompt            F5=Refresh          F6=Create
 F9=Retrieve      F10=Command entry    F23=More options    F24=More keys
```

Figure B-13   Work with Objects Using PDM display.

The third option from the **PDM** Main menu, *Work with members,* allows the programmer to access file members and is most often used to access source members in a source file. A screen similar to the one shown in Figure B-14 allows the programmer to specify the file and members to be displayed. The example specifies the QRPGSRC file in the SMYERS library and requests that all members be displayed.

```
                      Specify Members to Work With
Type choices, press Enter.
    File . . . . . . . . . .      QRPGSRC       Name, F4 for list
      Library . . . . . . .       SMYERS        *LIBL, *CURLIB, name
    Member:
      Name  . . . . . . . .       *ALL          *ALL, name, *generic*
      Type  . . . . . . . .       *ALL          *ALL, type, *generic*, *BLANK

 F3=Exit     F4=Prompt     F5=Refresh      F12=Cancel
```

Figure B-14   Specify Members to Work With display.

Similar to other major list displays, Figure B-15 shows standard options listed above the member display. Note that option **2** now specifies **Edit** instead of **Change.** Selecting option 2 will initiate an **SEU** (*Source Entry Utility*) session using the member indicated.

```
                       Work with Members Using PDM
  File . . . . . .    QRPGSRC
    Library . . . .    SMYERS             Position to  . . . . ._____
  Type options, press Enter.
    2=Edit           3=Copy        4=Delete       5=Display      6=Print
    7=Rename         8=Display description        9=Save         13=Change text ...
  Opt  Member    Type      Text
  __   APR820    RPG       AP Vendor Maintenence
  __   ARR121    RPG       AR Status Report
  __   COMRPT023 RPG       COMMISSION REPORT
  __   HOLDFLAG1 RPG       release records for tape
  __   OER726    RPG       Order Entry Quote List
  __   OER729    RPG       Order Entry Purge Quote File
  __   PRR327    RPG       Payroll Time Card Edit Report
  __   SAR010    RPG       Sales Analysis  Weekly Sales Report
  __   SAR045    RPG       Sales Analysis  On-line Inquiry
                                                              More...
  Parameters or command
  ===> _____

  F3=Exit        F4=Prompt        F5=Refresh        F6=Create
  F9=Retrieve    F10=Command entry  F23=More options  F24=More keys
```

Figure B-15   Work with Members Using PDM display.

Other useful options exist. If the programmer were to press **F23** (*More options*), a different set of standard options will appear, as shown in Figure B-16. Option **14** can be used to compile a source member (the create command to be used is determined by the *Type* field displayed next to the member name). If the source member is for a display file (type **DSPF**), then option **17** could be used to initiate an **SDA** (*Screen Design Aid*) session. If the source member is for a printer file, option **19** could be used to initiate an **RLU** (*Report Layout Utility*) session.

With its flexible user-defined options and simple list format, the Programming Development Manager can be a powerful tool for the programmer to use. The programmer is encouraged to explore **PDM** and become familiar with its various capabilities.

```
                       Work with Members Using PDM
  File . . . . . .    QRPGSRC
    Library . . . .    SMYERS             Position to  . . . . ._____
  Type options, press Enter.
    14=Compile        16=Run procedure      17=Change using SDA
    19=Change using RLU  25=Find string ...
  Opt  Member    Type      Text
  __   APR820    RPG       AP Vendor Maintenence
  __   ARR121    RPG       AR Status Report
  __   COMRPT023 RPG       COMMISSION REPORT
  __   HOLDFLAG1 RPG       release records for tape
  __   OER726    RPG       Order Entry Quote List
  __   OER729    RPG       Order Entry Purge Quote File
  __   PRR327    RPG       Payroll Time Card Edit Report
  __   SAR010    RPG       Sales Analysis  Weekly Sales Report
  __   SAR045    RPG       Sales Analysis  On-line Inquiry
                                                              More...
  Parameters or command
  ===> _____

  F3=Exit        F4=Prompt        F5=Refresh        F6=Create
  F9=Retrieve    F10=Command entry  F23=More options  F24=More keys
```

Figure B-16   Work with Members Using PDM display.

appendix c

Data File Utility (DFU)

The AS/400 *Data File Utility,* better known as **DFU,** allows the programmer to quickly generate an interactive program to add, delete, and change records in a database file. To access this utility, the programmer enters the **STRDFU** (*Start Data File Utility*) command from any command entry line. A menu similar to the one shown in Figure C-1 will be displayed.

```
                    AS/400 Data File Utility (DFU)
        Select one of the following:
            1. Run a DFU program
            2. Create a DFU program
            3. Change a DFU program
            4. Delete a DFU program
            5. Update data using temporary program



        Selection or command
        ===> 5
        F3=Exit    F4=Prompt    F9=Retrieve    F12=Cancel
                                          (C) COPYRIGHT IBM CORP. 1981, 1991.
```

Figure C-1   DFU Main menu.

DFU programs may be created and stored for later use. This is a good idea if the programmer intends to use the **DFU** program frequently. However, the programmer most often uses a **DFU** program to fix an occasional problem or to create test data. Under those circumstances, the **DFU** program is not intended for repeated use. A temporary **DFU** may be created by selecting option **5** from the **DFU** Main menu.

The programmer is then prompted with a screen similar to the one shown in Figure C-2 to specify the data file and member to be updated. Either a physical file or a logical file may be specified here.

The file's database definition is used to construct the temporary program. After a brief wait, during which time the **DFU** program is being generated, a screen will appear. If the file already contains data, **DFU** assumes that the programmer wishes to change an existing record. The **DFU** program will therefore present a record selection screen similar to the one shown in Figure C-3, and the default processing mode will be *CHANGE.* However, if the file does not contain any records, **DFU** will assume that the programmer intends to enter data and will present a screen similar to the one shown in Figure C-5, and

```
                    Update Data Using Temporary Program
    Type choices, press Enter.
       Data file . . . . . . . . .   CUSTOMERS    Name, F4 for list
          Library . . . . . . . . .   SMYERS      Name, *LIBL, *CURLIB
       Member  . . . . . . . . . .   CUSTOMERS    Name, *FIRST, F4 for list




    F3=Exit      F4=Prompt      F12=Cancel
```

Figure C-2   Data File Selection screen.

the default processing mode will be *ADD*. For purposes of this example, the programmer has chosen a file that already contained several records of test data.

```
    WORK WITH DATA IN A FILE              Mode . . . . :   CHANGE
    Format . . . . :   CUSTOMERS          File . . . . :   CUSTOMERS
    CUST#:                  ____




    F3=Exit                 F5=Refresh         F6=Select format
    F9=Insert               F10=Entry          F11=Change
```

Figure C-3   Record Selection screen.

First, a correction will be made to a customer's record. The programmer enters the desired customer number, in this case **11111,** on the Record Selection Screen. This key value is used to locate the appropriate customer record. If the file selected for processing was not a keyed access file, the Record Selection Screen would allow the programmer to specify the relative record number of the desired record. Either way, a record from the file is retrieved and displayed on a screen similar to the one shown in Figure C-4.

```
    WORK WITH DATA IN A FILE              Mode . . . . :   CHANGE
    Format . . . . :   CUSTOMERS          File . . . . :   CUSTOMERS
    CUST#:             11111
    LAST NAME:         LONGFELLOW
    FIRST NAME:        HENRY
    MIDDLE INITIAL:    W
    ADDRESS LINE 1:    88 HIAWATHA DRIVE
    ADDRESS LINE 2:
    CITY:              WILLOWTON
    STATE:             PA
    ZIP CODE:          01624

    F3=Exit                 F5=Refresh         F6=Select format
    F9=Insert               F10=Entry          F11=Change
```

Figure C-4   Record Update screen.

Data in any of the underlined fields may be changed. The programmer needs only to type the corrected data into the appropriate fields and press the ENTER key for the record correction to occur. Then the programmer is returned to the Record Selection Screen (Figure C-3).

As noted along the bottom of each screen, several command function keys are available throughout the **DFU** program processing. Pressing **F3** will end the **DFU** program, and pressing **F5** will clear entries made in data fields and reset them to their original values. **F6** will allow the programmer to change to a different screen format (this option does not apply for the temporary **DFU** because only one format is generated). **F9, F10,** and **F11** allow the programmer to change processing modes. To enter additional test records, the programmer now presses **F10** to switch to *ENTRY* mode. The **DFU** program now displays a screen similar to the one shown in Figure C-5.

```
WORK WITH DATA IN A FILE                    Mode . . . . :   ENTRY
   Format . . . . :   CUSTOMERS             File . . . . :   CUSTOMERS
   CUST#:                _____
   LAST NAME:            _____
   FIRST NAME:          _____
   MIDDLE INITIAL: _
   ADDRESS LINE 1:      _____
   ADDRESS LINE 2:      _____
   CITY:                _____
   STATE:               __
   ZIP CODE:            ____


   F3=Exit              F5=Refresh           F6=Select format
   F9=Insert            F10=Entry            F11=Change
```

Figure C-5   Add Record screen.

The programmer may now enter data in the fields provided (as shown in Figure C-6). When the ENTER key is pressed, the record will be added to the file.

```
WORK WITH DATA IN A FILE                    Mode . . . . :   ENTRY
   Format . . . . :   CUSTOMERS             File . . . . :   CUSTOMERS
   CUST#:                22220
   LAST NAME:            STEVENSON
   FIRST NAME:          ROBERT
   MIDDLE INITIAL: L
   ADDRESS LINE 1:      127 GREEN FARM RD.
   ADDRESS LINE 2:      _____
   CITY:                TOWNSEND
   STATE:               VT
   ZIP CODE:            22213


   F3=Exit              F5=Refresh           F6=Select format
   F9=Insert            F10=Entry            F11=Change
```

Figure C-6   Add Record screen.

To delete a record from a file via **DFU,** the programmer must enter the *DELETE* mode. To do this the programmer presses **F23.** Once in the *DELETE* mode, a screen similar to the one displayed in Figure C-7 allows the programmer to select the record to be deleted.

```
WORK WITH DATA IN A FILE                    Mode . . . . :   DELETE
   Format . . . . :   CUSTOMERS             File . . . . :   CUSTOMERS
   CUST#:                _____




   F3=Exit              F5=Refresh           F6=Select format
   F9=Insert            F10=Entry            F11=Change
```

Figure C-7   Delete Record screen.

DFU retrieves the specified record and displays it for visual verification on a screen similar to the one shown in Figure C-8. If this is not the correct record, the programmer may cancel the record deletion by pressing **F12** and returning to the Delete Record Selection screen (Figure C-7). Otherwise, to physically remove the record, the programmer must confirm the deletion by pressing **F23**.

```
WORK WITH DATA IN A FILE               Mode . . . . :    DELETE
Format . . . . :    CUSTOMERS          File . . . . :    CUSTOMERS
CUST#:              32247
LAST NAME:          EMERSON
FIRST NAME:         RALPH
MIDDLE INITIAL:     W
ADDRESS LINE 1:     726 GREAT POND DRIVE
ADDRESS LINE 2:
CITY:               WALDON
STATE:              MA
ZIP CODE:           60490
Record deletion pending

    F3=Exit            F5=Refresh          F6=Select format
    F9=Insert          F10=Entry           F11=Change
```

Figure C-8 Delete Record screen.

The programmer may toggle between functions by pressing **F10** (for *ENTRY* mode), **F11** (for *CHANGE* mode), and **F23** (for *DELETE* mode). All modifications are immediately reflected in the file.

When the programmer has completed all of the file modifications, he or she may end the **DFU** program by pressing **F3**. A screen summarizing the processing (see Figure C-9) will be displayed. Pressing the ENTER key will allow the **DFU** processing to complete, and an audit listing of the programmer's transactions will be printed.

```
                            End Data Entry
    Number of records processed
        Added  . . . . . :         1
        Changed  . . . . :         1
        Deleted  . . . . :         1

    Type choice, press Enter.
        End data entry . . . . . . .    Y        Y=Yes,  N=No


    F3=Exit        F12=Cancel
```

Figure C-9 End Data Entry screen.

appendix d

Screen Design Aid Utility (SDA)

The *Screen Design Aid* (**SDA**) utility provides an easy method to design, create, and maintain *display files, menus,* and *online help information.* Because the user does not need to know the complex and detailed syntax required when the *Source Entry Utility* (**SEU**) is used to create and maintain display files, the processes are simplified with **SDA.**

SDA may be accessed by any of the following methods.

1. From any menu that includes a command line by typing the Control Language (CL) command **STRSDA** and pressing ENTER.
2. Selecting Option 9 on the PM and pressing ENTER. Unless otherwise set up, the PM may be accessed by entering the CL command **STRPGMMNU** on the command line on any menu and pressing ENTER.
3. Selecting Option **17** when in the PDM (**PDM**) utility and pressing ENTER. **PDM** may be accessed by entering **STRPDM** on the command line of any display and pressing ENTER.

Upon entering the **SDA** environment, the first menu that displays is shown in Figure D-1.

```
                        AS/400 Screen Design Aid (SDA)

      Select one of the following:

           1. Design screens
           2. Design menus
           3. Test display files













      Selection or command
      ===> 1

      F1=Help    F3=Exit    F4=Prompt    F9=Retrieve    F12=Cancel
                                         (C) COPYRIGHT IBM CORP. 1981, 1992.
```

Figure D-1   Initial **SDA** display with Option **1** selected.

This initial menu includes the following options:

1. <u>Design screens</u>—Controls the creation or maintenance of the record(s) in a display file.
2. <u>Design menus</u>—Controls the creation and maintenance of interactive menus.
3. <u>Test display files</u>—Controls the testing of successfully compiled display files and menus.

Steps in the Creation of a Display File

The following steps create a display file with one-record format:

1. Select Option **1** (*Design screens*)—type **1** on the command line (Figure D-1).
2. Press the ENTER key, and the display shown in Figure D-2 will appear.

```
                              Design Screens

    Type choices, press Enter.

        Source file . . . . . . . .    QDDSSRC      Name, F4 for list

          Library . . . . . . . . .    SMYERS       Name, *LIBL, *CURLIB

        Member  . . . . . . . . . .    SMSDA2       Name, F4 for list




    F3=Exit      F4=Prompt       F12=Cancel
```

Figure D-2   Design Screens display with variables entered.

Definitions of the entries in the display in Figure D-2 are explained below.

- <u>Source file</u>—The IBM default is QDDSSRC; the installation has the option of assigning their own base source files.
- <u>Library</u>—The default is *LIBL or the user may enter the specific library in which the display file's source will be stored.
- <u>Member</u>—The name of the display file to be created is entered on this line. If an existing display file is to be changed, **F4** may be pressed for a list of the files in the library specified on the preceding line.
- The three command keys listed at the bottom of the display provide the following control:
- <u>F3 = Exit</u>—Returns control to the previous screen without executing the current changes (if any).
- <u>F4 = Prompt</u>—Displays list of existing files as explained above.
- <u>F12 = Cancel</u>—Cancels any entries and returns control to the previous screen.

Press ENTER, and the *Work with Display Record* screen shown in Figure D-3 will display.

```
                        Work with Display Records

     File . . . . . . :    QDDSSRC              Member . . . . . . . :   SMSDA2
       Library . . . . :    SMYERS              Source type . . . :      DSPF

     Type options, press Enter.
       1=Add              2=Edit comments       3=Copy          4=Delete
       7=Rename           8=Select keywords     12=Design image

     Opt  Order    Record        Type     Related Subfile   Date        DDS Error
     1             SMSDA2R
        (No records in file)




                                                                        Bottom
       F3=Exit                    F12=Cancel         F14=File-level keywords
       F15=File-level comments    F17=Subset         F24=More keys
```

Figure D-3   Work with Display Records screen.

Assuming that *File Level* keywords are required for the example display file to be created, **F14** must be pressed to display the screen shown in Figure D-4.

```
                        Select File Keywords
     Member . . . . :   SMSDA2

     Type choices, press Enter.
                                         Y=Yes
        General keywords . . . . . . . .   Y
        Indicator keywords . . . . . . .   Y
        Print keywords . . . . . . . . .   Y
        Help keywords . . . . . . . . .
        Display sizes . . . . . . . . . .
        Alternate keywords . . . . . . .
        DBCS conversion . . . . . . . . .
        Window Borders . . . . . . . . .




       F3=Exit    F12=Cancel
```

Figure D-4   Select File Keywords display with three options (*General, Indicator, Print keywords*) selected.

In response to the *General keywords* selection, type **Y** on the *General, Indicator, and Print keywords* lines to access each of those displays sequentially. Press the ENTER key, and the *Select General Keywords* display shown in Figure D-5 will appear.

```
                        Select General Keywords

     Member . . . :   SMSDA2

     Type choices, press Enter.
                                                  Keyword   Y=Yes   Indicators/+
        Invite devices for later read . . . . . . INVITE    _       __ __ __
        Allow graphics . . . . . . . . . . . . .  ALWGPH    _       __ __ __
```

Figure D-5   Select General Keywords display.

```
┌─────────────────────────────────────────────────────────────────────────┐
│                                                                           │
│   Sound alarm on messages . . . . . . . . .    MSGALARM    _   __ __ __ __│
│   Separate indicators area . . . . . . . .     INDARA      _              │
│   Manage display in S/36 mode . . . . . . .    USRDSPMGT   _              │
│   Allow blanks  . . . . . . . . . . . . . .    CHECK(AB)   _              │
│   Move cursor right-left, top-bottom  . . .    CHECK(RLTB) _              │
│   Move cursor right to left . . . . . . . .    CHECK(RL)   _              │
│   Change input defaults . . . . . . . . . .    CHGINPDFT   Y              │
│     Select parameters . . . . . . . . . . .                Y              │
│   Write error messages to subfile . . . . .    ERRSFL                     │
│   Reference database file . . . . . . . . .    REF         SMPF1____  Name │
│     Library . . . . . . . . . . . . . . . .                SMYERS___  Name │
│     Record  . . . . . . . . . . . . . . . .                SMPF1R___  Name │
│   Record to pass unformatted data . . . . .    PASSRCD     _____   Name │
│                                                                           │
│   F3=Exit   F12=Cancel                                                    │
└─────────────────────────────────────────────────────────────────────────┘
```

Figure D-5   Select General Keywords display. (Continued)

The display default (underline for variables) is changed by entering a **Y** (*Yes*) for the **CHGINPDFT** (*Change Input Defaults*) keyword entry. Selection of this option will override any default display attributes in all of the record formats in the display file. Specific display attributes are assigned at the *File Level* by entering **Y** for the *Select parameters* response and pressing ENTER. The screen shown in Figure D-6 will appear where one or more display attributes may be selected. Note that *Column separators* (**CS**) has been selected, which will display dots indicating the size of the variable fields (not constants) in the record format of the example display file.

```
┌─────────────────────────────────────────────────────────────────────────┐
│                          Select Display Attributes_                       │
│                                                                           │
│   Constant . . . :                                                        │
│   Length . . . . :                         Row . . . :     Column . . . :│
│                                                                           │
│   Type choices, press Enter.                                              │
│                                            Keyword  Y=Yes  Indicators/+   │
│     Field conditioning . . . . . . . . . .                                │
│     Display attributes:                    DSPATR                         │
│       High intensity . . . . . . . . . . .   HI      _     __ __ __ __    │
│       Reverse image . . . . . . . . . . .    RI      _                    │
│       Column separators . . . . . . . . .    CS      Y     __ __ __ __    │
│       Blink . . . . . . . . . . . . . . .    BL      _     __ __ __ __    │
│       Nondisplay . . . . . . . . . . . . .   ND      _     __ __ __ __    │
│       Underline . . . . . . . . . . . . .    UL      _     __ __ __ __    │
│       Position cursor . . . . . . . . . .    PC      _     __ __ __ __    │
│                                                                           │
│                                                                           │
│   F3=Exit   F12=Cancel                                                    │
└─────────────────────────────────────────────────────────────────────────┘
```

Figure D-6   Select Display Attributes display.

If database file field names are to be used in the display file, the related physical file name must be entered on the *Reference database file* **REF** line of the display shown in Figure D-5. Note that to the right of the **REF** keyword, **SMPF1** is specified by the programmer. **SMYERS** is entered for the *Library* selection and **SMPF1R** (physical file's record name) for the *Record* selection.

Pressing the ENTER key displays the *Define Indicator Keywords* screen illustrated in Figure D-7. Note that *Command Attention Key 3* (**CA03**) is assigned indicator **03** for EOJ (end-of-job control in the RPG/400 program). *Command Function Key 2* (**CF02**) is assigned indicator **02** for ENTER DATA control, and *Command Attention Key 5* (**CA05**)

```
                          Define Indicator Keywords

   Member . . . :   SMSDA2

   Type keywords and parameters, press Enter.
     Conditioned keywords:        CFnn CAnn CLEAR PAGEDOWN/ROLLUP PAGEUP/ROLLDOWN
                                  HOME HELP HLPRTN
     Unconditioned keywords:      INDTXT VLDCMDKEY


   Keyword   Indicators/+ Resp Text
   CA03____ ___ ___ ___   03  EOJ
   CF02____ ___ ___ ___   02  ENTER DATA
   CA05____ ___ ___ ___   05  REFRESH




                                                                    Bottom
   F3=Exit   F12=Cancel
```

Figure D-7 Define Indicator Keywords display with command keys/indicators specified.

indicator **05,** for REFRESH processing. Any command key and related indicators could be specified for the required screen controls. However, recall that **CA** (*Command Attention*) defines function keys *which do not pass data to or from the display file to the RPG/400 program,* whereas, **CF** (*Command Function) keys do pass data.* Pressing ENTER advances control to the Define Print Keywords display shown in Figure D-8.

```
                          Define Print Keywords

   Member . . . :   SMSDA2

   Type choices, press Enter.
                                          Keyword
     Enable keyword . . . . . . . . . .   PRINT   Y          Y=Yes
        Indicators . . . . . . . . . .           __ __ __

     Program handles print:
        Response indicator . . . . . .           _          01-99
        Text . . . . . . . . . . . .                        _____

     System handles print:
        Print file . . . . . . . . . .           _____ Name, *PGM
        Library  . . . . . . . . . .              _____ Name,
                                                             *LIBL, *CURLIB
     Leave print file open until
        display file is closed . . . .   OPENPRT  _          Y=Yes

   F3=Exit   F12=Cancel
```

Figure D-8 Define Print Keywords display with **PRINT** option selected.

The letter **Y** entered on the *Enable keyword PRINT* line enables the Print Screen key, which when pressed will print the image of the record format currently displayed. Pressing ENTER *twice* returns control back to the *Work with Display Records* screen.

Before a screen is designed, a record must be defined in the display file to store the coding entries. To add a record to the display file, **1** (for *Add*) must be entered in the *Opt* field of the Work with Display Records screen as shown in Figure D-9.

```
                   Work with Display Records

   File . . . . . . :   QDDSSRC           Member . . . . . . :   SMSDA2
     Library . . . . :     SMYERS         Source type  . . . :   DSPF

   Type options, press Enter.
     1=Add              2=Edit comments      3=Copy          4=Delete
     7=Rename           8=Select keywords    12=Design image

   Opt  Order   Record        Type      Related Subfile   Date       DDS Error

    1    10     _____       _____



                                                               Bottom
   F3=Exit                  F12=Cancel      F14=File-level keywords
   F15=File-level comments  F17=Subset      F24=More keys
```

Figure D-9   Work with Display Records screen with option **1** (Add) specified to add a record format.

Pressing ENTER displays the Add New Record screen illustrated in Figure D-10. Previously entered variables including the source file name, library name, member name, source type, and so forth are included in this display.

```
                      Add New Record

   File . . . . . . :   QDDSSRC           Member . . . . . . :   SMSDA2
     Library . . . . :     SMYERS         Source type  . . . :   DSPF

   Type choices, press Enter.

     New record . . . . . . . . . . . . . . .   SMSDA2R     Name

     Type . . . . . . . . . . . . . . . . . .   RECORD      RECORD, USRDFN
                                                            SFL,    SFLMSG
                                                            WINDOW, WDWSFL



   F3=Exit      F5=Refresh      F12=Cancel
```

Figure D-10   Add New Record display.

Unless entered on the previous display, a record name must be specified for the *New record* response and RECORD for *Type*. Pressing ENTER returns control back to the *Work with Display Record* screen shown in Figure D-11.

```
                   Work with Display Records

   File . . . . . . :   QDDSSRC           Member . . . . . . :   SMSDA2
     Library . . . . :     SMYERS         Source type  . . . :   DSPF

   Type options, press Enter.
     1=Add              2=Edit comments      3=Copy          4=Delete
     7=Rename           8=Select keywords    12=Design image
```

Figure D-11   Work with Display Record with option **12** (Design image) selected.

```
     Opt   Order    Record        Type      Related Subfile    Date          DDS Error

     12     10      SMSDA2R       RECORD                       08/14/95




                                                                             Bottom
 F3=Exit                       F12=Cancel     F14=File-level keywords
 F15=File-level comments       F17=Subset     F24=More keys
```

Figure D-11 Work with Display Record with option **12** (Design image) selected. (Continued)

At this point in the display file's creation, the named record format may be designed ("painted") on the CRT. From the *Work with Display Record* screen, entering **12** in the *Opt* field for Option **12** (Design image) and pressing ENTER will display the blank Work Screen shown in Figure D-12.

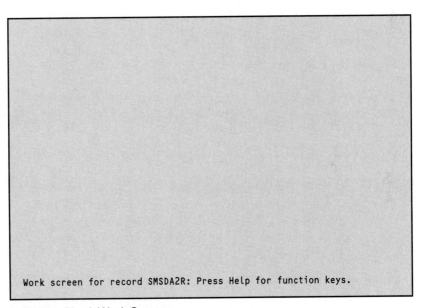

```
 Work screen for record SMSDA2R: Press Help for function keys.
```

Figure D-12 Blank Work Screen.

Then, to extract the physical file's fields to be used in the display file's record format, **F10** must be pressed to access the *Select Database Files* display shown in Figure D-13. Because a database file was referenced in the *Select General Keywords* display in Figure D-5, the variables (*Database File, Library,* and *Record*) are carried over to this display.

Because the display file record is to provide the input to an RPG/400 *add* program, option **2** was selected. If *inquiry*-only processing was required, option **3** would be specified. On the other hand, if *update* processing was supported, option **4** (both) would be required. Option **2, 3,** or **4** will access all of the fields in the related physical file. If, however, only some of the fields included in the physical file were needed, **1** would be entered as the option. After pressing ENTER, a list of the fields in the physical file's record format would display, from which the user could select only the fields needed for the display file's record format.

```
                          Select Database Files

Type options and names, press Enter.
  1=Display database field list
  2=Select all fields for input (I)
  3=Select all fields for output (O)
  4=Select all fields for both (B) input and output

 Option    Database File   Library      Record
   2         SMPF1          SMYERS       SMPD1R

 F3=Exit       F4=Prompt       F12=Cancel
```

Figure D-13 Select Database Files display with option **2** (Select all fields for input) specified.

Pressing ENTER returns control back to the blank *Work Screen* with the physical file's fields displayed horizontally across the bottom as shown in Figure D-14. If more fields were included that could fit across the row, a + (plus sign) would appear at the right of the field list. Any other fields may be displayed by pressing the Page Down key.

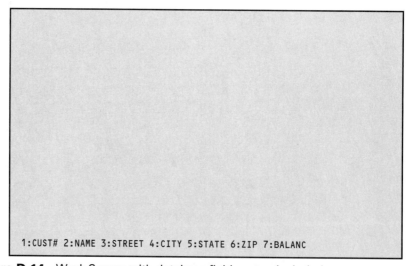

```
1:CUST# 2:NAME 3:STREET 4:CITY 5:STATE 6:ZIP 7:BALANC
```

Figure D-14 Work Screen with database field names included.

The user begins the layout process by entering constants and variables on the screen. Because the physical file referenced in Figure D-5 provides the field names, field sizes, and field constants, the "painting" process is simplified. To illustrate the relationship between the physical file and the display file, the record format of the physical file SMPF1 is presented in Figure D-15.

To provide a more detailed description of the data items, each field includes a **COLHDG** (*Column Heading*) keyword. The text included in a **COLHDG** keyword is the constant for the related field. If the **COLHDG** keywords were not specified, field names would be used as the constants.

```
                                      Data Description Source
SEQNBR    *...+....1....+....2....+....3....+....4....+....5....+....6....+....7....+
  100    A                                        UNIQUE
  200    A          R SMPF1R
  300    A            CUST#         5A             COLHDG('CUSTOMER NO')
  400    A            NAME         20A             COLHDG('CUSTOMER NAME')
  500    A            STREET       20A             COLHDG('STREET ADDRESS')
  600    A            CITY         20A             COLHDG('CITY ADDRESS')
  700    A            STATE         2A             COLHDG('STATE ADDRESS')
  800    A            ZIP          5P 0            COLHDG('ZIP CODE')
  900    A            BALANC       8P 2            COLHDG('BALANCE')
 1000    A          K CUST#
```

Figure D-15 Physical file (SMPF1) record format.

In the *Work Screen* shown in Figure D-16, all of the constant and field entries for the display file record are entered before the ENTER key is pressed. At the option of the programmer, each item may be separately entered and ENTER pressed after every entry.

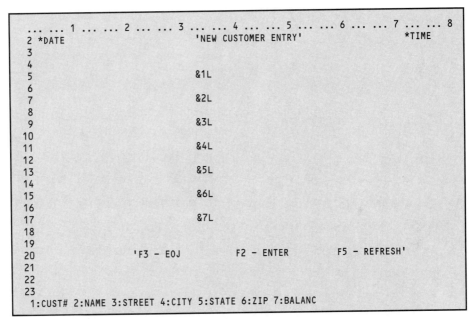

Figure D-16 Work Screen with all of the constants and fields specified (before EN-TER is pressed).

The following syntax is included in the *Work Screen* for building the display file's record:

1. When the *Work Screen* displays, the cursor will be positioned at row 1, column 2. Note that *row 1, column 1* is reserved by **SDA** for a Record Identification Code and cannot be used. The cursor may be moved to any position on the screen by up, down, right, or left arrow keys.

2. Pressing **F14** will access a "ruler" which displays vertical row and horizontal column numbers as shown in Figure D-16. The position of the cursor determines where the vertical row and column numbers appear. For this display, the cursor was positioned at Row 1, Column 2. The "ruler" may be disabled by pressing **F14** again.

3. A field for the system date is specified by the reserved word ***DATE** (upper or

lower case) and the system time by ***TIME.** The format for ***DATE** is MM/DD/YY and ***TIME,** HH:MM:SS.

4. The constant NEW CUSTOMER ENTRY is enclosed in single quotes. Constants may be entered without the quotes; however, if the entry has to be moved to another position on the screen, each word would have to be individually moved. In contrast, if a multiple word constant is included in leading and ending quotes, it can be moved as a unit. The same restrictions apply to the deletion of constants or assignment of display attributes (underlining, reverse image, highlighting, and so forth).

5. **&1L** through **&7L** reference the fields specified at the bottom of the screen. In addition to the field size, type (numeric or character), and usage (**I, O,** or **B**), the text in the **COLHDG** keyword included in the physical file will be displayed to the left of the related field format as shown in Figure D-17.

    If the **COLHDG** text was to be included at the right of the field format, entries **&1R** through **&7R** would be specified. On the other hand, if the **COLHDG** text was to be included over the field formats, **&1C** through **&7C** would be entered. Note that all of the items are not required to have the same format. Each field may be individually formatted.

6. The row of constants at the bottom of the screen are enclosed as a group within single quotes.

```
... ... 1 ... ... 2 ... ... 3 ... ... 4 ... ... 5 ... ... 6 ... ... 7 ... ... 8
2 DD/DD/DD                              NEW CUSTOMER ENTRY                    TT:TT:TT
3
4
5                     CUSTOMER NO:  IIIII
6
7                   CUSTOMER NAME:  IIIIIIIIIIIIIIIIIIII
8
9                  STREET ADDRESS:  IIIIIIIIIIIIIIIIIIII
10
11                   CITY ADDRESS:  IIIIIIIIIIIIIIIIIIII
12
13                  STATE ADDRESS:  II
14
15                       ZIP CODE:  33333-
16
17                        BALANCE:  33333333-
18
19
20                 F3 - EOJ              F2 - ENTER           F5 - REFRESH
21
22
23
24
```

Figure D-17 Work Screen display after all entries are made and ENTER key is pressed.

When the ENTER key is pressed, the *Work Screen* presented in Figure D-17 is redisplayed in the format shown.

Notice that the following conditions have occurred:

1. ***DATE** and ***TIME** items are displayed in an edited format.
2. Single quotes around each constant have disappeared.
3. The **COLHDG** text included in the field definitions in the physical file SMPF1 is included at the left of each variable and terminated with an **SDA**-supplied colon. If the **COLHDG** keyword was not specified for each data item, the field names would be used as the related constant.

4. The horizontal line of the field names at the bottom of the screen have disappeared.

5. Because the fields were specified to support input in the *Select Database Files* display in Figure D-13, the character fields are identified by **I**s and the numeric fields by **3**s. If output was selected, **O**s would be assigned to the character fields and **6**s to the numeric. On the other hand, if both (input and output) was selected, the character fields would be identified by **B**s and the numeric by **9**s.

Because the numeric fields were defined in the physical file as packed, a minus sign is included in the low-order position in the display of the *ZIP* and *BALANC* fields. The sign position does not increase the field size of the data stored on disk.

Moving Screen Items

Screen items (constants or variables) may be moved by the following methods.

1. The > (greater than) symbol will move an item to the right the number of columns equal to the number of > characters specified after the ENTER key is pressed.

2. The < (less than) symbol will move an item to the left the number of columns equal to the number of < characters specified after the ENTER key is pressed.

3. Typing a **-** (hyphen) before an item and an = (equal sign) somewhere on a used area on the screen will move the item beginning at the = location after ENTER is pressed.

When using any of the move functions, basic screen creation rules must be followed: at least one space must be included between items and they may not overlap each other. A sign position included at the end of a numeric field is considered a character, and anything following it must include at least one leading space.

Deleting Screen Items

Any screen item previously entered may be deleted by typing an upper- or lowercase **D** before it and pressing ENTER.

Specifying Display Attributes

Display attributes for constants or variables may be assigned by entering the related attribute letter in the space preceding the item and pressing ENTER. Figure D-18 lists the letter equivalents for each display attribute.

Letter	Display Attribute
H	Highlight
R	Reverse Image
S	Column Separators (dots)
B	Blink
U	Underline (default for variables)
N	Nondisplay

Figure D-18   Display attribute letter equivalents.

Another method to assign display attributes requires that an * (asterisk) be entered in the space before a screen item. After ENTER is pressed, the *Select Field Keywords*

```
                       Select Field Keywords

    Constant  . . . :   NEW CUSTOMER ENTRY
    Length  . . . . :   18                    Row . . . :  2   Column . . . :  34

    Type choices, press Enter.

                                           Y=Yes   For Field Type
        Display attributes  . . . . . . .    Y     All except Hidden
        Colors  . . . . . . . . . . . . .          All except Hidden


        General keywords  . . . . . . . .          All types



        TEXT keyword  . . . . . . . . .    _____
        ____

    F3=Exit    F12=Cancel
```

Figure D-19   Select Field Keywords screen with display attributes option selected.

display shown in Figure D-19 will appear. Note that the name of the field, its length, and Row/Column position on the screen are included at the top of the display. To access the *Select Display Attributes* screen shown in Figure D-20, where one or more attributes may be selected, **Y** must be entered on the *Display attribute* line and ENTER pressed.

From the *Select Display Attributes* screen illustrated in Figure D-20, one or more compatible display attributes may be selected by specifying **Y** on the related line(s). Pressing ENTER will return control to the *Work Screen* with the attributes enabled. Additional attributes, which cannot be assigned on the *Work Screen,* such as Protect Field, Position Cursor, and Modified Tag, may be specified on the *Select Display Attribute* or *Select Field Keywords* (General keywords line) displays.

```
                       Select Display Attributes

    Constant  . . . :   NEW CUSTOMER ENTRY
    Length  . . . . :   18                    Row . . . :  2   Column . . . :  34

    Type choices, press Enter.


                                          Keyword   Y=Yes    Indicators/+
        Field conditioning . . . . . . . . . . .                       ___ ___ ___
        Display attributes:               DSPATR
          High intensity . . . . . . . . . . .     HI       _       ___ ___ ___
          Reverse image  . . . . . . . . . . .     RI       _       ___ ___ ___
          Column separators  . . . . . . . . .     CS       _       ___ ___ ___
          Blink  . . . . . . . . . . . . . . .     BL       _       ___ ___ ___
          Nondisplay . . . . . . . . . . . . .     ND               ___ ___ ___
          Underline  . . . . . . . . . . . . .     UL       Y       ___ ___ ___
          Position cursor  . . . . . . . . . .     PC       _       ___ ___ ___



    F3=Exit    F12=Cancel
```

Figure D-20   Select Display Attributes screen with one selection specified (**UL**).

Deleting Display Attributes

Any attribute assigned to an item (constant or variable) may be deleted by typing a − (minus sign) in the space before the item, followed by the attribute letter over the first character of the item and pressing ENTER. If more than one attribute had been assigned and all were to be deleted, the same procedure would be followed except that the letter **A** would replace the individual attribute characters.

Adding Independent Fields

Fields not included in a related database may be added to the *Work Screen* by the syntax detailed in Figure D-21. After the required format is typed and ENTER pressed, the item is displayed as shown in the *Result* column.

```
Screen
  Entry        Result              Comment

 +I(10)     IIIIIIIIII      Character defined input field

 +O(12)     000000000000    Character defined output field

 +B(8)      BBBBBBBB        Character defined input/output (both)
                            field

 +3(5,0)    33333-          Numeric defined input field

 +6(6,2)    6666.66         Numeric defined output field

 +9(5,0)    99999-          Numeric defined input/output (both)
                            field
          |  |
          |  └─ Field size and decimal position for numeric items
          └──── Field type (character I, O, B) and (numeric 3, 6, 9)

 Note: 3s define numeric input, 6s numeric output, and 9s numeric
       input/output (both) fields.
```

Figure D-21   Screen entries to add independent fields.

An example of adding a field, **+3(7,0),** to the current *Work Screen* is illustrated in Figure D-22.

```
... ... 1 ... ... 2 ... ... 3 ... ... 4 ... ... 5 ... ... 6 ... ... 7 ... ... 8
 2 DD/DD/DD                   NEW CUSTOMER ENTRY                    TT:TT:TT
 3
 4
 5         CUSTOMER NO:  IIIII
 6
 7       CUSTOMER NAME:  IIIIIIIIIIIIIIIIIIII
 8
 9      STREET ADDRESS:  IIIIIIIIIIIIIIIIIIII
10
11        CITY ADDRESS:  IIIIIIIIIIIIIIIIIIII
12
13       STATE ADDRESS:  II                      ┌──────────────────┐
14                                               │ Attributes of the│
15           ZIP CODE:  33333-                   │ added input field│
16                                               └──────────────────┘
17            BALANCE:  33333333-    'CREDIT LIMIT:' +3(7,0)
18
19
20         F3 - EOJ          F2 - ENTER        F5 - REFRESH
21
22
23
```

Figure D-22   Work Screen with field addition syntax specified.

```
 ... ... 1 ... ... 2 ... ... 3 ... ... 4 ... ... 5 ... ... 6 ... ... 7 ... ... 8
 2 DD/DD/DD                         NEW CUSTOMER ENTRY                    TT:TT:TT
 3
 4
 5              CUSTOMER NO:  IIIII
 6
 7            CUSTOMER NAME:  IIIIIIIIIIIIIIIIIIII
 8
 9           STREET ADDRESS:  IIIIIIIIIIIIIIIIIIII
10
11            CITY ADDRESS:  IIIIIIIIIIIIIIIIIIII
12
13            STATE ADDRESS: II
14                                                          ┌─────────────────┐
15                ZIP CODE:  33333-                         │ Format of the   │
16                                                          │ dded field      │
17               BALANCE:  33333333-     CREDIT LIMIT:  3333333-──────────────┘
18
19
20              F3 - EOJ           F2 - ENTER         F5 - REFRESH
21
22              ┌──────────────┐
23              │ SDA supplied │
 1:FLD001───────│ field name   │
                └──────────────┘
```

Figure D-23 Work Screen after add field is entered and the ENTER key pressed.

After ENTER is pressed, the *Work Screen* is redisplayed with the "added" field formatted as shown in Figure D-23.

Note that an **SDA**-supplied field name, FLD001, is included at the lower-left corner of the screen. Additional user-defined "add" fields would be assigned FLD002, FLD003, and so forth.

Default field names may be changed by placing the cursor in the space preceding the field. Pressing **F4** will display the *Work with Fields* screen. To access the field name to be changed, press the Roll Up key until the field name to be changed is found. Figure D-24 illustrates the *Work with Fields* display <u>after</u> field FLD001 has been changed to LIMIT.

```
                            Work with Fields

     Record . . . :   SMSDA2R

     Type information, press Enter.
       Number of fields to roll . . . . . . . . . . . . . . . . .    6

     Type options, change values, press Enter.
       1=Select keywords    4=Delete field


     Option   Order   Field      Type Use  Length  Row/Col  Ref Condition  Overlap
       _        190   CREDIT LIM   C         13    17 050
       _        200   LIMIT──┐     I        7,0    17 066
              ┌───────────────┴────┐
              │ Field name changed │
              │ from FLD001 to LIMIT│
              │ by programmer      │
              └────────────────────┘
                                                                  Bottom
     Add                        H          Hidden
     Add                        M          Message
     Add                        P          Program-to-system

     F3=Exit   F6=Sort by row/column   F12=Cancel
```

Figure D-24 Work with Fields display after a default "add" field name (FLD001) is changed to LIMIT.

Specifying Error Messages

Error messages may be specified for field items by placing an asterisk in the space before the field. Pressing ENTER will display the *Select Field Keywords* display shown in Figure D-25.

```
                           Select Field Keywords

      Field . . . . . :   CUST#          Usage . . :  I
      Length . . . . :   5              Row . . . :  5    Column . . . :  33

      Type choices, press Enter.
                                      Y=Yes   For Field Type
        Display attributes . . . . . . .         All except Hidden
        Colors . . . . . . . . . . . .   _       All except Hidden
        Keying options . . . . . . . .   _       Input or Both
        Validity check . . . . . . . .   _       Input or Both, not float
        Input keywords . . . . . . . .   _       Input or Both
        General keywords . . . . . . .   _       All types

        Database reference . . . . . .   _       Hidden, Input, Output, Both
        Error messages . . . . . . . .   Y       Input, Output, Both



        TEXT keyword . . . . . . . . .   CUSTOMER NO_____


     F3=Exit   F12=Cancel
```

Figure D-25 Select Field Keywords display after **Y** is entered for Error messages choice.

Typing a **Y** on the *Error messages* line and pressing ENTER will display the *Define Error Messages* screen presented in Figure D-26. For this example, an error message is assigned to the CUST# field. Indicator **99** is entered for the *Indicator/+* response; the message **DUPLICATE KEY** for the *ERRMSG—Message Text* entry; and **99** for the *Ind* column entry.

The *Indicator/+* **99** entry is assigned at the option of the programmer. Because the database file was defined as supporting only **UNIQUE** keys (refer to Figure D-15), any attempt to add a record with CUST# key value already stored in the file will cause a pro-

```
                         Define Error Messages

      Field . . . . . :   CUST#          Usage . . :  I
      Length . . . . :   5              Row . . . :  5    Column . . . :  33

      Type parameters, press Enter.

        Indicators/+      ERRMSG - Message Text                    More  Ind
        99 ___  ___       DUPLICATE KEY                            ____  99




                                                                   Bottom


        Indicators/+      ERRMSGID  File        Library    Ind   Name




                                                                   Bottom

     F3=Exit   F12=Cancel
```

Figure D-26 Define Error Messages display after entries are specified.

cessing error. To control this, the **WRITE** statement in the related RPG/400 program must include **99** in columns 56–57 of the calculation instruction. When a duplicate key is tested, **99** will be set on by the program and cause the error message **DUPLICATE KEY** to display on line 24 of the screen. The **99** entry for the *Ind* column entry will set the indicator off after the Reset key is pressed. Pressing ENTER *twice* will return control to the *Work Screen*.

Changing a Field's Keying Options

When a numeric field is stored as packed and is subsequently referenced in a display file, a sign position will be included after the last digit. Under some conditions, this may be confusing to the user. In the example presented here, *ZIP* (zip code) was defined as packed in the physical file and when displayed will include a sign position in the low-order position as shown previously in Figure D-17.

The sign position may be deleted on the displayed field by entering an asterisk in the space preceding the *ZIP* field and pressing ENTER. *The Select Field Keywords* screen will display and the *Keying options* selection made by entering a **Y** on the related line as shown in Figure D-27.

```
                        Select Field Keywords


      Field . . . . . :  ZIP              Usage . . :  I
      Length . . . . :  5,0              Row . . . :  15   Column . . . :  33


   Type choices, press Enter.

                                        Y=Yes   For Field Type
      Display attributes . . . . . . .    _      All except Hidden
      Colors . . . . . . . . . . . .      _      All except Hidden
      Keying options . . . . . . . .      Y      Input or Both
      Validity check . . . . . . . .      _      Input or Both, not float
      Input keywords . . . . . . . .      _      Input or Both
      General keywords . . . . . . .      _      All types

      Database reference . . . . . .      _      Hidden, Input, Output, Both
      Error messages . . . . . . . .      _      Input, Output, Both




      TEXT keyword . . . . . . . . .    ZIP CODE _____


   F3=Exit    F12=Cancel
```

Figure D-27   Select Field Keywords display after option is entered.

Pressing ENTER again displays the *Select Keying Options* screen shown in Figure D-28. Entering a **Y** for the *Keyboard shift* attribute response and pressing ENTER will delete the sign position in the *ZIP* field and return control back to the *Work Screen*.

```
                        Select Keying Options


      Field . . . . . :  ZIP              Usage . . :  I
      Length . . . . :  5,0              Row . . . :  15   Column . . . :  33

   Type choices, press Enter.

                                         Keyword   Y=Yes  Indicators/+
      Keying options:                     CHECK
        Mandatory entry . . . . . . . . .   ME       _    ___ ___ ___
        Automatic record advance . . . . . ER       _    ___ ___ ___
```

Figure D-28   Select Keying Options display after **Y** is entered.

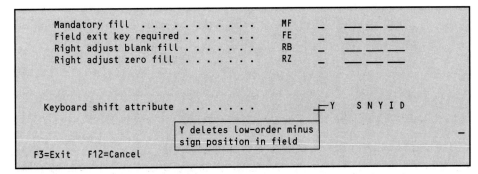

Figure D-28 Select Keying Options display after **Y** is entered. (Continued)

Saving and Compiling a Display File

To save the DDS source code, press **F3** until the *Exit SDA Work Screen* shown in Figure D-29 displays.

```
                        Exit SDA Work Screen

   Select one of the following:

        1. Save work since last Enter and exit work screen
        2. Exit without saving any work done on the work screen
        3. Resume work screen session













   Selection
      1

   F12=Cancel
```

Figure D-29 Exit SDA Work Screen with selection **1** specified.

Selecting 1 and pressing ENTER will display the *Save DDS–Create Display File* screen shown in Figure D-30.

```
                    Save DDS - Create Display File

   Type choices, press Enter.

        Save DDS source . . . . . . . . . . . .    Y           Y=Yes
          Source file . . . . . . . . . . . .      QDDSSRC     F4 for list
          Library . . . . . . . . . . . . . .      SMYERS      Name, *LIBL ...
        Member . . . . . . . . . . . . . . . .      SMSDA2      F4 for list
        Text . . . . . . . . . . . . . . . . .      sda example

        Create display file . . . . . . . . . .    Y           Y=Yes
          Prompt for parameters . . . . . . . .                 Y=Yes
          Display file . . . . . . . . . . . .      SMSDA2      F4 for list
          Library . . . . . . . . . . . . . .       SMYERS      Name, *CURLIB
          Replace existing file . . . . . . . .                 Y=Yes
```

Figure D-30 Save DDS—Create Display file screen.

```
┌─────────────────────────────────────────────────────────────────────────┐
│                                                                           │
│      Submit create job in batch . . . . . . .    Y          Y=Yes         │
│                                                                           │
│      Specify additional                                                   │
│         save or create options . . . . . . . .   _          Y=Yes         │
│                                                                           │
│    F3=Exit   F4=Prompt   F12=Cancel                                       │
│                                                                           │
└─────────────────────────────────────────────────────────────────────────┘
```

Figure D-30   Save DDS—Create Display file screen. (Continued)

After the defaults are taken or changes made, pressing ENTER twice will save, compile, and create an object (if there are no terminal errors). A listing that may be reviewed and/or printed will be generated in the user's print queue.

Every feature of **SDA** has not been introduced (e.g., menus and subfiles) in this appendix. For a comprehensive discussion of **SDA,** refer to the newest release of IBM's *AS/400 SDA* manual.

Testing a Display File's Record Format

After the display file has been successfully compiled, any record format included may be tested by the *Test display files* option (**3**) on the AS/400 Screen Design Aid (SDA) display shown in Figure D-31.

```
┌─────────────────────────────────────────────────────────────────────────┐
│                                                                           │
│                       AS/400 Screen Design Aid (SDA)                      │
│                                                                           │
│    Select one of the following:                                           │
│                                                                           │
│         1. Design screens                                                 │
│         2. Design menus                                                    │
│         3. Test display files                                             │
│                                                                           │
│                                                                           │
│                                                                           │
│                                                                           │
│                                                                           │
│    Selection or command                                                   │
│    ===> 3                                                                 │
│                                                                           │
│    F1=Help   F3=Exit   F4=Prompt   F9=Retrieve   F12=Cancel               │
│                                       (C) COPYRIGHT IBM CORP. 1981, 1992.  │
└─────────────────────────────────────────────────────────────────────────┘
```

Figure D-31   AS/400 Screen Design Aid (SDA) display with option **3** selected.

The *Test display files* option supports the following functions:

1. Tests record formats in the display file to observe how they appear on the screen
2. Tests any data validation checks of input fields
3. Displays the values in the input buffer that pass data and indicator status
4. Displays the values in the output buffer and the status (ON or OFF) of the indicator(s)

To advance to the next display, press ENTER. The *Test Display File* screen shown in Figure D-32 will display where the user must respond to the prompts: *Display File,*

```
                          Test Display File

 Type choices, press Enter.

       Display file . . . . . . . . . . . .   SMSDA2     Name, F4 for list
         Library  . . . . . . . . . . . . .   SMYERS     Name,
                                                         *LIBL ...
       Record to be tested  . . . . . . . .   SMSDA2R    Name,
                                                         F4 for list
       Additional records to display . . . .  _____   Name




  F3=Exit     F4=Prompt     F12=Cancel
```

Figure D-32   Test Display File screen with required entries.

Library, and *Record to be tested.* An entry (or entries) may be made for the *Additional records to display* prompt if the display file includes more than one record and additional formats are to be tested.

If the name of the display file record format to be tested is not known, a list of the record name(s) may be displayed by pressing **F4.**

Pressing ENTER will display the *Set Test Output Data* screen shown in Figure D-33. Because the display file's record format was defined to process *input* only (from the display file to the RPG/400 program), no fields are included in the *output* buffer. The ***IN99 Field** entry identifies the conditioning indicator (**99**) specified with the **ERRMSG** keyword in the display file. Note that the status of the **99** indicator is passed from the RPG/400 program (included with the **WRITE** instruction to test for duplicate records) to the display file. Consequently, it is automatically specified as output. The **0** entry under the *Value* column indicates that the **99** indicator is OFF. If *Output* and/or *Both* fields were defined, the related field name(s) and their display format would be included in the *Set Test Output Data* display.

```
                        Set Test Output Data

   Record . . . :  SMSDA2R

   Type indicators and output field values, press Enter.

   Field       Value
   *IN99       0:




                                                            Bottom

  F3=Exit    F12=Cancel
```

Figure D-33   Set Test Output Data display.

```
  8/14/95                      NEW CUSTOMER ENTRY                    9:53:00


                 CUSTOMER NO:  98765

               CUSTOMER NAME:  MICKEY THE MOOSE

              STREET ADDRESS:  1 DEER LANE

                CITY ADDRESS:  YELLOWSTONE

               STATE ADDRESS:  WY

                   ZIP CODE:   19901

                   BALANCE:    250000        CREDIT LIMIT:      3000


                 F3 - EOJ          F2 - ENTER        F5 - REFRESH
```

Figure D-34 Work screen after data is entered.

Pressing ENTER will display the *Work screen* shown in Figure D-34.

After the test data is entered, as shown in Figure D-34, and **F2** is pressed, the *Display Test Input Data* screen shown in Figure D-35 will appear.

```
                          Display Test Input Data

      Record . . . :   SMSDA2R

      View indicators and input field values.

      Field        Value
      *IN03        0:
      *IN02        1:
      *IN05        0:
      *IN99        0:
      CUST#        98765:
      NAME         MICKEY THE MOOSE    :
      STREET       1 DEER LANE         :
      CITY         YELLOWSTONE         :
      STATE        WY:
      ZIP          19901:
      BALANC       00250000:
      LIMIT        0003000:
                                                                      Bottom
      Press Enter to continue

      F3=Exit   F12=Cancel      F14=Display input buffer
```

Figure D-35 Display Test Input Data screen.

Examine Figure D-35 and note the following:

1. The status (**0** for OFF and **1** for ON) of the indicators defined in the record format is included. Because **F2** was pressed, the related ***IN02** indicator is **1** (ON) and indicators ***IN03** and ***IN05** are **0** (OFF).
2. The field values entered are included. Note that the **:** (colon) at the end of each field is a delimiter indicating its size.

When the test is completed, pressing **F3** several times will exit SDA.

Index

* Asterisk character;
    asterisk fill in an edit word, 75–76
    asterisk for source code comments, 39
** (RPG/400 control statement);
    with compile time tables, 267–68
    with compile time arrays, 302–03
*ALL 'x...' (figurative constant), 106–07
*BLANK/*BLANKS (figurative constants),
        106–07
*HIVAL (figurative constant), 106–07
*IN keyword, 109–10
*INxx keyword, 109–10
*LIKE DEFN operation, 120–21
*LOCK, 256–57
*LOVAL (figurative constant), 106–07
*NAMVAR (named variable), 256
*NONE (logical file), 510–12
*OFF (status of an indicator), 106–07
*ON (status of an indicator), 106–07
*ZEROS/*ZEROS (figurative constants), 106–07

A

Adding records to a physical file; 392–93
ADDROUT (address out) files;
    Creation by a sort, 621, 623
    File Description Specifications syntax, 626–27
    Extension Specifications syntax, 626–27
Alphanumeric;
    Fields, 13
    Literals, 182–83

Array editing (numeric);
    with edit codes, 314
    with edit words, 313
    with indexing, 314–15
Array lookup;
    LOKUP operation, 318–20
    by indexing, 320–21
    positionally, 319–20
Array processing;
    consecutively, 308–11
    multi-dimensional (defined), 300
    multi-dimensional (OCUR operation),
        327–34
    randomly, 318–21
    sorting, 334–35
Array run time errors, 322
Array types and loading;
    compile time arrays, 301–05
    pre-run time arrays, 301, 303–05
    run time arrays, 301, 305–08
ASCII coding set, 131
AS/400;
    models, 1
    operating system, 2

B

Blank after (letter B in column 39 of an output
        instruction), 215

Thanks to the cooperation of TRIDENT SOFTWARE, INC., a microcomputer version of an RPG/400 compiler is available to users of this textbook.

Offer includes the following:
1. Individual TS/RPG RPG compiler (student version) - The student version includes: Pre-compiled Data Files for each lab assignment, RPG compiler and Runtime System, Source Entry Utility (SEU), Programmer's Menu, Spooled Printer Output Queue to view compiles and reports before printing, and an Interactive Debugger. Pre-compiled DFUs exist for each data file, and the data for each lab is included in the files to save time keying all the data into the file. You still have the ability to run the pre-compiled DFUs for viewing or altering data file contents.
2. Individual TS/RPG compiler (full version) - The Full Development System is not intended as an RPG tutorial. Previous knowledge of RPG is assumed. Systems developed on the Full Systems may be executed on other PCs not containing a Full System by installation of a Run-Time only system. The TS/RPG Development Package includes SEU (Source Entry Utility), SDA (Screen Design Aid), Command Processor & Prompter, Programmer's Menu, Print Queues, Keyboard Mapping, RPG & DDS Compilers, and a Run-Time System.

How to order

Complete the order form and mail
it with your payment to:
   TRIDENT SOFTWARE, INC.
   P.O. Box 5608
   Hamden, CT 06518
Fax: (203) 223-1125
VISA or Mastercard phone orders call 203-877-9018 or 203-877-4331.

Hardware Requirements

IBM or compatible computer
640K memory, Hard disk
DOS 3.1 or greater
Operation system 286 or greater

All prices subject to change without notice

	Price	Quantity	Total
Individual Student Version:	$75	_____	_____
Individual Full Development System:	$495	_____	_____
Site license - Full Dev System Only:	$4800	_____	_____
Shipping and Handling:	$6	_____	_____
Connecticut residents add 6% sales tax:			_____
Order total:			$ _____

Mastercard or Visa:_____   Expires: _____

Signature (required for charging): _____
Please specify diskette format: 5 1/4 (HD) _____   3 1/2 (HD) _____

VERY IMPORTANT For student version orders please specify the title and author of the book you are using on the line below:

_____

School/Company: _____

Name: _____

Title: _____

Address: _____

City: _____

State/Zip: _____

Telephone: _____
Please allow 3-4 weeks for delivery except for phone orders.